Main Currents of Western Thought

READINGS IN WESTERN EUROPEAN INTELLECTUAL HISTORY FROM THE MIDDLE AGES TO THE PRESENT

Main Currents OF

EDITED
WITH INTERPRETATIVE ESSAYS
AND NOTES BY

Franklin Le Van Baumer
YALE UNIVERSITY

Western Thought

READINGS IN WESTERN EUROPEAN

INTELLECTUAL HISTORY FROM THE

MIDDLE AGES TO THE PRESENT

Fourth Edition

Yale University Press

NEW HAVEN AND LONDON

Set in Linotype Janson type and printed in the United
States of America.

Library of Congress Cataloging in Publication Data

Baumer, Franklin Le Van, ed.
  Main currents of Western thought.

  Bibliography: p.
  1. Europe—Intellectual life—Addresses, essays,
lectures. I. Title.
CB203.B35   1978   940   77-90945
ISBN 0-300-02233-6 (pbk.)

20   19   18   17   16   15   14

TO

MY WIFE

Preface to the Fourth Edition

*M*ain Currents of Western Thought, though it remains substantially the same book it was at its inception, has undergone extensive revision in successive editions since 1952. The second edition of 1964 performed major surgery on the twentieth-century part, called Age of Anxiety. The third edition of 1970 made major changes, not only in the selections but in the organization of the nineteenth century portion, which was retitled Century of Becoming. At that time I also rewrote the essay on the nineteenth century and part of the essay on the Enlightenment of the eighteenth century, and provided an addendum to the essay on the twentieth century.

In this fourth edition, published by the Yale University Press, I have done three things: trimmed, extended, and updated the Bibliographical Note, which is essential for a book like this; completely rewritten the essay on the twentieth century; and added a considerable number of new selections.

A French friend who saw the third edition was surprised by the absence of Pascal and Malraux. I pointed out to him that *Main Currents* was not intended to be an anthology of only great writers. My idea from the first was to choose selections for their representativeness— language used, ideas popular at the time, and so forth—rather than necessarily for their greatness. Nevertheless, I have put Pascal back in where he was in the first edition, under the heading "Science and Religion" in the seventeenth-century section. Malraux I have not put in because, while he is undoubtedly important and symptomatic, he is also an elusive writer, hard to quote out of complete context.

Other new selections include a brief but significant passage from Luther on the bondage of the will, which may be compared with some of Erasmus's observations on the same subject. Hugo Grotius appears in the seventeenth-century section for the first time. The eighteenth-century chapter "God and Nature" has been split into two, one called "Deism and Atheism" and the other "Nature." The latter compares ideas of Voltaire, Holbach, and Diderot.

A number of changes have been made in the nineteenth-century section. The chapter formerly called "Romanticism" has been renamed "Romanticism and Idealism" and includes new selections from Schelling and Herder. A new chapter entitled "Realism" has been inserted, in which the painter Gustave Courbet speaks his piece briefly on that subject. And under the final division "Toward the Twentieth Century" excerpts from Henri Bergson's *Creative Evolution* follow Fouillée in order to strengthen the selections dealing with "the reaction against positivism."

Finally, Rudolf Bultmann and Dietrich Bonhoeffer are now represented, under "Religion and Skepticism" in the twentieth-century part; and Werner Heisenberg's important statement on the idea of nature in the new physics has also been added to this part.

Thanks go especially to Edward Tripp, Editor in Chief of the Yale University Press, who encouraged me to do this fourth edition; to Steven Ozment for bibliographical suggestions; and as always to my wife for her help and guidance.

FRANKLIN L. BAUMER

New Haven, Connecticut

Preface to the First Edition

$\mathcal{T}$HE NEED for such a volume as this became patent to the author in the course of teaching western European intellectual history to Yale undergraduates. Intellectual history has caught the imagination of both teacher and student in American universities. But where can one find reading in "typical" documents; reading, together with running commentary which will serve as a springboard for further reading, and as a basis for discussion and interpretation? Of course, there are the great libraries, but not everybody has easy access to them, and even where there is access, students need lamps to light their way. There are also anthologies of literature and "source books" in the history of philosophy, political theory, and science, but these are restricted to special fields and make no attempt to get at the "climate of opinion." The only extant work that attempts to meet this need is the two-volume *Introduction to Contemporary Civilization in the West* (Columbia University Press, 1946). This is a very useful compilation, but it lacks tight organization and does not do justice to the twentieth century. It is also rather too exclusively preoccupied with the "great books." The author hopes that his book may go at least partway toward filling a gap for teacher and student, and, it may even be hoped, the general reader. He also hopes that the techniques employed herein may be useful, and the interpretations provocative to the scholar of intellectual history.

Approximately six-sevenths of the book consists of readings in important documents of western European intellectual history. Somewhat more space has been allotted to the twentieth century than to the other "periods," because of its contemporary interest. It goes without saying that the documents selected do not, and in any event could not, tell the whole story. The reader who complains that this or that idea is but slightly represented, if at all, should remember that not everything can be crowded into one volume. If space had permitted, I should certainly have included some documents on the social context of ideas, as well as additional material on intellectual institutions and the communication of ideas. For obvious reasons—lack of space, the cost of permissions, and the difficulty of making effective brief quotations—pictorial art and *belles lettres* have had to be largely forgone. Many of the documents included are, I believe, not well known, and some others have never before been translated. But the readings have been selected for their typicality rather than quaintness, and there is throughout a liberal sprinkling of the *vulgarisateurs* as well as the creative minds. The history of educational theory and art criticism receive some representation—both fields that deserve ploughing. For these reasons I fancy that this is no mere anthology. The attempt throughout has been to organize the readings around a number of themes which seem to the author to be of consequence in the intellectual history of the West.

The eight essays which make up the rest of the book aim to interpret the climates of opinion in which the documents were written. As interpretative essays, they necessarily assume some knowledge on the part of the reader. They should be read in conjunction with some general work like J. H. Randall's *Making of the Modern Mind* or Crane Brinton's *Ideas and Men* (from which, incidentally, they sometimes dissent), and more special monographs. The first essay, the longest in the book, describes the terminology, problems, and methods of intellectual history, and explains the author's reasons for periodizing as he has done. Later essays, necessarily brief, set forth some of the author's impressions of various phases of Western thought, together with some of his impressions of the main currents running through the whole. Without in the least attempting to expound a philosophy of history, these essays aim to stimulate thought, to provoke discussion, and to provide the impetus for the construction of a philosophy.

FRANKLIN L. BAUMER

New Haven, Conn.

Contents

PART *Two:* AGE OF *Science*

I. *THE SCIENTIFIC REVOLUTION*

II. THE ENLIGHTENMENT

III. CENTURY OF BECOMING

PART *Three:* AGE OF *Anxiety*

Contents

Main Currents OF *Western Thought*

READINGS IN WESTERN EUROPEAN
INTELLECTUAL HISTORY FROM THE
MIDDLE AGES TO THE PRESENT

Methodology and Interpretation

Main Currents of Western Thought attempts, by means of historical documents and interpretative essays, to tell the story of some of the more remarkable adventures of the "western mind" from the High Middle Ages to our present Age of Anxiety. For anyone with an iota of imagination, this story should be immensely exciting. It tells of at least two major shifts in emphasis within the same culture over a span of seven- to eight-hundred years. It tells of the adventures of a host of intellectuals, of their unceasing efforts to advance knowledge and to explain, in the light of their milieu and the body of knowledge at their disposal, this mysterious universe, to solve the riddle of human existence, and to outline desirable and workable social objectives. This story has to do primarily with Europe and Europeans, but it pertains to America and Americans in so far as they have participated in the mind and culture of the West.

I

SINCE the story told here is a story in intellectual history—Francis Bacon once said that the history of the world without such history seemed to him "as the statue of Polyphemus with his eye out"—it is important, at the outset, to say what intellectual history is, and to describe its methodology and working concepts. Intellectual history is a comparatively new discipline. Historically, it descends from German *Geistesgeschichte* which in turn grew out of the Hegelian tradition of the nineteenth century. From *Geistesgeschichte* (one of those untranslatable German words) the intellectual historian borrows some of his terminology—witness the terms *Weltanschauung* (world-view) and *Zeitgeist* (spirit of the times)—and some of his assumptions. He is worth his salt.

however, only when he subjects these terms and assumptions to searching analysis, not hesitating to modify or reject those which the facts do not appear to support. As of the moment, intellectual history is both popular and suspect. It is suspect by the specialists and the cruder sort of Marxists who contemptuously dismiss ideas as the mere rationalization of class interests. The more formidable criticism comes from the specialists who say that intellectual history is not sufficiently specialized (it cuts across too many fields); that it cannot be studied as history ought to be studied, *i.e.*, scientifically, objectively, without obtruding the historian's bias or interpretation on the materials.[1] Nevertheless, as I suggested in the preface, intellectual history currently enjoys something like a vogue on both sides of the Atlantic. One reason for this vogue is that the twentieth century understands, as perhaps no former century understood quite so well, the power of ideas and ideologies. A deeper reason is that after a century and more of intensive fact-finding in the various fields of knowledge, a good many puzzled people are asking that more attention be paid to the integration of the facts. Scientific research must go on, they say, but along with analysis there must be synthesis. Now intellectual history deals with large blocks of material, drawing its information from a great many special fields. It tries to find out whether the parts of a civilization add up to a whole. Thus, along with Gestalt psychology, cultural anthropology, and Whitehead's philosophy of organism, all of which emphasize the "whole," it is one of the signs of the times.

But what, precisely, is intellectual history? Perhaps it will be useful to say, first of all, *what it is not*. It is not the history of religion or philosophy or science or literature, although it draws upon all of these. The history of the single discipline tends to treat its subject *in vacuo*, without reference to the social environment, often without reference to what was going on in other fields of knowledge. It should further be noted that the literary historian, for instance, faces a very different problem from that of the intellectual historian. He resists, quite rightly, the tendency to treat literature as merely the reflection of the ideas prevalent at a given time in history. Literature, he will tell you, relates to the timeless world of the imagination as well as to the time-spirit.

Nor is intellectual history quite the same thing as the "history of ideas." The trouble with the history of ideas, at least as it has been developed by its leading exponent, Arthur O. Lovejoy, is its frequently excessive atomism. Lovejoy has performed a great service in cautioning against oversimplifications and facile generalizations, but in some, though by no means all, of his essays he literally cuts the ground out from under the intellectual historian. In his well-known essay "On the Discrimination

---

[1] This is a paraphrase of a statement in a letter I received from a former student of mine who writes from Oxford that intellectual history is still "rather frowned upon here."

of Romanticisms," for instance, he concludes that "the word 'romantic' has come to mean so many things that, by itself, it means nothing." [2] The historian of ideas will also select a single idea, the "great chain of being," usury, or some other idea, and trace its history through a number of centuries.

The intellectual historian, on the other hand, studies clusters of ideas, ideologies, rather than single ideas. To employ a convenient term coined in the seventeenth century, he studies "climates of opinion" and the way they change from age to age, from generation to generation. Furthermore, he studies these climates in relation to the milieu or social context, and as they become objectified in institutions. He believes, for example, that phenomena like the redistribution of property in Tudor England, increasing economic prosperity, frequent plague years, and short life expectancy help to explain the Tudor Englishman's peculiar tension with respect to the claims of two worlds. He tries to understand the role that the French *philosophes* of the eighteenth century played in the creation of new institutions during the revolutionary era.

"Climate of opinion" is, admittedly, an elusive term and requires careful definition. Perhaps the best way to define it is to give examples. In his excellent biography of Richard Oastler, C. H. Driver remarks that by most educated Englishmen of the early nineteenth century, both inside and outside Parliament, "the suggestion of labor regulation was regarded as manifestly preposterous" [3]—which is to say that the climate of opinion simply would not support such an idea. Another example: the two years when James I and Charles I ascended the throne of England happened also to be bad plague years. When I recently told a group of graduate students that some contemporaries interpreted this coincidence as a sign of God's displeasure with the Stuarts, or of his judgment upon the English people for their sins, I was greeted with laughter. Obviously, what might have seemed a perfectly reasonable explanation of events in the early seventeenth century, can scarcely be taken seriously today. Did the general belief in witches and witchcraft mean that sixteenth-century Europeans were superstitious? Not at all. Witchcraft was a perfectly logical deduction from their view of the universe.

What these examples show is that men live in an intellectual as well as physical climate which permits certain ideas and attitudes to survive and grow, while stunting the growth of others. Simply described, the climate of opinion means the complex of assumptions in terms of which the majority of men in a given society think and talk and act; the idiom they use to express themselves, the ways they have of explaining phenomena. This climate can easily be oversimplified. The temptation to generalize the "mind" of an age from the works of a handful of great men (Leo-

[2] *Essays in the History of Ideas* (Baltimore, 1948), p. 232.
[3] *Tory Radical* (New York, 1946), p. 248.

nardo, Descartes) must be resisted, as must the temptation to treat that "mind" as a static quantity which is not constantly undergoing modification. The exponents of *Geistesgeschichte* too often simply assumed a unitary "spirit of the times" to which all the aspects of civilization must be related. This was Oswald Spengler's fallacy. In characterizing a culture by means of a single idea, he failed to see that this idea called up its opposite, and that in every culture, groups representing different and even conflicting points of view live side by side. However, with these cautions the intellectual historian makes it his business to describe climates of opinion, without the concept of which he would, indeed, work to no purpose.

Another way of characterizing intellectual history is to say that it is the history of the "intellectual class." Elsewhere I have described this class as including "not only the comparatively small group of really profound and original thinkers, not only the professional philosophers, scientists, theologians, and scholars in general, but also the creative literary men and artists, the popularizers, and the intelligent reading public." [4] Obviously, this is not the Marxist conception of a united, class-conscious group at war with other groups. The intellectual class is nothing more nor less than "man thinking" in a variety of different ways. Some cultures, our own included, have a suspicion of intellectuals, but no one can deny that the intellectual has an important social function. He articulates (who else?) what other people feel to be real. He organizes and "explains" the universe. He acts as society's best critic, constantly setting new goals for it to achieve. He expands and broadens the human experience. Intellectual history, then, concerns itself primarily with the "inner world of thought" of the intellectual class, and it believes that this inner world has not a little to do with what transpires in the "outer world of action."

As a comparatively new discipline, intellectual history has by no means perfected its methodology. The method I have worked out, and which has proved to be fairly satisfactory, involves the analysis and comparison of climates of opinion in terms of certain categories: focus or foci of intellectual interest, keywords and symbols, the methods of knowledge in use, the dominant views of God and nature, man and society, the mood of the times (whether, for instance, it is hopeful or the reverse). This is the method used in putting together the documents in this book. A few examples will suffice to illustrate the method. Intellectual history can be studied, for instance, in terms of changing words and symbols. In a century like the sixteenth new words were forcing their way into the general vocabulary, and old words were falling into disuse. Similarly, new symbols—Bible, king, witch—tended, at least in the Protestant countries,

[4] "Intellectual History and its Problems," *Journal of Modern History*, vol. XXI (Chicago, 1949), p. 192.

to displace old symbols such as sacrament, images, vestments, charms and amulets. This is a process that is going on all the time, and it tells us a great deal about the thinking being done. Changing foci of intellectual interest can be measured in any number of ways—by reference to "best-seller" lists of books, school curricula, the clusters of great men and the cultural achievements which give an age its reputation, the sociology of professions. In his *History of the University of Cambridge*, Bass Mullinger says, on rather good evidence, that in Elizabethan England theology was absorbing to itself "the best brain-power of the age." [5] Fontenelle's funeral orations on the scientists of his time, several of which have been translated for this volume, supply some evidence that in the late seventeenth and early eighteenth centuries a not inconsiderable segment of the "brain-power" was shifting to the natural sciences.

Another method, which amounts to much the same thing, is to study the different branches of thought in relation to one another. This method provides a yardstick for determining, at any particular moment in history, the degree of intellectual integration. Is there a prestige science upon which the other "sciences" are drawing for their concepts and imagery, or are the sciences visibly compartmentalized or specialized? Obviously, these methods have their pitfalls. One has to be careful not to assume too much unity of thought, not to over-generalize for the sake of artistic and dramatic effect. One has to avoid dividing intellectual history into water-tight "periods" for the sake of neatness. But if we see the pitfalls, we can keep from falling into them and use these methods with some hope of success.

No discussion of methodology would be complete without also considering the attitude of the historian toward the materials he studies. Several years ago a student in my graduate seminar wrote a paper for me on Elizabethan Puritanism. He had obviously worked hard on it, got his facts straight and written them up well. But the paper was not first-rate because of his attitude toward his materials. He unconsciously condescended to these Puritans and evidently regarded their concern over predestination, church government, and the like as somewhat ridiculous. In other words, he lacked what the German philosopher Wilhelm Dilthey has called "sympathetic understanding" of the historical object. He studied it entirely from the outside, without entering sympathetically and imaginatively into its spirit. Dilthey maintained that the "cultural sciences" (studies dealing with man: history, political science, religion, literature, etc.) and the natural sciences required different methodologies. In the former there is a natural identity between the scholar and his object of study, which is man. Hence, if the cultural scientist wishes to understand his object, he must not merely observe it objectively but must interpret it sympathetically, by bringing his own living experience to

[5] (Cambridge, 1884), vol. II, p. 415.

bear upon it. The intellectual historian who would, for instance, understand Martin Luther must have a living interest in religion.[6]

I would go even farther than Dilthey and say that the intellectual historian must have a kind of commitment to the ideas and ideologies he studies in history. I do not mean commitment in Kierkegaard's sense that only a practicing Christian can understand Christianity. I mean personal involvement in the big intellectual debates of the past. I mean the conviction that these debates can tell him something about himself and the nature of reality. There are two ways of studying Calvin's doctrine of predestination. One way is to describe it accurately, and from the outside, as a "historical" phenomenon. This is good as far as it goes, but the subject only comes alive when we see that Calvin, however right or wrong he may have been, was grappling with a problem of existence that concerns us all. The history that is written is too often a parade of facts, external to and abstract from the experience of human beings. This is why so many people have dismissed it as antiquarianism. But the method outlined here suggests a way of studying history scientifically, and yet with a view to the human situation.

II

THE INTERPRETATION of western European intellectual history raises still other problems. One of the knottiest of these is the problem of periodization. The materials of this book have been organized under three "ages," and each of the first two ages is more or less subdivided into "periods." This scheme of periodization provides the basis for an interpretation. But is the historian justified in thinking of history in terms of periods?

Frankly, I do not see how the historian can avoid periodizing, but when he does so, I think he should know what he is doing. He should realize, and honestly admit, that periodization (barbarous term, but what better?) is merely a working concept, a practical device for interpreting the data of history. Inevitably, it represents to some extent an abstraction from reality. The historian should also recognize that there can be no such thing as a definitive periodization which will be acceptable to all times and all groups. "Every man is his own historian": this is especially true when the historian goes beyond the facts to interpret the facts. History channels through the mind of the historian who, however great be his talent and learning, sees through the glass of his times and his individual personality. Therefore, while he has his special insights, he will never perceive the whole truth, and his scheme of periodizing will al-

[6] On Dilthey's ideas, see Hajo Holborn, "Wilhelm Dilthey and the Critique of Historical Reason," *Journal of the History of Ideas*, vol. XI (New York, 1950), pp. 93–118.

ways be, at least in part, the construct of his special *aperçu*. In this sense, history is every bit as much an art as a science.

Historians have always periodized. But it is probably true to say that the concept of periodization arose more or less simultaneously with "classical" physics. Classical physics conceived of matter not as process or activity, but as dead stuff which one could cut up into chunks for the purpose of observation and manipulation. Similarly, the historian cut cross-sections through history, and to account for change (the equivalent of motion in physics) clumsily invented revolutions and sudden catastrophes. With the advent of an evolutionary mode of thinking, however, he came to see that the reality of history was flux, that life as a whole was continually in a process of becoming. It then became theoretically impossible to take a still photograph of history at any given instant of time. In periodizing, therefore, the historian frankly admits that he is using a purely practical device for determining the points at which certain types of thought or action, already evolving into something different, become dominant in society. Without such a device history would be nothing but an undifferentiated mass of isolated facts.

Also requiring a word of explanation is the "unit of historical study" employed in this book. Ten years ago our unit would probably have been the nation. But recent world events have made us realize, what Spengler and H. G. Wells realized years ago, that the nation is a part of a much larger cultural whole. No one in his senses doubts the existence of national habits of thinking and behaving, nor of those other interest groups which Marx called classes. But neither can anyone deny that bourgeois and proletariat, Englishmen, Germans, Frenchmen, and Italians participate in a wider cultural community traditionally known as "the West." The West, then, is our unit of historial study: the West to which the United States is affiliated, but which up to very recently western and central Europe chiefly exemplified; the West as differentiated from Hindu, Chinese, Mohammedan, and Russian civilization.

Having bared our premises and defined our terms, it now becomes possible to explain the way the materials have been organized, and to suggest an interpretation. Western European intellectual history from the Middle Ages to the present may profitably be studied under three large headings, designated in this book as Age of Religion, Age of Science, and Age of Anxiety. The weakest of these three terms is obviously the last, which has psychological undertones, and which is in any case rather nondescript. But any other term that might have been chosen—unreason, disillusion, conflict, confusion—would be open to similar objections. "Anxiety" is a convenient term for classifying a good many of the extraordinary mental phenomena of twentieth-century Europe. The historian does not need to apologize for not being able to divinize, as Spengler has done, the real meaning of our times. Some future historian will see the twentieth century in a perspective which, at this moment of writing, it is impossible to have.

Some people might prefer the Marxist concept of aristocratic, bourgeois, and proletarian ages. This would have required a somewhat different chronology and would have connoted, even though that would not have been my intention, a teleological vision of history. But the main objection to it, and in the end it proved to be insurmountable, is that most thinking simply cannot be explained on narrow class lines. St. Simon's division of western history into theological, metaphysical, and positivist periods is more persuasive, but the periodization here used seemed to me to best fit the facts as I understood them. Chronologically, the Age of Religion extends from the twelfth and thirteenth centuries to the first part of the seventeenth, the Age of Science from the seventeenth to the twentieth. As has been suggested, no single date or man, or even generation or century, marks a sudden break with past modes of thinking. The seventeenth century was a watershed only in the sense that at that time science (in the modern sense) was beginning to capture the imagination of a considerable segment of the intellectual class. Obviously, there were "scientists" before 1600, and obviously, in the eighteenth and nineteenth centuries there were a great many educated as well as uneducated people who continued to think, or who came back to thinking, of life in religious terms. What is in question is the dominant trend of thinking which, as has been said, never lacks an opposition. Each of these three ages also has its subdivisions which should likewise be construed not so much as temporal periods but as ways of thinking. The Renaissance, for instance, cannot really be dated. The Renaissance was a way of thinking characteristic of a certain group of intellectuals called humanists who flourished in the fifteenth and sixteenth centuries. To avoid further misunderstanding the medieval and eighteenth-century documents have purposely been described by the terms "medieval Christian world-view" and "Enlightenment" rather than "medieval mind" and "age of reason," because the documents in question do not purport to summarize *all* facets of thought during those centuries, but only those that the author deems to have been at the center of the thinking being done.

From the foregoing the reader will perhaps have guessed the author's criteria for periodization. They are principally these two: the sense that people have, at different times in history, of what is real and therefore worth doing; and the way they explain the events which come within their ken. Until well into the seventeenth century, during the period called the Age of Religion, resort was normally had to a supernatural explanation of the big events and often the small events too—from the wheeling of the planets in their courses and the phenomenon of death to the blight on cattle. After the seventeenth century the naturalistic mode became steadily more common than the theological, so that G. H. Lewes could observe with perfect accuracy in the mid-nineteenth century that of all the possible modes of explaining phenomena, "the scientific daily gains strength" while the theological and metaphysical "daily" lose their hold upon men.[7] In our own time there has been a noticeable tendency to temper the scientific explanation, to which Aldous Huxley attests when he says in *Ends and Means* that science has ignored many important aspects of reality "and concentrated its attention upon such aspects of the world as it could deal with by means of arithmetic, geometry and the higher branches of mathematics." [8]

Two examples will illustrate the changing sense of the real in history. Cardinal Newman tells us in his *Apologia pro Vita Sua* that from early childhood he mistrusted the reality of material phenomena. He felt isolated, he says, from the objects that surrounded him. Small wonder, then, that the teaching of the Church Fathers, Clement and Origen, should have come like music to his inward ear—the teaching that "the exterior world, physical and historical, was but the manifestation to our senses of realities greater than itself." For John Locke, on the other hand, it is quite clear that the real world was the world of objects and human beings. There may be another world, but we cannot know it. Let men, he writes in his journal, direct their major efforts to knowing the causes and effects of things "in their power," concentrating upon "the improvement of such arts and inventions, engines, and utensils, as might best contribute to their continuation in [this world] with conveniency and delight." [9]

In Newman and Locke, we have two sharply contrasting metaphysics which were broadly characteristic of the Ages of Religion and Science. The one, call it the Platonic, believes that the supreme reality consists of ideal forms, eternal ideas, God. The other, call it the Baconian, focuses upon the world that man can perceive by his senses and measure by mathematics. Convinced that nature is a parable, the first metaphysic looks for the meaning of the parable and tries to establish rapport with the powerful being behind things visible. The second attempts the scientific analysis and control of man's physical and social environment. The chief thing, then, that differentiates the two ages is the modern concept of power, or as Francis Bacon called it, the Kingdom of Man. Arthur Koestler maintains that in the present age there is a movement away from the "Commissar's," *i.e.*, the engineer's, point of view back to that of the "Yogi." Perhaps it would be more accurate to say that much of the intellectual anxiety observable in Europe today stems from the fact that probably the majority of educated people believe neither in Plato's other world *nor* in Bacon's magnificent vision of what this world might become.

[7] See below, p. 491.
[8] (New York and London, 1937), p. 309.
[9] See below, p. 297.

Is the story told by this book one of progress or decay or cycles? Hardly a year passes but what some new book appears on the decline of the West "since the Renaissance," "since Descartes," or, according to one of very recent vintage, "since the nominalist philosophers of the fourteenth century"! Most of these books have been written by people who believe that the scientific picture of reality has wrecked the Western world. I do not share this belief. Science has certainly given us valuable insights into reality and, what is perhaps beyond dispute, has provided us with useful techniques for controlling our environment. But in developing these insights and techniques westerners may have all but lost others which are equally important for their well-being. The tale told in these pages is therefore neither one of unmitigated progress or decay. Nor is it a cyclical interpretation, for history cannot *sui generis* repeat itself. Intellectual history delineates man's restless quest for truth and happiness. Every age is creative in the sense that it perceives and records in its thought some aspect, more or less important, of reality. No age, however great, sees reality whole, no age has a monopoly of the truth, for the reason that *a price has to be paid for creativity*. By encouraging certain forms of creation, an age discourages others. In proportion as it opens up new vistas, it closes down on others.

The question of *why* this is so, why, in history, old patterns of thought dissolve to be replaced by new patterns, poses the final problem which we must do something to unravel. This is the problem of intellectual or cultural change, and we have all experienced it in our own lives. Who does not know that the "sons," or at least the more intelligent sons, of our generation, and by inference every generation, think differently from the "fathers"? Ideas that horrify the fathers come perfectly natural to the sons. The sons have knowledge which the fathers refuse to discuss. The fathers themselves modify their opinions. Why should this be so?

The problem obviously requires a careful definition of terms. "Knowledge" is of two sorts. There is positive knowledge which we have come to associate particularly with the natural sciences and the technical aspects of any branch of learning. Then there are social ideas, and beliefs and opinions about man and the universe, as to which, as Bertrand Russell puts it, "pure reason is silent." [10] Now I imagine few people will deny that once a culture has decided that, for instance, intensive research in the physical sciences is worth doing, the progress in knowledge in that field is explicable very largely in terms of its own internal history. Our problem therefore centers on the second kind of knowledge which, because it is less cumulative and more "oscillatory," would seem to depend much more upon extra-theoretical and environmental factors. When we discuss ideational change, we must also be quite clear as to whether we mean ideas as they are hatched in the mind of some great intellect or

[10] *A History of Western Philosophy* (New York, 1945), p. 787.

leader, or ideas that win wide acceptance and become a social force.

On this point it is perhaps useful to distinguish between ideas and ideologies. It is not always possible to explain the birth of a new idea in terms of the originator's social position or interest group. In Martin Luther's case, for example, there was actually tension between his master idea (the priesthood of all believers) and the class to which he belonged (the priesthood). On the other hand, Luther's ideas could never have become an ideology if they had not appealed to an appreciable number of people in his society. What the sociologists of knowledge call *Realfactoren* (political conflict, economics, the social context) do act as the selective agencies of ideas, retarding or quickening their diffusion. This thesis can go wrong, however, if it is too closely identified with Marx's concept of class, or if it is construed to deny altogether the autonomous role of ideas in history. Any thoughtful person living in the twentieth century knows only too well that the "class" to which he belongs is not the sole determinant, nor even perhaps the most important determinant, of his thinking. War, and the threat of war, inevitably colors his whole mental picture. And with regard to the autonomous role of ideas, Max Weber has demonstrated, to my satisfaction at least, how the Protestant Reformation unwittingly produced a type of personality with traits useful to modern capitalism.

Ultimately, the problem of the "how" and "why" of intellectual change is insoluble in terms of any single factor. External events cause alterations in mental perspective, but who can deny that ideas and ideologies influence events? Intellectual change is not wholly dialectical (logical, rational) as Hegel supposed. Neither, however, is it wholly due to innovations in the environment because, as has been suggested, ideologies generate consequences that are not wholly the result of factors external to them. Until we have discovered the philosopher's stone, we can but conclude that ideological change is an extraordinarily complex thing, resulting from the concatenation of a variety of causes. It would appear to depend upon the accumulation of small changes in emphasis, which come about almost imperceptibly within a larger framework of ideas. Eventually these changes combine to bring that framework crashing down. But in the final analysis we have to admit that there is something that eludes us, some clue the lack of which prevents us from understanding the problem as we would like.

III

WHY do we study intellectual history? For one thing, it provides us with a map of the long road we have travelled to get where we are. We think and behave the way we do because we have traversed this road, and not some other road. Intellectual history also throws a good deal of light on the nature of man: man's limitations and potentialities, the way he adapts himself mentally to new situations. If extended to other areas of the world, it can perhaps suggest more intelligent ways of handling contemporary political problems. What the experts in international relations sorely need is a really profound knowledge of the intellectual and cultural traditions of the countries they deal with. If, in addition to the information they have about oil wells and uranium deposits and "power politics," they had this kind of knowledge, they would be in a much better position to predict how nations and their statesmen will behave in a given situation. But of all the uses of intellectual history, surely the most important is the help it can give us in our perennial quest for a meaningful philosophy of life.

As Dilthey would say, intellectual history can help us to become free men. We are not free so long as we live in the illusion that the ideas of our age, country, and interest group are absolute, for all times and places. Nor are we free so long as we remain imprisoned in our own little segment of time, cut off from the rich intellectual experience of the human race. To become free, we must therefore face the fact that ideas are relative to a particular time and group, that they are constantly undergoing change. We must then pass beyond this knowledge of historical relativism to an appreciation of the world-views of past generations. Of course, the men of the past were, like ourselves, creatures of their times. But for the very reason that they *were* limited, because they were reared in a different tradition from our own and were called upon to solve different problems, they had their special insights. Because they focused upon a particular aspect of the world, they had perspectives of which we could hardly be aware without their help. Thus, we can learn from the medieval Catholics and Elizabethans and *philosophes*, even though in certain respects we may think we have advanced beyond them.

In a word, intellectual history gives knowledge akin to that of great art. It widens our mental horizons and deepens our emotional responses. It makes us realize that we live in a world of flux but that we can transcend the flux. Upon such knowledge as we derive from its study, we can begin to build a meaningful philosophy of life and to become free in the fullest sense.

PART One:

AGE OF Religion

Understanding is the reward of faith. Therefore seek not to understand that thou mayest believe, but believe that thou mayest understand.

St. Augustine, ON THE GOSPEL OF ST. JOHN

1. THE MEDIEVAL CHRISTIAN WORLD-VIEW

The final happiness of man consists in the contemplation of truth. . . . This is sought for its own sake, and is directed to no other end beyond itself.

St. Thomas Aquinas, SUMMA CONTRA GENTILES

May my soul die the death which belongs to the angels; so that, departing from the remembrance of things present, and being divested not only of desire for, but also of the haunting ideas and images of, things corporeal and inferior, it may enter into pure relations with those in which is the image and likeness of purity.

Bernard of Clairvaux, SERMON ON THE ECSTASY THAT IS CALLED CONTEMPLATION

There are two powers by which this world is ruled, namely, the sacred authority of the priests and the royal power. Of these, that of the priests is the more weighty, since they have to render an account for even kings in the divine judgment.

Pope Gelasius I, LETTER TO EMPEROR ANASTASIUS

The human race we have distributed into two parts, the one consisting of those who live according to man, the other of those who live according to God. And these we also mystically call the two cities, or the two communities of men, of which the one is predestined to reign eternally with God, and the other to suffer eternal punishment with the devil.

St. *Augustine*, THE CITY OF GOD

The Medieval Christian World-View

*V*ALUE judgments on the so-called Middle Ages depend on the point of view. The concept of a "middle" age originated with a long line of debunkers from the Italian humanists of the fourteenth century to the French rationalists of the eighteenth. Petrarch may have been the first to designate as "dark" the thousand-year stretch of history following the decline of Rome, but the now familiar idea of a tripartite division of history (ancient—medieval—modern) did not fully crystallize until the first great century of modern science, the seventeenth. During the Enlightenment this idea obtained wide currency. To Voltaire the Middle Ages, far from constituting one of the "four happy ages of history," signified an era of barbarism, irrationality, and superstition. It was generally believed that the study of medieval history had no utility except possibly to remind men of their stupidities. Said Voltaire in his *Essay on Customs:* "It is necessary to know the history of that age only in order to scorn it." "To be learned about [the Middle Ages]," Bolingbroke wrote in 1735, "is a ridiculous affectation in any man who means to be useful to the present age. Down to this aera let us read history: from this aera, and down to our own time, let us study it." [1] From this debunking tradition has stemmed a formidable set of judgments, mostly mistaken, on medieval thought and culture: for instance, that prior to the Renaissance reason was "in prison," that medieval intellectuals had no interest in science or knowledge of the ancient classics, that medieval civilization was, in fact, a gigantic swindle.

Reacting against the excessive rationalism of the Enlightenment, the romantics of the early nineteenth century reversed this judgment and peopled the Middle Ages with chivalric knights, pious monks, singing troubadours, skilled craftsmen, and jolly peasants dancing around the Maypole. In *Past and Present* Thomas Carlyle, for instance, contrasted the

[1] *Letters on the Study of History, Works* (Dublin, 1793), vol. II, p. 343.

"Mammon-Gospel" of modern England unfavorably with the social out-look of the twelfth century. And John Ruskin recorded a revolution in artistic taste when he wrote of Gothic architecture that, unlike the Greek and Roman, it is "clothed with a power that can awe the mightiest, and exalt the loftiest of human spirits: an architecture that kindles every faculty in its workman, and addresses every emotion in its beholder." [2]

Of course, the romantic idealization of the Middle Ages was just as much a perversion of historic truth as the debunking. But if we had to choose between the romantics and the debunkers, we should choose the romantics—because, for all their exaggeration, they at least appreciated the inappropriateness of the term "middle ages," and understood that tra-dition alone could justify its continued use. Thanks partly to their en-thusiasm, partly to the labors of medieval scholars, we can now see the "high" Middle Ages of the twelfth and thirteenth centuries for what it was: a great civilization, which produced the universities, scholasticism, the ideal of chivalry, Gothic art, and some of the loftiest works of the human spirit. No one in his senses will deny what Henry Osborn Taylor called "the spotted actuality" in all this—indeed, what age has ever suc-ceeded in living up to its highest ideals? But neither will anyone now deny (I hope) that on its intellectual and cultural side the Middle Ages marks a *beginning,* and not a mere barren interim between "ancient" and "modern." Medieval historians have recently discovered in the Middle Ages the roots of modern secular civilization. But more important for our purposes, the Middle Ages created the Christian world-view, which did not spend its full strength until the Enlightenment, and which, for better or for worse depending on the point of view, has influenced Western thought and action ever since.

II

To UNDERSTAND the mind of the High Middle Ages we have to know its social context. The twelfth and thirteenth cen-turies witnessed the beginnings of a social revolution: the revival of town life after centuries of stagnation, the steady rise of population, the genesis of political consolidation (especially in France, England, and Spain), technological improvements in agriculture and manufacture. Yet J. H. Randall's characterization of this society as "a pioneer society, just strug-gling out of a long past of bitter toil for a bare subsistence" [3] still stands. The economy was still basically agrarian. The towns themselves were semi-rural, and were, in any case, but islands in the midst of a vast agrarian sea where the daily round of manorial existence went on without notice-

[2] *The Stones of Venice* (New York, 1860), vol. III, p. 215.
[3] *The Making of the Modern Mind* (Cambridge, Mass., 1940), p. 13.

able change. In few towns had the capitalistic mode of production and exchange yet supplanted the gild system. Life expectancy was low, and science did not know how to deal effectively with famine and epidemic. It requires no great stretch of the imagination to see in these conditions one of the causes for the contemporary strength of the Christian Church. Francis Bacon once observed that atheism flourishes in "learned times, specially with peace and prosperity, for troubles and adversities do more bow men's minds to religion." [4] He might have added that the rise of the Church to a position of cultural dominance coincided with the "Dark Ages" of political decentralization and economic and population decline, and with the continuation, to some extent, of adverse living conditions in the twelfth and thirteenth centuries.

High medieval thought reflects both the nascent social revolution and the agrarian-ecclesiastical civilization. Without the urban revival, the "twelfth-century Renaissance"—the revival of Aristotle and Greek and Arabic science and Roman law, the new mental curiosity and the high level of intellectual sophistication attained in scholastic debate—is simply unthinkable. On the other hand, the intellectual and spiritual prestige of the Church of Hildebrand and Pope Innocent III guaranteed that most of the thinking should be done within a religious framework, and that a major attempt should be made (witness St. Thomas Aquinas and Dante) to explain all knowledge in a religious synthesis. Town and court had only just begun to threaten the clerical monopoly of education, and if the monastery was commencing to lose some of its intellectual lustre, its place was at first taken by the cathedral school and university (in the case of Paris at least, a clerically controlled institution). The intellectual class, small in an age when comparatively few people could even read and write, consisted largely of clergymen, although admittedly not all clergymen were equally clerical-minded. Ernst Troeltsch therefore exaggerates only a little when he says that art and science remained for a long time "closely connected with the Church; in fact, there were no independent secular values of civilization at all which might have felt and claimed a Divine right to exist apart from the Church and her ideals. The only sovereignty that existed was that of the Church; there was no sovereignty of the State, nor of economic production, nor of science or art." [5]

Of the main body of medieval thought it can therefore be said that, to a degree seldom equalled before or since, it was authoritarian, theocentric and theocratic. Other descriptive terms would certainly be "ecclesiastical," "dualism" (in the Platonic rather than the Cartesian sense), "organism," and "hierarchy." Let us see in detail what these words mean. Medieval thought was *authoritarian* in the sense that it usually had recourse to authority—the theology of the Church and a select list of books

[4] *Essays*, "Of Atheism."
[5] *The Social Teachings of the Christian Churches* (London, 1931), vol. I. p. 252.

including the Scriptures and Plato and Aristotle (shorn of his heresies)—
for its fundamental premises about the world and man. To be sure, the
history of medieval rationalism would fill a large volume, and reason
sometimes contradicted authority. "Nothing should be believed, save
only that which either is self-evident, or can be deduced from self-evident
propositions"; "Theology rests upon fables," were among the 219 propositions condemned in 1277 by the Bishop of Paris who had become
alarmed at the spread of Averroist opinions in the University of Paris.
Ordinarily, however, reason did not clash with authority, but remained
content to speculate on neutral subjects, or else to elucidate and buttress
the central faith. Indeed, the main point about the school of St. Thomas
Aquinas is its assumption that reason and revelation must, in the end,
come to the same thing. The greatest of the medieval philosophers made
it his business to harmonize Aristotelianism with Christian theology, and
thus to demonstrate to "gentiles" and doubters that reason supported the
authoritative tradition. In his opinion, reason properly exercised will rise
to the knowledge of divine things, and will show that revealed truth (admittedly "above reason") is neither irrational nor improbable. Evidently,
few medieval intellectuals conceived of knowledge in the modern way,
as something expanding and hypothetical. Relying ultimately upon authority past and present, they believed themselves to be already in possession of all the truths that mattered. This is the real significance of those
"summas" and "mirrors" in which they delighted, *e.g.*, Aquinas's *Summa
theologica* and Vincent of Beauvais's *Speculum majus* which embraced
universal knowledge in a single book. How else explain the great vogue
of philosophy in the schools—philosophy which, unlike the particular
sciences, sought to survey and co-ordinate the whole range of human
knowledge.

The prestige of theology, the "realistic" (in the Platonic sense) persuasion of most of the scholastics, the widely acclaimed superiority of
the *vita contemplativa*, all attest to the *theocentric* bias in medieval
thought. Theology or sacred doctrine clearly ranked first in the hierarchy of learning. "Theology," said St. Thomas, "transcends other sciences." "One speculative science is said to be worthier than another, by
reason of its certitude, or the dignity of its matter. In both respects this
science surpasses other speculative sciences, because the others have certitude from the natural light of human reason, which may err; but this has
certitude from the light of the divine knowledge, which cannot be deceived; likewise by reason of the dignity of its matter." Theology dictated much of the art and history of the Middle Ages, and if philosophy
was not exactly its handmaiden, it often fused with it and had to be content to play second fiddle. Theology ranked first because it dealt with
first and last things—God, the purpose of creation, man's destiny; things
concerning which the natural reason alone could never have sufficient

knowledge. Of course, this theocentrism by no means precluded interest in man and nature. Medieval thought made man the point of the universe, relating the whole creation to his struggle for salvation. And far from discouraging natural science, the Christian Aristotelians made the knowledge of sensibles a prerequisite for philosophical synthesis. Beginning in the twelfth and thirteenth centuries, decorative art, moreover, began to evince considerable interest in natural objects for their own sake. Nevertheless, in medieval humanism man gained dignity only through his relation to the deity. And there can really be no question that for all but a few, the main scientific interest focused on the "final" rather than the "secondary" causes—on *why* rather than *how* nature functioned as it did. This, and its dependence on Aristotle, explains why the Middle Ages made such slow progress toward modern concepts of science.

The strong dash of "realism" in medieval thought further illustrates its theocentricity. By realism is meant, not the modern but the Platonic (and also Aristotelian) doctrine that the objects of sense perception participate in higher realities. Behind our familiar world the scholastics (nominalists excepted) perceived a supersensible world of Ideas and Forms which gave meaning to, and drew into actuality what was only potential in matter. On this view, sense objects are not merely what they seem to be, but are symbols of a more real world of Ideas and Forms of which God is the archetype. Thus, the words of Scripture convey more than the literal meaning—according to St. Jerome, says William Durandus, "we ought to study Holy Scriptures in three ways: firstly, according to the letter; secondly, after the allegory, that is the spiritual meaning; thirdly, according to the blessedness of the future." Similarly, the Eucharist—by the doctrine of transubstantiation of 1215—was said to consist not only of the "accidents" of the bread and wine, but also of the "substance," the real body and blood of the Lord, which the senses cannot perceive. Everywhere they looked medieval people saw visible signs of an invisible order. Papacy and Empire embodied the divine unity on earth. In the institution of chivalry the knight's sword signified the cross, his spear truth, and so on. A book like William Durandus's *Rationale divinorum officiorum* riots in symbol and figure, and so does the plastic art of the cathedrals. "The church," Durandus wrote, "consisteth of four walls, that is, is built on the doctrine of the Four Evangelists"; "the foundation is faith, which is conversant with unseen things"; "the door of the church is Christ," also the lamp and altar. Medieval art, says a modern art historian, "implies a profoundly idealistic view of the scheme of the universe, and the conviction that both history and nature must be regarded as vast symbols." [6]

This same metaphysic supported asceticism and the sense of the miraculous, and it explains why medieval intellectuals extolled the con-

[6] Émile Mâle, *Religious Art in France. XIII Century* (London, 1913), p. 15.

templative life. The story of Mary and Martha in Luke 10:38–42 was a favorite among medieval writers, and of the two sisters they infinitely preferred the contemplative Mary to the active Martha. For did not Jesus himself say that Mary had chosen the best part: Mary, who fixed her gaze on the face of the Lord, contemplating the eternal truth behind the appearances. And did not Aristotle also say in the tenth book of the *Ethics* (a work much quoted in the thirteenth century) that happiness stood "in perfect rest," that contemplative speculation excelled even virtuous action because it aimed "at no end beyond itself." The contemplation of a static and more than mortal truth—*this* was the ideal of both mystic and philosopher, and it shows how little they grasped the modern conception of knowledge as the means to control and power.

It is true that extreme "realism" began to decline as Aristotelian metaphysics took hold in the schools of the twelfth and thirteenth centuries. Aristotle, as is well known, brought the Ideas or Forms down to earth and made them work with and in material phenomena. Hence, those scholastics who followed Aristotle closely associated form with matter and grounded knowledge in sensory perception. It should be noted, however, that by no means all the intellectuals became Aristotelians, and what is more important, that the Aristotelian system itself was teleological and theological. The universe, as the Christian Aristotelian envisaged it, had an immaterial cause. God created primary matter and the forms *ex nihilo* (here the account in Genesis was preferred to Aristotle). God was "the efficient, the exemplar and the final cause of all things" who moved creatures to achieve the several ends or purposes for which they were fitted. God constructed the universe on a hierarchical rather than a democratic model. The same laws did not apply everywhere in the cosmos. Between its two parts there existed qualitative differences, the sublunary world of the four elements exhibiting rectilinear motion and hence mutability and decay, the celestial world of the stars circular motion and hence changelessness. The cosmic hierarchy presupposed a psychological hierarchy, the great "chain of being" stretching from God down through the angels and man to the animals and inanimate nature. Man represented the nodal link in this chain; man the microcosm who partook of the nature of both the angels and animals, man for whom the rest of nature had been created. It goes without saying that the creation was not all that there was. Beyond creation was the real world, the supersensory world of God, toward whom all creatures, and especially man, were straining, and in whom they had their being and meaning.

Theocentricity does not necessarily argue *theocracy* but in the High Middle Ages it generally did. Theocracy means literally the rule of society by God and God's agents. More generally, it connotes a social philosophy based upon theological premises in which religion embraces all aspects of human activity and allows no independent secular values to exist. The theocratic ideal owed its wide acceptance to the fact that it rationalized, to some extent, the actual social scene: the feudal class structure, the absence of organized nationality, the pre-capitalistic economy of most of the towns, and, principally, the rise to power of the sacramental Church. The Church had not always had this ideal. In the early Middle Ages it commonly took the ascetic view that Christ's kingdom was not of this world, that salvation depended upon flight from a world unalterably evil. But as it broadened its missionary effort and acquired feudal properties and successfully asserted its independence, in the Hildebrandine period, of the state, it began to aspire to be "not a sect, but a civilization." [7] It now argued that the world could not be wholly bad since God had created it, and that the Church must therefore do what it could to organize society on Christian principles. Its claim to theocratic powers rested on the new sacramental theory that divine grace operated objectively through the sacraments—*ex opere operato*, St. Thomas said, and not primarily *ex opere operantis*, and that no one save a duly ordained priest could administer them. "There is indeed one universal Church of the faithful, outside which no one at all is saved." The Church mediated salvation. Should it not therefore determine what pertained to salvation and thus direct the whole of society?

Medieval social theorists commonly described society on the analogy of the human body. Society, like the human body, was said to consist of organs or parts (clergy, nobility, workers), each of which had its separate function to perform in the life of the whole. On this theory, society was more than the sum of its individual parts. The individual existed but only as part of a class, which in turn had being only in the life of the larger organism, the *Corpus Christianum*. In this system the only equality was religious equality. Hierarchy or "degree" in society corresponded to hierarchy in the cosmos. It followed from the organic analogy, for obviously some organs have functions qualitatively superior to others. It was also explained by Adam's Fall which introduced sin into the world and doomed the majority of men to a menial existence, which they must endure humbly and patiently. The new bourgeoisie did not fit so easily into this snug pattern, but the theocrats devised rules for them too. Economic conduct was declared to be an aspect of personal conduct and hence subject to Christian morality. Avarice is a deadly sin. The merchant must therefore charge for his product only a "just price" which would enable him to live decently in his station. The value of a pair of shoes is not subjective (to be set by the individual seller) but objective (to be fixed by state, town, or gild according to Christian principles).

Medieval theory emphasized social harmony rather than struggle. The modern social reformer would say that it tried to preserve the *status quo* by making it appear to be the unalterable will of God. However that may

[7] R. H. Tawney, *Religion and the Rise of Capitalism* (London, 1933), p. 19.

be, its stated aim was to eliminate competition between individuals, classes, and states by stressing the common search for God. The ideal was a Christian *Pax Romana. Sacerdotium* (the papal Church) and *regnum* (the temporal rulers, chiefly the Holy Roman Emperor), the former being superior to the latter as the soul excels the body, co-operated to achieve on earth a semblance of the unity of the Godhead.

III

MEDIEVAL Christendom took its philosophy of history from St. Augustine. In the *City of God*—and also in Eusebius of Caesarea's *Ecclesiastical History* and Orosius's *History against the Pagans* —we see history unroll according to divine plan. St. Augustine repudiated the classical conception of time as cyclical recurrence, without beginning or end. "The classical view of the world is a view of things visible, while the Christian 'view' of the world is, after all, not a view but a matter of hope and faith in things invisible." [8] According to St. Augustine, God created time simultaneously with the world (5,611 years before the capture of Rome by the Goths, in Eusebius's reckoning), and would terminate it with the Last Judgment. There were various schemes of periodization: Eusebius posited three epochs of history, Augustine six corresponding to the six days of Creation, with a seventh as the Sabbath of eternity. But all agreed that time had meaning. Like everything else in creation, human history had a definite purpose or goal. And nobody questioned the absolute decisiveness of Eden and Calvary. In Eden, Adam committed the original sin which condemned the whole human race to perdition. Christ's atonement on the cross for man's sin, and the subsequent foundation of the Church, won God's forgiveness and gave man his second chance. The medieval doctrine of the nature of man made it clear, however, that neither the first Adam nor the second (Christ) determined man's fate completely. Despite its protestations to the contrary, the authoritative Church Council of Orange of 529 really took the semi-Pelagian rather than the Augustinian position. By Adam's sin man's free will was declared to be "attenuated" but not extinguished. "This we believe according to the Catholic faith, that with the grace received through baptism aiding and cooperating, all who are baptized in Christ can and ought, *if they will strive faithfully,*[9] to fulfill what pertains to the salvation of the soul." In other words, human choice also counted in the historical drama of salvation. To sum up, the medieval philosophy of history focused on God's Providence and man's pilgrimage toward the ultimate *telos,* paying scant attention to "secondary causes" or secular

[8] Karl Löwith, *Meaning in History* (Chicago, 1949), pp. 165-6.
[9] My italics.

events as such. History was the record, not of progress in earthly happiness, but of man's struggle, inevitably involving suffering, to overcome evil and find God.

It must not be supposed, however, that medieval religious thought dealt only in fear and gloom. The fear is there, no question about it: one has only to look at the forbidding representations of the Apocalypse and the Last Judgment in the cathedrals. But there was also plenty of "Christian optimism," notably in Christian prayer and theology. The note of penitential dread so conspicuous in early medieval prayer gives way to a mood of joyful thanksgiving and mystical love of God in the prayers of Bernard of Clairvaux and St. Francis of Assisi. And theology repudiated the pessimistic teaching of Manicheism which represented the world as the creation of the King of Darkness, and history as a conflict between the forces of darkness and light. The God of Christian theology not only made the world good, he ruled the world—he *cared*, as not even Aristotle's God cared, about what happened to it, and especially to man.

Readings

1. *Fundamental Assumptions*

ST. THOMAS AQUINAS: *On the Contemplative Life* *

> The Dominican Thomas Aquinas (1225–74) was the greatest philosopher and theologian of the medieval Church. He was canonized in 1323 and pronounced the "Angelic Doctor" by Pope Pius V in 1567. The following selections are from the *Summa Theologica* and *Summa contra Gentiles*, his two most important works, of which more below (see under "Christian Aristotelianism").

WE MUST now consider the active life in comparison with the contemplative life, under which head there are four points of inquiry: (1) Which of them is of greater import or excellence? (2) Which of them has the greater merit? (3) Whether the contemplative life is hindered by the active life? (4) Of their order. . . .

. . . Our Lord said (Luke x. 42): *Mary hath chosen the best part, which shall not be taken away from her*. Now Mary figures the contemplative life. Therefore the contemplative life is more excellent than the active.

I answer that, Nothing prevents certain things being more excellent in themselves, whereas they are surpassed by another in some respect. Accordingly we must reply that the contemplative life is simply more excellent than the active: and the Philosopher proves this by eight reasons (*Ethic*. x. 7, 8). The first is, because the contemplative life becomes man according to that which is best in him, namely the intellect, and according

* The quotations from the English translation of the *Summa Theologica* of St. Thomas Aquinas are reproduced with the permission of Benziger Brothers, Inc., publishers and copyright owners. Vol. II, pp. 1942–5.

From St. Thomas Aquinas: *Summa contra Gentiles*, trans. by the English Dominican Fathers, vol. III, pt. I, pp. 78–9. Copyright 1928 by Burns Oates & Washbourne Ltd. Reprinted by permission of Burns Oates & Washbourne Ltd.

to its proper objects, namely things intelligible; whereas the active life is occupied with externals. Hence Rachel, by whom the contemplative life is signified, is interpreted *the vision of the principle*, whereas as Gregory says (*Moral.* vi. 37) the active life is signified by Lia who was blear-eyed. —The second reason is because the contemplative life can be more continuous, although not as regards the highest degree of contemplation, as stated above (Q. 180, A. 8, *ad* 2; Q. 181, A. 4, *ad* 3), wherefore Mary, by whom the contemplative life is signified, is described as *sitting* all the time *at the Lord's feet*.—Thirdly, because the contemplative life is more delightful than the active; wherefore Augustine says (*De Verb. Dom. Serm.* ciii) that *Martha was troubled, but Mary feasted*.—Fourthly, because in the contemplative life man is more self-sufficient, since he needs fewer things for that purpose; wherefore it was said (Luke x. 41): *Martha, Martha, thou art careful and art troubled about many things*.—Fifthly, because the contemplative life is loved more for its own sake, while the active life is directed to something else. Hence it is written (Ps. xxvi. 4): *One thing I have asked of the Lord, this will I seek after, that I may dwell in the house of the Lord all the days of my life, that I may see the delight of the Lord*.—Sixthly, because the contemplative life consists in leisure and rest, according to Ps. xlv. 11, *Be still and see that I am God*.—Seventhly, because the contemplative life is according to Divine things, whereas active life is according to human things; wherefore Augustine says (*De Verb. Dom. Serm.* xiv): "*In the beginning was the Word*": to Him was Mary hearkening: "*The Word was made flesh*": Him was Martha serving.—Eighthly, because the contemplative life is according to that which is most proper to man, namely his intellect; whereas in the works of the active life the lower powers also, which are common to us and brutes, have their part; wherefore (Ps. xxxv. 7) after the words, *Men and beasts Thou wilt preserve, O Lord*, that which is special to man is added (*verse* 10): *In Thy light we shall see light*.

Our Lord adds a ninth reason (Luke x. 42) when He says: *Mary hath chosen the best part, which shall not be taken away from her*, which words Augustine (*De Verb. Dom. Serm.* ciii) expounds thus: *Not,—Thou hast chosen badly but,—She has chosen better. Why better? Listen, —Because it shall not be taken away from her. But the burden of necessity shall at length be taken from thee: whereas the sweetness of truth is eternal*. . . .

Reply Obj. 2. The contemplative life consists in a certain liberty of mind. For Gregory says (*Hom.* iii, *in Ezech.*) that *the contemplative life obtains a certain freedom of mind, for it thinks not of temporal but of eternal things*. And Boëthius says (*De Consol.* v. 2): *The soul of man must needs be more free while it continues to gaze on the Divine mind, and less so when it stoops to bodily things*. Wherefore it is evident that the active life does not directly command the contemplative life, but prescribes certain works of the active life as dispositions to the contemplative life; which it accordingly serves rather than commands. Gregory refers to this when he says (*loc. cit. in Ezech.*) that *the active life is bondage, whereas the contemplative life is freedom.*

Reply Obj. 3. Sometimes a man is called away from the contemplative life to the works of the active life on account of some necessity of the present life, yet not so as to be compelled to forsake contemplation altogether. Hence Augustine says (*De Civ. Dei*, xix. 19): *The love of truth seeks a holy leisure, the demands of charity undertake an honest toil,* the work namely of the active life. *If no one imposes this burden upon us we must devote ourselves to the research and contemplation of truth, but if it be imposed on us, we must bear it because charity demands it of us. Yet even then we must not altogether forsake the delights of truth, lest we deprive ourselves of its sweetness, and this burden overwhelm us.* Hence it is clear that when a person is called from the contemplative to the active life, this is done by way not of subtraction but of addition. . . .

We proceed thus to the Second Article:—
Objection 1. It would seem that the active life is of greater merit than the contemplative. For merit implies relation to meed; and meed is due to labor, according to 1 Cor. iii. 8, *Every man shall receive his own reward according to his own labor.* Now labor is ascribed to the active life, and rest to the contemplative life; for Gregory says (*Hom.* xiv, *in Ezech.*): *Whosoever is converted to God must first of all sweat from labor, i.e. he must take Lia, that afterwards he may rest in the embraces of Rachel so as to see the principle.* Therefore the active life is of greater merit than the contemplative. . . .

Reply Obj. 1. External labor conduces to the increase of the accidental reward; but the increase of merit with regard to the essential reward consists chiefly in charity, whereof external labor borne for Christ's sake is a sign. Yet a much more expressive sign thereof is shown when a man, renouncing whatsoever pertains to this life, delights to occupy himself entirely with Divine contemplation. . . .

. . . Gregory says (*Moral.* vi. 37): *Those who wish to hold the fortress of contemplation, must first of all train in the camp of action.*

I answer that, The active life may be considered from two points of view. First, as regards the attention to and practice of external works: and thus it is evident that the active life hinders the contemplative, in so far as it is impossible for one to be busy with external action and at the same time give oneself to Divine contemplation. Secondly, active life may be considered as quieting and directing the internal passions of the soul; and from this point of view the active life is a help to the contemplative, since the latter is hindered by the inordinateness of the internal passions. Hence Gregory says (*loc. cit.*): *Those who wish to hold the fortress of contemplation must first of all train in the camp of action. Thus after careful study they will learn whether they no longer wrong their neighbor, whether they bear with equanimity the wrongs their neighbors do to them, whether their soul is neither overcome with joy in the presence of temporal goods, nor cast down with too great a sorrow when those goods are withdrawn. In this way they will know when they withdraw within themselves, in order to explore spiritual things, whether they no longer carry with them the shadows of the things corporeal, or, if these follow them, whether they prudently drive them away.* Hence the work of the active life conduces to the contemplative, by quelling the interior passions which give rise to the phantasms whereby contemplation is hindered.

* * *

Accordingly if man's ultimate happiness consists not in external things, which are called goods of chance; nor in goods of the body; nor in goods of the soul, as regards the sensitive faculty; nor as regards the intellective faculty, in the practice of moral virtue; nor as regards intellectual virtue in those which are concerned about action, namely art and prudence; it remains for us to conclude that man's ultimate happiness consists in the contemplation of the truth.

For this operation alone is proper to man, and none of the other animals communicates with him therein.

Again. This is not directed to anything further as its end: since the contemplation of the truth is sought for its own sake.

Again. By this operation man is united to things above him, by becoming like them: because of all human actions this alone is both in God and in separate substances. Also, by this operation man comes into contact with those higher beings, through knowing them in any way whatever.

Besides, man is more self-sufficing for this operation, seeing that he stands in little need of the help of external things in order to perform it.

Further. All other human operations seem to be directed to this as their end. Because perfect contemplation requires that the body should be disencumbered, and to this effect are directed all the products of art that are necessary for life. Moreover, it requires freedom from the disturbance caused by the passions, which is achieved by means of the moral virtues and prudence; and freedom from external disturbance, to which all the regulations of the civil life are directed. So that, if we consider the matter rightly, we shall see that all human occupations are brought into the service of those who contemplate the truth. Now, it is not possible that man's ultimate happiness consist in contemplation based on the understanding of first principles: for this is most imperfect, as being universal and containing potential knowledge of things. Moreover, it is the beginning and not the end of human study, and comes to us from nature, and not through the study of the truth. Nor does it consist in contemplation based on the sciences that have the lowest things for their object: since happiness must consist in an operation of the intellect in relation to the highest objects of intelligence. It follows then that man's ultimate happiness consists in wisdom, based on the consideration of divine things. It is therefore evident by way of induction that man's ultimate happiness consists solely in the contemplation of God, which conclusion was proved above by arguments.

Statutes of New College, Oxford *

The statutes of New College, Oxford, dated 1400, illustrate the normally accepted hierarchy of knowledge in the Middle Ages. Although twelve of the seventy fellows were assigned to civil law, astronomy, and medicine, the dominance of sacred studies is clearly manifest. Moreover, all the fellows were "scholars clerks," clerks who at the age of fifteen took the clerical tonsure. The statutes of this "new" college were the model for English college statutes up to the Reformation.

Book of the Statutes of the College of the Blessed Mary of Winchester in Oxford, commonly called New College.

IN THE name of the Holy and Undivided Trinity, Father, Son and Holy Ghost, also of the most blessed Mary the glorious Virgin and of all the Saints of God. We William of Wykeham, by divine sufferance bishop of Winchester . . . , out of the goods of fortune, which out of the grace of His fulness He has given us abundantly in this life, have with apostolic and royal authority ordained, instituted, founded and established two everlasting colleges; namely, one everlasting college of poor and needy scholars clerks who are to study and become proficient in divers sciences and faculties in the school of the University of Oxford in the diocese of Lincoln, commonly called Seinte Mary College of Wynchestre in Oxenford; and another everlasting college of other poor and needy scholars clerks who are to study grammar near the city of Winchester, likewise called Seinte Mary College of Wynchestre, to the praise, glory and honour of the name of the Crucified and the most glorious Mary His mother, the maintenance and exaltation of the Christian faith, the profit

* From Arthur F. Leach: *Educational Charters and Documents 598 to 1909*, pp. 349–53, 355–7. Copyright 1911 by Cambridge University Press. Reprinted by permission of Cambridge University Press.

of Holy Church, the increase of divine worship, and the liberal arts, sciences and faculties, as in our deeds and letters patent made for the ordering, institution and foundation of the same colleges more fully appears. And so we wishing to make establish and also ordain certain things which now occur to us which we think necessary and useful for our said college at Oxford for the scholars clerks and other persons and the possessions and goods of the same college and their healthful regulation, and which are thought to regard their learning, increase and profit, first invoking the name of Christ, for their future and everlasting remembrance proceed thus.

Rubric 1. Of the whole number of the scholars clerks, priests, and other ministers of the chapel of the said college at Oxford, and the particular number of those studying in the same in different sciences and faculties.

In the first place then, that the Holy Writ or page, the mother and mistress of all the other sciences, may more freely and beyond the rest extend its tents, and that the faculty of both laws, namely canon and civil, may peacefully fight alongside of her, and that philosophy may not be wanting to give its dye to the rest, we decree and also ordain that our said college at Oxford shall consist in and of the number of one warden and seventy poor needy scholars clerks to study in the said sciences and faculties, and as the college itself will consist of divers persons whom it will collect into one, so in the same college there shall, by God's grace, flourish different sciences and faculties, namely, of philosophy, civil and canon law, and above all that Christ may be preached more fervently and frequently, and that the faith and worship of God's name may be increased and more strongly supported, beyond all of holy theology; that so the praise of God may be spread, the church directed, and strength and fervour of the Christian religion grow hotter, and all knowledge and virtue be increased in strength; also that we may relieve in part, though in truth we cannot wholly cure, that general disease of the clerical army, which we have seen grievously wounded through the want of clergy caused by plagues, wars and other miseries of the world, in compassion for its sad desolation; to this in our small way we willingly spend our labours. . . .

We have therefore decreed that of the scholars clerks aforesaid it shall be the duty of ten, and they shall be bound, to attend lectures on civil law, and another ten on canon law and to study effectively in the three separate law faculties, unless this is impracticable for the reasons stated below. . . .

[Similar provision that if the number of canonists is not full the number may be made up with civilians, so long as there are not more than twenty altogether in both laws.]

The rest of the number, namely fifty, shall severally diligently attend lectures in and learn arts, or philosophy and theology. We allow however that two of them may employ themselves and attend to the science of medicine, as long as he shall be an actually regent doctor in that faculty, and two others the science of astronomy only.

We do not wish however that anyone should turn to the faculty of medicine without the will and consent of the warden and the dean of the faculty of theology, and that only if he has first really incepted in the faculty or science of arts, and completed the course prescribed in the University of Oxford. And we wish that these students in the faculty of medicine, unless actually regent doctors in the same faculty, shall pass to the study of theology and become proficient in the same;

Decreeing and also ordaining that above and beyond the number of one warden and seventy scholars aforesaid there shall be always and continuously ten priests and three clerks, paid servants of the chapel aforesaid, daily serving in the same, of sufficient learning and good standing and upright life, having good voices and sufficiently instructed in reading and singing; also sixteen boys sufficiently taught to read and sing, as is below more fully expressed in our other statutes.

ST. AUGUSTINE: *Enchiridion* *

St. Augustine (354–430) is well known as one of the four great teachers or Fathers of Latin Christendom. Together with Ambrose, Jerome, and Pope Gregory the Great he exerted, through his voluminous writings, a tremendous influence on medieval thought. His career from teacher of Latin rhetoric to Christian convert is recorded in his famous *Confessions*. He became bishop of Hippo in north Africa and composed numerous works of Christian apologetics, including the *City of God* which demonstrated God's providence in history. The *Enchiridion*, written in 421 and widely read in the Middle Ages, was a "handbook" of Christian doctrine, an epitome of the Christian epic.

Chapter IV. *The questions propounded by Laurentius.*

You are anxious, you say, that I should write a sort of handbook for you, which you might always keep beside you, containing answers to the questions you put, viz.: what ought to be man's chief end in life; what he ought, in view of the various heresies, chiefly to avoid; to what extent

* St. Augustine: *Works*, ed. by Rev. Marcus Dods (Edinburgh: T. & T. Clark; 1871–7), vol. IX, pp. 177–81, 194–5, 200, 214–15, 220–1, 235, 244, 253, 257–8.

religion is supported by reason; what there is in reason that lends no support to faith, when faith stands alone; what is the starting-point, what the goal, of religion; what is the sum of the whole body of doctrine; what is the sure and proper foundation of the catholic faith. Now, undoubtedly, you will know the answers to all these questions, if you know thoroughly the proper objects of faith, hope, and love. For these must be the chief, nay, the exclusive objects of pursuit in religion. He who speaks against these is either a total stranger to the name of Christ, or is a heretic. These are to be defended by reason, which must have its starting point either in the bodily senses or in the intuitions of the mind. And what we have neither had experience of through our bodily senses, nor have been able to reach through the intellect, must undoubtedly be believed on the testimony of those witnesses by whom the Scriptures, justly called divine, were written; and who by divine assistance were enabled, either through bodily sense or intellectual perception, to see or to foresee the things in question.

Chapter V. *Brief answers to these questions.*

Moreover, when the mind has been imbued with the first elements of that faith which worketh by love, it endeavours by purity of life to attain unto sight, where the pure and perfect in heart know that unspeakable beauty, the full vision of which is supreme happiness. Here surely is an answer to your question as to what is the starting-point, and what the goal: we begin in faith, and are made perfect by sight. This also is the sum of the whole body of doctrine. But the sure and proper foundation of the catholic faith is Christ. "For other foundation," says the apostle, "can no man lay than that is laid, which is Jesus Christ."

Chapter VII. *The Creed and the Lord's Prayer demand the exercise of faith, hope, and love.*

For you have the Creed and the Lord's Prayer. What can be briefer to hear or to read? What easier to commit to memory? When, as the result of sin, the human race was groaning under a heavy load of misery, and was in urgent need of divine compassion, one of the prophets, anticipating the time of God's grace, declared: "And it shall come to pass, that whosoever shall call on the name of the Lord shall be delivered." Hence the Lord's Prayer. But the apostle, when, for the purpose of commending this very grace, he had quoted this prophetic testimony, immediately added: "How then shall they call on Him in whom they have not believed?" Hence the Creed. In these two you have those three graces exemplified: faith believes, hope and love pray. But without faith the two last cannot exist, and therefore we may say that faith also prays. Whence it is written: "How shall they call on Him in whom they have not believed?"

> Chapter IX. *What we are to believe. In regard to nature it is not necessary for the Christian to know more than that the goodness of the Creator is the cause of all things.*

When, then, the question is asked what we are to believe in regard to religion, it is not necessary to probe into the nature of things, as was done by those whom the Greeks call *physici;* nor need we be in alarm lest the Christian should be ignorant of the force and number of the elements,—the motion, and order, and eclipses of the heavenly bodies; the form of the heavens, the species and the natures of animals, plants, stones, fountains, rivers, mountains; about chronology and distances; the signs of coming storms; and a thousand other things which those philosophers either have found out, or think they have found out. For even these men themselves, endowed though they are with so much genius, burning with zeal, abounding in leisure, tracking some things by the aid of human conjecture, searching into others with the aids of history and experience, have not found out all things; and even their boasted discoveries are oftener mere guesses than certain knowledge. It is enough for the Christian to believe that the only cause of all created things, whether heavenly or earthly, whether visible or invisible, is the goodness of the Creator, the one true God; and that nothing exists but Himself that does not derive its existence from Him; and that He is the Trinity—to wit, the Father, and the Son begotten of the Father, and the Holy Spirit proceeding from the same Father, but one and the same Spirit of Father and Son.

> Chapter XXVI. *Through Adam's sin his whole posterity were corrupted, and were born under the penalty of death, which he had incurred.*

Thence, after his sin, he was driven into exile, and by his sin the whole race of which he was the root was corrupted in him, and thereby subjected to the penalty of death. And so it happens that all descended from him, and from the woman who had led him into sin, and was condemned at the same time with him,—being the off-spring of carnal lust on which the same punishment of disobedience was visited,—were tainted with the original sin, and were by it drawn through divers errors and sufferings into that last and endless punishment which they suffer in common with the fallen angels, their corrupters and masters, and the partakers of their doom. And thus "by one man sin entered into the world, and death by sin; and so death passed upon all men, for that all have sinned." By "the world" the apostle, of course, means in this place the whole human race.

Chapter XXVII. *The state of misery to which Adam's sin reduced mankind, and the restoration effected through the mercy of God.*

Thus, then, matters stood. The whole mass of the human race was under condemnation, was lying steeped and wallowing in misery, and was being tossed from one form of evil to another, and, having joined the faction of the fallen angels, was paying the well-merited penalty of that impious rebellion. For whatever the wicked freely do through blind and unbridled lust, and whatever they suffer against their will in the way of open punishment, this all evidently pertains to the just wrath of God. But the goodness of the Creator never fails either to supply life and vital power to the wicked angels (without which their existence would soon come to an end); or, in the case of mankind, who spring from a condemned and corrupt stock, to impart form and life to their seed, to fashion their members, and through the various seasons of their life, and in the different parts of the earth, to quicken their senses, and bestow upon them the nourishment they need. For He judged it better to bring good out of evil, than not to permit any evil to exist.

Chapter XXXIII. *Men, being by nature the children of wrath, needed a Mediator. In what sense God is said to be angry.*

. . . Now, as men were lying under this wrath by reason of their original sin, and as this original sin was the more heavy and deadly in proportion to the number and magnitude of the actual sins which were added to it, there was need for a Mediator, that is, for a reconciler, who, by the offering of one sacrifice, of which all the sacrifices of the law and the prophets were types, should take away this wrath. Wherefore the apostle says: "For if, when we were enemies, we were reconciled to God by the death of His Son, much more, being reconciled, we shall be saved by His life." Now when God is said to be angry, we do not attribute to Him such a disturbed feeling as exists in the mind of an angry man; but we call His just displeasure against sin by the name "anger," a word transferred by analogy from human emotions. But our being reconciled to God through a Mediator, and receiving the Holy Spirit, so that we who were enemies are made sons ("For as many as are led by the Spirit of God, they are the sons of God"): this is the grace of God through Jesus Christ our Lord.

Chapter LVI. *The Holy Spirit and the Church. The Church is the temple of God.*

And now, having spoken of Jesus Christ, the only Son of God, our Lord, with the brevity suitable to a confession of our faith, we go on to say that we believe also in the Holy Ghost,—thus completing the Trinity which constitutes the Godhead. Then we mention the Holy Church. And thus we are made to understand that the intelligent creation, which constitutes the free Jerusalem, ought to be subordinate in the order of speech to the Creator, the Supreme Trinity: for all that is said of the man Christ Jesus has reference, of course, to the unity of the person of the Only-begotten. Therefore the true order of the Creed demanded that the Church should be made subordinate to the Trinity, as the house to Him who dwells in it, the temple to God who occupies it, and the city to its builder. And we are here to understand the whole Church, not that part of it only which wanders as a stranger on the earth, praising the name of God from the rising of the sun to the going down of the same, and singing a new song of deliverance from its old captivity; but that part also which has always from its creation remained stedfast to God in heaven, and has never experienced the misery consequent upon a fall. This part is made up of the holy angels, who enjoy uninterrupted happiness; and (as it is bound to do) it renders assistance to the part which is still wandering among strangers: for these two parts shall be one in the fellowship of eternity, and now they are one in the bonds of love, the whole having been ordained for the worship of the one God.

Chapter LXIV. *Pardon of sin extends over the whole mortal life of the saints, which, though free from crime, is not free from sin.*

But the angels even now are at peace with us when our sins are pardoned. Hence, in the order of the Creed, after the mention of the Holy Church is placed the remission of sins. For it is by this that the Church on earth stands: it is through this that what had been lost, and was found, is saved from being lost again. For, setting aside the grace of baptism, which is given as an antidote to original sin, so that what our birth imposes upon us, our new birth relieves us from (this grace, however, takes away all the actual sins also that have been committed in thought, word, and deed): setting aside, then, this great act of favour, whence commences man's restoration, and in which all our guilt, both original and actual, is washed away, the rest of our life from the time that we have the use of reason provides constant occasion for the remission of sins, however great may be our advance in righteousness. For the sons of God, as long as they live in this body of death, are in conflict with death. And although it is truly said of them, "As many as are led by the Spirit of God, they are the sons of God," yet they are led by the Spirit of God, and as the sons of God advance towards God under this drawback, that they are led also by their own spirit, weighted as it is by the corruptible body; and that, as the sons of men, under the influence of human affections, they fall back to their old level, and so sin. There is a difference, however. For although every crime is a sin, every sin is not a crime. And so we say that the life of holy men, as long as they remain in this mortal body, may be found without crime; but, as the Apostle John says, "If we say that we have no sin, we deceive ourselves, and the truth is not in us."

Chapter LXV. *God pardons sins, but on condition of penitence, certain times for which have been fixed by the law of the Church.*

But even crimes themselves, however great, may be remitted in the Holy Church; and the mercy of God is never to be despaired of by men who truly repent, each according to the measure of his sin. And in the act of repentance, where a crime has been committed of such a nature as to cut off the sinner from the body of Christ, we are not to take account so much of the measure of time as of the measure of sorrow; for a broken and a contrite heart God doth not despise. But as the grief of one heart is frequently hid from another, and is not made known to others by words or other signs, when it is manifest to Him of whom it is said, "My groaning is not hid from Thee," those who govern the Church have rightly appointed times of penitence, that the Church in which the sins are remitted may be satisfied; and outside the Church sins are not remitted. For the Church alone has received the pledge of the Holy Spirit, without which there is no remission of sins—such, at least, as brings the pardoned to eternal life.

Chapter LXXXIV. *The resurrection of the body gives rise to numerous questions.*

Now, as to the resurrection of the body,—not a resurrection such as some have had, who come back to life for a time and died again, but a resurrection to eternal life, as the body of Christ Himself rose again,—I do not see how I can discuss the matter briefly, and at the same time give a satisfactory answer to all the questions that are ordinarily raised about it. Yet that the bodies of all men—both those who have been born and those who shall be born, both those who have died and those who shall die—shall be raised again, no Christian ought to have the shadow of a doubt.

Chapter XCIX. *As God's mercy is free, so His judgments are just, and cannot be gainsaid.*

Now after commending the mercy of God, saying, "So it is not of him that willeth, nor of him that runneth, but of God that showeth mercy," that he might commend His justice also (for the man who does not obtain mercy finds, not iniquity, but justice, there being no iniquity with God), he immediately adds: "For the scripture saith unto Pharaoh, Even for this same purpose have I raised thee up, that I might show my power in thee, and that my name might be declared throughout all the earth." And then he draws a conclusion that applies to both, that is, both to His mercy and His justice: "Therefore hath He mercy on whom He will have mercy, and whom He will He hardeneth." "He hath mercy" of His great goodness, "He hardeneth" without any injustice; so that neither can he that is pardoned glory in any merit of his own, nor he that is condemned complain of anything but his own demerit. For it is grace alone that separates the redeemed from the lost, all having been involved in one common perdition through their common origin.

Chapter CXI. *After the resurrection there shall be two distinct kingdoms, one of eternal happiness, the other of eternal misery.*

After the resurrection, however, when the final, universal judgment has been completed, there shall be two kingdoms, each with its own distinct boundaries, the one Christ's, the other the Devil's; the one consisting of the good, the other of the bad,—both, however, consisting of angels and men. The former shall have no will, the latter no power, to sin, and neither shall have any power to choose death; but the former shall live truly and happily in eternal life, the latter shall drag a miserable existence in eternal death without the power of dying; for the life and the death shall both be without end. But among the former there shall be degrees of happiness, one being more pre-eminently happy than another; and among the latter there shall be degrees of misery, one being more endurably miserable than another.

Chapter CXVIII. *The four stages of the Christian's life, and the four corresponding stages of the Church's history.*

When, sunk in the darkest depths of ignorance, man lives according to the flesh, undisturbed by any struggle of reason or conscience, this is his first state. Afterwards, when through the law has come the knowledge of sin, and the Spirit of God has not yet interposed His aid, man, striving to live according to the law, is thwarted in his efforts and falls into conscious sin, and so, being overcome of sin, becomes its slave ("for of whom a man is overcome, of the same is he brought in bondage"); and thus the effect produced by the knowledge of the commandment is this, that sin worketh in man all manner of concupiscence, and he is involved in the additional guilt of wilful transgression, and that is fulfilled which is written: "The law entered that the offence might abound." This is man's second state. But if God has regard to him, and inspires him with faith in God's help, and the Spirit of God begins to work in him, then the mightier power of love strives against the power of the flesh; and although there is still in the man's own nature a power that fights against him (for his disease is not completely cured), yet he lives the life of the just by faith, and lives in righteousness so far as he does not yield to evil lust, but conquers it by the love of holiness. This is the third state of a man of good hope; and he who by stedfast piety advances in this course, shall attain at last to peace, that peace which, after this life is over, shall be perfected in the repose of the spirit, and finally in the resurrection of the body. Of these four different stages the first is before the law, the second is under the law, the third is under grace, and the fourth is in full and perfect peace. Thus, too, has the history of God's people been ordered according to His pleasure who disposeth all things in number, and measure, and weight.

St. Thomas Aquinas: *On the Sacraments and the Priesthood* *

. . . Augustine says (*Contra Faust.* xix): *It is impossible to keep men together in one religious denomination, whether true or false, except they be united by means of visible signs or sacraments.* But it is necessary for salvation that men be united together in the name of the one true religion. Therefore sacraments are necessary for man's salvation.

I answer that, Sacraments are necessary unto man's salvation for three reasons. The first is taken from the condition of human nature which is such that it has to be led by things corporeal and sensible to things spiritual and intelligible. Now it belongs to Divine providence to provide for each one according as its condition requires. Divine wisdom, therefore, fittingly provides man with means of salvation, in the shape of corporeal and sensible signs that are called sacraments.

The second reason is taken from the state of man who in sinning subjected himself by his affections to corporeal things. Now the healing remedy should be given to a man so as to reach the part affected by disease. Consequently it was fitting that God should provide man with

* The quotations from the English translation of the *Summa Theologica* of St. Thomas Aquinas are reproduced with the permission of Benziger Brothers, Inc., publishers and copyright owners. Vol. II, p. 2352; vol. III, pp. 2626, 2635.

a spiritual medicine by means of certain corporeal signs; for if man were offered spiritual things without a veil, his mind being taken up with the material world would be unable to apply itself to them.

The third reason is taken from the fact that man is prone to direct his activity chiefly towards material things. Lest, therefore, it should be too hard for man to be drawn away entirely from bodily actions, bodily exercise was offered to him in the sacraments, by which he might be trained to avoid superstitious practices, consisting in the worship of demons, and all manner of harmful action, consisting in sinful deeds.

*   *   *

. . . It is written (Matth. xvi. 19): *To thee will I give the keys of the kingdom of heaven.*

Further, every dispenser should have the keys of the things that he dispenses. But the ministers of the Church are the dispensers of the divine mysteries, as appears from 1 Cor. iv. 1. Therefore they ought to have the keys.

I answer that, In material things a key is an instrument for opening a door. Now the door of the kingdom is closed to us through sin, both as to the stain and as to the debt of punishment. Wherefore the power of removing this obstacle is called a key. Now this power is in the Divine Trinity by authority; hence some say that God has the key of *authority*. But Christ Man had the power to remove the above obstacle, through the merit of His Passion, which also is said to open the door; hence some say that He has the keys of *excellence*. And since *the sacraments of which the Church is built, flowed from the side of Christ while He lay asleep on the cross,* the efficacy of the Passion abides in the sacraments of the Church. Wherefore a certain power for the removal of the aforesaid obstacle is bestowed on the ministers of the Church, who are the dispensers of the sacraments, not by their own, but by a Divine power and by the Passion of Christ. This power is called metaphorically the Church's key, and is the key of *ministry*.

*   *   *

. . . Ambrose says (*De Poenit.* i): *This right,* viz. of binding and loosing, *is granted to priests alone.*

Further, by receiving the power of the keys, a man is set up between the people and God. But this belongs to the priest alone, who *is ordained . . . in the things that appertain to God, that he may offer up gifts and sacrifices for sins* (Heb. v. 1). Therefore only priests have the keys.

I answer that, There are two kinds of key. One reaches to heaven itself directly, by remitting sin and thus removing the obstacles to the entrance into heaven; and this is called the key of *Order*. Priests alone have this key, because they alone are ordained for the people in the things which appertain to God directly. The other key reaches to heaven, not directly but through the medium of the Church Militant. By this key a man goes to heaven, since, by its means, a man is shut out from or admitted to the fellowship of the Church Militant, by excommunication or absolution. This is called the key of *jurisdiction* in the external court, wherefore even those who are not priests can have this key, e.g. archdeacons, bishops elect, and others who can excommunicate. But it is not properly called a key of heaven, but a disposition thereto.

WILLIAM DURANDUS: *The Symbolism of Churches and Church Ornaments* *

William Durandus (*c.* 1220–96) was a prominent churchman of his time, a teacher and writer on canon law, an office-holder under two popes, Bishop of Mende in 1286. His *Rationale Divinorum Officiorum*, composed toward the end of his life, epitomizes the symbolical thinking of the Middle Ages.

ALL things, as many as pertain to offices and matters ecclesiastical, be full of divine significations and mysteries, and overflow with a celestial sweetness. . . .

*   *   *

Now, in Holy Scriptures there be divers senses: as historic, allegoric, tropologic, and anagogic. . . .

History is *things signified by words:* as when a plain relation is made how certain events took place: as when the children of Israel, after their deliverence from Egypt, made a Tabernacle to the LORD. . . .

Allegory is when one thing is said and another meant: as when by one deed another is intended: which other thing, if it be visible, the whole is simply an allegory, if invisible and heavenly, an *anagoge.* Also an allegory is when one state of things is described by another: as when the Patience of Christ, and the Sacraments of the Church is set forth by mystical words or deeds. As in that place: THERE SHALL COME FORTH A ROD OF THE STEM OF JESSE, AND A BRANCH SHALL GROW OUT OF HIS ROOTS: which is, in plain language, The Virgin Mary shall be born of the family of David, who was the son of Jesse. . . .

Tropology is an injunction unto morality: or a moral speech, either with a symbolical or an obvious bearing, devised to evince and instruct our behaviour. *Symbolical;* as where he saith, LET THY GARMENTS BE AL-

* William Durandus: *The Symbolism of Churches and Church Ornaments,* trans. by J. M. Neale and B. Webb (Leeds: T. W. Green; 1843, pp. 3, 8–10, 24–5, 53, 58–60, 87–8, 96, 149.

WAYS WHITE: AND LET THE OIL OF THY HEAD NEVER FAIL. That is, let all thy works be pure, and charity never fail from thy mind. And again, It is fit that David should slay the Goliath within us: that is, that humbleness may subdue our pride. *Obvious* as in that saying "DEAL THY BREAD TO THE HUNGRY."...

Anagoge is so called from *ana*, which is upwards, and *goge*, a leading: as it were an upward leading. Whence the anagogic sense is that which leadeth from the visible to the invisible: as light, made the first day, signifieth a thing invisible, namely the angelic nature which was made in the beginning. *Anagoge*, therefore, is that sense which leadeth the mind upwards to heavenly things: that is to the TRINITY and the Orders of Angels, and speaketh concerning future rewards, and the future life which is in the Heaven: and it useth both obvious and mystical expressions; obvious, as in that saying, BLESSED ARE THE PURE IN HEART: FOR THEY SHALL SEE GOD: mystical, as that, BLESSED ARE THEY THAT HAVE MADE WHITE THEIR ROBES: THAT THEY MAY HAVE RIGHT UNTO THE TREE OF LIFE, AND ENTER IN THROUGH THE GATE INTO THE CITY. Which signifieth, Blessed are they who make pure their thoughts, that they may have a right to see GOD, WHO IS THE WAY, THE TRUTH, AND THE LIFE: and after the example of the Fathers, enter into the kingdom of heaven.

* * *

The arrangement of a material church resembleth that of the human body: the Chancel, or place where the Altar is, representeth the head: the Transepts, the hands and arms, and the remainder,—towards the west,—the rest of the body. The sacrifice of the Altar denoteth the vows of the heart. Furthermore, according to Richard de Sancto Victore, the arrangement of a church typifieth the three states in the Church: of virgins, of the continent, of the married. The Sanctuary is smaller than the Chancel, and this than the Nave: because the virgins are fewer in number than the continent, and these than the married. And the Sanctuary is more holy than the Chancel; and the Chancel than the Nave: because the order of virgins is more worthy than that of the continent, and the continent more worthy than the married.

Furthermore, the church consisteth of four walls, that is, is built on the doctrine of the Four Evangelists; and hath length, breadth, and height: the height representeth courage,—the length fortitude, which patiently endureth till it attaineth its heavenly Home; the breadth is charity, which, with long suffering, loveth its friends in GOD, and its foes for GOD; and again, its height is the hope of future retribution, which despiseth prosperity and adversity, hoping TO SEE THE GOODNESS OF THE LORD IN THE LAND OF THE LIVING.

Again, in the Temple of GOD, the foundation is Faith, which is conversant with unseen things: the roof, Charity, WHICH COVERETH A MUL-

TITUDE OF SINS. The door, Obedience, of which the LORD saith, IF THOU WILT ENTER INTO LIFE, KEEP THE COMMANDMENTS. The pavement, humility, of which the Psalmist saith, MY SOUL CLEAVETH TO THE PAVEMENT.

*   *   *

Pictures and ornaments in churches are the lessons and the scriptures of the laity. Whence Gregory: It is one thing to adore a picture, and another by means of a picture historically to learn what should be adored. For what writing supplieth to him which can read, that doth a picture supply to him which is unlearned, and can only look. Because they who are uninstructed, thus see what they ought to follow: and *things* are read, though letters be unknown. . . .

Represented in the Cradle, the artist commemorateth His Nativity: on the bosom of His Mother, His Childhood: the painting or carving His Cross signifieth His Passion: (and sometimes the sun and moon are represented on the Cross itself, as suffering an eclipse:) when depicted on a flight of steps, His Ascension is signified: when on a state or lofty throne, We be taught His present power: as if He said, ALL THINGS ARE GIVEN TO ME IN HEAVEN AND IN EARTH: according to that saying, I SAW THE LORD SITTING UPON HIS THRONE: that is, reigning over the angels: as the text, WHICH SITTETH UPON THE CHERUBIN. . . .

Sometimes the twenty-four Elders are painted around the Saviour, according to the Vision of the said John, with WHITE GARMENTS, AND THEY HAVE ON THEIR HEADS CROWNS OF GOLD. By which are signified the Doctors of the Old and New Testament; which are twelve, on account of Faith in the Holy Trinity preached through the *four* quarters of the world: or twenty-four, on account of good works, and the keeping of the Gospels.

*   *   *

You must know that bells, by the sound of which the people assembleth together to the church to hear, and the Clergy to preach, IN THE MORNING THE MERCY OF GOD AND HIS POWER BY NIGHT, do signify the silver trumpets, by which under the Old Law the people was called together unto sacrifice. . . .

Also bells be rung at processions, that the evil spirits may hear them and flee, as shall be said hereafter. For they do fear when the trumpets of the Church Militant, that is the bells, be heard, like as a Tyrant doth fear when he heareth on his own land the trumpets of any potent king his foe.

*   *   *

Without the reliques of Saints, or, where they cannot be had, without the Body of CHRIST, there is no consecration of a fixed Altar: but there may be of a travelling or portable one. Reliques in truth are, after the example of both Testaments, evidences of the suffering of Martyrs and lives of Confessors; which things be left to us as examples. These we enclose in a case, because we retain them, in order to imitate them, in our heart. . . .

But the solemn carrying of reliques is in imitation of what is read in the XXV chapter of Exodus; In the ark of the Testament there were two golden rings, going through the whole thickness of the wood, and through these were put the staves of Shittim wood overlaid with gold, by which the ark was borne. And before the Bishop entereth the church he goeth round it with the reliques in order that they may be protectors of that church.

2. *Aspects of Medieval Philosophy and Cosmology*

A. AUGUSTINIANISM

St. Augustine: *Confessions* *

> Medieval thought was deeply Platonic. The following selections from the *Confessions* show how St. Augustine approached Christianity by way of Neoplatonism. They also epitomize his doctrine of illumination, the psychological ascent of the soul from the knowledge of temporal things to the contemplation of the Platonic forms.

> *Faith is the basis of human life; man cannot discover that truth which Holy Scripture has disclosed.*

FROM this, however, being led to prefer the Catholic doctrine, I felt that it was with more moderation and honesty that it commanded things to be believed that were not demonstrated (whether it was that they could be demonstrated, but not to any one, or could not be demonstrated at all), than was the method of the Manichaeans, where our credulity was mocked by audacious promise of knowledge, and then so many most fabulous and absurd things were forced upon belief because they were not capable of demonstration. After that, O Lord, Thou, by little and little, with most gentle and most merciful hand, drawing and calming my heart, didst persuade me,—taking into consideration what a multiplic-

* St. Augustine: *Works*, ed. by Rev. Marcus Dods (Edinburgh: T. & T. Clark; 1871–77), vol. XIV, pp. 117–19, 157–8, 162–5, 169–73.

ity of things which I had never seen, nor was present when they were enacted, like so many of the things in secular history, and so many accounts of places and cities which I had not seen; so many of friends, so many of physicians, so many now of these men, now of those, which unless we should believe, we should do nothing at all in this life; lastly, with how unalterable an assurance I believed of what parents I was born, which it would have been impossible for me to know otherwise than by hearsay,—taking into consideration all this, Thou persuadedst me that not they who believed Thy books (which, with so great authority, Thou hast established among nearly all nations), but those who believed them not were to be blamed; and that those men were not to be listened unto who should say to me, "How dost thou know that those Scriptures were imparted unto mankind by the Spirit of the one true and most true God?" For it was this same thing that was most of all to be believed, since no wranglings of blasphemous questions, whereof I had read so many amongst the self-contradicting philosophers, could once wring the belief from me that Thou art,—whatsoever Thou wert, though what I knew not,—or that the government of human affairs belongs to Thee.

Thus much I believed, at one time more strongly than another, yet did I ever believe both that Thou wert, and hadst a care of us, although I was ignorant both what was to be thought of Thy substance, and what way led, or led back to Thee. Seeing, then, that we were too weak by unaided reason to find out the truth, and for this cause needed the authority of the holy writings, I had now begun to believe that Thou wouldest by no means have given such excellency of authority to those Scriptures throughout all lands, had it not been Thy will thereby to be believed in, and thereby sought.

*　　　*　　　*

Divine things are the more clearly manifested to him who withdraws into the recesses of his heart.

And being thence warned to return to myself, I entered into my inward self, Thou leading me on; and I was able to do it, for Thou wert become my helper. And I entered, and with the eye of my soul (such as it was) saw above the same eye of my soul, above my mind, the Unchangeable Light. Not this common light, which all flesh may look upon, nor, as it were, a greater one of the same kind, as though the brightness of this should be much more resplendent, and with its greatness fill up all things. Not like this was that light, but different, yea, very different from all these. Nor was it above my mind as oil is above water, nor as heaven above earth; but above it was, because it made me, and I below it, because I was made by it. He who knows the Truth knows that Light; and he that knows it knoweth eternity. Love knoweth it.

*　　　*　　　*

Above his changeable mind, he discovers the unchangeable Author of Truth.

And I marvelled that I now loved Thee, and no phantasm instead of Thee. And yet I did not merit to enjoy my God, but was transported to Thee by Thy beauty, and presently torn away from Thee by mine own weight, sinking with grief into these inferior things. This weight was carnal custom. Yet was there a remembrance of Thee with me; nor did I any way doubt that there was one to whom I might cleave, but that I was not yet one who could cleave unto Thee; for that the body which is corrupted presseth down the soul, and the earthly dwelling weigheth down the mind which thinketh upon many things. And most certain I was that Thy "invisible things from the creation of the world are clearly seen, being understood by the things that are made, even Thy eternal power and Godhead." For, inquiring whence it was that I admired the beauty of bodies whether celestial or terrestrial, and what supported me in judging correctly on things mutable, and pronouncing, "This should be thus, this not,"—inquiring, then, whence I so judged, seeing I did so judge, I had found the unchangeable and true eternity of Truth, above my changeable mind. And thus, by degrees, I passed from bodies to the soul, which makes use of the senses of the body to perceive; and thence to its inward faculty, to which the bodily senses represent outward things, and up to which reach the capabilities of beasts; and thence, again, I passed on to the reasoning faculty, unto which whatever is received from the senses of the body is referred to be judged, which also, finding itself to be variable in me, raised itself up to its own intelligence, and from habit drew away my thoughts, withdrawing itself from the crowds of contradictory phantasms; that so it might find out that light by which it was besprinkled, when, without all doubting, it cried out, "that the unchangeable was to be preferred before the changeable;" whence also it knew that unchangeable, which, unless it had in some way known, it could have had no sure ground for preferring it to the changeable. And thus, with the flash of a trembling glance, it arrived at that which is. And then I saw Thy invisible things understood by the things that are made. But I was not able to fix my gaze thereon; and my infirmity being beaten back, I was thrown again on my accustomed habits, carrying along with me naught but a loving memory thereof, and an appetite for what I had, as it were, smelt the odour of, but was not yet able to eat.

* * *

He rejoices that he proceeded from Plato to the Holy Scriptures, and not the reverse.

But having then read those books of the Platonists, and being admonished by them to search for incorporeal truth, I saw Thy invisible things understood by those things that are made; and though repulsed, I perceived what that was, which through the darkness of my mind I was not allowed to contemplate,—assured that Thou wert, and wert infinite, and yet not diffused in space finite or infinite; and that Thou truly art, who art the same ever, varying neither in part nor motion; and that all other things are from Thee, on this most sure ground alone, that they are. Of these things was I indeed assured, yet too weak to enjoy Thee. I chattered as one well skilled; but had I not sought Thy way in Christ our Saviour, I would have proved not skilful, but ready to perish. For now, filled with my punishment, I had begun to desire to seem wise; yet mourned I not, but rather was puffed up with knowledge. For where was that charity building upon the "foundation" of humility, "which is Jesus Christ"? Or, when would these books teach me it? Upon these, therefore, I believe, it was Thy pleasure that I should fall before I studied Thy Scriptures, that it might be impressed on my memory how I was affected by them; and that afterwards when I was subdued by Thy books, and when my wounds were touched by Thy healing fingers, I might discern and distinguish what a difference there is between presumption and confession, —between those who saw whither they were to go, yet saw not the way, and the way which leadeth not only to behold but to inhabit the blessed country. For had I first been moulded in Thy Holy Scriptures, and hadst Thou, in the familiar use of them, grown sweet unto me, and had I afterwards fallen upon those volumes, they might perhaps have withdrawn me from the solid ground of piety; or, had I stood firm in that wholesome disposition which I had thence imbibed, I might have thought that it could have been attained by the study of those books alone.

What he found in the sacred books which are not to be found in Plato.

Most eagerly, then, did I seize that venerable writing of Thy Spirit, but more especially the Apostle Paul; and those difficulties vanished away, in which he at one time appeared to me to contradict himself, and the text of his discourse not to agree with the testimonies of the Law and the Prophets. And the face of that pure speech appeared to me one and the same; and I learned to "rejoice with trembling." So I commenced, and found that whatsoever truth I had there read was declared here with the recommendation of Thy grace; that he who sees may not so glory as if he had not received not only that which he sees, but also that he can see (for what hath he which he hath not received?); and that he may not only be admonished to see Thee, who art ever the same, but also may be healed, to hold Thee; and that he who from afar off is not able to see, may still walk on the way by which he may reach, behold, and possess Thee. For though a man "delight in the law of God after the inward man," what shall he do with that other law in his members which warreth against the law of his mind, and bringeth him into captivity to the law of sin, which is in his members? For Thou art righteous, O Lord, but we have sinned and committed iniquity, and have done wickedly, and Thy hand is grown heavy upon us, and we are justly delivered over unto that ancient sinner, the governor of death; for he induced our will to be like his will, whereby he remained not in Thy truth. What shall "wretched man" do? "Who shall deliver him from the body of this death," but Thy grace only, "through Jesus Christ our Lord," whom Thou hast begotten co-eternal, and createdst in the beginning of Thy ways, in whom the Prince of this world found nothing worthy of death, yet killed he Him, and the handwriting which was contrary to us was blotted out? This those writings contain not. Those pages contain not the expression of this piety,—the tears of confession, Thy sacrifice, a troubled spirit, "a broken and a contrite heart," the salvation of the people, the espoused city, the earnest of the Holy Ghost, the cup of our redemption. No man sings there, Shall not my soul be subject unto God? For of Him cometh my salvation for He is my God and my salvation, my defender, I shall not be further moved. No one there hears Him calling, "Come unto me all ye that labour." They scorn to learn of Him, because He is meek and lowly of heart; for "Thou hast hid those things from the wise and prudent, and hast revealed them unto babes." For it is one thing, from the mountain's wooded summit to see the land of peace, and not to find the way thither,—in vain to attempt impassable ways, opposed and waylaid by fugitives and deserters, under their captain the "lion" and the "dragon"; and another to keep to the way that leads thither, guarded by the host of the heavenly general, where they rob not who have deserted the heavenly army, which they shun as torture. These things did in a wonderful manner sink into my bowels, when I read that "least of Thy apostles," and had reflected upon Thy works, and feared greatly.

B. CHRISTIAN ARISTOTELIANISM

ST. THOMAS AQUINAS: *Summa contra Gentiles* and *Summa Theologica* *

In his two greatest works, the *Summa contra Gentiles* and the *Summa Theologica*, selections from which follow, St. Thomas attempted the

* From St. Thomas Aquinas: *Summa contra Gentiles*, trans. by the English Dominican Fathers, vol. I, pp. 4–5, 9–11, 14, 23–4, 32–3, 100–01, 191. Copyright 1924 by Burns Oates & Washbourne Ltd. Reprinted by permission of Burns Oates & Washbourne Ltd.

The quotations from the English translation of the *Summa Theologica* of St. Thomas Aquinas are reproduced with the permission of Benziger Brothers, Inc., publishers synthesis of Aristotle and Christian theology. The first (c. 1260) was written for philosophers, primarily unbelievers, whereas the second, which he left unfinished, was intended for theological students. By the middle of the thirteenth century the corpus of Aristotle's works was well known in the West, and St. Thomas realized that Christianity must come to terms with it if it were not to lose the confidence of the educated classes. The Thomist synthesis encountered much opposition and did not become truly authoritative for Catholics until the sixteenth century.

"The Philosopher" to whom St. Thomas constantly refers in the text is, of course, Aristotle.

Of Reason and Faith

Now in those things which we hold about God there is truth in two ways. For certain things that are true about God wholly surpass the capability of human reason, for instance that God is three and one: while there are certain things to which even natural reason can attain, for instance that God is, that God is one, and others like these, which even the philosophers proved demonstratively of God, being guided by the light of natural reason.

That certain divine truths wholly surpass the capability of human reason, is most clearly evident. For since the principle of all the knowledge which the reason acquires about a thing, is the understanding of that thing's essence, because according to the Philosopher's teaching the principle of a demonstration is *what a thing is*, it follows that our knowledge about a thing will be in proportion to our understanding of its essence. Wherefore, if the human intellect comprehends the essence of a particular thing, for instance a stone or a triangle, no truth about that thing will surpass the capability of human reason. But this does not happen to us in relation to God, because the human intellect is incapable by its natural power of attaining to the comprehension of His essence: since our intellect's knowledge, according to the mode of the present life, originates from the senses: so that things which are not objects of sense cannot be comprehended by the human intellect, except in so far as knowledge of them is gathered from sensibles. Now sensibles cannot lead our intellect to see in them what God is, because they are effects unequal to the power of their cause. And yet our intellect is led by sensibles to the divine knowledge so as to know about God that He is, and other such truths, which need to be ascribed to the first principle. Accordingly some divine truths are attainable by human reason, while others altogether surpass the power of human reason.

* * *

It may appear to some that those things which cannot be investigated by reason ought not to be proposed to man as an object of faith: because divine wisdom provides for each thing according to the mode of its nature. We must therefore prove that it is necessary also for those things which surpass reason to be proposed by God to man as an object of faith.

For no man tends to do a thing by his desire and endeavour unless it be previously known to him. Wherefore since man is directed by divine providence to a higher good than human frailty can attain in the present life, as we shall show in the sequel, it was necessary for his mind to be bidden to something higher than those things to which our reason can reach in the present life, so that he might learn to aspire, and by his endeavours to tend to something surpassing the whole state of the present life. And this is especially competent to the Christian religion, which alone promises goods spiritual and eternal: for which reason it proposes many things surpassing the thought of man: whereas the old law which contained promises of temporal things, proposed few things that are above human inquiry. It was with this motive that the philosophers, in order to wean men from sensible pleasures to virtue, took care to show that there are other goods of greater account than those which appeal to the senses, the taste of which things affords much greater delight to those who devote themselves to active or contemplative virtues.

Again it is necessary for this truth to be proposed to man as an object of faith in order that he may have truer knowledge of God. For then alone do we know God truly, when we believe that He is far above all that man can possibly think of God, because the divine essence surpasses man's natural knowledge, as stated above. Hence by the fact that certain things about God are proposed to man, which surpass his reason, he is strengthened in his opinion that God is far above what he is able to think.

There results also another advantage from this, namely, the checking of presumption which is the mother of error. For some there are who presume so far on their wits that they think themselves capable of measuring the whole nature of things by their intellect, in that they esteem all things true which they see, and false which they see not. Accordingly, in order that man's mind might be freed from this presumption, and seek the truth humbly, it was necessary that certain things far surpassing his intellect should be proposed to man by God.

Yet another advantage is made apparent by the words of the Philosopher (10 *Ethic.*). For when a certain Simonides maintained that man should neglect the knowledge of God, and apply his mind to human affairs, and declared that *a man ought to relish human things, and a mortal, mortal things:* the Philosopher contradicted him, saying that *a man ought to devote himself to immortal and divine things as much as he can.* Hence he says (11 *De Animal.*) that though it is but little that we perceive of higher substances, yet that little is more loved and desired than all the knowledge we have of lower substances.

    *   *   *

Now though the aforesaid truth of the Christian faith surpasses the ability of human reason, nevertheless those things which are naturally instilled in human reason cannot be opposed to this truth. For it is clear that those things which are implanted in reason by nature, are most true, so much so that it is impossible to think them to be false. Nor is it lawful to deem false that which is held by faith, since it is so evidently confirmed by God. Seeing then that the false alone is opposed to the true, as evidently appears if we examine their definitions, it is impossible for the aforesaid truth of faith to be contrary to those principles which reason knows naturally.

Again. The same thing which the disciple's mind receives from its teacher is contained in the knowledge of the teacher, unless he teach insincerely, which it were wicked to say of God. Now the knowledge of naturally known principles is instilled into us by God, since God Himself is the author of our nature. Therefore the divine Wisdom also contains these principles. Consequently whatever is contrary to these principles, is contrary to the divine Wisdom; wherefore it cannot be from God. Therefore those things which are received by faith from divine revelation cannot be contrary to our natural knowledge.

Of God

Having shown then that it is not futile to endeavour to prove the existence of God, we may proceed to set forth the reasons whereby both philosophers and Catholic doctors have proved that there is a God. In the first place we shall give the arguments by which Aristotle sets out to prove God's existence: and he aims at proving this from the point of view of movement, in two ways.

The *first way* is as follows. Whatever is in motion is moved by another: and it is clear to the sense that something, the sun for instance, is in motion. Therefore it is set in motion by something else moving it. Now that which moves it is itself either moved or not. If it be not moved, then the point is proved that we must needs postulate an immovable mover: and this we call God. If, however, it be moved, it is moved by another mover. Either, therefore, we must proceed to infinity, or we must come to an immovable mover. But it is not possible to proceed to infinity. Therefore it is necessary to postulate an immovable mover. . . .

The Philosopher proceeds in a *different way* in 2 *Metaph.* to show that it is impossible to proceed to infinity in efficient causes, and that we must come to one first cause, and this we call God. This is how he proceeds.

In all efficient causes following in order, the first is the cause of the intermediate cause, and the intermediate is the cause of the ultimate, whether the intermediate be one or several. Now if the cause be removed, that which it causes is removed. Therefore if we remove the first the intermediate cannot be a cause. But if we go on to infinity in efficient causes, no cause will be first. Therefore all the others which are intermediate will be removed. Now this is clearly false. Therefore we must suppose *the existence of a first efficient cause:* and this is God. . . .

Another argument in support of this conclusion is adduced by Damascene from the government of things: and the same reasoning is indicated by the Commentator in *2 Phys.* It runs as follows. It is impossible for contrary and discordant things to accord in one order always or frequently except by someone's governance, whereby each and all are made to tend to a definite end. Now we see that in the world things of different natures accord in one order, not seldom and fortuitously, but always or for the most part. Therefore it follows that there is *someone by whose providence the world is governed.* And this we call God.

* * *

Moreover. Whatever tends definitely to an end, either prescribes that end to itself, or that end is prescribed to it by another: else it would not tend to this end rather than to that. Now natural things tend to definite ends, for they do not pursue their natural purposes by chance, since in that case those purposes would not be realized always or for the most part, but seldom, for of such is chance. Since then they do not prescribe the end to themselves, for they do not apprehend the notion of end, it follows that the end is prescribed to them by another, Who is the author of nature. This is He Who gives being to all, and Who necessarily exists of Himself, Whom we call God, as shown above. Now He would be unable to prescribe nature its end unless He were intelligent. Therefore God is intelligent.

Moreover. Whatever is imperfect originates from something perfect: because the perfect naturally precedes the imperfect, as act precedes potentiality. Now the forms that exist in particular things are imperfect, since their existence is limited and does not extend to the full universality of their nature. Wherefore they must needs originate from certain perfect and not limited forms. Now such forms are impossible except as an object of the understanding, since no form is found in a state of universality except in the intellect. Consequently those forms must be intelligent if they are subsistent, for in no other way can they be operative. Therefore it follows that God Who is the first subsistent act, from which all others derive, is intelligent.

* * *

In like manner it follows that love is in God as an act of His will.

For it belongs properly to the nature of love that the lover wills the good of the beloved. Now God wills His own and others' good, as stated above. Accordingly then God loves both Himself and other things.

Again. True love requires one to will another's good as one's own. For a thing whose good one wills merely as conducive to another's good, is loved accidentally: thus he who wills wine to be preserved that he may drink it, or who loves a man that he may be useful or pleasing to him, loves the wine or the man accidentally, but himself properly speaking. Now God loves each thing's good as its own, since He wills each thing to be in as much as it is good in itself: although He directs one to the profit of another. God therefore truly loves both Himself and other things.

Of the Divine Creation and Government

. . . God is the first exemplar cause of all things. In proof whereof we must consider that if for the production of anything an exemplar is necessary, it is in order that the effect may receive a determinate form. For an artificer produces a determinate form in matter by reason of the exemplar before him, whether it is the exemplar beheld externally, or the exemplar interiorly conceived in the mind. Now it is manifest that things made by nature receive determinate forms. This determination of forms must be reduced to the divine wisdom as its first principle, for divine wisdom devised the order of the universe, which order consists in the variety of things. And therefore we must say that in the divine wisdom are the types of all things, which types we have called ideas—*i.e.*, exemplar forms existing in the divine mind (Q. 15, A. 1). And these ideas, though multiplied by their relations to things, in reality are not apart from the divine essence, according as the likeness to that essence can be shared diversely by different things. In this manner therefore God Himself is the first exemplar of all things.

*   *   *

The distinction of things has been ascribed to many causes. For some attributed the distinction to matter, either by itself or with the agent. Democritus, for instance, and all the ancient natural philosophers, who admitted no cause but matter, attributed it to matter alone; and in their opinion the distinction of things comes from chance according to the movement of matter. Anaxagoras, however, attributed the distinction and multitude of things to matter and to the agent together; and he said that the intellect distinguishes things by extracting what is mixed up in matter.

But this cannot stand, for two reasons. First, because, as was shown above (Q. 44, A. 2), even matter itself was created by God. Hence we must reduce whatever distinction comes from matter to a higher cause. Secondly, because matter is for the sake of the form, and not the form for the matter, and the distinction of things comes from their proper forms. Therefore the distinction of things is not on account of the matter; but rather, on the contrary, created matter is formless, in order that it may be accommodated to different forms.

Others have attributed the distinction of things to secondary agents, as did Avicenna, who said that God by understanding Himself, produced the first intelligence; in which, forasmuch as it was not its own being, there is necessarily composition of potentiality and act, as will appear later (Q. 50, A. 3). And so the first intelligence, inasmuch as it understood the first cause, produced the second intelligence; and in so far as it understood itself as in potentiality it produced the heavenly body, which causes movement, and inasmuch as it understood itself as having actuality it produced the soul of the heavens.

But this opinion cannot stand, for two reasons. First, because it was shown above (Q. 45, A. 5) that to create belongs to God alone, and hence what can be caused only by creation is produced by God alone— viz., all those things which are not subject to generation and corruption. Secondly, because, according to this opinion, the universality of things would not proceed from the intention of the first agent, but from the concurrence of many active causes; and such an effect we can describe only as being produced by chance. Therefore, the perfection of the universe, which consists of the diversity of things, would thus be a thing of chance, which is impossible.

Hence we must say that the distinction and multitude of things come from the intention of the first agent, who is God. For He brought things into being in order that His goodness might be communicated to creatures, and be represented by them; and because His goodness could not be adequately represented by one creature alone, He produced many and diverse creatures, that what was wanting to one in the representation of the divine goodness might be supplied by another. For goodness, which in God is simple and uniform, in creatures is manifold and divided; and hence the whole universe together participates the divine goodness more perfectly, and represents it better than any single creature whatever.

*   *   *

Now if we wish to assign an end to any whole, and to the parts of that whole, we shall find, first, that each and every part exists for the sake of its proper act, as the eye for the act of seeing; secondly, that less honorable parts exist for the more honorable, as the senses for the intellect, the lungs for the heart; and, thirdly, that all parts are for the perfection of the whole, as the matter for the form, since the parts are, as it were, the matter of the whole. Furthermore, the whole man is on account of an extrinsic end, that end being the fruition of God. So, therefore, in the parts of the universe also every creature exists for its own proper act and perfection, and the less noble for the nobler, as those creatures that are less noble than man exist for the sake of man, whilst each and every creature exists for the perfection of the entire universe. Furthermore, the entire universe, with all its parts, is ordained towards God as its end, inasmuch as it imitates, as it were, and shows forth the Divine goodness, to the glory of God. Reasonable creatures, however, have in some special and higher manner God as their end, since they can attain to Him by their own operations, by knowing and loving Him. Thus it is plain that the Divine goodness is the end of all corporeal things.

*   *   *

For the same reason is God the ruler of things as He is their cause, because the same gives existence as gives perfection; and this belongs to government. Now God is the cause not indeed only of some particular kind of being, but of the whole universal being, as proved above (A. 44, AA. 1, 2). Wherefore, as there can be nothing which is not created by God, so there can be nothing which is not subject to His government. . . .

Foolish therefore was the opinion of those who said that the corruptible lower world, or individual things, or that even human affairs, were not subject to the Divine government. These are represented as saying, *God hath abandoned the earth* (Ezech. ix. 9).

Reply Obj. 1. These things are said to be under the sun which are generated and corrupted according to the sun's movement. In all such things we find chance: not that everything is casual which occurs in such things; but that in each one there is an element of chance. And the very fact that an element of chance is found in those things proves that they are subject to government of some kind. For unless corruptible things were governed by a higher being, they would tend to nothing definite, especially those which possess no kind of knowledge. . . .

Reply Obj. 2. Government implies a certain change effected by the governor in the things governed. Now every movement is the act of a movable thing, caused by the moving principle, as is laid down *Phys.* iii. 3. And every act is proportionate to that of which it is an act. Consequently, various movable things must be moved variously, even as regards movement by one and the same mover. Thus by the one art of the Divine governor, various things are variously governed according to their variety. Some, according to their nature, act of themselves, having dominion over their actions; and these are governed by God, not only in this, that they are moved by God Himself, Who works in them interiorly; but also in this, that they are induced by Him to do good and to fly from evil, by precepts and prohibitions, rewards and punishments. But irrational creatures which do not act but are acted upon, are not thus governed by God. Hence, when the Apostle says that *God hath no care for oxen*, he does not wholly withdraw them from the Divine government, but only as regards the way in which rational creatures are governed.

* * *

. . . Augustine says (*Contra Faust. xxvi. ibid.*):*God sometimes does things which are contrary to the ordinary course of nature.*

I answer that, From each cause there results a certain order to its effects, since every cause is a principle; and so, according to the multiplicity of causes, there results a multiplicity of orders, subjected one to the other, as cause is subjected to cause. Wherefore a higher cause is not subjected to a cause of a lower order; but conversely. An example of this may be seen in human affairs. On the father of a family depends the order of the household; which order is contained in the order of the city; which order again depends on the ruler of the city; while this last order depends on that of the king, by whom the whole kingdom is ordered.

If therefore we consider the order of things depending on the first cause, God cannot do anything against this order; for, if He did so, He would act against His foreknowledge, or His will, or His goodness. But if we consider the order of things depending on any secondary cause, thus God can do something outside such order; for He is not subject to the order of secondary causes; but, on the contrary, this order is subject to Him, as proceeding from Him, not by a natural necessity, but by the choice of His own will; for He could have created another order of things. Wherefore God can do something outside this order created by Him, when He chooses, for instance by producing the effects of secondary causes without them, or by producing certain effects to which secondary causes do not extend. So Augustine says (*Contra Faust. xxvi. ibid.*): *God acts against the wonted course of nature, but by no means does He act against the supreme law; because He does not act against Himself.* . . .

. . . Nothing is called a miracle by comparison with the Divine Power; because no action is of any account compared with the power of God, according to Isa. xl. 15: *Behold the Gentiles are as a drop from a bucket, and are counted as the smallest grain of a balance.* But, a thing is called a miracle by comparison with the power of nature which it surpasses. So the more the power of nature is surpassed, the greater is the miracle. Now the power of nature is surpassed in three ways: firstly, in the substance of the deed, for instance, if two bodies occupy the same place, or if the sun goes backwards; or if a human body is glorified: such things nature is absolutely unable to do; and these hold the highest rank among miracles. Secondly, a thing surpasses the power of nature, not in the deed, but in that wherein it is done; as the raising of the dead, and giving sight to the blind, and the like; for nature can give life, but not to the dead; and such hold the second rank in miracles. Thirdly, a thing surpasses nature's power in the measure and order in which it is done; as when a man is cured of a fever suddenly, without treatment or the usual process of nature; or as when the air is suddenly condensed into rain, by Divine power without a natural cause, as occurred at the prayers of Samuel and Elias; and these hold the lowest place in miracles. Moreover, each of these kinds has various degrees, according to the different ways in which the power of nature is surpassed.

Of Man

. . . It is written (Ecclus. xv. 14): *God made man from the beginning, and left him in the hand of his own counsel;* and the gloss adds: *That is of his free-will.*

I answer that, Man has free-will: otherwise counsels, exhortations, commands, prohibitions, rewards and punishments would be in vain. In order to make this evident, we must observe that some things act without judgment; as a stone moves downwards; and in like manner all things which lack knowledge. And some act from judgment, but not a free judgment; as brute animals. For the sheep, seeing the wolf, judges it a thing to be shunned, from a natural and not a free judgment, because it judges, not from reason, but from natural instinct. And the same thing is to be said of any judgment of brute animals. But man acts from judgment, because by his apprehensive power he judges that something should be avoided or sought. But because this judgment, in the case of some particular act, is not from a natural instinct, but from some act of comparison in the reason, therefore he acts from free judgment and retains the power of being inclined to various things. For reason in contingent matters may follow opposite courses, as we see in dialectic syllogisms and rhetorical arguments. Now particular operations are contingent, and therefore in such matters the judgment of reason may follow opposite courses, and is not determinate to one.

*   *   *

. . . Man's nature may be looked at in two ways: first, in its integrity, as it was in our first parent before sin; secondly, as it is corrupted in us after the sin of our first parent. Now in both states human nature needs the help of God as First Mover, to do or wish any good whatsoever, as stated above (A. 1). But in the state of integrity, as regards the sufficiency of the operative power, man by his natural endowments could wish and do the good proportionate to his nature, such as the good of acquired virtue; but not surpassing good, as the good of infused virtue. But in the state of corrupt nature, man falls short of what he could do by his nature, so that he is unable to fulfill it by his own natural powers. Yet because human nature is not altogether corrupted by sin, so as to be shorn of every natural good, even in the state of corrupted nature it can, by virtue of its natural endowments, work some particular good, as to build dwellings, plant vineyards, and the like; yet it cannot do all the good natural to it, so as to fall short in nothing; just as a sick man can of himself make some movements, yet he cannot be perfectly moved with the movements of one in health, unless by the help of medicine he be cured.

And thus in the state of perfect nature man needs a gratuitous strength superadded to natural strength for one reason, viz., in order to do and wish supernatural good; but for two reasons, in the state of corrupt nature, viz., in order to be healed, and furthermore in order to carry out works of supernatural virtue, which are meritorious. Beyond this, in both states man needs the Divine help, that he may be moved to act well.

* * *

. . . The Apostle says (Rom. vi. 23): *The grace of God is life everlasting.* And as a gloss says, this is said *that we may understand that God, of His own mercy, leads us to everlasting life.*

I answer that, Acts conducing to an end must be proportioned to the end. But no act exceeds the proportion of its active principle; and hence we see in natural things, that nothing can by its operation bring about an effect which exceeds its active force, but only such as is proportionate to its power. Now everlasting life is an end exceeding the proportion of human nature, as is clear from what we have said above (Q. 5, A. 5). Hence man, by his natural endowments, cannot produce meritorious works proportionate to everlasting life; and for this a higher force is needed, viz., the force of grace. And thus without grace man cannot merit everlasting life; yet he can perform works conducing to a good which is natural to man, as *to toil in the fields, to drink, to eat, or to have friends,* and the like, as Augustine says in his third *Reply to the Pelagians.*

Reply Obj. 1. Man, by his will, does works meritorious of everlasting life; but as Augustine says, in the same book, for this it is necessary that the will of man should be prepared with grace by God.

* * *

. . . It is written (Jer. xxxi. 16): *There is a reward for thy work.* Now a reward means something bestowed by reason of merit. Hence it would seem that a man may merit from God.

I answer that, Merit and reward refer to the same, for a reward means something given anyone in return for work or toil, as a price for it.

Hence, as it is an act of justice to give a just price for anything received from another, so also is it an act of justice to make a return for work or toil. Now justice is a kind of equality, as is clear from the Philosopher (*Ethic.* v. 3), and hence justice is simply between those that are simply equal; but where there is no absolute equality between them, neither is there absolute justice, but there may be a certain manner of justice, as when we speak of a father's or a master's right (*ibid.* 6), as the Philosopher says. And hence where there is justice simply, there is the character of merit and reward simply. But where there is no simple right, but only relative, there is no character of merit simply, but only relatively, in so far as the character of justice is found there, since the child merits something from his father and the slave from his lord.

Now it is clear that between God and man there is the greatest inequality: for they are infinitely apart, and all man's good is from God. Hence there can be no justice of absolute equality between man and God, but only of a certain proportion, inasmuch as both operate after their own manner. Now the manner and measure of human virtue is in man from God. Hence man's merit with God only exists on the presupposition of the Divine ordination, so that man obtains from God, as a reward of his operation, what God gave him the power of operation for, even as natural things by their proper movements and operations obtain that to which they were ordained by God; differently, indeed, since the rational creature moves itself to act by its free-will, hence its action has the character of merit, which is not so in other creatures.

Reply Obj. 1. Man merits, inasmuch as he does what he ought, by his free-will; otherwise the act of justice whereby anyone discharges a debt would not be meritorious.

Reply Obj. 2. God seeks from our goods not profit, but glory, *i.e.*, the manifestation of His goodness; even as He seeks it also in His own works. Now nothing accrues to Him, but only to ourselves, by our worship of Him. Hence we merit from God, not that by our works anything accrues to Him, but inasmuch as we work for His glory.

C. EXPERIMENTAL SCIENCE

ROGER BACON: *Opus Majus* *

Roger Bacon (*c.* 1212–92), a learned Franciscan friar and theologian who did most of his work at Oxford, is chiefly noted for his writings in natural science, and for his employment of the experimental method. At the request of his intimate friend, Pope Clement IV, he composed a

* From Roger Bacon: *Opus Majus*, trans. by R. B. Burke, vol. I, pp. 4–5, 36; vol. II, pp. 583–7. Copyright 1928 by University of Pennsylvania Press. Reprinted by permission of University of Pennsylvania Press.

series of works on astronomy, physics, and optics, the most important being the *Opus Majus*, from which selections follow. Later, however, owing it would seem to his outspoken attack on scholasticism, he was summoned to Rome and probably imprisoned.

Now there are four chief obstacles in grasping truth, which hinder every man, however learned, and scarcely allow any one to win a clear title to learning, namely, submission to faulty and unworthy authority, influence of custom, popular prejudice, and concealment of our own ignorance accompanied by an ostentatious display of our knowledge. . . . Therefore nothing is more necessary of consideration than the positive condemnation of those four errors through the chosen arguments of wise men which shall prove irrefutable. Inasmuch as the wise unite the first three together and condemn them, and since the fourth, owing to its exceptional folly, needs special treatment, I shall first attempt to show the banefulness of the three. But although authority be one of those, I am in no way speaking of that solid and sure authority, which either by God's judgment has been bestowed upon his Church, or which springs from the merit and dignity of an individual among the Saints, the perfect philosophers, and other men of science, who up to the limit of human utility are expert in the pursuit of science; but I am speaking of that authority, which without divine consent many in this world have unlawfully seized, not from the merit of their wisdom but from their presumption and desire of fame—an authority which the ignorant throng concedes to many to its own destruction by the just judgment of God. For according to Scripture "owing to the sins of the people frequently the hypocrite rules"; for I am speaking of the sophistical authorities of the irrational multitude, men who are authorities in an equivocal sense, even as the eye carved in stone or painted on canvas has the name but not the quality of an eye.

* * *

Accordingly after the four general causes of all human error have been banished to the lower regions and have been completely removed from this plea, I wish to show in this second part that there is one wisdom that is perfect and that this is contained in the Scriptures. From the roots of this wisdom all truth has sprung. I say, therefore, that one science is the mistress of the others, namely, theology, to which the remaining sciences are vitally necessary, and without which it cannot reach its end. The excellence of these sciences theology claims for her own law, whose nod and authority the rest of the sciences obey. Or better, there is only one perfect wisdom, which is contained wholly in the Scriptures, and is to be unfolded by canon law and philosophy. I make this statement since the exposition of divine truth is made through those sciences. For it is itself unfolded as it were in the palm with these sciences, and yet it gathers within its own grasp all wisdom; since all wisdom has been given by one God, to one world, for one purpose. Therefore this wisdom from its own triple arrangement will obtain unity. But the way of salvation is single, although there are many steps; but wisdom is the way to salvation. For every consideration of a man that does not belong to his salvation is full of blindness, and leads down to the darkness of hell; for which reason many sages famous in this world have been condemned, because they did not have the true wisdom, but an apparent and a false one, whence reckoning themselves wise they became fools according to the Scripture. But Augustine, speaking concerning the Scriptures, says in the second book on Christian Doctrine, if elsewhere there is truth, it is found here; if there is a hurtful thing, it is here condemned.

*   *   *

Having laid down fundamental principles of the wisdom of the Latins so far as they are found in language, mathematics, and optics, I now wish to unfold the principles of experimental science, since without experience nothing can be sufficiently known. For there are two modes of acquiring knowledge, namely, by reasoning and experience. Reasoning draws a conclusion and makes us grant the conclusion, but does not make the conclusion certain, nor does it remove doubt so that the mind may rest on the intuition of truth, unless the mind discovers it by the path of experience; since many have the arguments relating to what can be known, but because they lack experience they neglect the arguments, and neither avoid what is harmful nor follow what is good. For if a man who has never seen fire should prove by adequate reasoning that fire burns and injures things and destroys them, his mind would not be satisfied thereby, nor would he avoid fire, until he placed his hand or some combustible substance in the fire, so that he might prove by experience that which reasoning taught. But when he has had actual experience of combustion his mind is made certain and rests in the full light of truth. Therefore reasoning does not suffice, but experience does. . . .

He therefore who wishes to rejoice without doubt in regard to the truths underlying phenomena must know how to devote himself to experiment. For authors write many statements, and people believe them through reasoning which they formulate without experience. Their reasoning is wholly false. For it is generally believed that the diamond cannot be broken except by goat's blood, and philosophers and theologians misuse this idea. But fracture by means of blood of this kind has never been verified, although the effort has been made; and without that blood it can be broken easily. For I have seen this with my own eyes, and this is necessary, because gems cannot be carved except by fragments of this stone. . . . Moreover, it is generally believed that hot water freezes more quickly than cold water in vessels, and the argument in support of this is advanced that contrary is excited by contrary, just like enemies meeting each other. But it is certain that cold water freezes more quickly for any one who makes the experiment. . . .

But experience is of two kinds; one is gained through our external senses, and in this way we gain our experience of those things that are in the heavens by instruments made for this purpose, and of those things here below by means attested by our vision. Things that do not belong in our part of the world we know through other scientists who have had experience of them. As, for example, Aristotle on the authority of Alexander sent two thousand men through different parts of the world to gain experimental knowledge of all things that are on the surface of the earth, as Pliny bears witness in his Natural History. This experience is both human and philosophical, as far as man can act in accordance with the grace given him; but this experience does not suffice him, because it does not give full attestation in regard to things corporeal owing to its difficulty, and does not touch at all on things spiritual. It is necessary, therefore, that the intellect of man should be otherwise aided, and for this reason the holy patriarchs and prophets, who first gave sciences to the world, received illumination within and were not dependent on sense alone. The same is true of many believers since the time of Christ. For the grace of faith illuminates greatly, as also do divine inspirations, not only in things spiritual, but in things corporeal and in the sciences of philosophy; as Ptolemy states in the Centilogium, namely, that there are two roads by which we arrive at the knowledge of facts, one through the experience of philosophy, the other through divine inspiration, which is far the better way, as he says.

Moreover, there are seven stages of this internal knowledge, the first of which is reached through illuminations relating purely to the sciences. The second consists in the virtues. For the evil man is ignorant, as Aristotle says in the second book of the Ethics. Moreover, Algazel says in his Logic that the soul disfigured by sins is like a rusty mirror, in which the species of objects cannot be seen clearly; but the soul adorned with virtues is like a well-polished mirror, in which the forms of objects are clearly seen. . . .

The third stage consists in the seven gifts of the Holy Spirit, which Isaiah enumerates. The fourth consists in the beatitudes, which the Lord defines in the Gospels. The fifth consists in the spiritual senses. The sixth consists in fruits, of which is the peace of God which passes all understanding. The seventh consists in raptures and their states according to the different ways in which people are caught up to see many things of which it is not lawful for a man to speak. And he who has had diligent training in these experiences or in several of them is able to assure himself and others not only in regard to things spiritual, but also in regard to all human sciences. Therefore since all the divisions of speculative philosophy proceed by arguments, which are either based on a point from authority or on the other points of argumentation except this division which I am now examining, we find necessary the science that is called experimental. I wish to explain it, as it is useful not only to philosophy, but to the knowledge of God, and for the direction of the whole world; just as in the preceding divisions I showed the relationship of the languages and sciences to their end, which is the divine wisdom by which all things are disposed.

D. MYSTICISM

DIONYSIUS THE PSEUDO-AREOPAGITE: *The Mystical Theology* *

"Dionysius" (fifth century) was one of those early writers like Boethius and St. Augustine who profoundly influenced medieval thought. He claimed to be St. Paul's Athenian convert Dionysius, but from his references to the doctrines of the Neoplatonist Proclus it is believed that he was an ecclesiastic, probably Syrian, of the fifth century. He was the prototype of Christian mystical theology. Through the Latin translation by the philosopher Scotus Erigena in the ninth century, his treatise *On the Divine Names* was communicated to the West. St. Thomas Aquinas quotes him frequently. *The Mystical Theology* was freely translated into English in the fourteenth century at the height of the mystical movement.

TRINITY, which exceedeth all Being, Deity, and Goodness! Thou that instructeth Christians in Thy heavenly wisdom! Guide us to that topmost height of mystic lore which exceedeth light and more than exceedeth knowledge, where the simple, absolute, and unchangeable mysteries of heavenly Truth lie hidden in the dazzling obscurity of the secret Silence, outshining all brilliance with the intensity of their darkness, and surcharging our blinded intellects with the utterly impalpable and invisible fairness of glories which exceed all beauty! Such be my prayer; and thee, dear Timothy, I counsel that, in the earnest exercise of mystic contemplation, thou leave the senses and the activities of the intellect and all things that the senses or the intellect can perceive, and all things in this world of nothingness, or in that world of being, and that, thine understanding being laid to rest, thou strain (so far as thou mayest) towards

* From C. E. Rolt: *Dionysius the Areopagite,* pp. 191–4. Copyright 1920 by Society for Promoting Christian Knowledge. Reprinted by permission of Society for Promoting Christian Knowledge.

an union with Him whom neither being nor understanding can contain. For, by the unceasing and absolute renunciation of thyself and all things, thou shalt in pureness cast all things aside, and be released from all, and so shalt be led upwards to the Ray of that divine Darkness which exceedeth all existence.

These things thou must not disclose to any of the uninitiated, by whom I mean those who cling to the objects of human thought, and imagine there is no super-essential reality beyond, and fancy that they know by human understanding Him that has made Darkness His secret place. And, if the Divine Initiation is beyond such men as these, what can be said of others yet more incapable thereof, who describe the Transcendent Cause of all things by qualities drawn from the lowest order of being, while they deny that it is in any way superior to the various ungodly delusions which they fondly invent in ignorance of this truth? That while it possesses all the positive attributes of the universe (being the universal Cause), yet in a stricter sense It does not possess them, since It transcends them all, wherefore there is no contradiction between affirming and denying that It has them inasmuch as It precedes and surpasses all deprivation, being beyond all positive and negative distinctions?

Such at least is the teaching of the blessed Bartholomew. For he says that the subject-matter of the Divine Science is vast and yet minute, and that the Gospel combines in itself both width and straitness. Methinks he has shown by these his words how marvellously he has understood that the Good Cause of all things is eloquent yet speaks few words, or rather none; possessing neither speech nor understanding because it exceedeth all things in a super-essential manner, and is revealed in Its naked truth to those alone who pass right through the opposition of fair and foul, and pass beyond the topmost altitudes of the holy ascent and leave behind them all divine enlightenment and voices and heavenly utterances and plunge into the Darkness where truly dwells, as saith the Scripture, that One Which is beyond all things. For not without reason is the blessed Moses bidden first to undergo purification himself and then to separate himself from those who have not undergone it; and after all purification hears the many-voiced trumpets and sees many lights flash forth with pure and diverse-streaming rays, and then stands separate from the multitudes and with the chosen priests presses forward to the topmost pinnacle of the Divine Ascent. Nevertheless he meets not with God Himself, yet he beholds—not Him indeed (for He is invisible)—but the place wherein He dwells. And this I take to signify that the divinest and the highest of the things perceived by the eyes of the body or the mind are but the symbolic language of things subordinate to Him who Himself transcendeth them all. Through these things His incomprehensible presence is shown walking upon those heights of His holy places which are perceived by the mind; and then It breaks forth, even from the things

that are beheld and from those that behold them, and plunges the true
initiate unto the Darkness of Unknowing wherein he renounces all the
apprehensions of his understanding and is enwrapped in that which is
wholly intangible and invisible, belonging wholly to Him that is beyond
all things and to none else (whether himself or another), and being
through the passive stillness of all his reasoning powers united by his
highest faculty to Him that is wholly Unknowable, of whom thus by a
rejection of all knowledge he possesses a knowledge that exceeds his
understanding.

Unto this Darkness which is beyond Light we pray that we may come,
and may attain unto vision through the loss of sight and knowledge,
and that in ceasing thus to see or to know we may learn to know that
which is beyond all perception and understanding (for this emptying
of our faculties is true sight and knowledge). . . .

E. THE PTOLEMAIC UNIVERSE

DANTE ALIGHIERI: *The Banquet* *

> Dante Alighieri (1265–1321) has been alternately called exemplar of the
> ecclesiastical culture of the Middle Ages, and father of the Italian
> Renaissance. In any event, his greatest work is a classic statement of the
> medieval world-view: Henry Osborne Taylor calls the *Divine Comedy*
> a *Summa salvationis* just as St. Thomas Aquinas's masterpeice was a
> *Summa theologica*. In the unfinished *Convito* or *Banquet* Dante similarly
> aimed to write a *Summa* of universal knowledge. Lady Philosophy, he
> tells us, will rule his mature life as the Lady Beatrice had done his youth.
> And upon referring to Venus, he plunges into a disquisition on cosmol-
> ogy which "represents the prevailing views of his time as to the structure
> of the world."

I SAY, then, that there are many different opinions as to the number
and position of the heavens, although at last the truth be found. Aristotle (following only the ancient ignorance of the astrologers) believed
that there were only eight heavens, of which the outer one, containing
all the rest, was that of the Fixed Stars, that is, the eighth sphere; and
that beyond that was none other. . . .

Ptolemy afterwards, perceiving that the eighth sphere had more than
one motion (seeing that its revolution varied from the true circuit, which
turns only from east to west), and constrained by the principles of philosophy (which necessarily demanded a perfectly simple *Primum Mo-*

---

* *The Banquet of Dante Alighieri*, trans. by Katherine Hillard (London: Kegan
Paul, Trench & Co.; 1889), pp. 63–7, 69–72, 75–6, 80–1, 106–07, 121–2, 153–5.

bile), supposed another heaven to exist beyond that of the Fixed Stars, which made this revolution from east to west. This revolution, I say, was completed in about twenty-four hours, that is, in twenty-three hours and fourteen parts of the fifteen of another [hour], roughly calculated. So that according to him, and according to that which is received in astrology and in philosophy since these movements were seen, the movable heavens are nine; and their position is plain and determined, as the art of perspective, arithmetic, and geometry proves to our senses and our reason, and of which our senses have other testimony. . . .

And the order of position [of the heavens] is this, that the first one enumerated is that where the Moon is; the second that where Mercury is; the third that where Venus is; the fourth that where the Sun is; the fifth that where Mars is; the sixth that where Jupiter is; the seventh that where Saturn is; the eighth that where the Fixed Stars are; the ninth is that which is not perceptible to sense (except by the motion spoken of above), and which is called by many the Crystalline, that is, the diaphanous, or wholly transparent. However, beyond all these, the Catholics place the Empyrean Heaven, which is as much as to say the Heaven of *Flame*, or *Luminous* Heaven; and they hold it to be immovable, because it has within itself, in every part, that which its matter demands. And this is the reason that the *Primum Mobile* moves with immense velocity; because the fervent longing of all its parts to be united to those of this [tenth and] most divine and quiet heaven, makes it revolve with so much desire that its velocity is almost incomprehensible. And this quiet and peaceful heaven is the abode of that Supreme Deity who alone doth perfectly behold Himself. This is the abode of the beatified spirits, according to the holy Church, who cannot lie; and Aristotle also seems to think so, if rightly understood, in the first of *The Heavens and Earth*. This is the supreme edifice of the universe, in which all the world is included, and beyond which is nothing; and it is not in space, but was formed solely in the Primal Mind, which the Greeks called *Protonoe*. This is that magnificence of which the Psalmist spake, when he says to God, "Thy magnificence is exalted above the heavens." And thus, summing up what has been here discussed, it seems that there are ten heavens, of which that of Venus is the third; and this will be spoken of in the place where I intend to explain it. . . .

Since it has been demonstrated in the preceding chapter what this third heaven is, and how it is ordered within itself, it remains to show who they are who move it. Therefore be it known, in the first place, that these are Substances separate from matter, that is, Intelligences, whom the common people call Angels. And of these creatures, as of the heavens, different [writers] have held different opinions, although the truth is now known. There were certain philosophers, among whom seems to have been Aristotle in his *Metaphysics* (although in the first of the *Heaven and Earth* he appears incidentally to think otherwise), who believed that there were only as many of these [Intelligences] as there were circulations of the heavens, and no more; saying that other than these would exist eternally in vain, without effectuality; which were impossible, seeing that their being consists in their effectuality.

There were others like Plato, a most excellent man, who maintained that there are not only as many Intelligences as there are motions of the heavens, but also as many as there are kinds of things; such as one kind for all men, another for gold, another for treasures, and so on; and they say that as the Intelligences are the generators of these [motions], each of its own, so these other [Intelligences] are the generators of all other things, and the exemplars each of their own kind; and Plato calls them *Ideas*, which is as much as to say *forms*, and *universal natures*. The heathen called them gods and goddesses (although they had not so philosophical an understanding of them as Plato had), and adored their images, and built to them great temples—as to Juno, whom they called the goddess of power; to Vulcan, whom they called the god of fire; to Pallas, or Minerva, whom they called the goddess of wisdom; and to Ceres, whom they called the goddess of grain. . . .

And although the above opinions were well grounded upon human reason, and no little experience, the truth was not yet seen of them [the heathen], both through fault of reason and fault of teaching; because by reason alone we can see that the aforesaid creatures are much more numerous than are those effects of theirs which men are able to understand. And one reason is this: no one doubts, neither philosopher, nor heathen, nor Jew, nor Christian, nor any other sect, that they [these creatures] are full of all blessedness—all, or the greater part; and that the state of these blessed ones is most perfect. Whence, as that which is here [in this world] human nature has not only one beatitude but two, that of the social [or active] and that of the contemplative life, it would be irrational for us to consider these [celestial creatures] as having the blessedness of active, that is, social life, in the government of the world. and not as having that of the contemplative, the which is more excellent and more divine. And because they who have the beatitude of government cannot have the other also, because their intellect is one and perpetual, there must be others apart from this ministry, who live solely in contemplation. And because this life is more divine, and the more divine a thing is the more it resembles God, it is evident that this life is more beloved of God; and if more beloved, the greater hath been His bounty to it; and the greater His bounty, the more living creatures hath He given to this life than to the other. By which we conclude that the number of those whose effect is not evident, is very much the larger. . . .

Our Saviour said with His own lips that the Father could give Him many legions of angels. Nor did He deny it, when it was said to Him that the Father had commanded the angels to minister unto Him and serve Him. Therefore it is proved to us that these creatures exist in immense numbers; because His Spouse and Secretary, the Holy Church (of whom Solomon says, "Who is this that cometh up from the wilderness, full of delights, leaning upon her Beloved?"), says, believes, and preaches that these most noble creatures are almost innumerable; and she divides them into three hierarchies, that is to say, three holy, or rather divine, principalities; and each hierarchy has three orders; so that the Church holds and maintains that there are nine orders of spiritual creatures. . . .

Again, all this heaven moves and revolves with the epicycle from east to west, once in every day; which movement, whether it be caused by some Intelligence, or by the rush of the *Primum Mobile*, God knows, for to me it seems presumptuous to judge. These motive Powers guide by their thought alone the revolutions over which each one presides. The most noble form of the heaven, having within itself this principle of passivity, revolves at the touch of the motive force willing it so to move, and I say *touch*, not in a corporeal sense, of the power that is brought to bear on it. And these motive Powers are they who are understood to be addressed, and to whom I speak.

*   *   *

Here we must reflect upon a comparison between the order of the heavens and that of the sciences. For, as has been said above, the seven heavens nearest to us are those of the planets; then there are two heavens above these, movable, and one over all the rest, motionless. To the first seven correspond the seven sciences of the *Trivium* and *Quadrivium*, that is *Grammar*, Dialectics, Rhetoric, Arithmetic, Music, Geometry, and Astrology. To the eighth sphere, that is, to the Starry Heaven, correspond Natural Science, called *Physics*, and the first of sciences called *Metaphysics*; to the ninth sphere corresponds Moral Science; and to the Quiet Heaven corresponds Divine Science, which is called Theology. . . .

Again, the Empyrean Heaven, by its peace, resembles the Divine Science, which is full of all peace; which suffers no dispute whatsoever of opinions or sophistical arguments, by reason of the most excellent certitude of its subject, which is God. And of this He said to His disciples, "My peace I give unto you: my peace I leave with you," giving and bequeathing to them His doctrine, which is this science of which I speak. And of it Solomon says, "There are threescore queens, and fourscore concubines, and youthful handmaids without number. My dove, my undefiled, is but one." He calls all the [other] sciences queens, and faithful servants, and handmaids; and this he calls a *dove*, because it is without blemish of strife; and this he calls *perfect*, because it makes us behold perfectly that Truth in which our soul finds rest.

*   *   *

I say, then, "*The sun, that daily circleth round the world*"; and here we must know, that we may understand this perfectly, how the world is circled by the sun. And first I would say that by the *world* I do not mean here the whole body of the universe, but only this division of sea and land; following the common usage, which so designates it. Whence some say, "This man has seen all the world," meaning this division of the sea and land.

This world Pythagoras and his followers asserted to be one of the stars, and believed that there was another opposite to it, and exactly corresponding to it; and this he called *Antictona,* and said the two were both contained in one sphere which revolved from east to west, and on account of this revolution the sun was made to circle round us, and was now seen and then not seen. And he said that fire was between these two [stars], asserting that it was a more noble element than water and earth [of which these worlds are composed], and asserting the middle place to be the noblest of those occupied by the four simple bodies [or elements]. And therefore he said that fire, when it appeared to rise, in reality descended to this centre.

But Plato was of another opinion, and wrote in one of his books, called *Timaeus,* that the earth, with the sea, was actually the centre of all [the universe] but that its circumference revolved round its centre, following the first movement of the heavens; but very slowly, owing to the grossness of its matter, and its exceeding distance from the *Primum Mobile.*

These opinions are reproved as false in the second *Of Heaven and Earth,* by that glorious Philosopher to whom Nature has most completely revealed her secrets; and by him it is there proved that this world, that is, our earth, stands still and fixed to all eternity. And the reasons Aristotle gives to controvert these opinions, and to affirm the truth, it is not my intention to relate here; because it is quite enough for those to whom I speak, to know on his great authority that this earth is immovable, and does not revolve, and that, with the sea, it is the centre of the heavens.

The heavens revolve continually around this centre, as we see; . . .

3. *The Idea of a Christian Society*

JOHN OF SALISBURY: *The Statesman's Book* *

John of Salisbury (*c.* 1115-80) was one of the great scholars of his age and an international churchman. He served as secretary to Thomas Becket, Archbishop of Canterbury, whom he supported in his struggle

* From John of Salisbury: *The Statesman's Book,* trans. by John Dickinson, pp. 3, 33-4, 64-5, 243-4, 258. Copyright 1927 by Alfred A. Knopf, Inc. Reprinted by permission of Appleton-Century-Crofts, Inc.

with Henry II, and later became Bishop of Chartres. His *Policraticus* (1159), which was the first systematic treatise on political philosophy to appear in the Middle Ages, is noteworthy as a compendium of stock ideas, widely held then and for a long time thereafter.

BETWEEN a tyrant and a prince there is this single or chief difference, that the latter obeys the law and rules the people by its dictates, accounting himself as but their servant. It is by virtue of the law that he makes good his claim to the foremost and chief place in the management of the affairs of the commonwealth and in the bearing of its burdens; and his elevation over others consists in this, that whereas private men are held responsible only for their private affairs, on the prince fall the burdens of the whole community.

* * *

Now there are certain precepts of the law which have a perpetual necessity, having the force of law among all nations and which absolutely cannot be broken with impunity. . . . Let the whitewashers of rulers now come forward, and let them whisper, or if this is too little, let them trumpet abroad that the prince is not subject to the law, and that whatsoever is his will and pleasure, not merely in establishing law according to the model of equity, but absolutely and free from all restrictions, has the force of law. Let them thus, if they so desire and dare, make of their king, whom they except from the obligations of the law, a very outlaw, and still I will maintain not merely in the teeth of their denials but in the teeth of all the world, that kings are bound by this law.

* * *

The prince is first of all to make a thorough survey of himself, and diligently study the condition of the whole body of the commonwealth of which he is the representative, and in whose place he stands. A commonwealth, according to Plutarch, is a certain body which is endowed with life by the benefit of divine favor, which acts at the prompting of the highest equity, and is ruled by what may be called the moderating power of reason. Those things which establish and implant in us the practice of religion, and transmit to us the worship of God (here I do not follow Plutarch, who says "of the Gods") fill the place of the soul in the body of the commonwealth. And therefore those who preside over the practice of religion should be looked up to and venerated as the soul of the body. For who doubts that the ministers of God's holiness are His representatives? Furthermore, since the soul is, as it were, the prince of the body, and has rulership over the whole thereof, so those whom our author calls the prefects of religion preside over the entire body.

Augustus Caesar was to such a degree subject to the priestly power of the pontiffs that in order to set himself free from this subjection and have no one at all over him, he caused himself to be created a pontiff of Vesta, and thereafter had himself promoted to be one of the gods during his own life-time. The place of the head in the body of the commonwealth is filled by the prince, who is subject only to God and to those who exercise His office and represent Him on earth, even as in the human body the head is quickened and governed by the soul. The place of the heart is filled by the Senate, from which proceeds the initiation of good works and ill. The duties of eyes, ears, and tongue are claimed by the judges and the governors of provinces. Officials and soldiers correspond to the hands. Those who always attend upon the prince are likened to the sides. Financial officers and keepers (I speak now not of those who are in charge of the prisons, but of those who are keepers of the privy chest) may be compared with the stomach and intestines, which, if they become congested through excessive avidity, and retain too tenaciously their ac- cumulations, generate innumerable and incurable diseases, so that through their ailment the whole body is threatened with destruction. The hus- bandmen correspond to the feet, which always cleave to the soil, and need the more especially the care and foresight of the head, since while they walk upon the earth doing service with their bodies, they meet the more often with stones of stumbling, and therefore deserve aid and pro- tection all the more justly since it is they who raise, sustain, and move forward the weight of the entire body. Take away the support of the feet from the strongest body, and it cannot move forward by its own power, but must creep painfully and shamefully on its hand, or else be moved by means of brute animals.

*   *   *

Those are called the feet who discharge the humbler offices, and by whose services the members of the whole commonwealth walk upon solid earth. Among these are to be counted the husbandmen, who always cleave to the soil, busied about their plough-lands or vineyards or pas- tures or flower-gardens. To these must be added the many species of cloth-making, and the mechanic arts, which work in wood, iron, bronze and the different metals; also the menial occupations, and the manifold forms of getting a livelihood and sustaining life, or increasing household property, all of which, while they do not pertain to the authority of the governing power, are yet in the highest degree useful and profitable to the corporate whole of the commonwealth. All these different occupa- tions are so numerous that the commonwealth in the number of its feet exceeds not only the eight-footed crab but even the centipede, and be- cause of their very multitude they cannot be enumerated; for while they are not infinite by nature, they are yet of so many different varieties that no writer on the subject of offices or duties has ever laid down particular precepts for each special variety. But it applies generally to each and all of them that in their exercise they should not transgress the limits of the law, and should in all things observe constant reference to the public utility. For inferiors owe it to their superiors to provide them with service, just as the superiors in their turn owe it to their inferiors to provide them with all things needful for their protection and succor. Therefore Plutarch says that that course is to be pursued in all things which is of advantage to the humbler classes, that is to say to the multitude; for small numbers always yield to great. Indeed the reason for the institution of magistrates was to the end that subjects might be protected from wrongs, and that the commonwealth itself might be "shod," so to speak, by means of their services. For it is as it were "unshod" when it is exposed to wrongs,—than which there can be no more disgraceful pass of affairs to those who fill the magistracies. For an afflicted people is a sign and proof of the goutiness, so to speak, of the prince. Then and then only will the health of the commonwealth be sound and flourishing when the higher members shield the lower, and the lower respond faithfully and fully in like measure to the just demands of their superiors, so that each and all are as it were members one of another by a sort of reciprocity, and each regards his own interest as best served by that which he knows to be most advantageous for the others.

* * *

For myself, I am satisfied and persuaded that loyal shoulders should uphold the power of the ruler; and not only do I submit to his power patiently, but with pleasure, so long as it is exercised in subjection to God and follows His ordinances. But on the other hand if it resists and opposes the divine commandments, and wishes to make me share in its war against God; then with unrestrained voice I answer back that God must be preferred before any man on earth. Therefore inferiors should cleave and cohere to their superiors, and all the limbs should be in subjection to the head; but always and only on condition that religion is kept inviolate.

St. Thomas Aquinas: *On the Governance of Rulers* *

St. Thomas's *De Regimine Principum* (c. 1260?) is typical of a great many such medieval treatises proffering advice to rulers (it is addressed to the King of Cyprus). Having discussed the need for government

* From St. Thomas Aquinas: *On the Governance of Rulers*, trans. by G. B. Phelan, pp. 53-4, 58-62, 64-6. Copyright 1949 by Mediaeval Studies of Toronto, Inc. Reprinted by permission of Mediaeval Studies of Toronto, Inc.

and the superiority of monarchy, St. Thomas launches into the following discourse on the duties of rulers.

THE NEXT point to be considered is what the kingly office is and what qualities the king should have. Since things which are in accordance with art are an imitation of the things which are in accordance with nature (from which we accept the rules to act according to reason), it seems best that we learn about the kingly office from the pattern of the regime of nature.

In things of nature there is both a universal and a particular government. The former is God's government Whose rule embraces all things and Whose providence governs them all. The latter is found in man and it is much like the divine government. Hence man is called a *microcosmos*. Indeed there is a similitude between both governments in regard to their form; for just as the universe of corporeal creatures and all spiritual powers come under the divine government, in like manner the members of the human body and all the powers of the soul are governed by reason. Thus, in a proportionate manner, reason is to man what God is to the world. Since, however, man is by nature a social animal living in a multitude, as we have pointed out above, the analogy with the divine government is found in him not only in this way that one man governs himself by reason, but also in that the multitude of men is governed by the reason of one man. This is what first of all constitutes the office of a king. . . .

Therefore let the king recognize that such is the office which he undertakes, namely, that he is to be in the kingdom what the soul is in the body, and what God is in the world. If he reflect seriously upon this, a zeal for justice will be enkindled in him when he contemplates that he has been appointed to this position in place of God, to exercise judgment in his kingdom; further, he will acquire the gentleness of clemency and mildness when he considers as his own members those individuals who are subject to his rule.

*   *   *

Just as the founding of a city or kingdom may suitably be learned from the way in which the world was created, so too the way to govern may be learned from the divine government of the world.

Before going into that, however, we should consider that to govern is to lead the thing governed in a suitable way towards its proper end. Thus a ship is said to be governed when, through the skill of the pilot, it is brought unharmed and by a direct route to harbour. Consequently, if a thing be directed to an end outside itself (as a ship to the harbour), it is the governor's duty, not only to preserve the thing unharmed, but further to guide it towards this end. . . .

But as long as man's mortal life endures there is an extrinsic good for him, namely, final beatitude which is looked for after death in the enjoyment of God, for as the Apostle says: "As long as we are in the body we are far from the Lord." Consequently the Christian man, for whom that beatitude has been purchased by the blood of Christ, and who, in order to attain it, has received the earnest of the Holy Ghost, needs another and spiritual care to direct him to the harbour of eternal salvation, and this care is provided for the faithful by the ministers of the church of Christ.

Now the same judgment is to be formed about the end of society as a whole as about the end of one man. If, therefore, the ultimate end of man were some good that existed in himself, then the ultimate end of the multitude to be governed would likewise be for the multitude to acquire such good, and persevere in its possession. If such an ultimate end either of an individual man or a multitude were a corporeal one, namely, life and health of body, to govern would then be a physician's charge. If that ultimate end were an abundance of wealth, then knowledge of economics would have the last word in the community's government. If the good of the knowledge of truth were of such a kind that the multitude might attain to it, the king would have to be a teacher. It is, however, clear that the end of a multitude gathered together is to live virtuously. For men form a group for the purpose of *living well* together, a thing which the individual man living alone could not attain, and *good life* is virtuous life. Therefore, virtuous life is the end for which men gather together. The evidence for this lies in the fact that only those who render mutual assistance to one another in living well form a genuine part of an assembled multitude. If men assembled merely to live, then animals and slaves would form a part of the civil community. Or, if men assembled only to accrue wealth, then all those who traded together would belong to one city. Yet we see that only such are regarded as forming one multitude as are directed by the same laws and the same government to live well.

Yet through virtuous living man is further ordained to a higher end, which consists in the enjoyment of God, as we have said above. Consequently, since society must have the same end as the individual man, it is not the ultimate end of an assembled multitude to live virtuously, but through virtuous living to attain to the possession of God.

If this end could be attained by the power of human nature, then the duty of a king would have to include the direction of men to it. We are supposing, of course, that he is called king to whom the supreme power of governing in human affairs is entrusted. Now the higher the end to which a government is ordained, the loftier that government is. Indeed, we always find that the one to whom it pertains to achieve the final end commands those who execute the things that are ordained to that end.

For example, the captain, whose business it is to regulate navigation, tells the shipbuilder what kind of ship he must construct to be suitable for navigation; and the ruler of a city, who makes use of arms, tells the blacksmith what kind of arms to make. But because a man does not attain his end, which is the possession of God, by human power but by divine—according to the words of the Apostle: "By the grace of God life ever-lasting"—, therefore the task of leading him to that last end does not pertain to human but to divine government.

Consequently, government of this kind pertains to that king who is not only a man, but also God, namely, our Lord Jesus Christ, Who by making men sons of God brought them to the glory of Heaven. This then is the government which has been delivered to Him and which "shall not be destroyed," on account of which He is called, in Holy Writ, not Priest only, but King. As Jeremias says: "The king shall reign and he shall be wise." Hence a royal priesthood is derived from Him, and what is more, all those who believe in Christ, in so far as they are His members, are called kings and priests.

Thus, in order that spiritual things might be distinguished from earthly things, the ministry of this kingdom has been entrusted not to earthly kings but to priests, and most of all to the chief priest, the successor of St. Peter, the Vicar of Christ, the Roman Pontiff. To him all the kings of the Christian People are to be subject as to our Lord Jesus Christ Himself. For those to whom pertains the care of intermediate ends should be subject to him to whom pertains the care of the ultimate end, and be directed by his rule.

*   *   *

. . . it clearly follows that, just as the king ought to be subject to the divine government administered by the office of priesthood, so he ought to preside over all human offices, and regulate them by the rule of his government.

Now anyone on whom it devolves to do something which is ordained to another thing as to its end is bound to see that his work is suitable to that end; thus, for example, the armourer so fashions the sword that it is suitable for fighting, and the builder should so lay out the house that it is suitable for habitation. Therefore, since the beatitude of heaven is the end of that virtuous life which we live at present, it pertains to the king's office to promote the good life of the multitude in such a way as to make it suitable for the attainment of heavenly happiness, that is to say, he should command those things which lead to the happiness of Heaven and, as far as possible, forbid the contrary. . . . Thus the king, taught the law of God, should have for his principal concern the means by which the multitude subject to him may live well.

This concern is threefold: first of all, to establish a virtuous life in the multitude subject to him; second, to preserve it once established; and third, having preserved it, to promote its greater perfection.

For an individual man to lead a good life two things are required. The first and most important is to act in a virtuous manner (for virtue is that by which one lives well); the second, which is secondary and instrumental, is a sufficiency of those bodily goods whose use is necessary for virtuous life. Yet the unity of man is brought about by nature, while the unity of multitude, which we call peace, must be procured through the efforts of the ruler. Therefore, to establish virtuous living in a multitude three things are necessary. First of all, that the multitude be established in the unity of peace. Second, that the multitude thus united in the bond of peace, be directed to acting well. For just as a man can do nothing well unless unity within his members be presupposed, so a multitude of men lacking the unity of peace will be hindered from virtuous action by the fact that it is fighting against itself. In the third place, it is necessary that there be at hand a sufficient supply of the things required for proper living, procured by the ruler's efforts.

St. Thomas Aquinas: *On Heresy* *

> The following selections are from St. Thomas's article "On heresy" in the *Summa Theologica*. His views on the subject were basically those of St. Augustine who had preached the text, "Compel them to come in" (Luke 14: 21-3). However, the thirteenth century introduced the death penalty, to which Augustine had objected.

Now a heretic is one who devises or follows false or new opinions. Therefore heresy is opposed to the truth, on which faith is founded; and consequently it is a species of unbelief.

I answer that, The word heresy as stated in the first objection denotes a choosing. Now choice as stated above (I–II, Q. 13, A. 3) is about things directed to the end, the end being presupposed. Now, in matters of faith, the will assents to some truth, as to its proper good, as was shown above (Q. 4, A. 3): wherefore that which is the chief truth, has the character of last end, while those which are secondary truths, have the character of being directed to the end.

Now, whoever believes, assents to someone's words; so that, in every form of belief, the person to whose words assent is given seems to hold the chief place and to be the end as it were; while the things by holding which one assents to that person hold a secondary place. Consequently

* The quotations from the English translation of the *Summa Theologica* of St. Thomas Aquinas are reproduced with the permission of Benziger Brothers, Inc., publishers and copyright owners. Vol. II, pp. 1224-7.

he that holds the Christian faith aright, assents, by his will, to Christ, in those things which truly belong to His doctrine.

Accordingly there are two ways in which a man may deviate from the rectitude of the Christian faith. First, because he is unwilling to assent to Christ; and such a man has an evil will, so to say, in respect of the very end. This belongs to the species of unbelief in pagans and Jews. Secondly, because, though he intends to assent to Christ, yet he fails in his choice of those things wherein he assents to Christ, because he chooses, not what Christ really taught, but the suggestions of his own mind.

Therefore heresy is a species of unbelief, belonging to those who profess the Christian faith, but corrupt its dogmas.

* * *

. . . The Apostle says (Tit. iii. 10, 11): *A man that is a heretic, after the first and second admonition, avoid: knowing that he, that is such an one, is subverted.*

I answer that, With regard to heretics two points must be observed: one, on their own side, the other, on the side of the Church. On their own side there is the sin, whereby they deserve not only to be separated from the Church by excommunication, but also to be severed from the world by death. For it is a much graver matter to corrupt the faith which quickens the soul, than to forge money, which supports temporal life. Wherefore if forgers of money and other evil-doers are forthwith condemned to death by the secular authority, much more reason is there for heretics, as soon as they are convicted of heresy, to be not only excommunicated but even put to death.

On the part of the Church, however, there is mercy which looks to the conversion of the wanderer, wherefore she condemns not at once, but *after the first and second admonition,* as the Apostle directs: after that, if he is yet stubborn, the Church no longer hoping for his conversion, looks to the salvation of others, by excommunicating him and separating him from the Church, and furthermore delivers him to the secular tribunal to be exterminated thereby from the world by death. For Jerome commenting on Gal. v. 9, *A little leaven,* says: *Cut off the decayed flesh, expel the mangy sheep from the fold, lest the whole house, the whole paste, the whole body, the whole flock, burn, perish, rot, die. Arius was but one spark in Alexandria, but as that spark was not at once put out, the whole earth was laid waste by its flame.*

Reply Obj. 1. This very modesty demands that the heretic should be admonished a first and second time: and if he be unwilling to retract, he must be reckoned as already *subverted,* as we may gather from the words of the Apostle quoted above.

DANTE ALIGHIERI: *Of Monarchy* *

Dante's *De Monarchia* was at once a tract for the times and a political utopia. Driven into exile by the party of Pope Boniface VIII, which gained control of Florence in 1302, he wrote it in part as a protest against the papal claims to temporal power. But the book is also a superb statement of the medieval dream of Christian universalism, and a fine example of the scholastic way of arguing about politics.

FIRST, therefore, we must see what is it that is called Temporal Monarchy, in its idea, so to speak, and according to its purpose. Temporal Monarchy, then, or, as men call it, the Empire, is the government of one prince above all men in time, or in those things and over those things which are measured by time. Three great questions are asked concerning it. First, there is the doubt and the question, is it necessary for the welfare of the world? Secondly, did the Roman people take to itself by right the office of Monarchy? And thirdly, does the authority of Monarchy come from God directly, or only from some other minister or vicar of God?

Now, since, every truth, which is not itself a first principle, becomes manifest from the truth of some first principle, it is therefore necessary in every inquiry to have a knowledge of the first principle involved, to which by analysis we may go back for the certainty of all the propositions which are afterwards accepted. And since this treatise is an inquiry, we must begin by examining the first principle on the strength of which deductions are to rest. . . .

Now, therefore, we must see what is the end of the whole civil order of men; and when we have found this, then, as the Philosopher says in his book to Nicomachus, the half of our labour will have been accomplished. And to render the question clearer, we must observe that as there is a certain end for which nature makes the thumb, and another, different from this, for which she makes the whole hand, and again another for which she makes the arm, and another different from all for which she makes the whole man; so there is one end for which she orders the individual man, and another for which she orders the family, and another end for the city, and another for the kingdom, and finally an ultimate one for which the Everlasting God, by His art which is nature, brings into being the whole human race. And this is what we seek as a first principle to guide our whole inquiry. . . .

It has thus been sufficiently set forth that the proper work of the human race, taken as a whole, is to set in action the whole capacity of that

* The 'De Monarchia' of Dante, trans. by F. J. Church (London: Macmillan & Co.; 1879), pp. 2–5, 8–10, 13–16, 99–101, 127–8.

understanding which is capable of development: first in the way of speculation, and then, by its extension, in the way of action. And seeing that what is true of a part is true also of the whole, and that it is by rest and quiet that the individual man becomes perfect in wisdom and prudence; so the human race, by living in the calm and tranquillity of peace, applies itself most freely and easily to its proper work; a work which, according to the saying; "Thou hast made him a little lower than the angels," is almost divine. Whence it is manifest that of all things that are ordered to secure blessings to men, peace is the best. . . .

Now that we have declared these matters, it is plain what is the better, nay the best, way in which mankind may attain to do its proper work. And consequently we have seen the readiest means by which to arrive at the point, for which all our works are ordered, as their ultimate end; namely, the universal peace, which is to be assumed as the first principle for our deductions. As we said, this assumption was necessary, for it is as a sign-post to us, that into it we may resolve all that has to be proved, as into a most manifest truth.

As therefore we have already said, there are three doubts, and these doubts suggest three questions, concerning Temporal Monarchy, which in more common speech is called the Empire; and our purpose is, as we explained, to inquire concerning these questions in their given order, and starting from the first principle which we have just laid down. The first question, then, is whether Temporal Monarchy is necessary for the welfare of the world; and that it is necessary can, I think, be shown by the strongest and most manifest arguments; for nothing, either of reason or of authority, opposes me. Let us first take the authority of the Philosopher in his Politics. There, on his venerable authority, it is said that where a number of things are arranged to attain an end, it behoves one of them to regulate or govern the others, and the others to submit. And it is not only the authority of his illustrious name which makes this worthy of belief, but also reason, instancing particulars. . . .

Further, the whole human race is a whole with reference to certain parts, and, with reference to another whole, it is a part. For it is a whole with reference to particular kingdoms and nations, as we have shown; and it is a part with reference to the whole universe, as is manifest without argument. Therefore, as the lower portions of the whole system of humanity are well adapted to that whole, so that whole is said to be well adapted to the whole which is above it. It is only under the rule of one prince that the parts of humanity are well adapted to their whole, as may easily be collected from what we have said; therefore it is only by being under one Princedom, or the rule of a single Prince, that humanity as a whole is well adapted to the Universe, or its Prince, who is the One God. And it therefore follows that Monarchy is necessary for the welfare of the world.

And all is well and at its best which exists according to the will of the first agent, who is God. This is self-evident, except to those who deny that the divine goodness attains to absolute perfection. Now, it is the intention of God that all created things should represent the likeness of God, so far as their proper nature will admit. Therefore was it said: "Let us make man in our image, after our likeness." And though it could not be said that the lower part of creation was made in the image of God, yet all things may be said to be after His likeness, for what is the whole universe but the footprint of the divine goodness? The human race, therefore, is well, nay at its best state, when, so far as can be, it is made like unto God. But the human race is then most made like unto God when most it is one; for the true principle of oneness is in Him alone. Wherefore it is written: "Hear, O Israel; the Lord thy God is one God." But the race of man is most one when it is united wholly in one body, and it is evident that this cannot be, except when it is subject to one prince. Therefore in this subjection mankind is most made like unto God, and, in consequence, such a subjection is in accordance with the divine intention, and it is indeed well and best for man when this is so, as we showed at the beginning of this chapter.

Again, things are well and at their best with every son when he follows, so far as by his proper nature he can, the footsteps of a perfect father. Mankind is the son of heaven, which is most perfect in all its works; for it is "man and the sun which produce man," according to the second book on Natural Learning. The human race, therefore, is at its best when it imitates the movements of heaven, so far as human nature allows. And since the whole heaven is regulated with one motion, to wit, that of the *primum mobile*, and by one mover, who is God, in all its parts, movements, and movers (and this human reason readily seizes from science); therefore, if our argument be correct, the human race is at its best state when, both in its movements, and in regard to those who move it, it is regulated by a single Prince, as by the single movement of heaven, and by one law, as by the single motion. Therefore it is evidently necessary for the welfare of the world for there to be a Monarchy, or single Princedom, which men call the Empire. And this thought did Boethius breathe when he said: "Oh happy race of men, if your hearts are ruled by the love which rules the heaven."

Wherever there is controversy, there ought to be judgment, otherwise there would be imperfection without its proper remedy, which is impossible; for God and Nature, in things necessary, do not fail in their provisions. But it is manifest that there may be controversy between any two princes, where the one is not subject to the other, either from the fault of themselves, or even of their subjects. Therefore between them there should be means of judgment. And since, when one is not subject to the other, he cannot be judged by the other (for there is no rule of equals over equals), there must be a third prince of wider jurisdiction, within the circle of whose laws both may come. Either he will or he will not be a Monarch. If he is, we have what we sought; if not, then this one again will have an equal, who is not subject to his jurisdiction, and then again we have need of a third. And so we must either go on to infinity, which is impossible, or we must come to that judge who is first and highest; by whose judgment all controversies shall be either directly or indirectly decided; and he will be Monarch or Emperor.

*   *   *

They [the advocates of papal monarchy] also bring forward that saying in Matthew of Christ to Peter: "Whatsoever thou shalt bind on earth shall be bound in heaven; and whatsoever thou shalt loose on earth shall be loosed in heaven"; which also, from the text of Matthew and John, they allow to have been in like manner said to all the Apostles. From this they argue that it has been granted by God to the successor of Peter to be able to bind and to loose all things; hence they infer that he can loose the laws and decrees of the Empire, and also bind laws and decrees for the temporal power; and, if this were so, this conclusion would rightly follow.

But we must draw a distinction touching their major premiss. Their syllogism is in this form. Peter could loose and bind all things; the successor of Peter can do whatever Peter could do; therefore the successor of Peter can bind and can loose all things: whence they conclude that he can bind and can loose the decrees and the authority of the Empire.

Now I admit the minor premiss; but touching the major premiss I draw a distinction. The universal "everything" which is included in "whatever" is not distributed beyond the extent of the distributed term. If I say "all animals run," "all" is distributed so as to include everything which comes under the class "animal." But if I say "all men run," then "all" is only distributed so as to include every individual in the class "man"; and when I say "every grammarian runs," then is the distribution even more limited.

Therefore we must always look to see what it is that is to be included in the word "all," and when we know the nature and extent of the distributed term, it will easily be seen how far the distribution extends. Therefore, when it is said "whatsoever thou shalt bind," if "whatsoever" bore an unlimited sense, they would speak truly, and the power of the Pope would extend even beyond what they say; for he might then divorce a wife from her husband, and marry her to another while her first husband was yet alive, which he can in no wise do. He might even absolve me when impenitent, which God Himself cannot do.

Therefore it is manifest that the distribution of the term in question is not absolute, but in reference to something. What this is will be sufficiently clear if we consider what power was granted to Peter. Christ said to Peter: "To thee will I give the keys of the kingdom of heaven"—that is, "I will make thee the doorkeeper of the kingdom of heaven." And then He adds: "Whatsoever," which is to say "all that"—to wit, all that has reference to this duty—"thou shalt have power to bind and to loose." And thus the universal which is implied in "whatsoever" has only a limited distribution, referring to the office of the keys of the kingdom of heaven.

* * *

It is therefore clear that the authority of temporal Monarchy comes down, with no intermediate will, from the fountain of universal authority; and this fountain, one in its unity, flows through many channels out of the abundance of the goodness of God.

And now, methinks, I have reached the goal which I set before me. I have unravelled the truth of the questions which I asked: whether the office of Monarchy was necessary to the welfare of the world; whether it was by right that the Roman people assumed to themselves the office of Monarchy; and, further, that last question, whether the authority of the Monarch springs immediately from God, or from some other. Yet the truth of this latter question must not be received so narrowly as to deny that in certain matters the Roman Prince is subject to the Roman Pontiff. For that happiness, which is subject to mortality, in a sense is ordered with a view to the happiness which shall not taste of death. Let, therefore, Caesar be reverent to Peter, as the first-born son should be reverent to his father, that he may be illuminated with the light of his father's grace, and so may be stronger to lighten the world over which he has been placed by Him alone, who is the ruler of all things spiritual as well as temporal.

RAMÓN LULL: *The Book of the Order of Chivalry* *

> Ramón Lull (*c.* 1235–1315) was the son of a distinguished Majorcan soldier. In 1266, after having lived the life of a worldling at the court of James II of Aragon, he had a vision of the crucified Christ. Thenceforth he devoted his life to the conversion of the Saracens, journeying several times to Africa, composing numerous treatises in refutation of heathenism, and finally suffering the death of a martyr, being stoned to

death by Saracens. It was probably during his residence at the College of the Holy Trinity in Majorca, which he founded for the teaching of Arabic to monks, that he wrote *The Book of the Order of Chivalry* (1276–86).

UNTO the praising and divine glory of God, which is lord and sovereign king above and over all things celestial and worldly, we begin this book of the order of chivalry for to show that like God, the prince almighty which ruleth above the seven planets that make the course celestial and have power and seignory in government and ordaining the bodies terrestrial and earthly, that in likewise ought the kings, princes and great lords to have puissance and seignory upon the knights. And the knights by similitude ought to have power and domination over the people of middle rank.

*   *   *

Of the office that pertaineth to a knight

The office of a knight is the end and the beginning wherefore began the order of chivalry. Then if a knight use not his office, he is contrary to his order and to the beginning of chivalry aforesaid: by the which contrarity he is not a true knight, howbeit that he bear the name. For such a knight is more vile than the smith or the carpenter that do their office as they ought to do and have learned. The office of a knight is to maintain and defend the holy faith catholic, by the which God the Father sent his son into the world to take human flesh in the glorious virgin our lady saint Mary. . . . Then in likewise as our lord God hath chosen the clerks for to maintain the holy faith catholic with scripture and reasons against the miscreants and non-believers, in likewise God of glory hath chosen knights because that by force of arms they vanquish the miscreants which daily labor for to destroy holy church. And such knights God holdeth them for his friends honored in this world and in that other when they keep and maintain the faith by the which we expect to be saved. . . . Many there be that have offices which God hath given to them in this world to the end that by them he should be served and honored, but the most noble and the most honorable offices that be, be the offices of clerks and of knights. . . .

So much noble is chivalry that every knight ought to be governor of a great country or land. But there be so many knights that the land may not suffice to signify that one ought to be lord of all things. The emperor ought to be a knight and lord of knights, but because that the emperor may not by himself govern all knights it behooveth that he have under him kings that be knights, to the end that they aid and help to maintain the order of chivalry. And the kings ought to have under them dukes, earls, viscounts and other lords. And under the barons ought to be knights. . . .

The office of a knight is to maintain and defend his lord worldly or earthly, for a king nor no high baron hath no power to maintain right in his men without aid and help. Then if any man do against the commandment of his king or prince, it behooveth that the knights aid their lord . . . , and therefore the evil knight which sooner helpeth another man that would put down his lord from the seignory that he ought to have upon him, he followeth not the office by which he is called a knight. By the knights ought to be maintained and kept justice. . . . Knights ought to take coursers to joust and to go to tourneys, to hold open table, to hunt at harts, boars and other wild beasts. For in doing these things the knights exercize them to arms for to maintain the order of knighthood. . . . And thus, as all these things aforesaid pertain to a knight as touching his body, in like wise justice, wisdom, charity, loyalty, truth, humility, strength, hope, swiftness and all other virtues similarly pertain to a knight as touching his soul, and therefore the knight that useth the things that pertain to the order of chivalry as touching his body, and hath none of these virtues that pertain to chivalry touching his soul is not the friend of the order of knighthood. . . .

The office of a knight is to maintain the land, for because that the dread of the common people have of the knights, they labor and cultivate the earth for fear lest they should be destroyed. And by the dread of the knights they fear the kings, princes and lords by whom they have their power. . . .

The office of a knight is to maintain and defend women, widows and orphans, and men diseased and not puissant nor strong. For like as custom and reason is that the greatest and most mighty help the feeble and less, and that they have recourse to the great, right so is the order of chivalry, because she is great, honorable and mighty, be in succor and in aid to them that be under him, and less mighty and less honored than he is. . . .

The office of a knight is to have a castle and horse for to keep the highways, and for to defend them that labor on the lands and the earth, and they ought to have towns and cities for to hold right [administer justice] to the people, and for to assemble in a place men of many diverse crafts, which be much necessary to the ordinance of this world to keep and maintain the life of man and of woman.

    In what manner a squire ought to be received into the order of chivalry

At the beginning that a squire ought to enter into the order of chivalry, him behooveth that he confess him of his faults that he hath done against God, and ought to receive chivalry in intention that in the same he serve our lord God which is glorious. And if he be clean out of sin, he ought to receive his saviour. For to make and dub a knight, it appertaineth the day of some great feast, as Christmas, Easter, Whitsuntide, or on such day solemn, because that by the honor of the feast assemble much people in that place where the squire ought to be dubbed knight, and God ought to be adored and prayed that he give to him grace for to live well after the order of chivalry. The squire ought to fast the vigil of the same feast in the honor of the saint of whom the feast is made that day, and he ought to go to church for to pray God and ought to wake the night and be in his prayers, and ought to hear the word of God. . . . On the morning after the feast in the which he is to be dubbed, him behooveth that he do a mass to be sung solemnly, and the squire ought to come before the altar and offer to the priest, which holdeth the place of our lord to the honor of whom he must oblige and submit himself, to keep the honor of chivalry with all his power. In that same day ought to be made a sermon in which should be recounted and declared the twelve articles in which is founded the holy faith catholic, the ten commandments and the seven sacraments, and the other things that pertain to the faith. . . .

[Then] the squire ought to kneel before the altar, and lift up to God his eyes corporal and spiritual and his hands to heaven, and the knight ought to gird him in sign of chastity, justice and of charity, with his sword. The knight ought to kiss the squire and to give him a palm, because that he be remembering of that which he receiveth and promiseth, and of the great charge in which he is obliged and bounden, and of the great honor that he receiveth by the order of chivalry. And after when the knight spiritual, that is the priest, and the knight earthly have done that pertaineth to their office as touching to the making of a new knight, the new knight ought to ride through the town and to show him to the people, to the end that all man know and see that he is newly made knight.

Of the significance of the arms of a knight

As the vestments of the priest when he singeth the mass hath some significance which concordeth to his office, and the office of priesthood and of chivalry have great concordance, therefore the order of chivalry requireth that all that which is needful to a knight as touching the use of his office have some significance, by the which is signified the nobleness of chivalry and his order.

Unto a knight is given a sword which is made in semblance of the cross for to signify how our lord God vanquished in the cross the death of human lineage, and to the which he was judged for the sin of our first father Adam. All in likewise a knight ought to vanquish and destroy the enemies of the cross by the sword. For chivalry is to maintain justice. And therefore is the sword made cutting on both sides to signify that the knight ought with the sword maintain chivalry and justice. To a knight is given a spear for to signify truth. For truth is a thing right and even. And that truth ought to go before falseness. And the iron or head of the spear signifieth strength which truth ought to have above falseness. And the pennon signifieth that truth showeth to all faith and hath no dread nor fear of falseness nor of treachery, etc.

St. Thomas Aquinas: *On the Ethics of Trading* *

In the following selections from the *Summa Theologica* St. Thomas Aquinas sums up the dominant attitude of the Middle Ages that trading, like every other form of human occupation, is subject to religious ethics. His comment upon the famous Deuteronomic law, which permitted the Jews to take usury from foreigners but not from blood brothers of the tribe, is especially noteworthy.

Of Cheating, Which is Committed in Buying and Selling

WE MUST now consider those sins which relate to voluntary commutations. First, we shall consider cheating, which is committed in buying and selling: secondly, we shall consider usury, which occurs in loans. . . .

We proceed thus to the First Article:—
Objection 1. It would seem that it is lawful to sell a thing for more than its worth. In the commutations of human life, civil laws determine that which is just. Now according to these laws it is just for buyer and seller to deceive one another (Cod., IV, xliv, *De Rescind. Vend.* 8, 15): and this occurs by the seller selling a thing for more than its worth, and the buyer buying a thing for less than its worth. Therefore it is lawful to sell a thing for more than its worth. . . .

On the contrary, It is written (Matth. vii. 12): *All things . . . whatsoever you would that men should do to you, do you also to them.* But no man wishes to buy a thing for more than its worth. Therefore no man should sell a thing to another man for more than its worth.

I answer that, It is altogether sinful to have recourse to deceit in order to sell a thing for more than its just price, because this is to deceive one's neighbor so as to injure him. Hence Tully says (*De offic.* iii. 15): *Contracts should be entirely free from double-dealing: the seller must not impose upon the bidder, nor the buyer upon one that bids against him.*

* The quotations from the English translation of the *Summa Theologica* of St. Thomas Aquinas are reproduced with the permission of Benziger Brothers, Inc., publishers and copyright owners. Vol. II, pp. 1513–14, 1516–21.

But, apart from fraud, we may speak of buying and selling in two ways. First, as considered in themselves, and from this point of view, buying and selling seem to be established for the common advantage of both parties, one of whom requires that which belongs to the other, and vice versa, as the Philosopher states (*Polit.* i. 3). Now whatever is established for the common advantage, should not be more of a burden to one party than to another, and consequently all contracts between them should observe equality of thing and thing. Again, the quality of a thing that comes into human use is measured by the price given for it, for which purpose money was invented, as stated in *Ethic.* v. 5. Therefore if either the price exceed the quantity of the thing's worth, or, conversely, the thing exceed the price, there is no longer the equality of justice: and consequently, to sell a thing for more than its worth, or to buy it for less than its worth, is in itself unjust and unlawful. . . .

Reply Obj. 1. As stated above (I–II, Q. 96, A. 2) human law is given to the people among whom there are many lacking virtue, and it is not given to the virtuous alone. Hence human law was unable to forbid all that is contrary to virtue; and it suffices for it to prohibit whatever is destructive of human intercourse, while it treats other matters as though they were lawful, not by approving of them, but by not punishing them. Accordingly, if without employing deceit the seller disposes of his goods for more than their worth, or the buyer obtain them for less than their worth, the law looks upon this as licit, and provides no punishment for so doing, unless the excess be too great, because then even human law demands restitution to be made, for instance if a man be deceived in regard to more than half the amount of the just price of a thing.

On the other hand the Divine law leaves nothing unpunished that is contrary to virtue. Hence, according to the Divine law, it is reckoned unlawful if the equality of justice be not observed in buying and selling: and he who has received more than he ought must make compensation to him that has suffered loss, if the loss be considerable. I add this condition, because the just price of things is not fixed with mathematical precision, but depends on a kind of estimate, so that a slight addition or subtraction would not seem to destroy the equality of justice. . . .

We proceed thus to the Fourth Article:—

Objection 1. It would seem that it is not lawful, in trading, to sell a thing for a higher price than we paid for it. . . .

On the contrary, Augustine commenting on Ps. lxx. 15, *Because I have not known learning,* says: *The greedy tradesman blasphemes over his losses; he lies and perjures himself over the price of his wares. But these are vices of the man, not of the craft, which can be exercised without these vices.* Therefore trading is not in itself unlawful.

I answer that, A tradesman is one whose business consists in the exchange of things. According to the Philosopher (*Polit.* i. 3), exchange of things is twofold; one, natural as it were, and necessary, whereby one commodity is exchanged for another, or money taken in exchange for a commodity, in order to satisfy the needs of life. Such like trading, properly speaking, does not belong to tradesmen, but rather to housekeepers or civil servants who have to provide the household or the state with the necessaries of life. The other kind of exchange is either that of money for money, or of any commodity for money, not on account of the necessities of life, but for profit, and this kind of exchange, properly speaking, regards tradesmen, according to the Philosopher (*Polit.* i. 3). The former kind of exchange is commendable because it supplies a natural need: but the latter is justly deserving of blame, because, considered in itself, it satisfies the greed for gain, which knows no limit and tends to infinity. Hence trading, considered in itself, has a certain debasement attaching thereto, in so far as, by its very nature, it does not imply a virtuous or necessary end. Nevertheless gain which is the end of trading, though not implying, by its nature, anything virtuous or necessary, does not, in itself, connote anything sinful or contrary to virtue: wherefore nothing prevents gain from being directed to some necessary or even virtuous end, and thus trading becomes lawful. Thus, for instance, a man may intend the moderate gain which he seeks to acquire by trading for the upkeep of his household, or for the assistance of the needy: or again, a man may take to trade for some public advantage, for instance, lest his country lack the necessaries of life, and seek gain, not as an end, but as payment for his labor.

Of the Sin of Usury

We proceed thus to the First Article:—

Objection 1. It would seem that it is not a sin to take usury for money lent. For no man sins through following the example of Christ. But Our Lord said of Himself (Luke xix. 23): *At My coming I might have exacted it,* i.e. the money lent, *with usury.* Therefore it is not a sin to take usury for lending money.

Obj. 2. Further, according to Ps. xviii. 8, *The law of the Lord is unspotted,* because, to wit, it forbids sin. Now usury of a kind is allowed in the Divine law, according to Deut. xxiii. 19, 20. *Thou shalt not fenerate* [lend upon usury] *to thy brother money, nor corn, nor any other thing, but to the stranger:* nay more, it is even promised as a reward for the observance of the Law, according to Deut. xxviii. 12: *Thou shalt fenerate to many nations, and shalt not borrow of any one.* Therefore it is not a sin to take usury.

Obj. 3. Further, in human affairs justice is determined by civil laws. Now civil law allows usury to be taken. Therefore it seems to be lawful. . . .

On the contrary, It is written (Exod. xxii. 25): *If thou lend money to any of thy people that is poor, that dwelleth with thee, thou shalt not be hard upon them as an extortioner, nor oppress them with usuries.*

I answer that, To take usury for money lent is unjust in itself, because this is to sell what does not exist, and this evidently leads to inequality which is contrary to justice. . . .

Reply Obj. 2. The Jews were forbidden to take usury from their brethren, i.e. from other Jews. By this we are given to understand that to take usury from any man is evil simply, because we ought to treat every man as our neighbor and brother, especially in the state of the Gospel, whereto all are called. Hence it is said without any distinction in Ps. xiv. 5: *He that hath not put out his money to usury*, and (Ezech. xviii. 8): *Who hath not taken usury.* They were permitted, however, to take usury from foreigners, not as though it were lawful, but in order to avoid a greater evil, lest, to wit, through avarice to which they were prone according to Is. lvi. 11, they should take usury from the Jews who were worshippers of God. . . .

A lender may without sin enter an agreement with the borrower for compensation for the loss he incurs of something he ought to have, for this is not to sell the use of money but to avoid a loss. It may also happen that the borrower avoids a greater loss than the lender incurs, wherefore the borrower may repay the lender with what he has gained. But the lender cannot enter an agreement for compensation, through the fact that he makes no profit out of his money: because he must not sell that which he has not yet and may be prevented in many ways from having. . . .

He who lends money transfers the ownership of the money to the borrower. Hence the borrower holds the money at his own risk and is bound to pay it all back: wherefore the lender must not exact more. On the other hand he that entrusts his money to a merchant or craftsman so as to form a kind of society, does not transfer the ownership of his money to them, for it remains his, so that at his risk the merchant speculates with it, or the craftsman uses it for his craft, and consequently he may lawfully demand as something belonging to him, part of the profits derived from his money.

4. *The "Theology of History"*

BISHOP OTTO OF FREISING: *The Two Cities* *

Bishop Otto of Freising (*c.* 1114–58) was of royal lineage and one of the great German ecclesiastics of his time. He became abbot of the

* From Otto, Bishop of Freising: *The Two Cities*, trans. by C. C. Mierow, pp.

Cistercian monastery of Morimund and bishop of Freising, and participated in the disastrous crusade of the Emperor Conrad III. For the main outlines of his philosophy of history, as laid down in his *Chronicle of Universal History to the Year 1146* A.D. (or as he preferred to call it, *The History of the Two Cities*) he was deeply indebted to St. Augustine's *City of God* and Paulus Orosius's *Seven Books of Histories directed against the Pagans,* an epitome of universal history from Adam to the year 417.

Prologue of the First Book

IN PONDERING long and often in my heart upon the changes and vicissitudes of temporal affairs and their varied and irregular issues, even as I hold that a wise man ought by no means to cleave to the things of time, so I find that it is by the faculty of reason alone that one must escape and find release from them. For it is the part of a wise man not to be whirled about after the manner of a revolving wheel, but through the stability of his powers to be firmly fashioned as a thing foursquare. Accordingly, since things are changeable and can never be at rest, what man in his right mind will deny that the wise man ought, as I have said, to depart from them to that city which stays at rest and abides to all eternity? This is the City of God, the heavenly Jerusalem, for which the children of God sigh while they are set in this land of sojourn, oppressed by the turmoil of the things of time as if they were oppressed by the Babylonian captivity. For, inasmuch as there are two cities—the one of time, the other of eternity; the one of the earth, earthy, the other of heaven, heavenly; the one of the devil, the other of Christ—ecclesiastical writers have declared that the former is Babylon, the latter Jerusalem.

But, whereas many of the Gentiles have written much regarding one of these cities, to hand down to posterity the great exploits of men of old (the many evidences of their merits, as they fancied), they have yet left to us the task of setting forth what, in the judgment of our writers, is rather the tale of human miseries. There are extant in this field the famous works of Pompeius Trogus, Justin, Cornelius [*i.e.,* Tacitus], Varro, Eusebius, Jerome, Orosius, Jordanes, and a great many others of our number, as well as of their array, whom it would take too long to enumerate; in those writings the discerning reader will be able to find not so much histories as pitiful tragedies made up of mortal woes. We believe that this has come to pass by what is surely a wise and proper dispensation of the Creator, in order that, whereas men in their folly desire to cleave to earthly and transitory things, they may be frightened away from them by their own vicissitudes, if by nothing else, so as to be directed by the wretchedness of this fleeting life from the creature to a knowledge of the Creator. But we, set down as it were at the end of time, do not so much read of the miseries of mortals in the books of the writers named above as find them for ourselves in consequence of the experiences of our own time. For, to pass over other things, the empire of the Romans, which in Daniel is compared to iron on account of its sole lordship—monarchy, the Greeks call it—over the whole world, a world subdued by war, has in consequence of so many fluctuations and changes, particularly in our day, become, instead of the noblest and the foremost, almost the last. So that, in the words of the poet, scarcely

"a shadow of its mighty name remains."

For being transferred from the City [Rome] to the Greeks [the Byzantine Empire], from the Greeks to the Franks, from the Franks to the Lombards, from the Lombards again to the German Franks, that empire not only became decrepit and senile through lapse of time, but also, like a once smooth pebble that has been rolled this way and that by the waters, contracted many a stain and developed many a defect. The world's misery is exhibited, therefore, even in the case of the chief power in the world, and Rome's fall foreshadows the dissolution of the whole structure.

But what wonder if human power is changeable, seeing that even mortal wisdom is prone to slip? We read that in Egypt there was so great wisdom that, as Plato states, the Egyptians called the philosophers of the Greeks childish and immature. Moses also, the giver of the law, "with whom Jehovah spake as a man speaketh unto his friend," and whom He filled with wisdom divine, was not ashamed to be instructed in all the wisdom of Egypt. Did not that great patriarch, appointed by God the father of nations, Abraham, a man trained in the learning of the Chaldeans and endowed with wisdom, did he not, when called by God, desert his former manner of life [*i.e.*, go to Egypt] and yet not lay aside his wisdom? And yet Babylon the great, not only renowned for wisdom, but also "the glory of kingdoms, the beauty of the Chaldeans' pride," has become, in the words of the prophecy of Isaiah, without hope of restoration, a shrine of owls, a house of serpents and of ostriches, the lurking-place of creeping things. Egypt too is said to be in large measure uninhabitable and impassable. The careful student of history will find that learning was transferred from Egypt to the Greeks, then to the Romans, and finally to the Gauls and the Spaniards. And so it is to be observed that all human power or learning had its origin in the East, but is coming to an end in the West, that thereby the transitoriness and decay of all things human may be displayed. This, by God's grace, we shall show more fully in what follows.

Since, then, the changeable nature of the world is proved by this and like evidence, I thought it necessary . . . to compose a history whereby through God's favor I might display the miseries of the citizens of

Babylon and also the glory of the kingdom of Christ to which the citizens of Jerusalem are to look forward with hope, and of which they are to have a foretaste even in this life. I have undertaken therefore to bring down as far as our own time, according to the ability that God has given me, the record of the conflicts and miseries of the one city, Babylon; and furthermore, not to be silent concerning our hopes regarding that other city, so far as I can gather hints from the Scriptures, but to make mention also of its citizens who are now sojourning in the worldly city. In this work I follow most of all those illustrious lights of the Church, Augustine and Orosius, and have planned to draw from their fountains what is pertinent to my theme and my purpose. The one of these [Augustine] has discoursed most keenly and eloquently on the origin and the progress of the glorious City of God and its ordained limits, setting forth how it has ever spread among the citizens of the world, and showing which of its citizens or princes stood forth preëminent in the various epochs of the princes or citizens of the world. The other [Orosius], in answer to those who, uttering vain babblings, preferred the former times to Christian times, has composed a very valuable history of the fluctuations and wretched issues of human greatness, the wars and the hazards of wars, and the shifting of thrones, from the foundation of the world down to his own time. Following in their steps I have undertaken to speak of the Two Cities in such a way that we shall not lose the thread of history, that the devout reader may observe what is to be avoided in mundane affairs by reason of the countless miseries wrought by their unstable character, and that the studious and painstaking investigator may find a record of past happenings free from all obscurity.

Nor do I think that I shall be justly criticized if, coming after such great men—men so wise and so eloquent—I shall presume in spite of my ignorance to write, since I have both epitomized those things of which they themselves spoke profusely and at length, and have detailed, in however rude a style, the deeds which have been performed by citizens of the world since their time, whether to the advantage of the Church of God or to its hurt. Nor shall I believe that I ought to be assailed by that verse in which the writer of satire says:

"All of us, taught or untaught, are everywhere writers of poems."

For it is not because of indiscretion or frivolity, but out of devotion, which always knows how to excuse ignorance, that I, though I am without proper training, have ventured to undertake so arduous a task. Nor can anyone rightfully accuse me of falsehood in matters which—compared with the customs of the present time—will appear incredible, since down to the days still fresh in our memory I have recorded nothing save what I found in the writings of trustworthy men, and then only a few instances out of many. For I should never hold the view that these men are to be held in contempt if certain of them have preserved in their writings the apostolic simplicity, for, as overshrewd subtlety sometimes kindles error, so a devout rusticity is ever the friend of truth.

As we are about to speak, then, concerning the sorrow-burdened insecurity of the one city and the blessed permanence of the other, let us call upon God, who endures with patience the turbulence and confusion of this world, and by the vision of himself augments and glorifies the joyous peace of that other city, to the end that by His aid we may be able to say the things which are pleasing to Him.

Prologue of the Third Book

Not unmindful of my promise, beloved brother, I shall not hesitate to complete the discussion of the Two Cities, already brought down to the times of Caesar Octavianus with such style as I had at my command, particularly since we have now come to Christian times, and by God's grace I shall speak the more willingly as I shall now be able, because of growing faith, to speak more fully of the City of God. For heretofore, though I had at my command much regarding the citizens of the world, I was in position to say but little about the citizens of Christ, because from the time of the first man to Christ almost the whole world (except a few of the Israelitish race), led astray by error, given over to empty superstitions, ensnared by the mocking devices of demons and caught in the toils of the world, is found to have fought under the leadership of the devil, the prince of this world. "But when the fulness of the time came, God sent forth his Son" into the world to lead back into the highway mortal men, who were wandering like the brutes through trackless and devious places. By taking upon himself the form of a man He proffered mortal men a highway; to recall those who were utterly astray from the error of falsehood to the light of reason, He revealed Himself as the truth; to make over anew the perishing He showed Himself as the true life, saying "I am the way, and the truth, and the life," as though He were saying, "You are wandering astray; come therefore to me who am the way. That you may tread this way undismayed, learn that I am the truth. And if you have no provision for the journey, realize that I am the life.". . .

But at the very outset the question may properly be raised why the Saviour of all men was willing to be born at the end of the ages which Paul calls "the fulness of the time"; and why He permitted the whole Gentile world to perish in the sin of unbelief in so many past ages. Who that is circumscribed by the corruptible flesh of mortals would venture to inquire into the cause of this dispensation set away in the most profound and righteous treasures of the judgments of God; who, I say, would venture, seeing that the apostle says, "O the depth of the riches both of the wisdom and the knowledge of God! how unsearchable are his judgments, and his ways past finding out!" and so forth? What then shall we do? If we cannot understand we are not to be silent, are we? In that case who will reply to the defamers, stay the assailants and above all confute those who seek by argument and by the force of words to destroy the faith that is in us? Accordingly we cannot comprehend the secret counsels of God and yet we are frequently obliged to attempt an explanation of them. What? Are we to attempt an explanation of things which we are unable to understand? We can render explanations, human explanations to be sure, though we may still be unable to comprehend God's own explanations. And so it comes to pass that while we speak of theological matters, since we lack the language appropriate to these matters, we who are but men use our own terms and in speaking of the great God employ mortal expressions with the more assurance because we have no doubt that He understands the formulas we devise. For who understands better than He who created? Hence it follows that, although God is called ineffable, He yet desires us to say much in His praise. Therefore, since He is called ineffable, after a certain fashion He is seen to be effable. As Augustine says, this contradiction in terms can better be resolved by silent faith than by wordy disputation. And another has said: "Let what is beyond words be revered through the agency of silence."

So then "If God," as the Apostle says, "endured with much long-suffering vessels of wrath fitted unto destruction," if, desiring to reveal unto His Church the riches of His goodness, He permitted the city of the world to have long temporal prosperity in the free exercise of its own will, He is not to be blamed either because He abandoned that city to its own devices or because to His chosen people—chastised by contrast with that city of the world—He revealed the riches of His goodness. For on the one hand if He permits men to do what they themselves at all events desire to do, He cannot justly be accused by them; and on the other hand He should be greatly praised and revered by those whom, as He bestows on them His grace without price, He deters from such things as they wish to do to their own hurt and prevents from bringing such intentions to accomplishment. He cannot be said to be acting unjustly if in accordance with justice He does not bestow His grace, even as He must be believed to be acting only in mercy when He imparts it without price to whom He will. And so, if He abandoned so many ages of the past, not by forcing them into sin but by not giving them what was His own—with this purpose, that by the example of those that had gone before He might reveal to future generations what must be avoided by them, that they might render thanks unto their Saviour—if, I say, with this purpose He abandoned them to their own will, both that they might learn what they could do by themselves without Him and that when redeemed they might learn in addition what they possessed by their Saviour's mercy, then as He could not justly be blamed by the former, even so He gave the latter abundant reason whereby He ought rightly to be loved by them.

There is besides a reason why Christ wished to be born at this time rather than at any other, namely in the sixth age and when the world was united under the sway of the Romans and organized as a whole under Augustus Caesar. For inasmuch as he willed to be made flesh in order to atone for the sin of our first parent, who, putting away the delights of paradise, preferred to inhabit the land of the curse at the caprice of his own will, it was most fitting that this be done in the sixth age rather than in any other, because He also created that first man on the sixth day. Nor ought He to have been made flesh in an early age of men. For the men that were descended from these sinful parents, men whose nature, marred by disobedience, made them more inclined and prone to evil, who as yet were making no use of their reasoning powers, and were roaming about rather in the manner of wild, brute beasts—the natural goodness within them being obscured,—these men, I say, had not learned to live companionably with one another, to be moulded by laws, to be adorned with virtues, and to be lighted by the power of reason to the knowledge of the truth. Hence we have most shameful stories and even more shameful deeds, most monstrous recitals and still more monstrous acts, regarding all of which I think I have said enough in what has preceded. Since men were thus devoid of reason, incapable of receiving the truth, unacquainted with justice and with laws, how could they receive, how understand, how comprehend the laws and the most lofty precepts about life that were to be given by Christ? And so the Law was given first that it might be suited to their feeble intellects and might support the infancy of the world not with solid food but with milk. Then as this age gradually grew and made progress—partly through the association of men dwelling together, partly through the putting together of their wisdom for the purpose of establishing laws, and partly through the agency of the wisdom and of the teachings of the philosophers—it was fitting that the Saviour of all should appear in the flesh and establish new laws for the world at the time when, as I have said, the whole world had now bowed before the power of the Romans, and had been moulded by the wisdom of the philosophers, and the minds of men were suited to grasp more lofty precepts about right living.

The Eighth Book

It remains now to tell in this eighth book about the third state, namely, how the one City is to attain to the highest blessedness, the other to fail and to descend to the utmost misery, when the most righteous Judge shall, at the last judgment, examine and shall decide the case of each city. Because, as Solomon says, before destruction the heart is constantly exalted, before honor is constantly humbled, I think it appropriate to tell by way of preface what humiliation precedes this glory of His City, what transient exaltation under Antichrist goes before this downfall of the evil city—insofar as it is possible to reach conclusions from the authoritative books. For thus after the dense darkness of the persecutions the eternal day of eternal peace will appear the most delightful, and after the approving smile of this world the grievous storm of punishments and the eternal night will appear the more terrible, inasmuch as the hope of that glory makes present troubles light, the fear of that doom detracts from this temporal pleasure (if there be any such) because it is fleeting.

* * *

. . . that the time of persecution is to continue for three years and a half —just as long indeed, as the Lord's ministry—is indicated in veiled fashion by the fact that it is stated, also by a prophet: "Until a time and times and half a time." It is more clearly declared on the authority of the Apocalypse: "the holy city shall they tread under foot forty and two months." The Lord intimates that, by reason of the enormity of the persecution, this short time has been provided by a most merciful judge for the elect's sake, when He says, "Except those days had been shortened, no flesh would have been saved, but for the elect's sake those days shall be shortened."

When the head of the impious city shall be smitten, the Jews, that unbelieving people, seeing that they have been deceived will, it is believed, be converted, in accordance with the following saying of the prophet: "If the number of the children of Israel be as the sand of the sea, it is the remnant that shall be saved." After this a time for repentance remains—a time whose length is hidden from all mortals. Then when all those things which have been foretold shall have been brought to completion, and strange signs shall have been revealed in the sun, the moon, the stars and the sea—when all men shall be fainting for fear, and for expectation of the things which are to come upon the whole world— then the destruction of the evil city, and the increase of the City of Christ, and the day of the Lord are at hand, in accordance with the word of truth which, sweetly consoling God's own people, says: "When ye see these things coming to pass, know ye that the kingdom of God is nigh." Without doubt, the Kingdom "cometh as a thief in the night" (that is, unforeseen) while, once more according to the word of the Lord, men shall be eating and drinking, marrying and giving in marriage. We must believe that these matters are so ordered not in cruelty but in wisdom, through the wise providence of the Creator, that we may ever be found in fear of the coming of the Judge, ever prepared to render an account.

* * *

After these things shall have come to pass the Lord will, beyond doubt, come for the judgment and for the final sifting of both cities. He will come to judge, moreover, in the form in which He previously came to be judged, that with even justice the world may find a severe judge in Him whom previously with haughty mind it despised when He came humbly in the flesh. Hence we have the prophetic saying, "They shall look on him whom they pierced." For "the Father," judging not in His own person, "hath given all judgment unto the Son," in order that Him whom (though He was innocent) He had exposed to all manner of insult and to the cross, He may now make the Lord of "things in heaven and things on earth and things under the earth," ordaining Him to be "the Judge of the living and the dead." Yet, while to the just His human form will appear merciful, to the wicked He will be the more bright and terrible as He before seemed to them obscure and deserving of contempt.

*   *   *

Now we must inquire what the blessedness of that country is. For we must not suppose that souls, after they have been stripped from the body, or after they have taken up spiritual bodies and are not inferior to the angelic spirits in purity and in rank, find delight in external things as men do in this life. Accordingly, whenever Holy Scripture says that their spirits are refreshed and affected by flowering and verdant meadows, by pleasant places, by the singing of birds, by fragrant things (such as cinnamon and balsam), such expressions should, it is clear, be interpreted spiritually rather than carnally. And yet, for the sake of the simple—who must be nourished on mild, not on solid food, whose understanding is not yet exercised and who cannot as yet comprehend spiritual delights—these things are frequently set down by certain teachers that the simple may thus be directed through the visible to the understanding and discovery of the invisible. The blessedness of the saints then lies in beholding their Creator, in accordance with that saying of the Lord, "This is life eternal, that they should know thee the true God, and him whom thou didst send, even Jesus Christ"; of course we must understand the words "with the Holy Spirit" who proceedeth from both [the Father and the Son]. "This," he says, "is life eternal." For what else is life eternal than purest blessedness? For if the life were temporary it would not be blessed since it would be rendered anxious lest it come to an end. Again, however long in duration, it could not be called blessed unless it were free from the defect of misery of every kind and abounded in every sort of happiness, or if it were marred by any sort of blemish. That life therefore is eternal and blessed, blessed and eternal, "that they should know thee the true God, and him whom thou didst send, even Jesus Christ." Observe that he said that the enjoyment of blessedness is the knowledge of divinity. Hence it is to no purpose that certain people strive in this life to comprehend the divine nature, which is seen by saints in this life only with difficulty as "in a mirror" and "in a riddle," since it is promised that it is to be seen and fully understood by them only in the life to come. The saints therefore find their delight in the wholly ecstatic and eternally blessed vision of God, in accordance with the saying of the Psalmist, "He who gave the law shall give his benediction, they shall go from strength to strength, the God of gods shall be seen in Zion."

A stubborn and still undecided battle has been long raging on the field of my thoughts for the supremacy of one of the two men within me.

Petrarch, LETTER TO DIONIGI DE'ROBERTI

2. THE RENAISSANCE

He whose character I am seeking to mould should be a "wise man" in the Roman sense, that is, one who reveals himself as a true statesman, not in the discussions of the study, but in the actual practice and experience of life.

Quintilian, INSTITUTES OF ORATORY

Fortune, many times in the very midst of our race, at other times near the end, disappointeth our frail and vain purposes, sometimes drowneth them before they can once come to have a sight of the haven afar off.

Castiglione, THE COURTIER

So, Reader, I am myself the subject of my book.

Montaigne, ESSAYS

All barbarism, all corruption, all Latin adulterate which blind folly brought into this world and with the same hath poisoned the old Latin speech and the very Roman tongue which in the time of Tully and Sallust and Virgil and Terence was used, which also St. Jerome and St. Ambrose and St. Augustine learned in their times—I say that all such abuse which the later blind world brought in which may be called blotterature rather than literature I utterly banish out of this school and charge the Masters that they teach unto the children such authors that hath with wisdom joined the pure chaste eloquence.

John Colet, STATUTES OF ST. PAUL'S SCHOOL

The Renaissance

$\mathcal{O}$F THE Renaissance John Addington Symonds wrote in 1875: "It is the history of the attainment of self-conscious freedom by the human spirit manifested in the European races. . . . The arts and the inventions, the knowledge and the books, which suddenly became vital at the time of the Renaissance, had long lain neglected on the shores of the Dead Sea which we call the Middle Ages." The Renaissance, said Symonds, represented the first act in that great drama of liberty "which we nations of the present are still evolving in the establishment of the democratic idea." [1] This is the "classic" concept of the Renaissance, which historians generally accepted until very recently, and which the textbooks have immortalized. The Italian humanists themselves laid the foundations for this concept, with their threefold periodization of history (ancient—medieval—modern) and their use of the metaphor of "rebirth." But the classic expression of the classic concept came only with the publication in 1860 of Jacob Burckhardt's masterly *Civilization of the Renaissance in Italy*. For the Swiss historian, as for his English contemporary, the Renaissance represented the first chapter of modern history: the revolt of the individual against the authoritarianism, collectivism, and asceticism of the Middle Ages. Burckhardt wrote his essay partly as a tract for his own times. He believed in progress, yet he deplored the growing uniformity and philistinism of modern culture. The modern world would profit, he thought, by being reminded of its spiritual antecedents in the Renaissance.

In recent years this interpretation has undergone considerable revision. The impact of evolutionary thinking on historians, and the growth of medieval research, has tended to blur the lines between the Middle Ages and the Renaissance, and to play down the decisiveness of the Renaissance in intellectual and cultural history. The titles of two books show

[1] *Renaissance in Italy* (New York, 1935), vol. I, pp. 6, 8.

how the wind has been blowing: C. H. Haskins's *Renaissance of the Twelfth Century* (1927) and Huizinga's *Waning of the Middle Ages* (1919). Medievalists like Haskins push the Renaissance back into the Middle Ages. Huizinga, studying the culture of fifteenth-century Burgundy, finds the Middle Ages in the Renaissance. The latter tendency has been carried to the extreme by Douglas Bush who eschews "picturesque contrasts between the religiosity of the Middle Ages and the paganism of the Renaissance," and E. M. W. Tillyard who, in his *Elizabethan World Picture*, refers to the Renaissance as "that phase of culture which nowadays tends ever more to lose its identity and to turn out to be simply the late Middle Ages." [2]

My own view is—and I do not think that this is a mere quibble of words—that the Renaissance belongs to the Age of Religion but not to the Middle Ages. The revisionists are right in supposing that the Renaissance was, on the whole, less anti-religious and, one might add, less congenial to natural science than is sometimes supposed. But this does not mean that it was medieval. There were, of course, medieval survivals, but the Renaissance humanists lived to a very considerable extent in a world of their own making. This world was emphatically not the world of Bernard of Clairvaux or St. Thomas Aquinas, but on the other hand, neither was it the world of Francis Bacon and Galileo and Descartes. In certain ways, the Renaissance bore witness to the light of modern science, but it was not that light. Generally speaking—there are exceptions to the rule—the humanists worked within a humanistic-religious, rather than a scientific, framework of ideas. They ridiculed the scholastics and criticized the Church, but they did not lack cosmic piety, and they mostly all assumed, if they did not always emphasize, the main outlines of the Christian world-view.

II

THE RENAISSANCE, it should be noted, coincided with the decline of medieval institutions. The Church, because of the Babylonian Captivity, the Great Schism, and the territorial ambitions of the Italianate Papacy, was losing spiritual prestige. The towns were emancipating themselves from, and in some regions extending their control over, the feudal country. Within the towns, especially those towns like Florence engaging in international trade, the medieval guilds were losing ground to the bankers and capitalistic entrepreneurs. Politically, as Machiavelli tells us, this was the age of the prince, of the

[2] D. Bush, *The Renaissance and English Humanism* (Toronto, 1939), p. 28; E. M. W. Tillyard, *The Elizabethan World Picture* (London, 1943), p. 41. For Renaissance interpretation in general, see W. K. Ferguson, *The Renaissance in Historical Thought* (Cambridge, Mass., 1948).

condottiere and upstart despot in Italy, of the "new monarchy" in the north. Everywhere *novi homines* were pushing their way into positions of economic and political power.

This is to say that the Renaissance intellectuals lived in much more of a lay world than their medieval predecessors; a world, furthermore, in which tradition and custom were crumbling. Between the fourteenth and sixteenth centuries the Church lost its monopoly of culture. The new intelligentsia were mostly laymen, of middle-class and even base social origins. Patronage came not only from ecclesiastics and feudal aristocrats, but from the new great who employed artists and writers to perpetuate their fame. The most important of the new intellectual institutions, the classical schools, were largely founded and governed by lay patrons.

This socio-economic interpretation, so popular in recent years, by no means explains all the facets of Renaissance thought. It does not explain why its most brilliant achievements came in the humanities rather than the sciences, nor why religious feeling persisted to such a marked degree. All the same, the change in intellectual tone from the Middle Ages to the Renaissance *is* unmistakable, and there cannot be much doubt that it was related to contemporary social change. Conspicuously among the transalpine (Italian), but also among the cisalpine intellectuals, the accent was on the humanistic: on man and his everyday world; on the practical and the concrete as opposed to the abstract; on the individualistic rather than the collectivistic; on the active rather than the contemplative. Knowledge, once united under the aegis of theology, broke up into its several compartments. If it usually bore the trademark of antiquity, this was because Greece and Rome represented the one great humanistic culture to which the new humanists could refer. In any event, humanism of the type described is not the sort of thinking that one associates with a predominantly clerical and agrarian society.

The Renaissance was not a great age of philosophy, but what philosophy it produced bears an unmistakably humanistic stamp. The great medieval debate over universals, the problem of knowledge which arose to plague the philosophers of science of the seventeenth and eighteenth centuries, left the Renaissance cold. Humanists like Erasmus condemned all philosophy that did not bear directly upon human ethics. While not so universally condemnatory, others—Pico, for instance, the Florentine Platonists, and even the neo-Aristotelian Pomponazzi—chose to debate the nature of man, the measure of his freedom of will, and the immortality of his soul. In an age of economic and political opportunity, it is not surprising that they should take an almost Pelagian view of human nature. "Not undeservedly is man called the microcosm or the little world. Therefore some have said that man is a great marvel, since he is the whole world and convertible into every nature, since power has been given him to attain whatever property he may prefer." However, the deduction from this and a great many similar statements seems not invariably to have been man's power to control external events. The humanists were keenly aware of the tricks that Fate or Fortune might, and frequently did, play upon them. By freedom of will they ordinarily meant therefore man's capacity to achieve dignity and virtue amidst the perils of human existence, in the teeth of political and economic vicissitudes. The new thing in their teaching was more negative than positive: by emphasizing man's protean nature, they, in effect, rejected the doctrine of the Fall and man's inherent sinfulness. In defending the immortality of the soul, the Florentine Platonists likewise upheld man's individuality against the collectivistic view of the Averroists, then widely held in the Venetian universities, that men live on after death only as moments in the single Intellect of mankind.

Optimism about human nature led the humanists to put great emphasis on education. "Nature," they said, is a divine capacity, but it needs "nurture" to develop its highest potentialities. "Believe me," said Erasmus, "men are not born, they are made." "Educatio superat omnia." "Handle the wax whilst it is soft, mould the clay whilst it is moist, dye the fleece before it gathers stains." "Nature," wrote the Italian Guazzo, "always tendeth to the best: so that of good parents, ought naturally to come good children, and if it fall out sometimes otherwise, the fault is not to be imputed to nature. For if one look advisedly into the matter, he shall see that for the most part it happeneth not by the birth, but by the bringing up." Working from this premise, the humanists flooded the bookstalls with treatises on education and became great builders of schools. This was perhaps their most original intellectual contribution.

The type of man they wished to produce reflects the age they lived in. He was Cicero's statesman, Quintilian's "good man skilled in speaking": in short, a man fitted, by virtue of his moral and intellectual excellence, to be a good citizen or "governor" in one of the new territorial states of Europe. In filling out their ideal man, it was only natural that the humanists should have recourse to ancient example. Rome represented the greatest civilization of which they had knowledge, and to reproduce her statesmen and orators would be to usher in a new golden age. It was characteristic of the humanists that they thought of social reform primarily in terms of new men rather than new institutions. Alberti, Palmieri, Erasmus, Sir Thomas Elyot—in fact, all the educators —approached politics from the standpoint of the individual. The most sophisticated expression of this personality-cult was *The Courtier* of Baldassare Castiglione. To be a proper adornment of a prince's court and to give good and faithful advice to his prince, the would-be courtier must first become, in Castiglione's view, his highest attainable self. The reverse of a specialist, he must develop all his faculties, observing the classical rule of proportion or harmony between the claims of heart, head, and body.

The titles of some of the "courtesy" books—*The Education of a Christian Prince, The Courtier, The Governor, The Complete Gentleman*—reveal how very aristocratic the Renaissance ideal of education was. Yet it was aristocracy in a new key: aristocracy by talent (Italian: *virtù*) rather than birth, for room had to be made for the *novi homines* who were displacing the feudal nobility. Few of the humanists had any belief in education for all and sundry, but they admired more "*Nobility Dative,* being truly derived and raised for itself, than that which is *Native* and descended from another." [3] The humanists generally also preferred the active to the contemplative life. In this respect they followed Cicero and Quintilian rather than the *Nicomachean Ethics*. Thus, Palmieri ranked the solitary religious life well below the "civil life" of conscious citizenship, and Alberti declared the studious life to be incomplete if divorced from the public good.

To the modern educator the Renaissance curriculum or course of studies may seem "unprogressive." But we must not read it out of context. In its day it signified a radical innovation, and its *intention* was clearly practical. If it lacked modern subjects (science, the vernacular languages, modern history), it substituted for what were regarded as medieval abstractions the humanistic wisdom of the ancient world. Rhetoric (the study of antique literature and oratory) crowded out logic. Philosophy meant ethics. Ancient history, treated biographically, taught examples of virtue and vice. All these studies were meant to be guides to high-minded action in a world growing ever more Machiavellian. When we remember that the humanists lived under the spell of antiquity, we can readily understand why their education emphasized the knowledge to be got out of books rather than first-hand observation.

The individual and the human scene loom equally large in the other fields of Renaissance thought. The historians brought into sharp focus the communes and nation-states and recorded the decisive role that great individuals played in their development. In political thought, especially Italian, the tendency was toward more realistic analysis. Machiavelli, for instance, deliberately determined not to write about princes and principalities "which have never been seen or known to exist in reality." He would compound his recipe for political success not from the abstractions of theology and natural law, but from his own observations and what he had read in ancient history. Machiavelli allowed the individual considerable latitude to control his political destiny, but he too had a healthy respect for "fortune." "I think it may be true that fortune is the ruler of half our actions, but that she allows the other half or a little less

[3] Thomas Milles, *The Catalogue of Honor or Treasury of the Nobility peculiar and proper to the Isle of Great Britain* (London, 1610), Epilogue.

to be governed by us." He also shared the widespread belief of the Renaissance that history went in cycles. Most of the humanists were conscious of living in a time of great cultural revival (Machiavelli, however, was not one of these), but they did not think it could last.

Consciousness of individuality is perhaps most graphically displayed in literature and the fine arts. In the personal love poetry, in the great Elizabethan drama, in the sculpture of Donatello or the painting of Masaccio or Leonardo, the individual stands out, largely or wholly divested of the allegory in which the Gothic artist had so often submerged him. Because it was the best possible vehicle for humanism, painting became the dominant art. Both painting and sculpture declared their independence from architecture with which, under the patronage of the Church, they had been united in the Middle Ages. Thus, the arts exhibit that same tendency toward compartmentalization which we have observed in political thought and philosophy. Furthermore, Renaissance painting—and art criticism—stressed the individual part more than the whole, the landscapes, for example, usually serving only as settings for the human figure. It is similarly fascinating to watch the new drama of the sixteenth century gradually shake off its dependence on the miracle and morality play. Compare the York cycle or *The Summoning of Everyman* with Kyd's *Spanish Tragedy*, or better still, Shakespeare's "histories" and tragedies, and *The Shoemaker's Holiday*. In the latter the old machinery of abstract virtues and vices has given way to the blank-verse drama featuring the actions and passions of the individual personality. Moreover, the scene has shifted—at least in many cases—to the courts of real princes living in recent English history, and to London trade life and the rustic village. In Elizabethan England, the Renaissance all but drove the old morality play out of existence.

III

EARLIER in this essay it was said that Renaissance thought, while not essentially medieval, belonged to the Age of Religion. In the light of the above evidence, how can this be so? The answer comes from the fact that so much of the humanism of the times was "Christian humanism"—a type of religious piety which suited an increasingly lay society better than medieval religion.

To demonstrate the religious side of Renaissance thought requires no straining of the evidence. Doubtless, Bush exaggerates when he states that at the Renaissance the pagan tradition did not overthrow the Christian tradition but was absorbed by it,[4] but there is a strong element of truth in what he says. Theology, to be sure, was losing its control over

[4] *The Renaissance and English Humanism*, p. 34.

philosophy, the arts, and political and historical thinking. There was also a spirit of criticism in the air: criticism of priests and monks and friars (Boccaccio, Rabelais); criticism of medieval texts such as the Vulgate Bible and the Donation of Constantine; criticism of ecclesiastical customs, prayers to the saints, pilgrimages, and the like. Nor did scepticism lack advocates in thinkers like Pomponazzi who denied the immortality of the soul, and Montaigne who, influenced by the ancient Sceptics, had the rafters of his library inscribed with the sayings of Sextus Empiricus. To call Machiavelli's political analysis pagan rather than Christian does the pagans an injustice, for it was not only secular and unreligious, but also unmoral.

However, the main body of humanists would certainly have agreed with Francis Bacon when he wrote that "a little philosophy inclineth man's mind to atheism, but depth in philosophy bringeth men's minds about to religion." Atheism—and indeed, religious scepticism—always remained on the lunatic fringe of humanist thinking, even in Italy. Even Pomponazzi restored with one hand what he took away with the other: he denied personal immortality on philosophical grounds but accepted it as an article of religious faith—or at least so he said. Montaigne, for all his scepticism, remained a loyal son of the Roman Church. The point is, that although there may have been considerable religious indifference in the Renaissance, almost nobody seriously suggested an alternative to the Christian world-view, and very few professed doubts about the main teachings of the Church. The best of the humanists worked to deepen rather than to undermine man's religious life. The cultivation of *pietas literata* ("wise and eloquent piety") constituted the central aim of the educators from Vittorino da Feltre to John Sturm. Along with grammar and rhetoric, the school timetables invariably called for instruction in the catechism, daily prayers, and Sunday sermons, to which were often added in the sixteenth century, knowledge of the "holy" tongues and Bible reading. Most of the humanists, I think it is safe to say, continued to live securely within the Aristotelian-Christian universe of purpose and striving, and assumed a moral order in which evil actions brought down retribution from on high. This is the philosophy underlying Shakespeare's two tetralogies on English history (*Richard II* to *Henry V*, *Henry VI, Part I* to *Richard III*), and Sir Walter Raleigh's *History of the World*. If further proof were needed of Renaissance religiosity, one could mention the mental conflict experienced by so many of the humanists. Petrarch, for instance, confesses to being torn apart inside by the claims of two worlds. "A stubborn and still undecided battle has been long raging on the field of my thoughts for the supremacy of one of the two men within me." Petrarch's "two men" are the spiritual man described in St. Augustine's *Confessions,* and the worldly man lusting after literary fame and the beauties of nature. If Petrarch's schizophrenia indicates his modernity, it also clearly argues his acute awareness of the religious side of man's nature.

As previously noted, however, Renaissance religious thought was no mere continuation of medieval religion. In fact, the Christian humanists, particularly the group of Meaux in France, and Erasmus and his English friends, deplored scholasticism—"blotterature" rather than "literature" is how John Colet, the Dean of St. Paul's, described it, and he preached a return to the simple religion of Christian antiquity. "Christian humanism" may be defined as a fusion of the "philosophy of Christ," as Erasmus called it, with the moral wisdom of Greece and Rome, the emphasis being on the practical and concrete: ethics rather than theology and dogma, inner piety rather than outer church observance. Under Erasmus's leadership, it became a program of reform designed to renovate Western society from top to bottom.

Sir Thomas More's *Utopia* bitterly attacks the acquisitive society of western Europe in 1516: the new statemanship represented by the warring princes, the new economics of the commercial capitalists and rack-renting landlords, and, by implication at least, the new spirit of rapacity in the Church.[5] To combat these conditions the Christian humanists proposed a broad program of reeducation. Lefèvre d'Étaples and Erasmus devoted their scholarship to bringing out improved editions of the Bible and of the early Church Fathers, hoping in this way to get men back to the pure *fontes* of Christianity. John Colet's lectures at Oxford on St. Paul's Epistles admirably illustrate the primarily practical and ethical aim of the group. Colet largely broke with the allegorizing tradition, stressing the literal meaning and drawing from the text its human lessons rather than its theology. All of the New Testament except the parables, Colet wrote in another place, "has the sense that appears on the surface, nor is one thing said and another meant, but the very thing is meant which is said, and the sense is wholly literal." Colet also castigated the clergy for their ignorance and lack of morals, notably in his famous Convocation sermon of 1511, and founded a new school at St. Paul's to inculcate Christian humanism. The emphasis was again on new men rather than new institutions (new educational institutions excepted). The Christian humanists hoped to train "Christian knights" to go forth into the world and to animate church and state alike with Roman *philanthropia* and Christian *agape*. This was their answer to the political anarchy described in Machiavelli's *Prince* and to the religious anarchy soon to overtake Europe in the Protestant Reformation.

In conclusion, it needs to be said that the Renaissance did not flicker out at the Reformation, but on the contrary, either fused with that movement or else ran a course parallel or antipathetic to it. In either case it fed into what was to become the main stream of Western thought.

[5] See R. W. Chambers, *Thomas More* (New York, 1935), pp. 131–6.

If it can be safely bracketed with the Age of Religion, it nevertheless helped to undermine Christianity by demonstrating that the Logos had operated in pagan antiquity as well as during the Christian era; in addition it undermined by its tendency to separate philosophy and religion, which made Christianity appear to some to be intellectually indefensible. If its spirit was, on the whole, anti-scientific, it nevertheless contributed to the coming scientific revolution by reviving some of the ancient texts (Hippocrates, Galen, Euclid, Archimedes), and by removing from nature some of the stigma of original sin. By its preference for primitive to medieval Christianity, it undoubtedly prepared the way directly for the Protestant Reformation.

$$\mathscr{Readings}$$

1. *Mental Conflict*

Francesco Petrarch: *My Secret* *

Francesco Petrarch (1304–74), son of a Florentine notary, was the most celebrated humanist of his century. An avid collector of classical manuscripts, he composed a number of books in honor of illustrious ancients. He also wrote a series of love poems. The *Secretum* (*c.* 1342) however, is a work of a different order. It is a dialogue between himself and St. Augustine, whose thought he became addicted to, and whose *Confessions* he often carried in his pocket.

S. Augustine. The desire of all good cannot exist without thrusting out every lower wish. You know how many different objects one longs for in life. All these you must first learn to count as nothing before you can rise to the desire for the chief good; which a man loves less when along with it he loves something else that does not minister to it.

Petrarch. I recognise the thought.

S. Augustine. How many men are there who have extinguished all their passions, or, not to speak of extinguishing, tell me how many are there who have subdued their spirit to the control of Reason, and will dare to say, "I have no more in common with my body; all that once seemed so pleasing to me is become poor in my sight. I aspire now to joys of nobler nature"?

Petrarch. Such men are rare indeed. And now I understand what those difficulties are with which you threatened me.

S. Augustine. When all these passions are extinguished, then, and not

* From *Petrarch's Secret*, trans. by W. H. Draper, pp. 25–6, 64–5, 108–09, 124–5, 172, 176, 184–5. Copyright 1911 by Chatto & Windus. I have tried in vain to reach Mr. S. M. Draper to whom the copyright reverted.

till then, will desire be full and free. For when the soul is uplifted on one side to heaven by its own nobility, and on the other dragged down to earth by the weight of the flesh and the seductions of the world, so that it both desires to rise and also to sink at one and the same time, then, drawn contrary ways, you find you arrive nowhither.

Petrarch. What, then, would you say a man must do for his soul to break the fetters of the world, and mount up perfect and entire to the realms above?

S. Augustine. What leads to this goal is, as I said in the first instance, the practice of meditation on death and the perpetual recollection of our mortal nature.

* * *

S. Augustine. Do you remember with what delight you used to wander in the depth of the country? Sometimes, laying yourself down on a bed of turf, you would listen to the water of a brook murmuring over the stones; at another time, seated on some open hill, you would let your eye wander freely over the plain stretched at your feet; at others, again, you enjoyed a sweet slumber beneath the shady trees of some valley in the noontide heat, and revelled in the delicious silence. Never idle, in your soul you would ponder over some high meditation, with only the Muses for your friends—you were never less alone than when in their company, and then, like the old man in Virgil who reckoned himself

> "As rich as kings, when, at the close of day,
> Home to his cot he took his happy way,
> And on his table spread his simple fare,
> Fresh from the meadow without cost or care,"

you would come at sunset back to your humble roof; and, contented with your good things, did you not find yourself the richest and happiest of mortal men?

Petrarch. Ah, well-a-day! I recall it all now, and the remembrance of that time makes me sigh with regret.

S. Augustine. Why—why do you speak of sighing? And who, pray, is the author of your woes? It is, indeed, your own spirit and none other which too long has not dared to follow the true law of its nature, and has thought itself a prisoner only because it would not break its chain. Even now it is dragging you along like a runaway horse, and unless you tighten the rein it will rush you to destruction. Ever since you grew tired of your leafy trees, of your simple way of life, and society of country people, egged on by cupidity, you have plunged once more into the midst of the tumultuous life of cities. I read in your face and speech what a happy and peaceful life you lived; for what miseries have you not endured since then? Too rebellious against the teachings of experience, you still hesitate!

* * *

Petrarch. Alas, alas, I am more wretched then I thought. Do you mean to tell me my soul is still bound by two chains of which I am unconscious?

S. Augustine. All the same they are plain enough to see; but, dazzled by their beauty, you think they are not fetters but treasures; and, to keep to the same figure, you are like some one who, with hands and feet fast bound in shackles of gold, should look at them with delight and not see at all that they are shackles. Yes, you yourself with blinded eyes keep looking at your bonds; but, oh strange delusion! you are charmed with the very chains that are dragging you to your death, and, what is most sad of all, you glory in them!

Petrarch. What may these chains be of which you speak?

S. Augustine. Love and glory.

* * *

S. Augustine. She [Laura] has detached your mind from the love of heavenly things and has inclined your heart to love the creature more than the Creator: and that one path alone leads, sooner than any other, to death.

Petrarch. I pray you make no rash judgment. The love which I feel for her has most certainly led me to love God.

S. Augustine. But it has inverted the true order.

Petrarch. How so?

S. Augustine. Because every creature should be dear to us because of our love for the Creator. But in your case, on the contrary, held captive by the charm of the creature, you have not loved the Creator as you ought. You have admired the Divine Artificer as though in all His works He had made nothing fairer than the object of your love, although in truth the beauty of the body should be reckoned last of all.

* * *

Petrarch. Well do I know that old story bandied about by the philosophers, how they declare that all the earth is but a tiny point, how the soul alone endures for infinite millions of years, how fame cannot fill either the earth or the soul, and other paltry pleas of this sort, by which they try to turn minds aside from the love of glory. But I beg you will produce some more solid arguments than these, if you know any; for experience has shown me that all this is more specious than convincing. I do not think to become as God, or to inhabit eternity, or embrace heaven and earth. Such glory as belongs to man is enough for me.

That is all I sigh after. Mortal myself, it is but mortal blessings I desire.

S. Augustine. Oh, if that is what you truly mean, how wretched you are! If you have no desire for things immortal, if no regard for what is eternal, then you are indeed wholly of the earth earthy: then all is over for you; no hope at all is left. . . .

Petrarch. I do not think my way of looking at it is so unreasonable as you imagine. My principle is that, as concerning the glory which we may hope for here below, it is right for us to seek while we are here below. One may expect to enjoy that other more radiant glory in heaven, when we shall have there arrived, and when one will have no more care or wish for the glory of earth. Therefore, as I think, it is in the true order that mortal men should first care for mortal things; and that to things transitory things eternal should succeed; because to pass from those to these is to go forward in most certain accordance with what is ordained for us, although no way is open for us to pass back again from eternity to time.

S. Augustine. O man, little in yourself, and of little wisdom! Do you, then, dream that you shall enjoy every pleasure in heaven and earth, and everything will turn out fortunate and prosperous for you always and everywhere? But that delusion has betrayed thousands of men thousands of times, and has sunk into hell a countless host of souls. Thinking to have one foot on earth and one in heaven, they could neither stand here below nor mount on high. . . .

S. Augustine. Which foot you mean to hobble on, I do not know. You seem inclined to leave yourself derelict, rather than your books.

As for me, I shall do my duty, with what success depends on you; but at least I shall have satisfied my conscience. Throw to the winds these great loads of histories; the deeds of the Romans have been celebrated quite enough by others, and are known by their own fame. Get out of Africa and leave it to its possessors. You will add nothing to the glory of your Scipio or to your own. He can be exalted to no higher pinnacle, but you may bring down his reputation, and with it your own. Therefore leave all this on one side, and now at length take possession of yourself; and to come back to our starting-point, let me urge you to enter upon the meditation of your last end, which comes on step by step without your being aware. Tear off the veil; disperse the shadows; look only on that which is coming; with eyes and mind give all your attention there: let nought else distract you. Heaven, Earth, the Sea—these all suffer change. What can man, the frailest of all creatures, hope for?

2. *New Interests and New Emphases*

A. ITALIAN HUMANISTS AND THEIR PATRONS

VESPASIANO DA BISTICCI: *Lives of Illustrious Men of the Fifteenth Century* *

Vespasiano da Bisticci (1421–98) was a Florentine bookseller and one of the leading bibliophiles of his age. He purchased Greek and Latin manuscripts for great patrons of the *litterae humaniores,* and the scribes in his renowned *bottega* helped to meet the growing demand for copies of the ancient classics. His *Lives* include thumb-nail sketches of great ecclesiastical patrons of the arts like Pope Nicholas V, statesmen like Cosimo de Medici, the banker and ruler of Florence, and a score of humanists. They were written, as he himself tells us, "that their fame may not perish."

Cosimo de Medici (1389–1464)

So GREAT was his knowledge of all things, that he could find some matter of discussion with men of all sorts; he would talk literature with a man of letters and theology with a theologian, being well versed therein through his natural liking, and for the reading of the Holy Scripture. With philosophy it was just the same, also with astrology, of which he had complete knowledge from having practised it with Maestro Pagolo and other astrologers. Indeed, he put faith in it, and always made use of it in his affairs. He took kindly notice of all musicians, and delighted greatly in their art. He had dealings with painters and sculptors and had in his house works of divers masters. He was especially inclined towards sculpture and showed great favour to all worthy craftsmen, being a good friend to Donatello and all sculptors and painters; and because in his time the sculptors found scanty employment, Cosimo, in order that Donatello's chisel might not be idle, commissioned him to make the pulpits of bronze in S. Lorenzo and the doors of the sacristy. He ordered the bank to pay every week enough money to Donatello for his work and for that of his four assistants. . . .

Cosimo was always liberal, especially to men of merit. The majority of men who affect letters, without any other profitable employ, are poor in goods; men like Friar Ambrogio degli Agnoli, a man of religion, very

* From *The Vespasiano Memoirs,* trans. by William George and Emily Waters, pp. 223–4, 227–8, 351–3, 395–7, 400–1, 416–18. Copyright 1926 by Routledge and Kegan Paul Ltd. Reprinted by permission of Routledge and Kegan Paul Ltd.

holy and devoted to his order. Cosimo helped his monastery in all its needs, and a day seldom passed when he did not repair to the Agnoli, where he would find Nicolao Nicoli and Lorenzo his own brother, and would spend several hours with them. . . .

Nicolao had spent most of his substance in books and wanted for necessaries—as we may read in his Life. Cosimo, hearing of this, bade him not stint himself and told him that the bank had been ordered to advance him what he wanted, which the cashier would pay on receiving his bill. Nicolao duly took advantage of Cosimo's liberality; most praiseworthy because it served the needs of so illustrious a man as Nicolao. During his life he drew from the bank five hundred ducats, thus making a good show before the world, which he could hardly have done but for Cosimo, who, when he went to Verona to avoid the plague, took with him no buffoons or heralds but Nicolao Nicoli and Messer Carlo d'Arezzo with whom he could discuss literature. Cosimo made no demand on Nicolao for the five hundred ducats, having always treated this loan as a gift, and in this fashion he succoured all good and learned men in their need. They are indeed good men who practise liberality like Cosimo.

Nicolao Nicoli (d. 1437)

Nicolao was well born, one of the four sons of a rich merchant, all of whom became merchants. In his youth Nicolao, by his father's wish, entered trade, wherefore he could not give his time to letters as he desired. After his father's death he left his brothers so as to carry out his aims. He was the master of a good fortune and took up Latin letters, in which he soon became proficient. . . .

He was a man of upright life who favoured virtue and censured vice. He collected a fine library, not regarding the cost, and was always searching for rare books. He bought all these with the wealth which his father had left, putting aside only what was necessary for his maintenance. He sold several of his farms and spent the proceeds on his library. He was a devoted Christian, . . . If he heard of students going to Greece or to France or elsewhere he would give them the names of books which they lacked in Florence, and procure for them the help of Cosimo de Medici who would do anything for him. When it happened that he could only get the copy of a book he would copy it himself, either in current or shaped characters, all in the finest script, as may be seen in San Marco, where there are many books from his hand in one lettering or the other. He procured at his own expense the works of Tertullian and other writers which were not in Italy. He also found an imperfect copy of Ammianus Marcellinus and wrote it out with his own hand. The *De Oratore* and the *Brutus* were sent to Nicolao from Lombardy, having been brought by the envoys of Duke Filippo when they went to ask for peace in the time of Pope Martin. The book was found in a chest in a very old church; this chest had not been opened for a long time, and they found the book, a very ancient example, while searching for evidence concerning certain ancient rights. *De Oratore* was found broken up, and it is through the care of Nicolao that we find it perfect to-day. He also rediscovered many sacred works and several of Tully's orations. . . .

Nicolao always encouraged promising students to follow a literary life, and he nobly aided all those who showed merit in providing them with teachers and books, for in his time teachers and books were not so numerous as they are to-day. It may be said that he was the reviver of Greek and Latin letters in Florence; they had for a long time lain buried, and although Petrarch, Dante and Boccaccio had done something to rehabilitate them, they had not reached that height which they attained through Nicolao's cultivation of them for divers reasons. . . .

Nicolao patronised painters, sculptors and architects as well as men of letters, and he had a thorough knowledge of their crafts; he especially favoured Pippo di Ser Brunellesco, Donatello, Luca della Robbia, Lorenzo di Bartolaccio and was on intimate terms with them. He was a true connoisseur of all fine things. Friar Ambrogio, Messer Poggio and Carlo d'Arezzo were his friends, and it was through him that these men of genius became public teachers in Florence in the time of Pope Eugenius. He was on terms of friendship with all the learned men of Italy, and he corresponded with them both at home and abroad.

After having done so many good deeds, and gathered together a vast number of books on all the liberal arts in Greek and Latin, he desired that these should be made accessible to everyone. He directed that, after his death, they should continue to be at the service of all, so in his will he designated forty citizens to see that the books in question should be made a public library in order that all might use them. There were eight hundred volumes of Greek and Latin. He gave directions to these forty citizens that these books should be given to Cosimo de Medici for the library of San Marco, in fulfilment of the wishes of the testator, that they should remain in a public place for the use of those who might want to consult them.

Poggio Bracciolini (1380–1454)

Messer Poggio was born at Terranuova, a Florentine village. His father sent him to the University, where he remained as a teacher, being very learned in the Latin tongue and well conversant with Greek. He was an excellent scribe in ancient characters, and in his youth he was wont to write for a living, providing himself thus with money for the purchase of books and for his other needs. It is well known that the court of Rome is a place where distinguished men may find a position and reward for their activity, and thither he accordingly went, and when his quickness of wit had become known, he was appointed apostolic secretary. Afterwards he opened a scrivener's office, and in these two vocations was known as a man of integrity and good repute. He had no mind to enter the priesthood, or to accept ecclesiastical preferment, but he took as wife a lady of the noblest blood of Florence, one of the Buondelmonti, and by her had four sons and one daughter. . . .

When the Council of Constance was assembled, Poggio went thither, and was besought by Nicolao and other learned men not to spare himself trouble in searching through the religious houses in these parts for some of the many Latin books which had been lost. He found six Orations of Cicero, and, as I understood him to say, found them in a heap of waste paper amongst the rubbish. He found the complete works of Quintillian, which had hitherto been only known in fragments, and as he could not obtain the volume he spent thirty-two days in copying it with his own hand: this I saw in the fairest manuscript. Every day he filled a copybook with the text. He found Tully's *De Oratore*, which had been long lost and was known only in parts, Silius Italicus, *De secundo bello punico*, in heroic verse, Marcus Manilius on Astronomy, written in verse, and the poem of Lucretius, *De rerum Natura*, all works of the highest importance. Also the *Argonauticon* of Valerius Flaccus in verse, the comments of Asconius-Pedianus on certain of Cicero's Orations, Columella on Agriculture, Cornelius Celsus on Medicine, the *Noctium Atticarum* of Agellius, some additional works of Tertullian, the *Silvae* of Statius in verse, and Eusebius, *De Temporibus*, with manuscript additions by Girolamo and Prospero. Next at Constance he found Tully's letters to Atticus, but of these I have no information, and Messer Lionardo and Messer Poggio together discovered the last twelve comedies of Plautus, which Gregorio Corero, Poggio and certain others amended and set in the order which they still follow. The Verrine orations of Cicero also came from Constance and were brought to Italy by Lionardo and Poggio. Thus it may be seen how many noble works we possess through the efforts of these scholars, and how much we are indebted to them; and how greatly the students of our own time have been enlightened by their discoveries. There was no copy of Pliny in Italy; but, news having been brought to Nicolao that there was a fine and perfect one at Lubeck in Germany, he worked so effectively through Cosimo de Medici that he, by the agency of a kinsman of his living there, bargained with the friars who owned it, giving them a hundred Rhenish ducats in exchange for the book.

Matteo Palmieri (d. 1433)

Matteo di Marco Palmieri, a Florentine, was of middle-class birth. He was the founder of his house and ennobled it by his worthy life. He took up the study of Latin and became a good scholar. In the course of his studies he won a high position in the city, and ultimately enjoyed all the honours it could give. Both within and without the city he was engaged in divers offices and missions. . . . On account of his merits he was sent as ambassador to King Alfonso's court, where, through his learning and wisdom, he was received with honour. There were many literary men in Naples who knew Matteo by his works. . . .

He wrote in excellent style, both in Latin and Italian. . . . He wrote a book in Italian in which he taught how to rule both the public and the family; it is in the form of a dialogue, dedicated to Messer Alessandro degli Alessandri. Last he wrote some Italian verses in the manner of Dante, called Città di Vita, a work which cost him much labour, as the subject was a very difficult one; there are fine passages in it in which he shows his talent. However it may be, he went astray in this book while writing of religion, because he had no knowledge of sacred things, and the chief mistakes are those which he makes in dealing with those matters which are opposed to our religion. This is the lot of those who, as St. Paul says, would be wise in the things of this life; they have gone mad with the madness of the world, for of a truth those may be called mad who lose the knowledge of God through straying from His path. Matteo almost certainly fell into this error through ignorance, for at the end of this work he admits to the Church that on no account did he desire to go astray, and lets the Church approve what was right and disapprove of what was wrong.

B. THE CONCEPT OF A "RENAISSANCE"

GIORGIO VASARI: *The Lives of the Painters* *

> Giorgio Vasari (1511–74), an architect and painter of some note, is chiefly famous for his *Lives of the Painters, Sculptors, and Architects.* In this work, first published in 1550, Vasari treated the history of Italian Renaissance art, from its first revolt against medieval art to Michelangelo, as an organic whole, proceeding through three well defined stages. The following passage is from Vasari's Preface.

I THINK that anyone who will take the trouble to consider the matter carefully will arrive at the same conclusion as I have, that art owes its

* From Giorgio Vasari: *The Lives of the Painters Sculptors and Architects,* vol. I, pp. 5–6, 9–10, 12, 17–19. Copyright 1927 by J. M. Dent & Sons Ltd. Reprinted by permission of J. M. Dent & Sons Ltd.

Taken from *The Lives of the Painters Sculptors and Architects,* by Giorgio Vasari, Translated by Everyman's Library, published by E. P. Dutton & Co., Inc., New York.

origin to Nature herself, that this beautiful creation the world supplied the first model, while the original teacher was that divine intelligence which has not only made us superior to the other animals, but like God Himself, if I may venture to say it. In our own time it has been seen, as I hope to show quite shortly, that simple children, roughly brought up in the wilderness, have begun to draw by themselves, impelled by their own natural genius, instructed solely by the example of these beautiful paintings and sculptures of Nature. Much more then is it probable that the first men, being less removed from their divine origin, were more perfect, possessing a brighter intelligence, and that with Nature as a guide, a pure intellect for master, and the lovely world as a model, they originated these noble arts, and by gradually improving them brought them at length, from small beginnings, to perfection. I do not deny that there must have been an originator, since I know quite well that there must have been a beginning at some time, due to some individual. . . .

But we will now pass over these matters, which are too vague on account of their antiquity, and we will proceed to deal with clearer questions, namely, the rise of the arts to perfection, their decline and their restoration or rather renaissance, and here we stand on much firmer ground. The practice of the arts began late in Rome, if the first figures were, as reported, the image of Ceres made of the metal of the possessions of Spurius Cassius, who was condemned to death without remorse by his own father, because he was plotting to make himself king. But although the arts of painting and sculpture continued to flourish until the death of the last of the twelve Caesars, yet they did not maintain that perfection and excellence which had characterised them before, as we see by the buildings of the time under successive emperors. The arts declined steadily from day to day, until at length by a gradual process they entirely lost all perfection of design. Clear testimony to this is afforded by the works in sculpture and architecture produced in Rome in the time of Constantine. . . .

As Fortune, when she has brought men to the top of the wheel, either for amusement or because she repents, usually turns them to the bottom, it came to pass after these things that almost all the barbarian nations rose in divers parts of the world against the Romans, the result being the speedy fall of that great empire, and the destruction of everything, notably of Rome herself. That fall involved the complete destruction of the most excellent artists, sculptors, painters and architects, burying them and their arts under the débris and ruins of that most celebrated city. . . . But the most harmful and destructive force which operated against these fine arts was the fervent zeal of the new Christian religion, which, after long and sanguinary strife, had at length vanquished and abolished the old faith of the heathen, by means of a number of miracles and by the sincerity of its acts. Every effort was put forth to remove and utterly extirpate the smallest things from which errors might arise, and thus not only were the marvellous statues, sculptures, paintings, mosaics and ornaments of the false pagan gods destroyed and thrown down, but also the memorials and honours of countless excellent persons, to whose distinguished merits statues and other memorials had been set up in public by a most virtuous antiquity. . . .

Then new architects arose who created that style of building, for their barbarous nations, which we call Gothic, and produced some works which are ridiculous to our modern eyes, but appeared admirable to theirs. . . .

Yet some rising spirits, aided by some quality in the air of certain places, so far purged themselves of this crude style that in 1250 Heaven took compassion on the fine minds that the Tuscan soil was producing every day, and directed them to the original forms. For although the preceding generations had before them the remains of arches, colossi, statues, pillars or carved stone columns which were left after the plunder, ruin and fire which Rome had passed through, yet they could never make use of them or derive any profit from them until the period named. Those who came after were able to distinguish the good from the bad, and abandoning the old style they began to copy the ancients with all ardour and industry. That the distinction I have made between old and ancient may be better understood, I will explain that I call ancient the things produced before Constantine at Corinth, Athens, Rome and other renowned cities, until the days of Nero, Vespasian, Trajan, Hadrian and Antoninus; the old works are those which are due to the surviving Greeks from the days of S. Silvester, whose art consisted rather of tinting than of painting. . . .

Up to the present, I have discoursed upon the origin of sculpture and painting, perhaps more at length than was necessary at this stage. I have done so, not so much because I have been carried away by my love for the arts, as because I wish to be of service to the artists of our own day, by showing them how a small beginning leads to the highest elevation, and how from so noble a situation it is possible to fall to utterest ruin, and consequently, how these arts resemble nature as shown in our human bodies; and have their birth, growth, age and death, and I hope by this means they will be enabled more easily to recognise the progress of the renaissance of the arts, and the perfection to which they have attained in our own time. And again, if ever it happens, which God forbid, that the arts should once more fall to a like ruin and disorder, through the negligence of man, the malignity of the age, or the decree of Heaven, which does not appear to wish that the things of this world should remain stationary, these labours of mine . . . may maintain the arts in life, or, at any rate, encourage the better spirits to provide them with every assistance. . . .

C. THE AUTHORITY OF THE ANCIENTS

FRANCESCO PETRARCH: *Letters to Classical Authors* *

Included in Petrarch's voluminous correspondence are a number of letters addressed to classical authors, several of which follow. These letters show clearly the enthusiasm of the fourteenth-century humanist for the literature of Latin antiquity.

To Marcus Tullius Cicero

O THOU great father of Roman eloquence! Not only I, but all who take delight in the elegance of the Latin tongue render thee great thanks. Thou art the fountain-head from which we draw the vivifying waters for our meadows. We frankly confess that we have been guided by thee, assisted by thy judgments, enlightened by thy radiance; and, finally, that it was under thy auspices, so to speak, that I have gained this ability as a writer (such as it is), and that I have attained my purpose.

For the realms of poetry, however, there was at hand a second guide. The nature of the case demanded that there should be two leaders—one whom I might follow in the unencumbered ways of prose, and the other in the more restricted paths of poetry. It was necessary that there should be two men whom I should admire, respectively, for their eloquence and their song. . . .

Dost thou ask who that other guide is? Thou wilt know the man at once, if thou art merely reminded of his name. It is Publius Vergilius Maro, a citizen of Mantua, of whom thou didst prophesy such great things. For we have read that when thou, then advanced in years, hadst admired some youthful effort of his, thou didst inquire its author's name, and that, having seen the young man, thou didst express thy great delight. And then, drawing on thy unexhausted fount of eloquence, thou didst pronounce upon him a judgment which, though mingled with self-praise, was nevertheless both honorable and splendid for him: "Rome's other hope and stay." This sentence, which he thus heard fall from thy lips, pleased the youth to such a degree, and was so jealously treasured in his mind, that twenty years later, when thou hadst long since ended this earthly career, he inserted it word for word into his divine poem.

* From *Petrarch's Letters to Classical Authors*, trans. by Mario Emilio Cosenza, pp. 22-5, 43-4, 84-5, 100-01. Copyright 1910 by University of Chicago Press. Reprinted by permission of University of Chicago Press.

And if it had been thy lot to see this work, thou wouldst have rejoiced that from the first blossom thou hadst made such accurate prediction of future success. Thou wouldst, moreover, have congratulated the Latin Muses, either for leaving but a doubtful superiority to the arrogant Greek Muses, or else for winning over them a decisive victory. There are defenders for both these opinions, I grant thee. And yet, if I have come to know thee from thy works—and I feel that I know thee as intimately as if I had always lived with thee—I should say that thou wouldst have been a stern defender of the latter view, and that, just as thou hadst already granted to Latium the palm in oratory, thou wouldst have done likewise in the case of poetry.

To Seneca

I derive great enjoyment from speaking with you, O illustrious characters of antiquity. Each succeeding age has suffered your works to remain in great neglect; but our own age is quite content, in its ignorance, with a dearth that has become extraordinary. For my part, I daily listen to your words with more attention than can be believed; and so, perchance, I shall not be considered impertinent in desiring you in your turn to listen to me once.

I am fully aware that thou art to be numbered among those whose names are illustrious. Were I unable to gather this from any other source, I should still learn it from a great foreign authority. Plutarch, a Greek and the tutor of Emperor Trajan, in comparing the renowned men of his country with those of ours, opposed Marcus Varro to Plato and Aristotle (the former of whom the Greeks call divine, the latter inspired), Vergil to Homer, and Marcus Tullius to Demosthenes. He finally dared to discuss even the vexed question of military leaders, in the treatment of which he was not hampered by the respect due to his great pupil. In one department of learning, however, he did not blush to acknowledge that the genius of the Greeks was distinctly inferior, saying that he knew not whom to place on a par with thee in the field of moral philosophy. Great praise this, especially from the mouth of a man proud of his race, and a startling concession, seeing that he had opposed his Alexander the Macedon to our Julius Caesar.

To Quintilian

I had formerly heard of thy name, and had read something of thine, wondering whence it was that thou hadst gained renown for keen insight. It is but recently that I have become acquainted with thy talents. Thy work entitled the *Institutes of Oratory* has come into my hands, but alas how mangled and mutilated! I recognized therein the hand of time— the destroyer of all things—and thought to myself, "O Destroyer, as usual thou dost guard nothing with sufficient care except that which it were a gain to lose. O slothful and haughty Age, is it thus that thou dost hand down to us men of genius, though thou dost bestow most tender care on the unworthy? O sterile-minded and wretched men of today, why do you devote yourselves to learning and writing so many things which it were better to leave unlearned, but neglect to preserve this work intact?"

However, this work caused me to estimate thee at thy true worth. As regards thee I had long been in error, and I rejoice that I have now been corrected. I saw the dismembered limbs of a beautiful body, and admiration mingled with grief seized me. Even at this moment, indeed, thy work may be resting intact in someone's library, and, what is worse, with one who perhaps has not the slightest idea of what a guest he is harboring unawares. Whosoever more fortunate than I will discover thee, may he be sure that he has gained a work of great value, one which, if he be at all wise, he will consider among his chief treasures.

In these books (whose number I am ignorant of, but which must doubtless have been many) thou hast had the daring to probe again a subject treated with consummate skill by Cicero himself when enriched by the experience of a lifetime. Thou hast accomplished the impossible. Thou didst follow in the footsteps of so great a man, and yet thou didst gain new glory, due not to the excellence of imitation but to the merits of the original doctrines propounded in thine own work. By Cicero, the orator was prepared for battle; by thee he is molded and fashioned, with the result that many things seem to have been either neglected or unheeded by Cicero.

To Titus Livy

I should wish (if it were permitted from on high) either that I had been born in thine age or thou in ours; in the latter case our age itself, and in the former I personally should have been the better for it. I should surely have been one of those pilgrims who visited thee. For the sake of seeing thee I should have gone not merely to Rome, but indeed, from either Gaul or Spain I should have found my way to thee as far as India. As it is, I must fain be content with seeing thee as reflected in thy works —not thy whole self, alas, but that portion of thee which has not yet perished, notwithstanding the sloth of our age. We know that thou didst write one hundred and forty-two books on Roman affairs. With what fervor, with what unflagging zeal must thou have labored; and of that entire number there are now extant scarcely thirty.

Oh, what a wretched custom is this of wilfully deceiving ourselves! I have said "thirty," because it is common for all to say so. I find, however, that even from these few there is one lacking. They are twenty-nine in all, constituting three decades, the first, the third, and the fourth, the last of which has not the full number of books. It is over these small remains that I toil whenever I wish to forget these regions, these times, and these customs. Often I am filled with bitter indignation against the morals of today, when men value nothing except gold and silver, and desire nothing except sensual, physical pleasures. If these are to be considered the goal of mankind, then not only the dumb beasts of the field, but even insensible and inert matter has a richer, a higher goal than that proposed to itself by thinking man. But of this elsewhere.

It is now fitter that I should render thee thanks, for many reasons indeed, but for this in especial: that thou didst so frequently cause me to forget the present evils, and transfer me to happier times. As I read, I seem to be living in the midst of the Cornellii Scipiones Africani, of Laelius, Fabius Maximus, Metellus, Brutus and Decius, of Cato, Regulus, Cursor, Torquatus, Valerius Corvinus, Salinator, of Claudius, Marcellus, Nero, Aemilius, of Fulvius, Flaminius, Attilius, Quintius, Curius, Fabricius, and Camillus.

D. INDIVIDUALISM AND THE NATURE OF MAN

PICO DELLA MIRANDOLA: *Oration on the Dignity of Man* *

Giovanni Pico, count of Mirandola (1463–94), was one of the best educated men of the Italian Renaissance. Familiar with Latin and Greek, friend to the humanists, associated for a time with the Platonists of the Florentine Academy, he was also versed in scholasticism, Hebrew and Arabic, and vernacular Italian literature. His *Oration on the Dignity of Man* was probably written in 1486, as the introduction to a disputation in Rome to which he invited all comers. Pope Innocent VIII, however, suspended the disputation, and a papal commission adjudged heretical some of the nine hundred theses Pico proposed to defend.

I HAVE read in the records of the Arabians, reverend Fathers, that Abdala the Saracen, when questioned as to what on this stage of the world, as it were, could be seen most worthy of wonder, replied: "There is nothing to be seen more wonderful than man." In agreement with this opinion is the saying of Hermes Trismegistus: "A great miracle, Asclepius, is man." But when I weighed the reason for these maxims, the many grounds for the excellence of human nature reported by many men failed to satisfy me—that man is the intermediary between creatures, the intimate of the gods, the king of the lower beings, by the acuteness of his senses, by the discernment of his reason, and by the light of his intelligence the interpreter of nature, the interval between fixed eternity and fleeting time, and (as the Persians say) the bond, nay, rather, the marriage song of the world, on David's testimony but little lower than the angels. Admittedly great though these reasons be, they are not the principal grounds, that is, those which may rightfully claim for themselves the privilege of the highest admiration. For why should we not admire more the angels themselves and the blessed choirs of heaven? At last it seems to me I have come to understand why man is the most fortunate of creatures and consequently worthy of all admiration and what precisely is that rank which is his lot in the universal chain of Being —a rank to be envied not only by brutes but even by the stars and by minds beyond this world. It is a matter past faith and a wondrous one. Why should it not be? For it is on this very account that man is rightly called and judged a great miracle and a wonderful creature indeed.

2. But hear, Fathers, exactly what this rank is and, as friendly auditors, conformably to your kindness, do me this favor. God the Father, the supreme Architect, had already built this cosmic home we behold, the most sacred temple of His godhead, by the laws of His mysterious wisdom. The region above the heavens He had adorned with Intelligences, the heavenly spheres He had quickened with eternal souls, and the excrementary and filthy parts of the lower world He had filled with a multitude of animals of every kind. But, when the work was finished, the Craftsman kept wishing that there were someone to ponder the plan of so great a work, to love its beauty, and to wonder at its vastness. Therefore, when everything was done (as Moses and Timaeus bear witness), He finally took thought concerning the creation of man. But there was not among His archetypes that from which He could fashion a new offspring, nor was there in His treasure-houses anything which He might bestow on His new son as an inheritance, nor was there in the seats of all the world a place where the latter might sit to contemplate the universe. All was now complete; all things had been assigned to the highest, the middle, and the lowest orders. But in its final creation it was not the part of the Father's power to fail as though exhausted. It was not the part of His wisdom to waver in a needful matter through poverty of counsel. It was not the part of His kindly love that he who was to praise God's divine generosity in regard to others should be compelled to condemn it in regard to himself.

3. At last the best of artisans ordained that that creature to whom He had been able to give nothing proper to himself should have joint possession of whatever had been peculiar to each of the different kinds of being. He therefore took man as a creature of indeterminate nature and,

assigning him a place in the middle of the world, addressed him thus: "Neither a fixed abode nor a form that is thine alone nor any function peculiar to thyself have we given thee, Adam, to the end that according to thy longing and according to thy judgment thou mayest have and possess what abode, what form, and what functions thou thyself shalt desire. The nature of all other beings is limited and constrained within the bounds of laws prescribed by Us. Thou, constrained by no limits, in accordance with thine own free will, in whose hand We have placed thee, shalt ordain for thyself the limits of thy nature. We have set thee at the world's center that thou mayest from thence more easily observe whatever is in the world. We have made thee neither of heaven nor of earth, neither mortal nor immortal, so that with freedom of choice and with honor, as though the maker and molder of thyself, thou mayest fashion thyself in whatever shape thou shalt prefer. Thou shalt have the power to degenerate into the lower forms of life, which are brutish. Thou shalt have the power, out of thy soul's judgment, to be reborn into the higher forms, which are divine."

4. O supreme generosity of God the Father, O highest and most marvelous felicity of man! To him it is granted to have whatever he chooses, to be whatever he wills. Beasts as soon as they are born (so says Lucilius) bring with them from their mother's womb all they will ever possess. Spiritual beings, either from the beginning or soon thereafter, become what they are to be for ever and ever. On man when he came into life the Father conferred the seeds of all kinds and the germs of every way of life. Whatever seeds each man cultivates will grow to maturity and bear in him their own fruit. If they be vegetative, he will be like a plant. If sensitive, he will become brutish. If rational, he will grow into a heavenly being. If intellectual, he will be an angel and the son of God. And if, happy in the lot of no created thing, he withdraws into the center of his own unity, his spirit, made one with God, in the solitary darkness of God, who is set above all things, shall surpass them all. Who would not admire this our chameleon? Or who could more greatly admire aught else whatever?

DESIDERIUS ERASMUS: *On the Education of Children* *

The Dutchman Desiderius Erasmus (1466–1536; of whom more below, see under "Christian Humanism"), was perhaps the leading educator of his time. Among his educational tracts was the *De Pueris statim ac liberaliter instituendis* (1529), in which he voiced his optimism about the nature of man and his belief in the omnipotence of "training."

* From W. H. Woodward: *Desiderius Erasmus*, pp. 186–7, 191, 195–6. Copyright 1904 by Cambridge University Press. Reprinted by permission of Cambridge University Press.

Now it is the possession of Reason which constitutes a Man. If trees or wild beasts grow, men, believe me, are fashioned. Men in olden time who led their life in forests, driven by the mere needs and desires of their natures, guided by no laws, with no ordering in communities, are to be judged rather as savage beasts than as men. For Reason, the mark of humanity, has no place where all is determined by appetite. It is beyond dispute that a man not instructed through reason in philosophy and sound learning is a creature lower than a brute, seeing that there is no beast more wild or more harmful than a man who is driven hither and thither by ambition, or desire, anger or envy, or lawless temper. Therefore do I conclude that he that provides not that his own son may presently be instructed in the best learning is neither a man nor the son of a man. . . . Nature, in giving you a son, presents you, let me say, a rude, unformed creature, which it is your part to fashion so that it may become indeed a man. If this fashioning be neglected you have but an animal still: if it be contrived earnestly and wisely, you have, I had almost said, what may prove a being not far from a God.

*   *   *

Can anything be more deplorable than to have to admit that, whilst an unreasoning animal performs by instinct its duty towards its offspring, Man, the creature of Reason, is blind to what he owes to Nature, to parental responsibilty, and to God? But I will now consider definitely the three conditions which determine individual progress. They are Nature, Training and Practice. By *Nature*, I mean, partly, innate capacity for being trained, partly, native bent towards excellence. By *Training*, I mean the skilled application of instruction and guidance. By *Practice*, the free exercise on our own part of that activity which has been implanted by Nature and is furthered by Training. Nature without skilled Training must be imperfect, and Practice without the method which Training supplies leads to hopeless confusion.

*   *   *

By the *nature* of a man we mean, as a rule, that which is common to Man as such: the characteristic, namely, of being guided by Reason. But we may mean something less broad than this: the characteristic peculiar to each personality, which we may call individuality. Thus one child may shew a native bent to Mathematics, another to Divinity, another to Rhetoric, or Poetry, another to War. So strongly disposed are certain types of mind to certain studies that they cannot be won to others; the very attempt in that direction sets up a positive repulsion. . . .

The Master will be wise to observe such natural inclination, such individuality, in the early stages of child life, since we learn most easily the things which conform to it. It is not, I believe, a vain thing to try and infer from the face and bearing of a boy what disposition he will show. Nature has not omitted to give us marks for our guidance in this respect.

HENRY PEACHAM: *The Complete Gentleman* *

Henry Peacham (1576–1644) was a schoolmaster and, for a time, tutor to the sons of the Earl of Arundel, to the second of whom *The Complete Gentleman* (1622) is dedicated. This book is a typical specimen of the "courtesy" books which appeared with regular frequency from the fifteenth to the seventeenth centuries. Like Castiglione's *Courtier*, it epitomizes the evolution of the medieval knight into the domesticated "complete" man of the Renaissance.

I HERE present you [William Howard, son of the Earl of Arundel and Surrey] with the first and plainest directions (though but as so many keys to lead you into far fairer rooms) and the readiest method I know for your studies in general, and to the attaining of the most commendable qualities that are requisite in every noble or gentleman. Nothing doubting, but that after you have herein seen the worth and excellence of learning, how much it addeth to Nobility; what errors are hourly committed through ignorance; how sweet a thing it is to converse with the wisest of all ages by history; to have insight into the most pleasing and admirable sciences of the mathematics, poetry, picture, heraldry, &c. (whereof I here entreat together with the most commendable exercise of the body; with other general directions for carriage, travel, &c.) you will entertain this discourse, as Ulysses did Minerva at his elbow: as your guide to knowledge; the ground, not only of the sweetest, but the happiest life.

* * *

If we consider rightly the frame of the whole universe and method of the all-excellent wisdom in her work: as creating the forms of things infinitely divers, so according to dignity of essence or virtue in effect, we must acknowledge the same to hold a sovereignty, and transcendent predominance, as well of rule as place, each over either. Among the heavenly bodies we see the nobler orbs, and of greatest influence to be raised aloft, the less effectual, depressed. Of elements, the fire the most pure and operative to hold the highest place: in compounded bodies, of things as well sensible, as insensible, there runneth a vein of excellence proceeding from the form, ennobling (in the same kind) some other above the rest.

The lion we say is king of beasts, the eagle chief of birds; the whale and whirl-pool among fishes, Jupiter's oak the forest's king. Among flowers, we most admire and esteem the rose: among fruit, the pomeroy and queen-apple: among stones, we value above all the diamond; metals, gold and silver: and since we knew these to transfer their inward excellence and virtues to their species successively, shall we not acknowledge a nobility in man of greater perfection, of nobler form, and prince of these? . . .

Surely, to believe that Nature (rather the God of Nature) produceth not the same among ourselves, is to question the rarest work-mistress of ignorance or partiality, and to abase ourselves beneath the beast. *Nobility* then (taken in the general sense) is nothing else than a certain eminency, or notice taken of some one above the rest, for some notable act performed, be it good or ill; and in that sense are *nobilis* and *ignobilis* usually among the Latin poets taken. More particularly, and in the genuine sense, *Nobility* is the honor of blood in a race or lineage, conferred formerly upon some one or more of that family, either by the prince, the laws, customs of that land or place, whereby either out of knowledge, culture of the mind, or by some glorious action performed, they have been useful and beneficial to the commonwealths and places where they live.

For since all virtue consisteth in action, and no man is born for himself, we add, beneficial and useful to his country; for hardly they are to be admitted for noble, who (though of never so excellent parts) consume their light, as in a dark lantern, in contemplation, and a stoical retiredness. . . .

Besides, nobility being inherent and natural, can have (as the diamond) the luster but only from itself: honors and titles externally conferred, are but attendant upon desert, and are but as apparel, and the drapery to a beautiful body.

Memorable, as making to our purpose, is that speech of Sigismund the Emperor, to a doctor of the civil law, who when he had received knighthood at the Emperor's hands, left forthwith the society of his fellow doctors, and kept company altogether with the knights: which the Emperor well observing, smiling (before the open assembly) said unto him; fool, who preferrest knighthood before learning and thy degree; I can make a thousand knights in one day, but cannot make a doctor in a thousand years. Now for as much as the weal public of every estate, is preserved *armis* & *consilio*, this fair tree by two main branches spreadeth herself into the military and civil discipline; under the first I place valor and greatness of spirit: under the other, justice, knowledge of the law, which is *consilii fons;* magnificence, and eloquence.

For true fortitude and greatness of spirit were ennobled (we read)

Iphicrates, that brave Athenian, who overthrew in a set battle the Lacedemonians, stopped the fury of Epaminondas, and became lieutenant general to Artazerzes King of Persia, yet but the son of a poor cobbler.

Eumenes, one of the best captains for valor and advice Alexander had, was the son of an ordinary carter.

Diocletian was the son of a scrivener, or book-binder: Valentinian, of a rope-maker; Maximius, of a smith; Pertinax, of a woodmonger; Servius Tullius, son of a bond-woman, thence his name Servius; Tarquinius Priscus, of a poor merchant, or rather pedler in Corinth; Hugh Capet, the first of that name, King of France, the son of a butcher in Paris. . . .

For magnificence, and obliging the places wherein they lived, by great benefits, were ennobled Tarquinius Priscus, a stranger and a banished man: and of later times, Cosimo di Medici in Florence, upon whose virtues, as upon a fair prospect, or some princely palace, give me leave a little, as a traveller to breathe myself, and show you afar off the fair turrets of his more than royal magnificence, being but a private man, as I find it recorded in his history by Machiavelli. This Cosimo (saith he) was the most esteemed, and most famous citizen (being no man of war) that ever had been in the memory of man, either in Florence, or any other city; because he did not only excel all others (of his time) in authority and riches, but also in liberality and wisdom. For among other qualities which advanced him to be chief of his country, he was more than other men liberal and magnificent, which liberality appeared much more after his death than before. For his son Piero found by his father's records, that there was not any citizen of estimation, to whom Cosimo had not lent great sums of money: and many times also he did lend to those gentlemen, whom he knew to have need. His magnificence appeared by divers his buildings: for within the city of Florence he builded the abbeys and temples of S. Marco, S. Lorenzo, and the monastery of S. Verdiana, and in the mountains of Fiesole, S. Girolamo, with the abbey thereto belonging. . . . And because his magnificent houses in Italy did not in his opinion make him famous enough, he builded in Jerusalem an hospital to receive poor and diseased pilgrims. In which work he consumed great sums of money. And albeit these buildings, and every other his actions were princely, and that in Florence he lived like a prince; yet so governed by wisdom, as he never exceeded the bounds of civil modesty. For in his conversation, in riding, in marrying his children and kinsfolk, he was like unto all other modest and discreet citizens; because he well knew, that extraordinary things, which are of all men with admiration beheld, do procure more envy, than those which without ostentation be honestly covered, I omit, as followeth shortly after, his great and excessive charge in entertaining of learned men of all professions, to instruct the youth of Florence: his bounty to Argiropolo a Grecian, and Marsilio Ficino (whom he maintained for the exercise of his own studies in his house, and gave him goodly lands near his house of Carraggi), men in that time of singular learning, because virtue rears him rather to wonder than imitation.

To proceed, no less respect and honor is to be attributed to eloquence, whereby so many have raised their esteem and fortunes, as able to draw civility out of barbarism, and sway whole kingdoms by leading with Celtic Hercules, the rude multitude by the ears. Mark Anthony contending against Augustus for the Roman Empire, assured himself he could never obtain his purpose while Cicero lived, therefore he procured his death. . . . Much therefore it concerneth princes, not only to countenance honest and eloquent orators, but to maintain such near about them, as no mean props (if occasion serve) to uphold a state, and the only keys to bring in tune a discordant commonwealth.

*   *   *

Since learning then is an essential part of nobility, as unto which we are beholden, for whatsoever dependeth on the culture of the mind; it followeth, that who is nobly born, and a scholar withal, deserveth double honor, . . . for hereby as an ensign of the fairest colors, he is afar off discerned, and winneth to himself both love and admiration, heightening with skill his image to the life, making it precious, and lasting to posterity. . . .

Rome saw her best days under her most learned kings and emperors: as Numa, Augustus, Titus, Antoninus, Constantine, Theodosius, and some others. Plutarch giveth the reason: learning (saith he) reformeth the life and manners, and affordeth the wholesomest advice for the government of a commonwealth. I am not ignorant, but that (as all goodness else) she hath met with her mortal enemies, the champions of ignorance, as Licinius gave for his mot or poetry: *Pestes Reipublicae literae;* and Lewis the eleventh, King of France, would ever charge his son to learn no more Latin than this, *Qui nescit dissimulare, nescit regnare;* but these are the fancies of a few, and those of ignorant and corrupted judgments.

LEO BATTISTA ALBERTI: *Treatise on Painting* *

Leo Battista Alberti (1404–72) was one of those "universal" men of the Renaissance who made all knowledge their province. The architect of the church of S. Francesco at Rimini, he also wrote a treatise on the family and composed poems and plays. His *Treatise on Painting*, together with two companion works on architecture and sculpture, mark the first formulation of conscious principles of art.

* *The Painting of Leon Battista Alberti* (London: Thomas Eldin; 1726), pp. 1, 11, 13, 15, 17–19, 21, 23–5.

[IN THIS BOOK] I shall think I have done enough if painters, when they read me, can gain some information in this difficult subject which has not, as I know of, been discussed hitherto by any author. . . .

Is not painting the mistress of all others arts, or at least their principal ornament? . . .

There is hardly any art in which as well the ignorant as the skillful are employed either in learning or practicing it with so much delight to themselves. If I may be allowed to mention myself; whenever for my pleasure and recreation I sit down to paint, which I very often do when my affairs will permit, I am so intent upon my work and receive so much delight from it, that three or four hours are gone before I imagine it. Thus we see that this art affords pleasure while you cultivate it, and honor, wealth and perpetual fame when you attain to perfection in it. . . . Have always before your eyes, you that desire to excel in painting, the honor and fame which the ancients obtained by it. . . .

We divide painting into three parts [the outline, the composition, and the coloring of the picture]. . . . Composition is that part of drawing, by which the several parts of the picture are joined together to form a whole. The greatest work of the painter is, not a colossus, but a history. The parts of a history are bodies; the parts of a body are the members; the parts of the members are superficies. . . . In the composition of the superficies beauty and gracefulness is chiefly to be aimed at. How this is to be attained, I have as yet been able to discover no method more certain that to study Nature, than to observe long and diligently how that wonderful Artist proceeds in compounding the superficies in the most beautiful members. . . .

The first thing that delights us in a piece of history is the number and variety of the objects: for as in meats and music what is new and exuberant always pleases, as perhaps from other causes, so particularly because it differs from what we have been constantly used to; so the mind takes a pleasure in all other kinds of variety and abundance: and for this reason in painting also a variety of figures and of colors is grateful. . . . Indeed I am pleased with all manner of abundance that will suit the subject represented: for this detains the eye of the beholder, and obliges him to admire the richness of the painter's fancy. But then I would have this abundance set off by variety, and preserve at the same time a due moderation and dignity. . . . But as variety is pleasing in any story, a picture is more particularly so when the positions and attitudes of the several figures are very different one from the other. . . . I would have no two figures in the same action or attitude. . . .

As in representing these motions [of the body] truth and probability is sometimes transgressed, I will here set down some observations relating to the situation and motion of the members which I have borrowed from nature, in order to show with how much moderation we ought to make use of these motions. I have observed in man, that in all his attitudes he brings his whole body under his head, as the most weighty of all the members. Thus if he rests his whole body upon one foot, that foot, like the base of a column, is always perpendicularly under his head, etc. . . . I have observed from nature, that the hands are seldom raised higher than the head, nor the elbow above the shoulder, nor the foot higher than the knee, nor generally is one foot removed from the other farther than the length of one of those feet. . . .

[With regard to coloring] let the painter make light and shade his principal study. Let him observe that upon that part of the superficie where the rays of light fall, the color must be as bright and strong as possible; and as the light diminishes and sinks by degrees, the same color must be made darker and darker, etc. . . .

I wish the painter to be as learned as may be in all the liberal arts; but what I particularly desire in him is some knowledge in geometry. I am entirely of the opinion of Pamphilus, a most ancient and eminent painter, who first taught the art to gentleman's sons, who declared it as his sentiment, that one who was ignorant of geometry could never make a good painter. . . .

Demetrius, an ancient painter, fell short of perfection because he was more curious to express the strict resemblance of things, than to mark their peculiar beauties. We should therefore make collections of the most commended parts of the most lovely bodies, and by no means neglect applying ourselves with the greatest industry to learn, know and express what is beautiful: which though it be the most difficult part of all, because everything that is beautiful is not to be found in one single subject, but lies scattered and dispersed among several; yet we must spare no pains in finding it out and making ourselves masters of it. . . . Everything therefore that we are to paint, let us copy from nature and from that part of nature too which has most beauty and dignity.

E. THE NEW EDUCATION

LIONARDO BRUNI: *Concerning the Study of Literature* *

The *De Studiis et Literis* of the Italian humanist Lionardo Bruni d'Arezzo (d. 1443) expresses admirably the humanist admiration of ancient literature and the attention paid by the Renaissance to the education of women. It was written around 1405 in the form of a letter to the accomplished Baptista di Montefeltro, daughter of the Count of Urbino.

* From W. H. Woodward: *Vittorino da Feltre and other Humanist Educators*, pp. 124-32. Copyright 1897 by Cambridge University Press. Reprinted by permission of Cambridge University Press.

THE FOUNDATIONS of all true learning must be laid in the sound and thorough knowledge of Latin: which implies study marked by a broad spirit, accurate scholarship, and careful attention to details. Unless this solid basis be secured it is useless to attempt to rear an enduring edifice. Without it the great monuments of literature are unintelligible, and the art of composition impossible. To attain this essential knowledge we must never relax our careful attention to the grammar of the language, but perpetually confirm and extend our acquaintance with it until it is thoroughly our own. We may gain much from Servius, Donatus and Priscian, but more by careful observation in our own reading, in which we must note attentively vocabulary and inflexions, figures of speech and metaphors, and all the devices of style, such as rhythm, or antithesis, by which fine taste is exhibited. To this end we must be supremely careful in our choice of authors, lest an inartistic and debased style infect our own writing and degrade our taste; which danger is best avoided by bringing a keen, critical sense to bear upon select works, observing the sense of each passage, the structure of the sentence, the force of every word down to the least important particle. In this way our reading reacts directly upon our style.

You may naturally turn first to Christian writers, foremost amongst whom, with marked distinction, stands Lactantius, by common consent the finest stylist of the post-classical period. Especially do I commend to your study his works, '*Adversus falsam Religionem,*' '*De via Dei,*' and '*De opificio hominis.*' After Lactantius your choice may lie between Augustine, Jerome, Ambrose, and Cyprian; should you desire to read Gregory of Nazianzen, Chrysostom, and Basil, be careful as to the accuracy of the translations you adopt. Of the classical authors Cicero will be your constant pleasure: how unapproachable in wealth of ideas and of language, in force of style, indeed, in all that can attract in a writer! Next to him ranks Vergil, the glory and the delight of our national literature. Livy and Sallust, and then the chief poets, follow in order. The usage of these authors will serve you as your test of correctness in choice of vocabulary and of constructions. . . .

But the wider question now confronts us, that of the subject matter of our studies, that which I have already called the realities of fact and principle, as distinct from literary form. Here, as before, I am contemplating a student of keen and lofty aspiration to whom nothing that is worthy in any learned discipline is without its interest. But it is necessary to exercise discrimination. In some branches of knowledge I would rather restrain the ardour of the learner, in others, again, encourage it to the uttermost. Thus there are certain subjects in which, whilst a modest proficiency is on all accounts to be desired, a minute knowledge and excessive devotion seem to be a vain display. For instance, subleties of

Arithmetic and Geometry are not worthy to absorb a cultivated mind, and the same must be said of Astrology. . . .

What Disciplines then are properly open to her? In the first place she has before her, as a subject peculiarly her own, the whole field of religion and morals. The literature of the Church will thus claim her earnest study. Such a writer, for instance, as St. Augustine affords her the fullest scope for reverent yet learned inquiry. Her devotional instinct may lead her to value the help and consolation of holy men now living; but in this case let her not for an instant yield to the impulse to look into their writings, which, compared with those of Augustine, are utterly destitute of sound and melodious style, and seem to me to have no attraction whatever.

Moreover, the cultivated Christian lady has no need in the study of this weighty subject to confine herself to ecclesiastical writers. Morals, indeed, have been treated of by the noblest intellects of Greece and Rome. What they have left to us upon Continence, Temperance, Modesty, Justice, Courage, Greatness of Soul, demands your sincere respect. You must enter into such questions as the sufficiency of Virtue to Happiness; or whether, if Happiness consist in Virtue, it can be destroyed by torture, imprisonment or exile; whether, admitting that these may prevent a man from being happy, they can be further said to make him miserable. Again, does Happiness consist (with Epicurus) in the presence of pleasure and the absence of pain: or (with Xenophon) in the consciousness of uprightness: or (with Aristotle) in the practice of Virtue? These inquiries are, of all others, most worthy to be pursued by men and women alike; they are fit material for formal discussion and for literary exercise. Let religion and morals, therefore, hold the first place in the education of a Christian lady.

But we must not forget that true distinction is to be gained by a wide and varied range of such studies as conduce to the profitable enjoyment of life, in which, however, we must observe due proportion in the attention and time we devote to them.

First amongst such studies I place History: a subject which must not on any account be neglected by one who aspires to true cultivation. For it is our duty to understand the origins of our own history and its development; and the achievements of Peoples and of Kings.

For the careful study of the past enlarges our foresight in contemporary affairs and affords to citizens and to monarchs lessons of incitement or warning in the ordering of public policy. From History, also, we draw our store of examples of moral precepts.

In the monuments of ancient literature which have come down to us History holds a position of great distinction. We specially prize such authors as Livy, Sallust and Curtius; and, perhaps even above these,

Julius Caesar; the style of whose Commentaries, so elegant and so limpid, entitles them to our warm admiration. Such writers are fully within the comprehension of a studious lady. For, after all, History is an easy subject: there is nothing in its study subtle or complex. It consists in the narration of the simplest matters of fact which, once grasped, are readily retained in the memory.

The great Orators of antiquity must by all means be included. Nowhere do we find the virtues more warmly extolled, the vices so fiercely decried. From them we may learn, also, how to express consolation, encouragement, disuasion or advice. . . .

. . . familiarity with the great poets of antiquity is [also] essential to any claim to true education. For in their writings we find deep speculations upon Nature, and upon the Causes and Origins of things, which must carry weight with us both from their antiquity and from their authorship. Besides these, many important truths upon matters of daily life are suggested or illustrated. All this is expressed with such grace and dignity as demands our admiration. . . .

We know, however, that in certain quarters—where all knowledge and appreciation of Letters is wanting—this whole branch of Literature, marked as it is by something of the Divine, and fit, therefore, for the highest place, is decried as unworthy of study. But when we remember the value of the best poetry, its charm of form and the variety and interest of its subject-matter, when we consider the ease with which from our childhood up it can be committed to memory, when we recall the peculiar affinity of rhythm and metre to our emotions and our intelligence, we must conclude that Nature herself is against such headlong critics. . . . Plato and Aristotle studied the poets, and I decline to admit that in practical wisdom or in moral earnestness they yield to our modern critics. They were not Christians, indeed, but consistency of life and abhorrence of evil existed before Christianity and are independent of it.

LEONARDO DA VINCI: *On Painting as an Art* *

The following jottings by Leonardo da Vinci (1452–1519) have been thought to be (in their entirety, for only a selection is printed here) the famous artist's introduction to his *Treatise on Painting*. It seems more likely, however, that Leonardo made them in connection with some sort of battle of the arts among the humanists at the court of

* From *The Literary Works of Leonardo da Vinci*, ed. by Jean Paul Richter, Vol. I, pp. 33–4, 37–8, 54, 59–60, 67. Copyright 1939 by Oxford University Press. Reprinted by permission of Gisela M. A. Richter.

Ludovico the Moor, Duke of Milan. In any case they represent Leonardo's challenge to traditional conceptions, claiming for painting an
honored place among the Liberal Arts and even asserting her superiority
in certain respects to the other arts.

PAINTING has every right to complain of being driven out from the number of Liberal Arts, since she is a true daughter of nature and employs
the noblest of all the senses. It was wrong, oh writers, to leave her out
from the number of Liberal Arts, because she deals not only with the
works of nature but extends over an infinite number of things which
nature never created. . . .

As the scribes have had no knowledge of the science of painting they
could not assign to it its rightful place or share; and painting does not
display her accomplishment in words; therefore she was classed below
the sciences, through ignorance—but she does not thereby lose any
of her divine quality. . . .

They say that knowledge born of experience is mechanical, but that
knowledge born and consummated in the mind is scientific, while knowledge born of science and culminating in manual work is semi-
mechanical. But to me it seems that all sciences are vain and full of errors
that are not born of experience, mother of all certainty, and that are not
tested by experience, that is to say, that do not at their origin, middle,
or end pass through any of the five senses. (For if we are doubtful about
the certainty of things that pass through the senses how much more
should we question the many things against which these senses rebel,
such as the nature of God and the soul and the like, about which there
are endless disputes and controversies.) . . . This the deceptive purely
speculative sciences cannot achieve. If you say that these true sciences
that are founded on observation must be classed as mechanical because
they do not accomplish their end, without manual work, I reply that all
arts that pass through the hands of scribes are in the same position, for
they are a kind of drawing which is a branch of painting.

Astronomy and the other sciences also entail manual operations although they have their beginning in the mind, like painting, which
arises in the mind of the contemplator but cannot be accomplished without manual operation. The scientific and true principles of painting
first determine what is a shaded object, what is direct shadow, what is
cast shadow, and what is light, that is to say, darkness, light, colour, body,
figure, position, distance, nearness, motion, and rest. These are understood by the mind alone and entail no manual operation; and they
constitute the science of painting which remains in the mind of its contemplators; and from it is then born the actual creation, which is far
superior in dignity to the contemplation or science which precedes it.

*   *   *

If you despise painting, which is the sole imitator of all visible works of nature, you certainly will be despising a subtle invention which brings philosophy and subtle speculation to bear on the nature of all forms— sea and land, plants and animals, grasses and flowers—which are enveloped in shade and light. Truly painting is a science, the true-born child of nature. For painting is born of nature; to be more correct we should call it the grandchild of nature, since all visible things were brought forth by nature and these, her children, have given birth to painting. Therefore we may justly speak of it as the grandchild of nature and as related to God.

* * *

Painting can be shown to be philosophy because it deals with the motion of bodies in the promptitude of their actions, and philosophy too deals with motion. . . .

Painting extends to the surfaces, colours, and shapes of all things created by nature; while philosophy penetrates below the surface in order to arrive at the inherent properties, but it does not carry the same conviction, and in this is unlike the work of the painter who apprehends the foremost truth of these bodies as the eye errs less. . . . .

And as the geometrician reduces every area circumscribed by lines to the square and every body to the cube; and arithmetic does likewise with its cubic and square roots, these two sciences do not extend beyond the study of continuous and discontinuous quantities; but they do not deal with the quality of things which constitutes the beauty of the works of nature and the ornament of the world.

F. THE NEW POLITICS

NICCOLO MACHIAVELLI: *The Discourses on Titus Livy* *

Machiavelli's big book was *The Discourses on Titus Livy*. His better known *Prince* was merely a particular application to early sixteenth-century Italy of the general principles of politics formulated in the *Discourses*. Both books were written in 1513, shortly after Machiavelli's enforced retirement upon the downfall of the Florentine Republic. As second chancellor and secretary to the department of war and the interior in the Republic, Machiavelli (1469–1527) had ample opportunity to observe firsthand the workings of Italian and European statecraft. To his writing he also brought wide reading in the classics, particularly ancient history which he believed could serve as a mirror for contemporary rulers and states.

* *The Historical, Political, and Diplomatic Writings of Niccolo Machiavelli*, trans. by C. E. Detmold (Boston and New York: Houghton Mifflin Company; 1891), vol. II, pp. 93–4, 120–1, 129–31, 210–11, 232–3, 259, 421.

ALTHOUGH the envious nature of men, so prompt to blame and so slow to praise, makes the discovery and introduction of any new principles and systems as dangerous almost as the exploration of unknown seas and continents, yet, animated by that desire which impels me to do what may prove for the common benefit of all, I have resolved to open a new route, which has not yet been followed by any one, and may prove difficult and troublesome, but may also bring me some reward in the approbation of those who will kindly appreciate my efforts. . . .

When we consider the general respect for antiquity, and how often— to say nothing of other examples—a great price is paid for some fragments of an antique statue, which we are anxious to possess to ornament our houses with, or to give to artists who strive to imitate them in their own works; and when we see, on the other hand, the wonderful examples which the history of ancient kingdoms and republics presents to us, the prodigies of virtue and of wisdom displayed by the kings, captains, citizens, and legislators who have sacrificed themselves for their country,—when we see these, I say, more admired than imitated, or so much neglected that not the least trace of this ancient virtue remains, we cannot but be at the same time as much surprised as afflicted. The more so as in the differences which arise between citizens, or in the maladies to which they are subjected, we see these same people have recourse to the judgments and the remedies prescribed by the ancients. The civil laws are in fact nothing but decisions given by their jurisconsults, and which, reduced to a system, direct our modern jurists in their decisions. And what is the science of medicine, but the experience of ancient physicians, which their successors have taken for their guide? And yet to found a republic, maintain states, to govern a kingdom, organize an army, conduct a war, dispense justice, and extend empires, you will find neither prince, nor republic, nor captain, nor citizen, who has recourse to the examples of antiquity! This neglect, I am persuaded, is due less to the weakness to which the vices of our education have reduced the world, than to the evils caused by the proud indolence which prevails in most of the Christian states, and to the lack of real knowledge of history, the true sense of which is not known, or the spirit of which they do not comprehend. Thus the majority of those who read it take pleasure only in the variety of the events which history relates, without ever thinking of imitating the noble actions, deeming that not only difficult, but impossible; as though heaven, the sun, the elements, and men had changed the order of their motions and power, and were different from what they were in ancient times.

Wishing, therefore, so far as in me lies, to draw mankind from this error, I have thought it proper to write upon those books of Titus Livius that have come to us entire despite the malice of time; touching upon all those matters which, after a comparison between the ancient and modern events, may seem to me necessary to facilitate their proper understanding. In this way those who read my remarks may derive those advantages which should be the aim of all study of history.

* * *

It is the duty of princes and heads of republics to uphold the foundations of the religion of their countries, for then it is easy to keep their people religious, and consequently well conducted and united. And therefore everything that tends to favor religion (even though it were believed to be false) should be received and availed of to strengthen it; and this should be done the more, the wiser the rulers are, and the better they understand the natural course of things. Such was, in fact, the practice observed by sagacious men; which has given rise to the belief in the miracles that are celebrated in religions, however false they may be. For the sagacious rulers have given these miracles increased importance, no matter whence or how they originated; and their authority afterwards gave them credence with the people. . . .

And certainly, if the Christian religion had from the beginning been maintained according to the principles of its founder, the Christian states and republics would have been much more united and happy than what they are. Nor can there be a greater proof of its decadence than to witness the fact that the nearer people are to the Church of Rome, which is the head of our religion, the less religious are they. And whoever examines the principles upon which that religion is founded, and sees how widely different from those principles its present practice and application are, will judge that her ruin or chastisement is near at hand. But as there are some of the opinion that the well-being of Italian affairs depends upon the Church of Rome, I will present such arguments against that opinion as occur to me; two of which are most important, and cannot according to my judgment be controverted. The first is, that the evil example of the court of Rome has destroyed all piety and religion in Italy, which brings in its train infinite improprieties and disorders; for as we may presuppose all good where religion prevails, so where it is wanting we have the right to suppose the very opposite. We Italians then owe to the Church of Rome and to her priests our having become irreligious and bad; but we owe her a still greater debt, and one that will be the cause of our ruin, namely, that the Church has kept and still keeps our country divided. And certainly a country can never be united and happy, except when it obeys wholly one government, whether a republic or a monarchy, as is the case in France and in Spain; and the sole cause why Italy is not in the same condition, and is not governed by either one republic or one sovereign, is the Church; for having acquired and holding a temporal dominion, yet she has never had sufficient power or courage to enable her to seize the rest of the country and make herself sole sovereign of all Italy. And on the other hand she has not been so feeble that the fear of losing her temporal power prevented her from calling in the aid of a foreign power to defend her against such others as had become too powerful in Italy.

*   *   *

Reflecting now as to whence it came that in ancient times the people were more devoted to liberty than in the present, I believe that it resulted from this, that men were stronger in those days, which I believe to be attributable to the difference of education, founded upon the difference of their religion and ours. For, as our religion teaches us the truth and the true way of life, it causes us to attach less value to the honors and possessions of this world; whilst the Pagans, esteeming those things as the highest good, were more energetic and ferocious in their actions. We may observe this also in most of their institutions, beginning with the magnificence of their sacrifices as compared with the humility of ours, which are gentle solemnities rather than magnificent ones, and have nothing of energy or ferocity in them, whilst in theirs there was no lack of pomp and show, to which was superadded the ferocious and bloody nature of the sacrifice by the slaughter of many animals, and the familiarity with this terrible sight assimilated the nature of men to their sacrificial ceremonies. Besides this, the Pagan religion deified only men who had achieved great glory, such as commanders of armies and chiefs of republics, whilst ours glorifies more the humble and contemplative men than the men of action. Our religion, moreover, places the supreme happiness in humility, lowliness, and a contempt for worldly objects, whilst the other, on the contrary, places the supreme good in grandeur of soul, strength of body, and all such other qualities as render men formidable; and if our religion claims of us fortitude of soul, it is more to enable us to suffer than to achieve great deeds.

These principles seem to me to have made men feeble, and caused them to become an easy prey to evil-minded men, who can control them more securely, seeing that the great body of men, for the sake of gaining Paradise, are more disposed to endure injuries than to avenge them. And although it would seem that the world has become effeminate and Heaven disarmed, yet this arises unquestionably from the baseness of men, who have interpreted our religion according to the promptings of indolence rather than those of virtue. For if we were to reflect that our religion permits us to exalt and defend our country, we should see that according to it we ought also to love and honor our country, and prepare ourselves so as to be capable of defending her.

*   *   *

. . . those republics which have thus preserved their political existence uncorrupted do not permit any of their citizens to be or to live in the manner of gentlemen, but rather maintain amongst them a perfect equality, and are the most decided enemies of the lords and gentlemen that exist in the country; so that, if by chance any of them fall into their hands, they kill them, as being the chief promoters of all corruption and troubles.

And to explain more clearly what is meant by the term gentlemen, I say that those are called gentlemen who live idly upon the proceeds of their extensive possessions, without devoting themselves to agriculture or any other useful pursuit to gain a living. Such men are pernicious to any country or republic; but more pernicious even than these are such as have, besides their other possessions, castles which they command, and subjects who obey them. This class of men abound in the kingdom of Naples, in the Roman territory, in the Romagna, and in Lombardy; whence it is that no republic has ever been able to exist in those countries, nor have they been able to preserve any regular political existence, for that class of men are everywhere enemies of all civil government. And to attempt the establishment of a republic in a country so constituted would be impossible. The only way to establish any kind of order there is to found a monarchical government; for where the body of the people is so thoroughly corrupt that the laws are powerless for restraint, it becomes necessary to establish some superior power which, with a royal hand, and with full and absolute powers, may put a curb upon the excessive ambition and corruption of the powerful.

* * *

It may perhaps appear to some that I have gone too far into the details of Roman history before having made any mention of the founders of that republic, or of her institutions, her religion, and her military establishment. Not wishing, therefore, to keep any longer in suspense the desires of those who wish to understand these matters, I say that many will perhaps consider it an evil example that the founder of a civil society, as Romulus was, should first have killed his brother, and then have consented to the death of Titus Tatius, who had been elected to share the royal authority with him; from which it might be concluded that the citizens, according to the example of their prince, might, from ambition and the desire to rule, destroy those who attempt to oppose their authority. This opinion would be correct, if we do not take into consideration the object which Romulus had in view in committing that homicide. But we must assume, as a general rule, that it never or rarely happens that a republic or monarchy is well constituted, or its old institutions entirely reformed, unless it is done by only one individual; it is even necessary that he whose mind has conceived such a constitution should be alone in carrying it into effect. A sagacious legislator of a republic, therefore, whose object is to promote the public good, and not his private interests, and who prefers his country to his own successors, should concentrate all authority in himself; and a wise mind will never censure any one for having employed any extraordinary means for the purpose of establishing a kingdom or constituting a republic. It is well that, when the act accuses him, the result should excuse him; and when the result is good, as in the case of Romulus, it will always absolve him from blame. For he is to be reprehended who commits violence for the purpose of destroying, and not he who employs it for beneficent purposes.

* * *

I believe it to be most true that it seldom happens that men rise from low condition to high rank without employing either force or fraud, unless that rank should be attained either by gift or inheritance. Nor do I believe that force alone will ever be found to suffice, whilst it will often be the case that cunning alone serves the purpose; as is clearly seen by whoever reads the life of Philip of Macedon, or that of Agathocles the Sicilian, and many others, who from the lowest or most moderate condition have achieved thrones and great empires. Xenophon shows in his Life of Cyrus the necessity of deception to success: the first expedition of Cyrus against the king of Armenia is replete with fraud, and it was deceit alone, and not force, that enabled him to seize that kingdom. And Xenophon draws no other conclusion from it than that a prince who wishes to achieve great things must learn to deceive. Cyrus also practised a variety of deceptions upon Cyaxares, king of the Medes, his maternal uncle; and Xenophon shows that without these frauds Cyrus would never have achieved the greatness which he did attain. Nor do I believe that there was ever a man who from obscure condition arrived at great power by merely employing open force; but there are many who have succeeded by fraud alone, as, for instance, Giovanni Galeazzo Visconti in taking the state and sovereignty of Lombardy from his uncle, Messer Bernabo. And that which princes are obliged to do in the beginning of their rise, republics are equally obliged to practise until they have become powerful enough so that force alone suffices them. And as Rome employed every means, by chance or choice, to promote her aggrandizement, so she also did not hesitate to employ fraud; nor could she have practised a greater fraud than by taking the course we have explained above of making other peoples her allies and associates, and under that title making them slaves, as she did with the Latins and other neighboring nations.

* * *

For where the very safety of the country depends upon the resolution to be taken, no considerations of justice or injustice, humanity or cruelty, nor of glory or of shame, should be allowed to prevail. But putting all other considerations aside, the only question should be, What course will save the life and liberty of the country? The French follow this maxim by words and deeds in defending the majesty of their king and the greatness of France; for nothing excites their impatience more than to hear any one say that such or such a thing is discreditable to the king. For they say that their king can suffer no shame from any resolutions he may take, whether in good or in ill fortune; for whether he be victor or vanquished is a matter that only concerns the king.

G. THE CRITICAL SPIRIT

Lorenzo Valla: *On the Forgery of the Donation of Constantine* *

> The humanist Lorenzo Valla (*c.* 1406–57) exemplifies the critical side of the Italian Renaissance. His discourse exposing the forgery of the Donation of Constantine (1440) is only the most famous of his attacks on spurious documents of the Middle Ages. He wrote it when he was secretary to Alfonso V, King of Aragon, Sicily, and Naples, and it may be regarded as part of the latter's campaign against the pope for further Italian territories. The Donation (now believed to have been forged in the papal chancellary in the eighth century) recorded the Emperor Constantine's gift of the western half of the Roman Empire to Pope Sylvester I, in gratitude for being cured of leprosy. Needless to say, Valla got into trouble with the Inquisition, but he later became Apostolic Writer to Pope Nicholas V!

I know that for a long time now men's ears are waiting to hear the offense with which I charge the Roman pontiffs. It is, indeed, an enormous one, due either to supine ignorance, or to gross avarice which is the slave of idols, or to pride of empire of which cruelty is ever the companion. For during some centuries now, either they have not known that the Donation of Constantine is spurious and forged, or else they themselves forged it, and their successors walking in the same way of deceit as their elders have defended as true what they knew to be false, dishonoring the majesty of the pontificate, dishonoring the memory of ancient pontiffs, dishonoring the Christian religion, confounding everything with murders, disasters and crimes. They say the city of Rome is theirs, theirs the kingdom of Sicily and of Naples, the whole of Italy, the Gauls, the Spains, the Germans, the Britons, indeed the whole West; for all these

* From Christopher B. Coleman, ed.: *The Treatise of Lorenzo Valla on the Donation of Constantine*, pp. 25–7, 65–71, 95–7, 177–9, 183. Copyright 1922 by Yale University Press. Reprinted by permission of Yale University Press.

are contained in the instrument of the Donation itself. So all these are yours, supreme pontiff? And it is your purpose to recover them all? To despoil all kings and princes of the West of their cities or compel them to pay you a yearly tribute, is that your plan?

I, on the contrary, think it fairer to let the princes despoil you of all the empire you hold. For, as I shall show, that Donation whence the supreme pontiffs will have their right derived was unknown equally to Sylvester and to Constantine. . . .

[Having discussed the inherent improbability of Constantine's ever having made the "Donation," Valla proceeds thus:] Come now! Was Sylvester ever in possession? Who dispossessed him? For he did not have possession permanently, nor did any of his successors, at least till Gregory the Great, and even he did not have possession. One who is not in possession and cannot prove that he has been disseized certainly never did have possession, and if he says he did, he is crazy. You see, I even prove that you are crazy! Otherwise, tell who dislodged the Pope? Did Constantine himself, or his sons, or Julian, or some other Caesar? Give the name of the expeller, give the date, from what place was the Pope expelled first, where next, and so in order. . . .

I ask whether you can adduce any witnesses of these events, any writers. None, you answer. And are you not ashamed to say that it is likely that Sylvester possessed—even cattle, to say nothing of men!

But since you cannot [prove anything], I for my part will show that Constantine, to the very last day of his life, and thereafter all the Caesars in turn, did have possession [of the Roman Empire], so that you will have nothing left even to mutter. . . .

To say nothing of other monuments and temples in the city of Rome, there are extant gold coins of Constantine's after he became a Christian, with inscriptions, not in Greek, but in Latin letters, and of almost all the Emperors in succession. There are many of them in my possession with this inscription for the most part, under the image of the cross, "Concordia orbis [The Peace of the World]." What an infinite number of coins of the supreme pontiffs would be found if you ever had ruled Rome! But none such are found, neither gold nor silver, nor are any mentioned as having been seen by any one. And yet whoever held the government at Rome at that time had to have his own coinage: doubtless the Pope's would have borne the image of the Savior or of Peter. . . .

[Valla next analyzes the document itself and finds it a forgery on internal evidence:] I will not speak here of the barbarisms in [the forger's] language when he says "chief over the priests" instead of chief of the priests; when he puts in the same sentence "extiterit" and "existat" [confusing meanings, moods and tenses]; when, having said "in the whole earth," he adds again "of the whole world," as though he wished to include something else, or the sky, which is part of the world, though a good part of the earth even was not under Rome; when he distinguishes between providing for "the faith" of Christians and providing for their "stability," as though they could not coexist; when he confuses "ordain" and "decree.". . .

How in the world—this is much more absurd, and impossible in the nature of things—could one speak of Constantinople as one of the patriarchal sees, when it was not yet a patriarchate, nor a see, nor a Christian city, nor named Constantinople, nor founded, nor planned! For the "privilege" was granted, so it says, the third day after Constantine became a Christian; when as yet Byzantium, not Constantinople, occupied that site. . . .

[In the document Constantine is made to say: "On the churches of the blessed apostles Peter and Paul, for the providing of lights, we have conferred landed estates of possessions, and have enriched them with different objects." Valla remarks:] O you scoundrel! Were there in Rome churches, that is, temples, dedicated to Peter and Paul? Who had constructed them? Who would have dared to build them, when, as history tells us, the Christians had never had anything but secret and secluded meeting-places? And if there had been any temples at Rome dedicated to these apostles, they would not have called for such great lights as these to be set up in them; they were little chapels, not sanctuaries; little shrines, not temples; oratories in private houses, not public places of worship. So there was no need to care for the temple lights, before the temples themselves were provided.

* * *

But why need I say more in this case, absolutely self-evident as it is? I contend that not only did Constantine not grant such great possessions, not only could the Roman pontiff not hold them by prescription, but that even if either were a fact, nevertheless either right would have been extinguished by the crimes of the possessors, for we know that the slaughter and devastation of all Italy and of many of the provinces has flowed from this single source. . . .

Wherefore I declare, and cry aloud, nor, trusting God, will I fear men, that in my time no one in the supreme pontificate has been either a faithful or a prudent steward, but they have gone so far from giving food to the household of God that they have devoured it as food and a mere morsel of bread! And the Pope himself makes war on peaceable people, and sows discord among states and princes. . . . The Pope not only enriches himself at the expense of the republic, . . . but he enriches himself at the expense of even the church and the Holy Spirit as old Simon Magus himself would abhor doing. And when he is reminded of this and is reproved by good people occasionally, he does not deny it, but openly admits it, and boasts that he is free to wrest from its occupants by any means whatever the patrimony given the church by Constantine. . . .

If only I may sometime see, and indeed I can scarcely wait to see it, especially if it is brought about by my counsel, if only I may see the time when the Pope is the vicar of Christ alone, and not of Caesar also! If only there would no longer be heard the fearful cry, "Partisans for the Church," "Partisans against the Church," "The Church against the Perugians," "against the Bolognese"! It is not the church, but the Pope, that fights against Christians; the church fights against "spiritual wickedness in high places." Then the Pope will be the Holy Father in fact as well as in name, Father of all, Father of the church; nor will he stir up wars among Christians, but those stirred up by others he, through his apostolic judgment and papal prerogative, will stop.

3. *Christian Humanism*

DESIDERIUS ERASMUS

It has been said of Erasmus that he was to the educated world of his age, what Petrarch was to the fourteenth century, and Voltaire to the eighteenth. His great proficiency in the pagan classics and the Christian Fathers earned for him the title "Prince of Humanists." Although technically a monk and ordained priest, he lived the life of a travelling scholar, consorting with the intelligentsia of all the Western countries.

From his voluminous writings there emerges a clear-cut program of reform—religious, political, and educational—to which the majority of northern humanists in the early sixteenth century were pledged. The following selections from five of his major works describe his diagnosis and cure for the ills of European society on the eve of the Reformation.

I.

In *The Praise of Folly* (1509), his best known work, Erasmus diagnosed the evils of contemporary society in the manner of the Greek satirist Lucian. Although written in Latin, as indeed were all his works, it was widely read, passing through twenty-seven editions in his own lifetime. In the book the female goddess Folly is speaking, claiming all classes of men as her dominion.*

* From *Praise of Folly* by Desiderius Erasmus, translated by Leonard F. Dean, Packard and Company, 1946. Pp. 88–9, 94–7, 101–02, 107, 109–12.

You may think I am speaking more rashly than truly. Very well, let us examine the behavior of men, and it will become evident how much they owe me, and how widely I am imitated by all classes of society. . . .

The merchants, however, are the biggest fools of all. They carry on the most sordid business and by the most corrupt methods. Whenever it is necessary, they will lie, perjure themselves, steal, cheat, and mislead the public. Nevertheless, they are highly respected because of their money. There is no lack of flattering friars to kowtow to them and call them Right Honorable in public. The motive of the friars is clear enough: they are after some of the loot. . . .

After the lawyers come the philosophers, who are reverenced for their beards and the fur on their gowns. They announce that they alone are wise, and that the rest of men are only passing shadows. Their folly is a pleasant one. They frame countless worlds, and measure the sun, moon, stars, and spheres as with thumb and line. They unhesitatingly explain the causes of lightning, winds, eclipses, and other inexplicable things. One would think that they had excess to the secrets of nature, who is the maker of all things, or that they had just come from a council of the gods. Actually, nature laughs uproariously at them all the time. The fact that they can never explain why they constantly disagree with each other is sufficient proof that they do not know the truth about anything. They know nothing at all, yet profess to know everything. They are ignorant even of themselves, and are often too absent-minded or near-sighted to see the ditch or stone in front of them. At the same time, they assert that they can see ideas, universals, pure forms, original matter, and essences— things so shadowy that I doubt if Lynceus could perceive them. They show their scorn of the layman whenever they produce their triangles, quadrangles, circles, and other mathematical forms, lay one on another or entangle them into a labyrinth, then maneuver letters as if in battle formation, and presently reverse the arrangement. It is all designed to fool the uninitiated. Among these philosophers are some who predict future events by consulting the stars, and others who promise even greater wonders. And these fortunate fellows find people to believe them.

Perhaps it would be wise to pass over the theologians in silence. That short-tempered and supercilious crew is as unpleasant to deal with as Lake Camarina or *Anagyris foetida*. They may attack me with an army of six hundred syllogisms; and if I do not recant, they will proclaim me a heretic. With this thunderbolt they terrify the people they don't like. They are extremely reluctant to acknowledge my benefits to them, which are nevertheless considerable. Their opinion of themselves is so great that they behave as if they were already in heaven; they look down pityingly on other men as so many worms. A wall of imposing defini- tions, conclusions, corollaries, and explicit and implicit propositions protects them. They have so many hideouts that even Vulcan could not catch them with his net. They escape through distinctions, and cut knots as easily as with a double-bitted axe from Tenedos. They are full of big words and newly-invented terms.

They explain (to suit themselves) the most difficult mysteries: how the world was created and set in order; through what channels original sin has passed to successive generations; by what means, in what form, and for how long the perfect Christ was in the womb of the Virgin; and how accidents subsist in the Eucharist without their subject. But these are nothing. Here are questions worthy of these great and reputedly illuminated theologians. If they encounter these questions they will have to extend themselves. Was divine generation at a particular instant? Are there several son-ships in Christ? Is this a possible proposition: God the Father hates the Son? Could God have assumed the form of a woman, a devil, an ass, a gourd, a stone? If so, how could the gourd have preached, performed miracles, and been crucified? What would Peter have consecrated if he had administered the sacrament when Christ's body hung on the Cross? And was Christ at that moment a man? After the resurrection will it be forbidden to eat and drink? (They are providing now against hunger and thirst!) These subtleties are countless, and include even more refined propositions dealing with instants of time, opinions, relations, accidents, quiddities, entities, which no one can discern unless, like Lynceus, he can see in blackest darkness things that are not there.

There are in addition those moral maxims, or rather, contradictions, that make the so-called Stoic paradoxes seem like child's play. For example: it is less of a sin to cut the throats of a thousand men than to stitch a poor man's shoe on Sunday; it is better to commit the whole world to destruction than to tell a single lie, even a white one. These subtlest of subtleties are made more subtle by the methods of the scholastic philosophers. It is easier to escape from a maze than from the tangles of Realists, Nominalists, Thomists, Albertists, Occamists, and Scotists, to name the chief ones only. There is so much erudition and obscurity in the various schools that I imagine the apostles themselves would need some other spiritual assistance if they were to argue these topics with modern theologians. . . .

Next to the theologians in happiness are those who commonly call themselves "the religious" and "monks." Both are complete misnomers, since most of them stay as far away from religion as possible, and no people are seen more often in public. These monks would be very doleful if I did not relieve them in many ways. They are so detested that it is considered bad luck if one crosses your path, and yet they are highly pleased with themselves. They cannot read, and so they consider it the height of piety to have no contact with literature. In church, when they bray out the psalms they have memorized without understanding, they think they are anointing God's ears with the blandest oil. Most of them capitalize on their dirt and poverty by whining for food from door to door. They push into inns, ships, and public conveyances, to the great disadvantage of the regular beggars. These smooth fellows simply explain that by their very filth, ignorance, boorishness, and insolence they enact the lives of the apostles for us.

It is amusing to see how they do everything by rule, almost mathematically. Any slip is a sacrilege. Each shoe-string must have so many knots and must be of a certain color; the habit precisely trimmed; the girdle of the proper material and so many straws wide; the cowl of a prescribed style and size; the hair so many fingers long; and a regulated number of hours for sleep. Anyone can see that this equality is really very unequal in view of the variations in constitution and temperament; and yet on the basis of such nonsense they judge outsiders to be worthless. They even condemn each other, these professors of apostolic charity, making an extraordinary stir if a habit is belted incorrectly or if its color is a shade too dark. Some are so scrupulously religious that they will dress only in an outer garment of Cilician goat's hair and an inner garment of Milesian wool; others insist on linen on top of wool. The monks of certain orders recoil in horror from money, as if it were poison, but not from wine or women. They take extreme pains, not in order to be like Christ, but to be unlike each other. This explains their great delight in names. Those of one order are pleased to call themselves Cordeliers, and among them, in turn, some are Coletes, some Minors, some Minims, some Crutched. In addition, there are Benedictines, Bernardines, Bridgetines, Augustinians, Williamists, and Jacobines—as if it were not enough to be called Christians.

Most of them consider one heaven an inadequate reward for their devotion to ceremony and traditional details. They forget that Christ will condemn all of this and will call for a reckoning of that which He has prescribed, namely, charity. . . .

And now it gives me pleasure to speak of kings and nobles. They worship me openly and frankly, as becomes gentlemen. Indeed, what life would be more wretched or unenviable than theirs if they had even a particle of wisdom? . . .

For some time now, popes, cardinals, and bishops have avidly imitated the courtly way of life, and have even gone beyond it. A bishop might well recall that his alb, the white symbol of sincerity, is meant to remind him to lead a pure life; that his two-horned miter, its peaks bound by one knot, is presumed to signify a perfect understanding of the Old and New Testaments; that covering his hands with gloves indicates a clean administration of the sacrament, free from all worldly taint; that the crozier is for one who is vigilant in tending the flock entrusted to him;

and that the cross borne before him signifies victory over all carnal passions. If he would consider things like that, would he not lead a sad and troubled life? But as it is, bishops fare very well because they look after themselves. As for the sheep, the bishops either leave their care to Christ, or turn it over to suffragans, as they are called, or to other substitutes. They never give a thought to the meaning of the word *bishop*—labor, vigilance, and solicitude—, except when money is to be made, and then they are bishops indeed, overlooking nothing. . . .

Finally, if the Supreme Pontiffs, who are the vicars of Christ, tried to imitate His life, His poverty, labors, teaching, His cross and contempt for life; if they stopped to consider the meaning of the title of Pope, a Father, or the epithet Most Holy, who on earth would be more overwhelmed? Who would purchase that office at the cost of every effort? Who would retain it by the sword, by poison, and by every other way? If wisdom should come to Popes, what comforts it would deprive them of! Did I say wisdom? Even that grain of sense which Christ speaks of would do it. It would deprive them of all wealth, honor, and possessions; all the triumphal progresses, offices, dispensations, tributes, and indulgences; the many horses, mules, and retainers; in short, it would deprive them of all their pleasures. These few words comprehend a multitude of worldly goods. In their place wisdom would bring vigils, fasts, tears, prayers, sermons, studies, sighs, and a thousand similar trials. And think of the hardship on all those copyists and notaries, all those advocates, promoters, secretaries, muleteers, grooms, bankers, and pimps—I was about to add a softer but, perhaps, a naughtier name. In short, all those who bring shame—I mean fame—to the Roman See would have to beg for their bread. This would be terribly inhuman, and, even worse, those very princes of the church and true lights of the world would be reduced to a staff and a wallet.

As it is now, they turn over whatever work there is to Peter and Paul, who have ample time for it. The splendor and the pleasure, however, they take care of personally. And so, with my assistance, it comes about that almost no one lives more comfortably or with fewer worries. They think that they satisfy Christ perfectly if they act the part of bishops by means of mysterious and showy finery, blessings and cursings, and the titles of Beatitude, Reverence, and Holiness. To work miracles is primitive, obsolete, and out of date; to teach the people is a drudgery; to interpret the Scriptures is pedantry; to pray is futile and lazy; to shed tears is weak and depressing; to live in poverty is base; to be excelled is shameful, and scarcely worthy of one who will hardly allow the greatest king to kiss his sacred foot; and finally, to die is unpleasant, to die on the cross a disgrace.

The only things left are the weapons and sweet benedictions of which Paul speaks. The popes are sufficiently generous with these. I mean the interdictions, excommunications, re-excommunications, anathematizations, pictured damnations, and the terrible bolt of the papal bull, which by a flicker hurls the souls of men to the depths of hell. Our Christian fathers and vicars of Christ wield the bolt against no one with more zeal than against those who are moved by the devil to nibble at and diminish the patrimony of Peter. He said, "We have forsaken all, and followed Thee"; yet they give the name of patrimony to lands, towns, tributes, taxes, and riches. They fight for these things with fire and sword, inflamed by Christian zeal, and not without shedding Christian blood. They look on themselves as true apostles, defending the bride of Christ, and scattering what they are pleased to call her enemies. As if the church had more deadly enemies than impious popes who by their silence cause Christ to be forgotten, who use His laws to make money, who adulterate His word with forced interpretations, and who crucify Him with their corrupt life!

2.

— Basic to Erasmus's program of reform was education—education in the moral writings of antiquity, the Church Fathers, and the Scriptures. Erasmus's Christian humanism, *i.e.*, the identity between antique pagan and Christian moral precepts, is nowhere better seen than in "The Religious Banquet." This is one of the dialogues in his enormously popular *Colloquies*, which were composed between 1497 and 1533, and designed as a textbook of Latin style for young students. The interlocutors who appear in the following selections from the dialogue are named Chrysoglottus, Eusebius (at whose home they sup), and Nephalius.*

Ch. If I were not afraid that by my loquacity I should divert you from eating your dinners, and did think it were lawful to intermix anything out of profane authors with sacred discourses, I would venture to propose something that I read to-day, not so much with perplexity, as with a singular delight.

Eu. Whatsoever is pious, and conduces to good manners, ought not to be called profane. The first place must indeed be given to the authority of the Scriptures; but nevertheless, I sometimes find some things said or written by the ancients, nay, even by the heathens, nay, by the poets themselves, so chastely, so holily, and so divinely, that I cannot persuade myself but that when they wrote them they were divinely inspired; and perhaps the spirit of Christ diffuses itself farther than we imagine; and that there are more saints than we have in our catalogue. To confess freely among friends, I cannot read Tully "On Old Age," "On

* *The Whole Familiar Colloquies of D. Erasmus,* trans. by N. Bailey (London: Hamilton, Adams, & Co.; 1877), pp. 96–9.

Friendship," his "Offices," or his "Tusculan Questions," without kissing the book, and veneration for that divine soul. And on the contrary, when I read some of our modern authors, treating of politics, economics, and ethics, good God! how cold they are in comparison of these? Nay, how do they seem to be insensible of what they write themselves? So that I had rather lose Scotus, and twenty more such as he, than one Cicero or Plutarch. Not that I am wholly against them neither, but because, by the reading of the one I find myself become better; whereas I rise from the other I know not how coldly affected to virtue, but most violently inclined to cavil and contention; therefore never fear to propose it, whatsoever it is.

Ch. Although all Tully's books of philosophy seem to breathe out something divine, yet that treatise on old age that he wrote in old age, seems to me to be according to the Greek proverb: the song of the dying swan. I was reading it to-day, and these words pleasing me above the rest, I got them by heart: "Should it please God to give me a grant to begin my life again from my very cradle, and once more to run over the course of my years I have lived, I would not upon any terms accept of it. Nor would I, having in a manner finished my race, run it over again from the starting place to the goal. For what pleasure has this life in it? Nay, rather, what pain has it not? But if there were not, there would be undoubtedly in it satiety or trouble. I am not for bewailing my past life as a great many, and learned men too, have done; nor do I repent that I have lived, because I have lived so that I am satisfied I have not lived in vain. And when I leave this life, I leave it as an inn, and not as a place of abode. For Nature has given us our bodies as an inn to lodge in, and not to dwell in. Oh! glorious day will that be, when I shall leave this rabble rout and defilements of the world behind me, to go to that society and world of spirits!" Thus far out of Cato. What could be spoken more divinely by a Christian? I wish all the discourses of our monks, even with their holy virgins, were such as the dialogue of this aged pagan with the pagan youths of his time. . . .

Neph. . . . as for Cato's speech, although it be an excellent one, methinks there is more boldness and arrogance in it than becomes a Christian. Indeed, I never read anything in a heathen that comes nearer to a Christian than what Socrates said to Crito a little before he drank his poison: "Whether I shall be approved or not in the sight of God I cannot tell; but this I am certain of, that I have most affectionately endeavoured to please Him; and I have a good hope that He will accept of my endeavours." This great man was diffident of his own performances; but so that being conscious to himself of the propensity of his inclination to obey the divine will, he conceived a good hope that God, of His goodness, would accept him for the honesty of his intentions. Indeed, it was a wonderful elevation of mind in a man that knew not Christ, nor the

Holy Scriptures. And, therefore, I can scarce forbear when I read such things of such men, but cry out, "*Sancte Socrates, ora pro nobis,* Saint Socrates, pray for us." *Ch.* And I have much ado sometimes to keep myself from entertaining good hopes of the souls of Virgil and Horace. *Neph.* But how unwillingly have I seen many Christians die? Some put their trust in things not to be confided in; others breathe out their souls in desperation, either out of a consciousness of their lewd lives, or by reason of scruples that have been injected into their minds, even in their dying hours, by some indiscreet men, die almost in despair.

3.

In 1516 Erasmus published his Greek New Testament which, though certainly faulty in scholarship, dramatized his belief that reform depended upon wide knowledge of an accurate version of the Scriptures. In 1519 he got out a Latin translation which differed considerably from the standard Vulgate Bible of St. Jerome. The following selection is from his famous preface in which he argued for the translation of the Bible into the vernacular.*

It must needs be a high and excellent thing, and no trifle which that heavenly and marvelous master [Christ] came to teach openly. Why do we not go about to know, search and try out with a godly curiosity this fruitful Philosophy? Since that this kind of wisdom, being so profound and inscrutable that utterly it damneth and confoundeth as foolish all the wisdom of this world, may be gathered out of so small books as out of most pure springs. And that with much less labor than the doctrine of Aristotle out of so many brawling and contentious books, or of such infinite commentaries which do so much dissent. . . .

I do greatly dissent from those men which would not that the scripture of Christ should be translated into all tongues that it might be read diligently of the private and secular men and women. As though Christ had taught such dark and insensible things that they could scant be understood of a few divines. Or else as though the pith and substance of the Christian religion consisted chiefly in this, that it be not known. Peradventure it were most expedient that the councils of kings should be kept secret, but Christ would that his councils and mysteries should be spread abroad as much as is possible. I would desire that all women should read the gospel and Paul's epistles, and I would to God they were translated into the tongues of all men. So that they might not only be read and known of the Scots and Irishmen, but also of the Turks and Saracens. Truly it is one degree to good living, yea the first (I had almost

* Erasmus: *An exhortation to the diligent studye of scripture* (Hesse: Hans Luft; 1529), no pagination. I have modernized the spelling.

said the chief) to have a little sight in the scripture, though it be but a gross knowledge and not yet consummate. Be it in case that some would laugh at it, yea and that some should err and be deceived, I would to God the plowman would sing a text of the scripture at his plowing, and that the weaver at his loom with this would drive away the tediousness of time. I would the wayfaring man with this pastime would assuage the weariness of his journey. And to be short I would that all the communication of the Christian should be of the scripture, for in a manner such are we ourselves as our daily tales are.

4.

The thirteenth chapter of Erasmus's *Enchiridion Militis Christiani* (Handbook or Dagger of a Christian Knight, 1503) is an epitome of his "philosophy of Christ" which he urged as an antidote to the external religion of his time. The following selection is from the abridgement of the *Enchiridion* by Myles Coverdale, Bishop of Exeter (1545).*

The mystery therefore in all things ought to be looked upon, as well when we consider the outward creatures and works of God, as in the study of his holy scriptures: the spirit whereof, and not the bare letter, must specially be searched out, and the allegories handled, not dreamingly or unfruitfully, neither with subtle disputations, (after the manner of our divines that are too much addict to Aristotle,) but well favouredly, after the example of the old doctors. For inasmuch as it is the Spirit that giveth life and liberty, therefore in all manner letters, and in all our acts, we must have respect to the Spirit and fruits thereof, and not to the flesh and his fruits; wishing rather to be privily allowed in the sight of God, than openly in the sight of man; rather to worship God in spirit and verity, than otherwise; rather to eat Christ's flesh and drink his blood spiritually, than only with the mouth: rather to be quickened, and to have life in the Spirit, than, hanging St. John's gospel or an *Agnus Dei* about our necks, to rejoice in any carnal thing, where the Spirit is not present; rather to be one spirit with the Spirit of Christ, to be one body with his, to be a quick member of his church, than without fruit to say or hear many masses; rather to have a clean and sunny mind, and to study to walk with Christ in new life, than to have the body washed, touched with salt, anointed, or sprinkled with holy water; rather to represent and follow the virtuous and blessed doctrine of saints, yea, to counterfeit Christ in them, than to rejoice in touching their relics, to honour their bones, or to be buried in a grey friar's coat; rather to express the lively and very image of Christ, set forth in his own doctrine and living, than

* *Writings and Translations of Myles Coverdale*, ed. by George Pearson (Cambridge: Cambridge University Press; 1844), pp. 511-12.

to creep to the cross, or to have at home a piece of the wood that it was made of; rather to ascend to more perfectness of the Spirit, to grow in perfect love and charity, and to offer an humble and contrite heart unto God, than to have confidence in carnal things, or superstitious ceremonies, traditions, and inventions of men; rather to do the things that the eyes of God require, than to please the eyes of men; rather to procure the quietness and innocency of the mind, and to seek the nourishment thereof by the true hearing, seeing, and feeling of the word of God on the soul, than by the outward senses of the body; rather with inward medicines to heal the hurts of the soul, and by the wings of love to fly up to the Spirit, than, creeping on the ground with unclean beasts, to be still unlearned in the mysteries of Christ, or to be destitute of the sweet liquors that cometh of him.

5.

In the *Institutio principis Christiani* (Education of a Christian Prince, 1516) Erasmus sketched his program for political and social, as distinguished from ecclesiastical reform. The *Institutio* was addressed to the future Emperor Charles V.*

Plato is nowhere more painstaking than in the training of his guardians of the state. He does not wish them to excel all others in wealth, in gems, in dress, in statues and attendants, but in wisdom alone. He says that no state will ever be blessed unless the philosophers are at the helm, or those to whom the task of government falls embrace philosophy. By "philosophy" I do not mean that which disputes concerning the first beginnings, of primordial matter, of motion and infinity, but that which frees the mind from the false opinions and the vicious predilections of the masses and points out a theory of government according to the example of the Eternal Power.

*   *   *

Christian theology attributes three prime qualities to God—the highest power, the greatest wisdom, the greatest goodness. In so far as you can you should make this trinity yours. . . .

As God is good in all his beneficence and does not need the attendant services of anyone nor ask any recompense, so it should be with the prince who is really great—who is the likeness of the Eternal Prince. He should freely do works of kindness for everyone without thought of compensation or glory. God placed a beautiful likeness of Himself in

* From Erasmus: *The Education of a Christian Prince*, trans. and ed. by L. K. Born, pp. 133–4, 140, 158–9, 170, 200–01, 212–13, 217–18, 238, 251. Copyright 1936 by Columbia University Press. Reprinted by permission of Columbia University Press.

the heavens—the sun. Among mortal men he set up a tangible and living image of himself—the king. The sun is freely shared by all and imparts its light to the rest of the heavenly bodies. The prince should be readily accessible for all the needs of his people. He should be a virgin source of wisdom in himself, so that he may never become benighted, however blind everyone else may be.

God is swayed by no emotions, yet he rules the universe with supreme judgment. The prince should follow His example in all his actions, cast aside all personal motives, and use only reason and judgment. God is sublime. The prince should be removed as far as possible from the low concerns of the common people and their sordid desires.

*   *   *

. . . the chief hope for a good prince is from his education, which should be especially looked to. . . . Hence, from the very cradle, as it were, the mind of the future prince, while still open and unmolded, must be filled with salutary thoughts. Then the seeds of morality must be sown in the virgin soil of his spirit so that little by little they may grow and mature through age and experience, to remain firmly implanted throughout the course of life.

*   *   *

. . . as soon as the elements of language have been taught, he [the tutor] should set forth the *Proverbs* of Solomon, *Ecclesiasticus*, and the *Book of Wisdom*, not with the idea that the boy may be tormented with the four senses (*sensus*) of the theologian by a vaunting interpreter, but that he may fitly show in a few words whatever pertains to the functions of a good prince. . . . Later take the Gospels. . . . In the third place, read the *Apophthegmata* of Plutarch and then his *Morals,* for nothing can be found purer than these works. I should also prefer his *Lives* to those of anyone else. After Plutarch, I would readily assign the next place to Seneca, whose writings are wonderfully stimulating and excite one to enthusiasm for [a life of] moral integrity, raise the mind of the reader from sordid cares, and especially decry tyranny everywhere. From the *Politics* of Aristotle and from the *Offices* of Cicero many passages that are worth knowing can well be culled out. But Plato is the most venerable source of such things—in my opinion at least. Cicero has followed him in part in his work *The Laws;* that entitled *The Republic* is lost.

Now I shall not deny that a great fund of wisdom may be gathered from reading the historians, but you will also draw out the very essence of destruction from these same sources unless you are forearmed and read with discretion. Be on guard lest the names of writers and leaders celebrated by the approval of centuries deceive you. Herodotus and

Xenophon were both pagans and often set forth the worst types of prince, even if they did write history, the one to give pleasure through his narrative, the other to show the picture of an exceptional leader. Sallust and Livy tell us many things very clearly and everything very learnedly to be sure, but they do not weigh all that they tell, and they approve some things which are by no means to be approved for a Christian prince. When you hear about Achilles, Xerxes, Cyrus, Darius, and Julius Caesar, do not be carried away and deluded by the great names. You are hearing about great raging robbers, for that is what Seneca has called them on various occasions.

* * *

The good prince ought to have the same attitude toward his subjects, as a good *paterfamilias* toward his household—for what else is a kingdom but a great family? What is the king if not the father to a great multitude? . . .

A prince who is about to assume control of the state must be advised at once that the main hope of a state lies in the proper education of its youth. This Xenophon wisely taught in his *Cyropaedia*. Pliable youth is amenable to any system of training. Therefore the greatest care should be exercised over public and private schools and over the education of the girls, so that the children may be placed under the best and most trustworthy instructors and may learn the teachings of Christ and that good literature which is beneficial to the state. As a result of this scheme of things, there will be no need for many laws or punishments, for the people will of their own free will follow the course of right. . . .

The prince should try to prevent too great an inequality of wealth. I should not want to see anyone deprived of his goods, but the prince should employ certain measures to prevent the wealth of the multitude being hoarded by a few. Plato did not want his citizens to be too rich, neither did he want them extremely poor, for the pauper is of no use and the rich man will not use his ability for public service. . . .

A good prince will tax as lightly as possible those commodities which are used even by the poorest members of society; e.g., grain, bread, beer, wine, clothing, and all the other staples without which human life could not exist. But it so happens that these very things bear the heaviest tax in several ways; in the first place, by the oppressive extortion of the tax farmers, commonly called *assisiae*, then by import duties which call for their own set of extortionists, and finally by the monopolies by which the poor are sadly drained of their funds in order that the prince may gain a mere trifling interest.

As I have brought out, the best way of increasing the prince's treasury is to follow the old proverb, "Parsimony is a great revenue," and carefully check expenditures. However, if some taxation is absolutely necessary and the affairs of the people render it essential, barbarous and foreign goods should be heavily taxed because they are not the essentials of livelihood but the extravagant luxuries and delicacies which only the wealthy enjoy; for example, linen, silks, dyes, pepper, spices, unguents, precious stones, and all the rest of that same category. But by this system only those who can well afford it feel the pinch. They will not be reduced to straightened circumstances as a result of this outlay but perchance may be made more moderate in their desires so that the loss of money may be replaced by a change for the better in their habits.

*   *   *

Among all Christian princes there is at once a very firm and holy bond because of the very fact that they are Christian. Why, then, is there a need to conclude so many treaties every day as if everyone were the enemy of everyone else and human agreements were essential to gain what Christ could not [accomplish]? When a matter is transacted through many written agreements, it is a proof that it is not done in the best faith and we often see it happen that many lawsuits arise as a result of these agreements which were prepared for the very purpose of preventing litigation. When good faith is a party and the business is between honest men, there is no need for many painstaking contracts. When the transaction is between dishonest men and not made in good faith, these very agreements produce grounds for suit. . . .

Plato calls it sedition, not war, when Greeks war with Greeks; and if this should happen, he bids them fight with every restraint. What term should we apply, then, when Christians engage in battle with Christians, since they are united by so many bonds to each other? What shall we say when on account of a mere title, on account of a personal grievance, on account of a stupid and youthful ambition, a war is waged with every cruelty and carried on during many years?

Some princes deceive themselves that any war is certainly a just one and that they have a just cause for going to war. We will not attempt to discuss whether war is ever just; but who does not think his own cause just? Among such great and changing vicissitudes of human events, among so many treaties and agreements which are now entered into, now rescinded, who can lack a pretext—if there is any real excuse—for going to war? But the pontifical laws do not disapprove all war. Augustine approves of it in some instances, and St. Bernard praises some soldiers. But Christ himself and Peter and Paul everywhere teach the opposite. Why is their authority less with us than that of Augustine or Bernard? Augustine in one or two places does not disapprove of war, but the whole philosophy of Christ teaches against it.

The just shall live by faith.

St. Paul, EPISTLE TO THE ROMANS, I, 13.

𝒟. *THE CONFESSIONAL AGE*

Hence all we who believe in Christ are kings and priests in Christ. . . . Here you will ask: "If all who are in the Church are priests, by what character are those, whom we now call priests, to be distinguished from the laity?" I reply: By the use of these words, "priest," "clergy," "spiritual person," "ecclesiastic," an injustice has been done, since they have been transferred from the remaining body of Christians to those few, who are now, by a hurtful custom, called ecclesiastics.

Martin Luther, ON CHRISTIAN LIBERTY

The Body of Scripture is a doctrine sufficient to live well. It comprehendeth many holy sciences. . . . The principal science is Theology. Other attendants or handmaids [being] Ethics, Economics, Politics, Ecclesiastical discipline, Academy [Education].

William Perkins, A GOLDEN CHAIN

Let every soul be in subjection to the higher powers: for there is no power but of God; and the powers that be are ordained of God. Therefore he that resisteth the power, withstandeth the ordinance of God.

St. Paul, EPISTLE TO THE ROMANS, XIII, 1–2.

New presbyter is but old priest writ large.
James I of England

The Protestant Reformation

"WHOEVER examines the principles upon which that religion [Christianity] is founded, and sees how widely different from those principles its present practice and application are, will judge that her ruin or chastisement is near at hand." Thus wrote Machiavelli in 1513. Four years later Martin Luther nailed his ninety-five theses to the door of the Castle Church in Wittenberg, and within a generation Roman Catholicism had lost half of Europe to the "Protestants."

I

JUST what the Protestant Reformation signified intellectually and culturally is a matter for debate. Broadly speaking, there have been three major interpretations. Liberal and nationalist historians of the nineteenth century tied in the Reformation with the idea of progress. For Michelet and Guizot and Froude it represented a phase of the revolt against medieval tyranny and superstition, a link in the chain reaction that set off the French Revolution and secured the modern freedoms. This view has persisted in a good many of our general histories—in books like J. B. Bury's *History of Freedom of Thought* [1] and in textbooks of modern European history which commonly begin with the Renaissance and Reformation. Other historians have reversed this judgment, describing the Reformation, in Nietzsche's characteristic over-statement, as "a reaction of old-fashioned minds against the Italian Renaissance." Living in a secular climate, Edward Gibbon was struck by the similarities, rather than the differences, between Protestant and medieval Catholic modes of thought. "After a fair discussion," so reads an *obiter dictum*

[1] (New York, 1913). Bury's table of contents reads, in part, as follows: "Chapter III. Reason in Prison (The Middle Ages); Chapter IV. Prospect of Deliverance (The Renaissance and the Reformation); Chapter VI. The Growth of Rationalism (Seventeenth and Eighteenth Centuries)."

in the *Decline and Fall of the Roman Empire*, "we shall rather be surprised by the timidity, than scandalized by the freedom, of our first reformers." "The nature of the tiger was the same, but he was gradually deprived of his teeth and fangs." [2] While not quite believing that "the nature of the tiger was the same," many historians now feel that the Reformation was less a repudiation than a modification and simplification of the medieval religious system. On this view, the real break in Western culture came, not in the sixteenth century, but in the age of Galileo and Descartes and Newton.

Ernst Troeltsch, the great German church historian, struck a balance between these two views, and, all things considered, he best interprets the facts. Troeltsch distinguished between the intentions of the reformers and the indirect consequences of their intentions. On the one hand, he points out that Luther and Calvin were essentially religious men who aimed to reform individuals and society along religious lines. The differences between the Protestant world and the "modern" world are profound. To read democracy, *laissez-faire* capitalism, free thought, and science back into the reformers is utterly to mistake their intentions. On the other hand, "the great significance of Protestantism for the arising of the modern world is incontestable." [3] Many of the major developments in modern politics, science, and art arose quite independently of Protestantism. But the Reformation also contributed its bit—indirectly—to "the making of the modern mind" by its attack on the ecclesiastical hierarchy, its individualism, and in various other ways to be noted below. Troeltsch's term "the Confessional Age" aptly describes the sixteenth century. It was an age of rival religious confessions, both Catholic and Protestant. From the rivalry between the sects, but also to some extent from the inner nature of Protestantism itself and from independent secular movements, arose a civilization which would have shocked Luther and Calvin. The Confessional Age was the last phase of the great Age of Religion.

II

THE conservative side of the Reformation should be patent to anyone who studies the life-history of the reformers and their creeds. Take Luther, for instance. Attempts to explain Luther as the product of economics and the champion of middle-class interests are unconvincing to the point of absurdity. As Roland Bainton says of him, he was "so much a gothic figure that his faith may be called the last great flowering of the religion of the Middle Ages." [4] Throughout his life Luther's central interest was religion. We miss the point about him unless

[2] Chapter 54.
[3] Troeltsch, *Protestantism and Progress* (New York, 1912), p. 41.
[4] *Here I Stand* (New York, 1950), p. 25.

we see that the great reality for him was God and God's supreme importance for the individual. The familiar world of the senses, of princes and burghers and peasants, of political and social forms, was important to him only in so far as it related to his central interest. When he visited Rome in 1510, he had eyes to see neither the natural scenery nor the ruins of antiquity nor Renaissance art, but only the churches and shrines. To use Arthur Koestler's phrase, Luther and the reformers of the sixteenth century had a vivid sense of the "Man-Universe" relationship, comparatively little sense of the "Man-Society" relationship.

The new thing about Luther, the thing that ultimately brought him into conflict with the Church of Rome, was not the problem with which he wrestled in the monasteries of Erfurt and Wittenberg, but the solution to the problem. Even the solution was not really new, but was a throwback to Pauline and Augustinian theology. Like so many of his contemporaries, Luther trembled at the thought of death, dreaded the day when he should come before the bar of God the Judge. To save his soul he became a monk, and for eight years tried the Catholic "way of self-help," wearing himself out in the strict observance of the monastic rule, praying to the saints, confessing his sins. When this did not work and he reached the point of desperation, he suddenly found his release in the Bible upon which he had been invited to lecture at the University of Wittenberg. In Paul's Epistle to the Romans he read that "the just shall live by his faith." From the double meaning of the Greek word "justice," Luther construed this statement to mean that God suspended sentence against sinners and saved their souls by giving them faith—faith in his promise to save through Christ the Mediator. "Thereupon I felt myself to be reborn and to have gone through open doors into paradise." In plain language, Luther now taught both a God of love and a pessimistic anthropology. Man, wretched sinner, can never merit salvation by a virtuous life, by "good works." Divine grace alone can save him. Luther narrowed the competence of human reason and denied man's freedom of will. His conception of human nature was neither of the Renaissance nor of medieval scholasticism. But he was closer in spirit to St. Thomas than to Erasmus or John Locke.

The case of Luther raises a fundamental question for students of intellectual history. Why study Luther? A certain Luther scholar says frankly that he studies the man not for his philosophy—Goethe and Nietzsche, he says, have put Luther in the shade—but for his mastery of the German language. But surely we might also study Luther because we have an existential concern in the problems he posed. Luther was not merely representative of a phase of Western thought, now hopelessly outmoded. Luther had insights into the structure of the universe—for instance, when he said: "We cannot reach heaven until we first descend into hell"; or: "Philosophy ought to be content to investigate matter, its primary and secondary qualities, and to distinguish accidents from the substance. Concerning causes it is unable to reach any certainty." Doubtless, statements like these have to be decoded, translated into the language of our own times. Doubtless, there is much in Luther that we cannot accept, or even understand. But Luther said things out of the depths of his experience that we can build into our own philosophy of life. The same thing goes for Machiavelli or Descartes or Nietzsche or any other man of unusual perception.

Luther is not the only evidence of the essential conservatism of the Reformation. Compare the Protestant creeds of the sixteenth century (the Lutheran Augsburg Confession, the Anglican Thirty-nine Articles, etc.) with the decrees of the Roman Catholic Council of Trent, and you find that beneath all their anathematizations of each other lay a common core of belief. Consult that "Summa" of Protestant theology, Calvin's *Institutes of the Christian Religion,* and you see at once how much of the medieval tradition stuck fast to the Genevan reformer. The Protestants believed firmly in all the general features of the Christian Epic. In their world, as in the Middle Ages, supernatural revelation, miracles, and witches were taken for granted. In the sixteenth century, the majority stressed faith rather than reason, opposed religious toleration, and were indifferent, and sometimes hostile, to natural science and free inquiry.

Clearly, Protestantism belonged to the same genus of thought as medieval Catholicism. The Protestant world differed from the "modern" world in at least two fundamental respects. In the first place, as Troeltsch has pointed out, sixteenth-century Protestantism stood for a "church civilization," *i.e.,* a civilization in which an infallible and historic church claims the right to regulate society (either directly, or indirectly through the state) from the standpont of supernatural revelation. "Out of her bosom [the visible church] there can be no hope of remission of sins, or any salvation. . . . It is always fatally dangerous to be separated from the church." We do not generally associate this kind of thinking with Calvin, but this passage is from the *Institutes.* And from the title to save souls followed logically the claim to discipline men in all their worldly activities, whether in education or politics and business. The radical Protestant sects—the Anabaptists, Unitarians, and Mennonites—do not fit into this pattern, as we shall see. But for the churches of the right, which constituted the main body of Protestants, the ideal was of the kind described. The modern world, on the other hand, has in large part repudiated supernatural revelation and, along with it, ecclesiastical authority. For theology it has substituted rationalism, science, and the state, or simply the free individual. Whereas the "church civilization" aims to bring society into harmony with truths already established, the modern world has bent every effort to discover new truths.

A second important difference between the two worlds is that whereas the one regarded life *sub specie aeternitatis,* the other has largely limited its interests to the present life. The first attitude begot asceticism, although it might be of a different type from Catholic asceticism, and a relative indifference to new political and social forms. "Change from within," St. Paul's birth of the new Adam, was what counted most. Since the seventeenth and eighteenth centuries, however, the ideal has been "world-affirmation," and from this attitude stemmed the hope of the ideal transformation of the world, the belief in progress. At any rate this has been true of the modern world up to our present Age of Anxiety.

III

I well remember a seminar in which, after I had expounded the Reformation along these lines, a Catholic priest remarked: "But that is not the Reformation." He was partially right, of course. Were we not to turn the coin over and see the other side, we should see only part of the picture. The Reformation was no mere medieval reform movement, such as the Cluniac reform of the tenth century or the Franciscan movement of the thirteenth. Somebody has said that the word "new" was used more times in the sixteenth century than in the preceding thousand years. Whether this is true or not, the Protestants certainly coined new slogans which had explosive effects on the society into which they were flung. From these slogans—justification by faith, the priesthood of all believers, the supremacy of the Bible, Christian liberty—it is not difficult to see why the Protestants picked up strength among the princes and bourgeois and even the humanists. Protestantism was primarily and fundamentally a religious reform, but it owed its popularity and growth in large part to powerful lay movements which ran parallel with it. There can be no doubt that something *in* Protestant thought itself appealed to the most progressive elements of Western society. The Reformation was a primitivist movement which preached a return to the simple standards of the Bible and the early Christian community. But not infrequently in history primitivism serves as a lever for dislodging traditional forces and allowing others to take over. This is what the Reformation accomplished, and there is considerable irony in the situation. The reformers contributed to individualism, although none of them were individualists in the modern sense; to nationalism, although they hoped to restore Christian unity; to democracy, although hardly any of them were democrats; to the "capitalistic spirit," although they were extremely suspicious of capitalists; indeed, to the secularization of society, although their aim was exactly the reverse.

Sixteenth-century Protestant individualism was mainly religious. It meant neither the Renaissance doctrine of the free development of the individual's capacities, nor the political liberalism of later times. A study of Calvin's Geneva will disabuse anyone of the notion that Protestantism anticipated the "rights of man," or anything like. The citizen of the new Israel had to belong to the established church of his community and to attend its services. He had no free choice of what to believe—"separatism," "nonconformity," "dissent" were taboo in respectable Protestant, as well as Catholic, circles. He must live his life and conduct his business in strictly prescribed ways. Calvin preached discipline—discipline for the greater glory of God, according to an objective standard of truth, the Bible, as interpreted by the ministers and enforced by the city council. Freedom, in Protestant terminology, meant primarily emancipation *from* the Romish yoke *to* the service of God in the manner decreed by the reformers.

This "Christian liberty," however, undoubtedly paved the way for the more extreme individualism of the modern world. When Luther declared that popes and church councils might err, he invited men to question the infallibility of all institutions. When he said that the efficacy of the sacrament depended upon the faith of the recipient, he put the burden of salvation upon the individual rather than the institution. Contrary to their intentions, the reformers weakened the fabric of institutional religion, and thereby institutionalism in general. They made everyman a priest, thereby effectually destroying the middleman between the individual and his God. "Christian," in John Bunyan's *Pilgrim's Progress*, pursuing his lonely way, without help of priests or sacraments, toward the Celestial City was a typical Protestant. Likewise the Puritan diarist who in the secret of his closet recorded his daily struggle with sin. Unlike the medieval monk who followed the rule of his order, the Puritan had to work out his own rules and assume responsibility for them.

Anglicanism probably did the most of all the right-wing Protestant communions to promote intellectual freedom. The Elizabethan divines tried to discover a doctrinal formula that would be acceptable to all shades of religious opinion in England. The result was the Anglican *"via media"* which distinguished between things necessary, and things unnecessary or "indifferent" (*adiaphora*) to salvation. The Bible established the former, which all men were required to believe. The Bible, however, neither commanded nor prohibited the *adiaphora*—things like episcopal church government, vestments, praying to the saints, which could therefore vary according to the custom of the country. In the Anglican system the collective community (the king in parliament), not the individual, determined the ecclesiastical customs to be established by law and observed. But by its minimal theology, its deliberately vague doctrinal phraseology, its category of non-essentials to salvation, it undoubtedly tempered the severity of Calvinist Biblicism and widened the area of individual choice. The presence on English soil of a number of competing sects (Anglicans, Presbyterians, Separatists) stimulated religious toleration and intellectual freedom. In Germany, where the princes succeeded in stamping out the Anabaptists in the early sixteenth century, a new religious orthodoxy set in. But elsewhere in Europe, in Holland and to a lesser extent in France, the story was the same as in England. In the interests of peace and prosperity the state was obliged to tolerate religious dissent, and the friction between orthodox and dissenters created an atmosphere of free, if bitter, discussion.

Politically, the Reformation had similarly far-reaching effects. Protestantism, as has been said, was not primarily a political movement. But the reformers could not very well avoid defining their position with respect to the powers that be, and in the field of church government they evolved novel forms which had important political consequences. On the whole, sixteenth-century Protestantism proved to be a buttress to absolutism and nationalism. This does not mean that the reformers themselves were either absolutists or chauvinists. Even Luther, in whom some people profess to see the devil behind Bismarck and Hitler, qualified the state's power and preached passive resistance under certain conditions. The practical situation, however, made it almost a foregone conclusion that the early Protestants should fall back on the princes as their natural allies. They needed some power sufficiently strong to maintain the "true" religion against the papists on the right, and the Protestant lunatic fringe on the left. The princes alone could supply this power. Consequently, the Protestants erected a cult of royal authority and, at least in Lutheran Germany, Scandinavia, and England, virtually made the church a department of state. Romans 13 became their favorite political text: "the powers that be are ordained of God." Hence, in the extravagant language of William Tyndale's *Obedience of a Christian Man*, the king might not be resisted, "yea, even though he were an infidel."

The logic of Protestant theology also militated in favor of the princes. The chief obstacle to the secular state had been the sacramental power of the priesthood. By the Catholic sacrament of orders the priest had stamped upon him an indelible character which made him different from other men. He received thereby the keys of the kingdom—the power to absolve men of their sins and to sacrifice Christ in the mass. Upon these sacerdotal powers were based his claim to exemption from civil jurisdiction and the pretensions of the Church to temporal power. The Reformation destroyed this distinction between clergy and laity. Luther reduced the number of sacraments from seven to two, and converted the priest into a minister whose sole title to distinction was his "function," not his "office." An Elizabethan observer testifies to "the general contempt of the ministry" in the late sixteenth century, the lack of respect for church and churchyard, the difficulty of getting enough learned men to staff the Anglican ministry.[5] Laymen in general, and the state in particular, profited by this declining prestige of the ministry. In countries like England the bishops became state functionaries, and the crown and laity together plundered church properties. Thus did the Protestant doctrine of the priesthood of all believers lead to secularization, which was the last thing the reformers intended.

In the long run Protestantism made a real contribution to democracy as well as absolutism. "The congregation," it has been said, "was the school of democracy." It is noteworthy that an Elizabethan bishop denounced the leader of the English Presbyterians, Thomas Cartwright, for his "popularity" or "democratic sovereignty." Cartwright denied the charge. Nevertheless, the Calvinist scheme of church government rested upon the theory that spiritual sovereignty resides in the members of the church and their representatives—and not in pope or bishops or king. In the belief that they were restoring the ancient state of the church, the Calvinists postulated the popular election of ministers and lay participation in church government, through the institution of the eldership. The radical Protestants—the "Anabaptists" and "separatists"—went the Calvinists one better. They maintained that church membership itself must be voluntary. Troeltsch calls theirs the "sect-type," as contrasted with the "church-type" of Christian organization. The "sect-type" aims, not to comprehend the whole community, but to separate from the community in order to establish a "holy" church consisting only of tried Christians. Obviously, in such a church, membership can and must be purely voluntary.

Prior to the seventeenth century few Protestants applied these principles to politics or society. But there can be no doubt that a great many people were becoming accustomed to democratic ways in the congregations. We should also remember that wherever circumstances seemed to call for it, even sixteenth-century Protestant political thory could be quite radical. Catholic governments in England (Mary Tudor) and Scotland (Mary Stuart) evoked a flood of pamphlets, by John Knox and others, preaching the right of rebellion. Similarly, in France, in the heat of the religious wars, the boldest of the Huguenots sniped at the Catholic Henry III with theories of contractual government and individual rights. The "outs" in Elizabethan England, the Puritans, were less radical, but even they eventually carried their fight to the floor of parliament where they demanded free speech for members and the right to legislate matters traditionally reserved for the royal prerogative. Politically, Calvinism proved to be the most intransigent of all the Protestant confessions. "New

[5] William Harrison, *Description of England* (London, 1577), "Of the Ancient and Present Estate of the Church of England."

presbyter is but old priest writ large"—when James I of England made this statement, he was remembering the headaches given him by the Scottish kirk, and Calvin's theory of the separation of church and state, which poised the church as a powerful critic of state policy.

If Max Weber is right, Calvinism also helped to engender the "spirit of capitalism" in the West. There has been a good deal of misunderstanding of what Weber meant to say in his celebrated *Protestant Ethic and the Spirit of Capitalism*, and much of the criticism levelled at him is therefore hardly to the point. Weber did not mean that the reformers loved capitalists, or that the capitalistic system was the product of the Reformation. He did not turn Marx upside down and preach the "psychological determination of economic events." Weber merely contended that Protestant ethical teaching played *a* role, albeit an important role, in the formation and expansion of the "capitalistic spirit"—meaning by capitalistic spirit not simple avarice, but the businessman's conviction that it was his *duty* to work hard and increase his capital, and to avoid carefree pleasure. Weber's whole argument turned on the Protestant doctrine of the "calling." The Protestants abolished the monastic vocation and charged all men to labor in the world. God himself labors, and he expects men to work hard and not to while away their time in idle chanting and contemplation. Sloth is as dangerous to the soul as avarice. In Calvinism the businessman's calling became as respectable, as religiously significant, as any other. Like the statesman, the lord and the peasant, the bourgeois might use his calling as a means for promoting God's greater glory on earth. Calvin praised the "economic virtues" of diligence, thrift, and frugality. In Weber's view, this side of the Protestant ethic encouraged the accumulation of capital and the organization of business on rational lines. "He that hath a calling hath an office of profit and honor"; "Drive thy business!"; "If time be of all things the most precious, wasting of time must be the greatest prodigality"—maxims like these from Benjamin Franklin's *Poor Richard's Almanac* derived from the Protestant ethic. So, one might surmise, did a recent statement by an American track star who is also a Protestant minister: "In footracing, as in everyday life, the Lord expects each of us to make an all-out effort. That's why I run every mile to the limit of my ability, keeping nothing back."

Tawney believes, and rightly, that Weber underestimated the disciplinary aspects of sixteenth-century Calvinism. Calvinism grew up largely in cities and it assumed the credit system that made modern business possible, but it brooked no nonsense from businessmen, either in their callings or their private lives. Weber also failed to consider sufficiently the possible impact of economic and social needs on Protestant thought itself. But Weber was right in his main contention, that the Reformation had economic consequences that were unforeseen by the reformers themselves. As Tawney himself has written: "Calvin did for the *bourgeoisie* of the sixteenth century what Marx did for the proletariat of the nineteenth." [6]

The Reformation related to the modern world in one other respect, which has been largely overlooked. The tendency in Protestantism was to emphasize the practical and concrete, as opposed to the metaphysical and mysterious. One stumbles across evidence of this tendency in a hundred places. Like the Christian humanists, the Protestants stressed ethics rather than metaphysics. For the philosophical and theological speculations of the schools they had only contempt. What counted in their philosophy was the birth of the new man and ethical conduct. Note their concern—particularly the Calvinist's concern—for church organization and the implementation of the new Israel on earth. The only great polemical book produced by the Anglican Reformation was Richard Hooker's *Laws of Ecclesiastical Polity*, which, as its title implies, dealt largely with ecclesiastical structure and politics. As we have seen, the Protestants largely eschewed contemplation for practical divinity and busyness in the life of the community. Of course, they believed in the miraculous, in the great miracle of justification, but they took the miracle out of the mass and made the altar into a communion table. In contrast to medieval Catholicism, which believed in the daily occurrence of miracles, the Protestants took the position that the age of miracles had closed with the great Church Fathers. With regard to the interpretation of Scripture they again followed the Christian humanist line which rejected the tropological, allegorical, and analogical senses and sought for literal meaning and historical understanding. William Tyndale who translated the Bible into English declared that "the Scripture hath but one sense, which is the literal sense, and that literal sense is the root and ground of all, and the anchor that never faileth, whereunto if thou cleave thou canst never err or go out of the way."

In its general world-outlook and clear sense of an extra dimension in human life, the Protestant Reformation belonged to the Age of Religion. But the Protestant distrust of intellectual theorizing and partiality for common sense helped to build the bridge to the scientific empiricism of the modern world. By their preoccupation with practical living, the Protestants unwittingly increased the tension, already so noticeable during the Renaissance, between the claims of two worlds.

[6] *Religion and the Rise of Capitalism* (London, 1933), pp. 111–12.

Readings

1. *First Principles of the Protestant Reformation*

The Religious Experience of Thomas Bilney *

> The following document, a letter written by an English priest to the Bishop of London in 1527, describes a type of religious experience which must have been fairly common in the early sixteenth century. Thomas Bilney (1495?–1531) was no Lutheran, but his account of his "conversion" reads remarkably like that experienced by Martin Luther somewhat earlier at Erfurt and Wittenberg. Bilney was one of a little band of "Cambridge Reformers" who went about attacking the notion of salvation by good works. Arrested and brought to trial by Bishop Tunstal, he declared that he did not "wittingly" teach the doctrines of Luther, and accepted the papal supremacy. But after once recanting, he became a relapsed heretic and was executed in 1531.

To THE reverend father in Christ, Cuthbert, bishop of London, Thomas Bilney wisheth health in Christ, with all submission due unto such a prelate:

In this behalf, most reverend father in Christ, I think myself most happy that it is my chance to be called to examination before your reverence, for that you are of such wisdom and learning, of such integrity of life, which all men do confess to be in you, that even yourself cannot choose (if you do not too lightly esteem God's gifts in you), as often as you shall remember the great things which God hath done unto you, but straightways secretly in your heart, to his high praise say, 'He that is mighty hath done great things unto me, and holy is his name.' I rejoice, that I have now happened upon such a judge, and with all my heart give thanks unto God, who ruleth all things.

* *The Acts and Monuments of John Foxe*, ed. by Rev. S. R. Cattley (London: R. B. Seeley and W. Burnside; 1837–41), vol. IV, pp. 633–6.

And albeit (God is my witness) I know not myself guilty of any error in my sermons, neither of any heresy or sedition, which divers do slander me of, seeking rather their own lucre and advantage, than the health of souls: notwithstanding I do exceedingly rejoice, that it is so foreseen by God's divine providence, that I should be brought before the tribunal seat of Tonstal, who knoweth as well as any other, that there will never be wanting a Jannes and a Jambres, who will resist the truth; that there shall never be lacking some Elymas, who will go about to subvert the straight ways of the Lord; and finally, that some Demetriuses, Pithonises, Balaams, Nicolaitans, Cains, and Ishmaels, will be always at hand, who will greedily hunt and seek after that which pertaineth unto themselves, and not that which pertaineth to Jesus Christ. . . .

But if any man seeketh to reduce those who were gone astray, into the fold of Christ, that is, the unity of faith, by and by there rise up certain against him, which are named pastors, but indeed are wolves; which seek no other thing of their flock, but the milk, wool, and fell, leaving both their own souls, and the souls of their flock, unto the devil.

These men, I say, rise up like unto Demetrius, crying out, 'This heretic dissuadeth and seduceth much people every where, saying, that they are not gods, which are made with hands.' These are they, these I say, most reverend father! are they, who, under the pretence of presecuting heretics, follow their own licentious lives; enemies unto the cross of Christ, who can suffer and bear any thing rather than the sincere preaching of Christ crucified for our sins. These are they unto whom Christ threateneth eternal damnation, when he saith, 'Wo be unto you scribes, Pharisees, and hypocrites! which shut up the kingdom of heaven before men, and you yourselves enter not in, neither suffer those which would enter, to come in.' These are they that have come in another way to the charge of souls, as it appeareth; 'For if any man,' saith Christ, 'come in by me, he shall be saved; and shall come in, and go out, and find pasture.' These men do not find pasture, for they never teach and draw others after them, that they should enter by Christ, who alone is the door whereby we must come unto the Father; but set before the people another way, persuading them to come unto God through good works, oftentimes speaking nothing at all of Christ, thereby seeking rather their own gain and lucre, than the salvation of souls: in this point being worse than those who upon Christ (being the foundation) do build wood, hay and straw. These men confess that they know Christ, but by their deeds they deny him.

These are those physicians upon whom that woman that was twelve years vexed with the bloody flux had consumed all that she had, and felt no help, but was still worse and worse, until such time as she came at last unto Christ; and after she had once touched the hem of his vesture, through faith she was so healed, that by and by she felt the same in her body. O mighty power of the most Highest! which I also, miserable sinner, have often tasted and felt, who, before I could come unto Christ, had even likewise spent all that I had upon those ignorant physicians; that is to say, unlearned hearers of confession; so that there was but small force of strength left in me (who of nature was but weak), small store of money, and very little wit or understanding: for they appointed me fastings, watching, buying of pardons, and masses; in all which things (as I now understand) they sought rather their own gain, than the salvation of my sick and languishing soul.

But at last I heard speak of Jesus, even then when the New Testament was first set forth by Erasmus; which when I understood to be eloquently done by him, being allured rather by the Latin than by the word of God (for at that time I knew not what it meant), I bought it even by the providence of God, as I do now well understand and perceive: and at the first reading (as I well remember) I chanced upon this sentence of St. Paul (O most sweet and comfortable sentence to my soul!) in 1 Tim. i., 'It is a true saying, and worthy of all men to be embraced, that Christ Jesus came into the world to save sinners; of whom I am the chief and principal.' This one sentence, through God's instruction and inward working, which I did not then perceive, did so exhilarate my heart, being before wounded with the guilt of my sins, and being almost in despair, that immediately I felt a marvellous comfort and quietness, insomuch 'that my bruised bones leaped for joy.'

After this, the Scripture began to be more pleasant unto me than the honey or the honey-comb; wherein I learned, that all my travails, all my fasting and watching, all the redemption of masses and pardons, being done without trust in Christ, who only saveth his people from their sins; these, I say, I learned to be nothing else but even (as St. Augustine saith) a hasty and swift running out of the right way; or else much like to the vesture made of fig leaves, wherewithal Adam and Eve went about in vain to cover themselves, and could never before obtain quietness and rest, until they believed in the promise of God, that Christ, the seed of the woman, should tread upon the serpent's head: neither could I be relieved or eased of the sharp stings and bitings of my sins, before I was taught of God that lesson which Christ speaketh of in John iii.: 'Even as Moses exalted the serpent in the desert, so shall the Son of Man be exalted, that all which believe on him, should not perish, but have life everlasting.' . . .

And therefore, with all my whole power I teach, that all men should first acknowledge their sins, and condemn them, and afterwards hunger and thirst for that righteousness whereof St. Paul speaketh, 'The righteousness of God, by faith in Jesus Christ, is upon all them which believe in him; for there is no difference: all have sinned, and lack the glory of God, and are justified freely through his grace, by the redemption which is in Jesus Christ:' which whosoever doth hunger or thirst for, without doubt they shall at length so be satisfied, that they shall not hunger and thirst for ever.

But, forasmuch as this hunger and thirst were wont to be quenched with the fulness of man's righteousness, which is wrought through the faith of our own elect and chosen works, as pilgrimages, buying of pardons, offering of candles, elect and chosen fasts, and oftentimes superstitious; and finally all kind of voluntary devotions (as they call them), against which God's word speaketh plainly in Deut. iv., v. 2, saying, 'Thou shalt not do that which seemeth good unto thyself; but that which I command thee for to do, that do thou, neither adding to, neither diminishing any thing from it.' Therefore, I say, oftentimes I have spoken of those works, not condemning them (as I take God to my witness), but reproving their abuse; making the lawful use of them manifest even unto children; exhorting all men not so to cleave unto them, that they, being satisfied therewith, should loathe or wax weary of Christ, as many do: in whom I bid your fatherhood most prosperously well to fare.

And this is the whole sum. If you will appoint me to dilate more at large the things here touched, I will not refuse to do it, so that you will grant me time (for to do it out of hand I am not able for the weakness of my body); being ready always, if I have erred in any thing, to be better instructed.

Philip Melanchthon: *Common Topics* *

Philip Melanchthon (1497–1560) was the first great Protestant theologian. Called at the age of twenty-one to be professor of Greek at the University of Wittenberg, he was soon swept up in the Lutheran movement whose fundamental principles he expounded in his *Loci communes rerum theologicarum*. In the first edition of this work (1521) Melanchthon closely followed Luther, expressing contempt for Aristotle and humanistic wisdom. But in later revisions, which appeared from 1535 on, he tried to reconcile reason and revelation, Aristotle and Christian doctrine, in the manner of the scholastic theologians. Melanchthon is also noted as the author of the Augsburg Confession of 1530, the earliest confessional statement of Protestant doctrine. The following selections are from the *Loci communes* of 1521.

THE PRINCIPAL topics of Christian discipline are indicated in order that youths may understand both what things are to be sought out in the Scriptures, as well as learn under what base hallucinations they labor

* From Philip Melanchthon: *Loci Communes*, trans. by C. L. Hill, pp. 64–5, 67–71, 75–6, 80, 85–7, 89, 144, 169–72, 178, 202, 204. Copyright 1944 by Meador Publishing Company. Reprinted by permission of Meador Publishing Company.

everywhere in theological science, who have handed down to us the subtle pratings of Aristotle, instead of the doctrine of Christ.

I am indeed treating everything sparingly and briefly, due to the fact that I am discharging the duty of an Index rather than a commentary. Hence, I am only stating the nomenclature of the topics, to which that person roaming through the Divine Scriptures may be directed. I do not wish to lead them away from scriptures to some obscure and intricate argument of my own; but if possible that I might incite them to the Scriptures.

For on the whole, I am not quite equal to the commentaries, not even to those of the Ancients. So far from that am I, that I would not by any longer writings of mine, restrain anyone from the study of the Canonical Scripture. On the contrary, I would desire nothing quite so much if it were possible, as that all Christians be thoroughly conversant with divine letters alone, and be wholly transformed into their nature. For since the Godhead has expressed its most complete image in them, it cannot from any other source be more surely or correctly known. He is mistaken who seeks the form of Christianity in any other source than Canonical Scripture. For indeed how much do the Commentaries lack the purity of Canonical Scripture? In Canonical Scripture, one will find nothing but what is worthy of honor, while in the Commentaries how many things depend upon the valuation of human reason! . . .

. . . there is no reason why we should put much labor on the greatest topics such as, God, on the Unity and Trinity of God, on the great mystery of Creation, and on the mode of Incarnation. I ask you, what did the Scholastic theologians gain so many years ago, when they busied themselves with these topics alone? Did they not, as Paul says, become vain in their disquisitions, while joking a whole lifetime about universals, formalities, connotations and I know not what other meaningless words? And moreover, their folly might have gone unnoticed had not their foolish disputations for a time obscured to us the Gospel and the Benefits of Christ. . . .

Whoever is ignorant of the remaining topics such as the power of sin, the law and grace, I do not see how I may call him a Christian. For by them is Christ properly known, if indeed this is to know Christ, to wit, to know his benefits and not as they teach, to perceive his natures and the mode of his incarnation. Unless one knows why Christ took upon himself human flesh and was crucified, what advantage would accrue from having learned his life's history? Or on the other hand, is it of no consequence for a physician to have become acquainted with the kinds, colors and properties of plants, in order to know their native power? Accordingly it behooves us to become acquainted with Christ who has been given as a remedy for us, or to use the language of Scripture, "for our salvation," in some other way than that exhibited by the Scholastics.

Precisely this is Christian knowledge, to know what the law demands, whence you may seek the power to discharge the injunctions of the law, whence you may seek pardon for sin, how you may arouse a wavering mind against the Devil, the flesh and the world, and finally how you may console a dejected conscience. Of course the Scholastics teach such things, do they not? In the Epistle to the Romans, when he drew up a compendium of Christian doctrine, did Paul the author philosophize about the mysteries of the Trinity, the mode of the Incarnation or about "creation active and passive?" On the contrary, what does Paul do? He reasons most certainly about the Law, Sin, and Grace.

On Sin

The older Pelagians can be rooted out with less difficulty than can the newer Pelagians of modern times. For the latter, although they do not deny the fact of original sin, yet they do deny that it is the power of original sin that causes all human works and all human attempts to be sins. Therefore my treatment of this locus on the power and energy of original sin will be rather extended.

Original sin is a certain living energy at no time bearing any fruit save vices. For when is it that the human soul does not burn with evil desire, wherein things most disgraceful and offensive are not even checked? Avarice, hate, ambition, envy, emulation, the flames of lusts, anger! Who is there that does not sometime or other feel them? Arrogance, pride, a Pharisaic tumor, contempt of God, distrust of Him, blasphemy, while the chief affections but a few feel.

There are some who in outward appearance live right honorable lives. They have nothing in which to glory, seeing indeed that their souls are subject to those disgraceful and wretched affections which they do not perceive. . . .

Granted that there was some constancy manifested in a Socrates, chastity in a Zenocrates, temperance in a Zeno! Nevertheless because they were in impure minds, nay because they took origin in self-love, and out of desire for praise, these shadows of the virtues should be regarded as vices and not real virtues. Socrates was tolerant, but a lover of glory or else prided himself for his virtue. Cato was brave, but it was because he loved praise. Moreover God pours out upon the nations the shadows of such virtues, and upon the ungodly and on anyone who does not otherwise have the form, he bestows riches and similar gifts.

Now while the entire human reason marvels at this outer mask and spectre of virtue, our pseudo-theologians deceived by blind natural judgment, have commended unto us philosophic studies, philosophic virtues, and the merits of external works. But what do the philosophers in general teach (if there be any who teach well), but reliance on self and self-love? Take M. T. Cicero in his work *De Finibus* for instance. Now he estimates the whole scheme of virtue by self-love and self-regard. And, too, what pride and arrogance are to be found in Plato! . . .

Philosophy looks only upon the external masks of man, whereas Holy Writ discerns the innermost and incomprehensible affections.

When a man is dominated by these, Holy Writ judges his works according to the affections. For since in all our works we seek our own personal gains, our works are necessarily true sins.

On the Law and the Gospel

Of the whole of Scripture there are two parts: the law and the gospel. The law indicates the sickness, the gospel the remedy. To use Paul's words, the law is a minister of death, while the gospel is a minister of life and peace. "The strength of sin is the law," I Cor. 15:56, the gospel is the power or strength of salvation to everyone that believes. Nor has the Scripture so narrated law and gospel in such a manner that one would regard as gospel what Matthew, Mark, Luke and John have written, and as law what Moses has recorded. But the plan of the gospel is scattered; there are promises in both the Old and New Testaments. And again, laws are scattered throughout all the books of the Old and New Testaments. . . .

Just as the law is the knowledge of sin, so likewise is the gospel the promise of grace and righteousness. Moreover, because the words grace and righteousness, and certainly the gospel are to be considered, I must in this place subjoin the principles of grace and righteousness. For in this manner, the nature of the gospel can be more fully understood.

Indeed, I ask, who can rightly expostulate on this point with the Scholastics who have so foully abused that sacrosanct word grace when they use it, to express the quality that is in the minds of the saints? And above all especially the Thomists, who posited quality or grace in the very nature of the mind: that faith, hope and love are in the powers of the mind. And even here too, how anile and how foolish are their disputes about the powers of the mind! But let those impious men become exceedingly filthy; let those despisers of the gospel suffer anguish for their buffoonery and jest. . . .

Away with Aristotelian figments about qualities! For grace is nothing (if it is to be most exactly defined) but the benevolence of God toward us, or the will of God that has commiserated us. Therefore, the word "grace" does not signify some quality in us, but rather the will of God itself, or the benevolence of God toward us.

On Justification by Faith

We are justified, when mortified by the law, we are raised up by the word of grace that is promised in Christ, or in the gospel that forgives sins; and when we cling to Christ nothing doubting but that the righteousness of Christ is our righteousness, that his satisfaction is our expiation, that his resurrection is ours. In a word, nothing doubting that our sins are forgiven and that God loves and cherishes us. Our works however good they may be do not constitute our righteousness. For righteousness is faith alone in the mercy and grace of God in Jesus Christ. That is what Paul means when he says: "The just live by faith.". . .

Whatsoever kind the works may be: eating, drinking, working with the hand, teaching, I add that even they are plainly sins. You should not look at works: look at the promise of the mercy of God with trust in him doubting nothing, but that you have in heaven not a judge, but a father who cares for you just as human parents care for their children. But if there were no signification of the divine will toward us other than the fact that he has willed to be called father in that prayer which we daily pray, this alone should be sufficient argument that nothing is demanded of us before our faith. Now since God so often demands faith, since he so often approves of it alone, since he has commended it unto us by rich promises and in addition by the death of his son, why do we not commit ourselves to such a great mercy as this, and believe it? Scholastic theology has taught human works and satisfactions, for faith, for an anchor of consciences. May God destroy that scandal of his church! . . .

Now this fact must be considered also: that just as works are the fruits of the Spirit, they are also indications, testimonies, and signs of it. Christ says as much in Matt. 7:16: "By their fruits ye shall know them." For hyprocrisy cannot forever be dissembled, and faith unable not to assert itself to most eagerly serve God as a pious son serves a pious father. For when by faith we have tasted of the mercy of God, and have known the divine goodness through the word of the gospel which pardons our sins and promises grace, the soul cannot but love God in return and be joyful, and express its gratitude by some mutual kindness as it were for such great mercy. . . .

It is evident from this, how the love of God and the love of neighbor which they call "Caritas," proceed from faith. For the very knowledge of the mercy of God causes us to love God in return. It causes us of our own accord to subject ourselves to all creatures and this is "love of neighbor."

Moreover, hope also is a work of faith. For faith is that by which the word is believed, while hope is that by which one awaits what has already been promised through the word.

On Christian Liberty

Finally: Christianity is liberty, because those who have not the spirit of Christ can by no means do the law, and are guilty of the curses of the law.

They who have been renewed by the spirit of Christ, going of their own accord even without the law dictating, are led to do those things which the law has ordered. The will of God is the law. And the Holy Spirit is but the living will of God and a motion. Wherefore when we have been regenerated by the Spirit of God which is the living will of God, we will already of our own accord, the very things which the law has demanded. . . .

. . . liberty does not mean that we do not do the law, but that we will and desire spontaneously from our hearts that which the law demands. This is exactly what no man could do formerly. . . .

You have it to what extent we are free from the decalogue. In the first place, that although sinners yet it cannot condemn those who are in Christ; then secondly, that those who are in Christ are driven by the Spirit to do the law, and by the Spirit do it. They love and fear God, administer to the necessities of their neighbors, and desire those very things which the law has demanded, and would do them even had no law been given. For their will, to be sure the Spirit, is nothing other than a living law. . . .

In Romans 6, 7, and 8, Paul gives a long disputation about this freedom, teaching that only the new man is free. Hence, we are free insofar as we have been renewed. Insofar as we are flesh and age, we are under the law; although what is left of the old, is condoned in believers for the same of their faith. In a word, as far as we believe, we are free; and as far as we show diffidence, we are under the law.

On the Sacraments

I have said that the gospel is the promise of grace. Moreover next to promises is the place of signs. For in the Scriptures signs are added to the promises for a mark. These signs remind us of the promises and are sure testimonies of the divine will toward us. They also bear witness that of a certainty we will receive what God has promised unto us. Gross errors are made in the use of signs. For when the schools dispute about the difference between the sacraments of the Old and the New Testaments they deny that the sacraments of the Old Testament had any power to justify. They attribute to the New Testament sacraments (though by a manifest error) the power to justify. For faith alone justifies. . . .

In the gospel moreover, Christ has instituted two signs, to wit, baptism and the Table of the Lord. For I judge sacramental signs to be those that have been divinely given as tokens of God's grace. For we men cannot institute a sign of the divine will toward us, nor refer those signs as signifying the divine will, which Scripture has referred to another. I wonder the more, what has entered the minds of the Sophists, especially since they would attribute our justification to signs, to cause them to reckon among signs those things of which the Scripture does not mention even one word. For whence has the priestly order been invented? And too, God never instituted marriage to be a proper sign of grace. The rite of unction is older than the sign of grace. Luther has copiously treated this matter in his "Babylonian Captivity." From it you may seek a more exact discussion of this subject. But this is the sum of the matter: grace is not signified with certainty and indeed properly, except by those signs which have been divinely transmitted. Thus only those which have been added to the divine promises can be rightly called sacramental signs. The ancients were accustomed to say here that sacraments consist of things and words. The thing is the sign, the words the promise of grace.

MARTIN LUTHER: *On the Babylonish Captivity of the Church* *

In 1520 Martin Luther (1483–1546), soon to be excommunicated by the pope for heresy and put under the ban of the Holy Roman Empire, attacked the Roman Church in a series of powerful pamphlets. The best known of these, circulated widely throughout Germany, were the *Address to the Nobility of the German Nation, The Freedom of a Christian Man,* and *On the Babylonish Captivity of the Church.* The latter blasted the sacramental system, notably the sacrament of orders upon which the priestly power depended, and rejected all the sacraments but two, baptism and the Lord's Supper.

Of Orders

OF THIS sacrament the Church of Christ knows nothing; it was invented by the church of the Pope. It not only has no promise of grace, anywhere declared, but not a word is said about it in the whole of the New Testament. Now it is ridiculous to set up as a sacrament of God that which can nowhere be proved to have been instituted by God. Not that I consider that a rite practised for so many ages is to be condemned; but I would not have human inventions established in sacred things, nor should it be allowed to bring in anything as divinely ordained, which has not been divinely ordained; lest we should be objects of ridicule to our adversaries. . . .

Which of the ancient Fathers has asserted that by these words priests were ordained? Whence then this new interpretation? It is because it has been sought by this device to set up a source of implacable discord, by

* *First Principles of the Reformation,* trans. by H. Wace and C. A. Buchheim (Philadelphia: Lutheran Publication Society; 1885), pp. 227–8, 232, 236–7.

which clergy and laity might be placed farther asunder than heaven and earth, to the incredible injury of baptismal grace and confusion of evangelical communion. Hence has originated that detestable tyranny of the clergy over the laity, in which, trusting to the corporal unction by which their hands are consecrated, to their tonsure, and to their vestments, they not only set themselves above the body of lay Christians, who have been anointed with the Holy Spirit, but almost look upon them as dogs, unworthy to be numbered in the Church along with themselves. Hence it is that they dare to command, exact, threaten, drive, and oppress, at their will. In fine, the sacrament of orders has been and is a most admirable engine for the establishment of all those monstrous evils which have hitherto been wrought, and are yet being wrought, in the Church. In this way Christian brotherhood has perished; in this way shepherds have been turned into wolves, servants into tyrants, and ecclesiastics into more than earthly beings.

How if they were compelled to admit that we all, so many as have been baptized, are equally priests? We are so in fact, and it is only a ministry which has been entrusted to them, and that with our consent. They would then know that they have no right to exercise command over us, except so far as we voluntarily allow of it. Thus it is said: "Ye are a chosen generation, a royal priesthood, a holy nation." (1 Pet. ii. 9.) Thus all we who are Christians are priests; those whom we call priests are ministers chosen from among us to do all things in our name; and the priesthood is nothing else than a ministry. . . .

As far then as we are taught from the Scriptures, since what we call the priesthood is a ministry, I do not see at all for what reason a man who has once been made priest cannot become a layman again, since he differs in no wise from a layman, except by his ministerial office. But it is so far from impossible for a man to be set aside from the ministry, that even now this punishment is constantly inflicted on offending priests, who are either suspended for a time, or deprived for ever of their office. For that fiction of an indelible character has long ago become an object of derision. I grant that the Pope may impress this character, though Christ knows nothing of it, and for this very reason the priest thus consecrated is the lifelong servant and bondsman, not of Christ, but of the Pope, as it is at this day. But, unless I deceive myself, if at some future time this sacrament and figment fall to the ground, the Papacy itself will scarcely hold its ground, and we shall recover that joyful liberty in which we shall understand that we are all equal in every right, and shall shake off the yoke of tyranny and know that he who is a Christian has Christ, and he who has Christ has all things that are Christ's, and can do all things—on which I will write more fully and more vigorously when I find that what I have here said displeases my friends the papists.

MARTIN LUTHER: *The Papacy at Rome* *

The Papacy at Rome, also published in 1520, justified Luther's declaration at the Leipzig Disputation of 1519 that salvation did not depend upon belief in the divine supremacy of the Roman pope. It was written in rebuttal of a book by a Franciscan friar, Augustine von Alveld, appointed by the Bishop of Merseburg to defend the Petrine supremacy against Luther.

THIS then is the question: Whether the papacy at Rome, possessing the actual power over all Christendom (as they say), is of divine or of human origin, and this being decided, whether it is possible for Christians to say that all other Christians in the world are heretics and apostates, even if they agree with us in holding to the same baptism, Sacrament, Gospel, and all the articles of faith, but merely do not have their priests and bishops confirmed by Rome, or, as it is now, buy such confirmation with money and let themselves be mocked and made fools of like the Germans. Such are the Muscovites, Russians, Greeks, Bohemians, and many other great peoples in the world. . . .

I find three strong arguments by which this fruitful and noble little book of the Romanist at Leipzig attacks me.

The first, and by far the strongest, is, that he calls me names—a heretic, a blind, senseless fool, one possessed by the devil, a serpent, a poisonous reptile, and many other names of similar import; not simply once, but throughout the book, almost on every page. Such reproaches, slanders and calumnies are of no account in other books. But when a book is made at Leipzig, and issued from the cloister of the barefoot friars, by a Romanist of the high and holy observance of St. Francis, such names are not merely fine examples of moderation, but likewise strong arguments with which to defend papal power, indulgences, Scripture, faith and the Church. It is not necessary that any one of these should be proved by Scripture or by reason; it is quite enough that they have been put down in his book by a Romanist and holy observant of the order of St. Francis. . . .

The second argument, to express it tersely, is that of natural reason.

This is the argument: A. Every community on earth, if it is not to fall to pieces, must have a bodily head, under the true head, which is Christ.

B. Inasmuch as all Christendom is one community on earth, it must have a head, which is the pope.

This argument I have designated with the letters A and B for the sake

* From Martin Luther: *Works*, trans. by A. Steimle and others, vol. I, p. 340, 344–6, 363, 373–4, 381–2. Copyright 1915 by A. J. Holman Company. Reprinted by permission of United Lutheran Publication House.

of clearness, and also to show that this Romanist has learned his A-B-C all the way down to B. However, to answer this argument: Since the question is whether the pope's power is by divine right, is it not a bit ridiculous that human reason (that ability which is drawn from experience in temporal things) is brought in and placed on a level with the divine law, especially since it is the intention of this poor presumptuous mortal to bring the divine law against me. For the teachings of human experience and reason are far below the divine law. The Scriptures expressly forbid us to follow our own reason, Deuteronomy xii, "Ye shall not do . . . every man whatsoever is right in his own eyes"; for human reason ever strives against the law of God, as Genesis vi. says: "Every thought and imagination of man's heart is only evil continually." Therefore the attempt to establish or defend divine order with human reason, unless that reason has previously been established and enlightened by faith, is just as futile as if I would throw light upon the sun with a lightless lantern, or rest a rock upon a reed. For Isaiah vii. makes reason subject to faith, when it says: "Except ye believe, ye shall not have understanding or reason." It does not say, "Except ye have reason, ye shall not believe.". . .

Now comes the third argument, in which the high majesty of God is made a target, and the Holy Spirit becomes a liar and a heretic, so that by all means the contention of the Romanists may be upheld.

The third argument is taken from the Scriptures, just as the second was taken from reason and the first from folly, so that everything may be done in proper order. . . .

Now let us see how these pious people treat the holy words of Christ in this case. Christ says to St. Peter, Matthew xvi: "Thou art, or art called, Peter; and on the P e t r a m (i.e., on the rock) I will build My Church. And I will give unto thee the keys of the kingdom of heaven, and whatsoever thou shalt bind on earth, shall be bound in heaven, and whatsoever thou shalt loose on earth, shall be loosed in heaven." From these words they have claimed the keys for St. Peter alone; but the same Matthew has barred such erroneous interpretation in the xviii. chapter, where Christ says to all in common, "Verily, I say unto you, whatsoever ye shall bind on earth, shall be bound in heaven, and whatsoever ye shall loose on earth, shall be loosed in heaven." It is clear that Christ here interprets His own words, and in this xviii. chapter explains the former xvi.; namely, that the keys are given to St. Peter in the stead of the whole Church, and not for his own person. Thus also John, in the last chapter, "He breathed on them and said, Receive ye the Holy Ghost; whosesoever sins ye remit, they are remitted unto them, and whosoever sins ye retain, they are retained." To maintain the sole authority of St. Peter, when there are two texts against one, many men have labored in vain. But the Gospel is too clear, and they have had to admit until now that in the first passage nothing special was given to St. Peter for his own person. . . .

Now the greater part of the Roman communion, and even some of the popes themselves, have forsaken the faith wantonly and without struggle, and live under the power of Satan, as is plainly to be seen, and thus the papacy often has been under the dominion of the gates of hell. And should I speak quite openly, this same Roman authority, ever since the time it has presumed to soar over all Christendom, not only has never attained its purpose, but has become the cause of nearly all the apostasy, heresy, discord, sects, unbelief and misery in Christendom, and has never freed itself from the gates of hell. And if there were no other passage to prove that Roman authority was of human and not of divine right, this passage alone would be sufficient, where Christ says, the gates of hell shall not prevail against His building on the rock. Now the gates of hell offttimes had the papacy in their power, at times the pope was not a pious man, and the office was occupied by a man without faith, without grace, without good works; which God would never have permitted if the papacy were meant in Christ's word concerning the rock. For then He would not be true to His promise, nor fulfil His own word; therefore the rock, and the building of Christ founded upon it, must be something entirely different from the papacy and its external Church.

MARTIN LUTHER: *On the Bondage of the Will* *

> The debate between Erasmus and Luther epitomizes the central point at issue between Christian humanists and Lutherans. Luther called it "the vital spot"; it concerned the nature of man, the extent to which the "natural man" could freely contribute to his own eternal salvation. Erasmus, taking the late Scholastic (and semi-Pelagian) position, argued for freedom of the will in his diatribe by that title of 1524. Luther argued to the contrary in *On the Bondage of the Will*, published the following year. The debate foreclosed any hope of reconciliation between the two great Christian leaders.

. . . WE do everything by necessity, and nothing by free choice, since the power of free choice is nothing and neither does nor can do good in the absence of grace. . . . It follows now that free choice is plainly a divine term and can be properly applied to none but the Divine Majesty alone; for he alone can do and does (as the psalmist says

* From *Luther and Erasmus: Free Will and Salvation*, trans. and ed. by E. Gordon Rupp, Philip S. Watson, A. N. Marlow, and B. Drewery. Volume XVII, The Library of Christian Classics. Copyright 1969 by The Westminster Press. Used by permission.

[Ps. 115:3]) whatever he pleases in heaven and on earth. If this is attributed to men, it is no more rightly attributed than if divinity itself also were attributed to them, which would be the greatest possible sacrilege. Theologians therefore ought to have avoided this term when they wished to speak of human ability, leaving it to be applied to God alone. They should, moreover, have removed it from the lips and language of men, treating it as a kind of sacred and venerable name for their God. And if they attributed any power at all to men, they should teach that it must be called by another name than free choice. . . .

But if we are unwilling to let this term go altogether—though that would be the safest and most God-fearing thing to do—let us at least teach men to use it honestly, so that free choice is allowed to man only with respect to what is beneath him and not what is above him. That is to say, a man should know that with regard to his faculties and possessions he has the right to use, to do, or to leave undone, according to his own free choice, though even this is controlled by the free choice of God alone, who acts in whatever way he pleases. On the other hand in relation to God, or in matters pertaining to salvation or damnation, a man has no free choice, but is a captive, subject and slave either of the will of God or the will of Satan. . . .

I will here bring this little book to an end, though I am prepared if need be to carry the debate farther. However, I think quite enough has been done here to satisfy the godly and anyone who is willing to admit the truth without being obstinate. For if we believe it to be true that God foreknows and predestines all things, that he can neither be mistaken in his foreknowledge nor hindered in his predestination, and that nothing takes place but as he wills it (as reason itself is forced to admit), then on the testimony of reason itself there cannot be any free choice in man or angel or any creature. . . .

Similarly, if we believe that original sin has so ruined us that even in those who are led by the Spirit it causes a great deal of trouble by struggling against the good, it is clear that in a man devoid of the Spirit there is nothing left that can turn toward the good, but only toward evil.

Again, if the Jews, who pursued righteousness to the utmost of their powers, rather ran headlong into unrighteousness, while the Gentiles, who pursued ungodliness, attained righteousness freely and unexpectedly, then it is also manifest from this very fact and experience that man without grace can will nothing but evil.

To sum up: if we believe that Christ has redeemed men by his blood, we are bound to confess that the whole man was lost; otherwise, we should make Christ either superfluous or the redeemer of only the lowest part of man, which would be blasphemy and sacrilege. . . .

2. *The Calvinistic System*

JOHN CALVIN: *Institutes of the Christian Religion* *

John Calvin (1509–64) came to Geneva from France in 1536 and soon established himself, although not without serious opposition, as the spiritual leader of the city. He soon succeeded in making Geneva the capital of militant Protestantism in Europe. If his *Institutes of the Christian Religion*, expanded to eighty chapters in 1559, was not the Bible of Protestantism, it was for perhaps the majority of Protestants its *Summa Theologica.*

God and Man

TRUE and substantial wisdom principally consists of two parts, the knowledge of God, and the knowledge of ourselves. But, while these two branches of knowledge are so intimately connected, which of them precedes and produces the other, is not easy to discover. For, in the first place, no man can take a survey of himself but he must immediately turn to the contemplation of God, in whom he "lives and moves;" since it is evident that the talents which we possess are not from ourselves, and that our very existence is nothing but a subsistence in God alone. These bounties, distilling to us by drops from heaven, form, as it were, so many streams conducting us to the fountain-head. Our poverty conduces to a clearer display of the infinite fulness of God. Especially, the miserable ruin, into which we have been plunged by the defection of the first man, compels us to raise our eyes towards heaven, not only as hungry and famished, to seek thence a supply for our wants, but, aroused with fear, to learn humility. For, since man is subject to a world of miseries, and has been spoiled of his divine array, this melancholy exposure discovers an immense mass of deformity: every one, therefore, must be so impressed with a consciousness of his own infelicity, as to arrive at some knowledge of God. Thus a sense of our ignorance, vanity, poverty, infirmity, depravity, and corruption, leads us to perceive and acknowledge that in the Lord alone are to be found true wisdom, solid strength, perfect goodness, and unspotted righteousness; and so, by our imperfections, we are excited to a consideration of the perfections of God, Nor can we really aspire toward him, till we have begun to be displeased with ourselves. For who would not gladly rest satisfied with himself? where is the man not actually absorbed in self-complacency, while he remains unacquainted with his true situation, or content with his own endowments, and ig-

* From John Calvin: *Institutes of the Christian Religion*, trans. by John Allen, vol. I, pp. 46–7, 75–6, 78–80, 618–19, 648–9; vol. II, pp. 140–2, 149, 220–1, 224, 371, 410–16. Copyright 1932 by Westminster Press. Reprinted by permission of Westminster Press.

norant or forgetful of his own misery? The knowledge of ourselves, therefore, is not only an incitement to seek after God, but likewise a considerable assistance towards finding him.

Predestination

The covenant of life not being equally preached to all, and among those to whom it is preached not always finding the same reception, this diversity discovers the wonderful depth of the Divine judgment. Nor is it to be doubted that this variety also follows, subject to the decision of God's eternal election. If it be evidently the result of the Divine will, that salvation is freely offered to some, and others are prevented from attaining it,—this immediately gives rise to important and difficult questions, which are incapable of any other explication, than by the establishment of pious minds in what ought to be received concerning election and predestination—a question, in the opinion of many, full of perplexity; for they consider nothing more unreasonable, than that, of the common mass of mankind, some should be predestinated to salvation, and others to destruction. But how unreasonably they perplex themselves will afterwards appear from the sequel of our discourse. Besides, the very obscurity which excites such dread, not only displays the utility of this doctrine, but shows it to be productive of the most delightful benefit. We shall never be clearly convinced as we ought to be, that our salvation flows from the fountain of God's free mercy, till we are acquainted with his eternal election, which illustrates the grace of God by this comparison, that he adopts not all promiscuously to the hope of salvation, but gives to some what he refuses to others. Ignorance of this principle evidently detracts from the Divine glory, and diminishes real humility. But according to Paul, what is so necessary to be known, never can be known, unless God, without any regard to works, chooses those whom he has decreed. "At this present time also, there is a remnant according to the election of grace. And if by grace, then it is no more of works; otherwise, grace is no more grace. But if it be of works, then it is no more grace; otherwise, work is no more work." If we need to be recalled to the origin of election, to prove that we obtain salvation from no other source than the mere goodness of God, they who desire to extinguish this principle, do all they can to obscure what ought to be magnificently and loudly celebrated, and to pluck up humility by the roots. In ascribing the salvation of the remnant of the people to the election of grace, Paul clearly testifies, that it is then only known that God saves whom he will of his mere good pleasure, and does not dispense a reward to which there can be no claim. They who shut the gates to prevent any one from presuming to approach and taste this doctrine, do no less injury to man than to God; for nothing else will be sufficient to produce in us suitable humility, or to impress us with a due sense of our great obligations to God. Nor is there any other basis for solid confidence, even according to the authority of Christ, who, to deliver us from all fear, and render us invincible amidst so many dangers, snares, and deadly conflicts, promises to preserve in safety all whom the Father has committed to his care. Whence we infer, that they who know not themselves to be God's peculiar people will be tortured with continual anxiety; and therefore, that the interest of all believers, as well as their own, is very badly consulted by those who, blind to the three advantages we have remarked, would wholly remove the foundation of our salvation. And hence the Church rises to our view, which otherwise, as Bernard justly observes, could neither be discovered nor recognized among creatures, being in two respects wonderfully concealed in the bosom of a blessed predestination, and in the mass of a miserable damnation. But before I enter on the subject itself, I must address some preliminary observations to two sorts of persons. The discussion of predestination—a subject of itself rather intricate—is made very perplexed, and therefore dangerous, by human curiosity, which no barriers can restrain from wandering into forbidden labyrinths, and soaring beyond its sphere, as if determined to leave none of the Divine secrets unscrutinized or unexplored. As we see multitudes every where guilty of this arrogance and presumption, and among them some who are not censurable in other respects, it is proper to admonish them of the bounds of their duty on this subject. First, then, let them remember that when they inquire into predestination, they penetrate the inmost recesses of Divine wisdom, where the careless and confident intruder will obtain no satisfaction to his curiosity, but will enter a labyrinth from which he will find no way to depart. For it is unreasonable that man should scrutinize with impunity those things which the Lord has determined to be hidden in himself; and investigate, even from eternity, that sublimity of wisdom which God would have us to adore and not comprehend, to promote our admiration of his glory. . . .

In conformity, therefore, to the clear doctrine of the Scripture, we assert, that by an eternal and immutable counsel, God has once for all determined, both whom he would admit to salvation, and whom he would condemn to destruction. We affirm that this counsel, as far as concerns the elect, is founded on his gratuitous mercy, totally irrespective of human merit; but that to those whom he devotes to condemnation, the gate of life is closed by a just and irreprehensible, but incomprehensible, judgment. In the elect, we consider calling as an evidence of election, and justification as another token of its manifestation, till they arrive in glory, which constitutes its completion. As God seals his elect by vocation and justification, so by excluding the reprobate from the knowledge of his name and the sanctification of his Spirit, he affords an indication of the judgment that awaits them.

The Scriptures

Before I proceed any further, it is proper to introduce some remarks on the authority of the Scripture, not only to prepare the mind to regard it with due reverence, but also to remove every doubt. For, when it is admitted to be a declaration of the word of God, no man can be so deplorably presumptuous, unless he be also destitute of common sense and of the common feelings of men, as to dare to derogate from the credit due to the speaker. But since we are not favoured with daily oracles from heaven, and since it is only in the Scriptures that the Lord hath been pleased to preserve his truth in perpetual remembrance, it obtains the same complete credit and authority with believers, when they are satisfied of its divine origin, as if they heard the very words pronounced by God himself. The subject, indeed, merits a diffuse discussion, and a most accurate examination. But the reader will pardon me, if I attend rather to what the design of this work admits, than to what the extensive nature of the present subject requires. But there has very generally prevailed a most pernicious error, that the Scriptures have only so much weight as is conceded to them by the suffrages of the Church; as though the eternal and inviolable truth of God depended on the arbitrary will of men. . . .

But such cavillers are completely refuted even by one word of the Apostle. He testifies that the church is "built upon the foundation of the apostles and prophets." If the doctrine of the prophets and apostles be the foundation of the Church, it must have been certain, antecedently to the existence of the Church. Nor is there any foundation for this cavil, that though the Church derive its origin from the Scriptures, yet it remains doubtful what writings are to be ascribed to the prophets and apostles, unless it be determined by the Church. For if the Christian Church has been from the beginning founded on the writings of the prophets and the preaching of the apostles, wherever that doctrine is found, the approbation of it has certainly preceded the formation of the Church; since without it the Church itself had never existed. . . .

It must be maintained, as I have before asserted, that we are not established in the belief of the doctrine till we are indubitably persuaded that God is its Author. The principal proof, therefore, of the Scriptures is every where derived from the character of the Divine Speaker. The prophets and apostles boast not of their own genius, or any of those talents which conciliate the faith of the hearers; nor do they insist on arguments from reason; but bring forward the sacred name of God, to compel the submission of the whole world. We must now see how it appears, not from probable supposition, but from clear demonstration, that this use of the divine name is neither rash nor fallacious. Now, if we wish to consult the true interest of our consciences; that they may not be unstable and wavering, the subjects of pepetual doubt; that they may not hesitate at the smallest scruples,—this persuasion must be sought from a higher source than human reasons, or judgments, or conjectures—even from the secret testimony of the Spirit. . . .

Let it be considered, then, as an undeniable truth, that they who have been inwardly taught by the Spirit, feel an entire acquiescence in the Scripture, and that it is self-authenticated, carrying with it its own evidence, and ought not to be made the subject of demonstration and arguments from reason; but it obtains the credit which it deserves with us by the testimony of the Spirit. For though it conciliate our reverence by its internal majesty, it never seriously affects us till it is confirmed by the Spirit in our hearts. Therefore, being illuminated by him, we now believe the divine original of the Scripture, not from our own judgment or that of others, but we esteem the certainty, that we have received it from God's own mouth by the ministry of men, to be superior to that of any human judgment, and equal to that of an intuitive perception of God himself in it.

The Christian Life

Although the Divine law contains a most excellent and well-arranged plan for the regulation of life, yet it has pleased the heavenly Teacher to conform men by a more accurate doctrine to the rule which he had prescribed in the law. And the principle of that doctrine is this—that it is the duty of believers to "present their bodies a living sacrifice, holy, acceptable unto God;" and that in this consists the legitimate worship of him. Hence is deduced an argument for exhorting them, "Be not conformed to this world; but be ye transformed by the renewing of your mind, that ye may prove what is that will of God." This is a very important consideration, that we are consecrated and dedicated to God; that we may not hereafter think, speak, meditate, or do any thing but with a view to his glory. For that which is sacred cannot, without great injustice towards him, be applied to unholy uses. If we are not our own, but the Lord's, it is manifest both what error we must avoid, and to what end all the actions of our lives are to be directed. We are not our own; therefore neither our reason nor our will should predominate in our deliberations and actions. We are not our own; therefore let us not propose it as our end, to seek what may be expedient for us according to the flesh. We are not our own; therefore let us, as far as possible, forget ourselves and all things that are ours. On the contrary, we are God's; to him, therefore, let us live and die. We are God's; therefore let his wisdom and will preside in all our actions. We are God's; towards him, therefore, as our only legitimate end, let every part of our lives be directed. O, how great a proficiency has that man made, who, having been taught that he is not his own, has taken the sovereignty and government of himself from his own reason, to surrender it to God! For as compliance with their own inclinations leads men most effectually to ruin, so to place no dependence on our own knowledge or will, but merely to follow the guidance of the

Lord, is the only way of safety. Let this, then, be the first step, to depart from ourselves, that we may apply all the vigour of our faculties to the service of the Lord. By service I mean, not that only which consists in verbal obedience, but that by which the human mind, divested of its natural carnality, resigns itself wholly to the direction of the Divine Spirit. Of this transformation, which Paul styles a renovation of the mind, though it is the first entrance into life, all the philosophers were ignorant. For they set up Reason as the sole directress of man; they think that she is exclusively to be attended to; in short, to her alone they assign the government of the conduct. But the Christian philosophy commands her to give place and submit to the Holy Spirit, so that now the man himself lives not, but carries about Christ living and reigning within him. . . .

But there is no way more certain or concise, than what we derive from a contempt of the present life, and meditation on a heavenly immortality. For thence follow two rules. The first is, "that they that have wives be as though they had none; and they that buy, as though they possessed not; and they that use this world, as not abusing it;" according to the direction of Paul: the second, that we should learn to bear penury with tranquillity and patience, as well as to enjoy abundance with moderation. He who commands us to use this world as though we used it not, prohibits not only all intemperance in eating and drinking, and excessive delicacy, ambition, pride, haughtiness, and fastidiousness in our furniture, our habitations, and our apparel, but every care and affection, which would either seduce or disturb us from thoughts of the heavenly life, and attention to the improvement of our souls. Now, it was anciently and truly observed by Cato, That there is a great concern about adorning the body, and a great carelessness about virtue; and it is an old proverb, That they who are much engaged in the care of the body, are generally negligent of the soul. Therefore, though the liberty of believers in external things cannot be reduced to certain rules, yet it is evidently subject to this law, That they should indulge themselves as little as possible; that, on the contrary, they should perpetually and resolutely exert themselves to retrench all superfluities and to restrain luxury; and that they should diligently beware lest they pervert into impediments things which were given for their assistance. . . .

The Scripture has also a third rule, by which it regulates the use of earthly things; of which something was said, when we treated of the precepts of charity. For it states, that while all these things are given to us by the Divine goodness, and appointed for our benefit, they are, as it were, deposits intrusted to our care, of which we must one day give an account. We ought, therefore, to manage them in such a manner that this alarm may be incessantly sounding in our ears, "Give an account of thy stewardship." Let it also be remembered by whom this account is demanded; that it is by him who has so highly recommended abstinence, sobriety, frugality, and modesty; who abhors profusion, pride, ostentation, and vanity; who approves of no other management of his blessings, than such as is connected with charity; who has with his own mouth already condemned all those pleasures which seduce the heart from chastity and purity, or tend to impair the understanding. . . .

Every thing pertaining to the perfect rule of a holy life, the Lord has comprehended in his law, so that there remains nothing for men to add to that summary. And he has done this, first, that, since all rectitude of life consists in the conformity of all our actions to his will, as their standard, we might consider him as the sole Master and Director of our conduct; and secondly, to show that he requires of us nothing more than obedience.

Ecclesiastical Discipline

That by the faith of the gospel Christ becomes ours, and we become partakers of the salvation procured by him, and of eternal happiness, has been explained in the preceding Book. But as our ignorance and slothfulness, and, I may add, the vanity of our minds, require external aids, in order to the production of faith in our hearts, and its increase and progressive advance even to its completion, God has provided such aids in compassion to our infirmity; and that the preaching of the gospel might be maintained, he has deposited this treasure with the Church. He has appointed pastors and teachers, that his people might be taught by their lips; he has invested them with authority; in short, he has omitted nothing that could contribute to a holy unity of faith, and to the establishment of good order. First of all, he has instituted Sacraments, which we know by experience to be means of the greatest utility for the nourishment and support of our faith. . . .

But as our present design is to treat of the *visible* Church, we may learn even from the title of *mother*, how useful and even necessary it is for us to know her; since there is no other way of entrance into life, unless we are conceived by her, born of her, nourished at her breast, and continually preserved under her care and government till we are divested of this mortal flesh, and "become like the angels." For our infirmity will not admit of our dismission from her school; we must continue under her instruction and discipline to the end of our lives. It is also to be remarked, that out of her bosom there can be no hope of remission of sins, or any salvation. . . . The paternal favour of God, and the peculiar testimony of the spiritual life, are restricted to his flock, to teach us that it is always fatally dangerous to be separated from the Church. . . .

The discipline of the Church . . . must be despatched in a few words, that we may proceed to the remaining subjects. Now, the discipline depends chiefly on the power of the keys, and the spiritual jurisdiction. To make this more easily understood, let us divide the Church into two principal orders—the clergy and the people. I use the word *clergy* as the common, though improper, appellation of those who execute the public ministry in the Church. We shall, first, speak of the common discipline to which all ought to be subject; and in the next place we shall proceed to the clergy, who, beside this common discipline, have a discipline peculiar to themselves. But as some have such a hatred of discipline, as to abhor the very name, they should attend to the following consideration: That if no society, and even no house, though containing only a small family, can be preserved in a proper state without discipline, this is far more necessary in the Church, the state of which ought to be the most orderly of all. As the saving doctrine of Christ is the soul of the Church, so discipline forms the ligaments which connect the members together, and keep each in its proper place. Whoever, therefore, either desire the abolition of all discipline, or obstruct its restoration, whether they act from design or inadvertency, they certainly promote the entire dissolution of the Church. For what will be the consequence, if every man be at liberty to follow his own inclinations? . . .

The first foundation of discipline consists in the use of private admonitions; that is to say, that if any one be guilty of a voluntary omission of duty, or conduct himself in an insolent manner, or discover a want of virtue in his life, or commit any act deserving of reprehension, he should suffer himself to be admonished; and that every one should study to admonish his brother, whenever occasion shall require; but that pastors and presbyters, beyond all others, should be vigilant in the discharge of this duty, being called by their office, not only to preach to the congregation, but also to admonish and exhort in private houses, if in any instances their public instructions may not have been sufficiently efficacious; as Paul inculcates, when he says, that he "taught publicly and from house to house," and protests himself to be "pure from the blood of all men," having "ceased not to warn every one night and day with tears." For the doctrine then obtains its full authority and produces its due effect, when the minister not only declares to all the people together what is their duty to Christ, but has the right and means of enforcing it upon them whom he observes to be inattentive, or not obedient to the doctrine. If any one either obstinately reject such admonitions, or manifest his contempt of them by persisting in his misconduct; after he shall have been admonished a second time in the presence of witnesses, Christ directs him to be summoned before the tribunal of the Church, that is, the assembly of the elders, and there to be more severely admonished by the public authority, that if he reverence the Church, he may submit and obey; but if this do not overcome him, and he still persevere in his iniquity, our Lord then commands him, as a despiser of the Church, to be excluded from the society of believers. . . .

Now, there are three ends proposed by the Church in those corrections, and in excommunication. The first is, that those who lead scandalous and flagitious lives, may not, to the dishonour of God, be numbered among Christians; as if his holy Church were a conspiracy of wicked and abandoned men. For as the Church is the body of Christ, it cannot be contaminated with such foul and putrid members without some ignominy being reflected upon the Head. . . . The second end is, that the good may not be corrupted, as is often the case, by constant association with the wicked. . . . The third end is, that those who are censured or excommunicated, confounded with the shame of their turpitude, may be led to repentance. . . .

From this discipline none were exempted; so that princes and plebeians yielded the same submission to it; and that with the greatest propriety, since it is evidently the discipline of Christ, to whom it is reasonable that all the sceptres and diadems of kings should be subject. Thus Theodosius when Ambrose excluded him from the privilege of communion, on account of a massacre perpetrated at Thessalonica, laid aside the ensigns of royalty with which he was invested, publicly in the Church bewailed his sin, which the deceitful suggestions of others had tempted him to commit, and implored pardon with groans and tears. For great kings ought not to think it any dishonour to prostrate themselves as suppliants before Christ the King of kings, nor ought they to be displeased at being judged by the Church. As they hear scarcely any thing in their courts but mere flatteries, it is the more highly necessary for them to receive correction from the Lord by the mouth of his *ministers;* they ought even to wish not to be spared by the *pastors,* that they may be spared by the Lord.

WALTER TRAVERS: *A Directory of Church Government* *

Walter Travers (1548?–1635) was one of the leading Puritan divines of Elizabethan England, and a friend of Calvin's successor in Geneva, Theodore Beza. In the 1580's he composed in Latin a book of ecclesiastical discipline for the English Presbyterians. It was hoped that eventually this discipline would supplant the Anglican establishment as the law of the land. This book was subsequently translated into English under the title *A Directory of Church Government,* and published in 1644.

THE DISCIPLINE of Christ's church, that is necessary for all times, is delivered by Christ, and set down in the Holy Scriptures; therefore the true and lawful discipline is to be fetched from thence, and from thence alone. And that which resteth upon any other foundation ought to be esteemed unlawful and counterfeit.

Of all particular churches, there is one and the same right, order, and

* Daniel Neal: *The History of the Puritans* (London: T. Tegg and Son; 1837), vol. III, pp. 491-2, 494, 496-8.

form: therefore also no one may challenge to itself any power over others: nor any right which doth not alike agree to others.

The ministers of public charges, in every particular church, ought to be called and appointed to their charges by a lawful ecclesiastical calling, such as hereafter is set down.

All these, for the divers regard of their several kinds, are of equal power amongst themselves.

No man can be lawfully called to public charge in any church, but he that is fit to discharge the same. And none is to be accounted fit, but he that is endued with the common gifts of all the godly; that is, with faith, and a blameless life: and farther also, with those that are proper to that ministry wherein he is to be used, and necessary for the executing of the same; whereupon, for trial of those gifts, some convenient way and examination are to be used.

The party to be called must first be elected: then he is to be ordained to that charge whereunto he is chosen, by the prayers of that church whereunto he is to be admitted; the mutual duties of him and of the church being before laid open.

The ministers of the church are, first, they that are ministers of the word. In their examination, it is specially to be taken heed unto, that they be apt to teach, and tried men, not utterly unlearned, nor newly planted and converted to the faith.

Now these ministers of the word are, first, pastors, which do administer the word and sacraments; then, teachers, which are occupied in wholesome doctrine.

Besides, there are also elders, which watch over the life and behaviour of every man; and deacons, which have care over the poor.

Farther, in every particular church there ought to be a presbytery, which is a consistory, and, as it were, a senate of elders. Under the name of elders here are contained, they who in the church minister doctrine, and they who are properly called elders.

By the common counsel of the eldership, all things are directed that belong to the state of their church. First, such as belong to the guidance of the whole body of it in the holy and common assembly, gathered together in the name of the Lord, that all things may be done in them duly, orderly, and to edification. 2. Then also such as pertain to particular persons. First, to all the members of that church, that the good may enjoy all the privileges that belong unto them; that the wicked may be corrected with ecclesiastical censures, according to the quality of the fault, private and public, by admonishing and by removing either from the Lord's supper by suspension (as it is commonly called,) or out of the church by excommunication. The which belong specially to the ministers of public charge in the church to their calling, either to be begun or ended, and ended either by relieving or punishing them, and that for a time by suspension, or altogether by deposition.

For directing of the eldership, let the pastors be set over it; or if there be more pastors than one in the same church, let the pastors do it in their turns.

But yet in all the greater affairs of the church, as in excommunicating of any, and in choosing and deposing of church-ministers, nothing may be concluded without the knowledge and consent of the church.

Particular churches ought to yield mutual help one to another; for which cause they are to communicate amongst themselves.

The end of this communicating together is, that all things in them may be so directed, both in regard of doctrine, and also of discipline, as by the word of God they ought to be.

Therefore the things that belong hereunto are determined by the common opinion of those who meet so to communicate together; and whatsoever is to be amended, furthered, or procured, in any of those several churches that belong to that assembly. Wherein albeit no particular church hath power over another, yet every particular church of the same resort, meeting and counsel, ought to obey the opinion of more churches with whom they communicate.

For holding of these meetings and assemblies, there are to be chosen, by every church belonging to that assembly, principal men from among the elders, who are to have their instructions from them, and so to be sent to the assembly. There must also be a care had, that the things they shall return to have been godly agreed on by the meetings, be diligently observed by the churches.

* * *

Let him that shall preach choose some part of the canonical Scripture to expound, and not of the Apocrypha. Farther, in his ordinary ministry, let him not take postils, as they are called but some, whole book of the Holy Scripture, especially of the New Testament, to expound in order: in choice whereof regard is to be had both of the minister's ability, and of the edification of the church.

He that preacheth must perform two things: the first, that his speech be uncorrupt; which is to be considered both in regard of the doctrine, that it be holy, sound, wholesome and profitable to edification; not devilish, heretical, leavened, corrupt, fabulous, curious, or contentious; and also in respect of the manner of it, that it be proper to the place which is handled, that is, which either is contained plainly in the very words; or if it be gathered by consequent, that the same be fit and clear, and such as may rise upon the property of the word, grace of speech, and suit of the matter; and not be allegorical, strange, wrested, or far-fetched. Now let that which is such, and chiefly which is fittest for the times and occasions of the church, be delivered. Farther, let the explication, confirmation, enlargement, and application, and the whole treatise and handling of it, be in the vulgar tongue; and let the whole confirmation and proof be made by arguments, testimonies, and examples, taken only out of the Holy Scriptures, applied fitly, and according to the natural meaning of the places that are alleged.

The second thing to be performed by him that preacheth, is a reverend gravity; this is considered first in the style, phrase, and manner of speech, that it be spiritual, pure, proper, simple, and applied to the capacity of the people; nor such as human wisdom teacheth, nor savouring of new-fangledness, nor either so affectate as it may serve for pomp and ostentation, or so careless and base, as becometh not ministers of the word of God. Secondly, it is also to be regarded as well in ordering the voice, in which a care must be had, that (avoiding the keeping always of one tone) it may be equal, and both rise and fall by degrees: as also in ordering the gesture, wherein (the body being upright) the guiding and ordering the whole body is to follow the voice, there being avoided in it all unseemly gestures of the head, or other parts, and often turning of the body to divers sides. Finally, let the gesture be grave, modest, and seemly, not utterly none, nor too much neither, like the gestures of players or fencers.

*   *   *

Let children be instructed in schools, both in other learning, and especially in the catechism, that they may repeat it by heart, and understand it: when they are so instructed, let them be brought to the Lord's supper, after they have been examined by the minister, and allowed by him.

*   *   *

Let the elders know every particular house and person of the church, that they may inform the minister of the condition of every one, and the deacons of the sick and poor, that they may take care to provide for them: they are not to be perpetual; neither yet easily to be changed.

*   *   *

In the consistory the most voices are to be yielded unto. In it only ecclesiastical things are to be handled. Of them, first they are to be dealt with such as belong to the common direction of the public assembly, in the order of liturgy, or divine service, sermon, prayers, sacraments, marriages, and burials. Then with such also as pertain to the oversight of every one, and their particular deeds. Farther, they are to cause such things as shall be thought meet, to be registered and written in a book.

*   *   *

None is to be complained of unto the consistory, unless first the matter being uttered with silencing the parties' names, if it seem meet so to be done by the judgment of the consistory.

In private and less faults, the precept of Christ, Matt. xviii. is to be kept.

Greater and public offences are to be handled by the consistory. Farther, public offences are to be esteemed, first, Such as are done openly before all, or whomsoever, the whole church knowing of it. Secondly,

Such as be done in a public place, albeit few know it. Thirdly, That are made such by pertinacity and contempt. Fourthly, That for the heinousness of the offence are to be punished with some grievous civil punishment.

They that are to be excommunicated, being in public charge in the church, are to be deposed also from their charges. They also are to be discharged that are unfit for the ministry, by reason of their ignorance, or of some incurable disease; or by any other such cause, are disabled to perform their ministry: but in the room of such as are disabled by means of sickness or age, let another be placed without the reproach of him that is discharged; and farther, so as the reverence of the ministry may remain unto him, and he may be provided for, liberally and in good order.

When there is question concerning a heretic complained of to the consistory, straight let two or three neighbour ministers be called, men godly and learned, and free from that suspicion, by whose opinion he may be suspended, till such time as the conference may take knowledge of his cause.

The obstinate, after admonition by the consistory, though the fault have not been so great, are to be suspended from the communion; and if they continue in their obstinacy, this shall be the order to proceed to their excommunication. Three several sabbath-days after the sermon, publicly let be declared the offence committed by the offender. The first sabbath let not the offender's name be published: the second let it be declared, and withal a certain day of the week named, to be kept for that cause in fasting and prayer: the third let warning be given of his excommunicating to follow the next sabbath after, except there may be shewed some sufficient cause to the contrary: so upon the fourth sabbath day, let the sentence of excommunication be pronounced against him, that his spirit may be saved in the day of the Lord.

He that hath committed great offences, opprobrious to the church, and to be grievously punished by the magistrate's authority; albeit he profess his repentance in words, yet for the trial thereof, and to take away the offence, let him for a time be kept from the communion; which how often and how long it is to be done, let the consistory, according to their discretion, determine; after which, if the party repent, he is brotherly to be received again, but not until he have openly professed his repentance before the church, by consent whereof he should have been excommunicated.

The Holy Community of Northampton, England *

> There is on record a remarkable attempt to realize in an English market town Calvin's conception of the Holy Community. In 1571 the ministers

* John Strype: *Annals of the Reformation* (Oxford: Clarendon Press; 1824), vol. II, pt. II, pp. 133-6.

and ruling oligarchy of Northampton, England, issued a series of orders for the disciplining of its inhabitants which are reminiscent of Calvin's own *Ordonnances ecclésiastiques* for Geneva (1541). These orders were published with the consent of the Bishop of Peterborough and the justices of the peace within the county and town.

I. THE SINGING and playing of organs, beforetime accustomed in the quire, is put down, and the common prayer there accustomed to be said, brought down into the body of the church among the people, before whom the same is used according to the queen's book, with singing psalms before and after the sermon.

II. There is in the chief church every Tuesday and Thursday, from nine of the clock until ten in the morning, read a lecture of the scripture, beginning with the confession in the Book of Common Prayer, and ending with prayer and confession of the faith.

III. There is in the same church, every Sunday and holyday, after morning prayer, a sermon, the people singing the psalm before and after.

IV. The service be ended in every parish church by nine of the clock in the morning, every Sunday and holyday; to the end the people may resort to the sermon in the same church. And that every minister give warning to the parishioners in the time of common prayer, to repair to the sermon there; except they have a sermon in their own parish church.

V. That after prayers done, in the time of sermon or catechising, none sit in the streets, or walk up and down abroad, or otherwise occupy themselves vainly, upon such penalties as shall be appointed.

VI. The youth, at the end of evening prayer, every Sunday and holyday, (before all the elder people,) are examined in a portion of Calvin's catechism, which by the reader is expounded unto them; and holdeth an hour.

VII. There is a general communion once every quarter, in every parish church, with a sermon; which is by the minister at common prayer warned four several Sundays before every communion, with exhortation to the people to prepare for that day.

VIII. One fortnight before each communion, the minister with the churchwardens maketh a circuit from house to house, to take the names of the communicants, and to examine the state of their lives. Among whom if any discord be found, the parties are brought before the mayor and his brethren, being assisted by the preacher and other gentlemen. Before whom there is reconcilement made, or else correction, or putting the party from the communion, which will not live in charity.

IX. Immediately after the communion, the minister, &c. returneth to every house, to understand who have not received the communion, according to the common order taken; and certifieth it to the mayor, &c.

who, with the minister, examineth the matter, and useth means of persuasion to induce them to their duties.

X. Every communion day each parish hath two communions; the one for servants and officers, to begin at five of the clock in the morning, with a sermon of an hour, and to end at eight: the other for masters and dames, &c. to begin at nine the same day, with like sermon, and to end at twelve. . . .

XII. There is on every other Saturday, and now every Saturday, from nine to eleven of the clock in the morning, an exercise of the ministers both of town and country, about the interpretation of scriptures. The ministers speaking one after another, do handle some text; and the same openly among the people. That done, the ministers do withdraw themselves into a privy place, there to confer among themselves, as well touching doctrine as good life, manners, and other orders meet for them. There is also a weekly assembly every Thursday, after the lecture, by the mayor and his brethren, assisted with the preacher, minister, and other gentlemen, appointed to them by the bishop, for the correction of discord made in the town: as for notorious blasphemy, whoredom, drunkenness, railing against religion, or preachers thereof; scolds, ribalds, or such like. Which faults are each Thursday presented unto them in writing by certain sworn men, appointed for that service in each parish. So by the bishop's authority and the mayor's joined together, being assisted with certain other gentlemen in the commission of the peace, evil life is corrected, God's glory set forth, and the people brought in good obedience. . . .

XVII. There is hereafter to take place, order that all ministers of the shire, once every quarter of the year, upon one month's warning given, repair to the said town; and there, after a sermon in the church heard, to withdraw themselves into a place appointed within the said church; and there privately to confer among themselves of their manners and lives. Among whom if any be found in fault, for the first time, exhortation is made to him among all the brethren to amend. And so likewise the second and third time, by complaint from all the brethren, he is committed unto the bishop for his correction.

3. Radical Protestantism

Menno Simons *

Menno Simons (1496–1561) was the leader of the radical sect of Mennonites in Holland and northwest Germany. Menno went through one

* *The Complete Works of Menno Simons*, Eng. trans. (Elkhart, Indiana: John F. Funk and Brothers; 1871), vol. I, p. 29; vol. II, pp. 37–8, 215, 345–6.

of those soul-struggles that were so common in the early sixteenth century. In 1535, as the result of reading the New Testament and Anabaptist tracts, he abandoned the Roman priesthood to become an evangelical preacher. The New Testament was the yardstick by which he measured everything. On its authority he rejected war, oaths, and capital punishment. As the following selections from several of his pamphlets show, he followed the Anabaptists in teaching the radical doctrine of a "separated" church, membership in which depended upon individual religious experience.

The Church

THOSE who are one with Christ in Spirit, love and life; who teach that which was commanded by Christ, such as repentance and the peaceable gospel of grace, which he himself received of God, and taught to the world, all those who hear, believe, keep and fulfill the same in true fear, are the church of Christ, the truly believing, christian church, the body and bride of Christ, the ark of the Lord, the mount and paradise, the house, people, city and temple of God, the spiritual Eve, flesh of Christ's flesh and bone of his bone, children of God, the chosen generation, the spiritual seed of Abraham, children of the promise, branches and trees of righteousness, sheep of the heavenly pasture, kings and priests, a holy begotten people which is God's own. Besides, they are chosen to proclaim the darkness into his marvelous light, Col. 1:14; 1 Cor. 12:27; Heb. 12:22; Matt. 5:14; 2 Cor. 6:16; 11:5; Eph. 5:30; 1 Pet. 2:9; Rom. 9:8; Isa. 61:3; Ps. 95:7; 79:13; Rev. 1:6; 1 Pet. 2:9.

All those who have not the Spirit, love and life of Christ, nor sincerely desire them, have no share in the glorious Jerusalem of God, that is, in Christ's church; no matter whether they be teacher or disciple, prince or subject, man or woman; besides they have neither prayer, nor God, nor Christ, nor promise, nor remission of sins, nor any sure consolation in eternal life, so long as they do not sincerely repent, receive God's word, and fulfill it in the true fear, as Christ himself says, "He that believeth not is already condemned," Jn. 3:18. . . .

All the evangelical Scriptures teach us that the church of Christ was and is, in doctrine, life and worship, a people separated from the world. It also was in the times of the Old Testament, 2 Cor. 6:17; 1 Peter 2:9, 10; Exod. 19:12.

Since the church always was and shall be a separate people, as has been heard, and since it is as clear as the meridian sun, that for centuries no difference has been made between the church and the world, but that they have been indiscriminately blended together in baptism, Supper, life and worship, which is so plainly contrary to all Scripture, therefore we feel ourselves constrained by the Spirit and word of God, and not of our own account, to gather together, to the praise of Jesus Christ and to the salvation of our neighbors, and not unto us, but unto the Lord a pious and penitent church or community from all untrue and deceiving sects of the whole world, not contrary to the doctrine and example of Christ Jesus and the apostles, as Gellius falsely accuses us, but according to the Spirit, doctrine and example of Jesus Christ, manifested unto us; yea, gather them *patiently* under the cross of misery, in spite of all the violence and gates of hell, and not by force of arms and persecution as is the custom of the world, but separate them from it, as the Scriptures teach, that they may be an admonition, example and reproach to the impenitent world as has already been heard.

Baptism

My worthy, kind brethren, because the holy, christian baptism is a washing of regeneration, according to the doctrine of Paul, therefore none can be washed therewith, to the pleasure and will of God, but those alone who are regenerated through the word of God; for we are not regenerated because of baptism, as may be perceived in the infants who have been baptized; but we are baptized because we are regenerated by faith in God's word, as regeneration is not the result of baptism, but baptism the result of regeneration. This cannot well be controverted by any man, by force of the Scriptures. . . .

Luther writes, that children should be baptized on account of their own faith, and adds, "If children had no faith, then their baptism would be blaspheming the sacrament," &c. It appears to me, to be a great error in this learned man, through whose writings at first the Lord effected much good, that he maintained that children, without knowledge and understanding, had faith, while the Scriptures teach so plainly, that they know not good from evil, that they cannot discern right from wrong, and he (Luther) says that faith is dormant and concealed in children even as in a believing person who is asleep, till they arrive at the years of understanding. If Luther writes this as his sincere opinion, he writes much in vain concerning faith and its power, but if he writes to please men, may God have mercy upon him, for I know of a truth it is only human reason and the invention of man; but it shall not make void the word and ordinance of the Lord. We do not read in Scripture that the Apostles baptized a single believer while asleep. They baptized those who were awake, and not the slumbering. Why then do they baptize their children before that sleeping faith awakes and is confessed by them? . . .

Since we have not a single command in the Scriptures that infants are to be baptized, or that the apostles did practice it; we modestly confess, with a good conscience, that infant baptism is but human invention; a selfish notion; a perversion of the ordinance of Christ; a manifest abomination, standing in the holy place, where it ought, properly, not to be, Matt. 24:15.

ROBERT BARCLAY: *An Apology for the Quakers* *

Robert Barclay (1648–90) was the outstanding Quaker theologian of the seventeenth century. Most of the followers of George Fox belonged to the lower classes, but Barclay was an aristocrat and scholar who made it his life work to demonstrate that Quaker teachings were intellectually respectable. Both he and his father revolted from the Calvinistic Kirk in Scotland and joined the Society of Friends. His most considerable work was the *Apology* which was published in Amsterdam in 1676. The following selections are from the section entitled "Of Immediate Revelation," in which Barclay expounds the Quaker doctrine of the "inner light."

SEEING *no man knoweth the Father but the Son, and he to whom the Son revealeth him;* and seeing *the revelation of the Son is* in *and* by *the Spirit;* therefore the testimony of the Spirit is that alone by which the true knowledge of God hath been, is, and can be only revealed; who as, by the moving of his own Spirit, he disposed the *chaos* of this world into that wonderful order in which it was in the beginning, and created man a living soul, to rule and govern it, so by the revelation of the same Spirit he hath manifested himself all along unto the sons of men, both patriarchs, prophets, and apostles; which revelations of God by the Spirit, whether by outward voices and appearances, dreams, or inward objective manifestations in the heart, were of old the formal object of their faith, and remain yet so to be; since *the object of the saints' faith is the same in all ages, though held forth under divers administrations.* Moreover, these divine inward revelations, which we make absolutely necessary for the building up of true faith, neither do nor can ever contradict the outward testimony of the scriptures, or right and sound reason. Yet from hence it will not follow, that these divine revelations are to be subjected to the test, either of the outward testimony of the scriptures, or of the natural reason of man, as to a more noble or certain rule and touch-stone; for this divine revelation, and inward illumination, is that which is evident and clear of itself, forcing, by its own evidence and clearness, the well-disposed understanding to assent, irresistibly moving the same thereunto, even as the common principles of natural truths do move and incline the mind to a natural assent: as, *that the whole is greater than its part; that two contradictories can neither be both true, nor both false.* . . .

We then trust to and confide in this Spirit, because we know, and certainly believe, that it can only lead us aright, and never mislead us; and from this certain confidence it is that we affirm, that no revelation com-

* Robert Barclay: *An Apology for the true Christian Divinity* (New York: Samuel Wood and Sons; 1831), pp. 18–19, 63–7.

ing from it can ever contradict the scripture's testimony nor right reason: not as making this a more certain rule to ourselves, but as condescending to such, who not discerning the revelations of the Spirit, as they proceed purely from God, will try them by these *mediums*. Yet those that have their spiritual senses, and can savour the things of the Spirit, as it were *in prima instantia*, i.e. at the first blush, can discern them without, or before they apply them either to scripture or reason; just as a good *astronomer* can calculate an eclipse infallibly, by which he can conclude (if the order of nature continue, and some strange and unnatural revolution intervene not) there will be an eclipse of the sun or moon such a day, and such an hour; yet can he not persuade an ignorant rustic of this, until he visibly see it. So also a *mathematician* can infallibly know, by the rules of art, that the three angles of a right triangle are equal to two right angles; yea, can know them more certainly than any man by measure. And some *geometrical demonstrations* are by all acknowledged to be infallible, which can be scarcely discerned or proved by the senses; yet if a *geometer* be at the pains to certify some ignorant man concerning the certainty of his art, by condescending to measure it, and make it obvious to his senses, it will not thence follow, that that measuring is so certain as the demonstration itself, or that the demonstration would be uncertain without it.

But to make an end, I shall add one argument to prove, that this inward, immediate, objective revelation, which we have pleaded for all along, is the only sure, certain, and unmoveable foundation of all *Christian faith;* which argument, when well weighed, I hope will have weight with all sorts of Christians, and it is this:

That which all professors of *Christianity*, of what kind soever, are forced ultimately to recur unto, when pressed to the last; that for and because of which all other foundations are recommended, and accounted worthy to be believed, and without which they are granted to be of no weight at all, must needs be the only most true, certain, and unmoveable foundation of all Christian faith.

But inward, immediate, objective revelation by the Spirit, is that which all professors of *Christianity*, of what kind soever, are forced ultimately to recur unto, &c.

Therefore, &c.

The proposition is so evident, that it will not be denied; the assumption shall be proved by parts.

And First, as to the *Papists*, they place their foundation in the judgment of the *church* and *tradition*. If we press them to say, Why they believe as the *church* doth? their answer is, *Because the church is always led by the infallible Spirit*. So here the *leading of the Spirit* is the utmost foundation. Again, if we ask them, Why we ought to trust *tradition?* they answer, *Because these traditions were delivered us by the doctors and fathers of the church; which doctors and fathers, by the revelation of the Holy Ghost, commanded the church to observe them.* Here again all ends in the revelation of the Spirit.

And for the *Protestants* and *Socinians*, both which acknowledge the scriptures to be the foundation and rule of their faith; the one as subjectively influenced by the Spirit of God to use them, the other as managing them with and by their own reason; ask both, or either of them, Why they trust in the *scriptures*, and take them to be their rule? their answer is, *Because we have in them the mind of God delivered unto us by those to whom these things were inwardly, immediately, and objectively revealed by the Spirit of God;* and not because this or that man wrote them, but because the *Spirit of God* dictated them.

It is strange then that men should render that so uncertain and dangerous to follow, upon which alone the certain ground and foundation of their own faith is built; or that they should shut themselves out from that holy fellowship with God, which only is enjoyed in the Spirit, in which we are commanded both to walk and live.

If any reading these things find themselves moved, by the strength of these scripture-arguments, to assent and believe such revelations necessary, and yet find themselves strangers to them, which, as I observed in the beginning, is the cause that this is so much gainsaid and contradicted, let them know, that it is not because it is ceased to become the privilege of every true Christian that they do not feel it, but rather because they are not so much Christians by nature as by name; and let such know, that the secret *light* which shines in the heart, and reproves unrighteousness, is the small beginning of the revelation of God's Spirit, which was first sent into the world to reprove it of sin, *John* xvi. 8. And as by forsaking iniquity thou comest to be acquainted with that heavenly voice in thy heart, thou shalt feel, as the old man, or the natural man, that savoureth not the things of God's kingdom, is put off, with his evil and corrupt affections and lusts; I say, thou shalt feel the new man, or the spiritual birth and babe raised, which hath its spiritual senses, and can see, feel, taste, handle, and smell the things of the Spirit; but till then the knowledge of things spiritual is but as an historical faith. But as the description of the light of the sun, or of curious colours to a blind man, who, though of the largest capacity, cannot so well understand it by the most acute and lively description, as a child can by seeing them; so neither can the natural man, of the largest capacity, by the best words, even scripture-words, so well understand the *mysteries of God's kingdom*, as the least and weakest child who tasteth them, by having them revealed *inwardly* and *objectively* by the Spirit.

Wait then for this in the small revelation of that pure light which first reveals things more known; and as thou becomest fitted for it, thou shalt receive more and more, and by a living experience easily refute their ignorance, who ask, How dost thou know that thou art actuated by the Spirit of God? Which will appear to thee a question no less ridiculous, than to ask one whose eyes are open, How he knows the sun shines at noon-day?

4. *The Catholic Reformation*

Ignatius Loyola and Jesuit Education *

> The Society of Jesus, confirmed by papal bull in 1540, was the heart and soul of the Catholic (or Counter) Reformation. Almost from the beginning, the Jesuit leaders appreciated the importance of education for combating Protestantism and spreading the Catholic faith throughout the world. Accordingly, Part IV of *The Constitutions of the Society of Jesus*, written by the founder and first General of the Society, St. Ignatius Loyola (1491–1556), formulated general rules for Jesuit colleges and universities, for the instruction of laymen ("externs") as well as future priests and missionaries. The famous *Ratio Studiorum*, issued to the Society by General Aquaviva in 1599, became the official Jesuit pedagogical guide down to the suppression of the Society in 1773. At the time it was issued there were already over 300 Jesuit colleges in existence.

The Constitutions of the Society of Jesus, Part IV

SINCE the direct objective at which the Society aims is to help the souls of its members and of the neighbor to attain to the final end for which they were created, and since in addition to setting a good moral example, learning and methods of presenting it are necessary for the attaining of this end, therefore, after it seems that a fitting foundation for self-denial and for the necessary progress in virtue has been laid for those who have been admitted to probation, the education in letters and of the manner of utilizing them, so that they can aid to a better knowledge and service of God, our Creator and Lord, will be treated. . . .

It is for this purpose that the Society embraces colleges and sometimes even universities or *Studia generalia*, to which they may go who give a good indication of their character in the houses, while they are on probation, and yet are not sufficiently instructed in the doctrine necessary for our Rule, and where they may be instructed in this doctrine and in other things which pertain to the aid of souls. First, therefore, we shall treat of those things which pertain to the college, and then of what belongs to

* By permission from *St. Ignatius and the Ratio Studiorum*, edited by Edward A. Fitzpatrick. Copyright, 1933. McGraw-Hill Book Co., Inc. Pp. 49, 51, 64, 68–70, 81, 100, 106–07, 155–6, 160–1, 167–8, 170.

the university with the help which the Divine Wisdom will deign to grant us for His own glory and praise.

*   *   *

Besides the sacraments of confession and communion (to which they shall go every eight days) and besides Mass which they shall hear every day, they are to devote one hour a day to the recitation of the Office of the Blessed Virgin, and to examining their consciences twice a day, together with other prayers according to each one's devotion to fill up the mentioned hour if it is not already filled. Let them do all according to the command and judgment of their Superiors to whom they owe obedience in the place of Christ. . . .

Since the aim of the doctrine which is studied in this Society is with the aid of Divine grace to further the interests of their own souls and the souls of their neighbors, this, therefore, shall be the measure in general and for particular persons. From this measure therefore let it be decided what studies ours shall devote themselves to and how far they shall go in them. Speaking in general, the humane letters of the different tongues, and logic, natural and moral philosophy, metaphysics, and theology both scholastic and what is called "positive" (Explanation B), and sacred Scripture will conduce toward this end, and those who are sent to the colleges will pursue the studies of these faculties.

(Explanation B) If in college there is not sufficient time to read the Councils, the Decrees, the Holy Doctors, and the other books on morals, after they have left the colleges each one can in private study and with the approval of his Superiors finish them, especially if he has laid a solid foundation in scholastic philosophy. . . .

Let them follow in each faculty that teaching which is safer and more approved (Explanation E) and the authors who teach it; the responsibility for this will be in the hands of the Rector (who is to follow what shall be determined in the whole Society to be for the greater glory of God).

(Explanation E) No lectures should be given on those parts of books of humane letters which are contrary to virtue. The Society may use the rest as the "spoils of the Egyptians." The works of Christians, even though they may be good, are not to be read if the author is bad, lest some become attached to the author. . . .

Taking into account with due reason not only the progress in letters of our Scholastics but also the progress in letters and morals of externs whom we take to be instructed in our colleges, let public schools be opened where it can be done conveniently, at least in the liberal arts. In regard to the more advanced disciplines, schools may be opened according to the needs of the locality in which our colleges are situated, always keeping before our eyes what would be more pleasing to God. . . .

*   *   *

Since the aim of the Society and of its pursuits is to help the neighbor to a knowledge and love of God and to the salvation of their souls, and since for this end the chief means is the faculty of theology, the universities of the Society will lean most heavily upon this department, and it will treat thoroughly through suitable professors what pertain to scholastic doctrine and to the Sacred Scriptures and even as much of positive theology as is appropriate to our end (not touching, however, on that part of the Canons which gives rise to litigation).

And since instruction in theology and the application of it (especially in these times) demands a knowledge of the humane letters both Latin and Greek and of the Hebrew tongue, suitable professors in these subjects also, and in sufficient numbers, shall be secured. Professors of other languages may also be secured such as Chaldaic, Arabic, Indian, when these seem necessary or useful for the mentioned end, taking into account difference of country and the reasons which suggest the study of these languages. . . .

In general (as was said in treating of colleges), those books are to form the subject of lectures which are considered in any subject to be of solid and sound doctrine. Those are not to be touched whose doctrine or whose authors are suspect. In each university these ought to be listed. In theology the Old and New Testament are to be lectured upon, and the scholastic doctrine of St. Thomas, and in that part of theology which is called "positive" those authors are to be chosen who seem to contribute most to our aim. . . .

In regard to the books in the classical languages of Latin and Greek let the universities as well as the colleges, as far as possible, abstain from reading to youths books in which there is anything that can hurt good morals (Explanation D), unless the objectionable words and subjects are expurgated.

(Explanation D) If some cannot be expurgated at all, as Terence, then they should not be read at all; lest the kind of subjects offend the purity of souls.

In logic and natural philosophy, moral philosophy, and metaphysics, the doctrine of Aristotle is to be followed.

Ratio Studiorum of 1599

Rules for the Professor of Sacred Scripture

1. *Special Attention to Literal Meaning.*—He shall realize that his duties are to explain sacred literature piously, learnedly, and seriously, according to the true and literal meaning, in order to strengthen true faith in God and the establishment of sound morals.

2. *The Vulgate Edition.*—Among his other duties, it is especially important that he defend the version adopted by the Church. . . .

4. *Hebrew and Greek Text.*—He shall present examples from the

Hebrew and Greek, when it is advantageous, but briefly; but he shall do this only when some difference between these and the Vulgate edition needs to be reconciled, or when the idioms of the other languages afford greater insight or understanding. . . .

6. *Following Explanations of Popes and Councils.*—If the canons of Popes or Councils, especially General Councils, indicate the literal meaning of any passage, he shall defend this as literal; he shall not add any other literal meanings, unless led by unusually strong conjectures. If they set forth, according to custom, any meaning with a view to strengthening any dogma of faith, he shall teach this meaning as certain, whether literal or mystic.

7. *Following the Footsteps of the Fathers.*—He shall reverently follow the footsteps of the holy Fathers; if he finds them agreed on any literal or allegorical interpretation, especially when their words are clear, and if they professedly consider any point in Scripture or dogma, he shall not differ from them; if he does not find any such, then from their various explanations he shall select one toward which the Church has shown partiality for many years. . . .

Rules for the Professor of Scholastic Theology

1. *Duty.*—He shall realize that it is his duty to join a well-founded subtlety in disputation with an orthodox faith and devotion in such a way that the former shall especially serve the latter.

2. *Following St. Thomas.*—All members of our Order shall follow the teaching of St. Thomas in scholastic theology, and consider him as their special teacher; they shall center all their efforts in him so that their pupils may esteem him as highly as possible. However, they should realize that they are not confined to him so closely that they are never permitted to depart from him in any matter, since even those who especially profess to be Thomists occasionally depart from him, and it would not befit the members of our Order to be bound to St. Thomas more tightly than the Thomists themselves. . . .

5. *Regard for Faith and Devotion.*—In teaching, he shall first have regard for strengthening faith and fostering devotion. Wherefore, in those questions which St. Thomas does not explicitly treat, no one shall teach anything which does not accord with the interpretation of the Church and with her traditions, or which tends to weaken the foundation of true devotion. . . .

Rules for the Professor of Philosophy

1. *Purpose.*—Since the arts and the natural sciences prepare the mind for theology and help to a perfect knowledge and use of it and of themselves aid in reaching this end, the instructor, seeking in all things sincerely the honor and glory of God, shall so treat them as to prepare his

hearers and especially ours for theology and stir them up greatly to the knowledge of their Creator.

2. *How Far Aristotle Is to Be Followed.*—In matters of any importance let him not depart from Aristotle unless something occurs which is foreign to the doctrine which academies everywhere approve of; much more if it is opposed to the orthodox faith, and if there are any arguments of this or any other philosopher against the faith, he will endeavor earnestly to refute them according to the Lateran Council.

3. *Authors Hostile to Christianity.*—He shall not read without careful selection or bring into class interpreters of Aristotle who are out of harmony with the Christian religion and he will take care that his students do not become influenced by them.

4. *Averroes.*—For this reason he shall not treat of the digressions of Averroes (and the same judgment holds for others of this kind) in any separate treatise, and if anything good is to be cited from him, let him bring it out without praise and, if possible, let him show that he has taken it from some other source. . . .

5. And in order that the second year may be given up entirely to physics towards the end of the first year he will begin a rather full disputation about science and into this disputation he will bring the prolegomena to physics, such as the divisions of the sciences, abstractions, theories, practices, sub-alternation, and likewise the different methods of proceeding in physics and mathematics which Aristotle treats in the second book of *Physics*. And finally whatever is said about definition in the second book of the *De anima.* . . .

10. *What is to be given or omitted the second year.*—In the second year he will explain eight books of the physics, the books *De coelo* and the first book *De generatione*. In the eight books of the physics the text of books 6 and 7 will be given in summary, and also the text of the first book from that part which deals with the opinions of the ancients. In the eighth book let him not take any disputation about the number of intelligences or about liberty or about infinity of the prime mover, but these matters will be discussed in metaphysics, and only according to the opinion of Aristotle. . . .

5. *Protestantism and Politics*

Richard Hooker: *The Laws of Ecclesiastical Polity* *

Richard Hooker (1554?–1600) was the chief literary and scholarly ornament of the Church of England under Queen Elizabeth. His great work,

* Richard Hooker: *Works*, ed. by John Keble (Oxford: Oxford University Press; 1845), vol. III, pp. 327–30, 340–4, 366–7.

The Laws of Ecclesiastical Polity (first four books, 1594), was written at Archbishop Whitgift's request, as a defence of the Elizabethan religious establishment against the Puritans. But far from being merely a tract for the times, it represented a philosophical discussion of the whole problem of political order and obedience. The following selections are from the eighth book, not published until after Hooker's death, in which he discusses the validity of the Royal Supremacy in ecclesiastical affairs.

WE COME now to the last thing whereof there is controversy moved, namely *the power of supreme jurisdiction*, which for distinction's sake we call *the power of ecclesiastical dominion*.

It was not thought fit in the Jew's commonwealth, that the exercise of supremacy ecclesiastical should be denied unto him, to whom the exercise of chiefty civil did appertain; and therefore their kings were invested with both. . . .

According to the pattern of which example, the like power in causes ecclesiastical is by the laws of this realm annexed unto the crown. And there are which imagine, that kings, being mere lay persons, do by this means exceed the lawful bounds of their calling. Which thing to the end that they may persuade, they first make a necessary separation perpetual and personal between the Church and the commonwealth. Secondly, they so tie all kind of power ecclesiastical unto the Church, as if it were in every degree their only right which are by proper spiritual function termed Church-governors, and might not unto Christian princes in any wise appertain.

To lurk under shifting ambiguities and equivocations of words in matters of principal weight, is childish. A church and a commonwealth we grant are things in nature the one distinguished from the other. A commonwealth is one way, and a church another way, defined. In their opinion the church and the commonwealth are corporations, not distinguished only in nature and definition, but in subsistence perpetually severed; so that they which are of the one can neither appoint nor execute in whole nor in part the duties which belong unto them which are of the other, without open breach of the law of God, which hath divided them, and doth require that being so divided they should distinctly and severally work, as depending both upon God, and not hanging one upon the other's approbation for that which either hath to do. . . .

We hold, that seeing there is not any man of the Church of England but the same man is also a member of the commonwealth; nor any man a member of the commonwealth, which is not also of the Church of England; therefore as in a figure triangular the base doth differ from the sides thereof, and yet one and the selfsame line is both a base and also a side; a side simply, a base if it chance to be the bottom and underlie the rest: so, albeit properties and actions of one kind do cause the name of a commonwealth, qualities and functions of another sort the name of a Church to be given unto a multitude, yet one and the selfsame multitude may in such sort be both, and is so with us, that no person appertaining to the one can be denied to be also of the other. Contrariwise, unless they against us should hold, that the Church and the commonwealth are two, both distinct and separate societies, of which two, the one comprehendeth always persons not belonging to the other; that which they do they could not conclude out of the difference between the Church and the commonwealth; namely, that bishops may not meddle with the affairs of the commonwealth, because they are governors of another corporation, which is the Church; nor kings with making laws for the Church, because they have government not of this corporation, but of another divided from it, the commonwealth; and the walls of separation between these two must for ever be upheld. They hold the necessity of personal separation, which clean excludeth the power of one man's dealing in both; we of natural, which doth not hinder, but that one and the same person may in both bear a principal sway. . . .

Wherefore to end this point, I conclude: First, that under dominions of infidels, the Church of Christ, and their commonwealth, were two societies independent. Secondly, that in those commonwealths where the bishop of Rome beareth sway, one society is both the Church and the commonwealth; but the bishop of Rome doth divide the body into two diverse bodies, and doth not suffer the Church to depend upon the power of any civil prince or potentate. Thirdly, that within this realm of England the case is neither as in the one, nor as in the other of the former two: but from the state of pagans we differ, in that with us one society is both the Church and commonwealth, which with them it was not; as also from the state of those nations which subject themselves to the bishop of Rome, in that our Church hath dependency upon the chief in our commonwealth, which it hath not under him. In a word, our estate is according to the pattern of God's own ancient elect people, which people was not part of them the commonwealth, and part of them the Church of God, but the selfsame people whole and entire were both under one chief Governor, on whose supreme authority they did all depend.

Now the drift of all that hath been alleged to prove perpetual separation and independency between the Church and the commonwealth is, that this being held necessary, it might consequently be thought, that in a Christian kingdom he whose power is greatest over the commonwealth may not lawfully have supremacy of power also over the Church, as it is a church; that is to say, so far as to order and dispose of spiritual affairs, as the highest uncommanded commander in them. Whereupon it is grown a question, whether power ecclesiastical over the Church, power of dominion in such degree as the laws of this land do grant unto the sovereign governor thereof, may by the said supreme Head and Governor lawfully be enjoyed and held? For resolution wherein, we are, first, to define what the power of dominion is: then to shew by what right: after what sort: in what measure: with what conveniency: according unto whose example Christian kings may have it. And when these generalities are opened, to examine afterwards how lawful that is which we in regard of dominion do attribute unto our own: namely, the title of headship over the Church, so far as the bounds of this kingdom do reach: the prerogative of calling and dissolving greater assemblies, about spiritual affairs public: the right of assenting unto all those orders concerning religion, which must after be in force as laws: the advancement of principal church-governors to their rooms of prelacy: judicial authority higher than others are capable of: and exemption from being punishable with such kind of censures as the platform of reformation doth teach that they ought to be subject unto.

Without order there is no living in public society, because the want thereof is the mother of confusion, whereupon division of necessity followeth, and out of division, inevitable destruction. The Apostle therefore giving instruction to public societies, requireth that all things be orderly done. Order can have no place in things, unless it be settled amongst the persons that shall by office be conversant about them. And if things or persons be ordered, this doth imply that they are distinguished by degrees. For order is a gradual disposition.

The whole world consisting of parts so many, so different, is by this only thing upheld; he which framed them hath set them in order. Yea, the very Diety itself both keepeth and requireth for ever this to be kept as a law, that wheresoever there is a coagmentation of many, the lowest be knit to the highest by that which being interjacent may cause each to cleave unto other, and so all to continue one.

This order of things and persons in public societies is the work of polity, and the proper instrument thereof in every degree is power; power being that ability which we have of ourselves, or receive from others, for performance of any action. If the action which we are to perform be conversant about matter of mere religion, the power of performing it is then spiritual; and if that power be such as hath not any other to overrule it, we term it dominion, or power supreme, so far as the bounds thereof do extend.

When therefore Christian kings are said to have spiritual dominion or supreme power in ecclesiastical affairs and causes, the meaning is, that within their own precincts and territories they have authority and power to command even in matters of Christian religion, and that there is no higher nor greater that can in those causes over-command them, where they are placed to reign as kings. But withal we must likewise note that their power is termed supremacy, as being the highest, not simply without exception of any thing. For what man is there so brain-sick, as not to except in such speeches God himself, the King of all the kings of the earth? Besides, where the law doth give him dominion, who doubteth but that the king who receiveth it must hold it of and under the law? . . .

Unto which supreme power in kings two kinds of adversaries there are that have opposed themselves: one sort defending, "that supreme power in causes ecclesiastical throughout the world appertaineth of divine right to the, bishop of Rome:" another sort, that the said power belongeth "in every national church unto the clergy thereof assembled." We which defend as well against the one as the other, "that kings within their own precincts may have it," must shew by what right it may come unto them.

First, unto me it seemeth almost out of doubt and controversy, that every independent multitude, before any certain form of regiment established, hath, under God's supreme authority, full dominion over itself, even as a man not tied with the bond of subjection as yet unto any other, hath over himself the like power. God creating mankind did endue it naturally with full power to guide itself, in what kind of societies soever it should choose to live. A man which is born lord of himself may be made another's servant: and that power which naturally whole societies have, may be derived into many, few, or one, under whom the rest shall then live in subjection. . . .

Concerning therefore the matter whereof we have hitherto spoken, let it stand for our final conclusion, that in a free Christian state or kingdom, where one and the selfsame people are the Church and the commonwealth, God through Christ directing that people to see it for good and weighty considerations expedient that their sovereign lord and governor in causes civil have also in ecclesiastical affairs a supreme power; forasmuch as the light of reason doth lead them unto it, and against it God's own revealed law hath nothing: surely they do not in submitting themselves thereunto any other than that which a wise and religious people ought to do.

A Defense of Liberty against Tyrants *

> The authorship of the *Vindiciae contra tyrannos* (1579) is still an open question. But regardless of who wrote it, whether it was Hubert Languet, Philippe du Plessis-Mornay, or some other French Huguenot, it certainly represents a landmark in the history of revolutionary literature. The book reflects the views of the so-called "monarchomachs" who during the French religious wars defended the Huguenots against Catholic sovereigns bent on destroying them.

Now we read of two sorts of covenants at the inaugurating of kings, the first between God, the king, and the people, that the people might be the people of God. The second, between the king and the people, that the people shall obey faithfully, and the king command justly. We will treat hereafter of the second, and now speak of the first. . . .

The principal points of the covenants were chiefly these.

That the king himself, and all the people should be careful to honour and serve God according to His will revealed in His word, which, if they performed, God would assist and preserve their estates: as in doing the contrary, he would abandon, and exterminate them, which does plainly appear by the conferring of divers passages of holy writ. . . .

Now, although the form, both of the church and the Jewish kingdom be changed, for that which was before enclosed within the narrow bounds of Judaea is now dilated throughout the whole world; notwithstanding the same things may be said of Christian kings, the gospel having succeeded the law, and Christian princes being in the place of those of Jewry. There is the same covenant, the same conditions, the same punishments, and if they fail in the accomplishing, the same God Almighty, revenger of all perfidious disloyalty; and as the former were bound to keep the law, so the other are obliged to adhere to the doctrine of the Gospel, for the advancement whereof these kings at their anointing and receiving, do promise to employ the utmost of their means. . . .

. . . now for that we see that God invests kings into their kingdoms, almost in the same manner that vassals are invested into their fees by their sovereign, we must needs conclude that kings are the vassals of God, and deserve to be deprived of the benefit they receive from their lord if they commit felony, in the same fashion as rebellious vassals are of their estates. These premises being allowed, this question may be easily resolved; for if God hold the place of sovereign Lord, and the king as vassal, who dare deny but that we must rather obey the sovereign than the vassal? If God commands one thing, and the king commands the contrary, what is that proud man that would term him a rebel who refuses to obey the king, when else he must disobey God? . . .

It is then lawful for Israel to resist the king, who would overthrow the law of God and abolish His church; and not only so, but also they ought to know that in neglecting to perform this duty, they make themselves culpable of the same crime, and shall bear the like punishment with their king.

If their assaults be verbal, their defence must be likewise verbal; if the sword be drawn against them, they may also take arms, and fight either with tongue or hand, as occasion is: yea, if they be assailed by surprisals, they may make use both of ambuscades and countermines, there being no rule in lawful war that directs them for the manner, whether it be by open assailing their enemy, or by close surprising; provided always that they carefully distinguish between advantageous stratagems, and perfidious treason, which is always unlawful.

But I see well, here will be an objection made. What will you say? That a whole people, that beast of many heads, must they run in a mutinous disorder, to order the business of the commonwealth? What address or direction is there in an unruly and unbridled multitude? What counsel or wisdom, to manage the affairs of state?

When we speak of all the people, we understand by that, only those who hold their authority from the people, to wit, the magistrates, who are inferior to the king, and whom the people have substituted, or established, as it were, consorts in the empire, and with a kind of tribunitial authority, to restrain the encroachments of sovereignty, and to represent the whole body of the people. We understand also, the assembly of the estates, which is nothing else but an epitome, or brief collection of the kingdom, to whom all public affairs have special and absolute reference; such were the seventy ancients in the kingdom of Israel, amongst whom the high priest was as it were president, and they judged all matters of greatest importance, those seventy being first chosen by six out of each tribe, which came out of the land of Egypt, then the heads or governors or provinces. In like manner the judges and provosts of towns, the captains of thousands, the centurions and others who commanded over families, the most valiant, noble, and otherwise notable personages, of whom was composed the body of the states, assembled divers times as it plainly appears by the word of the holy scripture. . . .

But here presents itself another question, the which deserves to be considered, and amply debated in regard of the circumstance of time. Let us put the case that a king seeking to abolish the law of God, or ruin the church, that all the people or the greatest part yield their consent, that all the princes or the greatest number of them make no reckoning; and, notwithstanding, a small handful of people, to wit, some of the princes and magistrates desire to preserve the law of God entirely and inviolably, and to serve the Lord purely: what may it be lawful for them to do if the king seek to compel those men to be idolaters, or will take from them the exercise of true religion? . . .

We have formerly said that the king did swear to keep the law of God, and promised to the uttermost of his power to maintain the church; that the people of Israel considered in one body, covenanting by the high priest, made the same promise to God. Now, at this present, we say that all the towns and all the magistrates of these towns, which are parts and portions of the kingdom, promise each of them on his own behalf, and in express terms, the which all towns and Christian communalties have also done, although it has been but with a tacit consent.

*   *   *

We have shewed before that it is God that does appoint kings, who chooses them, who gives the kingdom to them: now we say that the people establish kings, puts the sceptre into their hands, and who with their suffrages, approves the election. God would have it done in this manner, to the end that the kings should acknowledge, that after God they hold their power and sovereignty from the people. . . .

Now, seeing that the people choose and establish their kings, it follows that the whole body of the people is above the king. . . .

In a commonwealth, commonly compared to a ship, the king holds the place of pilot, the people in general are owners of the vessel, obeying the pilot, whilst he is careful of the public good; as though this pilot neither is nor ought to be esteemed other than servant to the public. . . .

We have shewed already, that in the establishing of the king, there were two alliances or covenants contracted: the first between God, the king, and the people, of which we have formerly treated; the second, between the king and the people, of which we must now say somewhat. After that Saul was established king, the royal law was given him, according to which he ought to govern. David made a covenant in Hebron before the Lord, that is to say, taking God for witness, with all the ancients of Israel, who represented the whole body of the people, and even then he was made king. . . .

It is certain, then, that the people by way of stipulation, require a performance of covenants. The king promises it. Now the condition of a stipulator is in terms of law more worthy than of a promiser. The people ask the king, whether he will govern justly and according to the laws? He promises he will. Then the people answer, and not before, that whilst he governs uprightly, they will obey faithfully. The king therefore promises simply and absolutely, the people upon condition: the which failing to be accomplished, the people rest according to equity and reason, quit from their promise.

In the first covenant or contract there is only an obligation to piety: in the second, to justice. In that the king promises to serve God religiously: in this, to rule the people justly. By the one he is obliged with the utmost of his endeavours to procure the glory of God: by the other, the profit of the people. In the first, there is a condition expressed, "if thou keep my commandments": in the second, "if thou distribute justice equally to every man." God is the proper revenger of deficiency in the former, and the whole people the lawful punisher of delinquency in the latter, or the representative body thereof, who have assumed to themselves the protection of the people. . . .

First, the law of nature teaches and commands us to maintain and defend our lives and liberties, without which life is scant worth the enjoying, against all injury and violence. Nature has imprinted this by instinct in dogs against wolves, in bulls against lions, betwixt pigeons and sparrow-hawks, betwixt pullen and kites, and yet much more in man against man himself, if man become a beast: and therefore he who questions the lawfulness of defending oneself, does, as much as in him lies, question the law of nature. To this must be added the law of nations, which distinguishes possessions and dominions, fixes limits, and makes out confines, which every man is bound to defend against all invaders. . . .

There is, besides this, the civil law, or municipal laws of several countries which governs the societies of men, by certain rules, some in one manner, some in another. . . . If, therefore, any offer either by fraud or force to violate this law, we are all bound to resist him, because he wrongs that society to which we owe all that we have, and would ruin our country, to the preservation whereof all men by nature, by law and by solemn oath, are strictly obliged: insomuch that fear or negligence, or bad purposes, make us omit this duty, we may justly be accounted breakers of the laws, betrayers of our country, and contemners of religion. Now as the laws of nature, of nations, and the Civil commands us to take arms against such tyrants; so, is there not any manner of reason that should persuade us to the contrary; neither is there any oath, covenant, or obligation, public or private, of power justly to restrain us; therefore the meanest private man may resist and lawfully oppose such an intruding tyrant.

6. *Persecution and Toleration*

THEODORE BEZA: *Life of Calvin* *

> Theodore Beza (1519–1605), French lawyer and theologian, was Calvin's associate and successor in the church of Geneva. In his *Life of Calvin*, he tells the story of Calvin's denunciation of the heretic Michael Servetus, who was burned at the stake at Geneva for rejecting infant baptism and denying the doctrine of the Trinity; of the defence of Servetus by the liberals, Sebastian Castellio, professor of Greek at Basle, and the Unitarian Lelio Sozini; of Beza's own support of Calvin's position in his book *On Heretics* (1554). The "factious" referred to at the beginning of Beza's account were the malcontents, led by the powerful Perrin family, who chafed under Calvin's iron rule of the city.

THE FOLLOWING year, viz., 1553, while the malice of the factious, which was hastening to its close, was so boisterous, that not only the Church,

* *Tracts relating to the Reformation by John Calvin*, trans. by Henry Beveridge (Edinburgh: Edinburgh Printing Company; 1844), vol. I, pp. lx–lxi, lxiv–lxvi.

but even the Republic itself, was brought into extreme jeopardy, they proceeded to such lengths with clamour and menaces, and, in fine, by oppressing the liberty of the good, that they changed the ancient edicts with regard to the appointment of senators, (on this subject, the good afterwards took the greater care to provide for themselves, the Lord favouring them therein,) expelled some from the Senate, and pretending fear of the foreign exiles, deprived them of all weapons, except their swords, when they happened to go beyond the city; so that it seemed nothing could prevent them from accomplishing the design for which they had long agitated, as they had every thing in their power. And even at this time Satan furnished them with another occasion. For that declared enemy of the sacred Trinity, that is, of the whole Godhead, and therefore a monster compounded of all heresies, however rank and portentous,—I mean Michael Servetus,—after he had wandered up and down for several years, professing medicine, concealing himself under the name of Michael Villanovanus, had circulated his blasphemies, which he afterwards published at Vienne in a thick volume. The printer was one Arnoldi, a bookseller in Lyons, and what is called the corrector for the press was one William Guerot, who had formerly been devoted to the factious among the Genevese, but a few months before had left Geneva for Lyons, to avoid punishment for fornification and other crimes. Servetus having published this large volume of blasphemy, and having, for that reason, been imprisoned at Vienne, escaped I know not how, and, by a kind of fatality, came to Geneva, intending to pass through it for some more distant place, had he not been providentially recognized by Calvin, to whom he was well known long before, and on his information to the magistracy consigned to prison. The contest which then arose, and the important matters to which they related, are most fully explained in a work published with that view. The result of the whole was, that this abandoned man, (into whose ear one of the factious, an assessor of the then Praetor, was said to have whispered something which confirmed him in his wickedness,) being betrayed by his own vain confidence, was convicted of impiety and endless blasphemies, conformably to the opinion of all the Swiss churches. On the 27th of October, the unhappy man, who gave no sign of repentance, was burned alive. . . .

Thus the whole of this year was spent in contention with the wicked, and in defence both of doctrine and discipline, and everywhere with a prosperous issue, if we except the wound which not only England but all Christian churches received by the death of the most religious King Edward. Yet in this very year Calvin was so diligent a student that he published his excellent Commentary upon John. I may here be permitted (I wish it were without cause) to say of Servetus, what the ancient Fathers who spoke from experience, wrote concerning that twin monster, Paul Samosatenus and Arius of Alexandria, viz., that with them originated those fires by which the whole churches of Christendom were afterwards in a blaze. For punishment was most deservedly inflicted on Servetus at Geneva, not because he was a sectary, but a monstrous compound of mere impiety and horrid blasphemy, with which he had for the whole period of thirty years, by word and writing, polluted both heaven and earth. Even now it is impossible to say how much the influence of Satan has been increased by that flame which seized first upon Poland, then Transylvania and Hungary, and I fear may have proceeded farther still. Indeed, it would seem that Servetus prophesied under the influence of a Satanic spirit, when taking a passage of the Apocalypse and interpreting it in his usual way, he placed it in front of his book: "There was great war in heaven—Michael and his angels fighting with the dragon.". . .

Scarcely, therefore, were the ashes of that unhappy man cold when questions began to be agitated concerning the punishment of heretics— some maintaining that they ought indeed to be coerced, but could not justly be put to death; others, as if the nature of heresy could not be clearly ascertained from the Word of God, or as if it were lawful to judge in academic fashion of all the heads of religion, maintaining that heretics ought to be left to the judgment of God only. This opinion was defended even by some good men, who were afraid that if a different view were adopted they might seem to sanction the cruelty of tyrants against the godly. The chief abettors of that opinion (and they were thereby pleading their own cause) were Sebastian Castellio and Laelius Socinus; the latter, indeed, more secretly, but the former more openly, having in a certain treatise, which he prefixed to his translation, or rather perversion, of the sacred books, plainly studied to deprive the Divine Word of clear authority, and expressly maintained, in his Annotations on the First Epistle of Corinthians, as if for the express purpose of leading us away from the written Word as imperfect, that Paul had taught his perfect disciples—(who they were I know not)—a more recondite theology than he had delivered in his writings. Calvin having, in the beginning of the year 1554, drawn up a full refutation of the doctrine of Servetus, which was subscribed by all his colleagues; and having also added reasons, showing why and how far it was the duty of magistrates, after due investigation, to punish heretics, these men opposed him with a farrago, raked together partly from misquotations from the writings of pious doctors, and partly from the lucubrations of certain fanatics, otherwise of unknown name. The farrago bore to be written by one Martin Bellius. This was Castellio himself, although he afterwards swore it was not. The name of the town where it was said to be published was also fictitious. To that libellous production, containing not that error only, but teeming with many other blasphemies, I wrote an answer, with the view of relieving Calvin from the trouble, while occupied with far better business; I mean in writing his most learned Commentaries on Genesis and others, of which we will afterwards speak, and in warding off the dangers which threatened his church.

LEONARD BUSHER: *Religion's Peace* *

> Leonard Busher (b. 1571?) describes himself as a "citizen of London." He was probably the son of a Walloon refugee named Domynic Busher. At the time that he wrote *Religions Peace: or a Plea for Liberty of Conscience* (1614) he was living in Holland, as a Baptist exile from England. The book was dedicated to James I and the English Parliament, and was a remarkable plea for the religious liberty not merely of his own group but of all men.

THEREFORE may it please your majesty and parliament to understand that, by fire and sword, to constrain princes and peoples to receive that one true religion of the gospel, is wholly against the mind and merciful law of Christ, dangerous both to king and state, a means to decrease the kingdom of Christ, and a means to increase the kingdom of antichrist; as these reasons following do manifest. . . .

(As) kings and bishops cannot command the wind, so they cannot command faith; *and as the wind bloweth where it listeth, so is every man that is born of the Spirit.* You may force men to church against their consciences, but they will believe as they did afore, when they come there; for God giveth a blessing only to his own ordinance, and abhorreth antichrist's. . . .

I read that Constantine the emperor, called the great, wrote to the bishop of Rome, that he would not force and constrain any man to the faith, but only admonish, and commit the judgment to God. Christ's kingdom is not of this world, therefore may it not be purchased nor defended with the weapons of this world, but by his word and Spirit. No other weapons hath he given to his church, which is his spiritual kingdom. Therefore Christ saith, *He that will not hear the church, let him be to thee as a heathen and a publican.* He saith not, burn, banish, or imprison him; that is antichrist's ordinance. And though a man be an heretic, yet ought he not to be burnt, but to be rejected, *after once or twice admonition*—that is, cast out of the church.

But as in the church of Rome, people of all sorts are by persecution forced thereinto by the bishops and ministers thereof; so it is in the church of England also. Which showeth that the bishops and ministers of Rome and England are of one spirit, in gathering people to their faith

* *Tracts on Liberty of Conscience and Persecution*, Hanserd Knollys Society (London: J. Haddon; 1846), pp. 17–19, 24–5, 28–9, 33–4, 42, 50–3, 64, 68.

and church, which is the spirit of Satan, who knoweth well that his kingdom, the false church, would greatly decay, if persecution were laid down. . . .

And though tares have overgrown the wheat, yet Christ will have them let alone till harvest, *lest while you go about to pluck up the tares, you pluck up also the wheat with them;* as your predecessors have done, who thought they had gathered up the tares and burned them, but you see now that they have burned the wheat instead of tares. Wherefore in all humility and Christian modesty, I do affirm, that through the unlawful weed-hook of persecution, which your predecessors have used, and by your majesty and parliament is still continued, there is such a quantity of wheat plucked up, and such a multitude of tares left behind, that the wheat which remains cannot yet appear in any right visible congregation.

Certain Reasons against Persecution

Eighthly—Because if freedom of conscience be not set up, and persecution laid down, then all the king's subjects, and all strangers inhabiting the land, that shall believe the apostolic faith, must depart the land to some free country; or else abide the danger of burning, banishing, hanging, and imprisoning. The first will be a great impoverishing and weakening of our land, besides a loss of the faithfullest subjects and friends. The second will provoke the Lord to wrath, by spilling the blood of his faithful servants, ambassadors, and witnesses; and also open the mouths of all strangers, to speak yet more lamentably of the cruel and bloody persecution of our land.

Ninthly—because if persecution continue, then the king and state shall have, against their will, many dissemblers in authority and office, both in court, city, and country. . . .

And the king and parliament may please to permit all sorts of Christians; yea, Jews, Turks, and pagans, so long as they are peaceable, and no malefactors, as is above mentioned; which, if they be found to be, under two or three witnesses, let them be punished according to God's word. Also, if any be found to be willing liars, false accusers, false allegers and quoters of the scriptures, or other men's writings—as some men willingly do—let them be punished according to right and justice; it is due desert, and no persecution. But let God's word have its full and free passage among them all, even to the end of their lives, in all bountifulness, longsufferance, and patience; knowing that it is ordained of God's rich mercy, to lead the infidels and such as err unto repentance and amendment, out of the snare of the devil, of whom they are taken and deceived. . . .

Further, I beseech his right excellent majesty and parliament to observe, that persecution was the occasion that the apostolic church was at first scattered and driven into the wilderness, that is, desert places of the world; whither she fled to save herself from the rage and tyranny of antichrist, and his apostles and ministers, the first authors of persecution under the gospel. Therefore his majesty and parliament may please to consider, that so long as persecution continue, so long will the apostolic church continue scattered and persecuted into the secret places of this world. And no marvel, for her faith and discsipline is as offensive, as odious, and as unwelcome unto antichrist and his bishops and ministers now, as it was then; as their burning, banishing, hanging, and imprisoning do witness even unto this day. . . .

But permission of conscience, and freedom and liberty of the gospel, will no way be dangerous to the king or state, if such like rules as these be observed:— . . .

7. That for the more peace and quietness, and for the satisfying of the weak and simple, among so many persons differing in religion, it be lawful for every person or persons, yea, Jews and papists, to write, dispute, confer and reason, print and publish any matter touching religion, either for or against whomsoever; always provided they allege no fathers for proof of any point of religion, but only the holy scriptures.

Neither yet to reproach or slander one another, nor any other person or persons, but with all love, gentleness, and peaceableness, inform one another, to the glory of God, honour of the king and state, and to their own good and credit. . . .

Why, then, should those that have the truth, and those that would have the truth, be afraid of error? Seeing truth discovereth dark and dangerous ways of error, though abroad in open books, even as light discovereth dark and dangerous places, though abroad in open highways. And as the more dark and dangerous the ways be, the more necessary and needful will light be found of all that travel; so the more dark and dangerous the errors be, the more needful and profitable will truth be found of all that would travel to heaven.

But some may object and say, 'Let all this be granted, yet it is no wisdom, we think, to bring dangerous errors into the light, that so many men may stumble at them; which being not brought to light, would not be so much as known to some.'

I answer, no more than a rock that lieth hid under water, which, for want of bringing into the light, many men may make shipwreck thereon, and so stumble or fall, nevertheless, though it be not so much as known to them before. Therefore, as a rock in the seas, though not so much as known to some, yet, for want of being made known, many men stumble and fall thereon, and so perish, both men and goods: so an error, though not so much as known to some, yet, for want of being made known, many men may stumble and fall thereon, and so perish, both bodies and souls, the which is more lamentable. And as rocks in the seas, the more they manifest themselves, so errors in the world, the more they manifest themselves, the more furtherance in the way to heaven. And you shall understand, that errors being brought to the light of the word of God, will vanish as darkness before the light of a torch. Even as the chaff before the wind cannot stand, so error before truth cannot abide. Therefore it is no hindrance, but a great furtherance, to have all erroneous rocks in the haven to heaven, make known and published. . . .

[Good bishops might defend religious toleration on, among other grounds, that] "thereby great benefit and commodity, will redound both to your majesty and to all your subjects, within your highness's dominions, by the great commerce, in trade and traffic, both of Jews and all people: which now, for want of liberty of conscience, are forced and driven elsewhere.". . .

Therefore as the king would not have his subjects to take away his life, because he is contrary to them in religion; so let not the king take away his subjects' lives, because they are contrary to the king in religion. And as you would not that men should force you to a religion against your consciences, so do not you force men to a religion against their consciences. And as it is the duty of subjects to seek the conversion of their king and state by the word of God, and not his and their destruction by fire and sword; so it is the duty of the king and state to seek the conversion of their subjects by the word of God, and not their destruction by fire and sword, as the pope and his prelates do teach; whose vassals therein, both emperors and kings, as well as people, have been a long time, both to the destruction of themselves and their subjects.

Jean Bodin: *The Republic* *

The *Six livres de la république* of the French lawyer Jean Bodin (1530–96) was the most important book on political theory written in the sixteenth century. The thesis of this book, published in 1576 in the midst of the French religious wars and only four years after the Massacre of St. Bartholomew, was that strong monarchy alone could solve the problem of political order. But like the Politiques, Bodin believed that the monarchy would only ruin itself by trying to suppress the Huguenots. He therefore advocated religious toleration, primarily for reasons of state rather than religion.

* John Bodin: *The Six Bookes of a Commonweale*, trans. by Richard Knolles (London: G. Bishop; 1606), p. 382, 537–40.

IT MAY be that the consent and agreement of the nobility and people in
a new religion or sect may be so puissant and strong, as that to repress or
alter the same should be a thing impossible, or at leastwise marvelous
difficult, without the extreme peril and danger of the whole estate. In
which case the best advised princes and governors of Commonweals do
imitate the wise pilots, who when they cannot attain unto the port by
them desired, direct their course to such port as they may: Yea and oft
times quite changing their course, give way unto the storms and tempests,
lest in seeking too much to put into the desired haven, they suffer shipwreck. Wherefore that religion or sect is to be suffered, which without
the hazard and destruction of the state cannot be taken away: The health
and welfare of the Commonweal being the chief thing the law respecteth.
Wherefore *Constans* the emperor suffered the companies and colleges of
the Arians, not so much for the love and affection he bore towards them,
as divers have written, but so in quiet to preserve his subjects and estate.
And *Theodosius* the Great being himself a Catholic, and always contrary to the Arians' opinion, yet bore with their religion, which he
could by no means suppress, maintaining both the one sort and the
other in peace and obedience. And after him *Zeno* the emperor, to
reconcile the companies of all sorts of religions among themselves and
together with the Commonweal, commanded an edict . . . of union
and tranquility or quietness to be published. After whose example
Anastasius caused the law of forgetfulness to be set forth, cherishing the
grave and modest preachers, and removing such as were of vehement
and turbulent spirits. . . .

I will not here in so great variety of people so much differing among
themselves in religion, take upon me to determine which of them is the
best (howbeit that there can be but one such, one truth, and one divine
law, by the mouth of God published), but if the prince, well assured of
the truth of his religion, would draw his subjects thereunto, divided into
sects and factions, he must not therein (in mine opinion) use force: (For
that the minds of men the more they are forced, the more forward and
stubborn they are; and the greater punishment that shall be inflicted
upon them, the less good is to be done; the nature of man being commonly such as may of itself be led to like of anything, but never enforced so to do), but rather it behoveth the prince so persuaded of the
truth of his religion, without fainting or dissembling, to profess and follow the same, still devoutly serving the almighty God: by which means
he shall both turn the will and minds of his subjects unto the admiration
and imitation of himself, and at length also pluck up even the very roots
of all sects and opinions: In which doing he shall not only avoid com-
motions, troubles, and civil wars, but lead also his straying subjects unto
the port of health. . . .

The great emperor of the Turks doth with as great devotion as any prince in the world honour and observe the religion by him received from his ancestors, and yet detesteth he not the strange religions of others; but to the contrary permitteth every man to live according to his conscience: yea and what more is, near unto his palace at Pera, suffereth four divers religions, *viz.* that of the Jews, that of the Christians, that of the Grecians, and that of the Mohammedans: and besides that, sendeth alms unto the Calogers or religious monks, dwelling upon the mountain Athos (being Christians) to pray for him: as did *Augustus* to the Jews, to whom he ordinarily sent his alms and perpetual sacrifices to Jerusalem, which he commanded to be there daily made for the health of himself, and of the Commonweal. For why the people of ancient time were persuaded, as were the Turks, all sorts of religions which proceed from a pure mind, to be acceptable unto the gods. And albeit that the Romans easily admitted not strange religions into their Commonweals . . . , yet for all that did they easily suffer every man privately within the city to use his own manner and fashion, and his own religion: yea the Romans themselves received into the city the sacrifices of *Isis* and of *Esculapius*, and suffered the Pantheon to be dedicated to all the gods. Only the Jews of all people detested strange ceremonies: whereby they provoked the hatred of all people against them. . . .

Wicked and strange rites and ceremonies, and such other as the greater part of the subjects of greatest power detest, I think it good and profitable to have them kept out of the Commonweal. For the preservation of the subjects' love amongst themselves, which is especially nourished and maintained by their consent and agreement in matters of religion: yet if the same religion be liked of by the opinion of neighbour nations, and of many of the subjects, then ought it not only with punishments not to be restrained, but also so much as may be provided, that if it may not without sedition be publicly professed, yet that no man be forbidden the private exercise of such his religion. For otherwise it shall come to pass, that they which are destitute of the exercise of their religion, and withal distasted of the religion of the others, shall become altogether Atheists (as we daily see) and so after that they have once lost the fear of God, tread also under foot both the laws and magistrates, and so inure themselves to all kinds of impieties and villanies, such as is impossible by man's laws to be redressed. . . . For they are much deceived, which think Commonweals to be better kept in order by men's commands and laws, than by the fear of God his judgments. For as the greatest tyranny is nothing so miserable as an Anarchy, when as there is neither prince nor magistrate, none that obeyeth, neither yet any that commandeth, but that all men live as they list at liberty in all looseness of life, without fear of punishment. So the greatest superstition that is, is not by much any thing so detestable as Atheism. And truly they (in mine opinion)

offend much, which think that the same punishment is to be appointed
for them that make many gods, and them that would have none at all:
or that the infinity of gods admitted, the almighty and everliving God is
thereby taken away. For that superstition how great soever it be, doth
yet hold men in fear and awe, both of the laws and of the magistrates, as
also in mutual duties and offices one of them towards another: whereas
meer Atheism doth utterly root out of men's minds all the fear of doing
evil. Wherefore two inconveniences propounded, Superstition (I say)
and Atheism, we must still decline the greater: yet when we may not
publicly use the true religion, which still consisteth in the worshipping
of one almighty and everlasting God: lest by condemning of the religion
which is publicly received, we should seem to allure or stir the subjects
unto impiety or sedition, it is better to come unto the public service, so
that the mind still rest in the honour and reverence of one almighty and
ever living God.

7. *Protestantism and Capitalism*

JOHN CALVIN: *Letter on Usury* *

"Calvin on Deuteronomy became a Gospel of the modern era." In his
famous letter to his friend Sachinus in 1545 Calvin destroyed the absolute Deuteronomic prohibition and sanctioned usury that did not bite
the poor. In so doing, he adapted religious teaching to the needs of the
modern business community.

I HAVE not yet essayed what could fitly be answered to the question put
to me: but I have learned by the example of others with how great
danger this matter is attended. For if all usury is condemned, tighter
fetters are imposed on the conscience than the Lord himself would wish.
Or if you yield in the least, with that pretext very many will at once
seize upon unlicensed freedom, which can then be restrained by no
moderation or restriction. Were I writing to you alone, I would fear this
the less; for I know your good sense and moderation: but as you ask
counsel in the name of another, I fear, lest he may allow himself far more
than I would wish by seizing upon some word; yet confident that you
will look closely into his character, and from the matter which is here
treated judge what is expedient, and to what extent, I will open my
thoughts to you.

* *Economic Tracts* (New York: Society for Political Education; 1882), no. 4,
pp. 33–6.

And first I am certain that by no testimony of Scripture is usury wholly condemned. For the sense of that saying of Christ, which is usually regarded as clear and evident, 'Lend, hoping for nothing again' (Luke vi. 35), has up to this time been perverted; the same as in another passage, when speaking of splendid feasts and that desire of the rich to be received in turn, he commands them rather to summon to these feasts, the blind, the lame, and other needy men, who lie at the cross-roads, and have not the power to make a like return. Christ, wishing to restrain man's abuse of lending, commands them to lend to those from whom there is no hope of receiving or regaining anything; and his words ought to be interpreted, that while he would command loans to the poor without expectation of repayment or the receipt of interest, he did not mean at the same time to forbid loans being made to the rich with interest; any more than in the injunction to invite the poor to our feasts, he did not imply that the mutual invitation of friends to feasts is in consequence to be prohibited. Again the law of Moses (Deut. xxiii. 19), was political, and should not influence us beyond what justice and philanthropy will bear. It could be wished that all usury, and the name itself, were first banished from the earth. But as this cannot be accomplished, it should be seen, what can be done for the public good. Certain passages of Scripture remain, in the Prophets and Psalms, in which the Holy Spirit inveighs against usury. Thus, a city is described as wicked because usury was practiced in the forum and streets; but as the Hebrew word means *frauds* in general, this cannot be interpreted so strictly. But if we concede that the prophet there mentions usury by name, it is not a matter of wonder that among the great evils which existed, he should attack usury. For wherever gains are farmed out, there are generally added, as inseparable concomitants, cruelty, and numberless other frauds and deceits. On the other hand it is said in praise of a pious and holy man, "that he putteth not out his money to usury" (Psa. xv. 5). Indeed it is very rare for the same man to be honest and yet be a usurer. Ezekiel goes even further (Eze. xxii. 12). For, enumerating the crimes which inflamed the wrath of the Lord against the Jews he uses two words: one of which means *usury*, and is derived from a root meaning to *consume*; the other word means *increase* or *addition*; doubtless because one devoted to his private gain, takes or rather extorts it from the loss of his neighbor. It is clear that the prophets spoke even more harshly of usury, because it was forbidden by name among the Jews: and when therefore it was practiced against the express command of God, it merited even heavier censure. But when it is said, that, as the cause of our union (*i.e.*, situation) is the same, the same prohibition of usury should be retained, I answer, that there is some difference in what pertains to the civil state (then and now?). Because the surroundings of the place in which the Lord placed the Jews, as well as other circumstances, tended to this, that it might be easy for them to deal among themselves without usury, while our union (or situation) to-day is a very different one in many respects. Therefore usury is not wholly forbidden among us, except it be repugnant both to justice and to charity.

Money does not, it is said, beget money? What does the sea beget? What does a house, from the letting of which I receive a rent? Is money really born from roofs and walls? But on the other hand both the earth produces, and something is brought from the sea which afterwards produces money, and the convenience of a house can be bought or sold for money. If therefore more profit can be derived from trading through the employment of money, than from the produce of a farm, the purpose of which is subsistance, should not who lets some barren farm to a farmer, receiving in return a price, or part of the produce, be approved, and one who loans money to be used for producing profit, be condemned? and when any one buys a farm with money, does not that money produce other money yearly? And whence is derived the profit of the merchant? You will say from his diligence and industry. Who doubts that idle money is wholly useless? Who asks a loan of me does not intend to keep what he receives idle by him. Therefore the profit does not arise from that money, but from the produce that results from its use, or employment. I therefore conclude that usury must be judged not by a particular passage of Scripture, but simply by the rules of equity. This will be made clearer by an example. Let us imagine a rich man with large possessions in farms and rents, but with little money. Another man, not so rich, nor with such large possessions as the first, has more ready money. The latter being about to buy a farm with his own money is asked for a loan by the wealthier man. He who makes the loan may stipulate for a rent or interest for his money, and further, that the farm shall be mortgaged to him until the principal is repaid, but until it is repaid he will be content with the interest or usury on the loan. Why, then, shall this contract with a mortgage, but only for the profit of the money, be condemned, when a much harsher, it may be, of leasing or renting a farm at a large annual rent, is approved? And what else is it than to treat God like a child, when we judge of objects by mere words, and not from their nature? As if virtue can be distinguished from vice by the form of words.

It is not my intention to fully examine the matter here. I wished only to show what you should consider more carefully. You should remember this, that the importance of the question lies not in words, but in the thing itself.

RICHARD BAXTER: *A Christian Directory* *

Richard Baxter (1615–91) was a prominent Puritan minister who, for the sake of religious unity, preferred to remain within the Church of England. His *Christian Directory* (1673) has been called "a Puritan *Summa Theologica* and *Summa Moralis* in one." Divided into four parts, Ethics, Economics, Ecclesiastics, and Politics, it aimed to give practical directions to men, including businessmen, in the pursuit of their professions or "callings." It may have originated in Baxter's attempt to answer practical questions put to him by the members of his congregation at Kidderminster.

Take heed of Idleness, and be wholly taken up in diligent business, of your lawful callings, when you are not exercised in the more immediate service of God. David in his *idleness* or *vacancy* catcht those sparks of lust, which in his troubles and military life he was preserved from. Idleness is the soil, the culture, and the opportunity of Lust. The *idle* person goeth to School to the Devil: He sets all other employment aside, that the Devil may have time to teach him and treat with him and sollicit him to evil: Do you wonder that he is thinking on lustful objects, or that he is taken up in feasting and drinking, in chambering and wantonness? why he hath nothing else to do. Whereas a laborious diligent person hath a *body subdued* and hardned against the *mollities,* the effeminateness of the wanton; and a *mind employed* and taken up with better things: Leave thy *body* and *mind* no *leisure* to think of tempting filthy objects, or to look after them. As *Hierome* saith, *Facito aliquid operis, ut semper Diabolus inveniat te occupatum: Be still doing some work, that the Devil may always find thee busie.* And do not for thy fleshly ease *remit* thy *labours* and indulge thy flesh. Rise early and go late to bed, and put thy self upon a *Necessity* of *diligence* all the day: *undertake* and *engage* thy self, in as much business as thou art able to go through, that if thou *wouldst*, thou maist not be *able* to give any indulgence to the flesh: For if thou be not still pressed by *necessity*, Lust will serve it self by *idleness*, and the *flesh will lye down* if it feel not the *spur:* Therefore are the Rich and idle more lustful and filthy than the poor labouring people.

*   *   *

Proportion the time of your sleep aright (if it be in your power) *that you waste not your pretious morning hours sluggishly in your Bed.* Let the time of your sleep be rationally fitted to your health and labor, and not sensually to your slothful pleasure. About six hours is meet for

* Richard Baxter: *A Christian Directory* (London: Robert White; 1678), vol. I, p. 111, 336, 378; vol. II, pp. 77–9.

healthful people, and seven hours for the less healthful, and eight for the more weak and aged, ordinarily. The morning hours are to most the preciousest of all the day, for all our duties; especially servants that are scanted of time, must take it then for Prayer, if possible, lest they have none at all. . . .

Follow the labors of your calling painfully and diligently. From hence will follow many commodities. 1. You will shew that you are not sluggish and servants to your flesh, as those that cannot deny its ease; and you will further the mortification of all fleshly lusts and desires, which are fed by ease and idleness. 2. You will keep out idle thoughts from your mind, which swarm in the minds of idle persons. 3. You will scape the loss of precious Time, which idle persons are daily guilty of. 4. You will be in a course of obedience to God, when the slothful are in a constant sin of omission. 5. You may have the more time to spare for holy exercises, if you follow your labor close when you are at it; when idle persons can have no time for Prayer or Reading, because they lose it by loitering at their work, and leave their business still behind hand. 6. You may expect Gods blessing for the comfortable provision for your selves and families, and to have to give to them that need, when the slothful are in want themselves, and cast by their want into abundance of temptations, and have nothing to do good with. 7. And it will also tend to the health of your bodies, which will make them the fitter for the service of your Souls. When slothfulness wasteth time, and health, and estate, and wit, and grace, and all. . . .

Keep up a high esteem of Time; and be every day more careful that you lose none of your Time, than you are that you lose none of your Gold or Silver: And if vain recreations, dressings, feastings, idle talk, unprofitable company, or sleep, be any of them Temptations to rob you of any of your Time, accordingly heighten your watchfulness and firm resolutions against them. Be not more careful to escape Thieves and Robbers, than to escape that *person* or *action* or course of life, that would rob you of any of your Time. And for the Redeeming of Time especially see, not only that you be never idle, but also that you be doing the *Greatest Good* that you can do, and prefer not a *less* before a *Greater.*

Eat and drink with temperance, and thankfulness: for health and not for unprofitable pleasure.

＊   ＊   ＊

Especially be sure that you live not out of a calling, that is, such a stated course of employment, in which you may best be serviceable to God. Disability indeed is an unresistible impediment. Otherwise no man must either *live idlely*, or content himself with doing some little charres as a recreation or on the by: but every one that is able, must be *statedly*, and *ordinarily* imployed in such work, as is serviceable to God, and the common Good. Question. *But will not wealth excuse us? Answer.* It may excuse you from some sordid sort of work, by making you more serviceable in other: but you are no more excused from service and work of one kind or other, than the poorest man: Unless you think that God *requireth least,* where He *giveth most.* . . . Question. *But may I not cast off the world, that I may only think of my salvation? Answer.* You may cast off all such excess of worldly cares or business as unnecessarily hinder you in spiritual things: But you may not cast off all *bodily employment* and *mental labour* in which you may serve the common Good. Every one that is a member of Church or Common-wealth must employ their parts to the utmost for the good of the Church and Common-wealth: *Publick service* is Gods *greatest service.* To neglect this, and say, I will pray and meditate, is as if your servant should refuse your *greatest* work, and tye himself to some lesser easie part: And God hath commanded you some way or other to labour for your daily bread, and not to live as drones on the sweat of others only. Innocent *Adam* was put into the Garden of *Eden to dress it:* And fallen man must *eat his bread in the sweat of his brows:* Gen. 3. 19. And he that *will not work must be forbidden to eat,* 2 Thes. 3. 6, 10, 12. And indeed it is necessary to our selves, for the health of our *bodies,* which will grow diseased with idleness; and for the help of our *souls,* which will *fail if the body fail:* And man in flesh must have work for his body as well as for his soul: And he that will do nothing but pray. and *Meditate,* it's like will (by sickness or Melancholy) be disabled e're long either to pray or meditate: Unless he have a body extraordinary strong.

Be very watchful redeemers of your Time, and make conscience of every hour and minute, that you lose it not, but spend it in the best and most serviceable manner that you can. Of this I intend to speak more particularly anon; and therefore shall here add no more.

Watchfully and resolutely avoid the entanglements and diverting occasions, by which the tempter will be still endeavouring to waste your time and hinder you from your work. Know what is the principal service that you are called to, and avoid avocations: especially Magistrates and Ministers, and those that have *great* and *publick* work, must here take heed. For if you be not very *wise* and *watchful,* the Tempter will draw you before you are aware, into such a multitude of diverting cares or businesses, that shall seem to be your *duties,* as shall make you almost unprofitable in the world. You shall have this or that little thing that must be done, and this or that friend that must be visited or spoke to, and this or that civility that must be performed; so that trifles shall detain you from all considerable works. I confess friends must not be neglected, nor civilities be denied: but our *Greatest duties* having the *Greatest necessity,* all things must give place to them in their proper season.

*   *   *

It is lawful and meet to look at the commodity of your Calling in the third place, (that is, *after the publick good, and after your personal good of soul and bodily health.*) Though it is said, Prov. 23. 4. *Labour not to be rich:* the meaning is, that you make not Riches your chief end: Riches for our fleshly ends must not ultimately be intended or sought. But in subordination to higher things they may: That is, you may labour in that manner as tendeth most to your success and lawful gain: You are bound to improve all your Masters Talents: But then your *end* must be, that you may be the better provided to do God service, and may do the more good with what you have. If God shew you a way in which you may lawfully get more than in another way, (without wrong to your soul, or to any other) if you refuse this, and choose the less gainful way, you cross one of the ends of your Calling, and you refuse to be Gods Steward, and to accept his gifts, and use them for him when he requireth it: You may labour to be *Rich for God,* though not for the *flesh* and sin.

THOMAS WILSON: *A Discourse upon Usury* *

Whether they condemned all interest, or, like Calvin, sanctioned some interest, all the Protestant divines of the sixteenth century were agreed that economics was a branch of religious ethics. But Tawney points out that while the divines argued, their flank was turned "by the growth of a body of opinion which argued that economics were one thing and ethics another." This is the point of view advanced by the Elizabethan business man in Thomas Wilson's *Discourse upon Usury* (1572). Wilson (1526–81), as became a civil lawyer and Secretary in the Tudor welfare state, makes the characters in his dialogue, the doctor and lawyer as well as the merchant, bow in the end to the preacher's condemnation of economic individualism. But "Gromel-gayner," who represents the order of things to come, has his say, and what he says is, in effect, that "trade is one thing, religion another."

Gromel Gainer's or the Merchant's Oration

AND I, for my part, am against you all that will have no usury, or will make the gain over little. For, I pray you, what trade or bargaining can there be among merchants, or what lending or borrowing among all men, if you take away the assurance and the hope of gain? What man is so mad to deliver his money out of his own possession for naught? or who is he that will not make of his own the best he can? or who is he that will lend to others and want himself? You see all men now are so wise, that none will lend for moonshine in the water; and therefore, if you forbid gain, you destroy intercourse of merchandise, you overthrow bargaining, and you bring all trading betwixt man and man to such confusion, as either man will not deal, or else they will say they cannot tell how to deal one with another.

I have been a doer in this world these 30 winters, and as fresh an occupier as another, and yet never found I better or more assured gain than by putting out my money for gain, the same being always the best and easiest trade that could be in the world. And in a dead time when there is no occupying, either by restraint or through wars, what would you merchants to do otherwise than to turn the penny and to live by their money? For if they should spend still on the stock without lending it for gain, or barratting any whit at all, I do fear the best of us all (I mean such as live by our money) would soon shut up our doors, and play the bankrupts, which were a most abominable shame, and a great dishonor to this realn. Do not you know that we are ever called upon in time of need, to lend to the prince, for maintenance of the state? Have not noblemen money of us, and all other gentlemen of service, whensoever they have need? And when is it that they have not need of us, great need, god knows, full often and many a time? Yea, need must always be, and men shall ever have need. And where is money to be had in time of need, if the city should fail? Many men talk of Robin Hood, that did never shoot in his bow. Is not London the queen's chamber? Are not we then chamberlains to her majesty, people always ready to spend not only our goods, but also our lives in her service? So that, if we were not, the state, as I take it, should hardly stand, or perhaps not be in so good case as it is at this present.

We lend not for usury, but for interest, and by exchange, and I think no man can disallow either interest or exchange. I pray you, if an ambassador shall have cause to travel in the affairs of the state, or the Queen's agent occasion to pay great sums of money abroad in other countries beyond the seas, what will you have done, if the exchange were not? How can great masses of money be carried to far countries, if bills of exchange be not current? Or who will be so mad to pay thousands in another country for moonshine in the water, to have nothing for his pains, but only his labor for his travail? Hope of gain makes men industrious, and, where no gain is to be had, men will not take pains. And as good it is to sit idle and do nothing, as to take pains and have nothing. Merchants' doings must not thus be overthwarted by preachers and others, that can not skill of their dealings. And this over great curiosity of some to meddle in other men's matter, I must tell you plain, it is even the very right way to undo all in the end. Therefore say what you will, I will live and amend, so as I may live every day better and better, by any means, I care not how. Yea, I will make hard shift with the world, and strain my conscience narrowly, before I will either starve or beg, both I and my children after me. Provided always that I will not come within the compass of positive laws: and this I know well, that by all laws a man may take as much for his own wares as he can get, and it is no sin for one man to deceive another in bargaining, so that it be not too much beyond god's prohibition, and a bargain is a bargain, let men say what they like. Such your straight prohibitions and strange preciseness, my masters, do make men weary of their lives. You may as well forbid buying and selling, as forbid taking interest for money; for, I pray you, what difference is there between the one and the other? I do buy a piece of land for £500 this day, and sell it tomorrow, or within six months after, for £600; and I do lend likewise £500 at the same time that I do buy land, and do receive within six months after £600 again for my £500 so lent. What difference is there between these two dealings? God amend you, my masters of the Clergy, and you Civilians also.

8. *The Philosophy of History*

Sir Walter Raleigh: *The History of the World* *

> In 1603 Sir Walter Raleigh (1552–1618), the explorer and court favorite of Queen Elizabeth, was convicted of conspiring against the new king, James I. During his long imprisonment in the Tower, Raleigh planned and partly wrote an ambitious *History of the World*, a fragment of which was published in 1614. This work has been called "the culminating document" of Renaissance and Reformation historiography in England. The following selection is from Raleigh's preface.

To ME it belongs in the first part of this preface, following the common and approved custom of those who have left the memories of time past to after-ages, to give, as near as I can, the same right to history which they have done. Yet seeing therein I should but borrow other men's words, I will not trouble the reader with the repetition. True it is, that among many other benefits, for which it hath been honoured, in this one it triumpheth over all human knowledge, that it hath given us life in our understanding, since the world itself had life and beginning, even to this day: yea it hath triumphed over time, which, besides it, nothing but eternity hath triumphed over: for it hath carried our knowledge over the vast and devouring space of so many thousands of years, and given so fair and piercing eyes to our mind, that we plainly behold living now, as if we had lived then, that great world, *magni Dei sapiens opus*, "the

* Sir Walter Raleigh: *Works* (Oxford: Oxford University Press; 1829), vol. II, pp. v–vi, viii–xi, xiii–xvi, xlii–xliv.

wise work," saith Hermes, "of a great God," as it was then, when but new to itself. By it, I say, it is, that we live in the very time when it was created; we behold how it was governed; how it was covered with waters, and again repeopled; how kings and kingdoms have flourished and fallen; and for what virtue and piety God made prosperous, and for what vice and deformity he made wretched, both the one and the other. And it is not the least debt which we owe unto history, that it hath made us acquainted with our dead ancestors; and, out of the depth and darkness of the earth, delivered us their memory and fame. In a word, we may gather out of history a policy no less wise than eternal; by the comparison and application of other men's fore-passed miseries with our own like errors and ill deservings. . . .

For seeing the first books of the following story have undertaken the discourse of the first kings and kingdoms; and that it is impossible for the short life of a preface to travel after and overtake far-off antiquity, and to judge of it; I will for the present examine what profit hath been gathered by our own kings, and their neighbour princes: who having beheld, both in divine and human letters, the success of infidelity, injustice, and cruelty, have (notwithstanding) planted after the same pattern.

True it is, that the judgments of all men are not agreeable; nor (which is more strange) the affection of any one man stirred up alike with examples of like nature; but every one is touched most with that which most nearly seemeth to touch his own private, or otherwise best suiteth with his apprehension. But the judgments of God are for ever unchangeable; neither is he wearied by the long process of time, and won to give his blessing in one age to that which he hath cursed in another. Wherefore those that are wise, or whose wisdom, if it be not great, yet is true and well grounded, will be able to discern the bitter fruits of irreligious policy, as well among those examples that are found in ages removed far from the present, as in those of latter times. And that it may no less appear by evident proof, than by asseveration, that ill doing hath always been attended with ill success; I will here, by way of preface, run over some examples, which the work ensuing hath not reached.

Among our kings of the Norman race, we have no sooner passed over the violence of the Norman Conquest, than we encounter with a singular and most remarkable example of God's justice upon the children of Henry the First. For that king, when both by force, craft, and cruelty, he had dispossessed, overreached, and lastly made blind and destroyed his elder brother Robert duke of Normandy, to make his own sons lords of this land; God cast them all, male and female, nephews and nieces, (Maud excepted,) into the bottom of the sea, with above a hundred and fifty others that attended them; whereof a great many were noble, and of the king dearly beloved.

To pass over the rest, till we come to Edward the Second. It is certain that after the murder of that king, the issue of blood then made, though it had some times of stay and stopping, did again break out; and that so often, and in such abundance, as all our princes of the masculine race (very few excepted) died of the same disease. And although the young years of Edward the Third made his knowledge of that horrible fact no more than suspicious; yet in that he afterwards caused his own uncle the earl of Kent to die, for no other offence than the desire of his brother's redemption, whom the earl as then supposed to be living, (the king making that to be treason in his uncle, which was indeed treason in himself, had his uncle's intelligence been true;) this, I say, made it manifest, that he was not ignorant of what had passed, nor greatly desirous to have had it otherwise; though he caused Mortimer to die for the same.

This cruelty the secret and unsearchable judgment of God revenged on the grandchild of Edward the Third: and so it fell out, even to the last of that line, that in the second or third descent they were all buried under the ruins of those buildings, of which the mortar had been tempered with innocent blood. For Richard the Second, who saw both his treasures, his chancellor, and his steward, with divers others of his counsellors, some of them slaughtered by the people, others in his absence executed by his enemies; yet he always took himself for over-wise to be taught by examples. The earls of Huntington and Kent, Montague and Spencer, who thought themselves as great politicians in those days as others have done in these, hoping to please the king and to secure themselves by the murder of Gloucester, died soon after, with many other their adherents, by the like violent hands; and far more shamefully than did that duke. And as for the king himself, (who, in regard of many deeds, unworthy of his greatness, cannot be excused, as the disavowing himself by breach of faith, charters, pardons, and patents,) he was in the prime of his youth deposed, and murdered by his cousin-german and vassal, Henry of Lancaster, afterwards Henry the Fourth.

This king, whose title was weak, and his obtaining the crown traitorous; who brake faith with the lords at his landing, protesting to intend only the recovery of his proper inheritance; brake faith with Richard himself, and brake faith with all the kingdom in parliament, to whom he swore that the deposed king should live. After that he had enjoyed this realm some few years, and in that time had been set upon on all sides by his subjects, and never free from conspiracies and rebellions; he saw (if souls immortal see and discern any things after the body's death) his grandchild Henry the Sixth, and his son the prince, suddenly, and without mercy, murdered; the possession of the crown (for which he had caused so much blood to be poured out) transferred from his race, and by the issues of his enemies worn and enjoyed; enemies, whom by his own practice he supposed that he had left no less powerless, than the succession of the kingdom questionless, by entailing the same upon his own issues by parliament. And out of doubt, human reason could have judged no otherwise, but that these cautious provisions of the father, seconded by the valour and signal victories of his son Henry the Fifth, had buried the hopes of every competitor under the despair of all reconquest and recovery. I say, that human reason might so have judged, were not this passage of Casaubon also true: *Dies, hora, momentum, evertendis dominationibus sufficit, quae adamantinis credebantur radicibus esse fundatae:* "A day, an hour, a moment is enough to overturn the things that seemed to have been founded and rooted in adamant.". . .

To Edward the Fourth succeeded Richard the Third, the greatest master in mischief of all that forewent him. . . . And what success had Richard himself, after all these mischiefs and murders, policies and counterpolicies to Christian religion; and after such time as with a most merciless hand he had pressed out the breath of his nephews and natural lords, other than the prosperity of so short a life, as it took end ere himself could well look over and discern it? The great outcry of innocent blood obtaining at God's hands the effusion of his, who became a spectacle of shame and dishonour both to his friends and enemies.

This cruel king Henry the Seventh cut off; and was therein (no doubt) the immediate instrument of God's justice. A politic prince he was, if ever there were any . . . Howsoever, the taking off of Stanley's head, who set the crown on his, and the death of the young earl of Warwick, son to George duke of Clarence, shews, as the success also did, that he held somewhat of the errors of his ancestors; for his possession in the first line ended in his grandchildren, as that of Edward the Third and Henry the Fourth had done. . . .

For seeing God, who is the author of all our tragedies, hath written out for us and appointed us all the parts we are to play; and hath not, in their distribution, been partial to the most mighty princes of the world; that gave unto Darius the part of the greatest emperor and the part of the most miserable beggar, a beggar begging water of an enemy, to quench the great drought of death; that appointed Bajazet to play the grand signior of the Turks in the morning, and in the same day the footstool of Tamerlane, (both which parts Valerian had also played, being taken by Sapores;) that made Bellisarius play the most victorious captain, and lastly, the part of a blind beggar; of which examples many thousands may be produced: why should other men, who are but as the least worms, complain of wrongs? . . .

But it is now time to sound a retreat; and to desire to be excused of this long pursuit: and withal, that the good intent which hath moved me to draw the picture of time past (which we call history) in so large a table, may also be accepted in place of a better reason.

The examples of divine Providence every where found (the first divine histories being nothing else but a continuation of such examples) have persuaded me to fetch my beginning from the beginning of all things; to wit, creation. For though these two glorious actions of the Almighty be so near, and, as it were, linked together, that the one necessarily implieth the other: creation inferring providence, (for what father forsaketh the child that he hath begotten?) and providence presupposing creation; yet many of those that have seemed to excel in worldly wisdom have gone about to disjoin this coherence; the Epicure denying both creation and providence, but granting that the world had a beginning; the Aristotelian granting providence, but denying both the creation and the beginning.

PART *Two:*

AGE OF *Science*

The heavens declare the glory of God;
And the firmament showeth his handiwork.
NINETEENTH PSALM

4. THE SCIENTIFIC REVOLUTION

From these and all long errors of the way,
In which our wandring predecessors went,
And like th'old Hebrews many years did stray
In deserts but of small extent,
Bacon, like Moses, led us forth at last,
The barren wilderness he past,
Did on the very border stand
Of the bless'd promis'd land,
And from the mountains top of his exalted wit,
Saw it himself, and shew'd us it.
Abraham Cowley, TO THE ROYAL SOCIETY

After I had spent some years in those Notional
Studies. . . . I began to think CUI BONO, and to
consider what these things would signify in the
world of action and business.
Joseph Glanvill, PLUS ULTRA

No wonder they [the ancients] should outstrip us in those arts which are conversant in polishing and adorning their language, because they bestowed all their time and pains in cultivating of them. . . . But those arts are by wise men censured as far inferior to the study of things, words being but the picture of things.

John Ray, LETTER, DECEMBER 15, 1690

The Scientific Revolution

*I*N HIS book *The Origins of Modern Science* Professor Butterfield of Cambridge writes that the "scientific revolution" of the sixteenth and seventeenth centuries "outshines everything since the rise of Christianity and reduces the Renaissance and Reformation to the rank of mere episodes, mere internal displacements, within the system of medieval Christendom." "It looms so large as the real origin both of the modern world and of the modern mentality that our customary periodisation of European history has become an anachronism and an encumbrance." [1] This view can no longer be seriously questioned. The scientific achievements of the century and a half between the publication of Copernicus's *De Revolutionibus Orbium Celestium* (1543) and Newton's *Principia* (1687) marked the opening of a new period of intellectual and cultural life in the West, which I shall call the Age of Science. What chiefly distinguished this age from its predecessor was that science—meaning by science a body of knowledge, a method, an attitude of mind, a metaphysic (to be described below)—became the directive force of Western civilization, displacing theology and antique letters. Science made the world of the spirit, of Platonic Ideas, seem unreliable and dim by comparison with the material world. In the seventeenth century it drove revealed Christianity out of the physical universe into the region of history and private morals; to an ever growing number of people in the two succeeding centuries it made religion seem outmoded even there. Science invaded the schools, imposed literary canons, altered the world-picture of the philosophers, suggested new techniques to the social theorists. It changed profoundly man's attitude toward custom and tradition, enabling him to declare his independence of the past, to look down condescendingly upon the "ancients," and to envisage a rosy future. The Age of Science made the intoxicating discovery that melioration de-

[1] (London, 1950), p. viii.

pends, not upon "change from within" (St. Paul's birth of the new man), but upon "change from without" (scientific and social mechanics).

I

SOME people will perhaps object that there was no such thing as a "scientific revolution" in the sixteenth and seventeenth centuries. They will say that history does not work that way, that the new science was not "revolutionary," but the cumulative effect of centuries of trial and error among scientists. But if by "scientific revolution" is meant the occasion when science became a real intellectual and cultural force in the West, this objection must surely evaporate. The evidence is rather overwhelming that sometime between 1543 and 1687, certainly by the late seventeenth century, science captured the interest of the intellectuals and upper classes. Francis Bacon's ringing of a bell to call the wits of Europe together to advance scientific learning did not go unheeded. Note the creation of new intellectual institutions to provide a home for science—the *Academia del Cimento* at Florence (1661), the Royal Society at London (1662), the *Académie des Sciences* at Paris (1666), the Berlin Academy (1700), to mention only the most important. These scientific academies signified the advent of science as an organized activity. Note the appearance of a literature of popular science, of which Fontenelle's *Plurality of Worlds* is only one example, and of popular lectures on scientific subjects.[2] Note the movement for educational reform sponsored by Bacon and the Czech John Amos Comenius, who denounced the traditional education for its exclusive emphasis upon "words rather than things" (literature rather than nature itself). Evidently, by the end of the seventeenth century the prejudice against "mechanical" studies as belonging to practical rather than high mental life had all but disappeared. Bacon complained in 1605 that "matters mechanical" were esteemed "a kind of dishonour unto learning to descend to inquiry or meditation upon." But the Royal Society included in its roster a number of ecclesiastics and men of fashion. The second marquis of Worcester maintained a laboratory and published a book of inventions in 1663. Not a few men appear to have been "converted" from an ecclesiastical to a scientific career, and, as Butterfield notes, to have carried the gospel into the byways, with all the zest of the early Christian missionaries.

To account historically for the scientific revolution is no easy task. The problem becomes somewhat more manageable, however, if we exclude from the discussion the specific discoveries of the scientists. Only the internal history of science can explain how Harvey, for example, discovered the circulation of the blood, or Newton the universal law of gravita-

[2] See below, p. 303.

tion. But certain extrascientific factors were plainly instrumental in causing so many people to be simultaneously interested in "nature," and, moreover, to think about nature in the way they did. Professor Whitehead reminds us that one of these factors was medieval Christianity itself and medieval scholasticism. Medieval Christianity sponsored the Greek, as opposed to the primitive, idea of a rationally ordered universe which made the orderly investigation of nature seem possible. Scholasticism trained western intellectuals in exact thinking. The Renaissance and the Protestant Reformation also prepared the ground for the scientific revolution—not by design, but as an indirect consequence of their thinking. As I have previously noted, humanism and Protestantism represented a movement toward the concrete. Erasmus preferred ethics to the metaphysical debates of the philosophers and theologians. The Protestants reduced the miraculous element in institutional Christianity and emphasized labor in a worldly calling. Furthermore, by attacking scholastic theology with which Aristotle was bound up, they made it easier for scientists to think about physics and astronomy in un-Aristotelian terms. As E. A. Burtt has noted of Copernicus, these men lived in a mental climate in which people generally were seeking new centers of reference. Copernicus, the architect of the heliocentric theory of the universe, was a contemporary of Luther and Archbishop Cranmer, who moved the religious center from Rome to Wittenberg and Canterbury. In the sixteenth century the economic center of gravity was similarly shifting from the Mediterranean to the English Channel and the Atlantic Ocean. The revival of ancient philosophies and ancient texts at the Renaissance also sharpened the scientific appetite. The Platonic and Pythagorean revival in fifteenth-century Italy undoubtedly did a good deal to accustom scientists to think of the universe in mathematical, quantitative terms. The translation of Galen and Archimedes worked the last rich vein of ancient science, and made it abundantly clear that the ancients had frequently disagreed on fundamentals, thus necessitating independent investigation. By their enthusiasm for natural beauty, the humanists helped to remove from nature the medieval stigma of sin, and thus to make possible the confident pronouncement of the scientific movement that God's Word could be read not only in the Bible but in the great book of nature.

But no one of these factors, nor all of them together, could have produced the scientific revolution. One is instantly reminded of Bacon's statement that "by the distant voyages and travels which have become frequent in our times, many things in nature have been laid open and discovered which may let in new light upon philosophy." The expansion of Europe, and increased travel in Europe itself, not only stimulated interest in nature but opened up to the West the vision of a "Kingdom of Man" upon earth. Much of Bacon's imagery was borrowed from the geographical discoveries: he aspired to be the Columbus of a new inʋtellectual world, to sail through the Pillars of Hercules (symbol of the old knowledge) into the Atlantic Ocean in search of new and more useful knowledge. Bacon, however, failed to detect the coincidence of the scientific revolution with commercial prosperity and the rise of the middle class. Doubtless, the Marxist Professor Hessen greatly oversimplified when he wrote that "Newton was the typical representative of the rising bourgeoisie, and in his philosophy he embodies the characteristic features of his class." [3] The theoretical scientists had mixed motives. Along with a concern for technology, they pursued truth for its own sake, and they sought God in his great creation. All the same, it is not stretching the imagination too far to see a rough correspondence between the mechanical universe of the seventeenth-century philosophers and the bourgeois desire for rational, predictable order. Science and business were a two-way street. If science affected business, so did business affect science—by its businesslike temper and its quantitative thinking, by its interest in "matter" and the rational control of matter.

II

THE SCIENTIFIC revolution gave birth to a new conception of knowledge, a new methodology, and a new world-view substantially different from the old Aristotelian-Christian world-view. Its end-product was a new view of history which, in the eighteenth century, acted as a solvent of the traditional European social structure.

The history of the word "science" throws considerable light on the new meaning given to "knowledge" in the seventeenth century. In the Middle Ages the seven liberal "sciences" were often used synonymously with the seven liberal "arts." Theology was queen of the sciences. But in an article for the *Dublin Review* in 1867, W. G. Ward writes that he will use the word science "in the sense which Englishmen so commonly give to it; as expressing physical and experimental science, to the exclusion of the theological and metaphysical." [4] Since the seventeenth century, "science" or "knowledge" had obviously undergone a considerable restriction of meaning. Knowledge now meant exact knowledge: what you know for certain, and not what may possibly or even probably be. Knowledge is what can be clearly apprehended by the mind, or measured by mathematics, or demonstrated by experiment. Galileo came close to saying this when he declared that without mathematics "it is impossible to comprehend a single word of [the great book of the universe]"; likewise Descartes when he wrote that "we ought never to allow our-

---

[3] B. Hessen, "The Social and Economic Roots of Newton's *Principia*," in *Science at the Cross-Roads* (London, 1931), pp. 182-3.

[4] Quoted in *New English Dictionary on Historical Principles*, article "science."

selves to be persuaded of the truth of anything unless on the evidence of our Reason." The distinction between "primary" and "secondary qualities" in seventeenth-century metaphysics carried the same implication. To Galileo, Descartes, and Robert Boyle those mathematical qualities that inhered in objects (size, weight, position, etc.) were "primary," *i.e.*, matters of real knowledge; whereas all the other qualities that our senses tell us are in objects (color, odor, taste, etc.) were "secondary," less real because less amenable to measurement. The inference of all this is plain: knowledge pertains to "natural philosophy" and possibly social theory, but not to theology or the older philosophy or poetry which involve opinion, belief, faith, but not knowledge. The Royal Society actually undertook to renovate the English language, by excluding from it metaphors and pulpit eloquence which conveyed no precise meaning. The "enthusiasm" of the religious man became suspect as did the "sixth sense" of the poet who could convey pleasure but not knowledge.

"Knowledge" also frequently connoted utility in the seventeenth century. "The end of knowledge," says Thomas Hobbes, "is power; and . . . the scope of all speculation is the performance of some action, or thing to be done." "The principal end why we are to get knowledge here," writes Locke, "is to make use of it for the benefit of ourselves and others in this world." This was the burden of much of Francis Bacon's writings, of, for example, the *New Atlantis* in which the scientists of the mythical Solomon's House labor for "the enlarging of the bounds of human empire, to the effecting of all things possible." Both the Royal Society and the *Académie des Sciences* applied themselves vigorously to the immediate "relief of man's estate." Committees were appointed to study the problems of industrial science, shipping, and ballistics, and students of mechanics made improvements in clocks and watches and helped to make possible the invention of the first steam-engine.

From Bacon's time on, the point was also frequently made that knowledge is cumulative and tentative. Bacon stressed the cumulative nature of science when he called for the "advancement" of learning, decrying the defeatism of his contemporaries who believed that the ancients had discovered all that there was to be known about the natural world. Robert Hooke emphasized its tentativeness when he declared in 1663 that although the ultimate design of the Royal Society was to compile a complete system of natural philosophy, "in the meantime" it would admit no hypothesis, "nor dogmatically define, nor fix axioms of scientifical things," until they had been elucidated "by mature debate and clear arguments, chiefly such as are deduced from legitimate experiments."

This gingerly handling of hypotheses goes to the very heart of the new method which accompanied the new conception of knowledge in the seventeenth century. Whether they advocated the experimental method (Bacon) or the mathematical (Descartes), or a mixture of both (Galileo,

Newton), the many new books on scientific method had in common a healthy distrust of over-hasty generalizations about nature. In this respect they linked up with the nominalists of the late Middle Ages who had attacked the abstract universals of the scholastic "realists." Bacon's *Novum Organum* summarizes a good many aspects of the revolt against scholasticism. He calls the scholastic philosophers "rationalists" who, like spiders, spin webs out of themselves without ever referring to nature itself. The common logic (the Aristotelian syllogism), he says, can only fix and establish errors because it is never applied to the first principles of the sciences. He deplored the wild admixture of theology and philosophy with science: to found science upon sacred writ is to seek the dead among the living; the search for final causes in science is as sterile as a nun dedicated to God.

Bacon was a better critic than builder. His "inductive method," which he offered as a substitute for scholastic logic, could never have produced the new astronomy and the new mathematical physics. In these sciences, as distinguished from the biological sciences, the primary requisite was not observation and experiment, but a brand new way of thinking (quantitative, mathematical, non-Aristotelian thinking) about the physical universe. The new laws of motion formulated by Galileo, Descartes, and Newton entailed a degree of abstraction from nature which Bacon, had he been acquainted with them, might have compared with scholastic hypotheses. But in his methodical doubt of ancient methods and ideas Bacon expressed a general sentiment. However much he and Descartes might disagree in other respects, they agreed that these ideas were as so many "idols" that possessed the minds of men and prevented them from acquiring the kind of knowledge they desired. The times demanded the reconstruction of the edifice of knowledge from the ground up—by mathematical reasoning or experiment (as opposed to common sense or the appeal to ordinary appearances), or both, as the case might be, but certainly not by bowing down and worshipping Aristotle, or by consulting Genesis or the book of Job.

The odd thing about the scientific revolution is that for all its avowed distrust of hypotheses and systems, it created its own system of nature, or world-view. "I perceive," says the "Countess" in Fontenelle's popular dialogue of 1686, "Philosophy is now become very Mechanical." "I value [this universe] the more since I know it resembles a Watch, and the whole order of Nature the more plain and easy it is, to me it appears the more admirable." Descartes and other philosophers of science in the seventeenth century constructed a mechanical universe which resembled the machines—watches, pendulum clocks, steam engines—currently being built by scientists and artisans. However, it was not the observation of actual machines but the new astronomy and physics that made it possible to picture the universe in this way. The "Copernican revolution" de-

stroyed Aristotle's "celestial world" of planets and stars which, because
they were formed of a subtle substance having no weight, behaved differently from bodies on earth and in the "sublunary world." The new
laws of motion formulated by a succession of physicists from Kepler to
Newton explained the movement of bodies, both celestial and terrestrial, entirely on mechanical and mathematical principles. According
to the law of inertia, the "natural" motion of bodies was in a straight line
out into Euclidean space. The planets were pulled into their curvilinear
orbits by gravitation which could operate at tremendous distances, and
which varied inversely as the square of the distance.

Thus, the universe pictured by Fontenelle's Countess was very different
from that of Dante in the thirteenth, or Richard Hooker in the sixteenth
century. Gone was the Aristotelian-Christian universe of purposes, forms,
and final causes. Gone were the spirits and intelligences which had been
required to push the skies daily around the earth. The fundamental features of the new universe were numbers (mathematical quantities) and
invariable laws. It was an economical universe in which nature did nothing in vain and performed its daily tasks without waste. In such a universe
the scientist could delight and the bourgeois could live happily ever after
—or at least up to the time of Darwin. The fact that nature appeared to
have no spiritual purpose—Descartes said that it would continue to exist
regardless of whether there were any human beings to think it—was more
than compensated for by its dependability. Philosophy had indeed become very mechanical. Descartes kept God to start his machine going,
and Newton did what he could to save the doctrine of providence. But
for all practical purposes, God had become the First Cause, "very well
skilled in mechanics and geometry." And the rage for mechanical explanation soon spread beyond the confines of physics to encompass the biological and social sciences. Thus did Descartes regard animals as a piece
of clockwork, Robert Boyle the human body as a "matchless engine."

Under the circumstances, one would logically expect there to have
been warfare between science and religion in the seventeenth century.
But such was not the case. To be sure, some theologians expressed dismay
at the downfall of Aristotelianism, and the Roman Church took steps to
suppress Copernicanism when Giordano Bruno interpreted it to mean an
infinite universe and a plurality of worlds. But the majority of the
scientists and popularizers of science were sincerely religious men—not
a few were actually ecclesiastics—who either saw no conflict or else
went to some lengths to resolve it. Science itself was commonly regarded
as a religious enterprise. Science, the Book of Nature, was said to reveal
God's power in his works even as the Bible revealed his will—"the viewing of the works of God," Bishop Burnet said at Boyle's funeral, "gives
insensibly a greatness to the Soul." Bacon and Descartes understood perfectly well the "limitations of science." If Bacon warned theologians off

science's preserve, he showed himself equally anxious to reserve for theology its own sphere of influence. He concludes his survey of secular knowledge in *De Augmentis Scientiarum* with the categorical statement that "belief is more worthy than knowledge." If we are disposed to consider sacred theology, he says, "we must quit the small vessel of human reason, and put ourselves on board the ship of the church; which alone possesses the divine needle for justly shaping the course." I interpret Descartes to have meant somewhat the same thing by his famous "dualism." As is well known, Descartes divided the world into two parts: the external world of mathematical objects which was strictly controlled by mechanical laws, and the internal world of the "I," the thinking substance. By so doing, he clearly exempted from mechanization not only God, but the human soul and the whole realm of spiritual things. The type of thinking represented by these men advocated living on two levels of experience: the level of rational and scientific experience, and the level of religious faith.

In the final analysis, however, the new thing in seventeenth-century thought was the dethronement of theology from its proud position as the sun of the intellectual universe. Bacon and Descartes and Newton lived in an age that was finding it increasingly difficult to reconcile science and religion. To save the best features of both they effected a shaky compromise. For all practical purposes they eliminated religious purpose from nature—thus allowing science to get on with its work, while leaving religion in control of private belief and morals. By their insistence that religious truth itself must pass the tests of reason and reliable evidence, John Locke and the rationalists further reduced theology's prerogatives. Bacon was prepared to believe the word of God "though our reason be shocked at it." But not Locke: " 'I believe because it is impossible,' might," he says, "in a good man, pass for a sally of zeal, but would prove a very ill rule for men to choose their opinions or religion by." Good Christian though Locke might be, his teaching had the effect of playing down the supernatural aspects of religion, of equating religion with simple ethics. From his *Reasonableness of Christianity* (1695) and John Toland's *Christianity not Mysterious* (1696) it was only a step to the "natural religion" of the eighteenth-century *philosophes*.

The scientific revolution also changed Western man's historical perspective. Up to the seventeenth century it was commonly believed that man and nature had degenerated from an original perfect state. "We are born ruinous" was John Donne's lament in 1611. And like mankind,

> . . . so is the world's whole frame
> Quite out of joint, almost created lame:
> For, before God had made up all the rest,
> Corruption entered, and depraved the best.

In the course of the century, however, the intellectual vanguard repudiated the idea of degeneration, claiming the abiding strength of the forces of nature, and equality of brains with the ancients. Undoubtedly, the commercial revolution and the restoration of political order after a series of religious and civil wars contributed to the mounting optimism. But it was chiefly the scientific revolution—the spectacular achievements of the scientists and their demonstration of the invariable laws of nature—that emboldened the "moderns" to assert their equality with, and even superiority to, the ancients. As Joseph Glanvill said in his *Plus Ultra: or, the Progress and Advancement of Knowledge since the Days of Aristotle* (1668): the ancients were men of excellent wit, but their "way" was not right. "The unfruitfulness of those methods of science, which in so many centuries never brought the world so much practical, beneficial knowledge as would help toward the cure of a cut finger, is a palpable argument." These seventeenth-century "moderns" never quite grasped the idea of moral and social progress. But by their proclamation of intellectual progress, they laid the ghost of the pristine Golden Age and encouraged the *philosophes* of the next century to envisage the progress of mankind on all fronts.

Readings

1. *New Focus of Intellectual Interest*

Bishop Sprat: *History of the Royal Society* *

> Thomas Sprat (1635–1713), Bishop of Rochester and Dean of West-minster, wrote the first history of the Royal Society, which was incorporated in 1662. His *History of the Royal Society of London, For the Improving of Natural Knowledge* was published in 1667. Following a brief discussion of ancient and modern philosophy and the beginnings of the Society, Sprat describes as follows its membership and the general interest it elicited.

As FOR what belongs to the *Members* themselves that are to constitute the *Society:* It is to be noted, that they have freely admitted Men of different Religions, Countries, and Professions of Life. This they were oblig'd to do, or else they would come far short of the Largeness of their own Declarations. For they openly profess, not to lay the Foundation of an *English, Scotch, Irish, Popish,* or *Protestant* Philosophy; but a Philosophy of *Mankind.*

* * *

But, though the *Society* entertains very many Men of *particular Professions,* yet the far greater Number are *Gentlemen,* free and unconfin'd. By the Help of this there was hopeful Provision made against *two Corruptions* of Learning, which have been long complain'd of, but never remov'd: The *one,* that *Knowledge* still degenerates to consult *present Profit* too soon; the *other,* that *Philosophers* have been always *Masters* and *Scholars;* some imposing, and all the other submitting; and not as equal Observers without Dependence.

* * *

* Thomas Sprat: *History of the Royal Society of London* (London: S. Chapman; 1722), pp. 62–3, 67, 71–3, 76, 124–33.

[Critics object that there will be "scarce enough Men of philosophical Temper" to fill up the Society. To which Sprat replies] That this Scruple is of no Force, in Respect of *the Age wherein we live.* For now the Genius of *Experimenting* is so much dispers'd, that even in this *Nation,* if there were one or two more such *Assemblies* settled, there could not be wanting able Men enough to carry them on. All Places and Corners are now busie and warm about this Work: and we find many noble Rarities to be every Day given in not only by the Hands of learned and profess'd Philosophers; but from the Shops of *Mechanicks;* from the Voyages of *Merchants;* from the Ploughs of *Husbandmen;* from the Sports, the Fishponds, the Parks, the Gardens of *Gentlemen;* . . . It seems strange to me, that Men should conspire to believe all things more perplex'd, and difficult, than indeed they are. This may be shewn in most other Matters; but in this particular in hand, it is most evident. Men did generally think, that no Man was fit to meddle in Matters of this Consequence, but he that had bred himself up in a long Course of Discipline for that Purpose; that had the Habit, the Gesture, the Look of a Philosopher: Whereas Experience, on the contrary, tells us, that greater Things are produc'd by the *free* way, than the *formal.* This Mistake may well be compar'd to the Conceit we had of *Soldiers,* in the beginning of the civil Wars. None was thought worthy of that Name, but he that could shew his Wounds, and talk aloud of his Exploits in the *Low Countries:* Whereas the whole Business of fighting, was afterwards chiefly perform'd by *untravel'd Gentlemen, raw Citizens,* and *Generals* that had scarce ever before seen a Battle. But to say no more, it is so far from being a Blemish, that it is rather the Excellency of this Institution, that *Men of various Studies* are introduc'd. For so there will be always many sincere Witnesses standing by, whom Self-love will not persuade to report falsely, nor Heat of Invention carry to swallow a Deceit too soon; as having themselves no Hand in the making of the Experiment, but only in the *Inspection.* So cautious ought Men to be, in pronouncing even upon Matters of Fact. The whole Care is not to be trusted to *single* Men; not to a *Company* all of *one Mind;* not to *Philosophers;* not to *devout* and religious Men *alone.*

*   *   *

By this they have broken down the Partition-wall, and made a fair Entrance, for *all Conditions of Men* to engage in these Studies; which were heretofore affrighted from them, by a groundless Apprehension of their Chargeableness and Difficulty. Thus they have form'd that *Society,* which intends a *Philosophy,* for the Use of *Cities,* and not for the Retirements of *Schools,* to resemble the *Cities* themselves; which are compounded of all Sorts of Men, of the *Gown,* of the *Sword,* of the *Shop,* of the *Field,* of the *Court,* of the *Sea;* all mutually assisting each other.

*   *   *

There now remains to be added in this third Part of my *Narration,* an Account of the *Incouragements* they have receiv'd from abroad, and at home. . . .

It is evident, that this *searching Spirit,* and this Affection to *sensible Knowledge,* does prevail in most Countries round about us. 'Tis true, the Conveniences for such Labours are not equal in all Places. Some want the Assistance of others *Hands;* some the Contribution of others *Purses;* some the Benefit of excellent *Instruments,* some the *Patronage* of the Civil *Magistrates:* But yet according to their several *Powers,* they are every where intent on such *practical Studies.* And the most considerable Effects of such Attempts throughout *Europe* have been still recommended to this *Society,* by their *Authors,* to be examin'd, approv'd, or corrected.

The Country, that lyes next to *England* in its Situation is *France;* and that is also the nearest to it, in its Zeal for the Promotion of *Experiments.* In that Kingdom, the *Royal Society* has maintain'd a perpetual Intercourse, with the most eminent Men of *Art* of all Conditions; and has obtain'd from them, all the Help which might justly be hop'd for, from the *Vigour,* and *Activity,* and *Readiness* of Mind, which is natural to that People. From their *Physicians, Chirurgeons,* and *Anatomists,* it has receiv'd many faithful *Relations* of extraordinary *Cures;* from their most judicious *Travellers* the Fruits of their *Voyages;* from their most famous *Mathematicians,* diverse *Problems,* which have been solv'd many different Ways; from their *Chymists* the effects of their *Fires;* and from others of their best *Observers,* many Rarities, and Discourses of their *Fruits, Silk, Wine, Bread, Plants, Salt,* and such natural Productions of their Soil. And to instance once for all, it has been affectionately invited to a mutual *Correspondence* by the *French Academy* of *Paris.* . . .

In *Italy* the *Royal Society* has an excellent Privilege of receiving and imparting *Experiments,* by the Help of one of their own *Fellows,* who has the Opportunity of being *Resident* there for them, as well as for the *King.* From thence they have been earnestly invited to a mutual Intelligence, by many of their most *noble Wits,* but chiefly by the *Prince Leopoldo,* Brother to the great Duke of *Tuscany;* who is the Patron of all the *inquisitive Philosophers* of *Florence;* from whom there is coming out under his Name an Account of their Proceedings call'd *Ducal Experiments.* This Application to the *Royal Society* I have mention'd, because it comes from that Country, which is seldom wont to have any great Regard to the *Arts* of these *Nations,* that lye on this side of their Mountains.

In *Germany,* and its neighbouring Kingdoms, the *Royal Society* has met with great Veneration; as appears by several Testimonies in their late *printed Books,* which have been submitted to its Censure; by many *Curiosities* of *Mechanick Instruments,* that have been transmitted to it; and by the *Addresses* which have been sent from their *Philosophical Inquirers.* For which Kinds of Enterprizes the Temper of the *German* Nation is admirably fit, both in respect of their peculiar Dexterity in all sorts of manual *Arts,* and also in Regard of the plain and unaffected Sincerity of their *Manners;* wherein they so much resemble the *English,* that we seem to have deriv'd from them the Composition of our *Minds,* as well as to have descended from their *Race.*

In the *Low-Countries,* their Interest, and Reputation has been establish'd, by the Friendship of some of their chief learned Men, and principally of *Hugenius.* This Gentleman has bestow'd his Pains, on many Parts of the *Speculative,* and *practical Mathematicks,* with wonderful Successes. And particularly his applying the Motion of *Pendulums* to Clocks, and Watches, was an excellent *Invention.* For thereby there may be a Means found out of bringing the *Measures* of *Time,* to an exact *Regulation;* of which the Benefits are infinite. In the Prosecution of such *Discoveries,* he has often requir'd the Aid of this Society; he has receiv'd the Light of their *Trials,* and a Confirmation of his own, and has freely admitted their *Alterations* or *Amendments.* And this learned Correspondence with him, and many others, is still continued, even at this present Time, in the Breach between our *Countries:* Their great Founder, and Patron still permitting them to maintain the Traffick of *Sciences,* when all other *Commerce* is intercepted. Whence we may guess, what may be expected from the peaceful Part of our *King's Reign,* when his very Wars are manag'd without Injury to the *Arts* of *Civil Knowledge.*

But not to wander any farther in Particulars, it may perhaps in *general* be safely computed, that there has been as large a Communication of Foreign *Arts,* and *Inventions* to the *Royal Society,* within this small Compass of Time, as ever before did pass over the *English* Chanel, since the very first Transportation of *Arts* into our *Island.* . . .

It would be a useless Pomp to reckon up a *Catalogue* of their *Names;* especially seeing they are already recorded with Gratitude, in a more lasting *Monument,* the *Register* of the *Society.* Only it will not, I think, be amiss, if I mention the Visit of one *Prince,* because it may afford us a profitable Observation. When the Duke of *Brunswick* and *Lunenburgh* was introduc'd into their weekly *Assembly,* and had subscrib'd his Name to their *Statutes;* there was according to the Custom, one of the *Fellows* appointed, to interpret to him, what Experiments were produc'd, and examin'd at that Meeting. But his *Highness* told them, that it was not necessary they should put themselves to that Trouble; for he well understood our Language, having been drawn to the Study of it, out of a Desire of reading our *Philosophical Books.* . . .

I now come to relate, what *Incouragements* this Design has receiv'd at home in its native Soil. And I will assure my *Reader,* that the *Original* of the *Royal Society* has found a general *Approbation* within ourselves, and that the most prudent Men of all Professions and Interests, have shewn by their Respects to these hopeful Beginnings, that there is a *Reverence* due to the first Trials and Intentions, as well as to the last Accomplishment of generous Attempts.

Of our chief and most wealthy *Merchants* and *Citizens*, very many have assisted it with their Presence; and thereby have added the industrious, punctual, and active *Genius* of Men of *Traffick*, to the quiet, sedentary, and reserv'd Temper of Men of *Learning*. They have contributed their *Labours;* they have help'd their *Correspondence;* they have employ'd their *Factors* Abroad to answer their *Inquiries;* they have laid out in all Countries for *Observations;* they have bestow'd many considerable Gifts on their *Treasury* and Repository. And chiefly there is one *Bounty* to be here inserted, which for the singular Benefit that may be expected from it, deserves the *Applause* and *Imitation* of this and future Times. It is the *Establishment* made by Sir *John Cutler*, for the reading on *Mechanicks*, in the Place where the *Royal Society* shall meet. This is the first *Lecture* that has been founded of this Kind, amidst all the vast *Munificence* of so many *Benefactors to Learning* in this latter Age.

* * *

Of our *Nobility* and *Gentry*, the most noble and *illustrious* have condescended to labour here with their *Hands*, to impart their *Discoveries*, to propose their *Doubts*, to assist and defray the *Charge* of their *Trials*. And this they have done with such a universal Agreement, that it is almost the only thing, wherein the *Nobility* of all the three Kingdoms are *united*. In their *Assemblies* for making Laws they are separated; in their Customs and Manners of Life they differ; and in their Humours too, they are thought not much of kin to each other. But in the *Royal Society* the *Scotch*, the *Irish*, the *English* Gentry do meet, and communicate, without any Distinction of *Countries* or Affections. From hence no doubt very much *political*, as well as *philosophical* Benefit will arise. . . .

Of our *Ministers of State at home*, and our *Embassadors abroad*, there have been very few employ'd, who are not *Fellows* of the *Royal Society:* and especially these latter have bestow'd their Pains in *foreign Courts*, to collect *Relations* and Secrets of Nature, as well as of State: For which Service their Way of Life is most convenient, by the Generality of their Converse, the *Privileges* and *Freedom* of their *Dispatches*, and the usual Resort of the most knowing and inquisitive Men to their Company.

Our greatest *Captains* and *Commanders* have inroll'd their *Names* in this Number, and have regarded these *Studies:* which are not, as other Parts of *Learning*, to be call'd the *Studies of the Gown;* for they do as well become the Profession of a *Soldier*, or any other Way of Life. . . .

Of our *Churchmen* the greatest and the most *Reverend*, by their Care and Passion, and Endeavours in advancing this *Institution,* have taken off the unjust Scandal from *Natural* Knowledge, that it is an Enemy to *Divinity*. By the perpetual *Patronage* and *Assistance* they have afforded the *Royal Society*, they have confuted the false Opinions of those Men, who believe that *Philosophers* must needs be *irreligious:* they have shewn, that in our *Veneration* of *God's almighty Power*, we ought to imitate the manner of our Respect to *earthly Kings*. For as the greater their *Dominion* is, the more Observance is wont to be given to their nearest Servants and Officers: so the Greatness of the *Divine Majesty* is best to be worship'd, by the due honouring and observing of *Nature*, which is his immediate Servant, and the universal *Minister* of his *Pleasure*.

But I make haste to that, which ought to be esteem'd the very *Life* and Soul of this *Undertaking*, the Protection and Favour of the *King* and the *Royal Family*. When the *Society* first address'd themselves to his *Majesty*, he was pleas'd to express much Satisfaction, that this Enterprise was begun in *his Reign:* he then represented to them the Gravity and Difficulty of their Work, and assur'd them of all the kind Influence of his *Power* and *Prerogative*. Since that he has frequently committed many Things to their *Search:* he has refer'd many foreign *Rarities* to their *Inspection:* he has recommended many domestick *Improvements* to their Care: he has demanded the Result of their *Trials*, in many Appearances of *Nature:* he has been present, and assisted with his own Hands, at the performing of many of their *Experiments*, in his *Gardens*, his *Parks*, and on the *River*.

FONTENELLE: *Eulogies of Scientists* *

> Bernard le Bouvier de Fontenelle (1657–1757) is best known as a popularizer of the new science of the seventeenth century. He became secretary of the French Academy of Sciences whose history he wrote in 1733. His *Eloges des Académiciens*, composed between 1708 and 1719, testifies to the growing prestige of science and scientists in the seventeenth century. It consists of a series of brief biographies of members of the Academy, most of whom Fontenelle knew personally.

Louis Carré

Louis CARRÉ was born July 26, 1663, of a good farmer of Clofontaine near Nangis in Brie. His father made him study to be a priest, but he did not feel called to the priesthood. Out of filial obedience he studied theology for three years, at the end of which time, because he refused to take orders, his father refused to support him in Paris. Very often people become priests in order to save themselves from indigence; he preferred indigence to holy orders. . . .

* Fontenelle: *Eloges historiques des Académiciens* (Paris: Bernard Brunet; 1742), vol. I, pp. 145–7, 210–13, 301–02, 389–93; vol. II, pp. 448–9, 451–2. My translation.

His bad fortune produced a great good. He sought a refuge and found one in the home of Malebranche, who took him to write under him. From the dark Scholastic Philosophy, he was suddenly transported to the source of a luminous and brilliant Philosophy [Cartesianism]; in it he saw everything change face, and a new Universe was revealed to him.

Du Verney

Guichard Joseph du Verney was born at Feurs in Forez, August 5, 1648 of Jacques du Verney, doctor of the same town, and Antoinette Pittre. His classes over, he studied medicine at Avignon for five years, and in 1667 set out for Paris to which he felt called by his talents.

Scarcely had he arrived in this great city than he went to the home of the famous Abbé Bourdelot, who held conferences of men of letters of all kinds. He made for them an anatomy of the brain, and others at the learned doctor Denys', where they also assembled. He demonstrated what had been discovered by Stenon, Swammerdam, Graaf, and the other great anatomists, and he soon acquired a reputation.

Besides his learning, already great and rare for his age, what contributed a great deal to putting him promptly in vogue was the eloquence with which he spoke on these matters. This eloquence was comprised not only of clarity, exactness, and order—all the cold perfections which dogmatic subjects demand; it was a fire in his expression and manner, and a precision in his pronunciation which would almost have sufficed for an orator. . . .

When those who had charge of the Dauphin's education thought of giving him a knowledge of natural philosophy, they conferred upon the Academy of Sciences the honor of appointing from their body the ones who would have this function. The Academy appointed M. Roëmer for general experiments, and M. du Verney for anatomy. The latter prepared his projects in Paris and transported them to Saint-Germain or Versailles. There he found a formidable audience, the Dauphin surrounded by the Duke of Montausier, the Bishop of Meaux, M. Huet since become Bishop of Avranches, and M. de Cordemoi, all of whom . . . were very learned and capable of judging what was new to them. The anatomical demonstrations succeeded so well with the young prince that he sometimes offered not to go hunting if they could be continued after his dinner.

Lémery

Nicholas Lémery was born at Rouen, November 17, 1645, of Julian Lémery, prosecutor in the Parlement of Normandy and a Protestant.

[After studying chemistry in Paris and Montpellier, and looking up the most skillful chemists all over France] he returned to Paris in 1672. At that time Conferences were held in the homes of divers individuals. Those who had a taste for the true sciences assembled in small groups like rebels who conspired against ignorance and the dominant prejudices. Such were the Assemblies of M. the Abbé Bourdelot, physician of Prince Condé, and those of M. Justel. M. Lémery appeared and scintillated at all of these. He joined forces with M. Martin, the Prince's apothecary, and making use of his friend's laboratory at the Hotel Condé, he offered a course in chemistry which soon won for him the honor of being known and esteemed by the Prince, in whose house he worked. He was often sent for to Chantilly, where the hero, surrounded by intelligent and learned people, lived in a manner that would have made Caesar envious.

At length M. Lémery wished to have his own laboratory and to be independent. . . . In the rue Galande where he went to live he opened public courses. His laboratory was less a room than a cellar, and almost a magic cavern, lighted only by the gleam of furnaces. Nevertheless the concourse of the world there was so great that he scarcely had any room for his operations. His auditors included the most famous names, Rohaut Bernier, Auzout, Regis, Tournefort. Even women, carried along by the fashion, had the audacity to show themselves at these learned assemblies. At the same time M. du Verney offered equally brilliant courses in anatomy, and all the nations of Europe filled them with students. In one year they included forty Scotchmen who had come to Paris especially to study under these two masters, and who returned home as soon as their courses were finished.

Regis

Pierre-Silvain Regis was born in 1632. . . . His father lived nobly and was rich enough, but he had a great many children and M. Regis, who was one of the younger sons, found himself with little fortune.

After having performed brilliantly in the humanities and philosophy at the Jesuit school in Cahors, he studied theology in the University of that town because he was destined for the ecclesiastical state; and in four years he became so skillful that the University urged him to take the doctorate, offering to defray all his expenses. But he did not believe he was worthy of it because he had not studied at the Sorbonne at Paris. He went there; but disgusted by the excessive length of what a celebrated professor said on the single question of the hour of the institution of the Eucharist, and having been struck by the Cartesian Philosophy, which he became acquainted with at the lectures of M. Rohaut, he attached himself entirely to this philosophy whose charm, even independent of its novelty, could not fail to appeal to a spirit like his. . . .

M. Regis . . . went to establish the new philosophy at Toulouse by public debates which he began to hold there in 1665. He had an agreeable facility of speaking, and the gift of adapting abstract matters to the capacity of his auditors. Soon the whole town was roused by the new philosophy; savants, magistrates, ecclesiastics, everybody hastened to hear him, even the ladies making part of the crowd; and if someone could share with him the glory of this great success, it could be only the great Descartes whose discoveries he announced. A thesis maintaining pure Cartesianism and dedicated to one of the first ladies of Toulouse, whom M. Regis had made a very skillful Cartesian, was defended in a public debate over which he presided. The debate was in French and the lady herself resolved several knotty problems. By these means they were able to effect a more complete abjuration of the ancient philosophy. The gentlemen of Toulouse, sensible of the instruction and light that M. Regis had brought them, settled on him a public pension, an event almost unbelievable in our customs and which seems to belong to ancient Greece. . . .

Tournefort

Joseph Pitton de Tournefort was born at Aix in Provence June 5, 1656, of Pierre Pitton, squire of Tournefort, and Aimare de Fagouë, of a noble Parisian family.

He went to the college of the Jesuits at Aix. Like all the other students, he was put to work studying Latin, but as soon as he saw plants he longed to be a botanist. He wanted to know their names, he carefully marked their differences, and sometimes he missed his classes in order to herborize in the country and study nature instead of the language of the anient Romans. . . .

He had small taste for what they taught him in philosophy. He found that it had nothing to do with nature which he so loved to observe, but rather with vague and abstract ideas. . . . He discovered in the study of his father the philosophy of Descartes, then little known in Provence, and immediately recognized it for what he was looking for. He had to read it surreptitiously, but it was with that much more ardor. And his father who was opposed to so useful a study gave him, without realizing it, an excellent education.

As his father intended him for the church, he made him study theology and even put him in a seminary. But his natural destination prevailed. He had to see plants, and so he pursued his dear studies, whether in a rather curious garden belonging to an apothecary of Aix, or in the neighbouring fields, or on hill tops. . . .

He had scarcely less passion for anatomy and chemistry than for botany. Finally physic and medicine laid claim to him with such strength that theology, which unjustly possessed him, had to give him up. He was encouraged by the example of a paternal uncle, a very skillful and much esteemed doctor, and the death of his father in 1677 left him entirely free to follow his inclination.

2. *The New Science*

A. GEOGRAPHY AND THE EXPANSION OF EUROPE

MICHEL DE MONTAIGNE: *Of Cannibals* *

Michel de Montaigne (1533–92) was a member of the minor French nobility. At the age of thirty-eight he resigned from the Parlement of Bordeaux to live the life of a retired scholar in his family château. There he collected one of the largest private libraries of his time, and composed the famous *Essays*, which record the impressions of human nature and beliefs of a philosophical sceptic. The essay "Of Cannibals," a few brief excerpts from which follow, shows the sceptical trend of thought into which Montaigne drifted when reflecting upon the overseas discoveries.

WHEN King Pyrrhus passed over into Italy, having surveyed the ordering of the army the Romans sent out against him, he said, "I do not know what kind of barbarians these may be (for so the Greeks called all foreign nations), but the disposition of this army that I see has nothing of the barbarous in it." As much did the Greeks say of the army which Flaminius brought into their country, *and also Philip, when he beheld from an eminence the order and distribution of the Roman camp formed in his kingdom under Publius Sulpicius Galba.* Thus it appears how cautious men ought to be about clinging to vulgar opinions, and that we should judge by the method of reason and not by common report.

I had dwelling with me for a long time a man who had lived ten or twelve years in that other world which has been discovered in our time, in that place where Villegaignon landed, which he called Antarctic France. This discovery of so vast a country seems to be worthy of consideration. . . .

This man that I had was a plain ignorant fellow, which is a character likely to bear true witness; for your clever men are much more curious observers, and notice more things, but they gloss them; and to give the greater weight to their interpretation and make it persuasive, they cannot forbear a little to alter the story; they never represent things to you simply as they are, but bend and mask them according to the appearance which they had for them; and to gain faith for their

---

* Reprinted from *The Essays of Michel de Montaigne*, translated by Jacob Zeitlin, by permission of Alfred A. Knopf, Inc. Copyright 1934, 1935, 1936, by Alfred A. Knopf, Inc. Vol. I, pp. 179–o, 181–3.

judgment, and to induce you to accept it, are willing to add something of their own to the matter, to expand it and amplify it. We need either a very truthful man or one so simple that he has not wherewithal to build and to give a colour of truth to false stories, and who has espoused no theories. Such was my man; and besides, he has at divers times brought to me several seamen and merchants whom he knew on that voyage. I therefore content myself with his information, without inquiring what the cosmographers say about it. . . .

. . . I find that there is nothing barbarous and savage in this nation, as far as I have been informed, except that everyone calls barbarism that which is not his own usage; as, indeed, we seem to have no other level of truth and reason than the example and pattern of the opinions and practices of the country wherein we live. There one finds always the perfect religion, the perfect government, the most perfected and accomplished usage in all things. They are savages in the same sense that we say fruits are wild, which nature produces by herself and in her usual course; whereas in truth, we ought rather to call wild those whose natures we have changed by our artifice and diverted from the common order. . . .

These nations, then, seem to me to be so far barbarous as they have received very little fashioning from human wit, and are still very near to their original simplicity. The laws of Nature govern them still, very little debased with any mixture of ours; but they are in such a state of purity that I am sometimes vexed that the knowledge of them did not come earlier, at a time when there were men better able to judge of them than we are. I am sorry that Lycurgus and Plato did not know them; for it seems to me that what we now actually see in those nations, does not only surpass all the pictures with which the poets have adorned the golden age and all their inventions in feigning a happy state of man, but even the conceptions and the very desire of philosophy. They could not imagine so pure and simple an innocence as we by experience see to be in them; nor could they have believed that human society could be maintained with so little artifice and human cementing. This is a nation, I should say to Plato, wherein there is no manner of traffic, no knowledge of letters, no science of numbers, no name of magistrate or political superiority, no use of service, no riches or poverty, no contracts, no successions, no partitions of property, no employments but those of leisure, no respect of kinship save the common ties, no clothing, no agriculture, no metal, no use of corn or wine. The very words that signify lying, treachery, dissimulation, avarice, envy, detraction, pardon, never heard of. How far distant from this perfection would he find the republic of his imagination: *"viri a diis recentes," "mortals fresh from the gods."*

JOSEPH GLANVILL: *Plus Ultra* *

Joseph Glanvill (1636–80), Anglican divine and member of the Royal Society, wrote a number of essays championing experimental science and defending it from the charge of atheism. The title of his book, *Plus Ultra: or, the Progress and Advancement of Knowledge since the Days of Aristotle, in an Account of some of the most remarkable late Improvements of practical, useful Learning* (1668), is self-explanatory.

Geography

IN THIS the Ancients were exceedingly defective. And Aristotle knew the World, by the same figure his Scholar conquer'd it. 'Tis noted by the ingenious Varenius, that the most general and necessary things in this Science were then unknown; as, The Habitableness of the torrid Zone; The flux and reflux of the Sea; The diversity of Winds; The Polar propertie of the Magnet; The true dimension of the Earth. They wanted Descriptions of remote Countries, concerning which both the Greeks and Romans had very fabulous Relations. They knew not that the Earth was encompassed by the Sea, and might be Sailed round. They were totally ignorant of America, and both the North and South parts of this Hemisphere; yea, and understood very little of the remoter places of their own Asia. Japan, the Java's, the Philippicks, and Borneo, were either not at all known, or exceeding imperfectly of old: But all these are familiar to the latter Times. Mexico and Peru, and the vast Regions of those mighty Empires, with the many Isles of the Great Sea are disclosed. The frozen North, the torrid Line, and formerly unknown South, are visited, and by their numerous Inhabitants found not to be so inhospitable and unkind to men, as Antiquity believed. The Earth hath been rounded by Magellan, Drake, and Candish. The great Motion of the Sea is vulgar, and its varieties inquiring every day: The diversities of Winds stated, and better understood: The Treasure of hidden Vertues in the Loadstone, found and used. The Spicy Islands of the East, as also those of the remote South and North, frequented, and the knowledge of that People and those Countries transmitted to us, with their Riches; The most distant being Parts Travell'd and Describ'd. Our Navigation is far greater, our Commerce is more general, our Charts more exact, our Globes more accurate, our Travels more remote, our Reports more intelligent and sincere; and consequently, our Geography far more perfect, than it was in the elder Times of Polybius and Possidonius, yea than in those of Ptolemy, Strabo, and Pomponius Mela, who lived among the Caesars. And if It was so short in the flourishing Times of the Roman Empire, how was it before, in the days of Aristotle and the Graecians? We have an Instance of it in the Great Macedonian, who thought the bounds of

* Joseph Glanvill: *Plus Ultra* (London: J. Collins; 1668), pp. 48–50.

his Conquests to be the end of the World; when there were Nations enough beyond them, to have eaten up the Conqueror, with his proud and triumphant Armies. So that here also Modern Improvements have been great; and you will think so, if you compare the Geographical Performances of Gemma Frisius, Mercator, Ortelius, Stevinus, Bertius, and Guil. Blaeu, with the best Remains of the most celebrated Geographers of the more ancient Ages.

MELCHISÉDECH THÉVENOT: *Collection of Voyages* *

Melchisédech Thévenot (1620–92) was one of those responsible for the foundation of the French Academy of Sciences. His main interest was geography, and in his capacity as king's librarian he lectured on the subject and made collections of voyages. The following selection is from his preface to the *Recueil de voyages* (1681).

THE DESIRE to know the world is natural to us. . . . Almost all the nations have had geographers: the Persians and Arabs had as many as the Greeks and Latins, and the geography of China is as exact as that which the latter have left to us. There were so many descriptions of the world in the time of Augustus that Strabo apologizes for writing on a subject discussed by so many able people. Three or four centuries after Strabo, Ptolemy makes the same excuses, as though the subject had been exhausted by that time. But the great voyages of recent times have revealed to us an expanse of the world greater than that described by the Greeks, Romans, and Orientals. From these voyages we know that the ancients were almost always mistaken in what they have told us about the places to which their empires did not extend. If we reckon the extent of their discoveries in the world and in the history of nature, we owe as much knowledge to these recent voyagers as to all those who preceded them. They have disabused us of the error which St. Augustine shared with many great and saintly persons, that the tropics could not have been populated after the universal deluge. From the voyagers we have learned that the torrid zone is one of the most delightful parts of the earth and one of the most densely populated, by men and all kinds of animals. A great many men of letters have been exercised by another difficulty posed by these voyages, namely the origin of the people discovered in America. But they have not availed themselves of the most convincing of proofs: which is the chief reason why I have inserted in the fourth volume of this collection the history of the Mexicans by figures, from which I get the proof. In these figures or histories the years are marked in a manner peculiar to the peoples of Asia, the Chinese, Tartars, and Japanese. I do not

* *Recueil de Voyages de M' Thévenot* (Paris: E. Michallet; 1681), pp. 1–7. My translation.

know of any other peoples than these who have counted their years by cycles. And since this manner is subtle, and since the Americans of today are very simple, there is a good deal of reason to believe that the latter descended from another nation. . . .

I will be told that it is impossible to imagine how these peoples could have crossed the great ocean and made such a long journey. But those who make this objection forget about the great changes which can occur on the globe of the earth. . . . The slightest change in its center can cause upheavals—turn valleys into mountains, and mountains into valleys —which appear so great to men because of their presumption in measuring great and little by what they can do, and the duration of time by the duration of their own life. . . .

Lucretius, Ovid, Strabo and Pliny noticed and spoke about ships, anchors, shells, and remains of marine fish which they saw with astonishment on mountains. But men of letters could have explained these phenomena more satisfactorily if they had taken the trouble to examine them on the spot. Without going very far, those of us Frenchmen who would like to be enlightened in this matter can see, one league from Paris, below the walls of the park belonging to M. du Harlay, attorney-general of the Parlement of Paris, some very good evidence of one of these great upheavals. I can show you beds of shells, remains and bones of fish which are only to be found in the ocean—convincing proof that the sea, which is now about forty leagues away, formerly extended to that point. . . .

From this fact one can deduce many important consequences, not only for the knowledge of the earth but also for the chronology of the world: for although we cannot say exactly at what time similar deposits were laid down, it is certainly true that to find two or three above one another (as one sees them under the foundations of some towns which were placed there more than three thousand years ago) is good evidence that there have been changes in the earth unnoticed by history. . . . Whether the opinion of the Septuagint (Septantes) and the "Roman Martyrology" on the age of the world is more probable than that of the rabbis is something to think about. For the present it is enough for me to show how the migration of Asiatics to America might have come about.

B. THE NEW ASTRONOMY

NICHOLAS COPERNICUS: *Commentariolus* *

Nicholas Copernicus (1473–1543) was born in Poland, the son of a prosperous merchant and official of the Hanseatic town of Thorn. Like so many other scholars of his time, he went to Italy where he studied under Maria de Novara, Professor of Mathematics and Astronomy at Bologna. From Novara he caught the spirit of the Platonic and Pythagorean revival which criticized the Ptolemaic system for its lack of mathematical simplicity. From the ancient philosophers whose works he read, he conceived the possibilty of the earth's mobility and an alternative theory of celestial phenomena. His great work describing this theory, the *De Revolutionibus Orbium Celestium*, was not published until the year of his death, but some years before he set down his astronomical assumptions in a brief sketch (*Commentariolus*), a part of which follows.

OUR ancestors assumed, I observe, a large number of celestial spheres for this reason especially, to explain the apparent motion of the planets by the principle of regularity. For they thought it altogether absurd that a heavenly body, which is a perfect sphere, should not always move uniformly. They saw that by connecting and combining regular motions in various ways they could make any body appear to move to any position.

Callippus and Eudoxus, who endeavored to solve the problem by the use of concentric spheres, were unable to account for all the planetary movements; they had to explain not merely the apparent revolutions of the planets but also the fact that these bodies appear to us sometimes to mount higher in the heavens, sometimes to descend; and this fact is incompatible with the principle of concentricity. Therefore it seemed better to employ eccentrics and epicycles, a system which most scholars finally accepted.

Yet the planetary theories of Ptolemy and most other astronomers, although consistent with the numerical data, seemed likewise to present no small difficulty. For these theories were not adequate unless certain equants were also conceived; it then appeared that a planet moved with uniform velocity neither on its deferent nor about the center of its epicycle. Hence a system of this sort seemed neither sufficiently absolute nor sufficiently pleasing to the mind.

Having become aware of these defects, I often considered whether there could perhaps be found a more reasonable arrangement of circles, from which every apparent inequality would be derived and in which everything would move uniformly about its proper center, as the rule of absolute motion requires. After I had addressed myself to this very difficult and almost insoluble problem, the suggestion at length came to me how it could be solved with fewer and much simpler constructions than were formerly used, if some assumptions (which are called axioms) were granted me. They follow in this order.

1. There is no one center of all the celestial circles or spheres.

2. The center of the earth is not the center of the universe, but only of gravity and of the lunar sphere.

3. All the spheres revolve about the sun as their mid-point, and therefore the sun is the center of the universe.

4. The ratio of the earth's distance from the sun to the height of the firmament is so much smaller than the ratio of the earth's radius to its distance from the sun that the distance from the earth to the sun is imperceptible in comparison with the height of the firmament.

5. Whatever motion appears in the firmament arises not from any motion of the firmament, but from the earth's motion. The earth together with its circumjacent elements performs a complete rotation on its fixed poles in a daily motion, while the firmament and highest heaven abide unchanged.

6. What appear to us as motions of the sun arise not from its motion but from the motion of the earth and our sphere, with which we revolve about the sun like any other planet. The earth has, then, more than one motion.

7. The apparent retrograde and direct motion of the planets arises not from their motion but from the earth's. The motion of the earth alone, therefore, suffices to explain so many apparent inequalities in the heavens. . . .

Let no one suppose that I have gratuitously asserted, with the Pythagoreans, the motion of the earth; strong proof will be found in my exposition of the circles. For the principal arguments by which the natural philosophers attempt to establish the immobility of the earth rest for the most part on the appearances; it is particularly such arguments that collapse here, since I treat the earth's immobility as due to an appearance.

The celestial spheres are arranged in the following order. The highest is the immovable sphere of the fixed stars, which contains and gives position to all things. Beneath it is Saturn, which Jupiter follows, then Mars. Below Mars is the sphere on which we revolve; then Venus, last is Mercury. The lunar sphere revolves about the center of the earth and moves with the earth like an epicycle. In the same order also, one planet surpasses another in speed of revolution, according as they trace greater or smaller circles. Thus Saturn completes its revolution in thirty years, Jupiter in twelve, Mars in two and one-half, and the earth in one year; Venus in nine months, Mercury in three.

C. THE NEW PHYSICS

ROGER COTES: *Preface to Sir Isaac Newton's* Principia *

Sir Isaac Newton brought out a second edition of his *Principia* (*The Mathematical Principles of Natural Philosophy*) in 1713. The preface

* Sir Isaac Newton: *The Mathematical Principles of Natural Philosophy*, trans. by Andrew Motte (London: B. Motte; 1729), pp. 1–8, 10–13.

was written by his friend Roger Cotes (1682–1716), mathematician and professor of astronomy and natural philosophy at Cambridge. Cotes's summary of the Newtonian system—of the modern law of inertia, gravitation, the uniformity of nature, etc.—shows how far the new physics had travelled from Aristotelian principles.

THOSE who have treated of natural philosophy, may be nearly reduced to three classes. Of these some have attributed to the several species of things, specific and occult qualities; on which, in a manner unknown, they make the operations of the several bodies to depend. The sum of the doctrine of the Schools derived from *Aristotle* and the Peripatetics is herein contained. They affirm that the several effects of bodies arise from the particular natures of those bodies. But whence it is that bodies derive those natures they don't tell us; and therefore they tell us nothing. And being entirely employed in giving names to things, and not in searching into things themselves, we may say that they have invented a philosophical way of speaking, but not that they have made known to us true philosophy. . . .

There is left then the third class, which profess experimental philosophy. These indeed derive the causes of all things from the most simple principles possible; but then they assume nothing as a principle, that is not proved by phaenomena. They frame no hypotheses, nor receive them into philosophy otherwise than as questions whose truth may be disputed. They proceed therefore in a two-fold method, synthetical and analytical. From some select phaenomena they deduce by analysis the forces of nature, and the more simple laws of forces; and from thence by synthesis shew the constitution of the rest. This is that incomparably best way of philosophizing, which our renowned author most justly embraced before the rest; and thought alone worthy to be cultivated and adorned by his excellent labours. Of this he has given us a most illustrious example, by the explication of the System of the World, most happily deduced from the Theory of Gravity. That the virtue of gravity was found in all bodies, others suspected, or imagined before him; but he was the only and the first philosopher that could demonstrate it from appearances, and make it a solid foundation to the most noble speculations.

* * *

Therefore that we may begin our reasoning from what is most simple and nearest to us; let us consider a little what is the nature of gravity with us on Earth, that we may proceed the more safely when we come to consider it in the heavenly bodies, that lie at so vast a distance from us. It is now agreed by all philosophers that all circumterrestrial bodies gravitate towards the Earth. That no bodies really light are to be found, is now confirmed by manifold experience. That which is relative levity, is not true levity, but apparent only; and arises from the preponderating gravity of the contiguous bodies.

Moreover, as all bodies gravitate towards the Earth, so does the Earth again towards bodies. That the action of gravity is mutual, and equal on both sides, is thus proved. . . .

This is the nature of gravity upon Earth; let us now see what it is in the Heavens.

That every body perseveres in its state either of rest, or of moving uniformly in a right line, unless in so far as it is compelled to change that state by forces impressed, is a law of nature universally received by all philosophers. But from thence it follows that bodies which move in curve lines, and are therefore continually going off from the right lines that are tangents to their orbits, are by some continued force retained in those curvilinear paths. Since then the Planets move in curvilinear orbits there must be some force operating, by whose repeated actions they are perpetually made to deflect from the tangents. . . .

From what has been hitherto said, it is plain that the Planets are retained in their orbits by some force perpetually acting upon them; it is plain that that force is always directed towards the centres of their orbits; it is plain that its efficacy is augmented with the nearness to the centre, and diminished with the same; and that it is augmented in the same proportion with which the square of the distance is diminished, and diminished in the same proportion with which the square of the distance is augmented. . . .

Because the revolutions of the primary Planets about the Sun, and of the secondary about Jupiter and Saturn, are phaenomena of the same kind with the revolution of the Moon about the Earth; and because it has been moreover demonstrated that the centripetal forces of the primary Planets are directed towards the centre of the Sun, and those of the secondary towards the centres of Jupiter and Saturn, in the same manner as the centripetal force of the Moon is directed towards the centre of the Earth; and since besides, all these forces are reciprocally as the squares of the distances from the centres, in the same manner as the centripetal force of the Moon is as the square of the distance from the Earth; we must of course conclude, that the nature of all is the same. Therefore as the Moon gravitates towards the Earth, and the Earth again towards the Moon; so also all the secondary Planets will gravitate towards their primary, and the primary Planets again towards their secondary; and so all the primary towards the Sun; and the Sun again towards the primary.

Therefore the Sun gravitates towards all the Planets, and all the Planets towards the Sun. . . .

That the attractive virtue of the Sun is propagated on all sides to prodigious distances, and is diffused to every part of the wide space that surrounds it, is most evidently shewn by the motion of the Comets; which coming from places immensely distant from the Sun, approach very near to it; and sometimes so near, that in their perihelia they almost touch its body. The theory of these bodies was altogether unknown to astronomers, till in our own times our excellent author most happily discovered it, and demonstrated the truth of it by most certain observations. So that it is now apparent that the Comets move in conic sections having their foci in the Sun's centre, and by radii drawn to the Sun describe areas proportional to the times. But from these phaenomena it is manifest, and mathematically demonstrated, that those forces, by which the Comets are retained in their orbits, respect the Sun, and are reciprocally proportional to the squares of the distances from its centre. Therefore the Comets gravitate towards the Sun; and therefore the attractive force of the Sun not only acts on the bodies of the Planets, placed at given distances and very nearly in the same plane, but reaches also to the Comets in the most different parts of the heavens, and at the most different distances. This therefore is the nature of gravitating bodies, to propagate their force at all distances to all other gravitating bodies.

*   *   *

The foregoing conclusions are grounded on this axiom which is received by all philosophers; namely that effects of the same kind, that is, whose known properties are the same, take their rise from the same causes and have the same unknown properties also. For who doubts, if gravity be the cause of the descent of a stone in *Europe*, but that it is also the cause of the same descent in *America?* . . .

Since then all bodies, whether upon Earth or in the Heavens, are heavy, so far as we can make any experiments or observations concerning them; we must certainly allow that gravity is found in all bodies universally. And in like manner as we ought not to suppose that any bodies can be otherwise than extended, moveable or impenetrable; so we ought not to conceive that any bodies can be otherwise than heavy. The extension, mobility and impenetrability of bodies become known to us only by experiments; and in the very same manner their gravity becomes known to us. All bodies we can make any observations upon, are extended, moveable and impenetrable; and thence we conclude all bodies, and those we have no observations concerning, to be extended and moveable and impenetrable. So all bodies we can make observations on, we find to be heavy; and thence we conclude all bodies, and those we have no observations of, to be heavy also. If any one should say that the bodies of the fixed Stars are not heavy because their gravity is not yet observed; they may say for the same reason that they are neither extended, nor moveable nor impenetrable, because these affections of the fixed Stars are not yet observed. In short, either gravity must have a place among the primary qualities of all bodies, or extension, mobility and impenetrability must not.

D. THE NEW PHYSIOLOGY

WILLIAM HARVEY: *On the Motion of the Heart and Blood* *

William Harvey (1578–1657) has been called the father of modern physiology. He studied at Padua where Vesalius, Colombo, and Fabricius had preceded him. There he learned to question the authorities, to distrust final causes in science, and to make dissections and experiments. Harvey was a royalist in politics, but he overthrew the physiology of Galen in his great work on the circulation of the blood, *Exercitatio Anatomica de Motu Cordis et Sanguinis* (1628), which was addressed to the Royal College of Physicians.

WERE not the work indeed presented through you, my learned friends, I should scarce hope that it could come out scatheless and complete; for you have in general been the faithful witnesses of almost all the instances from which I have either collected the truth or confuted error; you have seen my dissections, and at my demonstrations of all that I maintain to be objects of sense, you have been accustomed to stand by and bear me out with your testimony. And as this book alone declares the blood to course and revolve by a new route, very different from the ancient and beaten pathway trodden for so many ages, and illustrated by such a host of learned and distinguished men, I was greatly afraid lest I might be charged with presumption did I lay my work before the public at home, or send it beyond seas for impression, unless I had first proposed its subject to you, had confirmed its conclusions by ocular demonstrations in your presence, had replied to your doubts and objections, and secured the assent and support of our distinguished President. For I was most intimately persuaded, that if I could make good my proposition before you and our College, illustrious by its numerous body of learned individuals, I had less to fear from others; I even ventured to hope that I should have the comfort of finding all that you had granted me in your sheer love of truth, conceded by others who were philosophers like yourselves. For true philosophers, who are only eager for truth and knowledge, never regard themselves as already so thoroughly informed, but

* *The Works of William Harvey*, trans. by R. Willis (London: Sydenham Society; 1847), pp. 5–7, 31–2, 45–7.

that they welcome further information from whomsoever and from whencesoever it may come; nor are they so narrow-minded as to imagine any of the arts or sciences transmitted to us by the ancients, in such a state of forwardness or completeness, that nothing is left for the ingenuity and industry of others; very many, on the contrary, maintain that all we know is still infinitely less than all that still remains unknown; nor do philosophers pin their faith to others' precepts in such wise that they lose their liberty, and cease to give credence to the conclusions of their proper senses. Neither do they swear such fealty to their mistress Antiquity, that they openly, and in sight of all, deny and desert their friend Truth. . . .

My dear colleagues, I had no purpose to swell this treatise into a large volume by quoting the names and writings of anatomists, or to make a parade of the strength of my memory, the extent of my reading, and the amount of my pains; because I profess both to learn and to teach anatomy, not from books but from dissections; not from the positions of philosophers but from the fabric of nature. . . .

*   *   *

From these and other observations of the like kind, I am persuaded it will be found that the motion of the heart is as follows:

First of all, the auricle contracts, and in the course of its contraction throws the blood, (which it contains in ample quantity as the head of the veins, the store-house and cistern of the blood,) into the ventricle, which being filled, the heart raises itself straightway, makes all its fibres tense, contracts the ventricles, and performs a beat, by which beat it immediately sends the blood supplied to it by the auricle into the arteries; the right ventricle sending its charge into the lungs by the vessel which is called vena arteriosa, but which, in structure and function, and all things else, is an artery; the left ventricle sending its charge into the aorta, and through this by the arteries to the body at large.

These two motions, one of the ventricles, another of the auricles, take place consecutively, but in such a manner that there is a kind of harmony or rhythm preserved between them, the two concurring in such wise that but one motion is apparent, especially in the warmer blooded animals, in which the movements in question are rapid. Nor is this for any other reason than it is in a piece of machinery, in which, though one wheel gives motion to another, yet all the wheels seem to move simultaneously; or in that mechanical contrivance which is adapted to firearms, where the trigger being touched, down comes the flint, strikes against the steel, elicits a spark, which falling among the powder, it is ignited, upon which the flame extends, enters the barrel, causes the explosion, propels the ball, and the mark is attained—all of which incidents, by reason of the celerity with which they happen, seem to take place in the twinkling of an eye.

* * *

Thus far I have spoken of the passage of the blood from the veins into the arteries, and of the manner in which it is transmitted and distributed by the action of the heart; points to which some, moved either by the authority of Galen or Columbus, or the reasonings of others, will give in their adhesion. But what remains to be said upon the quantity and source of the blood which thus passes, is of so novel and unheard-of character, that I not only fear injury to myself from the envy of a few, but I tremble lest I have mankind at large for my enemies, so much doth wont and custom, that become as another nature, and doctrine once sown and that hath struck deep root, and respect for antiquity influence all men: Still the die is cast, and my trust is in my love of truth, and the candour that inheres in cultivated minds. And sooth to say, when I surveyed my mass of evidence, whether derived from vivisections, and my various reflections on them, or from the ventricles of the heart and the vessels that enter into and issue from them, the symmetry and size of these conduits,—for nature doing nothing in vain, would never have given them so large a relative size without a purpose,—or from the arrangement and intimate structure of the valves in particular, and of the other parts of the heart in general, with many things besides, I frequently and seriously bethought me, and long revolved in my mind, what might be the quantity of blood which was transmitted, in how short a time its passage might be effected, and the like; and not finding it possible that this could be supplied by the juices of the ingested aliment without the veins on the one hand becoming drained, and the arteries on the other getting ruptured through the excessive charge of blood, unless the blood should somehow find its way from the arteries into the veins, and so return to the right side of the heart; I began to think whether there might not be A MOTION, AS IT WERE, IN A CIRCLE. Now this I afterwards found to be true; and I finally saw that the blood, forced by the action of the left ventricle into the arteries, was distributed to the body at large, and its several parts, in the same manner as it is sent through the lungs, impelled by the right ventricle into the pulmonary artery, and that it then passed through the veins and along the vena cava, and so round to the left ventricle in the manner already indicated. . . .

The heart, consequently, is the beginning of life; the sun of the microcosm, even as the sun in his turn might well be designated the heart of the world; for it is the heart by whose virtue and pulse the blood is moved, perfected, made apt to nourish, and is preserved from corruption and coagulation; it is the household divinity which, discharging its function, nourishes, cherishes, quickens the whole body, and is indeed the foundation of life, the source of all action.

3. *Redefinition of Knowledge: New Goals and Methods of Science*

FRANCIS BACON *

> Francis Bacon (1561–1626) was a "universal man," lawyer, courtier, holder of high public office under James I, author of essays and histories, popularizer of science. Taking all knowledge as his province, he planned early in life a *magnum opus* on the arts and sciences which he never completed. The following selections are from parts of this *Instauratio Magna* (*Great Renewal*), specifically from *The Advancement of Learning* (1605), the first book of aphorisms of *Novum Organum* (1620), and the preface to the whole work.

BUT the greatest error of all the rest is the mistaking or misplacing of the last or furthest end of knowledge. For men have entered into a desire of learning and knowledge, sometimes upon a natural curiosity and inquisitive appetite; sometimes to entertain their minds with variety and delight; sometimes for ornament and reputation; and sometimes to enable them to victory of wit and contradiction; and most times for lucre and profession; and seldom sincerely to give a true account of their gift of reason, to the benefit and use of men: as if there were sought in knowledge a couch, whereupon to rest a searching and restless spirit; or a terrace, for a wandering and variable mind to walk up and down with a fair prospect; or a tower of state, for a proud mind to raise itself upon; or a fort or commanding ground, for strife and contention; or a shop, for profit or sale; and not a rich storehouse, for the glory of the Creator and the relief of man's estate. But this is that which will indeed dignify and exalt knowledge, if contemplation and action may be more nearly and straitly conjoined and united together than they have been; a conjunction like unto that of the two highest planets, Saturn the planet of rest and contemplation, and Jupiter the planet of civil society and action.

*   *   *

* Francis Bacon: *Works*, ed. by James Spedding, R. L. Ellis, and D. D. Heath (London: Longman and Co.: 1857–62), vol. III, p. 294; vol. IV, pp. 20–1, 48–50, 53–5, 62–3, 72–4, 77–82, 87–93, 114–15.

Aphorism
XI

As the sciences which we now have do not help us in finding out new works, so neither does the logic which we now have help us in finding out new sciences.

XII

The logic now in use serves rather to fix and give stability to the errors which have their foundation in commonly received notions than to help the search after truth. So it does more harm than good.

XIII

The syllogism is not applied to the first principles of sciences, and is applied in vain to intermediate axioms; being no match for the subtlety of nature. It commands assent therefore to the proposition, but does not take hold of the thing.

XIV

The syllogism consists of propositions, propositions consist of words, words are symbols of notions. Therefore if the notions themselves (which is the root of the matter) are confused and over-hastily abstracted from the facts, there can be no firmness in the superstructure. Our only hope therefore lies in a true induction.

XIX

There are and can be only two ways of searching into and discovering truth. The one flies from the senses and particulars to the most general axioms, and from these principles, the truth of which it takes for settled and immoveable, proceeds to judgment and to the discovery of middle axioms. And this way is now in fashion. The other derives axioms from the senses and particulars, rising by a gradual and unbroken ascent, so that it arrives at the most general axioms last of all. This is the true way, but as yet untried.

XXXVIII

The idols and false notions which are now in possession of the human understanding, and have taken deep root therein, not only so beset men's minds that truth can hardly find entrance, but even after entrance obtained, they will again in the very instauration of the sciences meet and trouble us, unless men being forewarned of the danger fortify themselves as far as may be against their assaults.

XXXIX

There are four classes of Idols which beset men's minds. To these for distinction's sake I have assigned names,—calling the first class *Idols of the Tribe;* the second, *Idols of the Cave;* the third, *Idols of the Market-place;* the fourth, *Idols of the Theatre.*

XL

The formation of ideas and axioms by true induction is no doubt the proper remedy to be applied for the keeping off and clearing away of idols. To point them out, however, is of great use; for the doctrine of Idols is to the Interpretation of Nature what the doctrine of the refutation of Sophisms is to common Logic.

XLI

The Idols of the Tribe have their foundation in human nature itself; and in the tribe or race of men. For it is a false assertion that the sense of man is the measure of things. On the contrary, all perceptions as well of the sense as of the mind are according to the measure of the individual and not according to the measure of the universe. And the human understanding is like a false mirror, which, receiving rays irregularly, distorts and discolours the nature of things by mingling its own nature with it.

XLII

The Idols of the Cave are the idols of the individual man. For every one (besides the errors common to human nature in general) has a cave or den of his own, which refracts and discolours the light of nature; owing either to his own proper and peculiar nature; or to his education and conversation with others; or to the reading of books, and the authority of those whom he esteems and admires; or to the differences of impressions, accordingly as they take place in a mind preoccupied and predisposed or in a mind indifferent and settled; or the like. So that the spirit of man (according as it is meted out to different individuals) is in fact a thing variable and full of perturbation, and governed as it were by chance. Whence it was well observed by Heraclitus that men look for sciences in their own lesser worlds, and not in the greater or common world.

XLIII

There are also Idols formed by the intercourse and association of men with each other, which I call Idols of the Marketplace, on account of the commerce and consort of men there. For it is by discourse that men associate; and words are imposed according to the apprehension of the vulgar. And therefore the ill and unfit choice of words wonderfully obstructs the understanding. Nor do the definitions or explanations wherewith in some things learned men are wont to guard and defend themselves, by any means set the matter right. But words plainly force and overrule the understanding, and throw all into confusion, and lead men away into numberless empty controversies and idle fancies.

XLIV

Lastly, there are Idols which have immigrated into men's minds from
the various dogmas of philosophies, and also from wrong laws of demonstration. These I call Idols of the Theatre; because in my judgment all
the received systems are but so many stage-plays, representing worlds
of their own creation after an unreal and scenic fashion. Nor is it only
of the systems now in vogue, or only of the ancient sects and philosophies, that I speak; for many more plays of the same kind may yet be
composed and in like artificial manner set forth; seeing that errors the
most widely different have nevertheless causes for the most part alike.
Neither again do I mean this only of entire systems, but also of many
principles and axioms in science, which by tradition, credulity, and
negligence have come to be received.

LXI

. . . [What I propose] leaves the honour of the ancients untouched. For
they are no wise disparaged—the question between them and me being
only as to the way. For as the saying is, the lame man who keeps the
right road outstrips the runner who takes a wrong one. Nay it is obvious
that when a man runs the wrong way, the more active and swift he is the
further he will go astray.

But the course I propose for the discovering of sciences is such as
leaves but little to the acuteness and strength of wits, but places all wits
and understandings nearly on a level. For as in the drawing of a straight
line or a perfect circle, much depends on the steadiness and practice of
the hand, if it be done by aim of hand only, but if with the aid of rule
or compass, little or nothing; so is it exactly with my plan.

LXXI

The sciences which we possess come for the most part from the
Greeks. For what has been added by Roman, Arabic, or later writers is
not much nor of much importance; and whatever it is, it is built on the
foundation of Greek discoveries. Now the wisdom of the Greeks was
professorial and much given to disputations; a kind of wisdom most adverse to the inquisition of truth. . . .

Nor should we omit that judgment, or rather divination, which was
given concerning the Greeks by the Ægyptian priest,—that "they were
always boys, without antiquity of knowledge or knowledge of antiquity." Assuredly they have that which is characteristic of boys; they are
prompt to prattle, but cannot generate; for their wisdom abounds in
words but is barren of works. . . .

LXXII

Nor does the character of the time and age yield much better signs than the character of the country and nation. For at that period there was but a narrow and meagre knowledge either of time or place; which is the worst thing that can be, especially for those who rest all on experience. For they had no history, worthy to be called history, that went back a thousand years; but only fables and rumours of antiquity. And of the regions and districts of the world they knew but a small portion. . . . In our times on the other hand both many parts of the New World and the limits on every side of the Old World are known, and our stock of experience has increased to an infinite amount. . . .

LXXIII

Of all signs there is none more certain or more noble than that taken from fruits. For fruits and words are as it were sponsors and sureties for the truth of philosophies. Now, from all these systems of the Greeks, and their ramifications through particular sciences, there can hardly after the lapse of so many years be adduced a single experiment which tends to relieve and benefit the condition of man, and which can with truth be referred to the speculations and theories of philosophy.

LXXVIII

In times no less than in regions there are wastes and deserts. For only three revolutions and periods of learning can properly be reckoned; one among the Greeks, the second among the Romans, and the last among us, that is to say, the nations of Western Europe; and to each of these hardly two centuries can justly be assigned. The intervening ages of the world, in respect of any rich or flourishing growth of the sciences, were unprosperous. For neither the Arabians nor the Schoolmen need be mentioned; who in the intermediate times rather crushed the sciences with a multitude of treatises, than increased their weight. And therefore the first cause of so meagre a progress in the sciences is duly and orderly referred to the narrow limits of the time that has been favourable to them.

LXXIX

In the second place there presents itself a cause of great weight in all ways; namely, that during those very ages in which the wits and learning of men have flourished most, or indeed flourished at all, the least part of their diligence was given to natural philosophy. Yet this very philosophy it is that ought to be esteemed the great mother of the sciences. For all arts and all sciences, if torn from this root, though they may be polished and shaped and made fit for use, yet they will hardly grow. Now it is well known that after the Christian religion was received and

grew strong, by far the greater number of the best wits applied themselves to theology; that to this both the highest rewards were offered,
and helps of all kinds most abundantly supplied; and that this devotion to
theology chiefly occupied that third portion or epoch of time among us
Europeans of the West; and the more so because about the same time
both literature began to flourish and religious controversies to spring up.
In the age before, on the other hand, during the continuance of the
second period among the Romans, the meditations and labours of philosophers were principally employed and consumed on moral philosophy,
which to the Heathen was as theology to us. Moreover in those times
the greatest wits applied themselves very generally to public affairs; the
magnitude of the Roman empire requiring the services of a great number
of persons. Again, the age in which natural philosophy was seen to
flourish most among the Greeks, was but a brief particle of time; for
in early ages the Seven Wise Men, as they were called, (all except
Thales) applied themselves to morals and politics; and in later times,
when Socrates had drawn down philosophy from heaven to earth, moral
philosophy became more fashionable than ever, and diverted the minds
of men from the philosophy of nature. . . .

LXXX

To this it may be added that natural philosophy, even among those
who have attended to it, has scarcely ever possessed, especially in these
later times, a disengaged and whole man (unless it were some monk
studying in his cell, or some gentleman in his country-house), but that
it has been made merely a passage and bridge to something else. And so
this great mother of the sciences has with strange indignity been degraded to the offices of a servant; having to attend on the business of
medicine or mathematics, and likewise to wash and imbue youthful and
unripe wits with a sort of first dye, in order that they may be the fitter
to receive another afterwards. Meanwhile let no man look for much
progress in the sciences—especially in the practical part of them—unless
natural philosophy be carried on and applied to particular sciences, and
particular sciences be carried back again to natural philosophy.

LXXXII

And an astonishing thing it is to one who rightly considers the matter,
that no mortal should have seriously applied himself to the opening and
laying out of a road for the human understanding direct from the sense,
by a course of experiment orderly conducted and well built up; but that
all has been left either to the mist of tradition, or the whirl and eddy of
argument, or the fluctuations and mazes of chance and of vague and ill-
digested experience.

LXXXIII

This evil however has been strangely increased by an opinion or conceit, which though of long standing is vain and hurtful; namely, that the dignity of the human mind is impaired by long and close intercourse with experiments and particulars, subject to sense and bound in matter. . . .

LXXXIV

Again, men have been kept back as by a kind of enchantment from progress in the sciences by reverence for antiquity, by the authority of men accounted great in philosophy, and then by general consent. Of the last I have spoken above.

As for antiquity, the opinion touching it which men entertain is quite a negligent one, and scarcely consonant with the word itself. For the old age of the world is to be accounted the true antiquity; and this is the attribute of our own times, not of that earlier age of the world in which the ancients lived; and which, though in respect of us it was the elder, yet in respect of the world it was the younger. And truly as we look for greater knowledge of human things and a riper judgment in the old man than in the young, because of his experience and of the number and variety of the things which he has seen and heard and thought of; so in like manner from our age, if it but knew its own strength and chose to essay and exert it, much more might fairly be expected than from the ancient times, inasmuch as it is a more advanced age of the world, and stored and stocked with infinite experiments and observations.

Nor must it go for nothing that by the distant voyages and travels which have become frequent in our times, many things in nature have been laid open and discovered which may let in new light upon philosophy. And surely it would be disgraceful if, while the regions of the material globe,—that is, of the earth, of the sea, and of the stars,—have been in our times laid widely open and revealed, the intellectual globe should remain shut up within the narrow limits of old discoveries.

And with regard to authority, it shows a feeble mind to grant so much to authors and yet deny time his rights, who is the author of authors, nay rather of all authority. For rightly is truth called the daughter of time, not of authority.

LXXXIX

Neither is to be forgotten that in every age Natural Philosophy has had a troublesome adversary and hard to deal with; namely, superstition, and the blind and immoderate zeal of religion. . . .

Lastly, you will find that by the simpleness of certain divines, access to any philosophy, however pure, is well nigh closed. Some are weakly afraid lest a deeper search into nature should transgress the permitted limits of sobermindedness; wrongfully wresting and transferring what is said in holy writ against those who pry into sacred mysteries, to the hidden things of nature, which are barred by no prohibition. Others with more subtlety surmise and reflect that if second causes are unknown everything can more readily be referred to the divine hand and rod; a point in which they think religion greatly concerned; which is in fact nothing else but to seek to gratify God with a lie. Others fear from past example that movements and changes in philosophy will end in assaults on religion. And others again appear apprehensive that in the investigation of nature something may be found to subvert or at least shake the authority of religion, especially with the unlearned. But these two last fears seem to me to savour utterly of carnal wisdom; as if men in the recesses and secret thoughts of their hearts doubted and distrusted the strength of religion and the empire of faith over the sense, and therefore feared that the investigation of truth in nature might be dangerous to them. But if the matter be truly considered, natural philosophy is after the word of God at once the surest medicine against superstition, and the most approved nourishment for faith, and therefore she is rightly given to religion as her most faithful handmaid, since the one displays the will of God, the other his power.

XCII

But by far the greatest obstacle to the progress of science and to the undertaking of new tasks and provinces therein, is found in this—that men despair and think things impossible. For wise and serious men are wont in these matters to be altogether distrustful; considering with themselves the obscurity of nature, the shortness of life, the deceitfulness of the senses, the weakness of the judgment, the difficulty of experiment and the like; and so supposing that in the revolution of time and of the ages of the world the sciences have their ebbs and flows; that at one season they grow and flourish, at another wither and decay, yet in such sort that when they have reached a certain point and condition they can advance no further. If therefore any one believes or promises more, they think this comes of an ungoverned and unripened mind, and that such attempts have prosperous beginnings, become difficult as they go on, and end in confusion. . . .

And therefore it is fit that I publish and set forth those conjectures of mine which make hope in this matter reasonable; just as Columbus did, before that wonderful voyage of his across the Atlantic, when he gave the reasons for his conviction that new lands and continents might be discovered besides those which were known before; which reasons, though rejected at first, were afterwards made good by experience, and were the causes and beginnings of great events.

XCV

Those who have handled sciences have been either men of experiment or men of dogmas. The men of experiment are like the ant; they only collect and use: the reasoners resemble spiders, who make cobwebs out of their own substance. But the bee takes a middle course; it gathers its material from the flowers of the garden and of the field, but transforms and digests it by a power of its own. Not unlike this is the true business of philosophy; for it neither relies solely or chiefly on the powers of the mind, nor does it take the matter which it gathers from natural history and mechanical experiments and lay it up in the memory whole, as it finds it; but lays it up in the understanding altered and digested. Therefore from a closer and purer league between these two faculties, the experimental and the rational, (such as has never yet been made) much may be hoped.

CXXIX

Further, it will not be amiss to distinguish the three kinds and as it were grades of ambition in mankind. The first is of those who desire to extend their own power in their native country; which kind is vulgar and degenerate. The second is of those who labour to extend the power of their country and its dominion among men. This certainly has more dignity, though not less covetousness. But if a man endeavour to establish and extend the power and dominion of the human race itself over the universe, his ambition (if ambition it can be called) is without doubt both a more wholesome thing and a more noble than the other two. Now the empire of man over things depends wholly on the arts and sciences. For we cannot command nature except by obeying her. . . .

Lastly, if the debasement of arts and sciences to purposes of wickedness, luxury, and the like, be made a ground of objection, let no one be moved thereby. For the same may be said of all earthly goods; of wit, courage, strength, beauty, wealth, light itself, and the rest. Only let the human race recover that right over nature which belongs to it by divine bequest, and let power be given it; the exercise thereof will be governed by sound reason and true religion.

*　　*　　*

And now having said my prayers I turn to men; to whom I have certain salutory admonitions to offer and certain fair requests to make. My first admonition (which was also my prayer) is that men confine the sense within the limits of duty in respect of things divine: for the sense is like the sun, which reveals the face of earth, but seals and shuts up the face of heaven. My next, that in flying from this evil they fall not into the opposite error, which they will surely do if they think that the inquisition of nature is in any part interdicted or forbidden. For it was not that pure and uncorrupted natural knowledge whereby Adam gave names to the creatures according to their propriety, which gave occasion to the fall. It was the ambitious and proud desire of moral knowledge to judge of good and evil, to the end that man may revolt from God and give laws to himself, which was the form and manner of the temptation. . . .

Lastly, I would address one general admonition to all; that they consider what are the true ends of knowledge, and that they seek it not either for pleasure of the mind, or for contention, or for superiority to others, or for profit, or fame, or power, or any of these inferior things; but for the benefit and use of life; and that they perfect and govern it in charity. For it was from lust of power that the angels fell, from lust of knowledge that man fell; but of charity there can be no excess, neither did angel or man ever come in danger by it.

The requests I have to make are these. Of myself, I say nothing; but in behalf of the business which is in hand I entreat men to believe that it is not an opinion to be held, but a work to be done; and to be well assured that I am labouring to lay the foundation, not of any sect or doctrine, but of human utility and power. Next, I ask them to deal fairly by their own interests, and laying aside all emulations and prejudices in favour of this or that opinion, to join in consultation for the common good; and being now freed and guarded by the securities and helps which I offer from the errors and impediments of the way, to come forward themselves and take part in that which remains to be done. Moreover, to be of good hope, nor to imagine that this Instauration of mine is a thing infinite and beyond the power of man, when it is in fact the true end and termination of infinite error; and seeing also that it is by no means forgetful of the conditions of mortality and humanity, (for it does not suppose that the work can be altogether completed within one generation, but provides for its being taken up by another); and finally that it seeks for the sciences not arrogantly in the little cells of human wit, but with reverence in the greater world.

RENÉ DESCARTES: *Discourse on Method* *

> The best known work of the French philosopher René Descartes (1596–1650) is his *Discourse on the Method of rightly conducting the Reason and seeking Truth in the Sciences* (1637). The first part of the *Discourse* tells us how he became disillusioned with his scholastic education

* *The Method, Meditations, and Selections from the Principles of Descartes,* trans. by John Veitch (Edinburgh and London: W. Blackwood and Sons; 1887), pp. 11–20, 32–5, 37, 40, 60–1, 75–6.

under the Jesuits at La Flèche, and how he resolved to abandon the study of letters and to seek knowledge in "the great book of the world," *i.e.*, by travel. The selections below pick up the narrative at this point.

IT IS true that, while busied only in considering the manners of other men, I found here, too, scarce any ground for settled conviction, and remarked hardly less contradiction among them than in the opinions of the philosophers. So that the greatest advantage I derived from the study consisted in this, that, observing many things which, however extravagant and ridiculous to our apprehension, are yet by common consent received and approved by other great nations, I learned to entertain too decided a belief in regard to nothing of the truth of which I had been persuaded merely by example and custom: and thus I gradually extricated myself from many errors powerful enough to darken our Natural Intelligence, and incapacitate us in great measure from listening to Reason. But after I had been occupied several years in thus studying the book of the world, and in essaying to gather some experience, I at length resolved to make myself an object of study, and to employ all the powers of my mind in choosing the paths I ought to follow; an undertaking which was accompanied with greater success than it would have been had I never quitted my country or my books.

I was then in Germany, attracted thither by the wars in that country, which have not yet been brought to a termination; and as I was returning to the army from the coronation of the Emperor, the setting in of winter arrested me in a locality where, as I found no society to interest me, and was besides fortunately undisturbed by any cares or passions, I remained the whole day in seclusion, with full opportunity to occupy my attention with my own thoughts. Of these one of the very first that occurred to me was, that there is seldom so much perfection in works composed of many separate parts, upon which different hands have been employed, as in those completed by a single master. Thus it is observable that the buildings which a single architect has planned and executed, are generally more elegant and commodious than those which several have attempted to improve, by making old walls serve for purposes for which they were not originally built. Thus also, those ancient cities which, from being at first only villages, have become, in course of time, large towns, are usually but ill laid out compared with the regularly constructed towns which a professional architect has freely planned on an open plain; so that although the several buildings of the former may often equal or surpass in beauty those of the latter, yet when one observes their indiscriminate juxtaposition, there a large one and here a small, and the consequent crookedness and irregularity of the streets, one is disposed to allege that chance rather than any human will guided by reason, must have led to such an arrangement. And if we consider that nevertheless there have been at all times certain officers whose duty it was to see that private buildings contributed to public ornament, the difficulty of reaching high perfection with but the materials of others to operate on, will be readily acknowledged. In the same way I fancied that those nations which, starting from a semi-barbarous state and advancing to civilisation by slow degrees, have had their laws successively determined, and, as it were, forced upon them simply by experience of the hurtfulness of particular crimes and disputes, would by this process come to be possessed of less perfect institutions than those which, from the commencement of their association as communities, have followed the appointments of some wise legislator. . . . In the same way I thought that the sciences contained in books, (such of them at least as are made up of probable reasonings, without demonstrations,) composed as they are of the opinions of many different individuals massed together, are farther removed from truth than the simple inference which a man of good sense using his natural and unprejudiced judgment draws respecting the matters of his experience. And because we have all to pass through a state of infancy to manhood, and have been of necessity, for a length of time, governed by our desires and preceptors, (whose dictates were frequently conflicting, while neither perhaps always counselled us for the best,) I farther concluded that it is almost impossible that our judgments can be so correct or solid as they would have been, had our Reason been mature from the moment of our birth, and had we always been guided by it alone.

It is true, however, that it is not customary to pull down all the houses of a town with the single design of rebuilding them differently, and thereby rendering the streets more handsome; but it often happens that a private individual takes down his own with the view of erecting it anew, and that people are even sometimes constrained to this when their houses are in danger of falling from age, or when the foundations are insecure. With this before me by way of example, I was persuaded that it would indeed be preposterous for a private individual to think of reforming a state by fundamentally changing it throughout, and overturning it in order to set it up amended; and the same I thought was true of any similar project for reforming the body of the Sciences, or the order of teaching them established in the Schools: but as for the opinions which up to that time I had embraced, I thought that I could not do better than resolve at once to sweep them wholly away, that I might afterwards be in a position to admit either others more correct, or even perhaps the same when they had undergone the scrutiny of Reason. I firmly believed that in this way I would much better succeed in the conduct of my life, than if I built only upon old foundations, and leant upon principles which, in my youth, I had taken upon trust For although I recognised various difficulties in this undertaking, these were not, however, without remedy, nor once to be compared with such as attend the slightest reformation in public affairs. Large bodies, if once overthrown, are with great difficulty set up again, or even kept erect when once seriously shaken, and the fall of such is always disastrous. Then if there are any imperfections in the constitutions of states, (and that many such exist the diversity of constitutions is alone sufficient to assure us,) custom has without doubt materially smoothed their inconveniences, and has even managed to steer altogether clear of, or insensibly corrected a number which sagacity could not have provided against with equal effect; and, in fine, the defects are almost always more tolerable than the change necessary for their removal; in the same manner that highways which wind among mountains, by being much frequented, become gradually so smooth and commodious, that it is much better to follow them than to seek a straighter path by climbing over the tops of rocks and descending to the bottoms of precipices.

Hence it is that I cannot in any degree approve of those restless and busy meddlers who, called neither by birth nor fortune to take part in the management of public affairs, are yet always projecting reforms; and if I thought that this Tract contained aught which might justify the suspicion that I was a victim of such folly, I would by no means permit its publication. I have never contemplated anything higher than the reformation of my own opinions, and basing them on a foundation wholly my own. And although my own satisfaction with my work has led me to present here a draft of it, I do not by any means therefore recommend to every one else to make a similar attempt. . . .

For my own part, I should doubtless have belonged to the latter class, had I received instruction from but one master, or had I never known the diversities of opinion that from time immemorial have prevailed among men of the greatest learning. But I had become aware, even so early as during my college life, that no opinion, however absurd and incredible, can be imagined, which has not been maintained by some one of the philosophers; and afterwards in the course of my travels I remarked that all those whose opinions are decidedly repugnant to ours are not on that account barbarians and savages, but on the contrary that many of these nations make an equally good, if not a better, use of their Reason than we do. I took into account also the very different character which a person brought up from infancy in France or Germany exhibits, from that which, with the same mind originally, this individual would have possessed had he lived always among the Chinese or with savages, and the circumstance that in dress itself the fashion which pleased us ten years ago, and which may again, perhaps, be received into favour before ten years have gone, appears to us at this moment extravagant and ridiculous.

I was thus led to infer that the ground of our opinions is far more custom and example than any certain knowledge. . . .

Among the branches of Philosophy, I had, at an earlier period, given some attention to Logic, and among those of the Mathematics to Geometrical Analysis and Algebra,—three Arts or Sciences which ought, as I conceived, to contribute something to my design. But, on examination, I found that, as for Logic, its syllogisms and the majority of its other precepts are of avail rather in the communication of what we already know, or even as the Art of Lully, in speaking without judgment of things of which we are ignorant, than in the investigation of the unknown; and although this Science contains indeed a number of correct and very excellent precepts, there are, nevertheless, so many others, and these either injurious or superfluous, mingled with the former, that it is almost quite as difficult to effect a severance of the true from the false as it is to extract a Diana or a Minerva from a rough block of marble. . . . By these considerations I was induced to seek some other Method which would comprise the advantages of the three and be exempt from their defects. And as a multitude of laws often only hampers justice, so that a state is best governed when, with few laws, these are rigidly administered; in like manner, instead of the great number of precepts of which Logic is composed, I believed that the four following would prove perfectly sufficient for me, provided I took the firm and unwavering resolution never in a single instance to fail in observing them.

The *first* was never to accept anything for true which I did not clearly know to be such; that is to say, carefully to avoid precipitancy and prejudice, and to comprise nothing more in my judgment than what was presented to my mind so clearly and distinctly as to exclude all ground of doubt.

The *second*, to divide each of the difficulties under examination into as many parts as possible, and as might be necessary for its adequate solution.

The *third*, to conduct my thoughts in such order that, by commencing with objects the simplest and easiest to know, I might ascend by little and little, and, as it were, step by step, to the knowledge of the more complex; assigning in thought a certain order even to those objects which in their own nature do not stand in a relation of antecedence and sequence.

And the *last*, in every case to make enumerations so complete, and reviews so general, that I might be assured that nothing was omitted.

The long chains of simple and easy reasonings by means of which geometers are accustomed to reach the conclusions of their most difficult demonstrations, had led me to imagine that all things, to the knowledge of which man is competent, are mutually connected in the same way, and that there is nothing so far removed from us as to be beyond our reach, or so hidden that we cannot discover it, provided only we abstain from accepting the false for the true, and always preserve in our thoughts the order necessary for the deduction of one truth from another. And I had little difficulty in determining the objects with which it was necessary to commence, for I was already persuaded that it must be with the simplest and easiest to know, and, considering that of all those who have hitherto sought truth in the Sciences, the mathematicians alone have been able to find any demonstrations, that is, any certain and evident reasons, I did not doubt but that such must have been the rule of their investigations. I resolved to commence, therefore, with the examination of the simplest objects, not anticipating, however, from this any other advantage than that to be found in accustoming my mind to the love and nourishment of truth, and to a distaste for all such reasonings as were unsound.

*   *   *

I am in doubt as to the propriety of making my first meditations in the place above mentioned matter of discourse; for these are so metaphysical, and so uncommon, as not, perhaps, to be acceptable to every one. And yet, that it may be determined whether the foundations that I have laid are sufficiently secure, I find myself in a measure constrained to advert to them. I had long before remarked that, in relation to practice, it is sometimes necessary to adopt, as if above doubt, opinions which we discern to be highly uncertain, as has been already said; but as I then desired to give my attention solely to the search after truth, I thought that a procedure exactly the opposite was called for, and that I ought to reject as absolutely false all opinions in regard to which I could suppose the least ground for doubt, in order to ascertain whether after that there remained aught in my belief that was wholly indubitable. Accordingly, seeing that our senses sometimes deceive us, I was willing to suppose that there existed nothing really such as they presented to us, and because some men err in reasoning, and fall into paralogisms, even on the simplest matters of Geometry, I, convinced that I was as open to error as any other, rejected as false all the reasonings I had hitherto taken for demonstrations; and finally, when I considered that the very same thoughts (presentations) which we experience when awake may also be experienced when we are asleep, while there is at that time not one of them true, I supposed that all the objects (presentations) that had ever entered into my mind when awake, had in them no more truth than the illusions of my dreams. But immediately upon this I observed that, whilst I thus wished to think that all was false, it was absolutely necessary that I, who thus thought, should be somewhat; and as I observed that this truth, *I think, hence I am,* was so certain and of such evidence, that no ground of doubt, however extravagant, could be alleged by the Sceptics capable of shaking it, I concluded that I might, without scruple, accept it as the first principle of the Philosophy of which I was in search.

* * *

In the next place, from reflecting on the circumstance that I doubted, and that consequently my being was not wholly perfect, (for I clearly saw that it was a greater perfection to know than to doubt,) I was led to inquire whence I had learned to think of something more perfect than myself; and I clearly recognised that I must hold this notion from some Nature which in reality was more perfect. As for the thoughts of many other objects external to me, as of the sky, the earth, light, heat, and a thousand more, I was less at a loss to know whence these came; for since I remarked in them nothing which seemed to render them superior to myself, I could believe that, if these were true, they were dependencies on my own nature, in so far as it possessed a certain perfection, and, if they were false, that I held them from nothing, that is to say, that they were in me because of a certain imperfection of my nature. But this could not be the case with the idea of a Nature more perfect than myself; for to receive it from nothing was a thing manifestly impossible; and, because it is not less repugnant that the more perfect should be an effect of, and dependence on the less perfect, than that something should proceed from nothing, it was equally impossible that I could hold it from myself: accordingly, it but remained that it had been placed in me by a Nature which was in reality more perfect than mine, and which even possessed within itself all the perfections of which I could form any idea; that is to say, in a single word, which was God. . . .

. . . recurring to the examination of the idea of a Perfect Being, I found that the existence of the Being was comprised in the idea in the same way that the equality of its three angles to two right angles is comprised in the idea of a triangle, or as in the idea of a sphere, the equidistance of all points on its surface from the centre, or even still more clearly; and that consequently it is at least as certain that God, who is this Perfect Being, is, or exists, as any demonstration of Geometry can be.

* * *

For, in fine, whether awake or asleep, we ought never to allow ourselves to be persuaded of the truth of anything unless on the evidence of our Reason. And it must be noted that I say of our *Reason*, and not of our imagination or of our senses: thus, for example, although we very clearly see the sun, we ought not therefore to determine that it is only of the size which our sense of sight presents; and we may very distinctly imagine the head of a lion joined to the body of a goat, without being therefore shut up to the conclusion that a chimaera exists; for it is not a dictate of Reason that what we thus see or imagine is in reality existent; but it plainly tells us that all our ideas or notions contain in them some truth; for otherwise it could not be that God, who is wholly perfect and veracious, should have placed them in us.

* * *

But as soon as I had acquired some general notions respecting Physics, and beginning to make trial of them in various particular difficulties, had observed how far they can carry us, and how much they differ from the principles that have been employed up to the present time, I believed that I could not keep them concealed without sinning grievously against the law by which we are bound to promote, as far as in us lies, the general good of mankind. For by them I perceived it to be possible to arrive at knowledge highly useful in life; and in room of the Speculative Philosophy usually taught in the Schools, to discover a Practical, by means of which, knowing the force and action of fire, water, air, the stars, the heavens, and all the other bodies that surround us, as distinctly as we know the various crafts of our artizans, we might also apply them in the same way to all the uses to which they are adapted, and thus render ourselves the lords and possessors of nature. And this is a result to be desired, not only in order to the invention of an infinity of arts, by which we might be enabled to enjoy without any trouble the fruits of the earth, and all its comforts, but also and especially for the preservation of health, which is without doubt, of all the blessings of this life, the first and fundamental one; for the mind is so intimately dependent upon the condition and relation of the organs of the body, that if any means can ever be found to render men wiser and more ingenious than hitherto, I believe that it is in Medicine they must be sought for. It is true that the science of Medicine, as it now exists, contains few things whose utility is very remarkable: but without any wish to depreciate it, I am confident that there is no one, even among those whose profession it is, who does not admit that all at present known in it is almost nothing in comparison of what remains to be discovered; and that we could free ourselves from an infinity of maladies of body as well as of mind, and perhaps also even from the debility of age, if we had sufficiently ample knowledge of their causes, and of all the remedies provided for us by Nature.

* * *

And if I write in French, which is the language of my country, in preference to Latin, which is that of my preceptors, it is because I expect that those who make use of their unprejudiced natural Reason will be better judges of my opinions than those who give heed to the writings of the ancients only; and as for those who unite good sense with habits of study, whom alone I desire for judges, they will not, I feel assured, be so partial to Latin as to refuse to listen to my reasonings merely because I expound them in the vulgar Tongue.

JOHN LOCKE: *Journal* *

> From 1675 to 1688 the English philosopher John Locke (1632–1704) kept a journal in which he recorded his thoughts on a variety of subjects. The following passages are from two short treatises entered under the year 1677, and entitled "Knowledge, its Extent and Measure" and "Study."

OUR minds are not made as large as truth, nor suited to the whole extent of things; amongst those that come within its reach, it meets with a great many too big for its grasp, and there are not a few that it is fair to give up as incomprehensible. . . . This state of our minds, however remote from the perfection whereof we ourselves have an idea, ought not, however, to discourage our endeavours in the search of truth, or make us think we are incapable of knowing any thing, because we cannot understand all things. We shall find that we are sent out into the world furnished with those faculties that are fit to obtain knowledge, and knowledge sufficient, if we will but confine it within those purposes, and direct it to those ends, which the constitution of our nature, and the circumstance of our being, point out to us. If we consider ourselves in the condition we are in the world, we cannot but observe that we are in an estate, the necessities whereof call for a constant supply of meat, drink, clothing, and defence from the weather; and our conveniences demand yet a great deal more. To provide these things, Nature furnishes us only with the material, for the most part rough, and unfitted to our use; it requires labour, art, and thought, to suit them to our occasions; and if the knowledge of man had not found out ways to shorten the labour, and improve several things which seem not, at first sight, to be of any use to us, we should spend all our time to make a scanty provision for a poor and miserable life. . . . Here, then, is a large field for knowledge, proper for the use and advantage of men in this world; viz. to find out new inventions of dispatch to shorten or ease our labour, or applying sagaciously together several agents and materials, to procure new and beneficial productions fit for our use, whereby our stock of riches (i.e. things useful for the conveniences of our life,) may be increased, or better preserved: and for such discoveries as these the mind of man is well fitted; though, perhaps, the essence of things, their first original, their

* Peter King: *The Life of John Locke* (London: H. Colburn and R. Bentley; 1830), vol. I, pp. 161–5, 196–8.

secret way of working, and the whole extent of corporeal beings, be as far beyond our capacity as it is beside our use; and we have no reason to complain that we do not know the nature of the sun or stars, that the consideration of light itself leaves us in the dark, and a thousand other speculations in Nature, since, if we knew them, they would be of no solid advantage to us, nor help to make our lives the happier, they being but the useless employment of idle or over-curious brains, which amuse themselves about things out of which they can by no means draw any real benefit. So that, if we will consider man as in the world, and that his mind and faculties were given him for any use, we must necessarily conclude it must be to procure him the happiness which this world is capable of; which certainly is nothing else but plenty of all sorts of those things which can with most ease, pleasure, and variety, preserve him longest in it: so that, had mankind no concernment but in the world, no apprehensions of any being after this life, they need trouble their heads with nothing but the history of nature, and an inquiry into the qualities of the things in the mansion of the universe which hath fallen to their lot, and, being well-skilled in the knowledge of material causes and effect of things in their power, directing their thoughts to the improvement of such arts and inventions, engines, and utensils, as might best contribute to their continuation in it with conveniency and delight, they might well spare themselves the trouble of looking any farther; they need not perplex themselves about the original frame or constitution of the universe, drawing the great machine into systems of their own contrivance, and building hypotheses, obscure, perplexed, and of no other use but to raise dispute and continual wrangling: For what need have we to complain of our ignorance in the more general and foreign parts of nature, when all our business lies at home? Why should we bemoan our want of knowledge in the particular apartments of the universe, when our portion here only lies in the little spot of earth where we and all our concernments are shut up? Why should we think ourselves hardly dealt with, that we are not furnished with compass nor plummet to sail and fathom that restless, unnavigable ocean, of the universal matter, motion, and space?

*   *   *

It is of great use in the pursuit of knowledge not to be too confident, nor too distrustful of our own judgment, nor to believe we can comprehend all things nor nothing. He that distrusts his own judgment in every thing, and thinks his understanding not to be relied on in the search of truth, cuts off his own legs that he may be carried up and down by others, and makes himself a ridiculous dependant upon the knowledge of others, which can possibly be of no use to him. . . . On the other side, he that thinks his understanding capable of all things, mounts upon wings of his own fancy, though indeed Nature never meant him any, and so venturing into the vast expanse of incomprehensible verities, only makes good the fable of Icarus, and loses himself in the abyss. We are here in the state of mediocrity; finite creatures, furnished with powers and faculties very well fitted to some purposes, but very disproportionate to the vast and unlimited extent of things. . . .

That which seems to me to be suited to the end of man, and lie level to his understanding, is the improvement of natural experiments for the conveniences of this life, and the way of ordering himself so as to attain happiness in the other—*i.e.* moral philosophy, which, in my sense, comprehends religion too, or a man's whole duty.

BISHOP SPRAT: *On Style and Expression* *

THUS they [the Royal Society] have directed, judg'd, conjectur'd upon, and improved *Experiments*. But lastly, in these, and all other Businesses, that have come under their Care; there is one thing more, about which the *Society* has been most solicitous; and that is, the Manner of their *Discourse;* which, unless they had been very watchful to keep in due Temper, the whole Spirit and Vigour of their *Design* had been soon eaten out, by the Luxury and Redundance of *Speech.* The ill Effects of this Superfluity of Talking, have already overwhelm'd most other *Arts* and *Professions;* insomuch, that when I consider the Means of *happy Living,* and the Causes of their Corruption, I can hardly forbear recanting what I said before; and concluding, that *Eloquence* ought to be banish'd out of all *civil Societies,* as a thing fatal to Peace and good Manners. To this Opinion I should wholly incline, if I did not find, that it is a Weapon, which may be as easily procur'd by *bad* Men, as *good;* and that, if these should only cast it away, and those retain it; the *naked Innocence* of Virtue would be, upon all Occasions, expos'd to the *armed Malice* of the Wicked. . . .

Who can behold, without Indignation, how many Mists and Uncertainties, these specious *Tropes* and *Figures* have brought on our Knowledge? How many Rewards, which are due to more profitable and difficult *Arts,* have been still snatch'd away by the easie Vanity of *fine Speaking!* For now I am warm'd with this just Anger, I cannot withhold my self, from betraying the Shallowness of all these seeming Mysteries; upon which, we *Writers,* and *Speakers,* look so big. And in few Words, I dare say, that of all the Studies of Men, nothing may be sooner obtain'd, than this vicious Abundance of *Phrase,* this Trick of *Metaphors,*

* Thomas Sprat: *History of the Royal Society of London* (London: S. Chapman; 1722), pp. 111–13.

this Volubility of *Tongue*, which makes so great a Noise in the World. But I spend Words in Vain; for the Evil is now so inveterate, that it is hard to know whom to *blame*, or where to begin to *reform*. We all value one another so much, upon this beautiful Deceit; and labour so long after it, in the Years of our Education; that we cannot but ever after think kinder of it, than it deserves. . . .

They [the Royal Society] have therefore been more rigorous in putting in Execution the only Remedy, that can be found for this *Extravagance;* and that has been a constant Resolution, to reject all the Amplifications, Digressions, and Swellings of Style; to return back to the primitive Purity and Shortness, when Men deliver'd so many *Things*, almost in an equal Number of *Words*. They have exacted from all their Members, a close, naked, natural way of Speaking; positive Expressions, clear Senses; a native Easiness; bringing all Things as near the mathematical Plainness as they can; and preferring the Language of Artizans, Countrymen, and Merchants, before that of Wits, or Scholars.

SIR WILLIAM PETTY: *Tractate on Education* *

Sir William Petty (1623–87), physician, professor of anatomy, surveyor, inventor, social scientist, was one of the original members of the Royal Society. He coined the term "political arithmetic" and used vital statistics in his writings on population and trade during the Restoration. His tractate on education, or *The Advice of W. P. to Mr. Samuel Hartlib for the Advancement of some particular parts of Learning*, was published in 1648. It was one of many pieces of its kind in the seventeenth century, resembling Bacon's *New Atlantis* and Campanella's *City of the Sun*.

AND now we shall think of whetting our tools and preparing sharp instruments for this hard work [the advancement of learning], by delivering our thoughts concerning education, which are

1. That there be instituted literary work-houses, where children may be taught as well to do something toward their living, as to read and write.

That all children of above seven years old may be presented to this kind of education. . . .

That since few children have need of reading before they know, or can be acquainted with the things they read of, or of writing, before their thoughts are worth the recording, or they are able to put them into any form, much less of learning languages, when there be books enough for

* William Petty: *The Advice of W. P. to Mr. Samuel Hartlib* (London; 1648), pp. 3–9, 17–18, 22–3. I have modernized the spelling.

their present use in their own mother tongue; our opinion is, that those things . . . be deferred awhile, and others more needful for them . . . be studied before them. We wish therefore that the scholars be taught to observe and remember all sensible objects and actions, whether they be natural or artificial, which the educators must upon all occasions expound unto them. . . .

[That they be taught reading, writing, drawing, and foreign languages by improved methods.]

That the elements of arithmetic and geometry be by all studied, being not only of great and frequent use in all human affairs but also sure guides and helps to Reason. . . .

That all children, though of the highest rank, be taught some gentle Manufacture in their minority, such as are

Making mathematical instruments, dials, and how to use them in astronomical observations.

Making watches and other trochilic motions.

Limning and painting on glass or in oil colors.

Engraving, etching, carving, embossing and molding in sundry matters.

The lapidary's art of knowing, cutting and setting jewels.

Grinding of glasses dioptrical and catoprical.

Botanics and gardening.

Making musical instruments.

Navigation and making models for building and rigging of ships.

Architecture and making models for houses.

Chemistry, refining metals and counterfeiting jewels.

Anatomy, making skeletons and excarnating bowels.

Making mariners' compasses, globes, and other magnetic devices.

And all for these reasons:

1. They shall be less subject to be cheated by artificers.

2. They will become more industrious in general.

3. They will certainly bring to pass most excellent works, being as gentlemen, ambitious to excel ordinary workmen.

4. The *Resp. Artium* will be much advanced, when such as are rich and able, are also willing to make luciferous experiments.

5. It may engage them to be patrons of arts.

6. It will keep them from worse occasions of spending their time and estates.

*   *   *

In the next place for the Advancement of all Mechanical Arts and Manufactures, we wish that there were erected a Gymnasium Mechanicum or a College of Tradesmen wherein we would that one at least of every trade (but the prime, most ingenious workman, the most desirous to improve his art) might be allowed therein a handsome dwelling rent free, which with the credit of being admitted into this Society, and the quick sale which certainly they would have of their commodities, when all men would repair thither, as to a market of rare and exquisite pieces of workmanship, would be a sufficient motive to attract the very ablest mechanics, and such as we have described, to desire a fellowship in this College.

From this institution we may clearly hope . . . that all trades will miraculously prosper, and new inventions would be more frequent than new fashions of clothes and household-stuff. Here would be the best and most effectual opportunities and means for writing a History of Trades in perfection and exactness, and what experiments and stuff would all those shops and operations afford to active and philosophical heads, out of which to extract that interpretation of nature whereof there is so little, and that so bad as yet extant in the world?

Within the walls of this gymnasium or college should be a Noscocomium Academicum according to the most exact and perfect idea thereof, a complete *Theatrum Botanicum*, stalls and cages for all strange beasts and birds . . . ; here should be . . . models of all great and noble engines, with designs and platforms of gardens and buildings. The most artificial fountains and waterworks, a library of select books, an astronomical observatory for celestial bodies and meteors, large pieces of ground for several experiments of agriculture, galleries of the rarest paintings and statues, with the fairest globes and geographical maps of the best descriptions, and so far as is possible, we would have this place to be the epitome or abstract of the whole world. . . . We wish that a society of men might be instituted as careful to advance arts as the Jesuits are to propagate their religion for the government and managing of it.

But what relish will there be in all those dainties whereof we have spoken if we want a palate to taste them, which certainly is health, the most desirable of all earthly blessings, and how can we in any reason expect health when there are so many great difficulties in the curing of diseases and no proportionable course taken to remove them? We shall therefore pursue the means of acquiring the public good and comfort of mankind a little further, and vent our conceits concerning a Noscocomium Academicum or an hospital to cure the infirmities both of physician and patient.

[There follows a detailed description of the medical research to be undertaken in the college. Petty then goes on to describe the books that should be written and used in the schools.]

We recommend therefore in the first place . . . the compiling of a work whose title might justly be *Vellus Aureum sive Facultatum*

Luciferarum discriptio Magna, wherein all the practiced ways of getting
a subsistence and whereby men raise their fortunes, may be at large declared. And among these, we wish that the History of Arts or Manufactures might first be undertaken as the most pleasant and profitable of
all the rest, wherein should be described the whole process of manual
operations and applications of one natural thing to another, with the
necessary instruments and machines, whereby every piece of work is
elaborated and made to be what it is, unto which work bare words being
not sufficient, all instruments and tools must be pictured, and colors
added when the descriptions cannot be made intelligible without
them. . . .

[Among the advantages of writing such a history are these:]

3. Scholars and such as love to ratiocinate will have more and better
matter to exercise their wits upon, whereas now they puzzle and tire
themselves about mere words and chimerical notions.

7. All men in general that have wherewithal will be venturing at our
Vellus Aureum, by making of experiments: and whether thereby they
thrive or no . . . they shall nevertheless more and more discover nature.

11. We see that all countries where manufactures and trades flourish,
as Holland, etc. become potent and rich. For how can it otherwise be?
when the revenues of the state shall be increased by new and more
customs, all beggars . . . and even thieves and robbers (made for want
of better employment) shall be set on work, barren grounds made fruitful, wet dry and dry wet, when even hogs and more indocile beasts shall
be taught to labor, when all vile materials shall be turned to noble uses,
when one man or horse shall do as much as three, and everything improved to strange advantages.

12. There would not then be so many fustian and unworthy preachers
in divinity, so many pettifoggers in the law, so many quacks in physic, so
many grammaticasters in country schools, and so many lazy serving men
in gentlemen's houses, when every man might learn to live otherwise in
more plenty and honor. For all men desirous to take pains might by this
book survey all the ways of subsistence, and choose out of them all,
one that best suits his own genius and abilities.

4. The "Mechanical" Philosophy

FONTENELLE: *Plurality of Worlds* *

Fontenelle's *Entretiens sur la Pluralité des Mondes* (1686) is a popular
exposition of the universe in terms of the systems of Copernicus, Giordano Bruno, and Descartes. It is a dialogue between Fontenelle and a

* Fontenelle: *A Plurality of Worlds,* trans. by John Glanvill (London: R.
Bently; 1695), preface (no pagination), pp. 7-11, 14-19, 25-6, 34-5, 86, 125-6, 149.

fashionable French lady who eschew love to discuss astronomy as they walk in the lady's garden for six successive evenings.

MY PURPOSE is to discourse of Philosophy, but not in a Philosophical manner; and to raise it to such a pitch, that it shall not be too dry and insipid a Subject to please Gentlemen; nor too mean and trifling to entertain Scholars.

* * *

I have chosen that part of Philosophy which is most like to excite Curiosity; for what can more concern us, than to know how this World which we inhabit, is made; and whether there be any other Worlds like it, which are also inhabited as this is?

* * *

There remains no more to be said in this Preface; but to a sort of People who perhaps will not be easily satisfy'd; not but that I have good reasons to give 'em, but because the best that can be given, will not content 'em; they are those scrupulous Persons, who imagine, that the placing Inhabitants any where, but upon the Earth, will prove dangerous to Religion: I know how excessively tender some are in Religious Matters, and therefore I am very unwilling to give any offence in what I publish to People, whose opinion is contrary to that I maintain: But Religion can receive no prejudice by my System, which fills an infinity of Worlds with Inhabitants, if a little errour of the Imagination be but rectify'd. When 'tis said the Moon is inhabited, some presently fancy that there are such Men, there, as we are; and Church-Men, without any more ado, think him an Atheist, who is of that opinion. None of *Adam's* Posterity ever travel'd so far as the Moon, nor were any Colonies ever sent thither; the Men then that are in the Moon, are not the Sons of *Adam:* And here again Theology would be puzled, if there should be Men any where, that never descended from him. . . . Let none now think that I say there are no Men in the Moon, purposely to avoid the Objection made against me; for it appears 'tis impossible there should be any Men there, according to that Idea I have fram'd of that infinite diversity and variety, which is to be observed in the works of Nature; This Idea runs through the whole Book, and cannot be contradicted by any Philosopher: And to think there may be more Worlds than one, is neither against Reason, or Scripture. If God glorify'd himself in making one World, the more Worlds he made, the greater must be his Glory: But I do not declare these Ideas to be Articles of my Faith; when I do, I hope I shall have the same *Liberty* as the rest of my Neighbours.

* * *

. . . I fancy to my self, that Nature very much resembleth an Opera, where you stand, you do not see the Stage as really it is; but it is plac'd with advantage, and all the Wheels and Movements are hid, to make the Representation the more agreeable: Nor do you trouble your self how, or by what means the Machines are moved, tho' certainly an Engineer in the Pit is affected with what doth not touch you; he is pleas'd with the motion, and is demonstrating to himself on what it depends, and how it comes to pass. This Engineer then is like a Philosopher, tho' the difficulty is greater on the Philosopher's part, the Machines of the Theatre being nothing so curious as those of Nature, which disposeth her Wheels and Springs so out of sight, that we have been long a guessing at the Movement of the Universe. Suppose then the Sages at an Opera, the *Pithagoras's*, the *Plato's*, the *Aristotle's*, and all the Wise Men, who have made such a noise in the World, for these many Ages: We will suppose 'em at the Representation of *Phaeton*, where they see the aspiring Youth lifted up by the Winds, but do not discover the Wires by which he mounts, nor know they any thing of what is done behind the Scenes. Would you have all these Philosophers own themselves to be stark Fools, and confess ingenuously they know not how it comes to pass: No, no, they are not called Wise Men for nothing; tho', let me tell you, most of their Wisdom depends upon the ignorance of their Neighbours. Every man presently gives his Opinion, and how improbable so ever, there are Fools enough of all sorts to believe 'em: One tells you *Phaeton* is drawn up by a hidden Magnetick Vertue, no matter where it lies; and perhaps the grave Gentleman will take pet, if you ask him the Question. Another says, *Phaeton* is compos'd of certain Numbers that make him mount; and after all, the Philosopher knows no more of those numbers than a sucking Child of *Algebra:* A third tells you, *Phaeton* hath a secret love for the top of the Theatre, and like a true Lover cannot be at rest out of his Mistresses Company, with an hundred such extravagant fancies, that a Man must conclude the Old Sages were very good Banterers: But now comes Monsieur *Descartes*, with some of the Moderns, and they tell you *Phaeton* ascends, because a greater weight than he descends; so that now we do not believe a Body can move without it is push'd and forc'd by another body, and as it were drawn by Cords, so that nothing can rise or fall but by the means of a Counterpoise; he then that will see Nature really as she is, must stand behind the Scenes at the Opera. I perceive, *said the Countess*, Philosophy is now become very Mechanical. So Mechanical, *said I*, that I fear we shall quickly be asham'd of it; they will have the World to be in great, what a Watch is in little; which is very regular, and depends only upon the just disposing of the several parts of the Movement. But pray tell me, Madam, had you not formerly a more sublime Idea of the Universe? Do you not think you did then honour it more than it deserv'd? For most have the less esteem of it since they have pretended to know it. I am not of their opinion, *said she*, I value it the more since I know it resembles a Watch, and the whole order of Nature the more plain and easie it is, to me it appears the more admirable.

I know not, *said I*, who hath inspir'd you with these solid Notions, but I am certain there are few that have them besides your self, People generally admire what they do not comprehend, they have a Veneration for Obscurity, and look upon Nature while they do not understand her, as a kind of Magick, and despise her below Legerdemain, when once they are acquainted with her; but I find you, Madam, so much better dispos'd, that I have nothing to do but to draw the Curtain, and shew you the World.

*　　*　　*

. . . before I expound the first Systeme, I would have you observe, we are all naturally like that Mad-man at *Athens*, who fancy'd all the Ships were his that came into the Port *Pyraeum:* Nor is our Folly less extravagant, we believe all things in Nature design'd for our use; and do but ask a Philosopher, to what purpose there is that prodigious company of fix'd Stars, when a far less number would perform the service they do us? He answers coldly, they were made to please our Sight, Upon this Principle they imagin'd the Earth rested in the Centre of the Universe, while all the Celestial Bodies (which were made for it) took the pains to turn round to give light to it. . . . But why, *said the Countess*, interrupting me, do you dislike this Systeme? It seems to me very Clear and Intelligible. However, Madam, *said I*, I will make it plainer; for should I give it you as it came from *Ptolomy* its Author, or from some who have since study'd it, I should fright you, I fancy, instead of diverting you. Since the Motions of the Planets are not so regular, but that sometimes they go faster, sometimes slower, sometimes are nearer the Earth, and sometimes farther from it; the Ancients did invent I do not know how many Orbs or Circles involv'd one within another, which they thought would salve all Objections; this confusion of Circles was so great, that at that time when they knew no better, a certain King of *Arragon*, a great Mathematician, but not much troubled with Religion, said, *That had God consulted him when he made the World, he would have told him how to have fram'd it better.* The fancy was very Atheistical, and no doubt the Instructions he would have given the Almighty, was the suppressing those Circles with which they had clog'd the Celestial Motions, and the taking away two or three superfluous Heavens which they had placed above the fixed Stars; for these Philosophers to explain the Motion of the Celestial Bodies, had above the uppermost Heaven (which we see,) found another of Crystal, to influence and give Motion to the inferior Heavens; and wherever they heard of another Motion, they presently clap'd up a Crystal Heaven which cost 'em nothing. . . . [but] by the observations of these latter Ages it is now out of doubt, that *Venus* and *Mercury* turn round the Sun, and not round the Earth, according to the Antient Systeme, which is now every where exploded, and all the *Ipse Dixits* not worth a rush. But that which I am going to lay down, will salve all, and is so clear, that the King of *Arragon* himself may spare his Advice. Methinks, *saith the Countess*, your Philosophy is a kind of Out-cry, where he that offers to do the work cheapest, carries it from all the rest. 'Tis very true, *said I*, Nature is a great Huswife, she always makes use of what costs least, let the difference be never so inconsiderable; and yet this frugality is accompany'd with an extraordinary magnificence, which shines thro' all her works; that is, she is magnificent in the Design, but frugal in the Execution; and what can be more praise-worthy, than a great design accomplish'd with a little Expence? But in our Ideas we turn things topsy-turvy, we place our thrift in the Design, and are at ten times more charge in Workmanship than it requires, which is very ridiculous: Imitate Nature then, *saith she*, in your Systeme, and give me as little trouble as you can to comprehend you. Fear it not, Madam, *said I*, we have done with our impertinencies: Imagine then a German call'd *Copernicus* confounding every thing, tearing in pieces the beloved Circles of Antiquity, and shattering their Crystal Heavens like so many Glass-Windows, seiz'd with the noble Rage of Astronomy, he snatcheth up the Earth from the Centre of the Universe, sends her packing, and placeth the Sun in the Centre to which it did more justly belong, the Planets no longer turn round the Earth, and do not inclose it in the Circles they describe; if they give us light, it is but by chance, and as they meet us in their way. All now turns round the Sun, the Earth her self goes round the Sun, and *Copernicus* to punish the Earth for her former Lazyness, makes her contribute all he can to the Motion of the Planets and Heavens, and now stripp'd of all the heavenly Equipage with which she was so gloriously attended, she hath nothing left her but the Moon, which still turns round about her. . . .

*   *   *

. . . the Earth, at the same time that she advanceth on the Circle which in a Years space she makes round the Sun, in twenty four hours she turns round her self; so that in twenty four hours every part of the Earth loseth the Sun, and recovers him again, and as it turns towards the Sun, it seems to rise, and as it turns from him, it seems to fall. It is very pleasant, *said she*, that the Earth must take all upon her self, and the Sun do nothing. And when the Moon, the other Planets, and the fix'd Stars seem to go over our Heads every twenty four hours, you'll say that too is only Fancy? Pure Fancy, *said I*, which proceeds from the same cause, for the Planets compleat their Courses round the Sun at unequal times, according to their unequal distances, and that which we see to Day answer to a certain Point in the Zodiack or Circle of the fix'd Stars, to morrow we see answer to another point, because it is advanced on its own Circle as well as we are advanced upon ours. We move, and the Planets move too, which must make a great alteration; so that what seems irregular in the Planets, proceeds only from our Motion, when in truth they are all very irregular: I will suppose 'em so, *said the Countess,* but I would not have their Regularity put the Earth to so great trouble; methinks you exact too much Activity from so ponderous a Mass. But, *said I,* had you rather that the Sun and all the Stars, which are vast great Bodies, should in twenty four Hours travel such an infinity of Miles, and make so prodigious a *Tour* as they needs must, if the Earth did not turn round it self every twenty four Hours?

*   *   *

Ticho Brahe, who had fix'd the Earth in the Centre of the World, turn'd the Sun round the Earth, and the rest of the Planets round the Sun; for since the new discoveries, there was no way left to have the Planets turn round the Earth. But the Countess, who had a quick apprehension, said, she thought it was too affected, among so many great Bodies, to exempt the Earth only from turning round the Sun; that it was improper to make the Sun turn round the Earth, when all the Planets turn round the Sun; and that tho' this Systeme was to prove the immobility of the Earth, yet she thought it very improbable: So we resolv'd to stick to *Copernicus,* whose Opinion we thought most Uniform, Probable, and Diverting.

*   *   *

Well, Madam, *said I,* Since the Sun, which is now immoveable, hath left off being a Planet; and the Earth, which turns round him, is now become one, you will not be surprized when you hear that the Moon is an Earth too, and that she is inhabited as ours is.

*   *   *

The Moon, to all appearance, is inhabited, why should not *Venus* be so too? You are so full of your Whys, and your Wherefores, *says she,* interrupting me, that I fancy you are sending Colonies to all the Planets. You may be certain, so I will, *I reply'd,* for I see no reason to the contrary; we find that all the Planets are of the same nature, all obscure Bodies, which receive no Light but from the Sun, and then send it to one another; their Motions are the same, so that hitherto they are alike; and yet if we are to believe that these vast Bodies are not inhabited, I think they were made but to little purpose; why should Nature be so partial, as to except only the Earth?

*   *   *

I perceive, *says the Countess,* where you would carry me; you are going to tell me, that if the fix'd Stars are so many Suns, and our Sun the Centre of a Vortex that turns round him, why may not every fix'd Star be the Centre of a Vortex that turns round the fix'd Star? Our Sun enlightens the Planets; why may not every fix'd Star have Planets to which they give light? You have said it, *I reply'd,* and I will not contradict you.

You have made the Universe so large, *says she,* that I know not where I am, or what will become of me; what is it all to be divided into heaps confusedly, one among another? Is every Star the Centre of a Vortex, as big as ours? Is that vast space which comprehends our Sun and Planets, but an inconsiderable part of the Universe? and are there as many such spaces, as there are fix'd Stars? I protest it is dreadful. Dreadful, Madam, *said I;* I think it very pleasant, when the Heavens were a little blue Arch, stuck with Stars; methought the Universe was too strait and close, I was almost stifled for want of Air, but now it is enlarg'd in height and breadth, and a thousand Vortex's taken in; I begin to breath with more freedom, and think the Universe to be incomparably more magnificent than it was before. Nature hath spar'd no cost, even to profuseness, and nothing can be so glorious, as to see such a prodigious number of Vortex's, whose several centres are possess'd by a particular Sun, which makes the Planets turn round it.

*   *   *

Oh, Madam, *said I,* there is a great deal of time required to ruine a World. Grant it, *said she,* yet 'tis but time that is required. I confess it, *said I;* all this immense mass of Matter that composes the Universe, is in perpetual Motion, no part of it excepted; and since every part is moved, you may be sure that changes must happen sooner or later; but still in times proportioned to the Effect. The Ancients were pleasant Gentlemen, to imagine that the Celestial Bodies were in their own Nature unchangeable, because they observed no change in them; but they did not live long enough to confirm their Opinion by their own Experience; they were Boys in comparison of us.

ROBERT BOYLE: *On the Corpuscular Philosophy* *

Robert Boyle (1627–91), physicist, chemist, philosopher, member of the Royal Society, is best known for his book, *The Sceptical Chemist* (1661) in which he attacked the Aristotelian theory of the four ele-

* *The Works of the Honourable Robert Boyle* (London: J. and F. Rivington; 1772), vol. I, pp. 355–6; vol. III, pp. 14–16, 608–09; vol. IV, pp. 72–3; vol. V, p. 245.

ments. The following description of nature as an "automaton" or "self-moving engine" is pieced together from six of his minor treatises.

I CONSIDERED, that the Atomical and Cartesian hypotheses, though they differed in some material points from one another, yet in opposition to the Peripatetic and other vulgar doctrines they might be looked upon as one philosophy: for they agree with one another, and differ from the schools in this grand and fundamental point, that not only they take care to explicate things intelligibly; but that whereas those other philosophers give only a general and superficial account of the phaenomena of nature from certain substantial forms, which the most ingenious among themselves confess to be incomprehensible, and certain real qualities, which knowing men of other persuasions think to be likewise unintelligible; both the Cartesians and the Atomists explicate the same phaenomena by little bodies variously figured and moved. I know, that these two sects of modern naturalists disagree about the notion of body in general, and consequently about the possibility of a true vacuum; as also about the origin of motion, the indefinite divisibleness of matter, and some other points of less importance than these: but in regard that some of them seem to be rather metaphysical than physiological notions, and that some others seem rather to be requisite to the explication of the first origin of the universe, than of the phaenomena of it, in the state wherein we now find it; in regard of these, I say, and some other considerations, and especially for this reason, that both parties agree in deducing all the phaenomena of nature from matter and local motion; I esteemed that, notwithstanding these things, wherein the Atomists and the Cartesians differed, they might be thought to agree in the main, and their hypotheses might by a person of a reconciling disposition be looked on as, upon the matter, one philosophy. Which because it explicates things by corpuscles, or minute bodies, may (not very unfitly) be called corpuscular; though I sometimes style it the Phaenician philosophy, because some antient writers inform us, that not only before *Epicurus* and *Democritus*, but even before *Leucippus* taught in *Greece*, a Phaenician naturalist was wont to give an account of the phaenomena of nature by the motion and other affections of the minute particles of matter. Which because they are obvious and very powerful in mechanical engines, I sometimes also term it the mechanical hypothesis or philosophy.

By such considerations then, and by this occasion, I was invited to try, whether, without pretending to determine the above-mentioned controverted points, I could, by the help of the corpuscular philosophy, in the sense newly given of that appellation, associated with chymical experiments, explicate some particular subjects more intelligibly, than they are wont to be accounted for, either by the schools or the chymists. And however since the vulgar philosophy is yet so vulgar, that it is still in great request with the generality of scholars; and since the mechanical philosophers have brought so few experiments to verify their assertions: and the chymists are thought to have brought so many on the behalf of theirs, that of those, that have quitted the unsatisfactory philosophy of the schools, the greater number, dazzled as it were by the experiments of Spagyrists, have imbraced their doctrines instead of those they deserted: for these reasons, I say, I hoped I might at least do no unseasonable piece of service to the corpuscular philosophers, by illustrating some of their notions with sensible experiments, and manifesting, that the things by me treated of may be at least plausibly explicated without having recourse to inexplicable forms, real qualities, the four peripatetic elements, or so much as the three chymical principles.

* * *

That, before I descend to particulars, I may, *Pyrophilus*, furnish you with some general apprehension of the doctrine (or rather the hypothesis) which is to be collated with, and to be either confirmed or disproved by the historical truths that will be delivered concerning particular qualities (and forms); I will assume the person of a Corpuscularian, and here at the entrance give you (in a general way) a brief account of the hypothesis itself, as it concerns the origin of qualities (and forms). . . .

I. I agree with the generality of philosophers so far as to allow, that there is one catholick or universal matter common to all bodies, by which I mean a substance extended, divisible, and impenetrable.

II. But because this matter being in its own nature but one, the diversity we see in bodies must necessarily arise from somewhat else than the matter they consist of. And since we see not how there could be any change in matter, if all its (actual or designable) parts were perpetually at rest among themselves, it will follow, that to discriminate the catholick matter into variety of natural bodies, it must have motion in some or all its designable parts: and that motion must have various tendencies, that which is in this part of the matter tending one way, and that which is in that part tending another; as we plainly see in the universe or general mass of matter, there is really a great quantity of motion, and that variously determined, and that yet divers portions of matter are at rest.

That there is local motion in many parts of matter is manifest to sense; but how matter came by this motion was of old, and is still hotly disputed of: for the antient Corpuscularian philosophers (whose doctrine in most other points, though not in all, we are most inclinable to) not acknowledging an Author of the universe, were thereby reduced to make motion congenite to matter, and consequently coeval with it. But since local motion, or an endeavour at it, is not included in the nature of matter, which is as much matter when it rests as when it moves; and since we see that the same portion of matter may from motion be reduced to rest, and after it hath continued at rest, as long as other bodies do not put it out of that state, may by external agents be set a moving again; I, who am not wont to think a man the worse naturalist for not being an atheist, shall not scruple to say with an eminent philosopher of old, whom I find to have proposed among the *Greeks* that opinion (for the main) that the excellent *Des Cartes* has revived amongst us, that the origin of motion in matter is from God; and not only so, but that thinking it very unfit to be believed that matter barely put into motion, and then left to itself, should casually constitute this beautiful and orderly world: I think also further, that the wise Author of things did, by establishing the laws of motion among bodies, and by guiding the first motions of the small parts of matter, bring them to convene after the manner requisite to compose the world, and especially did contrive those curious and elaborate engines, the bodies of living creatures, endowing most of them with a power of propagating their species. But though these things are my persuasions, yet, because they are not necessary to be supposed here, where I do not pretend to deliver any compleat discourse of the principles of natural philosophy, but only to touch upon such notions as are requisite to explicate the origin of qualities and forms, I shall pass on to what remains, as soon as I have taken notice that local motion seems to be indeed the principal amongst second causes, and the grand agent of all that happens in nature: for though bulk, figure, rest, situation, and texture do concur to the phaenomena of nature, yet in comparison of motion they seem to be in many cases, effects, and in many others little better than conditions, or requisites, or causes *sine quibus non*, which modify the operation that one part of matter by virtue of its motion hath upon another; as in a watch, the number, the figure, and coaptation of the wheels and other parts is requisite to the shewing the hour, and doing the other things that may be performed by the watch; but till these parts be actually put into motion, all their other affections remain inefficacious. . . .

III. These two grand and most catholick principles of bodies, matter and motion, being thus established, it will follow, both that matter must be actually divided into parts, that being the genuine effect of variously determined motion, and that each of the primitive fragments, or other distinct and intire masses of matter, must have two attributes, its own magnitude, or rather size, and its own figure or shape. And since experience shews us (especially that which is afforded us by chymical operations, in many of which matter is divided into parts too small to be singly sensible) that this division of matter is frequently made into insensible corpuscles or particles, we may conclude, that the minutest fragments, as well as the biggest masses of the universal matter, are likewise endowed each with its peculiar bulk and shape. For being a finite body, its dimensions must be terminated and measurable: and though it may change its figure, yet for the same reason it must necessarily have some figure or other. So that now we have found out, and must admit three essential properties of each intire or undivided, though insensible part of matter; namely, magnitude (by which I mean not quantity in general, but a determined quantity, which we in *English* oftentimes call the size of a body) shape, and either motion or rest (for betwixt them two there is no mean). . . .

* * *

For though I do as freely and heartily, as the doctor himself, who, I dare say, does it very sincerely, admit, or rather assert an incorporeal being, that made and governs the world; yet all that I have endeavoured to do in the explication of what happens among inanimate bodies, is to shew, that supposing the world to have been at first made, and to be continually preserved by God's divine power and wisdom; and supposing his general concourse to the maintenance of the laws he has established in it, the phaenomena, I strive to explicate, may be solved mechanically, that is, by the mechanical affections of matter, without recourse to nature's abhorrence of a vacuum, to substantial forms, or to other incorporeal creatures. And therefore, if I have shewn, that the phaenomena, I have endeavoured to account for, are explicable by the motion, bigness, gravity, shape, and other mechanical affections of the small parts of liquors, I have done what I pretended; which was not to prove, that no angel or other immaterial creature could interpose in these cases; for concerning such agents, all that I need say, is, that in the cases proposed we have no need to recur to them. And this being agreeable to the generally owned rule about hypotheses, that *entia non sunt multiplicanda absque necessitate*, has been by almost all the modern philosophers of different sects thought a sufficient reason to reject the agency of intelligences, after *Aristotle*, and so many learned men, both mathematicians and others, had for many ages believed them the movers of the celestial orbs.

* * *

And now at length I come to consider that, which I observe the most to alienate other sects from the mechanical philosophy; namely, that they think it pretends to have principles so universal and so mathematical, that no other physical hypothesis can comport with it, or be tolerated by it.

But this I look upon as an easy, indeed, but an important mistake; because by this very thing, that the mechanical principles are so universal, and therefore applicable to so many things, they are rather fitted to include, than necessitated to exclude, any other hypothesis, that is founded in nature, as far as it is so. And such hypotheses, if prudently considered by a skilful and moderate person, who is rather disposed to unite sects than multiply them, will be found, as far as they have truth in them, to be either legitimately (though perhaps not immediately) deducible from the mechanical principles, or fairly reconcileable to them. For, such hypotheses will probably attempt to account for the phaenomena of nature, either by the help of a determinate number of material ingredients, such as the *tria prima* of the chymists, by participation whereof other bodies obtain their qualities; or else by introducing some general agents, as the Platonic soul of the world, or the universal spirit, asserted by some spagyrists; or by both these ways together.

Now, to dispatch first those, that I named in the second place; I consider, that the chief thing, that inquisitive naturalists should look after in the explicating of difficult phaenomena, is not so much what the agent is or does, as, what changes are made in the patient, to bring it to exhibit the phaenomena, that are proposed; and by what means, and after what manner, those changes are effected. So that the mechanical philosopher being satisfied, that one part of matter can act upon another but by virtue of local motion, or the effects and consequences of local motion, he considers, that as if the proposed agent be not intelligible and physical, it can never physically explain the phaenomena, so, if it be intelligible and physical, it will be reducible to matter, and some or other of those only catholick affections of matter, already often mentioned. And the indefinite divisibility of matter, the wonderful efficacy of motion, and the almost infinite variety of coalitions and structures, that may be made of minute and insensible corpuscles, being duly weighed, I see not, why a philosopher should think it impossible, to make out, by their help, the mechanical possibility of any corporeal agent, how subtil, or diffused, or active soever it be, that can be solidly proved to be really existent in nature, by what name soever it be called or disguised.

* * *

. . . if we consider the thing itself, by a free examen of the pretended explanations, that the vulgar philosophers are wont, by recurring to nature, to give of the phaenomena of the universe; we shall not easily look on those accounts, as meriting the name of explications. For to explicate a phaenomenon, it is not enough to ascribe it to one general efficient, but we must intelligibly shew the particular manner, how that general cause produces the proposed effect. He must be a very dull inquirer, who, demanding an account of the phaenomena of a watch, shall rest satisfied with being told, that it is an engine made by a watch-maker; though nothing be thereby declared of the structure and co-aptation of the spring, wheels, balance, and other parts of the engine, and the manner, how they act on one another, so as to co-operate to make the needle point out the true hour of the day. And (to improve to my present purpose an example formerly touched upon) as he, that knows the structure and other mechanical affections of a watch, will be able by them to explicate the phaenomena of it, without supposing, that it has a soul or life to be the internal principle of its motions or operations; so he, that does not understand the mechanism of a watch, will never be enabled to give a rational account of the operations of it, by supposing, as those of *China* did, when the Jesuits first brought watches thither, that a watch is an European animal, or living body, and endowed with a soul. This comparison seems not ill to befit the occasion of propounding it; but to second it by another, that is more purely physical, when a person, unacquainted with the mathematics, admires to see, that the sun rises and sets in winter in some parts of the horizon, and in summer in others, distant enough from them; that the day, in the former season, is, by odds shorter, than in the latter, and sometimes (as some days before the middle of *March* and of *September*) the days are equal to the night; that the moon is sometimes seen in conjunction with the sun, and sometimes in opposition to him; and, between those two states, is every day variously illuminated; and that sometimes one of those planets, and sometimes another, suffers an eclipse; this person, I say, will be much assisted to understand, how these things are brought to pass, if he be taught the clear mathematical elements of astronomy: but if he be of a temper to reject these explications, as too defective, it is not like that it will satisfy him, to tell him after *Aristotle* and the schoolmen, that the orbs of the sun and moon, and other coelestial spheres, are moved by angels or intelligences; since to refer him to such general and undetermined causes, will little, or not at all, assist him to understand, how the recited phaenomena are produced.

RENÉ DESCARTES: *The Principles of Philosophy* *

> In *The Principles of Philosophy* Descartes, in effect, declared nature to be a mathematical machine, devoid of purpose or beauty.

Part II

I. THE GROUNDS on which the existence of material things may be known with certainty. . . .

For we clearly conceive this matter as entirely distinct from God, and from ourselves, or our mind; and appear even clearly to discern that the idea of it is formed in us on occasion of objects existing out of our minds, to which it is in every respect similar. But since God cannot deceive us, for this is repugnant to his nature, as has been already remarked, we must unhesitatingly conclude that there exists a certain object extended in length, breadth, and thickness, and possessing all those properties which we clearly apprehend to belong to what is extended. And this extended substance is what we call body or matter. . . .

IV. That the nature of body consists not in weight, hardness, colour and the like, but in extension alone.

In this way we will discern that the nature of matter or body, consid-

* René Descartes: *The Meditations and Selections from the Principles of Philosophy*, trans. by John Veitch (Edinburgh: Sutherland and Knox; 1853), pp. 152–4, 164, 167–8, 176–8.

ered in general, does not consist in its being hard, or ponderous, or coloured, or that which affects our senses in any other way, but simply in its being a substance extended in length, breadth, and depth. . . . In the same way, it may be shown that weight, colour, and all the other qualities of this sort, which are perceived in corporeal matter, may be taken from it, itself meanwhile remaining entire: it thus follows that the nature of body depends on none of these.

*   *   *

XXII. It also follows that the matter of the heavens and earth is the same, and that there cannot be a plurality of worlds.

And it may also be easily inferred from all this that the earth and heavens are made of the same matter; and that even although there were an infinity of worlds, they would all be composed of this matter; from which it follows that a plurality of worlds is impossible, because we clearly conceive that the matter whose nature consists only in its being an extended substance, already wholly occupies all the imaginable spaces where these other worlds could alone be, and we cannot find in ourselves the idea of any other matter.

XXIII. That all the variety of matter, or the diversity of its forms, depends on motion.

There is therefore but one kind of matter in the whole universe, and this we know only by its being extended. All the properties we distinctly perceive to belong to it are reducible to its capacity of being divided and moved according to its parts; and accordingly it is capable of all those affections which we perceive can arise from the motion of its parts. For the partition of matter in thought makes no change in it; but all variation of it, or diversity of form, depends on motion.

Part III

II. That we ought to beware lest, in our presumption, we imagine that the ends which God proposed to himself in the creation of the world are understood by us.

The second is, that we should beware of presuming too highly of ourselves, as it seems we should do if we supposed certain limits to the world, without being assured of their existence either by natural reasons or by divine revelation, as if the power of our thought extended beyond what God has in reality made; but likewise still more if we persuaded ourselves that all things were created by God for us only, or if we merely supposed that we could comprehend by the power of our intellect the ends which God proposed to himself in creating the universe.

III. In what sense it may be said that all things were created for the sake of man.

For although, as far as regards morals, it may be a pious thought to believe that God made all things for us, seeing we may thus be incited to greater gratitude and love toward him; and although it is even in some sense true, because there is no created thing óf which we cannot make some use, if it be only that of exercising our mind in considering it, and honouring God on account of it, it is yet by no means probable that all things were created for us in this way that God had no other end in their creation; and this supposition would be plainly ridiculous and inept in physical reasoning, for we do not doubt but that many things exist, or formerly existed and have now ceased to be, which were never seen or known by man, and were never of use to him.

Part IV

CXCVIII. That by our senses we know nothing of external objects beyond their figure [or situation], magnitude, and motion. . . .
And we can easily conceive how the motion of one body may be caused by that of another, and diversified by the size, figure, and situation of its parts, but we are wholly unable to conceive how these same things (viz., size, figure, and motion), can produce something else of a nature entirely different from themselves, as, for example, those substantial forms and real qualities which many philosophers suppose to be in bodies; nor likewise can we conceive how these qualities or forms possess force to cause motions in other bodies. But since we know, from the nature of our soul, that the diverse motions of body are sufficient to produce in it all the sensations which it has, and since we learn from experience that several of its sensations are in reality caused by such motions, while we do not discover that anything besides these motions ever passes from the organs of the external senses to the brain, we have reason to conclude that we in no way likewise apprehend that in external objects, which we call light, colour, smell, taste, sound, heat or cold, and the other tactile qualities, or that which we call their substantial forms, unless as the various dispositions of these objects which have the power of moving our nerves in various ways.

CXCIX. That there is no phenomenon of nature whose explanation has been omitted in this treatise.

And thus it may be gathered, from an enumeration that is easily made, that there is no phenomenon of nature whose explanation has been omitted in this treatise; for beyond what is perceived by the senses, there is nothing that can be considered a phenomenon of nature. But leaving out of account motion, magnitude, figure, [and the situation of the parts of each body], which I have explained as they exist in body, we perceive nothing out of us by our senses except light, colours, smells, tastes, sounds, and the tactile qualities; and these I have recently shown to be nothing more, at least so far as they are known to us, than certain dispositions of the objects, consisting in magnitude, figure, and motion.

BENEDICT DE SPINOZA: *Ethics Demonstrated in the Geometrical Manner* *

The Jewish philosopher Spinoza's decision to change his name from Baruch to Benedict is symbolic of his intellectual career. Along with his Jewish name, Spinoza rejected the theological orthodoxy of the Amsterdam Synagogue which excommunicated him at the age of twenty-four. "Benedict" signified the free life of the mind. Deeply read in contemporary science and the philosophy of Descartes and Bruno, Spinoza (1637–77) saw more clearly than any of his contemporaries "what the Cartesian revolution had really done to man and his world." Owing to official censorship, his most important work, the *Ethica ordine geometrica demonstrata,* was not published until after his death. His aim was to establish ethics on a scientific basis, and he employed therefore the geometrical method of reasoning.

Concerning God

[SOME PEOPLE] think that God is a free cause, because he can, as they think, bring it about, that those things which we have said follow from his nature—that is, which are in his power, should not come to pass, or should not be produced by him. But this is the same as if they said, that God could bring it about, that it should not follow from the nature of a triangle, that its three interior angles should not be equal to two right angles; or that from a given cause no effect should follow, which is absurd.

Moreover, I will show below, without the aid of this proposition, that neither intellect nor will appertain to God's nature. . . .

If intellect and will appertain to the eternal essence of God, we must take these words in some significations quite different from those they usually bear. For intellect and will, which should constitute the essence of God, would perforce be as far apart as the poles from the human intellect and will, in fact, would have nothing in common with them but the name; there would be about as much correspondence between the two as there is between the Dog, the heavenly constellation, and a dog, an animal that barks. . . .

It follows solely from the perfection of God, that God never can decree, or never could have decreed anything but what is; that God did not exist before his decrees, and would not exist without them. . . .

Nothing, then, comes to pass in nature in contravention to her universal laws, nay, everything agrees with them and follows from them, for whatsoever comes to pass, comes to pass by the will and eternal decree

* *The Chief Works of Benedict de Spinoza,* translated by R. H. M. Elwes (Bohn's Philosophical Library, London: George Bell and Sons; 1891), vol. I, pp. 83–4; vol. II, pp. 60–1, 72, 74–9, 128–9.

of God; that is, as we have just pointed out, whatever comes to pass, comes to pass according to laws and rules which involve eternal necessity and truth; nature, therefore, always observes laws and rules which involve eternal necessity and truth, although they may not all be known to us, and therefore she keeps a fixed and immutable order. Nor is there any sound reason for limiting the power and efficacy of nature, and asserting that her laws are fit for certain purposes, but not for all; for as the efficacy and power of nature, are the very efficacy and power of God, and as the laws and rules of nature are the decrees of God, it is in every way to be believed that the power of nature is infinite, and that her laws are broad enough to embrace everything conceived by the Divine intellect; the only alternative is to assert that God has created nature so weak, and has ordained for her laws so barren, that he is repeatedly compelled to come afresh to her aid if He wishes that she should be preserved, and that things should happen as He desires: a conclusion, in my opinion, very far removed from reason. Further, as nothing happens in nature which does not follow from her laws, and as her laws embrace everything conceived by the Divine intellect, and lastly, as nature preserves a fixed and immutable order; it most clearly follows that miracles are only intelligible as in relation to human opinions, and merely mean events of which the natural cause cannot be explained by a reference to any ordinary occurrence, either by us, or at any rate, by the writer and narrator of the miracle. . . .

In the foregoing I have explained the nature and properties of God. . . . Yet there still remain misconceptions not a few, which might and may prove very grave hindrances to the understanding of the concatenation of things, as I have explained it above. I have therefore thought it worth while to bring these misconceptions before the bar of reason.

All such opinions spring from the notion commonly entertained, that all things in nature act as men themselves act, namely, with an end in view. It is accepted as certain, that God himself directs all things to a definite goal (for it is said that God made all things for man, and man that he might worship him). I will, therefore, consider this opinion, asking first, why it obtains general credence, and why all men are naturally so prone to adopt it? secondly, I will point out its falsity. . . . Men do all things for an end, namely, for that which is useful to them, and which they seek. Thus it comes to pass that they only look for a knowledge of the final causes of events, and when these are learned, they are content, as having no cause for further doubt. If they cannot learn such causes from external sources, they are compelled to turn to considering themselves, and reflecting what end would have induced them personally to bring about the given event, and thus they necessarily judge other natures by their own. Further, as they find in themselves and outside themselves many means which assist them not a little in their search for what is useful, for instance, eyes for seeing, teeth for chewing, herbs and animals for yielding food, the sun for giving light, the sea for breeding fish, &c., they come to look on the whole of nature as a means for obtaining such conveniences. Now as they are aware, that they found these conveniences and did not make them, they think they have cause for believing, that some other being has made them for their use. As they look upon things as means, they cannot believe them to be self-created; but, judging from the means which they are accustomed to prepare for themselves, they are bound to believe in some ruler or rulers of the universe endowed with human freedom, who have arranged and adapted everything for human use. . . . But in their endeavour to show that nature does nothing in vain, *i.e.*, nothing which is useless to man, they only seem to have demonstrated that nature, the gods, and men are all mad together. Consider, I pray you, the result: among the many helps of nature they were bound to find some hindrances, such as storms, earthquakes, diseases, &c.: so they declared that such things happen, because the gods are angry at some wrong done them by men, or at some fault committed in their worship. Experience day by day protested and showed by infinite examples, that good and evil fortunes fall to the lot of pious and impious alike; still they would not abandon their inveterate prejudice, for it was more easy for them to class such contradictions among other unknown things of whose use they were ignorant, and thus to retain their actual and innate condition of ignorance, than to destroy the whole fabric of their reasoning and start afresh. They therefore laid down as an axiom, that God's judgments far transcend human understanding. Such a doctrine might well have sufficed to conceal the truth from the human race for all eternity, if mathematics had not furnished another standard of verity in considering solely the essence and properties of figures without regard to their final causes. . . .

I have now sufficiently explained my first point. There is no need to show at length, that nature has no particular goal in view, and that final causes are mere human figments. . . . However, I will add a few remarks, in order to overthrow this doctrine of a final cause utterly. . . .

This doctrine does away with the perfection of God: for, if God acts for an object, he necessarily desires something which he lacks. Certainly, theologians and metaphysicians draw a distinction between the object of want and the object of assimilation; still they confess that God made all things for the sake of himself, not for the sake of creation. They are unable to point to anything prior to creation, except God himself, as an object for which God should act, and are therefore driven to admit (as they clearly must), that God lacked those things for whose attainment he created means, and further that he desired them.

We must not omit to notice that the followers of this doctrine, anxious to display their talent in assigning final causes, have imported a new method of argument in proof of their theory—namely, a reduction, not to the impossible, but to ignorance; thus showing that they have no other method of exhibiting their doctrine. For example, if a stone falls from a roof on to someone's head, and kills him, they will demonstrate by their new method, that the stone fell in order to kill the man; for, if it had not by God's will fallen with that object, how could so many circumstances (and there are often many concurrent circumstances) have all happened together by chance? Perhaps you will answer that the event is due to the facts that the wind was blowing, and the man was walking that way. "But why," they will insist, "was the wind blowing, and why was the man at that very time walking that way?" If you again answer, that the wind had then sprung up because the sea had begun to be agitated the day before, the weather being previously calm, and that the man had been invited by a friend, they will again insist: "But why was the sea agitated, and why was the man invited at that time?" So they will pursue their questions from cause to cause, till at last you take refuge in the will of God—in other words, the sanctuary of ignorance. . . .

On the Origin and Nature of the Emotions

Most writers on the emotions and on human conduct seem to be treating rather of matters outside nature than of natural phenomena following nature's general laws. They appear to conceive man to be situated in nature as a kingdom within a kingdom: for they believe that he disturbs rather than follows nature's order, that he has absolute control over his actions, and that he is determined solely by himself. They attribute human infirmities and fickleness, not to the power of nature in general, but to some mysterious flaw in the nature of man, which accordingly they bemoan, deride, despise, or, as usually happens, abuse. . . .

Such persons will, doubtless think it strange that I should attempt to treat of human vice and folly geometrically, and should wish to set forth with rigid reasoning those matters which they cry out against as repugnant to reason, frivolous, absurd, and dreadful. However, such is my plan. Nothing comes to pass in nature, which can be set down to a flaw therein; for nature is always the same, and everywhere one and the same in her efficacy and power of action; that is, nature's laws and ordinances, whereby all things come to pass and change from one form to another, are everywhere and always the same; so that there should be one and the same method of understanding the nature of all things whatsoever, namely, through nature's universal laws and rules. Thus the passions of hatred, anger, envy, and so on, considered in themselves, follow from this same necessity and efficacy of nature; they answer to certain definite causes, through which they are understood, and possess certain properties as worthy of being known as the properties of anything else, whereof the contemplation in itself affords us delight. I shall, therefore, treat of the nature and strength of the emotions according to the same method, as I employed heretofore in my investigations concerning God and the mind. I shall consider human actions and desires in exactly the same manner, as though I were concerned with lines, planes, and solids.

SIR ISAAC NEWTON: *Optics* *

> Like Galileo and Descartes, the great English physicist Sir Isaac Newton (1642–1727) pictured the universe as a machine, specifically as "a realm of masses, moving according to mathematical laws in space and time, under the influence of definite and dependable forces." However, it is equally clear that Newton thought this machine depended upon an ultimately non-mechanical principle. These two elements in his system, the mechanical and the non-mechanical, come out clearly in the following passages. The first short section is from his preface to the first edition of the *Principia* (1687), the rest from the *Opticks, or a Treatise of the Reflections, Refractions, Inflections and Colours of Light* (1704).

SINCE the ancients (as we are told by *Pappus*) made great account of the science of Mechanics in the investigation of natural things; and the moderns, laying aside substantial forms and occult qualities, have endeavoured to subject the phaenomena of nature to the laws of mathematics; I have in this treatise cultivated Mathematics, so far as it regards Philosophy. . . .

In the third book we give an example of this in the explication of the System of the World. For by the propositions mathematically demonstrated in the first books, we there derive from the celestial phaenomena, the forces of Gravity with which bodies tend to the Sun and the several Planets. Then from these forces by other propositions, which are also mathematical, we deduce the motions of the Planets, the Comets, the Moon, and the Sea. I wish we could derive the rest of the phaenomena of nature by the same kind of reasoning from mechanical principles. For I am induced by many reasons to suspect that they may all depend upon certain forces by which the particles of bodies, by some causes hitherto unknown, are either mutually impelled towards each other and cohere in regular figures, or are repelled and recede from each other; which forces being unknown, Philosophers have hitherto attempted the search of Na-

* Sir Isaac Newton: *The Mathematical Principles of Natural Philosophy*, trans. by Andrew Motte (London: B. Motte; 1729), vol. I, pp. A–A2; *Opticks* (London: W. & J. Innys; 1721), pp. 344–5, 375–81.

ture in vain. But I hope the principles here laid down will afford some light either to that, or some truer, method of Philosophy.

*   *   *

. . . the main Business of Natural Philosophy is to argue from Phaenomena without feigning Hypotheses, and to deduce Causes from Effects, till we come to the very first Cause, which certainly is not mechanical; and not only to unfold the Mechanism of the World, but chiefly to resolve these and such like Questions. What is there in places almost empty of Matter, and whence is it that the Sun and Planets gravitate towards one another, without dense Matter between them? Whence is it that Nature doth nothing in vain; and whence arises all that Order and Beauty which we see in the World? To what end are Comets, and whence is it that Planets move all one and the same way in Orbs concentrick, while Comets move all manner of ways in Orbs very excentrick, and what hinders the fix'd Stars from falling upon one another? How came the Bodies of Animals to be contrived with so much Art, and for what ends were their several Parts? Was the Eye contrived without Skill in Opticks, and the Ear without Knowledge of Sounds? How do the Motions of the Body follow from the Will, and whence is the Instinct in Animals? Is not the Sensory of Animals that place to which the sensitive Substance is present, and into which the sensible Species of Things are carried through the Nerves and Brain, that there they may be perceived by their immediate presence to that Substance? And these things being rightly dispatch'd, does it not appear from Phaenomena that there is a Being incorporeal, living, intelligent, omnipresent, who in infinite Space, as it were in his Sensory, sees the things themselves intimately, and thoroughly perceives them, and comprehends them wholly by their immediate presence to himself: Of which things the Images only carried through the Organs of Sense into our little Sensoriums, are there seen and beheld by that which in us perceives and thinks. And tho' every true Step made in this Philosophy brings us not immediately to the Knowledge of the first Cause, yet it brings us nearer to it, and on that account is to be highly valued. . . .

It seems probable to me, that God in the Beginning form'd Matter in solid, massy, hard, impenetrable, moveable Particles, of such Sizes and Figures, and with such other Properties, and in such Proportion to Space, as most conduced to the End for which he form'd them; and that these primitive Particles being Solids, are incomparably harder than any porous Bodies compounded of them; even so very hard, as never to wear or break in pieces: No ordinary Power being able to divide what God himself made one in the First Creation. . . .

It seems to me farther, that these Particles have not only a *Vis inertiae*, accompanied with such passive Laws of Motion as naturally result from that Force, but also that they are moved by certain active Principles, such as is that of Gravity, and that which causes Fermentation, and the Cohesion of Bodies. These Principles I consider not as occult Qualities, supposed to result from the specifick Forms of Things, but as general Laws of Nature, by which the Things themselves are form'd: their Truth appearing to us by Phaenomena, though their Causes be not yet discover'd. For these are manifest Qualities, and their Causes only are occult. And the *Aristotelians* gave the Name of occult Qualities not to manifest Qualities, but to such Qualities only as they supposed to lie hid in Bodies, and to be the unknown Causes of manifest Effects: Such as would be the Causes of Gravity, and of magnetick and electrick Attractions, and of Fermentations, if we should suppose that these Forces or Actions arose from Qualities unknown to us, and uncapable of being discovered and made manifest. Such occult Qualities put a stop to the Improvement of natural Philosophy, and therefore of late Years have been rejected. To tell us that every Species of Things is endow'd with an occult specifick Quality by which it acts and produces manifest Effects, is to tell us nothing: But to derive two or three general Principles of Motion from Phaenomena, and afterwards to tell us how the Properties and Actions of all corporeal Things follow from those manifest Principles, would be a very great step in Philosophy, though the Causes of those Principles were not yet discover'd: And therefore I scruple not to propose the Principles of Motion above mention'd, they being of very general Extent, and leave their Causes to be found out.

Now by the help of these Principles, all material Things seem to have been composed of the hard and solid Particles above mention'd, variously associated in the first Creation by the Counsel of an intelligent Agent. For it became him who created them to set them in order. And if he did so, it's unphilosophical to seek for any other Origin of the World, or to pretend that it might arise out of a Chaos by the mere Laws of Nature; though being once form'd, it may continue by those Laws for many Ages. For while Comets move in very excentrick Orbs in all manner of positions, blind Fate could never make all the Planets move one and the same way in Orbs concentrick, some inconsiderable Irregularities excepted which may have risen from the mutual Actions of Comets and Planets upon one another, and which will be apt to increase, till this System wants a Reformation. Such a wonderful Uniformity in the Planetary System must be allowed the Effect of Choice. And so must the Uniformity in the Bodies of Animals, they having generally a right and a left side shaped alike, and on either side of their Bodies two Legs behind, and either two Arms, or two Legs, or two Wings before upon their Shoulders, and between their Shoulders a Neck running down into a Backbone, and a Head upon it; and in the Head two Ears, two Eyes, a Nose, a Mouth, and a Tongue, alike situated. Also the first Contrivance of those very artificial Parts of Animals, the Eyes, Ears, Brain, Muscles, Heart, Lungs, Midriff, Glands, Larynx, Hands, Wings, Swimming Bladders, natural Spectacles, and other Organs of Sense and Motion; and the Instinct of Brutes and Insects, can be the effect of nothing else than the Wisdom and Skill of a powerful ever living Agent, who being in all Places, is more able by his Will to move the Bodies within his boundless uniform Sensorium, and thereby to form and reform the Parts of the Universe, than we are by our Will to move the Parts of our own Bodies. . . . And since Space is divisible *in infinitum,* and Matter is not necessarily in all places, it may be also allow'd that God is able to create Particles of Matter of several Sizes and Figures, and in several Proportions to Space, and perhaps of different Densities and Forces, and thereby to vary the Laws of Nature, and make Worlds of several sorts in several Parts of the Universe. At least, I see nothing of Contradiction in all this.

As in Mathematicks, so in Natural Philosophy, the Investigation of difficult Things by the Method of Analysis, ought ever to precede the Method of Composition. This Analysis consists in making Experiments and Observations, and in drawing general Conclusions from them by Induction, and admitting of no Objections against the Conclusions, but such as are taken from Experiments, or other certain Truths. For Hypotheses are not to be regarded in experimental Philosophy. And although the arguing from Experiments and Observations by Induction be no Demonstration of general Conclusions; yet it is the best way of arguing which the Nature of Things admits of, and may be looked upon as so much the stronger, by how much the Induction is more general. And if no Exception occur from Phaenomena, the Conclusion may be pronounced generally. But if at any time afterwards any Exception shall occur from Experiments, it may then begin to be pronounced with such Exceptions as occur. By this way of Analysis we may proceed from Compounds to Ingredients, and from Motions to the Forces producing them; and in general, from Effects to their Causes, and from particular Causes to more general ones, till the Argument end in the most general. This is the Method of Analysis: And the Synthesis consists in assuming the Causes discover'd, and establish'd as Principles, and by them explaining the Phaenomena proceeding from them, and proving the Explanations.

5. Science and Religion

GALILEO GALILEI: *On Theology as Queen of the Sciences* *

Galileo's Letter to the Grand Duchess Christina of Tuscany (1615), here reproduced in part, might be called a scientist's declaration of independence. Since 1611 the greatest scientist (1564–1642) had been under attack by certain churchmen for championing the Copernican theory of the universe, not merely as a mathematical hypothesis but as a physical fact. Replying to the attack in his famous letter, Galileo stated unequivocally what he considered to be the proper relations between theology and science.

SOME years ago, as Your Serene Highness well knows, I discovered in the heavens many things that had not been seen before our own age. The novelty of these things, as well as some consequences which followed from them in contradiction to the physical notions commonly held among academic philosophers, stirred up against me no small numbers of professors—as if I had placed these things in the sky with my own hands in order to upset nature and overturn the sciences. They seemed to forget that the increase of known truths stimulates the investigation, establishment, and growth of the arts; not their diminution or destruction.

Showing a greater fondness for their own opinions than for truth, they sought to deny and disprove the new things which, if they had cared to look for themselves, their own senses would have demonstrated to them. To this end they hurled various charges and published numerous writings filled with vain arguments, and they made the grave mistake of sprinkling these with passages taken from places in the Bible which they had failed to understand properly, and which were ill suited to their purposes. . . .

Persisting in their original resolve to destroy me and everything mine by any means they can think of, these men are aware of my views in astronomy and philosophy. They know that as to the arrangement of the parts of the universe, I hold the sun to be situated motionless in the center of the revolution of the celestial orbs while the earth rotates on its axis and revolves about the sun. They know also that I support this position not only by refuting the arguments of Ptolemy and Aristotle, but by producing many counterarguments; in particular, some

* From *Discoveries and Opinions of Galileo*, trans. by Stillman Drake, pp. 175, 177, 179, 182–3, 191–3, 203. Copyright © 1957 by Stillman Drake. Reprinted by permission of Doubleday & Company, Inc.

which relate to physical effects whose causes can perhaps be assigned in no other way. In addition there are astronomical arguments derived from many things in my new celestial discoveries that plainly confute the Ptomenaic system while admirably agreeing with and confirming the contrary hypothesis. Possibly because they are disturbed by the known truth of other propositions of mine which differ from those commonly held, and therefore mistrusting their defense so long as they confine themselves to the field of philosophy, these men have resolved to fabricate a shield for their fallacies out of the mantle of pretended religion and the authority of the Bible. These they apply, with little judgment, to the refutation of arguments that they do not understand and have not even listened to.

First they have endeavored to spread the opinion that such propositions in general are contrary to the Bible and are consequently damnable and heretical. . . . [And] they have had no trouble in finding men who would preach the damnability and heresy of the new doctrine from their very pulpits with unwonted confidence, thus doing impious and inconsiderate injury not only to that doctrine and its followers but to all mathematics and mathematicians in general. . . .

Now as to the false aspersions which they so unjustly seek to cast upon me, I have thought it necessary to justify myself in the eyes of all men, whose judgment in matters of religion and of reputation I must hold in great esteem. I shall therefore discourse of the particulars which these men produce to make this opinion detested and to have it condemned not merely as false but as heretical. To this end they make a shield of their hypocritical zeal for religion. They go about invoking the Bible, which they would have minister to their deceitful purposes. Contrary to the sense of the Bible and the intention of the holy Fathers, if I am not mistaken, they would extend such authorities until even in purely physical matters—where faith is not involved—they would have us altogether abandon reason and the evidence of our senses in favor of some biblical passage, though under the surface meaning of its words this passage may contain a different sense. . . .

. . . I think that in discussions of physical problems we ought to begin not from the authority of scriptural passages, but from sense-experiences and necessary demonstrations; for the holy Bible and the phenomena of nature proceed alike from the divine Word, the former as the dictate of the Holy Ghost and the latter as the observant executrix of God's commands. It is necessary for the Bible, in order to be accommodated to the understanding of every man, to speak many things which appear to differ from the absolute truth so far as the bare meaning of the words is concerned. But Nature, on the other hand, is inexorable and immutable; she never transgresses the laws imposed upon her, or cares a whit whether her abstruse reasons and methods of operation are understandable to men. For that reason it appears that nothing physical which sense-experience sets before our eyes, or which necessary demonstrations prove to us, ought to be called in question (much less condemned) upon the testimony of biblical passages which may have some different meaning beneath their words. For the Bible is not chained in every expression to conditions as strict as those which govern all physical effects; nor is God any less excellently revealed in Nature's actions than in the sacred statements of the Bible. . . .

I do not wish to place in the number of such lay writers some theologians whom I consider men of profound learning and devout behavior, and who are therefore held by me in great esteem and veneration. Yet I cannot deny that I feel some discomfort which I should like to have removed, when I hear them pretend to the power of constraining others by scriptural authority to follow in a physical dispute that opinion which they think best agrees with the Bible, and then believe themselves not bound to answer the opposing reasons and experiences. In explanation and support of this opinion they say that since theology is queen of all the sciences, she need not bend in any way to accommodate herself to the teachings of less worthy sciences which are subordinate to her; these others must rather be referred to her as to their supreme empress, changing and altering their conclusions according to her statutes and decrees. . . .

First, I question whether there is not some equivocation in failing to specify the virtues which entitle sacred theology to the title of "queen." It might deserve that name by reason of including everything that is learned from all the other sciences and establishing everything by better methods and with profounder learning. It is thus, for example, that the rules for measuring fields and keeping accounts are much more excellently contained in arithmetic and in the geometry of Euclid than in the practices of surveyors and accountants. Or theology might be queen because of being occupied with a subject which excels in dignity all the subjects which compose the other sciences, and because her teachings are divulged in more sublime ways.

That the title and authority of queen belongs to theology in the first sense, I think will not be affirmed by theologians who have any skill in the other sciences. None of these, I think, will say that geometry, astronomy, music, and medicine are much more excellently contained in the Bible than they are in the books of Archimedes, Ptolemy, Boethius, and Galen. Hence it seems likely that regal pre-eminence is given to theology in the second sense; that is, by reason of its subject and the miraculous communication of divine revelation of conclusions which could not be conceived by men in any other way, concerning chiefly the attainment of eternal blessedness.

Let us grant then that theology is conversant with the loftiest divine contemplation, and occupies the regal throne among sciences by dignity.

But acquiring the highest authority in this way, if she does not descend to the lower and humbler speculations of the subordinate sciences and has no regard for them because they are not concerned with blessedness, then her professors should not arrogate to themselves the authority to decide on controversies in professions which they have neither studied nor practiced. Why, this would be as if an absolute despot, being neither a physician nor an architect but knowing himself free to command, should undertake to administer medicines and erect buildings according to his whim—at grave peril of his poor patients' lives, and the speedy collapse of his edifices.

Again, to command that the very professors of astronomy themselves see to the refutation of their own observations and proofs as mere fallacies and sophisms is to enjoin something that lies beyond any possibility of accomplishment. For this would amount to commanding that they must not see what they see and must not understand what they know, and that in searching they must find the opposite of what they actually encounter. Before this could be done they would have to be taught how to make one mental faculty command another, and the inferior powers the superior, so that the imagination and the will might be forced to believe the opposite of what the intellect understands. I am referring at all times to merely physical propositions, and not to supernatural things which are matters of faith.

*   *   *

Besides, I question the truth of the statement that the church commands us to hold as matters of faith all physical conclusions bearing the stamp of harmonious interpretation by all the Fathers. . . . So far as I can find, all that is really prohibited is the "perverting into senses contrary to that of the holy Church or that of the concurrent agreement of the Fathers those passages, and those alone, which pertain to faith or ethics, or which concern the edification of Christian doctrine." . . . But the mobility or stability of the earth or sun is neither a matter of faith nor one contrary to ethics.

Blaise Pascal: *Selections* *

Blaise Pascal (1623–62) was one of the greatest mathematicians and scientists of his time. He was also a man of great religious sensitivity, the author of the famous *Pensées*, which were actually jottings or notes for a book he planned to write (but never completed) in defense of religion in a skeptical age. In the first of the selections below, from the preface to his treatise on the vacuum (1647?), Pascal speaks as a scientist who is trying to delimit the spheres of science and religion

* From *Great Shorter Works of Pascal*, trans. by Emile Cailliet and John C. Blankenagle. Copyright 1948 by The Westminster Press. Used by permission.
The Thoughts of Blaise Pascal, trans. by C. Kegan Paul (London: George Bell and Sons; 1890), pp. 102–03, 306–07.

according to modes of knowing. In the selections from the *Pensées* which follow, he speaks rather as a believing Christian, a Jansenist Catholic, opposed to the proud claims of the rationalists, including Descartes, to supply "metaphysical proofs" for the existence of God. Reason might lead to the God of the philosophers, but not to the living God of Abraham and St. Paul. Only the heart could intuit God, though by "the heart" Pascal meant to include knowledge and will as well as feeling.

Fragment of a Preface to the Treatise on the Vacuum

THE RESPECT for antiquity has today come to such a point in matters where it should have least influence that all its thoughts, its mysteries, and even its obscurities have been turned into oracles. Indeed, one can no longer submit innovations without jeopardy, and the text of an author suffices to bring the most cogent reasoning to naught.

Not that I would correct matters by substituting one vice for another or profess no esteem for the ancients because others hold them in too high esteem. I do not pretend to banish their authority in order to elevate reasoning alone, although there are those who desire to establish their authority solely at the expense of reasoning. . . .

In order to make this important distinction with proper care we must consider that some matters of knowledge depend on memory alone and are purely historical. Here the sole concern is to know what authors have written. Other matters of knowledge depend only on reasoning, and are entirely dogmatic. Here the aim is to seek and to discover hidden truths. Those which come under the first heading are as limited as the books that contain them. . . .

In matters where we merely seek to know what authors have written, as in history, geography, jurisprudence, languages, above all in theology, and finally in all those which have as their basic principle either simple facts or divine or human institutions, we must of necessity have recourse to their books, since these contain all that we can know about such matters.

If it is a matter of knowing who was the first king of France, in what place geographers located the prime meridian, what words are used in a dead language, and all such things, what means other than books can lead us to this knowledge? And who can add anything new to what they teach us about them, since we wish to know merely what they contain? It is authority alone that can enlighten us. But it is in theology that this authority has greatest weight because there it is inseparable from truth, and because only through it do we know truth. For if we desire to give complete assurance about matters which are most incomprehensible to reason, we need merely point to them in sacred books (similarly, when we wish to call attention to the uncertainty of the most plausible things, we need merely point out that they are not contained in these books). This is because these principles transcend nature and reason, and since the human mind is too feeble to arrive by its own efforts, it cannot attain such high understanding if it is not carried aloft by a force which is omnipotent and supernatural.

It is not the same with subjects which are self-evident to the senses and to reasoning; there authority is unnecessary; reason alone suffices to know them. Each has its separate jurisdiction; now the one has the advantage, and now the other reigns in its turn. But since subjects of this kind are adjusted to the range of the mind, it is entirely free to extend this range; its inexhaustible fecundity is constantly productive, and the sum total of its inventions may be without end and without interruption. . . .

It is thus that geometry, arithmetic, music, physics, medicine, architecture, and all the sciences, which are subject to experiment and to reasoning, must be augmented to become perfect. The ancients found them but roughly sketched by their predecessors, and we shall leave them to those who come after us in a better state than we received them. Since their perfection depends on time and toil, it is evident that our toil and our time would have achieved less for us if the labors of the ancients had been divorced from ours. Joined together, however, the two must produce a greater result than each by itself.

The clearing up of this difference must make us pity the blindness of those who offer only authority as their proof in matters of physics, instead of setting forth proofs based on reasoning or experimentation. And the clearing up of this difference must fill us with horror at the malice of others who, in theology, resort solely to reasoning instead of to the authority of the Scriptures and the [Church] Fathers. We must give heart to those timid people who dare not invent anything in physics, and we must confound the insolence of those foolhardy people who bring forth innovations in theology. . . .

Pensées

We know truth, not only by the reason, but also by the heart, and it is from this last that we know first principles; and reason, which has nothing to do with it, tries in vain to combat them. The sceptics who desire truth alone labour in vain. We know that we do not dream, although it is impossible to prove it by reason, and this inability shows only the weakness of our reason, and not, as they declare, the general uncertainty of our knowledge. For our knowledge of first principles, as *space, time, motion, number,* is as distinct as any principle derived from reason. And reason must lean necessarily on this instinctive knowledge of the heart, and must found on it every process. We know instinctively that there are three dimensions in space, and that numbers are infinite, and reason then shows that there are no two square numbers one of which is double of the other. We feel principles, we infer propositions, both with certainty, though by different ways. It is as useless and absurd for reason to demand from the heart proofs of first principles before it will admit them, as it would be for the heart to ask from reason a feeling of all the propositions demonstrated before accepting them.

This inability should serve then only to humiliate reason, which would fain judge of all things, but not to shake our certainty, as if only reason were able to instruct us. Would to God, on the contrary, that we never needed reason, and that we knew every thing by instinct and feeling! But nature has denied us this advantage, and has on the contrary, given us but little knowledge of this kind, all the rest can be acquired by reason only.

Therefore those to whom God has given Religion by an instinctive feeling, are very blessed, and justly convinced. But to those who have it not we can give it only by reasoning, waiting for the time when God shall impress it on their hearts, without which faith is human only, and useless for salvation. . . .

The heart has its reasons, which reason knows not, as we feel in a thousand instances. I say that the heart loves the universal Being naturally, and itself naturally, according as it gives itself to each, and it hardens itself against one or the other at its own will. You have rejected one and kept the other, does reason cause your love?

It is the heart which is conscious of God, not the reason. This then is faith; God sensible to the heart, not to the reason. . . .

JOHN LOCKE: *An Essay concerning Human Understanding* *

John Locke's *Essay concerning Human Understanding* (1690) is well known as a great landmark in the philosophy of empiricism. What is not so well known is that Book IV of the *Essay*, from which most of the following selections are taken, contains perhaps the most lucid statement on record of the controlling principles of the rationalist movement in religion, which marked as complete a break with Protestantism as Catholicism. Locke's remarks should be read in the context of religious warfare among the sects in seventeenth-century England.

Statement of Purpose

I ACKNOWLEDGE the age we live in is not the least knowing, and therefore not the most easy to be satisfied. . . . The commonwealth of learning is not at this time without master-builders, whose mighty designs, in ad-

* John Locke: *An Essay concerning Human Understanding* (Oxford: The Clarendon Press; 1894), vol. I, pp. 13–14, 27–8, 37–8, 121–2; vol. II, p. 387, 412–13, 415–16, 420–1, 423, 425–7, 430.

vancing the sciences, will leave lasting monuments to the admiration of posterity: but every one must not hope to be a Boyle or a Sydenham; and in an age that produces such masters as the great Huygenius and the incomparable Mr. Newton, with some others of that strain, it is ambition enough to be employed as an under-labourer in clearing the ground a little, and removing some of the rubbish that lies in the way to knowledge; which certainly had been very much more advanced in the world, if the endeavours of ingenious and industrious men had not been much cumbered with the learned but frivolous use of uncouth, affected, or unintelligible terms. . . .

[Locke proposes] to search out the bounds between opinion and knowledge; and examine by what measures, in things whereof we have no certain knowledge, we ought to regulate our assent and moderate our persuasion. In order whereunto I shall pursue this following method:—

First, I shall inquire into the original of those *ideas*, notions, or whatever else you please to call them, which a man observes, and is conscious to himself he has in his mind; and the ways whereby the understanding comes to be furnished with them.

Secondly, I shall endeavour to show what knowledge the understanding hath by those ideas; and the certainty, evidence, and extent of it.

Thirdly, I shall make some inquiry into the nature and grounds of *faith* or *opinion*: whereby I mean that assent which we give to any proposition as true, of whose truth yet we have no certain knowledge. And here we shall have occasion to examine the reasons and degrees of *assent*.

Epistemology

It is an established opinion amongst some men, that there are in the understanding certain *innate principles*; some primary notions, characters, as it were stamped upon the mind of man; which the soul receives in its very first being, and brings into the world with it. It would be sufficient to convince unprejudiced readers of the falseness of this supposition, if I should only show (as I hope I shall in the following parts of this Discourse) how men, barely by the use of their natural faculties, may attain to all the knowledge they have, without the help of any innate impressions; and may arrive at certainty, without any such original notions or principles. . . .

Let us then suppose the mind to be, as we say, white paper, void of all characters, without any ideas:—How comes it to be furnished? Whence comes it by that vast store which the busy and boundless fancy of man has painted on it with an almost endless variety? Whence has it all the *materials* of reason and knowledge? To this I answer, in one word, from EXPERIENCE. In that all our knowledge is founded; and from that it ultimately derives itself. Our observation employed either, about external sensible objects, or about the internal operations of our minds perceived and reflected on by ourselves, is that which supplies our understandings with all the *materials* of thinking. These two are the fountains of knowledge, from whence all the ideas we have, or can naturally have, do spring. . . .

Sense and intuition reach but a very little way. The greatest part of our knowledge depends upon deductions and intermediate ideas: and in those cases where we are fain to substitute assent instead of knowledge, and take propositions for true, without being certain they are so, we have need to find out, examine, and compare the grounds of their probability. In both these cases, the faculty which finds out the means, and rightly applies them, to discover certainty in the one, and probability in the other, is that which we call *reason*. . . .

Faith and Reason

By what has been before said of reason, we may be able to make some guess at the distinction of things, into those that are according to, above, and contrary to reason. 1. *According to reason* are such propositions whose truth we can discover by examining and tracing those ideas we have from sensation and reflection; and by natural deduction find to be true or probable. 2. *Above reason* are such propositions whose truth or probability we cannot by reason derive from those principles. 3. *Contrary to reason* are such propositions as are inconsistent with or irreconcilable to our clear and distinct ideas. Thus the existence of one God is according to reason; the existence of more than one God, contrary to reason; the resurrection of the dead, above reason. . . .

From these things thus premised, I think we may come to lay down *the measures and boundaries between faith and reason:* the want whereof may possibly have been the cause, if not of great disorders, yet at least of great disputes, and perhaps mistakes in the world. For till it be resolved how far we are to be guided by reason, and how far by faith, we shall in vain dispute, and endeavour to convince one another in matters of religion. . . .

Reason, therefore, here, as contradistinguished to *faith*, I take to be the discovery of the certainty or probability of such propositions or truths, which the mind arrives at by deduction made from such ideas which it has got by the use of its natural faculties: viz. by sensation or reflection.

Faith, on the other side, is the assent to any proposition, not thus made out by the deductions of reason, but upon the credit of the proposer, as coming from God, in some extraordinary way of communication. This way of discovering truths to men, we call *revelation*. . . .

In propositions whose certainty is built upon the clear perception of the agreement or disagreement of our ideas, attained either by immediate intuition, as in self-evident propositions, or by evident deductions of reason in demonstrations we need not the assistance of revelation, as necessary to gain our assent, and introduce them into our minds. Because the natural ways of knowledge could settle them there, or had done it already; which is the greatest assurance we can possibly have of anything, unless where God immediately reveals it to us: and there too our assurance can be no greater than our knowledge is, that it *is* a revelation from God. But yet nothing, I think, can, under that title, shake or overrule plain knowledge; or rationally prevail with any man to admit it for true, in a direct contradiction to the clear evidence of his own understanding. For, since no evidence of our faculties, by which we receive such revelations, can exceed, if equal, the certainty of our intuitive knowledge, we can never receive for a truth anything that is directly contrary to our clear and distinct knowledge; v.g. the ideas of one body and one place do so clearly agree, and the mind has so evident a perception of their agreement, that we can never assent to a proposition that affirms the same body to be in two distant places at once, however it should pretend to the authority of a divine revelation. . . . And therefore *no proposition can be received for divine revelation, or obtain the assent due to all such, if it be contradictory to our clear intuitive knowledge.* Because this would be to subvert the principles and foundations of all knowledge, evidence, and assent whatsoever: and there would be left no difference between truth and falsehood, no measures of credible and incredible in the world, if doubtful propositions shall take place before self-evident; and what we certainly know give way to what we may possibly be mistaken in. In propositions therefore contrary to the clear perception of the agreement or disagreement of any of our ideas, it will be in vain to urge them as matters of faith. They cannot move our assent under that or any other title whatsoever. For faith can never convince us of anything that contradicts our knowledge. . . .

But there being many things wherein we have very imperfect notions, or none at all; and other things, of whose past, present, or future existence, by the natural use of our faculties, we can have no knowledge at all; these, as being beyond the discovery of our natural faculties, and *above reason*, are, when revealed, *the proper matter of faith*. Thus, that part of the angels rebelled against God, and thereby lost their first happy state: and that [the dead shall rise, and live again]: these and the like, being beyond the discovery of reason, are purely matters of faith, with which reason has directly nothing to do. . . .

Thus far the dominion of faith reaches, and that without any violence or hindrance to reason; which is not injured or disturbed, but assisted and improved by new discoveries of truth, coming from the eternal fountain of all knowledge. Whatever God hath revealed is certainly true: no doubt can be made of it. This is the proper object of faith: but whether it be a *divine* revelation or no, reason must judge; which can never permit the mind to reject a greater evidence to embrace what is less evident, nor allow it to entertain probability in opposition to knowledge and certainty. There can be no evidence that any traditional revelation is of divine original, in the words we receive it, and in the sense we understand it, so clear and so certain as that of the principles of reason: and therefore *Nothing that is contrary to, and inconsistent with, the clear and self-evident dictates of reason, has a right to be urged or assented to as a matter of faith, wherein reason hath nothing to do.* Whatsoever is divine revelation, ought to overrule all our opinions, prejudices, and interest, and hath a right to be received with full assent. Such a submission as this, of our reason to faith, takes not away the landmarks of knowledge: this shakes not the foundations of reason, but leaves us that use of our faculties for which they were given us.

If the provinces of faith and reason are not kept distinct by these boundaries, there will, in matters of religion, be no room for reason at all; and those extravagant opinions and ceremonies that are to be found in the several religions of the world will not deserve to be blamed. For, to this crying up of faith in *opposition* to reason, we may, I think, in good measure ascribe those absurdities that fill almost all the religions which possess and divide mankind. For men having been principled with an opinion, that they must not consult reason in the things of religion, however apparently contradictory to common sense and the very principles of all their knowledge, have let loose their fancies and natural superstition; and have been by them led into so strange opinions, and extravagant practices in religion, that a considerate man cannot but stand amazed at their follies, and judge them so far from being acceptable to the great and wise God, that he cannot avoid thinking them ridiculous and offensive to a sober good man. So that, in effect, religion, which should most distinguish us from beasts, and ought most peculiarly to elevate us, as rational creatures, above brutes, is that wherein men often appear most irrational, and more senseless than beasts themselves. *Credo, quia impossibile est:* I believe, because it is impossible, might, in a good man, pass for a sally of zeal; but would prove a very ill rule for men to choose their opinions or religion by. . . .

Upon this occasion I shall take the liberty to consider *a third ground of assent,* which with some men has the same authority, and is as confidently relied on as either faith or reason; I mean *enthusiasm:* which, laying by reason, would set up revelation without it. Whereby in effect it takes away both reason and revelation, and substitutes in the room of them the ungrounded fancies of a man's own brain, and assumes them for a foundation both of opinion and conduct.

6. Seventeenth-Century Political Theories

HUGO GROTIUS: *The Law of War and Peace* *

The Dutch scholar Hugo Grotius (1583–1645) is best known for his *De Jure Belli ac Pacis* (1625). The chief purpose of this famous work, written while he was in exile in France and dedicated to Louis XIII, was to provide a system of law which could maintain some sort of community in the new world of competing sovereign states. Grotius first redefined natural law in essentially secular terms, as law based primarily on human reason. At the same time he resurrected the old *jus gentium* or law of nations, which, though based on custom and voluntary agreements rather than "nature," was nevertheless binding on states in both war and peace. Grotius prided himself on being strictly scientific in his thinking, arguing from self-evident axioms to conclusions on the geometric model. This method of thinking had great appeal in an age which was enamored of the *esprit géométrique*.

MANY have undertaken to expound or to summarize in commentaries or abridgments the civil law of Rome or of their own states. But few have treated of that law that exists between peoples, or between the rulers of peoples, whether based upon nature, or established by divine decree, or grown out of custom and tacit agreements; and no one as yet has discussed it in a comprehensive and systematic way, important as it is to mankind that this should be done. . . .

The work is all the more necessary because in our own time, as in the past, there is no lack of men who make light of this branch of the law, as if it were nothing but an empty name. On most men's lips are the words of Euphemus, quoted by Thucydides, that for a king or a free city nothing is wrong that is to their advantage. To this may be added a similar saying that for fortune's favorites might makes right; also, that a state cannot be run without some injustice. Moreover, the disputes that arise between nations or kings are in fact usually decided by Mars. And it is not only the ignorant who believe that war has nothing whatever to do with law, but men who are learned and wise often let fall remarks that support such an opinion. Nothing is more common than a contrast drawn between law and arms. . . .

But since it would be futile to discuss this kind of law, if actually it does not exist, it is incumbent on us to endorse and defend our work by refuting briefly this most serious error. So, to save us from having to

---

* Hugo Grotius: *The Law of War and Peace,* trans. by Louise Loomis (New York: published for the Classics Club by Walter J. Black, Inc.; 1949).

deal with a swarm of opponents, let us appoint one speaker for them all. And whom better could we choose than Carneades, who became so skillful in what his school considered the supreme art that he could muster the full power of his eloquence as easily to defend a falsehood as to defend a truth. He once undertook an attack on justice—in particular, that type of justice of which we are now speaking—and used this as his strongest argument: that laws were imposed by men on themselves in their own interest, varying as customs varied, and often altered by the same people as the times changed; that, accordingly, there was no such thing as a law of nature. . . .

Natural law is [in truth, however] a dictate of right reason, showing the moral necessity or moral baseness of any act according to its agreement or disagreement with rational nature, and indicating that such an act is therefore either commanded or forbidden by the author of nature, God. The acts for which such a dictate exists are in themselves either obligatory or unallowable, and therefore recognized as necessarily being either commanded or forbidden by God. This mark distinguishes natural law, not only from human law, but from ordained divine law, which does not command or forbid things that in themselves and by their own nature are either obligatory or unallowable, but by forbidding them makes them unallowable, or by commanding them obligatory. . . .

Now just as there are laws in each state that aim at securing some advantage for that state, so between all or most states some laws could be and indeed have been established by common consent, which look to the advantage not of single communities but of the whole great concourse of states. And this is the law we call the law of nations, whenever we distinguish it from natural law. . . .

If no community can subsist without law, as Aristotle showed by his famous illustration of brigand bands, surely the community that embraces the whole human race, or at least a great many nations, needs law. . . .

There are persons who imagine that all laws lose their authority in wartime, but such a theory we should never accept. Rather, we should declare it wrong to begin a war except for the enforcement of justice, and wrong to continue a war already begun, unless it is kept within the bounds of justice and good faith. Demosthenes well said that wars should be made only against those who cannot be restrained by courts of law. For legal judgments are effective against persons who know they are too weak to resist, and wars are our resort against those who are strong enough, or who think they are. Nonetheless, in order to be right, wars must be conducted as scrupulously as judicial proceedings habitually are. . . .

. . . I have now to explain briefly what helps I have used and with what care I have approached the task. In the first place, I have taken pains to refer for proofs of all my statements regarding the law of nature to certain ideas so unquestionably true that no one can deny them without doing violence to himself. For the principles of that law, if only you look at them fairly, are in themselves plain and evident, almost as clear as the things we perceive with our external senses. . . .

Further to prove the existence of this law of nature, I have called on the testimonies of philosophers, historians, poets, and, lastly, orators. Not that we should believe these men indiscriminately, for they were accustomed to serving the interests of their sect, their argument, or their cause. But whenever many of them at different times and in different places declared the same thing to be true, their unanimity must be ascribed to a universal cause, which, as we inquire into it, can be nothing else than a correct inference from the principles of nature, or some general consensus of opinion. The former means a law of nature, the latter a law of nations. The difference between these two kinds of law cannot be found in the testimonies just mentioned (for writers are apt to confuse the terms, law of nature and law of nations), but from the character of the content. A rule that cannot be deduced from fixed principles by a sure process of reasoning and that is yet apparently everywhere observed must have originated in the free will of mankind. . . .

If anyone supposes I have written with an eye to any of the controversies of our own age, either some that have already arisen or some that may be foreseen as likely to arise in the future, he does me an injustice. For I truthfully declare that, even as mathematicians view their figures abstracted from bodies, so I in my treatment of law have held my mind aloof from all particular events. . . .

BISHOP BOSSUET: *Politics drawn from the Holy Scriptures* *

The *Politique tirée des propres Paroles de l'Écriture sainte* was one of three treatises which Jacques Bénigne Bossuet (1627–1704) wrote for the edification of the dauphin, Louis XIV's son, whom he served as tutor from 1670 to 1681. The other two treatises dealt with the nature of God and man, and God's providence in history. The *Politique* described the rights and duties of a prince, and is an excellent specimen of the philosophy of the divine right of kings. Bossuet, who later became Bishop of Meaux, was one of the great orators and theologians of his age.

* *Oeuvres de Bossuet* (Paris: Firmin Didot Frères; 1862), vol. I, pp. 322–5, 333–4, 370, 383–4, 390. My translation, except for the Biblical quotations which are according to the King James version.

THERE are four qualities essential to royal authority. First, the royal authority is sacred; second, it is paternal; third, it is absolute; fourth, it is submitted to reason. . . .

*   *   *

We have already seen that all power comes from God.

The prince, St. Paul adds, "is a minister of God to thee for good. But if thou do that which is evil, be afraid; for he beareth not the sword in vain: for he is a minister of God, an avenger for wrath to him that doeth evil" (Romans 13:4).

Princes act then as ministers of God, and his lieutenants on earth. It is by them that he rules his empire. "And now ye think to withstand the kingdom of Jehovah in the hand of the sons of David" (II Chronicles 13:8).

Thus, as we have seen, the royal throne is not the throne of a man, but the throne of God himself. "Jehovah hath chosen Solomon my son to sit upon the throne of the kingdom of Jehovah over Israel" (I Chronicles 28:5). And again: "Then Solomon sat on the throne of Jehovah" (*ibid.* 29:23). . . .

It appears from all this that the person of kings is sacred, and that to make an attempt on their lives is a sacrilege.

God causes them to be anointed by his prophets with a sacred unction, in the same way that he causes pontiffs and his ministry to be anointed.

But even without the exterior application of this unction, they are sacred by their charge, being representatives of the divine majesty, deputed by his providence to the execution of his designs. . . .

St. Paul, after having said that the prince is the minister of God, concludes thus: "Wherefore ye must needs be in subjection, not only because of the wrath, but also for conscience' sake" (Romans 13:5). . . .

And again: "Servants, obey in all things your masters according to the flesh. . . . And whatsoever ye do, do it heartily, as to the Lord, and not unto men" (Colossians 3:22–3). . . .

If the apostle speaks thus of servitude, an unnatural state, what ought we to think of legitimate subjection to princes and magistrates who are the protectors of public liberty! . . .

Even when princes do not do their duty, we must respect their office and ministry. "Servants, be subject to your masters with all fear; not only to the good and gentle, but also to the froward" (I Peter 2:18).

There is then something religious in the respect we pay to the prince. The service of God and the respect for kings are one and the same thing; and St. Peter puts these two duties together: "Fear God. Honour the king" (I Peter 2:17). . . .

However, because their power comes from above, princes must not think that they are free to use it at their pleasure; rather must they use it with fear and discretion, as a thing which comes to them from God, and of which God will demand a strict account. . . .

Kings should therefore tremble while using their God-given power, and think what a horrible sacrilege it is to misuse it. . . .

* * *

The royal authority is paternal, and its proper character is goodness.

We have seen that kings hold their place from God, who is the true father of the human race. We have also seen that the first idea of power known to man was paternal power, and that kings were made on the model of fathers.

Everybody also agrees that the obedience which is owed to public power, is found, in the Decalogue, in the precept which obliges them to honor their parents.

It appears, from all this, that the name of king is a name of father, and that goodness is the most natural character of kings. . . .

* * *

The royal authority is absolute.

In order to render this term odious and insupportable, some people try to confuse absolute and arbitrary government. But there is nothing more different, as we shall see when we speak of justice.

The prince is accountable to no one for what he orders. . . .

We must obey princes as justice itself, without which there would be no order nor purpose in human affairs.

They are gods, and participate in the divine independence. . . .

Whoever becomes a sovereign prince, holds in his hands everything together, both the sovereign authority to judge, and all the forces of the state. . . .

* * *

Majesty is the image of the grandeur of God in the prince.

God is infinite, God is all. The prince, so far as he is prince, is not regarded as a particular man: he is a public personage, the whole state is in him; the will of the whole people is comprehended in his will. As in God are united all perfection and all virtue, just so all the power of particulars is united in the person of the prince. What grandeur that a single man contains so much of it!

The power of God makes itself felt in an instant from one end of the world to another: the royal power acts at the same time in the whole kingdom. It keeps the whole kingdom in its place, as God keeps the whole world.

Let God withdraw his hand, and the world will collapse; let authority cease in the kingdom, and everything will be in confusion.

* * *

The end of government is the good and conservation of the state. . . .

The good constitution of the body of the state consists in two things: in religion and justice: these are the interior and constitutive principles of states. By the one, we render to God what is due to him; and by the other, we render to men what belongs to them. . . .

The prince must employ his authority to destroy false religions in his state. . . .

He is the protector of the public peace which depends upon religion; and he must sustain his throne, of which it is the foundation, as we have seen. Those who would not suffer the prince to act strictly in matters of religion because religion ought to be free, are in impious error. Otherwise it would be necessary to suffer, among his subjects and in the whole state, idolatry, Mohammedanism, Judaism, every false religion; blasphemy, even atheism, and the greatest crimes, would go unpunished. . . .

Thomas Hobbes: *Leviathan* *

> In the *Leviathan, or the Matter, Form and Power of a Commonwealth, Ecclesiastical and Civil* (1651) the English philosopher Thomas Hobbes (1588–1679) applied the mathematical method to politics. It is therefore one of the first attempts at a science of politics. It was also a defense of monarchical absolutism, and must be read in the context of the English Civil Wars. On the meeting of the Long Parliament in 1640, Hobbes fled to Paris where he became mathematical tutor to the future Charles II. Since Hobbes's arguments could apply to any goverment in power, however, they pleased the royalists hardly more than the revolutionaries.

NATURE, the art whereby God hath made and governs the world, is by the "art" of man, as in many other things, so in this also imitated, that it can make an artificial animal. For seeing life is but a motion of limbs, the beginning whereof is in some principal part within; why may we not say, that all "automata" (engines that move themselves by springs and wheels as doth a watch) have an artificial life? For what is the "heart," but a "spring"; and the "nerves," but so many "strings"; and the "joints," but so many "wheels," giving motion to the whole body, such as was intended by the artificer? "Art" goes yet further, imitating that rational and most excellent work of nature, "man." For by art is created that great "Leviathan" called a "Commonwealth," or "State," in Latin *Civitas*, which is but an artificial man; though of greater stature and strength than the natural, for whose protection and defence is was intended; and in which the "sovereignty" is an artificial "soul," as giving life and motion to the whole body; the "magistrates," and other "officers" of judicature

* Thomas Hobbes: *Leviathan* (London: George Routledge and Sons; 1887), pp. 11, 52–3, 63–7, 82, 84–9, 211–12.

and execution, artificial "joints"; "reward" and "punishment," by which fastened to the seat of the sovereignty every joint and member is moved to perform his duty, are the "nerves," that do the same in the body natural; the "wealth" and "riches" of all the particular members, are the "strength"; *salus populi*, the "people's safety," its "business"; counsellors," by whom all things needful for it to know are suggested unto it, are the "memory"; "equity," and "laws," an artificial "reason," and "will"; "concord," "health"; "sedition," "sickness"; and "civil war," "death." Lastly, the "pacts" and "covenants," by which the parts of this body politic were at first made, set together, and united, resemble that "fiat," or the "let us make man," pronounced by God in the creation. To describe the nature of this artificial man, I will consider—

First, the "matter" thereof, and the "artificer"; both which is "man."

Secondly, "how," and by what "covenants" it is made; what are the "rights" and just "power" or "authority" of a "sovereign"; and what it is that "preserveth" or "dissolveth" it.

Thirdly, what is a "Christian Commonwealth.". . .

Of Man

So that in the first place, I put for a general inclination of all mankind, a perpetual and restless desire of power after power, that ceaseth only in death. And the cause of this is not always that a man hopes for a more intensive delight than he has already attained to, or that he cannot be content with a moderate power; but because he cannot assure the power and means to live well, which he hath present, without the acquisition of more. . . .

Nature hath made men so equal, in the faculties of the body and mind; as that though there be found one man sometimes manifestly stronger in body, or of quicker mind than another, yet when all is reckoned together, the difference between man and man, is not so considerable, as that one man can thereupon claim to himself any benefit, to which another may not pretend, as well as he. For as to the strength of body, the weakest has strength enough to kill the strongest, either by secret machination, or by confederacy with others, that are in the same danger with himself. . . .

So that in the nature of man, we find three principal causes of quarrel. First, competition; secondly, diffidence; thirdly, glory.

The first, maketh men invade for gain; the second, for safety; and the third, for reputation. The first use violence, to make themselves masters of other men's persons, wives, children, and cattle; the second, to defend them; the third, for trifles, as a word, a smile, a different opinion, and any other sign of undervalue, either direct in their persons, or by reflection in their kindred, their friends, their nation, their profession, or their name.

Hereby it is manifest, that during the time men live without a common power to keep them all in awe, they are in that condition which is called war; and such a war, as is of every man, against every man. . . .

Whatsoever therefore is consequent to a time of war, where every man is enemy to every man, the same is consequent to the time wherein men live without other security than what their own strength and their own invention shall furnish them withal. In such condition there is no place for industry, because the fruit thereof is uncertain, and consequently no culture of the earth; . . . no arts; no letters; no society; and, which is worst of all, continual fear and danger of violent death; and the life of man, solitary, poor, nasty, brutish, and short. . . .

To this war of every man, against every man, this also is consequent; that nothing can be unjust. The notions of right and wrong, justice and injustice, have there no place. Where there is no common power, there is no law: where no law, no injustice. Force and fraud, are in war the two cardinal virtues. Justice and injustice are none of the faculties neither of the body nor mind. If they were, they might be in a man that were alone in the world, as well as his senses, and passions. They are qualities that relate to men in society, not in solitude. It is consequent also to the same condition, that there be no propriety, no dominion, no "mine" and "thine" distinct; but only that to be every man's, that he can get; and for so long, as he can keep it. And thus much for the ill condition, which man by mere nature is actually placed in; though with a possibility to come out of it, consisting partly in the passions, partly in his reason.

The passions that incline men to peace, are fear of death; desire of such things as are necessary to commodious living; and a hope by their industry to obtain them. And reason suggesteth convenient articles of peace, upon which men may be drawn to agreement. These articles are they which otherwise are called the Laws of Nature. . . .

"The right of Nature," which writers commonly call *jus naturale*, is the liberty each man hath, to use his own power, as he will himself, for the preservation of his own nature; that is to say, of his own life; and consequently, of doing anything, which in his own judgment and reason he shall conceive to be the aptest means thereunto.

By "liberty," is understood, according to the proper signification of the word, the absence of external impediments: which impediments may oft take away part of a man's power to do what he would; but cannot hinder him from using the power left him, according as his judgment and reason shall dictate to him.

A "law of Nature," *lex naturalis*, is a precept or general rule, found out by reason, by which a man is forbidden to do that which is destructive of his life, or taketh away the means of preserving the same; and to omit that, by which he thinketh it may be best preserved. For though they that speak of this subject, use to confound *jus* and *lex*, "right" and "law": yet they ought to be distinguished; because "right," consisteth in liberty to do, or to forbear; whereas "law," determineth and bindeth to one of them; so that law and right differ as much as obligation and liberty; which in one and the same matter are inconsistent. . . .

The mutual transferring of right, is that which men call "contract."

Of Commonwealth

The final cause, end, or design of men, who naturally love liberty, and dominion over others, in the introduction of that restraint upon themselves, in which we see them live in commonwealths, is the foresight of their own preservation, and of a more contented life thereby; that is to say, of getting themselves out from that miserable condition of war, which is necessarily consequent . . . to the natural passions of men, when there is no visible power to keep them in awe, and tie them by fear of punishment to the performance of their covenants, and observation of [the] laws of Nature. . . .

A "Commonwealth" is said to be "instituted," when a "multitude" of men do agree, and "covenant, every one, with every one," that to whatsoever "man," or "assembly of men," shall be given by the major part, the "right" to "present" the person of them all, that is to say, to be their "representative"; every one, as well he that "voted for it," as he that "voted against it," shall "authorize" all the actions and judgments, of that man, or assembly of men, in the same manner, as if they were his own, to the end, to live peaceably amongst themselves, and be protected against other men.

From this institution of a commonwealth are derived all the "rights" and "faculties" of him, or them, on whom sovereign power is conferred by the consent of the people assembled.

First, because they covenant, it is to be understood, they are not obliged by former covenant, to anything repugnant hereunto. And consequently they that have already instituted a commonwealth, being thereby bound by covenant, to own the actions and judgments of one, cannot lawfully make a new covenant, amongst themselves, to be obedient to any other, in any thing whatsoever, without his permission. . . . And whereas some men have pretended for their disobedience to their sovereign, a new covenant, made not with men, but with God; this also is unjust: for there is no covenant with God but by mediation of somebody that representeth God's person; which none doth but God's lieutenant, who hath the sovereignty under God. But this pretence of covenant with God, is so evident a lie, even in the pretenders' own consciences, that it is not only an act of an unjust, but also of a vile and unmanly disposition.

Secondly, because the right of bearing the person of them all, is given to him they make sovereign, by covenant only of one to another, and not of him to any of them; there can happen no breach of covenant on the part of the sovereign: and consequently none of his subjects, by any pretence of forfeiture, can be freed from his subjection. . . .

Fourthly, because every subject is by this institution author of all the actions and judgments of the sovereign instituted, it follows, that whatsoever he doth it can be no injury to any of his subjects, nor ought he to be by any of them accused of injustice. For he that doth anything by authority from another doth therein no injury to him by whose authority he acteth: but by this institution of a commonwealth every particular man is author of all the sovereign doth. . . . It is true that they that have sovereign power may commit iniquity, but not injustice or injury in the proper signification.

Fifthly, and consequently to that which was said last, no man that hath sovereign power can justly be put to death, or otherwise in any manner by his subjects punished. For seeing every subject is author of the actions of his sovereign, he punisheth another for the actions committed by himself.

And because the end of this institution is the peace and defence of them all; and whosoever has right to the end has right to the means; it belongeth of right to whatsoever man or assembly that hath the sovereignty to be judge both of the means of peace and defence, and also of the hindrances and disturbances of the same, and to do whatsoever he shall think necessary to be done, both beforehand, for the preserving of peace and security, by prevention of discord at home and hostility from abroad; and, when peace and security are lost, for the recovery of the same. And therefore,

Sixthly, it is annexed to the sovereignty to be judge of what opinions and doctrines are averse and what conducing to peace; and consequently, on what occasions, how far, and what men are to be trusted withal, in speaking to multitudes of people, and who shall examine the doctrines of all books before they be published. For the actions of men proceed from their opinions, and in the well governing of opinions consisteth the well-governing of men's actions, in order to their peace and concord. And though in matter of doctrine nothing ought to be regarded but the truth; yet this is not repugnant to regulating the same by peace. For doctrine repugnant to peace can be no more true than peace and concord can be against the law of Nature. . . .

Seventhly, is annexed to the sovereignty, the whole power of prescribing the rules, whereby every man may know what goods he may enjoy, and what actions he may do, without being molested by any of his fellow-subjects; and this is it men call "propriety.". . .

Eighthly, is annexed to the sovereignty, the right of judicature. . . .

Ninthly, is annexed to the sovereignty, the right of making war and peace with other nations and commonwealths; that is to say, of judging when it is for the public good, and how great forces are to be assembled, armed, and paid for that end; and to levy money upon the subjects to defray the expenses thereof. . . .

These are the rights, which make the essence of sovereignty; and which are the marks whereby a man may discern in what man, or assembly of men, the sovereign power is placed and resideth. For these are incommunicable, and inseparable. . . . And so if we consider any one of the said rights, we shall presently see, that the holding of all the rest will produce no effect, in the conservation of peace and justice, the end for which all commonwealths are instituted. And this division is it, whereof it is said, "a kingdom divided in itself cannot stand": for unless this division precede, division into opposite armies can never happen. If there had not first been an opinion received of the greatest part of England, that these powers were divided betwen the King, and the Lords, and the House of Commons, the people had never been divided and fallen into this civil war; first betwen those that disagreed in politics; and after between the dissenters about the liberty of religion; which have so instructed men in this point of sovereign right, that there be few now in England that do not see that these rights are inseparable, and will be so generally acknowledged at the next return of peace. . . .

This great authority being indivisible, and inseparably annexed to the sovereignty, there is little ground for the opinion of them that say of sovereign kings, though they be *singulis majores*, of greater power than every one of their subjects, yet they be *universis minores*, of less power than them all together. For if by "all together," they mean not the collective body as one person, then "all together," and "every one," signify the same; and the speech is absurd. But if by "all together," they understand them as one person, which person the sovereign bears, then the power of all together, is the same with the sovereign's power; and so again the speech is absurd: which absurdity they see well enough, when the sovereignty is in an assembly of the people; but in a monarch they see it not; and yet the power of sovereignty is the same in whomsoever it be placed. . . .

But a man may here object, that the condition of subjects is very miserable; as being obnoxious to the lusts, and other irregular passions of him or them that have so unlimited a power in their hands. And commonly they that live under a monarch, think it the fault of monarchy; and they that live under the government of democracy, or other sovereign assembly, attribute all the inconvenience to that form of commonwealth; whereas the power in all forms, if they be perfect enough to protect them, is the same: not considering that the state of man can never be without some incommodity or other; and that the greatest, that in any form of government can possibly happen to the people in general, is scarce sensible, in respect of the miseries, and horrible calamities, that accompany a civil war, or that dissolute condition of masterless men, without subjection to laws, and a coercive power to tie their hands from rapine and revenge. . . .

Of a Christian Commonwealth

I define a "Church" to be "a company of men professing Christian religion, united in the person of one sovereign, at whose command they ought to assemble, and without whose authority they ought not to assemble." And because in all commonwealths that assembly, which is without warrant from the civil sovereign, is unlawful, that Church also which is assembled in any commonwealth that hath forbidden them to assemble, is an unlawful assembly.

It followeth also that there is on earth no such universal Church, as all Christians are bound to obey; because there is no power on earth to which all other commonwealths are subject. There are Christians in the dominions of several princes and states, but every one of them is subject to that commonwealth whereof he is himself a member; and consequently, cannot be subject to the commands of any other person. And therefore a Church, such a one as is capable to command, to judge, absolve, condemn, or do any other act, is the same thing with a civil commonwealth, consisting of Christian men; and is called a "civil state," for that the subjects of it are "men"; and a "Church," for that the subjects thereof are "Christians." "Temporal" and "spiritual" government are but two words brought into the world to make men see double, and mistake their "lawful sovereign." It is true that the bodies of the faithful, after the resurrection, shall be not only spiritual but eternal; but in this life they are gross and corruptible. There is therefore no other government in this life, neither of state, nor religion, but temporal; nor teaching of any doctrine, lawful to any subject, which the governor both of the state and of the religion forbiddeth to be taught. And that governor must be one; or else there must needs follow faction and civil war in the commonwealth between the "Church" and "State"; between "spiritualists" and "temporalists"; between the "sword of justice," and the "shield of faith": and which is more, in every Christian man's own breast, between the "Christian" and the "man." The doctors of the Church are called pastors; so also are civil sovereigns. But if pastors be not subordinate one to another, so as that there may be one chief pastor, men will be taught contrary doctrines, whereof both may be, and one must be false. Who that one chief pastor is, according to the law of Nature, hath been already shown; namely, that it is the civil sovereign. . . .

John Milton *

During the period of the English Civil Wars and the Interregnum the great Puritan poet John Milton (1608–74) raised his voice repeatedly

* *The Prose Works of John Milton*, ed. by J. A. St. John (London: H. G. Bohn; 1848–53), vol. II, pp. 8–13, 16, 55–6, 66, 68, 75, 81, 96–7.

in defence of "liberty." In *Areopagitica* (1644) he defended freedom of publication against the presbyterian Parliament which, by an order of June, 1643, had established a strict censorship of the press. The *Tenure of Kings and Magistrates* (1648–49), which was written to defend the execution of Charles I, argued down the philosophy of the divine right of kings.

Areopagitica

I DENY not, but that it is of greatest concernment in the church and commonwealth, to have a vigilant eye how books demean themselves, as well as men; and thereafter to confine, imprison, and do sharpest justice on them as malefactors; for books are not absolutely dead things, but do contain a progeny of life in them to be as active as that soul was whose progeny they are; nay, they do preserve as in a vial the purest efficacy and extraction of that living intellect that bred them. I know they are as lively, and as vigorously productive, as those fabulous dragon's teeth: and being sown up and down, may chance to spring up armed men. And yet, on the other hand, unless wariness be used, as good almost kill a man as kill a good book: who kills a man kills a reasonable creature, God's image; but he who destroys a good book, kills reason itself, kills the image of God, as it were, in the eye. Many a man lives a burden to the earth; but a good book is the precious life-blood of a master-spirit, embalmed and treasured up on purpose to a life beyond life. It is true, no age can restore a life, whereof, perhaps, there is no great loss; and revolutions of ages do not oft recover the loss of a rejected truth, for the want of which whole nations fare the worse. We should be wary, therefore, what persecution we raise against the living labours of public men, how we spill that seasoned life of man, preserved and stored up in books; since we see a kind of homicide may be thus committed, sometimes a martyrdom; and if it extend to the whole impression, a kind of massacre, whereof the execution ends not in the slaying of an elemental life, but strikes at the ethereal and fifth essence, the breath of reason itself; slays an immortality rather than a life. But lest I should be condemned of introducing licence, while I oppose licensing, I refuse not the pains to be so much historical, as will serve to shew what hath been done by ancient and famous commonwealths, against this disorder, till the very time that this project of licensing crept out of the inquisition, was catched up by our prelates, and hath caught some of our presbyters. . . .

I conceive . . . that when God did enlarge the universal diet of man's body, (saving ever the rules of temperance,) he then also, as before, left arbitrary the dieting and repasting of our minds; as wherein every mature man might have to exercise his own leading capacity. How great a virtue is temperance, how much of moment through the whole life of man! Yet God commits the managing so great a trust, without particular law or prescription, wholly to the demeanour of every grown man. . . . For those actions which enter into a man, rather than issue out of him, and therefore defile not, God uses not to captivate under a perpetual childhood of prescription, but trusts him with the gift of reason to be his own chooser. . . .

As therefore the state of man now is; what wisdom can there be to choose, what continence to forbear, without the knowledge of evil? He that can apprehend and consider vice with all her baits and seeming pleasures, and yet abstain, and yet distinguish, and yet prefer that which is truly better, he is the true warfaring Christian. I cannot praise a fugitive and cloistered virtue unexercised and unbreathed, that never sallies out and seeks her adversary, but slinks out of the race, where that immortal garland is to be run for, not without dust and heat. . . .

Suppose we could expel sin by this means; look how much we thus expel of sin, so much we expel of virtue: for the matter of them both is the same: remove that, and ye remove them both alike. This justifies the high providence of God, who, though he commands us temperance, justice, continence, yet pours out before us even to a profuseness all desirable things, and gives us minds that can wander beyond all limit and satiety. Why should we then affect a rigour contrary to the manner of God and of nature, by abridging or scanting those means, which books freely permitted, are both to the trial of virtue, and the exercise of truth? . . .

Truth and understanding are not such wares as to be monopolized and traded in by tickets, and statutes, and standards. We must not think to make a staple commodity of all the knowledge in the land, to mark and license it like our broad-cloth and our woolpacks. What is it but a servitude like that imposed by the Philistines, not to be allowed the sharpening of our own axes and coulters, but we must repair from all quarters to twenty licensing forges? . . .

And though all the winds of doctrine were let loose to play upon the earth, so truth be in the field, we do injuriously by licensing and prohibiting to misdoubt her strength. Let her and falsehood grapple; who ever knew truth put to the worse, in a free and open encounter? Her confuting is the best and surest suppressing. He who hears what praying there is for light and clear knowledge to be sent down among us, would think of other matters to be constituted beyond the discipline of Geneva, framed and fabricated already to our hands. . . .

For who knows not that truth is strong, next to the Almighty; she needs no policies, nor stratagems, nor licensings to make her victorious, those are the shifts and the defences that error uses against her power: give her but room, and do not bind her when she sleeps, for then she speaks not true. . . .

Yet is it not impossible that she may have more shapes than one? What else is all that rank of things indifferent, wherein truth may be on this side, or on the other, without being unlike herself? . . . What great purchase is this Christian liberty which Paul so often boasts of? His doctrine is, that he who eats or eats not, regards a day or regards it not, may do either to the Lord. How many other things might be tolerated in peace, and left to conscience, had we but charity, and were it not the chief stronghold of our hypocrisy to be ever judging one another? I fear yet this iron yoke of outward conformity hath left a slavish print upon our necks; the ghost of a linen decency yet haunts us. . . . We do not see that while we still affect by all means a rigid external formality, we may as soon fall again into a gross conforming stupidity, a stark and dead congealment of "wood and hay and stubble" forced and frozen together, which is more to the sudden degenerating of a church than many subdichotomies of petty schisms.

Not that I can think well of every light separation; or that all in a church is to be expected "gold and silver, and precious stones": it is not possible for man to sever the wheat from the tares, the good fish from the other fry; that must be the angels' ministry at the end of mortal things. Yet if all cannot be of one mind, as who looks they should be? this doubtless is more wholesome, more prudent, and more Christian, that many be tolerated rather than all compelled.

The Tenure of Kings and Magistrates

I shall here set down, from first beginning, the original of kings; how and wherefore exalted to that dignity above their brethren; and from thence shall prove, that turning to tyranny they may be as lawfully deposed and punished, as they were at first elected: this I shall do by authorities and reasons, not learnt in corners among schisms and heresies, as our doubling divines are ready to calumniate, but fetched out of the midst of choicest and most authentic learning, and no prohibited authors; nor many heathen, but Mosaical, Christian, orthodoxal, and, which must needs be more convincing to our adversaries, presbyterial.

No man, who knows aught, can be so stupid to deny, that all men naturally were born free, being the image and resemblance of God himself, and were, by privilege above all the creatures, born to command, and not to obey: and that they lived so, till from the root of Adam's transgression falling among themselves to do wrong and violence, and foreseeing that such courses must needs tend to the destruction of them all, they agreed by common league to bind each other from mutual injury, and jointly to defend themselves against any that gave disturbance or opposition to such agreement. Hence came cities, towns, and commonwealths. And because no faith in all was found sufficiently binding, they saw it needful to ordain some authority that might restrain by force and punishment what was violated against peace and common right.

This authority and power of self-defence and preservation being originally and naturally in every one of them, and unitedly in them all; for ease, for order, and lest each man should be his own partial judge, they communicated and derived either to one, whom for the eminence of his wisdom and integrity they chose above the rest, or to more than one, whom they thought of equal deserving: the first was called a king; the other, magistrates: not to be their lords and masters, (though afterward those names in some places were given voluntarily to such as had been authors of inestimable good to the people,) but to be their deputies and commissioners, to execute, by virtue of their intrusted power, that justice, which else every man by the bond of nature and of covenant must have executed for himself, and for one another. And to him that shall consider well, why among free persons one man by civil right should bear authority and jurisdiction over another, no other end or reason can be imaginable.

These for a while governed well, and with much equity decided all things at their own arbitrement; till the temptation of such a power, left absolute in their hands, perverted them at length to injustice and partiality. Then did they, who now by trial had found the danger and inconveniences of committing arbitrary power to any, invent laws, either framed or consented to by all, that should confine and limit the authority of whom they chose to govern them: that so man, of whose failing they had proof, might no more rule over them, but law and reason, abstracted as much as might be from personal errors and frailties. "While, as the magistrate was set above the people, so the law was set above the magistrate." When this would not serve, but that the law was either not executed, or misapplied, they were constrained from that time, the only remedy left them, to put conditions and take oaths from all kings and magistrates at their first instalment, to do impartial justice by law: who, upon those terms and no other, received allegiance from the people, that is to say, bond or covenant to obey them in execution of those laws, which they, the people, had themselves made or assented to. And this ofttimes with express warning, that if the king or magistrate proved unfaithful to his trust, the people would be disengaged. They added also counsellors and parliaments, not to be only at his beck, but, with him or without him, at set times, or at all times, when any danger threatened, to have care of the public safety. . . . That this and the rest of what hath hitherto been spoken is most true, might be copiously made appear through all stories, heathen and Christian; even of those nations where kings and emperors have sought means to abolish all ancient memory of the people's right by their encroachments and usurpations. But I spare long insertions, appealing to the German, French, Italian, Arragonian, English, and not least the Scottish histories. . . .

It being thus manifest, that the power of kings and magistrates is nothing else but what is only derivative, transferred, and committed to them in trust from the people to the common good of them all, in whom the power yet remains fundamentally, and cannot be taken from them, without a violation of their natural birthright. . . .

Secondly, that to say, as is usual, the king hath as good right to his crown and dignity as any man to his inheritance, is to make the subject no better than the king's slave, his chattel, or his possession that may be bought and sold: and doubtless, if hereditary title were sufficiently inquired, the best foundation of it would be found but either in courtesy or convenience. But suppose it to be of right hereditary, what can be more just and legal, if a subject for certain crimes be to forfeit by law from himself and posterity all his inheritance to the king, than that a king, for crimes proportional, should forfeit all his title and inheritance to the people? Unless the people must be thought created all for him, he not for them, and they all in one body inferior to him single; which were a kind of treason against the dignity of mankind to affirm.

Thirdly, it follows, that to say kings are accountable to none but God, is the overturning of all law and government. For if they may refuse to give account, then all covenants made with them at coronation, all oaths are in vain, and mere mockeries; all laws which they swear to keep, made to no purpose: for if the king fear not God, (as how many of them do not,) we hold then our lives and estates by the tenure of his mere grace and mercy, as from a god, not a mortal magistrate; a position that none but court-parasites or men besotted would maintain! . . .

Therefore kingdom and magistracy, whether supreme or subordinate, is called "a human ordinance," (1 Pet ii. 13, &c.,) which we are there taught is the will of God we should submit to, so far as for the punishment of evil-doers, and the encouragement of them that do well. "Submit," saith he, "as free men." "But to any civil power unaccountable, unquestionable, and not to be resisted, no, not in wickedness, and violent actions, how can we submit as free men?" "There is no power but of God," saith Paul; (Rom. xiii.;) as much as to say, God put it into man's heart to find out that way at first for common peace and preservation, approving the exercise thereof; else it contradicts Peter, who calls the same authority an ordinance of man. . . . Therefore Saint Paul in the forecited chapter tells us, that such magistrates he means, as are not a terror to the good, but to the evil; such as bear not the sword in vain, but to punish offenders, and to encourage the good. . . .

JOHN LOCKE: *A Letter concerning Toleration* *

The following *Letter concerning Toleration* was the first of four letters written by Locke on the subject. Written in Latin, probably in

* *The Works of John Locke* (London: Ward, Lock, and Co.; 1888), vol. III, pp. 5–7, 30–2.

1685, it was not published until 1689. It provided a philosophical basis for the famous Act of Toleration, passed by the English Parliament in that same year, which granted freedom of worship to Presbyterians, Congregationalists, Baptists, and Quakers.

I ESTEEM it above all things necessary to distinguish exactly the business of civil government from that of religion, and to settle the just bounds that lie between the one and the other. If this be not done, there can be no end put to the controversies that will be always arising between those that have, or at least pretend to have, on the one side, a concernment for the interest of mens souls, and on the other side, a care of the commonwealth.

The commonwealth seems to me to be a society of men constituted only for the procuring, the preserving, and the advancing their own civil interests.

Civil interests I call life, liberty, health, and indolency of body; and the possession of outward things, such as money, lands, houses, furniture, and the like.

It is the duty of the civil magistrate, by the impartial execution of equal laws, to secure unto all the people in general, and to every one of his subjects in particular, the just possession of these things belonging to this life. . . .

Now that the whole jurisdiction of the magistrate reaches only to these civil concernments; and that all civil power, right, and dominion, is bounded and confined to the only care of promoting these things, and that it neither can or ought in any manner to be extended to the salvation of souls; these following considerations seem unto me abundantly to demonstrate.

First, because the care of souls is not committed to the civil magistrate, any more than to other men. It is not committed unto him, I say, by God; because it appears not that God has ever given any such authority to one man over another, as to compel any one to his religion. Nor can any such power be vested in the magistrate by the consent of the people; because no man can so far abandon the care of his own salvation, as blindly to leave it to the choice of any other, whether prince or subject, to prescribe to him what faith or worship he shall embrace. For no man can, if he would, conform his faith to the dictates of another. All the life and power of true religion consists in the outward and full persuasion of the mind; and faith is not faith without believing. . . .

In the second place. The care of souls cannot belong to the civil magistrate, because his power consists only in outward force; but true and saving religion consists in the inward persuasion of the mind, without which nothing can be acceptable to God. And such is the nature of the understanding, that it cannot be compelled to the belief of any thing by outward force. Confiscation of estate, imprisonment, torments, nothing of that nature can have any such efficacy as to make men change the inward judgment that they have framed of things.

It may indeed be alleged, that the magistrate may make use of arguments, and thereby draw the heterodox into the way of truth, and procure their salvation. I grant it; but this is common to him with other men. In teaching, instructing, and redressing the erroneous by reason, he may certainly do what becomes any good man to do. Magistracy does not oblige him to put off either humanity or Christianity. But it is one thing to persuade, another to command; one thing to press with arguments, another with penalties. . . .

In the third place, the care of the salvation of mens souls cannot belong to the magistrate; because, though the rigour of laws and the force of penalties were capable to convince and change mens minds, yet would not that help at all to the salvation of their souls. For, there being but one truth, one way to heaven; what hope is there that more men would be led into it, if they had no other rule to follow but the religion of the court, and were put under a necessity to quit the light of their own reason, to oppose the dictates of their own consciences, and blindly to resign up themselves to the will of their governors, and to the religion, which either ignorance, ambition, or superstition had chanced to establish in the countries where they were born? . . .

Let us now consider what a church is. A church then I take to be a voluntary society of men, joining themselves together of their own accord, in order to the publick worshipping of God, in such a manner as they may judge acceptable to him, and effectual to the salvation of their souls.

I say, it is a free and voluntary society. Nobody is born a member of any church; otherwise the religion of parents would descend unto children, by the same right of inheritance as their temporal estates, and every one would hold his faith by the same tenure he does his lands; than which nothing can be imagined more absurd. Thus therefore that matter stands. No man by nature is bound unto any particular church or sect, but every one joins himself voluntarily to that society in which he believes he has found that profession and worship which is truly acceptable to God. . . .

[However] no opinions contrary to human society, or to those moral rules which are necessary to the preservation of civil society, are to be tolerated by the magistrate. . . .

Again: That church can have no right to be tolerated by the magistrate, which is constituted upon such a bottom, that all those who enter into it, do thereby *ipso facto*, deliver themselves up to the protection and service of another prince. For by this means the magistrate would give way to the settling of a foreign jurisdiction in his own country, and suffer his own people to be listed, as it were, for soldiers against his own government. . . .

Lastly, those are not at all to be tolerated who deny the being of God. Promises, covenants, and oaths, which are the bonds of human society, can have no hold upon an atheist. The taking away of God, though but even in thought, dissolves all. Besides also, those that by their atheism undermine and destroy all religion, can have no pretence of religion whereupon to challenge the privilege of a Toleration. As for other practical opinions, though not absolutely free from all error, yet if they do not tend to establish domination over others, or civil impunity to the church in which they are taught, there can be no reason why they should not be tolerated.

7. *"Ancients" and "Moderns"*

FONTENELLE: *Digression on the Ancients and Moderns* *

> Fontenelle's *Digression sur les Anciens et les Modernes* (1688) was the first book "to formulate the idea of the progress of knowledge as a complete doctrine."

THE WHOLE question of preeminence between the Ancients and Moderns is reduced to knowing if the trees of bygone days were larger than those of today. If they were, then Homer, Plato, and Demosthenes cannot be equalled in these last centuries: but if our trees are just as large, we can equal them.

Let us clarify this paradox. If the Ancients had more intellect than we, it is because the brains of those times were better ordered, formed of fibers more firm or more delicate, filled with more animal spirits; but by virtue of what would their brains have been better ordered? Then the trees would also have been larger and more beautiful; for if nature was younger and more vigorous, the trees as well as the brains of men must have felt this youth and vigor.

Let the admirers of the Ancients take a little care when they tell us that those people are the sources of good taste and reason, the luminaries destined to guide all other men; that we are intelligent only in proportion as we admire them, that nature exhausted itself in producing these great originals, that in truth they were of a different species. Physics does not agree with all these beautiful phrases. Nature uses a certain paste which is

---

* *Oeuvres diverses de M. de Fontenelle* (La Haye: Gosse & Neaulme; 1728), vol. II, p. 125, 127–30, 133–4, 137. My translation.

always the same, which it moulds and remoulds ceaselessly in a thousand ways, and from which it forms men, animals, and plants. And certainly it has not formed Plato, Demosthenes, and Homer from a clay finer nor better prepared than our philosophers, orators, and poets of today.

* * *

The centuries put no natural difference between men. Nor does climate which is too much alike in Greece, Italy, and France to make any sensible difference between the Greeks, the Latins, and ourselves. . . . Behold, then, all are perfectly equal, Ancients and Moderns, Greeks, Latins, and Frenchmen.

* * *

The partisans of the Ancients argue that since the Ancients invented everything they have a great deal more intellect than we. Not at all: they simply preceded us in time. . . . If we had been put in their place, we would have invented; if they in ours, they would have added to what they found invented. There is no great mystery about it.

* * *

I make allowances for the infinity of false views that the Ancients had, the bad reasonings they made, the foolishness they uttered. Such is our condition that we are not permitted to arrive all at once at something reasonable no matter what it is. Before that it is necessary that we go astray for a long time, that we pass by all sorts of errors and degrees of impertinences. One would think it would be easy to view the whole play of Nature as consisting of figures and the movement of bodies. Nevertheless, before coming to that view, it was necessary to try the Ideas of Plato, the Numbers of Pythagoras, the Qualities of Aristotle; and all that having been recognized as false, we have been reduced to trying the true system. I say we have been reduced because in truth there remained no other alternative, and it seems that we are forbidden to take as long a time as possible. We are obliged to the Ancients for having exhausted most of the false ideas we could have; it was absolutely necessary to pay to error and ignorance the tribute they paid, and we must not lack gratitude toward those who cleared the ground for us. . . .

What is basic to philosophy and affects everything else, I mean the method of reasoning, has been greatly perfected in this century. . . . It is Descartes, it seems to me, who has introduced this new method of reasoning, a great deal more estimable than his philosophy itself, a good part of which is false or very uncertain according to the proper rules he has taught us. A precision and accuracy, which up to the present have been scarcely known, now rules not only in our good works of physics and mathematics, but also in religion, morals, and criticism.

I am further persuaded that these works will go still farther. . . . Someday we too shall be Ancients, and will it not be very just that our posterity in its turn correct and surpass us, principally in the method of reasoning, which is a science apart, and the most difficult and least cultivated of all?

* * *

Doubtless Nature remembers perfectly well how she formed the head of Cicero and Titus Livy. She produces in every century potentially great men, but the centuries do not permit them all to exercise their talents. Barbarian invasions, governments either absolutely opposed or little favorable to the sciences and arts, prejudices and fantasies which can take an infinite number of different forms, such as the respect paid to cadavers in China which prevents the Chinese from studying anatomy, universal wars—circumstances such as these often establish for long periods ignorance and bad taste.

* * *

The comparison which we have just made of the men of all the centuries to a single man can be extended to our whole question of the Ancients and Moderns. A good cultivated mind is, so to speak, composed of all the minds of preceding centuries, it is a mind which has been formed during that whole time. Thus, that man who has lived since the beginning of the world up to the present has had his infancy in which he was occupied only with the most pressing needs of life, his youth in which he has succeeded well enough in the things of imagination, such as poetry and eloquence, and in which he has begun to reason, but with less solidity than fire. He is now in the age of virility, in which he reasons with more force and has more light than ever; but he would be even farther advanced if the passion of war had not occupied him for a long time, and if he had not professed scorn for the sciences to which he has finally returned.

It is unfortunate not to be able to push to its logical conclusion such an apt comparison, but I have to confess that this man will have no old age; he will always be equally capable of the things proper to his youth and more and more of those things which suit the age of virility. That is to say, to leave the allegory, that men will never degenerate, and that the sound views of all the good minds through the centuries will always be building upon each other.

* * *

If the great men of this century had charitable sentiments for posterity, they would warn it not to admire them too much, and always to aspire at least to equal them. Nothing arrests so much the progress of things, nothing limits minds so much as the excessive admiration of the Ancients. Because people bowed down to the authority of Aristotle and sought the truth only in his enigmatic writings and never in nature, not only did philosophy not advance in any way but it fell into an abyss of unintelligible ideas from which it has been extricated only with the greatest difficulty. Aristotle never produced a true philosophy, but he successfully prevented one from appearing. And the bad part of it is that once a fantasy of this kind has been established for a long time among men, centuries are required for breaking away from it, even after it has been recognized as ridiculous. It would be almost as disadvantageous if someday men were to become similarly infatuated with Descartes and put him in the place of Aristotle.

Know then thyself, presume not God to scan,
The proper study of mankind is man.

Alexander Pope, ESSAY ON MAN

2. THE ENLIGHTENMENT

What light has burst over Europe within the last
few years! It first illuminated almost all the princes
of the North; it has even come into the universities.
It is the light of common sense.

Voltaire, LAST REMARKS ON THE "THOUGHTS" OF M.
PASCAL

History in general is a collection of crimes, follies,
and misfortunes, among which we have now and
then met with a few virtues, and some happy times;
as we sometimes see a few scattered huts in a barren
desert.

Voltaire, ESSAY ON THE MANNERS AND SPIRIT OF
NATIONS

Posterity is for the philosopher what the other world
is for the religious man.

Diderot, LETTER TO FALCONET, FEBRUARY, 1766

If I knew something useful to my nation which would be ruinous to another, I would not propose it to my prince, because I am a man before I am a Frenchman, or (better still) because I am necessarily a man, and only by chance a Frenchman.

Montesquieu, PENSÉES

The Enlightenment

"CRISIS of the European conscience"—thus a French historian describes the ferment in the intellectual world between 1680 and 1715.[1] This "crisis" precipitated the "Enlightenment" of the eighteenth century. Crisis, of course, need not mean cataclysm. The Enlightenment marked no cataclysmic break with the past. It evolved out of the past, primarily out of the Renaissance and the scientific revolution of which it can be said to be the logical and historical culmination. Crisis simply means the turning point, the moment at which a large segment of the intellectual class became conscious of its opposition to theological and religious modes of thought. The declining years of the reign of Louis XIV in France, and in England the Restoration, witnessed the birth of a new world-view that, Carl Becker notwithstanding, differed profoundly from the world-view of medieval Catholics and Protestants. Becker quite correctly reminds us of the debt that the *philosophes* owed to medieval thought. But he obscures the "crisis" when he says that the *philosophes* "demolished the Heavenly City of St. Augustine only to rebuild it with more up-to-date materials."[2] Ernst Troeltsch more nearly represents the facts when he interprets the Enlightenment as "the beginning and foundation of the properly modern period of European culture and history, in contrast to the theretofore prevailing ecclesiastical and theological culture."[3] In the *salons* of eighteenth-century Paris and the French provinces, in the Masonic lodges and the coffee houses, the talk was of machines and social engineering, of natural laws and education and progress. To be sure, the *philosophes* did not have things all their own way. The upholders of the old faith fought a stubborn rear-guard action, and in the course of the century the "romantics" managed to mount a limited

[1] Paul Hazard, *La Crise de la Conscience Européenne* (Paris, 1935).
[2] Carl Becker, *The Heavenly City of the Eighteenth-Century Philosophers* (New Haven, Conn.: Yale University Press, 1932), p. 31.
[3] Quoted in Preserved Smith, *History of Modern Culture* (New York: Holt, Rinehart and Winston, 1930–34), vol. II, p. 360.

offensive against the Enlightenment. But the *philosophes* represented the wave of the future, and to the degree that historical periodization is ever valid, we can say that under their leadership the West definitely moved into the Age of Science.

A number of factors conjoined to make France, rather than England or Germany or Italy, the home of the Enlightenment: the decadence of the *ancien régime* under the three Louis; the increasing prosperity and self-consciousness of the middle classes; the absence of political barriers, which in Germany robbed would-be reformers of a national public; and the *philosophes* themselves. These *philosophes* (henceforth we will call them the "philosophers")—Voltaire, Diderot and the Encyclopedists, and expatriates like the Baron d'Holbach—constituted a new type of intellectual class. They were not philosophers in the technical and academic sense. Neither were they scholars or specialists, nor courtiers, nor "gentlemen." They were emphatically not of the ivory tower. Literary men, popularizers, and propagandists, they made their appeal to a newly awakened public opinion, against the powers that be, against the learned world of church and university. Fontenelle was their prototype, but they went farther than Fontenelle, for they wished not only to advance knowledge but also to change society—the educational and religious system, the economic and social system, and eventually even the political system. They did not foresee nor desire a revolution, but their pungent criticism and their thousand-and-one projects for social melioration undoubtedly helped to bring the *ancien régime* tumbling down.

Of the wide influence of the philosophers there cannot be the slightest doubt. Despite official censorship (by no means consistently ferocious, especially after Malesherbes took over its direction in 1750) their ideas got through to an ever increasing reading public. To begin with, they deliberately wrote in a style calculated to reach and amuse the average educated person. In her book on Germany, published in 1813,[4] Mme de Staël commented upon this social consciousness of the French intellectual. Whereas the German sacrifices the form of his thought to the matter, the Frenchman, she said, sacrifices the matter to the form so as to communicate it. Hence, the German excels in abstract and original thought, and the Frenchman excels in social thought which has a practical end in view. New intellectual institutions—the Parisian *salon*, which fostered an "esprit de conversation," the circulating library and popular newspaper, and the Society of Free Masons, which founded lodges all over Europe—provided channels for the flow of *philosophie* to a still wider audience. But in the final analysis the philosophers flourished because they articulated the hopes and fears of the middle classes who, in the phrase of the Abbé Sieyès, demanded "to be some-

[4] See p. 460 this text.

thing" socially and politically, as well as economically. "Give me leave
to say," says Mr. Sealand to Sir John Bevil in Sir Richard Steele's play
The Conscious Lovers, "that we merchants are a species of gentry that
have grown into the world this last century, and are as honourable, and
almost as useful, as you landed folks that have always thought yourselves so much above us." Not all the philosophers were bourgeois—
note the large number of abbés and renegade aristocrats among them,
nor were they narrowly class-conscious in the Marxist sense. But in their
attack on the *ancien régime* they necessarily championed the classes that
had "grown into the world this last century" and that desired accordingly "to be something." The eighteenth century was the century when
the French bourgeoisie became not only rich but self-conscious. They
comprised the core of the reading public for which the philosophers
wrote. They helped to pay the expenses of the avant-garde intellectuals
who now depended for their livelihood less upon the patronage of the
great and more upon public demand for their talent. "The privileged
and feudal intellectualism of the seventeenth century was passing into
the democratic intellectualism of the nineteenth century." [5] Without the
bourgeoisie, then, the philosophers could hardly have existed. On the
other hand, without the philosophers the bourgeoisie must have lacked
assurance and a philosophical basis.

I I

THIS social milieu, together with the Renaissance
and the scientific revolution, conditioned the "mind" of the Enlightenment. The philosophers were essentially humanitarians. They had no
sense of the reality of another world, no interest in plumbing spiritual
depths. Religious meditation and solitude they understood not at all.
How very droll to think that laziness can be a title to greatness and
action a lowering of our nature—thus did Voltaire reply, in effect, to his
favorite whipping boy, the Christian Pascal who, in his famous dictum,
said that man's misfortunes derive from not knowing how to sit quietly
in a room. The philosophers admired sociability and social action. More
than anything else they wanted to make this world a more comfortable
and agreeable place for man to live in. They strove manfully—and with
considerable success—to secure religious toleration and political justice
and educational reform and to abolish torture and witch hunts. Their
principal intellectual achievement was in the field of the human and
social sciences. The Enlightenment made quiet progress in the natural
sciences, particularly in chemistry and biology. But its chief claim to
originality rests upon its attempt to extend to man and society the

[5] W. L. Dorn, *Competition for Empire, 1740–63* (New York, 1940), p. 185.

methods and laws of the natural scientists. Man and man's world had become the measure of all things. The Enlightenment thus signified the profound secularization, almost beyond recovery, of Western thought and culture. Political and economic thinking had finally divested itself of religion. Morals could do without religious sanctions. Religion itself ceased to be mysterious.

The vocabulary of the philosophers provides a clue to the way their minds worked. Three words—"reason," "nature," and "progress"—appear with great frequency in their writing and talking. What did they mean? The eighteenth century is often called the "Age of Reason," but reason has been invoked in practically all ages and its special meaning in the Enlightenment must be clearly understood. Reason, particularly among the French, was partly Cartesian, and partly Lockean and Newtonian. Voltaire both praised and blamed Descartes. He blamed him for his *esprit de système* and his metaphysical errors. Nevertheless, "he taught the men of his time how to reason." Voltaire was thinking of Descartes' methodical doubt, which he hoped might be extended now beyond metaphysical ideas to social mores and institutions. Thus, reason meant, primarily, the critical reason that takes nothing on trust, is suspicious of authority, tradition, and revelation. It obviously differed profoundly from Thomistic reason.

It was also Lockean in its distrust of all intellectual "systems," including those erected by the Cartesians on the slender foundation of intuitive certainties and in the severe limits it put on its own operations. "Our minds are not made as large as truth, nor suited to the whole extent of things." [6] Rational knowledge, that is, could not transcend the empirical world. It was limited, as Immanuel Kant was later to say, to appearances. Yet within its sphere of competence the human reason or "understanding" was a reliable and powerful instrument, particularly when it made use of the method of analysis worked out by scientists like Newton. The philosophers hoped to employ this method, so successful in physics, to discover the laws of society as well as nature, to create a "social physics." Thus, reason meant, in the second place, the scientific reason as it was understood at that time.

Edmund Burke (and later on, Hippolyte Taine) attacked the philosophers for their *esprit géometrique*, that is, for presuming to solve problems, political as well as scientific, by means of "the naked reason," without reference to the facts of the case or history. This was not fair to the followers of Locke and Newton who prided themselves on their empiricism, hence on reasoning from particulars and by analyzing problems into their component parts before leaping to synthesis. Yet they were more Cartesian than they supposed. If they eschewed "the naked reason" and rejected innate ideas and final "systems" of knowledge, they were not at all averse from generalizing about the universe and man. In

[6] See p. 297 this text.

truth, their general assumptions frequently take one's breath away. They assumed (excepting sceptics like David Hume, of course) a universal law and order in material nature and man's rational capacity to comprehend it. They assumed the apriority of universal laws, of "natural laws" and "natural rights," in human society. Even Montesquieu, so observant of different political customs and constitutions, found a "spirit of the laws," that is, certain general principles, underlying the variety of the laws themselves. They assumed, in spite of obvious surface differences, a uniform human nature throughout the world. Reason in the Enlightenment, then, was at least as universalistic—one might even say, as rationalistic—as it was empiricist, although doubtless the latter element was becoming more conspicuous.

How rational did the philosophers think man was? It is not true that they ignored the passions or that they had an invariably good opinion of human nature. They sometimes spoke as though the human mind lacked autonomy or freedom. Was it not like a tabula rasa, as Locke said, or perhaps like a machine, more acted upon than acting? Later on, this became a standard complaint of the romantics who denounced the philosophers for making man a largely passive creature, lacking both creative reason and imagination. The truth is that they were not always consistent. Humanism pulled them one way and the logical demands of a mechanistic science another. But the palm lay with humanism. They all believed that virtue is knowledge, that progress came through enlightenment. Hence, man must be either (1) rational and moral by nature, as Voltaire and Diderot usually argued, or (2) capable of becoming so through environmental conditioning, principally through exposure to better laws and education. In either case man was malleable, educable, improvable, to that degree at least, rational, and not, as Christians like Pascal contended, permanently corrupt through original sin. "Pascal," said Condorcet, "is not right in depicting man's corruption as either general or natural and incurable. Errors of long standing have brutalized and corrupted him. But we must not despair too quickly, for by enlightening him, we can give him the courage to become better and happier."

"Nature," too, was rational. I am speaking now of non-human nature, the nature studied by the physical scientists, thought of as the "external world" since the time of Descartes. The philosophers further secularized that world. "Instead of raising the natural to the supernatural," Thomas Carlyle said, "the Philosophers strove to sink the supernatural to the natural." True, many of them tried not to be dogmatic about it in keeping with their stated empiricism. Nevertheless, few avoided projecting—and, I think, believing in—a "classical" nature, homogeneous, largely unchanging, ruled by universal and rational laws. This was a nature in which rational man could have confidence, although he could scarcely think of it as a home or as pulsing with "spirit" or a moral life like his own. Another interpretation, less influential than the Newtonian but anticipating the future, was currently being worked out by Diderot and the French materialists. The bold editor of the great *Encyclopedia*, challenged to bring life out of matter and influenced by a recent vitalist trend in the biological sciences, suggested a creative nature, constantly changing, and capable of producing new organic forms. Diderot and some of his friends were obviously moving from a static to a dynamic conception of nature.

"Progress," the third and last word to be considered, expressed the philosophers' view of history. It is not true that they had no sense of history, as has been claimed, or that they heaped indiscriminate abuse on the past. It is not true that they were invariably optimistic about the future. They had their pessimistic moments when they despaired of enlightening the canaille and wondered if the progress of science was compatible with progress in the arts. By comparison with other ages, however, our own included, they seem amazingly sanguine. This was because they lived just at that time in history when faith in the scientific reason was at flood tide, or nearly so. Reason was given an excellent chance of overcoming barbarism and superstition and of solving the great political and economic problems. The philosophers had none of that fear of the machine and distrust of human nature that was to become so characteristic of later times. Their mood, indeed, was frequently apocalyptic. By the year 2000 or 2440 the world would have been enlightened, united, and at peace—compare George Orwell's recent grisly prediction for the year 1984! "We are approaching one of the grand revolutions of the human race," Condorcet wrote in 1794. The future that lay just ahead would surely be "healthy, wealthy, and wise."

III

THE *ancien régime*, symbol of unenlightenment, alone stood between mankind and its goal. The philosophers therefore trained their big guns on this living relic of the past, blasting first its religion, and then its politics and economics. The Enlightenment marked the beginning of open warfare between "science" and theology in the West. Numerous witnesses, both Christian and non-Christian, testify to the substantial growth of religious infidelity during the century. Joseph Priestley, for instance, records in his *Memoirs* that when he visited Paris, he found all the philosophical persons to whom he was introduced "unbelievers in Christianity, and even professed atheists. Le Roi, the philosopher, told me that I was the only man of sense he knew that was a Christian." The attack on organized Christianity assumed its most violent form in France because of the special nature of the French Church. The point is not only that ecclesiasticism per se constituted an anachronism in an increasingly secular society. Ever since Louis XIV's Revocation of the Edict of Nantes in 1685, no one knew when the Church might swoop down on him for religious heterodoxy. Hatred of the Church that persecuted Jean Calas and others inspired much of the philosopher's talk about crushing "the infamous thing" and the feeling of moral superiority of atheists over religious fanatics. The Civil Constitution of the Clergy in 1790 and the systematic dechristianization of France during the Revolution merely represented the logical extension of this anti-clericalism. Philosophers all over Europe claimed, moreover, and not without justice, that religious fanaticism had had not a little to do with the chronic state of warfare in the West. Behind their deism lay the desire to find a simple religious creed to which all men could agree and that could restrain Catholics and Protestants from cutting each others' throats.

Of course, their antipathy to revealed religion was also ingrained in their intellectual presuppositions. In his discussion of miracles in the primitive Church, Edward Gibbon remarks in *The Decline and Fall of the Roman Empire* that "in modern times, a latent and even involuntary skepticism adheres to the most pious dispositions. . . . Accustomed long since to observe and to respect the invariable order of nature, our reason, or at least our imagination, is not sufficiently prepared to sustain the visible action of the Deity." Gibbon here testifies to what W. E. H. Lecky calls the "declining sense of the miraculous." The philosophers' view of nature precluded belief in the mysterious and miraculous. They rejected all miracles except the one great miracle of nature itself, all providence except a general providence. In his impertinent *Questions of Dr. Zapata*, Voltaire subjected the Bible to merciless criticism, thus laying the foundations for the "Higher Criticism" of the nineteenth century. Similarly, in the "offensive" fifteenth chapter of *The Decline and Fall*, Gibbon discussed the early history of Christianity as though it were a purely human phenomenon. The philosophers did not know it, but they caricatured revealed religion. They treated it as an imposture, fobbed off on an innocent public by rascally priests and tyrants, or alternatively as the product of fear or mental sickness.

Not many of them, however, became atheists. For revealed religion they substituted their own brand of natural religion, called "deism." Deism was watered-down theism, and it represented an attempt to construct a religion in keeping with modern science. Preserved Smith calls the deists "constitutional reformers who wished to retain the monarchical form of government, but to put it under the restraint of fixed, general laws." [7] They found it hard to conceive of things just starting, but on the other hand they could not believe that God had issued special revelations to chosen peoples. Like the neo-classical art critic who declared that the best art conforms to general principles that

[7] Preserved Smith, *History of Modern Culture* (New York: Holt, Rinehart and Winston; 1930–34), vol. II, p. 505.

everybody can understand, the deist looked for the kernel of religion contained within the husks of the positive faiths of the world. His principle was uniformitarianism. Whatever is uniform, that is, believed everywhere (the *consensus gentium*), is right. The reports of travellers confirmed the philosophers in their belief in a universal religion, natural to the Chinese and American Indians as well as the Europeans. This natural religion, this least common denominator of all the faiths, boiled down to simple ethics. God remained, but he was hardly a God to whom one could pray. The philosophers hoped that such a religion would ensure religious toleration.

As the century proceeded, the philosophers became increasingly critical of the political and economic, as well as ecclesiastical, aspects of the *ancien régime*. Taine derived the revolutionary spirit of the 1790's from the "classical spirit" of the philosophers. But the philosophers were not revolutionaries. Their liberalism consisted primarily in securing the individual from arbitrary interference in private life and in freeing him from what Adam Smith called "profusion of government." Rousseau's attack on private property as the root of all evil ran counter to their way of thinking. "The social laws established by the supreme Being prescribe uniquely the conservation of the *right of property*, and of the *liberty* which is inseparable from it." Likewise, this is true of Rousseau's democracy. They feared the uneducated multitude. Like the Erasmians of the early sixteenth century, the philosophers hoped to get reforms without any serious dislocation of the existing framework of government. Initially, they had some hopes of the reigning monarchs, but when the French "despots" refused to be enlightened they veered toward a mixed or "moderate" type of government that would "guarantee" civil liberties, as in England. Still later, especially after the American Revolution, the English system itself came under fire by democrats who professed to admire the Greek and Roman Republics. The Declaration of the Rights of Man and the Constitution of 1791, however, would probably have suited the majority very well indeed.

All the same, there is something to Taine's thesis. No doubt the eighteenth century witnessed some erosion of the natural law tradition and a progression toward a more empirical and utilitarian type of political thought. But much remained, as has been suggested, of the older apriorist rationalism. If the philosophers were not doctrinaires, they did have a penchant for referring political as well as other problems to general principles supposedly built into the structure of the universe: "natural rights" said to be anterior to society and universally valid, "natural law," "reason," and so forth. Was this mere rhetoric? Proof that it was not is contained in a key document, such as the Declaration of 1789, which, as everybody knows, commenced by asserting "the natural, inalienable, and sacred rights of man." This sort of rationalism, hardly based on empirical observation but proclaimed to the rafters for several generations, did, I believe, help to generate a spirit of revolution.

The social theory of the Enlightenment blazed new trails with its individualism and secularism. The philosophers lived at a time when liberty had superseded order as the great social problem. They therefore discussed politics and economics from the side of the individual rather than the state. For Jean Bodin, writing in the thick of the French religious wars of the sixteenth century, "sovereignty" was the panacea. For the philosophers it was liberty and equality. They were more nominalistic than Locke. Only the individual is a true "person"; the state is but a name, an artificial machine constructed by individual men for their mutual advantage. The individualism of the Enlightenment was a great leveler. Assuming the sameness of human nature everywhere, it equalized all men, ironing out national and cultural differences, destroying special privilege and social status. Furthermore, politics and economics were now discussed in a wholly secular context. The time had at last arrived when religion could be assumed to be one thing, politics and economics another. "Classical" economics dispensed altogether with theocratic presuppositions. Political liberalism followed Locke in rejecting the divine right of kings and the sacrosanctity, and hence fixity, of the social hierarchy. In Lecky's phrase, the stream of self-sacrifice was now passing from theology to politics.

Becker says that the eighteenth century was "an age of faith as well as of reason." [8] In the summing up, this is perhaps the most important thing to remember about the Enlightenment. The philosophers substituted a new faith for the old. Faith—enthusiastic faith—in reason, science, and the future replaced faith in revealed religion. "Posterity," said Diderot in a famous epigram, "is for the philosopher what the other world is for the religious man." Eighteenth-century palaver about the noble savage and the decline of civilization from an original state of nature should not obscure this fundamental belief in posterity. The eighteenth century is distinguished from all previous centuries, even the seventeenth, by its vision of an expanding future. Natural scientists and historians alike were giving up the old idea of stability and cyclical returns. The Comte de Buffon and Jean Lamarck foretold Charles Darwin in their attack on the immutability of species and their theories of the evolution of the earth and life. Similarly, Gotthold Lessing, in his *Education of the Human Race*, described the history of religion as an evolution from primitive animism and superstition to Christianity, and beyond Christianity. Clearly, as Herbert Butterfield puts it, the philosophers thought time was aiming at something. In Condorcet's "Tenth Epoch" mankind would be biologically, materially, and morally superior—in a word, mankind would be happy.

[8] Carl Becker, *The Heavenly City of the Eighteenth-Century Philosophers* (New Haven, Conn.: Yale University Press; 1932), p. 8.

Readings

1. *Spirit of the Enlightenment*

VOLTAIRE: *Letters on the English* *

Francois-Marie Arouet, "M. de Voltaire" (1694–1778) was the leading figure among the *philosophes*, the spearhead of the attack on the *Ancien Régime*. His *Lettres philosophiques sur les Anglais* (1734), which belongs to the early period of his career, explained England, her government, religion, and thought, to the French. In it he paid tribute to England's great men, notably Bacon, Locke, and Newton who, even more than Descartes, became the patron saints of the French Enlightenment.

On the Lord Bacon

NOT long since the trite and frivolous question following was debated in a very polite and learned company, viz., Who was the greatest man, Caesar, Alexander, Tamerlane, Cromwell, &c.?

Somebody answered that Sir Isaac Newton excelled them all. The gentleman's assertion was very just; for if true greatness consists in having received from heaven a mighty genius, and in having employed it to enlighten our own mind and that of others, a man like Sir Isaac Newton, whose equal is hardly found in a thousand years, is the truly great man. And those politicians and conquerors (and all ages produce some) were generally so many illustrious wicked men. That man claims our respect who commands over the minds of the rest of the world by the force of truth, not those who enslave their fellow-creatures: he who is acquainted with the universe, not they who deface it.

Since, therefore, you desire me to give you an account of the famous personages whom England has given birth to, I shall begin with Lord Bacon, Mr. Locke, Sir Isaac Newton, &c. Afterwards the warriors and Ministers of State shall come in their order.

* From the *Harvard Classics*, copyright 1910, by courtesy of P. F. Collier & Son Corporation. Vol. XXIV, pp. 99–106, 110–11, 113–15.

I shall confine myself to those things which so justly gained Lord Bacon the esteem of all Europe.

The most singular and the best of all his pieces is that which, at this time, is the most useless and the least read, I mean his *Novum Scientiarum Organum*. This is the scaffold with which the new philosophy was raised; and when the edifice was built, part of it at least, the scaffold was no longer of service.

The Lord Bacon was not yet acquainted with Nature, but then he knew, and pointed out, the several paths that lead to it. He had despised in his younger years the thing called philosophy in the Universities, and did all that lay in his power to prevent those societies of man instituted to improve human reason from depraving it by their quiddities, their horrors of the vacuum, their substantial forms, and all those impertinent terms which not only ignorance had rendered venerable, but which had been made sacred by their being ridiculously blended with religion.

He is the father of experimental philosophy. . . .

No one before the Lord Bacon was acquainted with experimental philosophy, nor with the several physical experiments which have been made since his time. Scarce one of them but is hinted at in his work, and he himself had made several. He made a kind of pneumatic engine, by which he guessed the elasticity of the air. He approached, on all sides as it were, to the discovery of its weight, and had very near attained it, but some time after Torricelli seized upon this truth. In a little time experimental philosophy began to be cultivated on a sudden in most parts of Europe. It was a hidden treasure which the Lord Bacon had some notion of, and which all the philosophers, encouraged by his promises, endeavoured to dig up.

On Mr. Locke

Perhaps no man ever had a more judicious or more methodical genius, or was a more acute logician than Mr. Locke, and yet he was not deeply skilled in the mathematics. This great man could never subject himself to the tedious fatigue of calculations, nor to the dry pursuit of mathematical truths, which do not at first present any sensible objects to the mind; and no one has given better proofs than he, that it is possible for a man to have a geometrical head without the assistance of geometry. Before his time, several great philosophers had declared, in the most positive terms, what the soul of man is; but as these absolutely knew nothing about it, they might very well be allowed to differ entirely in opinion from one another.

In Greece, the infant seat of arts and of errors, and where the grandeur as well as folly of the human mind went such prodigious lengths, the people used to reason about the soul in the very same manner as we do.

The divine Anaxagoras, in whose honour an altar was erected for his having taught mankind that the sun was greater than Peloponnesus, that snow was black, and that the heavens were of stone, affirmed that the soul was an aërial spirit, but at the same time immortal. Diogenes (not he who was a cynical philosopher after having coined base money) declared that the soul was a portion of the substance of God: an idea which we must confess was very sublime. Epicurus maintained that it was composed of parts in the same manner as the body.

Aristotle, who has been explained a thousand ways, because he is unintelligible, was of opinion, according to some of his disciples, that the understanding in all men is one and the same substance. . . .

With regard to the Fathers of the Church, several in the primitive ages believed that the soul was human, and the angels and God corporeal. Men naturally improve upon every system. St. Bernard, as Father Mabillon confesses, taught that the soul after death does not see God in the celestial regions, but converses with Christ's human nature only. However, he was not believed this time on his bare word; the adventure of the crusade having a little sunk the credit of his oracles. Afterwards a thousand schoolmen arose, such as the Irrefragable Doctor, the Subtile Doctor, the Angelic Doctor, the Seraphic Doctor, and the Cherubic Doctor, who were all sure that they had a very clear and distinct idea of the soul, and yet wrote in such a manner, that one would conclude they were resolved no one should understand a word in their writings. Our Descartes, born to discover the errors of antiquity, and at the same time to substitute his own; and hurried away by that systematic spirit which throws a cloud over the minds of the greatest men, thought he had demonstrated that the soul is the same thing as thought, in the same manner as matter, in his opinion, is the same as extension. He asserted, that man thinks eternally, and that the soul, at its coming into the body, is informed with the whole series of metaphysical notions: knowing God, infinite space, possessing all abstract ideas—in a word, completely endued with the most sublime lights, which it unhappily forgets at its issuing from the womb.

Father Malebranche, in his sublime illusions, not only admitted innate ideas, but did not doubt of our living wholly in God, and that God is, as it were, our soul.

Such a multitude of reasoners having written the romance of the soul, a sage at last arose, who gave, with an air of the greatest modesty, the history of it. Mr. Locke has displayed the human soul in the same manner as an excellent anatomist explains the springs of the human body. He everywhere takes the light of physics for his guide. He sometimes presumes to speak affirmatively, but then he presumes also to doubt. Instead of concluding at once what we know not, he examines gradually what we would know. He takes an infant at the instant of his birth; he traces, step by step, the progress of his understanding; examines what things he has in common with beasts, and what he possesses above them. Above all, he consults himself: the being conscious that he himself thinks.

"I shall leave," says he, "to those who know more of this matter than myself, the examining whether the soul exists before or after the organisation of our bodies. But I confess that it is my lot to be animated with one of those heavy souls which do not think always; and I am even so unhappy as not to conceive that it is more necessary the soul should think perpetually than that bodies should be for ever in motion."

With regard to myself, I shall boast that I have the honour to be as stupid in this particular as Mr. Locke. No one shall ever make me believe that I think always: and I am as little inclined as he could be to fancy that some weeks after I was conceived I was a very learned soul; knowing at that time a thousand things which I forgot at my birth; and possessing when in the womb (though to no manner of purpose) knowledge which I lost the instant I had occasion for it; and which I have never since been able to recover perfectly.

Mr. Locke, after having destroyed innate ideas; after having fully renounced the vanity of believing that we think always; after having laid down, from the most solid principles, that ideas enter the mind through the sense; having examined our simple and complex ideas; having traced the human mind through its several operations; having shown that all the languages in the world are imperfect, and the great abuse that is made of words every moment, he at last comes to consider the extent or rather the narrow limits of human knowledge.

On Descartes and Sir Isaac Newton

The progress of Sir Isaac Newton's life was quite different [from that of Descartes]. He lived happy, and very much honoured in his native country, to the age of fourscore and five years.

It was his peculiar felicity, not only to be born in a country of liberty, but in an age when all scholastic impertinences were banished from the world. Reason alone was cultivated, and mankind could only be his pupil, not his enemy. . . .

The opinion that generally prevails in England with regard to these new philosophers is, that the latter was a dreamer, and the former a sage.

Very few people in England read Descartes, whose works indeed are now useless. On the other side, but a small number peruse those of Sir Isaac, because to do this the student must be deeply skilled in the mathematics, otherwise those works will be unintelligible to him. But notwithstanding this, these great men are the subject of everyone's discourse. Sir Isaac Newton is allowed every advantage, whilst Descartes is not indulged a single one. According to some, it is to the former that we owe the discovery of a vacuum, that the air is a heavy body, and the invention of telescopes. In a word, Sir Isaac Newton is here as the Hercules of fabulous story, to whom the ignorant ascribed all the feats of ancient heroes.

* * *

Geometry was a guide he [Descartes] himself had in some measure fashioned, which would have conducted him safely through the several paths of natural philosophy. Nevertheless, he at last abandoned this guide, and gave entirely into the humour of forming hypotheses; and then philosophy was no more than an ingenious romance, fit only to amuse the ignorant. He was mistaken in the nature of the soul, in the proofs of the existence of a God, in matter, in the laws of motion, and in the nature of light. He admitted innate ideas, he invented new elements, he created a world; he made man according to his own fancy; and it is justly said, that the man of Descartes is, in fact, that of Descartes only, very different from the real one.

He pushed his metaphysical errors so far, as to declare that two and two make four for no other reason but because God would have it so. However, it will not be making him too great a compliment if we affirm that he was valuable even in his mistakes. He deceived himself, but then it was at least in a methodical way. He destroyed all the absurd chimeras with which youth had been infatuated for two thousand years. He taught his contemporaries how to reason, and enabled them to employ his own weapons against himself. If Descartes did not pay in good money, he however did great service in crying down that of a base alloy.

I indeed believe that very few will presume to compare his philosophy in any respect with that of Sir Isaac Newton. The former is an essay, the latter a masterpiece. But then the man who first brought us to the path of truth, was perhaps as great a genius as he who afterwards conducted us through it.

Descartes gave sight to the blind. These saw the errors of antiquity and of the sciences. The path he struck out is since become boundless. Robault's little work was, during some years, a complete system of physics; but now all the Transactions of the several academies in Europe put together do not form so much as the beginning of a system. In fathoming this abyss no bottom has been found.

The Encyclopedia *

The *Encyclopédie, ou Dictionnaire raisonné des Sciences, des Arts, et des Métiers* has been called "the greatest publishing venture of the

* *Encyclopédie, ou Dictionnaire raisonné des Sciences, des Arts, et des Métiers* (Genève: J. Pellet; 1778), vol. I, p. xxxv, liv–lviii; vol. III, p. 475; vol. XII, pp. 382–3; vol. XXV, pp. 667–9. My translation.

century." Begun in 1745 under the joint editorship of Denis Diderot (1713–84) and the mathematician Jean-le-Rond d'Alembert (1717–83), it was finally completed in 1780, a work of thirty-five volumes, twenty-one volumes of text, twelve of plates illustrating the trades and mechanical arts, and two of index. The aim of the work was to bring together in one place a summary of human knowledge in the spirit of the "Enlightenment." The following selections are from the Preliminary Discourse by d'Alembert, who makes some penetrating and often critical remarks about the philosophic spirit of the Age of Reason, two articles by Diderot, and the article "Philosopher" which may have been written by Dumarsais.

Preliminary Discourse

WHEN we consider the progress of the mind since that memorable epoch [the Renaissance], we find that it has followed a natural order. Classical scholarship came first, followed by belles-lettres, and finally philosophy. In truth, this order differs from that which ought to be observed by the man abandoned to his own light or bounded by the intercourse of his contemporaries, as we have principally considered him in the first part of this Discourse: indeed, we have shown that the isolated mind must meet in its route philosophy before belles-lettres. But on emerging from a long interval of ignorance which had been preceded by centuries of light, the regeneration of ideas, if one can speak in this way, was necessarily different from their primitive generation. . . .

Philosophy, which is the dominant taste of our century, seems by the progress it has made among us to wish to make up for lost time and to take revenge for the contempt which our fathers heaped upon it. This contempt has today fallen on erudition and it is no more just for having changed its object. We imagine that we have drawn from the works of the ancients everything that it is important for us to know; and on this ground we would willingly free from their pains those who still wish to consult them. . . . [But, in my opinion] it is being ignorant or presumptuous to believe . . . that there is no longer any advantage to be gained from the study and lessons of the ancients.

The custom of writing everything today in the vulgar tongue has doubtless helped to fortify this prejudice, and perhaps this custom is more pernicious than the prejudice itself. Our tongue having spread throughout all Europe, we have believed that it was time to substitute it for the Latin tongue, which since the renaissance of letters was that of our savants. I admit that it is much more excusable for a philosopher to write in French than for a Frenchman to make Latin verses; I even agree that this custom has helped to make enlightenment more general, if it has really reached the mind of a people rather than merely the surface. Nevertheless, there results from this an inconvenience which we ought to have foreseen. The savants of other nations, to whom we have given the example, have believed with reason that they would write still better in their language than in ours. . . . The custom of Latin, which we have ridiculed in matters of taste, could be very useful in works of philosophy which require clarity and precision, and which need a universal language and convention. It would be to our advantage to reestablish this custom, but there is no ground to hope that it will be. The abuse of which we dare to complain is too favorable to vanity and indolence for us to flatter ourselves that we can uproot it. The philosophers, like other writers, wish to be read, and especially by their nation. If they used a less familiar language, they would have fewer mouths to praise them, and one could not boast of understanding them. . . .

Nevertheless, philosophy, while thinking to please, appears not to have forgotten that it is principally made to teach; this is the reason why the taste for systems, more proper to flattering the imagination than to enlightening the reason, is today almost entirely banished from good works. One of our best philosophers [Condillac, in his *Traité des systèmes*] seems to have finally destroyed it. In bygone days the spirit of hypothesis and conjecture was very useful, and even necessary for the renaissance of philosophy; because then it was a question less of thinking well than of learning to think for oneself. But the times have changed, and a writer who would now praise systems would have come too late. The advantages which this spirit can now procure are too few to balance the inconveniences which result from it. . . . The spirit of system is in physics what metaphysics is in geometry. If it is sometimes necessary in order to put us on the road to truth, it is almost always incapable of leading us there by itself. Enlightened by the observation of nature, it can perhaps see dimly the causes of phenomena: but calculation is necessary to guarantee, so to speak, the existence of these causes, by determining exactly the effects which they can produce, and by comparing these effects with those which experience uncovers for us. Every hypothesis stripped of such help rarely acquires that degree of certitude which we must always look for in the natural sciences, but which is so seldom found in those frivolous conjectures which we honor by the name of systems. If he could have only systems of this kind, the principal merit of the physicist would be, properly speaking, to have the spirit of system but never to make any. With regard to the use of systems in the other sciences, a thousand experiences prove how dangerous they are. . . .

We abuse the best things. This philosophic spirit, so à la mode at the present time, which wishes to see everything and to suppose nothing, has spread over into belles-lettres. I maintain that it is hurtful to their progress, and it is difficult to conceal it. Our century, so given to calculation and analysis, seems to wish to introduce cold and didactic discussions into the things of sentiment. . . . Nevertheless, I must agree that this spirit of discussion has helped to free our literature from blind admiration of the ancients; it has taught us to esteem in them only the beauties that we would be constrained to admire in the moderns. But it is perhaps also to the same source that we owe I do not know what metaphysic of the heart which has taken possession of our theatres; if this metaphysic ought not to be banished from them entirely, still less ought it to be allowed to reign there. This anatomy of the soul has even slipped into our conversations; we no longer talk, we discuss formally; and our society has lost its principal charms, warmth and gaiety.

Let us not then be astonished that our works of imagination are in general inferior to those of the preceding century. . . . Altogether we have more principles by which to judge well, a greater fund of enlightenment, more good judges and fewer good works; we do not say of a book that it is good, but that it is the book of a man of understanding. It is thus that the century of Demetrius and Phalère succeeded immediately to that of Demosthenes, the century of Lucan and Seneca to that of Cicero and Virgil, and ours to that of Louis XIV.

Art

In examining the products of the arts, we observe that some were more the work of the mind than of the hand, and that to the contrary others were more the work of the hand than of the mind. Such is in part the origin of the preeminence which has been accorded to certain arts over others, and of the division that has been made of the arts into *liberal arts* and *mechanical arts*. This distinction, though well founded, has produced a bad effect by degrading some very estimable and useful people, and by strengthening in us I do not know what natural laziness, which has already disposed us only too much to believe that to give constant application to experiences and particular objects, sensible and material, was to derogate from the dignity of the human mind; and that to practice, or even to study, the mechanical arts, was to lower oneself to things the research of which is laborious, the meditation ignoble, the exposition difficult, the commerce dishonorable, the number inexhaustible, and the value negligible: . . . a prejudice which has tended to fill the cities with proud reasoners and useless contemplators, and the country with little ignorant tyrants, idle and disdainful. Bacon, one of the first geniuses of England, did not think thus; nor Colbert, one of the greatest ministers of France; nor the good minds and wise men of all times. Bacon regarded the history of the mechanical arts as the most important branch of true philosophy; he took care not to despise the practical. Colbert regarded the industry of peoples and the establishment of manufactures as the surest wealth of a kingdom. . . . Put on one side of the balance the real advantages of the most sublime sciences and the most honored arts, and on the other side those of the mechanical arts, and you will find that the reckoning we have made of them has not been distributed in just relationship to these advantages; and that we have praised a great deal more the men occupied in making us believe we were happy, than the men occupied in making us so indeed. What eccentricity in our judgments! We require that we be occupied usefully, and we despise useful men. . . .

Encyclopedia

One consideration especially which we ought not to lose sight of, is that if we banish man, the thinking and contemplative being, from the surface of the earth, this pathetic and sublime spectacle of nature becomes a scene melancholy and dumb. Silence and night take possession of the universe. Everything is transformed into a vast solitude in which unobserved phenomena move in an obscure and secret manner. It is the presence of man that makes the existence of beings interesting. Can we propose anything better in the history of these beings than to submit ourselves to this consideration? Why should we not introduce man into our work, as he is placed in the universe? Why should we not make him a common center? . . .

This is what has determined us to find in the principal faculties of man the general division to which we have subordinated our work. . . . Man is the unique point to which we must refer everything, if we wish to interest and please amongst considerations the most arid and details the most dry. Abstract from my existence and the happiness of my fellow human beings, and the rest of nature is of no consequence.

Philosopher

Reason is to the philosopher what grace is to the Christian.

Grace causes the Christian to act, reason the philosopher.

Other men are carried away by their passions, their actions not being preceded by reflection: these are the men who walk in darkness. On the other hand, the philosopher, even in his passions, acts only after reflection; he walks in the dark, but by a torch.

The philosopher forms his principles from an infinity of particular observations. Most people adopt principles without thinking of the observations that have produced them: they believe that maxims exist, so to speak, by themselves. But the philosopher takes maxims from their source; he examines their origin; he knows their proper value, and he makes use of them only in so far as as they suit him.

Truth is not for the philosopher a mistress who corrupts his imagination and whom he believes is to be found everywhere; he contents himself with being able to unravel it where he can perceive it. He does not confound it with probability; he takes for true what is true, for false what is false, for doubtful what is doubtful, and for probable what is only probable. He does more, and here you have a great perfection of the philosopher: when he has no reason by which to judge, he knows how to live in suspension of judgment. . . .

The philosophic spirit is, then, a spirit of observation and exactness, which relates everything to true principles; but the philosopher does not cultivate the mind alone, he carries his attention and needs farther. . . .

Our philosopher does not believe in exiling himself from this world, he does not believe that he is in enemy country; he wishes to enjoy with wise economy the goods which nature offers him; he wishes to find pleasure with others, and in order to find it, he must make it: thus he tries to be agreeable to those with whom chance and his choice have thrown him, and at the same time he finds what is agreeable to him. He is an honest man who wishes to please and to make himself useful.

The majority of the great, whose dissipations do not leave enough time to meditate, are savage toward those whom they do not believe to be their equals. The ordinary philosophers who meditate too much, or rather who meditate badly, are savage toward everybody; they flee men, and men avoid them. But our philosopher who knows how to strike a balance between retreat from and commerce with men, is full of humanity. He is Terence's Chrémès who feels that he is a man, and that humanity alone is interested in the good and bad fortune of his neighbour. *Homo sum, humani a me nihil alienum puto.*

It would be useless to remark here how jealous the philosopher is of everything calling itself honor and probity. Civil society is, so to speak, a divinity for him on earth; he burns incense to it, he honors it by probity, by an exact attention to his duties, and by a sincere desire not to be a useless or embarrassing member of it. The sentiments of probity enter as much into the mechanical constitution of the philosopher as the illumination of the mind. The more you find reason in a man, the more you find in him probity. On the other hand, where fanaticism and superstition reign, there reign the passions and anger. The temperament of the philosopher is to act according to the spirit of order or reason; as he loves society extremely, it is more important to him than to other men to bend every effort to produce only effects conformable to the idea of the honest man. . . .

This love of society, so essential to the philosopher, makes us see how very true was the remark of Marcus Aurelius: "How happy will the people be when kings are philosophers or philosophers are kings!"

LA CHALOTAIS: *Essay on National Education* *

Louis-René de Caradeuc de la Chalotais (1701–85) was, throughout his life, an intrepid opponent of Church and State in France. In his capacity

* From *French Liberalism and Education in the Eighteenth Century* by Francois de la Fontainerie. Copyright, 1932. Courtesy of McGraw-Hill Book Co. Pp. 53, 69–70, 73–4, 81, 83, 90–3, 112–13, 128–30, 132–3, 136, 143–5, 149–50.

as attorney-general of the Parlement of Brittany, he demanded the suppression of the Jesuits and frequently defied the authority of the crown, thus helping to sow the whirlwind. He was incarcerated and exiled by Louis XV but pardoned by Louis XVI. His *Essay on National Education* was one of many educational treatises in the eighteenth century, appearing in 1763, just one year after Rousseau's *Emile*.

General Principles

I CLAIM the right to demand for the Nation an education that will depend upon the State alone; because it belongs essentially to it, because every nation has an inalienable and imprescriptible right to instruct its members, and finally because the children of the State should be educated by members of the State.

* * *

The principles to be observed in teaching children should be the same as those by which Nature itself teaches them. Nature is the best of teachers.

It suffices then to observe how the first knowledge enters the minds of children and how grown men themselves acquire it.

Experience—against which it is vain to philosophize—teaches us that we possess at birth only an empty capacity which gradually fills itself, and that there are no other channels than sensation and reflection by which ideas can enter the mind.

It seems certain that man begins to acquire knowledge only when he begins to make use of his senses: his first sensation is his first knowledge.

Children are no more capable than older people of reflection other than by means of acquired ideas. Abstract ideas presuppose in the mind knowledge with which they may connect; they are called abstract only because they are derived from particular ideas. They must, consequently, be preceded in the order of teaching by particular ideas; just as in the order of Nature. You would never be able to make a person understand that the whole is greater than any part of it, unless he already had an idea of what is a part and what is a whole.

Thus the fundamental principle of every good method is to begin with what is perceptible, and proceed by degrees to what is intellectual; to attain what is complex by means of what is simple, and to make sure of facts before seeking causes.

* * *

All that needs to be known is not contained in books. There are a thousand things about which it is possible to learn by conversation, by usage and by practice; but only minds that are already somewhat trained can profit by this sort of instruction. Man is made for action, and he studies only in order to render himself capable of acting.

Almost all our philosophy and education can be expressed in these few words: it is the things themselves that it is important to know. Let us return to the true and the real; for in itself truth is nothing other than what is, what exists, and in our minds it is only the knowledge of existing things.

Such an aim is certainly more correct, and the way to it is straighter than the winding path by which the young people attain only the knowledge of words or of abstractions.

History

I should like to see composed for their use histories of every nation, of every century, and, above all, of the last centuries. I should wish the latter to be more detailed, and that they be read before the histories of more remote ages. I should also wish that the lives of famous men of all sorts be written, of men of all conditions and all professions: heroes, scholars, celebrated women and children, etc., and that vivid pictures be presented of great events, of memorable examples of vice or of virtue, of misfortune or of prosperity, etc. . . .

These histories and collections, in order to be useful, should be prepared by philosophers.

Natural Science and Mechanics

Nobody expects mechanics to be taught to children; but they cannot be accustomed too soon to observing simple machines which produce and facilitate motion, to noticing the perceptible effects of the lever, of wheels, of pulleys, of the screw, of the wedge and of balances. . . .

There is a rather imperfect book which has the title: *Description abrégée des principaux Arts & Métiers, & des instruments qui leur sont propres, le tout détaillé par figures*. The Academy is having printed a description of the arts. It is one of the most beautiful monuments that the present generation could leave to posterity.

Is it beyond the capacity of children to look over these books, to draw some of the figures contained in them? Would it be impossible to have in a college a room in which would be kept some iron or wooden models of machines? If there were in this room some cases containing objects pertaining to natural history, would not the children ask eagerly to see them? They would stroll around, they would be active and they would acquire knowledge at the same time. . . .

Would it be useless for them to know that the earth in its journey around the sun goes more than six hundred thousand leagues in an hour, or four hundred and sixteen in a minute; that a ball shot from a cannon would go at the rate of two thousand six hundred leagues in twenty-four hours, and thus the earth goes one hundred and fifty times as fast as a ball shot from a cannon?

Once again I ask, would there be any disadvantage in striking the minds of children with admiration and astonishment by the infinitely great and the infinitely small?

What an idea would this not give of the Being who has created everything! Would it be necessary to ask them, no matter what be their age, *Quis est qui creavit haec?*

Would it be necessary, after this knowledge had been for a long time inculcated, to prepare them to understand the weight of air, its elasticity, all the phenomena which physical science describes and all those which chemistry discovers? Would there be any danger in showing them that meat upon which flies deposit their eggs becomes wormy, whereas that upon which they do not deposit them does not become so?

Would not this fact, which their eyes could witness, lead them to think that everything is organized and has its germ? Would they not naturally conclude that a mushroom is the work of the wisdom of God, just as the world is?

Are there in the books of spiritual exercises reflections more pious than those that result from these observations and these experiments?

* * *

To learn to read, to write and to handle the pencil is the occupation of the first period; to learn to read well, to pronounce well, to write well and to define well is that of the second. I include always music, history, geography, mathematics, natural history and literature.

It is then that should be begun the study of Nature from Nature itself, and the study of the arts and manufactures in the workshops. It is then that to the facts of history which were learned in early childhood, should be added the general history of nations, and, what is no less useful, the history of the sciences and, above all, of the arts which are most closely connected with our needs.

To initiate the young people into the knowledge of these precious arts, it would be enough to show them the simplest machines, which it would afford them great pleasure to take apart and put together again. I am convinced that in proceeding by degrees it would be possible to succeed in making a child of twelve put together all the works of a clock or the springs of any other machine, and, consequently, make him understand its mechanism. Most of them require only eyes and a plan together with some knowledge of geometry. Several articles on the arts, in the *Encyclopédie* are masterpieces, and what there is about physics and the arts in the *Spectacle de la Nature* is excellent, but the dialogue is often poor. It would be desirable that some able members of the Academy should assume the task of preparing the elementary books which would be needed. . . .

Rules of Logic

One of the principal rules, and at the same time one which would remedy one of these defects, is to reject the suppositions of all systems of philosophy which are employed to explain things for which it would otherwise be impossible to account; to pronounce judgment only concerning things which are within our comprehension, concerning which we possess acquired knowledge, positive elements. When we do not possess these elements, or not enough of them to judge, reason requires that we suspend judgment.

The second rule, which is equally important to prevent the abuse of abstractions, is to fix and determine the ideas. The means of doing this is to reduce abstract and complex ideas to particular and simple ones, or to the elements which compose them. This is what is called to define; for definition is only the enumeration of the simple ideas comprised in a complex and abstract idea. . . .

The third rule is to make sure of facts before seeking causes, if we do not wish, as has often been said, to expose ourselves to ridicule by finding the reason for what does not exist. . . .

Metaphysics

Logic and criticism are instruments for learning to think. Metaphysics is the science of principles. It teaches us about the aims to which the faculties of man are directed, about their extent, their limitations and their use. It pertains to this science alone to determine what is truth, in what error consists, and what are the means of avoiding the latter. It shows by experience that everything reduces itself to sense perceptions, to immediate knowledge. With logic, it teaches us to discover truths, to deduce them from their veritable principles, to arrange them in order. In short it is the basis of all knowledge, of which it contains the term and the outline.

It demonstrates the existence of God and His attributes, and it justifies His providence. It establishes human liberty, natural laws and the immortality of the soul.

It reveals the weakness of the human mind; but it appreciates its strength. It proves that their reason is the sole natural means that the Author of their being has given to men to guide them, that all that is intelligible is in its province, that nothing is foreign to it but that which is incomprehensible, that it pertains to it to determine the nature and limits of authority, and, consequently, to indicate the cases and matters for submission, to weigh the motives for belief. It proves that to believe is to judge that reason obliges us to recognize, on the strength of external proofs, the existence or the properties of a being or an object, that thus it is its function to regulate the limits between itself and faith; because it precedes, accompanies and follows always a rational submission. . . .

The Spirit of Philosophy

From the continual practice of an exact logic and a good criticism founded upon the solid principles of an enlightened metaphysics, would result a spirit of philosophy.

This spirit of enlightenment is useful in everything, applicable to everything, and derives everything from its principles independently of opinions and customs.

The spirit of philosophy is different from philosophy, and is as superior to it as the spirit of geometry is to geometry or as the spirit of the laws is above the knowledge of the laws. It is the product and the aim of philosophy, which recognizes and discusses particular truths; whereas the spirit of philosophy appreciates them all.

Philosophy is a science; the spirit of philosophy comprises all the sciences.

Moral Philosophy and Religion

In the schools, moral philosophy is deferred until after the other branches of philosophy, and it has been reduced to a few useless questions of scholastic philosophy. It has been forgotten that of all the sciences, it is the most important, and that it is as susceptible of demonstration as any other.

Rules of conduct have their origin either in sound reason or in divine or human laws. The former dictates natural laws, or ethics properly calléd, which are equally divine and immutable; for the existence of a Divine Law-giver is no less necessary to moral philosophy than the existence of a Divine Creator is to natural philosophy. But the laws of ethics take precedence over all positive laws, both divine and human, and would, consequently, subsist even if these laws had never been declared.

It was true before Moses, and even among all the peoples who were deprived of the light of the Revelation, that we should do as much good and as little evil as possible to our fellow-men. . . .

It is not the written law which has revealed to men the turpitude and the terrible injustice of [foul] deeds. It is, at the same time, a natural as well as a divine law which is written in all hearts, and to which the conscience bears witness, says the Apostle. It is of all centuries, of all countries, of all nations, and, so to say, of all worlds. It is of this law that Cicero says: "It is born with us. We have not received it from our fathers, nor learned it from our teachers, nor read it in our books. We have taken it, derived it, imbibed it from Nature itself. It is a law of which we are not merely aware, but with which we are, so to say, penetrated and imbued."

Would it then be useless to recommend to men moral virtues that even pagans have so highly recommended?

Can there not be, and is there not in fact, a communion of morals even between peoples who differ most in religion? What is it that a Catholic, a Protestant, a Jew and a Mohammedan, who deal and traffic with each other, exact of each other reciprocally?

*   *   *

I have spoken of the moral law which precedes all positive laws, both divine and human. The teaching of the divine law concerns the Church; but the teaching of the moral law belongs to the State, and has always belonged to it. It existed before it was revealed, and, consequently, it does not depend upon Revelation, although it acquires its greatest force and its most powerful motives from its confirmation by Revelation.

Revelation is a fact. The moral law is based entirely upon right.

The distinction between virtue and vice, between right and wrong, as has been said, is derived from reason and from the very nature of things. Love of order cannot be absolutely extinguished in the heart of man, because it is not possible to renounce reason entirely.

Revelation adds supernatural motives. It promises rewards, and it foretells punishments. But even if it foretold neither punishments nor rewards, moral obligation would nevertheless subsist. It would exist even in the false hypothesis of unbelief. Saint Paul and Saint Augustine have said: *The faith and the prophesies will pass away, the intelligence will remain eternally* (I Corinth., ch. 13, v. 8).

It follows thence (according to the Abbé Gédoyn) that morals have been made to depend too much upon Revelation.

SIR JOSHUA REYNOLDS: *Discourses on Painting* *

> The following selections are from the discourses on art which the great English portrait painter, Sir Joshua Reynolds (1723–92), delivered to the students of the Royal Academy. In the third and fourth discourses he outlined the principles of the "grand style" as he conceived it. The seventh discourse dealt with the standards of artistic taste.

IT IS not easy to define in what this great style consists; nor to describe, by words, the proper means of acquiring it, if the mind of the Student should be at all capable of such an acquisition. Could we teach taste or genius by rules, they would be no longer taste and genius. But though there neither are, nor can be, any precise invariable rules for the exercise, or the acquisition, of these great qualities, yet we may truly say, that

* *The Literary Works of Sir Joshua Reynolds*, ed. by H. W. Beechey (London: H. G. Bohn; 1852), vol. I, pp. 332–3, 337–9, 344–5, 363, 414–15, 423–6.

they always operate in proportion to our attention in observing the works of Nature, to our skill in selecting, and to our care in digesting, methodising, and comparing our observations. There are many beauties in our art that seem, at first, to lie without the reach of precept, and yet may easily be reduced to practical principles. Experience is all in all: but it is not every one who profits by experience; and most people err, not so much from want of capacity to find their object, as from not knowing what object to pursue. This great ideal perfection and beauty are not to be sought in the heavens, but upon the earth. They are about us, and upon every side of us. But the power of discovering what is deformed in Nature, or, in other words, what is particular and uncommon, can be acquired only by experience; and the whole beauty and grandeur of the art consists, in my opinion, in being able to get above all singular forms, local customs, particularities, and details of every kind. . . .

When the Artist has by diligent attention acquired a clear and distinct idea of beauty and symmetry; when he has reduced the variety of nature to the abstract idea; his next task will be to become acquainted with the genuine habits of nature, as distinguished from those of fashion. For in the same manner, and on the same principles, as he has acquired the knowledge of the real forms of nature, distinct from accidental deformity, he must endeavour to separate simple chaste nature, from those adventitious, those affected and forced airs or actions, with which she is loaded by modern education. . . .

However the mechanic and ornamental arts may sacrifice to Fashion, she must be entirely excluded from the Art of Painting; the painter must never mistake this capricious challenging for the genuine offspring of nature; he must divest himself of all prejudices in favour of his age or country; he must disregard all local and temporary ornaments, and look only on those general habits which are every where and always the same; he addresses his works to the people of every country and every age, he calls upon posterity to be his spectators, and says, with Zeuxis, *In aeternitatem pingo.* . . .

To avoid this error, however, and to retain the true simplicity of nature, is a task more difficult than at first sight it may appear. The prejudices in favour of the fashions and customs that we have been used to, and which are justly called a second nature, make it too often difficult to distinguish that which is natural from that which is the result of education; they frequently even give a predilection in favour of the artificial mode; and almost every one is apt to be guided by those local prejudices, who has not chastised his mind, and regulated the instability of his affections by the eternal invariable idea of nature.

Here, then, as before, we must have recourse to the Ancients as instructors. It is from a careful study of their works that you will be enabled to attain to the real simplicity of nature. . . .

I have formerly observed that perfect form is produced by leaving out particularities, and retaining only general ideas: I shall now endeavour to show that this principle, which I have proved to be metaphysically just, extends itself to every part of the Art; that it gives what is called the *grand style*, to Invention, to Composition, to Expression, and even to Colouring and Drapery.

Invention, in Painting, does not imply the invention of the subject, for that is commonly supplied by the Poet or Historian. With respect to the choice, no subject can be proper that is not generally interesting. It ought to be either some eminent instance of heroic action or heroic suffering. There must be something, either in the action or in the object, in which men are universally concerned, and which powerfully strikes upon the public sympathy. . . .

On the whole, it seems to me that there is but one presiding principle which regulates and gives stability to every art. The works, whether of poets, painters, moralists, or historians, which are built upon general nature, live for ever; while those which depend for their existence on particular customs and habits, a partial view of nature, or the fluctuation of fashion, can only be coeval with that which first raised them from obscurity. Present time and future may be considered as rivals; and he who solicits the one must expect to be discountenanced by the other.

*   *   *

We will take it for granted, that reason is something invariable, and fixed in the nature of things; and without endeavouring to go back to an account of first principles, which for ever will elude our search, we will conclude, that whatever goes under the name of taste, which we can fairly bring under the dominion of reason, must be considered as equally exempt from change. If, therefore, in the course of this enquiry, we can show that there are rules for the conduct of the artist which are fixed and invariable, it follows of course, that the art of the connoisseur, or, in other words, taste, has likewise invariable principles. . . .

The first idea that occurs in the consideration of what is fixed in art, or in taste, is that presiding principle of which I have so frequently spoken in former discourses,—the general idea of nature. The beginning, the middle, and the end of every thing that is valuable in taste, is comprised in the knowledge of what is truly nature; for whatever notions are not conformable to those of nature, or universal opinion, must be considered as more or less capricious. . . .

I shall now say something on that part of *taste*, which as I have hinted to you before, does not belong so much to the external form of things, but is addressed to the mind, and depends on its original frame, or, to use the expression, the organization of the soul; I mean the imagination and the passions. The principles of these are as invariable as the former, and are to be known and reasoned upon in the same manner, by an appeal to common sense deciding upon the common feelings of mankind. This sense, and these feelings appear to me of equal authority, and equally conclusive. Now this appeal implies a general uniformity and agreement in the minds of men. It would be else an idle and vain endeavour to establish rules of art; it would be pursuing a phantom, to attempt to move affections with which we were entirely unacquainted. We have no reason to suspect there is a greater difference between our minds than between our forms; of which, though there are no two alike, yet there is a general similitude that goes through the whole race of mankind; and those who have cultivated their taste, can distinguish what is beautiful or deformed, or, in other words, what agrees with or deviates from the general idea of nature, in one case, as well as in the other.

The internal fabric of our minds, as well as the external form of our bodies, being nearly uniform; it seems then to follow of course, that as the imagination is incapable of producing any thing originally of itself, and can only vary and combine those ideas with which it is furnished by means of the senses, there will be necessarily an agreement in the imaginations, as in the senses of men. . . .

He therefore who is acquainted with the works which have pleased different ages and different countries, and has formed his opinion on them, has more materials, and more means of knowing what is analogous to the mind of man, than he who is conversant only with the works of his own age or country. What has pleased, and continues to please, is likely to please again: hence are derived the rules of art, and on this immoveable foundation they must ever stand.

2. *Deism and Atheism*

Pierre Bayle: *Historical and Critical Dictionary* *

Pierre Bayle (1647–1706) was the son of a French Huguenot minister. Converted to Roman Catholicism, he soon returned to his father's sect, but in his later life, which he spent in Holland, he became more or less of a freethinker and the foe of religious dogmatism in general. His most famous work, the *Dictionnaire Historique et Critique* (1697), was an enormously popular work in the eighteenth century which found its way into hundreds of private libraries and furnished materials for Voltaire and other *philosophes* in their warfare on organized Chris-

* Pierre Bayle: *An Historical and Critical Dictionary* (London: C. Harper; 1710), vol. II, pp. 1059–62; *Dictionnaire Historique et Critique* (Rotterdam: R. Leers; 1697), vol. I, p. 925. My translation of "Remarque D."

tianity. The following selection is from the scandalous article "David." The text is innocent enough but the footnotes and "remarks" contained inflammable material some of which had to be suppressed in later editions.

David

[IN THE text Bayle says that David was the youngest of the eight sons of Jesse the Bethlehemite, which prompts him to remark in a footnote]: Some modern rabbis say that when David was conceived, his father Jesse did not think that he lay with his wife, but with his servant maid, and thereby they explain the fifth verse of the fifty-first Psalm, wherein David affirms that he was shapen in iniquity, and that his mother conceived him in sin. . . . If the supposition of those rabbis was true, they would have reason to say that Jesse had committed adultery; but on the other side it must be said that he was not guilty of it, if believing honestly that he lay with his wife, he had got his servant maid with child. . . . Those who would adopt the impertinence of the rabbis concerning David's conception might easily admit another impertinent thing, which would be to place David in the number of illustrious bastards. . . .

[In the text Bayle says that King Saul asked his general, when he saw David go forth to fight Goliath, "Whose son is this youth?", upon which Bayle remarks in a footnote:] It is somewhat strange that Saul did not know David that day since this young man had played several times on his musical instruments before him, in order to disperse the black vapors that tormented him. If such a narrative as this should be found in Thucydides or Titus Livy, all the critics would unanimously conclude that the transcribers had transposed the pages, forgotten something in one place, repeated something in another, or inserted some additions in the author's work. But no such suspicions ought to be entertained of the Bible. Nevertheless some have been so bold as to pretend that all the chapters, or all the verses of the first book of Samuel, are not placed as they were at first. . . .

[In the text Bayle says that David was a holy son of the Church, over which he spread, by his works, a wonderful light of consolation and piety. "But he had his faults," which prompts Bayle to remark in a footnote:] The numbering of the people was a thing which God looked upon as a great sin. His love for the wife of Uriah, and the orders he gave to cause the same Uriah to be killed, are two very heinous crimes; but he expiated them by such an admirable repentance, that this passage of his life does not a little contribute to the instruction and edification of faithful souls. It teaches us the frailty of the saints; and it is a precept of vigilance: we learn thereby how to bewail our sins, and it is a very fine model. As to the remarks which certain critics would like to make in order to show that in other actions of his life he merits great blame, I suppress them in this edition [1702], all the more agreeably because some persons a great deal more learned than I in this sort of thing have assured me that these objections can easily be dismissed if we remember 1. that he was lawful king during the life of Saul; 2. that he had with him the great High Priest who consulted God in order to know what he must do; 3. that the order given to Joshua to exterminate the heathen of Palestine was still in effect; 4. that several other circumstances, taken from Scripture, can convince us of David's innocence in a conduct which, considered in general, looks bad and would be so today.

[In "Remark D" of the 1697 edition, subsequently suppressed, Bayle writes:] David having remained for some time in the capital city of King Akis with his little troop of six hundred warriors, feared to be obligated to this prince and begged him to assign him another residence. Akis designated the town of Siceleg. David transported his warriors there and did not let their swords rust. He often led them on expeditions and killed without pity men and women: he left only the animals alive and they were the only booty with which he returned. He was afraid that prisoners would reveal the mystery to King Akis; that is why he did not bring any back but wiped out both sexes. The mystery which he did not wish to be revealed was that these ravages were made, not on the lands of the Israelites, as he caused the king of Gath to believe, but on the lands of the ancient peoples of Palestine.

Frankly, this conduct was very bad; in order to cover up one fault, he committed a greater. He deceived a king to whom he was under obligation, and he exercised a prodigious cruelty to hide this trickery. If David had been asked: "By what authority do you do these things," what could he have answered? A private person like him, a fugitive who finds an asylum in the land of a neighbouring prince, is he in the right in committing hostilities on his own account, and without a commission from the sovereign of the country? Did David have such a commission? Did he not act contrary both to the intentions and interests of the king of Gath? Certainly if today a private person, no matter what his origin, conducted himself as David did in this case, he could not avoid acquiring a bad reputation. I know that the most illustrious heroes and most famous prophets of the Old Testament sometimes approved putting to the sword everything living; and for that reason if David had been authorized by the orders of some prophet, or if God had inspired him to behave thus, I would beware of calling what he did inhumanity: but it manifestly appears by the silence of the Scriptures that he did everything on his own authority. . . .

VOLTAIRE: *Philosophical Dictionary* *

Voltaire was at his satirical best in his *Dictionnaire philosophique* (begun in 1752, first published anonymously in 1764, and afterwards revised and expanded) in which he aimed to crush ecclesiastical orthodoxy ("Crush the Infamous Thing") and to outline his own theistic or deistic religious position.

Abbé

"WHERE are you going, *Monsieur l'Abbé?*" etc. Do you know that the word Abbé means *Father?* If you become a father you do a service to the state; surely you do the best work a man can do: you cause the birth of a thinking being. There is something divine in this act. But if you are *Monsieur l'Abbé* merely because you like your head shaved, wear a small collar, a short cloak, and to wait for a benefice, you don't deserve the name of Abbé.

The ancient monks gave this name to the superior they elected. The Abbé was their spiritual father. What different things do the same names mean at different times! The spiritual Abbé was a poor man at the head of several other poor men: but the poor spiritual fathers have since got incomes of two hundred, four hundred thousand francs, and today there are poor fathers in Germany who have a regiment of guards.

A poor man taking a vow of poverty and consequently becoming a sovereign! I have already said it; I must say it again a thousand times: this is intolerable. The laws protest against this abuse, religion is indignant at it, and the really poor who lack food and clothing cry to heaven at the door of *Monsieur l'Abbé*.

But I hear the abbés of Italy, Germany, Flanders, and Burgundy say: "Why shouldn't we accumulate wealth and honors, why shouldn't we become princes? After all, the bishops are. They were once poor like us; they have enriched themselves, they have elevated themselves; one of them has even become superior to kings; let us imitate them as much as we can."

Gentlemen, you are right. Overrun the land; it belongs to the strong man, or the clever who seize it. You have profited from times of ignorance, superstition, and insanity to despoil us of our inheritance and trample us under your feet, that you might fatten on the substance of the unfortunate. But tremble, lest the day of reason arrive.

* Voltaire: *Philosophical Dictionary*, trans. Peter Gay, Vol. I, pp. 57–8, 103–5, 240–1, 275; Vol. II, pp. 392–3, 418–19, 479–80, 495–6. Copyright 1962 by Basic Books, Inc. Reprinted by permission of Basic Books, Inc.

Atheist, Atheism

I should want no dealings with an atheist prince, whose interest it would be to have me pounded in a mortar: I am quite sure that I would be pounded. If I were sovereign, I should want no dealing with atheist courtiers, whose interest it would be to poison me: I should need to take an antidote every day at random. Hence it is absolutely necessary for princes and people to have profoundly engraved on their minds the idea of a supreme Being, creator, governor, rewarder, and avenger. . . .

What conclusion shall we draw from all this? That atheism is a most monstrous evil in those who govern; that it is the same in councilors, even though their lives be innocent, since they may influence men who hold office; that even though it is less disastrous than fanaticism, it is almost always fatal to virtue. Above all, let us add that there are fewer atheists today than ever, since philosophers have recognized that there is no vegetative being without germ, no germ without design, etc., and that pure grain does not come from rottenness.

Unphilosophical geometers have rejected final causes, but true philosophers accept them; and, as a well-known author has said, a catechist announces God to children, and Newton demonstrates him to the wise.

If there are atheists, who is responsible but the mercenary tyrants of souls who, as they provoke us against themselves with their impostures, compel some feeble spirits to deny the God whom these monsters dishonor? How often have the people's bloodsuckers driven the over-burdened citizens even to revolt against the king!

Men fattened on our substance cry out to us, "Be convinced that a she-ass spoke; believe that a fish swallowed a man and threw him up three days later safe and sound on the shore; don't doubt that the God of the universe ordered one Jewish prophet to eat shit (Ezekiel) and another prophet to buy two prostitutes and have children by them (Hosea)." These are the very words which they have the God of purity and truth pronounce: "Believe a hundred things either manifestly abominable or mathematically impossible: otherwise the God of mercy will burn you in the fires of hell, not only for millions of billions of centuries, but for all eternity, whether you have a body or whether you don't."

These unbelievable stupidities are revolting to feeble and rash minds as well as to firm and wise ones. The former say: "If our teachers portray God to us as the most senseless and the most barbarous of all beings, there is no God"; but they should say: "Since our teachers attribute to God their absurdities and rages, therefore God is the opposite of what they proclaim, therefore God is as wise and as good as they say he is mad and evil." That is what the wise conclude. But if a fanatic hears them, he denounces them to a magistrate, a sergeant of priests, and this sergeant has them burned on a slow fire, thinking that he is avenging and imitating the Divine Majesty, which he insults.

Divinity of Jesus

The Socinians, who are considered blasphemers, don't recognize the divinity of Jesus Christ. They dare to maintain, with the philosophers of antiquity, with the Jews, the Mohammedans, and so many other nations, that the idea of a God-man is monstrous, that the distance between a God and man is infinite, and that it is impossible for the infinite, immense, eternal Being to have been contained in a perishable body.

They have the effrontery to cite Eusebius, bishop of Caesarea, in support of their view. In his *Ecclesiastical History,* book I, chapter 11, he declares that it is absurd that the unbegotten, immutable nature of almighty God should take the form of a man. They cite the Church Fathers Justin and Tertullian, who said the same thing: Justin in his Dialogue with Tryphon, and Tertullian in his Discourse against Praxeas.

They cite St. Paul, who never calls Jesus Christ God, and who very often calls him man. They push audacity to the point of maintaining that the Christians spent three entire centuries inventing the apotheosis of Jesus, bit by bit, and that they raised this astonishing edifice only in imitation of the pagans, who had deified mortals. According to them, Jesus was at first regarded merely as a man inspired by God; later, as a creature more perfect than others. Some time later, as St. Paul says, he was given a place above the angels. He became an emanation of God manifested in time. This was not enough; they had him born before time itself. Finally, he was made God, consubstantial with God.

Crellius, Voquelsius, Alexander Natalis, Hornebeck, have supported all these blasphemies with arguments that astound the wise and pervert the feeble. It was Faustus Socinus above all who spread the seeds of this doctrine through Europe; and at the end of the sixteenth century it almost established a new Christian sect of which there were already more than three hundred brands.

Faith

What is faith? Is it to believe what appears quite evident? No: it is evident to me that there is a Being, necessary, eternal, supreme, intelligent; this is not a matter of faith, but of reason. I deserve no credit for thinking that this eternal, infinite Being, which I perceive as virtue and goodness itself, wishes me to be good and virtuous. Faith consists in believing, not what seems true, but what seems false to our understanding. By faith alone can the Asiatics believe in the journey of Mahomet to the seven planets, the incarnations of the god Fo, of Vishnu, of Xaca, of Brahma, of Sammonocodom, etc., etc., etc. They subordinate their understanding, they fear to investigate, they want neither to be impaled nor burned; they say: "I believe."

Miracles

A miracle, according to the real meaning of the word, is something admirable. Then everything is a miracle. The marvelous order of nature, the rotation of a hundred million globes around a million suns, the activity of light, the life of animals—these are perpetual miracles.

According to accepted notions, we call *miracle* the violation of these divine and eternal laws. Let there be an eclipse of the sun during a full moon, let a dead man walk five miles carrying his head in his arms, and we'll call that a miracle.

Some natural scientists maintain that there are no miracles in this sense of the word; and here are their arguments.

A miracle is the violation of mathematical, divine, immutable, eternal laws. By this very statement, a miracle is a contradiction in terms. A law cannot be immutable and violable at the same time. But, they may be asked, can't a law be suspended by its author, since it was established by God himself? They have the insolence to answer, No, that it is impossible for the infinitely wise Being to make laws in order to violate them. They say that he might unsettle his machine, but only to make it go better; however, it is clear that, being God, he made this immense machine as best he could: if he had seen some imperfections resulting from the nature of the material, he would have attended to that in the beginning; so he will never change anything in it.

Moreover, God cannot do anything without reason; now what reason could make him temporarily disfigure his own work?

For the sake of men, they will be told. Then, they reply, it would be at least for the sake of all men; for it is impossible to conceive Divine Nature working for some men in particular, and not for the whole human race; and even the human race is quite unimportant; it is much less than a small anthill in comparison with all the beings that fill infinity. Now isn't it the most absurd piece of folly to imagine that the infinite Being would reverse the eternal working of the immense activity which makes the whole universe move, all for the sake of three or four hundred ants on this little mud pile?

But let's suppose that God had wanted to single out a small number of men by special favors: would he need to change what he had established for all times and places? Surely he has no need for this change, this inconstancy, to favor his creatures: his favors are in his very laws. He has foreseen everything, arranged everything, for them; all obey irrevocably the force that he has impressed on nature forever.

Why should God perform a miracle? To realize a certain plan concerning a few living beings! He would then be saying: "I could not complete a certain plan, with the universe ordered as it now is according to my divine decrees, my eternal laws; I am going to change my eternal ideas, my immutable laws, to try to execute what I could not do with them." This would be an admission of his weakness, not his power. It would seem to be the most inconceivable contradiction in him. Therefore, to dare palm off miracles on God is really to insult him (if men can insult God); it's to tell him: "You are a weak and inconsistent being." It is therefore absurd to believe in miracles—in one way or another it dishonors Divinity.

Persecution

What is a persecutor? He is a man whose wounded pride and insane fanaticism stir up the princes or the magistrates against innocent men whose sole crime is their failure to agree with him. "Impudent fellow! You worship a God, you preach virtue, and you practice it; you have served men, and you have comforted them; you have settled the orphan, you have aided the poor; you have transformed the desert in which a few slaves dragged out a miserable life into fertile lands populated with happy families; but I have discovered that you despise me, and that you have never read my book of controversy; you know that I'm a rascal, that I forged the hand-writing of G***, that I robbed the ****; you might well reveal it; I must forestall you. So I'll go to the confessor of the prime minister, or the Podesta; I will show them, bending my head and twisting my mouth, that you have an erroneous opinion about the cells in which the seventy translators of the Septuagint were locked up; that ten years ago you even spoke rather disrespectfully about Tobias' dog, which you maintained was a spaniel while I'll prove to you that it was a greyhound; I'll denounce you as the enemy of God and men." Such is the language of the persecutor; and if these words don't exactly issue from his mouth, they are engraved in his heart with the cutting edge of fanaticism dipped in the gall of envy.

That's how the Jesuit Le Tellier dared to persecute cardinal de Noailles, and Jurieu persecuted Bayle.

When the Protestants in France began to be persecuted, Francis I, Henri II, and Francis II did not lie in wait for them, did not arm themselves with premeditated madness, and did not deliver these unfortunates to the flames to exercise vengeance on them. Francis I was too busy with the duchess d'Etampes, Henri II with his old Diane, and Francis II was too young. Who started these persecutions? Jealous priests, who fortified the prejudices of the magistrates and the policies of the ministers.

If the kings hadn't been deceived, if they had foreseen that persecution would produce fifty years of civil war, and that one half of the nation would be exterminated by the other, they would have put out with their tears the first stakes they allowed to be lighted.

O God of mercy! If any man resembles the malignant being who is portrayed as ceaselessly occupied with destroying your works, isn't it the persecutor?

Theist

The theist is a man firmly convinced of the existence of a supreme Being, as good as it is powerful, which has created all the extended, vegetating, feeling, and reflecting beings; which perpetuates their species, which punishes crimes without cruelty, and rewards virtuous actions with kindness.

The theist does not know how God punishes, how he protects, how he forgives; for he is not rash enough to flatter himself that he knows how God acts; but he knows that God does act and that he is just. The difficulties in the notion of Providence do not shake him in his faith, because they are only great difficulties and not disproofs; he submits himself to this Providence, although he merely perceives some of its effects and externals; and, judging things he does not see by the things he does see, he thinks that this Providence reaches into every place and time.

United in this principle with the rest of the universe, he does not embrace any of the sects, which all contradict one another. His religion is the most ancient and the most widespread; for the simple worship of God preceded all the systems of the world. He speaks a language all nations understand, while they don't understand each other. He has brothers from Peking to Cayenne and counts all sages among his brothers. He believes that religion consists neither in the opinions of an unintelligible metaphysics nor in vain display, but in worship and in justice. To do good—that is his worship; to submit to God—that is his doctrine. The Mahometan exclaims to him: "Take care if you don't make the pilgrimage to Mecca!" "Woe to you," a Franciscan tells him, "if you don't make a voyage to Our Lady of Loretto!" He laughs at Loretto and Mecca; but he helps the needy and he defends the oppressed.

Virtue

What is virtue? Doing good to your neighbor. . . .

What, you admit as virtues only those useful to your neighbor? Well, but how can I admit any others? We live in society; therefore nothing is truly good for us that isn't good for society. A hermit is sober and pious; he dresses in a hair shirt: all right, he is a saint; but I shall call him virtuous only when he performs some act of virtue from which other men benefit. . . . Virtue among men is a trade of kindnesses; the one who takes no part in this trade should not be counted. If this saint were in the world, he would doubtless do good there; but as long as he is not, the world will have good reason not to call him virtuous.

DAVID HUME: *On Miracles* *

David Hume (1711–76), the Scottish philosopher, is best known as the sceptic who undermined the principles of the Enlightenment. In his chief philosophical work, the *Treatise of Human Nature*, he denied that belief could be rationally grounded. But he argued like any *philosophe* in his attack on traditional religion. The following selection is from the famous chapter "Of Miracles" in the *Inquiry into Human Understanding* (1748).

I FLATTER myself that I have discovered an argument . . . , which, if just, will, with the wise and learned, be an everlasting check to all kinds of superstitious delusion, and consequently will be useful as long as the world endures; for so long, I presume, will the accounts of miracles and prodigies be found in all history, sacred and profane. . . .

A wise man proportions his belief to the evidence. . . .

A miracle is a violation of the laws of nature; and as a firm and unalterable experience has established these laws, the proof against a miracle, from the very nature of the fact, is as entire as any argument from experience can possibly be imagined. . . . Nothing is esteemed a miracle, if it ever happen in the common course of nature. It is no miracle that a man, seemingly in good health, should die on a sudden; because such a kind of death, though more unusual than any other, has yet been frequently observed to happen. But it is a miracle that a dead man should come to life; because that has never been observed in any age or country. There must, therefore, be an uniform experience against every miraculous event, otherwise the event would not merit that appellation. And as an uniform experience amounts to a proof, there is here a direct and full *proof*, from the nature of the fact, against the existence of any miracle. . . .

[Further] there is not to be found, in all history, any miracle attested by a sufficient number of men, of such unquestioned good sense, education, and learning, as to secure us against all delusion in themselves; of such undoubted integrity, as to place them beyond all suspicion of any design to deceive others; of such credit and reputation in the eyes of mankind, as to have a great deal to lose in case of their being detected in any falsehood. . . .

* *The Philosophical Works of David Hume* (Edinburgh: A. Black & W. Tait; 1826), vol. IV, pp. 128–9, 133–8, 141–2, 150.

Secondly, We may observe in human nature a principle which, if strictly examined, will be found to diminish extremely the assurance, which we might, from human testimony, have in any kind of prodigy. . . . The passion of *surprise* and *wonder,* arising from miracles, being an agreeable emotion, gives a sensible tendency towards the belief of those events from which it is derived. . . .

With what greediness are the miraculous accounts of travellers received, their descriptions of sea and land monsters, their relations of wonderful adventures, strange men, and uncouth manners? But if the spirit of religion join itself to the love of wonder, there is an end of common sense; and human testimony, in these circumstances, loses all pretensions to authority. A religionist may be an enthusiast, and imagine he sees what has no reality: He may know his narrative to be false, and yet persevere in it, with the best intentions in the world, for the sake of promoting so holy a cause: Or even where this delusion has not place, vanity, excited by so strong a temptation, operates on him more powerfully than on the rest of mankind in any other circumstances; and self-interest with equal force. . . .

The many instances of forged miracles and prophecies and supernatural events, which, in all ages, have either been detected by contrary evidence, or which detect themselves by their absurdity, prove sufficiently the strong propensity of mankind to the extraordinary and marvellous, and ought reasonably to beget a suspicion against all relations of this kind. . . .

Thirdly, It forms a strong presumption against all supernatural and miraculous relations, that they are observed chiefly to abound among ignorant and barbarous nations; or if a civilized people has ever given admission to any of them, that people will be found to have received them from ignorant and barbarous ancestors, who transmitted them with that inviolable sanction and authority which always attend received opinions. . . .

I may add, as a *fourth* reason, which diminishes the authority of prodigies, that there is no testimony for any, even those which have not been expressly detected, that is not opposed by any infinite number of witnesses; so that not only the miracle destroys the credit of testimony, but the testimony destroys itself. To make this the better understood, let us consider, that in matters of religion, whatever is different is contrary; and that it is impossible the religions of ancient Rome, of Turkey, of Siam, and of China, should all of them be established on any solid foundation. Every miracle, therefore, pretended to have been wrought in any of these religions, (and all of them abound in miracles), as its direct scope is to establish the particular system to which it is attributed; so has it the same force, though more indirectly, to overthrow every other system. In destroying a rival system, it likewise destroys the credit of those miracles on which that system was established, so that all the prodigies of different religions are to be regarded as contrary facts, and the evidences of these prodigies, whether weak or strong, as opposite to each other. . . .

Upon the whole, then, it appears, that no testimony for any kind of miracle has ever amounted to a probability, much less to a proof; and that, even supposing it amounted to a proof, it would be opposed by another proof, derived from the very nature of the fact which it would endeavour to establish. It is experience only which gives authority to human testimony; and it is the same experience which assures us of the laws of nature. When, therefore, these two kinds of experience are contrary, we have nothing to do but to subtract the one from the other, and embrace an opinion either on one side or the other, with that assurance which arises from the remainder. But according to the principle here explained, this subtraction with regard to all popular religions amounts to an entire annihilation; and therefore we may establish it as a maxim, that no human testimony can have such force as to prove a miracle, and make it a just foundation for any such system of religion.

BARON D'HOLBACH: *On Theology and Morality* *

> Baron d'Holbach (1723–89) was a German nobleman from the Palatinate who assumed French citizenship and married into a French family. He wrote scientific articles for the *Encyclopedia* and befriended and lent assistance to the *philosophes*. He was dubbed "personal enemy of God" for his atheism, and his *Système de la Nature*, published under a pseudonym in 1770, was called the "Bible of materialism." The reader should compare the following excerpts from this book with the excerpts from the same book in the succeeding section on Nature.

The Immortality of the Soul

THE MOST simple reflection upon the nature of his soul, ought to convince man that the idea of its immortality is only an illusion of the brain. Indeed, what is his soul, save the principle of sensibility? What is it to think, to enjoy, to suffer; is it not to feel? What is life, except it be the assemblage of modifications, the congregation of motion, peculiar to an organized being? Thus, as soon as the body ceases to live, its sensibility can no longer exercise itself; therefore it can no longer have ideas, nor in consequence thoughts. Ideas, as we have proved, can only reach man through his senses; now, how will they have it, that once

* Baron d'Holbach: *The System of Nature*, trans. by H. D. Robinson (Boston: J. P. Mendum; 1853), pp. 118–19, 263, 265, 280–81.

deprived of his senses, he is yet capable of receiving sensations, of having perceptions, of forming ideas? As they have made the soul of man a being separated from the animated body, wherefore have they not made life a being distinguished from the living body? Life in a body is the totality of its motion; feeling and thought make a part of this motion; thus, in the dead man, these motions will cease like all the others. . . .

An organized being may be compared to a clock, which, once broken, is no longer suitable to the use for which it was designed. To say, that the soul shall feel, shall think, shall enjoy, shall suffer, after the death of the body, is to pretend, that a clock, shivered into a thousand pieces, will continue to strike the hour, and have the faculty of marking the progress of time. Those who say, that the soul of man is able to subsist notwithstanding the destruction of the body, evidently support the position, that the modification of a body will be enabled to conserve itself, after the subject is destroyed: but this is completely absurd.

Theological and Natural Morality

We have hitherto seen the slender foundation of those ideas which men form to themselves of the Divinity; the little solidity there is in the proofs by which they suppose his existence: the want of harmony in the opinions they have formed of this being, equally impossible to be known to the inhabitants of the earth: we have shown the incompatibility of those attributes which theology assigns to him: we have proved that this being, whose name alone has the power of inspiring fear, is nothing but the shapeless fruit of ignorance, of an alarmed imagination, of enthusiasm, of melancholy: we have shown that the notions which men have formed of him, only date their origin from the prejudices of their infancy, transmitted by education, strengthened by habit, nourished by fear, maintained and perpetuated by authority. In short, every thing must have convinced us, that the idea of God so generally diffused over the earth, is no more than a universal errour of the human species. It remains now to examine if this errour be useful. . . .

Plato has said, that *virtue consisted in resembling God*. But where shall we find this God whom man ought to resemble? Is it in nature? Alas! he who is supposed to be the mover of it, diffuses indifferently over the human race great evils and great benefits; he is frequently unjust to the purest souls; he accords the greatest favours to the most perverse mortals; and if, as we are assured, he must show himself one day more equitable, we shall be obliged to wait for that time to regulate our conduct upon his own.

Shall it be in the revealed religions, that we shall draw up our ideas of virtue? Alas! do they not all appear to be in accord in announcing a despotic, jealous, vindictive, and selfish God, who knows no law, who follows his caprice in every thing, who loves or who hates, who chooses or reproves, according to his whim; who acts irrationally, who delights in carnage, rapine, and crime; who plays with his feeble subjects, who overloads them with puerile laws, who lays continual snares for them, who rigorously prohibits them from consulting their reason? What would become of morality, if men proposed to themselves such Gods for models.

It is, however, some Divinity of this temper which all nations adore. Thus, we see it is in consequence of these principles, that religion, in all countries, far from being favourable to morality, shakes it and annihilates it. It divides men in the room of uniting them; in the place of loving each other, and lending mutual succours one to the other, they dispute with each other, they despise each other, they hate each other, they persecute each other, and they frequently cut each others' throats for opinions equally irrational: the slightest difference in their religious notions, renders them from that moment enemies, separates their interests, and sets them into continual quarrels.

*   *   *

Every thing that has been advanced, evidently proves, that religious morality is an infinite loser, when compared with the morality of nature, with which it is found in perpetual contradiction. Nature invites man to love himself, to preserve himself, to incessantly augment the sum of his happiness: religion orders him to love only a formidable God, that deserves to be hated; to detest himself, to sacrifice to his frightful idol the most pleasing and legitimate pleasures of his heart. Nature tells man to consult reason, and to take it for his guide: religion teaches him that his reason is corrupted, that it is only a treacherous guide, given by a deceitful God to lead his creatures astray. Nature tells man to enlighten himself, to search after truth, to instruct himself in his duties: religion enjoins him to examine nothing, to remain in ignorance, to fear truth; it persuades him, that there are no relations more important than those which subsist between him and a being of whom he will never have any knowledge. Nature tells the being who is in love with his welfare, to moderate his passions, to resist them when they are destructive to himself, to counterbalance them by real motives borrowed from experience: religion tells the sensible being to have no passions, to be an insensible mass, or to combat his propensities by motives borrowed from the imagination, and variable as itself. Nature tells man to be sociable, to love his fellow-creatures, to be just, peaceable, indulgent, and benevolent, to cause or suffer his associates to enjoy their opinions: religion counsels him to fly society, to detach himself from his fellow-creatures, to hate them, when their imagination does not procure them dreams conformable to his own, to break the most sacred bonds to please his God, to torment, to afflict, to persecute, and to massacre those who will not be mad after his own manner. Nature tells man in society to cherish glory, to labour to render himself estimable, to be active, courageous, and industrious: religion tells him to be humble, abject, pusillanimous, to live in obscurity, to occupy himself with prayers, with meditations, and with ceremonies; it says to him, be useful to thyself, and do nothing for others. Nature proposes to the citizen for a model, men endued with honest, noble, energetic souls, who have usefully served their fellow-citizens; religion commends to them abject souls, extols pious enthusiasts, frantic penitents, fanatics, who, for the most ridiculous opinions, have disturbed empires. . . . Nature says to the philosopher, occupy thyself with useful objects, consecrate thy cares to thy country, make for it advantageous discoveries, calculated to perfectionate its condition: religion says to him, occupy thyself with useless reveries, with endless disputes, with researches suitable to sow the seeds of discord and carnage, and obstinately maintain opinions, which thou wilt never understand thyself. . . .

The citizen, or the man in society, is not less depraved by religion, which is always in contradiction with sound politics. Nature says to man, *thou art free, no power on earth can legitimately deprive thee of thy rights:* religion cries out to him, that he is a slave, condemned by his God to groan all his life under the iron rod of his representatives. Nature tells man to *love the country which gave him birth*, to serve it faithfully, to blend his interests with it against all those who shall attempt to injure it: religion orders him to obey, without murmuring, the tyrants who oppress his country, to serve them against it, to merit their favours, by enslaving their fellow-citizens, under their unruly caprices. Nevertheless, if the sovereign be not sufficiently devoted to his priests, religion quickly changes its language; it calls upon subjects to become rebels, it makes it a duty in them to resist their master, it cries out to them, that it is better to obey God than man. Nature tells princes they are men; that it is not their whim that can decide what is just, and what is unjust, *that the public will maketh the law:* religion, sometimes says to them, that they are Gods, to whom nothing in this world ought to offer resistance; sometimes it transforms them into tyrants whom enraged Heaven is desirous should be immolated to its wrath.

3. *Nature*

VOLTAIRE: *Newtonian Nature* *

Pierre de Maupertuis (1698–1759), French scientist and president of the Academy of Sciences at Berlin, said that the philosophers of his day formed two sects, one professing to see nature as the work of a divine Creator, the other wishing "to submit nature to an order purely material," excluding all intelligent agents including God, and banishing entirely final causes. Voltaire belonged to the first of these sects, as is shown in the excerpts below from his book of popular science, *Elements of the Philosophy of Newton* (1738). Holbach (see preceding section on Deism and Atheism) belonged to the second or materialist sect, as is shown in his *System of Nature*, also represented below.

THE WHOLE of the philosophy of Newton leads necessarily to the knowledge of a supreme Being, who has created all things, and disposed of them with perfect liberty. For if the universe be finite, or if there be a vacuum, matter exists not by necessity; it has therefore received existence from a freely acting cause. If matter gravitate, as is demonstrable, it does not appear to gravitate of its own nature, in like manner as it is extended of its own nature: it has, therefore, received the power or quality of gravitation from God. If the planets revolve in one direction rather than another, in a non-resisting space, the hand of their Creator must have directed their motions in that direction with an absolute liberty.

It were well if the pretended principles of Descartes conducted the mind in the like manner to the knowledge of its Creator. God forbid that, by the most horrible calumny, I should accuse that great man with despising that God, to whom he owed so much, and who had raised him above almost all the men of the age he lived in. I say only, that the ill use, to which he has sometimes applied his genius, has conducted his disciples to precipices, from which their master was far removed; I say that the Cartesian system has produced that of Spinoza: I say that I have known many whom the Cartesian doctrine have induced to admit no other God than the immensity of things, and on the contrary, that I never saw a Newtonian who was not a theist, in the strictest sense of the word.

When one is persuaded, with Descartes, that it is impossible for the universe to be finite, that the quantity of motion in the universe is ever

* Voltaire: *Works*, trans. by the Rev. David Williams et al (London: Fielding and Walker; 1780), Vol. LXIII, pp. 2–4.

equal and the same; when we presume to say, give me matter and motion and I will form a world; then, it must be confessed that these positions seem, by consequences too just, to exclude that of a Being sole infinite, sole author of motion, and sole author of the organisation of substances.

Many will perhaps be surprised that, of all the proofs of the existence of a God, that which is deduced from final causes should appear the strongest in the eyes of Newton. The design, or rather the designs varied to infinity, which shine forth in the most vast as well as in the most minute parts of the universe, form a demonstration, which, because dependent on sense, is almost despised by some philosophers; but in short, Newton concluded that the infinity of arguments, of which he saw more than any other man, were the work of an infinitely skilful artist. . . .

The atheists have called to their assistance the old axiom, that nothing can produce nothing, that one substance cannot produce another, that every thing is eternal and necessary.

Matter is necessary, said they, because it exists; motion is necessary, and nothing is at rest; and motion is so far necessary, that the moving forces are never lost in nature.

That which exists to day was in being yesterday; by the same argument it existed the day before, and so on; we may recur to an endless precession of days. There is no person as hardy as to say, that things will return to nothing, how then can we presume to say they came from nothing?

No less than the whole book of Clarke [the Boyle Lectures of Dr. Samuel Clarke, *The Being and Attributes of God*, 1704–1705] is necessary to answer these objections.

In a word, I do not know if there be a proof in metaphysics, more striking to the mind of man, than that admirable order that reigns throughout the world, or if there be a more convincing argument than this verse, *the heavens declare the glory of God*. And thus you see that Newton uses no other at the end of his Optics and his Principia. He found no reasoning more convincing and admirable in favour of the Divinity than that of Plato, who makes one of the persons in his dialogues say, You conclude that I have an intelligent soul, because you perceive order in my speech, and actions; believe then from the order you see in the world, that there is a sovereign and intelligent mind.

BARON D'HOLBACH: *A Materialist View of Nature* *

Preface

THE SOURCE of man's unhappiness is his ignorance of Nature. The pertinacity with which he clings to blind opinions imbibed in his infancy, which interweave themselves with his existence, the consequent prejudice that warps his mind, that prevents its expansion, that renders him the slave of fiction, appears to doom him to continual errour. He resembles a child destitute of experience, full of idle notions: a dangerous leaven mixes itself with all his knowledge: it is of necessity obscure, it is vacillating and false:—He takes the tone of his ideas on the authority of others, who are themselves in errour, or else have an interest in deceiving him. To remove this Cimmerian darkness, these barriers to the improvement of his condition; to disentangle him from the clouds of errour that envelop him, that obscure the path he ought to tread; to guide him out of this Cretan labyrinth, requires the clue of Ariadne, with all the love she could bestow on Theseus. It exacts more than common exertion; it needs a most determined, a most undaunted courage— it is never effected but by a persevering resolution to act, to think for himself; to examine with rigour and impartiality the opinions he has adopted. . . .

Man seeks to range out of his sphere: notwithstanding the reiterated checks his ambitious folly experiences, he still attempts the impossible; strives to carry his researches beyond the visible world; and hunts out misery in imaginary regions. He would be a metaphysician before he has become a practical philosopher. He quits the contemplation of realities to meditate on chimeras. He neglects experience to feed on conjecture, to indulge in hypothesis. He dares not cultivate his reason, because from his earliest days he has been taught to consider it criminal. He pretends to know his fate in the indistinct abodes of another life, before he has considered of the means by which he is to render himself happy in the world he inhabits: in short, man disdains the study of Nature, except it be partially. . . .

The most important of our duties, then, is to seek means by which we may destroy delusions that can never do more than mislead us. The remedies for these evils must be sought for in Nature herself; it is only in the abundance of her resources, that we can rationally expect to find antidotes to the mischiefs brought upon us by an ill-directed, by an over-powering enthusiasm. It is time these remedies were sought; it is

* Baron d'Holbach: *The System of Nature*, trans. by H. D. Robinson (Boston: J. P. Mendum; 1853), pp. viii–ix, 12–13, 15, 19–23.

time to look the evil boldly in the face, to examine its foundations, to scrutinize its super-structure: reason, with its faithful guide experience, must attack in their entrenchments those prejudices to which the human race has but too long been the victim. For this purpose reason must be restored to its proper rank,—it must be rescued from the evil company with which it is associated. . . .

Truth speaks not to these perverse beings [the enemies of the human race]:—her voice can only be heard by generous minds accustomed to reflection, whose sensibilities make them lament the numberless calamities showered on the earth by political and religious tyranny—whose enlightened minds contemplate with horrour the immensity, the ponderosity of that series of misfortunes with which errour has in all ages overwhelmed mankind.

Nature

The *civilized man*, is he whom experience and social life have enabled to draw from nature the means of his own happiness; because he has learned to oppose resistance to those impulses he receives from exterior beings, when experience has taught him they would be injurious to his welfare.

The *enlightened man*, is man in his maturity, in his perfection; who is capable of pursuing his own happiness; because he has learned to examine, to think for himself, and not to take that for truth upon the authority of others, which experience has taught him examination will frequently prove erroneous. . . .

It necessarily results, that man in his researches ought always to fall back on experience, and natural philosophy: These are what he should consult in his religion—in his morals—in his legislation—in his political government—in the arts—in the sciences—in his pleasures—in his misfortunes. Experience teaches that Nature acts by simple, uniform, and invariable laws. It is by his senses man is bound to this universal Nature; it is by his senses he must penetrate her secrets; it is from his senses he must draw experience of her laws. Whenever, therefore, he either fails to acquire experience or quits its path, he stumbles into an abyss, his imagination leads him astray. . . .

Man did not understand that Nature, equal in her distributions, entirely destitute of goodness or malice, follows only necessary and immutable laws, when she either produces beings or destroys them, when she causes those to suffer, whose organization creates sensibility; when she scatters among them good and evil; when she subjects them to incessant change—he did not perceive it was in the bosom of Nature herself, that it was in her abundance he ought to seek to satisfy his wants; for remedies against his pains; for the means of rendering himself happy: he expected to derive these benefits from imaginary beings, whom he erroneously imagined to be the authors of his pleasures, the cause of his misfortunes. From hence it is clear that to his ignorance of Nature, man owes the creation of those illusive powers under which he has so long trembled with fear; that superstitious worship, which has been the source of all his misery.

   * * *

  The universe, that vast assemblage of every thing that exists, presents only matter and motion: the whole offers to our contemplation nothing but an immense, an uninterrupted succession of causes and effects; some of these causes are known to us, because they strike immediately on our senses; others are unknown to us, because they act upon us by effects, frequently very remote from their original cause. . . .

  Observation and reflection ought to convince us, that every thing in Nature is in continual motion. . . . Thus, the idea of Nature necessarily includes that of motion. But, it will be asked, from whence did she receive her motion? Our reply is, from herself, since she is the great whole, out of which, consequently, nothing can exist. We say this motion is a manner of existence, that flows, necessarily, out of the essence of matter; that matter moves by its own peculiar energies; that its motion is to be attributed to the force which is inherent in itself; that the variety of motion, and the phenomena which result, proceed from the diversity of the properties, of the qualities, and of the combinations, which are originally found in the primitive matter, of which Nature is the assemblage.

  Natural philosophers, for the most part, have regarded as inanimate, or as deprived of the faculty of motion, those bodies which are only moved by the interposition of some agent, or exterior cause; they have considered themselves justified in concluding, that the matter which constitutes these bodies, is perfectly inert in its nature. They have not relinquished this errour, although they must have observed, that whenever a body is left to itself, or disengaged from those obstacles which oppose themselves to its descent, it has a tendency to fall, or to approach the centre of the earth, by a motion uniformly accelerated; they have rather chosen to suppose an imaginary exterior cause, of which they themselves had no correct idea, than admit that these bodies held their motion from their own peculiar nature.

  In like manner, although these philosophers saw above them an infinite number of immense globes, moving with great rapidity round a common centre, still they clung fast to their opinions; and never ceased to suppose chimerical causes for these movements, until the immortal NEWTON demonstrated that it was the effect of the gravitation of these celestial bodies towards each other. . . .

If they had viewed Nature uninfluenced by prejudice, they must have been long since convinced, that matter acts by its own peculiar energy, and needs not any exterior impulse to set it in motion. They would have perceived, that whenever mixed bodies were placed in a capacity to act on each other, motion was instantly engendered, and that these mixtures acted with a force capable of producing the most surprising effects. If filings of iron, sulphur and water be mixed together, these bodies thus capacitated to act on each other, are heated by degrees, and ultimately produce a violent combustion. If flour be wetted with water, and the mixture closed up, it will be found, after some little lapse of time, by the aid of a microscope, to have produced organized beings that enjoy life, of which the water and the flour were believed incapable: it is thus that inanimate matter can pass into life, or animate matter, which is in itself only an assemblage of motion. Reasoning from analogy, the production of a man, independent of the ordinary means, would not be more marvelous than that of an insect with flour and water. . . .

Those who admit a cause exterior to matter, are obliged to suppose, that this cause produced all the motion by which matter is agitated in giving it existence. This supposition rests on another, namely, that matter could begin to exist; a hypothesis that, until this moment, has never been demonstrated by any thing like solid proof. To produce from nothing, or the *Creation*, is a term that cannot give us the most slender idea of the formation of the universe; it presents no sense, upon which the mind can fasten itself.

Motion becomes still more obscure, when creation, or the formation of matter, is attributed to a *spiritual* being, that is to say, to a being which has no analogy, no point of contact, with it; to a being which has neither extent, nor parts, and cannot, therefore, be susceptible of motion, as we understand the term; this being only the change of one body relatively to another body, in which the body moved, presents successively different parts to different points of space. Moreover, as all the world are nearly agreed that matter can never be totally annihilated, or cease to exist, how can we understand, that that which cannot cease to be, could ever have had a beginning?

If, therefore, it be asked, whence came matter? it is a very reasonable reply to say, it has always existed. . . .

Let us, therefore, content ourselves with saying *that* which is supported by our experience, and by all the evidence we are capable of understanding; against the truth of which, not a shadow of proof such as our reason can admit, has ever been adduced; which has been maintained by philosophers in every age; which theologians themselves have not denied, but which many of them have upheld; namely, that *matter always existed; that it moves by virtue of its essence; that all the phenomena of Nature is ascribable to the diversified motion of the variety of matter she contains; and which, like the phenix, is continually regenerating out of her own ashes.*

DENIS DIDEROT: *Toward Evolution* *

Diderot (see preceding section on the Spirit of the Enlightenment), member of the Holbachian circle in Paris, was also a professed materialist. In the dialogues known as *D'Alembert's Dream* (1769), however, he went farther than even Holbach in speculating about a creative nature, constantly changing and possibly producing new species. Thus, Diderot belongs among the proto-evolutionists, advocating what the French have always called "transformism." Diderot was stimulated to speculate in this fashion by the contemporary vitalist trend in biological thinking, particularly by experiments that appeared to prove the spontaneous generation of life and nature's regenerative powers.

MLLE. DE L'ESPINASSE. At this point he [D'Alembert who is sick and dreaming] began to mumble something I couldn't quite make out—all about seeds, shreds of meat ground up in water, different races of animals that he saw being born or dying out. With his right hand he seemed to be imitating the tube of a microscope while with his left hand he tried to show, I think, the aperture of a vessel. He looked through the tube into the vessel and said: "Our Voltaire may make as many jokes about it as he likes, but Needham [English physiologist who believed in spontaneous generation] is right about his little eels; I have to believe the evidence of my own eyes and I can actually see them. My, what a swarm! Look how they dart back and forth! See them squirm!" Then he began comparing the vessel, in which he saw so many instantaneous births, with the whole universe, pretending to see in a single drop of water the history of the entire world. This idea struck him as a great one, he thought it altogether in the spirit of sound scientific procedure, which learns about large bodies by studying small ones, and he said: "In Needham's drop of water everything is over and done with in an instant. In the world at large the same phenomena occupy a little more time; but what is our human lifetime in comparison with the infinite duration of the universe? Less, surely, than this drop, which I take on the point of a needle, is in comparison with the boundless space that surrounds us. You have an infinite succession of little animals inside the fermenting atom, and the same infinite succession of

---

* From Diderot, *Rameau's Nephew and Other Works*, trans. by Jacques Barzun and Ralph H. Bowen (The Library of Liberal Arts, The Bobbs-Merrill Company, Inc., 1964), pp. 116–17, 118–19, 120.

tiny animals inside the other atom that is called the Earth. Who knows how many races of animals have preceded us? Who knows how many will follow the races that now exist? Everything changes, everything passes away—only the Whole endures. The world is perpetually beginning and ending; every moment is its beginning and its end; there has never been any other kind of world, and there never will be any other. . . ."

MLLE. DE L'ESPINASSE. . . : Who can tell what place we humans occupy in the chain of animal species? Who knows whether those deformed bipeds who are only four feet tall, and who are called men by those who visit the polar regions—who knows whether these creatures might not soon cease to be called men if they were only slightly more misshapen? Perhaps they are just the remnant of a race that is passing away. Who can say that the same thing is not true of any other species of animals? Who can be sure that the universe is not tending to degenerate into an inert and motionless. desposit of sediment? Who can tell how long such a state of inertia might last? Who knows what new species might once again arise from such a vast heap of sensitive, living particles? Why not just one kind of animal? How did the elephant originate? Perhaps this huge beast, as he appears to us now, was once only a single atom—we know that both elephants and atoms exist, and we need appeal only to motion and to the other various properties of matter. . . .

4. *Man*

VOLTAIRE: *On Evil and Free Will*

> Voltaire's conception of man was ambiguous and ambivalent. On the one hand, he upheld the dignity of man in opposition to the doctrine of original sin. On the other hand, the scientific revolution persuaded him to relinquish (albeit reluctantly) his humanistic belief in free will, and to think of man as a "machine" subject to uniform laws like the rest of nature. These two strains in his thought—we might call them the humanistic and the scientific—appear side by side in the following selections, the first of which is from the article "Méchant" in the *Philosophical Dictionary*, the second from an occasional piece entitled "Franc arbitre."

Evil *

PEOPLE clamor that human nature is essentially perverse, that man is born the child of the devil, and of evil. Nothing is more ill-advised; for,

* Voltaire: *Philosophical Dictionary*, trans. Peter Gay, Vol. II, pp. 377–80. Copyright 1962 by Basic Books, Inc. Reprinted by permission of Basic Books, Inc.

my friend, in preaching at me that everybody is born perverse, you warn me that you were born that way, that I must distrust you as I would a fox or a crocodile.—Oh, not at all, you tell me; I have been regenerated, I am neither heretic nor infidel, you can trust me.—But then the rest of mankind, which is either heretical or what you call infidel, must be nothing but an assemblage of monsters; and every time you talk to a Lutheran or a Turk, you may be sure that they will rob you and kill you: for they are children of the devil; they were born evil; one was not regenerated, and the other has degenerated. It would be much more reasonable, much nobler, to say to men: "You were all born good; see how frightful it would be to corrupt the purity of your being." We should treat mankind as we should treat all men individually. Does a canon lead a scandalous life? Say to him: "Is it possible that you should dishonor the dignity of a canon?" One can remind a man of the robe that he has the honor to be king's councilor, and that he should set an example. One says to a soldier to encourage him: "Remember that you are with the regiment of Champagne." One should say to every individual: "Remember your dignity as a man."

And in fact, whatever we may say, we always come back to that; for what does this phrase mean, so frequently employed in all nations: *Return to yourself?* If you were born a child of the Devil, if you were criminal from the start, if your blood had been formed of an infernal liqueur, the phrase *return to yourself* would mean: consult, follow your diabolic nature, be an impostor, thief, assassin—that is your father's law.

Man is not born evil; he becomes evil, as he becomes sick. Physicians appear and tell him: "You were born sick." It is quite certain that these physicians, whatever they say and whatever they do, won't cure him if his malady is inherent in his nature; and these logicians are quite sick themselves.

Gather together all the children of the universe; you will see in them nothing but innocence, gentleness, and fear; had they been born evil, malevolent, cruel, they would give some sign of it, as small snakes try to bite and small tigers try to tear something to pieces. But since Nature has given men no more offensive weapons than it has to pigeons and rabbits, it couldn't have given them an instinct that inclines them to destructiveness.

Man, then is not born evil. Why then are some of them infected with this plague of malevolence? It's because those who are at their head have the malady and communicate it to the rest of mankind, just as a woman attacked by the sickness Christopher Columbus brought back from America spread that poison from one end of Europe to the other. The first ambitious man corrupted the earth.

You will tell me that this first monster merely brought out the germ of pride, plunder, fraud, cruelty, which is in all men. I admit that as a general rule most of our brothers can acquire these qualities; but does everybody have the putrid fever, the stone, and the gravel because everybody is exposed to it?

There are entire nations which are not evil: the Philadelphians, the Banians, have never killed anybody; the Chinese, the people of Tonking, Laos, Siam, even Japan, haven't known war for more than a hundred years. In the towns of Rome, Venice, Paris, London, Amsterdam, we scarcely see once in ten years one of those great crimes which shock human nature, although these are towns in which cupidity, the mother of all crimes, is extreme.

If men were essentially evil, if they were all born the subjects of a being as malevolent as it is unhappy, who inspired them with all this frenzy to avenge his own torment, we would see husbands murdered by their wives, and fathers by their children every morning, as we see, at the dawn of each day, hens strangled by a marten who has come to suck their blood.

* * *

There is, then, infinitely less evil in this world than people say and believe. To be sure, there is still too much: we see horrible misfortunes and crimes; but the pleasure of complaining and exaggerating is so great that at the slightest scratch you cry out that the world runs over with blood. Have you been deceived? Then all men are perjurers. A melancholy soul who has suffered some injustice sees the universe covered with the damned, as a young voluptuary, having supper with his lady after the opera, can't imagine that there are unfortunate men.

Free Will *

From the commencement of the time in which men began to reason, philosophers have agitated this question, which theologians have rendered unintelligible by their absurd subtleties upon grace. Locke is perhaps the first, who, without having the arrogance of announcing a general principle, has examined human nature by analysis. It has been disputed for three thousand years, whether the will is free or not; Locke shows, that the question is absurd, and that liberty cannot belong to the will any more than colour and motion.

What is meant by the expression to be free? It signifies power, or rather it has no sense at all. To say that the will *can*, is in itself as ridiculous as if we said that it is yellow, or blue, round or square. Will is will, and liberty is power. Let us gradually examine the chain of what passes within us, without confusing our minds with any scholastic terms, or antecedent principle.

It is proposed to you to ride on horseback, it is absolutely necessary for you to make a choice, for it is very clear that you must either

* Voltaire: *A Philosophical Dictionary* (London: J. Hunt; 1824), Vol. III, pp. 254–56. The editor wrongly included this piece in the *Dictionary*.

go or not; there is no medium, you must absolutely do the one or the other. So far it is demonstrated that the will is not free. You will get on horseback? why? Because I will to do so, an ignoramus will say. This reply is an absurdity, nothing can be done without reason or cause. Your will then is caused by what? the agreeable idea which is presented to your brain; the predominant, or determinate idea; but, you will say, cannot I resist an idea which predominates over me? No, for what would be the cause of your resistance? an idea by which your will is swayed still more despotically.

You receive your ideas, and, therefore, receive your will. You will then necessarily; consequently, the word liberty belongs not to will in any sense.

You ask me, how thought and will are formed within you? I answer, that I know nothing about it. I no more know how ideas are created, than I know how the world was formed. We are only allowed to grope in the dark in reference to all that inspires our incomprehensible machine.

Will, then, is not a faculty which can be called free. A free-will is a word absolutely void of sense; and that which scholars have called in-difference, that is to say, will without cause, is a chimera, unworthy to be combatted.

In what then consists liberty? In the power of doing what we will? I would go into my cabinet, the door is open, I am free to enter. But say you, if the door is shut and I remain where I am, I remain freely? Let us explain ourselves;—you then exercise the power that you possess of remaining, you possess this power, but not the power of going out.

Liberty, then, on which so many volumes have been written, reduced to its proper sense, is only the power of acting.

In what sense must the expression "this man is free" be spoken? In the same sense in which we use the words health, strength, and happi-ness. Man is not always strong, healthy, or happy. A great passion, a great obstacle, may deprive him of his liberty, or power of action.

The words liberty and free-will are, then, abstractions, general terms, like beauty, goodness, justice. These terms do not signify that all men are always handsome, good, and just, neither are they always free.

Further, liberty being only the power of acting,—what is this power? It is the effect of the constitution, and the actual state of our organs. Leibnitz would solve a problem of geometry, but falls into an apoplexy: he certainly has not the liberty to solve his problem. A vigorous young man, passionately in love, who holds his willing mistress in his arms, is he free to subdue his passion? doubtless not. He has the power of enjoying, and has not the power to abstain. Locke is then very right in calling liberty, power. When can this young man abstain, notwithstand-ing the violence of his passion? when a stronger idea shall determine the springs of his soul and body to the contrary.

But how? have other animals the same liberty, the same power? Why not? They have sense, memory, sentiment, and perceptions like ourselves; they act spontaneously as we do. They must also, like us, have the power of acting by virtue of their perception, and of the play of their organs.

We exclaim,—if it be thus, all things are machines merely; everything in the universe is subjected to eternal laws. Well, would you have everything rendered subject to a million of blind caprices? Either all is the consequence of the nature of things, or, all is the effect of the eternal order of an absolute master; in both cases we are only wheels to the machine of the world.

CLAUDE-ADRIEN HELVÉTIUS: *On Man* *

> Claude-Adrien Helvétius (1715–71) used the large fortune he amassed as a tax collector to protect the *philosophes* and maintain a distinguished salon in Paris. His two principal works, *De l'esprit* (1758) and *De l'homme* (published posthumously in 1772) brought down on him the condemnation of the Catholic authorities and the Parlement of Paris. His belief in equality was too extreme even for Diderot, but his sensationalist psychology and environmentalism were shared to a degree by all the *philosophes*.

THE UNDERSTANDING is nothing more than the assemblage of our ideas. Our ideas, says Locke, come to us by the senses; and from this principle, as from mine, it may be concluded that our understanding is nothing more than an acquisition.

To regard it as a mere gift of nature, or the effect of a particular organization, without being able to name the organ by which it is produced, is to bring back to philosophy the occult qualities; it is to believe without proof, and judge at a venture.

History and experience equally inform us that the understanding is independent of the greater or less acuteness of the senses; that men of different constitutions are susceptible of the same passions and the same ideas.

The principles of Locke, far from contradicting this opinion, confirm it; they prove that education makes us what we are; that men the more resemble each other as their instructions are more similar; and consequently that a German resembles a Frenchman more than an Asiatic; and

* Helvétius: *A Treatise on Man*, trans. by W. Hooper (London: Vernor, Hood and Sharpe; 1810), vol. I, pp. 3, 6, 8–9, 92–4, 284, 286–8; vol. II, pp. 205–06, 423, 434–5, 448–9, 473–4, 476–7.

another German more than a Frenchman; and in short, if the understandings of men be very different, it is because none of them have the same education.

Such are the facts on which I have composed this work; I offer it with more confidence to the public, as the analogy of my principles with those of Locke assure me of their truth. . . .

What is a science? A series of propositions which all relate to one general and original principle. Is morality a science? Yes; if in corporeal sensation I have discovered the sole principle of which all the precepts of morality are the necessary consequences. It is an evident proof of the truth of this principle, that it explains all the modes of being of mankind, that it developes the causes of their understanding, their stupidity, their love, their hatred, their errors and contradictions. This principle ought to be the more easily and universally adopted, as the existence of corporeal sensibility is a fact allowed by all, as the idea of it is clear, the notion distinct, the expression determinate, and, lastly, as no error can mix itself with so simple an axiom.

Corporeal sensibility seems to have been given to men as a tutelar angel, charged to watch incessantly over their preservation. Let men be happy; this perhaps is the sole view of nature, and the sole principle of morality. When the laws are good, private interest will never be destructive of that of the public: every one will be employed in pursuing his felicity; every one will be fortunate and just; because every one will perceive that his happiness depends upon that of his neighbour. . . .

Pleasure and pain are the bonds by which private interest may be always united with that of the nation: they both take their source from corporeal sensibility. The sciences of morality and legislation cannot therefore be any thing else than deductions from this simple principle.

*   *   *

If it be true that the talents and the virtues of a people determine their power and their happiness, no question can be more important than this: *are the talents and virtues of each individual, the effect of his organisation, or of the education he receives?*

I am of the latter opinion, and propose to prove here what perhaps is only advanced in the Treatise on the Understanding (Helvétius's *De l'esprit*, 1758). If I can demonstrate that man is, in fact, nothing more than the product of his education, I shall doubtless reveal an important truth to mankind. They will learn, that they have in their own hands the instrument of their greatness and their felicity, and that to be happy and powerful nothing more is requisite than to perfect the science of education. . . .

Man is born ignorant; he is not born a fool; and it is not even without labour that he is made one. To be such, and to be able to extinguish in himself his natural lights, art and method must be used; instruction must heap on him error upon error; more he reads, the more numerous must be the prejudices he contracts. . . .

We are astonished at the age the Greeks and Romans acquired maturity. What various talents did they display in their adolescence? At twenty, Alexander, already a man of letters and a great general, undertook the conquest of the East. At the same age Scipio and Hannibal formed the greatest projects, and executed the most difficult enterprises. Before the age of maturity Pompey, the conqueror of Europe, Asia, and Africa, had filled the earth with his glory. Now how did these Greeks and Romans become at once men of letters, orators, generals, and ministers of state? How did they qualify themselves for all sorts of employments in their republics, exercise them, and even frequently abdicate them, at an age when no one in our days is capable of assuming them? Were the men of antiquity different from the moderns? Was their organisation more perfect? No doubtless. For in the sciences, and the arts of navigation, physics, mechanics, the mathematics, &c. we know that the moderns excel the ancients.

The superiority the latter have for so long a time preserved in morality, politics, and legislation, is therefore to be regarded as the effect of their education. The instruction of youth was not then confided to scholastics, but philosophers. The object of these philosophers was to form heroes and great politicians. The story of the pupil was reflected on the master; that was his reward.

The object of an instructor is no longer the same. What interest has he in exalting the mind and soul of his pupils? None. What is his aim? To weaken their natural abilities, to make them superstitious; to disjoint, if I may be allowed the expression, the wings of their genius; to stifle in their minds all true science, and in their hearts every patriotic virtue.

The golden ages of these school divines were the ages of ignorance, whose darkness, before the time of Luther and Calvin, covered the earth. Then, says an English philosopher, superstition reigned over all nations, "Men were changed, like Nebuchadnezzar, into brutes, and being like mules, bridled, saddled, and loaded with heavy burdens, they groaned under the weight of superstition; but at last some of these mules began to kick, and throw off at once their loads and their riders."

*   *   *

Two opinions concerning this subject divide the learned of the present age. Some maintain that, *The understanding is the effect of a certain sort of interior temperament and organisation.* But no one has, by a series of observations, yet determined the sort of organs, temperament, or nourishment that produces the understanding. This assertion being vague and destitute of proof, is then reduced to this, *The understanding is the effect*

of an unknown cause, or occult quality, to which is given the name of
temperament or organisation.

Quintilian, Locke, and I, say:

The inequality in minds or understandings, is the effect of a known
cause, and this cause is the difference of education. . . .

Experience then proves that the character and spirit of a people change
with the form of government; and that a different government gives by
turns, to the same nation, a character noble or base, firm or fickle, courageous or cowardly. Men therefore are endowed at their birth, either
with no disposition, or with dispositions to all vices and all virtues; they
are therefore nothing more than the produce of their education. If the
Persian have no idea of liberty, and the savage no idea of servitude, it is
the effect of their different instruction. . . .

Whoever says that men do not easily change their characters by constraint, only says that habits long established are not to be destroyed in
an instant.

The man of ill humour preserves his character, because he has always
some inferior on whom he can exercise his ill nature. But let him be kept
a long time in the presence of a lion or a tyrant, and there is no doubt but
a continued restraint, transformed into a habit, will soften his character.
In general, as long as we are young enough to contract new habits, the
only incurable faults, and vices, are those that we cannot correct without
employing means of which morals, laws, or customs do not allow the
practice. There is nothing impossible to education; it makes the bear
dance. . . .

Man is born without ideas and without passions, but he is born an
imitator and docile to example; consequently it is to instruction he owes
his habits and his character. Now I ask, why habits contracted during a
certain time, cannot at length be effaced by contrary habits. How many
people do we see change their character with their rank, according to
the different place they occupy at court, and in the ministry; in short,
according to the change that happens in their situation.

*   *   *

The almost universal unhappiness of man, and of nations, arises from
the imperfections of their laws, and the too unequal partition of their
riches. There are in most kingdoms only two classes of citizens, one of
which want necessaries, and the other riot in superfluities.

The former cannot gratify their wants but by excessive labour: such
labour is a natural evil for all; and to some it is a punishment.

The second class live in abundance, but at the same time in the anguish
of discontent. Now discontent is an evil almost as much to be dreaded as
indigence.

Most countries, therefore, must be peopled by the unfortunate. What would be done to make them happy? Diminish the riches of some; augment that of others; put the poor in such a state of ease, that they may by seven or eight hours' labour abundantly provide for the wants of themselves and their families. It is then, that a people will become as happy as they can be.

*　　*　　*

There are few good patriots; few citizens that are always just: Why? Because men are not educated to be just; because the present morality, as I have just said, is nothing more than a jumble of gross errors and contradictions; because to be just a man must have discernment, and they obscure in children the most obvious conceptions of the natural law.

But are children capable of conceiving adequate ideas of justice? This I know, that if by the aid of a religious catechism we can engrave on the memory of a child articles of faith that are frequently the most absurd, we might consequently, by the aid of a moral catechism, there engrave the precepts of an equity, which daily experience would prove to be at once useful and true. . . .

The interest of the clergy, like that of every other body, changes according to time, place, and circumstance. Therefore every morality whose principles are fixed will never be adopted by the priesthood; they require one whose precepts being obscure and contradictory, and consequently variable, may be adapted to all the several positions in which they may find themselves.

The priest requires an arbitrary morality, that allows him to legitimate to-day the action he will declare infamous to-morrow.

Unhappy is the nation that confides the education of the people to the priests! . . .

5. *Society*

VOLTAIRE: *Philosophical Dictionary* *

Country

IT IS lamentable, that to be a good patriot we must become the enemy of the rest of mankind. That good citizen the ancient Cato always gave it as his opinion, that Carthage must be destroyed: "Delenda est Carthago."

* Voltaire: *A Philosophical Dictionary* (London: J. Hunt; 1824), vol. II, pp. 327–8; vol. III, p. 381; vol. IV, pp. 186–7, 354; vol. VI, pp. 272–4, 276–7, 279.

To be a good patriot is to wish our own country enriched by commerce, and powerful by arms; but such is the condition of mankind, that to wish the greatness of our own country is often to wish evil to our neighbours. He who could bring himself to wish that his country shall always remain as it is, would be a citizen of the universe.

Government

In the time of William the Third it [the English constitution] was rebuilt of stone. Philosophy destroyed fanaticism, which convulses to their centres states even the most firm and powerful. We cannot easily help believing that a constitution which has regulated the rights of king, lords, and people, and in which every individual finds security, will endure as long as human institutions and concerns shall have a being.

We cannot but believe, also, that all states not established upon similar principles, will experience revolutions.

The English constitution has in fact arrived at that point of excellence, in consequence of which every man is restored to those natural rights, which, in nearly all monarchies, they are deprived of. These rights are, entire liberty of person and property; freedom of the press; the right of being tried in all criminal cases by a jury of independent men; the right of being tried only according to the strict letter of the law; and the right of every man to profess, unmolested, what religion he chooses, while he renounces offices, which the members of the Anglican or established church alone can hold. These are denominated privileges. And, in truth, invaluable privileges they are in comparison with the usages of most other nations of the world! To be secure on lying down that you shall rise in possession of the same property with which you retired to rest; that you shall not be torn from the arms of your wife, and from your children, in the dead of night, to be thrown into a dungeon or buried in exile in a desert; that, when rising from the bed of sleep, you will have the power of publishing all your thoughts; and that, if you are accused of having either acted, spoken, or written wrongly, you can be tried only according to law. These privileges attach to every one who sets his foot on English ground. A foreigner enjoys perfect liberty to dispose of his property and person; and, if accused of any offence, he can demand that half the jury shall be composed of foreigners.

I will venture to assert, that, were the human race solemnly assembled for the purpose of making laws, such are the laws they would make for their security.

Intolerance

Read the article on "Intolerance" in the great Encyclopedia. Read the treatise on toleration composed on occasion of the dreadful assassination of John Calas, a citizen of Toulouse; and if, after that, you allow of persecution in matters of religion, compare yourself at once to Ravaillac. Ravaillac, you know, was highly intolerant.

The following is the substance of all the discourses ever delivered by the intolerant.

You monster! who will be burnt to all eternity in the other world, and whom I will myself burn as soon as ever I can in this; you really have the insolence to read De Thou and Bayle, who have been put into the index of prohibited authors at Rome! When I was preaching to you in the name of God, how Samson had killed a thousand men with the jawbone of an ass, your head, still harder than the arsenal from which Samson obtained his arms, showed me by a slight movement from left to right that you believed nothing of what I said. And when I stated, that the devil Asmodeus, who out of jealousy twisted the necks of the seven husbands of Sarah among the Medes, was put in chains in Upper Egypt, I saw a small contraction of your lips, in Latin called cachinnus (a grin) which plainly indicated to me, that in the bottom of your soul you held the history of Asmodeus in derision.

And as for you, Isaac Newton; Frederick the great, king of Prussia and elector of Brandenburgh; John Locke; Catherine, empress of Russia, victorious over the Ottomans; John Milton; the beneficent sovereign of Denmark; Shakspeare; the wise king of Sweden; Leibnitz; the august house of Brunswick; Tillotson; the emperor of China; the parliament of England; the Council of the great Mogul; in short, all you who do not believe one word which I have taught in my courses on divinity, I declare to you, that I regard you all as pagans and publicans, as, in order to en-grave it on your unimpressible brains, I have often told you before. You are a set of callous miscreants; you will all go to the gehenna where the worm dies not and the fire is not quenched; for I am right, and you are all wrong; and I have grace, and you have none. I confess three devotees in my neighbourhood, while you do not confess a single one; I have exe-cuted the mandates of bishops, which has never been the case with you; I have abused philosophers in the language of the fish-market, while you have protected, imitated, or equalled them; I have composed pious de-famatory libels, stuffed with infamous calumnies, and you have never so much as read them. I say mass every day in Latin for fourteen sous, and you are never even so much as present at it, any more than Cicero, Cato, Pompey, Caesar, Horace, or Virgil, were ever present at it;—conse-quently you deserve each of you to have your right hand cut off, your tongue cut out, to be put to the torture, and at last burnt at a slow fire; for God is merciful.

Such, without the slightest abatement, are the maxims of the intolerant, and the sum and substance of all their books. How delightful to live with such amiable people!

Liberty of the Press

In general, we have as natural a right to make use of our pen as our language, at our peril, risk, and fortune. I know many books which fatigue, but I know of none which have done real evil. Theologians, or pretended politicians, cry—"Religion is destroyed, the government is lost, if you print certain truths or certain paradoxes. Never attempt to think, till you have demanded permission from a monk or an officer. It is against good order for a man to think for himself. Homer, Plato, Cicero, Virgil, Pliny, Horace, never published anything but with the approbation of the doctors of the Sorbonne and of the holy Inquisition."

"See into what horrible decay the liberty of the press brought England and Holland. It is true that they possess the commerce of the whole world, and that England is victorious on sea and land; but it is merely a false greatness, a false opulence: they hasten with long strides to their ruin. An enlightened people cannot subsist."

Toleration

What is toleration? It is the appurtenance of humanity. We are all full of weakness and errors; let us mutually pardon each other our follies,—it is the first law of nature.

When, on the exchange of Amsterdam, of London, of Surat, or of Bassora, the Guebre, the Banian, the Jew, the Mahometan, the Chinese Deist, the Brahmin, the Christian of the Greek Church, the Roman Catholic Christian, the Protestant Christian, and the Quaker Christian, traffic together, they do not lift the poniard against each other, in order to gain souls for their religion. Why then have we been cutting one another's throats almost without interruption since the first council of Nice?

*   *   *

It is clear that every private individual who persecutes a man, his brother, because he is not of the same opinion, is a monster. This admits of no difficulty. But the government, the magistrates, the princes!—how do they conduct themselves towards those who have a faith different from their own? If they are powerful foreigners, it is certain that a prince will form an alliance with them. The Most Christian Francis I. will league himself with the Mussulmans against the Most Catholic Charles V. Francis I. will give money to the Lutherans in Germany, to support them in their rebellion against their emperor; but he will commence, as usual, by having the Lutherans in his own country burnt. He pays them in Saxony from policy; he burns them at Paris from policy. But what follows? Persecutions make proselytes. France will soon be filled with new Protestants. At first they will submit to be hanged, afterwards they will hang in their turn. There will be civil wars; then Saint Bartholomew will come; and this corner of the world will be worse than all that the ancients and moderns have ever said of hell.

Blockheads, who have never been able to render a pure worship to the God who made you! Wretches, whom the example of the Noachides, the Chinese literati, the Parsees, and of all the wise, has not availed to guide! Monsters, who need superstitions, just as the gizzard of a raven needs carrion! We have already told you—and we have nothing else to say—if you have two religions among you, they will massacre each other; if you have thirty, they will live in peace.

* * *

Such was the practice for a long time in a great part of the world; but now, when so many sects are balanced by their power, what side must we take among them? Every sect, we know, is a mere title of error; while there is no sect of geometricians, of algebraists, of arithmeticians; because all the propositions of geometry, algebra, and arithmetic, are true. In all the other sciences, one may be mistaken. What Thomist or Scotist theologian can venture to assert seriously that he goes upon sure grounds?

* * *

Let us consider, that throughout English America, which constitutes nearly the fourth part of the known world, entire liberty of conscience is established; and provided a man believes in a God, every religion is well received; notwithstanding which, commerce flourishes and population increases.

BARON DE MONTESQUIEU: *The Spirit of the Laws* *

Charles de Secondat, baron de la Brède et de Montesquieu (1689–1755) studied law and became successively counselor and president of the Parlement of Bordeaux. However, he devoted most of his time to scientific research, frequenting the salons of Paris, travelling, and writing books. His *Lettres persanes* (1721) was a witty satire on French institutions under the guise of letters written home by two fictitious Persian visitors in Paris. In preparation for his great work *L'Esprit des lois* (1748) Montesquieu studied a large number of actual constitutions, both ancient and modern. For him, as for Voltaire and others among his contemporaries, England, which he visited in 1729, was the symbol of political freedom.

Of Laws in General

LAWS, in their most general signification, are the necessary relations arising from the nature of things. In this sense, all beings have their laws; the

* *The Complete Works of M. de Montesquieu* (London: T. Evans; 1777), vol. I, pp. 1–4, 8, 197–205, 207, 209–12.

Deity his laws, the material world its laws, the intelligences superior to man their laws, the beasts their laws, man his laws. . . .

There is then a primitive reason; and laws are the relations subsisting between it and different beings, and the relations of these to one another.

God is related to the universe as creator and preserver: the laws by which he created all things are those by which he preserves them. He acts according to these rules, because he knows them; he knows them, because he made them; and he made them, because they are relative to his wisdom and power.

Since we observe that the world, though formed by the motion of matter, and void of understanding, subsists through so long a succession of ages, its motions must certainly be directed by invariable laws: and, could we imagine another, it must also have constant rules, or it would inevitably perish.

Thus the creation, which seems an arbitrary act, supposeth laws as invariable as those of the fatality of the atheists. It would be absurd to say, that the Creator might govern the world without those rules, since without them it could not subsist. . . .

Particular intelligent beings may have laws of their own making; but they have some likewise which they never made. Before there were intelligent beings, they were possible; they had therefore possible relations, and consequently possible laws. Before laws were made, there were relations of possible justice. To say that there is nothing just or unjust, but what is commanded or forbidden by positive laws, is the same as saying that, before the describing of a circle, all the radii were not equal.

We must therefore acknowledge relations of justice antecedent to the positive law by which they are established. . . .

Man, as a physical being, is, like other bodies, governed by invariable laws. . . . Such a being might every instant forget his Creator; God has therefore reminded him of his duty by the laws of religion. Such a being is liable every moment to forget himself; philosophy has provided against this by the laws of morality. Formed to live in society, he might forget his fellow-creatures; legislators have, therefore, by political and civil laws, confined him to his duty. . . .

Law in general is human reason, inasmuch as it governs all the inhabitants of the earth; the political and civil laws of each nation ought to be only the particular cases in which human reason is applied.

They should be adapted in such a manner to the people for whom they are framed, that it is a great chance if those of one nation suit another.

They should be relative to the nature and principle of each government; whether they form it, as may be said of political laws; or whether they support it, as in the case of civil institutions.

They should be relative to the climate of each country, to the quality of its soil, to its situation and extent, to the principal occupation of the natives, whether husbandmen, huntsmen, or shepherds: they should have a relation to the degree of liberty which the constitution will bear, to the religion of the inhabitants, to their inclinations, riches, numbers, commerce, manners, and customs. In fine, they have relations to each other, as also to their origin, to the intent of the legislator, and to the order of things on which they are established; in all which different lights they ought to be considered.

This is what I have undertaken to perform in the following work. These relations I shall examine, since all these together constitute what I call the *Spirit of Laws*.

Of Political Liberty and the Constitution of England

Democratic and aristocratic states are not in their own nature free. Political liberty is to be found only in moderate governments; and even in these it is not always found. It is there only when there is no abuse of power: but constant experience shews us that every man invested with power is apt to abuse it, and to carry his authority as far as it will go. Is it not strange, though true, to say, that virtue itself has need of limits?

To prevent this abuse, it is necessary, from the very nature of things, power should be a check to power. A government may be so constituted as no man shall be compelled to do things to which the law does not oblige him, nor forced to abstain from things which the law permits. . . .

The political liberty of the subject is a tranquility of mind arising from the opinion each person has of his safety. In order to have this liberty, it is requisite the government be so constituted as one man need not be afraid of another.

When the legislative and executive powers are united in the same person, or in the same body of magistrates, there can be no liberty; because apprehensions may arise, lest the same monarch or senate should enact tyrannical laws, to execute them in a tyrannical manner.

Again, there is no liberty if the judiciary power be not separated from the legislative and executive. Were it joined with the legislative, the life and liberty of the subject would be exposed to arbitrary control; for the judge would be then the legislator. Were it joined to the executive power, the judge might behave with violence and oppression.

There would be an end of every thing, were the same man, or the same body, whether of the nobles or of the people, to exercise those three powers, that of enacting laws, that of executing the public resolutions, and of trying the causes of individuals.

* * *

The judiciary power ought not to be given to a standing senate; it should be exercised by persons taken from the body of the people, at certain times of the year, and consistently with a form and manner pre-

scribed by law, in order to erect a tribunal that should last only so long
as necessity requires.

By this method, the judicial power, so terrible to mankind, not being
annexed to any particular state or profession, becomes, as it were, invisible. People have not then the judges continually present to their view;
they fear the office, but not the magistrate. . . .

But, though the tribunals ought not to be fixed, the judgments ought;
and to such a degree, as to be ever conformable to the letter of the law.
Were they to be the private opinion of the judge, people would then live
in society without exactly knowing the nature of their obligations.

* * *

As, in a country of liberty, every man who is supposed a free agent
ought to be his own governor, the legislative power should reside in the
whole body of the people. But, since this is impossible in large states, and
in small ones is subject to many inconveniences, it is fit the people should
transact by their representatives what they cannot transact by themselves.

The inhabitants of a particular town are much better acquainted with
its wants and interests than with those of other places; and are better
judges of the capacity of their neighbours than of that of the rest of their
countrymen. The members, therefore, of the legislature should not be
chosen from the general body of the nation; but it is proper, that, in every
considerable place, a representative should be elected by the inhabitants.

The great advantage of representatives is, their capacity of discussing
public affairs. For this, the people collectively are extremely unfit, which
is one of the chief inconveniences of a democracy. . . .

All the inhabitants of the several districts ought to have a right of
voting at the election of a representative, except such as are in so mean
a situation as to be deemed to have no will of their own.

* * *

In such a state, there are always persons distinguished by their birth,
riches, or honours: but, were they to be confounded with the common
people, and to have only the weight of a single vote, like the rest, the
common liberty would be their slavery, and they would have no interest
in supporting it, as most of the popular resolutions would be against them.
The share they have, therefore, in the legislature ought to be proportioned to their other advantages in the state; which happens only when
they form a body that has a right to check the licentiousness of the people, as the people have a right to oppose any encroachment of theirs.

The legislative power is, therefore, committed to the body of the
nobles, and to that which represents the people; each having their assemblies and deliberations apart, each their separate views and interests. . . .

The body of the nobility ought to be hereditary. In the first place, it is so in its own nature; and, in the next, there must be a considerable interest to preserve its privileges: privileges, that, in themselves, are obnoxious to popular envy, and of course, in a free state, are always in danger.

But, as an hereditary power might be tempted to pursue its own particular interests, and forget those of the people, it is proper, that, where a singular advantage may be gained by corrupting the nobility, as in the laws relating to the supplies, they should have no other share in the legislation than the power of rejecting, and not that of resolving.

*   *   *

The executive power ought to be in the hands of a monarch, because this branch of government, having need of dispatch, is better administered by one than by many: on the other hand, whatever depends on the legislative power, is oftentimes better regulated by many than by a single person. . . .

Were the legislative body to be a considerable time without meeting, this would likewise put an end to liberty. For, of two things, one would naturally follow; either that there would be no longer any legislative resolutions, and then the state would fall into anarchy; or that these resolutions would be taken by the executive power, which would render it absolute. . . .

But, if the legislative power, in a free state, has no right to stay the executive, it has a right, and ought to have the means, of examining in what manner its laws have been executed; an advantage which this government has over that of Crete and Sparta, where the Cosmi and the Ephori gave no account of their administration.

But, whatever may be the issue of that examination, the legislative body ought not to have a power of arraigning the person, nor, of course, the conduct, of him who is entrusted with the executive power. His person should be sacred, because, as it is necessary, for the good of the state, to prevent the legislative body from rendering themselves arbitrary, the moment he is accused or tried there is an end of liberty.

In this case, the state would be no longer a monarchy, but a kind of republic, though not a free government. But, as the person, intrusted with the executive power, cannot abuse it without bad counsellors, and such as hate the laws as ministers, though the laws protect them, as subjects these men may be examined and punished: an advantage which this government has over that of *Gnidus*, where the law allowed of no such thing as calling the *Amymones* to account, even after their administration; and therefore the people could never obtain any satisfaction for the injuries done them. . . .

The executive power, pursuant to what has been already said, ought to have a share in the legislature by the power of rejecting; otherwise it would soon be stripped of its prerogative. But, should the legislative power usurp a share of the executive, the latter would be equally undone.

If the prince were to have a part in the legislature by the power of resolving, liberty would be lost. But, as it is necessary he should have a share in the legislature for the support of his own prerogative, this share must consist in the power of rejecting. . . .

Were the executive power to determine the raising of public money otherwise than by giving its consent, liberty would be at an end; because it would become legislative in the most important point of legislation. . . .

To prevent the executive power from being able to oppress, it is requisite that the armies with which it is intrusted should consist of the people, and have the same spirit as the people, as was the case at Rome till the time of *Marius*. To obtain this end, there are only two ways; either that the persons employed in the army should have sufficient property to answer for their conduct to their fellow-subjects, and be enlisted only for a year, as was customary at Rome; or, if there should be a standing-army composed chiefly of the most despicable part of the nation, the legislative power should have a right to disband them as soon as it pleased; the soldiers should live in common with the rest of the people; and no separate camp, barracks, or fortress, should be suffered.

* * *

In perusing the admirable treatise of Tacitus on the manners of the Germans, we find it is from that nation the English have borrowed the idea of their political government. This beautiful system was invented first in the woods. . . .

It is not my business to examine whether the English actually enjoy this liberty, or not. Sufficient it is for my purpose to observe, that it is established by their laws; and I inquire no farther.

Neither do I pretend by this to undervalue other governments, nor to say that this extreme political liberty ought to give uneasiness to those who have only a moderate share of it. How should I have any such design; I who think that even the highest refinement of reason is not always desirable, and that mankind generally find their account better in mediums than in extremes?

JEAN JACQUES ROUSSEAU: *The Social Contract* *

Jean Jacques Rousseau (1712–78) "marked the end of the compromise with the *Ancien Régime*." The doctrine enunciated in *The Social Con-*

* Taken from *The Social Contract & Discourses*, by Jean Jacques Rousseau, translated by G. D. H. Cole, published by E. P. Dutton & Co., Inc., New York. Also reprinted by permission of J. M. Dent & Sons, Ltd. Pp. 3–5, 7–8, 10–16, 26, 110–15.

tract (1762)—the social contract and the "general will"—helped to foment the French Revolution and enrich the democratic tradition. However, Rousseau quarrelled with the *philosophes* as well as the *Ancien Régime*. He has been styled, and with good reason, the Prophet of Romanticism (note his emphasis on feeling in the *Confessions* and *Émile*). And in political philosophy he broke with the tradition of individualism which stemmed from Locke.

I MEAN to inquire if, in the civil order, there can be any sure and legitimate rule of administration, men being taken as they are and laws as they might be. In this inquiry I shall endeavour always to unite what right sanctions with what is prescribed by interest, in order that justice and utility may in no case be divided. . . .

 Man is born free; and everywhere he is in chains. One thinks himself the master of others, and still remains a greater slave than they. How did this change come about? I do not know. What can make it legitimate? That question I think I can answer.

If I took into account only force, and the effects derived from it, I should say: 'As long as a people is compelled to obey, and obeys, it does well; as soon as it can shake off the yoke, and shakes it off, it does still better; for, regaining its liberty by the same right as took it away, either it is justified in resuming it, or there was no justification for those who took it away.' But the social order is a sacred right which is the basis of all other rights. Nevertheless, this right does not come from nature, and must therefore be founded on conventions. . . .

The First Societies and Slavery

Grotius denies that all human power is established in favour of the governed, and quotes slavery as an example. His usual method of reasoning is constantly to establish right by fact. It would be possible to employ a more logical method, but none could be more favourable to tyrants.

It is then, according to Grotius, doubtful whether the human race belongs to a hundred men, or that hundred men to the human race: and, throughout his book, he seems to incline to the former alternative, which is also the view of Hobbes. On this showing, the human species is divided into so many herds of cattle, each with its ruler, who keeps guard over them for the purpose of devouring them. . . .

The reasoning of Caligula agrees with that of Hobbes and Grotius. Aristotle, before any of them, had said that men are by no means equal naturally, but that some are born for slavery, and others for dominion.

Aristotle was right; but he took the effect for the cause. Nothing can be more certain than that every man born in slavery is born for slavery. Slaves lose everything in their chains, even the desire of escaping from them: they love their servitude, as the comrades of Ulysses loved their brutish condition. If then there are slaves by nature, it is because there have been slaves against nature. Force made the first slaves, and their cowardice perpetuated the condition. . . .

Since no man has a natural authority over his fellow, and force creates no right, we must conclude that conventions form the basis of all legitimate authority among men.

If an individual, says Grotius, can alienate his liberty and make himself the slave of a master, why could not a whole people do the same and make itself subject to a king? . . .

It will be said that the despot assures his subjects civil tranquillity. Granted; but what do they gain, if the wars his ambition brings down upon them, his insatiable avidity, and the vexatious conduct of his ministers press harder on them than their own dissensions would have done? What do they gain, if the very tranquillity they enjoy is one of their miseries? Tranquillity is found also in dungeons; but is that enough to make them desirable places to live in? . . .

To say that a man gives himself gratuitously, is to say what is absurd and inconceivable; such an act is null and illegitimate, from the mere fact that he who does it is out of his mind. To say the same of a whole people is to suppose a people of madmen; and madness creates no right.

Even if each man could alienate himself, he could not alienate his children: they are born men and free; their liberty belongs to them, and no one but they has the right to dispose of it. . . .

To renounce liberty is to renounce being a man, to surrender the rights of humanity and even its duties. For him who renounces everything no indemnity is possible. Such a renunciation is incompatible with man's nature; to remove all liberty from his will is to remove all morality from his acts. . . .

The Social Compact

Even if I granted all that I have been refuting, the friends of despotism would be no better off. There will always be a great difference between subduing a multitude and ruling a society. Even if scattered individuals were successively enslaved by one man, however numerous they might be, I still see no more than a master and his slaves, and certainly not a people and its ruler; I see what may be termed an aggregation, but not an association; there is as yet neither public good nor body politic. . . .

A people, says Grotius, can give itself to a king. Then, according to Grotius, a people is a people before it gives itself. The gift is itself a civil act, and implies public deliberation. It would be better, before examining the act by which a people gives itself to a king, to examine that by which it has become a people; for this act, being necessarily prior to the other, is the true foundation of society. . . .

I suppose men to have reached the point at which the obstacles in the way of their preservation in the state of nature show their power of resistance to be greater than the resources at the disposal of each individual for his maintenance in that state. That primitive condition can then subsist no longer; and the human race would perish unless it changed its manner of existence.

But, as men cannot engender new forces, but only unite and direct existing ones, they have no other means of preserving themselves than the formation, by aggregation, of a sum of forces great enough to overcome the resistance. These they have to bring into play by means of a single motive power, and cause to act in concert.

This sum of forces can arise only where several persons come together: but, as the force and liberty of each man are the chief instruments of his self-preservation, how can he pledge them without harming his own interests, and neglecting the care he owes to himself? This difficulty, in its bearing on my present subject, may be stated in the following terms:

'The problem is to find a form of association which will defend and protect with the whole common force the person and goods of each associate, and in which each, while uniting himself with all, may still obey himself alone, and remain as free as before.' This is the fundamental problem of which the *Social Contract* provides the solution.

The clauses of this contract . . . may be reduced to one—the total alienation of each associate, together with all his rights, to the whole community; for, in the first place, as each gives himself absolutely, the conditions are the same for all; and, this being so, no one has any interest in making them burdensome to others. . . .

Finally, each man, in giving himself to all, gives himself to nobody; and as there is no associate over which he does not acquire the same right as he yields others over himself, he gains an equivalent for everything he loses, and an increase of force for the preservation of what he has.

If then we discard from the social compact what is not of its essence, we shall find that it reduces itself to the following terms:

'*Each of us puts his person and all his power in common under the supreme direction of the general will, and, in our corporate capacity, we receive each member as an indivisible part of the whole.*'

At once, in place of the individual personality of each contracting party, this act of association creates a moral and collective body, composed of as many members as the assembly contains voters, and receiving from this act its unity, its common identity, its life, and its will. This public person, so formed by the union of all other persons, formerly took the name of *city*, and now takes that of *Republic* or *body politic;* it is called by its members *State* when passive, *Sovereign* when active, and *Power* when compared with others like itself. Those who are associated in it take collectively the name of *people*, and severally are called *citizens*, as sharing in the sovereign power, and *subjects*, as being under the laws of the State. . . .

The Sovereign

The Sovereign, being formed wholly of the individuals who compose it, neither has nor can have any interest contrary to theirs; and consequently the sovereign power need give no guarantee to its subjects, because it is impossible for the body to wish to hurt all its members. We shall also see later on that it cannot hurt any in particular. The Sovereign, merely by virtue of what it is, is always what it should be.

This, however, is not the case with the relation of the subjects to the Sovereign, which, despite the common interest, would have no security that they would fulfil their undertakings, unless it found means to assure itself of their fidelity.

In fact, each individual, as a man, may have a particular will contrary or dissimilar to the general will which he has as a citizen. His particular interest may speak to him quite differently from the common interest: his absolute and naturally independent existence may make him look upon what he owes to the common cause as a gratuitous contribution, the loss of which will do less harm to others than the payment of it is burdensome to himself; and, regarding the moral person which constitutes the state as a *persona ficta*, because not a man, he may wish to enjoy the rights of citizenship without being ready to fulfil the duties of a subject. The continuance of such an injustice could not but prove the undoing of the body politic.

In order then that the social compact may not be an empty formula, it tacitly includes the undertaking, which alone can give force to the rest, that whoever refuses to obey the general will shall be compelled to do so by the whole body. This means nothing less than that he will be forced to be free; for this is the condition which, by giving each citizen to his country, secures him against all personal dependence. In this lies the key to the working of the political machine; this alone legitimizes civil undertakings, which, without it, would be absurd, tryannical, and liable to the most frightful abuses.

The Civil State

The passage from the state of nature to the civil state produces a very remarkable change in man, by substituting justice for instinct in his conduct, and giving his actions the morality they had formerly lacked. Then only, when the voice of duty takes the place of physical impulses and right of appetite, does man, who so far had considered only himself, find that he is forced to act on different principles, and to consult his reason before listening to his inclinations. Although, in this state, he deprives himself of some advantages which he got from nature, he gains in return others so great, his faculties are so stimulated and developed, his ideas so extended, his feelings so ennobled, and his whole soul so uplifted, that, did not the abuses of this new condition often degrade him below that which he left, he would be bound to bless continually the happy moment which took him from it for ever, and, instead of a stupid and unimaginative animal, made him an intelligent being and a man.

Let us draw up the whole account in terms easily commensurable. What man loses by the social contract is his natural liberty and an unlimited right to everything he tries to get and succeeds in getting; what he gains is civil liberty and the proprietorship of all he possesses. If we are to avoid mistake in weighing one against the other, we must clearly distinguish natural liberty, which is bounded only by the strength of the individual, from civil liberty, which is limited by the general will; and possession, which is merely the effect of force or the right of the first occupier, from property, which can be founded only on a positive title.

We might, over and above all this, add, to what man acquires in the civil state, moral liberty, which alone makes him truly master of himself; for the mere impulse of appetite is slavery, while obedience to a law which we prescribe to ourselves is liberty. . . .

The Limits of the Sovereign Power

From whatever side we approach our principle, we reach the same conclusion, that the social compact sets up among the citizens an equality of such a kind, that they all bind themselves to observe the same conditions and should therefore all enjoy the same rights. Thus, from the very nature of the compact, every act of Sovereignty, i.e. every authentic act of the general will, binds or favours all the citizens equally; so that the Sovereign recognizes only the body of the nation, and draws no distinctions between those of whom it is made up. . . .

We can see from this that the sovereign power, absolute, sacred, and inviolable as it is, does not and cannot exceed the limits of general conventions, and that every man may dispose at will of such goods and liberty as these conventions leave him; so that the Sovereign never has a right to lay more charges on one subject than on another, because, in that case, the question becomes particular, and ceases to be within its competency.

Civil Religion

Religion, considered in relation to society, which is either general or particular, may also be divided into two kinds: the religion of man, and that of the citizen. The first, which has neither temples, nor altars, nor rites, and is confined to the purely internal cult of the supreme God and the eternal obligations of morality, is the religion of the Gospel pure and simple, the true theism, what may be called natural divine right or law. The other, which is codified in a single country, gives it its gods, its own tutelary patrons; it has its dogmas, its rites, and its external cult prescribed by law; outside the single nation that follows it, all the world is in its sight infidel, foreign, and barbarous; the duties and rights of man extend for it only as far as its own altars. . . .

The second is good in that it unites the divine cult with love of the laws, and, making country the object of the citizens' adoration, teaches them that service done to the State is service done to its tutelary gods. It is a form of theocracy, in which there can be no pontiff save the prince, and no priests save the magistrates. To die for one's country then becomes martyrdom; violation of its laws, impiety; and to subject one who is guilty to public execration is to condemn him to the anger of the gods; *Sacer estod.*

On the other hand, it is bad in that, being founded on lies and error, it deceives men, makes them credulous and superstitious, and drowns the true cult of the Divinity in empty ceremonial. It is bad, again, when it becomes tyrannous and exclusive, and makes a people bloodthirsty and intolerant, so that it breathes fire and slaughter, and regards as a sacred act the killing of every one who does not believe in its gods. The result is to place such a people in a natural state of war with all others, so that its security is deeply endangered.

There remains therefore the religion of man or Christianity—not the Christianity of to-day, but that of the Gospel, which is entirely different. By means of this holy, sublime, and real religion all men, being children of one God, recognize one another as brothers, and the society that unites them is not dissolved even at death.

But this religion, having no particular relation to the body politic, leaves the laws in possession of the force they have in themselves without making any addition to it; and thus one of the great bonds that unite society considered in severalty fails to operate. Nay, more, so far from binding the hearts of the citizens to the State, it has the effect of taking them away from all earthly things. I know of nothing more contrary to the social spirit. . . .

Christianity as a religion is entirely spiritual, occupied solely with heavenly things; the country of the Christian is not of this world. He does his duty, indeed, but does it with profound indifference to the good or ill success of his cares. Provided he has nothing to reproach himself with, it matters little to him whether things go well or ill here on earth. If the State is prosperous, he hardly dares to share in the public happiness, for fear he may grow proud of his country's glory; if the State is languishing, he blesses the hand of God that is hard upon His people. . . .

But I am mistaken in speaking of a Christian republic; the terms are mutually exclusive. Christianity preaches only servitude and dependence.

Its spirit is so favourable to tyranny that it always profits by such a regime. True Christians are made to be slaves, and they know it and do not much mind: this short life counts for too little in their eyes. . . .

Now, it matters very much to the community that each citizen should have a religion. That will make him love his duty; but the dogmas of that religion concern the State and its members only so far as they have reference to morality and to the duties which he who professes them is bound to do to others. . . .

There is therefore a purely civil profession of faith of which the Sovereign should fix the articles, not exactly as religious dogmas, but as social sentiments without which a man cannot be a good citizen or a faithful subject. While it can compel no one to believe them, it can banish from the State whoever does not believe them—it can banish him, not for impiety, but as an antisocial being. . . .

The dogmas of civil religion ought to be few, simple, and exactly worded, without explanation or commentary. The existence of a mighty, intelligent, and beneficent Divinity, possessed of foresight and providence, the life to come, the happiness of the just, the punishment of the wicked, the sanctity of the social contract and the laws: these are its positive dogmas. Its negative dogmas I confine to one, intolerance, which is a part of the cults we have rejected.

Those who distinguish civil from theological intolerance are, to my mind, mistaken. The two forms are inseparable. It is impossible to live at peace with those we regard as damned; to love them would be to hate God who punishes them: we positively must either reclaim or torment them. Wherever theological intolerance is admitted, it must inevitably have some civil effect; and as soon as it has such an effect, the Sovereign is no longer Sovereign even in the temporal sphere: thenceforth priests are the real masters, and kings only their ministers.

Now that there is and can be no longer an exclusive national religion, tolerance should be given to all religions that tolerate others, so long as their dogmas contain nothing contrary to the duties of citizenship. But whoever dares to say: 'Outside the Church is no salvation,' ought to be driven from the State, unless the State is the Church, and the prince the pontiff. Such a dogma is good only in a theocratic government; in any other, it is fatal. The reason for which Henry IV is said to have embraced the Roman religion ought to make every honest man leave it, and still more any prince who knows how to reason.

MARQUIS DE CONDORCET: *The Progress of the Human Mind* *

The following passage from the "Ninth Epoch" of the Marquis de Condorcet's *Esquisse d'un Tableau historique des Progrès de L'esprit humain* (1793–4) is a popular statement of the individualistic political philosophy of the *philosophes* which traced its lineage from John Locke. Condorcet, however, was a democrat whereas Voltaire and Montesquieu had compromised with the *Ancien Régime* to the extent of preserving individual rights under an enlightened or constitutional monarchy. He praises Rousseau's "general will," the collectivistic aspect of which he seems not to have noticed. Born of noble parents, Condorcet (1743–94) started out as a distinguished mathematician and ended up as a political pamphleteer. With the advent of the French Revolution he became a prominent member of the Girondist party and served for a time as president of the Legislative Assembly.

AND now we arrive at the period when philosophy, the most general and obvious effects of which we have before remarked, obtained an influence on the thinking class of men, and these on the people and their governments, that, ceasing any longer to be gradual, produced a revolution in the entire mass of certain nations, and gave thereby a secure pledge of the general revolution one day to follow that shall embrace the whole human species.

After ages of error, after wandering in all the mazes of vague and defective theories, writers upon politics and the law of nations at length arrived at the knowledge of the true rights of man, which they deduced from this simple principle: that *he is a being endowed with sensation, capable of reasoning upon and understanding his interests, and of acquiring moral ideas.*

They saw that the maintenance of his rights was the only object of political union, and that the perfection of the social art consisted in preserving them with the most entire equality, and in their fullest extent. They perceived that the means of securing the rights of the individual, consisting of general rules to be laid down in every community, the power of choosing these means, and determining these rules, could vest only in the majority of the community: and that for this reason, as it is impossible for any individual in this choice to follow the dictates of his own understanding, without subjecting that of others, the will of the majority is the only principle which can be followed by all, without infringing upon the common equality.

* Condorcet: *The Progress of the Human Mind* (Philadelphia: Lang and Ustick; 1796), pp. 185–8, 190.

Each individual may enter into a previous engagement to comply with the will of the majority, which by this engagement becomes unanimity; he can however bind nobody but himself, nor can he bind himself except so far as the majority shall not violate his individual rights, after having recognised them.

Such are at once the rights of the majority over individuals, and the limits of these rights; such is the origin of that unanimity, which renders the engagement of the majority binding upon all; a bond that ceases to operate when, by the change of individuals, this species of unanimity ceases to exist. There are objects, no doubt, upon which the majority would pronounce perhaps oftener in favour of error and mischief, than in favour of truth and happiness; still the majority, and the majority only, can decide what are the objects which cannot properly be referred to its own decision; it can alone determine as to the individuals whose judgment it resolves to prefer to its own, and the method which these individuals are to pursue in the exercise of their judgment; in fine, it has also an indispensable authority of pronouncing whether the decisions of its officers have or have not wounded the rights of all.

From these simple principles men discovered the folly of former notions respecting the validity of contracts between a people and its magistrates, which it was supposed could only be annulled by mutual consent, or by a violation of the conditions by one of the parties; as well as of another opinion, less servile, but equally absurd, that would chain a people for ever to the provisions of a constitution when once established, as if the right of changing it were not the security of every other right, as if human institutions, necessarily defective, and capable of improvement as we become enlightened, were to be condemned to an eternal monotony. Accordingly the governors of nations saw themselves obliged to renounce that false and subtle policy, which, forgetting that all men derive from nature an equality of rights, would sometimes measure the extent of those which it might think proper to grant by the size of territory, the temperature of the climate, the national character, the wealth of the people, the state of commerce and industry; and sometimes cede them in unequal portions among the different classes of society, according to their birth, their fortune, or their profession, thereby creating contrary interests and jarring powers, in order afterwards to apply correctives, which, but for these institutions, would not be wanted, and which, after all, are inadequate to the end.

It was now no longer practicable to divide mankind into two species, one destined to govern, the other to obey, one to deceive, the other to be dupes: the doctrine was obliged universally to be acknowledged, that all have an equal right to be enlightened respecting their interests, to share in the acquisition of truth, and that no political authorities appointed by the people for the benefit of the people, can be entitled to retain them in ignorance and darkness.

These principles, which were vindicated by the generous Sydney, at the expense of his blood, and to which Locke gave the authority of his name, were afterwards developed with greater force, precision, and extent by Rousseau, whose glory it is to have placed them among those truths henceforth impossible to be forgotten or disputed. . . .

Hence it appears to be one of the rights of man that he should employ his faculties, dispose of his wealth, and provide for his wants in whatever manner he shall think best. The general interest of the society, so far from restraining him in this respect, forbids, on the contrary, every such attempt; and in this department of public administration, the care of securing to every man the rights which he derives from nature, is the only sound policy, the only control which the general will can exercise over the individuals of the community.

DUPONT DE NEMOURS: *On the Origin and Progress of a New Science* *

Pierre Samuel Dupont de Nemours (1739–1817), French economist and statesman, first applied the term "Physiocracy" to the group of economists headed by Dr. Quesnay. For him, political economy or economic liberalism was a corollary of natural philosophy: hence the term "Physiocracy." Dupont edited two journals, in which the principles of Physiocracy were developed, and for which he contributed articles on the history of economics, equitable taxation, against monopolies and the restriction of the grain trade, and universal education. In 1774 he entered the French government as Turgot's adviser and also served under Vergennes, helping to negotiate the Anglo-French commercial treaty of 1786. During the early stages of the Revolution he represented Nemours but in 1792 was forced into hiding because he was a monarchist. *De l'Origine et des Progrès d'une Science nouvelle,* from which the following selections are taken, was published in 1768.

MONTESQUIEU, so worthy in every respect to teach the human race, has told us that the principles of government ought to change according to the form of its constitution—without showing us what is the primitive basis, the common object of every constitution of government. . . .

Nevertheless, men are not united by chance into civil societies. It is not without reason that they have extended the natural chain of re-

· * Dupont de Nemours: *De l'Origine et des Progrès d'une Science nouvelle* (London and Paris: Desaint; 1768), pp. 6–11, 16–19, 25–31, 68–9, 78, 81–2. My translation.

ciprocal duties and submitted to a sovereign authority. They had, and they have, an end *essentially* marked out by their nature which makes them behave in this way. Now their physical constitution, and that of other beings by whom they are surrounded, does not allow the means to this end to be arbitrary; for there can be nothing arbitrary in the physical acts conducing to a determined end. One can reach a point only by the road that leads to it.

There is, then, a *necessary* route for achieving the object of association between men, and the formation of political bodies. There is, then, *an order*, natural, essential and general, which comprises the constitutive and fundamental laws of all societies; *an order* which could not be entirely abandoned without effecting the dissolution of society and soon the absolute destruction of the human race.

This is what Montesquieu did not see. . . .

*   *   *

About thirty years ago a man of the most vigorous genius [François Quesnay], practiced in profound meditations, already known by excellent works and by his success in an art [medicine] requiring great skill in observing and respecting nature, concluded that *physical* laws are not limited to those which have heretofore been studied in our colleges and academies; and that when nature gives to the ants, bees and beavers the faculty of submitting themselves by a common accord and by their proper interest to a good, stable and uniform government, she does not refuse to man the power of enjoying the same advantage. Animated by the importance of this view and by the prospect of the great consequences that could be deduced from it, he applied his whole mind to the research of the physical laws relative to society; and at last succeeded in assuring himself of the immovable basis of these laws, in grasping their entirety, in developing their logical sequence, in deducing from them results. The whole formed a doctrine very new, very far removed from the prejudices adopted by the general ignorance, and very much above the scope of vulgar men, whose habit, contracted in youth, of exercising only their memory, stifles the power of using their judgment.

However, the moment was not absolutely favorable for publishing this doctrine. The illustrious M. DE GOURNAY, intendant of commerce, guided, like QUESNAY, only by the exactness of his genius, arrived at the same time by a different route at much the same practical results. He began to lay them before the supreme administrators, and to mould by his conversations and counsels some young and worthy magistrates who are today the honor and hope of the nation; while Doctor *Quesnay* wrote articles for the *Encyclopedia* on "Farmers and Grains" which mark the first public works in which he commenced to expound the science which he owed to his discoveries. Soon after, the latter invented the *Tableau économique,* that astonishing formula which describes the birth, distribution and reproduction of riches, and which serves to calculate, with so much certainty, promptness and precision, the effect of all operations relative to riches. This formula, his explication, and *the general maxims of political economy* which the author joined to it, were printed with learned notes at the palace of Versailles in 1758. . . .

I would esteem myself very happy if I could here present worthily a clear and succinct idea of the principal truths, the sequence of which, discovered by Doctor QUESNAY, is so excellently and clearly developed in this sublime book [*The Natural and Essential Order of Political Societies* by M. de la Rivière, another political economist]. The conviction which they have for a long time carried in my mind prevents me from resisting the desire to attempt this enterprise, which is perhaps beyond my resources. . . .

[There follows a brief description of some of the "principal truths" of the Physiocrats]:

I

THERE is a natural society, anterior to every convention between men, founded on their constitution, physical needs, and obviously common interest.

In this primitive state men have reciprocal *rights* and *duties* by an *absolute* justice, because they stem from physical necessity and are in consequence *absolute* for their existence.

No rights without duties, and no duties without rights.

The *rights* of every man, anterior to conventions, are the *liberty* to provide for his subsistence and well-being, the *proprietorship* of his person and of the things acquired by the work of his person.

His *duties* are work in order to provide for his needs, and respect for the liberty, and personal and movable property of others.

Conventions are entered into between men for the sole purpose of recognizing and guaranteeing mutually these rights and duties established by God himself. . . .

II

THE SPONTANEOUS productions of land and sea are not enough to support a numerous population, nor to procure for man all the pleasures of which he is desirous.

The nature of man invincibly leads him to propagate his species, to procure pleasures, and to flee suffering and privation as much as possible.

Nature, then, prescribes to man the art of increasing production, the cultivation of the land, in order to better his lot, and in order to supply abundantly the needs of increasing families. . . .

IV

THE MORE consumer production is increased, the more men can procure pleasures, and in consequence the more they are happy.

The more men are happy, the more the population increases.

It is in this way that the prosperity of all humanity is related to the greatest possible *net yield* and to the best possible state of landed proprietors.

V

. . . it is necessary that there be the greatest possible *liberty* in the use of all personal, movable and landed property, and the greatest possible *security* in the possession of what one acquires by the use of this property.

To restrict this liberty would be to diminish the net yield of cultivation, and consequently the interest that one takes in cultivation, the total of consumer production, and population.

To commit this outrage would be to declare war on one's fellows, to violate the rights and to fail in the duties instituted by the Creator, to oppose his decrees as much as our feebleness can, to commit a crime of lese majesty divine and human.

The general liberty of enjoying the whole extent of his rights of property supposes necessarily for each individual the entire security of this enjoyment, and obviously proscribes every use of the faculties of some against the property of others.

No property without liberty, no liberty without security.

VI

IN ORDER that there be the greatest possible liberty in the use, and the greatest possible security in the enjoyment of personal, movable and landed property, it is necessary that men united in *society* mutually guarantee this property and protect it reciprocally by all their physical strength.

This mutual guarantee and protection is what properly constitutes *society*.

VIII

THE SOVEREIGN authority is not established in order *to make Laws;* for *the Laws are all made* by the hand of the one who created *rights and duties.*

The *social Laws* established by the supreme Being prescribe uniquely the conservation of the *right of property,* and of the *liberty* which is inseparable from it.

The Decrees of Sovereigns which we call *positive Laws* ought to be only *declaratory acts of these essential Laws of the social order.*

If the Decrees of Sovereigns were contradictory to the *Laws of the social order,* if they forbade that property to be respected, if they ordered the harvests to be burned and little children to be sacrificed, they would not be *Laws* but insane acts which would be obligatory upon no one.

There is therefore a natural and unimpeachable Judge of the decrees even of Sovereigns; and this Judge is *the evidence of their conformity or opposition to the natural Laws of the social* order. . . .

XIX

HEREDITARY Monarchy presents the most perfect form of Government, when it is joined to the establishment of the co-proprietorship of the public in the net yield of all goods, in such proportion that the revenue of the fisc is the largest possible, without the condition of the landed proprietors ceasing to be the best that can be had in society.

*   *   *

Such is the précis of this doctrine which exposes, according to the nature of man, the *necessary* laws of a Government made for man and proper to man in all climates and countries. . . .

Would one believe that in spite of the evidence of the Sovereign truths, the thread of which we have just followed and which manifest to us the laws of this *physiocratic* Government; would one believe that there are still to be found men and writers who say it is not true that God has established a natural order which ought to serve as a rule for society. . . .

ADAM SMITH: *The Wealth of Nations* *

Adam Smith (1723–90), British economist, professor of moral philosophy at Glasgow University, has been called "the first great theorist of

* Adam Smith: *An Inquiry into the Nature and Causes of the Wealth of Nations,* edited by James E. Thorold Rogers (Oxford: The Clarendon Press; 1869), vol. I, pp. 15, 125, 349, 359–60; vol. II, pp. 1, 23–5, 28–9, 272–3.

that stage of capitalist enterprise which we call the domestic system." His immensely popular and influential *Wealth of Nations* was published in 1776, and it was indeed a declaration of economic liberty against the "mercantile" system and craft gild regulation.

IN CIVILIZED society [man] stands at all times in need of the co-operation and assistance of great multitudes, while his whole life is scarce sufficient to gain the friendship of a few persons. In almost every other race of animals each individual, when it is grown up to maturity, is entirely independent, and in its natural state has occasion for the assistance of no other living creature. But man has almost constant occasion for the help of his brethren, and it is in vain for him to expect it from their benevolence only. He will be more likely to prevail if he can interest their self-love in his favour, and show them that it is for their own advantage to do for him what he requires of them. Whoever offers to another a bargain of any kind, proposes to do this. Give me that which I want, and you shall have this which you want, is the meaning of every such offer; and it is in this manner that we obtain from one another the far greater part of those good offices which we stand in need of. It is not from the benevolence of the butcher, the brewer, or the baker, that we expect our dinner, but from their regard to their own interest. We address ourselves, not to their humanity but to their self-love, and never talk to them of our own necessities but of their advantages. Nobody but a beggar chooses to depend chiefly upon the benevolence of his fellow-citizens. . . .

The policy of Europe, by not leaving things at perfect liberty, occasions [many great inequalities].

It does this chiefly in the three following ways. First, by restraining the competition in some employments to a smaller number than would otherwise be disposed to enter into them; secondly, by increasing it in others beyond what it naturally would be; and, thirdly, by obstructing the free circulation of labour and stock, both from employment to employment and from place to place.

First, The policy of Europe occasions a very important inequality in the whole of the advantages and disadvantages of the different employments of labour and stock, by restraining the competition in some employments to a smaller number than might otherwise be disposed to enter into them.

The exclusive privileges of corporations are the principal means it makes use of for this purpose.

The exclusive privilege of an incorporated trade necessarily restrains the competition, in the town where it is established, to those who are free of the trade. To have served an apprenticeship in the town, under a master properly qualified, is commonly the necessary requisite for obtaining this freedom. The bye-laws of the corporation regulate sometimes the number of apprentices which any master is allowed to have, and almost always the number of years which each apprentice is obliged to serve. The intention of both regulations is to restrain the competition to a much smaller number than might otherwise be disposed to enter into the trade. The limitation of the number of apprentices restrains it directly. A long term of apprenticeship restrains it more indirectly, but as effectually, by increasing the expense of education. . . .

But though the profusion of government must, undoubtedly, have retarded the natural progress of England towards wealth and improvement, it has not been able to stop it. The annual produce of its land and labour is, undoubtedly, much greater at present than it was either at the Restoration or at the Revolution. The capital, therefore, annually employed in cultivating this land, and in maintaining this labour, must likewise be much greater. In the midst of all the exactions of government, this capital has been silently and gradually accumulated by the private frugality and good conduct of individuals, by their universal, continual, and uninterrupted effort to better their own condition. It is this effort, protected by law and allowed by liberty to exert itself in the manner that is most advantageous, which has maintained the progress of England towards opulence and improvement in almost all former times, and which, it is to be hoped, will do so in all future times. . . .

In some countries the interest of money has been prohibited by law. But as something can everywhere be made by the use of money, something ought everywhere to be paid for the use of it. This regulation, instead of preventing, has been found from experience to increase the evil of usury; the debtor being obliged to pay, not only for the use of the money, but for the risk which his creditor runs by accepting a compensation for that use. He is obliged, if one may say so, to insure his creditor from the penalties of usury.

In countries where interest is permitted, the law, in order to prevent the extortion of usury, generally fixes the highest rate which can be taken without incurring a penalty. This rate ought always to be somewhat above the lowest market price, or the price which is commonly paid for the use of money by those who can give the most undoubted security. If this legal rate should be fixed below the lowest market rate, the effects of this fixation must be nearly the same as those of a total prohibition of interest. The creditor will not lend his money for less than the use of it is worth, and the debtor must pay him for the risk which he runs by accepting the full value of that use. . . .

[The mercantile system is based on the false but "popular" notion that] "wealth consists in money, or in gold and silver." . . .

The two principles being established, however, that wealth consisted in gold and silver, and that those metals could be brought into a country which had no mines only by the balance of trade, or by exporting to a greater value than it imported, it necessarily became the great object of political economy to diminish as much as possible the importation of foreign goods for home consumption, and to increase as much as possible the exportation of the produce of domestic industry. Its two great engines for enriching the country, therefore, were restraints upon importation, and encouragements to exportation.

The restraints upon importation were of two kinds.

First, restraints upon the importation of such foreign goods for home consumption as could be produced at home, from whatever country they were imported.

Secondly, restraints upon the importation of goods of almost all kinds from those particular countries with which the balance of trade was supposed to be disadvantageous.

Those different restraints consisted sometimes in high duties, and sometimes in absolute prohibitions.

Exportation was encouraged sometimes by drawbacks, sometimes by bounties, sometimes by advantageous treaties of commerce with sovereign states, and sometimes by the establishment of colonies in distant countries. . . .

That this monopoly of the home market frequently gives great encouragement to that particular species of industry which enjoys it, and frequently turns towards that employment a greater share of both the labour and stock of the society than would otherwise have gone to it, cannot be doubted. But whether it tends either to increase the general industry of the society, or to give it the most advantageous direction, is not, perhaps, altogether so evident. . . .

The annual revenue of every society is always precisely equal to the exchangeable value of the whole annual produce of its industry, or rather is precisely the same thing with that exchangeable value. As every individual, therefore, endeavours as much as he can both to employ his capital in the support of domestic industry, and so to direct that industry that its produce may be of the greatest value, every individual necessarily labours to render the annual revenue of the society as great as he can. He generally, indeed, neither intends to promote the public interest, nor knows how much he is promoting it. By preferring the support of domestic to that of foreign industry, he intends only his own security; and by directing that industry in such a manner as its produce may be of the greatest value, he intends only his own gain, and he is in this, as in many other cases, led by an invisible hand to promote an end which was no part of his intention. Nor is it always the worse for the society that it was no part of it. By pursuing his own interest he frequently promotes that of the society more effectually than when he really intends to promote it. I have never known much good done by those who affected to trade for the public good. It is an affectation, indeed, not very common among merchants, and very few words need be employed in dissuading them from it.

What is the species of domestic industry which his capital can employ, and of which the produce is likely to be of the greatest value, every individual, it is evident, can, in his local situation, judge much better than any statesman or lawgiver can do for him. The statesman, who should attempt to direct private people in what manner they ought to employ their capitals, would not only load himself with a most unnecessary attention, but assume an authority which could safely be trusted, not only to no single person, but to no council or senate whatever, and which would nowhere be so dangerous as in the hands of a man who had folly and presumption enough to fancy himself fit to exercise it.

To give the monopoly of the home market to the produce of domestic industry, in any particular art or manufacture, is in some measure to direct private people in what manner they ought to employ their capitals, and must, in almost all cases, be either a useless or a hurtful regulation. If the produce of domestic can be brought there as cheap as that of foreign industry, the regulation is evidently useless. If it cannot, it must generally be hurtful. It is the maxim of every prudent master of a family, never to attempt to make at home what it will cost him more to make than to buy. The tailor does not attempt to make his own shoes, but buys them of the shoemaker. . . .

What is prudence in the conduct of every private family, can scarce be folly in that of a great kingdom. If a foreign country can supply us with a commodity cheaper than we ourselves can make it, better buy it of them with some part of the produce of our own industry, employed in a way in which we have some advantage. The general industry of the country, being always in proportion to the capital which employs it, will not thereby be diminished, no more than that of the above-mentioned artificers, but only left to find out the way in which it can be employed with the greatest advantage. It is certainly not employed to the greatest advantage, when it is thus directed towards an object which it can buy cheaper than it can make. . . .

All systems either of preference or of restraint, therefore, being thus completely taken away, the obvious and simple system of natural liberty establishes itself of its own accord. Every man, as long as he does not violate the laws of justice, is left perfectly free to pursue his own interest his own way, and to bring both his industry and capital into competition with those of any other man, or order of men. The sovereign is completely discharged from a duty, in the attempting to perform which he must always be exposed to innumerable delusions, and for the proper performance of which no human wisdom or knowledge could ever be sufficient—the duty of superintending the industry of private people, and of directing it towards the employments most suitable to the interest of the society. According to the system of natural liberty, the sovereign has only three duties to attend to; three duties of great importance, indeed, but plain and intelligible to common understandings: first, the duty of protecting the society from the violence and invasion of other independent societies; secondly, the duty of protecting, as far as possible, every member of the society from the injustice or oppression of every other member of it, or the duty of establishing an exact administration of justice; and, thirdly, the duty of erecting and maintaining certain public works and certain public institutions, which it can never be for the interest of any individual, or small number of individuals, to erect and maintain; because the profit could never repay the expense to any individual or small number of individuals, though it may frequently do much more than repay it to a great society.

6. *The Idea of Progress*

GIAMBATTISTA VICO: *The New Science* *

It hardly seems necessary to point out that not everybody believed in progress in the eighteenth century. Perhaps the most conspicuous among those who did not was Giambattista Vico (1668–1744), philosopher and professor of rhetoric at the University of Naples and author of *New Science concerning the Common Nature of the Nations* (first edition, 1725). Vico harked back to the ancient idea of historical cycles. But he did more; he anticipated modern ideas of historicism and history as a science. So, though his period of influence did not begin until the next century, he should be thought of as having seminal as well as traditional ideas about nature and the "course" of history.

BUT in the night of thick darkness enveloping the earliest antiquity, so remote from ourselves, there shines the eternal and never failing light of a truth beyond all question: that the world of civil society has certainly been made by men, and that its principles are therefore to be found within the modifications of our own human mind. Whoever reflects on this cannot but marvel that the philosophers should have bent

* Reprinted from Thomas G. Bergin and Max H. Fisch: *The New Science of Giambattista Vico*. Revised translation of the third edition (1744). Copyright 1968 by Cornell University, 1961 by Thomas Goddard Bergin and Max Harold Fisch, 1948 by Cornell University. Used by permission of Cornell University Press.

all their energies to the study of the world of nature, which, since God made it, He alone knows; and that they should have neglected the study of the world of nations, or civil world, which, since men had made it, men could come to know. This abberation was a consequence of that infirmity of the human mind by which, immersed and buried in the body, it naturally inclines to take notice of bodily things, and finds the effort to attend to itself too laborious; just as the bodily eye sees all objects outside itself but needs a mirror to see itself.

Now since this world of nations has been made by men, let us see in what institutions all men agree and always have agreed. For these institutions will be able to give us the universal and eternal principles (such as every science must have) on which all nations were founded and still preserve themselves. . . .

*   *   *

This New Science or metaphysic, studying the common nature of nations in the light of divine providence, discovers the origins of divine and human institutions among the gentile nations, and thereby establishes a system of the natural law of the gentes, which proceeds with the greatest equality and constancy through the three ages which the Egyptians handed down to us as the three periods through which the world has passed up to their time. These are: (1) The age of the gods, in which the gentiles believed they lived under divine governments, and everything was commanded them by auspices and oracles, which are the oldest institutions in profane history. (2) The age of the heroes, in which they reigned everywhere in aristocratic commonwealths, on account of a certain superiority of nature which they held themselves to have over the plebs. (3) The age of men, in which all men recognized themselves as equal in human nature, and therefore there were established first the popular commonwealths and then the monarchies, both of which are forms of human government.

In harmony with these three kinds of nature and government, three kinds of language were spoken which compose the vocabulary of this Science: (1) That of the time of the families when gentile men were newly received into humanity. This, we shall find, was a mute language of signs and physical objects having natural relations to the ideas they wished to express. (2) That spoken by means of heroic emblems, or similitudes, comparisons, images, metaphors, and natural descriptions, which make up the great body of the heroic language which was spoken at the time the heroes reigned. (3) Human language using words agreed upon by the people, a language of which they are absolute lords, and which is proper to the popular commonwealths and monarchical states; a language whereby the people may fix the meaning of the laws by which the nobles as well as the plebs are bound. Hence, among all nations, once the laws had been put into the vulgar tongue, the science of laws passed from the control of the nobles. Hitherto, among all nations, the nobles, being also priests, had kept the laws in a secret language as a sacred thing. That is the natural reason for the secrecy of the laws among the Roman patricians until popular liberty arose. . . .

Along with these three languages—proper to the three ages in which three forms of government prevailed, conforming to three types of civil natures, which succeed one another as the nations run their course —we find there went also in the same order a jurisprudence suited to each in its time.

Of these (three types of jurisprudence) the first was a mystic theology, which prevailed in the period when the gentiles were commanded by the gods. . . .

The second was the heroic jurisprudence, all verbal scrupulosity (in which Ulysses was manifestly expert). This jurisprudence looked to what the Roman jurisconsults called civil equity and we call reason of state. . . .

The last type of jurisprudence was that of natural equity, which reigns naturally in the free commonwealths, in which the people, each for his own particular good (without understanding that it is the same for all), are led to command universal laws. They naturally desire these laws to bend benignly to the least details of matters calling for equal utility. . . .

*   *   *

But as the popular states became corrupt, so also did the philosophies. They descended to skepticism. Learned fools fell to calumniating the truth. Thence arose a false eloquence, ready to uphold either of the opposed sides of a case indifferently. Thus it came about that, by abuse of eloquence like that of the tribunes of the plebs at Rome, when the citizens were no longer content with making wealth the basis of rank, they strove to make it an instrument of power. And as furious south winds whip up the sea, so these citizens provoked civil wars in their commonwealths and drove them to total disorder. Thus they caused the commonwealths to fall from a perfect liberty into the perfect tyranny of anarchy or the unchecked liberty of the free peoples, which is the worst of all tyrannies. . . .

But if the peoples are rotting in that ultimate civil disease and cannot agree on a monarch from within, and are not conquered and preserved by better nations from without, then providence for their extreme ill has its extreme remedy at hand. For such peoples, like so many beasts, have fallen into the custom of each man thinking only of his own private interests and have reached the extreme of delicacy, or better of pride, in which like wild animals they bristle and lash out at the slightest displeasure. Thus no matter how great the throng and press of their bodies, they live like wild beasts in a deep solitude of spirit and will, scarcely any two being able to agree since each follows his own pleasure or caprice. By reason of all this, providence decrees that, through obstinate factions and desperate civil wars, they shall turn their cities into forests and the forests into dens and lairs of men. In this way, through long centuries of barbarism, rust will consume the misbegotten subtleties of malicious wits that have turned them into beasts made more inhuman by the barbarism of reflection than the first men had been made by the barbarism of sense. . . . Hence peoples who have reached this point of premeditated malice, when they receive this last remedy of providence and are thereby stunned and brutalized, are sensible no longer of comforts, delicacies, pleasures, and pomp, but only of the sheer necessities of life. And the few survivors in the midst of an abundance of the things necessary for life naturally become sociable and, returning to the primitive simplicity of the first world of peoples, are again religious, truthful, and faithful. Thus providence brings back among them the piety, faith, and truth which are the natural foundations of justice as well as the graces and beauties of the eternal order of God. . . .

JOSEPH PRIESTLEY *

> Joseph Priestley (1733–1804) was a Christian *philosophe* who hobnobbed with French and English free-thinkers but who defended Christianity against the atheists. His Christianity was, however, of the liberal type exemplified earlier by Locke and Toland. He was at one and the same time an experimental chemist of some distinction, a nonconformist minister, and a political liberal. The following selections are from his *Lectures on History* (1788) and *An Essay on the first Principles of Government, and on the Nature of Political, Civil, and Religious Liberty* (1768).

SINCE, in the greatest part of the works of God, we see plain marks of wise and kind intention, we never think we ought to give up our belief of the wisdom and goodness of God, because we are not able to see how every appearance in nature is reconcileable with them; and if this be our maxim in the investigation of the works of nature, much more ought it to be so in scanning the ways of God in the course of his providence; this being a subject in itself much more obscure, and to which our faculties, for the reasons given above, are much more unequal. Let an historian,

* Joseph Priestley: *Lectures on History* (Birmingham: J. Johnson; 1788), pp. 530–2; *Essay on Government* (London: J. Johnson; 1771), pp. 1–5.

therefore, attend to every instance of improvement, and a better state of things being brought about, by the events which are presented to him in history, and let him ascribe those events to an *intention* in the Divine Being to bring about that better state of things by means of those events; and if he cannot see the same benevolent tendency in all other appearances let him remain in suspence with regard to them.

Let the person, then, who would trace the conduct of Divine Providence, attend to every advantage which the present age enjoys above ancient times, and see whether he cannot perceive marks of things being in a progress towards a state of greater perfection. Let him particularly attend to every event which contributes to the propagation of religious knowledge; and lastly, let him carefully observe all the evils which mankind complain of, and consider whether they be not either remedies of greater evils, or, supposing the general constitution of things unalterable, the necessary means of introducing a greater degree of happiness than could have been brought about by any other means; at least, whether they be not, in fact, subservient to a state of greater happiness. I shall make a few observations upon each of these heads, in order to assist you in your farther enquiries into this important subject.

That the state of the world at present, and particularly the state of Europe, is vastly preferable to what it was in any former period, is evident from the very first view of things. A thousand circumstances shew how inferior the ancients were to the moderns in religious knowledge, in science in general, in government, in laws, both the laws of nations, and those of particular states, in arts, in commerce, in the conveniences of life, in manners, and in consequence of all these, in *happiness*. Almost all these particulars have been demonstrated in the course of these lectures. I shall, therefore, confine myself, in this place, to two particulars, comprehended under the general subject of laws and government, in which the superiority of the internal constitution of modern states above those of the ancients will appear to great advantage, and those are, *personal security* and *personal liberty*.

* * *

Man derives two capital advantages from the superiority of his intellectual powers. The first is, that, as an individual, he possesses a certain comprehension of mind, whereby he contemplates and enjoys the past and the future, as well as the present. This comprehension is enlarged with the experience of every day; and by this means the happiness of man, as he advances in intellect, is continually less dependent on temporary circumstances and sensations.

The next advantage resulting from the same principle, and which is, in many respects, both the cause and effect of the former, is, that the human species itself is capable of a similar and unbounded improvement;

whereby mankind in a later age are greatly superior to mankind in a former age, the individuals being taken at the same time of life. Of this progress of the species, brute animals are more incapable than they are of that relating to individuals. No horse of this age seems to have any advantage over horses of former ages; and if there be any improvement in the species, it is owing to our manner of breeding and training them. But a man at this time, who has been tolerably well educated, in an improved christian country, is a being possessed of much greater power, to be, and to make happy, than a person of the same age, in the same, or any other country, some centuries ago. And, for this reason, I make no doubt, that a person some centuries hence will, at the same age, be as much superior to us.

The great instrument in the hand of divine providence, of this progress of the species towards perfection, is *society*, and consequently *government*. In a state of nature the powers of any individual are dissipated by an attention to a multiplicity of objects. The employments of all are similar. From generation to generation every man does the same that every other does, or has done, and no person begins where another ends; at least, general improvements are exceedingly slow, and uncertain. This we see exemplified in all barbarous nations, and especially in countries thinly inhabited, where the connections of the people are slight, and consequently society and government very imperfect; and it may be seen more particularly in North America, and Greenland. Whereas a state of more perfect society admits of a proper distribution and division of the objects of human attention. In such a state, men are connected with and subservient to one another; so that, while one man confines himself to one single object, another may give the same undivided attention to another object.

Thus the powers of all have their full effect; and hence arise improvements in all the conveniences of life, and in every branch of knowledge. In this state of things, it requires but a few years to comprehend the whole preceding progress of any one art or science; and the rest of a man's life, in which his faculties are the most perfect, may be given to the extension of it. If, by this means, one art or science should grow too large for an easy comprehension, in a moderate space of time, a commodious subdivision will be made. Thus all knowledge will be subdivided and extended; and *knowledge*, as Lord *Bacon* observes, being *power*, the human powers will, in fact, be enlarged; nature, including both its materials, and its laws, will be more at our command; men will make their situation in this world abundantly more easy and comfortable; they will probably prolong their existence in it, and will grow daily more happy, each in himself, and more able (and, I believe, more disposed) to communicate happiness to others. Thus, whatever was the beginning of this world, the end will be glorious and paradisaical, beyond what our imaginations can now conceive. Extravagant as some may suppose these views to be, I think I could show them to be fairly suggested by the true theory of human nature, and to arise from the natural course of human affairs. But, for the present, I wave this subject, the contemplation of which always makes me happy.

MARQUIS DE CONDORCET: *The Progress of the Human Mind* *

It is one of the ironies of history that Condorcet wrote his optimistic Esquisse *in hiding, while under sentence of death by the Jacobin-controlled Revolutionary Convention of 1793 and 1794.*

Introduction

THE RESULT of [my work] will be to show, from reasoning and from facts, that no bounds have been fixed to the improvement of the human faculties; that the perfectibility of man is absolutely indefinite; that the progress of this perfectibility, henceforth above the control of every power that would impede it, has no other limit than the duration of the globe upon which nature has placed us. The course of this progress may doubtless be more or less rapid, but it can never be retrograde; at least while the earth retains its situation in the system of the universe, and the laws of this system shall neither effect upon the globe a general overthrow, nor introduce such changes as would no longer permit the human race to preserve and exercise therein the same faculties, and find the same resources. . . .

Every thing tells us that we are approaching the era of one of the grand revolutions of the human race. . . .

Tenth Epoch: Future Progress of Mankind

If man can predict, almost with certainty, those appearances of which he understands the laws; if, even when the laws are unknown to him, experience of the past enables him to foresee, with considerable probability, future appearances; why should we suppose it a chimerical undertaking to delineate, with some degree of truth, the picture of the future destiny of mankind from the results of its history? The only foundation of faith in the natural sciences is the principle, that the general laws, known or unknown, which regulate the phenomena of the universe, are regular and constant; and why should this principle, applicable to the other operations of nature, be less true when applied to the development of the intellectual and moral faculties of man? In short, as opinions formed from experience, relative to the same class of objects, are the only rule by

* Condorcet: *The Progress of the Human Mind* (Philadelphia: Lang and Ustick; 1796), pp. 11–12, 22–3, 250–1, 259–60, 265–6, 268, 270–3, 275, 278–9, 281–2, 288–93.

which men of soundest understanding are governed in their conduct, why should the philosopher be proscribed from supporting his conjectures upon a similar basis, provided he attribute to them no greater certainty than the number, the consistency, and the accuracy of actual observations shall authorise?

Our hopes, as to the future condition of the human species, may be reduced to three points: the destruction of inequality between different nations; the progress of equality in one and the same nation; and lastly, the real improvement of man.

Will not every nation one day arrive at the state of civilization attained by those people who are most enlightened, most free, most exempt from prejudices, as the French, for instance, and the Anglo-Americans? Will not the slavery of countries subjected to kings, the barbarity of African tribes, and the ignorance of savages gradually vanish? Is there upon the face of the globe a single spot the inhabitants of which are condemned by nature never to enjoy liberty, never to exercise their reason?

*   *   *

In tracing the history of societies we have had occasion to remark, that there frequently exists a considerable distinction between the rights which the law acknowledges in the citizens of a state, and those which they really enjoy; between the equality established by political institutions, and that which takes place between the individual members; and that to this disproportion was chiefly owing the destruction of liberty in the ancient republics, the storms which they had to encounter, and the weakness that surrendered them into the power of foreign tyrants.

Three principal causes may be assigned for these distinctions: inequality of wealth, inequality of condition between him whose resources of subsistence are secured to himself and descendable to his family, and him whose resources are annihilated with the termination of his life, or rather of that part of his life in which he is capable of labour; and lastly, inequality of instruction.

It will therefore behoove us to shew, that these three kinds of real inequality must continually diminish; but without becoming absolutely extinct, since they have natural and necessary causes, which it would be absurd as well as dangerous to think of destroying; nor can we attempt even to destroy entirely their effects, without opening at the same time more fruitful sources of inequality, and giving to the rights of man a more direct and more fatal blow.

It is easy to prove that fortunes naturally tend to equality, and that their extreme disproportion either could not exist, or would quickly cease, if positive law had not introduced factitious means of amassing and perpetuating them; if an entire freedom of commerce and industry were brought forward to supersede the advantages which prohibitory laws and fiscal rights necessarily give to the rich over the poor; if duties upon every sort of transfer and convention, if prohibitions to certain kinds, and the tedious and expensive formalities prescribed to other kinds; if the uncertainty and expense attending their execution had not palsied the efforts of the poor, and swallowed up their little accumulations; if political institutions had not laid certain prolific sources of opulence open to a few, and shut them against the many. . . .

Instruction, properly directed, corrects the natural inequality of the faculties, instead of strengthening it, in like manner as good laws remedy the natural inequality of the means of subsistence; or as, in societies whose institutions shall have effected this equality, liberty, though subjected to a regular government, will be more extensive, more complete, than in the independence of savage life. Then has the social art accomplished its end, that of securing and extending for all the enjoyment of the common rights which impartial nature has bequeathed to all.

* * *

The energy, the real extent of the human intellect may remain the same; but the instruments which it can employ will be multiplied and improved; but the language which fixes and determines the ideas will acquire more precision and compass; and it will not be here, as in the science of mechanics, where, to increase the force, we must diminish the velocity; on the contrary, the methods by which genius will arrive at the discovery of new truths, augment at once both the force and the rapidity of its operations.

* * *

If we pass to the progress of the arts, those arts particularly the theory of which depends on these very same sciences, we shall find that it can have no inferior limits; that their processes are susceptible of the same improvement, the same simplifications, as the scientific methods; that instruments, machines, looms, will add every day to the capabilities and skill of man—will augment at once the excellence and precision of his works, while they will diminish the time and labour necessary for executing them; and that then will disappear the obstacles that still oppose themselves to the progress in question, accidents which will be foreseen and prevented; and lastly, the unhealthiness at present attendant upon certain operations, habits and climates.

* * *

It may, however, be demanded, whether, amidst this improvement in industry and happiness, where the wants and faculties of men will continually become better proportioned, each successive generation possess more various stores, and of consequence in each generation the number of individuals be greatly increased; it may, I say, be demanded, whether these principles of improvement and increase may not, by their continual operation, ultimately lead to degeneracy and destruction? Whether the number of inhabitants in the universe at length exceeding the means of existence, there will not result a continual decay of happiness and population, and a progress towards barbarism, or at least a sort of oscillation between good and evil? . . .

Supposing the affirmative, supposing it actually to take place, there would result from it nothing alarming, either to the happiness of the human race, or its indefinite perfectibility; if we consider, that prior to this period the progress of reason will have walked hand in hand with that of the sciences; that the absurd prejudices of superstition will have ceased to infuse into morality a harshness that corrupts and degrades, instead of purifying and exalting it; that men will then know, that the duties they may be under relative to propagation will consist not in the question of giving *existence* to a greater number of beings, but *happiness;* will have for their object, the general welfare of the human species; of the society in which they live; of the family to which they are attached; and not the puerile idea of encumbering the earth with useless and wretched mortals.

*   *   *

Among the variety, almost infinite, of possible systems, in which the general principles of equality and natural rights should be respected, have we yet fixed upon the precise rules of ascertaining with certainty those which best secure the preservation of these rights, which afford the freest scope for their exercise and enjoyment, which promote most effectually the peace and welfare of individuals, and the strength, repose, and prosperity of nations?

The application of the arithmetic of combinations and probabilities to these sciences, promises an improvement by so much the more considerable, as it is the only means of giving to their results an almost mathematical precision, and of appreciating their degree of certainty or probability.

*   *   *

In manner as the mathematical and physical sciences tend to improve the arts that are employed for our most simple wants, so is it not equally in the necessary order of nature that the moral and political sciences should exercise a similar influence upon the motives that direct our sentiments and our actions? . . .

What vicious habit can be mentioned, what practice contrary to good faith, what crime even, the origin and first cause of which may not be traced in the legislation, institutions, and prejudices of the country in which we observe such habit, such practice, or such crime to be committed?

In short, does not the well-being, the prosperity, resulting from the progress that will be made by the useful arts, in consequence of their being founded upon a sound theory, resulting, also, from an improved legislation, built upon the truths of the political sciences, naturally dispose men to humanity, to benevolence, and to justice? Do not all the observations, in fine, which we proposed to develop in this work prove, that the moral goodness of man, the necessary consequence of his organization, is, like all his other faculties, susceptible of an indefinite improvement? and that nature has connected, by a chain which cannot be broken, truth, happiness, and virtue?

* * *

The people being more enlightened, and having resumed the right of disposing for themselves of their blood and their treasure, will learn by degrees to regard war as the most dreadful of all calamities, the most terrible of all crimes. The first wars that will be superseded, will be those into which the usurpers of sovereignty have hitherto drawn their subjects for the maintenance of rights pretendedly hereditary.

Nations will know, that they cannot become conquerors without losing their freedom; that perpetual confederations are the only means of maintaining their independence; that their object should be security, and not power. By degrees commercial prejudices will die away; a false mercantile interest will lose the terrible power of imbuing the earth with blood, and of ruining nations under the idea of enriching them. As the people of different countries will at last be drawn into closer intimacy, by the principles of politics and morality, as each, for its own advantage, will invite foreigners to an equal participation of the benefits which it may have derived either from nation or its own industry, all the causes which produce, envenom, and perpetuate national animosities, will one by one disappear, and will no more furnish to warlike insanity either fuel or pretext.

Institutions, better combined than those projects of perpetual peace which have occupied the leisure and consoled the heart of certain philosophers, will accelerate the progress of this fraternity of nations; and wars, like assassinations, will be ranked in the number of those daring atrocities, humiliating and loathsome to nature; and which fix upon the country or the age whose annals are stained with them, an indelible opprobrium.

* * *

We have hitherto considered [man] as possessing only the same natural faculties, as endowed with the same organization. How much greater would be the certainty, how much wider the compass of our hopes, could we prove that these natural faculties themselves, that this very organization, are also susceptible of melioration? And this is the last question we shall examine.

The organic perfectibility or deterioration of the classes of the vegetable, or species of the animal kingdom, may be regarded as one of the general laws of nature.

This law extends itself to the human race; and it cannot be doubted that the progress of the sanative art, that the use of more wholesome food and more comfortable habitations, that a mode of life which shall develop the physical powers by exercise, without at the same time impairing them by excess; in fine, that the destruction of the two most active causes of deterioration, penury and wretchedness on the one hand, and enormous wealth on the other, must necessarily tend to prolong the common duration of man's existence, and secure him a more constant health and a more robust constitution. It is manifest that the improvement of the practice of medicine, become more efficacious in consequence of the progress of reason and the social order, must in the end put a period to transmissible or contagious disorders, as well to those general maladies resulting from climate, aliments, and the nature of certain occupations. Nor would it be difficult to prove that this hope might be extended to almost every other malady, of which it is probable we shall hereafter discover the most remote causes. Would it even be absurd to suppose this quality of melioration in the human species as susceptible of an indefinite advancement; to suppose that a period must one day arrive when death will be nothing more than the effect either of extraordinary accidents, or of the slow and gradual decay of the vital powers; and that the duration of the middle space, of the interval between the birth of man and this decay, will itself have no assignable limit? Certainly man will not become immortal; but may not the distance between the moment in which he draws his first breath, and the common term when, in the course of nature, without malady or accident, he finds it impossible any longer to exist, be necessarily protracted? . . .

But may not our physical faculties, the force, the sagacity, the acuteness of the senses, be numbered among the qualities, the individual improvement of which it will be practicable to transmit? An attention to the different breeds of domestic animals must lead us to adopt the affirmative of this question, and a direct observation of the human species itself will be found to strengthen the opinion.

Lastly, may we not include in the same circle the intellectual and moral faculties? May not our parents, who transmit to us the advantages or defects of their conformation, and from whom we receive our features and shape, as well as our propensities to certain physical affections, transmit to us also that part of organization upon which intellect, strength of understanding, energy of soul or moral sensibility depend? Is it not probable that education, by improving these qualities, will at the same time have an influence upon, will modify and improve this organization itself? Analogy, an investigation of the human faculties, and even some facts, appear to authorise these conjectures, and there to enlarge the boundary of our hopes.

Such are the questions with which we shall terminate the last division of our work. And how admirably calculated is this view of the human race, emancipated from its chains, released alike from the dominion of chance, as well as from that of the enemies of its progress, and advancing with a firm and indeviate step in the paths of truth, to console the philosopher lamenting the errors, the flagrant acts of injustice, the crimes with which the earth is still polluted? It is the contemplation of this prospect that rewards him for all his efforts to assist the progress of reason and the establishment of liberty. He dares to regard these efforts as a part of the eternal chain of the destiny of mankind; and in this persuasion he finds the true delight of virtue, the pleasure of having performed a durable service, which no vicissitude will ever destroy in a fatal operation calculated to restore the reign of prejudice and slavery. This sentiment is the asylum into which he retires, and to which the memory of his persecutors cannot follow him: he unites himself in imagination with man restored to his rights, delivered from oppression, and proceeding with rapid strides in the path of happiness; he forgets his own misfortunes while his thoughts are thus employed; he lives no longer to adversity, calumny and malice, but becomes the associate of these wiser and more fortunate beings whose enviable condition he so earnestly contributed to produce.

The community is a fictitious *body*, composed of the individual persons who are considered as constituting as it were its *members*. The interest of the community then is, what?—the sum of the interests of the several members who compose it.

Jeremy Bentham, PRINCIPLES OF MORALS AND
LEGISLATION

3. *CENTURY OF BECOMING*

In nine cases out of ten, the individual is the architect of his own good fortune and the rise of one man by honest means, furnishes a ground of hope to all.

MECHANIC'S MAGAZINE

If there is any idea that properly belongs to our century, . . . it is, as it seems to me, the idea of progress, conceived as a general law of history and the future of humanity.

A. Javary, DE L'IDÉE DE PROGRÈS

"The struggle for existence," and "Natural selection," have become household words and every-day conceptions. . . . To any one who studies the signs of the times, the emergence of the philosophy of Evolution . . . is the most portentous event of the nineteenth century.

Thomas Henry Huxley, ON THE RECEPTION OF
THE "ORIGIN OF SPECIES"

The whole history of mankind . . . has been a history of class struggles, contests between exploiting and exploited, ruling and oppressed classes. . . . This proposition is destined to do for history what Darwin's theory has done for biology. . . .

Friedrich Engels, PREFACE TO THE COMMUNIST MANIFESTO

Century of Becoming

$\mathscr{O}$N THE eve of the battle of Jena (1806) a young professor of philosophy at the nearby University hailed the new century as a "birth-time" or "period of transition." It is hardly surprising that Hegel and other young intellectuals should have thought of their times as such. They were living in a revolutionary epoch in which old ways of thinking, as well as old institutions, were tottering and collapsing. But, as Hegel said, it was one thing to see the new-born child, but quite another to visualize what it would grow up to be. What would the nineteenth century actually be like?

In retrospect it seems ironic that so many of Hegel's contemporaries, regardless of party affiliations, should have looked forward confidently to a new age of organic belief. According to the currently fashionable theory expounded by the fantastic, yet often perceptive, Comte de Saint-Simon (1760–1825), history observes an alternativity of "organic" and "critical" periods. Each organic period, that is, one in which men do not live in doubt but are united by firm convictions, is succeeded by a critical or transitional period characterized by disunity and destruction. In the Saint-Simonian scheme the eighteenth-century Enlightenment figured as the tail-end of the most recent critical period that began with the Reformation and ended by destroying the religious synthesis of the Christian Middle Ages. The nineteenth century marked the commencement of a new organic period that would be based not on supernatural religion but on science and that would constitute a step forward, possibly the final step, in the progress of the human race. "The philosophy of the eighteenth century has been critical; that of the nineteenth century will be inventive and constructive," Saint-Simon predicted. Many others who did not share his faith in science, Thomas Carlyle, for instance, and Hegel, agreed substantially with his optimistic prognostication.

But alas, an organic period was precisely what the nineteenth century did not turn out to be. To the contrary, it became the most critical period to date, not only in the Saint-Simonian but in a new and more radical sense. Matthew Arnold was one of the first to sense the extreme "multitudinousness" of nineteenth-century thought and to perceive that it was spreading from society to the individual, splitting his mind, and depriving him of the ability to see life as a whole. Doubtless, this "anarchy," affecting the individual now as well as society, was much more pronounced at the end of the century than at the beginning. It was, however, far advanced at mid-century, as two such different observers as Arnold and John Stuart Mill bear witness. Mill had not abandoned his Saint-Simonian dream of a new sort of organic unity. Yet he was making the same point as Arnold, namely that uncertainty of mind (or "congestion of the brain" as Arnold also called it) was on the increase and that it was attributable to the sheer weight of knowledge in the new age, the welter of ideas, facts, and impressions with which the individual mind had to cope. Mill made the following entry in his diary for January 13, 1854: "Those who should be the guides of the rest [the better educated classes], see too many sides to every question. They hear so much said, or find that so much can be said, about everything, that they feel no assurance of the truth of anything." Arnold's Empedocles (*Empedocles on Etna*, 1853) was just such a man as Mill was talking about. Empedocles likened the human soul to a mirror hung by the gods on a cord in space, tossed by every gust, reflecting a thousand impressions.

> Hither and thither spins
> The wind-borne, mirroring soul,
> A thousand glimpses wins,
> And never sees a whole;
> Looks once, and drives elsewhere, and leaves its last employ.[1]

A remark made by the French scholar and critic Ernest Renan at almost exactly the same time suggests another and deeper reason why the nineteenth century became so "critical." "The great progress of criticism," he wrote in the preface to his doctoral dissertation, "has been *to substitute the category of becoming for the category of being*, the conception of the relative for that of the absolute, movement for immobility." [2] One is reminded of what John Dewey said much later apropos of Darwinism, that it had brought about a transfer of interest

---

[1] *Empedocles on Etna* was, to be sure, one of Arnold's most negative poems. Soon thereafter he turned essayist in order to propose a cure for the "anarchy" of his times (see selections from *Culture and Anarchy*, pp. 503–506 this text).

[2] Ernest Renan, *Averroes et l'Averroïsme* (Paris, 1852), p. ii. Italics are editorial, except for the words "devenir" and "être."

from the permanent to the changing and thus transformed the whole logic of knowledge, including the treatment of morals, politics, and religion. But Renan had observed this logic at work before Darwin. "Formerly," he went on to say, "everything was considered as being; one spoke of philosophy, law, politics, art, poetry, in an absolute manner; now everything is considered as in the process of becoming (*en voie de se faire*)." For Renan this was the essence of the "historical method" as opposed to the "dogmatic method," and he was not wrong to single it out as the characteristic mark or feature of nineteenth-century thinking. Thanks partly to developments, already noted, within the Enlightenment itself and to certain new emphases in the Romantic Movement, and also, partly no doubt, to rapid changes effected by the French and Industrial Revolutions, men were beginning to see everything—nature, man, society, God—in a new light, *sub specie temporis*, as not simply changing but developing into or *becoming* something different. This new category of thinking explains many of the regnant ideas of the nineteenth century and even to some extent its peculiar malaise. It explains, for instance, the longing for infinity so noticeable in the romantics, and the Fichtean Ego "endlessly striving." It explains the Hegelian conception of thinking as properly dialectical, and of the world as "a becoming" rather than a system of fixed entities. It explains the new historicism with its accent on the changes wrought by time and its aversion to the old natural law tradition. It even explains, at least partly, the new doctrines of evolution in both animate and inanimate nature. It was an essentially "critical" mode of thinking, destructive of the fixities or of anything fixed. It was, of course, not necessarily pessimistic; in fact, it might and often did promise better things to come. But in the end its historical effect was more corrosive than not, for it involved thinking men in a morass of relativism. Relativism became a considerable problem for a considerable number of thinking men toward the end of the century, and relativism, one might suppose, was the acme of what Saint-Simon meant by criticism. It is this end effect that more than anything else justifies us in speaking of the nineteenth century as a "period of criticism" *par excellence*, and also as a prelude to our own.

II

YET the nineteenth century was by no means *only* a period of criticism (or Age of Becoming) and to leave it at that would be to miss a great deal. To get it in sharper focus one probably needs to jettison the Saint-Simonian concepts and find others less rigid and simplistic. There are, it seems to me, two different, and more valid, ways of looking at the nineteenth century that are not mutually exclusive. The first is to see it as a continuation of the eighteenth-century Enlightenment, as a further extension and expansion of the latter's world-view in an industrial age. On this view the nineteenth century marked the culmination of modernity, that is, the spread to wider circles than ever before of that "modern" view of life that, as we have seen, began to be formulated in the Battle between the Ancients and Moderns in the seventeenth century. Modernity triumphed at last in the New Enlightenment of Auguste Comte and Ernest Renan, Jeremy Bentham, John Stuart Mill, and his father, James Mill, and the Young Hegelians. Here is where Saint-Simon's instinct was essentially correct. He understood better than most—far better than Hegel, for instance—that the new century would belong, like no century before it, to the scientists, industrialists, and engineers. He exaggerated the power of science to restore unity to Western thought. Nevertheless, his comparison of the human mind to "a vast building" dominated initially by priests but gradually taken over by scientists is not far from the mark, especially if applied to the "positivist" decades of the century. Scientism peaked during those middle years. Moreover, despite the later "revolt against positivism," its prestige remained high to the end of the century and beyond.

A second and equally valid way of viewing nineteenth-century thought is to see in it the emergence of another kind of modernity, closer to our own, not at all like what Saint-Simon was talking about. It is noteworthy that the romantics of the 1790's had already begun to use the word "modern" in a different sense; in fact, they turned it on its head and made it denote, among other things, subjective expression in poetry as opposed to "classical" objectivism. They were obviously bored with the Moderns as well as the Ancients and determined to build their own universe, one that, as they thought, would reflect more faithfully the inner and even unconscious shades of human experience. To the degree that romantic views of nature and man caught on, the nineteenth century marked new beginnings rather than merely the continuation or culmination of a predominantly scientific and rationalistic type of culture. Much of nineteenth-century thought conceals the inherent antagonism between these two modernities. Attempts were even made to mediate between them, as by Comte, whose Positivism had its romantic side; John Stuart Mill, who admired both Samuel Taylor Coleridge and Bentham; and others. But toward the end the new modernity, if we may call it such, became more pronounced, and considerably more negative than in the earlier days of the Romantic Movement. It now involved a really serious running-down of confidence, not only in the Christian verities, but also in most of those things in which the true "Modern" had come to believe: rational man, a rational universe, knowledge itself, or the power of knowledge to produce virtue and human happiness. *The new meaning of the Period*

It is important, as has been intimated, not to exaggerate this trend, which can hardly have been dominant even in the 1890's. Yet even as sober a judge of "opinion" as the historian A. V. Dicey noted the disintegration of established beliefs of all kinds in the latter part of the century that he coupled, although perhaps not too sharply, with "the apotheosis of instinct" in the new view of human nature and the "historical method," which had become an all but universal way of looking at ideas and institutions.[3] Apostles of the positivist modernity were still very much in evidence, and maybe in the majority, in 1890. But there were more critics now, and more apostates and ironists. Among the latter were the novelist and critic Anatole France, whose *Garden of Epicurus* of 1895 so well captures the spirit of this latter-day modernity, and his mentor Renan. Renan, so hopeful of science in his youth and so delighted with "becoming," soured in his old age. He seriously wondered if scientific criticism had not gone too far and destroyed the illusions men so obviously need to produce a viable civilization. "We have eaten the fruits of the tree of science," wrote Anatole France, "and there remains in our mouths a taste of ashes." What would Saint-Simon have said if he could have heard the New Moderns talking? At the very least, would he not have had to alter his chronology, as Lenin felt obliged to alter the chronology of the Marxist revolution. To fit the facts, would he not have had to extend the "critical period" of modern history down farther and perhaps tack onto it an additional Age of Irony. Would he have been able to stick to his conviction that a new "organic period," based on faith in science, was imminent? There were still a good many people at the end of the century, as at the beginning, who kept the faith. But it was just then, also, that Anatole France and some others were beginning to contemplate the irrationality of man and even "the tragic absurdity of living" in the universe revealed by science.[4]

III

THE nineteenth century had many facets. It makes sense therefore to break it down into a number of styles of thought or subperiods. I have organized the readings around four of these that were indubitably of major importance. The first is romanti-

[3] A. V. Dicey, *Lectures on the Relation between Law and Public Opinion in England, in the Nineteenth Century* (London, 1905).
[4] See Anatole France's essay entitled "Pourquoi sommes-nous tristes?"

cism, which reached its apogee between the last decades of the eighteenth century and about 1830 or 1840. Like other movements in thought, it assumed different forms in different countries, and there was disagreement, too, as to what the word itself meant. Nevertheless, it had a discernible core. On the negative side it represented a revolt against the rational-empirical and "neo-classical" culture of the Enlightenment, which seemed to the romantics to provide an altogether too mean and narrow view of the world. Diderot's world, said Carlyle, was only "a half-world, distorted into looking like a whole." "Fractional," "partial," "insignificant," and "poor" were the adjectives he used to describe it. It should be emphasized that romanticism was no mere literary or artistic movement, although it did exalt the artistic genius and with spectacular results. The Romantic Movement plumbed all of man's deepest problems and eventually came up with new views of "Man, Nature, and Society," as William Wordsworth proposed doing in his philosophic poem *The Excursion*. It tried to restore man's sense of "the Infinite," although not necessarily by going back to the traditional churches. It tried to breach the dualism between man and nature by putting "spirit," that is, divinity and moral purpose, back into nature and history. It gave man himself enlarged faculties in order to discover truth beyond the empirical world and to "imagine" and create worlds of his own. It deepened man's historical sense, his sense of a present with important links to the past, and of profound differences between nations and peoples. In a word, it shook the foundations.

I have adopted the term "New Enlightenment" for the second movement because it seems to me to have been a continuation, in spirit if not always in doctrine, of the eighteenth-century Enlightenment. Chronologically, it ran more or less in tandem with the Romantic Movement until mid-century. Although not uninfluenced by the latter, particularly by its historicism, its spirit and aims were quite different. "The French *philosophes* of the eighteenth century were the example we sought to imitate," said John Stuart Mill of the Philosophical Radicals of the 1820's. Mill's mentor Bentham was suckled on Hume and David Hartley, Helvétius, and Adam Smith. Similarly, Comte cannot really be understood without reference to the "positivism" of the Old Enlightenment and Condorcet and Saint-Simon. The affinities between the Young Hegelians in Germany and the Enlightenment, even their own *Aufklärung*, were not nearly so tight. Yet they, too, carried the torch in their attack on tradition—mostly traditional religion in the first generation (David Friedrich Strauss and Ludwig Feuerbach), but also traditional social and economic ideas in the second (Karl Marx and Friedrich Engels)—in the name of reason or philosophy or, more and more now, of history. True, they were more historical-minded (but not more traditional-minded) than the old philosophers, closer to the romantics in that one respect if in no other. But in general they all believed in the superseding of religion by a more up-to-date "philosophy" or "science." Politically, these three prongs of the movement were miles apart. The Benthamites were liberals, the French Positivists generally conservatives, the Young Hegelians either apolitical or socialists or communists. But like their spiritual forbears they had faith, all of them, in the progress of humanity toward a brighter future. Some among them, indeed, had begun to think of progress not as a hope or aspiration but as "a general law of history and the future of humanity." [5]

"The Darwinian World," as I have called the next section, was perhaps not distinct from the New Enlightenment except for its greater emphasis on evolution and the "survival of the fittest." Darwin became a household word, said Thomas Henry Huxley. And indeed he did, and surprisingly soon after 1859, despite opposition from clerics and even some scientists. Everybody, especially in England and Germany, began talking about the ideas in *The Origin of Species* and *The Descent of Man*. There was evolution before Darwin, of course, going back at least to his grandfather Erasmus Darwin, but the point is that it did not become à la mode until the time of the grandson. Now the suspicion became widespread that everything under creation was constantly evolving, that perhaps nothing was exempted from the law of flux, not even religion or "fundamental" principles of ethics and political life. The effect of this "cosmic impermanence" could be exhilarating. "We were intellectually intoxicated" by it all, says George Bernard Shaw of the young intellectuals of that time; Darwinism seemed "a glorious enlightenment and emancipation" from outmoded religious ideas. But to many, including eventually Shaw himself, it struck a chill in the heart. The trouble lay not so much in the idea of evolution per se as in the mechanism of evolution as Darwin was popularly supposed to have explained it. Natural selection seemed to banish mind or any sort of "design" from the universe and to bring the jungle back in domestic, and especially, international politics. Shaw and many others protested in the name of humanity, idealism, Butlerism, "creative evolution," and so on.[6]

So in a sense nineteenth-century positivism, especially as wrapped up in Darwinian concepts, created its own gravediggers; or, more precisely, helped to establish a very different kind of mental climate. It is not easy to describe that climate because it centered on no single idea or even cluster of ideas. The philosophic "revolt against positivism," which actually began in the 1860's, represented only one aspect of it. Seen in

[5] Auguste Javary, *De l'idée de progrès* (Paris, 1851), p. 1.
[6] Shaw's preface to his play *Back to Methusaleh*, although written later (1921), is a good source for the intellectual ferment of Darwinian times. Shaw was one of the young intellectuals of whom he speaks.

broader outline, it presaged new and sometimes disturbing views of the world and man. These views were not necessarily pessimistic, although there was a good deal of *fin-de-siècle* pessimism: witness, for example, the remarkable vogue of Arthur Schopenhauer's philosophy after mid-century, books like Max Nordau's *Degeneration* of 1893, and the Decadent Movement in literature. Clearly, however, the new climate's mood was not optimistic either, at least not in the Enlightenment sense. It was as though the scales had begun to fall from men's eyes. The philosopher Friedrich Nietzsche, for instance, pronounced the death of God and predicted terrible days ahead for a culture lacking a religious base. Others had second thoughts about science, not turning their backs on it but seeing it realistically, perhaps for the first time, as a destroyer of illusions, illusions possibly needed by a culture to survive. A new crop of psychologists and social thinkers detected more clearly than before the strong irrational streak in human nature and the role, not specially stressed in major nineteenth-century philosophies of history, played by unreason and "myth" in history. Whatever else it was, this was not Enlightenment optimism. Here, in the closing decades of the century known for its Hegels and Comtes and Mills, were sown the seeds of a new type of modernity, more ironic, as I have suggested, than the type epitomized by the Enlightenment, old or new. Was the *fin-de-siècle* an Age of Iron or Irony? It was both, of course, but it was the irony that anticipated the Age of Anxiety to come. That is why I have preferred to call this fourth and final section "Toward the Twentieth Century." It is indicative of what lay ahead.

IV

IN CONCLUSION, I should like to make two further observations about the nineteenth century as a whole. The first is that it was the European Century *par excellence*. Soon after World War I, Paul Valéry questioned if Europe, in view of its suicidal "domestic" politics, could hold its world preeminence for long. Could it possibly remain what it still seemed, "the elect portion of the terrestrial globe, the pearl of the sphere, the brain of a vast body"? This question would be raised many times thereafter, especially after World War II, and a spate of books would be written bemoaning "the end of European history" ("end" in the sense of superiority or clear-cut dominance over the rest of the world). But in the nineteenth century Europe and Europeans were never prouder of their achievements. History was customarily written as though Europe (or some portion thereof, some one or more nations, because this was the heyday of European nationalism) were indeed the center of the universe where all the new and creative things were going on. This seemed true even to so jaundiced an observer as the historian Jacob Burckhardt who feared the onset of barbarism inside materialistic Europe. It was a sign that irony had not yet corroded self-confidence, at least vis-à-vis the rest of the world.

Within Europe itself, however, there was a significant shift in the balance of intellectual power. Comte, at the conclusion of his lectures on Positive Philosophy, spoke of western Europe and what he expected each of five main constituent nations to contribute to the "impending philosophical regeneration." What Comte missed, although he paid lip service to her "natural aptitude for systematic generalization," was Germany's rise as an intellectual power. France and England had dominated "Enlightenment" culture. In the nineteenth century, however, Germany rose to equality with these two nations and even surpassed them in some fields. She excelled in the "natural" as well as the "cultural" sciences. It is tempting to relate this intellectual upsurge to extraordinary political events, to Germany's achievement of national unification and eventually European hegemony. In truth, however, it began much earlier with the Sturm und Drang of Goethe and Schiller, the Romantic Movement (so important in Germany), and the Idealist philosophy of Immanuel Kant and his successors. Still known primarily as a nation of philosophers in Hegel's day, the Germans went on to be leaders in all the other fields of thought, notably in historical scholarship and the history and psychology of religion, but also in the more precise and "nomothetic" sciences, including physics and the new experimental psychology. In the nineteenth century, intellectual currents radiated out from Germany to the other countries as they had not done since the Reformation.

"Wonderful Century!" That was what the scientist Alfred Russel Wallace called the nineteenth century as he looked back over it toward the end of his life. Wonderful, certainly, but increasingly unsettling too, thanks partly to the very idea of evolution that he and Darwin sponsored simultaneously; thanks also to the need to get used to living in a world of perpetual evolution or "becoming"; thanks to the growing multitude of ideas, which Arnold noted, and the mounting "criticism" not only of the old culture of Europe but also of the new, which since the days of Newton had seemed to so many to be the chief hope of the world. The nineteenth century, wonderful though it might have been, was indeed an Age of Becoming.

Readings

1. Romanticism and Idealism

MADAME DE STAËL: *Germany* *

Madame de Staël (1776–1817) was a novelist and writer of some reputation during the Napoleonic period. Daughter of the Swiss financier Necker, who served as financial adviser to Louis XVI, she fled from France during the French Revolution and became a leader of the moderate liberal emigrés. Upon the fall of Robespierre she returned, only to incur, a little later, the animosity of Napoleon who, for her outspoken political opinions, condemned her books and exiled her person. *De L'Allemagne* (1813) celebrated the rising tide of what she called "romanticism" in literature, philosophy, and the arts, of which she regarded Germany as the leader.

IT MIGHT be said with reason that the French and the Germans are at the two extremes of the moral chain; since the former regard all ideas as moving from exterior objects; the latter, all impressions as proceeding from pre-conceived ideas. These two nations, nevertheless, agree together pretty well in their social relations; but none can be more opposite in their literary and philosophical systems. Intellectual Germany is hardly known to France: very few men of letters among us have troubled themselves about her. . . .

For these reasons I believed that there might be some advantage in making known that country in which, of all Europe, study and meditation have been carried so far, that it may be considered as the native land of thought.

Literature

The word *romantic* has been lately introduced in Germany, to designate that kind of poetry which is derived from the songs of the Trouba-

* Baroness Staël Holstein: *Germany* (London: John Murray; 1814), vol. I, pp. 4–5, 304, 311–12, 355–7; vol. II, pp. 371–2, 394; vol. III, pp. 17–18, 38–9, 42, 46–9, 93–4, 376, 379, 386–7.

dours; that which owes its birth to the union of chivalry and Christianity. If we do not admit that the empire of literature has been divided between paganism and Christianity, the north and the south, antiquity and the middle ages, chivalry and the institutions of Greece and Rome, we shall never succeed in forming a philosophical judgment of ancient and of modern taste.

* * *

Some French critics have asserted, that German literature is still in its infancy; this opinion is entirely false: men who are best skilled in the knowledge of languages, and the works of the ancients, are certainly not ignorant of the defects and advantages attached to the species of literature which they either adopt or reject; but their character, their habits, and their modes of reasoning, have led them to prefer that which is founded on the recollection of chivalry, on the wonders of the middle ages, to that which has for its basis the mythology of the Greeks. The literature of romance is alone capable of farther improvement, because, being rooted in our own soil, that alone can continue to grow and acquire fresh life: it expresses our religion; it recalls our history; its origin is ancient, although not of classical antiquity. Classic poetry, before it comes home to us, must pass through our recollections of paganism: that of the Germans is the Christian aera of the fine arts; it employs our personal impressions to excite strong and vivid emotions; the genius by which it is inspired addresses itself immediately to our hearts, and seems to call forth the spirit of our own lives, of all phantoms at once the most powerful and the most terrible.

* * *

It is said there are persons who discover springs, hidden under the earth, by the nervous agitation which they cause in them: in German poetry, we often think we discover that miraculous sympathy between man and the elements. The German poet comprehends nature not only as a poet, but as a brother; and we might almost say, that the bonds of family union connect him with the air, the water, flowers, trees—in short, all the primary beauties of the creation.

There is no one who has not felt the undefinable attraction which we experience when looking on the waves of the sea, whether from the charm of their freshness, or from the ascendancy which an uniform and perpetual motion insensibly acquires over our transient and perishable existence. This ballad of Goethe's ["The Fisherman"] admirably expresses the increasing pleasure we derive from contemplating the pure waters of a flowing stream: the measure of the rhythm and harmony is made to imitate the motion of the waves, and produces an analogous effect on the imagination. The soul of nature discovers itself to us in every place, and under a thousand different forms. The fruitful country and the unpeopled desert, the sea as well as the stars, are all subjected to the same laws; and man contains within himself sensations and occult powers, which correspond with the day, with the night, and with the storm; it is this secret alliance of our being with the wonders of the universe, which gives to poetry its true grandeur. The poet knows how to restore the union between the natural and the moral world: his imagination forms a connecting tie between the one and the other.

* * *

When I began the study of German literature, it seemed as if I was entering on a new sphere, where the most striking light was thrown on all that I had before perceived only in a confused manner. For some time past, little has been read in France except memoirs and novels, and it is not wholly from frivolity, that we are become less capable of more serious reading, but because the events of the revolution have accustomed us to value nothing but the knowledge of men and things: we find in German books, even on the most abstract subjects, that kind of interest which confers their value upon good novels, and which is excited by the knowledge which they teach us of our own hearts. The peculiar character of German literature, is to refer every thing to an interior existence; and as that is the mystery of mysteries, it awakens an unbounded curiosity.

* * *

The new school maintains the same system in the fine arts, as in literature, and affirms that Christianity is the source of all modern genius; the writers of this school also characterize, in a new manner, all that in Gothic architecture agrees with the religious sentiments of Christians. It does not follow however from this, that the moderns can and ought to construct Gothic churches; neither art nor nature admit of repetition: it is only of consequence to us, in the present silence of genius, to lay aside the contempt which has been thrown on all the conceptions of the middle ages; it certainly does not suit us to adopt them, but nothing is more injurious to the development of genius, than to consider as barbarous every thing that is original.

Philosophy

The soul is a fire that darts its rays through all the senses: it is in this fire that existence consists: all the observations and all the efforts of philosophers ought to turn towards this point of individuality—the centre and the moving power of our sentiments and our ideas. . . .

Love is the instructor who teaches us more certainly what belongs to the mysteries of the soul, than the utmost metaphysical subtilty. We never attach ourselves to this or that qualification of the object of our preference; and every madrigal reveals a great philosophical truth, when it says—"I love I know not why!" for this "I know not why," is that collective character, and that harmony, which we recognise by love, by admiration, by all the sentiments which reveal to us what is most deep and most secret in the heart of another.

The method of analysis, which can only examine by division, applies itself like the dissecting-knife to dead nature; but it is a bad instrument to teach us to understand what is living; and if we feel a difficulty in verbally defining that animated conception which represents whole objects to our mind, it is precisely because that conception clings more closely to the very essence of things. To divide, in order to comprehend, is a sign of weakness in philosophy; as to divide, in order to rule, is a sign of weakness in political power.

*   *   *

Descartes, Pascal, and Malebranche, had much more resemblance to the German philosophers than the French writers of the eighteenth century; but Malebranche and the Germans differ in this, that the one lays down as an article of faith what the others reduce into a scientific theory: —the one aims at clothing the forms inspired by his imagination in a dogmatic dress, because he is afraid of being accused of enthusiasm; while the others, writing at the end of an aera when analysis has been extended to every object of study, know that they are enthusiasts, and are solely anxious to prove that reason and enthusiasm are of one accord.

If the French had followed the metaphysical bias of their great men of the seventeenth century, they would now have entertained the same opinions as the Germans; for in the progress of philosophy Leibnitz is the natural successor of Descartes and Malebranche, and Kant of Leibnitz.

England had great influence over the writers of the eighteenth century; the admiration which they felt for that country inspired them with the wish of introducing into France her liberty and her philosophy. English philosophy was then only void of danger when united with the religious sentiments of that people, with their liberty, and with their obedience to the laws. In the bosom of a nation where Newton and Clarke never pronounced the name of God without bowing their heads, let the metaphysical systems have been ever so erroneous, they could not be fatal. That which is every way wanting in France, is the feeling and habit of veneration; and the transition is there very quick from the examination which may enlighten, to the irony which reduces every thing to dust.

*   *   *

External objects, it was said, are the cause of all our impressions; nothing then appears more agreeable than to give ourselves up to the physical world, and to come, self-invited guests, to the banquet of nature; but by degrees the internal source is dried up, and even as to the imagination that is requisite for luxury and pleasure, it goes on decaying to such a degree, that very shortly man will not retain soul enough to relish any enjoyment, of however material a nature.

* * *

The philosophical system, adopted in any country, exerts a great influence over the direction of mind; it is the universal model after which all thought is cast;—those persons even, who have not studied the system, conform, unknowingly, to the general disposition which it inspires. We have seen for nearly a hundred years past, in Europe, the growth and increase of a sort of scoffing scepticism, the foundation of which is the species of metaphysics that attributes all our ideas to our sensations. The first principle in this philosophy is, not to believe any thing which cannot be proved like a fact or a calculation: in union with this principle is contempt for all that bears the name of exalted sentiment; and attachment to the pleasures of sense. These three points of the doctrine include all the sorts of irony, of which religion, sensibility, and morals, can become the object.

Bayle, whose learned Dictionary is hardly read by people of the world, is nevertheless the arsenal from which all the pleasantries of scepticism have been drawn; Voltaire has given them a pungency by his wit and elegance; but the foundation of all this jesting is, that every thing, not as evident as a physical experiment, ought to be reckoned in the number of dreams and idle thoughts.

* * *

The day on which it was said, there are no mysteries in the world, or at all events it is unnecessary to think about them; all our ideas come by the eyes and by the ears, and the palpable only is the true;—on that day the individuals who enjoyed all their senses in perfect health believed themselves the genuine philosophers. We hear it incessantly said, by those who have ideas enough to get money when they are poor, and to spend it when they are rich, that they only possess a reasonable philosophy, and that none but enthusiasts would dream of any other. In effect, our sensations teach this philosophy alone; and if we can gain no knowledge except by their means, every thing that is not subject to the evidence of matter must bear the name of folly.

If it was admitted, on the contrary, that the soul acts by itself, and that we must draw up information out of ourselves to find the truth, and that this truth cannot be seized upon, except by the aid of profound meditation, because it is not within the range of terrestrial experience; the whole course of men's minds would be changed; they would not disdainfully reject the most sublime thoughts, because they demand a close attention; but that which they found insupportable would be the superficial and the common; for emptiness grows at length singularly burthensome.

*   *   *

I do not certainly flatter myself that I have been able, in a few pages, to give an account of a system which, for twenty years, has occupied all thinking heads in Germany; but I hope to have said enough to show the general spirit of the philosophy of Kant, and to enable me to explain, in the following chapters, the influence which it has had upon literature, science, and morality.

In order to reconcile experimental and ideal philosophy, Kant has not made the one subordinate to the other, but he has given to each of the two, separately, a new degree of force. Germany was threatened by that cold doctrine which regarded all enthusiasm as an error, and classed amongst prejudices those sentiments which form the consolation of our existence. It was a great satisfaction for men, at once so philosophical and so poetical, so capable of study and of exaltation, to see all the fine affections of the soul defended with the strictness of the most abstract reasonings. The force of the mind can never be long in a negative state; that is, it cannot long consist principally, in not believing, in not understanding, and in what it disdains. We must have a philosophy of belief, of enthusiasm, a philosophy which confirms by reason, what sentiment reveals to us.

Of the Contemplation of Nature

The labours of philosophers, of learned men, and of poets, in Germany, aim at diminishing the dry power of argumentation, without in the least obscuring knowledge. It is thus that the imagination of the ancient world may be born again, like the phoenix, from the ashes of all errors.

The greater number of naturalists have attempted to explain Nature like a good government, in which every thing is conducted according to wise principles of administration; but it is in vain that we try to transfer this prosaic system to creation. Neither the terrible, nor even the beautiful, can be explained by this circumscribed theory; and Nature is by turns too cruel and too magnificent to permit us to subject her to that sort of calculation which directs our judgment in the affairs of this world.

*   *   *

The contemplation of Nature overwhelms our thoughts. We feel ourselves in a state of relation with her, which does not depend upon the good or evil which she can do; but her visible soul endeavours to find ours in her bosom, and holds converse with us. When darkness alarms us, it is not always the peril to which it exposes us that we dread, but it is the sympathy of night with every sort of privation, or grief, with which we are penetrated. The sun, on the contrary, is like an emanation from the Deity, like a glorious messenger, who tells us that our prayer is heard: his rays descend upon the earth not only to direct the labours of man, but to express a feeling of love for Nature.

* * *

The true final causes of nature are these relations with our soul and our immortal destiny. Physical objects themselves have a destination which is not bounded by the contracted existence of man below; they are placed here to assist in the development of our thoughts to the work of our moral life. The phaenomena of nature must not be understood according to the laws of matter alone, however well combined those laws may be; they have a philosophical sense and a religious end, of which the most attentive contemplation will never know the extent.

SAMUEL TAYLOR COLERIDGE: *On Reason and Understanding* *

In his work, Samuel Taylor Coleridge (1772-1834), poet and philosopher, sums up two very important aspects of the romantic revolt: (1) its dissatisfaction with certain aspects of Enlightenment philosophy, especially the theory of a passive mind, and (2) its attempt to build a new theory that would at once give the mind a greater creative power and make possible a wider and more "spiritual" view of the universe. Both aspects stand out in his famous distinctions between "Reason" and "Understanding" (derived from German usage, particularly in Jacobi and Kant, of the words *Vernunft* and *Verstand*) and "Imagination" and "Fancy." The following three selections come from a letter written to Thomas Poole on March 23, 1801, a volume of essays entitled *The Friend* (1809), and the thirteenth chapter of the *Biographia Literaria* (1817).

MY DEAR FRIEND,—I received your kind letter of the 14th. I was agreeably disappointed in finding that you had been interested in the letter respecting Locke. . . . Be not afraid that I shall join the party of the *Little-ists*. I believe that I shall delight you by the detection of their artifices. *Now Mr. Locke was the founder of this sect, himself a perfect Little-ist.*

My opinion is thus: that deep thinking is attainable only by a man of deep feeling, and that all truth is a species of revelation. The more I

* From E. H. Coleridge (ed.): *Letters of Samuel Taylor Coleridge* (Boston and New York: Houghton, Mifflin and Company; 1895), Vol. I, pp. 350–352; W. G. T. Shedd (ed.): *The Complete Works of Samuel Taylor Coleridge* (New York: Harper and Brothers; 1884), Vol. II, pp. 144–145; Vol. III, pp. 363–64.

understand of Sir Isaac Newton's works, the more boldly I dare utter to my own mind, and therefore to *you*, that I believe the souls of five hundred Sir Isaac Newtons would go to the making up of a Shakespeare or a Milton. But if it please the Almighty to grant me health, hope, and a steady mind (always the three clauses of my hourly prayers), before my thirtieth year I will thoroughly understand the whole of Newton's works. At present I must content myself with endeavouring to make myself entire master of his easier work, that on Optics. I am exceedingly delighted with the beauty and neatness of his experiments, and with the accuracy of his *immediate* deductions from them; but the opinions founded on these deductions, and indeed his whole theory is, I am persuaded, so exceedingly superficial as without impropriety to be deemed false. Newton was a mere materialist. *Mind*, in his system, is always *passive*,—a lazy *Looker-on* on an external world. If the mind be not *passive*, if it be indeed made in God's Image, and that, too, in the sublimest sense, the *Image of the Creator*, there is ground for suspicion that any system built on the passiveness of the mind must be false, as a system. . . .

* * *

I should have no objection to define reason with Jacobi and with his friend Hemsterhuis, as an organ bearing the same relation to spiritual objects, the universal, the eternal, and the necessary, as the eye bears to material and contingent *phenomena*. But then it must be added, that it is an organ identical with its appropriate objects. Thus, God, the soul, eternal truth, &c., are the objects of reason; but they are themselves reason. We name God the Supreme Reason; and Milton says,—

—whence the soul
Reason receives, and reason is her being.

Whatever is conscious self-knowledge is reason: and in this sense it may be safely defined the organ of the supersensuous; even as the understanding wherever it does not possess or use the reason, as its inward eye, may be defined the conception of the sensuous, or the faculty by which we generalize and arrange the *phenomena* of perception; that faculty, the functions of which contain the rules and constitute the possibility of outward experience. In short, the understanding supposes something that is understood. This may be merely its own acts or forms, that is, formal logic; but real objects, the materials of substantial knowledge, must be furnished, I might safely say revealed, to it by organs of sense. The understanding of the higher brutes has only organs of outward sense, and consequently material objects only; but man's understanding has likewise an organ of inward sense, and therefore the power of acquainting itself with invisible realities or spiritual objects. This organ is his reason.

* * *

The Imagination then I consider either as primary, or secondary. The primary Imagination I hold to be the living power and prime agent of all human perception, and as a repetition in the finite mind of the eternal act of creation in the infinite I AM. The secondary Imagination I consider as an echo of the former co-existing with the conscious will, yet still as identical with the primary in the *kind* of its agency, and differing only in *degree* and in the *mode* of its operation. It disolves, diffuses, dissipates, in order to re-create: or where this process is rendered impossible, yet still at all events it struggles to idealize and to unify. It is essentially *vital*, even as all objects (*as* objects) are essentially fixed and dead.

FANCY, on the contrary, has no other counters to play with but fixities and definites. The fancy is indeed no other than a mode of memory emancipated from the order of time and space; while it is blended with, and modified by that empirical phenomenon of the will, which we express by the word Choice. But equally with the ordinary memory the Fancy must receive all its materials ready made from the law of association.

VICOMTE DE CHATEAUBRIAND: *The Genius of Christianity* *

François René, Vicomte de Chateaubriand (1768–1848) was one of the leaders of the reaction against the French Revolution and a leading literary figure in the France of Napoleon. In his *Memoirs* he describes his return, after an experiment in freethinking, to the religion of his mother, and his determination to destroy the influence of Voltaire. His best known work, *The Genius of Christianity* (1802), was opportunely published on the eve of Napoleon's re-establishment of the Catholic Church in France.

Of Mysteries

THERE is nothing beautiful, pleasing, or grand in life, but that which is more or less mysterious. The most wonderful sentiments are those which produce impressions difficult to be explained.

* * *

We perceive at the first glance, that, in regard to mysteries, the Christian religion has a great advantage over the religions of antiquity.

* Chateaubriand: *The Genius of Christianity*, trans. by C. I. White (Baltimore: J. Murphy & Co.; 1862), p. 51, 53–4, 139–40, 172–3, 291, 384–7, 467–8.

The mysteries of the latter bore no relation to man, and afforded, at the utmost, but a subject of reflection to the philosopher or of song to the poet. Our mysteries, on the contrary, speak directly to the heart; they comprehend the secrets of our existence. The question here is not about a futile arrangement of numbers, but concerning the salvation and felicity of the human race. Is it possible for man, whom daily experience so fully convinces of his ignorance and frailty, to reject the mysteries of Jesus Christ? They are the mysteries of the unfortunate!

The Trinity, which is the first mystery presented by the Christian faith, opens an immense field for philosophic study, whether we consider it in the attributes of God, or examine the vestiges of this dogma, which was formerly diffused throughout the East. It is a pitiful mode of reasoning to reject whatever we cannot comprehend.

Of God and Nature

There is a God. The plants of the valley and the cedars of the mountain bless his name; the insect hums his praise; the elephant salutes him with the rising day; the bird glorifies him among the foliage; the lightning bespeaks his power, and the ocean declares his immensity. Man alone has said, "There is no God."

Has he then in adversity never raised his eyes toward heaven? has he in prosperity never cast them on the earth? Is Nature so far from him that he has not been able to contemplate its wonders; or does he consider them as the mere result of fortuitous causes? But how could chance have compelled crude and stubborn materials to arrange themselves in such exquisite order?

It might be asserted that man is the *idea of God displayed*, and the universe *his imagination made manifest*. They who have admitted the beauty of nature as a proof of a supreme intelligence, ought to have pointed out a truth which greatly enlarges the sphere of wonders. It is this: motion and rest, darkness and light, the seasons, the revolutions of the heavenly bodies, which give variety to the decorations of the world, are successive only in appearance, and permanent in reality. The scene that fades upon our view is painted in brilliant colors for another people; it is not the spectacle that is changed, but the spectator. Thus God has combined in his work absolute duration and progressive duration. The first is placed in time, the second in space; by means of the former, the beauties of the universe are one, infinite, and invariable; by means of the latter, they are multiplied, finite, and perpetually renewed. Without the one, there would be no grandeur in the creation; without the other, it would exhibit nothing but dull uniformity.

Here time appears to us in a new point of view; the smallest of its fractions becomes a complete whole, which comprehends all things, and in which all things transpire, from the death of an insect to the birth of a world; each minute is in itself a little eternity. Combine, then, at the same moment, in imagination, the most beautiful incidents of nature; represent to yourself at once all the hours of the day and all the seasons of the year, a spring morning and an autumnal morning, a night spangled with stars and a night overcast with clouds, meadows enamelled with flowers, forests stripped by the frosts, and fields glowing with their golden harvests; you will then have a just idea of the prospect of the universe. While you are gazing with admiration upon the sun sinking beneath the western arch, another beholds it emerging from the regions of Aurora. By what inconceivable magic does it come, that this aged luminary, which retires to rest, as if weary and heated, in the dusky arms of night, is at the very same moment that youthful orb which awakes bathed in dew, and sparkling through the gray curtains of the dawn? Every moment of the day the sun is rising, glowing at his zenith, and setting on the world; or rather our senses deceive us, and there is no real sunrise, noon, or sunset. The whole is reduced to a fixed point, from which the orb of day emits, at one and the same time, three lights from one single substance. This triple splendor is perhaps the most beautiful incident in nature; for, while it affords an idea of the perpetual magnificence and omnipresence of God, it exhibits a most striking image of his glorious Trinity.

*   *   *

I am nothing; I am only a simple, solitary wanderer, and often have I heard men of science disputing on the subject of a Supreme Being, without understanding them; but I have invariably remarked, that it is in the prospect of the sublime scenes of nature that this unknown Being manifests himself to the human heart. One evening, after we had reached the beautiful waters that bathe the shores of Virginia, there was a profound calm, and every sail was furled. I was engaged below, when I heard the bell that summoned the crew to prayers. I hastened to mingle my supplications with those of my travelling companions. The officers of the ship were on the quarter-deck with the passengers, while the chaplain, with a book in his hand, was stationed at a little distance before them; the seamen were scattered at random over the poop; we were all standing, our faces toward the prow of the vessel, which was turned to the west.

The solar orb, about to sink beneath the waves, was seen through the rigging, in the midst of boundless space; and, from the motion of the stern, it appeared as if it changed its horizon every moment. A few clouds wandered confusedly in the east, where the moon was slowly rising. The rest of the sky was serene; and toward the north, a waterspout, forming a glorious triangle with the luminaries of day and night and glistening with all the colors of the prism, rose from the sea, like a column of crystal supporting the vault of heaven.

He had been well deserving of pity who would not have recognised in this prospect the beauty of God. When my companions, doffing their tarpaulin hats, entoned with hoarse voice their simple hymn to Our Lady of Good Help, the patroness of the seas, the tears flowed from my eyes in spite of myself. How affecting was the prayer of those men, who, from a frail plank in the midst of the ocean, contemplated the sun setting behind the waves! How the appeal of the poor sailor to the Mother of Sorrows went to the heart! The consciousness of our insignificance in the presence of the Infinite,—our hymns, resounding to a distance over the silent waves,—the night approaching with its dangers, —our vessel, itself a wonder among so many wonders,—a religious crew, penetrated with admiration and with awe,—a venerable priest in prayer,—the Almighty bending over the abyss, with one hand staying the sun in the west, with the other raising the moon in the east, and lending, through all immensity, an attentive ear to the feeble voice of his creatures,—all this constituted a scene which no power of art can represent, and which it is scarcely possible for the heart of man to feel.

The Christian Religion a Passion

Not satisfied with enlarging the sphere of the passions in the drama and the epic poem, the Christian religion is itself a species of passion, which has its transports, its ardors, its sighs, its joys, its tears, its love of society and of solitude. This, as we know, is by the present age denominated *fanaticism*. We might reply in the words of Rousseau, which are truly remarkable in the mouth of a philosopher: "Fanaticism, though sanguinary and cruel, is nevertheless a great and powerful passion, which exalts the heart of man, which inspires him with a contempt of death, which gives him prodigious energy, and which only requires to be judiciously directed in order to produce the most sublime virtues. On the other hand, irreligion, and a *reasoning and philosophic* spirit in general, strengthens the attachment to life, debases the soul and renders it effeminate, concentrates all the passions in the meanness of private interest, in the abject motive of self, and thus silently saps the real foundations of all society; for so trifling are the points in which private interests are united, that they will never counterbalance those in which they oppose one another."

Gothic Churches

It is even curious to remark how readily the poets and novelists of this infidel age, by a natural return toward the manners of our ancestors, introduce dungeons, spectres, castles, and Gothic churches, into their fictions,—so great is the charm of recollections associated with religion and the history of our country. Nations do not throw aside their ancient customs as people do their old clothes. Some part of them may be discarded; but there will remain a portion, which with the new manners will form a very strange mixture.

In vain would you build Grecian temples, ever so elegant and well-lighted, for the purpose of assembling the *good people* of St. Louis and Queen Blanche, and making them adore a *metaphysical God;* they would still regret those *Notre Dames* of Rheims and Paris,—those venerable cathedrals, overgrown with moss, full of generations of the dead and the ashes of their forefathers; they would still regret the tombs of those heroes, the Montmorencys, on which they loved to kneel during mass; to say nothing of the sacred fonts to which they were carried at their birth. The reason is that all these things are essentially interwoven with their manners; that a monument is not venerable, unless a long history of the past be, as it were, inscribed beneath its vaulted canopy, black with age. For this reason, also, there is nothing marvellous in a temple whose erection we have witnessed, whose echoes and whose domes were formed before our eyes. God is the eternal law; his origin, and whatever relates to his worship, ought to be enveloped in the night of time.

You could not enter a Gothic church without feeling a kind of awe and a vague sentiment of the Divinity. You were all at once carried back to those times when a fraternity of cenobites, after having meditated in the woods of their monasteries, met to prostrate themselves before the altar and to chant the praises of the Lord, amid the tranquillity and the silence of night. Ancient France seemed to revive altogether; you beheld all those singular costumes, all that nation so different from what it is at present; you were reminded of its revolutions, its productions, and its arts. The more remote were these times the more magical they appeared, the more they inspired ideas which always end with a reflection on the nothingness of man and the rapidity of life. . . .

. . . every thing in a Gothic church reminds you of the labyrinths of a wood; every thing excites a feeling of religious awe, of mystery, and of the Divinity.

The two lofty towers erected at the entrance of the edifice overtop the elms and yew-trees of the churchyard, and produce the most picturesque effect on the azure of heaven. Sometimes their twin heads are illumined by the first rays of dawn; at others they appear crowned with a capital of clouds or magnified in a foggy atmosphere. The birds themselves seem to make a mistake in regard to them, and to take them for the trees of the forests; they hover over their summits, and perch upon their pinnacles. But, lo! confused noises suddenly issue from the top of these towers and scare away the affrighted birds. The Christian architect, not content with building forests, has been desirous to retain their murmurs; and, by means of the organ and of bells, he has attached to the Gothic temple the very winds and thunders that roar in the recesses of the woods. Past ages, conjured up by these religious sounds, raise their venerable voices from the bosom of the stones, and are heard in every corner of the vast cathedral. The sanctuary re-echoes like the cavern of the ancient Sibyl; loud-tongued bells swing over your head, while the vaults of death under your feet are profoundly silent.

Of Ruins

We were one day walking behind the palace of the Luxembourg, and were accidentally led to the very same Carthusian convent which Fontanes has celebrated. We beheld a church the roof of which had fallen in; the lead had been stripped from the windows, and the doorways blocked with upright planks. Most of the other buildings of the monastery no longer existed. Long did we stroll among the sepulchral stones of black marble scattered here and there upon the ground; some were completely dashed in pieces, others still exhibited some vestiges of inscriptions. We advanced into the inner cloister; there grew two wild plum-trees amid high grass and rubbish. On the walls were to be seen paintings half effaced, representing events in the life of St. Bruno; a dial-plate was left on one of the sides of the church; and in the sanctuary, instead of that hymn of peace formerly chanted in honor of the dead, was heard the grating of instruments employed in sawing the tombstones.

The reflections which occurred to us in this place may be made by any of our readers. We left it with a wounded heart, and entered the contiguous suburb without knowing whither we went. Night came on. As we were passing between the two lofty walls in a lonely street, all at once the sound of an organ struck our ear, and the words of that triumphal hymn, *Laudate Dominum omnes gentes*, issued from a neighboring church; it happened to be the octave of Corpus Christi. It is impossible to express the emotion excited in us by these religious strains; it seemed as if we heard a voice from heaven saying, "O thou of little faith, why mournest thou as those without hope? Thinkest thou that I change my mind like men? that I forsake because I punish? Instead of arraigning my decrees, follow the example of these faithful servants, who bless my chastening hand even under the ruins beneath which I crush them."

We entered the church just at the moment when the priest was pronouncing the benediction. Old men, poor women, and children, were on their knees. We knelt down among them; our tears flowed, and from the bottom of our heart we said, "Forgive us, O Lord, if we murmured on beholding the desolation of thy temple; forgive our overwhelmed reason! Man himself is but a decayed edifice, a wreck of sin and death; his lukewarm love, his wavering faith, his limited charity, his imperfect sentiments, his insufficient thought, his broken heart,—in short, all things about him,—are but ruins!"

F. W. J. VON SCHELLING: *On Nature and Art* *

Friedrich Wilhelm von Schelling (1775–1854) has been called "the philosopher of romanticism." In the main he acquired this reputation from his *Naturphilosophie*, developed early in opposition to Fichte's conception of nature as mere obstacle to ego. In the passages below, taken from his Munich lecture of 1807 on "The Philosophy of Art," he first compares his idea of nature with some previous ideas. He then goes on to explain the relation between nature and art, a subject dear to the romantic heart. Schelling had close relations with the German romantics, and Coleridge mentions him, along with Kant, as the German philosopher from whom he drew inspiration. Schelling occupied professorial posts in five universities, including Jena, Munich, and Berlin.

To SOME, nature is nothing more than the dead aggregate of an indeterminate host of objects, or the space in which things are packed as in a case; to another, merely the ground whence he draws his nourishment and sustenance. To the inspired inquirer alone is nature the holy and ever-creating primal energy of the world, which begets and actively produces all things from itself.

That principle would, indeed, have a higher import, if it taught art to imitate this creative energy; but there can be little doubt how it was meant to be understood, when one is acquainted with the general condition of the sciences at the time of its appearance. Strange, indeed, would it be, if that which denied all life in nature should hold that life up for imitation to art. Of them, the words of the deep-thinking man were true:—"Your lying philosophy has annihilated nature; wherefore do you demand that we should imitate her—that you may have the new pleasure of exerting the same tyranny on her disciples?"

Nature was to them, not merely a dumb, but a totally dead image, in whose inmost recesses was implanted no living word; a hollow scaffolding of forms, from which an equally hollow image was to be transferred to canvass or marble. This was, indeed, the right theory for the more ancient and rough races; as they saw not the godlike in nature, they derived idols from her; while for the penetrating Hellenist, who

* F. W. J. von Schelling: *The Philosophy of Art*, trans. by A. Johnson (London: John Chapman; 1845), pp. 3–5, 8–10.

everywhere recognised the traces of this living creative energy, nature produced gods indeed. . . .

Never, then, with him to whom nature appears as dead, will that divine, and, as it were, chymical process, succeed, from which, as from a purifying fire, flows the pure gold of beauty.

The general aspect of this relation to nature was not altered when the unsatisfying character of the principle became more generally felt; not even by the noble foundation of new theory and knowledge laid by J. Winkelmann. He, indeed, gave the soul her whole sphere of action in art, and elevated it from an unworthy dependence to a more intellectual freedom.

Impressed in the most lively manner by the beauty of form in the works of antiquity, he taught that the production of the ideal; and a nature more elevated than the actual, with intellectual expression, was the highest aim of art.

We will inquire, however, in what sense this surpassing the actual was by the greater number understood; and it is evident that with this theory also nature was still looked upon as mere product, and things as lifeless presences, and that thereby the idea of a living and creative nature was by no means awakened.

Thus neither could those ideal forms be animated by any positive conceptions of their being or nature.

If those of common life were dead for the dead beholder, these were not less so. If no self-development of the former were possible, neither was there of the latter.

The object of imitation was altered, but imitation remained; the lofty works of antiquity took the place of nature, from which the student busied himself to take the outward form, but without the spirit that filled it. They, indeed, are unapproachable—more so than the works of nature; they leave us also colder than nature, unless we bring with us that intellectual eye which can penetrate their veil and perceive the living energy within them.

On the other hand, however, artists since this time have acquired a certain ideal aim and notions of a more than material beauty; but these notions were but beautiful words, to which no deeds corresponded. If the earlier practice of art begat bodies without souls, this theory taught the secret of the soul, but not that of the body. The theory, as is usual, passed over with hurried steps to the other side. The living mid-point was not yet found. . . .

Nature meets us everywhere; at first, in forms more or less hard and undeveloped; like that serious and quiet beauty, that wins not the attention by striking peculiarities—which attracts not the eye of all.

How can we, as it were, intellectually melt these apparently hard forms, that the pure energy of things may flow together with that of our souls, and both gush forth together in one stream? . . .

Thus rough matter strives, as it were blindly, after regular shape, and unconsciously assumes pure stereometric forms, which, indeed, belong to the realm of conception, and are somewhat of spirituality in matter. The stars are instinct with the most exalted science of number and measure, which they, without a conception of these things, put into practice in their movements. More evident, though not self-conscious, appears the living perception in animals, which we therefore see accomplish innumerable works, far nobler than themselves, without deliberation on their part: the bird, enraptured with music, excels itself in soul-filling tones; the small, art-gifted creature, without practice or instruction, perfects light works of architecture; but all are led by an overpowering spirit, which lightens indeed in solitary flashes of knowledge, but nowhere comes forth as the full sun, as it does in man.

This effective science is, in nature and art, the bond between conception and form, between body and soul. Every single thing is preceded by an eternal conception schemed in the infinite understanding; but by what means does this conception pass into actuality and embodiment? Only through the creative intelligence, which is as necessarily combined with the infinite understanding, as that essence, which comprehends the idea of immaterial beauty, is combined with that which embodies it in the mind of the artist.

If that artist is to be accounted happy and before all praiseworthy, to whom the gods have granted this creative spirit, so will that work of art appear in the same measure excellent, in which this unalloyed energy of creation and activity of nature is shown us as in an outline.

It has long been perceived that, in art, all things are not performed with a full consciousness; that with the conscious activity an unconscious energy must unite itself; that the perfect union and reciprocal interpenetration of the two is that which accomplishes the highest in art; works wanting this seal of unconscious power are recognised by the evident want of a self-sufficing life, independent of the producing life; while on the contrary, where this operates, art gives to its productions, together with the highest clearness of the understanding, that inscrutable reality by which they resemble works of nature.

The position of the artist, in relation to nature, should be continually made clear by the declaration that art, really to be art, should at first withdraw itself from nature, and only in the last accomplishment return to her. The true meaning of this seems to be no other than the following:—In all things in nature the living principle appears only blindly effective;—if it were so with the artist, he would not be distinguishable from nature itself. If it were his wish consciously to subordinate himself to nature, and to repeat things present with a slavish truth, he would produce masks (larvae) indeed, but no works of art. Thus he must remove himself from the result, from the creature, that he may elevate himself to the creative energy, and spiritually seize on that.

By this means he elevates himself into the region of pure ideas; he foresakes the creature, that he may regain it with thousand-fold interest, and in this sense certainly to return to nature.

The artist should indeed, above all things, imitate that spirit of nature, which, working in the core of things, speaks by form and shape, as if by symbols; and only in so far as he seizes this spirit, and vitally imitates it, has he himself created anything of truth! . . .

WILLIAM BLAKE: *Annotations to Sir Joshua Reynolds's "Discourses"* *

> Lone wolf though he was, William Blake (1757–1827) yet typifies several aspects of the romantic revolt against the Enlightenment. He was a religious mystic, a lyrical and symbolic poet, and an artist who refused to imitate nature. In the following jottings, written down about 1808, he expressed his contempt for the sort of art criticism typified by Sir Joshua Reynolds.

THIS Man was Hired to Depress Art.

This is the Opinion of Will Blake: my Proofs of this Opinion are given in the following Notes. . . .

Reynolds's Opinion was that Genius May be Taught & that all Pretence to Inspiration is a Lie & a Deceit, to say the least of it. For if it is a Deceit, the whole Bible is Madness. This Opinion originates in the Greeks' calling the Muses Daughters of Memory. . . .

"But as mere enthusiasm will carry you but a little way."

Mere Enthusiasm is the All in All! Bacon's Philosophy has Ruin'd England. Bacon is only Epicurus over again. . . .

The Man who never in his Mind & Thoughts travel'd to Heaven Is No Artist.

Artists who are above a plain Understanding are Mock'd & Destroy'd by this President of Fools. . . .

It is Evident that Reynolds Wish'd none but Fools to be in the Arts & in order to this, he calls all others Vague Enthusiasts or Madmen.

What has Reasoning to do with the Art of Painting? . . .

Knowledge of Ideal Beauty is Not to be Acquired. It is Born with us. Innate Ideas are in Every Man, Born with him; they are truly Himself.

* From *The Writings of William Blake*, ed. by Geoffrey Keynes, vol. III, p. 5, 15, 20, 23–5, 34, 41, 46, 48. Copyright 1925 by The Nonesuch Press, Ltd. Reprinted by the permission of The Nonesuch Press, Ltd.

The Man who says that we have No Innate Ideas must be a Fool & Knave, Having No Con-Science or Innate Science. . . .

One Central Form composed of all other Forms being Granted, it does not therefore follow that all other Forms are Deformity.

All Forms are Perfect in the Poet's Mind, but these are not Abstracted nor compounded from Nature, but are from Imagination. . . .

What is General Nature? is there Such a Thing? what is General Knowledge? is there such a Thing? Strictly Speaking all Knowledge is Particular. . . .

Passion & Expression is Beauty Itself. The Face that is Incapable of Passion & Expression is deformity Itself. Let it be Painted & Patch'd & Praised & Advertised for Ever, it will only be admired by Fools. . . .

If Art was Progressive We should have had Mich. Angelos & Rafaels to Succeed & to Improve upon each other. But it is not so. Genius dies with its Possessor & Comes not again till Another is Born with It. . . .

Reynolds Thinks that Man Learns all that he knows. I say on the Contrary that Man Brings All that he has or can have Into the World with him. Man is Born Like a Garden ready Planted & Sown. This World is too poor to produce one Seed. . . .

God forbid that Truth should be Confined to Mathematical Demonstration! . . .

Here is a Plain Confession that he Thinks Mind & Imagination not to be above the Mortal & Perishing Nature. Such is the End of Epicurean or Newtonian Philosophy; it is Atheism.

EDMUND BURKE: *Reflections on the Revolution in France* *

"All circumstances taken together," said the great English statesman Edmund Burke (1729–97), "the French Revolution is the most astonishing that has hitherto happened in the world." Burke did not like the Revolution: it violated everything he knew about politics and human nature. Consequently, he proceeded to demolish it in the *Reflections* (1790), the book which best elucidates his "philosophy of conservatism."

You will observe, that, from Magna Charta to the Declaration of Right, it has been the uniform policy of our Constitution to claim and assert our liberties as an *entailed inheritance* derived to us from our fore-fathers, and to be transmitted to our posterity,—as an estate specially belonging to the people of this kingdom, without any reference whatever to any other more general or prior right. By this means our Constitution preserves an unity in so great a diversity of its parts. We

* Edmund Burke: *Works* (Boston: Little, Brown and Company; 1865), vol. III, pp. 274–6, 307–13, 345–7, 358–9.

have an inheritable crown, an inheritable peerage, and a House of Commons and a people inheriting privileges, franchises, and liberties from a long line of ancestors.

This policy appears to me to be the result of profound reflection,—or rather the happy effect of following Nature, which is wisdom without reflection, and above it. A spirit of innovation is generally the result of a selfish temper and confined views. People will not look forward to posterity, who never look backward to their ancestors. Besides, the people of England well know that the idea of inheritance furnishes a sure principle of conservation, and a sure principle of transmission, without at all excluding a principle of improvement. It leaves acquisition free; but it secures what it acquires. Whatever advantages are obtained by a state proceeding on these maxims are locked fast as in a sort of family settlement, grasped as in a kind of mortmain forever. By a constitutional policy working after the pattern of Nature, we receive, we hold, we transmit our government and our privileges, in the same manner in which we enjoy and transmit our property and our lives. The institutions of policy, the goods of fortune, the gifts of Providence, are handed down to us, and from us, in the same course and order. Our political system is placed in a just correspondence and symmetry with the order of the world, and with the mode of existence decreed to a permanent body composed of transitory parts,—wherein, by the disposition of a stupendous wisdom, moulding together the great mysterious incorporation of the human race, the whole, at one time, is never old or middle-aged or young, but, in a condition of unchangeable constancy, moves on through the varied tenor of perpetual decay, fall, renovation, and progression. Thus, by preserving the method of Nature in the conduct of the state, in what we improve we are never wholly new, in what we retain we are never wholly obsolete. By adhering in this manner and on those principles to our forefathers, we are guided, not by the superstition of antiquarians, but by the spirit of philosophic analogy. In this choice of inheritance we have given to our frame of polity the image of a relation in blood: binding up the Constitution of our country with our dearest domestic ties; adopting our fundamental laws into the bosom of our family affections; keeping inseparable, and cherishing with the warmth of all their combined and mutually reflected charities, our state, our hearths, our sepulchres, and our altars.

Through the same plan of a conformity to Nature in our artificial institutions, and by calling in the aid of her unerring and powerful instincts to fortify the fallible and feeble contrivances of our reason, we have derived several other, and those no small benefits, from considering our liberties in the light of an inheritance. Always acting as if in the presence of canonized forefathers, the spirit of freedom, leading in itself to misrule and excess, is tempered with an awful gravity. This idea of a liberal descent inspires us with a sense of habitual native dignity, which prevents that upstart insolence almost inevitably adhering to and disgracing those who are the first acquirers of any distinction. By this means our liberty becomes a noble freedom. It carries an imposing and majestic aspect. It has a pedigree and illustrating ancestors. . . .

They [English and French revolutionaries] despise experience as the wisdom of unlettered men; and as for the rest, they have wrought under ground a mine that will blow up, at one grand explosion, all examples of antiquity, all precedents, charters, and acts of Parliament. They have "the rights of men." Against these there can be no prescription; against these no argument is binding: these admit no temperament and no compromise: anything withheld from their full demand is so much of fraud and injustice. Against these their rights of men let no government look for security in the length of its continuance, or in the justice and lenity of its administration. . . .

Far am I from denying in theory, full as far is my heart from withholding in practice, (if I were of power to give or to withhold,) the *real* rights of men. In denying their false claims of right, I do not mean to injure those which are real, and are such as their pretended rights would totally destroy. If civil society be made for the advantage of man, all the advantages for which it is made become his right. It is an institution of beneficence; and law itself is only beneficence acting by a rule. Men have a right to live by that rule; they have a right to justice, as between their fellows, whether their fellows are in politic function or in ordinary occupation. They have a right to the fruits of their industry, and to the means of making their industry fruitful. They have a right to the acquisitions of their parents, to the nourishment and improvement of their offspring, to instruction in life and to consolation in death. Whatever each man can separately do, without trespassing upon others, he has a right to do for himself; and he has a right to a fair portion of all which society, with all its combinations of skill and force, can do in his favor. In this partnership all men have equal rights; but not to equal things. He that has but five shillings in the partnership has as good a right to it as he that has five hundred pounds has to his larger proportion; but he has not a right to an equal dividend in the product of the joint stock. And as to the share of power, authority, and direction which each individual ought to have in the management of the state, that I must deny to be amongst the direct original rights of man in civil society; for I have in my contemplation the civil social man, and no other. It is a thing to be settled by convention. . . .

Government is not made in virtue of natural rights, which may and do exist in total independence of it,—and exist in much greater clearness, and in a much greater degree of abstract perfection: but their abstract perfection is their practical defect. By having a right to everything they want everything. Government is a contrivance of human wisdom to provide for human *wants*. Men have a right that these wants should be provided for by this wisdom. Among these wants is to be reckoned the want, out of civil society, of a sufficient restraint upon their passions. . . .

The science of constructing a commonwealth, or renovating it, or reforming it, is, like every other experimental science, not to be taught *a priori*. Nor is it a short experience that can instruct us in that practical science; because the real effects of moral causes are not always immediate, but that which in the first instance is prejudicial may be excellent in its remoter operation, and its excellence may arise even from the ill effects it produces in the beginning. . . .

The nature of man is intricate; the objects of society are of the greatest possible complexity: and therefore no simple disposition or direction of power can be suitable either to man's nature or to the quality of his affairs. When I hear the simplicity of contrivance aimed at and boasted of in any new political constitutions, I am at no loss to decide that the artificers are grossly ignorant of their trade or totally negligent of their duty. The simple governments are fundamentally defective, to say no worse of them. If you were to contemplate society in but one point of view, all these simple modes of polity are infinitely captivating. In effect each would answer its single end much more perfectly than the more complex is able to attain all its complex purposes. But it is better that the whole should be imperfectly and anomalously answered than that while some parts are provided for with great exactness, others might be totally neglected, or perhaps materially injured, by the over-care of a favorite member.

The pretended rights of these theorists are all extremes; and in proportion as they are metaphysically true, they are morally and politically false. . . .

We are not the converts of Rousseau; we are not the disciples of Voltaire; Helvetius has made no progress amongst us. Atheists are not our preachers; madmen are not our lawgivers. We know that *we* have made no discoveries, and we think that no discoveries are to be made, in morality,—nor many in the great principles of government, nor in the ideas of liberty, which were understood long before we were born altogether as well as they will be after the grave has heaped its mould upon our presumption, and the silent tomb shall have imposed its law on our pert loquacity. In England we have not yet been completely embowelled of our natural entrails: we still feel within us, and we cherish and cultivate, those inbred sentiments which are the faithful guardians, the active monitors of our duty, the true supporters of all liberal and manly morals. We have not been drawn and trussed, in order that we may be filled, like stuffed birds in a museum, with chaff and rags, and paltry, blurred shreds of paper about the rights of man. We preserve the whole of our feelings still native and entire, unsophisticated by pedantry and infidelity. We have real hearts of flesh and blood beating in our bosoms. We fear God; we look up with awe to kings, with affection to Parliaments, with duty to magistrates, with reverence to priests, and with respect to nobility. Why? Because, when such ideas are brought before our minds, it is *natural* to be so affected. . . .

We are afraid to put men to live and trade each on his own private stock of reason; because we suspect that the stock in each man is small, and that the individuals would do better to avail themselves of the general bank and capital of nations and of ages. . . .

But one of the first and most leading principles on which the commonwealth and the laws are consecrated is lest the temporary possessors and life-renters in it, unmindful of what they have received from their ancestors, or of what is due to their posterity, should act as if they were the entire masters; that they should not think it amongst their rights to cut off the entail or commit waste on the inheritance, by destroying at their pleasure the whole original fabric of their society: hazarding to leave to those who come after them a ruin instead of an habitation,—and teaching these successors as little to respect their contrivances as they had themselves respected the institutions of their forefathers. By this unprincipled facility of changing the state as often and as much and in as many ways as there are floating fancies or fashions, the whole chain and continuity of the commonwealth would be broken; no one generation could link with the other; men would become little better than the flies of a summer. . . .

To avoid, therefore, the evils of inconstancy and versatility, ten thousand times worse than those of obstinacy and the blindest prejudice, we have consecrated the state, that no man should approach to look into its defects or corruptions but with due caution; that he should never dream of beginning its reformation by its subversion; that he should approach to the faults of the state as to the wounds of a father, with pious awe and trembling solicitude. . . .

Society is, indeed, a contract. Subordinate contracts for objects of mere occasional interest may be dissolved at pleasure; but the state ought not to be considered as nothing better than a partnership agreement in a trade of pepper and coffee, calico or tobacco, or some other such low concern, to be taken up for a little temporary interest, and to be dissolved by the fancy of the parties. It is to be looked on with other reverence; because it is not a partnership in things subservient only to the gross animal existence of a temporary and perishable nature. It is a partnership in all science, a partnership in all art, a partnership in every virtue and in all perfection. As the ends of such a partnership cannot be obtained in many generations, it becomes a partnership not only between those who are living, but between those who are living, those who are dead, and those who are to be born. Each contract of each particular state is but a clause in the great primeval contract of eternal society, linking the lower with the higher natures, connecting the visible and invisible world, according to a fixed compact sanctioned by the inviolable oath which holds all physical and all moral natures each in their appointed place. . . .

JOHANN GOTTFRIED VON HERDER: *On Historicism* *

Herder (1744–1803), proto-romantic, friend of Goethe, and for a long time court preacher in Weimar, wrote many works on language, literature, theology, and history. *Yet Another Philosophy of History* (1774), from which the following excerpts are taken, is one of the earliest and best expressions of what today we call historicism. Therein Herder went against the grain of Enlightenment thought to deny the immutability of human nature and to assert the individuality of each *Volk* or culture and its place, an honorable place, in the scheme of history as a whole.

. . . No one in the world feels the weakness of general characterization more than I do. If one depicts a whole people, an age, an area, whom has one depicted? If one groups into one mass the peoples and periods which succeed each other eternally like the waves of the sea, what has one described? To whom does the descriptive term apply? Finally, one brings all of it together into nothing but a *general word*, whereby each individual thinks and feels as he will. How imperfect the means of description! How great the ease of misunderstanding! . . .

The general, philosophical, philanthropical tone of our century wishes to extend "our own ideal" of virtue and happiness to each distant nation, to even the remotest age in history. But can one such single ideal act as an arbiter praising or condemning other nations or periods, their customs and laws; can it remake them after its own image? Is good not dispersed over the earth? Since one form of mankind and one region could not encompass it, it has been distributed in a thousand forms, changing shape like an eternal Proteus throughout continents and centuries. . . .

Because it [the Middle Ages] comes between the Romans and us— *quanti viri*—some have treated it with derision; others, somewhat adventurously minded, have exalted it above everything; but it seems to me that it is neither more nor less than a "particular state of the world,"

* From F. M. Barnard: *Herder on Social and Political Culture* (Cambridge: Cambridge University Press, 1969), pp. 187, 191–92, 209, 214, 215–16.

whose advantages and disadvantages should not be compared with those of preceding ages: it took its point of departure from these ages, but by ceaseless transformation and aspiration became uniquely itself—on a grand scale.

We can read of the dark sides of this period in any book. Every classical litterateur who takes our regimented century for the *ne plus ultra* of mankind finds occasion to reproach whole centuries for barbarism, wretched constitutional law, superstition and stupidity, lack of manners and taste, and to mock their schools, country seats, temples, monasteries, town halls, guilds, cottages and houses. At the same time, he shouts the praises of the light of our century, or, rather, of its frivolity and exuberance, its warmth in theory and coldness in practice, its apparent strength and freedom, and its real mortal weakness and exhaustion under the weight of unbelief, despotism, and luxury. All the books of our Voltaires, Humes, Robertsons and Iselins are, to the delight of their contemporaries, full of beautiful accounts of how the enlightenment and improvement of the world, philosophy and order, emerged from the bleaker epochs of theism and spiritual despotism. All this is both true and untrue. It is true if, like a child, one holds one colour against another, if one wishes to contrive a bright, contrasty little picture—there is, alas, so much light in our century! It is untrue, if one considers the earlier epoch according to its intrinsic nature and aims, its pastimes and mores, and especially as the instrument of the historical process. . . .

How wretchedly primitive was the age [again, the Middle Ages; Herder, of course, here resorts to sarcasm] in which nationality and national character still existed; and, with it, hatred and hostility towards the foreigner, self-centered parochialism, prejudice, attachment to the soil where one was born and in which one was buried; a native mentality, a narrow span of ideas—eternal barbarism! With us, thank God, national character is no more! We love each and every one, or rather, we can dispense with love; for we simply *get on* with one another, being all equally polite, well-mannered and even-tempered. To be sure, we no longer have a fatherland or any kinship feelings; instead, we are all philanthropic citizens of the world. The princes speak French, and soon everybody will follow their example; and, then, behold, perfect bliss; the golden age, when all the world will speak one tongue, one universal language, is dawning again! There will be one flock and one shepherd! National cultures, where are you? . . .

As a rule, the philosopher is never more of an ass than when he most confidently wishes to play God, when with remarkable assurance, he pronounces on the perfection of the world, wholly convinced that everything moves just so, in a nice, straight line, that every succeeding generation reaches perfection in a completely linear progression, according to *his* ideals of virtue and happiness. It so happens that he is always the *ratio ultima*, the last, the highest, link in the chain of being, the very culmination of it all. "Just see to what enlightenment, virtue and happiness the world has swung! And here, behold, am I at the top of the pendulum, the gilded tongue of the world's scales!" . . .

He has not considered—this omniscient philosopher—that there can be a great, divine plan for the whole human race which a single creature cannot survey, since it is not he, philosopher or monarch of the eighteenth century though he be, who matters in the last resort. Whilst each actor has only one role in each scene, one sphere in which to strive for happiness, each scene forms part of a whole, a whole unknown and invisible to the individual, self-centered actor, but evident to the spectator from his vantage point and through his ability to see the sequence of the total performance.

See the entire universe from heaven to earth! What are the means, what the ends? Is not everything a means to a million ends? Is not everything an end for a million means? The chain of an almighty and omniscient goodness is twisted and tangled a thousand times; but each link in the chain has its own place—it is attached to the chain, but is unaware of the end to which the chain is finally attached. Everyone is under the illusion that he himself is the centre, is sensitive to everything around him only so far as it directs its rays or its waves towards this centre—a fine illusion! But where is the outer circumference of all these waves, rays and apparent centres? What is it for?

Is it likely to be otherwise in the history of the human race? Are all the waves, and all the times to come, likely to be something other than the blueprint of the almighty wisdom? If the dwelling down to its smallest detail manifests itself as the handiwork of God, would it not be so with the history of its inhabitants? The dwelling is only décor, a painting of one scene, one view! The history of its inhabitants, on the other hand, is an unending drama with many scenes, God's epic through all centuries, continents and generations, a fable with a thousand variations full of immense meaning. . . .

FRIEDRICH KARL VON SAVIGNY: *Two Schools of Legal Thought* *

Friedrich Karl von Savigny (1779–1861) was a famous German jurist who held the chair of Roman Law at the University of Berlin and was appointed High Chancellor or head of the judicial system in Prussia in 1842. He was one of the founders of the *Zeitschrift für geschichtliche Rechtswissenschaft*, a journal which became the organ of the new

* *Zeitschrift für geschichtliche Rechtswissenschaft* (Berlin: Nicolai; 1815), pp. 2–4, 5–7. My translation, with the assistance of Heinz Lubasz.

"historical" school of law which opposed the demand for a civil code on the French pattern and the "revolutionary" doctrine of natural law. The following selections, which describe the "two schools" of legal thought, are from Savigny's introductory article in the first number of the *Zeitschrift:* "On the purpose of this Journal" (1815).

ONE of these schools [of legal thought] may adequately be termed the *historical.* On the other hand, it is hardly possible to find a positive name for the other, since it is unanimous only in its opposition to the first; while apart from this it manifests itself in the most various and contradictory forms, proclaiming itself to be now philosophy and law of nature, now plain common sense. We will, then, for lack of a better term, call it the *unhistorical* school. But the antithesis between these schools of jurisprudence cannot be thoroughly understood so long as one's attention is confined to this legal science of ours: for the antithesis is of a quite general nature, manifesting itself to a greater or lesser extent in all things human, and most of all in everything relating to the constitution and government of states.

This, then, is the general question: in what relationship does the past stand to the present, or "becoming" to "being"? As to this, the one school teaches that every age creates, freely and arbitrarily, its own mode of life, its own universe—good and happy or bad and unhappy in proportion to its insight and its strength. In this task the consideration of past ages, too, is not to be disdained, since from them might be learned how they fared in the course of their own experience; so that history is a collection of moral and political examples. But this contemplation of the past is considered as nevertheless only one of many auxiliary sciences, with which true genius might well dispense.

According to the teaching of the other school, there is no such thing as a completely separate and isolated human existence; rather, that which may be regarded as separate is, when viewed from a different side, part of a greater whole. Thus, every single human being must be thought of as the member, at once, of a family, a people, and a state; every generation of a people, as the continuation and development of all times past. Precisely for these reasons any view other than this is one-sided, and, if it claims exclusive validity, false and pernicious. If this is so, then every age does *not* create its own universe freely and arbitrarily, but creates it in intimate partnership with the whole past. Every generation, therefore, must acknowledge some heritage, which yet is at once necessary and free: necessary to the extent that it is not dependent on the particular caprice of the present; free because it proceeds just as little from any particular alien caprice (such as the master's command to his slave), but much rather is created by the higher nature of the people as a continuously growing, developing whole. Indeed, of this higher Folk the present generation is a part, which wills and acts in and with this whole, so that whatever is created by the whole may be considered as freely created by the part also. History then becomes not merely a collection of examples, but the sole means to a true understanding of our own situation. Whoso maintains this historical position thus in addition pronounces judgment upon the opposite position. There is no question here of a choice between good and bad, the recognition of some heritage being good, its rejection bad but equally possible. Rather, this rejection of that which is anteriorly given is strictly impossible—it inevitably controls and governs us, and, while we can be deceived about it, we can do nothing to alter it. He who is thus deceived, and means to exercise his particular free will—while only that higher, collective freedom is possible—he surrenders even his noblest claims: he is a slave, who fancies himself a king, while he could at least be a free man. . . .

If we apply this general statement of the antithesis between the historical and the unhistorical view to jurisprudence, it will not be difficult to determine the nature of the two above-mentioned schools. The historical school supposes the substance of the law to be created by the whole of the nation's past; yet not through arbitrary will—so that this or any other could be the substance of the law—but emanating from the innermost being of the nation and its history. The deliberate function of every generation must, however, be directed towards the examination, rejuvenation, and maintenance of the substance of the law, handed down as it is through an inner necessity. The unhistorical school, on the other hand, supposes that the law is created arbitrarily at every instant by those who are invested with legislative power, quite independently of the law of the past, and merely on the basis of the strongest conviction of the present moment. That at any one instant the whole law is not organized afresh and quite differently from the preceding system can be explained by this school only by asserting that the law-giver was too indolent properly to do his duty, that he must by chance have considered as still valid the legal views of the precious instant. Everyone will perceive how sharp is the conflict between these schools, if he attempts the application of these principles to particular cases. The calling of the legislative power, that of the judge, especially the scientific treatment of the law—everything becomes radically different according as one holds to the one or the other of these views.

GEORG WILHELM FRIEDRICH HEGEL: *Lectures on the Philosophy of History* *

Georg Wilhelm Friedrich Hegel (1770–1831), the great Idealist philosopher, did not belong to the so-called "Romantic school" in Germany. Nevertheless, he struck some characteristic romantic notes in his work. Although a great rationalist, his "reason" was more like *Vernunft* than *Verstand* (see selection from Coleridge). And in his lectures on the philosophy of history, delivered at Berlin between 1822 and 1831, he exhibited a strong historical sense, put "Spirit" (as opposed to "Matter") at the heart of the historical process, and stressed the role played by great individuals. Hegel's enormous influence on subsequent thought, especially on the Young Hegelians, including Marx, is well known.

LIKE the soul-conductor Mercury, the Idea is in truth, the leader of peoples and of the World; and Spirit, the rational and necessitated will of that conductor, is and has been the director of the events of the World's History. To become acquainted with Spirit in this its office of guidance, is the object of our present undertaking. . . .

The only Thought which Philosophy brings with it to the contemplation of History, is the simple conception of *Reason;* that Reason is the Sovereign of the World; that the history of the world, therefore, presents us with a rational process. This conviction and intuition is a hypothesis in the domain of history as such. In that of Philosophy it is no hypothesis. It is there proved by speculative cognition, that Reason —and this term may here suffice us, without investigating the relation sustained by the Universe to the Divine Being,—is *Substance*, as well as *Infinite Power;* its own *Infinite Material* underlying all the natural and spiritual life which it originates, as also the *Infinite Form,*—that which sets this Material in motion. On the one hand, Reason is the *substance* of the Universe; viz. that by which and in which all reality has its being and subsistence. On the other hand, it is the *Infinite Energy* of the Universe; since Reason is not so powerless as to be incapable of producing anything but a mere ideal, a mere intention—having its place outside reality, nobody knows where; something separate and abstract, in the heads of certain human beings. . . .

If the clear idea of Reason is not already developed in our minds, in beginning the study of Universal History, we should at least have the

* Georg Wilhelm Friedrich Hegel: *Lectures on the Philosophy of History*, J. Sibree (trans.) (London: H. G. Bohn; 1857), pp. 8–11, 18–20, 31, 40–42, 45, 54–58, 66.

firm, unconquerable faith that Reason *does* exist there; and that the World of intelligence and conscious volition is not abandoned to chance, but must shew itself in the light of the self-cognizant Idea. . . .

* * *

The nature of Spirit may be understood by a glance at its direct opposite—*Matter*. As the essence of Matter is Gravity, so, on the other hand, we may affirm that the substance, the essence of Spirit is Freedom. . . . Matter has its essence out of itself; Spirit is *self-contained existence*. Now this is Freedom, exactly. For if I am dependent, my being is referred to something else which I am not; I cannot exist independently of something external. I am free, on the contrary, when my existence depends upon myself. This self-contained existence of Spirit is none other than self-consciousness—consciousness of one's own being. Two things must be distinguished in consciousness; first, the fact *that I know;* secondly, *what I know*. In *self* consciousness these are merged in one; for Spirit *knows itself*. It involves an appreciation of its own nature, as also an energy enabling it to realise itself; to make itself *actually* that which it is *potentially*. According to this abstract definition it may be said of Universal History, that it is the exhibition of Spirit in the process of working out the knowledge of that which it is potentially. And as the germ bears in itself the whole nature of the tree, and the taste and form of its fruits, so do the first traces of Spirit virtually contain the whole of that History. . . .

The History of the world is none other than the progress of the consciousness of Freedom; a progress whose development according to the necessity of its nature, it is our business to investigate.

The general statement given above, of the various grades in the consciousness of Freedom—and which we applied in the first instance to the fact that the Eastern nations knew only that *one* is free; the Greek and Roman world only that *some* are free; whilst *we* know that all men absolutely (man *as man*) are free,—supplies us with the natural division of Universal History, and suggests the mode of its discussion.

* * *

[The "particular aims" of "great historical men"] involve those large issues which are the will of the World-Spirit. They may be called Heroes, inasmuch as they have derived their purposes and their vocation, not from the calm, regular course of things, sanctioned by the existing order; but from a concealed fount—one which has not attained to phenomenal, present existence,—from that inner Spirit, still hidden beneath the surface, which, impinging on the outer world as on a shell, bursts it in pieces, because it is another kernel than that which belonged to the shell in question. They are men, therefore, who appear to draw the impulse of their life from themselves; and whose deeds have produced a condition of things and a complex of historical relations which appear to be only *their* interest, and *their* work.

Such individuals had no consciousness of the general Idea they were unfolding, while prosecuting those aims of theirs; on the contrary, they were practical, political men. But at the same time they were thinking men, who had an insight into the requirements of the time—*what was ripe for development.*

*   *   *

It must further be understood that all the worth which the human being possesses—all spiritual reality, he possesses only through the State. For his spiritual reality consists in this, that his own essence—Reason—is objectively present to him, that it possesses objective immediate existence for him. Thus only is he fully conscious; thus only is he a partaker of morality—of a just and moral social and political life. For Truth is the Unity of the universal and subjective Will; and the Universal is to be found in the State, in its laws, its universal and rational arrangements. The State is the Divine Idea as it exists on Earth. We have in it, therefore, the object of History in a more definite shape than before; that in which Freedom obtains objectivity, and lives in the enjoyment of this objectivity. For Law is the objectivity of Spirit; volition in its true form. Only that will which obeys law, is free; for it obeys itself—it is independent and so free. When the State or our country constitutes a community of existence; when the subjective will of man submits to laws,—the contradiction between Liberty and Necessity vanishes. The Rational has necessary existence, as being the reality and substance of things, and we are free in recognizing it as law, and following it as the substance of our own being. The objective and the subjective will are then reconciled, and present one identical homogeneous whole. For the morality (Sittlichkeit) of the State is not of that ethical (moralische) reflective kind, in which one's own conviction bears sway; this latter is rather the peculiarity of the modern time, while the true antique morality is based on the principle of abiding by one's duty [to the state at large]. . . .

The development *in extenso* of the Idea of the State belongs to the Philosophy of Jurisprudence; but it must be observed that in the theories of our time various errors are current respecting it, which pass for established truths, and have become fixed prejudices. We will mention only a few of them, giving prominence to such as have a reference to the object of our history.

The error which first meets us is the direct contradictory of our principle that the state presents the realization of Freedom; the opinion, viz., that man is free by *nature*, but that in *society*, in the State—to which nevertheless he is irresistibly impelled—he must limit this natural freedom. . . .

If the principle of regard for the individual will is recognized as the only basis of political liberty, viz., that nothing should be done by or for the State to which all the members of the body politic have not given their sanction, we have, properly speaking, no *Constitution*.

*   *   *

Summing up what has been said of the State, we find that we have been led to call its vital principle, as actuating the individuals who compose it,—Morality. The State, its laws, its arrangements, constitute the rights of its members; its natural features, its mountains, air, and waters, are *their* country, their fatherland, their outward material property; the history of this State, *their* deeds; what their ancestors have produced, belongs to them and lives in their memory. All is their possession, just as they are possessed by it; for it constitutes their existence, their being.

Their imagination is occupied with the ideas thus presented, while the adoption of these laws, and of a fatherland so conditioned is the expression of their will. It is this matured totality which thus constitutes *one* Being, the spirit of *one* People. To it the individual members belong; each unit is the Son of his Nation, and at the same time—in as far as the State to which he belongs is undergoing development—the Son of his Age. None remains behind it, still less advances beyond it. This spiritual Being (the Spirit of his Time) is his; he is a representative of it; it is that in which he originated, and in which he lives. Among the Athenians the word Athens had a double import; suggesting primarily, a complex of political institutions, but no less, in the second place, that Goddess who represented the Spirit of the People and its unity. . . .

The remark next in order is, that each particular National genius is to be treated as only One Individual in the process of Universal History. For that history is the exhibition of the divine, absolute development of Spirit in its highest forms,—that gradation by which it attains its truth and consciousness of itself. The forms which these grades of progress assume are the characteristic "National Spirits" of History; the peculiar tenor of their moral life, of their Government, their Art, Religion, and Science. To realize these grades is the boundless impulse of the World-Spirit—the goal of its irresistible urging; for this division into organic members, and the full development of each, is its Idea. . . .

The mutations which history presents have been long characterized in the general, as an advance to something better, more perfect. The changes that take place in Nature—how infinitely manifold soever they may be—exhibit only a perpetually self-repeating cycle; in Nature there happens "nothing new under the sun," and the multiform play of its phenomena so far induces a feeling of *ennui;* only in those changes which take place in the region of Spirit does anything new arise. This peculiarity in the world of mind has indicated in the case of man an altogether different destiny from that of merely natural objects—in which we find always one and the same stable character, to which all change reverts;—namely, a *real* capacity for change, and that for the better,—an impulse of *perfectibility*. . . .

The principle of *Development* involves also the existence of a latent germ of being—a capacity or potentiality striving to realise itself. This formal conception finds actual existence in Spirit; which has the History of the World for its theatre, its possession, and the sphere of its realization. It is not of such a nature as to be tossed to and fro amid the superficial play of accidents, but is rather the absolute arbiter of things; entirely unmoved by contingencies, which, indeed, it applies and manages for its own purposes. . . . That development (of *natural organisms*) takes place in a direct, unopposed, unhindered manner. Between the Idea and its realization—the essential constitution of the original germ and the conformity to it of the existence derived from it—no disturbing influence can intrude. But in relation to Spirit it is quite otherwise. The realization of *its* Idea is mediated by consciousness and will; these very faculties are, in the first instance, sunk in their primary *merely* natural life; the first object and goal of their striving is the realization of their merely natural destiny,—but which, since it is Spirit that animates it, is possessed of vast attractions and displays great power and moral richness. Thus Spirit is at war with itself; it has to overcome itself as its most formidable obstacle. That development which in the sphere of Nature is a peaceful growth, is in that of Spirit, a severe, a mighty conflict with itself. What Spirit really strives for is the realization of its Ideal being; but in doing so, it hides that goal from its own vision, and is proud and well satisfied in this alienation from it.

Its expansion, therefore, does not present the harmless tranquillity of mere growth, as does that of organic life, but a stern reluctant working against itself. It exhibits, moreover, not the mere formal conception of development, but the attainment of a definite result. The goal of attainment we determined at the outset: it is Spirit in its *completeness*, in its essential nature, *i.e.*, Freedom.

* * *

Universal history—as already demonstrated—shews the development of the consciousness of Freedom on the part of Spirit, and of the consequent realization of that Freedom. This development implies a gradation—a series of increasingly adequate expressions or manifestations of Freedom, which result from its Idea. The logical, and—as still more prominent—the *dialectical* nature of the Idea in general, viz. that it is self-determined—that it assumes successive forms which it successively transcends; and by this very process of transcending its earlier stages, gains an affirmative, and, in fact, a richer and more concrete shape;—this necessity of its nature, and the necessary series of pure abstract forms which the Idea successively assumes—is exhibited in the department of *Logic*. Here we need adopt only one of its results, viz. that every step in the process, as differing from any other, has its determinate peculiar principle. In history this principle is idiosyncrasy of Spirit—peculiar National Genius. It is within the limitations of this idiosyncrasy that the spirit of the nation, concretely manifested, expresses every aspect of its consciousness and will—the whole cycle of its realization.

2. *The New Enlightenment*

A. ENGLISH UTILITARIANISM AND LIBERALISM

JEREMY BENTHAM: *On the Principle of Utility* *

Jeremy Bentham's *An Introduction to the Principles of Morals and Legislation* (1780) laid the predicates for the Utilitarian Movement in England. Bentham (1748–1832) aimed to establish first principles or laws in those areas, as Newton had done for the physical sciences. His principle of utility, which owed much to Hume and Helvétius, was actually an axiom of human nature. Hence, his science can be said to be deductive in the manner of geometry, rather than inductive, and to involve quantification, that is, the famous "felicific calculation" described in the following excerpts.

I. Nature has placed mankind under the governance of two sovereign masters, *pain* and *pleasure*. It is for them alone to point out what we

* Jeremy Bentham: *An Introduction to the Principles of Morals and Legislation* (London: E. Wilson; 1823), Vol. I, pp. 1–5, 13, 30, 49–50, 52; Vol. II, pp. 30–31.

ought to do, as well as to determine what we shall do. On the one hand the standard of right and wrong, on the other the chain of causes and effects, are fastened to their throne. They govern us in all we do, in all we say, in all we think: every effort we can make to throw off our subjection, will serve but to demonstrate and confirm it. In words a man may pretend to abjure their empire: but in reality he will remain subject to it all the while. The *principle of utility* recognises this subjection, and assumes it for the foundation of that system, the object of which is to rear the fabric of felicity by the hands of reason and of law. Systems which attempt to question it, deal in sounds instead of sense, in caprice instead of reason, in darkness instead of light.

But enough of metaphor and declamation: it is not by such means that moral science is to be improved.

II. The principle of utility is the foundation of the present work: it will be proper therefore at the outset to give an explicit and determinate account of what is meant by it. By the principle of utility is meant that principle which approves or disapproves of every action whatsoever, according to the tendency which it appears to have to augment or diminish the happiness of the party whose interest is in question: or, what is the same thing in other words, to promote or to oppose that happiness. I say of every action whatsoever; and therefore not only of every action of a private individual, but of every measure of government.

III. By utility is meant that property in any object, whereby it tends to produce benefit, advantage, pleasure, good or happiness, (all this in the present case comes to the same thing) or (what comes again to the same thing) to prevent the happening of mischief, pain, evil, or unhappiness to the party whose interest is considered: if that party be the community in general, then the happiness of the community: if a particular individual, then the happiness of that individual.

IV. The interest of the community is one of the most general expressions that can occur in the phraseology of morals: no wonder that the meaning of it is often lost. When it has a meaning, it is this. The community is a fictitious *body*, composed of the individual persons who are considered as constituting as it were its *members*. The interest of the community then is, what?—the sum of the interests of the several members who compose it.

V. It is in vain to talk of the interest of the community, without understanding what is the interest of the individual. A thing is said to promote the interest, or to be *for* the interest, of an individual, when it tends to add to the sum total of his pleasures: or, what comes to the same thing, to diminish the sum total of his pains.

VI. An action then may be said to be conformable to the principle of utility, or, for shortness sake, to utility, (meaning with respect to the community at large) when the tendency it has to augment the happiness of the community is greater than any it has to diminish it.

VII. A measure of government (which is but a particular kind of action, performed by a particular person or persons) may be said to be conformable to or dictated by the principle of utility, when in like manner the tendency which it has to augment the happiness of the community is greater than any which it has to diminish it.

*   *   *

If the principle of utility be a right principle to be governed by, and that in all cases, it follows from what has been just observed, that whatever principle differs from it in any case must necessarily be a wrong one. To prove any other principle, therefore, to be a wrong one, there needs no more than just to show it to be what it is, a principle of which the dictates are in some point or other different from those of the principle of utility: to state it is to confute it. . . .

A great multitude of people are continually talking of the Law of Nature; and then they go on giving you their sentiments about what is right and what is wrong: and these sentiments, you are to understand, are so many chapters and sections of the Law of Nature.

Instead of the phrase, Law of Nature, you have sometimes, Law of Reason, Right Reason, Natural Justice, Natural Equity, Good Order. Any of them will do equally well. This latter is most used in politics. The three last are much more tolerable than the others, because they do not very explicitly claim to be any thing more than phrases. . . . On most occasions, however, it will be better to say *utility: utility* is clearer, as referring more explicitly to pain and pleasure. . . .

*   *   *

Pleasures then, and the avoidance of pains, are the *ends* which the legislator has in view: it behoves him therefore to understand their *value*. Pleasures and pains are the *instruments* he has to work with: it behoves him therefore to understand their force, which is again, in other words, their value.

To a person considered *by himself*, the value of a pleasure or pain considered *by itself*, will be greater or less according to the four following circumstances:

1. Its *intensity*.
2. Its *duration*.
3. Its *certainty* or *uncertainty*.
4. Its *propinquity* or *remoteness*. . . .

Sum up all the values of all the *pleasures* on the one side, and those of all the pains on the other. The balance, if it be on the side of pleasure, will give the *good* tendency of the act upon the whole, with respect to the interests of that *individual* person; if on the side of pain, the *bad* tendency of it upon the whole.

Take an account of the *number* of persons whose interests appear to be concerned; and repeat the above process with respect to each. *Sum up* the numbers expressive of the degrees of *good* tendency, which the act has, with respect to each individual, in regard to whom the tendency of it is *good* upon the whole: do this again with respect to each individual, in regard to whom the tendency of it is *bad* upon the whole. Take the *balance;* which, if on the side of pleasure, will give the general *good tendency* of the act, with respect to the total number or community of individuals concerned; if on the side of pain, the general *evil tendency*, with respect to the same community.

*   *   *

There are some, perhaps, who, at first sight, may look upon the nicety employed in the adjustment of such rules, as so much labour lost: for gross ignorance, they will say, never troubles itself about laws, and passion does not calculate. But the evil of ignorance admits of cure: and as to the proposition that passion does not calculate this, like most of these very general and oracular propositions, is not true. When matters of such importance as pain and pleasure are at stake, and these in the highest degree (the only matters, in short, that can be of importance) who is there that does not calculate? Men calculate, some with less exactness, indeed, some with more: but all men calculate. I would not say, that even a madman does not calculate. Passion calculates, more or less, in every man. . . .

JOHN STUART MILL: *Autobiography* *

In the following passage the great English liberal John Stuart Mill (1806–73), describes with admirable clarity and terseness the credo of the "Philosophical Radicals" who in the 1820's and 1830's banded

* John Stuart Mill: *Autobiography* (London: Longmans; 1875), pp. 105–9, 225–6, 273–4.

together to propagate the social philosophy of Bentham, James Mill, Thomas Malthus, and David Ricardo. By the time he came to write his autobiography, during the last five years of his life, Mill had personally moved quite a way from the views here expressed, but they remained, nevertheless, the basis of classic liberalism in the nineteenth century.

BUT though none of us, probably, agreed in every respect with my father, his opinions, as I said before, were the principal element which gave its colour and character to the little group of young men who were the first propagators of what was afterwards called "Philosophic Radicalism." Their mode of thinking was not characterized by Benthamism in any sense which has relation to Bentham as a chief or guide, but rather by a combination of Bentham's point of view with that of the modern political economy, and with the Hartleian metaphysics. Malthus's population principle was quite as much a banner, and point of union among us, as any opinion specially belonging to Bentham. This great doctrine, originally brought forward as an argument against the indefinite improvability of human affairs, we took up with ardent zeal in the contrary sense, as indicating the sole means of realizing that improvability by securing full employment at high wages to the whole labouring population through a voluntary restriction of the increase of their numbers. The other leading characteristics of the creed, which we held in common with my father, may be stated as follows:

In politics, an almost unbounded confidence in the efficacy of two things: representative government, and complete freedom of discussion. So complete was my father's reliance on the influence of reason over the minds of mankind, whenever it is allowed to reach them, that he felt as if all would be gained if the whole population were taught to read, if all sorts of opinions were allowed to be addressed to them by word and in writing, and if by means of the suffrage they could nominate a legislature to give effect to the opinions they adopted. He thought that when the legislature no longer represented a class interest, it would aim at the general interest, honestly and with adequate wisdom; since the people would be sufficiently under the guidance of educated intelligence, to make in general a good choice of persons to represent them, and having done so, to leave to those whom they had chosen a liberal discretion. Accordingly aristocratic rule, the government of the Few in any of its shapes, being in his eyes the only thing which stood between mankind and an administration of their affairs by the best wisdom to be found among them, was the object of his sternest disapprobation, and a democratic suffrage the principal article of his political creed, not on the ground of liberty, Rights of Man, or any of the phrases, more or less significant, by which, up to that time, democracy had usually been defended, but as the most essential of "securities for good government." In this, too, he held fast only to what he deemed essentials; he was comparatively indifferent to monarchical or republican forms—far more so than Bentham, to whom a king, in the character of "corrupter-general," appeared necessarily very noxious. Next to aristocracy, an established church, or corporation of priests, as being by position the great depravers of religion, and interested in opposing the progress of the human mind, was the object of his greatest detestation. . . . In psychology, his fundamental doctrine was the formation of all human character by circumstances, through the universal Principle of Association, and the consequent unlimited possibility of improving the moral and intellectual condition of mankind by education. Of all his doctrines none was more important than this, or needs more to be insisted on. . . .

These various opinions were seized on with youthful fanaticism by the little knot of young men of whom I was one: and we put into them a sectarian spirit, from which, in intention at least, my father was wholly free. What we (or rather a phantom substituted in the place of us) were sometimes, by a ridiculous exaggeration, called by others, namely a "school," some of us for a time really hoped and aspired to be. The French *philosophes* of the eighteenth century were the example we sought to imitate, and we hoped to accomplish no less results. No one of the set went to so great excesses in this boyish ambition as I did; which might be shown by many particulars, were it not an useless waste of space and time. . . .

> Philosophically, Mill was an empiricist, and he saw the closest connection between the empirical theory of knowledge and political liberalism, just as, conversely, he believed philosophical "intuitionism" (as he called it), that is, German philosophy since Kant and the philosophy of Coleridge as well as Sir William Hamilton, to be a support for political conservatism and reactionism. This conviction, common to many English liberals, stands out clearly in the last chapter in which he tells about completing *A System of Logic* (1843), which is his important book on scientific method. Incidentally, these passages reveal that by that time Mill had jettisoned the "Geometric method" of Bentham and his father.

. . . The German, or *à priori* view of human knowledge, and of the knowing faculties, is likely for some time longer (though it may be hoped in a diminishing degree) to predominate among those who occupy themselves with such inquiries, both here and on the Continent. But the "System of Logic" supplies what was much wanted, a text-book of the opposite doctrine—that which derives all knowledge from experience, and all moral and intellectual qualities principally from the direction given to the associations. I make as humble an estimate as anybody of what either an analysis of logical processes, or any possible canons of evidence, can do by themselves, towards guiding or rectifying the operations of the understanding. Combined with other requisites, I certainly do think them of great use; but whatever may be the practical value of a true philosophy of these matters, it is hardly possible to exaggerate the mischiefs of a false one. The notion that truths external to the mind may be known by intuition or consciousness, independently of observation and experience, is, I am persuaded, in these times, the great intellectual support of false doctrines and bad institutions. By the aid of this theory, every inveterate belief and every intense feeling, of which the origin is not remembered, is enabled to dispense with the obligation of justifying itself by reason, and is erected into its own all-sufficient voucher and justification. There never was such an instrument devised for consecrating all deep-seated prejudices. . . .

Now, the difference between these two schools of philosophy, that of Intuition, and that of Experience and Association, is not a mere matter of abstract speculation; it is full of practical consequences, and lies at the foundation of all the greatest differences of practical opinion in an age of progress. The practical reformer has continually to demand that changes be made in things which are supported by powerful and widely-spread feelings, or to question the apparent necessity and indefeasibleness of established facts; and it is often an indispensable part of his argument to show, how those powerful feelings had their origin, and how those facts came to seem necessary and indefeasible. There is therefore a natural hostility between him and a philosophy which discourages the explanation of feelings and moral facts by circumstances and association, and prefers to treat them as ultimate elements of human nature; a philosophy which is addicted to holding up favourite doctrines as intuitive truths, and deems intuition to be the voice of Nature and of God, speaking with an authority higher than that of our reason. In particular, I have long felt that the prevailing tendency to regard all the marked distinctions of human character as innate, and in the main indelible, and to ignore the irresistible proofs that by far the greater part of those differences, whether between individuals, races, or sexes, are such as not only might but naturally would be produced by differences in circumstances, is one of the chief hindrances to the rational treatment of great social questions, and one of the greatest stumbling blocks to human improvement. This tendency has its source in the intuitional metaphysics which characterized the reaction of the nineteenth century against the eighteenth, and it is a tendency so agreeable to human indolence, as well as to conservative interests generally, that unless attacked at the very root, it is sure to be carried to even a greater length than is really justified by the more moderate forms of the intuitional philosophy. That philosophy, not always in its moderate forms, had ruled the thought of Europe for the greater part of a century. . . .

SAMUEL SMILES: *Self-help* *

> The optimistic "gospel according to Smiles," which is set forth in *Self-help* (1859), enjoyed an enormous vogue in Europe and outside of Europe. Of Dr. Samuel Smiles (1812–1904) the obituary in *The Athenaeum* said: "The number of his years is important. For he saw the rise of railways and shared the common belief that the lines which fell on all the pleasant places of England secured prosperity for the population, that the steamships put men into touch with the Isles of the Blest, and that mechanics meant the millennium." Smiles was a doctor of medicine, editor of the *Leeds Times*, secretary of two English railways, and writer of many popular books on the order of *Self-help*.

"HEAVEN helps those who help themselves," is a well-worn maxim, embodying in a small compass the results of vast human experience. The spirit of self-help is the root of all genuine growth in the individual; and, exhibited in the lives of many, it constitutes the true source of national vigor and strength. Help from without is often enfeebling in its effects, but help from within invariably invigorates. Whatever is done for *men* or classes, to a certain extent takes away the stimulus and necessity of doing for themselves; and where men are subjected to over-guidance and over-government, the inevitable tendency is to render them comparatively helpless.

Even the best institutions can give a man no active aid. Perhaps the utmost they can do is, to leave him *free* to develop himself and improve his individual condition. But in all times men have been prone to believe that their happiness and well-being were to be secured by means of institutions rather than by their own conduct. Hence the value of legislation as an agent in human advancement has always been greatly over-estimated. To constitute the millionth part of a legislature, by voting for one or two men once in three or five years, however conscientiously this duty may be performed, can exercise but little active influence upon any man's life and character. Moreover, it is every day becoming more clearly understood, that the function of government is negative and restrictive, rather than positive and active; being resolvable

* Samuel Smiles: *Self-help* (Boston: Ticknor and Fields; 1860), pp. 15–17, 67–8, 167–9, 189, 191–2, 265–7, 279.

principally into protection,—protection of life, liberty and property. Hence the chief "reforms" of the last fifty years have consisted mainly in abolitions and disenactments. But there is no power of law that can make the idle man industrious, the thriftless provident, or the drunken sober; though every individual can be each and all of these if he will, by the exercise of his own free powers of action and self-denial. Indeed, all experience serves to prove that the worth and strength of a state depend far less upon the form of its institutions than upon the character of its men. For the nation is only the aggregate of individual conditions, and civilization itself is but a question of personal improvement.

National progress is the sum of individual industry, energy, and uprightness, as national decay is of individual idleness, selfishness, and vice. What we are accustomed to decry as great social evils, will, for the most part, be found to be only the outgrowth of our own perverted life; and though we may endeavour to cut them down and extirpate them by means of law, they will only spring up again with fresh luxuriance in some other form, unless the individual conditions of human life and character are radically improved. If this view be correct, then it follows that the highest patriotism and philanthropy consist, not so much in altering laws and modifying institutions, as in helping and stimulating men to elevate and improve themselves by their own free and independent action as individuals.

*   *   *

Fortune has often been blamed for her blindness; but fortune is not so blind as men are. Those who look into practical life will find that fortune is invariably on the side of the industrious, as the winds and waves are on the side of the best navigators. Success treads on the heels of every right effort; and though it is possible to overestimate success to the extent of almost deifying it, as is sometimes done, still, in any worthy pursuit, it is meritorious. Nor are the qualities necessary to insure success at all extraordinary. They may, for the most part, be summed up in these two,—common sense and perseverance. Genius may not be necessary, though even genius of the highest sort does not despise the exercise of these common qualities. The very greatest men have been among the least believers in the power of genius, and as worldly wise and persevering as successful men of the commoner sort. Some have even defined genius to be only common sense intensified. A distinguished teacher and president of a college spoke of it as the power of making efforts. John Foster held it to be the power of lighting one's own fire. Buffon said of genius,—It is patience.

*   *   *

Practical industry, wisely and vigorously applied, never fails of success. It carries a man onward and upward, brings out his individual character, and powerfully stimulates the action of others. All may not rise equally, yet each, on the whole, very much according to his deserts. "Though all cannot live on the piazza," as the Tuscan proverb has it, "every one may feel the sun."

We have already referred to some illustrious Commoners raised from humble to elevated positions by the power of application and industry; and we might point to even the Peerage itself as affording equally instructive examples. One reason why the peerage of England has succeeded so well in retaining its vigor and elasticity, arises from the fact that, unlike the peerages of other countries, it has been fed from time to time by the best industrial blood of the country—the very "liver, heart, and brain of Britain.". . .

The great bulk of our peerage is comparatively modern, so far as the titles go; but it is not the less noble that it has been recruited to so large an extent from the ranks of honorable industry. In olden times, the wealth and commerce of London, conducted as it was by energetic and enterprising men, was a prolific source of peerages. Thus, the earldom of Cornwallis was founded by Thomas Cornwallis, the Cheapside merchant; that of Essex by William Capel, the draper; and that of Craven by William Craven, the merchant tailor. The modern Earl of Warwick is not descended from "the Kingmaker," but from William Greville, the woolstapler; whilst the modern dukes of Northumberland find their head, not in the Percies, but in Hugh Smithson, a respectable London apothecary.

*   *   *

The cultivation of this quality is of the greatest importance; resolute determination in the pursuit of worthy objects being the foundation of all true greatness of character. Energy enables a man to force his way through irksome drudgery and dry details, and carries him onward and upward in every station in life. It accomplishes more than genius, with not one half the disappointment and peril. It is not even eminent talent that is required to insure success in any pursuit so much as purpose,—not merely the power to achieve, but the will to labor energetically and perseveringly. Hence energy of will may be defined to be the very central power of character in a man,—in a word, it is the Man himself. It gives impulse to his every action, and soul to every effort. True hope is based on it,—and it is hope that gives the real perfume to life.

*   *   *

It is *will*,—force of purpose,—that enables a man to do or be whatever he sets his mind on being or doing. A holy man was accustomed to say,

"Whatever you wish, that you are: for such is the force of our will, joined to the Divine, that whatever we wish to be, seriously, and with a true intention, that we become. No one ardently wishes to be submissive, patient, modest, or liberal, who does not become what he wishes." The story is told of a working carpenter, who was observed one day planing a magistrate's bench, which he was repairing, with more than usual carefulness, and when asked the reason, he replied, "Because I wish to make it easy against the time when I come to sit upon it myself." And singularly enough, the man actually lived to sit upon that very bench as a magistrate.

Whatever theoretical conclusions logicians may have formed as to the freedom of the will, each individual feels that practically he is free to choose between good and evil,—that he is not like a mere straw thrown upon the water to mark the direction of the current, but that he has within him the power of a strong swimmer, and is capable of striking out for himself, of buffeting with the waves, and directing to a great extent his own independent course. There is no absolute constraint upon our volitions, and we feel and know that we are not bound, as by a spell, with reference to our actions. It would paralyze all desire of excellence were we to think otherwise. The entire business and conduct of life, with its domestic rules, its social arrangements, and its public institutions, proceed upon the practical conviction that the will is free. Without this where would be responsibility?—and what the advantage of teaching, advising, preaching, reproof, and correction? What were the use of laws, were it not the universal belief, as it is the universal fact, that men obey them or not, very much as they individually determine? In every moment of our life, conscience is proclaiming that our will is free. It is the only thing that is wholly ours, and it rests solely with ourselves individually, whether we give it the right or the wrong direction. Our habits or our temptations are not our masters, but we of them. Even in yielding, conscience tells us we might resist; and that were we determined to master them, there would not be required for that purpose a stronger resolution than we know ourselves to be capable of exercising.

*   *   *

Any class of men that lives from hand to mouth will ever be an inferior class. They will necessarily remain impotent and helpless, hanging on to the skirts of society, the sport of times and seasons. Having no respect for themselves, they will fail in securing the respect of others. In commercial crises, such men must inevitably go to the wall. Wanting that husbanded power which a store of savings, no matter how small, invariably gives them, they will be at every man's mercy, and, if possessed of right feelings, they cannot but regard with fear and trembling the future possible fate of their wives and children. "The world," once said Mr. Cobden to the working men of Huddersfield, "has always been divided into two classes,—those who have saved, and those who have spent,—the thrifty and the extravagant. The building of all the houses, the mills, the bridges, and the ships, and the accomplishment of all other great works which have rendered man civilized and happy, has been done by the savers, the thrifty; and those who have wasted their resources have always been their slaves. It has been the law of nature and of Providence, that this should be so; and I were an impostor if I promised any class that they would advance themselves if they were improvident, thoughtless, and idle."

Equally sound was the advice given by Mr. Bright to an assembly of working men at Rochdale, in 1847, when, after expressing his belief that "so far as honesty was concerned, it was to be found in pretty equal amount among all classes," he used the following words: "There is only one way that is safe for any man, or any number of men, by which they can maintain their present position if it be a good one, or raise themselves above it if it be a bad one,—that is, by the practice of the virtues of industry, frugality, temperance, and honesty. There is no royal road by which men can raise themselves from a position which they feel to be uncomfortable and unsatisfactory, as regards their mental or physical condition, except by the practice of those virtues by which they find numbers amongst them are continually advancing and bettering themselves. What is it that has made, that has in fact created, the middle class in this country, but the virtues to which I have alluded? There was a time when there was hardly any class in England, except the highest, that was equal in condition to the poorest class at this moment. How is it that the hundreds of thousands of men, now existing in this our country, of the middle class, are educated, comfortable, and enjoying an amount of happiness and independence, to which our forefathers were wholly unaccustomed? Why, by the practice of those very virtues; for I maintain that there has never been in any former age as much of these virtues as is now to be found amongst the great middle class of our community. When I speak of the middle class, I mean that class which is between the privileged class, the richest, and the very poorest in the community; and I would recommend every man to pay no attention whatever to public writers or speakers, whoever they may be, who tell them that this class or that class, that this law or that law, that this government or that government, can do all these things for them. I assure you, after long reflection and much observation, that there is no way for the working classes of this country to improve their condition but that which so many of them have already availed themselves of,—that is, by the practice of those virtues, and by reliance upon themselves."

*   *   *

Many popular books have been written for the purpose of communicating to the public the grand secret of making money. But there is no secret whatever about it, as the proverbs of every nation abundantly testify. "Many a little makes a meikle."—"Take care of the pennies and the pounds will take care of themselves."—"A penny saved is a penny gained."—"Diligence is the mother of good-luck."—"No pains no gains."—"No sweat no sweet."—"Sloth, the key of poverty."—"Work, and thou shalt have."—"He who will not work, neither shall he eat."—"The world is his, who has patience and industry."—"It is too late to spare when all is spent."—"Better go to bed supperless than rise in debt." —"The morning hour has gold in its mouth."—"Credit keeps the crown of the causeway." Such are specimens of the proverbial philosophy, embodying the hoarded experience of many generations, as to the best means of thriving in the world. They were current in people's mouths long before books were invented; and like other popular proverbs, they were the first codes of popular morals. Moreover they have stood the test of time, and the experience of every day still bears witness to their accuracy, force, and soundness.

HERBERT SPENCER: *Social Statics* *

> Herbert Spencer (1820–1903) has been called "the most self-confident representative of a self-confident age." In *Social Statics* (1851), the first of a long series of impressive tomes expounding his "Synthetic Philosophy," he announced the laws of "evolution" or progress. Spencer's background was religious non-conformist, and he was successively civil engineer, magazine editor, and free-lance writer.

ALL evil results from the non-adaptation of constitution to conditions. This is true of everything that lives. . . .

Equally true is it that evil perpetually tends to disappear. In virtue of an essential principle of life, this non-adaptation of an organism to its conditions is ever being rectified; and modification of one or both, continues until the adaptation is complete. Whatever possesses vitality, from the elementary cell up to man himself, inclusive, obeys this law. We see it illustrated in the acclimatization of plants, in the altered habits of domesticated animals, in the varying characteristics of our own race. . . .

Keeping in mind then the two facts, that all evil results from the non-adaptation of constitution to conditions; and that where this non-adaptation exists it is continually being diminished by the changing of constitution to suit conditions, we shall be prepared for comprehending the present position of the human race. . . .

Concerning the present position of the human race, we must therefore say, that man needed one moral constitution to fit him for his original state; that he needs another to fit him for his present state; and that he has been, is, and will long continue to be, in process of adaptation. By the term *civilization* we signify the adaptation that has already taken place. The changes that constitute *progress* are the successive steps of the transition. And the belief in human perfectibility, merely amounts to the belief, that in virtue of this process, man will eventually become completely suited to his mode of life. . . .

Progress, therefore, is not an accident, but a necessity. Instead of civilization being artificial, it is a part of nature; all of a piece with the development of the embryo or the unfolding of a flower. The modifications mankind have undergone, and are still undergoing, result from a law underlying the whole organic creation; and provided the human race continues, and the constitution of things remains the same, those modifications must end in completeness. . . .

There is another form under which civilization can be generalized. We may consider it as a progress towards that constitution of man and society required for the complete manifestation of every one's individuality. To be that which he naturally is—to do just what he would spontaneously do—is essential to the full happiness of each, and therefore to the greatest happiness of all. Hence, in virtue of the law of adaptation, our advance must be towards a state in which this entire satisfaction of every desire, or perfect fulfilment of individual life, becomes possible. . . .

In man we see the highest manifestation of this tendency. By virtue of his complexity of structure, he is furthest removed from the inorganic world in which there is least individuality. Again, his intelligence and adaptability commonly enable him to maintain life to old age—to complete the cycle of his existence; that is, to fill out the limits of this individuality to the full. Again, he is self-conscious; that is, he recognizes his own individuality. And, as lately shown, even the change observable in human affairs is still towards a greater development of individuality —may still be described as "a tendency to individuation."

But note lastly, and note chiefly, as being the fact to which the foregoing sketch is introductory, that what we call the moral law—the law of equal freedom, is the law under which individuation becomes perfect; and that ability to recognise and act up to this law, is the final endowment of humanity—an endowment now in process of evolution. The increasing assertion of personal rights, is an increasing demand that the external conditions needful to a complete unfolding of the individuality shall be respected. Not only is there now a consciousness of individuality, and an intelligence whereby individuality may be preserved; but there is a perception that the sphere of action requisite for due development of the individuality may be claimed; and a correlative desire to claim it. And when the change at present going on is complete —when each possesses an active instinct of freedom, together with an active sympathy—then will all the still existing limitations to individuality, be they governmental restraints, or be they the aggressions of men on one another, cease. Then, none will be hindered from duly unfolding their natures; for whilst every one maintains his own claims, he will respect the like claims of others. Then, there will no longer be legislative restrictions and legislative burdens; for by the same process these will have become both needless and impossible. Then, for the first time in the history of the world, will there exist beings whose individualities can be expanded to the full in all directions. And thus, as before said, in the ultimate man perfect morality, perfect individuation, and perfect life will be simultaneously realized.

ROBERT OWEN: *The New Moral World* *

> The next two selections sample the kinds of criticism to which laissez-faire liberalism was subjected. The first is by the "utopian" socialist Robert Owen (1771–1858), well known as the founder of model communities in England and the United States. Owen, although he was a self-made "captain of industry," attacked the economic side of liberalism. He was an environmentalist who believed human nature could be made over with the proper education and institutional arrangements. The following brief selection from *The Book of the New Moral Order* (1826–44) is a typical piece of utopian rhetoric.

THE time approaches, when, in the course of nature, the evil spirit of the world, engendered by ignorance and selfishness, will cease to exist, and when another spirit will arise, emanating from facts and experience, which will give a new direction to all the thoughts, feelings, and actions

---

* Robert Owen: *The Book of the New Moral World* (New York: G. Vale; 1845), pp. iii, v-vii.

of men, and which will create a new character of wisdom and benevolence for the human race.

The present work has been written to hasten the period of this all-important change, by explaining the cause of human evil, the means of removing it, and by unfolding a new moral world, in which evil, except as it will be recorded in the past sufferings of mankind, will be unknown; a new moral world, in which truth alone will govern all the affairs of men, and in which knowledge, unchecked by superstition or prejudice, will make an everlasting progress; a world in which justice, for the first time, will be done to human nature, by every feeling, faculty, and power, inherent in each child, being cultivated to its full extent; and cultivated, too, by the concentrated intelligence and goodness of the age. By these measures all the external circumstances, under the control of man, will be rearranged, and so wisely combined, that they will give full efficiency and excellence to every thought, feeling, and action, of the human race. . . .

The religious, moral, political, and commercial arrangements of society, throughout the world, have been based, from the commencement of history, upon an error respecting the nature of man; an error so grievous in its consequences, that it has deranged all the proceedings of society, made man irrational in his thoughts, feelings, and actions, and, consequently, more inconsistent, and perhaps more miserable, than any other animal.

This work is written to explain, first—the cause of this universal error, which has produced the derangement, degradation, and misery, of the human race; and secondly—to open to the present generation a new moral world founded on principles opposed to this error; and in which, the causes producing it will cease. In this new world, the inhabitants will attain a state of existence, in which a spirit of charity and affection will pervade the whole human race; man will become spiritualized, and happy amid a race of superior beings.

The knowledge which he will thus acquire of himself and of nature, will induce and enable him, through his self-interest, or desire for happiness, to form such superior external arrangements as will place him within a terrestrial paradise. . . .

The evils, also, which are now produced by the desire ignorantly created to obtain individual superiority in wealth, privileges, and honors, will not exist; but advantages much superior to these will be secured to all, and feelings of a higher character than individual distinctions can create, will be universally experienced.

Scientific arrangements will be formed to make wealth everywhere, and at all times, superabound beyond the wants or wishes of the human race, and all desire for individual accumulation, or any inequality of condition, will consequently cease.

The necessity for a never-ceasing supply of wealth for the use and enjoyment of all, and the right of each to produce and enjoy his fair share of it, will be obvious and admitted. . . .

With means thus ample to procure wealth with ease and pleasure to all, none will be so unwise as to desire to have the trouble and care of individual property. To divide riches among individuals in unequal proportions, or to hoard it for individual purposes, will be perceived to be as useless and as injurious as it would be to divide water or air into unequal quantities for different individuals, or that they should hoard them for their future use. . . .

None will be trained in idleness and uselessness to waste extravagantly the productions of others, to which no just law can give them a shadow of right or title; and no unjust law will be admitted into the code of the new moral world. None will be trained and set apart to attack, plunder, and murder, their fellow-men; this conduct will be known to be irrational, and the very essence of wickedness; nor yet, will any be trained to bargain with, or even to attempt to take advantage of another, or to desire individual privileges or distinctions of any kind. The individual who is trained to buy cheap, sell dear, and seek for individual benefits above his fellows, is thereby degraded—is unfitted to acquire superior qualities—is deprived of the finest feelings of our nature, and rendered totally incompetent to experience the highest enjoyments of human existence. . . .

MATTHEW ARNOLD: *Culture and Anarchy* *

> The great English poet and critic, Matthew Arnold (1822–88), son of Thomas Arnold, headmaster of Rugby, needs no introduction. About the time of the publication of *Culture and Anarchy* (1869) Arnold had turned from literature to social criticism, regarding it as his mission to bring "sweetness and light" to the "Philistine" middle classes. In its wider context his book is a diatribe on nineteenth-century liberal and bourgeois civilization.

IF CULTURE, then, is a study of perfection, and of harmonious perfection, general perfection, and perfection which consists in becoming something rather than in having something, in an inward condition of the mind and spirit, not in an outward set of circumstances,—it is clear that culture, instead of being the frivolous and useless thing which Mr.

* Matthew Arnold: *Culture and Anarchy* (London: Smith, Elder; 1869), pp. 14–20, 54–6, 67.

Bright, and Mr. Frederic Harrison, and many other liberals are apt to call it, has a very important function to fulfil for mankind. And this function is particularly important in our modern world, of which the whole civilisation is, to a much greater degree than the civilisation of Greece and Rome, mechanical and external, and tends constantly to become more so. But above all in our own country has culture a weighty part to perform, because here that mechanical character, which civilisation tends to take everywhere, is shown in the most eminent degree. Indeed nearly all the characters of perfection, as culture teaches us to fix them, meet in this country with some powerful tendency which thwarts them and sets them at defiance. The idea of perfection as an *inward* condition of the mind and spirit is at variance with the mechanical and material civilisation in esteem with us, and nowhere, as I have said, so much in esteem as with us. The idea of perfection as a *general* expansion of the human family is at variance with our strong individualism, our hatred of all limits to the unrestrained swing of the individual's personality, our maxim of "every man for himself." The idea of perfection as an *harmonious* expansion of human nature is at variance with our want of flexibility, with our inaptitude for seeing more than one side of a thing, with our intense energetic absorption in the particular pursuit we happen to be following. So culture has a rough task to achieve in this country, and its preachers have, and are likely long to have, a hard time of it, and they will much oftener be regarded, for a great while to come, as elegant or spurious Jeremiahs, than as friends and benefactors. . . .

Faith in machinery is, I said, our besetting danger; often in machinery most absurdly disproportioned to the end which this machinery, if it is to do any good at all, is to serve; but always in machinery, as if it had a value in and for itself. What is freedom but machinery? what is population but machinery? what is coal but machinery? what are railroads but machinery? what is wealth but machinery? what are religious organisations but machinery? Now almost every voice in England is accustomed to speak of these things as if they were precious ends in themselves, and therefore had some of the characters of perfection indisputably joined to them. I have once before noticed Mr. Roebuck's stock argument for proving the greatness and happiness of England as she is, and for quite stopping the mouths of all gainsayers. Mr. Roebuck is never weary of reiterating this argument of his, so I do not know why I should be weary of noticing it. "May not every man in England say what he likes?"—Mr. Roebuck perpetually asks; and that, he thinks, is quite sufficient, and when every man may say what he likes, our aspirations ought to be satisfied. But the aspirations of culture, which is the study of perfection, are not satisfied, unless what men say, when they may say what they like, is worth saying,—has good in it, and more good than bad. In the same way *The Times*, replying to some foreign strictures on the dress, looks, and behaviour of the English abroad, urges that the English ideal is that every one should be free to do and to look just as he likes. But culture indefatigably tries, not to make what each raw person may like, the rule by which he fashions himself; but to draw ever nearer to a sense of what is indeed beautiful, graceful, and becoming, and to get the raw person to like that. And in the same way with respect to railroads and coal. Every one must have observed the strange language current during the late discussions as to the possible failure of our supplies of coal. Our coal, thousands of people were saying, is the real basis of our national greatness; if our coal runs short, there is an end of the greatness of England. But what *is* greatness?—culture makes us ask. Greatness is a spiritual condition worthy to excite love, interest, and admiration; and the outward proof of possessing greatness is that we excite love, interest, and admiration. If England were swallowed up by the sea to-morrow, which of the two, a hundred years hence, would most excite the love, interest, and admiration of mankind,—would most, therefore, show the evidences of having possessed greatness,—the England of the last twenty years, or the England of Elizabeth, of a time of splendid spiritual effort, but when our coal, and our industrial operations depending on coal, were very little developed? . . .

Wealth, again, that end to which our prodigious works for material advantages are directed,—the commonest of commonplaces tells us how men are always apt to regard wealth as a precious end in itself; and certainly they have never been so apt thus to regard it as they are in England at the present time. Never did people believe anything more firmly, than nine Englishmen out of ten at the present day believe that our greatness and welfare are proved by our being so very rich. Now, the use of culture is that it helps us, by means of its spiritual standard of perfection, to regard wealth as but machinery, and not only to say as a matter of words that we regard wealth as but machinery, but really to perceive and feel that it is so. If it were not for this purging effect wrought upon our minds by culture, the whole world, the future as well as the present, would inevitably belong to the Philistines. The people who believe most that our greatness and welfare are proved by our being very rich, and who most give their lives and thoughts to becoming rich, are just the very people whom we call the Philistines. Culture says: "Consider these people, then, their way of life, their habits, their manners, the very tones of their voice; look at them attentively; observe the literature they read, the things which give them pleasure, the words which come forth out of their mouths, the thoughts which make the furniture of their minds; would any amount of wealth be worth having with the condition that one was to become just like these people by having it?" And thus culture begets a dissatisfaction which is of the highest possible value in stemming the common tide of men's thoughts in a wealthy and industrial community, and which saves the future, as one may hope, from being vulgarised, even if it cannot save the present.

* * *

In our common notions and talk about freedom, we eminently show our idolatry of machinery. Our prevalent notion is,—and I quoted a number of instances to prove it,—that it is a most happy and important thing for a man merely to be able to do as he likes. On what he is to do when he is thus free to do as he likes, we do not lay so much stress. Our familiar praise of the British Constitution under which we live, is that it is a system of checks,—a system which stops and paralyses any power in interfering with the free action of individuals. To this effect Mr. Bright, who loves to walk in the old ways of the Constitution, said forcibly in one of his great speeches, what many other people are every day saying less forcibly, that the central idea of English life and politics is *the assertion of personal liberty*. Evidently this is so; but evidently, also, as feudalism, which with its ideas and habits of subordination was for many centuries silently behind the British Constitution, dies out, and we are left with nothing but our system of checks, and our notion of its being the great right and happiness of an Englishman to do as far as possible what he likes, we are in danger of drifting towards anarchy. We have not the notion, so familiar on the Continent and to antiquity, of *the State* —the nation, in its collective and corporate character, entrusted with stringent powers for the general advantage, and controlling individual wills in the name of an interest wider than that of individuals.

* * *

Now, if culture, which simply means trying to perfect oneself, and one's mind as part of oneself, brings us light, and if light shows us that there is nothing so very blessed in merely doing as one likes, that the worship of the mere freedom to do as one likes is worship of machinery, that the really blessed thing is to like what right reason ordains, and to follow her authority, then we have got a practical benefit out of culture. We have got a much wanted principle, a principle of authority, to counteract the tendency to anarchy which seems to be threatening us.

B. POSITIVISM

AUGUSTE COMTE: *The Positive Philosophy* *

Basil Willey says of the French sociologist Auguste Comte (1798–1857) that he was "in a sense, the century in epitome." "Comte

* *The Positive Philosophy of Auguste Comte*, trans. by Harriet Martineau (London: J. Chapman; 1853), vol. I, pp. 1–3, 7; *A General View of Positivism*, trans. by J. H. Bridges (London: Trübner and Co.; 1865), pp. 348–50.

may be regarded as a nineteenth century Schoolman, and his system as a *Summa* based, not on dogmatic theology, but on dogmatic science." Comte's system was the so-called "Positive Philosophy" which he began to expound in articles and lectures in the 1820's. His famous "law" of the three stages in intellectual development was derived, at least in part, from Condorcet, his "spiritual father," and the Utopian socialist Saint-Simon. The following selections are from *The Positive Philosophy* (1830–42) and *A General View of Positivism* (1848).

In order to understand the true value and character of the Positive Philosophy, we must take a brief general view of the progressive course of the human mind, regarded as a whole; for no conception can be understood otherwise than through its history.

From the study of the development of human intelligence, in all directions, and through all times, the discovery arises of a great fundamental law, to which, it is necessarily subject, and which has a solid foundation of proof, both in the facts of our organization and in our historical experience. The law is this:—that each of our leading conceptions,—each branch of our knowledge,—passes successively through three different theoretical conditions: the Theological, or fictitious; the Metaphysical, or abstract; and the Scientific, or positive. In other words, the human mind, by its nature, employs in its progress three methods of philosophizing, the character of which is essentially different, and even radically opposed: viz., the theological method, the metaphysical, and the positive. Hence arise three philosophies, or general systems of conceptions on the aggregate of phenomena, each of which excludes the others. The first is the necessary point of departure of the human understanding; and the third is its fixed and definitive state. The second is merely a state of transition.

In the theological state, the human mind, seeking the essential nature of beings, the first and final causes (the origin and purpose) of all effects,—in short, Absolute knowledge,—supposes all phenomena to be produced by the immediate action of supernatural beings.

In the metaphysical state, which is only a modification of the first, the mind supposes, instead of supernatural beings, abstract forces, veritable entities (that is, personified abstractions) inherent in all beings, and capable of producing all phenomena. What is called the explanation of phenomena is, in this stage, a mere reference of each to its proper entity.

In the final, the positive state, the mind has given over the vain search after Absolute notions, the origin and destination of the universe, and the causes of phenomena, and applies itself to the study of their laws,—that is, their invariable relations of succession and resemblance. Reasoning and observation, duly combined, are the means of this knowledge. What is now understood when we speak of an explanation of facts is simply the establishment of a connection between single phenomena and some general facts, the number of which continually diminishes with the progress of science.

The Theological system arrived at the highest perfection of which it is capable when it substituted the providential action of a single Being for the varied operations of the numerous divinities which had been before imagined. In the same way, in the last stage of the Metaphysical system, men substitute one great entity (Nature) as the cause of all phenomena, instead of the multitude of entities at first supposed. In the same way, again, the ultimate perfection of the Positive system would be (if such perfection could be hoped for) to represent all phenomena as particular aspects of a single general fact;—such as Gravitation, for instance.

* * *

In mentioning just now the four principal categories of phenomena, —astronomical, physical, chemical, and physiological,—there was an omission which will have been noticed. Nothing was said of Social phenomena. Though involved with the physiological, Social phenomena demand a distinct classification, both on account of their importance and of their difficulty. They are the most individual, the most complicated, the most dependent on all others; and therefore they must be the latest, —even if they had no special obstacle to encounter. This branch of science has not hitherto entered into the domain of Positive philosophy. Theological and metaphysical methods, exploded in other departments, are as yet exclusively applied, both in the way of inquiry and discussion, in all treatment of Social subjects, though the best minds are heartily weary of eternal disputes about divine right and the sovereignty of the people. This is the great, while it is evidently the only gap which has to be filled, to constitute, solid and entire, the Positive Philosophy. Now that the human mind has grasped celestial and terrestrial physics,—mechanical and chemical; organic physics, both vegetable and animal,— there remains one science, to fill up the series of sciences of observation, —Social physics. This is what men have now most need of: and this it is the principal aim of the present work to establish.

* * *

All essential phases in the evolution of society answer to corresponding phases in the growth of the individual, whether it has proceeded spontaneously or under systematic guidance, supposing always that his development be complete. But it is not enough to prove the close connection which exists between all modes and degrees of human regeneration. We have yet to find a central point round which all will naturally meet. In this point consists the unity of Positivism as a system of life. Unless it can be thus condensed round one single principle, it will never wholly supersede the synthesis of Theology, notwithstanding its superiority in the reality and stability of its component parts, and in their homogeneity and coherence as a whole. There should be a central point in the system, towards which Feeling, Reason, and Activity alike converge. The proof that Positivism possesses such a central point will remove the last obstacle to its complete acceptance, as the guide of private or of public life.

Such a centre we find in the great conception of Humanity, towards which every aspect of Positivism naturally converges. By it the conception of God will be entirely superseded, and a synthesis be formed, more complete and permanent than that provisionally established by the old religions. Through it the new doctrine becomes at once accessible to men's hearts in its full extent and application. From their hearts it will penetrate their minds, and thus the immediate necessity of beginning with a long and difficult course of study is avoided, though this must of course be always indispensable to its systematic teachers.

This central point of Positivism is even more moral than intellectual in character; it represents the principle of Love upon which the whole system rests. It is the peculiar characteristic of the Great Being who is here set forth, to be compounded of separable elements. Its existence depends therefore entirely upon mutual Love knitting together its various parts. The calculations of self-interest can never be substituted as a combining influence for the sympathetic instincts.

Yet the belief in Humanity while stimulating Sympathy, at the same time enlarges the scope and vigour of the Intellect. For it requires high powers of generalization to conceive clearly of this vast organism, as the result of spontaneous co-operation, abstraction made of all partial antagonisms. Reason, then, has its part in this central dogma as well as Love. It enlarges and completes our conception of the Supreme Being, by revealing to us the external and internal conditions of its existence.

Lastly, our active powers are stimulated by it no less than our feelings and our reason. For since Humanity is so far more complex than any other organism, it will react more strongly and more continuously on its environment, submitting to its influence and so modifying it. Hence results Progress, which is simply the development of Order under the influence of Love.

Thus, in the conception of Humanity, the three essential aspects of Positivism, its subjective principle, its objective dogma, and its practical object, are united. Towards Humanity, who is for us the only true Great Being, we, the conscious elements of whom she is composed, shall henceforth direct every aspect of our life, individual or collective. Our thoughts will be devoted to the knowledge of Humanity, our affections to her love, our actions to her service.

G. H. LEWES: *The History of Philosophy from Thales to Comte* *

George Henry Lewes (1817–78) is best known for his liason with George Eliot whose genius for fiction he discovered and encouraged. He, however, enjoyed a considerable reputation in his own right for his work in physiology and psychology, his popular works on science and philosophy, and his *Life of Goethe*. His *History of Philosophy* (1867) was a revised edition of an earlier work entitled *Biographical History of Philosophy* which had a wide sale and which criticized all the metaphysical systems from the standpoint of Comte's Positivism.

PHILOSOPHY, as we have seen in the various phases of its history, has always had one aim, that of furnishing an Explanation of the world, of man and of society; but it has sought that aim by various routes. To solve the problems of existence, and to supply a rule of life, have constituted its purpose more or less avowed. Steady in this purpose, it has been vacillating in its means. . . .

With the creation of the Positive Philosophy this vacillation ceases. A new era has dawned. For the first time in history an Explanation of the world, society, and man, is presented which is thoroughly in accordance with accurate knowledge: having the reach of an all-embracing System, it condenses human knowledge into a Doctrine, and co-ordinates all the methods by which that knowledge has been reached, and will in future be extended. Its aim is the renovation of Society. Its basis is Science—the positive knowledge we have attained, and may attain, of all phenomena whatever. Its method is the Objective Method which has justified its supremacy by its results. Its superstructure is the hierarchy of the sciences—i.e. that distribution and co-ordination of general truths which transforms the scattered and independent sciences into an organic whole wherein each part depends on all that precede, and determines all that succeed.

The cardinal distinctions of this system may be said to arise naturally from the one aim of making all speculations homogeneous. Hitherto Theology while claiming certain topics as exclusively its own (even within the domain of knowledge) left vast fields of thought untraversed. It reserved to itself Ethics and History with occasional incursions into Psychology; but it left all cosmical problems to be settled by Science, and many psychological and biological problems to be settled by Metaphysics. On the other hand Science claiming absolute dominion over all cosmical and biological problems, left Morals and Politics to metaphysi-

* George Henry Lewes: *The History of Philosophy from Thales to Comte* (London: Longmans; 1867), vol. II, pp. 590–1, 593–5, 640–4.

cians and theologians, with only an occasional and incidental effort to bring these also under its sway. Thus while it is clear that society needs one Faith, one Doctrine, which shall satisfy the whole intellectual needs, on the other hand it is clear that such a Doctrine is impossible so long as three antagonistic lines of thought and three antagonistic modes of investigation are adopted. Such is, and has long been, the condition of Europe. A glance suffices to see that there is no one Doctrine *general* enough to embrace *all* knowledge, and sufficiently warranted by experience to carry irresistible conviction.

*   *   *

In the present state of things the speculative domain is composed of two very different portions,—general ideas and positive sciences. The general ideas are powerless because they are not positive: the positive sciences are powerless because they are not general. The new Philosophy is destined to put an end to this anarchy, by presenting a Doctrine which is *positive*, because elaborated from the sciences, and yet possessing all the desired *generality* of metaphysical doctrines, without possessing their vagueness, instability, and inapplicability.

How is this to be effected? Obviously by taking Science as the basis. The teaching of history is clear. Everywhere, Science with its all-conquering Methods is seen steadily advancing, drawing more and more subjects under its rule, yielding answers to more and more problems, while Theology and Metaphysics remain impotent to furnish satisfactory answers, and are constantly found in flagrant contradiction with the certainties of experience. There are but three modes of explaining phenomena, and of these the scientific daily gains strength, the other two daily lose their hold upon men. If the present anarchy is due to the simultaneous employment of three radically incompatible modes of thought, obviously the cessation of that anarchy must follow on the general adoption of only one of these modes of thought. The question is, which are we to select? When Theology was supreme there was unity in doctrine and unity in life. All men accepted the theological explanation of the world, man and society. But in proportion as knowledge advanced this explanation was discovered to be incessantly in contradiction with experience. If, therefore, we are to select the theological mode of thought as our guide, and the theological explanation of the Cosmos and Society as our doctrine, we must ignore all experience, sweep away all science, and appeal to the Pope or to the Archbishop of Canterbury for answers to the questions in Astronomy, Physics, Chemistry, Biology, and Sociology, which our pressing needs or speculative curiosity may force upon us. Is Europe prepared for this? Is any one nation prepared for it? Is any cultivated mind prepared for it?

The incompetence of Metaphysics has been clearly exhibited in this

History. Nothing, therefore, but Science remains. Nevertheless, Science itself only furnishes the basis. It must be transformed into a Philosophy before it can satisfy the higher needs. Even the encyclopaedic knowledge of a Humboldt was powerless, because it was scientific knowledge, not Philosophy; and because, moreover, even as scientific knowledge it had the fatal defect of incompleteness—it embraced cosmical, but excluded sociological speculations. Supposing Humboldt to have mastered, what he was far from conceiving, the philosophy of the cosmical sciences, he would still have left the great problem untouched, he would have failed to propound a homogeneous doctrine, since he would have left the vast and important field of moral speculation to theologians or metaphysicians. The completion of the scientific encyclopaedia was therefore a necessary preliminary; and this was effected by the creation of Sociology, as a science ranking with the cosmical sciences. This task was reserved for the genius of Auguste Comte. Having done this, he held in his hand the complete materials for an universal Philosophy. All human knowledge was now capable of being treated as a homogeneous and organic whole, one spirit, one method, and one aim presiding over each department.

* * *

Hitherto the History of Philosophy has been that of a long period of preparation. A new era dawns with the transformation of Science into Philosophy. Henceforward History will record development, not revolution—convergence of effort, not conflict. Each science has had its period of preparation, during which knowledge was accumulated, but no presiding conceptions gave unity to researches, no fixed methods enabled all men to assist in building one temple. Then came the change: each science was 'constituted,' separated from Common Knowledge, and the efforts of all labourers were convergent, the development was continuous. The constitution of the Positive Philosophy closes the period of preparation, and opens the period of evolution. It is far, very far from complete as a Doctrine. It will have to undergo many enlargements and modifications, advancing with the progress of discovery, and adapting itself flexibly to all the changes of scientific knowledge. But while it will thus need and will absorb the labours of future generations, it will continue in the same path, undisturbed by conflicts of principles.

This prophecy is not made in forgetfulness of the fact that at present the doctrine has no very extensive acceptance, and that even positive thinkers are not always willing to accept it. . . .

In France, at first sight, the signs seem unfavourable, since what little speculative activity exists there (out of Science) is markedly opposed to the positive spirit. The reaction against the 18th century still continues, and 'Materialism' is still the bugbear erected to warn men away from positive tendencies. In Germany, on the other hand, the old spiritualism is daily falling into discredit, and what are called materialistic opinions are rising into popularity. Nay, even in England there is no mistaking the strong current towards positive ideas, in spite of our theological impatience of whatever can be stigmatised as Materialism.

Materialism is an ugly word, which *connotes* certain opinions of very questionable validity held by some writers, and opinions both silly and immoral which are wantonly *attributed* to these writers by rash and reckless polemists. Be their opinions, however, what they may, the materialists have at least this important advantage, that they strive to get rid of all metaphysical entities, and seek an explanation of phenomena in the laws of phenomena. . . .

The reaction against the Philosophy of the Eighteenth Century was less a reaction against a doctrine proved to be incompetent than against a doctrine believed to be the source of frightful immorality. The reaction was vigorous, because it was animated by the horror which agitated Europe at the excesses of the French Revolution. Associated in men's minds with the saturnalia of the Terror, the philosophical opinions of Condillac, Diderot, and Cabanis were held responsible for the crimes of the Convention; and what might be true in those opinions was flung aside with what was false, without discrimination, without analysis, in fierce impetuous disgust. Every opinion which had what was called 'a taint of materialism,' or seemed to point in that direction, was denounced as an opinion necessarily leading to the destruction of all Religion, Morality, and Government. . . .

This history of the reaction in France is very instructive but it would require more space than can here be given adequately to narrate the story. Four streams of influence converged into one, all starting from the same source, namely, horror at the Revolutionary excesses. The Catholics, with the great Joseph de Maistre and M. de Bonald at their head, appealed to the religious sentiments; the Royalists, with Chateaubriand and Madame de Staël, appealed to the monarchical and literary sentiments; the metaphysicians, with Laromiguière, and Maine de Biran, and the moralists with Royer-Collard, one and all attacked the weak points of Sensationalism, and prepared the way for the enthusiastic reception of the Scotch and German philosophies. A glance at almost any of these writers will suffice to convince the student that their main purpose is to defend morality and order, which they believe to be necessarily imperilled by the philosophy they attack. The appeals to the prejudices and sentiments are incessant. Eloquence is made to supply the deficiencies of argument; emotion takes the place of demonstration. The hearer is charmed, roused, dazzled. He learns to associate all the nobler sentiments with spiritualistic doctrines, and all grovelling ideas with materialistic doctrines; till the one school becomes inseparably linked in his mind with emotions of reverence for whatever is lofty, profound, and noble, and the other with emotions of contempt for whatever is shallow and unworthy. The leaders of the reaction were men of splendid talents, and their work was eminently successful. But now that the heats of controversy have cooled, and all these debates have become historical, we who look at them from a distance can find in them no philosophical progress, no new elements added which could assist the evolution of Philosophy, and form a broader basis for future monuments. In political and literary history these attempts would claim a conspicuous position; in the History of Philosophy they deserve mention only as having made mankind aware of the limited nature of the eighteenth-century philosophy, and its extraordinary *lacunae*. Their office was critical, and has been fulfilled.

CLAUDE BERNARD: *An Introduction to the Study of Experimental Medicine* *

Claude Bernard's *Introduction* (1865) has been called the *Discourse on Method* of the nineteenth century. It might better be called "the credo of positivist science." Strictly speaking, the great physiologist (1813–78) was not a positivist in the sense of being a follower of Comte. Nevertheless, he shared with Comte a distrust of metaphysical systems and reiterated the latter's distinction between "laws" and "causes." His book was a plea for the extension of the experimental method to the life sciences. Note his emphasis on "determinism," which later evoked a philosophic "reaction" (see page 598 this text).

Belief in Science

The first condition to be fulfilled by men of science, applying themselves to the investigation of natural phenomena, is to maintain absolute freedom of mind, based on philosophic doubt. Yet we must not be in the least sceptical; we must believe in science, i.e., in determinism; we must believe in a complete and necessary relation between things, among the phenomena proper to living beings as well as in all others; but at the same time we must be thoroughly convinced that we know this relation only in a more or less approximate way, and that the theories we hold are far from embodying changeless truths. . . .

The absolute principle of experimental science is conscious and necessary determinism in the conditions of phenomena. So that, given no matter what natural phenomenon, experimenters can never acknowledge variation in the embodiment of this phenomenon, unless new conditions have at the same time occurred in its coming to pass; what is more, they have an *a priori* certainty, that these variations are determined by rigorous, mathematical relations. Experiment only shows us the form of phenomena; but the relation of a phenomenon to a definite cause is necessary and independent of experiment; it is necessarily mathematical and absolute. Thus we see that the principle of the criterion in experimental sciences is fundamentally identical with that of the mathematical sciences, since in each case the principle is expressed by a necessary and absolute relation between things. Only in the experimental sciences these relations are surrounded by numerous, complex and infinitely varied phenomena which hide them from our sight. With the help of experiment, we analyze, we dissociate these phenomena, in order to reduce them to more and more simple relations and conditions. In this way we try to lay hold on scientific truth, i.e., find the law that shall give us the key to all variations of the phenomena. Thus experimental analysis is our only means of going in search of truth in the natural sciences, and the absolute determinism of phenomena, of which we are conscious *a priori*, is the only criterion or principle which directs and supports us. . . .

. . . In short, science rejects the indeterminate; and in medicine, when we begin to base our opinions on medical tact, on inspiration, or on more or less vague intuition about things, we are outside of science and offer an example of that fanciful medicine which may involve the greatest dangers, by surrendering the health and life of the sick to the whims of an inspired ignoramus. True science teaches us to doubt and, in ignorance, to refrain. . . .

Our feelings lead us at first to believe that absolute truth must lie within our realm; but study takes from us, little by little, these chimerical conceits. Science has just the privilege of teaching us what we do not know, by replacing feeling with reason and experience and clearly showing us the present boundaries of our knowledge. But by a marvellous compensation, science, in humbling our pride, proportionately increases our power. Men of science who carry experimental analysis to the point of relatively determining a phenomenon doubtless see clearly their own ignorance of the phenomenon in its primary cause; but they have become its master; the instrument at work is unknown, but they can use it. This is true of all experimental sciences in which we can reach only relative or partial truths and know phenomena only in their necessary conditions. But this knowledge is enough to broaden our power over nature. Though we do not know the essence of phenomena, we can produce or prevent their appearance, because we can regulate their physico-chemical conditions. We do not know the essence of fire, of electricity, of light, and still we regulate their phenomena to our own advantage. We know absolutely nothing of the essence even of life; but we shall nevertheless regulate vital phenomena as soon as we know enough of their necessary conditions. Only in living bodies these conditions are much more complex and more difficult to grasp than in inorganic bodies; that is the whole difference.

To sum up, if our feeling constantly puts the question *why*, our reason shows us that only the question *how* is within our range; for the moment, then, only the question *how* concerns men of science and experimenters. . . .

Science and Philosophy

We have just said that knowledge of physiology is indispensable to physicians; we must therefore cultivate the physiological sciences, if we wish to further the development of experimental medicine. This is all the more necessary, because it is the only way to provide a foundation for scientific medicine, and unfortunately we are still far from the time when we shall see the scientific spirit generally prevailing among physicians. Now the absence of the scientific habit of mind is a serious hindrance, because it favors belief in occult forces, rejects determinism in vital phenomena, and leads to the notion that the phenomena of living beings are governed by mysterious, vital forces which are continually invoked. When an obscure or inexplicable phenomenon presents itself, instead of saying "I do not know," as every scientific man should do, physicians are in the habit of saying "This is life"; apparently without the least idea that they are explaining darkness by still greater darkness. We must therefore get used to the idea that science implies merely determining the conditions of phenomena; and we must always seek to exclude life entirely from our explanations of physiological phenomena as a whole. Life is nothing but a word which means ignorance, and when we characterize a phenomenon as vital, it amounts to saying that we do not know its immediate cause or its conditions. Science should always explain obscurity and complexity by clearer and simpler ideas. Now since nothing is more obscure, life can never explain anything. I emphasize this point, because I have seen even chemists at times appeal to life to explain certain physico-chemical phenomena peculiar to living beings. Thus the ferment in yeast is an organic, living material which has the property of converting sugar into alcohol, carbonic acid and several other products. I have sometimes heard it said that the property of decomposing sugar was due to the life inherent in a globule of yeast. This vitalistic explanation means nothing and explains nothing about the action of yeast. We do not know the nature of this property, but it must necessarily belong to the physico-chemical order and be as precisely defined as, for instance, the property of platinum sponge which produces a more or less analogous action that cannot be attributed to vital force. In a word, all the properties of living matter are, at bottom, either known and defined properties, in which case we call them physico-chemical properties, or else unknown and undefined properties, in which case we name them vital properties. Certainly a special force in living beings, not met with elsewhere, presides over their organization; but the existence of this force cannot in any way change our idea of the properties of organic matter,—matter which, when once created, is endowed with fixed and determinate, physico-chemical properties. Vital force is, therefore, an organizing and nutritive force; but it does not in any way determine the manifestation of the properties of living matter. In a word, physiologists and physicians must seek to reduce vital properties to physico-chemical properties, and not physico-chemical properties to vital properties. . . .

We said that experimental medicine is not a new system of medicine, but on the contrary is the negation of all systems. In fact, the advent of experimental medicine will cause all individual views to disappear from the science, to be replaced by impersonal and general theories which, as in other sciences, will be only a regular and logical coördination of facts furnished by experience.

Scientific medicine is certainly not yet well established to-day; but thanks to the experimental method which is permeating it more and more, it is tending to become an exact science. Medicine is in transition; the day of personal doctrines and systems is past, and little by little they will be replaced by theories embodying the present state of the science and showing from that point of view the results of all our efforts. But that must not make us believe that theories are ever absolute truths; they may always be improved, and so are always mobile. That is why I have been careful to say that we must not, as men often do, confuse advancing and perfectible progressive theories, which may be improved, with scientific methods and principles that are fixed and unshakable. We must remember that the one unchangeable scientific principle, in medicine as well as in the other experimental sciences, is the absolute determinism of phenomena. We gave the name of determinism to the immediate or determining cause of phenomena. We never act on the essence of natural phenomena, but only on their determining causes; and because we act thus, determinism differs from fatalism, on which we cannot act. Fatalism assumes that the manifestation of any phenomenon is necessary and independent of its conditions, while determinism is the condition necessary to a phenomenon, whose manifestation is free. When search for the causes determining phenomena is once posited as the fundamental principle of the experimental method, materialism, spiritualism, inert matter and living matter cease to exist; only phenomena are left, whose conditions we must determine, i.e., the conditions which play the part of immediate cause. Scientific determinism ceases here; there are only words beyond, which are of course necessary, but which may delude us if we are not constantly on guard against the traps which our minds perpetually set for themselves.

As experimental medicine, like all the experimental sciences, should not go beyond phenomena, it does not need to be tied to any system; it is neither vitalistic, nor animistic, nor organistic, nor solidistic, nor humoral; it is simply the science which tries to reach the immediate causes of vital phenomena in the healthy and in the morbid state. It has no reason, in fact, to encumber itself with systems, none of which can ever embody the truth.

In this connection it may be useful to recall, in a few words, the essential characteristics of the scientific method and to show how the ideas derived from it differ from systematic and doctrinal ideas. In the experimental method we never make experiments except to see or to prove, i.e., to control or verify. As a scientific method, the experimental method rests wholly on the experimental verification of a scientific hypothesis. We obtain this verification with the help, sometimes of a fresh observation (observational science), sometimes of an experiment (experimental science). In the experimental method, the hypothesis is a scientific idea that we submit to experiment. Scientific invention consists in the creation of fortunate and fertile hypotheses; these are suggested by the feeling or even the genius of the men of science who create them.

When an hypothesis is submitted to the experimental method, it becomes a theory, while if it is submitted to logic alone, it becomes a system. A system, then, is an hypothesis with which we have connected the facts logically with the help of reason, but without experimental, critical verification. A theory is a verified hypothesis, after it has been submitted to the control of reason and experimental criticism. The soundest theory is one that has been verified by the greatest number of facts. But to remain valid, a theory must be continually altered to keep pace with the progress of science and must be constantly resubmitted to verification and criticism as new facts appear.

If we consider a theory perfect and stop verifying it by daily scientific experience, it becomes a doctrine. A doctrine, then, is a theory which we regard as immutable, which we take as a starting point for later deduction, and which we believe we are no longer obliged to submit to experimental verification. . . .

As an experimenter, then, I avoid philosophic systems; but I cannot for that reason reject the philosophic spirit which, without being anywhere, is everywhere and, without belonging to any system, ought to reign, not only over all science but over all human knowledge. So even while avoiding philosophic systems, I like philosophers and greatly enjoy their converse. Indeed, from the scientific point of view, philosophy embodies the eternal aspiration of human reason toward knowledge of the unknown. Therefore philosophers always live in controversial questions and lofty regions, the upper boundaries of science. Hence they impart to scientific thought an enlivening and ennobling motion; they develop and fortify the mind by general intellectual exercise, while ceaselessly bearing it toward the inexhaustible solution of great problems; thus they nourish a kind of thirst for the unknown; the sacred fire of research must therefore never be extinguished in men of science. . . .

Philosophy and science, then, must never be systematic: without trying to dominate one another, they must unite. Their separation could only be harmful to the progress of human knowledge. Striving ever upward, philosophy makes science rise toward the cause or the source of things. It shows science that there are questions beyond it, torturing humanity, which it has not yet solved. Solid union between science and philosophy is useful to both: it lifts the one and confines the other. But if the bonds uniting philosophy to science should break, philosophy, lacking the support or the counterpoise of science would rise out of sight and be lost in the clouds, while science, without guidance and without high aspiration, would sail at random. . . .

EMILE ZOLA: *The Experimental Novel* *

> Emile Zola's essay *Le Roman Expérimental* (1880) might be called the *reductio ad absurdum* of positivist science because it attempted to carry the scientific spirit into literature itself and also to make it "experimental." Zola (1840–1902) was a leader of the Naturalist school of literature, the author of the celebrated Rougon-Macquart series of novels depicting "the natural and social history" of a family living under the Second Empire.

IN MY literary essays I have often spoken of the application of the experimental method to the novel and to the drama. The return to nature, the naturalistic evolution which marks the century, drives little by little all the manifestation of human intelligence into the same scientific path. Only the idea of a literature governed by science is doubtless a surprise, until explained with precision and understood. It seems to me necessary, then, to say briefly and to the point what I understand by the experimental novel.

I really only need to adapt, for the experimental method has been established with strength and marvelous clearness by Claude Bernard in his "Introduction à l'Étude de la Médecine Expérimentale." . . .

---

* Emile Zola: *The Experimental Novel and Other Essays*, Belle M. Sherman (trans.) (London: Cassell Publishing Co.; 1893), pp. 1, 8–9, 16–20, 23.

To return to the novel, we can easily see that the novelist is equally an observer and an experimentalist. The observer in him gives the facts as he has observed them, suggests the point of departure, displays the solid earth on which his characters' are to tread and the phenomena to develop. Then the experimentalist appears and introduces an experiment, that is to say, sets his characters going in a certain story so as to show that the succession of facts will be such as the requirements of the determinism of the phenomena under examination call for. Here it is nearly always an experiment "*pour voir*," as Claude Bernard calls it. The novelist starts out in search of a truth. I will take as an example the character of the *Baron Hulot*, in "Cousine Bette," by Balzac. The general fact observed by Balzac is the ravages that the amorous temperament of a man makes in his home, in his family, and in society. As soon as he has chosen his subject he starts from known facts; then he makes his experiment, and exposes *Hulot* to a series of trials, placing him amid certain surroundings in order to exhibit how the complicated machinery of his passions works. It is then evident that there is not only observation there, but that there is also experiment; as Balzac does not remain satisfied with photographing the facts collected by him, but interferes in a direct way to place his character in certain conditions, and of these he remains the master. The problem is to know what such a passion, acting in such a surrounding and under such circumstances, would produce from the point of view of an individual and of society; and an experimental novel, "Cousine Bette," for example, is simply the report of the experiment that the novelist conducts before the eyes of the public. In fact, the whole operation consists in taking facts in nature, then in studying the mechanism of these facts, acting upon them, by the modification of circumstances and surroundings, without deviating from the laws of nature. Finally, you possess knowledge of the man, scientific knowledge of him, in both his individual and social relations. . . .

Thus you see the progress which science has made. In the last century a more exact application of the experimental method creates physics and chemistry, which then are freed from the irrational and supernatural. Men discover that there are fixed laws, thanks to analysis, and make themselves masters of phenomena. Then a new point is gained. Living beings, in which the vitalists still admitted a mysterious influence, are in their turn brought under and reduced to the general mechanism of matter. Science proves that the existing conditions of all phenomena are the same in living beings as in inanimate; and from that time on physiology assumes little by little the certainty of chemistry and medicine. But are we going to stop there? Evidently not. When it has been proved that the body of man is a machine, whose machinery can be taken apart and put together again at the will of the experimenter, then we can pass to the passionate and intellectual acts of man. Then we shall enter into the domain which up to the present has belonged to physiology and literature; it will be the decisive conquest by science of the hypotheses of philosophers and writers. We have experimental chemistry and medicine; we shall have an experimental physiology, and later on an experimental novel. It is an inevitable evolution, the goal of which it is easy to see to-day. All things hang together; it is necessary to start from the determinism of inanimate bodies in order to arrive at the determinism of living beings; and since savants like Claude Bernard demonstrate now that fixed laws govern the human body, we can easily proclaim, without fear of being mistaken, the hour in which the laws of thought and passion will be formulated in their turn. A like determinism will govern the stones of the roadway and the brain of man. . . .

I certainly do not intend at this point to formulate laws. In the actual condition of the science of man the obscurity and confusion are still too great to risk the slightest synthesis. All that can be said is that there is an absolute determinism for all human phenomena. From that an investigation is a duty. . . .

Without daring, as I say, to formulate laws, I consider that the question of heredity has a great influence in the intellectual and passionate manifestations of man. I also attach considerable importance to the surroundings. . . . We have just seen the great importance given by Claude Bernard to the study of those inter-organic conditions which must be taken into account if we wish to find the determinism of phenomena in living beings. Well, then! in the study of a family, of a group of living beings, I think that the social condition is of equal importance. Some day the physiologist will explain to us the mechanism of the thoughts and the passions; we shall know how the individual machinery of each man works; how he thinks, how he loves, how he goes from reason to passion and folly; but these phenomena, resulting as they do from the mechanism of the organs, acting under the influence of an interior condition, are not produced in isolation or in the bare void. Man is not alone; he lives in society, in a social condition; and consequently, for us novelists, this social condition unceasingly modifies the phenomena. . . .

I have reached this point: the experimental novel is a consequence of the scientific evolution of the century; it continues and completes physiology, which itself leans for support on chemistry and medicine; it substitutes for the study of the abstract and the metaphysical man the study of the natural man, governed by physical and chemical laws, and modified by the influences of his surroundings; it is in one word the literature of our scientific age, as the classical and romantic literature corresponded to a scholastic and theological age. . . .

C. THE YOUNG HEGELIANS

DAVID FRIEDRICH STRAUSS: *The Life of Jesus* *

David Friedrich Strauss' *The Life of Jesus*, though the work of a young man, caused a great sensation when it first appeared in 1835–36. It has been called "a turning point in modern theology" for it raised the question—debated many times since—of who Jesus was: fact or fiction? In consequence of his radical conclusions Strauss (1808–74) was relieved of his teaching position at Tübingen and estopped by clerical opposition from accepting an appointment at the University of Zurich. He was much influenced by the Hegelian philosophy, which he had studied at Berlin, and in particular by Hegel's conception that philosophical and religious ideas were preceded by more primitive "mythical" presentations.

IT APPEARED to the author of the work, the first half of which is herewith submitted to the public, that it was time to substitute a new mode of considering the life of Jesus, in the place of the antiquated systems of supranaturalism and naturalism. This application of the term antiquated will in the present day be more readily admitted in relation to the latter system than to the former. For while the interest excited by the explanations of the miracles and the conjectural facts of the rationalists has long ago cooled, the commentaries now most read are those which aim to adapt the supranatural interpretation of the sacred history to modern taste. Nevertheless, in point of fact, the orthodox view of this history became superannuated earlier than the rationalistic, since it was only because the former had ceased to satisfy an advanced state of culture, that the latter was developed, while the recent attempts to recover, by the aid of a mystical philosophy, the supranatural point of view held by our forefathers, betray themselves, by the exaggerating spirit in which they are conceived, to be final, desperate efforts to render the past present, the inconceivable conceivable.

The new point of view, which must take the place of the above, is the mythical. This theory is not brought to bear on the evangelical history for the first time in the present work: it has long been applied to particular parts of that history, and is here only extended to its entire tenor. It is not by any means meant that the whole history of Jesus is to be represented as mythical, but only that every part of it is to be subjected to a critical examination, to ascertain whether it have not some admixture of the mythical. The exegesis of the ancient church set out from the double presupposition: first, that the gospels contained a

* David Friedrich Strauss: *The Life of Jesus*, trans. Marian Evans (New York: Calvin Blanchard; 1860), Vol. I, pp. 3–4, 69–71.

history, and secondly, that this history was a supernatural one. Rationalism rejected the latter of these presuppositions, but only to cling the more tenaciously to the former, maintaining that these books present unadulterated, though only natural, history. Science cannot rest satisfied with this half-measure: the other presupposition also must be relinquished, and the inquiry must first be made whether in fact, and to what extent, the ground on which we stand in the gospels is historical. This is the natural course of things, and thus far the appearance of a work like the present is not only justifiable, but even necessary.

It is certainly not therefore evident that the author is precisely the individual whose vocation it is to appear in this position. He has a very vivid consciousness that many others would have been able to execute such a work with incomparably superior erudition. Yet on the other hand he believes himself to be at least possessed of one qualification which especially fitted him to undertake this task. The majority of the most learned and acute theologians of the present day fail in the main requirement for such a work, a requirement without which no amount of learning will suffice to achieve anything in the domain of criticism, namely, the internal liberation of the feelings and intellect from certain religious and dogmatical presuppositions; and this the author early attained by means of philosophical studies. If theologians regard this absence of presupposition from his work, as unchristian: he regards the believing presuppositions of theirs as unscientific. Widely as in this respect the tone of the present work may be contrasted with the edifying devoutness and enthusiastic mysticism of recent books on similar subjects; still it will nowhere depart from the seriousness of science, or sink into frivolity; and it seems a just demand in return, that the judgments which are passed upon it should also confine themselves to the domain of science, and keep aloof from bigotry and fanaticism. . . .

*　　*　　*

The precise sense in which we use the expression *mythus*, applied to certain parts of the gospel history, is evident from all that has already been said; at the same time the different kinds and gradations of the mythi which we shall meet with in this history may here by way of anticipation be pointed out.

We distinguish by the name *evangelical mythus* a narrative relating directly or indirectly to Jesus, which may be considered not as the expression of a fact, but as the product of an idea of his earliest followers; such a narrative being mythical in proportion as it exhibits this character. The mythus in this sense of the term meets us, in the Gospel as elsewhere, sometimes in its pure form, constituting the substance of the narrative, and sometimes as an accidental adjunct to the actual history.

The pure mythus in the Gospel will be found to have two sources, which in most cases contributed simultaneously, though in different proportions, to form the mythus. The one source is, as already stated, the Messianic ideas and expectations existing according to their several forms in the Jewish mind before Jesus, and independently of him; the other is that particular impression which was left by the personal character, actions, and fate of Jesus, and which served to modify the Messianic idea in the minds of his people. The account of the Transfiguration, for example, is derived almost exclusively from the former source; the only amplification taken from the latter source being—that they who appeared with Jesus on the Mount spake of his decease. On the other hand, the narrative of the rending of the veil of the temple at the death of Jesus seems to have had its origin in the hostile position which Jesus, and his church after him, sustained in relation to the Jewish temple worship. Here already we have something historical, though consisting merely of certain general features of character, position etc.; we are thus at once brought upon the ground of the historical mythus.

The historical mythus has for its groundwork a definite individual fact which has been seized upon by religious enthusiasm, and twined around with mythical conceptions culled from the idea of the Christ. This fact is perhaps a saying of Jesus such as that concerning "fishers of men" or the barren fig-tree, which now appear in the Gospels transmuted into marvellous histories; or, it is perhaps a real transaction or event taken from his life; for instance, the mythical traits in the account of the baptism were built upon such a reality. Certain of the miraculous histories may likewise have had some foundation in natural occurrences, which the narrative has either exhibited in a supernatural light, or enriched with miraculous incidents.

All the species of imagery here enumerated may justly be designated as mythi, even according to the modern and precise definition of George, inasmuch as the unhistorical which they embody—whether formed gradually by tradition, or created by an individual author—is in each case the product of an *idea*. But for those parts of the history which are characterized by indefiniteness and want of connexion, by misconstruction and transformation, by strange combinations and confusion,—the natural results of a long course of oral transmission; or which, on the contrary, are distinguished by highly coloured and pictorial representations, which also seem to point to a traditionary origin;—for these parts the term *legendary* is certainly the more appropriate.

Lastly. It is requisite to distinguish equally from the mythus and the legend, that which, as it serves not to clothe an idea on the one hand, and admits not of being referred to tradition on the other, must be regarded as *the addition of the author*, as purely individual, and designed merely to give clearness, connexion, and climax, to the representation.

It is to the various forms of the unhistorical in the gospels that this enumeration exclusively refers; it does not involve the renunciation of the *historical* which they may likewise contain.

Having shown the possible existence of the mythical and the legendary in the gospels, both on extrinsic and intrinsic grounds, and defined their distinctive characteristics, it remains in conclusion to inquire how their actual presence may be recognized in individual cases?

The mythus presents two phases; in the first place it is not history; in the second it is fiction, the product of the particular mental tendency of a certain community. These two phases afford the one a negative, the other a positive criterion, by which the mythus is to be recognized.

Negative. That an account is not historical—that the matter related could not have taken place in the manner described is evident.

First. When the narration is irreconcileable with the known and universal laws which govern the course of events. Now according to these laws, agreeing with all just philosophical conceptions and all credible experience, the absolute cause never disturbs the chain of secondary causes by single arbitrary acts of interposition, but rather manifests itself in the production of the aggregate of finite causalities, and of their reciprocal action. When therefore we meet with an account of certain phenomena or events of which it is either expressly stated or implied that they were produced immediately by God himself (divine apparitions—voices from heaven and the like), or by human beings possessed of supernatural powers (miracles, prophecies), such an account is *in so far* to be considered as not historical. And inasmuch as, in general, the intermingling of the spiritual world with the human is found only in unauthentic records, and is irreconcileable with all just conceptions; so narratives of angels and of devils, of their appearing in human shape and interfering with human concerns, cannot possibly be received as historical.

LUDWIG FEUERBACH: *The Essence of Christianity* *

Ludwig Feuerbach's *The Essence of Christianity* (1841) created scarcely less of a sensation than Strauss' *The Life of Jesus.* Although influenced by Hegel—he went to hear Hegel lecture in Berlin and under Hegel's influence gave up theology for philosophy—Feuerbach (1804-72) nevertheless attacked the Hegelian philosophy as "the last refuge, the last rational support of theology." He explained God psychologically, as a projection of man's desires and needs, thus anticipating and influencing later critiques of religion by Marx and Freud.

* Ludwig Feuerbach: *The Essence of Christianity*, trans. Marian Evans (London: Trübner & Co.; 1881), pp. vii-ix, xi, xiii, 12-14, 20-1, 184.

THE CLAMOUR excited by the present work has not surprised me, and hence it has not in the least moved me from my position. On the contrary, I have once more, in all calmness, subjected my work to the severest scrutiny, both historical and philosophical. . . . It has no pretension to be anything more than a close translation, or, to speak literally, an empirical or historico-philosophical analysis, a solution of the enigma of the Christian religion. The general propositions which I premise in the Introduction are no *à priori*, excogitated propositions, no products of speculation; they have arisen out of the analysis of religion; they are only, as indeed are all the fundamental ideas of the work, generalisations from the known manifestations of human nature, and in particular of the religious consciousness,—facts converted into thoughts, *i.e.*, expressed in general terms, and thus made the property of the understanding. . . . I am nothing but a *natural philosopher in the domain of mind;* and the natural philosopher can do nothing without instruments, without material means. In this character I have written the present work, which consequently contains nothing else than the principle of a new philosophy verified practically, *i.e.*, *in concreto*, in application to a special object, but an object which has a universal significance: namely, to religion, in which this principle is exhibited, developed, and thoroughly carried out. This philosophy is essentially distinguished from the systems hitherto prevalent, in that it corresponds to the real, complete nature of man; but for that very reason it is antagonistic to minds perverted and crippled by a superhuman, *i.e.*, anti-human, anti-natural religion and speculation. . . .

*   *   *

. . . Thus in the first part I show that the true sense of Theology is Anthropology, that there is no distinction between the *predicates* of the divine and human nature, and, consequently, no distinction between the divine and human *subject*. . . .

Religion is the dream of the human mind. . . .

*   *   *

. . . And here may be applied, without any limitation, the proposition: The object of any subject is nothing else than the subject's own nature taken objectively. Such as are a man's thoughts and dispositions, such is his God; so much worth as a man has, so much and no more has his God. Consciousness of God is self-consciousness, knowledge of God is self-knowledge. By his God thou knowest the man, and by the man his God; the two are identical. Whatever is God to a man, that is his heart and soul; and conversely, God is the manifested inward nature, the expressed self of a man,—religion the solemn unveiling of a man's hidden treasures, the revelation of his intimate thoughts, the open confession of his love-secrets.

But when religion—consciousness of God—is designated as the self-consciousness of man, this is not to be understood as affirming that the religious man is directly aware of this identity; for, on the contrary, ignorance of it is fundamental to the peculiar nature of religion. To preclude this misconception, it is better to say, religion is man's earliest and also indirect form of self-knowledge. Hence, religion everywhere precedes philosophy, as in the history of the race, so also in that of the individual. Man first of all sees his nature as if *out of* himself, before he finds it in himself. His own nature is in the first instance contemplated by him as that of another being. Religion is the childlike condition of humanity; but the child sees his nature—man—out of himself; in childhood a man is an object to himself, under the form of another man. Hence the historical progress of religion consists in this: that what by an earlier religion was regarded as objective, is now recognised as subjective; that is, what was formerly contemplated and worshipped as God is now perceived to be something *human*. What was at first religion becomes at a later period idolatry; man is seen to have adored his own nature. Man has given objectivity to himself, but has not recognised the object as his own nature: a later religion takes this forward step; every advance in religion is therefore a deeper self-knowledge.

*   *   *

Religion, at least the Christian, is the relation of man to himself, or more correctly to his own nature (*i.e.*, his subjective nature); but a relation to it, viewed as a nature apart from his own. The divine being is nothing else than the human being, or, rather, the human nature purified, freed from the limits of the individual man, made objective—*i.e.*, contemplated and revered as another, a distinct being. All the attributes of the divine nature are, therefore, attributes of the human nature. . . .

The identity of the subject and predicate is clearly evidenced by the progressive development of religion, which is identical with the progressive development of human culture. So long as man is in a mere state of nature, so long is his god a mere nature-god—a personification of some natural force. Where man inhabits houses, he also encloses his gods in temples. The temple is only a manifestation of the value which man attaches to beautiful buildings. Temples in honour of religion are in truth temples in honour of architecture. With the emerging of man from a state of savagery and wildness to one of culture, with the distinction between what is fitting for man and what is not fitting, arises simultaneously the distinction between that which is fitting and that which is not fitting for God. God is the idea of majesty, of the highest dignity: the religious sentiment is the sentiment of supreme fitness. The later more cultured artists of Greece were the first to embody in the statues of the gods the ideas of dignity, of spiritual grandeur, of imperturbable repose and serenity. But why were these qualities in their view attributes, predicates of God? Because they were in themselves regarded by the Greeks as divinities. Why did those artists exclude all disgusting and low passions? Because they perceived them to be unbecoming, unworthy, unhuman, and consequently ungodlike. The Homeric gods eat and drink;—that implies eating and drinking is a divine pleasure. Physical strength is an attribute of the Homeric gods: Zeus is the strongest of the gods. Why? Because physical strength, in and by itself, was regarded as something glorious, divine. To the ancient Germans the highest virtues were those of the warrior; therefore their supreme god was the god of war, Odin,—war, "the original or oldest law." . . .

. . . God is pure absolute subjectivity released from all natural limits; he is what individuals ought to be and will be: faith in God is therefore the faith of man in the infinitude and truth of his own nature; the Divine Being is the subjective human being in his absolute freedom and unlimitedness.

Our most essential task is now fulfilled. We have reduced the supermundane, supernatural, and superhuman nature of God to the elements of human nature as its fundamental elements. Our process of analysis has brought us again to the position with which we set out. The beginning, middle and end of religion is MAN.

Karl Marx: *On Man and History* *

The following two statements are from the hand of the young Karl Marx (1818–83). The thoughts they contain, however, are basic to his mature system. The first, from the article, "Alienated Labor," in the Economic and Philosophical Manuscripts of 1844 (not published until 1932), contains the kernel of Marx's conception of human nature and what he thought capitalism had done to it. It explains why he thought communism was necessary. The second, from the unfinished "German Ideology" written jointly with Engels in 1845–46, is essentially a critique of the "German" or Hegelian philosophy of history. Both show how far Marx departed from, yet also how much he owed to, Hegel and the Young Hegelians of the first generation. For example,

* From Karl Marx *Early Writings*, translated and edited by T. B. Bottomore, pp. 120–126, 129–133. © T. B. Bottomore, 1963. Used by permission of McGraw-Hill Book Company and C. A. Watts & Co. Ltd. Karl Marx and Friedrich Engels, *The German Ideology*, R. Pascal (trans.) (New York: International Publishers; 1960), pp. 16, 30–31, 39–41. Used by permission of International Publishers.

he derived the concept of "alienation" from Hegel and Feuerbach, but he modified it to fit his own "humanistic," as opposed to "idealistic," views.

Alienated Man

WE HAVE begun from the presuppositions of political economy. We have accepted its terminology and its laws. We presupposed private property; the separation of labour, capital and land, as also of wages, profit and rent; the division of labour; competition; the concept of exchange value, etc. From political economy itself, in its own words, we have shown that the worker sinks to the level of a commodity, and to a most miserable commodity; that the misery of the worker increases with the power and volume of his production; that the necessary result of competition is the accumulation of capital in a few hands, and thus a restoration of monopoly in a more terrible form; and finally that the distinction between agricultural labourer and industrial worker, must disappear, and the whole of society divide into the two classes of property *owners* and *propertyless* workers. . . .

Let us not begin our explanation, as does the economist, from a legendary primordial condition. . . .

We shall begin from a *contemporary* economic fact. The worker becomes poorer the more wealth he produces and the more his production increases in power and extent. The worker becomes an ever cheaper commodity the more goods he creates. The *devaluation* of the human world increases in direct relation with the *increase in value* of the world of things. Labour does not only create goods; it also produces itself and the worker as a *commodity*, and indeed in the same proportion as it produces goods.

This fact simply implies that the object produced by labour, its product, now stands opposed to it as an *alien being*, as a *power independent* of the producer. The product of labour is labour which has been embodied in an object and turned into a physical thing; this product is an *objectification* of labour. The performance of work is at the same time its objectification. The performance of work appears in the sphere of political economy as a *vitiation* of the worker, objectification as a *loss* and as *servitude to the object*, and appropriation as *alienation*. . . .

All these consequences follow from the fact that the worker is related to the *product of his labour* as to an *alien* object. For it is clear on this presupposition that the more the worker expends himself in work the more powerful becomes the world of objects which he creates in face of himself, the poorer he becomes in his inner life, and the less he belongs to himself. It is just the same as in religion. The more of himself man attributes to God the less he has left in himself. The worker puts his life into the object, and his life then belongs no longer to himself but to the object. The greater his activity, therefore, the less he possesses. What is embodied in the product of his labour is no longer his own. The greater this product is, therefore, the more he is diminished. The *alienation* of the worker in his product means not only that his labour becomes an object, assumes an *external* existence, but that it exists independently, *outside himself,* and alien to him, and that it stands opposed to him as an autonomous power. The life which he has given to the object sets itself against him as an alien and hostile force. . . .

So far we have considered the alienation of the worker only from one aspect; namely, *his relationship with the products of his labour.* However, alienation appears not merely in the result but also in the *process* of *production,* within *productive activity* itself. How could the worker stand in an alien relationship to the product of his activity if he did not alienate himself in the act of production itself? The product is indeed only the *résumé* of activity, of production. Consequently, if the product of labour is alienation, production itself must be active alienation—the alienation of activity and the activity of alienation. The alienation of the object of labour merely summarizes the alienation in the work activity itself.

What constitutes the alienation of labour? First, that the work is external to the worker, that it is not part of his nature; and that, consequently, he does not fulfil himself in his work but denies himself, has a feeling of misery rather than well-being, does not develop freely his mental and physical energies but is physically exhausted and mentally debased. The worker, therefore, feels himself at home only during his leisure time, whereas at work he feels homeless. His work is not voluntary but imposed, *forced labour.* It is not the satisfaction of a need, but only a *means* for satisfying other needs. Its alien character is clearly shown by the fact that as soon as there is no physical or other compulsion it is avoided like the plague. External labour, labour in which man alienates himself, is a labour of self-sacrifice, or mortification. Finally, the external character of work for the worker is shown by the fact that it is not his own work but work for someone else, that in work he does not belong to himself but to another person. . . .

We arrive at the result that man (the worker) feels himself to be freely active only in his animal functions—eating, drinking and procreating, or at most also in his dwelling and in personal adornment—while in his human functions he is reduced to an animal. The animal becomes human and the human becomes animal. . . .

. . . This is *self-alienation* as against the above-mentioned alienation of the *thing.* . . .

. . . Alienated labour [also] turns nature . . . into an *alien* being and into a *means* for his *individual existence.* It alienates from man his own body, external nature, his mental life and his *human* life. A direct consequence of the alienation of man from the product of his labour, from his life activity and from his species-life, is that *man is alienated* from other *men*. When man confronts himself he also confronts *other* men. What is true of man's relationship to his work, to the product of his work and to himself, is also true of his relationship to other men, to their labour and to the objects of their labour.

In general, the statement that man is alienated from his species-life means that each man is alienated from others, and that each of the others is likewise alienated from human life.

Human alienation, and above all the relation of man to himself, is first realized and expressed in the relationship between each man and other men. Thus in the relationship of alienated labour every man regards other men according to the standards and relationships in which he finds himself placed as a worker. . . .

Let us now examine further how this concept of alienated labour must express and reveal itself in reality. If the product of labour is alien to me and confronts me as an alien power, to whom does it belong? If my own activity does not belong to me but is an alien, forced activity, to whom does it belong? To a being *other* than myself. And who is this being? The *gods?* It is apparent in the earliest stages of advanced production, e.g., temple building, etc. in Egypt, India, Mexico, and in the service rendered to gods, that the product belonged to the gods. But the gods alone were never the lords of labour. And no more was *nature*. . . .

The *alien* being to whom labour and the product of labour belong, to whose service labour is devoted, and to whose enjoyment the product of labour goes, can only be *man* himself. If the product of labour does not belong to the worker, but confronts him as an alien power, this can only be because it belongs to *a man other than the worker*. If his activity is a torment to him it must be a source of *enjoyment* and pleasure to another. Not the gods, nor nature, but only man himself can be this alien power over men. . . .

Thus, through alienated labour the worker creates the relation of another man, who does not work and is outside the work process, to this labour. The relation of the worker to work also produces the relation of the capitalist (or whatever one likes to call the lord of labour) to work. *Private property* is, therefore, the product, the necessary result, of *alienated labour*, of the external relation of the worker to nature and to himself. . . .

From the relation of alienated labour to private property it also follows that the emancipation of society from private property, from servitude, takes the political form of the *emancipation of the workers;* not in the sense that only the latter's emancipation is involved, but because this emancipation includes the emancipation of humanity as a whole. For all human servitude is involved in the relation of the worker to production, and all the types of servitude are only modifications or consequences of this relation. . . .

History

Since we are dealing with the Germans, who do not postulate anything, we must begin by stating the first premise of all human existence, and therefore of all history, the premise namely that men must be in a position to live in order to be able to "make history." But life involves before everything else eating and drinking, a habitation, clothing and many other things. The first historical act is thus the production of the means to satisfy these needs, the production of material life itself. . . .

In the whole conception of history up to the present this real basis of history has either been totally neglected or else considered as a minor matter quite irrelevant to the course of history. History must therefore always be written according to an extraneous standard; the real production of life seems to be beyond history, while the truly historical appears to be separated from ordinary life, something extra-superterrestrial. With this the relation of man to nature is excluded from history and hence the antithesis of nature and history is created. The exponents of this conception of history have consequently only been able to see in history the political actions of princes and States, religious and all sorts of theoretical struggles, and in particular in each historical epoch have had to share the *illusion of that epoch*. For instance, if an epoch imagines itself to be actuated by purely "political" or "religious" motives, although "religion" and "politics" are only forms of its true motives, the historian accepts this opinion. The "idea," the "conception" of these conditioned men about their real practice, is transformed into the sole determining, active force, which controls and determines their practice. . . . While the French and the English at least hold by the political illusion, which is moderately close to reality, the Germans move in the realm of the "pure spirit," and make religious illusion the driving force of history.

The Hegelian philosophy of history is the last consequence, reduced to its "finest expression," of all this German historiography, for which it is not a question of real, nor even of political, interests, but of pure thoughts. . . .

The ideas of the ruling class are in every epoch the ruling ideas: i.e. the class, which is the ruling material force of society, is at the same time its ruling intellectual force. The class which has the means of material production at its disposal, has control at the same time over the means of mental production, so that thereby, generally speaking, the ideas of those who lack the means of mental production are subject to it. The ruling ideas are nothing more than the ideal expression of the dominant material relationships, the dominant material relationships grasped as ideas; hence of the relationships which make the one class the ruling one, therefore the ideas of its dominance. The individuals composing the ruling class possess among other things consciousness, and therefore think. In so far, therefore, as they rule as a class and determine the extent and compass of an epoch, it is self-evident that they do this in their whole range, hence among other things rule also as thinkers, as producers of ideas, and regulate the production and distribution of the ideas of their age: thus their ideas are the ruling ideas of the epoch. For instance, in an age and in a country where royal power, aristocracy and bourgeoisie are contending for mastery and where, therefore, mastery is shared, the doctrine of the separation of powers proves to be the dominant idea and is expressed as an "eternal law." . . .

If now in considering the course of history we detach the ideas of the ruling class from the ruling class itself and attribute to them an independent existence, if we confine ourselves to saying that these or those ideas were dominant, without bothering ourselves about the conditions of production and the producers of these ideas, if we then ignore the individuals and world conditions which are the source of the ideas, we can say, for instance, that during the time that the aristocracy was dominant, the concepts honour, loyalty, etc., were dominant, during the dominance of the bourgeoisie the concepts freedom, equality, etc. The ruling class itself on the whole imagines this to be so. This conception of history, which is common to all historians, particularly since the eighteenth century, will necessarily come up against the phenomenon that increasingly abstract ideas hold sway, i.e. ideas which increasingly take on the form of universality. For each new class which puts itself in the place of one ruling before it, is compelled, merely in order to carry through its aim, to represent its interest as the common interest of all the members of society, put in an ideal form; it will give its ideas the form of universality, and represent them as the only rational, universally valid ones. The class making a revolution appears from the very start, merely because it is opposed to a *class*, not as a class but as the representative of the whole of society; it appears as the whole mass of society confronting the one ruling class. . . . Every new class, therefore, achieves its hegemony only on a broader basis than that of the class ruling previously, in return for which the opposition of the non-ruling class against the new ruling class later develops all the more sharply and profoundly. Both these things determine the fact that the struggle to be waged against this new ruling class, in its turn, aims at a more decided and radical negation of the previous conditions of society than could all previous classes which sought to rule.

This whole semblance, that the rule of a certain class is only the rule of certain ideas, comes to a natural end, of course, as soon as society

ceases at last to be organized in the form of class-rule, that is to say as
soon as it is no longer necessary to represent a particular interest as
general or "the general interest" as ruling.

FRIEDRICH ENGELS: *Herr Eugen Dühring's Revolution in Science* *

> In the following work, usually referred to as *Anti-Dühring* and
> published in 1878, Engels expounds the creed of "scientific socialism."
> Friedrich Engels (1820–95), son of a wealthy German cotton-spinner,
> is well known as the close friend and collaborator of Karl Marx.
> Engels spent most of his life in England, working in his father's
> business which had a factory near Manchester, and writing books on
> communism.

MODERN socialism is, in its content, primarily the product of the perception on the one hand of the class antagonisms existing in modern society,
between possessors and non-possessors, wage workers and bourgeois;
and on the other hand, of the anarchy ruling in production. In its
theoretical form, however, it originally appears as a further and ostensi-
bly more logical extension of the principles established by the great
French philosophers of the eighteenth century. Like every new theory,
it had at first to link itself on to the intellectual material which lay ready
to its hand, however deep its roots lay in economic facts.

The great men who in France were clearing the minds of men for the
coming revolution themselves acted in an extremely revolutionary fashion. They recognised no external authority of any kind. Religion, conceptions of nature, society, political systems, everything was subjected
to the most merciless criticism; everything had to justify its existence at
the bar of reason or renounce all claim to existence. The reasoning
intellect was applied to everything as the sole measure. It was the time
when, as Hegel says, the world was stood upon its head; first, in the
sense that the human head and the principles arrived at by its thought
claimed to be the basis of all human action and association; and then later
on also in the wider sense, that the reality which was in contradiction
with these principles was in fact turned upside down from top to
bottom. All previous forms of society and government, all the old ideas
handed down by tradition, were flung into the lumber-room as irrational; the world had hitherto allowed itself to be guided solely by
prejudices; everything in the past deserved only pity and contempt.

* Friedrich Engels: *Herr Eugen Dühring's Revolution in Science*, trans. by
Emile Burns (New York: International Publishers Co., Inc.; n. d.), pp. 23–4, 26–34.

Now for the first time appeared the light of day; henceforth, superstition, injustice, privilege and oppression were to be superseded by eternal truth, eternal justice, equality grounded in Nature and the inalienable rights of man.

We know today that this kingdom of reason was nothing more than the idealised kingdom of the bourgeoisie; that eternal justice found its realisation in bourgeois justice; that equality reduced itself to bourgeois equality before the law; that bourgeois property was proclaimed as one of the essential rights of man; and that the government of reason, the Social Contract of Rousseau, came into existence and could only come into existence as a bourgeois democratic republic. No more than their predecessors could the great thinkers of the eighteenth century pass beyond the limits imposed on them by their own epoch.

*   *   *

Meanwhile, along with and after the French philosophy of the eighteenth century, the newer German philosophy had arisen, culminating in Hegel. Its greatest merit was the re-adoption of dialectics as the highest form of thinking. . . .

When we reflect on Nature, or the history of mankind, or our own intellectual activity, the first picture presented to us is of an endless maze of relations and interactions, in which nothing remains what, where and as it was, but everything moves, changes, comes into being and passes out of existence. This primitive, naïve, yet intrinsically correct conception of the world was that of ancient Greek philosophy, and was first clearly formulated by Heraclitus: everything is and also is not, for everything is in *flux*, is constantly changing, constantly coming into being and passing away. But this conception, correctly as it covers the general character of the picture of phenomena as a whole, is yet inadequate to explain the details of which this total picture is composed; and so long as we do not understand these, we also have no clear idea of the picture as a whole. In order to understand these details, we must detach them from their natural or historical connections, and examine each one separately, as to its nature, its special causes and effects, etc. This is primarily the task of natural science and historical research. . . . The analysis of Nature into its individual parts, the grouping of the different natural processes and natural objects in definite classes, the study of the internal anatomy of organic bodies in their manifold forms—these were the fundamental conditions of the gigantic strides in our knowledge of Nature which have been made during the last four hundred years. But this method of investigation has also left us as a legacy the habit of observing natural objects and natural processes in their isolation, detached from the whole vast interconnection of things; and therefore not in their motion, but in their repose; not as essentially changing, but as fixed constants; not in their life, but in their death. And when, as was the case with Bacon and Locke, this way of looking at things was transferred from natural science to philosophy, it produced the specific limitations of last century, the metaphysical mode of thought.

* * *

Nature is the test of dialectics, and it must be said for modern natural science that it has furnished extremely rich and daily increasing materials for this test, and has thus proved that in the last analysis Nature's process is dialectical and not metaphysical. . . .

An exact representation of the universe, of its evolution and that of mankind, as well as of the reflection of this evolution in the human mind, can therefore only be built up in a dialectical way, taking constantly into account the general actions and reactions of becoming and ceasing to be, of progressive or retrogressive changes. And the more recent German philosophy worked with this standpoint from the first. Kant began his career by resolving the stable solar system of Newton and its eternal permanence—after the famous initial impulse had once been given—into a historical process: the formation of the sun and of all the planets out of a rotating nebulous mass. Together with this he already drew the conclusion that given this origin of the solar system, its ultimate dissolution was also inevitable. Half a century later his views were given a mathematical basis by Laplace, and another fifty years later the spectroscope proved the existence in space of such incandescent masses of gas in various stages of condensation.

This newer German philosophy culminated in the Hegelian system, in which for the first time—and this is its great merit—the whole natural, historical and spiritual world was presented as a process, that is, as in constant motion, change, transformation and development; and the attempt was made to show the internal interconnections in this motion and development. From this standpoint the history of mankind no longer appeared as a confused whirl of senseless deeds of violence, all equally condemnable before the judgment seat of the now matured philosophic reason, and best forgotten as quickly as possible, but as the process of development of humanity itself. It now became the task of thought to follow the gradual stages of this process through all its devious ways, and to trace out the inner regularities running through all its apparently fortuitous phenomena.

That Hegel did not succeed in this task is here immaterial. His epoch-making service was that he propounded it. It is indeed a task which no individual will ever be able to solve. Although Hegel—with Saint-Simon —was the most encyclopaedic mind of his age, yet he was limited, in the first place, by the necessarily restricted compass of his own knowledge, and, secondly, by the similarly restricted scope and depth of the knowledge and ideas of his age. But there was also a third factor. Hegel was an idealist, that is to say, the thoughts within his mind were to him not the more or less abstract images of real things and processes, but, on the contrary, things and their development were to him only the images made real of the "Idea" existing somewhere or other already before the world existed. This mode of thought placed everything on its head, and completely reversed the real connections of things in the world. And although Hegel grasped correctly and with insight many individual interconnections, yet, for the reasons just given, there is also much that in point of detail also is botched, artificial, laboured, in a word, wrong. The Hegelian system as such was a colossal miscarriage—but it was also the last of its kind. . . .

The realisation of the entire incorrectness of previous German idealism led necessarily to materialism, but, it must be noted, not to the simple metaphysical and exclusively mechanical materialism of the eighteenth century. Instead of the simple and naïvely revolutionary rejection of all previous history, modern materialism sees history as the process of the evolution of humanity, and its own problem as the discovery of the laws of motion of this process. The conception was prevalent among the French of the eighteenth century, as well as with Hegel, of Nature as a whole, moving in narrow circles and remaining immutable, with its eternal celestial bodies, as Newton taught, and unalterable species of organic beings, as Linnaeus taught. In opposition to this conception, modern materialism embraces the more recent advances of natural science, according to which Nature also has its history in time, the celestial bodies, like the organic species which under favourable circumstances people them, coming into being and passing away, and the recurrent circles, in so far as they are in any way admissible, assuming infinitely vaster dimensions. . . .

While, however, the revolution in the conception of Nature could only be carried through to the extent that research furnished the corresponding positive materials of knowledge, already much earlier certain historical facts had occurred which led to a decisive change in the conception of history. In 1831, the first working-class rising had taken place in Lyons; between 1838 and 1842 the first national workers' movement, that of the English Chartists, reached its height. The class struggle between proletariat and bourgeoisie came to the front in the history of the most advanced European countries, in proportion to the development there, on the one hand, of large-scale industry, and on the other, of the newly-won political domination of the bourgeoisie. Facts more and more forcibly stamped as lies the teachings of bourgeois economics as to the identity of the interests of capital and labour, as to the universal harmony and universal prosperity that free competition brings. All these things could no longer be ignored, any more than the French and English socialism which was their theoretical, even though extremely imperfect, expression. But the old idealist conception of history, which was not yet displaced, knew nothing of class struggles based on material interests, in fact knew nothing at all of material interests; production and all economic relations appeared in it only as incidental, subordinate elements in the "history of civilisation." The new facts made imperative a new examination of all past history, and then it was seen that all past history was the history of class struggles, that these warring classes of society are always the product of the modes of production and exchange, in a word, of the *economic* conditions of their time; that therefore the economic structure of society always forms the real basis from which, in the last analysis, is to be explained the whole superstructure of legal and political institutions, as well as of the religious, philosophical, and other conceptions of each historical period. Now idealism was driven from its last refuge, the philosophy of history; now a materialistic conception of history was propounded, and the way found to explain man's consciousness by his being, instead of, as heretofore, his being by his consciousness.

But the socialism of earlier days was just as incompatible with this materialist conception of history as the French materialist conception of Nature was with dialectics and modern natural science. It is true that the earlier socialism criticised the existing capitalist mode of production and its consequences, but it could not explain them, and so also could not get the mastery over them; it could only simply reject them as evil. But what had to be done was to show this capitalist mode of production on the one hand in its historical sequence and in its inevitability for a definite historical period, and therefore also the inevitability of its downfall, and on the other hand also to lay bare its essential character, which was still hidden, as its critics had hitherto attacked its evil consequences rather than the process of the thing itself. This was done by the discovery of *surplus value*. It was shown that the appropriation of unpaid labour is the basic form of the capitalist mode of production and of the exploitation of the worker effected through it; that even if the capitalist buys the labour power of his labourer at its full value as a commodity on the market, he yet extracts more value from it than he paid for; and that in the ultimate analysis this surplus value forms those sums of value from which are heaped up the constantly increasing masses of capital in the hands of the possessing classes. The process both of capitalist production and of the production of capital was explained.

These two great discoveries, the materialist conception of history and the revelation of the secret of capitalist production by means of surplus value, we owe to *Marx*. With these discoveries socialism became a science, which had in the first place to be developed in all its details and relations.

D. REALISM

GUSTAVE COURBET: *To a Group of Students* *

Gustave Courbet (1819–77) addressed the following letter, dated December 25, 1861, to a group of students who were dissatisfied with the academic art that they were being taught at the Ecole des Beaux Arts in Paris. Courbet expressed very clearly therein the new creed of *realism*, applicable to literature as well as painting, and opposed to other such "schools" of art as the historical and metaphysical-romantic. The anarchist-socialist Pierre-Joseph Proudhon noted the parallel between realism and positivism.

GENTLEMEN and dear friends,

You want to open a painting studio in which you can freely continue your artistic education and you have been kind enough to offer to place it under my direction. Before I give any answer, we must be clear on the meaning of that word DIRECTION. I can not lend myself to there being a question of professor and student in our relationship.

I should explain to you what I recently said to the Congress at Anvers: I do not have, and I can not have, students.

I who believe that every artist should be his own master, can not think of making myself into a professor.

I can not teach my art, nor the art of any school, because I deny that art can be taught and because, in other terms, I maintain that art is completely individual, and the talent of each artist is only the result of his own inspiration and his own study of tradition.

In addition I say that art or talent to an artist can only be (in my opinion) the means of applying his personal faculties to the ideas and the objects of the time in which he lives.

Especially, art in painting can only consist of the representation of objects that are visible and tangible to the artist.

No age can be depicted except by its own artists. I mean to say by the artists that have lived during it. I believe that the artists of one century are completely incompetent when it comes to depicting the objects of a preceding or future century, in other words, to paint either the past or the future.

It is in this sense that I deny the term historical art as applied to the

* From *From The Classicists to the Impressionists* by Elizabeth Gilmore Holt. Copyright 1966 by Elizabeth Gilmore Holt. Reprinted by permission of Doubleday & Company, Inc.

past. Historical art is, by its very essence, contemporary. Every age should have its artists, who will express it and depict it for the future. An age that has not been able to express itself through its own artists, does not have the right to be expressed by outside artists. This would be falsifying history. . . .

The true artists are those who take up their epoch at exactly the point to which it has been carried by preceding ages. To retreat is to do nothing, is to work without result, is to have neither understood nor profited from the lessons of the past. This explains why all archaic schools have always ended by reducing themselves to the most useless compilations.

I also believe that painting is an essentially CONCRETE art and can only consist of the representation of REAL AND EXISTING objects. It is a completely physical language that has as words all visible objects, and an ABSTRACT object, invisible and non-existent, is not part of painting's domain. Imagination in art consists in knowing how to find the most complete expression of an existing object, but never in imagining or in creating the object itself.

Beauty is in nature, and in reality is encountered under the most diverse forms. As soon as it is found, it belongs to art, or rather to the artist who is able to perceive it. As soon as beauty is real and visible, it has its own artistic expression. But artificiality has no business amplifying this expression. It can not enter into it without risking its distortion, and consequent weakening. The beauty based on nature is superior to all artistic conventions.

Here is the basis of my ideas in art. With such ideas, to think of opening a school in which conventional principles would be taught would be to return to the incomplete and banal premises which until now have everywhere directed modern art.

There can be no school, there are only painters. Schools only serve in the research on the analytical proceedings of art. No school can lead to synthesis in isolation. Painting can not, without falling into abstraction, allow one particular aspect of the art to dominate, whether it be drawing, color, composition, or any of the other multiple aspects whose total constitutes this art.

Therefore I can not pretend to open a school in which to mold students, to teach this or that partial tradition of art. I can only explain to artists, who will be my collaborators and not my students, the method according to which, in my opinion, one becomes a painter which I have myself followed from my beginnings, leaving to each one the complete direction of his own individuality, the full liberty of his personal expression in the application of this method. The founding of a common studio, bringing to mind the fruitful collaborations of the studios of the Renaissance, can certainly be useful in attaining this end and contribute to opening the phase of modern painting. To attain it, I will lend myself with eagerness to all that you wish of me. . . .

E. LIBERAL NATIONALISM

JOSEPH MAZZINI: *On the Duties of Man* *

Joseph Mazzini (1805–72) was a typical liberal nationalist of the mid-nineteenth century. A prophet of the *Risorgimento,* an admirer of Dante rather than Machiavelli, he spent his life (mostly in exile in England and France) propagandizing the Italian masses and plotting the overthrow of Austrian rule in Italy. His most representative work, *On the Duties of Man,* was first published as a series of articles in Italian-language journals in 1844 and 1858.

YOUR first duties—first as regards importance—are, as I have already told you, towards Humanity. You are *men* before you are either citizens or fathers. If you do not embrace the whole human family in your affection, if you do not bear witness to your belief in the Unity of that family, consequent upon the Unity of God, and in that fraternity among the peoples which is destined to reduce that unity to action; if, wheresoever a fellow-creature suffers, or the dignity of human nature is violated by falsehood or tyranny—you are not ready, if able, to aid the unhappy, and do not feel called upon to combat, if able, for the redemption of the betrayed or oppressed—you violate your law of life, you comprehend not that Religion which will be the guide and blessing of the future.

But what can each of you, singly, *do* for the moral improvement and progress of Humanity? You can from time to time give sterile utterance to your belief; you may, on some rare occasions, perform some act of *charity* towards a brother man not belonging to your own land;—no more. But charity is not the watchword of the Faith of the Future. The watchword of the faith of the future is *Association,* and fraternal co-operation of all towards a common aim; and this is as far superior to all charity, as the edifice which all of you should unite to raise would be superior to the humble hut each one of you might build alone, or with the mere assistance of lending and borrowing stone, mortar, and tools.

But, you tell me, you cannot attempt united action, distinct and divided as you are in language, customs, tendencies, and capacity. The individual is too insignificant, and Humanity too vast. The mariner of

* Mrs. Emilie Ashurst Venturi: *Joseph Mazzini: A Memoir* (London: Alexander & Shepheard; 1875), pp. 312–17.

Brittany prays to God as he puts to sea: *Help me, my God! my boat is so small and thy ocean so wide!* And this prayer is the true expression of the condition of each one of you, until you find the means of infinitely multiplying your forces and powers of action.

This means was provided for you by God when he gave you a country; when, even as a wise overseer of labour distributes the various branches of employment according to the different capacities of the workmen, he divided Humanity into distinct groups or nuclei upon the face of the earth, thus creating the germ of Nationalities. Evil governments have disfigured the divine design. Nevertheless you may still trace it, distinctly marked out—at least as far as Europe is concerned—by the course of the great rivers, the direction of the higher mountains, and other geographical conditions. They have disfigured it by their conquests, their greed, and their jealousy even of the righteous power of others; disfigured it so far that, if we except England and France—there is not perhaps a single country whose present boundaries correspond to that design.

These governments did not, and do not, recognise any country save their own families or dynasty, the egotism of caste. But the Divine design will infallibly be realized. Natural divisions, and the spontaneous, innate tendencies of the peoples, will take the place of the arbitrary divisions sanctioned by evil governments. The map of Europe will be redrawn. The countries of the Peoples, defined by the vote of free men, will arise upon the ruins of the countries of kings and privileged castes, and between these countries harmony and fraternity will exist. And the common work of Humanity, of general amelioration and the gradual discovery and application of its Law of life, being distributed according to local and general capacities, will be wrought out in peaceful and progressive development and advance. Then may each one of you, fortified by the power and the affection of many millions, all speaking the same language, gifted with the same tendencies, and educated by the same historical tradition, hope, even by your own single effort, to be able to benefit all Humanity.

O my brothers, love your Country! Our country is our Home, the house that God has given us, placing therein a numerous family that loves us, and whom we love; a family with whom we sympathise more readily, and whom we understand more quickly than we do others; and which, from its being centred round a given spot, and from the homogeneous nature of its elements, is adapted to a special branch of activity. Our country is our common workshop, whence the products of our activity are sent forth for the benefit of the whole world; wherein the tools and implements of labour we can most usefully employ are gathered together: nor may we reject them without disobeying the plan of the Almighty, and diminishing our own strength.

In labouring for our own country on the right principle, we labour for Humanity. Our country is the fulcrum of the lever we have to wield for the common good. If we abandon that fulcrum, we run the risk of rendering ourselves useless not only to humanity but to our country itself. Before men can *associate* with the nations of which humanity is composed, they must have a National existence. There is no true association except among equals. It is only through our country that we can have a recognised *collective* existence.

Humanity is a vast army advancing to the conquest of lands unknown, against enemies both powerful and astute. The peoples are the different corps, the divisions of that army. Each of them has its post assigned to it, and its special operation to execute; and the common victory depends upon the exactitude with which those distinct operations shall be fulfilled. Disturb not the order of battle. Forsake not the banner given to you by God. Wheresoever you may be, in the centre of whatsoever people circumstances may have placed you, be ever ready to combat for the liberty of that people should it be necessary, but combat in such wise that the blood you shed may reflect glory, not on yourselves alone, but on your country. Say not *I*, but *we*. Let each man among you strive to incarnate his country in himself. Let each man among you regard himself as a guarantee, responsible for his fellow-countrymen, and learn so to govern his actions as to cause his country to be loved and respected through him. Your country is the sign of the mission God has given you to fulfil towards Humanity. The faculties and forces of *all* her sons should be associated in the accomplishment of that mission. The true country is a community of free men and equals, bound together in fraternal concord to labour towards a common aim. You are bound to make it and to maintain it such. The country is not an *aggregation*, but an *association*. There is therefore no true country without an uniform right. There is no true country where the uniformity of that right is violated by the existence of castes, privilege, and inequality. Where the activity of a portion of the powers and faculties of the individual is either cancelled or dormant; where there is not a common Principle, recognised, accepted, and developed by all, there is no true nation, no People; but only a multitude, a fortuitous agglomeration of men whom circumstances have called together, and whom circumstances may again divide. In the name of the love you bear your country you must peacefully but untiringly combat the existence of privilege and inequality in the land that gave you life.

There is but one sole legitimate privilege, the privilege of Genius when it reveals itself united with virtue. But this is a privilege given by God, and when you acknowledge it and follow its inspiration, you do so freely, exercising your own reason and your own choice. Every privilege which demands submission from you in virtue of power, inheritance, or any other right than the Right common to all, is a usurpation and a tyranny which you are bound to resist and destroy.

Be your country your Temple. God at the summit; a people of equals at the base.

Accept no other formula, no other moral law, if you would not dishonour alike your country and yourselves. Let all secondary laws be but the gradual regulation of your existence by the progressive application of this supreme law. And in order that they may be such, it is necessary that *all* of you should aid in framing them. Laws framed only by a single fraction of the citizens, can never, in the very nature of things, be other than the mere expression of the thoughts, aspirations, and desires of that fraction; the representation, not of the Country, but of a third or fourth part, of a class or zone of the country.

The laws should be the expression of the *universal* aspiration, and promote the universal good. They should be a pulsation of the heart of the nation. The entire nation should, either directly or indirectly, legislate.

By yielding up this mission into the hands of a few, you substitute the egotism of one class for the Country, which is the union of all classes.

Country is not a mere zone of territory. The true country is the Idea to which it gives birth; it is the Thought of love, the sense of communion which unites in one all the sons of that territory.

So long as a single one amongst your brothers has no vote to represent him in the development of the national life, so long as there is one left to vegetate in ignorance where others are educated, so long as a single man, able and willing to work, languishes in poverty through want of work to do, you have no country in the sense in which country ought to exist—the country of all and for all.

Education, labour, and the franchise, are the three main pillars of the nation. Rest not until you have built them strongly up with your own labour and exertions.

Never deny your sister nations. Be it yours to evolve the life of your country in loveliness and strength; free from all servile fears or sceptical doubts; maintaining as its basis the People; as its guide the consequences of the principles of its Religious Faith, logically and energetically applied; its strength, the united strength of all; its aim, the fulfilment of the mission given to it by God.

And so long as you are ready to die for Humanity, the life of your country will be immortal.

3. *The Darwinian World*

A. DARWINISM

SIR CHARLES LYELL: *Principles of Geology* *

> Sir Charles Lyell (1797–1875) has rightly been called "the single greatest influence in the life of Charles Darwin." Darwin carried with him on the *Beagle* the first edition of the great geologist's *Principles of Geology* (1830). Without the "uniformitarian" hypothesis of nature, extended to geology in that work, and the "time revolution," suggested by it, Darwin might never have arrived at his own theory of evolution in animate nature.

WHEN we compare the result of observations in the last fifty years with those of the three preceding centuries, we cannot but look forward with the most sanguine expectations to the degree of excellence to which geology may be carried, even by the labours of the present generation. Never, perhaps, did any science, with the exception of astronomy, unfold, in an equally brief period, so many novel and unexpected truths, and overturn so many preconceived opinions. The senses had for ages declared the earth to be at rest, until the astronomer taught that it was carried through space with inconceivable rapidity. In like manner was the surface of this planet regarded as having remained unaltered since its creation, until the geologist proved that it had been the theatre of reiterated change, and was still the subject of slow but never-ending fluctuations. The discovery of other systems in the boundless regions of space was the triumph of astronomy; to trace the same system through various transformations—to behold it at successive eras adorned with different hills and valleys, lakes and seas, and peopled with new inhabitants, was the delightful meed of geological research. By the geometer were measured the regions of space, and the relative distances of the heavenly bodies;—by the geologist myriads of ages were reckoned, not by arithmetical computation, but by a train of physical events—a succession of phenomena in the animate and inanimate worlds—signs which convey to our minds more definite ideas than figures can do of the immensity of time. . . .

If we reflect on the history of the progress of geology, as explained in the preceding chapters, we perceive that there have been great fluctua-

---

* Sir Charles Lyell: *Principles of Geology* (London: John Murray; 1853), pp. 60–62, 64–65.

tions of opinion respecting the nature of the causes to which all former changes of the earth's surface are referable. The first observers conceived the monuments which the geologist endeavours to decipher to relate to an original state of the earth, or to a period when there were causes in activity, distinct, in kind and degree, from those now constituting the economy of nature. These views were gradually modified, and some of them entirely abandoned in proportion as observations were multiplied, and the signs of former mutations more skilfully interpreted. Many appearances, which had for a long time been regarded as indicating mysterious and extraordinary agency, were finally recognized as the necessary result of the laws now governing the material world; and the discovery of this unlooked-for conformity has at length induced some philosophers to infer, that, during the ages contemplated in geology, there has never been any interruption to the agency of the same uniform laws of change. The same assemblage of general causes, they conceive, may have been sufficient to produce, by their various combinations, the endless diversity of effects, of which the shell of the earth has preserved the memorials; and, consistently with these principles, the recurrence of analogous changes is expected by them in time to come. . . .

. . . The philosopher at last becomes convinced of the undeviating uniformity of secondary causes; and, guided by his faith in this principle, he determines the probability of accounts transmitted to him of former occurrences, and often rejects the fabulous tales of former times, on the ground of their being irreconcilable with the experience of more enlightened ages.

As a belief in the want of conformity in the causes by which the earth's crust has been modified in ancient and modern periods was, for a long time, universally prevalent, and that, too, amongst men who were convinced that the order of nature had been uniform for the last several thousand years, every circumstance which could have influenced their minds and given an undue bias to their opinions deserves particular attention. Now the reader may easily satisfy himself, that, however undeviating the course of nature may have been from the earliest epochs, it was impossible for the first cultivators of geology to come to such a conclusion, so long as they were under a delusion as to the age of the world, and the date of the first creation of animate beings. . . . Even when they conceded that the earth had been peopled with animate beings at an earlier period than was at first supposed, they had no conception that the quantity of time bore so great a proportion to the historical era as is now generally conceded. How fatal every error as to the quantity of time must prove to the introduction of rational views concerning the state of things in former ages, may be conceived by supposing the annals of the civil and military transactions of a great nation to be perused under the impression that they occurred in a period of one hundred instead of two thousand years. Such a portion of history would immediately assume the air of a romance; the events would seem devoid of credibility, and inconsistent with the present course of human affairs. A crowd of incidents would follow each other in thick succession. Armies and fleets would appear to be assembled only to be destroyed, and cities built merely to fall in ruins. There would be the most violent transitions from foreign or intestine war to periods of profound peace, and the works effected during the years of disorder or tranquility would appear alike superhuman in magnitude.

He who should study the monuments of the natural world under the influence of a similar infatuation, must draw a no less exaggerated picture of the energy and violence of causes, and must experience the same insurmountable difficulty in reconciling the former and present state of nature. If we could behold in one view all the volcanic cones thrown up in Iceland, Italy, Sicily, and other parts of Europe, during the last five thousand years, and could see the lavas which have flowed during the same period; the dislocations, subsidences, and elevations caused during earth-quakes; the lands added to various deltas, or devoured by the sea, together with the effects of devastation by floods, and imagine that all these events had happened in one year, we must form most exalted ideas of the activity of the agents, and the suddenness of the revolutions. Were an equal amount of change to pass before our eyes in the next year, could we avoid the conclusion that some great crisis of nature was at hand? If geologists, therefore, have misinterpreted the signs of a succession of events, so as to conclude that centuries were implied where the characters imported thousands of years, and thousands of years where the language of Nature signified millions, they could not, if they reasoned logically from such false premises, come to any other conclusion than that the system of the natural world had undergone a complete revolution.

We should be warranted in ascribing the erection of the great pyramid to superhuman power, if we were convinced that it was raised in one day; and if we imagine, in the same manner, a continent or mountain-chain to have been elevated, during an equally small fraction of the time which was really occupied in upheaving it, we might then be justified in inferring, that the subterranean movements were once far more energetic than in our own times. . . .

Charles Darwin *

"The idea of Evolution," says J. H. Randall, "of change, growth, and development, has been the most revolutionary notion in man's thought about himself and his world in the last hundred years." To the great English scientist Charles Darwin (1809–82), more than to any other single person, was due the spread of this idea, and the related idea of Natural Selection. The following selections are from Darwin's two most famous books, *The Origin of Species* (1859) and *The Descent of Man* (1871), which precipitated a storm in theological circles.

The Origin of Species

Historical Sketch

I will here give a brief sketch of the progress of opinion on the Origin of Species. Until recently the great majority of naturalists believed that species were immutable productions, and had been separately created. This view has been ably maintained by many authors. Some few naturalists, on the other hand, have believed that species undergo modification, and that the existing forms of life are the descendants by true generation of pre-existing forms. Passing over allusions to the subject in the classical writers, the first author who in modern times has treated it in a scientific spirit was Buffon. But as his opinions fluctuated greatly at different periods, and as he does not enter on the causes or means of the transformation of species, I need not here enter on details.

Lamarck was the first man whose conclusions on the subject excited much attention. This justly-celebrated naturalist first published his views in 1801; he much enlarged them in 1809 in his 'Philosophie Zoologique,' and subsequently, in 1815, in the Introduction to his 'Hist. Nat. des Animaux sans Vertebres.' In these works he upholds the doctrine that all species, including man, are descended from other species. He first did the eminent service of arousing attention to the probability of all change in the organic, as well as in the inorganic world, being the result of law, and not of miraculous interposition. Lamarck seems to have been chiefly led to his conclusion on the gradual change of species, by the difficulty of distinguishing species and varieties, by the almost perfect gradation of forms in certain groups, and by the analogy of domestic productions. With respect to the means of modification, he attributed something to the direct action of the physical conditions of life, something to the crossing of already existing forms, and much to use and disuse, that is, to

* Charles Darwin: *On the Origin of Species by Means of Natural Selection* (New York: D. Appleton and Company; 1878), pp. xiii–xiv, xix, 2–4; *The Descent of Man and Selection in Relation to Sex* (New York: D. Appleton and Company; 1871), vol. II, pp. 368–70, 372–5, 377–8, 386–7.

the effects of habit. To this latter agency he seems to attribute all the beautiful adaptations in nature;—such as the long neck of the giraffe for browsing on the branches of trees. But he likewise believed in a law of progressive development; and as all the forms of life thus tend to progress, in order to account for the existence at the present day of simple productions, he maintains that such forms are now spontaneously generated. . . .

Mr. Herbert Spencer, in an Essay (originally published in the 'Leader,' March 1852, and republished in his 'Essays' in 1858), has contrasted the theories of the Creation and the Development of organic beings with remarkable skill and force. He argues from the analogy of domestic productions, from the changes which the embryos of many species undergo, from the difficulty of distinguishing species and varieties, and from the principle of general gradation, that species have been modified; and he attributes the modification to the change of circumstances. The author (1855) has also treated Psychology on the principle of the necessary acquirement of each mental power and capacity by gradation.

Introduction

In considering the Origin of Species, it is quite conceivable that a naturalist, reflecting on the mutual affinities of organic beings, on their embryological relations, their geographical distribution, geological succession, and other such facts, might come to the conclusion that species had not been independently created, but had descended, like varieties, from other species. Nevertheless, such a conclusion, even if well founded, would be unsatisfactory, until it could be shown how the innumerable species inhabiting this world have been modified, so as to acquire that perfection of structure and coadaptation which justly excites our admiration. Naturalists continually refer to external conditions, such as climate, food, &c., as the only possible cause of variation. In one limited sense, as we shall hereafter see, this may be true; but it is preposterous to attribute to mere external conditions, the structure, for instance, of the woodpecker, with its feet, tail, beak, and tongue, so admirably adapted to catch insects under the bark of trees. In the case of the mistletoe, which draws its nourishment from certain trees, which has seeds that must be transported by certain birds, and which has flowers with separate sexes absolutely requiring the agency of certain insects to bring pollen from one flower to the other, it is equally preposterous to account for the structure of this parasite, with its relations to several distinct organic beings, by the effects of external conditions, or of habit, or of the volition of the plant itself.

It is, therefore, of the highest importance to gain a clear insight into the means of modification and coadaptation. At the commencement of my observations it seemed to me probable that a careful study of domesticated animals and of cultivated plants would offer the best chance of making out this obscure problem. Nor have I been disappointed; in this and in all other perplexing cases I have invariably found that our knowledge, imperfect though it be, of variation under domestication, afforded the best and safest clue. I may venture to express my conviction of the high value of such studies, although they have been very commonly neglected by naturalists.

From these considerations, I shall devote the first chapter of this Abstract to Variation under Domestication. We shall thus see that a large amount of hereditary modification is at least possible; and, what is equally or more important, we shall see how great is the power of man in accumulating by his Selection successive slight variations. I will then pass on to the variability of species in a state of nature; but I shall, unfortunately, be compelled to treat this subject far too briefly, as it can be treated properly only by giving long catalogues of facts. We shall, however, be enabled to discuss what circumstances are most favourable to variation. In the next chapter the Struggle for Existence amongst all organic beings throughout the world, which inevitably follows from the high geometrical ratio of their increase, will be considered. This is the doctrine of Malthus, applied to the whole animal and vegetable kingdoms. As many more individuals of each species are born than can possibly survive; and as, consequently, there is a frequently recurring struggle for existence, it follows that any being, if it vary however slightly in any manner profitable to itself, under the complex and sometimes varying conditions of life, will have a better chance of surviving, and thus be *naturally selected*. From the strong principle of inheritance, any selected variety will tend to propagate its new and modified form. . . . Although much remains obscure, and will long remain obscure, I can entertain no doubt, after the most deliberate study and dispassionate judgment of which I am capable, that the view which most naturalists until recently entertained, and which I formerly entertained—namely, that each species has been independently created—is erroneous. I am fully convinced that species are not immutable; but that those belonging to what are called the same genera are lineal descendants of some other and generally extinct species, in the same manner as the acknowledged varieties of any one species are the descendants of that species. Furthermore, I am convinced that Natural Selection has been the most important, but not the exclusive, means of modification.

The Descent of Man

The main conclusion arrived at in this work, and now held by many naturalists who are well competent to form a sound judgment, is that man is descended from some less highly-organized form. The grounds upon which this conclusion rests will never be shaken, for the close similarity between man and the lower animals in embryonic development, as well as in innumerable points of structure and constitution, both of high and of the most trifling importance—the rudiments which he retains, and the abnormal reversions to which he is occasionally liable—are facts which cannot be disputed. They have long been known, but until recently they told us nothing with respect to the origin of man. Now, when viewed by the light of our knowledge of the whole organic world, their meaning is unmistakable. The great principle of evolution stands up clear and firm, when these groups of facts are considered in connection with others, such as the mutual affinities of the members of the same group, their geographical distribution in past and present times, and their geological succession. It is incredible that all these facts should speak falsely. He who is not content to look, like a savage, at the phenomena of Nature as disconnected, cannot any longer believe that man is the work of a separate act of creation. He will be forced to admit that the close resemblance of the embryo of man to that, for instance, of a dog—the construction of his skull, limbs, and whole frame, independently of the uses to which the parts may be put, on the same plan with that of other mammals—the occasional reappearance of various structures, for instance, of several distinct muscles, which man does not normally possess, but which are common to the Quadrumana—and a crowd of analogous facts—all point in the plainest manner to the conclusion that man is the codescendant with other mammals of a common progenitor.

We have seen that man incessantly presents individual differences in all parts of his body and in his mental faculties. These differences or variations seem to be induced by the same general causes, and to obey the same laws as with the lower animals. In both cases similar laws of inheritance prevail. Man tends to increase at a greater rate than his means of subsistence; consequently he is occasionally subjected to a severe struggle for existence, and natural selection will have effected whatever lies within its scope. A succession of strongly-marked variations of a similar nature are by no means requisite; slight fluctuating differences in the individual suffice for the work of natural selection. We may feel assured that the inherited effects of the long-continued use or disuse of parts will have done much in the same direction with natural selection. Modifications formerly of importance, though no longer of any special use, will be long inherited. When one part is modified, other parts will change through the principle of correlation, of which we have instances in many curious cases of correlated monstrosities. Something may be attributed to the direct and definite action of the surrounding conditions of life, such as abundant food, heat, or moisture; and lastly, many characters of slight physiological importance, some indeed of considerable importance, have been gained through sexual selection. . . .

By considering the embryological structure of man—the homologies which he presents with the lower animals—the rudiments which he retains—and the reversions to which he is liable, we can partly recall in imagination the former condition of our early progenitors; and can approximately place them in their proper position in the zoological series. We thus learn that man is descended from a hairy quadruped, furnished with a tail and pointed ears, probably arboreal in its habits, and an inhabitant of the Old World. This creature, if its whole structure had been examined by a naturalist, would have been classed among the Quadrumana, as surely as would the common and still more ancient progenitor of the Old and New World monkeys. . . .

The greatest difficulty which presents itself, when we are driven to the above conclusion on the origin of man, is the high standard of intellectual power and of moral disposition which he has attained. But every one who admits the general principle of evolution, must see that the mental powers of the higher animals, which are the same in kind with those of mankind, though so different in degree, are capable of advancement. Thus the interval between the mental powers of one of the higher apes and of a fish, or between those of an ant and scale-insect, is immense. The development of these powers in animals does not offer any special difficulty; for with our domesticated animals, the mental faculties are certainly variable, and the variations are inherited. No one doubts that these faculties are of the utmost importance to animals in a state of nature. Therefore the conditions are favorable for their development through natural selection. The same conclusion may be extended to man; the intellect must have been all-important to him, even at a very remote period, enabling him to use language, to invent and make weapons, tools, traps, etc.; by which means, in combination with his social habits, he long ago became the most dominant of all living creatures. . . .

The development of the moral qualities is a more interesting and difficult problem. Their foundation lies in the social instincts, including in this term the family ties. These instincts are of a highly-complex nature, and in the case of the lower animals give special tendencies toward certain definite actions; but the more important elements for us are love, and the distinct emotion of sympathy. Animals endowed with the social instincts take pleasure in each other's company, warn each other of danger, defend and aid each other in many ways. These instincts are not extended to all the individuals of the species, but only to those of the same community. As they are highly beneficial to the species, they have in all probability been acquired through natural selection.

A moral being is one who is capable of comparing his past and future actions and motives—of approving of some and disapproving of others;

and the fact that man is the one being who with certainty can be thus designated makes the greatest of all distinctions between him and the lower animals. But in our third chapter I have endeavored to show that the moral sense follows, firstly, from the enduring and always present nature of the social instincts, in which respect man agrees with the lower animals; and secondly, from his mental faculties being highly active and his impressions of past events extremely vivid, in which respects he differs from the lower animals. Owing to this condition of mind, man cannot avoid looking backward and comparing the impressions of past events and actions. He also continually looks forward. Hence after some temporary desire or passion has mastered his social instincts, he will reflect and compare the now weakened impression of such past impulses with the ever-present social instinct; and he will then feel that sense of dissatisfaction which all unsatisfied instincts leave behind them. Consequently he resolves to act differently for the future—and this is conscience.

The belief in God has often been advanced as not only the greatest, but the most complete, of all the distinctions between man and the lower animals. It is, however, impossible, as we have seen, to maintain that this belief is innate or instinctive in man. On the other hand, a belief in all-pervading spiritual agencies seems to be universal; and apparently follows from a considerable advance in the reasoning powers of man, and from a still greater advance in his faculties of imagination, curiosity, and wonder. I am aware that the assumed instinctive belief in God has been used by many persons as an argument for His existence. But this is a rash argument, as we should thus be compelled to believe in the existence of many cruel and malignant spirits, possessing only a little more power than man; for the belief in them is far more general than that of a beneficent Deity. The idea of a universal and beneficent Creator of the universe does not seem to arise in the mind of man, until he has been elevated by long-continued culture.

He who believes in the advancement of man from some lowly-organized form, will naturally ask, "How does this bear on the belief in the immortality of the soul?" The barbarous races of man, as Sir J. Lubbock has shown, possess no clear belief of this kind; but arguments derived from the primeval beliefs of savages are, as we have just seen, of little or no avail. Few persons feel any anxiety from the impossibility of determining at what precise period in the development of the individual, from the first trace of the minute germinal vesicle to the child either before or after birth, man becomes an immortal being; and there is no greater cause for anxiety because the period in the gradually-ascending organic scale cannot possibly be determined.

I am aware that the conclusions arrived at in this work will be denounced by some as highly irreligious; but he who thus denounces them is bound to show why it is more irreligious to explain the origin of man as a distinct species by descent from some lower form, through the laws of variation and natural selection, than to explain the birth of the individual through the laws of ordinary reproduction. The birth both of the species and of the individual are equally parts of that grand sequence of events, which our minds refuse to accept as the result of blind chance. The understanding revolts at such a conclusion, whether or not we are able to believe that every slight variation of structure, the union of each pair in marriage, the dissemination of each seed, and other such events, have all been ordained for some special purpose. . . .

The main conclusion arrived at in this work, namely, that man is descended from some lowly-organized form, will, I regret to think, be highly distasteful to many persons. But there can hardly be a doubt that we are descended from barbarians. The astonishment which I felt on first seeing a party of Fuegians on a wild and broken shore will never be forgotten by me, for the reflection at once rushed into my mind—such were our ancestors. These men were absolutely naked and bedaubed with paint, their long hair was tangled, their mouths frothed with excitement, and their expression was wild, startled, and distrustful. They possessed hardly any arts, and, like wild animals, lived on what they could catch; they had no government, and were merciless to every one not of their own small tribe. He who has seen a savage in his native land will not feel much shame, if forced to acknowledge that the blood of some more humble creature flows in his veins. For my own part, I would as soon be descended from that heroic little monkey, who braved his dreaded enemy in order to save the life of his keeper; or from that old baboon, who, descending from the mountains, carried away in triumph his young comrade from a crowd of astonished dogs—as from a savage who delights to torture his enemies, offers up bloody sacrifices, practices infanticide without remorse, treats his wives like slaves, knows no decency, and is haunted by the grossest superstitions.

Man may be excused for feeling some pride at having risen, though not through his own exertions, to the very summit of the organic scale; and the fact of his having thus risen, instead of having been aboriginally placed there, may give him hopes for a still higher destiny in the distant future. But we are not here concerned with hopes or fears, only with the truth as far as our reason allows us to discover it. I have given the evidence to the best of my ability; and we must acknowledge, as it seems to me, that man with all his noble qualities, with sympathy which feels for the most debased, with benevolence which extends not only to other men but to the humblest living creature, with his godlike intellect which has penetrated into the movements and constitution of the solar system —with all these exalted powers—Man still bears in his bodily frame the indelible stamp of his lowly origin.

ALFRED RUSSEL WALLACE: *Darwinism* *

Alfred Russel Wallace (1823–1913) was a naturalist who, along with Darwin, originated the theory of natural selection. While doing field work in the Moluccas, he says that he began to think about Malthus's *Essay on Population* and "there suddenly flashed upon me the idea of the survival of the fittest." Wallace wrote out his ideas and sent them to Darwin in England who recognized therein the thesis upon which he had been working for twenty years. "I never saw a more striking coincidence," Darwin wrote to the geologist, Sir Charles Lyell. Wallace's essay was read, together with an abstract of Darwin's thesis, as a joint paper at the Linnaean Society, July 1, 1858. The following selections are from Wallace's book *Darwinism: an Exposition of the Theory of Natural Selection with some of its Applications* (1889).

THE POINT I wish especially to urge is this. Before Darwin's work appeared, the great majority of naturalists, and almost without exception the whole literary and scientific world, held firmly to the belief that *species* were realities, and had not been derived from other species by any process accessible to us; the different species of crow and of violet were believed to have been always as distinct and separate as they are now, and to have originated by some totally unknown process so far removed from ordinary reproduction that it was usually spoken of as "special creation." There was, then, no question of the origin of families, orders, and classes, because the very first step of all, the "origin of species," was believed to be an insoluble problem. But now this is all changed. The whole scientific and literary world, even the whole educated public, accepts, as a matter of common knowledge, the origin of species from other allied species by the ordinary process of natural birth. The idea of special creation or any altogether exceptional mode of production is absolutely extinct! Yet more: this is held also to apply to many higher groups as well as to the species of a genus, and not even Mr. Darwin's severest critics venture to suggest that the primeval bird, reptile, or fish must have been "specially created." And this vast, this totally unprecedented change in public opinion has been the result of the work of one man, and was brought about in the short space of twenty years! . . . we claim for Darwin that he is the Newton of natural history, and that, just so surely as that the discovery and demonstration by Newton of the law of gravitation established order in place of chaos and laid a sure foundation for all future study of the starry heavens, so surely has Darwin, by his discovery of the law of natural selection and his demonstration of the great principle of the preservation of useful variations in the struggle for life, not only thrown a flood of light on the process of development of the whole organic world, but also established a firm foundation for all future study of nature.

* * *

The theory of natural selection rests on two main classes of facts which apply to all organised beings without exception, and which thus take rank as fundamental principles or laws. The first is, the power of rapid multiplication in a geometrical progression; the second, that the offspring always vary slightly from the parents, though generally very closely resembling them. From the first fact or law there follows, necessarily, a constant struggle for existence; because, while the offspring always exceed the parents in number, generally to an enormous extent, yet the total number of living organisms in the world does not, and cannot, increase year by year. Consequently every year, on the average, as many die as are born, plants as well as animals; and the majority die premature deaths. They kill each other in a thousand different ways; they starve each other by some consuming the food that others want; they are destroyed largely by the powers of nature—by cold and heat, by rain and storm, by flood and fire. There is thus a perpetual struggle among them which shall live and which shall die; and this struggle is tremendously severe, because so few can possibly remain alive—one in five, one in ten, often only one in a hundred or even one in a thousand.

Then comes the question, Why do some live rather that others? If all the individuals of each species were exactly alike in every respect, we could only say it is a matter of chance. But they are not alike. We find that they vary in many different ways. Some are stronger, some swifter, some hardier in constitution, some more cunning. An obscure colour may render concealment more easy for some, keener sight may enable others to discover prey or escape from an enemy better than their fellows. Among plants the smallest differences may be useful or the reverse. The earliest and strongest shoots may escape the slug; their greater vigour may enable them to flower and seed earlier in a wet autumn; plants best armed with spines or hairs may escape being devoured; those whose flowers are most conspicuous may be soonest fertilised by insects. We cannot doubt that, on the whole, any beneficial variations will give the possessors of it a greater probability of living through the tremendous ordeal they have to undergo. There may be something left to chance, but on the whole *the fittest will survive*.

* * *

Our exposition of the phenomena presented by the struggle for existence may be fitly concluded by a few remarks on its ethical aspect. Now that the war of nature is better known, it has been dwelt upon by many writers as presenting so vast an amount of cruelty and pain as to be revolting to our instincts of humanity, while it has proved a stumbling-block in the way of those who would fain believe in an all-wise and benevolent ruler of the universe. Thus, a brilliant writer says: "Pain, grief, disease, and death, are these the inventions of a loving God? That no animal shall rise to excellence except by being fatal to the life of others, is this the law of a kind Creator? It is useless to say that pain has its benevolence, that massacre has its mercy. Why is it so ordained that bad should be the raw material of good? Pain is not the less pain because it is useful; murder is not less murder because it is conducive to development. Here is blood upon the hand still, and all the perfumes of Arabia will not sweeten it."

Even so thoughtful a writer as Professor Huxley adopts similar views. In a recent article on "The Struggle for Existence" he speaks of the myriads of generations of herbivorous animals which "have been tormented and devoured by carnivores"; of the carnivores and herbivores alike "subject to all the miseries incidental to old age, disease, and over-multiplication"; and of the "more or less enduring suffering," which is the need of both vanquished and victor. And he concludes that, since thousands of times a minute, were our ears sharp enough, we should hear sighs and groans of pain like those heard by Dante at the gate of hell, the world cannot be governed by what we call benevolence.

Now there is, I think, good reason to believe that all this is greatly exaggerated; that the supposed "torments" and "miseries" of animals have little real existence, but are the reflection of the imagined sensations of cultivated men and women in similar circumstances; and that the amount of actual suffering caused by the struggle for existence among animals is altogether insignificant. Let us, therefore, endeavour to ascertain what are the real facts on which these tremendous accusations are founded.

In the first place, we must remember that animals are entirely spared the pain we suffer in the anticipation of death—a pain far greater, in most cases, than the reality.

*   *   *

We have a horror of all violent and sudden death, because we think of the life full of promise cut short, of hopes and expectations unfulfilled, and of the grief of mourning relatives. But all this is quite out of place in the case of animals, for whom a violent and a sudden death is in every way the best. Thus the poet's picture of

> "Nature red in tooth and claw
>   With ravine"

is a picture the evil of which is read into it by our imaginations, the reality being made up of full and happy lives, usually terminated by the quickest and least painful of deaths.

On the whole, then, we conclude that the popular idea of the struggle for existence entailing misery and pain on the animal world is the very reverse of the truth. What it really brings about, is, the maximum of life and of the enjoyment of life with the minimum of suffering and pain. Given the necessity of death and reproduction—and without these there could have been no progressive development of the organic world,—it is difficult even to imagine a system by which a greater balance of happiness could have been secured. And this view was evidently that of Darwin himself, who thus concludes his chapter on the struggle for existence: "When we reflect on this struggle, we may console ourselves with the full belief that the war of nature is not incessant, that no fear is felt, that death is generally prompt, and that the vigorous, the healthy, and the happy survive and multiply."

B. DARWINISM, PHILOSOPHY, AND RELIGION

Thomas Henry Huxley: *On Agnosticism and Evolutionary Ethics* *

The following selections are from three works by Thomas Henry Huxley (1825–95), a scientist of considerable reputation and known as "Darwin's Bulldog," that is, as the foremost champion of the new evolutionary hypothesis. The first, from an essay of 1889, tells how he came to invent the term "Agnosticism." The Metaphysical Society to which he refers was formed in 1869 to debate the great issue of the day: science and religion. The second, from another essay titled "An Episcopal Trilogy" (1887), comments on the superiority, in certain respects, of "scientific ethics" to the ethics of orthodox Christianity. Finally, in *Evolution and Ethics* (1893), Huxley comes to grips directly with the implications of evolution for morals. His conclusion, it should be noted, was rather different from that of Sir Leslie Stephen (see p. 568 this text).

On Agnosticism

When I reached intellectual maturity and began to ask myself whether I was an atheist, a theist, or a pantheist; a materialist or an

* Thomas Henry Huxley: *Essays upon Some Controverted Questions* (New York: D. Appleton & Co.; 1892), pp. 241–43, 276–78, 281–82; *Evolution and Ethics* (London: Macmillan & Co.; 1894), pp. 49–50, 78–83, 85–86.

idealist; a Christian or a freethinker; I found that the more I learned and reflected, the less ready was the answer; until, at last, I came to the conclusion that I had neither art nor part with any of these denominations, except the last. The one thing in which most of these good people were agreed was the one thing in which I differed from them. They were quite sure they had attained a certain "gnosis,"—had, more or less successfully, solved the problem of existence; while I was quite sure I had not, and had a pretty strong conviction that the problem was insoluble. . . .

This was my situation when I had the good fortune to find a place among the members of that remarkable confraternity of antagonists, long since deceased, but of green and pious memory, the Metaphysical Society. Every variety of philosophical and theological opinion was represented there, and expressed itself with entire openness; most of my colleagues were -*ists* of one sort or another; and, however kind and friendly they might be, I, the man without a rag of a label to cover himself with, could not fail to have some of the uneasy feelings which must have beset the historical fox when, after leaving the trap in which his tail remained, he presented himself to his normally elongated companions. So I took thought, and invented what I conceived to be the appropriate title of "agnostic." It came into my head as suggestively antithetic to the "gnostic" of Church history, who professed to know so much about the very things of which I was ignorant; and I took the earliest opportunity of parading it at our Society, to show that I, too, had a tail, like the other foxes. To my great satisfaction, the term took; and when the *Spectator* had stood godfather to it, any suspicion in the minds of respectable people, that a knowledge of its parentage might have awakened, was, of course, completely lulled. . . .

"It is, and it ought to be," authoritatively declares [an] official representative of Christian ethics, "an unpleasant thing for a man to have to say plainly that he does not believe in Jesus Christ."

Whether it is so depends, I imagine, a good deal on whether the man was brought up in a Christian household or not. I do not see why it should be "unpleasant" for a Mahommedan or Buddhist to say so. But that "it ought to be" unpleasant for any man to say anything which he sincerely, and after due deliberation, believes, is, to my mind, a proposition of the most profoundly immoral character. I verily believe that the great good which has been effected in the world by Christianity has been largely counteracted by the pestilent doctrine on which all the Churches have insisted, that honest disbelief in their more or less astonishing creeds is a moral offense, indeed a sin of the deepest dye, deserving and involving the same future retribution as murder and robbery. If we could only see, in one view, the torrents of hypocrisy and cruelty, the lies, the slaughter, the violations of every obligation of humanity, which have flowed from this source along the course of the history of Christian nations, our worst imaginations of Hell would pale beside the vision.

A thousand times, no! It ought *not* to be unpleasant to say that which one honestly believes or disbelieves. That it so constantly is painful to do so, is quite enough obstacle to the progress of mankind in that most valuable of all qualities, honesty of word or of deed, without erecting a sad concomitant of human weakness into something to be admired and cherished. The bravest soldiers often, and very naturally, "feel it unpleasant" to go into action; but a court-martial which did its duty would make shortwork of the officer who promulgated the doctrine that his men ought to feel their duty unpleasant. . . .

It appears that Mr. Gladstone some time ago asked Mr. Laing if he could draw up a short summary of the negative creed; a body of negative propositions, which have so far been adopted on the negative side as to be what the Apostles' and other accepted creeds are on the positive; and Mr. Laing at once kindly obliged Mr. Gladstone with the desired articles—eight of them.

If any one had preferred this request to me I should have replied that, if he referred to agnostics, they have no creed; and, by the nature of the case, can not have any. Agnosticism, in fact, is not a creed, but a method, the essence of which lies in the rigorous application of a single principle. That principle is of great antiquity; it is as old as Socrates; as old as the writer who said, "Try all things, hold fast by that which is good"; it is the foundation of the Reformation, which simply illustrated the axiom that every man should be able to give a reason for the faith that is in him; it is the great principle of Descartes; it is the fundamental axiom of modern science. Positively the principle may be expressed: In matters of the intellect follow your reason as far as it will take you without regard to any other consideration. And negatively: In matters of the intellect do not pretend that conclusions are certain which are not demonstrated or demonstrable. That I take to be the agnostic faith, which if a man keep whole and undefiled, he shall not be ashamed to look the universe in the face, whatever the future may have in store for him.

On Science and Religion

The so-called religious world is given to a strange delusion. It fondly imagines that it possesses the monopoly of serious and constant reflection upon the terrible problems of existence; and that those who can not accept its shibboleths are either mere Gallios, caring for none of these things, or libertines desiring to escape from the restraints of morality. It does not appear to have entered the imaginations of these people that, outside their pale and firmly resolved never to enter it, there are thousands of men, certainly not their inferiors in character, capacity, or knowledge of the questions at issue, who estimate those purely spiritual elements of the Christian faith of which the Bishop of Manchester speaks as highly as the Bishop does; but who will have nothing to do with the Christian Churches, because in their apprehension and for them, the profession of belief in the miraculous, on the evidence offered, would be simply immoral.

So far as my experience goes, men of science are neither better nor worse than the rest of the world. Occupation with the endlessly great parts of the universe does not necessarily involve greatness of character, nor does microscopic study of the infinitely little always produce humility. We have our full share of original sin; need, greed, and vainglory beset us as they do other mortals; and our progress is, for the most part, like that of a tacking ship, the resultant of opposite divergencies from the straight path. But, for all that, there is one moral benefit which the pursuit of science unquestionably bestows. It keeps the estimate of the value of evidence up to the proper mark; and we are constantly receiving lessons, and sometimes very sharp ones, on the nature of proof. Men of science will always act up to their standard of veracity, when mankind in general leave off sinning; but that standard appears to me to be higher among them than in any other class of the community.

I do not know any body of scientific men who could be got to listen without the strongest expressions of disgusted repudiation to the exposition of a pretended scientific discovery, which had no better evidence to show for itself than the story of the devils entering a herd of swine, or of the fig-tree that was blasted for bearing no figs when "it was not the season of figs." Whether such events are possible or impossible, no man can say; but scientific ethics can and does declare that the profession of belief in them, on the evidence of documents of unknown date and of unknown authorship, is immoral. Theological apologists who insist that morality will vanish if their dogmas are exploded, would do well to consider the fact that, in the matter of intellectual veracity, science is already a long way ahead of the Churches; and, that, in this particular, it is exerting an educational influence on mankind of which the Churches have shown themselves utterly incapable.

On Implications of Evolution

As no man fording a swift stream can dip his foot twice into the same water, so no man can, with exactness, affirm of anything in the sensible world that it is. As he utters the words, nay, as he thinks them, the predicate ceases to be applicable; the present has become the past; the "is" should be "was." And the more we learn of the nature of things, the more evident is it that what we call rest is only unperceived activity;

that seeming peace is silent but strenuous battle. In every part, at every moment, the state of the cosmos is the expression of a transitory adjustment of contending forces; a scene of strife, in which all the combatants fall in turn. What is true of each part, is true of the whole. Natural knowledge tends more and more to the conclusion that "all the choir of heaven and furniture of the earth" are the transitory forms of parcels of cosmic substance wending along the road of evolution, from nebulous potentiality, through endless growths of sun and planet and satellite; through all varieties of matter; through infinite diversities of life and thought; possibly, through modes of being of which we neither have a conception, nor are competent to form any, back to the indefinable latency from which they arose. Thus the most obvious attribute of the cosmos is its impermanence. It assumes the aspect not so much of a permanent entity as of a changeful process, in which naught endures save the flow of energy and the rational order which pervades it. . . .

We are more than sufficiently familiar with modern pessimism, at least as a speculation. . . . We also know modern speculative optimism, with its perfectibility of the species, reign of peace, and lion and lamb transformation scenes; but one does not hear so much of it as one did forty years ago; indeed, I imagine it is to be met with more commonly at the tables of the healthy and wealthy, than in the congregations of the wise. The majority of us, I apprehend, profess neither pessimism nor optimism. We hold that the world is neither so good, nor so bad, as it conceivably might be; and, as most of us have reason, now and again, to discover that it can be. Those who have failed to experience the joys that make life worth living are, probably, in as small a minority as those who have never known the griefs that rob existence of its savour and turn its richest fruits into mere dust and ashes.

Further, I think I do not err in assuming that, however diverse their views on philosophical and religious matters, most men are agreed that the proportion of good and evil in life may be very sensibly affected by human action. I never heard anybody doubt that the evil may be thus increased, or diminished; and it would seem to follow that good must be similarly susceptible of addition or subtraction. Finally, to my knowledge, nobody professes to doubt that, so far forth as we possess a power of bettering things, it is our paramount duty to use it and to train all our intellect and energy to this supreme service of our kind.

Hence the pressing interest of the question, to what extent modern progress in natural knowledge, and, more especially, the general outcome of that progress in the doctrine of evolution, is competent to help us in the great work of helping one another?

The propounders of what are called the "ethics of evolution," when the "evolution of ethics" would usually better express the object of their speculations, adduce a number of more or less interesting facts and more or less sound arguments, in favour of the origin of the moral sentiments, in the same way as other natural phenomena, by a process of evolution. I have little doubt, for my own part, that they are on the right track; but as the immoral sentiments have no less been evolved, there is, so far, as much natural sanction for the one as the other. The thief and the murderer follow nature just as much as the philanthropist. . . .

There is another fallacy which appears to me to pervade the so-called "ethics of evolution." It is the notion that because, on the whole, animals and plants have advanced in perfection of organization by means of the struggle for existence and the consequent "survival of the fittest"; there-fore men in society, men as ethical beings, must look to the same process to help them towards perfection. I suspect that this fallacy has arisen out of the unfortunate ambiguity of the phrase "survival of the fittest." "Fittest" has a connotation of "best"; and about "best" there hangs a moral flavour. In cosmic nature, however, what is "fittest" depends upon the conditions. Long since, I ventured to point out that if our hemi-sphere were to cool again, the survival of the fittest might bring about, in the vegetable kingdom, a population of more and more stunted and humbler and humbler organisms, until the "fittest" that survived might be nothing but lichens, diatoms, and such microscopic organisms as those which give red snow its colour; while, if it became hotter, the pleasant valleys of the Thames and Isis might be uninhabitable by any animated beings save those that flourish in a tropical jungle. They, as the fittest, the best adapted to the changed conditions, would survive.

Men in society are undoubtedly subject to the cosmic process. As among other animals, multiplication goes on without cessation, and involves severe competition for the means of support. The struggle for existence tends to eliminate those less fitted to adapt themselves to the circumstances of their existence. The strongest, the most self-assertive, tend to tread down the weaker. But the influence of the cosmic process on the evolution of society is the greater the more rudimentary its civilization. Social progress means a checking of the cosmic process at every step and the substitution for it of another, which may be called the ethical process; the end of which is not the survival of those who may happen to be the fittest, in respect of the whole of the conditions which obtain, but of those who are ethically the best.

As I have already urged, the practice of that which is ethically best—what we call goodness or virtue—involves a course of conduct which, in all respects, is opposed to that which leads to success in the cosmic struggle for existence. In place of ruthless self-assertion it de-mands self-restraint; in place of thrusting aside, or treading down, all competitors, it requires that the individual shall not merely respect, but shall help his fellows; its influence is directed, not so much to the survival of the fittest, as to the fitting of as many as possible to survive. It repudiates the gladiatorial theory of existence. . . .

It is from neglect of these plain considerations that the fanatical individualism of our time attempts to apply the analogy of cosmic nature to society. Once more we have a misapplication of the stoical injunction to follow nature; the duties of the individual to the state are forgotten, and his tendencies to self-assertion are dignified by the name of rights. It is seriously debated whether the members of a community are justified in using their combined strength to constrain one of their number to contribute his share to the maintenance of it; or even to prevent him from doing his best to destroy it. The struggle for existence, which has done such admirable work in cosmic nature, must, it appears, be equally beneficent in the ethical sphere. Yet if that which I have insisted upon is true; if the cosmic process has no sort of relation to moral ends; if the imitation of it by man is inconsistent with the first principles of ethics; what becomes of this surprising theory?

Let us understand, once for all, that the ethical progress of society depends, not on imitating the cosmic process, still less in running away from it, but in combating it. It may seem an audacious proposal thus to pit the microcosm against the macrocosm and to set man to subdue nature to his higher ends; but I venture to think that the great intellectual difference between the ancient times with which we have been occupied and our day, lies in the solid foundation we have acquired for the hope that such an enterprise may meet with a certain measure of success. . . .

The theory of evolution encourages no millennial anticipations. If, for millions of years, our globe has taken the upward road, yet, some time, the summit will be reached and the downward route will be commenced. The most daring imagination will hardly venture upon the suggestion that the power and the intelligence of man can ever arrest the procession of the great year.

Moreover, the cosmic nature born with us and, to a large extent, necessary for our maintenance, is the outcome of millions of years of severe training, and it would be folly to imagine that a few centuries will suffice to subdue its masterfulness to purely ethical ends. Ethical nature may count upon having to reckon with a tenacious and powerful enemy as long as the world lasts. But, on the other hand, I see no limit to the extent to which intelligence and will, guided by sound principles of investigation, and organized in common effort, may modify the conditions of existence, for a period longer than that now covered by history. And much may be done to change the nature of man himself. The intelligence which has converted the brother of the wolf into the faithful guardian of the flock ought to be able to do something towards curbing the instincts of savagery in civilized men.

But if we may permit ourselves a larger hope of abatement of the essential evil of the world than was possible to those who, in the infancy of exact knowledge, faced the problem of existence more than a score of centuries ago, I deem it an essential condition of the realization of that hope that we should cast aside the notion that the escape from pain and sorrow is the proper object of life.

We have long since emerged from the heroic childhood of our race, when good and evil could be met with the same "frolic welcome"; the attempts to escape from evil, whether Indian or Greek, have ended in flight from the battle-field; it remains to us to throw aside the youthful over-confidence and the no less youthful discouragement of nonage. We are grown men, and must play the man strong in will

> *To strive, to seek, to find, and not to yield,*

cherishing the good that falls in our way, and bearing the evil, in and around us, with stout hearts set on diminishing it. So far, we all may strive in one faith towards one hope:

> *It may be that the gulfs will wash us down,*
> *It may be we shall touch the Happy Isles,*
> *. . . but something ere the end,*
> *Some work of noble note may yet be done.*

ERNST HAECKEL: *The Riddle of the Universe* *

Ernst Haeckel (1834–1919), biologist and professor at the University of Jena, did for Darwinism in Germany what Thomas Henry Huxley had done for it in England. By his ceaseless propaganda, he assured its success, and in *Die Welträtsel* (1899) and other books, applied the doctrine of evolution to the problems of philosophy and religion. His philosophy of "monism," which asserted the unity of organic and inorganic nature, deriving everything, life itself, from the chemical properties of carbon, was widely popular in his day.

The Law of Substance

THE SUPREME and all-pervading law of nature, the true and only cosmological law, is, in my opinion, *the law of substance;* its discovery and establishment is the greatest intellectual triumph of the nineteenth cen-

---

tury, in the sense that all other known laws of nature are subordinate to it. Under the name of "law of substance" we embrace two supreme laws of different origin and age—the older is the chemical law of the "conservation of matter," and the younger is the physical law of the "conservation of energy.". . .

The *law of the "persistence"* or *"indestructibility of matter,"* established by Lavoisier in 1789, may be formulated thus: The sum of matter, which fills infinite space, is unchangeable. A body has merely changed its form, when it seems to have disappeared. When coal burns, it is changed into carbonic-acid gas by combination with the oxygen of the atmosphere; when a piece of sugar melts in water, it merely passes from the solid to the fluid condition. In the same way, it is merely a question of change of form in the cases where a new body seems to be produced. A shower of rain is the moisture of the atmosphere cast down in the form of drops of water; when a piece of iron rusts, the surface layer of the metal has combined with water and with atmospheric oxygen, and formed a "rust," or oxyhydrate of iron. Nowhere in nature do we find an example of the production, or "creation," of new matter; nowhere does a particle of existing matter pass entirely away. . . .

We may formulate the *"law of the persistence of force"* or *"conservation of energy"* thus: The sum of force, which is at work in infinite space and produces all phenomena, is unchangeable. When the locomotive rushes along the line, the potential energy of the steam is transformed into the kinetic or actual energy of the mechanical movement. . . . The whole marvellous panorama of life that spreads over the surface of our globe is, in the last analysis, transformed sunlight. It is well known how the remarkable progress of technical science has made it possible for us to convert the different physical forces from one form to another; heat may be changed into molar movement, or movement of mass; this in turn into light or sound, and then into electricity, and so forth. Accurate measurement of the quantity of force which is used in this metamorphosis has shown that it is "constant" or unchanged. No particle of living energy is ever extinguished; no particle is ever created anew.

* * *

Once modern physics had established the law of substance as far as the simpler relations of inorganic bodies are concerned, physiology took up the story, and proved its application to the entire province of the organic world. It showed that all the vital activities of the organism—without exception—are based on a constant "reciprocity of force" and a correlative change of material, or metabolism, just as much as the simplest processes in "lifeless" bodies. Not only the growth and the nutrition of plants and animals, but even their functions of sensation and movement, their sense-action and psychic life, depend on the conversion of potential into kinetic energy, and *vice versa*. This supreme law dominates also those elaborate performances of the nervous system which we call, in the higher animals and man, "the action of the mind."

Our monistic view, that the great cosmic law applies throughout the whole of nature, is of the highest moment. For it not only involves, on its positive side, the essential unity of the cosmos and the causal connection of all phenomena that come within our cognizance, but it also, in a negative way, marks the highest intellectual progress, in that it definitely rules out the three central dogmas of metaphysics—God, freedom, and immortality. In assigning mechanical causes to phenomena everywhere, the law of substance comes into line with the universal law of causality.

The Idea of "Design"

Astronomy, cosmogony, geology, meterology, and inorganic physics and chemistry are now absolutely ruled by mechanical laws on a mathematical foundation. The idea of "design" has wholly disappeared from this vast province of science. At the close of the nineteenth century, now that this monistic view has fought its way to general recognition, no scientist ever asks seriously of the "purpose" of any single phenomenon in the whole of this great field. Is any astronomer likely to inquire seriously to-day into the purpose of planetary motion, or a mineralogist to seek design in the structure of a crystal? Does the physicist investigate the purpose of electric force, or the chemist that of atomic weight? We may confidently answer in the negative—certainly not, in the sense that God, or a purposive natural force, had at some time created these fundamental laws of the mechanism of the universe with a definite design, and causes them to work daily in accordance with his rational will. The anthropomorphic notion of a deliberate architect and ruler of the world has gone forever from this field; the "eternal, iron laws of nature" have taken his place.

But the idea of design has a very great significance and application in the *organic* world. We do undeniably perceive a purpose in the structure and in the life of an organism. The plant and the animal seem to be controlled by a definite design in the combination of their several parts, just as clearly as we see in the machines which man invents and constructs; as long as life continues the functions of the several organs are directed to definite ends, just as is the operation of the various parts of a machine. Hence it was quite natural that the older naïve study of nature, in explaining the origin and activity of the living being, should postulate a creator who had "arranged all things with wisdom and understanding," and had constructed each plant and animal according to the special purpose of its life. The conception of this "almighty creator of heaven and earth" was usually quite anthropomorphic; he created "everything after its kind." As long as the creator seemed to man to be of human shape, to think with his brain, see with his eyes, and fashion with his hands, it was possible to form a definite picture of this "divine engineer" and his artistic work in the great workshop of creation. This was not so easy when the idea of God became refined, and man saw in his "invisible God" a creator without organs—a gaseous being. Still more unintelligible did these anthropomorphic ideas become when physiology substituted for the conscious, divine architect an unconscious, creative "vital force"—a mysterious, purposive, natural force, which differed from the familiar forces of physics and chemistry, and only took these in part, during life, into its service. This vitalism prevailed until about the middle of the nineteenth century. Johannes Müller, the great Berlin physiologist, was the first to menace it with a destructive dose of facts. It is true that the distinguished biologist had himself (like all others in the first half of the century) been educated in a belief in this vital force, and deemed it indispensable for an elucidation of the ultimate sources of life; nevertheless, in his classical and still unrivalled *Manual of Physiology* (1833) he gave a demonstrative proof that there is really nothing to be said for this vital force. Müller himself, in a long series of remarkable observations and experiments, showed that most of the vital processes in the human organism (and in the other animals) take place according to physical and chemical laws, and that many of them are capable of mathematical determination. That was no less true of the animal functions of the muscles and nerves, and of both the higher and the lower sense-organs, than of the vegetal functions of digestion, assimilation, and circulation. Only two branches of the life of the organism, mental action and reproduction, retained any element of mystery, and seemed inexplicable without assuming a vital force. But immediately after Müller's death such important discoveries and advances were made in these two branches that the uneasy "phantom of vital force" was driven from its last refuge. By a very remarkable coincidence Johannes Müller died in the year 1858, which saw the publication of Darwin's first communication concerning his famous theory. The theory of selection solved the great problem that had mastered Müller—the question of the origin of orderly arrangements from purely mechanical causes.

Darwin, as we have often said, had a twofold immortal merit in the field of philosophy—firstly, the reform of Lamarck's theory of descent, and its establishment on the mass of facts accumulated in the course of the half-century; secondly, the conception of the theory of selection, which first revealed to us the true causes of the gradual formation of species. Darwin was the first to point out that the "struggle for life" is the unconscious regulator which controls the reciprocal action of heredity and adaptation in the gradual transformation of species; it is the great "selective divinity" which, by a purely "natural choice," without preconceived design, creates new forms, just as selective man creates new types by an "artificial choice" with a definite design.

*   *   *

In the philosophy of history,—that is, in the general reflections which historians make on the destinies of nations and the complicated course of political evolution—there still, prevails the notion of a "moral order of the universe." Historians seek in the vivid drama of history a leading design, an ideal purpose, which has ordained one or other race or state to a special triumph, and to dominion over the others. This teleological view of history has recently become more strongly contrasted with our monistic view in proportion as monism has proved to be the only possible interpretation of inorganic nature. Throughout the whole of astronomy, geology, physics, and chemistry there is no question to-day of a "moral order," or a personal God, whose "hand hath disposed all things in wisdom and understanding." And the same must be said of the entire field of biology, the whole constitution and history of organic nature, if we set aside the question of man for the moment. Darwin has not only proved by his theory of selection that the orderly processes in the life and structure of animals and plants have arisen by mechanical laws without any preconceived design, but he has shown us in the "struggle for life" the powerful natural force which has exerted supreme control over the entire course of organic evolution for millions of years. It may be said that the struggle for life is the "survival of the fittest" or the "victory of the best"; that is only correct when we regard the strongest as the best (in a moral sense). Moreover, the whole history of the organic world goes to prove that, besides the predominant advance towards perfection, there are at all times cases of retrogression to lower stages. Even Baer's notion of "design" has no moral feature whatever.

Do we find a different state of things in the history of peoples, which man, in his anthropocentric presumption, loves to call "the history of the world"? Do we find in every phase of it a lofty moral principle or a wise ruler, guiding the destinies of nations? There can be but one answer in the present advanced stage of natural and human history: No. The fate of those branches of the human family, those nations and races which have struggled for existence and progress for thousands of years, is determined by the same "eternal laws of iron" as the history of the whole organic world which has peopled the earth for millions of years.

SIR LESLIE STEPHEN: *The Science of Ethics* *

Sir Leslie Stephen (1832–1904) was one of the great Victorian agnostics, and his agnosticism impelled him, as it did so many of his
contemporaries, to try to discover a new sanction for ethics. Why
should a man be good if he did not believe in God? Stephen thought
he had found the answer in Darwinian science. Note that his *Science
of Ethics* (1882) followed *An Agnostic's Apology* (1876), which
stated his religious position. While still a don at Cambridge, Stephen
had read John Stuart Mill, Comte, and Spencer, as well as Darwin, and
he lost his belief in Christianity. He became one of the most celebrated literary historians and critics of his generation.

My ethical theory, then, when I first became the conscious proprietor
of any theory at all, was that of the orthodox utilitarians. J. S. Mill was
the Gamaliel at whose feet I sat, and whose authority was decisive with
me on this as on other matters. In this, of course, I was simply following
the example of the majority of the more thoughtful lads of my own
generation. At a later period my mind was stirred by the great impulse
conveyed through Mr. Darwin's *Origin of Species*. I shall always, I
hope, be proud to acknowledge the great intellectual debt which I, in
common with so many worthier disciples, owe to his writings. So far as
ethical problems were concerned, I at first regarded Mr. Darwin's
principles rather as providing a new armoury wherewith to encounter
certain plausible objections of the so-called Intrusionists, than as implying any reconstruction of the utilitarian doctrine itself. Gradually, however, I came to think that a deeper change would be necessary, and I
believe that this conviction came to me from a study of some of Mr.
Herbert Spencer's works. It became stronger during a subsequent attempt at a brief historical examination of the English moralists of the
eighteenth century. Whilst I was finishing that task, I read Mr. Henry
Sidgwick's *Methods of Ethics*, then just published. As I differ upon
many points from Mr. Sidgwick, and especially upon the critical point
of the relation of evolution to ethics, I am the more bound to express my
sincere admiration for his book. It set me thinking when it failed to
make me think with him. The result of my thinking was a resolution to
set down as systematically as I could a statement of the ethical theory
which had commended itself to me. I resolved to begin at the beginning
as well as I could, and trudge steadily through the alternate platitudes
and subtleties into which every moralist must plunge. My views were, of
course, more or less modified in the process, and though they have not
substantially changed, I hope that they have gained in consistency and
clearness. At any rate, my labours are embodied in the following pages,

* Sir Leslie Stephen: *The Science of Ethics* (London: Smith, Elder, & Co.;
1882), pp. 31–33, 35, 120, 123, 370–71, 450, 456–60.

which may be briefly described as an attempt to lay down an ethical doctrine in harmony with the doctrine of evolution so widely accepted by modern men of science. . . .

The Social Organism

A full realisation of this truth, which is of course a very old truth in substance, a perception that society is not a mere aggregate but an organic growth, that it forms a whole, the laws of whose growth can be studied apart from those of the individual atom, supplies the most characteristic postulate of modern speculation, and we may note its general bearing upon the problem before us. . . .

What advantage is gained by accepting this theory? The first gain is the simple recognition that there must be laws, and that there may be discoverable laws of social growth which are essentially relevant to our investigation, but which previous methods of inquiry have tended to ignore. So long as reasoning has been conducted upon the tacit assumption that social phenomena can be satisfactorily explained by studying their constituent atoms separately, attention was diverted from some most important principles. If we could have studied the body on the assumption that each organ had an independent vitality which required no reference to the other organs to make its laws of growth intelligible, we should gain a good deal by simply recognising the existence of the whole organism. There are cases in which we may study a number of units separately, and thence infer the properties of a whole figured from such units. There are other cases in which the properties of each part are so dependent upon the whole that it is impossible to understand them separately without reference to the properties of the whole. If the problems of human conduct really fall under the second category, and if at the same time we assume them to belong to the first, we shall manifestly neglect some essential conditions. . . . The theory of evolution brings out the fact that every organism, whether social or individual, represents the product of an indefinite series of adjustments between the organism and its environment. . . .

We may apply this briefly to the special problem before us. That problem is, in fact, to discover the scientific form of morality, or, in other words, to discover what is the general characteristic, so far as science can grasp it, of the moral sentiments. . . .

Social Tissue

I will venture to speak—applying an obvious analogy—of social "tissue." The tissue is built up of men, as the tissue of physiology is said to be built up of cells. Every society is composed of such tissue; and the social tissue can no more exist apart from such associations than the physiological tissue exist apart from the organs of living animals. The

distinction does not correspond to things separable as concrete phenomena, nor can it be compared to the distinction between a coat and the
cloth of which it is made; for unorganised social tissue does not exist,
and the tissue develops new properties according to the mode in which
it is arranged. Thus, if you will, the distinction may be regarded as
merely a logical device; and yet, without taking into account in some
form or other the fact which it is intended to describe, it seems impossible to give an adequate account of the process which we have to
consider.

The process is the social evolution. The typical organism is by our
assumption that organism which is best fitted for all the conditions of
life, or in other words, which has the strongest vitality. . . .

It is indeed clear that this process does not exclude the action of the
"struggle for existence." An invention, that is to say, is propagated, in
part at least, because the possession gives an advantage to the possessors.
When one people has big guns or effective steam-engines, another
people makes them in order to hold its own in the commercial and
political competition. But there is the important difference that the other
race *can* make them. If some animals acquire better teeth, their rivals
cannot at once improve their teeth in order to meet the new difficulty;
but men in the same social state can adopt the same inventions. And,
moreover, the process takes place in great part by a direct method. A
new discovery spreads through the social tissue as a fermentation spreads
through a continuous fluid. It is always regulated by the struggle for
existence. Beliefs which give greater power to their holders have so far a
greater chance of spreading as pernicious beliefs would disappear by
facilitating the disappearance of their holders. . . .

The Evolutionist Criterion

In this sense the growth of the social organism is precisely analogous
to that of the individual. The development of the animal implies the
slow acquisition of new instincts, which in time become part of its
organic constitution. Whilst they are not fully organised they determine
its conduct more or less by the pain and pleasure with which they are
associated, and they tend to become fixed as they imply on the whole a
superior or more efficient form of organisation. The moral instincts of
the society correspond in the same way to the social development, and
express at every instant the judgment formed of the happiness and
misery caused by corresponding modes of conduct. As they become
organised the whole society becomes more efficiently constituted, and its
standard of happiness is also modified. We may therefore say that at any
period the utilitarian judgment must be satisfied. Given a certain stage of
social development, the society will be in a healthier state and the
general happiness greater in proportion as it is moral. But since the

happiness itself changes as the society develops, we cannot compare the two societies at different stages as if they were more or less efficient machines for obtaining an identical product. . . .

The evolution theory necessarily assumes a variation of morality, but not an indefinite or arbitrary variability. And this may lead us to a further question. We must admit, of course, that the calculus of happiness will give different results at different periods. Qualities will be regarded as virtuous amongst savages which cease to be virtuous amongst civilised men. . . .

Conclusions

The first principle which I have sought to establish is, briefly, that a moral rule is a statement of a condition of social welfare. Intemperance, according to me, is proved to be immoral by the same methods which prove it to be unwholesome. Scientific observation shows that it is productive of diseased states either of the individual or of society. In great part the arguments are identical, and though the moralist has to go into questions not considered by the physiologist, he still uses the same methods. . . .

I come to the final question about morality, and the most difficult. Must we not go to transcendental considerations in order to find a sufficient motive for moral conduct? This brings us back to the previous argument. To say what morality is—I repeat the statement once more—is by no means the same thing as to enforce morality. It is not when one is approaching the last page of an ethical essay that one can have any illusions upon that point. Undoubtedly a man may have very clear conceptions about the nature of morality, and yet may receive from that circumstance a very slight impulse towards being himself moral. . . . A man may be forced to comply with external morality by some appeal to extrinsic motives; but to make him really moral we must stimulate the intrinsic motives. . . .

Here, in fact, arises a vast problem or series of problems at which only the briefest glance is possible. The relation between morality and religion suggests at once whole libraries of controversy and lifetimes of investigation. . . .

. . . A religion, so far as it is moral (for, of course, many religions have a very questionable relation to morality), must act by stimulating the intrinsic motives to morality. Further, it can act only through the genuine belief which it embodies; and thus when we wish to estimate the effect of a religion upon morality, we come at once to a further problem.

In what sense, we have to ask, is a belief the ultimate condition of conduct? We may, as it is easy to see, fall into great difficulties, unless we can say also what governs the belief. . . .

This, of course, applies to the case of so-called religious sanctions. Is the dread of hell the cause of abstinence from vice? It may no doubt be the immediate cause for the individual. If a man believes that drunkards will be damned, that is for him a sufficient cause for abstaining; and if you prove to him that hell is a fiction, he may become a drunkard. But this is an obviously inadequate account of the whole phenomenon. If this belief in hell were the result of scientific inquiry, if the tendency of drunkenness to produce damnation were proved like its tendency to produce delirium tremens, the explanation would be sufficient. We should say simply that the existence of a known place of torment was one of the causes which limited drunkenness. But if hell be an imaginary place we must necessarily go further. People are afraid of being damned for drunkenness, and therefore they do not drink. But why do they anticipate damnation as a consequence of drunkenness? Obviously they must think it hateful for some independent reason. They think that drunkards will be damned because they think drunkenness hateful; or at any rate, the belief in the damnation of drunkards has arisen from a perception of its other evil consequences. The supposed ultimate ground, therefore, of the dislike is itself a corollary from the dislike. We must distinguish between the social and the individual creed. A given person may be influenced solely by the belief which he has accepted from his neighbours, whether it be true or false. But the belief has been developed in the society from a perception of the evil, and is a product of that perception, not the determining cause.

Thus the true statement of the case will be, upon my theory, that the limiting and determining cause of the moral objection to vice is in all cases measured by the perception of the social evils which it causes. Whilst the society is permeated by a belief in the supernatural, this perception has to express itself in terms of the supernatural sanction. . . . But as the belief in such interference decays, the perception of the pernicious consequences which expressed itself in terms of hell may use a different language without being therefore less efficacious. . . .

C. SOCIAL DARWINISM

SIDNEY WEBB: *Fabian Essays in Socialism* *

The following two selections represent two different types of "social Darwinism." In the first, taken from Sidney Webb's historical essay in *Fabian Essays in Socialism* (1889), the idea of evolution, but not natural selection, is applied to social theory. Of course, Darwin was not the only influence on Webb (1859–1947). Webb was one of the

* From *Fabian Essays in Socialism*, pp. 29–33, 37–40, 43, 46–47, 52–57. Copyright 1931 by G. B. Shaw. Reprinted by permission of George Allen & Unwin Ltd.

founders of the Fabian Society and, like all Fabian socialists, was dedicated to "gradualism" rather than to socialism by revolution.

The Development of the Democratic Ideal

OWING mainly to the efforts of Comte, Darwin, and Herbert Spencer, we can no longer think of the ideal society as an unchanging State. The social ideal from being static has become dynamic. The necessity of the constant growth and development of the social organism has become axiomatic. No philosopher now looks for anything but the gradual evolution of the new order from the old, without breach of continuity or abrupt change of the entire social tissue at any point during the process. The new becomes itself old, often before it is consciously recognized as new. . . .

History not only gives the clue to the significance of contemporary events; it also enables us to understand those who have not yet found that clue. We learn to class men and ideas in a kind of geological order in time. The Comte de Paris gives us excellent proofs that in absolute monarchy lies the only safety of social order. He is a survival: the type flourished in the sixteenth century; and the splendid fossils of that age can be studied in any historic museum. Lord Bramwell will give cogent reasons for the belief that absolute freedom of contract, subject to the trifling exception of a drastic criminal law, will ensure a perfect State. His lordship is a survival from a nearer epoch: about 1840 this was as far as social science had got; and there are still persons who have learnt nothing of later date. . . .

The main stream which has borne European society towards Socialism during the past 100 years is the irresistible progress of Democracy. . . . There is every day a wider consensus that the inevitable outcome of Democracy is the control by the people themselves, not only of their own political organization, but, through that, also of the main instruments of wealth production; the gradual substitution of organized cooperation for the anarchy of the competitive struggle. . . . The economic side of the democratic ideal is, in fact, Socialism itself.

The Period of Anarchy

The result of the industrial revolution, with its dissolution of mediaevalism amid an impetuous reaction against the bureaucratic tyranny of the past, was to leave all the new elements of society in a state of unrestrained license. Individual liberty, in the sense of freedom to privately appropriate the means of production, reached its maximum at the commencement of the century. . . .

But this "acute outbreak of individualism, unchecked by the old restraints, and invested with almost a religious sanction by a certain soulless school of writers," was inevitable, after the economic blundering of governments in the eighteenth century. Prior to the scientific investigation of economic laws, men had naturally interfered in social arrangements with very unsatisfactory results. . . .

And so grew up the doctrine of what Professor Huxley has since called "Administrative Nihilism." It was the apotheosis of *Laisser Faire, Laisser Aller*.

The Intellectual and Moral Revolt, and Its Political Outlook

The first man who really made a dint in the individualist shield was Carlyle, who knew how to compel men to listen to him. Oftener wrong than right in his particular proposals, he managed to keep alive the faith in nobler ends than making a fortune in this world and saving one's soul in the next. Then came Maurice, Kingsley, Ruskin, and others who dared to impeach the current middle class cult; until finally, through Comte and John Stuart Mill, Darwin and Herbert Spencer, the conception of the Social Organism has at last penetrated to the minds, though not yet to the books, even of our professors of Political Economy.

Meanwhile, caring for none of these things, the practical man had been irresistibly driven in the same direction. In the teeth of the current Political Economy, and in spite of all the efforts of the millowning Liberals, England was compelled to put forth her hand to succour and protect her weaker members. Any number of Local Improvement Acts, Drainage Acts, Truck Acts, Mines Regulation Acts, Factory Acts, Public Health Acts, Adulteration Acts, were passing into law. . . .

Even in the fields still abandoned to private enterprise, its operations are thus every day more closely limited, in order that the anarchic competition of private greed, which at the beginning of the century was set up as the only infallibly beneficent principle of social action, may not utterly destroy the State. All this has been done by "practical" men, ignorant, that is to say, of any scientific sociology believing Socialism to be the most foolish of dreams, and absolutely ignoring, as they thought, all grandiloquent claims for social reconstruction. Such is the irresistible sweep of social tendencies, that in their every act they worked to bring about the very Socialism they despised; and to destroy the Individualist faith which they still professed. They builded better than they knew. . . .

The general failure to realize the extent to which our unconscious Socialism has already proceeded . . . is due to the fact that few know anything of local administration outside their own town. It is the municipalities which have done most to "socialize" our industrial life; and the municipal history of the century is yet unwritten. . . . Most of us know that the local governments have assumed the care of the roads, streets and bridges, once entirely abandoned to individual enterprise, as well as the lighting and cleansing of all public thoroughfares, and the provision of sewers, drains, and "storm-water courses.". . . It is in the provision of gas, water, and tramways, that local authorities organize labor on a large scale. . . .

The New Synthesis

It need hardly be said that the social philosophy of the time did not remain unaffected by the political evolution and the industrial development. Slowly sinking into men's minds all this while was the conception of a new social nexus, and a new end of social life. It was discovered (or rediscovered) that a society is something more than an aggregate of so many individual units—that it possesses existence distinguishable from those of any of its components. . . . Without the continuance and sound health of the social organism, no man can now live or thrive; and its persistence is accordingly his paramount end. His conscious motive for action may be, nay always must be, individual to himself; but where such action proves inimical to the social welfare, it must sooner or later be checked by the whole, lest the whole perish through the error of its member. The conditions of social health are accordingly a matter for scientific investigation. There is, at any moment, one particular arrangement of social relations which involves the minimum of human misery then and there possible amid the "niggardliness of nature." Fifty years ago it would have been assumed that absolute freedom in the sense of individual or "manly" independence, plus a criminal code, would spontaneously result in such an arrangement for each particular nation; and the effect was the philosophic apotheosis of *Laisser Faire*. To-day every student is aware that no such optimistic assumption is warranted by the facts of life. We know now that in natural selection at the stage of development where the existence of civilized mankind is at stake, the units selected from are not individuals, but societies. . . .

If we desire to hand on to the afterworld our direct influence, and not merely the memory of our excellence, we must take even more care to improve the social organism of which we form part, than to perfect our own individual developments. Or rather, the perfect and fitting development of each individual is not necessarily the utmost and highest cultivation of his own personality, but the filling, in the best possible way, of his humble function in the great social machine. We must abandon the self-conceit of imagining that we are independent units, and bend our jealous minds, absorbed in their own cultivation, to this subjection to the higher end, the Common Weal. . . .

The results of this development of Sociology is to compel a revision of the relative importance of liberty and equality as principles to be kept in view in social administration. In Bentham's celebrated "ends" to be aimed at in a civil code, liberty stands predominant over equality, on the ground that full equality can be maintained only by the loss of security for the fruits of labor. That exposition remains as true as ever; but the question for decision remains, how much liberty? . . . [The Benthamite] cannot escape the lesson of the century, taught alike by the economists, the statesmen, and the "practical men," that complete individual liberty, with unrestrained private ownership of the instruments of wealth production, is irreconcileable with the common weal. The free struggle for existence among ourselves menaces our survival as a healthy and permanent social organism. Evolution, Professor Huxley declares, is the substitution of consciously regulated co-ordination among the units of each organism, for blind anarchic competition. . . .

It was inevitable that the Democracy should learn this lesson. With the masses painfully conscious of the failure of Individualism to create a decent social life for four-fifths of the people, it might have been foreseen that Individualism could not survive their advent to political power. If private property in land and capital necessarily keeps the many workers permanently poor (through no fault of their own) in order to make the few idlers rich (from no merit of their own), private property in land and capital will inevitably go the way of the feudalism which it superseded. The economic analysis confirms the rough generalization of the suffering people. The history of industrial evolution points to the same result; and for two generations the world's chief ethical teachers have been urging the same lesson. No wonder the heavens of Individualism are rolling up before our eyes like a scroll and even the Bishops believe and tremble.

KARL PEARSON: *National Life from the Standpoint of Science* *

Karl Pearson's address to the Literary and Philosophical Society of Newcastle (November 19, 1900) begins with the question: Why had the British Empire suffered such military reverses earlier in the year in the Boer War? What had gone wrong, and how could the nation provide against graver crises in the future "when great nation meets great nation"? The answer, Pearson thought, was provided by Darwinian science. Pearson (1857–1936), it should be noted, was no crackpot chauvinist but one of England's foremost scientists, a professor of applied mathematics and mechanics and later of eugenics at University College, London, and the author of the widely read *Grammar of Science* (1892), which came out of his lectures.

* Karl Pearson: *National Life from the Standpoint of Science* (London: Adam and Charles Black; 1901), pp. 13–25, 34–5, 41–4. Used by permission of Adam and Charles Black Ltd.

FROM the standpoint of science there are two questions we can, or, rather, we *must*, ask. First: What, from the scientific standpoint, is the function of a nation? What part from the natural history aspect does the national organization play in the universal struggle for existence? And, secondly, What has science to tell us of the best methods of fitting the nation for its task?

To answer the latter question at all effectually, we must first consider what is the proper answer to be given to the former. I shall therefore endeavour to lay in broad outlines before you what I hold to be the scientific view of a nation, and of the relationship of nations to each other. . . .

I want you to look with me for awhile on mankind as a product of Nature, and subject to the natural influences which form its environment. I will, first, notice a point which bears upon man as upon all forms of animal life. The characters of both parents—their virtues, their vices, their capabilities, their tempers, their diseases—all devolve in due proportion upon their children. Some may say, "Oh yes; but we know such things are inherited." I fear that the great majority of the nation does not realize what inheritance means, or much that happens now would not be allowed to happen. Our knowledge of heredity has developed enormously in the last few years; it is no longer a vague factor of development, to be appealed to vaguely. Its intensity in a great variety of characters in a great many forms of life has been quantitatively determined, and we no longer stand even where we did ten years ago. The form of a man's head, his stature, his eye-colour, his temper, the very length of his life, the coat colour of horses and dogs, the form of the capsule of the poppy, the spine of the water-flea, these and other things are all inherited, and in approximately the same manner. Nay, if we extend the notion of like producing like, we shall find, as I have recently done, that the same laws are probably true for the mushroom and for the forest tree; that the principle of heredity runs with certainly no weakened intensity from the lowest to the highest organisms, and from their least to their most important characters. . . .

Now, if we once realize that this law of inheritance is as inevitable as the law of gravity, we shall cease to struggle against it. This does not mean a fatal resignation to the presence of bad stock, but a conscious attempt to modify the percentage of it in our own community and in the world at large. . . .

What I have said about bad stock seems to me to hold for the lower races of man. How many centuries, how many thousands of years, have the Kaffir and the Negro held large districts in Africa undisturbed by the white man? Yet their inter-tribal struggles have not yet produced a civilization in the least comparable with the Aryan. Educate and nurture them as you will, I do not believe that you will succeed in modifying the stock. History shows me one way, and one way only, in which a high state of civilization has been produced, namely, the struggle of race with race, and the survival of the physically and mentally fitter race. If you want to know whether the lower races of man can evolve a higher type, I fear the only course is to leave them to fight it out among themselves, and even then the struggle for existence between individual and individual, between tribe and tribe, may not be supported by that physical selection due to a particular climate on which probably so much of the Aryan's success depended.

If you bring the white man into contact with the black, you too often suspend the very process of natural selection on which the evolution of a higher type depends. . . .

You may possibly think that I am straying from my subject, but I want to justify natural selection to you. I want you to see selection as something which renders the inexorable law of heredity a source of progress, which produces the good through suffering, an infinitely greater good which far out-balances the very obvious pain and evil. Let us suppose the alternative were possible. Let us suppose we could prevent the white man, if we liked, from going to lands of which the agricultural and mineral resources are not worked to the full; then I should say a thousand times better for him that he should not go than that he should settle down and live alongside the inferior race. The only healthy alternative is that he should go, and completely drive out the inferior race. That is practically what the white man has done in North America. We sometimes forget the light that chapter of history throws on more recent experiences. Some 250 years ago there was a man who fought in our country against taxation without representation, and another man who did not mind going to prison for the sake of his religious opinions. As Englishmen we are proud of them both, but we sometimes forget that they were both considerable capitalists for their age, and started chartered companies in another continent. Well, a good deal went on in the plantations they founded, if not with their knowledge, with that at least of their servants and of their successors, which would shock us at the present day. But I venture to say that no man calmly judging will wish either that the whites had never gone to America, or would desire that whites and Red Indians were to-day living alongside each other as negro and white in the Southern States, as Kaffir and European in South Africa, still less that they had mixed their blood as Spaniard and Indian in South America. The civilization of the white man is a civilization dependent upon free white labour, and when that element of stability is removed it will collapse like those of Greece and Rome. I venture to assert, then, that the struggle for existence between white and red man, painful and even terrible as it was in its details, has given us a good far outbalancing its immediate evil. In place of the red man, contributing practically nothing to the work and thought of the world, we have a great nation, mistress of many arts, and able, with its youthful imagination and fresh, untrammelled impulses, to contribute much to the common stock of civilized man. Against that you have only to put the romantic sympathy for the Red Indian generated by the novels of Cooper and the poems of Longfellow, and then—see how little it weighs in the balance! . . .

. . . The struggle means suffering, intense suffering, while it is in progress; but that struggle and that suffering have been the stages by which the white man has reached his present stage of development, and they account for the fact that he no longer lives in caves and feeds on roots and nuts. This dependence of progress on the survival of the fitter race, terribly black as it may seem to some of you, gives the struggle for existence its redeeming features; it is the fiery crucible out of which comes the finer metal. You may hope for a time when the sword shall be turned into the plough-share, when American and German and English traders shall no longer compete in the markets of the world for their raw material and for their food supply, when the white man and the dark shall share the soil between them, and each till it as he lists. But, believe me, when that day comes, mankind will no longer progress; there will be nothing to check the fertility of inferior stock; the relentless law of heredity will not be controlled and guided by natural selection. Man will stagnate; and unless he ceases to multiply, the catastrophe will come again; famine and pestilence, as we see them in the East, physical selection instead of the struggle of race against race, will do the work more relentlessly, and, to judge from India and China, far less efficiently than of old. . . .

Here, I think, is the point where we reach the second great function of science in national life. The first function is to show us what national life means, and how the nation is a vast organism subject as much to the great forces of evolution as any other gregarious type of life. There is a struggle of race against race and of nation against nation. In the early days of that struggle it was a blind, unconscious struggle of barbaric tribes. At the present day, in the case of the civilized white man, it has become more and more the conscious, carefully directed attempt of the nation to fit itself to a continuously changing environment. The nation has to foresee how and where the struggle will be carried on; the maintenance of national position is becoming more and more a conscious preparation for changing conditions, an insight into the needs of coming environments.

This is the second important duty of science in relation to national life. It has to develop our brain-power by providing a training in method and by exercising our powers of cautious observation. It has to teach not only the leaders of our national life, but the people at large, to prepare for and meet the difficulties of new environments. . . .

It may be as well now to sum up my position as far as I have yet developed it. I have asked you to look upon the nation as an organized whole in continual struggle with other nations, whether by force of arms or by force of trade and economic processes. I have asked you to look upon this struggle of either kind as a not wholly bad thing; it is the source of human progress throughout the world's history. But if a nation is to maintain its position in this struggle, it must be fully provided with trained brains in every department of national activity, from the government to the factory, and have, if possible, *a reserve of brain and physique* to fall back upon in times of national crisis. . . .

You will see that my view—and I think it may be called the scientific view of a nation—is that of an organized whole, kept up to a high pitch of internal efficiency by insuring that its numbers are substantially recruited from the better stocks, and kept up to a high pitch of external efficiency by contest, chiefly by way of war with inferior races, and with equal races by the struggle for trade-routes and for the sources of raw material and of food supply. . . .

D. THE NEW NATIONALISM AND RACISM

HEINRICH VON TREITSCHKE: *Politics* *

It is not suggested that the following two selections were connected directly with Darwinism. The new bellicose nationalism and racism were, however, contemporary with, and flourished in, the Darwinian world. Nor should it be inferred that they were peculiar to Germans. Nevertheless, Heinrich von Treitschke (1834–96), historian and university professor, was one of the chief exponents of the new nationalism. A liberal in his youth, he devoted his mature years to extolling the mission of Prussia to unify Germany and of Bismarck's united Germany to lead Europe and the world. His magnum opus was his *History of Germany in the Nineteenth Century* (first volume 1879). The following selections are from his lectures on politics and the state, delivered at Berlin in the 1880's and 1890's.

THE STATE is the people, legally united as an independent entity. By the word "people" we understand briefly a number of families permanently

* From Heinrich von Treitschke: *Politics*, Blanche Dugdale and Torben de Bille (trans.), Vol. I, pp. 3–4, 10, 12–15, 19–24, 26, 28–29, 33–34, 60–61, 64–67. Copyright 1916 by Constable & Company Limited. Reprinted by permission of Constable & Company Limited.

living side by side. This definition implies that the State is primordial and necessary, that it is as enduring as history, and no less essential to mankind than speech. History, however, begins for us with the art of writing; earlier than this men's conscious recollection of the past cannot be reckoned with. Therefore everything which lies beyond this limit is rightly judged to be prehistoric. We, on the other hand, must deal here with man as an historical being, and we can only say that creative political genius is inherent in him, and that the State, like him, subsists from the beginning. The attempt to present it as something artificial, following upon a natural condition, has fallen completely into discredit. We lack all historical knowledge of a nation without a constitution. Wherever Europeans have penetrated they have found some form of State organization, rude though it may have been. This recognition of the primordial character of the State is very widespread at the present day, but was in fact discovered in the eighteenth century. Eichhorn, Niebuhr, and Savigny were the first to show that the State is the constituted people. It was indeed a familiar fact to the Ancients in their great and simple Age. For them the State was a divinely appointed order, the origins of which were not subject to inquiry.

*   *   *

If, then, political capacity is innate in man, and is to be further developed, it is quite inaccurate to call the State a necessary evil. We have to deal with it as a lofty necessity of Nature. Even as the possibility of building up a civilization is dependent upon the limitation of our powers combined with the gift of reason, so also the State depends upon our inability to live alone. This Aristotle has already demonstrated. The State, says he, arose in order to make life possible; it endured to make good life possible.

*   *   *

Ultramontanes and Jacobins both start with the assumption that the legislation of a modern State is the work of sinful man. They thus display their total lack of reverence for the objectively revealed Will of God, as unfolded in the life of the State.

*   *   *

. . . if we simply look upon the State as intended to secure life and property to the individual, how comes it that the individual will also sacrifice life and property to the State? It is a false conclusion that wars are waged for the sake of material advantage. Modern wars are not fought for the sake of booty. Here the high moral ideal of national honour is a factor handed down from one generation to another, enshrining something positively sacred, and compelling the individual to sacrifice himself to it. This ideal is above all price and cannot be reduced to pounds, shillings, and pence. Kant says, "Where a price can be paid, an equivalent can be substituted. It is that which is above price and which consequently admits of no equivalent, that possesses real value." Genuine patriotism is the consciousness of co-operating with the body-politic, of being rooted in ancestral achievements and of transmitting them to descendants. Fichte has finely said, "Individual man sees in his country the realisation of his earthly immortality."

This involves that the State has a personality, primarily in the juridical, and secondly in the politico-moral sense.

*　　*　　*

Treat the State as a person, and the necessary and rational multiplicity of States follows. Just as in individual life the ego implies the existence of the non-ego, so it does in the State. The State is power, precisely in order to assert itself as against other equally independent powers. War and the administration of justice are the chief tasks of even the most barbaric States. But these tasks are only conceivable where a plurality of States are found existing side by side. Thus the idea of one universal empire is odious—the ideal of a State co-extensive with humanity is no ideal at all. In a single State the whole range of culture could never be fully spanned; no single people could unite the virtues of aristocracy and democracy. All nations, like all individuals, have their limitations, but it is exactly in the abundance of these limited qualities that the genius of humanity is exhibited. The rays of the Divine light are manifested, broken by countless facets among the separate peoples, each one exhibiting another picture and another idea of the whole. Every people has a right to believe that certain attributes of the Divine reason are exhibited in it to their fullest perfection. . . .

The features of history are virile, unsuited to sentimental or feminine natures. Brave peoples alone have an existence, an evolution or a future; the weak and cowardly perish, and perish justly. The grandeur of history lies in the perpetual conflict of nations, and it is simply foolish to desire the suppression of their rivalry. Mankind has ever found it to be so. The Kingdoms of the Diadochi and the hellenized nations of the East were the natural reaction from the world-empire of Alexander. The extreme one-sidedness of the idea of nationality which has been formed during our century by countries big and small is nothing but the natural revulsion against the world-empire of Napoleon. The unhappy attempt to transform the multiplicity of European life into the arid uniformity of universal sovereignty has produced the exclusive sway of nationality as the dominant political idea. Cosmopolitanism has receded too far.

These examples show clearly that there is no prospect of a settlement of international contradictions. The civilization of nations as well as of individuals tends to specialization. The subtleties of personal character assert themselves proportionately to increase of culture, and with its growth even the differences between nations become more sharply defined. In spite of the increased facilities of communications between different countries, no blending of their peculiarities has taken place; on the contrary, the more delicate distinctions of national character are far more marked to-day than in the Middle Ages. . . .

Further, if we examine our definition of the State as "the people legally united as an independent entity," we find that it can be more briefly put thus: "The State is the public force for Offence and Defence." It is, above all, Power which makes its will to prevail, it is not the totality of the people as Hegel assumes in his deification of it. The nation is not entirely comprised in the State, but the State protects and embraces the people's life, regulating its external aspects on every side. It does not ask primarily for opinion, but demands obedience, and its laws must be obeyed, whether willingly or no. . . .

The State is not an Academy of Arts. If it neglects its strength in order to promote the idealistic aspirations of man, it repudiates its own nature and perishes. This is in truth for the State equivalent to the sin against the Holy Ghost, for it is indeed a mortal error in the State to subordinate itself for sentimental reasons to a foreign Power, as we Germans have often done to England.

We have described the State as an independent force. This pregnant theory of independence implies firstly so absolute a moral supremacy that the State cannot legitimately tolerate any power above its own, and secondly a temporal freedom entailing a variety of material resources adequate to its protection against hostile influences. Legal sovereignty, the State's complete independence of any other earthly power, is so rooted in its nature that it may be said to be its very standard and criterion. . . .

The notion of sovereignty must not be rigid, but flexible and relative, like all political conceptions. Every State, in treaty making, will limit its power in certain directions for its own sake. States which conclude treaties with each other thereby curtail their absolute authority to some extent. But the rule still stands, for every treaty is a voluntary curb upon the power of each, and all international agreements are prefaced by the clause "Rebus sic stantibus." No State can pledge its future to another. It knows no arbiter, and draws up all its treaties with this implied reservation. This is supported by the axiom that so long as international law exists all treaties lose their force at the very moment when war is declared between the contracting parties; moreover, every sovereign State has the undoubted right to declare war at its pleasure, and is consequently entitled to repudiate its treaties. Upon this constantly recurring alteration of treaties the progress of history depends; every State must take care that its treaties do not survive their effective value, lest another Power should denounce them by a declaration of war; for antiquated treaties must necessarily be denounced and replaced by others more consonant with circumstances.

It is clear that the international agreements which limit the power of a State are not absolute, but voluntary self-restrictions. Hence, it follows that the establishment of a permanent international Arbitration Court is incompatible with the nature of the State, which could at all events only accept the decision of such a tribunal in cases of second- or third-rate importance. When a nation's existence is at stake there is no outside Power whose impartiality can be trusted.

*　　*　　*

If we apply the test of "autarchy" we perceive that, as Europe is now constituted, the larger States are constantly gaining influence in proportion as our international system assumes a more and more aristocratic complexion. The time is not yet very distant when the adhesion or withdrawal of such States as Piedmont and Savoy could actually decide the fate of a coalition. To-day such a thing would be impossible. Since the Seven Years' War the domination of the five great Powers has been necessarily evolved. The big European questions are decided within this circle. Italy is on the verge of being admitted into it, but neither Belgium, Sweden, nor Switzerland have a voice unless their interests are directly concerned.

The entire development of European polity tends unmistakeably to drive the second-rate Powers into the background. . . .

On close examination then, it becomes clear that if the State is power, only that State which has power realizes its own idea, and this accounts for the undeniably ridiculous element which we discern in the existence of a small State. Weakness is not itself ridiculous, except when masquerading as strength.

*　　*　　*

When we begin to consider the aim of the State we are immediately confronted with the old vexed question which has needlessly fretted both the learned and the ignorant, namely—Should we look upon it as a means towards the private ends for which its citizens strive, or are those citizens means towards the great national ends of the State? The severely political outlook of the ancient world favoured the second alternative; the first is maintained by the modern social conception of the State, and the eighteenth century believed itself to have discovered in it the theory that the State should be treated only as an instrument to promote the aims of its citizens.

But, as Falstaff would say, this is "a question not to be asked," for ever since it has been considered at all, it has been universally agreed that the rights and duties of the State and its members are reciprocal. There can be no two opinions on that point. But parties which are bound together by mutual obligations and rights cannot stand to each other in the relations of means to an end, for means only exist to serve an end, and there can be no reciprocity between them. The Christian point of view has destroyed the ancient conception of the State, and the Christian would be false to himself if he did not reserve that immortal and intransitory something, which we call conscience, as his own private and peculiar possession.

In one of his greatest books, *The Foundations of the Metaphysics of Ethics*, Kant logically develops the principle that no human being may be used merely as an instrument, thereby recognizing the divinely appointed dignity of man. Conversely, to regard the State as nothing but a means for the citizens' ends is to place the subjective aspect too high. The greatness of the State lies precisely in its power of uniting the past with the present and the future; and consequently no individual has the right to regard the State as the servant of his own aims but is bound by moral duty and physical necessity to subordinate himself to it, while the State lies under the obligation to concern itself with the life of its citizens by extending to them its help and protection.

*   *   *

The next essential function of the State is the conduct of war. The long oblivion into which this principle had fallen is a proof of how effeminate the science of government had become in civilian hands. In our century this sentimentality was dissipated by Clausewitz, but a one-sided materialism arose in its place, after the fashion of the Manchester school, seeing in man a biped creature, whose destiny lies in buying cheap and selling dear. It is obvious that this idea is not compatible with war, and it is only since the last war that a sounder theory arose of the State and its military power.

Without war no State could be. All those we know of arose through war, and the protection of their members by armed force remains their primary and essential task. War, therefore, will endure to the end of history, as long as there is multiplicity of States. The laws of human thought and of human nature forbid any alternative, neither is one to be wished for. The blind worshipper of an eternal peace falls into the error of isolating the State, or dreams of one which is universal, which we have already seen to be at variance with reason.

Even as it is impossible to conceive of a tribunal above the State, which we have recognized as sovereign in its very essence, so it is likewise impossible to banish the idea of war from the world. It is a favourite fashion of our time to instance England as particularly ready for peace. But England is perpetually at war; there is hardly an instant in her recent history in which she has not been obliged to be fighting somewhere. The great strides which civilization makes against barbarism and unreason are only made actual by the sword. Between civilized nations also war is the form of litigation by which States make their claims valid. The arguments brought forward in these terrible law suits of the nations compel as no argument in civil suits can ever do. Often as we have tried by theory to convince the small States that Prussia alone can be the leader in Germany, we had to produce the final proof upon the battlefields of Bohemia and the Main.

Moreover war is a uniting as well as a dividing element among nations; it does not draw them together in enmity only, for through its means they learn to know and to respect each other's peculiar qualities. . . .

The grandeur of war lies in the utter annihilation of puny man in the great conception of the State, and it brings out the full magnificence of the sacrifice of fellow-countrymen for one another. In war the chaff is winnowed from the wheat. Those who have lived through 1870 cannot fail to understand Niebuhr's description of his feelings in 1813, when he speaks of how no one who has entered into the joy of being bound by a common tie to all his compatriots, gentle and simple alike, can ever forget how he was uplifted by the love, the friendliness, and the strength of that mutual sentiment.

It is war which fosters the political idealism which the materialist rejects. What a disaster for civilization it would be if mankind blotted its heroes from memory. The heroes of a nation are the figures which rejoice and inspire the spirit of its youth, and the writers whose words ring like trumpet blasts become the idols of our boyhood and our early manhood. He who feels no answering thrill is unworthy to bear arms for his country.

HOUSTON STEWART CHAMBERLAIN: *Foundations of the Nineteenth Century* *

Houston Stewart Chamberlain (1855–1926) was the son of a British admiral who adopted Germany as his country. Devoted to Wagner's music, he took up residence in Bayreuth and married the composer's daughter. In the *Foundations of the Nineteenth Century* (1899), which was written in German, he appears as a champion of Pan-Teutonism rather than the narrower Pan-Germanism of Dr. Ernst Hasse and the Pan-German League. The book sold widely in Germany and was popular at a later date with the Nazis.

RANKE had prophesied that our century would be a century of nationality; that was a correct political prognostic, for never before have the
nations stood opposed to each other so clearly and definitely as antagonistic unities. It has, however, also become a century of races, and that
indeed is in the first instance a necessary and direct consequence of
science and scientific thinking. I have already said at the beginning of
this introduction that science does not unite but dissects. That statement
has not contradicted itself here. Scientific anatomy has furnished such
conclusive proofs of the existence of physical characteristics distinguishing the races from each other that they can no longer be denied;
scientific philology has discovered between the various languages fundamental differences which cannot be bridged over; the scientific study of
history in its various branches has brought about similar results, especially by the exact determination of the religious history of each race, in
which only the most general of general ideas can raise the illusion of
similarity, while the further development has always followed and still
follows definite, sharply divergent lines. The so-called unity of the
human race is indeed still honoured as a hypothesis, but only as a
personal, subjective conviction lacking every material foundation. The
ideas of the eighteenth century with regard to the brotherhood of
nations were certainly very noble but purely sentimental in their origin;
and in contrast to these ideas to which the Socialists still cling, limping
on like reserves in the battle, stern reality has gradually asserted itself as
the necessary result of the events and investigations of our time.

*   *   *

To this day these two powers—Jews and Teutonic races—stand, wherever the recent spread of the Chaos has not blurred their features, now
as friendly, now as hostile, but always as alien forces face to face.

In this book I understand by "Teutonic peoples" the different North-
European races, which appear in history as Celts, Teutons (Germanen)
and Slavs, and from whom—mostly by indeterminable mingling—the
peoples of modern Europe are descended. It is certain that they belonged originally to a single family, as I shall prove in the sixth chapter;
but the Teuton in the narrower Tacitean sense of the word has proved
himself so intellectually, morally and physically pre-eminent among his
kinsmen, that we are entitled to make his name summarily represent the
whole family. The Teuton is the soul of our culture. Europe of to-day,
with its many branches over the whole world, represents the chequered
result of an infinitely manifold mingling of races: what binds us all
together and makes an organic unity of us is "Teutonic" blood. If we
look around, we see that the importance of each nation as a living power
to-day is dependent upon the proportion of genuinely Teutonic blood in
its population. Only Teutons sit on the thrones of Europe.—What

preceded in the history of the world we may regard as Prolegomena; true history, the history which still controls the rhythm of our hearts and circulates in our veins, inspiring us to new hope and new creation, begins at the moment when the Teuton with his masterful hand lays his grip upon the legacy of antiquity.

* * *

And as if the scientific rearing of animals and plants did not afford us an extremely rich and reliable material, whereby we may become acquainted not only with the conditions but with the importance of "race"! Are the so-called (and rightly so-called) "noble" animal races, the draught-horses of Limousin, the American trotter, the Irish hunter, the absolutely reliable sporting dogs, produced by chance and promiscuity? Do we get them by giving the animals equality of rights, by throwing the same food to them and whipping them with the same whip? No, they are produced by artificial selection and strict maintenance of the purity of the race. Horses and especially dogs give us every chance of observing that the intellectual gifts go hand in hand with the physical; this is specially true of the moral qualities: a mongrel is frequently very clever, but never reliable; morally he is always a weed. Continual promiscuity between two pre-eminent animal races leads without exception to the destruction of the pre-eminent characteristics of both. Why should the human race form an exception? . . . In spite of the broad common foundation, the human races are, in reality, as different from one another in character, qualities, and above all, in the degree of their individual capacities, as greyhound, bull-dog, poodle and Newfoundland dog. Inequality is a state towards which nature inclines in all spheres; nothing extraordinary is produced without "specialisation"; in the case of men, as of animals, it is this specialisation that produces noble races; history and ethnology reveal this secret to the dullest eye. Has not every genuine race its own glorious, incomparable physiognomy? . . .

If the men who should be the most competent to pronounce an opinion on the essence and significance of Race show such an incredible lack of judgment—if in dealing with a subject where wide experience is necessary for sure perception, they bring to bear upon it nothing but hollow political phrases—how can we wonder that the unlearned should talk nonsense even when their instinct points out the true path? For the subject has in these days aroused interest in widely various strata of society, and where the learned refuse to teach, the unlearned must shift for themselves. When in the fifties Count Gobineau published his brilliant work on the inequality of the races of mankind, it passed unnoticed: no one seemed to know what it all meant. Like poor Virchow men stood puzzled before a riddle. Now that the Century has come to an end things have changed: the more passionate, more impulsive element in the nations pays great and direct attention to this question.

*   *   *

Nothing is so convincing as the consciousness of the possession of Race. The man who belongs to a distinct, pure race, never loses the sense of it. The guardian angel of his lineage is ever at his side, supporting him where he loses his foothold, warning him like the Socratic Daemon where he is in danger of going astray, compelling obedience, and forcing him to undertakings which, deeming them impossible, he would never have dared to attempt. Weak and erring like all that is human, a man of this stamp recognises himself, as others recognise him, by the sureness of his character, and by the fact that his actions are marked by a certain simple and peculiar greatness, which finds its explanation in his distinctly typical and super-personal qualities. Race lifts a man above himself: it endows him with extraordinary—I might almost say supernatural—powers, so entirely does it distinguish him from the individual who springs from the chaotic jumble of peoples drawn from all parts of the world: and should this man of pure origin be perchance gifted above his fellows, then the fact of Race strengthens and elevates him on every hand, and he becomes a genius towering over the rest of mankind, not because he has been thrown upon the earth like a flaming meteor by a freak of nature, but because he soars heavenward like some strong and stately tree, nourished by thousands and thousands of roots—no solitary individual, but the living sum of untold souls striving for the same goal.

*   *   *

There is one point which I have not expressly formulated, but it is self-evident from all that I have said; the conception of Race has nothing in it unless we take it in the narrowest and not in the widest sense: if we follow the usual custom and use the word to denote far remote hypothetical races, it ends by becoming little more than a colourless synonym for "mankind"—possibly including the long-tailed and short-tailed apes: Race only has a meaning when it relates to the experiences of the past and the events of the present.

Here we begin to understand what nation signifies for race. It is almost always the nation, as a political structure, that creates the conditions for the formation of race or at least leads to the highest and most individual activities of race.

*   *   *

. . . since race is not a mere word, but an organic living thing, it follows as a matter of course that it never remains stationary; it is ennobled or it degenerates, it develops in this or that direction and lets this or that quality decay. This is a law of all individual life. But the firm national union is the surest protection against going astray: it signifies common memory, common hope, common intellectual nourishment; it fixes firmly the existing bond of blood and impels us to make it ever closer.

4. *Toward the Twentieth Century*

FRIEDRICH NIETZSCHE: *On the Death of God* *

The German philosopher Friedrich Nietzsche (1844–1900) descried and described better than almost any of his contemporaries the major changes that were overtaking the European mind toward the end of the–nineteenth century. Some of these changes he welcomed, and others, such as the new nationalism, he deplored. On the "Death of God," discussed at some length in *The Gay Science* (1882) from which the following excerpts are taken, he was ambivalent. He himself was quite cheerful about it, but at the same time he foresaw extremely hard times for a culture trying to live without a religion and without the morality dependent upon religion. There are hints all through these powerful passages of Nietzsche's own "philosophy of power," to be developed more fully the following year in his tone poem *Thus Spoke Zarathustra.*

108.

New Struggles.—After Buddha was dead people showed his shadow for centuries afterwards in a cave,—an immense frightful shadow. God is dead: but as the human race is constituted, there will perhaps be caves for millenniums yet, in which people will show his shadow.—And we—we have still to overcome his shadow!

124.

In the Horizon of the Infinite.—We have left the land and have gone aboard ship! We have broken down the bridge behind us,—nay, more, the land behind us! Well, little ship! look out! Beside thee is the ocean; it is true it does not always roar, and sometimes it spreads out like silk and gold and a gentle reverie. But times will come when thou wilt feel that it is infinite, and that there is nothing more frightful than infinity. Oh, the poor bird that felt itself free, and now strikes against the walls of this

* From *The Complete Works of Friedrich Nietzsche*, Dr. Oscar Levy (ed.) (New York: The Macmillan Company; 1924), Vol. X, pp. 151, 167–69, 275–76, 285–87, 308–09, 342–43, 345–46. Used by permission of George Allen and Unwin Ltd.

cage! Alas, if homesickness for the land should attack thee, as if there had been more *freedom* there,—and there is no "land" any longer!

125.

The Madman.—Have you ever heard of the madman who on a bright morning lighted a lantern and ran to the market-place calling out unceasingly: "I seek God! I seek God!"—As there were many people standing about who did not believe in God, he caused a great deal of amusement. Why! is he lost? said one. Has he strayed away like a child? said another. Or does he keep himself hidden? Is he afraid of us? Has he taken a sea-voyage? Has he emigrated?—the people cried out laughingly, all in a hubbub. The insane man jumped into their midst and transfixed them with his glances. "Where is God gone?" he called out. "I mean to tell you! *We have killed him,*—you and I! We are all his murderers! But how have we done it? How were we able to drink up the sea? Who gave us the sponge to wipe away the whole horizon? What did we do when we loosened this earth from its sun? Wither does it now move? Wither do we move? Away from all suns? Do we not dash on unceasingly? Backwards, sideways, forwards, in all directions? Is there still an above and below? Do we not stray, as through infinite nothingness? Does not empty space breathe upon us? Has it not become colder? Does not night come on continually, darker and darker? Shall we not have to light lanterns in the morning? Do we not hear the noise of the grave-diggers who are burying God? Do we not smell the divine putrefaction?—for even Gods putrefy! God is dead! God remains dead! And we have killed him! How shall we console ourselves, the most murderous of all murderers? The holiest and the mightiest that the world has hitherto possessed, has bled to death under our knife,—who will wipe the blood from us? With what water could we cleanse ourselves? What lustrums, what sacred games shall we have to devise? Is not the magnitude of this deed too great for us? Shall we not ourselves have to become Gods, merely to seem worthy of it? There never was a greater event,—and on account of it, all who are born after us belong to a higher history than any history hitherto!"—Here the madman was silent and looked again at his hearers; they also were silent and looked at him in surprise. At last he threw his lantern on the ground, so that it broke in pieces and was extinguished. "I come too early," he then said, "I am not yet at the right time. This prodigious event is still on its way, and is travelling,—it has not yet reached men's ears. Lightning and thunder need time, the light of the stars needs time, deeds need time, even after they are done, to be seen and heard. This deed is as yet further from them than the furthest star,—*and yet they have done it!*"—It is further stated that the madman made his way into different churches on the same day, and there intoned his *Requiem aeternam deo.*

When led out and called to account, he always gave the reply: "What are these churches now, if they are not the tombs and monuments of God?"

343.

What our Cheerfulness Signifies.—The most important of more recent events—that "God is dead," that the belief in the Christian God has become unworthy of belief—already begins to cast its first shadows over Europe. To the few at least whose eye, whose *suspecting* glance, is strong enough and subtle enough for this drama, some sun seems to have set, some old, profound confidence seems to have changed into doubt: our old world must seem to them daily more darksome, distrustful, strange and "old." In the main, however, one may say that the event itself is far too great, too remote, too much beyond most people's power of apprehension, for one to suppose that so much as the report of it could have *reached* them; not to speak of many who already knew *what* had taken place, and what must all collapse now that this belief had been undermined,—because so much was built upon it, so much rested on it, and had become one with it: for example, our entire European morality. This lengthy, vast and uninterrupted process of crumbling, destruction, ruin and overthrow which is now imminent: who has realised it sufficiently to-day to have to stand up as the teacher and herald of such a tremendous logic of terror, as the prophet of a period of gloom and eclipse, the like of which has probably never taken place on earth before? . . . Even we, the born riddle-readers, who wait as it were on the mountains posted 'twixt to-day and to-morrow, and engirt by their contradiction, we, the firstlings and premature children of the coming century, into whose sight especially the shadows which must forthwith envelop Europe *should* already have come—how is it that even we, without genuine sympathy for this period of gloom, contemplate its advent without any *personal* solicitude or fear? Are we still, perhaps, too much under the *immediate effects* of the event—and are these effects, especially as regards *ourselves*, perhaps, the reverse of what was to be expected—not at all sad and depressing, but rather like a new and indescribable variety of light, happiness, relief, enlivenment, encouragement, and dawning day? . . . In fact, we philosophers and "free spirits" feel ourselves irradiated as by a new dawn by the report that the "old God is dead"; our hearts overflow with gratitude, astonishment, presentiment and expectation. At last the horizon seems open once more, granting even that it is not bright; our ships can at last put out to sea in face of every danger; every hazard is again permitted to the discerner; the sea, *our* sea, again lies open before us; perhaps never before did such an "open sea" exist.

347.

Believers and their Need of Belief.—How much *faith* a person requires in order to flourish, how much "fixed opinion" he requires which he does not wish to have shaken, because he *holds* himself thereby—is a measure of his power (or more plainly speaking, of his weakness). Most people in old Europe, as it seems to me, still need Christianity at present, and on that account it still finds belief. For such is man: a theological dogma might be refuted to him a thousand times,—provided, however, that he had need of it, he would again and again accept it as "true,"—according to the famous "proof of power" of which the Bible speaks. Some have still need of metaphysics; but also the impatient *longing for certainty* which at present discharges itself in scientific, positivist fashion among large numbers of the people, the longing by all means to get at something stable (while on account of the warmth of the longing the establishing of the certainty is more leisurely and negligently undertaken):—even this is still the longing for a hold, a support; in short, the *instinct of weakness*, which, while not actually creating religions, metaphysics, and convictions of all kinds, nevertheless—preserves them. In fact, around all these positivist systems there fume the vapours of a certain pessimistic gloom, something of weariness, fatalism, disillusionment, and fear of new disillusionment—or else manifest animosity, ill-humour, anarchic exasperation, and whatever there is of symptom or masquerade of the feeling of weakness. . . . Belief is always most desired, most pressingly needed, where there is a lack of will: for the will, as emotion of command, is the distinguishing characteristic of sovereignty and power. That is to say, the less a person knows how to command, the more urgent is his desire for that which commands, and commands sternly,—a God, a prince, a caste, a physician, a confessor, a dogma, a party conscience. From whence perhaps it could be inferred that the two world-religions, Buddhism and Christianity, might well have had the cause of their rise, and especially of their rapid extension, in an extraordinary *malady of the will.* And in truth it has been so: both religions lighted upon a longing, monstrously exaggerated by malady of the will, for an imperative, a "Thou-shalt," a longing going the length of despair; but religions were teachers of fanaticism in times of slackness of will-power, and thereby offered to innumerable persons a support, a new possibility of exercising will, an enjoyment in willing. For in fact fanaticism is the sole "volitional strength" to which the weak and irresolute can be excited, as a sort of hypnotising of the entire sensory-intellectual system, in favour of the over-abundant nutrition (hypertrophy) of a particular point of view and a particular sentiment, which then dominates—the Christian calls it his *faith.* When a man arrives at the fundamental conviction that he *requires* to be commanded, he becomes "a believer." Reversely, one could imagine a delight and a power of self-determining, and a *freedom* of will, whereby a spirit could bid farewell to every belief, to every wish for certainty, accustomed as it would be to support itself on slender cords and possibilities, and to dance even on the verge of abysses. Such a spirit would be the *free spirit par excellence.*

357.

. . . To look upon nature as if it were a proof of the goodness and care of a God; to interpret history in honour of a divine reason, as a constant testimony to a moral order in the world and a moral final purpose; to explain personal experiences as pious men have long enough explained them, as if everything were a dispensation or intimation of Providence, something planned and sent on behalf of the salvation of the soul: all that is now *past*, it has conscience *against* it, it is regarded by all the more acute consciences as disreputable and dishonourable, as mendaciousness, femininism, weakness, and cowardice,—by virtue of this severity, if by anything, we are *good* Europeans, the heirs of Europe's longest and bravest self-conquest. When we thus reject the Christian interpretation, and condemn its "significance" as a forgery, we are immediately confronted in a striking manner with the *Schopenhauerian* question: *Has existence then a significance at all?*—the question which will require a couple of centuries even to be completely heard in all its profundity.

377.

We Homeless Ones.—Among the Europeans of to-day there are not lacking those who may call themselves homeless ones in a way which is at once a distinction and an honour; it is by them that my secret wisdom and *gaya scienza* is especially to be laid to heart! For their lot is hard, their hope uncertain; it is a clever feat to devise consolation for them. But what good does it do! We children of the future, how *could* we be at home in the present? We are unfavourable to all ideals which could make us feel at home in this frail, broken-down, transition period; and as regards the "realities" thereof, we do not believe in their *endurance*. The ice which still carries has become very thin: the thawing wind blows; we ourselves, the homeless ones, are an agency that breaks the ice, and the other too thin "realities." . . . We "preserve" nothing, nor would we return to any past age. . . . We are, in a word—and it shall be our word of honour!—*good Europeans*, the heirs of Europe, the rich, over-wealthy heirs, but too deeply obligated heirs of millenniums of European thought. As such, we have also outgrown Christianity, and are disinclined to it—and just because we have grown *out of* it, because our forefathers were Christians uncompromising in their Christian integrity, who willingly sacrificed possessions and positions, blood and country, for the sake of their belief. We—do the same. For what, then? For our unbelief? For all sorts of unbelief? Nay, you know better than that, my friends! The hidden *Yea* in you is stronger than all the Nays and Perhapses, of which you and your age are sick; and when you are obliged to put out to sea, you emigrants, it is—once more a *faith* which urges you thereto! . . .

WILHELM DILTHEY: *On Historical Relativism* *

The following brief excerpts from two treatises by Wilhelm Dilthey (1833–1911), the philosopher and historian of ideas, call attention to a problem that was understandably beginning to disturb some of the best minds toward the close of the nineteenth century. This problem, relativism (the relativity of men's ideas and convictions), stemmed from the growth of historicism or the historical spirit. Dilthey himself claimed to view this relativism as a "liberation" from fixed beliefs and absolutes. But even he admitted, toward the end of his life, the "anarchy of world views" into which the study of history had plunged the modern mind. Dilthey succeeded to Hegel's chair in philosophy at the University of Berlin in 1882.

"THE knife of historical relativism," I continued, "which has cut to pieces all metaphysics and religion, must also bring healing." . . .

"All *Weltanschauungen* arise from the objectification of the ways in which living man, perceiving and thinking, feeling and desiring, seeking to have his way with things, experiences the world. From the countless points of view in the sequence of generations arise objectifications without number. If someone of unprejudiced mind wishes to combine all that he can relive in himself, if he desires to look the world in the face in order to understand its inwardness, he is confronted by features which refuse to blend in a single interpretation." . . .

Every solution of the philosophical problems belongs from a historical point of view to a particular date and a particular situation at that date: man, the creature of time, so long as he works in time, finds the security of his existence in the fact that he lifts his creations out of the stream of time as something lasting: this illusion gives to his creative work a greater joy and power. Herein lies the perpetual contradiction between creative minds and the historical consciousness. It is natural to them to wish to forget the past and to disregard the better future that is coming: but the historical consciousness lives in the comprehension of all ages,

* From H. A. Hodges: *Wilhelm Dilthey: An Introduction* (New York: Oxford University Press; 1944), pp. 154–56. Reprinted by permission of Routledge & Kegan Paul Ltd.

and it observes in all creativity of individuals the accompanying relativity and transience. This contradiction is the secret trouble which present-day philosophy is silently bearing. . . .

But if for these reasons no metaphysic can satisfy the demands for scientific proof, yet philosophy still retains a firm point in the relation between the subject and his world, by virtue of which each attitude of the subject brings to expression one side of the universe. Philosophy cannot comprehend the world in its essence by means of a metaphysical system, and set forth this knowledge in a way that is universally valid; but as in all serious poetry there is disclosed an aspect of life which has not been seen before, as poetry in this way reveals to us the various sides of life in ever new works, as we do not possess a comprehensive view of life in any work of art and yet approximate to it by means of them all: so in the typical outlooks of philosophy we meet a world such as it appears when a powerful philosophical personality makes one of the attitudes to it predominate over the others and subordinates the other categories to the categories native to the one attitude. Thus from all the enormous labour of the metaphysical mind there remains the historical consciousness, which repeats that labour in itself and so experiences in it the inscrutable depths of the world. The last word of the mind which has run through all the outlooks is not the relativity of them all, but the sovereignty of the mind in face of each one of them, and at the same time the positive consciousness of the way in which, in the various attitudes of the mind, the one reality of the world exists for us.

ERNEST RENAN: *Second Thoughts about Science* *

> In 1845 Ernest Renan (1823–92) abruptly left the seminary of St. Sulpice in Paris, a convert, as he himself tells us, from Catholicism to "science." Three years later he wrote an optimistic book entitled *The Future of Science*, which, however, was not published until much later. The new preface of 1890 shows that by then Renan had second thoughts about science, not as "the only legitimate means of knowing," but for what science could be expected to know and for its effect on society. Renan, one of France's leading intellectuals and a great oriental scholar, is best known for his *Life of Jesus* (1863).

. . . My religion is now as ever the progress of reason, in other words the progress of science. But in looking over these pages of my youth, I often found a certain confusion which distorted certain deductions. . . .

The main error with which these old pages teem is an exaggerated

* Ernest Renan: *The Future of Science* (Boston: Roberts Brothers; 1891), pp. x, xii, xiv–xv, xviii–xx.

optimism which fails or is determined not to see that evil still exists and that we have to pay dearly, that is in privileges, the power that protects us against this evil. . . .

In attempting to strike a balance between what has remained merely so much vision and what has been realized in those dreams of half a century ago I must confess to a feeling of appreciable moral satisfaction. After all, I was right. Excepting a few disappointments progress has travelled on the lines laid down in my imagination. . . .

I perceived well enough that everything is accomplished in humanity and nature, that creation has no part nor parcel in the series of effects and causes. Too little of a naturalist to track the paths of life in the labyrinth which we see without seeing it, I was a determined evolutionist in all that appertains to the productions of humanity, language, literature, social forms, writings. I began to perceive that the morphological draughtboard of the vegetal and animal species was indeed the indication of a genesis; that everything is born in accordance with a design of which we can only see the obscure canvas. The aim of science is an immense development of which the cosmological sciences give us the first perceptible links, of which history proper shows us the last expansions. Like Hegel I made the mistake of being too confident in attributing to mankind a central part in the universe.

The whole of human development may be of no more consequence than the moss or lichen with which every moist surface is covered. To us, though, the history of man stands first and foremost, seeing that humanity alone creates the conscience of the universe. . . .

Historical science and its auxiliaries, philological sciences, have made immense conquests since I took to them so fondly forty years ago. . . .

The history of religion has been cleared up in its most important branches. It has become patent, not from *a priori* arguments, but from the very discussion of evidence that in the centuries open to men's researches there has been neither revelation nor supernatural fact. . . .

To sum up; if through the constant labour of the nineteenth century the knowledge of facts has considerably increased, the destiny of mankind has on the other hand become more obscure than ever. The serious thing is that we fail to perceive a means of providing humanity in the future with a catechism that will be acceptable henceforth, except on the condition of returning to a state of credulity. Hence, it is possible that the ruin of idealistic beliefs may be fated to follow hard upon the ruin of supernatural beliefs and that the real abasement of the morality of humanity will date from the day it has seen the reality of things. Chimeras have succeeded in obtaining from the good gorilla an astonishing moral effort; do away with the chimeras and part of the factitious energy they aroused will disappear. Even glory, as a motive-power implies in some respects immortality, the fruit of it generally coming only after death. Suppress the alcohol on which the workman has hitherto relied for his strength, but you must not ask him for the same amount of work.

Candidly speaking, I fail to see how, without the ancient dreams, the foundations of a happy and noble life are to be relaid. The hypothesis that the true sage would be he who, barring to himself all distant horizons, would confine himself to the perspective of mere vulgar gratification, this perspective, I say, is absolutely repugnant to us. However, man's happiness and noble aims have rested before now on false foundations. The wisest thing to do, then, is to go on enjoying the supreme gifts vouchsafed to us, life and the faculty of seeing the reality. Science will always remain the gratification of the noblest craving of our nature; curiosity; it will always supply man with the sole means of improving his lot. It protects him against error, though it may not reveal the truth to him, but there is an advantage in being certain of not being duped. Man fashioned according to this discipline is on the whole a better man than the instinctive man of the ages of faith. He is not subject to the errors to which the uncultured fatally yield, he is more enlightened, he commits fewer crimes, he is less sublime, but he is also less ridiculous. All this, it will be said, is not worth the heaven science takes away from us. First of all, who knows whether it does take it away; secondly people are none the poorer for being robbed of bogus shares and false banknotes. A little true science is better than a great deal of bad science. One is less liable to error by confessing one's ignorance than by fancying that one knows a great many things one knows not. . . .

Alfred Fouillée: *The Reaction against Positivism* *

> In the book from which these excerpts are taken, the French philosopher Alfred Fouillée (1838–1912) sums up admirably the philosophic climate of the late nineteenth century, especially the reaction that had set in, and the reasons why, against positivism. What makes Fouillée's account so valuable is that he himself was an eye witness and participant in the movement he describes. In his own work Fouillée strove to mediate between idealism and positivism. Among his best known works are *La liberté et le déterminisme* (1872), a subject then much in debate, and a number of books dealing with his central idea of the *idée-force* or the influence of ideas in history.

Never has philosophic teaching excited greater interest among youth than at the present time. . . . Like literature, philosophy has had its

* Alfred Fouillée: *Le mouvement idéaliste et la réaction contre la science positive*, Franklin Le Van Baumer (trans.) (Paris: Ancienne Librairie Germer Baillière et Cie; 1896), pp. vi, x–xi, xiii–xv, xvii–xix, xxi–xxvi, xxix.

symbolists and decadents; but if, underneath the exaggerations and deviations, one tries to penetrate to the real meaning of the present-day movement, one can say that in the domain of philosophy as in all others, *it is idealist.* . . .

If we go back to the origins of the contemporary movement we find that the most striking phenomenon, in the first half of our century, was the rise of positivist and humanitarian philosophy, brought into being by the scientific and social advances of the preceding century. The rapid progress of science, which had just come into possession of its true methods, and the parallel discrediting of theology and abstract metaphysics, seemed to open to humanity an epoch in which science would have the hegemony, in which the progress of knowledge and human industry would be pursued without limits. At the same time the French Revolution had witnessed a more or less successful application of the new conceptions. The idea of "society" grew at the same time as that of "science." It was therefore natural to look forward to the application of science even to the reorganization of society. Thus were produced, and then united in one principle, the two ruling conceptions of *positivism*. Descartes had already extended the domain of science to the whole of nature, but not to human society; he had provisionally put to the side, along with theology, the moral and political sciences. The extension of science to everything which had been hitherto excluded from its domain was the characteristic of the positivist movement. To be sure, theology and ontology lived on in the first half of the century, but without having before them a bright future. Theology battles still with the Chateaubriands, Maistres, Bonalds, Lamennais, but its influence is diminishing. The activity of metaphysics, represented especially by Victor Cousin and the eclectics, is not sufficiently profound. . . . Unfortunately, Cousin's rationalism remained too abstract, too thoroughly intellectual [that is, to combat successfully the positivist movement].

Vigny [Alfred de Vigny, the romantic poet] compares the cold rationalism of that time to the light of the moon which gives light without warmth. "One can distinguish objects by its light, but its entire strength would not evoke the slightest spark." The philosophy which little by little tended to become dominant, in spite of the efforts of the eclectic school, was a positivism shot through with agnosticism. The reduction of the transcendent to an unknowable, of the observable to the sole object of knowledge, such was the work of the first half of the century. The result was to hold to observable *facts* and their special *laws*. Everything which seemed irreducible to scientific treatment was dismissed to the realm of the unknowable: X.

In the second half of the century, an attempt has been made to reduce this "irreducible" by passing from a static to a more "dynamic" point of view. . . . It is especially the genesis of things and their development which now attract attention. Laplace's conception has been developed: the unsolvable nebulosities [*nébuleuses*] seem like worlds in formation; the so-called "firmament" now has a visible history and its solidity turns out to be founded on fluidity. The stars have different ages; stars and planets represent successive stages of cosmic formations. Lyell explains the history of the earth by the action of the same causes that we see at work today. Finally, in the domain of life, Darwin shows how species proceed one from the other. In philosophy as in science the new idea could not fail to appear: the idea of evolution. From then on, what one might call a dynamic positivism displaced the older static positivism; that is, the discontinuities which Auguste Comte believed definitive tend to be changed into a continuity of development. *The second half of our century is evolutionist.*

Auguste Comte had wanted to banish every hypothesis on the origin of things, essences, first and final causes, the indefinite reducibility of phenomena, the transformation of forces, the transmutation of species; he admitted only the research of the *how*, not that of the *why;* he declared that philosophic synthesis does not embrace the unity of nature as it really is in itself, but that it can be only a classification of the irreducible characteristics of phenomena as they appear to us. Evolutionism, on the contrary, admits the possibility of resolving, at least in the phenomenal order, the questions of origin and even of essence, of reducing phenomena, forces, species, of explaining their natural derivations by rising from the most simple and homogeneous phenomena to the most complex and heterogeneous.

A characteristic fact in this period is the reduction to zero, or almost to zero, of the theological movement which had still been so notable in the first part of the century. To theology succeeds "agnosticism" which in the new order seems the real victor. The Lamennais of the second half of the century is Ernest Renan, who limits himself to combining poetic recollections of his religious youth with an inconsistent Hegelianism, and who ends by reducing God to the category of the ideal. Catholicism no longer inspires anything comparable to its great output at the beginning of the century. In the majority of minds there remains scarcely anything except the "amorphous religion" of the Unknowable whose high priest is Herbert Spencer. The "theological state" is in manifest decay. It is not the same with metaphysics which seems to have inherited everything that theology has lost. Observe the current struggle between naturalism and idealism. As the movement of ideas accelerates, the second half of the nineteenth century presents two distinct periods, the one in which naturalism predominates, and toward 1855 even invades literature, the other in which idealism gains the upper hand.

The year 1851, which was in France the critical year of the century, had seen dashed all the dreams of social and religious reorganization, of liberty and universal fraternity. Force triumphed; we went backwards, the fact gave the lie to the idea. . . .

[At that time] minds remained abandoned for the most part either to a bloodless idealism or to a materialistic positivism. Join to these two the demoralizing action of Darwin's theories which, badly interpreted and extended beyond their legitimate limits, seemed the apology for might against right; and finally, the pessimistic theories of Schopenhauer and Hartmann which only served to increase the universal discouragement. The war of 1870 seemed to consecrate the final triumph of might over right, of fact over idea. In literature positivist realism triumphed with Zola and the Goncourts; painting became realistic with Courbet and Manet. History abandoned vast syntheses only to get lost, like the novelists, in the "document." To the politics of ideas had finally succeeded the positivist politics of facts, or better still, of "business."

Meanwhile the successors of Victor Cousin had not stopped fighting for idealism and spiritualism. In his fine books on materialism and the philosophical crisis, which would be followed later by important works on morals and final causes, M. Paul Janet boldly, from 1863 on, directed the effort of his dialectic against the positivism and materialism then in high favor. . . . M. Cournot, for his part, published original works, semi-positivist and semi-Kantian, on the foundations of knowledge. M M. Renouvier and Ravaisson succeeded in restoring to honor the philosophy of Kant, Aristotle, and Leibniz. In the last quarter of the century one at least sees a metaphysical and moral reaction set in against the abuses of a rationalism which a cloudy idealism had tempered so badly. M. Renouvier, a subtle and profound thinker, began to have a definite influence through his *Essays*, the first of which appeared in 1854, the others from 1859 to 1864, but especially through his *Critique philosophique*, an intransigently neo-Kantian work, but of high moral and social inspiration. Obstinate in defence of his own ideas, not very accessible to the ideas of others, measuring all by his own system, he criticized mercilessly everything that smacked of positivism, evolutionism, and determinism. In the end, by dint of repeating the same things week after week and in every possible form, he made a distinct impression with his doctrine of "indeterminist phenomenalism," combined with "apriorism" and the ethic of the "categorical imperative." Comte, Littré, Taine, Renan, and Spencer had no more indefatigable adversary than Renouvier. . . .

M. Félix Ravaisson's magisterial report on *The Philosophy of France in the Nineteenth Century*, drawn up on the occasion of the exposition of 1868, also stimulated the highest speculations of metaphysics. Opening up large perspectives, M. Ravaisson took as the center of his teaching an "absolute spiritualism," from which, however, he banished the idea of substance, that vain remainder of matter. Like Aristotle, he suspended the entire world on the pure act of thought. Of the attacks on Kant, M. Ravaisson took little account: metaphysics appeared to him, as to the predecessors and successors of Kant, the "science" par excellence. His philosophy, too well known to need review here, was not without analogy to the last philosophy of Schelling. . . .

All the other masters who taught philosophy at the Ecole Normale can claim the honor of having, in their turn, though in different ways and by other doctrines, contributed to the idealist movement. One of them [the reference is to Fouillée himself]—in order to follow the historical order—hoped to reconcile idealism and naturalism by bringing Plato's Ideas down from heaven to earth. He undertook to show how in each idea there resides a power [Fouillée's famous *idées-forces*] which is realized in proportion as it clearly conceives and desires its own realization; to restore to determinism the idea and desire of liberty; to reintegrate in the evolution of nature the psychic factors and states of conscience; to reestablish in the evolution of society not only rights, but the efficacious action of the ideal. A little later another philosopher [Emile Boutroux], who was profoundly versed in German philosophy and au courant of the progress of the sciences, strove to pierce the armor of mechanical necessity. He hoped thereby to make room for a spontaneity which revealed the "contingency of the laws of nature." Still others demonstrated the role the will played, whether in "moral certitude" or in "error." . . .

In these last years a new current has indeed been accentuated in philosophy which goes back to Lotze through the intermediation of M. Renouvier and M. Boutroux. The latter, in his fine thesis on *The Contingency of the Laws of Nature*, to which just now we made allusion, and later in his learned readings at the Ecole Normale and the Sorbonne, contested the principle of determinism. . . . An analogous inspiration is to be found in the remarkable work of M. Bergson on *Memory and Free Will* [*Les Donneés immédiates de la conscience*, 1889] in which the interior world of pure duration is contrasted with the exterior world of extension. This whole *philosophy of contingency* seems to be a mixture of neocriticism [Kantian] and English empiricism. . . . Uniting these two philosophies it has carried to new ground the struggle between determinism and indeterminism. A narrow evolutionism had threatened to lead determinism back to one of its particular forms, the mathematical and mechanical, that is to say, to materialism. It reduced the mental to the role of simple reflex, thereby explaining everything materialistically. Against this usurpation of mechanism, it was necessary to react. For that purpose two ways opened themselves. The first consisted in reintegrating the mental and its essential modes among the true factors of determinism, which thus became enlarged, was made more supple, and was vivified by its equivalence with the active life and to thought. Thus by adding to determinism, as its necessary complement, a mental factor and the idea of liberty, this way tried to give more complete satisfaction to those who feared the transformation of determinism into a mechanical and brutal fatalism, like that of Taine. . . . But another way still remained which seemed to lead further: that was to oppose to mechanism, not merely a psychic determinism but a phychic (and even physical) *indeterminism*, which resulted in putting into everything something unintelligible and unknowable, as a deep and always gushing source of reality. The philosophy of contingency has followed this second way. . . .

Like every reaction, the idealist movement has ended by overreaching itself. Some young philosophers believed they were doing a holy work by denying science itself or by reducing it to a subaltern role, in order to exalt both belief and action to spheres where criticism could no longer reach them. They professed so much skepticism at the beginning only to be all the more credulous at the end. . . .

It is, in short, by the development of its philosophy and science that one can judge an epoch and country, not by surface agitations. If to indifference in the matter of religion, now a chronic state of mind in France, we were to join indifference in philosophy, then indeed we should be in a state of degeneracy. Neither pure science nor pure literature would save us, for they could remedy neither the intellectual decline nor the moral disorganization. But we have seen how strong is the philosophic as well as the scientific movement in our country. Whether it is a question of idealist philosophy (principal object of this study) or of positivist philosophy, England and Germany alone can compare with France today in activity and vigor of thought. Moreover, we see mixing together more and more these two idealist and naturalist currents.

HENRI BERGSON: *Creative Evolution* *

Henri Bergson, born in 1859 (he died in 1941), was one of the chief philosophers of evolution. But because he descended from the "spiritual" school of French philosophy, which goes all the way back to Ravaisson and the Second French Empire, he emphasized the "freedom" involved in the evolutionary process. In this respect, in his refutation of mechanism and determinism, and in his exaltation of the creative vital process at work in the cosmos and in individual life, he was very much a part of the "reaction against positivism" described by Fouillée in the preceding selection. When he wrote *Creative Evolution* (1907), his best-known book, he was already famous as a professor of philosophy and an immensely popular lecturer at the Collège de France.

THE HISTORY of the evolution of life, incomplete as it yet is, already reveals to us how the intellect has been formed, by an uninterrupted progress, along a line which ascends through the vertebrate series up to man. It shows us in the faculty of understanding an appendage of the faculty of acting, a more and more precise, more and more complex and supple adaptation of the consciousness of living beings to the conditions of existence that are made for them. Hence should result this consequence that our intellect, in the narrow sense of the word, is intended to secure the perfect fitting of our body to its environment, to represent the relations of external things among themselves—in short, to think matter. Such will indeed be one of the conclusions of the present essay. We shall see that the human intellect feels at home among inanimate objects, more especially among solids, where our action finds its fulcrum and our industry its tools; that our concepts have been formed on the model of solids; that our logic is, pre-eminently, the logic of solids; that, consequently, our intellect triumphs in geometry, wherein is revealed the kinship of logical thought with unorganized matter, and where the intellect has only to follow its natural movement, after the lightest possible contact with experience, in order to go from discovery to discovery, sure that experience is following behind it and will justify it invariably.

But from this it must also follow that our thought, in its purely logical form, is incapable of presenting the true nature of life, the full meaning of the evolutionary movement. Created by life, in definite circumstances, to act on definite things, how can it embrace life, of which it is only an emanation or an aspect? Deposited by the evolutionary movement in the course of its way, how can it be applied to the evolutionary movement itself? As well contend that the part is equal to the whole, that the effect can reabsorb its cause, or that the pebble left on the beach displays the form of the wave that brought it there. In fact, we do indeed feel that not one of the categories of our thought —unity, multiplicity, mechanical causality, intelligent finality, etc.— applies exactly to the things of life: who can say where individuality begins and ends, whether the living being is one or many, whether it is the cells which associate themselves into the organism or the organism which dissociates itself into cells? In vain we force the living into this or that one of our molds. All the molds crack. Our reasoning, so sure of itself among things inert, feels ill at ease on this new ground. It would be difficult to cite a biological discovery due to pure reasoning.

And most often, when experience has finally shown us how life goes to work to obtain a certain result, we find its way of working is just that of which we should never have thought.

Yet evolutionist philosophy does not hesitate to extend to the things of life the same methods of explanation which have succeeded in the case of unorganized matter. It begins by showing us in the intellect a local effect of evolution, a flame, perhaps accidental, which lights up the coming and going of living beings in the narrow passage open to their action; and lo! forgetting what it has just told us, it makes of this lantern glimmering in a tunnel a Sun which can illuminate the world.

*   *   *

Of the discontinuous alone does the intellect form a clear idea.

*   *   *

Of immobility alone does the intellect form a clear idea.

*   *   *

The intellect is characterized by a natural inability to comprehend life.

Instinct, on the contrary, is molded on the very form of life. While intelligence treats everything mechanically, instinct proceeds, so to speak, organically. If the consciousness that slumbers in it should awake, if it were wound up into knowledge instead of being wound off into action, if we could ask and it could reply, it would give up to us the most intimate secrets of life.

*   *   *

Instinct is sympathy. If this sympathy could extend its object and also reflect upon itself, it would give us the key to vital operations—just as intelligence, developed and disciplined, guides us into matter. For—we cannot too often repeat it—intelligence and instinct are turned in opposite directions, the former toward inert matter, the latter toward life. Intelligence, by means of science, which is its work, will deliver up to us more and more completely the secret of physical operations; of life it brings us, and moreover only claims to bring us, a translation in terms of inertia. It goes all round life, taking from outside the greatest possible number of views of it, drawing it into itself instead of entering into it. But it is to the very inwardness of life that *intuition* leads us—by intuition I mean instinct that has become disinterested, self-conscious, capable of reflecting upon its object and of enlarging it indefinitely.

That an effort of this kind is not impossible, is proved by the existence in man of an aesthetic faculty along with normal perception. Our eye perceives the features of the living being, merely as assembled, not as mutually organized. The intention of life, the simple movement that runs through the lines, that binds them together and gives them significance, escapes it. The intention is just what the artist tries to regain, in placing himself back within the object by a kind of sympathy, in breaking down, by an effort of intuition, the barrier that space puts up between him and his model. It is true that this aesthetic intuition, like external perception, only attains the individual. But we can conceive an inquiry turned in the same direction as art, which would take life *in general* for its object, just as physical science, in following to the end the direction pointed out by external perception, prolongs the individual facts into general laws. No doubt this philosophy will never obtain a knowledge of its object comparable to that which science has of its own. Intelligence remains the luminous nucleus around which instinct, even enlarged and purified into intuition, forms only a vague nebulosity. But, in default of knowledge properly so called, reserved to pure intelligence, intuition may enable us to grasp what it is that intelligence fails to give us, and indicate the means of supplementing it.

GUSTAVE LE BON: *The Crowd-man* *

> *La psychologie des foules* (1895) by Gustave Le Bon, physician, social psychologist, and political conservative, appeared in the same year as Freud's (with Josef Breuer) *Studies in Hysteria*. It was also contemporaneous with several important studies of crowd psychology by Gabriel Tarde and Scipio Sighele. These and other books reveal a growing awareness in the late nineteenth century of irrational man and of the role played by the "unconscious" in human behaviour. Le Bon's book also reflects current interest in "crowds," observed by many with increasing apprehension from the French Revolution to the Third Republic.

ORGANISED crowds have always played an important part in the life of peoples, but this part has never been of such moment as at present. The substitution of the unconscious action of crowds for the conscious activity of individuals is one of the principal characteristics of the present age. . . .

Crowds, doubtless, are always unconscious, but this very unconsciousness is perhaps one of the secrets of their strength. In the natural world beings exclusively governed by instinct accomplish acts whose marvellous complexity astounds us. Reason is an attribute of humanity of too recent date and still too imperfect to reveal to us the laws of the unconscious, and still more to take its place. The part played by the

* Gustave Le Bon: *The Crowd* (New York: The Macmillan Company; 1930), pp. 5, 9–10, 13–15, 33–36, 73–75. Reprinted by permission of Ernest Benn Limited.

unconscious in all our acts is immense, and that played by reason very small. The unconscious acts like a force still unknown. . . .

The great upheavals which precede changes of civilisation, such as the fall of the Roman Empire and the foundation of the Arabian Empire, seem at first sight determined more especially by political transformations, foreign invasion, or the overthrow of dynasties. But a more attentive study of these events shows that behind their apparent causes the real cause is generally seen to be a profound modification in the ideas of the peoples. The true historical upheavals are not those which astonish us by their grandeur and violence. The only important changes whence the renewal of civilisations results, affect ideas, conceptions, and beliefs. The memorable events of history are the visible effects of the invisible changes of human thought. The reason these great events are so rare is that there is nothing so stable in a race as the inherited groundwork of its thoughts.

The present epoch is one of these critical moments in which the thought of mankind is undergoing a process of transformation.

Two fundamental factors are at the base of this transformation. The first is the destruction of those religious, political, and social beliefs in which all the-elements of our civilisation are rooted. The second is the creation of entirely new conditions of existence and thought as the result of modern scientific and industrial discoveries.

The ideas of the past, although half destroyed, being still very powerful, and the ideas which are to replace them being still in process of formation, the modern age represents a period of transition and anarchy.

It is not easy to say as yet what will one day be evolved from this necessarily somewhat chaotic period. What will be the fundamental ideas on which the societies that are to succeed our own will be built up? We do not at present know. . . . While all our ancient beliefs are tottering and disappearing, while the old pillars of society are giving way one by one, the power of the crowd is the only force that nothing menaces, and of which the prestige is continually on the increase. The age we are about to enter will in truth be the ERA OF CROWDS. . . .

How is it that these new characteristics are created? . . .

. . . A third cause, and by far the most important, determines in the individuals of a crowd special characteristics which are quite contrary at times to those presented by the isolated individual. I allude to that suggestibility of which, moreover, the contagion mentioned above is neither more nor less than an effect.

To understand this phenomenon it is necessary to bear in mind certain recent physiological discoveries. We know to-day that by various processes an individual may be brought into such a condition that, having entirely lost his conscious personality, he obeys all the suggestions of the operator who has deprived him of it, and commits acts in utter contradiction with his character and habits. The most careful observations seem to prove that an individual immersed for some length of time in a crowd in action soon finds himself—either in consequence of the magnetic influence given out by the crowd, or from some other cause of which we are ignorant—in a special state, which much resembles the state of fascination in which the hypnotised individual finds himself in the hands of the hypnotiser. The activity of the brain being paralysed in the case of the hypnotised subject, the latter becomes the slave of all the unconscious activities of his spinal cord, which the hypnotiser directs at will. The conscious personality has entirely vanished; will and discernment are lost. All feelings and thoughts are bent in the direction determined by the hypnotiser.

Such also is approximately the state of the individual forming part of a psychological crowd. He is no longer conscious of his acts. In his case, as in the case of the hypnotised subject, at the same time that certain faculties are destroyed, others may be brought to a high degree of exaltation. Under the influence of a suggestion, he will undertake the accomplishment of certain acts with irresistible impetuosity. This impetuosity is the more irresistible in the case of crowds than in that of the hypnotised subject, from the fact that, the suggestion being the same for all the individuals of the crowd, it gains in strength by reciprocity. The individualities in the crowd who might possess a personality sufficiently strong to resist the suggestion are too few in number to struggle against the current. At the utmost, they may be able to attempt a diversion by means of different suggestions. It is in this way, for instance, that a happy expression, an image opportunely evoked, have occasionally deterred crowds from the most bloodthirsty acts.

We see, then, that the disappearance of the conscious personality, the predominance of the unconscious personality, the turning by means of suggestion and contagion of feelings and ideas in an identical direction, the tendency immediately to transform the suggested ideas into acts; these we see, are the principal characteristics of the individual forming part of a crowd. He is no longer himself, but has become an automaton who has ceased to be guided by his will.

Moreover, by the mere fact that he forms part of an organised crowd, a man descends several rungs in the ladder of civilisation. Isolated, he may be a cultivated individual; in a crowd, he is a barbarian—that is, a creature acting by instinct. He possesses the spontaneity, the violence, the ferocity, and also the enthusiasm and heroism of primitive beings, whom he further tends to resemble by the facility with which he allows himself to be impressed by words and images—which would be entirely without action on each of the isolated individuals composing the crowd —and to be induced to commit acts contrary to his most obvious interests and his best-known habits. . . .

It cannot absolutely be said that crowds do not reason and are not to be influenced by reasoning.

However, the arguments they employ and those which are capable of influencing them are, from a logical point of view, of such an inferior kind that it is only by way of analogy that they can be described as reasoning.

The inferior reasoning of crowds is based, just as is reasoning of a high order, on the association of ideas, but between the ideas associated by crowds there are only apparent bonds of analogy or succession. . . .

The characteristics of the reasoning of crowds are the association of dissimilar things possessing a merely apparent connection between each other, and the immediate generalisation of particular cases. It is arguments of this kind that are always presented to crowds by those who know how to manage them. They are the only arguments by which crowds are to be influenced. A chain of logical argumentation is totally incomprehensible to crowds, and for this reason it is permissible to say that they do not reason or that they reason falsely, and are not to be influenced by reasoning. . . .

It would be superfluous to add that the powerlessness of crowds to reason aright prevents them displaying any trace of the critical spirit, prevents them, that is, from being capable of discerning truth from error, or of forming a precise judgment on any matter. Judgments accepted by crowds are merely judgments forced upon them and never judgments adopted after discussion. . . .

GRAHAM WALLAS: *Human Nature in Politics* *

> Like Le Bon, whom he in fact mentions, Graham Wallas (1858–1932) attacked the "intellectualist fallacy," particularly the assumption held by most nineteenth-century political thinkers that people can be counted on to behave rationally in politics. In attempting to link political theory to the new psychology, *Human Nature in Politics* (1908) was a pioneer work. Wallas, one of the early members of the Fabian Society, helped to plan the London School of Economics and Political Science and was named its first professor of political science.

THE only form of study which a political thinker of one or two hundred years ago would now note as missing is any attempt to deal with politics in its relation to the nature of man. The thinkers of the past, from Plato to Bentham and Mill, had each his own view of human nature, and they made those views the basis of their speculations on government. But no modern treatise on political science, whether dealing with institutions or

* From: *Human Nature in Politics* by Graham Wallas, Third Edition, Copyright, 1921, by F. S. Crofts & Co., Inc., pp. 12–14, 21–25, 98–99, 103–104, 110. Reprinted by permission of Appleton-Century-Crofts, Division of Meredith Corporation, and Constable and Company Limited.

finance, now begins with anything corresponding to the opening words of Bentham's *Principles of Morals and Legislation*—"Nature has placed mankind under the governance of two sovereign masters, pain and pleasure"; or to the "first general proposition" of Nassau Senior's *Political Economy*, "Every man desires to obtain additional wealth with as little sacrifice as possible." In most cases one cannot even discover whether the writer is conscious of possessing any conception of human nature at all.

It is easy to understand how this has come about. Political science is just beginning to regain some measure of authority after the acknowledged failure of its confident professions during the first half of the nineteenth century. Bentham's Utilitarianism, after superseding both Natural Right and the blind tradition of the lawyers, and serving as the basis of innumerable legal and constitutional reforms throughout Europe, was killed by the unanswerable refusal of the plain man to believe that ideas of pleasure and pain are the only sources of human motive. The "classical" political economy of the universities and the newspapers, the political economy of MacCulloch and Senior and Archbishop Whately, was even more unfortunate in its attempt to deduce a whole industrial polity from a "few simple principles" of human nature. . . .

When the struggle against "Political Economy" was at its height, Darwin's *Origin of Species* revealed a universe in which the "few simple principles" seemed a little absurd, and nothing has hitherto taken their place. . . .

For the moment, therefore, nearly all students of politics analyse institutions and avoid the analysis of man. The study of human nature by the psychologists has, it is true, advanced enormously since the discovery of human evolution, but it has advanced without affecting or being affected by the study of politics. . . .

Impulse and Instinct in Politics

Whoever sets himself to base his political thinking on a reexamination of the working of human nature, must begin by trying to overcome his own tendency to exaggerate the intellectuality of mankind.

We are apt to assume that every human action is the result of an intellectual process, by which a man first thinks of some end which he desires, and then calculates the means by which that end can be attained. An investor, for instance, desires good security combined with five per cent. interest. He spends an hour in studying with an open mind the price-list of stocks, and finally infers that the purchase of Brewery Debentures will enable him most completely to realise his desire. Given the original desire for good security, his act in purchasing the Debentures appears to be the inevitable result of his inference. The desire for good security itself may further appear to be merely an intellectual inference as to the means of satisfying some more general desire, shared by all mankind, for "happiness," our own "interest," or the like. The satisfaction of this general desire can then be treated as the supreme "end" of life, from which all our acts and impulses, great and small, are derived by the same intellectual process as that by which the conclusion is derived from the premises of an argument.

This way of thinking is sometimes called "common sense." A good example of its application to politics may be found in a sentence from Macaulay's celebrated attack on the Utilitarian followers of Bentham in the *Edinburgh Review* of March, 1829. This extreme instance of the foundation of politics upon dogmatic psychology is, curiously enough, part of an argument intended to show that "it is utterly impossible to deduce the science of government from the principles of human nature." "What proposition," Macaulay asks, "is there respecting human nature which is absolute and universally true? We know of only one: and that is not only true, but identical; that men always act from self-interest. . . . *When we see the actions of a man, we know with certainty what he thinks his interest to be.*" Macaulay believes himself to be opposing Benthamism root and branch, but is unconsciously adopting and exaggerating the assumption which Bentham shared with most of the other eighteenth and early nineteenth century philosophers—that all motives result from the idea of some preconceived end. . . .

The text-books of psychology now warn every student against the "intellectualist" fallacy which is illustrated by my quotation from Macaulay. Impulse, it is now agreed, has an evolutionary history of its own earlier than the history of those intellectual processes by which it is often directed and modified. Our inherited organisation inclines us to react in certain ways to certain stimuli because such reactions have been useful in the past in preserving our species. Some of the reactions are what we call specifically "instincts," that is to say, impulses towards definite acts or series of acts, independent of any conscious anticipation of their probable effects. Those instincts are sometimes unconscious and involuntary; and sometimes, in the case of ourselves and apparently of other higher animals, they are conscious and voluntary. But the connection between means and ends which they exhibit is the result not of any contrivance by the actor, but of the survival, in the past, of the "fittest" of many varying tendencies to act. . . .

Non-Rational Inference in Politics

The assumption—which is so closely interwoven with our habits of political and economic thought—that men always act on a reasoned opinion as to their interests, may be divided into two separate assumptions: first, that men always act on some kind of inference as to the best means of reaching a preconceived end, and secondly, that all inferences are of the same kind, and are produced by a uniform process of "reasoning."

In the two preceding chapters I dealt with the first assumption, and attempted to show that it is important for a politician to realise that men do not always act on inferences as to means and ends. I argued that men often act in politics under the immediate stimulus of affection and instinct, and that affection and interest may be directed towards political entities which are very different from those facts in the world around us which we can discover by deliberate observation and analysis.

In this chapter I propose to consider the second assumption, and to inquire how far it is true that men, when they do form inferences as to the result of their political actions, always form them by a process of reasoning. . . .

[The truth is] that most of the political opinions of most men are the result, not of reasoning tested by experience, but of unconscious or half-conscious inference fixed by habit. It is indeed mainly in the formation of tracks of thought that habit shows its power in politics. . . .

Some men even seem to reverence most those of their opinions whose origin has least to do with deliberate reasoning. When Mr. Barrie's Bowie Haggart said: "I am of opeenion that the works of Burns is of an immoral tendency. I have not read them myself, but such is my opeenion," he was comparing the merely rational conclusion which might have resulted from a reading of Burns' works with the conviction about them which he found ready-made in his mind, and which was the more sacred to him and more intimately his own, because he did not know how it was produced. . . .

Writers on the "psychology of the crowd" have pointed out the effect of excitement and numbers in substituting non-rational for rational inference. Any cause, however, which prevents a man from giving full attention to his mental processes may produce the phenomena of non-rational inference in an extreme degree. I have often watched in some small sub-committee the method by which either of the two men with a real genius for committee work whom I know could control his colleagues. The process was most successful towards the end of an afternoon, when the members were tired and somewhat dazed with the effort of following a rapid talker through a mass of unfamiliar detail. If at that point the operator slightly quickened the flow of his information, and slightly emphasised the assumption that he was being thoroughly understood, he could put some at least of his colleagues into a sort of walking trance, in which they would have cheerfully assented to the proposition that the best means of securing, *e.g.*, the permanence of private schools was a large and immediate increase in the number of public schools. . . .

GEORGES SOREL: *Myth in History* *

Reflections on Violence, from which the following excerpts are taken, originally appeared as journal articles (1906). They were later gathered together and published as a book for which the author provided a special introduction in the form of a letter to Daniel Halevy. This letter contains many of his key ideas: pessimism, anti-intellectualism (like Graham Wallas, he attacked the "intellectualist fallacy"), the decadence of the middle class, and especially the social myth and the role he thought it played in history. The text developed these ideas, enlarging on the general strike as the means of social revolution. His philosophy of history, although obviously influenced by Marx, was essentially un-Marxist. It owed something to the philosopher Henri Bergson, whom Sorel greatly admired. Georges Sorel (1847–1922), French engineer and syndicalist, is perhaps best remembered for the influence he is supposed to have had on fascist thinking through his idea of the "myth."

On Pessimism

MY *Reflections on Violence* have irritated many people on account of the pessimistic conception on which the whole of the study rests; but I know that you do not share this impression; you have brilliantly shown in your *Histoire de quatre ans* that you despise the deceptive hopes with which the weak solace themselves. We can then talk pessimism freely to each other, and I am happy to have a correspondent who does not revolt against a doctrine without which nothing very great has been accomplished in this world. I have felt for some time that Greek philosophy did not produce any great moral result, simply because it was, as a rule, very optimistic. Socrates was at times optimistic to an almost unbearable degree. . . .

The immense successes obtained by industrial civilisation has created the belief that, in the near future, happiness will be produced automatically for everybody. "The present century," writes Hartmann, "has for the last forty years only entered the third period of illusion. In the enthusiasm and enchantment of its hopes, it rushes towards the realisation of the promise of a new age of gold. Providence takes care that the anticipations of the isolated thinker do not disarrange the course of history by prematurely gaining too many adherents." He thinks that for this reason his readers will have some difficulty in accepting his criticism of the illusion of future happiness. The leaders of the contemporary world are pushed towards optimism by economic forces. . . .

---

* Georges Sorel: *Reflections on Violence*, T. E. Hulme (trans.) pp. 7–11, 22–24, 28–33, 35, 84–85, 130–136, 298–299. Copyright 1916 by George Allen & Unwin Ltd. Reprinted by permission of George Allen & Unwin Ltd.

The optimist in politics is an inconstant and even dangerous man, because he takes no account of the great difficulties presented by his projects; these projects seem to him to possess a force of their own, which tends to bring about their realisation all the more easily as they are, in his opinion, destined to produce the happiest results. He frequently thinks that small reforms in the political constitution, and, above all, in the personnel of the government, will be sufficient to direct social development in such a way as to mitigate those evils of the contemporary world which seem so harsh to the sensitive mind. . . .

Pessimism is quite a different thing from the caricatures of it which are usually presented to us; it is a philosophy of conduct rather than a theory of the world; it considers the *march towards deliverance* as narrowly conditioned, on the one hand, by the experimental knowledge that we have acquired from the obstacles which oppose themselves to the satisfaction of our imaginations (or, if we like, by the feeling of social determinism), and, on the other, by a profound conviction of our natural weakness. These two aspects of pessimism should never be separated, although, as a rule, scarcely any attention is paid to their close connection.

1. The conception of pessimism springs from the fact that literary historians have been very much struck with the complaints made by the great poets of antiquity on the subject of the griefs which constantly threaten mankind. There are few people who have not, at one time or another, experienced a piece of good fortune; but we are surrounded by malevolent forces always ready to spring out on us from some ambuscade and overwhelm us. Hence the very real sufferings which arouse the sympathy of nearly all men, even of those who have been more favourably treated by fortune; so that the literature of grief has always had a certain success throughout the whole course of history. But a study of this kind of literature would give us a very imperfect idea of pessimism. It may be laid down as a general rule, that in order to understand a doctrine it is not sufficient to study it in an abstract manner, nor even as it occurs in isolated people: it is necessary to find out how it has been manifested in historical groups; it is for this reason that I am here led to add the two elements that were mentioned earlier.

2. The pessimist regards social conditions as forming a system bound together by an iron law which cannot be evaded, so that the system is given, as it were, in one block, and cannot disappear except in a catastrophe which involves the whole. If this theory is admitted, it then becomes absurd to make certain wicked men responsible for the evils from which society suffers; the pessimist is not subject to the sanguinary follies of the optimist, infatuated by the unexpected obstacles that his projects meet with; he does not dream of bringing about the happiness of future generations by slaughtering existing egoists.

3. The most fundamental element of pessimism is its method of conceiving the path towards deliverance. A man would not go very far in the examination either of the laws of his own wretchedness or of fate, which so much shock the ingenuousness of our pride, if he were not borne up by the hope of putting an end to these tyrannies by an effort, to be attempted with the help of a whole band of companions. . . .

New Views of Man and History

In the course of this study one thing has always been present in my mind, which seemed to me so evident that I did not think it worth while to lay much stress on it—that men who are participating in a great social movement always picture their coming action as a battle in which their cause is certain to triumph. These constructions, knowledge of which is so important for historians, I propose to call myths; the syndicalist "general strike" and Marx's catastrophic revolution are such myths. As remarkable examples of such myths, I have given those which were constructed by primitive Christianity, by the Reformation, by the Revolution and by the followers of Mazzini. I now wish to show that we should not attempt to analyse such groups of images in the way that we analyse a thing into its elements, but that they must be taken as a whole, as historical forces, and that we should be especially careful not to make any comparison between accomplished fact and the picture people had formed for themselves before action. . . .

In employing the term myth I believed that I had made a happy choice, because I thus put myself in a position to refuse any discussion whatever with the people who wish to submit the idea of a general strike to a detailed criticism, and who accumulate objections against its practical possibility. It appears, on the contrary, that I had made a most unfortunate choice, for while some told me that myths were only suitable to a primitive state of society, others imagined that I thought the modern world might be moved by illusions analogous in nature to those which Renan thought might usefully replace religion. But there has been a worse misunderstanding than this even, for it has been asserted that my theory of myths was only a kind of lawyer's plea, a falsification of the real opinions of the revolutionaries, the *sophistry of an intellectualist.*

If this were true, I should not have been exactly fortunate, for I have always tried to escape the influence of that intellectualist philosophy, which seems to me a great hindrance to the historian who allows himself to be dominated by it. The contradiction that exists between this philosophy and the true understanding of events has often struck the readers of Renan. Renan is continually wavering between his own intuition, which was nearly always admirable, and a philosophy which cannot touch history without falling into platitudes; but, alas, he too often believed himself bound to think in accordance with the *scientific opinions* of his day.

The intellectualist philosophy finds itself unable to explain phenomena like the following—the sacrifice of his life which the soldier of Napoleon made in order to have had the honour of taking part in "immortal deeds" and of living in the glory of France, knowing all the time that "he would always be a poor man"; then, again, the extraordinary virtues shown by the Romans who resigned themselves to a frightful inequality and who suffered so much to conquer the world. . . .

The mind of man is so constituted that it cannot remain content with the mere observation of facts, but always attempts to penetrate into the inner reason of things. I therefore ask myself whether it might not be desirable to study this theory of myths more thoroughly, utilising the enlightenment we owe to the Bergsonian philosophy. . . .

Bergson asks us to consider the inner depths of the mind and what happens there during a creative moment. "There are," he says, "two different selves, one of which is, as it were, the external projection of the other, its spatial and, so to speak, social representation. We reach the former by deep introspection, which leads us to grasp our inner states as living things, constantly *becoming*, as states not amenable to measure. . . . But the moments at which we thus grasp ourselves are rare, and that is just why we are rarely free. The greater part of our time we live outside ourselves, hardly perceiving anything of ourselves but our own ghost, a colourless shadow. . . . Hence we live for the external world rather than for ourselves; we speak rather than think; we are acted rather than act ourselves. To act freely is to recover possession of oneself, and to get back into pure duration. . . .

It seems to me that this psychology of the deeper life must be represented in the following way. We must abandon the idea that the soul can be compared to something moving, which, obeying a more or less mechanical law, is impelled in the direction of certain given motive forces. To say that we are acting, implies that we are creating an imaginary world placed ahead of the present world and composed of movements which depend entirely on us. In this way our freedom becomes perfectly intelligible. Starting from a study of these artificial constructions which embrace everything that interests us, several philosophers, inspired by Bergsonian doctrines, have been led to formulate a rather startling theory. Edouard Le Roy, for example, says: "Our real body is the entire universe in as far as it is experienced by us. And what common sense more strictly calls our body is only the region of least unconsciousness and greatest liberty in this greater body, the part which we most directly control and by means of which we are able to act on the rest." But we must not, as this subtle philosopher constantly does, confuse a passing state of our willing activity with the stable affirmations of science.

These artificial worlds generally disappear from our minds without leaving any trace in our memory; but when the masses are deeply moved it then becomes possible to trace the outlines of the kind of representation which constitutes a social myth. . . .

As long as there are no myths accepted by the masses, one may go on talking of revolts indefinitely, without ever provoking any revolutionary movement; this is what gives such importance to the general strike and renders it so odious to socialists who are afraid of a revolution; they do all they can to shake the confidence felt by the workers in the preparations they are making for the revolution; and in order to succeed in this they cast ridicule on the idea of the general strike—the only idea that could have any value as a motive force. One of the chief means employed by them is to represent it as a Utopia; this is easy enough, because there are very few myths which are perfectly free from any Utopian element.

The revolutionary myths which exist at the present time are almost free from any such mixture; by means of them it is possible to understand the activity, the feelings and the ideas of the masses preparing themselves to enter on a decisive struggle; the myths are not descriptions of things, but expressions of a determination to act. A Utopia is, on the contrary, an intellectual product; it is the work of theorists who, after observing and discussing the known fact, seek to establish a model to which they can compare existing society in order to estimate the amount of good and evil it contains. It is a combination of imaginary institutions having sufficient analogies to real institutions for the jurist to be able to reason about them; it is a construction which can be taken to pieces, and certain parts of it have been shaped in such a way that they can (with a few alterations by way of adjustment) be fitted into approaching legislation. Whilst contemporary myths lead men to prepare themselves for a combat which will destroy the existing state of things, the effect of Utopias has always been to direct men's minds towards reforms which can be brought about by patching up the existing system; it is not surprising, then, that so many makers of Utopias were able to develop into able statesmen when they had acquired a greater experience of political life. A myth cannot be refuted, since it is, at bottom, identical with the convictions of a group, being the expression of these convictions in the language of movement; and it is, in consequence, unanalysable into parts which could be placed on the plane of historical descriptions. A Utopia, on the contrary, can be discussed like any other social constitution; the spontaneous movements it presupposes can be compared with the movements actually observed in the course of history, and we can in this way evaluate its verisimilitude; it is possible to refute Utopias by showing that the economic system on which they have been made to rest is incompatible with the necessary conditions of modern production. . . .

People who are living in this world of "myths," are secure from all refutation; this has led many to assert that Socialism is a kind of religion. For a long time people have been struck by the fact that religious convictions are unaffected by criticism, and from that they have concluded that everything which claims to be beyond science must be a religion. It has been observed also that Christianity tends at the present day to be less a system of dogmas than a Christian life, *i.e.*, a moral reform penetrating to the roots of one's being; consequently, a new analogy has been discovered between religion and the revolutionary Socialism which aims at the apprenticeship, preparation, and even reconstruction of the individual,—a gigantic task. But Bergson has taught us that it is not only religion which occupies the profounder region of our mental life; revolutionary myths have their place there equally with religion. . . .

The Myth of the General Strike

According to Marx, capitalism, by reason of the innate laws of its own nature, is hurrying along a path which will lead the world of to-day, with the inevitability of the evolution of organic life, to the doors of the world of tomorrow. This movement comprises a long period of capitalistic construction, and it ends by a rapid destruction, which is the work of the proletariat. Capitalism creates the heritage which Socialism will receive, the men who will suppress the present régime, and the means of bringing about this destruction, at the same time that it preserves the results obtained in production. Capitalism begets new ways of working; it throws the working class into revolutionary organisations by the pressure it exercises on wages; it restricts its own political basis by competition, which is constantly eliminating industrial leaders. Thus, after having solved the great problem of the organisation of labour, to effect which Utopians have brought forward so many naïve or stupid hypotheses, capitalism provokes the birth of the cause which will overthrow it, and thus renders useless everything that Utopians have written to induce enlightened people to make reforms; and it gradually ruins the traditional order, against which the critics of the idealists had proved themselves to be so deplorably incompetent. It might therefore be said that capitalism plays a part analogous to that attributed by Hartmann to The Unconscious in nature, since it prepares the coming of social reforms which it did not intend to produce. Without any coordinated plan, without any directive ideas, without any ideal of a future world, it is the cause of an inevitable evolution; it draws from the present all that the present can give towards historical development; it performs in an almost mechanical manner all that is necessary, in order that a new era may appear, and that this new era may break every link with the idealism of the present times, while preserving the acquisitions of the capitalistic economic system.

Socialists should therefore abandon the attempt (initiated by the Utopians) to find a means of inducing the enlightened middle class to prepare the *transition to a more perfect system of legislation;* their sole function is that of explaining to the proletariat the greatness of the revolutionary part they are called upon to play. . . .

These results could not be produced in any very certain manner by the use of ordinary language; use must be made of a body of images which, *by intuition alone,* and before any considered analyses are made, is capable of evoking as an undivided whole the mass of sentiments which corresponds to the different manifestations of the war undertaken by Socialism against modern society. The Syndicalists solve this problem perfectly, by concentrating the whole of Socialism in the drama of the general strike; there is thus no longer any place for the reconciliation of contraries in the equivocations of the professors; everything is clearly mapped out, so that only one interpretation of Socialism is possible. This method has all the advantages which "integral" knowledge has over analysis, according to the doctrine of Bergson: and perhaps it would not be possible to cite another example which would so perfectly demonstrate the value of the famous professor's doctrines.

The possibility of the actual realisation of the general strike has been much discussed; it has been stated that the Socialist war could not be decided in one single battle. To the people who think themselves cautious, practical, and scientific the difficulty of setting great masses of the proletariat in motion at the same moment seems prodigious; they have analysed the difficulties of detail which such an enormous struggle would present. It is the opinion of the Socialist-sociologists, as also of the politicians, that the general strike is a popular dream, characteristic of the beginnings of a working-class movement; we have had quoted against us the authority of Sidney Webb, who has decreed that the general strike is an illusion of youth, of which the English workers—whom the monopolists of sociology have so often presented to us as the depositaries of the true conception of the working-class movement—soon rid themselves. . . .

And yet without leaving the present, without reasoning about this future, which seems for ever condemned to escape our reason, we should be unable to act at all. Experience shows that the *framing of a future, in some indeterminate time,* may, when it is done in a certain way, be very effective, and have very few inconveniences; this happens when the anticipations of the future take the form of those myths, which enclose with them all the strongest inclinations of a people, of a party or of a class, inclinations which recur to the mind with the insistence of instincts in all the circumstances of life; and which give an aspect of complete reality to the hopes of immediate action by which, more easily than by any other method, men can reform their desires, passions, and mental activity. We know, moreover, that these social myths in no way prevent a man profiting by the observations which he makes in the course of his life, and form no obstacle to the pursuit of his normal occupations.

The truth of this may be shown by numerous examples.

The first Christians expected the return of Christ and the total ruin of the pagan world, with the inauguration of the kingdom of the saints, at the end of the first generation. The catastrophe did not come to pass, but Christian thought profited so greatly from the apocalyptic myth that certain contemporary scholars maintain that the whole preaching of Christ referred solely to this one point. The hopes which Luther and Calvin had formed of the religious exaltation of Europe were by no means realised; these fathers of the Reformation very soon seemed men of a past era; for present-day Protestants they belong rather to the Middle Ages than to modern times, and the problems which troubled them most occupy very little place in contemporary Protestantism. Must we for that reason deny the immense result which came from their dreams of Christian renovation? It must be admitted that the real developments of the Revolution did not in any way resemble the enchanting pictures which created the enthusiasm of its first adepts; but without those pictures would the Revolution have been victorious? Many Utopias were mixed up with the Revolutionary myth, because it had been formed by a society passionately fond of imaginative literature, full of confidence in the "science," and very little acquainted with the economic history of the past. The Utopias came to nothing; but it may be asked whether the Revolution was not a much more profound transformation than those dreamed of by the people who in the eighteenth century had invented social Utopias. In our own times Mazzini pursued what the wiseacres of his time called a mad chimera; but it can no longer be denied that, without Mazzini, Italy would never have become a great power, and that he did more for Italian unity than Cavour and all the politicians of his school.

A knowledge of what the myths contain in the way of details which will actually form part of the history of the future is then of small importance; they are not astrological almanacs; it is even possible that nothing which they contain will ever come to pass,—as was the case with the catastrophe expected by the first Christians. In our own daily life, are we not familiar with the fact that what actually happens is very different from our preconceived notion of it? And that does not prevent us from continuing to make resolutions. Psychologists say that there is heterogeneity between the ends in view and the ends actually realised: the slightest experience of life reveals this law to us, which Spencer transferred into nature, to extract therefrom his theory of the multiplication of effects.

The myth must be judged as a means of acting on the present; any attempt to discuss how far it can be taken literally as future history is devoid of sense. *It is the myth in its entirety which is alone important:* its parts are only of interest in so far as they bring out the main ideas. . . .

The conception of the general strike, engendered by the practice of violent strikes, admits the conception of an irrevocable overthrow. There is something terrifying in this which will appear more and more terrifying as violence takes a greater place in the mind of the proletariat. But, in undertaking a serious, formidable, and sublime work, Socialists raise themselves above our frivolous society and make themselves worthy of pointing out new roads to the world.

PART *Three:*

AGE OF *Anxiety*

We are living to-day under the sign of the collapse of civilization. The situation has not been produced by the war; the latter is only a manifestation of it. The spiritual atmosphere has solidified into actual facts, which again react on it with disastrous results in every respect.

Albert Schweitzer, THE PHILOSOPHY OF CIVILIZATION

Lord of all things, [man] is not lord of himself. He feels lost amid his own abundance. With more means at his disposal, more knowledge, more technique than ever, it turns out that the world to-day goes the same way as the worst of worlds that have been; it simply drifts. Hence the strange combination of a sense of power and a sense of insecurity which has taken up its abode in the soul of modern man.

Ortega y Gasset, THE REVOLT OF THE MASSES

Current events impress us with their irrationality. . . . The dominance of irrational forces in human nature has perhaps never been as complete as at the present moment.

Franz Alexander, OUR AGE OF UNREASON

The symbolic nature of the entities of physics is generally recognised; and the scheme of physics is now formulated in such a way as to make it almost self-evident that it is a partial aspect of something wider.
Sir Arthur Eddington, THE NATURE OF THE PHYSICAL
WORLD

Age of Anxiety

*I*N a striking essay written in 1919, one of France's literary lights called attention to a crisis that had overtaken the European mind in the twentieth century. Hamlet-like, Paul Valéry brooded on the greatness and decline of Europe, a subject to which he returned again and again until his death in 1945. The greatness was not in doubt. Valéry marvelled at the imbalance of political and intellectual power between Europe and the rest of the world up to the present. Small though it was in size, in reality only a little promontory on the great continent of Asia, Europe had led the world in thought and culture for centuries. Europe was "the elect portion of the terrestrial globe, the pearl of the sphere, the brain of a vast body." Europe's superiority rested on a happy combination of qualities—imagination and rigorous logic, skepticism and mysticism, above all an ardent and disinterested curiosity. "Everything came to Europe, and everything came from it. Or almost everything."[1]

"—until recently," said Valéry. The Great War had made him ponder deeply the fragility of civilizations, that of Europe as well as Nineveh, Babylon, and Persepolis. "We later civilizations . . . we too now know that we are mortal."[2] In fact, however, Europe's mortality, or at least decline, had begun, as Valéry now saw, long before World War I. Already by 1914 Europe had perhaps reached the limits of "modernism," which was characterized above all, Valéry thought, by disorder in the mind. By disorder he appears to have meant the lack of any fixed system of reference for living and thinking. This lack could be ascribed to "the free coexistence, in all her cultivated minds, of the most dissimilar ideas, the most contradictory principles of life and

[1] Paul Valéry, "The Crisis of the Mind," *Collected Works*, vol. 10 (New York, 1962), pp. 31-3.
[2] Ibid., p. 23.

647

learning. This is characteristic of a *modern* epoch." [3] The decline also owed much to politics, which had never been Europe's strong suit, a weakness for which the continent was now being punished. The export of European knowledge and applied science had enabled others to upset the inequality on which Europe's predominance had been based. For these and other causes Europe and *Homo europaeus* had succumbed at last to *anxiety* and *anguish*. The military crisis might be temporarily over, but the economic crisis remained, as did above all "the crisis of the mind" which was the most subtle cause of all and the most fateful for literature, philosophy, and aesthetics.

Thus Valéry, along with many of his contemporaries, announced the beginning of a new Age of Anxiety in European history. Before pursuing further that anxiety, which Valéry interpreted as a symptom of decline, it would be well for us to cast more than a passing glance at Europe's continuing intellectual greatness in the twentieth century. Despite his pessimism Valéry would have been the first to say that the greatness persisted, though not without signs of diminishment, through most of his lifetime. It is true that twentieth-century Europe lived to a large extent on the accumulated intellectual capital of past centuries. Some of its chief luminaries in science and philosophy, for example, were born and educated in the nineteenth century and did some of their most important work before 1914: Sigmund Freud (b. 1856), Max Planck (b. 1858), Alfred North Whitehead (b. 1861), Carl Jung (b. 1875), and Albert Einstein (b. 1879). It is also true that a serious brain drain to America and elsewhere began to set in with the rise of fascism in the 1920s and 1930s. Nevertheless, it cannot be gainsaid that there were major breakthroughs in at least three major areas of thought between 1900 and 1950: physical science, psychology, and philosophy.

The new quantum and relativity physics, said to constitute a "twin-revolution in the realms of the infinitely large and the infinitely small," [4] was comparable in its richness of new ideas to "classical" physics. It in fact upset some of the major presuppositions of the older physics. Because it could not be as readily pictured as the Newtonian world-machine, it was not equally accessible to the lay mind and did not have the same profound effect on the "other culture" of the humanities. Indeed, it reached the humanities chiefly in a roundabout way, by means of the awesome technology it made possible. In philosophical circles, however, it did certainly give rise to much new speculation about the nature and structure of matter, space and time, causation and predictability, the problem of knowledge, and even God. Between the materialistic science of the communists (as stated by Lenin in *Materialism*

[3] Ibid., p. 27.
[4] Arthur Koestler, *Arrow in the Blue* (New York, 1952).

and Empirio-Criticism, 1909) and the "idealistic" philosophy of science that now emerged in western Europe a great gulf was fixed.

Existentialism and psychoanalysis also constituted major break-throughs. Both had roots in the nineteenth century, as indeed did the new physics. But both flourished in twentieth-century soil because the climate—that of anxiety—was right. Both, moreover, because they pertained centrally to man rather than to electrons and wave lengths, quickly and deeply permeated the culture around them. Existentialism, called "the philosophy of the twentieth century," spilled over into literature and the drama. So did psychoanalysis, described by Thomas Mann as a "world movement," affecting every domain of the intellect, not only literature but also prehistory, mythology, folklore, religion, and pedagogy. "Indeed, it would be too much to say that I came to psychoanalysis. It came to me," [5] said this major novelist of the twentieth century.

It was existentialism's special distinction to provide philosophy with a new starting point for thinking, sharply different from the "objective" thinking characteristic of "modern" philosophy. True philosophy, according to such philosophers as Martin Heidegger and Jean-Paul Sartre, was the fruit of personal rather than impersonal thinking, of the thinker's involvement in a life-situation, and of caring deeply about that situation, rather than of the detached observation and logic so cherished by Idealism or scientific Positivism. The distinction of psychoanalysis was similarly to probe beneath abstract "reason" or the "ego" to find the emotional springs of thought and action. If psychoanalysis did not discover the unconscious, it did explore it thoroughly, especially in the systems of Freud and Carl Jung. Otto Rank, who was one of Freud's circle, rightly called the twentieth century the "age of psychology." For never before had psychology, now completely independent of philosophy, been so central to Europe's intellectual endeavor. Psychoanalysis, it should be noted, was but one of many contemporary schools of psychology. In addition to Freudians there were also Jungians, Adlerians, and behaviorists, to name only the best known. There was even a school of existential psychology led by the Swiss psychologist Ludwig Binswanger, correspondent and antagonist of Freud.

Nor does this list of three—physics, existentialism, and psychoanalysis—by any means exhaust the intellectual achievements of Europe between the two world wars. It would not be difficult to draw up a much longer list including logical positivism, still another creative movement in philosophy; Keynesian economics; all the new movements, some

---

[5] Thomas Mann, "Freud and the Future" (1936). Reprinted in Mann, *Essays of Three Decades* (New York, 1947).

highly experimental, in literature and art (especially the metaphysical novel and metaphysical poetry); and the new theologies, some of which, like "neoorthodoxy," did indeed recall older theologies, but others of which projected radically new points of view. The documents collected in this section record some of these "adventures of ideas."

Along with the greatness, however, went the decline or anxiety, as Valéry said. Not outsiders but Europeans themselves invented the term Age of Anxiety to describe what they thought was happening to them in the twentieth century. They themselves dwelt increasingly not on the growing enlightenment of their times, as so many had done in the eighteenth century, nor on Europe's continuing greatness, but on the anxiety they felt about their existence, their culture, and their destiny. "Today," said the theologian-philosopher Paul Tillich at midcentury, "it has become almost a truism to call our time an 'age of anxiety.' " [6] Tillich believed that anxiety infected even the greatest achievement of contemporary Europeans in literature, art, and philosophy. Europe, by his account, had entered its third great period of anxiety, comparable in intensity to that of the ancient world and the Reformation.

The special form of anxiety that Tillich perceived in twentieth-century Europe was the anxiety of meaninglessness. He traced it to the modern world's loss of a spiritual center which could provide answers to the question of the meaning of life. This was a common observation among those who still belonged to an identifiable religious group. Witness, for example, the early poetry of T. S. Eliot, especially "The Hollow Men" (1925), and the later poetry of W. H. Auden after he had recovered his religious belief. Auden was obsessed by the anxiety felt by the "lonelies" or sick souls of the modern world. In *The Age of Anxiety* (1947) he equated it with the suffering that comes from living without purpose or faith. His four characters, huddling together for warmth, go in search of The Quiet Kingdom, impelled by "a feeling of having lost their bearings, of a restless urge to find water." This sort of observation was not, however, peculiar to religious thinkers. The atheistic existentialists also related anxiety to man's consciousness of living in an "absurd" world. Unlike Tillich, they did not believe there were any essences decreed by God. But the knowledge that there were none caused anxiety because the responsibility for making whatever values there were devolved entirely on man. Man was free— free to choose without reference to God or an ideal world of essences—but his freedom was a "dread" freedom, involving crushing responsibility and the eternal threat of non-being.

The death of God was not the only observed cause of anxiety. Also

[6] Paul Tillich, *The Courage To Be* (New Haven, 1952). Note that Tillich's remark applied to America as well as Europe.

cited frequently were the death of man and the death of Europe; in fact, the death—or at least the toppling—of all the great modern idols: not only God and man, but also reason, science, progress, and history. Dire external events from 1914 to 1945 obviously had much to do with this fall of the idols, and consequently with anxiety. However, it is interesting to note that contemporary writers frequently used the fall and the anxiety to explain the events. Tillich did so, for example, in his explanation of the success of fascism. In a time of "total doubt" men escaped from freedom to an authority that promised meaning and imposed answers.[7] "Twentieth-century man," Arthur Koestler wrote shortly after World War II, "is a political neurotic because he has no answer to the question of the meaning of life, because socially and metaphysically he does not know where he belongs."[8] Anxiety, then, was thought to be generated, internally as well as externally, by that "crisis of the mind" that Valéry had detected in 1919 but that had been brewing for decades.

The fall of the idols requires further comment. It is paradoxical that science became an object of distrust and fear in a great age of science. This was because to many people science, once regarded as a cure-all, had come to signify machines, and machines now spelled impersonality, dehumanization, and the ability to wage total war. The new feeling about machines, still glorified by the Italian Futurists in the early part of the century, is recorded vividly in such books as Aldous Huxley's *Brave New World* (1933) and Virgil Gheorghiu's *The Twenty-fifth Hour* (1949). In the latter the machines created by science revolt against their human masters and enslave them. Samuel Butler's *Erewhon* (1872), a book with a similar theme, had a happier ending: men regained control over the machines. If science could not come to the relief of man's estate, at least not in the way Bacon had believed, neither could it provide an acceptable interpretation of the universe or found a morality. It was certainly no substitute for the religion that so many Europeans had lost.

Nor was man any longer a pillar of strength. André Malraux may have been the first to talk about "the death of man." In one of Malraux's early works of fiction an Asian writes to a European friend: "For you [Europeans] absolute reality was first God, then Man; but [now] Man [too] is dead, following God, and you search with anguish for something to which you can entrust his strange heritage."[9] What Malraux meant was that the "classical" image of rational man was dead or dying.

---

[7] Doubtless, Tillich borrowed the expression "escape from freedom" from Erich Fromm's famous book of 1941 by that title.

[8] Arthur Koestler, "A Guide to Political Neuroses," *The Trail of the Dinosaur* (New York, 1955), pp. 229–30.

[9] André Malraux, *La tentation de l'Occident* (Paris, 1926), letter no. 15.

But long before Malraux the Freudians had been saying that man was less rational than he knew, that he was suffering from neurosis, and that he was not master even in his own house, the psyche. Other images, equally unflattering to human self-esteem, emerged more or less simultaneously: sinful man, "the man without qualities," "the stranger," "the unnameable," etc.[10] Existential man could be either pathetic, subject to nausea (as in Sartre's early novel by that title), or heroic, defiant of gods and tyrants. But even when defiant—and successful—like Aegisthus in Sartre's later wartime play *The Flies*, he was still afflicted by cosmic anxiety. All of these and similar images surfaced in literature, and indeed changed the nature of literature. Because the "modern" picture of human nature was disintegrating, it became difficult to write novels and plays with old-fashioned heroes or even ordinary people with firm personality traits.

This skepticism extended to history, another erstwhile idol. The communists and fascists continued to have faith in history. This was one of the advantages they had over their rivals: they knew where history was taking them or where they were taking history, whereas "bourgeois" liberals discussed seriously the "decline of the West." William Inge, "the gloomy Dean" of Saint Paul's Cathedral in London, denounced the idea of progress as a "modern superstition." Instead of being progressive, history was perhaps cyclical, or at least liable to shipwreck at any time. In any case, there was no observable end to the great battle between freedom and destiny in history. Oswald Spengler, whose famous book on the "going under" of the West was published immediately after World War I, believed in destiny. Nothing could stop or delay the inexorable turning of a society from "culture" to "civilization," that is, from its phase of spiritual creativity to that of soullessness and materialism, and on to its eventual demise. Arnold Toynbee, less deterministic, thought that civilizations (he did not use the word pejoratively, as did Spengler) could always rally; still, it was a fact that twenty-five of the twenty-six great civilizations of the world had disappeared, and that the twenty-sixth, that of the West, had already entered its "time of troubles." Malraux, opposing Spengler, insisted on freedom in history, particularly through man's artistic creativity. Yet he too had a healthy respect for destiny, which he defined as the feeling man develops at certain times in history of not being in control, of not having goals; and he thought that destiny so defined had enlarged its empire in recent times. The representativeness of Valéry's plaint of 1919 —that "we later civilizations . . . we too know

[10] I have written at length about these images in the chapter entitled "Problematic Man" in my *Modern European Thought* (New York, 1977).

that we are mortal"—becomes apparent when we read these and smilar statements by his contemporaries.

Whither Europe in particular? The idol of Europe fell along with the idol of history. Valéry, despite his many essays on Europe's greatness, ended by harping more on its decline. Others like Spengler contemplated the permanent decline of Europe. Malraux thought that "the death of Europe" was premature. Who could match, even now after two world wars, Europe's "will to discovery and awareness," her great art, science, and literature? All, however, whatever their individual prognosis, agreed that henceforth Europe's intellectual and cultural achievements must be gauged in relation to what was being done elsewhere, in America or Asia. This may not seem an especially original insight. The point is that it was new for Europeans who, as Geoffrey Barraclough said, had been contemplating their navels for a long time. Henceforth, history must be written from a world viewpoint. European history and even Western history must not be studied in isolation. This was one of the points Spengler insisted on. He urged the replacement of a "Ptolemaic" by a "Copernican" viewpoint in history. His Copernican revolution consisted in treating Europe as one of a number of great cultures of world history, and not as the center of the historical universe around which all other cultures orbited.

But what of the larger question: upon what do all great cultures depend? How much does intellectual leadership depend on preponderant political and economic power? If it in fact does not depend on this power, Europe might continue to be, if not the sun of the world's intellectual universe, at least one of the most important planets—as I believe Europe has been since 1950, and will continue to be. The philosopher Alfred North Whitehead had some wise things to say on this subject.[11] A "live" and "high" civilization, he thought, was contingent upon a spirit of adventure. The latter was in turn contingent upon the amount of curiosity and self-criticism a society could generate, and upon explicit recognition of the need for free speculation, because all reasonably coherent points of view contribute to man's understanding of the universe. But such a society must also have "some transcendent aim," for lack of which people wallow in pleasure and corruption. It must have ultimate, even if "impracticable," ideals concerning the Good, the True, and the Beautiful toward which people are agreed that they should strive. Europe, one might add, was for many centuries the heir of ancient Greece in all these respects. After the "civil wars" from 1914 to 1945, the freedom, the self-criticism, and even much of the curiosity remain, though in a truncated Europe. But

[11] See especially Whitehead's *Adventures of Ideas* (New York, 1933).

is Europe still a particularly adventurous civilization now that it has been put on the defensive like late imperial Rome and is no longer an expanding world power? Above all, can Europeans ever recover the transcendent aims they once had? The answer to these questions is not determined or presently determinable. Surely the answer will be supplied in large measure not merely by a hypothetical shift in the political and economic balance of nations, but by the goals and ideals that Europeans set for themselves in the years to come.

$$\mathcal{R}eadings$$

1. *On the Meaning of the Twentieth Century*

PAUL TILLICH: *Age of Anxiety* *

> The following three selections register the grave concern of a theologian (Paul Tillich), a psychiatrist (Franz Alexander), and a philosopher (C. E. M. Joad) about recent developments in western thought and culture. Paul Tillich (1886–1965), one of the most impressive and influential Protestant theologians of the twentieth century, came to the U. S. A. in 1933 after having held academic posts at four German universities. *The Courage To Be*, from which the following excerpts are taken, grew out of the Terry Lectures delivered at Yale University.

. . . SOCIOLOGICAL analyses of the present period have pointed to the importance of anxiety as a group phenomenon. Literature and art have made anxiety a main theme of their creations, in content as well as in style. The effect of this has been the awakening of at least the educated groups to an awareness of their own anxiety, and a permeation of the public consciousness by ideas and symbols of anxiety. Today it has become almost a truism to call our time an "age of anxiety." This holds equally for America and Europe. . . .

. . . I suggest that we distinguish three types of anxiety according to the three directions in which nonbeing threatens being. Nonbeing threatens man's ontic self-affirmation, relatively in terms of fate, absolutely in terms of death. It threatens man's spiritual self-affirmation, relatively in terms of emptiness, absolutely in terms of meaninglessness. It threatens man's moral self-affirmation, relatively in terms of guilt, absolutely in terms of condemnation. The awareness of this threefold threat is anxiety appearing in three forms, that of fate and death (briefly, the anxiety of death), that of emptiness and loss of meaning (briefly, the anxiety of meaninglessness), that of guilt and condemnation (briefly, the anxiety of condemnation). In all three forms anxiety is existential in the sense that it belongs to existence as such and not to an abnormal state of mind as in neurotic (and psychotic) anxiety. . . .

The anxiety of meaninglessness is anxiety about the loss of an ultimate concern, of a meaning which gives meaning to all meanings. This anxiety is aroused by the loss of a spiritual center, of an answer, however symbolic and indirect, to the question of the meaning of existence. . . .

The distinction of the three types of anxiety is supported by the history of Western civilization. We find that at the end of ancient civilization ontic anxiety is predominant, at the end of the Middle Ages moral anxiety, and at the end of the modern period spiritual anxiety. But in spite of the predominance of one type the others are also present and effective. . . .

The breakdown of absolutism, the development of liberalism and democracy, the rise of a technical civilization with its victory over all enemies and its own beginning disintegration—these are the sociological presupposition for the third main period of anxiety. In this the anxiety of emptiness and meaninglessness is dominant. We are under the threat of spiritual nonbeing. . . .

It is significant that the three main periods of anxiety appear at the end of an era. The anxiety which, in its different forms, is potentially present in every individual becomes general if the accustomed structures of meaning, power, belief, and order disintegrate. These structures, as long as they are in force, keep anxiety bound within a protective system of courage by participation. The individual who participates in the institutions and ways of life of such a system is not liberated from his personal anxieties but he has means of overcoming them with well-known methods. In periods of great changes these methods no longer work. Conflicts between the old, which tries to maintain itself, often with new means, and the new, which deprives the old of its intrinsic power, produce anxiety in all directions. Nonbeing, in such a situation, has a double face, resembling two types of nightmare (which are perhaps, expressions of an awareness of these two faces). The one type is the anxiety of annihilating narrowness, of the impossibility of escape and the horror of being trapped. The other is the anxiety of annihilating openness, of infinite formless space into which one falls without a place to fall upon. Social situations like those described have the character both of a trap without exit and of an empty, dark, and unknown void. Both faces of the same reality arouse the latent anxiety of every individual who looks at them. Today most of us do look at them.

FRANZ ALEXANDER: *Our Age of Unreason* *

Like Tillich, Franz Alexander (1891–   ) came to the U. S. A. after a
career in Europe. He was born and trained in Budapest and was lecturer
at the Institute for Psychoanalysis in Berlin from 1921 to 1930. He became director of the Chicago Institute for Psychoanalysis in 1932.

THIS book has been written under the influence of rapid and profound
cultural changes in the years following the World War. I spent the
eleven years following the Versailles and Trianon Peace Treaties in
Europe, the next twelve years in the United States. In Europe I saw the
world of my youth rapidly disintegrate and standards and ideals which
had become second nature to me vanish. Like most European observers
of these eventful years I saw that a cultural epoch was in process of dissolution. What would follow was not clear, but much clearer was what
was specifically disappearing, the highest values I had known; science
and artistic creation for their own sakes, the gradual improvement of
human relations by the use of knowledge and reason were giving way
to a chaotic sense of insecurity, fear, and distrust among mechanically
minded men who had been corrupted by technical accomplishments.
Everyone expected the worst, was worried, strained, and was concerned
with himself, with his uncertain future, and with the pressing and
practical problems of the present. The maxim *Primum vivere deinde
philosophare* ("First live; then philosophize") became the ruling principle.

*   *   *

Current events impress us with their irrationality. We are witnessing
on an unprecedented scale the wholesale destruction of life and property. All this happens in an era of the utmost scientific enlightenment
and of the greatest technical achievements which, if intelligently used,
could render the life of all the inhabitants of the earth easier and more
carefree than ever before. There is little doubt that a council of economists and political scientists could work out a peaceful social organization and a rational world order which could satisfy the vital needs of
all. That such a rational world order is today, as in Plato's time, a utopia
is due to the fact that human relationships are not governed primarily
by reason but by essentially irrational emotional forces. The dominance
of irrational forces in human nature has perhaps never been as complete
as at the present moment. It is no wonder that in the face of current
world events many turn for an explanation to the psychiatrist, the specialist in irrational behavior.

The truth is that in our generation man has begun to lose his faith that he can improve his lot through technical advance alone. It is becoming a truism that the natural sciences have failed to increase human happiness and that their most obvious contribution has been to supply increasingly deadly weapons of destruction. The mastery of nature has proved more a curse than a blessing in the hands of men ignorant of their own personalities and of human relationships. The discrepancy between the development of the natural sciences and that of psychology and the social sciences is largely responsible for the disasters we are witnessing at present.

C. E. M. JOAD: *Decadence* *

The English philosopher Cyril E. M. Joad (1891–1953) was widely known as an analyst and critic of contemporary trends of thought. Among his many works were the autobiographical *Under the Fifth Rib, Guide to Modern Thought,* and *God and Evil* (see below, pp. 609–13). In *Decadence,* published in 1948, he arraigned modern society for its subjectivism—for its "dropping of the object" or loss of objective standards.

SPECULATION, at all times hazardous, is particularly so in a time like the present which wears the appearance of an interim age, an age in exile between two worlds, the one dead, the other trying, yet failing to be born. The late Hellenistic was another such age; the Alexandrian another. It may well be that these interim ages and the qualities associated with them constitute the clearest examples of what the common sense of mankind has always recognized as decadence. . . .

The characteristics of a decadent society are fairly constant. According to Palinurus's *Unquiet Grave* [a book by the English literary critic, Cyril Connolly, published in 1946] they are 'luxury, scepticism, weariness and superstition'. These, he says, being himself decadent and, therefore, sceptical, constitute 'the goal of all cultures', for 'the goal of all cultures is to decay through over-civilization'. I agree very largely with Palinurus's list of the stigmata of decadence; I venture to add a preoccupation with the self and its experiences, promoted by and promoting the subjectivist analysis of moral, aesthetic, metaphysical and theological judgements. . . .

. . . Subjectivism is perhaps the most distinctive belief of our age, or more precisely, it is the philosophical attitude which underlies a number of its distinctive beliefs. . . .

* From C. E. M. Joad: *Decadence*, pp. 421, 117, 104, 108–9. Copyright 1948 by Faber and Faber Limited. Reprinted by permission of A. D. Peters, Literary Agent for the Author's Estate.

. . . A subjectivist attitude to art and morality which analyses apparently objective aesthetic and moral judgments on subjectivist lines is naturally allied to Scepticism and Hedonism. Common to all three is the tendency to leave out 'the object'.

This leaving out of 'the object' is an essential part of my definition of decadence; it is also a pervasive characteristic of the intellectual climate of our time.

An Age Without Standards? It is often charged against the present age that it lacks standards. To what does the charge amount? First, in the sphere of religion, that the generation which came to maturity in the years between the wars lacks a creed. Broadly, it holds no beliefs of any kind about the fundamental nature and government of the universe. It is not that it doubts—doubt, at least, implies interest; but the contemporary generation does not think about the matters which fall within the province of religion one way or the other. Secondly, in the sphere of morals that it has no code. When the foundations of the Christian code in Christian belief were sapped, it was unlikely that the superstructure of morals which was raised upon them would indefinitely survive. Nor has it done so. It would, I think, be generally agreed that in this country, at least, the moral level of behaviour has further declined since the outbreak of the second world war. This decline has occurred not merely in the sphere of sexual morals; it is also to be observed in the practice of the specifically Christian virtues, in charity, mercy, pity, honesty and unselfishness. The decline had already begun before 1914 and each of the two wars has accelerated the process.

Thirdly, in the sphere of art, a lack of standards is said to be a noticeable characteristic of the movements which have made their appearance during the last three decades. Expressionism, Surrealism and Existentialism are, perhaps, the most distinctive of these movements. Of them it may be said that they have sought less to imitate or represent the external world than to express the moods of the artists and writers. Novelists wove atmospheres instead of constructing plots, while poets used verse as a vehicle for the out-pourings of agitated emotions and the intricacies of tortured thought. There have never been so many novelists, there have not often been so many poets; yet, judged by Victorian standards, there have been few great novels and fewer great poems. . . .

ORTEGA Y GASSET: *An Interregnum* *

The noted Spanish philosopher José Ortega y Gasset (1883–1955) is one of many contemporary writers who have characterized the twenti-

* From José Ortega y Gasset: *The Revolt of the Masses*, pp. 33–4, 36–7, 47–8, 195–6. Copyright © 1932 by W. W. Norton & Company, Inc., Copyright © 1960 by Teresa Carey. Selections reprinted by permission of the publisher.

eth century as "an interregnum." He did not think of it as decadent; it was too full of a sense of vitality and power. On the other hand, he noted (and deplored) its sense of insecurity, its rootlessness and lack of unifying standards. The following excerpts are taken from his best known book *The Revolt of the Masses,* which was first published in 1930.

. . . THERE have been, then, various periods in history which have felt themselves as having attained a full, definitive height, periods in which it is thought that the end of a journey has been reached, a long-felt desire obtained, a hope completely fulfilled. This is "the plenitude of the time," the full ripening of historic life. And, in fact, thirty years ago, the European believed that human life had come to be what it ought to be, what for generations previous it had been desiring to be, what it was henceforward always bound to be. These epochs of plenitude always regard themselves as the result of many other preparatory periods, of other times lacking in plenitude, inferior to their own, above which this time of full-flower has risen. . . .

Do we not here touch upon the essential difference between our time and that which has just passed away? Our time, in fact, no longer regards itself as definitive; on the contrary, it discovers, though obscurely, deep within itself an intuition that there are no such epochs, definitive, assured, crystallised for ever. Quite the reverse, the claim that a certain type of existence—the so-called "modern culture"—is definitive seems to us an incredible narrowing down and shutting out of the field of vision. And as an effect of this feeling we enjoy a delightful impression of having escaped from a hermetically sealed enclosure, of having regained freedom, of coming out once again under the stars into the world of reality, the world of the profound, the terrible, the unforeseeable, the inexhaustible, where everything is possible, the best and the worst. That faith in modern culture was a gloomy one. It meant that to-morrow was to be in all essentials similar to to-day, that progress consisted merely in advancing, for all time to be, along a road identical to the one already under our feet. Such a road is rather a kind of elastic prison which stretches on without ever setting us free. . . .

Over against this emotional state, is it not clear that the feelings of our time are more like the noisy joy of children let loose from school? Nowadays we no longer know what is going to happen to-morrow in our world, and this causes us a secret joy; because that very impossibility of foresight, that horizon ever open to all contingencies, constitute authentic life, the true fullness of our existence. This diagnosis, the other aspect of which, it is true, is lacking, stands in contrast to the plaints of decadence which wail forth in the pages of so many contemporary writers. . . .

*　　*　　*

. . . We live at a time when man believes himself fabulously capable of creation, but he does not know what to create. Lord of all things, he is not lord of himself. He feels lost amid his own abundance. With more means at its disposal, more knowledge, more technique than ever, it turns out that the world to-day goes the same way as the worst of worlds that have been; it simply drifts.

Hence the strange combination of a sense of power and a sense of insecurity which has taken up its abode in the soul of modern man. To him is happening what was said of the Regent during the minority of Louis XV: he had all the talents except the talent to make use of them. . . .

No one knows towards what centre human things are going to gravitate in the near future, and hence the life of the world has become scandalously provisional. Everything that to-day is done in private—even in one's inner conscience—is provisional, the only exception being certain portions of certain sciences. He will be a wise man who puts no trust in all that is proclaimed, upheld, essayed, and lauded at the present day. All that will disappear as quickly as it came. . . . Nothing of all that has any roots. . . . Life to-day is the fruit of an interregnum, of an empty space between two organisations of historical rule —that which was, that which is to be. For this reason it is essentially provisional. Men do not know what institutions to serve in truth. . . .

2. *Religion and Skepticism*

SIGMUND FREUD: *The Future of an Illusion* *

> *The Future of an Illusion* (1928) not only states concisely Sigmund Freud's main ideas about religion but typifies the twentieth-century "warfare between religion and psychiatry."

IN PAST ages, in spite of their incontrovertible lack of authenticity, religious ideas have exercised the very strongest influence on mankind. . . . We must ask where the inherent strength of these doctrines lies and to what circumstance they owe their efficacy, independent, as it is, of the acknowledgement of the reason.

I think we have sufficiently paved the way for the answer to both these questions. It will be found if we fix our attention on the psychical origin of religious ideas. These, which profess to be dogmas, are not the residue of experience or the final result of reflection; they are illusions, fulfilments of the oldest, strongest and most insistent

* From Sigmund Freud: *The Future of an Illusion*, pp. 51–5, 67–8, 84–6. Copyright 1928 by The Hogarth Press Ltd. Reprinted by permission of The Hogarth Press Ltd. and by permission of Liveright, Publishers, N. Y.

wishes of mankind; the secret of their strength is the strength of these wishes. We know already that the terrifying effect of infantile helplessness aroused the need for protection—protection through love—which the father relieved, and that the discovery that this helplessness would continue through the whole of life made it necessary to cling to the existence of a father—but this time a more powerful one. Thus the benevolent rule of divine providence allays our anxiety in face of life's dangers, the establishment of a moral world order ensures the fulfilment of the demands of justice, which within human culture have so often remained unfulfilled, and the prolongation of earthly existence by a future life provides in addition the local and temporal setting for these wish-fulfilments. Answers to the questions that tempt human curiosity, such as the origin of the universe and the relation between the body and the soul, are developed in accordance with the underlying assumptions of this system; it betokens a tremendous relief for the individual psyche if it is released from the conflicts of childhood arising out of the father complex, which are never wholly overcome, and if these conflicts are afforded a universally accepted solution.

When I say that they are illusions, I must define the meaning of the word. An illusion is not the same as an error, it is indeed not necessarily an error. . . . It is characteristic of the illusion that it is derived from men's wishes; in this respect it approaches the psychiatric delusion, but it is to be distinguished from this, quite apart from the more complicated structure of the latter. In the delusion we emphasize as essential the conflict with reality; the illusion need not be necessarily false, that is to say, unrealizable or incompatible with reality. . . . Thus we call a belief an illusion when wish-fulfilment is a prominent factor in its motivation, while disregarding its relations to reality, just as the illusion itself does.

If after this survey we turn again to religious doctrines, we may reiterate that they are all illusions, they do not admit of proof, and no one can be compelled to consider them as true or to believe in them. Some of them are so improbable, so very incompatible with everything we have laboriously discovered about the reality of the world, that we may compare them—taking adequately into account the psychological differences—to delusions. Of the reality value of most of them we cannot judge; just as they cannot be proved, neither can they be refuted. We still know too little to approach them critically. The riddles of the universe only reveal themselves slowly to our enquiry, to many questions science can as yet give no answer; but scientific work is our only way to the knowledge of external reality.

*   *   *

Let us consider the unmistakable character of the present situation. We have heard the admission that religion no longer has the same influence on men that it used to have (we are concerned here with European Christian culture). And this, not because its promises have become smaller, but because they appear less credible to people. Let us admit that the reason—perhaps not the only one—for this change is the increase of the scientific spirit in the higher strata of human society. Criticism has nibbled at the authenticity of religious documents, natural science has shown up the errors contained in them, and the comparative method of research has revealed the fatal resemblance between religious ideas revered by us and the mental productions of primitive ages and peoples.

The scientific spirit engenders a particular attitude to the problems of this world; before the problems of religion it halts for a while, then wavers, and finally here too steps over the threshold. In this process there is no stopping. The more the fruits of knowledge became accessible to men, the more widespread is the decline of religious belief, at first only of the obsolete and objectionable expressions of the same, then of its fundamental assumptions also.

*　　*　　*

[I believe] that it is worth while to make the experiment of a non-religious education. . . . I disagree . . . that man cannot in general do without the consolation of the religious illusion, that without it he would not endure the troubles of life, the cruelty of reality. Certainly this is true of the man into whom you have instilled the sweet—or bitter-sweet—poison from childhood on. But what of the other, who has been brought up soberly? Perhaps he, not suffering from neurosis, will need no intoxicant to deaden it. True, man will then find himself in a difficult situation. He will have to confess his utter helplessness and his insignificant part in the working of the universe; he will have to confess that he is no longer the centre of creation, no longer the object of the tender care of a benevolent providence. He will be in the same position as the child who has left the home where he was so warm and comfortable. But, after all, is it not the destiny of childishness to be overcome? Man cannot remain a child for ever; he must venture at last into the hostile world. This may be called 'education to reality'; need I tell you that it is the sole aim of my book to draw attention to the necessity for this advance?

KARL BARTH: *The Word of God and the Word of Man* *

Karl Barth (1886–1968), Swiss preacher and theologian, is the leader of the powerful "neo-orthodox" movement in contemporary Protestantism. Barth occupied chairs of theology in three German universities until the Nazis banished him from Germany as an undesirable alien. Since 1935 he has been professor of theology at Basel. The following selection on "The Righteousness of God" is from an address delivered in the Town Church of Aarau in 1916. In the second selection Barth traces briefly the historical lineage of his theology.

The Righteousness of God

"The voice of him that crieth in the wilderness, Prepare ye the way of the Lord, make straight in the desert a highway for our God. Every valley shall be exalted, and every mountain and hill shall be made law; and the crooked shall be made straight, and the rough places plain; and the glory of the Lord shall be revealed!" This is the voice of our conscience, telling us of the righteousness of God. And since conscience is the perfect interpreter of life, what it tells us is no question, no riddle, no problem, but a fact—the deepest, innermost, surest fact of life: God is righteous. Our only question is what attitude toward the fact we ought to take.

We shall hardly approach the fact with our critical reason. The reason sees the small and the larger but not the large. It sees the preliminary but not the final, the derived but not the original, the complex but not the simple. It sees what is human but not what is divine.

We shall hardly be taught this fact by men. . . .

We [on the other hand] suffer from unrighteousness. We dread it. All that is within us revolts against it. We know more about it, it is true, than we do about righteousness. We have constantly before us, in the great and small occurrences of life, in our own conduct and in that of others, another kind of will, a will which knows no dominant and inflexible idea but is grounded upon caprice, vagary, and self-seeking—a will without faithfulness, logic, or correlation, disunited and distraught within itself. The more sharply we look, the more clearly we see it. Of such are we, of such is life, of such is the world. The critical reason may come and prove to us that it has always been so and always must be so. But we have before our eyes the consequences of this unrighteous will—disquiet, disorder, and distress in forms minute and gross, obscure

* From Karl Barth: *The Word of God and the Word of Man*, trans. by Douglas Horton, pp. 9, 11–16, 18–19, 22–3, 25–7, 195–6. Copyright 1928 by Sidney A. Weston. Reprinted by permission of The Pilgrim Press.

and evident. We have before us the fiendishness of business competition and the world war, passion and wrongdoing, antagonism between classes and moral depravity within them, economic tyranny above and the slave spirit below. . . .

Oppressed and afflicted by his own unrighteousness and the unrighteousness of others, man—every man—lifts up from the depths of his nature the cry for righteousness, the righteousness of God. . . .

*　　*　　*

But now comes a remarkable turn in our relation with the righteousness of God. The trumpet of conscience sounds; we start with apprehension; we feel the touch of holiness upon us—but at first we do not dream of appealing beyond ourselves for help in our need and anxiety. Quite the opposite. "They said one to another, Go to, let us make brick, and burn them thoroughly. Let us build us a city and a tower whose top may reach unto heaven; and let us make a name, lest we be scattered abroad upon the face of the whole earth!" We come to our own rescue and build the tower of Babel. . . .

Shall we call this pride on our part? There is, as a matter of fact, something of pride in it. We are inwardly resentful that the righteousness we pant after is God's and can come to us only from God. We should like to take the mighty thing into our own hands and under our own management, as we have done with so many other things. It seems quite desirable that the righteousness without which we cannot exist should be controlled by our own will, whatever kind of will that may really be. We arrogate to ourselves, unquestioningly, the right to take up the tumultuous question, What shall we *do?* as if that were in any case the first and most pressing problem. Only let us be quick to put our hand to reform, sanitation, methods, cultural and religious endeavors of all sorts! Only to do "real work"! And before we know it, the trumpet blast of conscience has lost its disturbing tone. The anxiety in which we found ourselves when confronted by the dominant world-will has been gently changed into a prosperous sense of normality, and we have arrived again at reflection, criticism, construction, and organization. The longing for a new world has lost all its bitterness, sharpness, and restlessness, has become the joy of development, and now blossoms sweetly and surely in orations, donor's tablets, committee meetings, reviews, annual reports, twenty-five year anniversaries, and countless mutual bows. The righteousness of God itself has slowly changed from being the surest of facts into being the highest among various high ideals, and is now at all events our very own affair. This is evident in our ability now to hang it gayly out of the window and now to roll it up again, somewhat like a flag. *Eritis sicut Deus!* You may act as if you were God, you may with ease take his righteousness under your own management. This is certainly pride. . . .

Does it not make us blind and impenitent toward the deep real needs of existence? Is it not remarkable that the greatest atrocities of life—I think of the capitalistic order and of the war—can justify themselves on purely moral principles? The devil may also make use of morality. He laughs at the tower of Babel which we erect to him.

The righteousness of the state and of the law. A wonderful tower! A most necessary and useful substitute to protect us in some measure from certain unpleasant results of our unrighteous will! Very suitable for quieting the conscience! But what does the state really do for us? It can order and organize the self-seeking and capricious vagaries of the human will. It can oppose certain hindrances to this will by its regulations and intimidations. It can set up certain institutions—schools, for instance—for the refining and ennobling of it. A vast amount of respectable work goes into all of this; for the building of this one tower of the state, millions of valuable lives are offered and consumed—to what end? The righteousness of the state, for all its variety of form, fails to touch the inner character of the world-will at any point. By this will it is indeed dominated. The war again provides the striking illustration: were it really possible for the state to make men out of wild animals, would the state find it necessary by a thousand arts to make wild animals out of men? The devil may laugh at this tower of Babel, also. . . .

In the question, Is God righteous? our whole tower of Babel falls to pieces. In this now burning question it becomes evident that we are looking for a righteousness without God, that we are looking, in truth, for a god without God and against God—and that our quest is hopeless. It is clear that such a god is not God. He is not even righteous. He cannot prevent his worshipers, all the distinguished European and American apostles of civilization, welfare, and progress, all zealous citizens and pious Christians, from falling upon one another with fire and sword to the amazement and derision of the poor heathen in India and Africa. This god is really an unrighteous god, and it is high time for us to declare ourselves thorough-going doubters, sceptics, scoffers and atheists in regard to him. It is high time for us to confess freely and gladly: this god, to whom we have built the tower of Babel, is not God. He is an idol. He is dead.

God himself, the real, the living God, and his love which comes in glory! These provide the solution. We have not yet begun to listen quietly to what the conscience asks when it reminds us, in our need and anxiety, of the righteousness of God. We have been much too eager to do something ourselves. . . .

In the Bible this humility and this joy are called—faith. Faith means seeking not noise but quiet, and letting God speak within—the righteous God, for there is no other. And then God works in us. Then begins in us, as from a seed, but an unfailing seed, the new basic something which overcomes unrighteousness. Where faith is, in the midst of the old world of war and money and death, there is born a new spirit out of which grows a new world, the world of the righteousness of God. . . .

It remains to be seen whether the quaking of the tower of Babel which we are now experiencing will be violent enough to bring us somewhat nearer to the way of *faith*. Opportunity offers. We may take the new way. Or we may not. Sooner or later we shall. There is no other.

Contra Modernist Theology

Let me conclude this part of our discussion with a historical note. Those who accept the thoughts I have brought forward as germane to the essential facts thereby acknowledge themselves descendents of an ancestral line which runs back through *Kierkegaard* to *Luther* and *Calvin*, and so to *Paul* and *Jeremiah*. . . .

And to leave nothing unsaid, I might explicitly point out that this ancestral line—which I commend to you—does *not include Schleiermacher*. With all due respect to the genius shown in his work, I can *not* consider Schleiermacher a good teacher in the realm of theology because, so far as I can see, he is disastrously dim-sighted in regard to the fact that man as man is not only in *need* but beyond all hope of saving himself; that the whole of so-called religion, and not least the Christian religion, *shares* in this need; and that one can *not* speak of God simply by speaking of man in a loud voice. There are those to whom Schleiermacher's peculiar excellence lies in his having discovered a conception of religion by which he overcame Luther's so-called dualism and connected earth and heaven by a much needed bridge, upon which we may reverently cross. Those who hold this view will finally turn their backs if they have not done so already, upon the considerations I have presented. I ask only that they do not appeal *both* to Schleiermacher *and* the Reformers, *both* to Schleiermacher *and* the New Testament, *both* to Schleiermacher *and* the Old Testament prophets, but that from Schleiermacher back they look for another ancestral line. . . . The very names Kierkegaard, Luther, Calvin, Paul, and Jeremiah suggest what Schleiermacher never possessed, a clear and direct apprehension of the truth that man is made to serve *God* and not God to serve man. . . .

Rudolf Bultmann: *New Testament and Mythology* *

Next to Barth, Rudolf Bultmann (1884–1976) was perhaps the best known Protestant theologian of the post-World War I epoch in Europe. Two years older than Barth, he nonetheless did not achieve notoriety outside theological circles until the publication of his article "New Testament and Mythology" in 1941. This article set off the famous debate, which extended into the 1960's, over "demythologization." Unlike Barth, Bultmann tried to accommodate the New Testament to modern culture, yet without giving up its essential "kerygma" or Gospel message which he interpreted existentially rather than supernaturally or as objective knowledge.

THE COSMOLOGY of the New Testament is essentially mythical in character. The world is viewed as a three-storied structure, with the earth in the centre, the heaven above, and the underworld beneath. Heaven is the abode of God and of celestial beings—the angels. The underworld is hell, the place of torment. Even the earth is more than the scene of natural, everyday events, of the trivial round and common task. It is the scene of the supernatural activity of God and his angels on the one hand, and of Satan and his daemons on the other. These supernatural forces intervene in the course of nature and in all that men think and will and do. Miracles are by no means rare. Man is not in control of his own life. Evil spirits may take possession of him. Satan may inspire him with evil thoughts. Alternatively, God may inspire his thought and guide his purposes. He may grant him heavenly visions. He may allow him to hear his word of succour or demand. He may give him the supernatural power of his Spirit. History does not follow a smooth unbroken course; it is set in motion and controlled by these supernatural powers. . . .

All this is the language of mythology, and the origin of the various themes can be easily traced in the contemporary mythology of Jewish Apocalyptic and in the redemption myths of Gnosticism. To this extent *the kerygma is incredible to modern man, for he is convinced that the mythical view of the world is obsolete.* We are therefore bound to ask whether, when we preach the Gospel to-day, we expect our converts to accept not only the Gospel message, but also the

* From "New Testament and Mythology" by Rudolf Bultmann, in *Kerygma and Myth,* edited by Hans-Werner Bartsch, trans. by Reginald H. Fuller, (London, SPCK, New York, Harper & Row). Reproduced by permission of SPCK.

mythical view of the world in which it is set. If not, does the New Testament embody a truth which is quite independent of its mythical setting? If it does, theology must undertake the task of stripping the Kerygma from its mythical framework, of "demythologizing" it.

Can Christian preaching expect modern man *to accept the mythical view of the world as true?* To do so would be both senseless and impossible. It would be senseless, because there is nothing specifically Christian in the mythical view of the world as such. It is simply the cosmology of a pre-scientific age. . . .

For all our thinking to-day is shaped irrevocably by modern science. A blind acceptance of the New Testament mythology would be arbitrary, and to press for its acceptance as an article of faith would be to reduce faith to works. Wilhelm Herrmann pointed this out, and one would have thought that his demonstration was conclusive. It would involve a sacrifice of the intellect which could have only one result— a curious form of schizophrenia and insincerity. It would mean accepting a view of the world in our faith and religion which we should deny in our everyday life. Modern thought as we have inherited it brings with it criticism of *the New Testament view of the world.*

Man's knowledge and mastery of the world have advanced to such an extent through science and technology that it is no longer possible for anyone seriously to hold the New Testament view of the world— in fact, there is no one who does. What meaning, for instance, can we attach to such phrases in the creed as "descended into hell" or "ascended into heaven"? We no longer believe in the three-storied universe which the creeds take for granted. The only honest way of reciting the creeds is to strip the mythological framework from the truth they enshrine—that is, assuming that they contain any truth at all, which is just the question that theology has to ask. . . .

. . . The only relevant question for the theologian is the basic assumption on which the adoption of a biological as of every other *Weltanschauung* rests, and that assumption is the view of the world which has been moulded by modern science and the modern conception of human nature as a self-subsistent unity immune from the interference of supernatural powers. . . .

If the truth of the New Testament proclamation is to be preserved, the only way is to demythologize it. But our motive in so doing must not be to make the New Testament relevant to the modern world at all costs. The question is simply whether the New Testament message consists exclusively of mythology, or whether it actually demands the elimination of myth if it is to be understood as it is meant to be. . . .

. . . Can we recover the truth of the kerygma for men who do not think in mythological terms without forfeiting its character as kerygma?

An Existentialist Interpretation the Only Solution

The theological work which such an interpretation involves can be sketched only in the broadest outline and with only a few examples. We must avoid the impression that this is a light and easy task, as if all we have to do is to discover the right formula and finish the job on the spot. It is much more formidable than that. It cannot be done single-handed. It will tax the time and strength of a whole theological generation.

The mythology of the New Testament is in essence that of Jewish apocalyptic and the Gnostic redemption myths. A common feature of them both is their basic dualism, according to which the present world and its human inhabitants are under the control of daemonic, satanic powers, and stand in need of redemption. Man cannot achieve this redemption by his own efforts; it must come as a gift through a divine intervention. Both types of mythology speak of such an intervention: Jewish apocalyptic of an imminent world crisis in which this present aeon will be brought to an end and the new aeon ushered in by the coming of the Messiah, and Gnosticism of a Son. of God sent down from the realm of light, entering into this world in the guise of a man, and by his fate and teaching delivering the elect and opening up the way for their return to their heavenly home.

The meaning of these two types of mythology lies once more not in their imagery with its apparent objectivity but in the understanding of human existence which both are trying to express. In other words, they need to be interpreted existentially. . . .

Our task is to produce an existentialist interpretation of the dualistic mythology of the New Testament. . . . When, for instance, we read of daemonic powers ruling the world and holding mankind in bondage, does the understanding of human existence which underlies such language offer a solution to the riddle of human life which will be acceptable even to the non-mythological mind of to-day? Of course we must not take this to imply that the New Testament presents us with an anthropology like that which modern science can give us. It cannot be proved by logic or demonstrated by an appeal to factual evidence. Scientific anthropologies always take for granted a definite understanding of existence, which is invariably the consequence of a deliberate decision of the scientist, whether he makes it consciously or not. And that is why we have to discover whether the New Testament offers man an understanding of himself which will challenge him to a genuine existential decision. . . .

DIETRICH BONHOEFFER: *Toward "Death-of-God Theology"* *

Dietrich Bonhoeffer (1906–45), the young German theologian put to death by the Nazis, was critical of both Barth and Bultmann while also recognizing his debt to them. They did not go nearly far enough, he felt, in making religion "relevant to the man of today." In the following excerpts from letters he wrote from prison to a friend and to his family he was feeling his way toward a new sort of radical Christianity, which was afterwards called the "death-of-God theology," emphasizing Christ rather than God.

APRIL 30, 1944

You would be surprised, and perhaps even worried, by my theological thoughts and the conclusions that they lead to; and this is where I miss you most of all, because I don't know anyone else with whom I could so well discuss them to have my thinking clarified. What is bothering me incessantly is the question what Christianity really is, or indeed who Christ really is, for us today. The time when people could be told everything by means of words, whether theological or pious, is over, and so is the time of inwardness and conscience—and that means the time of religion in general. We are moving towards a completely religionless time; people as they are now simply cannot be religious any more. Even those who honestly describe themselves as 'religious' do not in the least act up to it, and so they presumably mean something quite different by 'religious.'

Our whole nineteen-hundred-year-old Christian preaching and theology rest on the 'religious *a priori*' of mankind. 'Christianity' has always been a form—perhaps the true form—of 'religion.' But if one day it becomes clear that this *a priori* does not exist at all, but was a historically conditioned and transient form of human self-expression, and if therefore man becomes radically religionless—and I think that that is already more or less the case (else how is it, for example, that this war, in contrast to all previous ones, is not calling forth any 'religious' reaction?)—what does that mean for 'Christianity'? It means that the foundation is taken away from the whole of what has up to now been our 'Christianity,' . . .

* Reprinted with permission of Macmillan Publishing Co., Inc., from *Letters and Papers from Prison*, revised, enlarged edition, by Dietrich Bonhoeffer. Pp. 279–280, 325–326, 360–361 and 381–382. Copyright 1953, 1967, 1971 by SCM Press, Ltd.

June 8, 1944

I'll try to define my position from the historical angle.

The movement that began about the thirteenth century (I'm not going to get involved in any argument about the exact date) towards the autonomy of man (in which I should include the discovery of the laws by which the world lives and deals with itself in science, social and political matters, art, ethics, and religion) has in our time reached an undoubted completion. Man has learnt to deal with himself in all questions of importance without recourse to the 'working hypothesis' called 'God.' In questions of science, art, and ethics this has become an understood thing at which one now hardly dares to tilt. But for the last hundred years or so it has also become increasingly true of religious questions; it is becoming evident that everything gets along without 'God'—and, in fact, just as well as before. As in the scientific field, so in human affairs generally, 'God' is being pushed more and more out of life, losing more and more ground. . . .

July 16, 1944

God as a working hypothesis in morals, politics, or science, has been surmounted and abolished; and the same thing has happened in philosophy and religion (Feuerbach!). For the sake of intellectual honesty, that working hypothesis should be dropped, or as far as possible eliminated. A scientist or physician who sets out to edify is a hybrid.

Anxious souls will ask what room there is left for God now; and as they know of no answer to the question, they condemn the whole development that has brought them to such straits. I wrote to you before about the various emergency exits that have been contrived; and we ought to add to them the *salto mortale* [death-leap] back into the Middle Ages. But the principle of the Middle Ages is heteronomy in the form of clericalism; a return to that can be a counsel of despair, and it would be at the cost of intellectual honesty. It's a dream that reminds one of the song *O wüsst'ich doch den Weg zurück, den weiten Weg ins Kinderland*. There is no such way—at any rate not if it means deliberately abandoning our mental integrity; the only way is that of Matt. 18.3, i.e. through repentance, through *ultimate* honesty.

And we cannot be honest unless we recognize that we have to live in the world *etsi deus non daretur*. And this is just what we do recognize—before God! God himself compels us to recognize it. So our coming of age leads us to a true recognition of our situation before God. God would have us know that we must live as men who manage our lives without him. The God who is with us is the God who forsakes us (Mark 15.34). The God who lets us live in the world without the working hypothesis of God is the God before whom we stand continually. Before God and with God we live without God. God lets himself be pushed out of the world on to the cross. He is weak and powerless in the world, and that is precisely the way, the only way, in which he is with us and helps us. Matt. 8.17 makes it quite clear that Christ helps us, not by virtue of his omnipotence, but by virtue of his weakness and suffering.

Here is the decisive difference between Christianity and all religions. Man's religiosity makes him look in his distress to the power of God in the world: God is the *deus ex machina*. The Bible directs man to God's powerlessness and suffering; only the suffering God can help. To that extent we may say that the development towards the world's coming of age outlined above, which has done away with a false conception of God, opens up a way of seeing the God of the Bible, who wins power and space in the world by his weakness. This will probably be the starting-point for our 'secular interpretation.' . . .

Outline for a Book

Who is God? Not in the first place an abstract belief in God, in his omnipotence etc. That is not a genuine experience of God, but a partial extension of the world. Encounter with Jesus Christ. The experience that a transformation of all human life is given in the fact that 'Jesus is there only for others.' His 'being there for others' is the experience of transcendence. It is only this 'being there for others,' maintained till death, that is the ground of his omnipotence, omniscience, and omnipresence. Faith is participation in this being of Jesus (incarnation, cross, and resurrection). Our relation to God is not a 'religious' relationship to the highest, most powerful, and best Being imaginable—that is not authentic transcendence—but our relation to God is a new life in 'existence for others,' through participation in the being of Jesus. The transcendental is not infinite and unattainable tasks, but the neighbour who is within reach in any given situation. God in human form—not, as in oriental religions, in animal form, monstrous, chaotic, remote, and terrifying, nor in the conceptual forms of the absolute, metaphysical, infinite, etc., nor yet in the Greek divine-human form of 'man in himself,' but 'the man for others,' and therefore the Crucified, the man who lives out of the transcendent.

JACQUES MARITAIN: *The Angelic Doctor* *

The French philosopher Jacques Maritain (1882–   ) is perhaps the leading light of the present-day Catholic Renaissance. A student of Bergson and a convert to Roman Catholicism, Maritain has devoted his mature life to diagnosing the disease of the modern mind, and to

* From Jacques Maritain: *The Angelic Doctor*, pp. 80–2, 109–14. Copyright 1931 by Dial Press, Inc. Reprinted by permission of Sheed and Ward Limited.

recommending as cure for the disease a return to the great tradition of Christian culture, especially as embodied by St. Thomas Aquinas. One of a score of considerable works, his *Angelic Doctor* (English title: *St. Thomas Aquinas*) was published in 1931.

THE DISTRESS of modern times, it was observed in the beginning of this essay, derives from the fact that culture, which is a certain perfection of man, has come to consider itself an ultimate end. It began by despising in its Cartesian or philosophical phase everything above the level of reason; it ends by despising reason itself, suffers both the law of the flesh and the spiritual vertigo which irrationality inevitably precipitates in the case of man. "The error of the modern world consists in its claim to ensure the dominance of reason over nature while refusing the dominance of supernature over reason." This is the reason why, even in the order of knowledge, the metaphysics referred to a moment ago remains an inadequate remedy. Another wisdom, more exalted and more divine, is born of love itself, through the gifts of the Holy Ghost. And it is for that mystical wisdom in the first place that our misery hungers and thirsts, because it alone is capable of satisfying our hunger and our thirst, being union in experience with divine things and a beginning of beatitude. And yet it still leaves us hungry and thirsty, because vision alone can fully satiate our desire with God.

St. John of the Cross is the great experimental doctor of such wisdom; St. Thomas Aquinas is its great theologian. And because he has defined more accurately than any other doctor the central truth which cannot be disregarded without dealing a mortal blow to contemplation, and Christianity itself—I mean the distinction between nature and grace, and their active compenetration, and the whole organism of the infused gifts —he provides a better explanation than any other of the true nature of mystical wisdom, and defends it better than any other against every counterfeit.

That is the greatest benefit we may expect from him from the point of view of the restoration of Christian culture; for, in the last resort, it is from that wisdom and contemplation that the whole Christian order on this earth depends.

The unity of a culture is determined in the first place and above all by a certain common philosophical structure, a certain metaphysical and moral attitude, a certain common scale of values, in a word, a certain common conception of the universe, of man and human life, of which social, linguistic, and juridical structures are, so to speak, the embodiment.

This metaphysical unity has long been broken—not certainly completely destroyed, but broken and as it were obliterated in the West. The drama of Western culture consists in the fact that its stock of common metaphysics has been reduced to an utterly inadequate minimum, so that only matter now holds it together, and matter is incapable of keeping anything together. The drama is all the more tragic for us because everything at the moment has to be recreated, everything to be put in place again in our European house. If a common philosophy succeeded in securing acceptance by an élite in Europe, it would be the beginning of the cure of the Western world.

*   *   *

The disease afflicting the modern world is in the first place a disease of the mind; it began in the mind, it has now attacked the roots of the mind. Is it surprising that the world should seem to us shrouded in darkness? *Si oculus tuus fuerit nequam, totum corpus tuum tenebrosum erit.*

Just as at the moment when the original sin was committed all the harmony of the human being was shattered, because the order that insists that the reason shall be subject to God had first been violated, so at the root of all our disorders there is apparent, in the first place and above all, a rupture in the supreme ordinations of the mind. The responsibility of philosophers in this respect is enormous. In the sixteenth century, and more particularly in the age of Descartes, the interior hierarchies of the virtue of reason were shattered. Philosophy abandoned theology to assert its own claim to be considered the supreme science, and, the mathematical science of the sensible world and its phenomena taking precedence at the same time over metaphysics, the human mind began to profess independence of God and being. Independence of God; that is to say, of the supreme Object of all intelligence, Whom it accepted only half-heartedly until it finally rejected the intimate knowledge of Him supernaturally procured by grace and revelation. Independence of being; that is to say, of the con-natural object of the mind as such, against which it ceased to measure itself humbly, until it finally undertook to deduce it entirely from the seeds of geometrical clarity which it conceived to be innate in itself.

We have difficulty in realizing that the ordered relation of the mind to its object should be thus shattered; we have difficulty in realizing—so material have we become—the frightful significance, sodden with blood and tears, of those few abstract words; we have difficulty in realizing the tremendous upheaval, the tremendous invisible catastrophe, thereby indicated. The mind is that "divine" activity, as Aristotle said, that prodigy of light and life, that supreme glory and perfection of created nature, through which we become immaterially all things, through which we shall one day posses our supernatural beatitude, the cause of all our actions on earth so far as they are human actions and of the rectitude of everything we do. Can we conceive what is the meaning for man of the disturbance of that life, which he carries in him and in which the divine light has its share? The revolution inaugurated by Descartes and continued by the philosophers of the eighteenth and nineteenth centuries, which merely let loose the destructive forces for ever active in the minds of the children of Adam, is an infinitely greater historical cataclysm than the most formidable upheavals of the crust of the earth or the economy of the nations.

Indocile to the object, to God, to being, the mind becomes also and to the same extent indocile to all human authority, a rebel against all tradition and spiritual continuity. It retires within its shell, shuts itself up in the incommunicability of the individual. And if you consider that *docibilitas*, the faculty of being taught, is an essential characteristic of the created mind—nay, rather of animal faculties themselves, inasmuch as they imitate and prepare the mind, so much so that Aristotle classifies animals according to that criterion, placing those that refuse to be taught on the lowest rung; if you also consider that such *docibilitas* is in our case the real root of social life—man being a political animal primarily because he needs other men to make progress in the work of the speculative and practical reason, which is his specific work—the inevitable conclusion is, on the one hand, that by losing its docility to human teaching and its docility also to the object, the mind in our time has proceeded in the direction of an absolutely brutal hardening and a progressive weakening of reason; and, on the other hand, that the most profound and at the same time most human bonds of social life must have simultaneously become by an unavoidable consequence gradually loosened and undone.

Three main symptoms of the disease afflicting the mind at the present day down to its very roots may be discerned at the point of evolution which speculation has reached since the great changes inaugurated by the Cartesian reform.

The mind imagines that it is giving proof of its own native strength by denying and rejecting as science first theology and then metaphysics; by abandoning any attempt to know the primary Cause and immaterial realities; by cultivating a more or less refined doubt which is an outrage both to the perception of the senses and the principles of reason, that is to say the very things on which all our knowledge depends. Such a presumptuous collapse of human knowledge may be described in one word: agnosticism.

The mind at the same time refuses to recognize the rights of primary Truth and repudiates the supernatural order, considering it impossible— and such a denial is a blow at all the interior life of grace. That may be described in a word as naturalism.

Lastly, the mind allows itself to be deceived by the mirage of a mythical conception of human nature, which attributes to that nature conditions peculiar to pure spirit, assumes that nature to be in each of us as perfect and complete as the angelic nature in the angel and therefore claims for us, as being in justice our due, along with complete domination over nature, the superior autonomy, the full self-sufficiency, the autarchy appropriate to pure forms. That may be described as individualism, giving the word its full metaphysical meaning, although *angelism* would be a more accurate description; such a term is justified by historical no less than by doctrinal considerations, because the ideal origin and metaphysical type of modern individualism are to be found in the Cartesian confusion between substance of whatever sort and the angelic monad.

I say that these three great errors are the symptoms of a really radical disease, for they attack the very root, the triple root, rational, religious and moral, of our life.

They were, to begin with, singularly latent and dissimulated, in the state of pure spiritual intentions. They are before us today, sparkling, oppressive, ubiquitous. Everybody sees and feels them, because their sharp unsparing point has passed from the mind into the very flesh of humanity.

Let it be observed once more, it is the integrity of natural reason, the singleness of the eye of the mind, to adapt the expression in the Gospel, the fundamental rectitude of common sense which is outraged by such errors. What a strange fate has befallen rationalism! Men emancipated themselves from all control to conquer the universe and reduce all things to the level of reason. And in the end they come to abandon reality, no longer dare to make use of ideas to adhere to being, forbid themselves the knowledge of anything beyond the sensible fact and the phenomenon of consciousness, dissolve every object of speculation in a great fluid jelly called Becoming or Evolution, conceive themselves barbarous if they do not suspect every first principle and every rational demonstration of naïveté, substitute for the effort of speculation and logical discernment a sort of refined play of instinct, imagination, intuition, visceral emotions, have lost the courage to form a judgment.

3. *Existentialism*

JEAN-PAUL SARTRE: *Existentialism* *

Jean-Paul Sartre (1905–   ) is the acknowledged leader of the "atheistic" existentialists. He holds a Ph.D. and has taught school in three French cities. During World War II he spent nine months in a German prison camp. He has broadcast his existentialist philosophy in philosophical works, plays, and novels. The following selections are from a lecture delivered by Sartre in Paris in 1945.

* From Jean-Paul Sartre: *Existentialism*, pp. 14–18, 21–2, 25–8, 34–5, 42–5, 60–1. Copyright 1947 by Philosophical Library, Inc. Reprinted by permission of Philosophical Library, Inc.

WHAT is meant by the term *existentialism?*

Most people who use the word would be rather embarrassed if they had to explain it, since, now that the word is all the rage, even the work of a musician or painter is being called existentialist. . . .

Actually, it is the least scandalous, the most austere of doctrines. It is intended strictly for specialists and philosophers. Yet it can be defined easily. What complicates matters is that there are two kinds of existentialist; first, those who are Christian, among whom I would include Jaspers and Gabriel Marcel, both Catholic; and on the other hand the atheistic existentialists, among whom I class Heidegger, and then the French existentialists and myself. What they have in common is that they think that existence precedes essence, or, if you prefer, that subjectivity must be the starting point.

Just what does that mean? Let us consider some object that is manufactured, for example, a book or a paper-cutter: here is an object which has been made by an artisan whose inspiration came from a concept. He referred to the concept of what a paper-cutter is and likewise to a known method of production, which is part of the concept, something which is, by and large, a routine. Thus, the paper-cutter is at once an object produced in a certain way and, on the other hand, one having a specific use; and one can not postulate a man who produces a paper-cutter but does not know what it is used for. Therefore, let us say that, for the paper-cutter, essence—that is, the ensemble of both the production routines and the properties which enable it to be both produced and defined —precedes existence. Thus, the presence of the paper-cutter or book in front of me is determined. Therefore, we have here a technical view of the world whereby it can be said that production precedes existence.

When we conceive God as the Creator, He is generally thought of as a superior sort of artisan. Whatever doctrine we may be considering, whether one like that of Descartes or that of Leibnitz, we always grant that will more or less follows understanding or, at the very least, accompanies it, and that when God creates He knows exactly what He is creating. Thus, the concept of man in the mind of God is comparable to the concept of paper-cutter in the mind of the manufacturer, and, following certain techniques and a conception, God produces man, just as the artisan, following a definition and a technique, makes a paper-cutter. Thus, the individual man is the realization of a certain concept in the divine intelligence.

In the eighteenth century, the atheism of the *philosophes* discarded the idea of God, but not so much for the notion that essence precedes existence. To a certain extent, this idea is found everywhere; we find it in Diderot, in Voltaire, and even in Kant. Man has a human nature; this human nature, which is the concept of the human, is found in all men, which means that each man is a particular example of a universal concept, man. In Kant, the result of this universality is that the wild-man, the natural man, as well as the bourgeois, are circumscribed by the same definition and have the same basic qualities. Thus, here too the essence of man precedes the historical existence that we find in nature.

Atheistic existentialism, which I represent, is more coherent. It states that if God does not exist, there is at least one being in whom existence precedes essence, a being who exists before he can be defined by any concept, and that this being is man, or, as Heidegger says, human reality. What is meant here by saying that existence precedes essence? It means that, first of all, man exists, turns up, appears on the scene, and, only afterwards, defines himself. If man, as the existentialist conceives him, is indefinable, it is because at first he is nothing. Only afterward will he be something, and he himself will have made what he will be. Thus, there is no human nature, since there is no God to conceive it. Not only is man what he conceives himself to be, but he is also only what he wills himself to be after this thrust toward existence.

*   *   *

The existentialists say at once that man is anguish. What that means is this: the man who involves himself and who realizes that he is not only the person he chooses to be, but also a law-maker who is, at the same time, choosing all mankind as well as himself, can not help escape the feeling of his total and deep responsibility.

*   *   *

When we speak of forlornness, a term Heidegger was fond of, we mean only that God does not exist and that we have to face all the consequences of this. The existentialist is strongly opposed to a certain kind of secular ethics which would like to abolish God with the least possible expense. About, 1880, some French teachers tried to set up a secular ethics which went something like this: God is a useless and costly hypothesis; we are discarding it; but, meanwhile, in order for there to be an ethics, a society, a civilization, it is essential that certain values be taken seriously and that they be considered as having an *a priori* existence. It must be obligatory, *a priori*, to be honest, not to lie, not to beat your wife, to have children, etc., etc. So we're going to try a little device which will make it possible to show that values exist all the same, inscribed in a heaven of ideas, though otherwise God does not exist. In other words—and this, I believe, is the tendency of everything called reformism in France—nothing will be changed if God does not exist. We shall find ourselves with the same norms of honesty, progress, and humanism, and we shall have made of God an outdated hypothesis which will peacefully die off by itself.

The existentialist, on the contrary, thinks it very distressing that God does not exist, because all possibility of finding values in a heaven of ideas disappears along with Him; there can no longer be an *a priori*

Good, since there is no infinite and perfect consciousness to think it. Nowhere is it written that the Good exists, that we must be honest, that we must not lie; because the fact is we are on a plane where there are only men. Dostoievsky said, "If God didn't exist, everything would be possible." That is the very starting point of existentialism. Indeed, everything is permissible if God does not exist, and as a result man is forlorn, because neither within him nor without does he find anything to cling to. He can't start making excuses for himself.

If existence really does precede essence, there is no explaining things away by reference to a fixed and given human nature. In other words, there is no determinism, man is free, man is freedom. On the other hand, if God does not exist, we find no values or commands to turn to which legitimize our conduct. So, in the bright realm of values, we have no excuse behind us, nor justification before us. We are alone, with no excuses.

That is the idea I shall try to convey when I say that man is condemned to be free. Condemned, because he did not create himself, yet, in other respects is free; because, once thrown into the world, he is responsible for everything he does. The existentialist does not believe in the power of passion. He will never agree that a sweeping passion is a ravaging torrent which fatally leads a man to certain acts and is therefore an excuse. He thinks that man is responsible for his passion.

* * *

Forlornness implies that we ourselves choose our being. Forlornness and anguish go together.

As for despair, the term has a very simple meaning. It means that we shall confine ourselves to reckoning only with what depends upon our will, or on the ensemble of probabilities which make our action possible. When we want something, we always have to reckon with probabilities. I may be counting on the arrival of a friend. The friend is coming by rail or street-car; this supposes that the train will arrive on schedule, or that the street-car will not jump the track. I am left in the realm of possibility; but possibilities are to be reckoned with only to the point where my action comports with the ensemble of these possibilities, and no further. The moment the possibilities I am considering are not rigorously involved by my action, I ought to disengage myself from them, because no God, no scheme, can adapt the world and its possibilities to my will. When Descartes said, "Conquer yourself rather than the world," he meant essentially the same thing.

* * *

Thus, I think we have answered a number of the charges concerning existentialism. You see that it can not be taken for a philosophy of quietism, since it defines man in terms of action; nor for a pessimistic description of man—there is no doctrine more optimistic, since man's destiny is within himself; nor for an attempt to discourage man from acting, since it tells him that the only hope is in his acting and that action is the only thing that enables a man to live. Consequently, we are dealing here with an ethics of action and involvement.

Nevertheless, on the basis of a few notions like these, we are still charged with immuring man in his private subjectivity. There again we're very much misunderstood. Subjectivity of the individual is indeed our point of departure, and this for strictly philosophic reasons. Not because we are bourgeois, but because we want a doctrine based on truth and not a lot of fine theories, full of hope but with no real basis. There can be no other truth to take off from than this: *I think; therefore, I exist*. . . .

Secondly, this theory is the only one which gives man dignity, the only one which does not reduce him to an object. The effect of all materialism is to treat all men, including the one philosophizing, as objects, that is, as an ensemble of determined reactions in no way distinguished from the ensemble of qualities and phenomena which constitute a table or a chair or a stone. We definitely wish to establish the human realm as an ensemble of values distinct from the material realm. But the subjectivity that we have thus arrived at, and which we have claimed to be truth, is not a strictly individual subjectivity, for we have demonstrated that one discovers in the *cogito* not only himself, but others as well. . . .

Hence, let us at once announce the discovery of a world which we shall call inter-subjectivity; this is the world in which man decides what he is and what others are.

* * *

. . . existentialist humanism. Humanism, because we remind man that there is no law-maker other than himself, and that in his forlornness he will decide by himself; because we point out that man will fulfill himself as man, not in turning toward himself, but in seeking outside of himself a goal which is just this liberation, just this particular fulfillment.

From these few reflections it is evident that nothing is more unjust than the objections that have been raised against us. Existentialism is nothing else than an attempt to draw all the consequences of a coherent atheistic position. It isn't trying to plunge man into despair at all. But if one calls every attitude of unbelief despair, like the Christians, then the word is not being used in its original sense. Existentialism isn't so atheistic that it wears itself out showing that God doesn't exist. Rather, it declares that even if God did exist, that would change nothing. There you've got our point of view. Not that we believe that God exists, but we think that the problem of His existence is not the issue. In this sense existentialism is optimistic, a doctrine of action, and it is plain dishonesty for Christians to make no distinction between their own despair and ours and then to call us despairing.

KARL JASPERS: *Way to Wisdom* *

Since 1950 Karl Jaspers, whom F. H. Heinemann called "the originator of the [existentialist] movement," has preferred not to be called a "philosopher of existence." Nevertheless, he still adheres to one of the fundamental tenets of Existentialism, namely that truth is (at least in part) subjectivity: that truth arises, not from the calm contemplation of the world as an object, but from intense personal experience in "ultimate situations" which force man to ask ultimate questions about himself—and to choose. It should be noted that Jaspers is not an "atheist" but a "transcendental" existentialist who seeks "essence" or being "beyond the world." Jaspers (1883–1969) was appointed professor of philosophy at Heidelberg in 1921 but lost his professorship during the Nazi regime. He returned to Heidelberg after the war.

AND now let us take a look at our human state. We are always in situations. Situations change, opportunities arise. If they are missed they never return. I myself can work to change the situation. But there are situations which remain essentially the same even if their momentary aspect changes and their shattering force is obscured: I must die, I must suffer, I must struggle, I am subject to chance, I involve myself inexorably in guilt. We call these fundamental situations of our existence ultimate situations. That is to say, they are situations which we cannot evade or change. Along with wonder and doubt, awareness of these ultimate situations is the most profound source of philosophy. In our day-to-day lives we often evade them, by closing our eyes and living as if they did not exist. We forget that we must die, forget our guilt, and forget that we are at the mercy of chance. We face only concrete situations and master them to our profit, we react to them by planning and acting in the world, under the impulsion of our practical interests. But to ultimate situations we react either by obfuscation or, if we really apprehend them, by despair and rebirth: we become ourselves by a change in our consciousness of being. . . .

The ultimate situations—death, chance, guilt, and the uncertainty of the world—confront me with the reality of failure. What do I do in the face of this absolute failure, which if I am honest I cannot fail to recognize?

The advice of the Stoic, to withdraw to our own freedom in the independence of the mind, is not adequate. The Stoic's perception of man's weakness was not radical enough. He failed to see that the mind in itself

* Karl Jaspers: *Way to Wisdom*, pp. 19-20, 22-3, 121. Copyright 1951 by Yale University Press. Reprinted by permission of Yale University Press.

is empty, dependent on what is put into it, and he failed to consider the possibility of madness. The Stoic leaves us without consolation; the independent mind is barren, lacking all content. He leaves us without hope, because his doctrine affords us no opportunity of inner transformation, no fulfilment through self-conquest in love, no hopeful expectation of the possible.

And yet the Stoics' striving is toward true philosophy. Their thought, because its source is in ultimate situations, expresses the basic drive to find a revelation of true being in human failure.

Crucial for man is his attitude toward failure: whether it remains hidden from him and overwhelms him only objectively at the end or whether he perceives it unobscured as the constant limit of his existence; whether he snatches at fantastic solutions and consolations or faces it honestly, in silence before the unfathomable. The way in which man approaches his failure determines what he will become.

In ultimate situations man either perceives nothingness or senses true being in spite of and above all ephemeral worldly existence. Even despair, by the very fact that it is possible in the world, points beyond the world.

Or, differently formulated, man seeks redemption. Redemption is offered by the great, universal religions of redemption. They are characterized by an objective guarantee of the truth and reality of redemption. Their road leads to an act of individual conversion. This philosophy cannot provide. And yet all philosophy is a transcending of the world, analogous to redemption. . . .

The desire to lead a philosophical life springs from the darkness in which the individual finds himself, from his sense of forlornness when he stares without love into the void, from his self-forgetfulness when he feels that he is being consumed by the busy-ness of the world, when he suddenly wakes up in terror and asks himself: What am I, what am I failing to do, what should I do?

That self-forgetfulness has been aggravated by the machine age. With its time clocks, its jobs, whether absorbing or purely mechanical, which less and less fulfil man as man, it may even lead man to feel that he is part of the machine, interchangeably shunted in here and there, and when left free, to feel that he is nothing and can do nothing with himself. And just as he begins to recover himself, the colossus of this world draws him back again into the all-consuming machinery of empty labour and empty leisure.

But man as such inclines to self-forgetfulness. He must snatch himself out of it if he is not to lose himself to the world, to habits, to thoughtless banalities, to the beaten track.

Philosophy is the decision to awaken our primal source, to find our way back to ourselves, and to help ourselves by inner action.

4. *Another Scientific Revolution*

PHILIPP FRANK: *On the Crisis in Science and Logical Positivism* *

> Philipp Frank (1884–1966), for many years professor of theoretical physics at Prague, since 1939 lecturer in physics and philosophy at Harvard, is one of the leaders of the "school" of logical positivism. In the following passages from *Modern Science and its Philosophy* (1949) he describes the "crisis in science" at the turn of the century and the historical background of the logical positivist movement.

AT THE time when the first chapter of this book was written (1907) I had just graduated from the University of Vienna as a doctor of philosophy in physics. But the domain of my most intensive interest was the philosophy of science. I used to associate with a group of students who assembled every Thursday night in one of the old Viennese coffee houses. We stayed until midnight and even later, discussing problems of science and philosophy. Our interest was spread widely over many fields, but we returned again and again to our central problem: How can we avoid the traditional ambiguity and obscurity of philosophy? How can we bring about the closest possible *rapprochement* between philosophy and science? By "science" we did not mean "natural science" only, but we included always social studies and the humanities. The most active and regular members of our group were, besides myself, the mathematician, Hans Hahn, and the economist, Otto Neurath. . . .

At that time a prominent French historian and philosopher of science, Abel Rey, published a book which later was to make a great impression upon me. At the turn of the century the decline of mechanistic physics was accompanied by a belief that the scientific method itself had failed to give us the "truth about the universe"; hence nonscientific and even antiscientific tendencies gained momentum. I quote some passages in which Rey describes this situation excellently and precisely.

Fifty years ago, he says, the explanation of nature was believed to be purely mechanical.

"It was postulated that physics was nothing but a complication of mechanics, a molecular mechanics. . . . Today (1907) it seems that the picture offered by the physical sciences has changed completely. The general unity is replaced by an extreme diversity, not only in the details, but in the leading and fundamental ideas . . . [This accounts for] what

* Reprinted by permission of the publishers from Philipp Frank, *Modern Science and its Philosophy*. Cambridge, Mass.: Harvard University Press, 1941–9. Pp. 1–5, 18–21, 25–6, 34–5, 41–2, 49–50.

is called the crisis of contemporary physics. Traditional physics assumed until the middle of the nineteenth century that it had only to continue its own path to become the metaphysics of matter. It ascribed to its theories an ontologic value, and these theories were all mechanistic. Traditional mechanistic physics was supposed, above and beyond the results of experience, to be the *real* cognition of the material universe. This conception was not a hypothetical description of our experience; it was a dogma.

"The criticism of the traditional mechanistic physics that was formulated in the second half of the nineteenth century weakened this assertion of the ontologic reality of mechanistic physics. Upon this criticism a philosophy of physics was established that became almost traditional toward the end of the nineteenth century. Science became nothing but a symbolic pattern, a frame of reference. Moreover, since this frame of reference varied according to the school of thought, it was soon discovered that actually nothing was referred that had not previously been fashioned in such a way that it could be so referred. Science became a work of art to the lover of pure science, a product of artisanship to the utilitarian. This attitude could quite rightly be interpreted as denying the possibility that science can exist. A science that has become simply a useful technique . . . no longer has the right to call itself science without distorting the meaning of the word. To say that science cannot be anything but this means to negate science in the proper sense of the word.

"The failure of the traditional mechanistic science . . . entails the proposition: 'Science itself has failed.' . . . We can have a collection of empirical recipes, we can even systematize them for the convenience of memorizing them, but we have no cognition of the phenomena to which this system or these recipes are applied."

Our group was formed during the period which was so eloquently described by Rey. His book was discussed frequently by us in the last years of my stay in Vienna (1908–1912). The problems raised and the results obtained are reflected partly in Chapter 2 of this book. The general reaction of our group to the intellectual and cultural situation depicted by Rey can be described as follows:

We recognized the gradual decline in the belief that mechanistic science would eventually embrace all our observations. This belief had been closely connected with the belief in progress in science and in the scientific conception of the world. Therefore, this decline brought about a noticeable uneasiness. Many people lost their faith in scientific method and looked for some other method which might yield a real understanding of the world. A great many people believed, or at least wanted to believe, that the time had come to return to the medieval ideas that may be characterized as the organismic conception of the world.

In the history of science and philosophy there have always been divergent opinions about the conditions under which we may say that a scientific theory has "explained" a certain range of observations. Some authors have maintained that only an explanation by mechanical causes and by the motion of material particles can satisfy our intellectual curiosity. Others have claimed that the reduction to mechanical causes is only a superficial explanation and not a real one. Some of the opponents of the mechanistic world view have stated that all phenomena must be interpreted in terms of the evolution of an "organic whole" in order really to understand them. The decline of the belief in mechanistic science seemed to favor this organismic view, which has been attractive to many because of its religious and social implications. In this way there had arisen at the turn of the century what some called a crisis in science or, more accurately, in the scientific conception of the world. For more than two centuries the idea of progress in science and human life had been connected with the advance of the mechanistic explanation of natural phenomena. Now science itself seemed to abandon this mechanistic conception, and the paradoxical situation arose that one could fight the scientific conception of the world in the name of the advance of science.

The sixteen chapters of this book have been written over a period of almost forty years. They are all meant to be contributions to one task: to break through the wall which has separated science and philosophy for about one and one-half centuries. The book reflects the methods by which this wall has been besieged in the twentieth century. During the last decades of the nineteenth century, a revolution in physical science started which has itself brought about a revolution in our general scientific thought. The methods that have been tried in the fight for the unity between science and philosophy have changed along with the advance of science. Two characteristic beliefs of nineteenth-century science broke down during its last decades; these were the belief that all phenomena in nature can be reduced to the laws of mechanics, and the belief that science will eventually reveal the "truth" about the universe. In the twentieth century the revolutionary changes in science developed with ever-increasing rapidity and intensity. It is no wonder that this rapid transformation of scientific thought has been accompanied by rapidly changing methods in the scientist's approach to philosophy and in the philosopher's views on science.

* * *

The years after 1917 saw, as has been mentioned, the establishment of Soviet power in Russia, the end of World War I, and the founding of new democracies in Central Europe, such as the Austrian, Czechoslovakian, and Polish republics. The event that had the greatest bearing at this time on the development of the philosophy of science, however, was the new general theory of relativity advanced by Einstein after 1916. In this theory Einstein derived his laws of motion and laws of the gravitational field from very general and abstract principles, the principles of equivalence and of relativity. His principles and laws were connections between abstract symbols: the general space-time coördinates and the ten potentials of the gravitational field. This theory seemed to be an excellent example of the way in which a scientific theory is built up according to the ideas of the new positivism. The symbolic or structural system is neatly developed and is sharply separated from the observational facts that are to be embraced. Then the system must be interpreted, and the prediction of facts that are observable must be made and the predictions verified by observation. There were three specific observational facts that were predicted: the bending of light rays and the red shift of spectral lines in a gravitational field, and the advance of the perihelion of Mercury.

However, if we compare Einstein's theory with previous physical theories, we note a certain difference in structure. It is after all only a difference in degree, but it directs our attention to a considerable change in the conception of physical theory.

Whatever conclusions may be drawn from them, Einstein's fundamental laws will describe motions in terms of the general space-time coördinates. Before the results of his theory can be verified by observation, it is necessary to know how statements about these general coördinates can be expressed in terms of observational facts. In traditional Newtonian physics, spatial coördinates and time intervals could be determined by the traditional methods of measuring length and time, by using yardsticks and clocks. However, the general coördinates in Einstein's theory are quantities that define the positions and motions of moving particles with respect to systems of reference that can possess all sorts of deformations, with variable rates of deformation at every point. No rigid and defined system of reference for space and time measurement is given as a general basis for the definition of the space and time coördinates. The methods of measurement must be developed along with the conclusions from the principles of the theory. What is the bearing of these facts upon our general conception of the structure of a scientific theory?

In nineteenth-century physics the translations of statements that contain abstract symbols of the theory—mass, distance, time interval, and the like—into observational facts did not cause much trouble. It was taken for granted that the straightness of a line, the temperature of a body, or the velocity of a motion could be measured. At least, it was not suspected that there was any difficulty in assuming that such measurements are possible. In Einstein's general theory of relativity, however, the description of the operations by which these quantities could be measured becomes a serious and complex task; it becomes an essential part of the theory. These descriptions of the operations by which abstract symbols, such as the general space-time coördinates, are connected with observational facts are called today "operational definitions," according to a terminology suggested by P. W. Bridgman.

As early as 1905, in his restricted theory of relativity, Einstein was well aware that the "operational definitions" are an essential part of his theory. Later he described the decisive alterations that were brought about by his new physical principles in the conception of a physical theory by stressing the fact that the connection between the symbols of the theory and the observational facts following from them is much longer, much more complex, and much more difficult to deal with than the connection assumed by nineteenth-century physics, to say nothing of the physics of the seventeenth and eighteenth centuries. The alteration brought about in the general conception of a scientific theory was a greater emphasis on the gap between the structural system and the experimental confirmation. Advancing a new theory now involved two tasks, both of which required great creative power: the invention of a structural system, and the working out of operational definitions for its symbols.

However, the great new idea in every new physical theory, according to Einstein, was the creation of the structural system. In this sense a physical theory describes "the structure of the world." This way of speaking could easily be interpreted as meaning that the symbols, which are the building stones of the structure, are also the "real building stones" of the universe and that the structure of the symbolic system is "the real structure of the world." Following Einstein's own interpretation of his conceptions, statements like "the theory describes the real structure of the world" mean that appropriate operational definitions enable us to derive from the symbolic system observational facts that check with our actual observations. Hence, the conception of physics advocated by the new positivism of Poincaré is altered by Einstein's conception in such a way that a theory remains an economical description of facts by means of a structure and operational definitions. . . .

The neo-Thomist and neo-Kantian schools reacted to the revolutionary changes that have arisen in science since the turn of the century by establishing a kind of "iron curtain" between science and philosophy. But none of these schools, and, as a matter of fact, none of the schools of traditional philosophy, of the idealistic or realistic type, were able to make a valuable contribution toward integrating the new science of the twentieth century into the general framework of human thought. . . .

Immediately after Einstein had published his general theory of relativity (1917), in which he advanced his new physics in full generality, writings appeared that did not attempt to integrate the new physics into traditional philosophy but to build up a new philosophy on the basis of that new science. These writings did not follow the reaction of traditional philosophy—of either the fundamentalist or the modernist types —to the new science. Theirs was a radical reaction in accordance with the words of the gospel:

"No man putteth new wine into old bottles; else the new wine will burst the bottles, and be spilled, and the bottles shall perish. But new wine must be put into new bottles; and both are preserved. No man also having drunk old wine straightway desireth new: for he saith, The old is better."

The old bottles were the patterns of traditional philosophy and the new wine was twentieth-century science. A group of men went in for new bottles. They did not borrow the framework of Thomistic or Kantian metaphysics but they borrowed a pattern that had grown up in the soil of modern science, the pattern of the "new positivism." While men like Poincaré and Duhem had used this pattern for strictly domestic consumption, to clear up their own back yard, the foundations of science, the new men who emerged after 1917 ventured to build up a new philosophy that was expected to replace the traditional systems of the Aristotelian or Kantian type.

The new movement started about the time when the first world war ended (1918). New democratic republics were established in Central Europe: Austria, Czechoslovakia, Poland, and the Weimar experiment in Germany. They offered a favorable soil for the evolution of a scientific world conception. A similar situation seemed to arise in Russia after the overthrow of the Czarist regime (1917). It is interesting to note how the turn from the democratic start to the establishment of a new authoritarianism was accompanied by a turn from the philosophy of the new positivism to a philosophy which was nearer to the Aristotelian and Kantian tradition. . . .

The men who had expanded the new positivism into a general logical basis of human thought—Schlick and Carnap—came now into personal contact with the original Viennese group, particularly with Hahn and Neurath, while my own contact was restricted to the time of the university vacations. As a result of the developing coöperation the new philosophy became more and more different from the traditional German philosophy. . . .

They had demonstrated logically that no scientific metaphysics is possible because metaphysical statements do not fit into the pattern that statements must have in order to be called true or false. But the social scientist Neurath investigated the meaning of metaphysical statements as social phenomena. He insisted with a certain ruthlessness that no formulation should be allowed to slip in that would "give comfort to the enemy," even if it would be admissible from the purely logical viewpoint. The whole original Viennese group was convinced that the elimination of metaphysics not only was a question of a better logic but was of great relevance for the social and cultural life. They were also convinced that the elimination of metaphysics would deprive the groups that we call today totalitarian of their scientific and philosophic basis and would lay bare the fact that these groups are actually fighting for special interests of some kind.

In the long thorough and intimate discussions that the Viennese group had with Schlick and Carnap, the point was made that the new philosophy must be built up in such a way that no misinterpretation in favor of metaphysics could occur. We all knew that misinterpretations were bound to happen if and when expressions like "real," "essential," "real building stone of the universe," were used in a loose way. Neurath even recommended, half jokingly, that an "index of prohibited words" should be set up. In a monograph on the "Foundations of the Social Sciences" he avoided, as he explicitly states, words like "entity," "essence," "mind," "matter," "reality," "thing.". . .

In the years 1930–31, there appeared the first volume of the journal *Erkenntnis* (Cognition), which became the main mouthpiece of our movement. The editors were R. Carnap and H. Reichenbach. The first issue began with the paper, "The Turn in Philosophy," by M. Schlick. I shall quote some lines in order to show that an optimistic belief in the new trend was the keynote of this journal. Schlick writes:

"I am convinced that we are in the middle of an altogether final turn in philosophy. I am justified, on good grounds, in regarding the sterile conflict of systems as settled. Our time, so I claim, possesses already the methods by which any conflict of this kind is rendered superfluous; what matters is only to apply these methods resolutely."

In the same year (1930) Schlick published a paper, "Personal Experience, Cognition, Metaphysics," in which he writes:

"All cognition of the being is achieved, in principle, by the methods of the special sciences; every other kind of ontology is empty talk. Metaphysics is impossible because its goals contradict one another. If the metaphysician longs only for personal experience, his longing can be satisfied by poetry and art—or by life itself. But if he longs for a personal experience of the transcendent, he confuses life and cognition, he chases futile shadows."

For Schlick, as we know, "cognition" is the construction of a system of symbols that denotes uniquely the world of facts. It is therefore fundamentally different from personal experience.

This strong optimistic feeling is psychologically the feeling of a turn. You can ride in a car at high speed and you do not feel anything so long as the velocity remains unchanged. But if a turn or an acceleration takes place, you experience a strong reaction. Today, the movement of logical positivism is no longer so conspicuous. It had produced a turn in philosophy, which afterwards moved in a new direction and rather smoothly. I quote a passage from a philosopher who is by no means a follower of what is now called logical positivism. C. West Churchman writes:

"Few can doubt the healthy impact that the positivist position has had upon modes of inquiry; it has sharply distinguished the schools of thought, and has raised a standard under which the proponents of experimental methods can fight their battles against a reactionary movement. To return to a prepositivistic viewpoint is to return to a prescientific viewpoint, to become a reactionary as an advocate of the indisputable power of the sovereign in the eyes of one with a democratic outlook.". . .

In the year 1936, just while the Congress for the Unity of Science was in session at Copenhagen, Professor Schlick was assassinated near his lecture hall in the University of Vienna by a student. At the court trial the attorney for the defendant pleaded extenuating circumstances because the student was indignant about Schlick's "vicious philosophy." Everyone who knew Schlick had been full of admiration for his noble, humane and restrained personality. The political implications of the expression "vicious philosophy" were obvious. The student received a ten-year prison term. When, however, two years later, the Nazi troops occupied Vienna and arrested a great many people, Schlick's murderer was released from prison.

The shots directed at Schlick were a dramatic indication of the dispersal of the Central European positivism that was taking place under the pressure of the advancing Nazi power. At the end of 1938 this process was completed. By far the greatest part of the Central Europeans who had worked along the lines of logical positivism had left their countries. The immediate reason was either to escape political persecution, or, in many cases, just the feeling that under the dictatorship of the Nazis there would be no place for a philosophy guided by logic and experience. The majority of the emigrants have lived since in the United States, a smaller part in Great Britain.

ARTHUR KOESTLER: *A Layman's View* *

In his autobiography Arthur Koestler (1905–   ), well known novelist and essayist, describes his first encounter with the new physics (roughly in 1930 when he became science editor of the *Vossische Zeitung*, an important German newspaper) and comments on "the philosophical upheaval" which accompanied it. For Koestler's encounter with Communism, see below, pp. 763–66.

. . . I THREW myself with enthusiasm into my new job. It was an ideal job, with unlimited possibilities for roaming through the domains of science and fantasy, from the electron to the spiral nebulae, from experiments in telepathy to the quest for the lost Atlantis. To be a science editor sounds like a rather dull occupation; I found it incomparably more exciting than that of a foreign correspondent or a war reporter. After four years of travel I had begun to tire of living in a whirl of colourful but undigested impressions, and of the superficiality of the type of journalism in which I had been engaged. I felt that during all this rush and bustle my mind had been free-wheeling; now, parallel to the reawakening of political interest, the questing, contemplative mood also reappeared. My new job made me turn back to my first youthful passion, to Science as a key to the ultimate mystery. . . .

The more I became engrossed in historical materialism, and in the dry schema of a world governed by the class struggles of Economic Man, the more romantic became, by a kind of backstroke process, my approach to science. This, however, was not a purely subjective reaction. Just at that time science itself was in the throes of a revolutionary crisis which was rapidly demolishing all familiar assumptions of thought, and replacing our traditional concepts of reality by a new, wildly futuristic picture of the world. The arrow in the blue no longer pursued its flight in a straight line through infinity; it followed an elliptical path through the curved space of a finite universe, and would eventually return to its point of origin from the opposite direction like a traveller on the earth always heading due east. . . .

During my science editorship, not only was the universe exploding, but the microcosmos, the inside of the atom, was in even worse fermentation. . . .

Even more important than this twin-revolution in the realms of the infinitely large and the infinitely small, was the philosophical upheaval which accompanied them, and which became known as "the crisis of causality." Absolute space and absolute time had already gone overboard; the third pillar of our traditional view of the world, the law of causal determination, now followed suit. The so-called Laws of Nature lost their solid character; they could no longer be regarded as expressing certainties, merely statistical probabilities. The rigid causal connections between "cause" and "effect" were loosened, softened up as it were; the physicist found himself living in a world where it was no longer possible for him to say: "Under such and such conditions this and that will happen"; he could merely say: "This and that is *likely* to happen." What he had regarded as universal laws now turned out to be mere rules of thumb, whose validity was limited to medium-sized phenomena; on the sub-atomic level determinism itself dissolved in a kind of blurred fringe, and all certainty had vanished from the universe.

This crisis had been brewing in the physicists' laboratories since the beginning of the century; but its full philosophical implications only became apparent around 1930. The law of Rutherford and Soddy, published in 1903, had already implied that the collapse of radio-active atoms was "spontaneous," that is, independent of the atom's physical state, position and environment; and that the most complete description of the atom's present condition in physical terms permitted no predictions regarding its future. Its destiny, in the words of Sir James Jeans, seemed determined "from inside and not from outside." The individual atom seemed to experience freedom at least in the sense that no explanation of its behaviour was possible in the language of physics. In 1917 Einstein showed that the right to "spontaneous" collapse had to be accorded *all* atoms. Then, between 1927 and '32, a series of swift blows put an end to the age-old illusion of a solid, rigid, causally determined world. Schroedinger's wave-mechanics implied that the exact whereabouts of an electron travelling through space could only be expressed in terms of probabilities; Heisenberg's "Uncertainty Relation" seemed to prove that the same ambiguity reigned with regard to electrons inside the atom, and moreover, that an exact determination of the position and momentum of such electrons was not only practically impossible but also theoretically *unthinkable*. Within a certain, though very narrow margin —Planck's quantum "h"—the data as such became blurred, events were undeterminable, and "measurement" was a meaningless term. . . .

This upheaval, which I witnessed so closely, had a profound influence on my spiritual development; but once again the lesson was slow to sink in, and its assimilation was not a conscious process. At sixteen, I had lived in a neatly arranged, comprehensible clockwork-universe whose last mystery was just about to be solved. At twenty-six I saw the arrogant self-confidence of the nineteenth century Scientist collapse, and the commandment "Thou shalt not make unto thee any graven image" acquire a new meaning with regard to curved space, electrons, wave-packets and a universe in permanent explosion. Since the Renaissance, the Ultimate Cause had gradually shifted from the heavens to the atomic nucleus, from the super-human to the sub-human level. But now it became clear that the working of this "destiny from below" was just as unfathomable in terms of man's spatio-temporal experience as "destiny from above" had been. I learnt a decisive lesson in intellectual modesty which, without my noticing it, counter-balanced the "total explanations" offered by Marxist philosophy.

In still another way my return to Science acted as a corrective to the Marxian "closed system." In that system the course of History appears rigidly determined by economic forces; individual responsibility has no place in it. Historical materialism is a typical product of the nineteenth century, in keeping with the mechanical clockwork-universe of its physics—a clockwork which, once it has somehow been wound up, will unrelentingly follow its preordained course. But this rigid schema was no longer in keeping with the twentieth century's conceptions of the physical world, of biological processes, psychological motivations. The philosophical part of the Marxian doctrine was, by the time I became acquainted with it, already an anachronism.

MAX PLANCK: *The Meaning and Limits of Exact Science* *

Max Planck (1858–1947) was perhaps the greatest of modern Germany's theoretical physicists. His Quantum Theory, which threw new light on the fundamental units of matter and energy of which the physical universe is composed, won for him an international reputation. The following selections are from a lecture delivered by Planck in 1941.

EXACT Science—what wealth of connotation these two words have! They conjure up a vision of a lofty structure, of imperishable slabs of stone firmly joined together, treasure-house of all wisdom, symbol and promise of the coveted goal for a human race thirsting for knowledge, longing for the final revelation of truth. And since knowledge always means power, too, with every new insight that Man gains into the forces at work in Nature, he always opens up also a new gateway to an ultimate mastery over them, to the possibility of harnessing these natural forces and making them obey his every command.

But this is not all—nor even the most important part of it. Man wants not only knowledge and power. He wants also a standard, a measure of his actions, a criterion of what is valuable and what is worthless. He wants an ideology and philosophy of life, to assure him of the greatest good on earth—peace of mind. And if religion fails to satisfy his longing, he will seek a substitute in exact science. I refer here merely to the endeavors of Monism, founded by outstanding scholars, philosophers and natural scientists, a school of thought which commanded high respect only as recently as a short generation ago.

Yet, in these our days hardly a word is being heard about the Monists, although the structure of their ideology was unquestionably erected to endure for a long time to come, and it started out on its career with high hopes and great promises. There must be something wrong somewhere! And in fact, if we take a closer look and scrutinize the edifice of exact science more intently, we must very soon become aware of the fact that it has a dangerously weak point—namely, its very foundation. Its foundation is not braced, reinforced properly, in every direction, so as to en-

* From Max Planck: *Scientific Autobiography and other Papers*, trans. by Frank Gaynor, pp. 80–2, 90, 95–103, 105–08. Copyright 1949 by Philosophical Library, Inc. Reprinted by permission of Philosophical Library, Inc.

able it to withstand external strains and stresses. In other words, exact science is not built on any principle of such universal validity, and at the same time of such portentous meaning, as to be fit to support the edifice properly. To be sure, exact science relies everywhere on exact measurements and figures, and is therefore fully entitled to bear its proud name, for the laws of logic and mathematics must undoubtedly be regarded as reliable. But even the keenest logic and the most exact mathematical calculation cannot produce a single fruitful result in the absence of a premise of unerring accuracy. Nothing can be gained from nothing.

*   *   *

The scientific world picture or the so-called phenomenological world is also not final and constant, but is in a process of constant change and improvement. . . .

The sensations produced by objects are private, and vary from one individual to another. But the world picture, the world of objects, is the same for all human beings, and we may say that the transition from the sense world to the world picture amounts to a replacement of a disordered subjective manifold by a constant objective order, or chance by law, and of variable appearance by stable substance.

The world of objects, in contrast to the sense world, is therefore called the *real world*. Yet, one must be careful when using the word, *real*. It must be taken here in a qualified sense only. For this word has the connotation of something absolutely stable, permanent, immutable, whereas the objects of the child's world picture could not rightly be claimed to be immutable. The toy is not immutable, it may break or burn. The electric lamp can be smashed to smithereens. This precludes their being called *real* in the sense just mentioned.

This sounds both self-evident and trivial. But we must bear in mind that in the case of the scientific world picture, where as we have seen, the situation is quite analogous, this state of affairs was by no means found to be self-evident. For just as to the child the toy is the true reality, so for decades and centuries the atoms were taken by science to constitute the true reality in natural processes. The atoms were considered to be that which remains immutable when an object is smashed or burned, thus representing permanency in the midst of all change— until one day, to everybody's astonishment, it was found that even atoms could change. Therefore, whenever in the sequel we refer to the "real world," we shall be using the word *real* primarily in a qualified, naïve sense, adjusted to the particular character of the dominant world picture, and we must constantly bear in mind that a change in the world picture may go hand in hand, simultaneously, with that which people call "real."

Every world picture is characterized by the real elements, of which it is composed. The real world of exact science, the scientific world picture, evolved from the real world of practical life. But even this world picture is not final, but changes all the time, step by step, with every advance of inquiry.

Such a stage of development is represented by that scientific world picture which today we are accustomed to call "classical." Its real elements, and hence its characteristic feature, were the chemical atoms. In our own day, scientific research, fructified by the theory of relativity and the quantum theory, stands at the threshold of a higher stage of development, ready to mould a new world picture for itself. The real elements of this coming world picture are no longer the chemical atoms, but electrons and protons, whose mutual interactions are governed by the velocity of light and by the elementary quantum of action. From today's point of view, therefore, we must regard the realism of the classical world picture as naïve. But nobody can tell whether some day in the future the same words will not be used in referring to our modern world picture, too. . . .

But the pursuit of this question will lead to a discovery which we must regard as the greatest of all the wonders previously mentioned. First of all, it must be noted that the continual displacement of one world picture by another is dictated by no human whim or fad, but by an irresistible force. Such a change becomes inevitable whenever scientific inquiry hits upon a new fact in nature for which the currently accepted world picture cannot account. To cite a concrete example, such a fact is the velocity of light in empty space, and another is the part played by the elementary quantum of action in the regular occurrence of all atomic processes. These two facts, and many more, could not be incorporated in the classical world picture, and consequently, the classical world picture had to yield its place to a new world picture.

This in itself is enough to make one wonder. But the circumstance which calls for ever greater wonderment, because it is not self-evidently a matter of course by any means, is that the new world picture does not wipe out the old one, but permits it to stand in its entirety, and merely adds a special condition for it. This special condition involves a certain limitation, but because of this very fact it simplifies the world picture considerably. In fact, the laws of classical mechanics continue to hold satisfactorily for all the processes in which the velocity of light may be considered to be infinitely great, and the quantum of action to be infinitely small. In this way we are able to link up in a general manner mechanics with electro-dynamics, to substitute energy for mass, and moreover, to reduce the building blocks of the universe from the ninety-two different atom types of the classical world picture to two—electrons and protons. Every material body consists of electrons and protons. The combination of a proton and an electron is either a neutron or a hydrogen atom, according as the electron becomes attached to the proton or circles about it. All the physical and chemical properties of a body may be deduced from the type of its structure.

The formerly accepted world picture is thus preserved, except for the fact that now it takes on the aspect of a special section of a still larger, still more comprehensive, and at the same time still more homogeneous picture. This happens in all cases within our experience. As the multitude of the natural phenomena observed in all fields unfolds in an ever richer and more variegated profusion, the scientific world picture, which is derived from them, assumes an always clearer and more definite form. The continuing changes in the world picture do not therefore signify an erratic oscillation in a zigzag line, but a progress, an improvement, a completion. In establishing this fact I have, in my opinion, indicated the basically most important accomplishment that scientific research can claim.

But what is the direction of this progress, and what is its ultimate goal? The direction, evidently, is the constant improvement of the world picture by reducing the real elements contained in it to a higher reality of a less naïve character. The goal, on the other hand, is the creation of a world picture, with real elements which no longer require an improvement, and therefore represent the ultimate reality. A demonstrable attainment of this goal will—or can—never be ours. But in order to have at least a name for it, for the time being, we call the ultimate reality "the real world," in the absolute, metaphysical sense of the word, *real*. This is to be construed as expressing the fact that the *real* world—in other words, objective nature—stands behind everything explorable. In contrast to it, the scientific world picture gained by experience—the *phenomenological* world—remains always a mere approximation, a more or less well divined model. As there is a material object behind every sensation, so there is a metaphysical reality behind everything that human experience shows to be real. Many philosophers object to the word, "*behind*." They say: "Since in exact science all concepts and all measures are reducible to sensations, in the last analysis the meaning of every scientific finding also refers only to the sense world, and it is inadmissible, or at least superfluous, to postulate the existence behind this world of a metaphysical world, totally inaccessible to direct scientific inquiry and examination." The only proper reply to this argument is, simply, that in the above sentence the word, *behind*, must not be interpreted in an external or spatial sense. Instead of "behind," we could just as well say, "*in*" or "*within*." Metaphysical reality does not stand spatially *behind* what is given in experience, but lies fully *within* it. "Nature is neither core nor shell—she is everything at once." The essential point is that the world of sensation is not the only world which may conceivably exist, but that there is still another world. To be sure, this other world is not directly accessible to us, but its existence is indicated, time and again, with compelling clarity, not only by practical life, but also by the labors of science. For the great marvel of the scientific world picture, becoming progressively more complete and perfect, necessarily impels the investigator to seek its ultimate form. And since one must assume the existence of that which one seeks, the scientist's assumption of the actual existence of a "real world," in the absolute sense of the word, eventually grows into a firm conviction which nothing can shake any more. This firm belief in the absolute *Real* in nature is what constitutes for him the given, self-evident premise of his work; it fortifies repeatedly his hope of eventually groping his way still a little nearer to the essence of objective Nature, and of thereby gaining further clues to her secrets.

* * *

But significant as the achievements may be, and near as the desired goal may seem, there always remains a gaping chasm, unbridgeable from the point of view of exact science, between the real world of phenomenology and the real world of metaphysics. This chasm is the source of a constant tension, which can never be balanced, and which is the inexhaustible source of the insatiable thirst for knowledge within the true research scientist. But at the same time, we catch here a glimpse of the boundaries which exact science is unable to cross. May its results be ever so deep and far-reaching, it can never succeed in taking the last step which would take it into the realm of metaphysics. The fact that although we feel inevitably compelled to postulate the existence of a *real world*, in the absolute sense, we can never fully comprehend its nature, constitutes the irrational element which exact science can never shake off, and the proud name, "Exact Science," must not be permitted to cause anybody to underestimate the significance of this element of irrationality. On the other hand, the very fact that science sets its own limits on the basis of scientific knowledge itself, appears well suited to strengthen everybody's confidence in the reliability of that knowledge, knowledge obtained on the basis of incontestable presupposition and with the help of rigorous experimental and theoretical methods. . . .

It is at this modest point that scientific research enters with its exact methods, and it works its way step by step from the specific to the always more general. To this end, it must set and continually keep its sights on the objective reality which it seeks, and in this sense exact science can never dispense with *Reality* in the metaphysical sense of the term. But the real world of metaphysics is not the starting point, but the goal of all scientific endeavor, a beacon winking and showing the way from an inaccessibly remote distance.

The assurance that every new discovery, and every new fact of knowledge gained from it, will bring us nearer to the goal, must compensate us for the numerous, and certainly not negligible, drawbacks which are necessarily created by the continual abatement of the intuitive character and ease of application of the world picture. In fact, the present scientific world picture, as against the original naïve world picture, shows an odd, almost alien aspect. The immediately experienced sense impressions, the primordial sources of scientific activity, have dropped totally out of the world picture, in which sight, hearing and touch no longer play a part. A glance into a modern scientific laboratory shows that the functions of these senses have been taken over by a collection of extremely complex, intricate and specialized apparatus, contrived and constructed for handling problems which can be formulated only with the aid of abstract concepts, mathematical and geometric symbols, and which often are beyond the layman's power of understanding.

ALFRED NORTH WHITEHEAD: *Science and the Modern World* *

Alfred North Whitehead (1861–1947), the great English philosopher who taught at Harvard 1924–37, hardly needs an introduction. In *Science and the Modern World* (1926), *Process and Reality* (1929), and elsewhere, Whitehead expounded his difficult philosophy of "organism," which, partly in the name of modern science, rejected the materialistic explanation of phenomena.

THE DOCTRINE which I am maintaining is that the whole concept of materialism only applies to very abstract entities, the products of logical discernment. The concrete enduring entities are organisms, so that the plan of the *whole* influences the very characters of the various subordinate organisms which enter into it. In the case of an animal, the mental states enter into the plan of the total organism and thus modify the plans of the successive subordinate organisms until the ultimate smallest organisms, such as electrons, are reached. Thus an electron within a living body is different from an electron outside it, by reason of the plan of the body. The electron blindly runs either within or without the body; but it runs within the body in accordance with its character within the body; that is to say, in accordance with the general plan of the body, and this plan includes the mental state. But the principle of modification is perfectly general throughout nature, and represents no property peculiar to living bodies. In subsequent lectures it will be ex-

* Alfred North Whitehead: *Science and the Modern World*. Copyright 1925 by The Macmillan Company and used with their permission. Pp. 115-16, 148-50, 157-8 (1937 ed.).

plained that this doctrine involves the abandonment of the traditional scientific materialism, and the substitution of an alternative doctrine of organism.

* * *

. . . we can now see that the adequacy of scientific materialism as a scheme of thought for the use of science was endangered. The conservation of energy provided a new type of quantitative permanence. It is true that energy could be construed as something subsidiary to matter. But, anyhow, the notion of *mass* was losing its unique pre-eminence as being the one final permanent quantity. Later on, we find the relations of mass and energy inverted; so that mass now becomes the name for a quantity of energy considered in relation to some of its dynamical effects. This train of thought leads to the notion of energy being fundamental, thus displacing matter from that position. But energy is merely the name for the quantitative aspect of a structure of happenings; in short, it depends on the notion of the functioning of an organism. The question is, can we define an organism without recurrence to the concept of matter in simple location? We must, later on, consider this point in more detail.

The same relegation of matter to the background occurs in connection with the electromagnetic fields. The modern theory presupposes happenings in that field which are divorced from immediate dependence upon matter. It is usual to provide an ether as a substratum. But the ether does not really enter into the theory. Thus again the notion of material loses its fundamental position. Also, the atom is transforming itself into an organism; and finally the evolution theory is nothing else than the analysis of the conditions for the formation and survival of various types of organisms. In truth, one most significant fact of this later period is the advance in biological sciences. These sciences are essentially sciences concerning organisms. During the epoch in question [the nineteenth century], and indeed also at the present moment, the prestige of the more perfect scientific form belongs to the physical sciences. Accordingly, biology apes the manner of physics. It is orthodox to hold, that there is nothing in biology but what is physical mechanism under somewhat complex circumstances.

One difficulty in this position is the present confusion as to the foundational concepts of physical science. This same difficulty also attaches to the opposed doctrine of vitalism. For, in this later theory, the fact of mechanism is accepted—I mean, mechanism based upon materialism—and an additional vital control is introduced to explain the actions of living bodies. It cannot be too clearly understood that the various physical laws which appear to apply to the behaviour of atoms are not mutually consistent as at present formulated. The appeal to mechanism on behalf of biology was in its origin an appeal to the well-attested self-consistent physical concepts as expressing the basis of all natural phenomena. But at present there is no such system of concepts.

Science is taking on a new aspect which is neither purely physical, nor purely biological. It is becoming the study of organisms. Biology is the study of the larger organisms; whereas physics is the study of the smaller organisms.

*   *   *

This rapid outline of a thoroughgoing organic theory of nature enables us to understand the chief requisites of the doctrine of evolution. The main work, proceeding during this pause at the end of the nineteenth century, was the absorption of this doctrine as guiding the methodology of all branches of science. By a blindness which is almost judicial as being a penalty affixed to hasty, superficial thinking, many religious thinkers opposed the new doctrine; although, in truth, a thoroughgoing evolutionary philosophy is inconsistent with materialism. The aboriginal stuff, or material, from which a materialistic philosophy starts is incapable of evolution. This material is in itself the ultimate substance. Evolution, on the materialistic theory, is reduced to the role of being another word for the description of the changes of the external relations between portions of matter. There is nothing to evolve, because one set of external relations is as good as any other set of external relations. There can merely be change, purposeless and unprogressive. But the whole point of the modern doctrine is the evolution of the complex organisms from antecedent states of less complex organisms. The doctrine thus cries aloud for a conception of organism as fundamental for nature. It also requires an underlying activity—a substantial activity—expressing itself in individual embodiments, and evolving in achievements of organism. The organism is a unit of emergent value, a real fusion of the characters of eternal objects, emerging for its own sake.

Thus in the process of analysing the character of nature in itself, we find that the emergence of organisms depends on a selective activity which is akin to purpose. The point is that the enduring organisms are now the outcome of evolution; and that, beyond these organisms, there is nothing else that endures. On the materialistic theory, there is material —such as matter or electricity—which endures. On the organic theory, the only endurances are structures of activity, and the structures are evolved.

SIR JAMES JEANS: *On Free-Will* *

It will be recalled that Koestler mentioned the "crisis of causality," *i.e.*, the problem of freedom and determinism as raised anew by modern physics (see above, p. 636–7). At the conclusion of his *Physics and Philosophy*, Sir James Jeans (1877–1946), British astronomer and physicist, makes some judicious remarks about this problem.

BEFORE the era of modern physics, it was a simple matter to define what we meant by causality and free-will. We supposed the world to consist of atoms and radiation; we imagined that precise positions could be assigned, in principle, to every atom and to every element of radiation, and the question of causality was simply whether, knowing these positions, it was possible in principle to predict the future course of events with certainty. The question of free-will was whether it was still possible to predict this course when consciousness and human volitions intervened in the picture.

But modern physics shows that these formulations of the questions have become meaningless. It is no longer possible to know the exact positions of particles or of elements of radiation, and, even if we could, it would still be impossible to predict what was going to happen next. So far as the inanimate world is concerned, we may picture a substratum below space and time in which the springs of events are concealed, and it may be that the future already lies hidden, but uniquely and inevitably determined, in this substratum. Such a hypothesis at least fits all the known facts of physics. But as we pass from the phenomenal world of space and time to this substratum, we seem, in some way we do not understand, to be passing from materialism to mentalism, and so possibly also from matter to mind. It may be then that the springs of events in this substratum include our own mental activities, so that the future course of events may depend in part on these mental activities.

At least the new physics has shown that the problems of causality and free-will are in need of a new formulation. If those who believe in freedom of the will could explain what they mean by freedom, and could show precisely where it differs from what we have called unconscious determinism, it is at least conceivable that what they want would be found in modern physics. The classical physics seemed to bolt and bar the door leading to any sort of freedom of the will; the new physics hardly does this; it almost seems to suggest that the door may be unlocked—if only we could find the handle. The old physics showed us a universe which looked more like a prison than a dwelling-place. The

* From Sir James Jeans: *Physics and Philosophy*, pp. 215–17. Copyright 1943 by Cambridge University Press. Reprinted by permission of Cambridge University Press.

new physics shows us a universe which looks as though it might conceivably form a suitable dwelling-place for free men, and not a mere shelter for brutes—a home in which it may at least be possible for us to mould events to our desires and live lives of endeavour and achievement.

Conclusion

There is a temptation to try to round off our discussion by summarizing the conclusions we have reached. But the plain fact is that there are no conclusions. If we must state a conclusion, it would be that many of the former conclusions of nineteenth-century science on philosophical questions are once again in the melting-pot.

Just because of this, we cannot state any positive conclusions of any kind, as for instance that materialism is dead, or that a deterministic interpretation of the world is obsolete, but we can say that determinism and freedom, matter and materialism need to be redefined in the light of our new scientific knowledge. When this has been done, the materialist must decide for himself whether the only kind of materialism which science now permits can be suitably labelled materialism, and whether the ghostly remains of matter should be labelled as matter or as something else; it is mainly a question of terminology.

What remains is in any case very different from the full-blooded matter and the forbidding materialism of the Victorian scientist. His objective and material universe is proved to consist of little more than constructs of our own minds. In this and in other ways, modern physics has moved in the direction of mentalism.

Again we can hardly say that the new physics justifies any new conclusions on determinism, causality or free-will, but we can say that the argument for determinism is in some respects less compelling than it seemed to be fifty years ago. There appears to be a case for reopening the whole question as soon as anyone can discover how to do so.

This may seem a disappointing harvest to have garnered from so extensive a field of new scientific activity, and from one, moreover, which comes so close to the territory of philosophy. Yet we may reflect that physics and philosophy are at most a few thousand years old, but probably have lives of thousands of millions of years stretching away in front of them. They are only just beginning to get under way, and we are still, in Newton's words, like children playing with pebbles on the sea-shore, while the great ocean of truth rolls, unexplored, beyond our reach. It can hardly be a matter for surprise that our race has not succeeded in solving any large part of its most difficult problems in the first millionth part of its existence. Perhaps life would be a duller affair if it had, for to many it is not knowledge but the quest for knowledge that gives the greater interest to thought—to travel hopefully is better than to arrive.

WERNER HEISENBERG: *The Idea of Nature in Contemporary Physics* *

The book from which the following excerpts are taken was originally entitled *Das Naturbild der heutigen Physik* (1955). In it Werner Heisenberg (1901–76), the distinguished German physicist, reviews briefly and compares ideas of nature from the Middle Ages to the twentieth century. He also discusses the Principle of Indeterminacy or Uncertainty, of which he was the chief architect (see also discussion of this principle by Arthur Koestler and Sir James Jeans in this same section). Heisenberg was awarded the Nobel Prize in 1932, and after World War II served as director of the Kaiser Wilhelm Institute for Physics in Berlin.

The Problem of Nature

Changes in the Investigator's Attitude to Nature

LET us first look back at the historical roots of modern science. When it was founded by Kepler, Galileo and Newton in the seventeenth century, there still prevailed the idea of nature of the Middle Ages. Nature was seen as God's creation. Nature was God's Work and it would have been thought senseless to ask questions about the material world without reference to God. . . .

Yet, within the course of a few decades, man's attitude to nature was to change radically. As scientists delved more deeply into the details of natural processes they realized, as in fact Galileo had been the first to do, that individual natural processes can be isolated from their context in order to be described and explained mathematically. At the same time it became clear how immense was the task confronting this new science. Thus, Newton no longer looked upon the world as a whole that could only be understood as God's work, and his attitude to nature is best summed up by his well-known statement: 'I do not know what I may appear to the world, but to myself I seem to have been only like a boy playing on the seashore, and diverting myself in now and then finding a smoother pebble or a prettier shell than ordinary, while the great ocean of truth lay all undiscovered before me.'

This change in the scientists' attitude to nature is perhaps best understood if we consider that, to Christian thought of the time, God

* Excerpts from *The Physicist's Conception of Nature* by Werner Heisenberg. Copyright 1955 by Rowohlt Taschenbuch Verlag, GmbH, 1958 by Hutchinson and Company (Publishers) Ltd. Reprinted by permission of Harcourt Brace Jovanovich, Inc.

seemed to be in a Heaven so high above the earth, that it became significant to look at the earth without reference to God. . . . The scientist was conforming with this tendency when, considering nature not only independently of God but even independently of man, he aimed at its 'objective' description or explanation. Yet it must be stressed that even for Newton the shell was important only because it stemmed from the great ocean of truth. Its observation was not yet a purpose in itself, but derived its significance from its connection with the ocean.

In the ensuing years the methods of Newtonian mechanics were applied successfully to ever greater realms of nature. Attempts were made to discover the details of natural processes by means of experiments, to observe them objectively and to understand the laws governing them. Scientists tried to formulate relationships mathematically, and to arrive at 'laws' which would hold without restriction in the entire cosmos. In this way they finally managed to harness the forces of nature to man's purposes. The magnificent development of mechanics in the eighteenth century, and of optics, thermodynamics and heat technology at the beginning of the nineteenth century are all evidence of the power of this approach.

Changes in the Meaning of the Word 'Nature'

Inasmuch as this kind of science was successful, it spread beyond the realm of daily experience into distant realms of nature, which could only be opened up properly by means of techniques which arose out of the development of science itself. Even in Newton's case, the decisive step had been his realization that the same laws of mechanics which governed the fall of a stone determined the motion of the moon about the earth; in other words, they could also be applied on a cosmic scale. In the period that followed, science began its victorious march on a broad front even into those distant realms of nature which could only be entered through technology, *i.e.*, by means of more or less complicated instruments. Astronomy, making use of ever better telescopes, conquered even wider cosmic spaces. From the behaviour of matter during chemical changes, chemistry tried to fathom processes on the atomic scale. Experiments with the induction machine and the Voltaic cell provided the first common knowledge of electrical phenomena not yet understood. Thus, there took place a slow change in the significance of 'nature' as a subject for investigation by science. It became a collective concept for all those realms of experience into which man could penetrate by means of science and technology, regardless of whether or not they appeared as 'nature' to his immediate perception. Even the phrase 'description of nature' lost more and more of its original significance of a living and meaningful account of nature. Increasingly it became to mean the mathematical description of nature, *i.e.*, an accurate and concise yet comprehensive collection of data about relations that hold in nature.

This semi-conscious extension of the concept of nature must not yet be considered a basic departure from the original aims of science, since, even in this wider field, the crucial concepts were still the same as those of ordinary experience. In the nineteenth century nature still appeared as a set of laws in space and time in which man and man's intervention in nature could be ignored in principle, if not in practice.

Matter was thought of in terms of its mass, which remained constant through all changes, and which required forces to move it. Because, from the eighteenth century onwards, chemical experiments could be classified and explained by the atomic hypothesis of ancient times, it appeared reasonable to take over the view of ancient philosophy that atoms were the real substance, the immutable building-stones of matter. Just as in the philosophy of Democritus, the differences in material qualities were considered to be merely apparent; smell or colour, temperature or viscosity, were not actual qualities of matter but resulted from the interaction of matter and our senses, and had to be explained by the arrangements and movements of atoms, and by the effect of these arrangements on our minds. It is thus that there arose the over-simplified world-view of nineteenth-century materialism: atoms move in space and time as the real and immutable substances, and it is their arrangement and motion that create the colourful phenomena of the world of our senses.

The Crisis of the Materialist Conception

The first, but not yet very dangerous, incursion into this world-view took place in the second half of the last century with the development of the theory of electricity, in which not matter but fields of force were considered to be the real explanation. . . .

But in our century it is just in this sphere that fundamental changes have taken place in the basis of atomic physics which have made us abandon the world-view of ancient atomic philosophy. It has become clear that the desired objective reality of the elementary particles is too crude an oversimplification of what really happens, and that it must give way to very much more abstract conceptions. For if we wish to form a picture of the nature of these elementary particles, we can no longer ignore the physical processes through which we obtain our knowledge of them. While, in observing everyday objects, the physical process involved in making the observation plays a subsidiary role only, in the case of the smallest building particles of matter, every process of observation produces a large disturbance. We can no longer speak of the behaviour of the particle independently of the process of observation. As a final consequence, the natural laws formulated mathematically in quantum theory no longer deal with the elementary particles themselves but with our knowledge of them. Nor is it any longer possible to ask whether or not these particles exist in space and time objectively, since the only processes we can refer to as taking place are those which represent the interplay of particles with some other physical system, *e.g.*, a measuring instrument.

Thus, the objective reality of the elementary particles has been strangely dispersed, not into the fog of some new ill-defined or still unexplained conception of reality, but into the transparent clarity of a mathematics that no longer describes the behaviour of the elementary particles but only our knowledge of this behaviour. The atomic physicist has had to resign himself to the fact that his science is but a link in the infinite chain of man's argument with nature, *and that it cannot simply speak of nature 'in itself.'* Science always presupposes the existence of man and, as Bohr has said, we must become conscious of the fact that we are not merely observers but also actors on the stage of life. . . .

Some of the most interesting general effects of modern atomic physics are the changes which it has brought about in the concept of natural laws. In the last few years many people have stated that modern atomic physics has abolished the law of cause and effect, or at least that it has shown the latter to be partially inoperative, and that we can no longer properly speak of processes determined by natural laws. . . . Determinism was still present in principle until Max Planck's famous discovery ushered in quantum theory. Planck, in his work on the theory of radiation, had originally encountered an element of uncertainty in radiation phenomena. He had shown that a radiating atom does not deliver up its energy continuously, but discreetly in bundles. This assumption of a discontinuous and pulse-like transfer of energy, like every other notion of atomic theory, leads us once more to the idea that the emission of radiation is a statistical phenomenon. However, it took two and a half decades before it became clear *that quantum theory actually forces us to formulate these laws precisely as statistical laws* and to depart radically from determinism. Since the work of Einstein, Bohr and Sommerfeld, Planck's theory has proved to be the key with which the door to the entire sphere of atomic physics could be opened. Chemical processes could be explained by means of the Rutherford-Bohr atomic model, and since then, chemistry, physics and astrophysics have been fused into unity. With the mathematical formulation of quantum-theoretical laws pure determinism had to be abandoned.

Since I cannot speak of the mathematical methods here, I should merely like to mention some aspects of the strange situation confronting the physicist in atomic physics.

We can express the departure from previous forms of physics by means of the so-called uncertainty relations. It was discovered that it was impossible to describe simultaneously both the position and the velocity of an atomic particle with any prescribed degree of accuracy. We can either measure the position very accurately—when the action of the instrument used for the observation obscures our knowledge of the velocity, or we can make accurate measurements of the velocity and forego knowledge of the position. The product of the two uncertainties can never be less than Planck's constant. This formulation makes it quite clear that we cannot make much headway with the concepts of Newtonian mechanics, since in the calculation of a mechanical process it is essential to know simultaneously the position and velocity at a particular moment, and this is precisely what quantum theory considers to be impossible. . . .

Even without entering into the mathematics of quantum theory these brief comments might have helped us to realize *that the incomplete knowledge of a system must be an essential part of every formulation in quantum theory*. Quantum theoretical laws must be of a statistical kind. To give an example: we know that the radium atom emits alpha-radiation. Quantum theory can give us an indication of the probability that the alpha-particle will leave the nucleus in unit time, but it cannot predict at what precise point in time the emission will occur, for this is uncertain in principle. We cannot even assume that new laws still to be discovered will allow us to determine this precise point in time; were this possible the alpha-particle could not also be considered to behave as a wave leaving the atomic nucleus, a fact which we can prove experimentally. The various experiments proving both the wave nature and also the particle nature of atomic matter create a paradox which forces us to devise a formulation of statistical laws. . . .

5. *The Nature of Man*

ERNST CASSIRER: *The Crisis in Man's Knowledge of Himself* *

In his *An Essay on Man*, here quoted, Ernst Cassirer (1874–1945), well known German philosopher and historian of philosophy, describes succinctly "the crisis in man's knowledge of himself" in the twentieth century. Subsequent excerpts in this section are a sampling of the bewildering and often contradictory views on man to which Cassirer alludes.

. . . OUR modern theory of man lost its intellectual center. We acquired instead a complete anarchy of thought. Even in the former times to be sure there was a great discrepancy of opinions and theories relating to this problem. But there remained at least a general orientation, a frame of reference, to which all individual differences might be referred. Metaphysics, theology, mathematics, and biology successively assumed the guidance for thought on the problem of man and determined the line of investigation. The real crisis of this problem manifested itself when such a central power capable of directing all individual efforts ceased to exist. The paramount importance of the problem was still felt in all the different branches of knowledge and inquiry. But an established authority to which one might appeal no longer existed. Theologians, scientists, politicians, sociologists, biologists, psychologists, ethnologists, economists all approached the problem from their own viewpoints. To combine or unify all these particular aspects and perspectives was impossible. And even within the special fields there was no generally accepted scientific principle. The personal factor became more and more prevalent, and the temperament of the individual writer tended to play a decisive role. *Trahit sua quemque voluptas:* every author seems in the last count to be led by his own conception and evaluation of human life.

That this antagonism of ideas is not merely a grave theoretical problem but an imminent threat to the whole extent of our ethical and cultural life admits of no doubt. In recent philosophical thought Max Scheler was one of the first to become aware of and to signalize this danger. "In no other period of human knowledge," declares Scheler, "has man ever become more problematic to himself than in our own days. We have a scientific, a philosophical, and a theological anthropology

---

* From Ernst Cassirer: *An Essay on Man*, pp. 21–2. Copyright 1944 by Yale University Press. Reprinted by permission of Yale University Press.

that know nothing of each other. Therefore we no longer possess any clear and consistent idea of man. The ever-growing multiplicity of the particular sciences that are engaged in the study of men has much more confused and obscured than elucidated our concept of man."

Such is the strange situation in which modern philosophy finds itself. No former age was ever in such a favorable position with regard to the sources of our knowledge of human nature. Psychology, ethnology, anthropology, and history have amassed an astoundingly rich and constantly increasing body of facts. Our technical instruments for observation and experimentation have been immensely improved, and our analyses have become sharper and more penetrating. We appear, nevertheless, not yet to have found a method for the mastery and organization of this material. When compared with our own abundance the past may seem very poor. But our wealth of facts is not necessarily a wealth of thoughts. Unless we succeed in finding a clue of Ariadne to lead us out of this labyrinth, we can have no real insight into the general character of human culture; we shall remain lost in a mass of disconnected and disintegrated data which seem to lack all conceptual unity.

SIGMUND FREUD

> The following selections from four separate works by Sigmund Freud (1856–1939) describe concisely some of the salient features of the great Viennese psychologist's conception of the nature and destiny of man. The four works are, in order: "One of the Difficulties of Psychoanalysis" (1917), *New Introductory Lectures on Psychoanalysis* (1933), "Analysis Terminable and Interminable" (1937), and *Civilization and Its Discontents* (1930).

Three Blows to Narcissism *

". . . I SHALL describe how the general narcissism of man, the self-love of humanity, has up to the present been three times severely wounded by the researches of science.

When the first promptings of curiosity about his dwelling-place, the earth, began to arise in him, man believed that it was the stationary centre of the universe, with the sun, moon and planets circling round it. With this he was naïvely following the dictates of his sense-perceptions, for he felt no movement of the earth, and wherever he had an unimpeded view he found himself in the centre of a circle that enclosed the whole world outside him. The central position of the earth was to him a token

* From Sigmund Freud: *Collected Papers*, trans. Joan Riviere, Vol. IV, pp. 350-2, 355. Copyright 1956 by The Hogarth Press Ltd. Reprinted by permission of The Hogarth Press Ltd. and Basic Books, Inc., Publishers.

of its sovereignty in the universe and it appeared to accord very well with his proclivity to regard himself as lord of the world.

The destruction of this narcissistic illusion is associated with the name and work of Copernicus in the sixteenth century. . . . When it achieved general recognition, the self-love of humanity suffered its first blow, the *cosmological* one.

In the course of his development towards culture man acquired a dominating position over his fellow-creatures in the animal kingdom. Not content with this supremacy, however, he began to place a gulf between his nature and theirs. He denied the possession of reason to them, and to himself he attributed an immortal soul, and made claims to a divine descent which permitted him to annihilate the bond of community between him and the animal kingdom. . . .

We all know that, little more than half a century ago, the researches of Charles Darwin, his collaborators and predecessors put an end to this presumption on the part of man. Man is not a being different from animals or superior to them; he himself originates in the animal race and is related more closely to some of its members and more distantly to others. The accretions he has subsequently developed have not served to efface the evidences, both in his physical structure and in his mental dispositions, of his parity with them. This was the second, the *biological* blow to human narcissism.

The third blow, which is psychological in nature, is probably the most wounding.

Although thus humbled in his external relations, man feels himself to be supreme in his own soul. Somewhere in the core of his ego he has developed an organ of observation to keep a watch on his impulses and actions and see that they accord with its demands. If they do not, they are inexorably prohibited and retracted. His inner perception, consciousness, gives the ego news of all the important occurrences in the mind's working, and the will, set in motion by these reports, carries out what the ego directs and modifies all that tends to accomplish itself independently. . . .

But two discoveries (by psychoanalysis)—that the life of the sexual instincts cannot be totally restrained, and that mental processes are in themselves unconscious and only reach the ego and come under its control through incomplete and untrustworthy perceptions—amount to a statement that *the ego is not master in its own house.* Together they represent the third wound inflicted on man's self-love, that which I call the *psychological* one. No wonder, therefore, that the ego shows no favour to psycho-analysis and persistently refuses to believe in it.

The Anatomy of the Mental Personality *

Super-ego, ego and id, then, are the three realms, regions or provinces into which we divide the mental apparatus of the individual; and it is their mutual relations with which we shall be concerned in what follows. . . .

You must not expect me to tell you much that is new about the id, except its name. It is the obscure inaccessible part of our personality; the little we know about it we have learnt from the study of dream-work and the formation of neurotic symptoms, and most of that is of a negative character, and can only be described as being all that the ego is not. We can come nearer to the id with images, and call it a chaos, a cauldron of seething excitement. We suppose that it is somewhere in direct contact with somatic processes, and takes over from them instinctual needs and gives them mental expression, but we cannot say in what substratum this contact is made. These instincts fill it with energy, but it has no organisation and no unified will, only an impulsion to obtain satisfaction for the instinctual needs, in accordance with the pleasure-principle. The laws of logic—above all, the law of contradiction—do not hold for processes in the id. . . .

Naturally, the id knows no values, no good and evil, no morality. The economic, or, if you prefer, the quantitative factor, which is so closely bound up with the pleasure-principle, dominates all its processes. . . . As regards a characterisation of the ego, in so far as it is to be distinguished from the id and the super-ego, we shall get on better if we turn our attention to the relation between it and the most superficial portion of the mental apparatus; which we call the Pcpt-cs (perceptual-conscious) system. This system is directed on to the external world, it mediates perceptions of it, and in it is generated, while it is functioning, the phenomenon of consciousness. It is the sense-organ of the whole apparatus, receptive, moreover, not only of excitations from without but also of such as proceed from the interior of the mind. One can hardly go wrong in regarding the ego as that part of the id which has been modified by its proximity to the external world and the influence that the latter has had on it, and which serves the purpose of receiving stimuli and protecting the organism from them, like the cortical layer with which a particle of living substance surrounds itself. This relation to the external world is decisive for the ego. The ego has taken over the task of representing the external world for the id, and so of saving it; for the id, blindly striving to gratify its instincts in complete disregard of the superior strength of outside forces, could not otherwise escape annihilation. . . . On behalf of the id, the ego controls the path of access to motility, but it interpolates between desire and action the procrastinating factor of thought, during which it makes use of the residues of experience stored up in memory. In this way it dethrones the pleasure-principle, which exerts undisputed sway over the processes in the id, and substitutes for it the reality-principle, which promises greater security and greater success. . . . In popular language, we may say that the ego stands for reason and circumspection, while the id stands for the untamed passions.

So far we have allowed ourselves to dwell on the enumeration of the merits and capabilities of the ego; it is time now to look at the other side of the picture. The ego is after all only a part of the id, a part purposively modified by its proximity to the dangers of reality. From a dynamic point of view it is weak; it borrows its energy from the id. . . . One might compare the relation of the ego to the id with that between a rider and his horse. The horse provides the locomotive energy, and the rider has the prerogative of determining the goal and of guiding the movements of his powerful mount towards it. But all too often in the relations between the ego and the id we find a picture of the less ideal situation in which the rider is obliged to guide his horse in the direction in which it itself wants to go. . . .

The proverb tells us that one cannot serve two masters at once. The poor ego has a still harder time of it; it has to serve three harsh masters; and has to do its best to reconcile the claims and demands of all three. These demands are always divergent and often seem quite incompatible; no wonder that the ego so frequently gives way under its task. The three tyrants are the external world, the super-ego and the id. When one watches the efforts of the ego to satisfy them all, or rather, to obey them all simultaneously, one cannot regret having personified the ego, and established it as a separate being. It feels itself hemmed in on three sides and threatened by three kinds of danger, towards which it reacts by developing anxiety when it is too hard pressed. Having originated in the experiences of the perceptual system, it is designed to represent the demands of the external world, but it also wishes to be a loyal servant of the id, to remain upon good terms with the id, to recommend itself to the id as an object, and to draw the id's libido on to itself. . . . On the other hand, its every movement is watched by the severe super-ego, which holds up certain norms of behaviour, without regard to any difficulties coming from the id and the external world; and if these norms are not acted up to, it punishes the ego with the feelings of tension which manifest themselves as a sense of inferiority and guilt. In this way, goaded on by the id, hemmed in by the super-ego, and rebuffed by reality, the ego struggles to cope with its economic task of reducing the forces and influences which work in it and upon it to some kind of harmony; and we may well understand how it is that we so often cannot repress the cry: "Life is not easy."

Eros and Thanatos *

Nothing impresses us more strongly in connection with the resistances encountered in analysis than the feeling that there is a force at work which is defending itself by all possible means against recovery and is clinging tenaciously to illness and suffering. We have recognized that part of this force is the sense of guilt and the need for punishment, and that is undoubtedly correct; we have localized it in the ego's relation to the super-ego. But this is only one element in it, which may be described as psychically bound by the super-ego and which we thus perceive. We may suppose that other portions of the same force are at work, either bound or free, in some unspecified region of the mind. If we consider the whole picture made up of the phenomena of the masochism inherent in so many people, of the negative therapeutic reaction and of the neurotic's sense of guilt, we shall have to abandon the belief that mental processes are governed exclusively by a striving after pleasure. These phenomena are unmistakable indications of the existence of a power in mental life which, according to its aim, we call the aggressive or destructive instinct and which we derive from the primal death-instinct of animate matter. It is not a question of an optimistic as opposed to a pessimistic theory of life. Only by the concurrent or opposing action of the two primal instincts—Eros and the death-instinct—never by one or the other alone, can the motley variety of vital phenomena be explained. . . .

I am well aware that the dualistic theory, according to which an instinct of death, destruction or aggression claims equal partnership with Eros as manifested in libido, has met with little general acceptance and has not really established itself even among psycho-analysts. My delight was proportionately great when I recently discovered that that theory was held by one of the great thinkers of ancient Greece. . . .

The theory of Empedocles which specially claims our attention is one which approximates closely to the psycho-analytical theory of the instincts. . . .

The Greek philosopher taught that there were two principles governing events in the life of the universe as in that of the mind, and that these principles were eternally in conflict with each other. He called them love and strife. Of these powers, which he really conceived of as "natural forces working like instincts, and certainly not intelligences with a conscious purpose", the one strives to unite the atoms of these four elements into a single unity, while the other seeks to dissolve these fusions and to separate the atoms of the elements. Empedocles conceives of the world-process as a continuous, never-ceasing alternation of periods in which the one or the other of the two fundamental forces triumphs, so that at one time love and, at another time, strife fulfils its purpose and governs the universe, after which the other, vanquished power asserts itself and in its turn prevails.

The two fundamental principles of Empedocles—love and strife—are, both in name and in function, the same as our two primal instincts, *Eros* and *Destructiveness,* the former of which strives to combine existing phenomena into ever greater unities, while the latter seeks to dissolve these combinations and destroy the structures to which they have given rise.

SIGMUND FREUD: *Civilization and Its Discontents* *

[FREUD asks] what the behaviour of men themselves reveals as the purpose and object of their lives, what they demand of life and wish to attain in it. The answer to this can hardly be in doubt: they seek happiness, they want to become happy and to remain so. There are two sides to this striving, a positive and a negative; it aims on the one hand at eliminating pain and discomfort, on the other at the experience of intense pleasures. In its narrower sense the word 'happiness' relates only to the last. Thus human activities branch off in two directions—corresponding to this double goal—according to which of the two they aim at realizing, either predominantly or even exclusively.

As we see, it is simply the pleasure-principle which draws up the programme of life's purpose. This principle dominates the operation of the mental apparatus from the very beginning; there can be no doubt about its efficiency, and yet its programme is in conflict with the whole world, with the macrocosm as much as with the microcosm. It simply cannot be put into execution, the whole constitution of things runs counter to it; one might say the intention that man should be 'happy' is not included in the scheme of 'Creation.' What is called happiness in its narrowest sense comes from the satisfaction—most often instantaneous—of pent-up needs which have reached great intensity, and by its very nature can only be a transitory experience. When any condition desired by the pleasure-principle is protracted, it results in a feeling only of mild comfort; we are so constituted that we can only intensely enjoy contrasts, much less intensely states in themselves. Our possibilities of happiness are thus limited from the start by our very constitution. It is much less difficult to be unhappy. Suffering comes from three quarters: from our own body, which is destined to decay and dissolution, and cannot even dispense with anxiety and pain as danger-signals; from the outer world, which can rage against us with the most powerful and pitiless forces of destruction; and finally from our relations with other men. The unhappiness which has this last origin we find perhaps more painful than any other; we tend to regard it more or less as a gratuitous addition, although it cannot be any less an inevitable fate than the suffering that proceeds from other sources. . . .

The bit of truth behind all this—one so eagerly denied—is that men are not gentle, friendly creatures wishing for love, who simply defend themselves if they are attacked, but that a powerful measure of desire for aggression has to be reckoned as part of their instinctual endowment. The result is that their neighbour is to them not only a possible helper or sexual object, but also a temptation to them to gratify their aggressiveness on him, to exploit his capacity for work without recompense, to use him sexually without his consent, to seize his possessions, to humiliate him, to cause him pain, to torture and to kill him. *Homo homini lupus;* who has the courage to dispute it in the face of all the evidence in his own life and in history? This aggressive cruelty usually lies in wait for some provocation, or else it steps into the service of some other purpose, the aim of which might as well have been achieved by milder measures. In circumstances that favour it, when those forces in the mind which ordinarily inhibit it cease to operate, it also manifests itself spontaneously and reveals men as savage beasts to whom the thought of sparing their own kind is alien. Anyone who calls to mind the atrocities of the early migrations, of the invasion by the Huns or by the so-called Mongols under Jenghiz Khan and Tamurlane, of the sack of Jerusalem by the pious Crusaders, even indeed the horrors of the last world-war, will have to bow his head humbly before the truth of this view of man.

The existence of this tendency to aggression which we can detect in ourselves and rightly presume to be present in others is the factor that disturbs our relations with our neighbours and makes it necessary for culture to institute its high demands. Civilized society is perpetually menaced with disintegration through this primary hostility of men towards one another. Their interests in their common work would not hold them together; the passions of instinct are stronger than reasoned interests. Culture has to call up every possible reinforcement in order to erect barriers against the aggressive instincts of men and hold their manifestations in check by reaction-formations in men's minds. Hence its system of methods by which mankind is to be driven to identifications and aim-inhibited love-relationships; hence the restrictions on sexual life; and hence, too, its ideal command to love one's neighbour as oneself, which is really justified by the fact that nothing is so completely at variance with original human nature as this. . . .

The Communists believe they have found a way of delivering us from this evil. Man is whole-heartedly good and friendly to his neighbour, they say, but the system of private property has corrupted his nature. The possession of private property gives power to the individual and thence the temptation arises to ill-treat his neighbour; the man who is excluded from the possession of property is obliged to rebel in hostility against the oppressor. If private property were abolished, all valuables held in common and all allowed to share in the enjoyment of them, ill-will and enmity would disappear from among men. Since all needs would be satisfied, none would have any reason to regard another as an enemy; all would willingly undertake the work which is necessary. I have no concern with any economic criticisms of the communistic system; I cannot enquire into whether the abolition of private property is advantageous and expedient. But I am able to recognize that psychologically it is founded on an untenable illusion. By abolishing private property one deprives the human love of aggression of one of its instruments, a strong one undoubtedly, but assuredly not the strongest. It in no way alters the individual differences in power and influence which are turned by aggressiveness to its own use, nor does it change the nature of the instinct in any way. This instinct did not arise as the result of property; it reigned almost supreme in primitive times when possessions were still extremely scanty; it shows itself already in the nursery when possessions have hardly grown out of their original anal shape; it is at the bottom of all the relations of affection and love between human beings—possibly with the single exception of that of a mother to her male child. Suppose that personal rights to material goods are done away with, there still remain prerogatives in sexual relationships, which must arouse the strongest rancour and most violent enmity among men and women who are otherwise equal. Let us suppose this were also to be removed by instituting complete liberty in sexual life, so that the family, the germ-cell of culture, ceased to exist; one could not, it is true, foresee the new paths on which cultural development might then proceed, but one thing one would be bound to expect and that is that the ineffaceable feature of human nature would follow wherever it led. . . .

In all that follows I take up the standpoint that the tendency to aggression is an innate, independent, instinctual disposition in man, and I come back now to the statement that it constitutes the most powerful obstacle to culture. At one point in the course of this discussion the idea took possession of us that culture was a peculiar process passing over human life and we are still under the influence of this idea. We may add to this that the process proves to be in the service of Eros, which aims at binding together single human individuals, then families, then tribes, races, nations, into one great unity, that of humanity. Why this has to be done we do not know; it is simply the work of Eros. These masses of men must be bound to one another libidinally; necessity alone, the advantages of common work, would not hold them together. The natural instinct of aggressiveness in man, the hostility of each one against all and of all against each one, opposes this programme of civilization. This instinct of aggression is the derivative and main representative of the death instinct we have found alongside of Eros, sharing his rule over the earth. And now, it seems to me, the meaning of the evolution of culture is no longer a riddle to us. It must present to us the struggle between Eros and Death, between the instincts of life and the instincts of destruction, as it works itself out in the human species. This struggle is what all life essentially consists of and so the evolution of civilization may be simply described as the struggle of the human species for existence. And it is this battle of the Titans that our nurses and governesses try to compose with their lullaby-song of Heaven!

CARL JUNG: *On the Collective Unconscious* *

> Next to Freud, Carl Jung (1875–1961) is probably the best known modern psychologist. Originally associated with Freud—he was in fact the first president of the International Psychoanalytic Association—he broke with the master early in his career and developed, in Zurich, his own "analytical psychology." Among his most original conceptions is that of the collective unconscious which is, among other things, the source of man's religious life. The following selections are from two essays by Jung, "Archetypes of the Collective Unconscious" (1934) and "On the Nature of the Psyche" (1946).

THE HYPOTHESIS of a collective unconscious belongs to the class of ideas that people at first find strange but soon come to possess and use as familiar conceptions. This has been the case with the concept of the unconscious in general. After the philosophical idea of the unconscious, in the form presented chiefly by Carus and von Hartmann, had gone down under the overwhelming wave of materialism and empiricism, leaving hardly a ripple behind it, it gradually reappeared in the scientific domain of medical psychology.

At first the concept of the unconscious was limited to denoting the state of repressed or forgotten contents. Even with Freud, who makes

* The Collected Works of C. J. Jung, vol. 8, The Structure and Dynamics of the Psyche, pp. 365-7, 372, 375, 380-1; vol. 9, The Archetypes and the Collective Unconscious, pt. 1, pp. 3-7. Copyright 1959 and 1960 by Bollingen Foundation, New York, N. Y. Reprinted by permission of Bollingen Foundation, New York, N. Y., and Routledge & Kegan Paul, Ltd.

the unconscious—at least metaphorically—take the stage as the acting subject, it is really nothing but the gathering place of forgotten and repressed contents, and has a functional significance thanks only to these. For Freud, accordingly, the unconscious is of an exclusively personal nature, although he was aware of its archaic and mythological thought-forms.

A more or less superficial layer of the unconscious is undoubtedly personal. I call it the *personal unconscious*. But this personal unconscious rests upon a deeper layer, which does not derive from personal experience and is not a personal acquisition but is inborn. This deeper layer I call the *collective unconscious*. I have chosen the term "collective" because this part of the unconscious is not individual but universal; in contrast to the personal psyche, it has contents and modes of behaviour that are more or less the same everywhere and in all individuals. It is, in other words, identical in all men and thus constitutes a common psychic substrate of a suprapersonal nature which is present in every one of us.

Psychic existence can be recognized only by the presence of contents that are *capable of consciousness*. We can therefore speak of an unconscious only in so far as we are able to demonstrate its contents. The contents of the personal unconscious are chiefly the *feeling-toned complexes*, as they are called; they constitute the personal and private side of psychic life. The contents of the collective unconscious, on the other hand, are known as *archetypes*.

The term "archetype" occurs as early as Philo Judaeus, with reference to the *Imago Dei* (God-image) in man. It can also be found in Irenaeus, who says: "The creator of the world did not fashion these things directly from himself but copied them from archetypes outside himself.". . . For our purposes this term is apposite and helpful, because it tells us that so far as the collective unconscious contents are concerned we are dealing with archaic or—I would say—primordial types, that is, with universal images that have existed since the remotest times. The term "représentations collectives," used by Lévy-Bruhl to denote the symbolic figures in the primitive view of the world, could easily be applied to unconscious contents as well, since it means practically the same thing. Primitive tribal lore is concerned with archetypes that have been modified in a special way. They are no longer contents of the unconscious, but have already been changed into conscious formulae taught according to tradition, generally in the form of esoteric teaching. This last is a typical means of expression for the transmission of collective contents originally derived from the unconscious.

Another well-known expression of the archetypes is myth and fairytale. But here too we are dealing with forms that have received a specific stamp and have been handed down through long periods of time. The term "archetype" thus applies only indirectly to the "représentations collectives," since it designates only those psychic contents which have not yet been submitted to conscious elaboration and are therefore an immediate datum of psychic experience. In this sense there is a considerable difference between the archetype and the historical formula that has evolved. Especially on the higher levels of esoteric teaching the archetypes appear in a form that reveals quite unmistakably the critical and evaluating influence of conscious elaboration. Their immediate manifestation, as we encounter it in dreams and visions, is much more individual, less understandable, and more naïve than in myths, for example. The archetype is essentially an unconscious content that is altered by becoming conscious and by being perceived, and it takes its colour from the individual consciousness in which it happens to appear.

What the word "archetype" means in the nominal sense is clear enough, then, from its relations with myth, esoteric teaching, and fairytale. But if we try to establish what an archetype is *psychologically*, the matter becomes more complicated. So far mythologists have always helped themselves out with solar, lunar, meteorological, vegetal, and other ideas of the kind. The fact that myths are first and foremost psychic phenomena that reveal the nature of the soul is something they have absolutely refused to see until now. Primitive man is not much interested in objective explanations of the obvious, but he has an imperative need—or rather, his unconscious psyche has an irresistible urge—to assimilate all outer sense experiences to inner, psychic events. It is not enough for the primitive to see the sun rise and set; this external observation must at the same time be a psychic happening: the sun in its course must represent the fate of a god or hero who, in the last analysis, dwells nowhere except in the soul of man. All the mythologized processes of nature, such as summer and winter, the phases of the moon, the rainy seasons, and so forth, are in no sense allegories of these objective occurrences; rather they are symbolic expressions of the inner, unconscious drama of the psyche which becomes accessible to man's consciousness by way of projection—that is, mirrored in the events of nature. The projection is so fundamental that it has taken several thousand years of civilization to detach it in some measure from its outer object. . . .

Primitive man impresses us so strongly with his subjectivity that we should really have guessed long ago that myths refer to something psychic. His knowledge of nature is essentially the language and outer dress of an unconscious psychic process. But the very fact that this process is unconscious gives us the reason why man has thought of everything except the psyche in his attempts to explain myths. He simply didn't know that the psyche contains all the images that have ever given rise to myths, and that our unconscious is an acting and suffering subject with an inner drama which primitive man rediscovers, by means of analogy, in the processes of nature both great and small.

*   *   *

Does this theory and this conception of man [the Freudian] contain anything valuable for our *Weltanschauung?* I hardly think so. It is the well-known rationalistic materialism of the late nineteenth century, which is the guiding principle of the interpretive psychology underlying Freud's psychoanalysis. . . .

Psychoanalysis has removed the veil from facts that were known only to a few, and has even made an effort to deal with them. But has it any new attitude to them? Has the deep impression produced lasting and fruitful results? Has it altered our picture of the world and thus added to our *Weltanschauung?* The *Weltanschauung* of psychoanalysis is a rationalistic materialism, the *Weltanschauung* of an essentially practical science—and this view we feel to be inadequate. When we trace a poem of Goethe's to his mother-complex, when we seek to explain Napoleon as a case of masculine protest, or St. Francis as a case of sexual repression, a sense of profound dissatisfaction comes over us. The explanation is insufficient and does not do justice to the reality and meaning of things. What becomes of beauty, greatness, and holiness? These are vital realities without which human existence would be superlatively stupid. . . .

Thus man is born with a complicated psychic disposition that is anything but a *tabula rasa.* Even the boldest fantasies have their limits determined by our psychic inheritance, and through the veil of even the wildest fantasy we can still glimpse the dominants that were inherent in the human mind from the very beginning. . . .

I have called the sphere of our psychic heritage the collective unconscious. The contents of consciousness are all acquired individually. If the human psyche consisted simply and solely of consciousness, there would be nothing psychic that had not arisen in the course of the individual's life. In that case we would seek in vain for any prior conditions or influences behind a simple parental complex. With the reduction to father and mother the last word would be said, for they are the figures that first influenced the conscious psyche to the exclusion of all else. But actually the contents of consciousness did not come into existence simply through the influence of the environment; they were also influenced and arranged by our psychic inheritance, the collective unconscious. . . .

If, in this lecture, I have helped you to recognize that the powers which men have always projected into space as gods, and worshipped with sacrifices, are still alive and active in our own unconscious psyche, I shall be content. This recognition should suffice to show that the manifold religious practices and beliefs which, from the earliest times, have played such an enormous role in history cannot be traced back to the whimsical fancies and opinions of individuals, but owe their existence far more to the influence of unconscious powers which we cannot neglect without disturbing the psychic balance. . . .

Seen in this light, analytical psychology is a reaction against the exaggerated rationalization of consciousness which, seeking to control nature, isolates itself from her and so robs man of his own natural history. He finds himself transplanted into a limited present, consisting of the short span between birth and death. The limitation creates a feeling that he is a haphazard creature without meaning, and it is this feeling that prevents him from living his life with the intensity it demands if it is to be enjoyed to the full. Life becomes stale and is no longer the exponent of the complete man. That is why so much unlived life falls into the unconscious. People live as though they were walking in shoes too small for them. That quality of eternity which is so characteristic of the life of primitive man is entirely lacking. Hemmed round by rationalistic walls, we are cut off from the eternity of nature. Analytical psychology seeks to break through these walls by digging up again the fantasy-images of the unconscious which our rationalism has rejected. These images lie beyond the walls; they are part of the nature *in us*, which apparently lies buried in our past and against which we have barricaded ourselves behind the walls of reason. Analytical psychology tries to resolve the resultant conflict not by going "back to Nature" with Rousseau, but by holding on to the level of reason we have successfully reached, and by enriching consciousness with a knowledge of man's psychic foundations.

ERICH FROMM: *Man for Himself* *

Erich Fromm (1900–   ), born and educated in Germany, was one of a number of European psychiatrists who migrated to the U. S. A. in the '30's. In demand as a university lecturer, he has also written a number of influential books, including *Escape from Freedom* (1941), which analyzed the psychological appeal of totalitarianism. Often classified as a neo-Freudian, he nevertheless differs significantly from Freud in his conception of the nature of man.

THE CONTEMPORARY human crisis has led to a retreat from the hopes and ideas of the Enlightenment under the auspices of which our political and economic progress had begun. The very idea of progress is called a childish illusion, and "realism," a new word for the utter lack of faith in

* From Erich Fromm: *Man for Himself*, pp. 4–5, 7, 210–12, 217. Copyright 1947 by Erich Fromm. Reprinted by permission of Holt, Rinehart and Winston, Inc.

man, is preached instead. The idea of the dignity and power of man, which gave man the strength and courage for the tremendous accomplishments of the last few centuries, is challenged by the suggestion that we have to revert to the acceptance of man's ultimate powerlessness and insignificance. This idea threatens to destroy the very roots from which our culture grew. . . .

I have written this book with the intention of reaffirming the validity of humanistic ethics. . . .

The position taken by humanistic ethics that man is able to know what is good and to act accordingly on the strength of his natural potentialities and of his reason would be untenable if the dogma of man's innate natural evilness were true. The opponents of humanistic ethics claim that man's nature is such as to make him inclined to be hostile to his fellow men, to be envious and jealous, and to be lazy, unless he is curbed by fear. Many representatives of humanistic ethics met this challenge by insisting that man is inherently good and that destructiveness is not an integral part of his nature.

Indeed, the controversy between these two conflicting views is one of the basic themes in Western thought. To Socrates, ignorance, and not man's natural disposition, was the source of evilness; to him vice was error. The Old Testament, on the contrary, tells us that man's history starts with an act of sin, and that his "strivings are evil from childhood on.". . .

These two threads remain interwoven in the texture of modern thought. The idea of man's dignity and power was pronounced by the enlightenment philosophy, by progressive, liberal thought of the nineteenth century, and most radically by Nietzsche. The idea of man's worthlessness and nothingness found a new, and this time entirely secularized, expression in the authoritarian systems in which the state of "society" became the supreme rulers, while the individual, recognizing his own insignificance, is supposed to find his fulfillment in obedience and submission. The two ideas, while clearly separated in the philosophies of democracy and authoritarianism, are blended in their less extreme forms in the thinking, and still more so in the feeling, of our culture. Today, we are adherents both of Augustine and Pelagius, of Luther and Pico della Mirandola, of Hobbes and Jefferson. We consciously believe in man's power and dignity, but—often unconsciously—we also believe in man's—and particularly our own—powerlessness and badness and explain it by pointing to "human nature.". . .

According to Freud destructiveness is inherent in all human beings. . . . It would seem [however] that the degree of destructiveness is proportionate to the degree to which the unfolding of a person's capacities is blocked. I am not referring here to occasional frustrations of this or that desire but to the blockage of spontaneous expression of man's sensory, emotional, physical, and intellectual capacities, to the thwarting of his productive potentialities. If life's tendency to grow, to be lived, is thwarted, the energy thus blocked undergoes a process of change and is transformed into life-destructive energy. Destructiveness is the outcome of unlived life. Those individual and social conditions which make for the blocking of life-furthering energy produce destructiveness which in turn is the source from which the various manifestations of evil spring. . . .

Provided we are right in assuming that destructiveness is a secondary potentiality in man which becomes manifest only if he fails to realize his primary potentialities, we have answered one of the objections to humanistic ethics. We have shown that man is not necessarily evil but becomes evil only if the proper conditions for his growth and development are lacking. The evil has no independent existence of its own, it is the absence of the good, the result of the failure to realize life. . . .

Prophecies of doom are heard today with increasing frequency. While they have the important function of drawing attention to the dangerous possibilities in our present situation they fail to take into account the promise which is implied in man's achievement in the natural sciences, in psychology, in medicine and in art. Indeed, these achievements portray the presence of strong productive forces which are not compatible with the picture of a decaying culture. Our period is a period of transition. The Middle Ages did not end in the fifteenth century, and the modern era did not begin immediately afterward. End and beginning imply a process which has lasted over four hundred years —a very short time indeed if we measure it in historical terms and not in terms of our life span. Our period is an end and a beginning, pregnant with possibilities.

If I repeat now the question raised in the beginning of this book, whether we have reason to be proud and to be hopeful, the answer is again in the affirmative, but with the one qualification which follows from what we have discussed throughout; neither the good nor the evil outcome is automatic or preordained. The decision rests with man. It rests upon his ability to take himself, his life and happiness seriously; on his willingness to face his and his society's moral problem. It rests upon his courage to be himself and to be for himself.

6. *New Social Perspectives*

A. COMMUNISM

VLADIMIR LENIN: *What Is to Be Done?* *

> In the Pamphlet *What Is to Be Done?* (1902) Vladimir Lenin (1870–
> 1924), the future architect of the Bolshevik Revolution in Russia, dis-
> cussed the problem of Communist party organization. Among other
> things, he discussed the question of freedom within the party, answer-
> ing the demand of revisionists like Bernstein for "freedom of criticism,"
> as opposed to what they called the "dogmatism" of orthodox Marxism.

"FREEDOM of criticism," this undoubtedly is the most fashionable slogan
at the present time, and the one most frequently employed in the controversies between the Socialists and democrats of all countries. At first
sight, nothing would appear to be more strange than the solemn appeals
by one of the parties to the dispute for freedom of criticism. Can it be
that some of the progressive parties have raised their voices against the
constitutional law of the majority of European countries which guaran-
tees freedom to science and scientific investigation? "Something must be
wrong here," an onlooker who has not yet fully appreciated the nature
of the disagreements among the controversialists will say, when he hears
this fashionable slogan repeated at every cross-road. . . .

"Freedom" is a grand word, but under the banner of Free Trade the
most predatory wars were conducted: under the banner of "free labour," the toilers were robbed. The term "freedom of criticism" contains the same inherent falsehood. Those who are really convinced that
they have advanced science, would demand, not freedom for the new
views to continue side by side with the old, but the substitution of the
old views by the new views. . . .

Thus we see that high-sounding phrases against the ossification of
thought, etc., conceal carelessness and helplessness in the development
of theoretical ideas. The case of the Russian Social-Democrats strikingly
illustrates the fact observed in the whole of Europe (and long ago observed in German Marxism) that the notorious freedom of criticism implies, not the substitution of one theory by another, but freedom from
every complete and thought-out theory; it implies eclecticism and absence of principle. Those who are in the least acquainted with the actual
state of our movement cannot but see that the spread of Marxism was
accompanied by a certain deterioration of theoretical standards. Quite

* Vladimir Lenin: *What Is to Be Done?* (New York: International Publishers
Co., Inc.; 1929), pp. 12, 14, 27, 40–1.

a number of people, with very little, and even totally lacking in, theoretical training, joined the movement for the sake of its practical significance and its practical successes. We can judge, therefore, how tactless *Rabocheye Dyelo* is when, with an air of invincibility, it quotes the statement of Marx that: "A single step of the real movement is worth a dozen programmes." To repeat these words in the epoch of theoretical chaos is sheer mockery. Moreover, these words of Marx are taken from his letter on the Gotha Programme, in which he *sharply condemns* eclecticism in the formulation of principles: "If you must combine," Marx wrote to the party leaders, "then enter into agreements to satisfy the practical aims of the movement, but do not haggle over principles, do not make 'concessions' in theory." This was Marx's idea, and yet there are people among us who strive—in his name!—to belittle the significance of theory.

Without a revolutionary theory there can be no revolutionary movement. . . .

Since there can be no talk of an independent ideology being developed by the masses of the workers in the process of their movement then *the only choice is:* Either bourgeois, or Socialist ideology. There is no middle course (for humanity has not created a "third" ideology, and, moreover, in a society torn by class antagonisms there can never be a non-class or above-class ideology). Hence, to belittle Socialist ideology *in any way,* to *deviate from it in the slightest degree* means strengthening bourgeois ideology. There is a lot of talk about spontaneity, but the *spontaneous* development of the labour movement leads to its becoming subordinated to bourgeois ideology, it means developing *according to the programme* of the *Credo,* for the spontaneous labour movement is pure and simple trade unionism, is *Nur-Gewerkschaftlerei,* and trade unionism means the ideological subordination of the workers to the bourgeoisie. Hence, our task, the task of Social-Democracy, is to *combat spontaneity,* to *divert* the labour movement, with its spontaneous trade-unionist striving, from under the wing of the bourgeoisie, and to bring it under the wing of revolutionary Social-Democracy.

Vladimir Lenin: *State and Revolution* *

> In *State and Revolution* (1917) Lenin describes the future—what will happen in Communist society once the "dictatorship of the proletariat" has displaced the bourgeois state by revolution.

THE DICTATORSHIP of the proletariat—*i.e.,* the organisation of the vanguard of the oppressed as the ruling class for the purpose of crushing

* Vladimir Lenin: *State and Revolution* (New York: International Publishers Co., Inc.; 1932), pp. 73, 75, 82–5.

the oppressors—cannot produce merely an expansion of democracy. *Together* with an immense expansion of democracy which *for the first time* becomes democracy for the poor, democracy for the people, and not democracy for the rich folk, the dictatorship of the proletariat produces a series of restrictions of liberty in the case of the oppressors, the exploiters, the capitalists. We must crush them in order to free humanity from wage-slavery; their resistance must be broken by force; it is clear that where there is suppression there is also violence, there is no liberty, no democracy.

Engels expressed this splendidly in his letter to Bebel when he said, as the reader will remember, that "as long as the proletariat still *needs* the state, it needs it not in the interests of freedom, but for the purpose of crushing its antagonists; and as soon as it becomes possible to speak of freedom, then the state, as such, ceases to exist.". . .

Only Communism renders the state absolutely unnecessary, for there is *no one* to be suppressed—"no one" in the sense of a *class*, in the sense of a systematic struggle with a definite section of the population. We are not Utopians, and we do not in the least deny the possibility and inevitability of excesses on the part of *individual persons*, nor the need to suppress *such* excesses. But, in the first place, no special machinery, no special apparatus of repression is needed for this; this will be done by the armed people itself, as simply and as readily as any crowd of civilised people, even in modern society, parts a pair of combatants or does not allow a woman to be outraged. And, secondly, we know that the fundamental social cause of excesses which consists in violating the rules of social life is the exploitation of the masses, their want and their poverty. With the removal of this chief cause, excesses will inevitably begin to "*wither away.*" We do not know how quickly and in what succession, but we know that they will wither way. With their withering way, the state will also *wither away*. . . .

Democracy is of great importance for the working class in its struggle for freedom against the capitalists. But democracy is by no means a limit one may not overstep; it is only one of the stages in the course of development from feudalism to capitalism, and from capitalism to Communism.

Democracy means equality. The great significance of the struggle of the proletariat for equality, and the significance of equality as a slogan, are apparent, if we correctly interpret it as meaning the abolition of *classes*. But democracy means only *formal* equality. Immediately after the attainment of equality for all members of society *in respect* of the ownership of the means of production, that is, of equality of labour and equality of wages, there will inevitably arise before humanity the question of going further from formal equality to real equality, *i.e.,* to realising the rule, "From each according to his ability; to each according to his needs." By what stages, by means of what practical measures humanity will proceed to this higher aim—this we do not and cannot know. But it is important to realise how infinitely mendacious is the usual bourgeois presentation of Socialism as something lifeless petrified, fixed once for all, whereas in reality, it is *only* with Socialism that there will commence a rapid, genuine, real mass advance, in which first the *majority* and then the whole of the population will take part—an advance in all domains of social and individual life.

Democracy is a form of the state—one of its varieties. Consequently, like every state, it consists in organised, systematic application of force against human beings. This on the one hand. On the other hand, however, it signifies the formal recognition of the equality of all citizens, the equal right of all to determine the structure and administration of the state. This, in turn, is connected with the fact that, at a certain stage in the development of democracy, it first rallies the proletariat as a revolutionary class against capitalism, and gives it an opportunity to crush, to smash to bits, to wipe off the face of the earth the bourgeois state machinery—even its republican variety: the standing army, the police, and bureaucracy; then it substitutes for all this a *more* democratic, but still a state machinery in the shape of armed masses of workers, which becomes transformed into universal participation of the people in the militia. . . .

[Eventually] the whole of society will have become one office and one factory, with equal work and equal pay.

But this "factory" discipline, which the proletariat will extend to the whole of society after the defeat of the capitalists and the overthrow of the exploiters, is by no means our ideal, or our final aim. It is but a *foothold* necessary for the radical cleansing of society of all the hideousness and foulness of capitalist exploitation, *in order to advance further.*

From the moment when all members of society, or even only the overwhelming majority, have learned how to govern the state *themselves,* have taken this business into their own hands, have "established" control over the insignificant minority of capitalists, over the gentry with capitalist leanings, and the workers thoroughly demoralised by capitalism—from this moment the need for any government begins to disappear. The more complete the democracy, the nearer the moment when it begins to be unnecessary. The more democratic the "state" consisting of armed workers, which is "no longer a state in the proper sense of the word," the more rapidly does *every* state begin to wither away.

For when *all* have learned to manage, and independently are actually managing by themselves social production, keeping accounts, controlling the idlers, the gentlefolk, the swindlers and similar "guardians of capitalist traditions," then the escape from this national accounting and control will inevitably become so increasingly difficult, such a rare exception, and will probably be accompanied by such swift and severe punishment (for the armed workers are men of practical life, not sentimental intellectuals, and they will scarcely allow any one to trifle with them), that very soon the *necessity* of observing the simple, fundamental rules of every-day social life in common will have become a *habit*.

The door will then be wide open for the transition from the first phase of Communist society to its higher phase, and along with it to the complete withering away of the state.

VLADIMIR LENIN: *On Socialism and Religion* *

The following selections are from an article written by Lenin in 1905.

RELIGION is one of the forms of spiritual oppression which everywhere weigh upon the masses who are crushed by continuous toil for others, by poverty and loneliness. The helplessness of the exploited classes in their struggle against the exploiters inevitably generates a belief in a better life after death, even as the helplessness of the savage in his struggle with nature gives rise to a belief in gods, devils, miracles, etc.

Religion teaches those who toil in poverty all their lives to be resigned and patient in this world, and consoles them with the hope of reward in heaven. As for those who live upon the labour of others, religion teaches them to be charitable in earthly life, thus providing a cheap justification for their whole exploiting existence and selling them at a reasonable price tickets to heavenly bliss. "Religion is the opium of the people." Religion is a kind of spiritual intoxicant, in which the slaves of capital drown their humanity and blunt their desires for some sort of decent human existence.

But a slave who has become conscious of his slavery, and who has risen to the height of fighting for his emancipation, has half ceased to be a slave. The class-conscious worker of to-day, brought up in big industry, and enlightened by town life, rejects religious prejudices with contempt. He leaves heaven to the priests and bourgeois hypocrites and fights for a better life for himself, here on earth. The modern proletariat ranges itself on the side of Socialism, which, with the help of science, is dispersing the fog of religion and is liberating the workers from their faith in a life after death, by rallying them to the present-day struggle for a better life here upon earth.

"Religion must be regarded as a private matter"; in these words the attitude of Socialists to religion is usually expressed. But we must define

* Vladimir Lenin: *Religion* (New York: International Publishers Co., Inc.; 1933), pp. 7–8, 10.

the meaning of these words precisely so as to avoid misunderstanding. We demand that religion be regarded as a private matter as far as the State is concerned, but under no circumstances can we regard it as a private matter with regard to our own Party.

*   *   *

Our programme is based entirely on scientific—to be more precise— upon a *materialist* world conception. In explaining our programme therefore we must necessarily explain the actual historical and economic roots of the religious fog. Our programme necessarily includes the propaganda of atheism. The publication of related scientific literature (which up till now has been strictly forbidden and persecuted by the autocratic feudal government) must now form one of the items of our party work. We shall now, probably, have to follow the advice which Engels once gave to the German Socialists—to translate and spread among the masses the enlightening atheist literature of the Eighteenth century.

Vladimir Lenin: *On Ethics* *

The following selection is from Lenin's speech to the Third All Russian Congress of the Young Communist League, October 3, 1920.

But is there such a thing as Communist ethics? Is there such a thing as Communist morality? Of course there is. It is frequently asserted that we have no ethics, and very frequently the bourgeoisie makes the charge that we Communists deny all morality. That is one of their methods of confusing the issue, of throwing dust into the eyes of the workers and peasants.

In what sense do we deny ethics, morals?

In the sense in which they are preached by the bourgeoisie, a sense which deduces these morals from god's commandments. Of course, we say that we do not believe in god. We know perfectly well that the clergy, the landlords, and the bourgeoisie all claimed to speak in the name of god, in order to protect their own interests as exploiters. Or, instead of deducing their ethics from the commandments of morality, from the commandments of god, they deduced them from idealistic or semi-idealistic phrases which in substance were always very similar to divine commandments.

We deny all morality taken from superhuman or non-class conceptions. We say that this is a deception, a swindle, a befogging of the minds

* Vladimir Lenin: *Religion* (New York: International Publishers Co., Inc.; 1933), pp. 47–8.

of the workers and peasants in the interests of the landlords and capitalists.

We say that our morality is wholly subordinated to the interests of the class struggle of the proletariat. We deduce our morality from the facts and needs of the class struggle of the proletariat.

The old society was based on the oppression of all the workers and peasants by the landlords and capitalists. We had to destroy this society. We had to overthrow these landowners and capitalists. But to do this, organisation was necessary. God could not create such organisation.

JOSEPH STALIN: *Dialectical and Historical Materialism* *

> Embedded in chapter four of the official *History of the Communist Party of the Soviet Union* is a brief essay by Joseph Stalin (1879–1953), Secretary General of the Soviet Communist Party from 1922–1953, Lenin's successor as ruler of Russia. This exposition contains the essence of "diamat" or the Communist theory of dialectical and historical materialism.

DIALECTICAL materialism is the world outlook of the Marxist-Leninist party. It is called dialectical materialism because its approach to the phenomena of nature, its method of studying and apprehending them, is *dialectical,* while its interpretation of the phenomena of nature, its conception of these phenomena, its theory, is *materialistic.*

Historical materialism is the extension of the principles of dialectical materialism to the study of social life, an application of the principles of dialectical materialism to the phenomena of the life of society, to the study of society and its history.

*   *   *

Dialectics comes from the Greek *dialego,* to discourse, to debate. In ancient times dialectics was the art of arriving at the truth by disclosing the contradictions in the argument of an opponent and overcoming these contradictions. There were philosophers in ancient times who believed that the disclosure of contradictions in thought and the clash of opposite opinions was the best method of arriving at the truth. This dialectical method of thought, later extended to the phenomena of nature, developed into the dialectical method of apprehending nature, which regards the phenomena of nature as being in constant movement and undergoing constant change, and the development of nature as the result of the development of the contradictions in nature, as the result of the interaction of opposed forces in nature.

* Joseph Stalin: *Dialectical and Historical Materialism* (New York: International Publishers Co., Inc.; 1940), pp. 5–9, 11–17, 19–24.

In its essence, dialectics is the direct opposite of metaphysics.

1. The principal features of the Marxist *dialectical method* are as follows:

(a) Contrary to metaphysics, dialectics does not regard nature as an accidental agglomeration of things, of phenomena, unconnected with, isolated from, and independent of, each other, but as a connected and integral whole, in which things, phenomena, are organically connected with, dependent on, and determined by, each other.

The dialectical method therefore holds that no phenomenon in nature can be understood if taken by itself, isolated from surrounding phenomena, inasmuch as any phenomenon in any realm of nature may become meaningless to us if it is not considered in connection with the surrounding conditions, but divorced from them; and that, vice versa, any phenomenon can be understood and explained if considered in its inseparable connection with surrounding phenomena, as one conditioned by surrounding phenomena.

(b) Contrary to metaphysics, dialectics holds that nature is not a state of rest and immobility, stagnation and immutability, but a state of continuous movement and change, of continuous renewal and development, where something is always arising and developing, and something always disintegrating and dying away.

The dialectical method therefore requires that phenomena should be considered not only from the standpoint of their interconnection and interdependence, but also from the standpoint of their movement, their change, their development, their coming into being and going out of being.

The dialectical method regards as important primarily not that which at the given moment seems to be durable and yet is already beginning to die away, but that which is arising and developing, even though at the given moment it may appear to be not durable, for the dialectical method considers invincible only that which is arising and developing.

"All nature," says Engels, "from the smallest thing to the biggest, from a grain of sand to the sun, from the protista to man, is in a constant state of coming into being and going out of being, in a constant flux, in a ceaseless state of movement and change.". . .

(c) Contrary to metaphysics, dialectics does not regard the process of development as a simple process of growth, where quantitative changes do not lead to qualitative changes, but as a development which passes from insignificant and imperceptible quantitative changes to open, fundamental changes, to qualitative changes; a development in which the qualitative changes occur not gradually, but rapidly and abruptly, taking the form of a leap from one state to another; they occur not accidentally but as the natural result of an accumulation of imperceptible and gradual quantitative changes.

The dialectical method therefore holds that the process of development should be understood not as movement in a circle, not as a simple repetition of what has already occurred, but as an onward and upward movement, as a transition from an old qualitative state to a new qualitative state, as a development from the simple to the complex, from the lower to the higher:

"Nature," says Engels, "is the test of dialectics, and it must be said for modern natural science that it has furnished extremely rich and daily increasing materials for this test, and has thus proved that in the last analysis nature's process is dialectical and not metaphysical, that it does not move in an eternally uniform and constantly repeated circle, but passes through a real history. Here prime mention should be made of Darwin, who dealt a severe blow to the metaphysical conception of nature by proving that the organic world of today, plants and animals, and consequently man too, is all a product of a process of development that has been in progress for millions of years." (*Socialism, Utopian and Scientific.*)

Describing dialectical development as a transition from quantitative changes to qualitative changes, Engels says:

"In physics . . . every change is a passing of quantity into quality, as a result of quantitative change of some form of movement either inherent in a body or imparted to it. For example, the temperature of water has at first no effect on its liquid state; but as the temperature of liquid water rises or falls, a moment arrives when this state of cohesion changes and the water is converted in one case into steam and in the other into ice.". . .

*   *   *

(d) Contrary to metaphysics, dialectics holds that internal contradictions are inherent in all things and phenomena of nature, for they all have their negative and positive sides, a past and a future, something dying away and something developing; and that the struggle between these opposites, the struggle between the old and the new, between that which is dying away and that which is being born, between that which is disappearing and that which is developing, constitutes the internal content of the process of development, the internal content of the transformation of quantitative changes into qualitative changes.

The dialectical method therefore holds that the process of development from the lower to the higher takes place not as a harmonious unfolding of phenomena, but as a disclosure of the contradictions inherent in things and phenomena, as a "struggle" of opposite tendencies which operate on the basis of these contradictions.

"In its proper meaning," Lenin says, "dialectics is the study of the contradiction *within the very essence of things.*" (*Philosophical Notebooks.*)

And further:

"Development is the 'struggle' of opposites." (*Materialism and Empirio-Criticism.*)

Such, in brief, are the principal features of the Marxist dialectical method.

It is easy to understand how immensely important is the extension of the principles of the dialectical method to the study of social life and the history of society, and how immensely important is the application of these principles to the history of society and to the practical activities of the party of the proletariat.

If there are no isolated phenomena in the world, if all phenomena are interconnected and interdependent, then it is clear that every social system and every social movement in history must be evaluated not from the standpoint of "eternal justice" or some other preconceived idea, as is not infrequently done by historians, but from the standpoint of the conditions which gave rise to that system or that social movement and with which they are connected.

The slave system would be senseless, stupid and unnatural under modern conditions. But under the conditions of a disintegrating primitive communal system, the slave system is a quite understandable and natural phenomenon, since it represents an advance on the primitive communal system.

The demand for a bourgeois-democratic republic when tsardom and bourgeois society existed, as, let us say, in Russia in 1905, was a quite understandable, proper and revolutionary demand, for at that time a bourgeois republic would have meant a step forward. But now, under the conditions of the U. S. S. R., the demand for a bourgeois-democratic republic would be a meaningless and counter-revolutionary demand, for a bourgeois republic would be a retrograde step compared with the Soviet republic.

Everything depends on the conditions, time and place.

It is clear that without such a *historical* approach to social phenomena, the existence and development of the science of history is impossible, for only such an approach saves the science of history from becoming a jumble of accidents and an agglomeration of most absurd mistakes.

Further, if the world is in a state of constant movement and development, if the dying away of the old and the upgrowth of the new is a law of development, then it is clear that there can be no "immutable" social systems, no "eternal principles" of private property and exploitation, no "eternal ideas" of the subjugation of the peasant to the landlord, of the worker to the capitalist.

Hence the capitalist system can be replaced by the socialist system, just as at one time the feudal system was replaced by the capitalist system.

Hence we must not base our orientation on the strata of society which are no longer developing, even though they at present constitute the predominant force, but on those strata which are developing and have a future before them, even though they at present do not constitute the predominant force.

*   *   *

Further, if the passing of slow quantitative changes into rapid and abrupt qualitative changes is a law of development, then it is clear that revolutions made by oppressed classes are a quite natural and inevitable phenomenon.

Hence the transition from capitalism to socialism and the liberation of the working class from the yoke of capitalism cannot be effected by slow changes, by reforms, but only by a qualitative change of the capitalist system, by revolution.

Hence, in order not to err in policy, one must be a revolutionary, not a reformist.

Further, if development proceeds by way of the disclosure of internal contradictions, by way of collisions between opposite forces on the basis of these contradictions and so as to overcome these contradictions, then it is clear that the class struggle of the proletariat is a quite natural and inevitable phenomenon.

*   *   *

As to Marxist philosophical materialism, it is fundamentally the direct opposite of philosophical idealism.

The principal features of Marxist philosophical *materialism* are as follows:

(a) Contrary to idealism, which regards the world as the embodiment of an "absolute idea," a "universal spirit," "consciousness," Marx's philosophical materialism holds that the world is by its very nature *material*, that the multifold phenomena of the world constitute different forms of matter in motion, that interconnection and interdependence of phenomena, as established by the dialectical method, are a law of the development of moving matter, and that the world develops in accordance with the laws of movement of matter and stands in no need of a "universal spirit.". . .

(b) Contrary to idealism, which asserts that only our mind really exists, and that the material world, being, nature, exists only in our mind, in our sensations, ideas and perceptions, the Marxist materialist philosophy holds that matter, nature, being, is an objective reality existing outside and independent of our mind; that matter is primary, since it is the source of sensations, ideas, mind, and that mind is secondary, derivative, since it is a reflection of matter, a reflection of being; that thought is a product of matter which in its development has reached a high degree of perfection, namely, of the brain, and the brain is the organ of thought; and that therefore one cannot separate thought from matter without committing a grave error. . . .

(c) Contrary to idealism, which denies the possibility of knowing the world and its laws, which does not believe in the authenticity of our knowledge, does not recognize objective truth, and holds that the world is full of "things-in-themselves" that can never be known to science, Marxist philosophical materialism holds that the world and its laws are fully knowable, that our knowledge of the laws of nature, tested by experiment and practice, is authentic knowledge having the validity of objective truth, and that there are no things in the world which are unknowable, but only things which are still not known, but which will be disclosed and made known by the efforts of science and practice.

* * *

It is easy to understand how immensely important is the extension of the principles of philosophical materialism to the study of social life, of the history of society, and how immensely important is the application of these principles to the history of society and to the practical activities of the party of the proletariat.

If the connection between the phenomena of nature and their interdependence are laws of the development of nature, it follows, too, that the connection and interdependence of the phenomena of social life are laws of the development of society, and not something accidental.

Hence social life, the history of society, ceases to be an agglomeration of "accidents," and becomes the history of the development of society according to regular laws, and the study of the history of society becomes a science.

Hence the practical activity of the party of the proletariat must not be based on the good wishes of "outstanding individuals," not on the dictates of "reason," "universal morals," etc., but on the laws of development of society and on the study of these laws.

Further, if the world is knowable and our knowledge of the laws of development of nature is authentic knowledge, having the validity of objective truth, it follows that social life, the development of society, is also knowable, and that the data of science regarding the laws of development of society are authentic data having the validity of objective truths.

Hence the science of the history of society, despite all the complexity of the phenomena of social life, can become as precise a science as, let us say, biology, and capable of making use of the laws of development of society for practical purposes.

Hence the party of the proletariat should not guide itself in its practical activity by casual motives, but by the laws of development of society, and by practical deductions from these laws.

Hence socialism is converted from a dream of a better future for humanity into a science.

Hence the bond between science and practical activity, between theory and practice, their unity, should be the guiding star of the party of the proletariat.

Further, if nature, being, the material world, is primary, and mind, thought, is secondary, derivative; if the material world represents objective reality existing independently of the mind of men, while the mind is a reflection of this objective reality, it follows that the material life of society, its being, is also primary, and its spiritual life secondary, derivative, and that the material life of society is an objective reality existing independently of the will of men, while the spiritual life of society is a reflection of this objective reality, a reflection of being.

Hence the source of formation of the spiritual life of society, the origin of social ideas, social theories, political views and political institutions, should not be sought for in the ideas, theories, views and political institutions themselves, but in the conditions of the material life of society, in social being, of which these ideas, theories, views, etc., are the reflection.

Hence, if in different periods of the history of society different social ideas, theories, views and political institutions are to be observed; if under the slave system we encounter certain social ideas, theories, views and political institutions, under feudalism others, and under capitalism others still, this is not to be explained by the "nature," the "properties" of the ideas, theories, views and political institutions themselves but by the different conditions of the material life of society at different periods of social development.

Whatever is the being of a society, whatever are the conditions of material life of a society, such are the ideas, theories, political views and political institutions of that society.

In this connection, Marx says:

"It is not the consciousness of men that determines their being, but, on the contrary, their social being that determines their consciousness." (*A Contribution to the Critique of Political Economy*.)

Hence, in order not to err in policy, in order not to find itself in the position of idle dreamers, the party of the proletariat must not base its activities on abstract "principles of human reason," but on the concrete conditions of the material life of society, as the determining force of social development; not on the good wishes of "great men," but on the real needs of development of the material life of society. . . .

It does not follow from Marx's words, however, that social ideas, theories, political views and political institutions are of no significance in the life of society, that they do nòt reciprocally affect social being, the development of the material conditions of the life of society. We have been speaking so far of the *origin* of social ideas, theories, views and political institutions, of *the way they arise*, of the fact that the spiritual life of society is a reflection of the conditions of its material life. As regards the *significance* of social ideas, theories, views and political institutions, as regards their *role* in history, historical materialism, far from denying them, stresses the role and importance of these factors in the life of society, in its history.

There are different kinds of social ideas and theories. There are old ideas and theories which have outlived their day and which serve the interests of the moribund forces of society. Their significance lies in the fact that they hamper the development, the progress of society. Then there are new and advanced ideas and theories which serve the interests of the advanced forces of society. Their significance lies in the fact that they facilitate the development, the progress of society; and their significance is the greater the more accurately they reflect the needs of development of the material life of society. . . .

Hence, in order to be able to influence the conditions of material life of society and to accelerate their development and their improvement, the party of the proletariat must rely upon such a social theory, such a social idea as correctly reflects the needs of development of the material life of society, and which is therefore capable of setting into motion broad masses of the people and of mobilizing them and organizing them into a great army of the proletarian party, prepared to smash the reactionary forces and to clear the way for the advanced forces of society.

B. FASCISM

Alfredo Rocco: *On the Political Doctrine of Fascism* *

> Alfredo Rocco (1875–1925) was a professor of law who became Minister of Justice in Mussolini's government. He helped to frame some of the fascist statutes and to reform the Italian legal code on fascist principles. The following selections are from a speech delivered at Perugia, August 30, 1925.

First of all let us ask ourselves if there is a political doctrine of Fascism; if there is any ideal content in the Fascist state. . . .

It is true that Fascism is, above all, action and sentiment and that such

* From Alfredo Rocco: *The Political Doctrine of Fascism*, pp. 394–6, 400–03, 405, 407–08, 411–12, 415. Reprinted by permission of Carnegie Endowment for International Peace.

it must continue to be. Were it otherwise, it could not keep up that immense driving force, that renovation power which it now possesses and would merely be the solitary meditation of a chosen few. Only because it is feeling and sentiment, only because it is the unconscious reawakening of our profound racial instinct, has it the force to stir the soul of the people, and to set free an irresistible current of national will. Only because it is action, and as such actualizes itself in a vast organization and in a huge movement, has it the conditions for determining the historical course of contemporary Italy.

But Fascism is thought as well and it has a theory, which is an essential part of this historical phenomenon, and which is responsible in a great measure for the successes that have been achieved. . . .

Modern political thought remained, until recently, both in Italy and outside of Italy under the absolute control of those doctrines which, proceeding from the Protestant Reformation and developed by the adepts of natural law in the 17th and 18th centuries, were firmly grounded in the institutions and customs of the English, of the American, and of the French Revolutions. Under different and sometimes clashing forms these doctrines have left a determining imprint upon all theories and actions both social and political, of the 19th and 20th centuries down to the rise of Fascism. The common basis of all these doctrines, which stretch from Languet, from Buchanan, and from Althusius down to Karl Marx, to Wilson and to Lenin is a social state concept which I shall call mechanical or atomistic.

Society according to this concept is merely a sum total of individuals, a plurality which breaks up into its single components. Therefore the ends of a society, so considered, are nothing more than the ends of the individuals which compose it and for whose sake it exists. An atomistic view of this kind is also necessarily anti-historical, inasmuch as it considers society in its spatial attributes and not in its temporal ones; and because it reduces social life to the existence of a single generation. Society becomes thus a sum of determined individuals, viz., the generation living at a given moment. This doctrine which I call atomistic and which appears to be anti-historical, reveals from under a concealing cloak a strongly materialistic nature. For in its endeavors to isolate the present from the past and the future, it rejects the spiritual inheritance of ideas and sentiments which each generation receives from those preceding and hands down to the following generation thus destroying the unity and the spiritual life itself of human society.

This common basis shows the close logical connection existing between all political doctrines; the substantial solidarity, which unites all the political movements, from Liberalism to Socialism, that until recently have dominated Europe. For these political schools differ from one another in their methods, but all agree as to the ends to be achieved.

All of them consider the welfare and happiness of individuals to be the goal of society, itself considered as composed of individuals of the present generation. All of them see in society and in its juridical organization, the state, the mere instrument and means whereby individuals can attain their ends. They differ only in that the methods pursued for the attainment of these ends vary considerably one from the other.

Thus the Liberals insist that the best manner to secure the welfare of the citizens as individuals is to interfere as little as possible with the free development of their activities and that therefore the essential task of the state is merely to coördinate these several liberties in such a way as to guarantee their coexistence. . . .

*   *   *

The true antithesis, not to this or that manifestation of the liberal-democratic-socialistic conception of the state but to the concept itself, is to be found in the doctrine of Fascism. . . .

I shall not try here to expound this doctrine but shall limit myself to a brief résumé of its fundamental concepts. . . .

Fascism replaces therefore the old atomistic and mechanical state theory which was at the basis of the liberal and democratic doctrines with an organic and historic concept. When I say organic I do not wish to convey the impression that I consider society as an organism after the manner of the so-called "organic theories of the state"; but rather to indicate that the social groups as fractions of the species receive thereby a life and scope which transcend the scope and life of the individuals identifying themselves with the history and finalities of the uninterrupted series of generations. . . .

*   *   *

At this juncture the antithesis between the two theories must appear complete and absolute. Liberalism, Democracy, and Socialism look upon social groups as aggregates of living individuals; for Fascism they are the recapitulating unity of the indefinite series of generations. For Liberalism, society has no purposes other than those of the members living at a given moment. For Fascism, society has historical and immanent ends of preservation, expansion, improvement, quite distinct from those of the individuals which at a given moment compose it; so distinct in fact that they may even be in opposition. Hence the necessity, for which the older doctrines make little allowance, of sacrifice, even up to the total immolation of individuals, in behalf of society; hence the true explanation of war, eternal law of mankind, interpreted by the liberal-democratic doctrines as a degenerate absurdity or as a maddened monstrosity.

For Liberalism, society has no life distinct from the life of the individuals, or as the phrase goes; solvitur in singularitates. For Fascism, the life of society overlaps the existence of individuals and projects itself into the succeeding generations through centuries and millennia. Individuals come into being, grow, and die, followed by others, unceasingly; social unity remains always identical to itself. For Liberalism, the individual is the end and society the means; nor is it conceivable that the individual, considered in the dignity of an ultimate finality, be lowered to mere instrumentality. For Fascism, society is the end, individuals the means, and its whole life consists in using individuals as instruments for its social ends. The state therefore guards and protects the welfare and development of individuals not for their exclusive interest, but because of the identity of the needs of individuals with those of society as a whole. We can thus accept and explain institutions and practices, which like the death penalty, are condemned by Liberalism in the name of the preëminence of individualism.

The fundamental problem of society in the old doctrines is the question of the rights of individuals. It may be the right to freedom as the Liberals would have it; or the right to the government of the commonwealth as the Democrats claim it, or the right to economic justice as the Socialists contend; but in every case it is the right of individuals, or groups of individuals (classes). Fascism on the other hand faces squarely the problem of the right of the state and of the duty of individuals. Individual rights are only recognized in so far as they are implied in the rights of the state. In this preëminence of duty we find the highest ethical value of Fascism. . . .

*   *   *

. . . Fascism insists that the government be entrusted to men capable of rising above their own private interests and of realizing the aspirations of the social collectivity, considered in its unity and in its relation to the past and future. Fascism therefore not only rejects the dogma of popular sovereignty and substitutes for it that of state sovereignty, but it also proclaims that the great mass of citizens is not a suitable advocate of social interests for the reason that the capacity to ignore individual private interests in favor of the higher demands of society and of history is a very rare gift and the privilege of the chosen few. Natural intelligence and cultural preparation are of great service in such tasks. Still more valuable perhaps is the intuitiveness of rare great minds, their traditionalism and their inherited qualities. This must not however be construed to mean that the masses are not to be allowed to exercise any influence on the life of the state. On the contrary, among peoples with a great history and with noble traditions, even the lowest elements of society possess an instinctive discernment of what is necessary for the welfare of the race, which in moments of great historical crises reveals itself to be almost infallible. It is therefore as wise to afford to this instinct the means of declaring itself as it is judicious to entrust the normal control of the commonwealth to a selected élite. . . .

. . . what I have already said is sufficient to show that the rise of a Fascist ideology already gives evidence of an upheaval in the intellectual field as powerful as the change that was brought about in the 17th and 18th centuries by the rise and diffusion of those doctrines of ius naturale which go under the name of "Philosophy of the French Revolution." The philosophy of the French Revolution formulated certain principles, the authority of which, unquestioned for a century and a half, seemed so final that they were given the attribute of immortality. The influence of these principles was so great that they determined the formation of a new culture, of a new civilization. Likewise the fervor of the ideas that go to make up the Fascist doctrine, now in its inception but destined to spread rapidly, will determine the course of a new culture and of a new conception of civil life. The deliverance of the individual from the state carried out in the 18th century will be followed in the 20th century by the rescue of the state from the individual. The period of authority, of social obligations, of "hierarchical" subordination will succeed the period of individualism, of state feebleness, of insubordination.

This innovating trend is not and cannot be a return to the Middle Ages. It is a common but an erroneous belief that the movement, started by the Reformation and heightened by the French Revolution, was directed against mediaeval ideas and institutions. Rather than as a negation, this movement should be looked upon as the development and fulfillment of the doctrines and practices of the Middle Ages. Socially and politically considered the Middle Ages wrought disintegration and anarchy; they were characterized by the gradual weakening and ultimate extinction of the state, embodied in the Roman Empire, driven first to the East, then back to France, thence to Germany, a shadow of its former self; they were marked by the steady advance of the forces of usurpation, destructive of the state and reciprocally obnoxious; they bore the imprints of a triumphant particularism. Therefore the individualistic and anti-social movement of the 17th and 18th centuries was not directed against the Middle Ages, but rather against the restoration of the state by great national monarchies. If this movement destroyed mediaeval institutions that had survived the Middle Ages and had been grafted upon the new states, it was in consequence of the struggle primarily waged against the state. The spirit of the movement was decidedly mediaeval. The novelty consisted in the social surroundings in which it operated and in its relation to new economic developments. The individualism of the feudal lords, the particularism of the cities and of the corporations had been replaced by the individualism and the particularism of the bourgeoisie and of the popular classes.

The Fascist ideology cannot therefore look back to the Middle Ages, of which it is a complete negation. The Middle Ages spell disintegration; Fascism is nothing if not sociality. It is if anything the beginning of the end of the Middle Ages prolonged four centuries beyond the end ordinarily set for them and revived by the social democratic anarchy of the past thirty years. If Fascism can be said to look back at all it is rather in the direction of ancient Rome whose social and political traditions at the distance of fifteen centuries are being revived by Fascist Italy. . . .

* * *

The Roman tradition, which was one of practice but not of theories— for Rome constructed the most solid state known to history with extraordinary statesmanship but with hardly any political writings—influenced considerably the founder of modern political science, Nicolo Machiavelli, who was himself in truth not a creator of doctrines but a keen observer of human nature who derived from the study of history practical maxims of political import. He freed the science of politics from the formalism of the scholastics and brought it close to concrete reality. His writings, an inexhaustible mine of practical remarks and precious observations, reveals dominant in him the state idea, no longer abstract but in the full historical concreteness of the national unity of Italy. Machiavelli therefore is not only the greatest of modern political writers, he is also the greatest of our countrymen in full possession of a national Italian consciousness. To liberate Italy, which was in his day "enslaved, torn and pillaged," and to make her more powerful, he would use any means, for to his mind the holiness of the end justified them completely. In this he was sharply rebuked by foreigners who were not as hostile to his means as they were fearful of the end which he propounded. He advocated therefore the constitution of a strong Italian state, supported by the sacrifices and by the blood of the citizens, not defended by mercenary troops; well-ordered internally, aggressive and bent on expansion. . . . Machiavelli was not only a great political authority, he taught the mastery of energy and will. Fascism learns from him not only its doctrines but its action as well. . . .

* * *

A powerful innovating movement, issuing from the war and of which Fascism is the purest expression, was to restore Italian thought in the sphere of political doctrine to its own traditions which are the traditions of Rome.

This task of intellectual liberation, now slowly being accomplished, is no less important than the political deliverance brought about by the

Fascist Revolution. It is a great task which continues and integrates the Risorgimento; it is now bringing to an end, after the cessation of our political servitude, the intellectual dependence of Italy.

Thanks to it, Italy again speaks to the world and the world listens to Italy. It is a great task and a great deed and it demands great efforts. To carry it through, we must, each one of us, free ourselves of the dross of ideas and mental habits which two centuries of foreign intellectualistic tradition have heaped upon us; we must not only take on a new culture but create for ourselves a new soul. We must methodically and patiently contribute something towards the organic and complete elaboration of our doctrine, at the same time supporting it both at home and abroad with untiring devotion. We ask this effort of renovation and collaboration of all fascists, as well as of all who feel themselves to be Italians. After the hour of sacrifice comes the hour of unyielding efforts. To our work, then, fellow countrymen, for the glory of Italy!

BENITO MUSSOLINI: *The Doctrine of Fascism* *

> Benito Mussolini (1883–1945), Duce of fascist Italy from 1922 to 1945, needs no introduction. The following selections are from his article entitled "The Doctrine of Fascism" which appeared in the *Italian Encyclopedia* of 1932.

THERE is no concept of the State which is not fundamentally a concept of life: philosophy or intuition, a system of ideas which develops logically or is gathered up into a vision or into a faith, but which is always, at least virtually, an organic conception of the world.

2. Thus Fascism could not be understood in many of its practical manifestations as a party organization, as a system of education, as a discipline, if it were not always looked at in the light of its whole way of conceiving life, a spiritualized way. The world seen through Fascism is not this material world which appears on the surface, in which man is an individual separated from all others and standing by himself, and in which he is governed by a natural law that makes him instinctively live a life of selfish and momentary pleasure. The man of Fascism is an individual who is nation and fatherland, which is a moral law, binding together individuals and the generations into a tradition and a mission, suppressing the instinct for a life enclosed within the brief round of pleasure in order to restore within duty a higher life free from the limits of time and space: a life in which the individual, through the denial of himself, through the sacrifice of his own private interests,

---

* From Michael J. Oakeshott: *The Social and Political Doctrines of Contemporary Europe*, pp. 164–8. Copyright 1939 by Cambridge University Press. Reprinted by permission of Cambridge University Press.

through death itself, realizes that completely spiritual existence in which his value as a man lies.

3. Therefore it is a spiritualized conception, itself the result of the general reaction of modern times against the flabby materialistic positivism of the nineteenth century. Anti-positivistic, but positive: not sceptical, nor agnostic, nor pessimistic, nor passively optimistic, as are, in general, the doctrines (all negative) that put the centre of life outside man, who with his free will can and must create his own world. Fascism desires an active man, one engaged in activity with all his energies: it desires a man virilely conscious of the difficulties that exist in action and ready to face them. It conceives of life as a struggle, considering that it behoves man to conquer for himself that life truly worthy of him, creating first of all in himself the instrument (physical, moral, intellectual) in order to construct it. Thus for the single individual, thus for the nation, thus for humanity. Hence the high value of culture in all its forms (art, religion, science), and the enormous importance of education. Hence also the essential value of work, with which man conquers nature and creates the human world (economic, political, moral, intellectual).

4. This positive conception of life is clearly an ethical conception. It covers the whole of reality, not merely the human activity which controls it. No action can be divorced from moral judgement; there is nothing in the world which can be deprived of the value which belongs to everything in its relation to moral ends. Life, therefore, as conceived by the Fascist, is serious, austere, religious: the whole of it is poised in a world supported by the moral and responsible forces of the spirit. The Fascist disdains the "comfortable" life.

5. Fascism is a religious conception in which man is seen in his immanent relationship with a superior law and with an objective Will that transcends the particular individual and raises him to conscious membership of a spiritual society. Whoever has seen in the religious politics of the Fascist regime nothing but mere opportunism has not understood that Fascism besides being a system of government is also, and above all, a system of thought.

6. Fascism is an historical conception, in which man is what he is only in so far as he works with the spiritual process in which he finds himself, in the family or social group, in the nation and in the history in which all nations collaborate. From this follows the great value of tradition, in memories, in language, in customs, in the standards of social life. Outside history man is nothing. Consequently Fascism is opposed to all the individualistic abstractions of a materialistic nature like those of the eighteenth century; and it is opposed to all Jacobin utopias and innovations. It does not consider that "happiness" is possible upon earth, as it appeared to be in the desire of the economic literature of the eight-

eenth century, and hence it rejects all teleological theories according to which mankind would reach a definitive stabilized condition at a certain period in history. This implies putting oneself outside history and life, which is a continual change and coming to be. Politically, Fascism wishes to be a realistic doctrine; practically, it aspires to solve only the problems which arise historically of themselves and that of themselves find or suggest their own solution. To act among men, as to act in the natural world, it is necessary to enter into the process of reality and to master the already operating forces.

7. Against individualism, the Fascist conception is for the State; and it is for the individual in so far as he coincides with the State, which is the conscience and universal will of man in his historical existence. It is opposed to classical Liberalism, which arose from the necessity of reacting against absolutism, and which brought its historical purpose to an end when the State was transformed into the conscience and will of the people. Liberalism denied the State in the interests of the particular individual; Fascism reaffirms the State as the true reality of the individual. And if liberty is to be the attribute of the real man, and not of that abstract puppet envisaged by individualistic Liberalism, Fascism is for liberty. And for the only liberty which can be a real thing, the liberty of the State and of the individual within the State. Therefore, for the Fascist, everything is in the State, and nothing human or spiritual exists, much less has value, outside the State. In this sense Fascism is totalitarian, and the Fascist State, the synthesis and unity of all values, interprets, develops and gives strength to the whole life of the people.

8. Outside the State there can be neither individuals nor groups (political parties, associations, syndicates, classes). Therefore Fascism is opposed to Socialism, which confines the movement of history within the class struggle and ignores the unity of classes established in one economic and moral reality in the State; . . .

9. Individuals form classes according to the similarity of their interests, they form syndicates according to differentiated economic activities within these interests; but they form first, and above all, the State, which is not to be thought of numerically as the sum-total of individuals forming the majority of a nation. And consequently Fascism is opposed to Democracy, which equates the nation to the majority, lowering it to the level of that majority; nevertheless it is the purest form of democracy if the nation is conceived, as it should be, qualitatively and not quantitatively, as the most powerful idea (most powerful because most moral, most coherent, most true) which acts within the nation as the conscience and the will of a few, even of One, which ideal tends to become active within the conscience and the will of all—that is to say, of all those who rightly constitute a nation by reason of nature, history or race, and have set out upon the same line of development and spiritual

formation as one conscience and one sole will. Not a race, nor a geo-graphically determined region, but as a community historically per-petuating itself, a multitude unified by a single idea, which is the will to existence and to power: consciousness of itself, personality.

10. This higher personality is truly the nation in so far as it is the State. It is not the nation that generates the State, as according to the old naturalistic concept which served as the basis of the political theories of the national States of the nineteenth century. Rather the nation is created by the State, which gives to the people, conscious of its own moral unity, a will and therefore an effective existence. The right of a nation to independence derives not from a literary and ideal conscious-ness of its own being, still less from a more or less unconscious and inert acceptance of a *de facto* situation, but from an active consciousness, from a political will in action and ready to demonstrate its own rights: that is to say, from a state already coming into being. The State, in fact, as the universal ethical will, is the creator of right.

11. The nation as the State is an ethical reality which exists and lives in so far as it develops. To arrest its development is to kill it. Therefore the State is not only the authority which governs and gives the form of laws and the value of spiritual life to the wills of individuals, but it is also a power that makes its will felt abroad, making it known and re-spected, in other words, demonstrating the fact of its universality in all the necessary directions of its development. It is consequently organiza-tion and expansion, at least virtually. Thus it can be likened to the human will which knows no limits to its development and realizes itself in testing its own limitlessness.

12. The Fascist State, the highest and most powerful form of person-ality, is a force, but a spiritual force, which takes over all the forms of the moral and intellectual life of man. It cannot therefore confine itself simply to the functions of order and supervision as Liberalism desired. It is not simply a mechanism which limits the sphere of the supposed liberties of the individual. It is the form, the inner standard and the discipline of the whole person; it saturates the will as well as the intelligence. Its principle, the central inspiration of the human person-ality living in the civil community, pierces into the depths and makes its home in the heart of the man of action as well as of the thinker, of the artist as well as of the scientist: it is the soul of the soul.

13. Fascism, in short, is not only the giver of laws and the founder of institutions, but the educator and promoter of spiritual life. It wants to remake, not the forms of human life, but its content, man, character, faith. And to this end it requires discipline and authority that can enter into the spirits of men and there govern unopposed. Its sign, therefore, is the Lictors' rods, the symbol of unity, of strength and justice.

BENITO MUSSOLINI: *On Myth* *

The following statement is embedded in a speech delivered by Mussolini at Naples, October 24, 1922.

WE HAVE created our myth. The myth is a faith, it is passion. It is not necessary that it shall be a reality. It is a reality by the fact that it is a good, a hope, a faith, that it is courage. Our myth is the Nation, our myth is the greatness of the Nation! And to this myth, to this grandeur, that we wish to translate into a complete reality, we subordinate all the rest.

ADOLF HITLER: *Mein Kampf* †

Mein Kampf is the autobiography of Adolph Hitler (1889–1945), the son of a minor Austrian customs official who later became Führer of the National Socialist party in Germany and Chancellor of the Third Reich. The book was first published in two volumes, in 1925 and 1927.

JUST as little as Nature desires a mating between weaker individuals and stronger ones, far less she desires the mixing of a higher race with a lower one, as in this case her entire work of higher breeding, which has perhaps taken hundreds of thousands of years, would tumble at one blow.

Historical experience offers countless proofs of this. It shows with terrible clarity that with any mixing of the blood of the Aryan with lower races the result was the end of the culture-bearer.

* * *

Thus the highest purpose of the folkish State is the care for the preservation of those racial primal elements which, supplying culture, create the beauty and dignity of a higher humanity. . . .

The folkish State, through this realization, has to direct its entire education primarily not at pumping in mere knowledge, but at the breeding of absolutely healthy bodies. Of secondary importance is the training of the mental abilities. But here again first of all the development of the character, especially the promotion of will power and determination, connected with education for joyfully assuming responsibility, and only as the last thing, scientific schooling.

Thereby the folkish State has to start from the presumption that a man, though scientifically little educated but physically healthy, who has a sound, firm character, filled with joyful determination and will power, is of greater value to the national community than an ingenious weakling.

*   *   *

A view of life which, by rejecting the democratic mass idea, endeavors to give this world to the best people, that means to the most superior men, has logically to obey the same aristocratic principle also within this people and has to guarantee leadership and highest influence within the respective people to the best heads. With this it does not build up on the idea of the majority, but on that of the personality.

*   *   *

After my joining the German Workers' Party, I immediately took over the management of the propaganda. . . . Propaganda had to precede far in advance of the organization and to win for the latter the human material to be utilized. . . .

The psyche of the great masses is not receptive to half measures or weakness.

Like a woman, whose psychic feeling is influenced less by abstract reasoning than by an undefinable, sentimental longing for complementary strength, who will submit to the strong man rather than dominate the weakling, thus the masses love the ruler rather than the suppliant, and inwardly they are far more satisfied by a doctrine which tolerates no rival than by the grant of liberal freedom; they often feel at a loss what to do with it, and even easily feel themselves deserted. . . .

The great masses' receptive ability is only very limited, their understanding is small, but their forgetfulness is great. As a consequence of these facts, all effective propaganda has to limit itself only to a very few points and to use them like slogans until even the very last man is able to imagine what is intended by such a word.

ALFRED ROSENBERG: *The Myth of the Twentieth Century* *

Next to Adolf Hitler's *Mein Kampf*, Alfred Rosenberg's best-selling *Der Mythus des 20. Jahrhunderts* (1930) ranked as the most authorita-

* From Alfred Rosenberg: *Der Mythus des 20. Jahrhunderts*, pp. 1–2, 114–15, 117–18, 629. Copyright 1930 by Hoheneichen Verlag. My translation from the 1936 edition. The German interests in the United States Copyright in this work were vested in the Alien Property Custodian in 1942, pursuant to law. The use of this material is by permission of his successor, the Attorney General of the United States, in the public interest under License No. JA-1464.

tive expression of the Nazi world-view. Rosenberg (1893–1946) held important posts in the Nazi government and edited the leading Nazi newspaper and monthly magazine.

ALL the contemporary struggles for power are outward expressions of an inner collapse. All the state systems of 1914 have already fallen, likewise social, ecclesiastical, and philosophical world-views and values. No high principle, no lofty idea rules unchallenged the life of the peoples. Group struggles against group, party against party, national values against international precepts, benumbed imperialism against spreading pacifism. Finance ensnares with golden nets states and peoples, the economy is primitivized, life is uprooted.

The World War, which marked the beginning of a world revolution in all spheres, showed the tragic fact that while millions sacrificed their lives, this sacrifice profited powers different from those for which the armies were ready to die. The dead of the war are the sacrifice to the catastrophe of an epoch that had become valueless, but they are at the same time . . . the martyrs of a new day and a new faith.

The blood that died begins to come alive. Under its mystical sign a new cell-structure of the German soul develops. Present and past suddenly appear in a new light, and for the future a new mission is revealed. History and the task of the future no longer mean the struggle of class against class, ecclesiastical dogma against secular creeds, but the putting asunder of blood and blood, race and race, folk and folk. And this means: the struggle of soul-value against soul-value.

The racial interpretation of history is an insight which will soon become self-evident. Meritorious men already serve it. Draymen will in the not-very-far-future be able to complete the building of the new world-picture.

But the values of the racial *soul* which are the driving forces behind the new world-picture, have not yet come to full consciousness. *Soul means race seen from the inside. And contrariwise is race the outer side of a soul.* To awaken to life the racial soul means to recognize it as the highest value, and under its dominion to assign to the other values their organic place, in state, art, and religion; that is the task of our century: out of a new life-myth to create a new type of man. For this task courage is needed, the courage of each individual, the courage of the whole rising generation, yes, and of many generations to come. For chaos is never banished by cowards, nor has a new world ever been built by weaklings. Whoever wishes to go forward must therefore burn his bridges behind him. Whoever sets out upon a great journey must leave behind his old household furniture. Whoever strives for the sublime must leave behind the lesser ideal. And to all doubts and questions the new man of the coming first *German* Reich knows only one answer: I am determined to do it!

*   *   *

Today there awakens a new faith: the myth of blood, the belief that to defend blood is to defend the divine nature of man: the faith, embodied in clearest knowledge, that the nordic blood represents that mystery which has replaced and overcome the old sacraments.

. . . Germanic Europe presented the world with the brightest ideal of manhood: the teaching of the value of character as the foundation of all morality, the paean of praise to the highest values of the nordic nature, to the idea of freedom of conscience and honor. . . .

This knowledge is the foundation of a new world-view, of a new-old theory of state; it is the myth of a new feeling of life, which alone will give us the strength to overthrow the usurped rule of the lower order of men and to create a distinctive morality penetrating all walks of life.

*   *   *

The life of a race, a folk, is not a philosophy that develops logically nor a process unwinding according to natural law, but is the expression of a mystical synthesis, an activity of the soul which can neither be explained by rational processes, nor made comprehensible by the analysis of causes and effects. . . . *In the final analysis every philosophy going beyond formal rational criticism is less a knowledge than an affirmation;* a spiritual and racial affirmation, an affirmation of the values of *character*.

*   *   *

Neither history nor the weaknesses of our heroes ought to be hushed up, but the eternal mythical elements which transcend them should be discerned and made clear. Thus will arise a series of great spirits: Odin, Siegfried, Widukind, Frederick II (the Hohenstaufen), Eckhart, Vogelweide, Luther, Frederick the Great, Bach, Goethe, Beethoven, Schopenhauer, Bismarck. . . . To serve this new evaluation is the mission of the schools of the coming Reich. It is its greatest, if not its only task in the next decades to make this evaluation self-evident to all Germans. But the schools still await a great teacher of German history with the will to a German future. He will come when the myth has become life.

C. DEMOCRACY IN A WORLD OF TENSIONS

The UNESCO Questionnaire on Ideological Conflicts concerning Democracy *

In 1947 UNESCO (United Nations Educational, Scientific and Cultural Organization) voted to investigate world conflicts concerning fundamental political concepts. Accordingly, a study of the idea of democracy was begun the following year. A questionnaire, prepared by Professor Arne Naess of the University of Oslo, was sent out to more than five hundred experts, the replies being collated and published in 1951. The following selection includes a portion of the questionnaire, together with some of Naess's "Conclusions" based upon an analysis of the replies. The questionnaire points up the conflict between "East" and "West," but the "Conclusions" suggest that between them there is at least verbal agreement on general aims. As the Committee of Experts puts it, "the unanimity which appears in the statement of aims is an impressive fact. For the first time in the history of the world, no doctrines are advanced as undemocratic."

THE PEOPLES of the world, laymen no less than experts, have never been more conscious of conflicts of convictions than in the years after World War II.

Ideological conflicts are present everywhere, between nations, within nations, between minds, within minds.

Few words have played a greater role in these conflicts than the word "democracy." What does it mean, connote, imply? Does it cover one and the same meaning to all and everybody, or is it just used to express whatever anybody thinks worth fighting for?

It has been the common watchword in two world wars. The victory of November, 1918, was said to be the victory of democracy. The common aim of the Allied Powers in World War II, as formulated by Roosevelt, Stalin, and Churchill at the Teheran Conference in December, 1943, was the establishment of "a world family of democratic nations." The declarations of Yalta in February and of Potsdam in August, 1945, both stressed the same principle: the Great Powers announced their intention of "meeting the political and economic problems of liberated Europe in accordance with democratic principles"; they made these principles the basis of their joint policy in Germany.

Did they mean the same by "democracy," the same by "democratic," when they used these words in these declarations? Did they only agree on the *words*, or did they agree on substance?

The events that have followed: the disagreements on elections in eastern Europe, the disagreements on the "new type democracies," the "people's democracies" established in these countries, the general disagreement within the United Nations Organization, have given ample evidence that the words did not connote any definite criteria *that could be agreed upon* in cases of concrete application of the principles laid down in the declarations of the Great Powers.

The disagreements have given rise to long series of ideological criticisms and countercriticisms; to give instances of cruder arguments it has, on the one hand, been claimed that "democracy" cannot thrive where free scope is given to racial discrimination and exploitation of toiling masses and colonial peoples, on the other, that "democracy" cannot exist where only one party takes part in elections and opposition is not tolerated.

What was the background of these violent disagreements? How were the divergencies in usage and interpretation of the word "democracy" to be clarified?

The problem is one of vast implications. It is not just a question of terminology. It has its background in contrasts of historical development, of social conditions, of political patterning, of ideological structuration, of public opinion formation, of education. It is deeply entangled in the immense cluster of problems raised by the impact of technology and industrial civilization on the lives of the peoples of the world; it is part of the general problem of world-integration under conditions never before experienced in the history of mankind. It is not only a problem of philosophy, of the normative basis of the relations between the individual and the state, it is a problem of war or peace.

A multitude of articles, pamphlets, and books published in the years since the end of World War II have attacked the problem. Philosophers, humanists, sociologists, political scientists, journalists, and statesmen have tried to analyze the divergencies and discuss the causes and responsibilities for the disagreements experienced in the concrete applications of principles once so heartily agreed upon.

But the problem has not yet been attacked on the international level, within the general framework of organized efforts toward international understanding.

It is the central aim of the inquiry launched by UNESCO to remedy this shortcoming, to organize *philosophically detached debates between nations, between opposed ideological camps:* to elucidate, through international exchanges of views, the divergencies of usage and interpretation, to analyze the normative foundations of those divergencies and to search for potential sources of reconciliation.

At this stage, the inquiry will concentrate on four clusters of problems which have seemed to be among the crucial ones in the controversies so far:

First, the general problem of the ambiguity and slogan-like character of the word "democracy": Are there divergent concepts covered by the word, what are the criteria of misuse, what historical basis is there for adopting one usage as the correct one and rejecting others?

Second, the general problem of the relations between "formal" democracy as an exclusively political concept and "real" democracy as a broad social *and* political concept: Does "democracy" connote universal and equal suffrage rights only, or does it even connote other rights to equality—educational, economic ones?

Third, the problem of tolerance, of the right of opposition: Does "democracy" connote the right of any group of any opinion whatsoever to take part in political life and influence public opinion, or are there limits to such rights, and what are these? Does "democracy" necessarily imply the existence of several parties? Does "democracy" imply the duty to fight any "antidemocratic" group?

Fourth, the problem of the normative bases of the divergencies of usage and interpretation manifest in current controversies: Do the divergencies reflect irreducible conflicts of value, or do they conceal deeper agreements and forces working toward reconciliation?

SOCIAL VERSUS POLITICAL DEMOCRACY

The opposition between a "narrow" political concept and a "broad" social concept of "democracy" became acute for the first time in the 1848 crisis in western Europe. The problems raised might be said to focus on the social and economic implications of the introduction of universal suffrage. Socialists and Communists conceived of "democracy" as logically and necessarily implying the extension of the equality of rights from the political to the social and economic field, i.e., the abolition of privileges, the reduction of class distinctions, and even the socialization of the means of production. The reaction among Liberals and Conservatives was to a large extent a terminological one; they made efforts to prove that the term "democracy" was exclusively a political one with no necessary implications whatever in the social and economic field. In a famous speech in the Assemblée Constituante on September 12, 1848, Alexis de Tocqueville gave vent to this line of opinion in these words: "No, gentlemen, democracy and socialism are not necessarily interconnected. They are not only different, they are opposed. Are you perchance trying to tell me that democracy consists in the creation of a more vexatious, more meddlesome and more restrictive form of government than any other, with the sole difference that you let the people elect it and make it act in the name of the people? But then what would you have done but confer on tyranny an air of legality which it did not possess and ensure for it the force and independence it lacked. Democracy extends the sphere of individual independence, socialism contracts it. Democracy gives to every man his full value, socialism makes of every man an agent, an instrument, a cipher. Democracy and socialism are linked only by the word 'equality'; but note the difference: Democracy wants equality in freedom, socialism wants equality in constraint and enslavement.". . .

The distinction stressed by de Tocqueville has been vigorously carried through in a long series of Western treatises on political philosophy and political science. In his classical work on *Modern Democracies*, the late Lord Bryce stated his position in the following way: ". . . Democracy—which is merely a form of government, not a consideration of the purposes to which government may be turned—has nothing to do with economic equality, which might exist under any form of government, and might possibly work more smoothly under some other form. . . . Political equality can exist either along with or apart from equality in property.". . .

The *attacks* upon this line of arguing have not lagged behind in violence.

The "formal" concept of democracy has been the subject of caustic analyses by Socialists and Communists, by Anarchists and Syndicalists. One of the most outstanding of these attacks was that launched by Lenin in the *State and Revolution:* "In capitalist society, under the conditions most favourable to its development, we have more or less complete democracy in the democratic republic. But this democracy is always restricted by the narrow framework of capitalist exploitation, and consequently always remains, in reality, a democracy for the minority, only for the possessing classes, only for the rich. Freedom in capitalist society always remains about the same as it was in the ancient Greek republics: freedom for the slave owners. Owing to the conditions of capitalist exploitation, the modern wage-slaves are also so crushed by want and poverty that "they cannot be bothered with politics"; in the ordinary peaceful course of events the majority of the population is debarred from participating in social and political life."

Quite along the same line is Stalin's comparison of bourgeois and Communist democracy in his speech on the Draft Constitution in 1936: "They talk of democracy. But what is democracy? Democracy in capitalist countries, where there are antagonistic classes, is, in the last analysis, democracy for the strong, democracy for the propertied minority. In the U. S. S. R., on the contrary, democracy is democracy for the working people, i.e., democracy for all."

What are, in your view, the crucial differences between the line of argumentation taken by de Tocqueville and Bryce and the line taken by

Lenin and Stalin? Do de Tocqueville and Lenin disagree on the relation between "democracy" and "liberty"; if so, of what nature is their disagreement?

Conclusions

The Lincoln formula affords a convenient point of departure for the analysis of ideological agreements on a "democracy." There is a general agreement that to serve the people in the broadest sense of the term, and ultimately the people of the earth, is the sole justification of government. Further, it is generally agreed that the people are served by giving the fullest possible access to the means by which each member can develop personal possibilities without jeopardizing the chances of others.

There is general doctrinal agreement that government should be "by the people," that is, that one should develop the most intense and widespread participation of the inhabitants in preparing, reaching, and carrying out decisions of importance to the welfare of the community. But it is also agreed that such participation is only possible if there is a minimum of general education and leisure and energy available for studies of the issues brought before the people. It is further agreed that in times of severe crisis, popular participation must be more or less reduced and opportunities of incitement to violent change of form of government curtailed.

From the unanimity on the principle of equal possibility of access to economic, educational, and cultural values flows an agreement that no individual should be allowed, by his particular talents or shrewdness, to reduce others to permanent dependence on him or to reduce permanently their and their offspring's access to economic, educational, and cultural values.

From the generally accepted broad interpretations of "people" flows a general rejection of race or color discrimination and a rejection of discriminations on the basis of religion, philosophical inclinations, or nobility of birth.

Implicit in the doctrines of government by the people and the appeals to knowledge as the guide to solution of questions of policy, there is a rejection of leadership on the basis of mystical insight of élites, of a *Führer* and *Gefolgschaft* following "the instincts of the pure blood."

There is no indication of disagreement on the opinion that there are in all ideological camps people who sincerely accept the foregoing doctrines, try to live up to their severe requirements and deplore the shortcomings of achievements so far realized.

The agreements thus listed make it possible to formulate severe criticism without leaving a common ground of accepted doctrines. The basic criticism will be that of inconsistency.

Even if the view were accepted, that mere lip service to the *common aspirations and principles* is the rule and sincerity the exception, their codification and the *increasing frequency of appeals to them* the world over by individuals and institutions on the national and international level, give to those who wish to propagate their sincere acceptance *a unique instrument* that should be tentatively perfected by research and worldwide educational drives.

D. UNITED EUROPE

WINSTON CHURCHILL: *On the Congress of Europe* *

Winston Churchill (1874–1965), Britain's great war leader during World War II, is the leading spokesman for a United Europe. He discussed the idea in speeches at Metz and Zürich in 1946. The following selection is from a speech delivered at The Hague, May 7, 1948, on the occasion of the meeting of the so-called Congress of Europe.

SINCE I spoke on this subject at Zürich in 1946, and since our British United Europe Movement was launched in January 1947, events have carried our affairs beyond our expectations. This cause was obviously either vital or merely academic. If it was academic, it would wither by the wayside; but if it was the vital need of Europe and the world in this dark hour, then the spark would start a fire which would glow brighter and stronger in the hearts and the minds of men and women in many lands. This is what has actually happened. Great governments have banded themselves together with all their executive power. The mighty republic of the United States has espoused the Marshall Plan. Sixteen European States are now associated for economic purposes; five have entered into close economic and military relationship. We hope that this nucleus will in due course be joined by the peoples of Scandinavia, and of the Iberian peninsula, as well as by Italy, who should now resume her full place in the comity of nations. . . .

We need not waste our time in disputes about who originated this idea of United Europe. There are many valid modern patents. There are many famous names associated with the revival and presentation of this idea, but we may all, I think, yield our pretensions to Henry of Navarre, King of France, who, with his great Minister Sully, between the years 1600 and 1607, laboured to set up a permanent committee representing the fifteen—now we are sixteen—leading Christian States of Europe. This body was to act as an arbitrator on all questions concerning religious conflict, national frontiers, internal disturbance, and

* From *Europe Unite. Speeches 1947 and 1948 by Winston Churchill*, pp. 310–317. Copyright 1950 by Houghton Mifflin Company. Reprinted by permission of Houghton Mifflin Company.

common action against any danger from the East, which in those days meant the Turks. This he called "The Grand Design." After this long passage of time we are the servants of the Grand Design.

This Congress has brought together leaders of thought and action from all the free countries of Europe. Statesmen of all political parties, leading figures from all the Churches, eminent writers, leaders of the professions, lawyers, chiefs of industry and prominent trade-unionists are gathered here. In fact a representative grouping of the most essential elements in the political, industrial, cultural and spiritual life of Europe is now assembled in this ancient hall. And although everyone has been invited in his individual capacity, nevertheless this Congress, and any conclusions it may reach, may fairly claim to be the voice of Europe. It is time indeed that that voice should be raised upon the scene of chaos and prostration, caused by the wrongs and hatreds of the past, and amid the dangers which lie about us in the present and cloud the future. We shall only save ourselves from the perils which draw near by forgetting the hatreds of the past, by letting national rancours and revenges die, by progressively effacing frontiers and barriers which aggravate and congeal our divisions, and by rejoicing together in that glorious treasure of literature, of romance, of ethics, of thought and toleration belonging to all, which is the true inheritance of Europe, the expression of its genius and honour, but which by our quarrels, our follies, by our fearful wars and the cruel and awful deeds that spring from war and tyrants, we have almost cast away. . . .

The Movement for European Unity must be a positive force, deriving its strength from our sense of common spiritual values. It is a dynamic expression of democratic faith based upon moral conceptions and inspired by a sense of mission. In the centre of our movement stands the idea of a Charter of Human Rights, guarded by freedom and sustained by law. It is impossible to separate economics and defence from the general political structure. Mutual aid in the economic field and joint military defence must inevitably be accompanied step by step with a parallel policy of closer political unity. It is said with truth that this involves some sacrifice or merger of national sovereignty. But it is also possible and not less agreeable to regard it as the gradual assumption by all the nations concerned of that larger sovereignty which can alone protect their diverse and distinctive customs and characteristics and their national traditions all of which under totalitarian systems, whether Nazi, Fascist, or Communist, would certainly be blotted out for ever.

Some time ago I stated that it was the proud mission of the victor nations to take the Germans by the hand and lead them back into the European family, and I rejoice that some of the most eminent and powerful Frenchmen have spoken in this sense. To rebuild Europe from its ruins and make its light shine forth again upon the world, we must first of all conquer ourselves. It is in this way only that the sublime, with its marvellous transmutations of material things, can be brought into our daily life. Europe requires all that Frenchmen, all that Germans, and all that every one of us can give. I therefore welcome here the German delegation, whom we have invited into our midst. For us the German problem is to restore the economic life of Germany and revive the ancient fame of the German race without thereby exposing their neighbours and ourselves to any rebuilding or reassertion of their military power of which we still bear the scars. United Europe provides the only solution to this two-sided problem and it is also a solution which can be implemented without delay. . . .

Nothing that we do or plan here conflicts with the paramount authority of a world organisation of the United Nations. On the contrary I have always believed, as I declared in the war, that a Council of Europe was a subordinate but necessary part of the world organisation. I thought at that time, when I had great responsibility, that there should be several regional councils, august but subordinate, that these should form the massive pillars upon which the world organisation would be founded in majesty and calm. This was the direction in which my hopes and thought lay three or four years ago. To take an example from the military sphere, with which our hard experiences have made us all familiar, the design for world government might have followed the system of three or more groups of armies—in this case armies of peace—under one supreme headquarters. Thus I saw the vast Soviet Union forming one of these great groups. The Council of Europe, including Great Britain linked with her Empire and Commonwealth, would be another. Thirdly, there was the United States and her sister republics in the Western Hemisphere with all their great spheres of interest and influence. . . .

To some extent events have moved in this direction, but not in the spirit or the shape that was needed. The western hemisphere already presents itself as a unit. Here at The Hague we are met to help our various Governments to create the new Europe. But we are all grieved and perplexed and imperilled by the discordant attitude and policy of the third great and equal partner, without whose active aid the world organisation cannot function, nor the shadow of war be lifted from the hearts and minds of men and nations. . . .

I have the feeling that after the second Thirty Years' War, for that is what it is, through which we have just passed, mankind needs and seeks a period of rest. After all, how little it is that the millions of homes in Europe represented here today are asking. What is it that all these wage-earners, skilled artisans, soldiers and tillers of the soil require, deserve, and may be led to demand? Is it not a fair chance to make a home, to reap the fruits of their toil, to cherish their wives, to bring up their children in a decent manner and to dwell in peace and safety, without fear or bullying or monstrous burdens or exploitations, however this may be imposed upon them? That is their heart's desire. That is what we mean to win for them.

President Roosevelt spoke of the Four Freedoms, but the one that matters most today is Freedom from Fear. Why should all these hard-working families be harassed, first in bygone times, by dynastic and religious quarrels, next by nationalistic ambitions, and finally by ideological fanaticism? Why should they now have to be regimented and hurled against each other by variously labelled forms of totalitarian tyranny, all fomented by wicked men, building their own predominance upon the misery and the subjugation of their fellow human beings? Why should so many millions of humble homes in Europe, aye, and much of its enlightenment and culture, sit quaking in dread of the policeman's knock? That is the question we have to answer here. That is the question which perhaps we have the power to answer here. After all, Europe has only to arise and stand in her own majesty, faithfulness and virtue, to confront all forms of tyranny, ancient or modern, Nazi or Communist, with forces which are unconquerable, and which if asserted in good time may never be challenged again. . . .

A high and a solemn responsibility rests upon us here this afternoon in this Congress of a Europe striving to be reborn. If we allow ourselves to be rent and disordered by pettiness and small disputes, if we fail in clarity of view or courage in action, a priceless occasion may be cast away for ever. But if we all pull together and pool the luck and the comradeship—and we shall need all the comradeship and not a little luck if we are to move together in this way—and firmly grasp the larger hopes of humanity, then it may be that we shall move into a happier sunlit age, when all the little children who are now growing up in this tormented world may find themselves not the victors nor the vanquished in the fleeting triumphs of one country over another in the bloody turmoil of destructive war, but the heirs of all the treasures of the past and the masters of all the science, the abundance and the glories of the future.

7. *The Intellectuals and Political Commitment*

JULIEN BENDA: *The Betrayal of the Intellectuals* *

> In a celebrated book, *The Betrayal of the Intellectuals* (1927), the
> French philosopher Julien Benda (1867–1956) accused modern intel-
> lectuals or "clerks" of abandoning the western tradition of speculative
> and disinterested thought for political partisanship. Though patently too
> sweeping Benda's indictment pinpoints a major phenomenon of in-
> tellectual life since the first World War: what later came to be called
> "engagement" or "commitment," particularly to the extremes of Right
> and Left.

IN ALL that I have said hitherto I have been considering only masses,
whether bourgeois or proletarian, kings, ministers, political leaders, all
that portion of the human species which I shall call 'the laymen', whose
whole function consists essentially in the pursuit of material interests,
and who, by becoming more and more solely and systematically realist,
have in fact only done what might be expected of them.

Side by side with this humanity . . . there existed until the last
half century another, essentially distinct humanity, which to a certain
extent acted as a check upon the former. I mean that class of men
whom I shall designate '*the clerks*', by which term I mean all those
whose activity essentially is *not* the pursuit of practical aims, all those
who seek their joy in the practice of an art or a science or metaphysical speculation, in short in the possession of non-material advantages,
and hence in a certain manner say: 'My kingdom is not of this world.'
Indeed, throughout history, for more than two thousand years until
modern times, I see an uninterrupted series of philosophers, men of
religion, men of literature, artists, men of learning (one might say
almost all during this period), whose influence, whose life, were in
direct opposition to the realism of the multitudes. To come down
specifically to the political passions—the 'clerks' were in opposition to
them in two ways. They were either entirely indifferent to these
passions, and, like Leonardo da Vinci, Malebranche, Goethe, set an
example of attachment to the purely disinterested activity of the mind
and created a belief in the supreme value of this form of existence; or,
gazing as moralists upon the conflict of human egotisms, like Erasmus,
Kant, Renan, they preached, in the name of humanity or justice, the
adoption of an abstract principle superior to and directly opposed to

these passions. Although these 'clerks' founded the modern State to the extent that it dominates individual egotisms, their activity undoubtedly was chiefly theoretical, and they were unable to prevent the laymen from filling all history with the noise of their hatreds and their slaughters; *but the 'clerks' did prevent the laymen from setting up their actions as a religion, they did prevent them from thinking themselves great men as they carried out these activities*. It may be said that, thanks to the 'clerks', humanity did evil for two thousand years, but honoured good. This contradiction was an honour to the human species, and formed the rift whereby civilization slipped into the world.

Now, at the end of the nineteenth century a fundamental change occurred: *the 'clerks' began to play the game of political passions*. The men who had acted as a check on the realism of the people began to act as its stimulators. This upheaval in the moral behaviour of humanity operated in several ways.

First of all the 'clerks' have adopted political passions. No one will deny that throughout Europe to-day the immense majority of men of letters and artists, a considerable number of scholars, philosophers, and 'ministers' of the divine, share in the chorus of hatreds among races and political factions. . . .

In the first place, the 'clerks' have set out to exalt the will of men to feel conscious of themselves as distinct from others, and to proclaim as contemptible every tendency to establish oneself in a universal. With the exception of certain authors like Tolstoi and Anatole France, whose teaching moreover is now looked on with contempt by most of their colleagues, all the influential moralists of Europe during the past fifty years, Bourget, Barrès, Maurras, Péguy, d'Annunzio, Kipling, the immense majority of German thinkers, have praised the efforts of men to feel conscious of themselves in their nation and race, to the extent that this distinguishes them from others and opposes them to others, and have made them ashamed of every aspiration to feel conscious of themselves as men in the general sense and in the sense of rising above ethnical aims. Those whose activity since the time of the Stoics had been devoted to preaching the extinction of national egotism in the interest of an abstract and eternal entity, set out to denounce every feeling of this kind and to proclaim the lofty morality of that egotism. . . .

The modern 'clerk' denounces the feeling of universalism, not only for the profit of the nation, but for that of a class. Our age has beheld moralists who have declared to the bourgeois world (or to the working classes) that, far from trying to check the feeling of their differences from others and to feel conscious of their common human nature, they should on the contrary try to feel conscious of this difference in all its profundity and irreducibleness, and that this effort is fine and noble, whereas every desire for union is here a sign of baseness and cowardice, and also of weakness of mind. This, as everyone knows, is the thesis of the 'Reflections on Violence', which has been praised by a whole galaxy of apostles of the modern soul. There is certainly something more novel in this attitude of the 'clerks' to class differences than in their attitude towards national differences. To discover the results of this teaching and the additional hatred (hitherto unknown) which it has given to either class in doing violence to its adversary, you have only to look at Italian Fascism for the bourgeois class, and at Russian Bolshevism for the working class.

ARTHUR KOESTLER: *Conversion to Communism* *

> Arthur Koestler (see above, pp. 691–94) is an example of the type of modern "clerk" whom Benda deplored. Four years after Benda's "j'accuse," Koestler joined the Communist Party which, however, he left in 1938. The following excerpts are from an essay he wrote years later for a cooperative volume entitled *The God That Failed*. Koestler, Ignazio Silone, and others explain therein why they were initially attracted to—but later repelled by—Communism. This essay should be read in connection with *Darkness at Noon* (1941), Koestler's powerful novel about the Soviet system of ideas.

I BECAME converted [to Communism] because I was ripe for it and lived in a disintegrating society thirsting for faith. But the day when I was given my Party card was merely the climax of a development which had started long before I had . . . heard the names of Marx and Lenin. Its roots reach back into childhood; and though each of us, comrades of the Pink Decade, had individual roots with different twists in them, we are products of, by and large, the same generation and cultural climate. It is this unity underlying diversity which makes me hope that my story is worth telling.

I was born in 1905 in Budapest; we lived there till 1919, when we moved to Vienna. Until the First World War we were comfortably off, a typical Continental middle-middle-class family: my father was the Hungarian representative of some old-established British and German textile manufacturers. In September, 1914, this form of existence, like so many others, came to an abrupt end; my father never found his feet

* From *The God That Failed*, edited by Richard Crossman, pp. 17–21, 23. Copyright 1949 by Richard Crossman. Reprinted by permission of Harper & Brothers and Hamish Hamilton Ltd.

again. He embarked on a number of ventures which became the more fantastic the more he lost self-confidence in a changed world. He opened a factory for radioactive soap; he backed several crank-inventions (everlasting electric bulbs, self-heating bed bricks and the like); and finally lost the remains of his capital in the Austrian inflation of the early 'twenties. I left home at twenty-one, and from that day became the only financial support of my parents.

At the age of nine, when our middle-class idyl collapsed, I had suddenly become conscious of the economic Facts of Life. As an only child, I continued to be pampered by my parents; but, well aware of the family crisis, and torn by pity for my father, who was of a generous and somewhat childlike disposition, I suffered a pang of guilt whenever they bought me books or toys. This continued later on, when every suit I bought for myself meant so much less to send home. Simultaneously, I developed a strong dislike of the obviously rich; not because they could afford to buy things (envy plays a much smaller part in social conflict than is generally assumed) but because they were able to do so without a guilty conscience. Thus I projected a personal predicament onto the structure of society at large. . . .

Thus sensitized by a personal conflict, I was ripe for the shock of learning that wheat was burned, fruit artificially spoiled and pigs were drowned in the depression years to keep prices up and enable fat capitalists to chant to the sound of harps, while Europe trembled under the torn boots of hunger-marchers and my father hid his frayed cuffs under the table. The frayed cuffs and drowned pigs blended into one emotional explosion, as the fuse of the archetype was touched off. We sang the "Internationale," but the words might as well have been the older ones: "Woe to the shepherds who feed themselves, but feed not their flocks."

In other respects, too, the story is more typical than it seems. A considerable proportion of the middle classes in central Europe was, like ourselves, ruined by the inflation of the 'twenties. It was the beginning of Europe's decline. This disintegration of the middle strata of society started the fatal process of polarization which continues to this day. The pauperized bourgeois became rebels of the Right or Left; Schickelgrüber and Djugashwili shared about equally the benefits of the social migration. Those who refused to admit that they had become déclassé, who clung to the empty shell of gentility, joined the Nazis and found comfort in blaming their fate on Versailles and the Jews. Many did not even have that consolation; they lived on pointlessly, like a great black swarm of tired winterflies crawling over the dim windows of Europe, members of a class displaced by history.

The other half turned Left, thus confirming the prophecy of the "Communist Manifesto":

> Entire sections of the ruling classes are . . . precipitated into
> the proletariat, or are at least threatened in their conditions of
> existence. They . . . supply the proletariat with fresh ele-
> ments of enlightenment and progress. . . .

I was ripe to be converted, as a result of my personal case-history;
thousands of other members of the intelligentsia and the middle classes
of my generation were ripe for it, by virtue of other personal case-
histories; but, however much these differed from case to case, they had
a common denominator; the rapid disintegration of moral values, of the
pre-1914 pattern of life in postwar Europe, and the simultaneous lure
of the new revelation which had come from the East.

I joined the Party (which to this day remains "the" Party for all of us
who once belonged to it) in 1931, at the beginning of that short-
lived period of optimism, of that abortive spiritual renaissance, later
known as the Pink Decade. The stars of that treacherous dawn were
Barbusse, Romain Rolland, Gide and Malraux in France; Piscator,
Becher, Renn, Brecht, Eisler, Säghers in Germany; Auden, Isherwood,
Spender in England; Dos Passos, Upton Sinclair, Steinbeck in the United
States. (Of course, not all of them were members of the Communist
Party.) The cultural atmosphere was saturated with Progressive Writers'
congresses, experimental theaters, committees for peace and against
Fascism, societies for cultural relations with the USSR, Russian films
and avant-garde magazines. It looked indeed as if the Western world,
convulsed by the aftermath of war, scourged by inflation, depression,
unemployment and the absence of a faith to live for, was at last going
to "construct at last a human justice.". . .

I began for the first time to read Marx, Engels and Lenin in earnest.
By the time I had finished with *Feuerbach* and *State and Revolution*,
something had clicked in my brain which shook me like a mental explosion. To say that one had "seen the light" is a poor description of the
mental rapture which only the convert knows (regardless of what faith
he has been converted to). The new light seems to pour from all directions across the skull; the whole universe falls into pattern like the stray
pieces of a jigsaw puzzle assembled by magic at one stroke. There is
now an answer to every question, doubts and conflicts are a matter of
the tortured past—a past already remote, when one had lived in dismal
ignorance in the tasteless, colorless world of those who *don't know*.
Nothing henceforth can disturb the convert's inner peace and serenity
—except the occasional fear of losing faith again, losing thereby what
alone makes life worth living, and falling back into the outer darkness,
where there is wailing and gnashing of teeth. This may explain how
Communists, with eyes to see and brains to think with, can still act in
subjective *bona fides*, anno Domini 1949. At all times and in all creeds

only a minority has been capable of courting excommunication and committing emotional harakiri in the name of an abstract truth.

JEAN-PAUL SARTRE: *Materialism and Revolution* *

Jean-Paul Sartre too has been sympathetic to the political Left. Yet he is critical of the "materialistic myth," *i.e.*, the metaphysic on which Communism is based, and seeks to substitute for it his own "philosophy of revolution." Sartre describes this philosophy, which has obvious affinities with his existentialism (see above, pp. 621–5), in a long article entitled "Materialism and Revolution," which appeared in *Les Temps Modernes* in 1946.

THIS, then, is the materialism they [the Communists] want me to choose, a monster, an elusive Proteus, a large, vague, contradictory semblance. I am asked to choose, this very day, in all intellectual freedom, in all lucidity, and that which I am to choose freely and lucidly ?·... with all my wits about me is a doctrine that destroys thought. I know that man has no salvation other than the liberation of the working class; I know this *before* being a materialist and from a plain inspection of the facts. I know that our intellectual interest lies with the proletariat. Is that a reason for me to demand of my thinking, which has led me to this point, that it destroy itself? Is that a reason for me to force it henceforth to abandon its criteria, to think in contradictions, to be torn between incompatible theses, to lose even the clear consciousness of itself, to launch forth blindly in a giddy flight that leads to faith? "Fall to thy knees and thou shalt believe," says Pascal. The materialist's effort is very closely akin to this. . . .

. . . A revolutionary philosophy ought to set aside the materialistic myth and endeavour to show: (1) That man is unjustifiable, that his existence is contingent, in that neither he nor any Providence has produced it; (2) That, as a result of this, any collective order established by men can be transcended towards other orders; (3) That the system of values current in a society reflects the structure of that society and tends to preserve it; (4) That it can thus always be transcended toward other systems which are not yet clearly perceived since the society of which they are the expression does not yet exist—but which are adumbrated and are, in a word, invented by the very effort of the members of society to transcend it.

* From Jean-Paul Sartre: *Literary and Philosophical Essays*, pp. 206–7, 219–20, 228, 233–4, 237. Copyright 1955 by Rider and Company. Reprinted by permission of Rider and Company and Editions Gallimard.

The oppressed person lives out his original contingency, and revolutionary philosophy must reckon with this. But in living out his contingency he accepts the *de facto* existence of his oppressors and the absolute value of the ideologies they have produced. He becomes a revolutionary only through a movement of transcendence which challenges these rights and this ideology. The revolutionary philosopher has, above all, to explain the possibility of this movement of transcendence. It is obvious that its source is not to be found in the individual's purely natural and material existence, since the individual turns back on this existence to judge it from the viewpoint of the future.

This possibility of *rising above* a situation in order to get a perspective on it (a perspective which is not pure knowledge, but an indissoluble linking of understanding and action) is precisely that which we call freedom. No materialism of any kind can ever explain it. A series of causes and effects may very well impel me to gesture or to behaviour which itself will be an effect and which will modify the state of the world; it cannot make me look back at my situation in order to grasp it in its totality. . . .

But, say the Marxists, if you teach man that he *is* free, you betray him; for he no longer needs to *become* free; can you conceive of a man free from birth who demands to be liberated? To this I reply that if man is not originally free, but determined once and for all, we cannot even conceive what his liberation might be. Some may say, "We will release human nature from its determining constraints." These people are fools.

What indeed can the nature of a man be, apart from that which he concretely is in his present existence? . . .

We must, at this point, repeat the following: The revolutionary, if he wishes to act, cannot regard historical events as the result of lawless contingencies; but he by no means demands that his path be cleared in advance; he wishes to clear it himself. Certain partial series, constancies and structural laws within determined social forms are what he needs in order to see ahead. If you give him more, everything fades away into ideas and history no longer has to be *made*, but rather to be *read*, day by day; the real becomes a dream.

We were called upon to choose between materialism and idealism, we were told that we would be unable to find a middle way between these two doctrines. Without preconceived ideas, we have allowed revolutionary demands to speak for themselves and we have seen that they trace, of themselves, the features of an odd sort of philosophy that dismisses idealism and materialism unsuited. The revolutionary act seemed to us, at first, the free act *par excellence*. Not free in an anarchist and individualist way at all; if that were true, the revolutionary, by the very nature of his situation, could only claim, with a greater or lesser degree of explicitness, the rights of the "exquisite class," that is, his integration with the upper social layers.

But as he demands, within the oppressed class and for the entire oppressed class, a more rational social status, his freedom resides in the act by which he demands the liberation of his whole class and, more generally, of all men. It springs from a recognition of other freedoms and it demands recognition on their part. Thus, from the beginning, it places itself on the level of solidarity. And the revolutionary act contains within itself the premises of a philosophy of freedom, or, rather, by its very existence it creates this philosophy. . . .

The revolutionary considers that he *builds* socialism, and since he has shaken off and overthrown all legal rights, he recognizes its existence only in so far as the revolutionary class invents, wills and builds it. And, in this sense, this slow, stern conquest of socialism is none other than the affirmation of human freedom in and through history. And precisely because man is free, the triumph of socialism is not at all certain. It does not lie at the end of the road, like a boundary-mark; it is *the* scheme formulated by humanity. It will be what men make it; it is the outcome of the soberness with which the revolutionary envisages his action. He feels responsible not only for the coming of a socialist republic in general, but for the particular character of this socialism as well.

Thus the philosophy of revolution, transcending both idealist thinking which is bourgeois and the myth of materialism which suited the oppressed masses for a while, claims to be the philosophy of *man* in the general sense.

ALBERT CAMUS: *On Rebellion* *

> Albert Camus (1913–60), perhaps best known for his great allegorical novel *The Plague* and recipient of the Nobel Prize for literature, very much believed in the writer's political commitment, but not to "revolution" in the Communist sense. To Communist "revolution" he opposed the idea of "revolt" or "rebellion." The following selections, which embody these ideas, are from two works by Camus, the first a lecture given at the University of Uppsala in 1957, the second the long philosophical essay entitled *The Rebel* (1951).

AN ORIENTAL wise man always used to ask the divinity in his prayers to be so kind as to spare him from living in an interesting era. As we are not wise, the divinity has not spared us and we are living in an interesting era. In any case, our era forces us to take an interest in it. The writers of today know this. If they speak up, they are criticized and attacked. If they become modest and keep silent, they are vociferously blamed for their silence.

In the midst of such din the writer cannot hope to remain aloof in order to pursue the reflections and images that are dear to him. Until the present moment, remaining aloof has always been possible in history. When someone did not approve, he could always keep silent or talk of something else. Today everything is changed and even silence has dangerous implications. The moment that abstaining from choice is itself looked upon as a choice and punished or praised as such, the artist is willy-nilly impressed into service. . . .

For a hundred and fifty years the writers belonging to a mercantile society, with but few exceptions, thought they could live in happy irresponsibility. They lived, indeed, and then died alone, as they had lived. But we writers of the twentieth century shall never again be alone. Rather, we must know that we can never escape the common misery and that our only justification, if indeed there is a justification, is to speak up, insofar as we can, for those who cannot do so. But we must do so for all those who are suffering at this moment, whatever may be the glories, past or future, of the States and parties oppressing them: for the artist there are no privileged torturers. This is why beauty, even today, especially today, cannot serve any party; it cannot serve, in the long or short run, anything but men's suffering or their liberty. The only really committed artist is he who, without refusing to take part in the combat, at least refuses to join the regular armies and remains a free-lance.

*   *   *

. . . The revolution of the twentieth century [*i.e.*, Communism] believes that it can avoid nihilism and remain faithful to true rebellion, by replacing God by history. In reality, it fortifies the former and betrays the latter. History in its pure form furnishes no value by itself. Therefore one must live by the principles of immediate expediency and keep silent or tell lies. Systematic violence, or imposed silence, calculation or concerted falsehood become the inevitable rule. Purely historical thought is therefore nihilistic: it whole-heartedly accepts the evil of history and in this way is opposed to rebellion. . . .

If, on the other hand, rebellion could found a philosophy it would be 'a philosophy of limits, of calculated ignorance, and of risk. He who does not know everything cannot kill everything. The rebel, far from making an absolute of history, rejects and disputes it, in the name of a concept that he has of his own nature. He refuses his condition, and his condition to a large extent is historical. Injustice, the transcience of time, death—all are manifest in history. In spurning them, history itself is spurned. . . .

The mystification peculiar to the mind which claims to be revolutionary today sums up and increases bourgeois mystification. It contrives, by the promise of absolute justice, the acceptance of perpetual injustice, of unlimited compromise, and of indignity. Rebellion itself only aspires to the relative and can only promise an assured dignity coupled with relative justice. It supposes a limit at which the community of man is established. Its universe is the universe of relative values. Instead of saying, with Hegel and Marx, that all is necessary, it only repeats that all is possible and that, at a certain point on the farthest frontier, it is worth making the supreme sacrifice for the sake of the possible. Between God and history, the yogi and the commissar, it opens a difficult path where contradictions may exist and thrive. Let us consider the two contradictions given as an example in this way.

A revolutionary action which wishes to be coherent in terms of its origins should be embodied in an active consent to the relative. It would express fidelity to the human condition. Uncompromising as to its means, it would accept an approximation as far as its ends are concerned and, so that the approximation should become more and more accurately defined, it would allow absolute freedom of speech. Thus it would preserve the common existence that justifies its insurrection. In particular, it would preserve as an absolute law the permanent possibility of self-expression. This defines a particular line of conduct in regard to justice and freedom. There is no justice in society without natural or civil rights as its basis. There are no rights without expression of those rights. If the rights are expressed without hesitation it is more than probable that, sooner or later, the justice they postulate will come to the world. . . . The revolution of the twentieth century has arbitrarily separated, for overambitious ends of conquest, two inseparable ideas. Absolute freedom mocks at justice. Absolute justice denies freedom. To be fruitful, the two ideas must find their limits in each other. No man considers that his condition is free if it is not at the same time just, nor just unless it is free. . . .

The same reasoning can be applied to violence. . . . Authentic arts of rebellion will only consent to take up arms for institutions that limit violence, not for those which codify it. A revolution is not worth dying for unless it assures the immediate suppression of the death penalty; not worth going to prison for unless it refuses in advance to pass sentence without fixed terms. . . .

. . . Historical absolutism is not efficacious, it is efficient; it has seized and kept power. Once it is in possession of power, it destroys the only creative reality. Uncompromising and limited action, springing from rebellion, upholds this reality and only tries to extend it farther and farther. . . .

There does exist for man, therefore, a way of acting and of thinking which is possible on the level of moderation to which he belongs. Every undertaking that is more ambitious than this proves to be contradictory. The absolute is not attained nor, above all, created through history. Politics is not religion, or if it is, then it is nothing but the Inquisition. How would society define an absolute? Perhaps everyone is looking for this absolute on behalf of all. But society and politics only have the responsibility of arranging everyone's affairs so that each will have the leisure and the freedom to pursue this common search. History can then no longer be presented as an object of worship. It is only an opportunity that must be rendered fruitful by a vigilant rebellion.

8. *Progress or Decay?*

Nicolas Berdyaev: *Reflections on Time and History* *

> Although his exact meaning is not always easy to grasp, it is clear that Nicolas Berdyaev (1874–1948), like so many of his contemporaries, was pessimistic about "time" and convinced that the "tragic conflict" of history can be resolved only outside of, or at the end of time. Mystic and religious philosopher, though originally a Marxist, Berdyaev was expelled from Russia in 1922 and spent most of the rest of his life in Paris where he wrote a number of books on the philosophy of history. The following selections are taken from his autobiography.

RUSSIAN thought has always been preoccupied with the problems of the philosophy of history, and my own keen interest in this subject developed in accordance with the tradition of Russian thought. In setting out to understand the nature of history I had one overwhelming impression, namely, that nothing seems to succeed in history and yet all things are significant in it. The meaning of history is beyond the confines of history. History has meaning because it comes to an end. Unending history, be it as progress or as regress, is the epitome of meaninglessness. Thus I arrived at the conclusion that the true philosophy of history is eschatological in nature: that is to say, the historical process ought to be understood in the light of the end. . . .

There is an individual eschatology and apocalypse, and there is an

* From Nicolas Berdyaev: *Dream and Reality*, pp. 294–6, 298. Copyright 1950 by Geoffrey Bles Ltd. Reprinted by permission of Geoffrey Bles Ltd.

historical eschatology and apocalypse; but the two intertwine: history and the end are my own history and my own end, and my own history and end affect the entire course and outcome of history. But this interdependence does not lend itself to clear-cut definition, for there is a tragic conflict between history, with its complex movements and agencies, and man, with his unique and irreducible personal destiny. I have frequently found myself resisting the pressure of historical processes because of their hostility and mercilessness towards man, because they arise and grow for the sake of inhuman and impersonal aims. History must come to an end, since it is incapable of resolving the problem of personality within its limits, and leads beyond them. This is one aspect of the historiographical theme.

The other aspect is marked by an experience of man's self-identification with history: I cannot extricate myself from the world, from humanity, from the social and cultural movements in the world, from the past, present and future. History takes place within me, for I am not an isolated entity existing by itself and for itself, but a microcosmos. My sense of history, then, involves these two experiences: the experience of history's hostile and alien character and of my implication in it. The tension inherent in this twofold experience can only be resolved in the end of history, which signifies a victory over all objectification and alienation—a victory by which man ceases to be determined from without. We are, however, in danger of objectifying the end itself, and imagine it as taking place in historical time. In point of fact, what is beyond history cannot be related to history in simply historical terms. The failure to see this proves a stumbling-block in the many attempts to interpret the Apocalypse. We may not be able to dispense altogether with time when thinking of its end, and yet this end cannot be a mere part of our broken time. It belongs to another order of existence; it must be the end of time itself if it is to be an end at all, however difficult it may be for us to think of something absolutely last. Thus the Apocalyptic angel swears that there should be time no longer. The flux of time is a symptom of the disrupted, fallen state of our world: "the new heaven and the new earth" betokens victory over this disrupting temporal flux, which splits human existence into extraneous moments and experiences, and the beginning of another time, which I have called "existential time," and which is not open to mathematical or astronomical measurements. . . .

Some people may still delude themselves with the idea that men are becoming richer and richer and are having a better and better time in virtue of that secret force called progress, but others are not so easily deceived. I too believe in progress, but a progress derived from the recognition of the possibility of true creative acts in history, not from evolutionary naturalism or determinism. But progress is, admittedly, a misleading word. History provides the stage for a tragic struggle in which both good and evil are engaged in an ever increasing and intense contest. It is this which moves and presses history towards the end, in which historic time will pass into existential time.

Man is nailed to the cross of time with its tormenting contradictions, and he cannot bear its apparently unending, relentless course. . . .

. . . A terrible judgment hangs over history and civilization—the imminent judgment over their human, all-too-human pathways. History shows constant signs of a fatal lapse from the human or divine-human to the sub-human or demonic. Out of his idolatrous and demonolatrous instincts man conjures up real demonic powers which in turn seize control of him. "The beast rising out of the sea" is a highly suggestive apocalyptic image of the last demonic attempts of the kingdom of Caesar to dominate and to enslave man and the world. The victory of the Lamb over the Beast is the victory of freedom and love over force and hatred. The Beast will then be cast once more into the abyss of hell and shackled, not to eternity, but to time: for hell is that which remains in time; that which, obsessed by its evil nightmares, does not pass into eternity.

W. R. INGE: *The Idea of Progress* *

> William Ralph Inge (1860–1954), the "gloomy" Dean of St. Paul's, London, is well known as the author of scholarly books in the history of religious mysticism, and works of Christian apologetics. *The Idea of Progress* was first delivered as a lecture at Oxford in 1920.

THE BELIEF in Progress, not as an ideal but as an indisputable fact, not as a task for humanity but as a law of Nature, has been the working faith of the West for about a hundred and fifty years.

*   *   *

In France, the chief home of this heady doctrine, the psychical temperature soon began to rise under its influence, till it culminated in the delirium of the Terror. The Goddess of Reason hardly survived Robespierre and his guillotine; but the belief in progress, which might otherwise have subsided when the French resumed their traditional pursuits—'rem militarem et argute loqui'—was reinforced by the industrial revolution, which was to run a very different course from that indicated by the theatrical disturbances at Paris between 1789 and 1794, the

---

* From W. R. Inge: *The Idea of Progress*, p. 3, 7–9, 13–16, 22–5. Copyright 1920 by The Clarendon Press, Oxford. Reprinted by permission of The Clarendon Press, Oxford.

importance of which has perhaps been exaggerated. In England above all, the home of the new industry, progress was regarded (in the words which Mr. Mallock puts into the mouth of a nineteenth-century scientist) as that kind of improvement which can be measured by statistics. This was quite seriously the view of the last century generally, and there has never been, nor will there ever be again, such an opportunity for gloating over this kind of improvement. . . .

But Herbert Spencer asserts the perfectibility of man with an assurance which makes us gasp. 'Progress is not an accident but a necessity. What we call evil and immorality must disappear. It is certain that man must become perfect.' 'The ultimate development of the ideal man is certain— as certain as any conclusion in which we place the most implicit faith; for instance, that all men will die.' 'Always towards perfection is the mighty movement—towards a complete development and a more un- mixed good.'

* * *

If we turn to history for a confirmation of the Spencerian doctrine, we find, on the contrary, that civilization is a disease which is almost invariably fatal, unless its course is checked in time. The Hindus and Chinese, after advancing to a certain point, were content to mark time; and they survive. But the Greeks and Romans are gone; and aristocracies everywhere die out. Do we not see to-day the complex organization of the ecclesiastic and college don succumbing before the simple squeezing and sucking organs of the profiteer and trade-unionist? If so-called civilized nations show any protracted vitality, it is because they are only civilized at the top. Ancient civilizations were destroyed by imported barbarians; we breed our own.

It is also an unproved assumption that the domination of the planet by our own species is a desirable thing, which must give satisfaction to its Creator. We have devastated the loveliness of the world; we have exterminated several species more beautiful and less vicious than our- selves; we have enslaved the rest of the animal creation, and have treated our distant cousins in fur and feathers so badly that beyond doubt, if they were able to formulate a religion, they would depict the Devil in human form. If it is progress to turn the fields and woods of Essex into East and West Ham, we may be thankful that progress is a sporadic and transient phenomenon in history. It is a pity that our biologists, instead of singing paeans to Progress and thereby stultifying their own specula- tions, have not preached us sermons on the sin of racial self-idolatry, a topic which really does arise out of their studies. '*L'anthropolatrie, voilà l'ennemi*,' is the real ethical motto of biological science, and a valuable contribution to morals.

It was impossible that such shallow optimism as that of Herbert Spencer should not arouse protests from other scientific thinkers. . . .

One recent thinker, who accepts Huxley's view that the nature of things is cruel and immoral, is willing to face the probability that we cannot resist it with any prospect of victory. Mr. Bertrand Russell, in his arresting essay, 'A Free Man's Worship,' shows us Prometheus again, but Prometheus chained to the rock and still hurling defiance against God. He proclaims the moral bankruptcy of naturalism, which he yet holds to be forced upon us. 'That man is the product of causes which had no prevision of the end they were achieving; that his origin, his growth, his hopes and fears, his loves and his beliefs, are but the outcome of accidental collocations of atoms; that no fire, no heroism, no intensity of thought and feeling, can preserve an individual beyond the grave; that all the labours of the ages, all the devotion, all the inspiration, all the noonday brightness of human genius, are destined to extinction in the vast death of the solar system, and that the whole temple of man's achievement must inevitably be buried beneath the débris of a universe in ruins—all these things, if not quite beyond dispute, are yet so nearly certain, that no philosophy which rejects them can hope to stand. Only within the scaffolding of these truths, only on the firm foundation of unyielding despair, can the soul's habitation henceforth be safely built.' Man belongs to 'an alien and inhuman world,' alone amid 'hostile forces.' What is man to do? The God who exists is evil; the God whom we can worship is the creation of our own conscience, and has no existence outside it. The 'free man' will worship the latter; and, like John Stuart Mill, 'to hell he will go.'

If I wished to critize this defiant pronouncement, which is not without a touch of bravado, I should say that so complete a separation of the real from the ideal is impossible, and that the choice which the writer offers us, of worshipping a Devil who exists or a God who does not, is no real choice, since we cannot worship either. But my object in quoting from this essay is to show how completely naturalism has severed its alliance with optimism and belief in progress. Professor Huxley and Mr. Russell have sung their palinode and smashed the old gods of their creed. No more proof is needed, I think, that the alleged law of progress has no scientific basis whatever.

*   *   *

Our optimists have not made it clear to themselves or others what they mean by progress, and we may suspect that the vagueness of the idea is one of its attractions. There has been no physical progress in our species for many thousands of years. The Cro-Magnon race, which lived perhaps twenty thousand years ago, was at least equal to any modern people in size and strength; the ancient Greeks were, I suppose handsomer and better formed than we are; and some unprogressive races, such as the Zulus, Samoans, and Tahitians, are envied by Europeans either for strength or beauty. Although it seems not to be true that the sight and hearing of civilized peoples are inferior to those of savages, we have certainly lost our natural weapons, which from one point of view is a mark of degeneracy. Mentally, we are now told that the men of the Old Stone Age, ugly as most of them must have been, had as large brains as ours; and he would be a bold man who should claim that we are intellectually equal to the Athenians or superior to the Romans. The question of moral improvement is much more difficult. Until the Great War few would have disputed that civilized man had become much more humane, much more sensitive to the sufferings of others, and so more just, more self-controlled, and less brutal in his pleasures and in his resentments. The habitual honesty of the Western European might also have been contrasted with the rascality of inferior races in the past and present. It was often forgotten that, if progress means the improvement of human nature itself, the question to be asked is whether the modern civilized man behaves better in the same circumstances than his ancestor would have done. Absence of temptation may produce an appearance of improvement; but this is hardly what we mean by progress, and there is an old saying that the Devil has a clever trick of pretending to be dead. It seems to me very doubtful whether when we are exposed to the same temptations we are more humane or more sympathetic or juster or less brutal than the ancients. Even before this war, the examples of the Congo and Putumayo, and American lynchings, proved that contact with barbarians reduces many white men to the moral condition of savages; and the outrages committed on the Chinese after the Boxer rebellion showed that even a civilized nation cannot rely on being decently treated by Europeans if its civilization is different from their own. During the Great War, even if some atrocities were magnified with the amiable object of rousing a good-natured people to violent hatred, it was the well-considered opinion of Lord Bryce's commission that no such cruelties had been committed for three hundred years as those which the Germans practised in Belgium and France. It was startling to observe how easily the blood-lust was excited in young men straight from the fields, the factory, and the counter, many of whom had never before killed anything larger than a wasp, and that in self-defence. . . .

We have, then, been driven to the conclusion that neither science nor history gives us any warrant for believing that humanity has advanced, except by accumulating knowledge and experience and the instruments of living. The value of these accumulations is not beyond dispute.

Attacks upon civilization have been frequent, from Crates, Pherecrates, Antisthenes, and Lucretius in antiquity to Rousseau, Walt Whitman, Thoreau, Ruskin, Morris, and Edward Carpenter in modern times. I cannot myself agree with these extremists. I believe that the accumulated experience of mankind, and his wonderful discoveries, are of great value. I only point out that they do not constitute real progress in human nature itself, and that in the absence of any real progress these gains are external, precarious, and liable to be turned to our own destruction, as new discoveries in chemistry may easily be.

OSWALD SPENGLER: *The Decline of the West* *

The Decline of the West, in which the German school teacher and free-lance writer Oswald Spengler (1880–1936) outlined his "Morphology of History," is not so much serious history as a reflection of the mood of the times. The book, widely discussed in the 1920's, was completed in 1914 but not published until after the First World War.

HERE, then, I lay it down that *Imperialism*, of which petrifacts such as the Egyptian empire, the Roman, the Chinese, the Indian may continue to exist for hundreds or thousands of years—dead bodies, amorphous and dispirited masses of men, scrap-material from a great history—is to be taken as the typical symbol of the passing away. Imperialism is Civilization unadulterated. In this phenomenal form the destiny of the West is now irrevocably set. The energy of culture-man is directed inwards, that of civilization-man outwards. And thus I see in Cecil Rhodes the first man of a new age. He stands for the political style of a far-ranging, Western, Teutonic and especially German future, and his phrase "expansion is everything" is the Napoleonic reassertion of the indwelling tendency of *every* Civilization that has fully ripened— Roman, Arab or Chinese. It is not a matter of choice—it is not the conscious will of individuals, or even that of whole classes or peoples that decides. The expansive tendency is a doom, something daemonic and immense, which grips, forces into service, and uses up the late mankind of the world-city stage, willy-nilly, or unaware.

*　　*　　*

Up to now everyone has been at liberty to hope what he pleased about the future. Where there are no facts, sentiment rules. But henceforward it will be every man's business to inform himself of what *can* happen and

* Reprinted from *The Decline of the West* by Oswald Spengler by permission of Alfred A. Knopf, Inc. Copyright 1926 by Alfred A. Knopf, Inc. Pp. 36-7, 39-40, 104, 356, 358–60 (1947 edition).

therefore of what with the unalterable necessity of destiny and irrespective of personal ideals, hopes or desires, *will* happen. When we use the risky word "freedom" we shall mean freedom to do, not this or that, but the necessary or nothing. The feeling that this is "just as it should be" is the hall-mark of the man of fact. To lament it and blame it is not to alter it. To birth belongs death, to youth age, to life generally its form and its allotted span. The present is a civilized, emphatically not a cultured time, and *ipso facto* a great number of life-capacities fall out as impossible. This may be deplorable, and may be and will be deplored in pessimist philosophy and poetry, but it is not in our power to make otherwise. It will not be—already it is not—permissible to defy clear historical experience and to expect, merely because we hope, that this will spring or that will flourish.

It will no doubt be objected that such a world-outlook, which in giving this certainty as to the outlines and tendency of the future cuts off all far-reaching hopes, would be unhealthy for all and fatal for many, once it ceased to be a mere theory and was adopted as a practical scheme of life by the group of personalities effectively moulding the future.

Such is not my opinion. We are civilized, not Gothic or Rococo, people; we have to reckon with the hard cold facts of a *late* life, to which the parallel is to be found not in Pericles's Athens but in Caesar's Rome. Of great painting or great music there can no longer be, for Western people, any question. Their architectural possibilities have been exhausted these hundred years. Only *extensive* possibilities are left to them. Yet, for a sound and vigorous generation that is filled with unlimited hopes, I fail to see that it is any disadvantage to discover betimes that some of these hopes must come to nothing. And if the hopes thus doomed should be those most dear, well, a man who is worth anything will not be dismayed.

* * *

Cultures are organisms, and world-history is their collective biography. Morphologically, the immense history of the Chinese or of the Classical Culture is the exact equivalent of the petty history of the individual man, or of the animal, or the tree, or the flower. For the Faustian vision, this is not a postulate but an experience; if we want to learn to recognize inward forms that constantly and everywhere repeat themselves, the comparative morphology of plants and animals has long ago given us the methods. In the destinies of the several Cultures that follow upon one another, grow up with one another, touch, overshadow, and suppress one another, is compressed the whole content of human history. And if we set free their shapes, till now hidden all too deep under the surface of a trite "history of human progress," and let them march past us in the spirit, it cannot but be that we shall succeed in distinguishing, amidst all that is special or unessential, the primitive culture-form, *the* Culture that underlies as ideal all the individual Cultures.

* * *

Each Culture, further, has *its own mode of spiritual extinction*, which is that which follows of necessity from its life as a whole. And hence Buddhism, Stoicism and Socialism are morphologically equivalent as end-phenomena.

* * *

Every soul has religion, which is only another word for its existence. All living forms in which it expresses itself—all arts, doctrines, customs, all metaphysical and mathematical form-worlds, all ornament, every column and verse and idea—are ultimately religious, and *must* be so. But from the setting-in of Civilization they *cannot* be so any longer. As the essence of every Culture is religion, so—and *consequently*—the essence of every Civilization is irreligion—the two words are synonymous. He who cannot feel this in the creativeness of Manet as against Velasquez, of Wagner as against Haydn, of Lysippus as against Phidias, of Theocritus as against Pindar, knows not what the best means in art. Even Rococo in its worldliest creations is still religious. But the buildings of Rome, even when they are temples, are irreligious; the one touch of religious architecture that there was in old Rome was the intrusive Magian-souled Pantheon, first of the mosques. The megalopolis itself, as against the old Culture-towns—Alexandria as against Athens, Paris as against Bruges, Berlin as against Nürnberg—is irreligious down to the last detail, down to the look of the streets, the dry intelligence of the faces. And, correspondingly, the ethical sentiments belonging to the form-language of the megalopolis are irreligious and soulless also. Socialism is the Faustian world-feeling become irreligious; . . .

It is this extinction of living inner religiousness, which gradually tells upon even the most insignificant element in a man's being, that becomes phenomenal in the historical world-picture at the turn from the Culture to the Civilization, the *Climacteric* of the Culture, as I have already called it, the time of change in which a mankind loses its spiritual fruitfulness for ever, and building takes the place of begetting. Unfruitfulness—understanding the word in all its direct seriousness—marks the brain-man of the megalopolis, as the sign of fulfilled destiny, and it is one of the most impressive facts of historical symbolism that the change manifests itself not only in the extinction of great art, of great courtesy, of great formal thought, of the great style in all things, but also quite carnally in the childlessness and "race-suicide" of the civilized and rootless strata, a phenomenon not peculiar to ourselves but already observed and deplored—and of course not remedied—in Imperial Rome and Imperial China.

As to the living representative of these new and purely intellectual creations, the men of the "New Order" upon whom every decline-time founds such hopes, we cannot be in any doubt. They are the fluid megalopolitan Populace, the rootless city-mass (oi polloi, as Athens called it) that has replaced the People, the Culture-folk that was sprung from the soil and peasantlike even when it lived in towns. They are the market-place loungers of Alexandria and Rome, the newspaper-readers of our own corresponding time; the "educated" man who then and now makes a cult of intellectual mediocrity and a church of advertisement; the man of the theatres and places of amusement, of sport and "best-sellers." It is this late-appearing mass and *not* "mankind" that is the object of Stoic and Socialist propaganda, and one could match it with equivalent phenomena in the Egyptian New Empire, Buddhist India and Confucian China.

Correspondingly, there is a characteristic form of public effect, the *Diatribe*. First observed as a Hellenistic phenomenon, it is an efficient form in *all* Civilizations. Dialectical, practical and plebian through and through, it replaces the old meaningful and far-ranging Creation the great man by the unrestrained Agitation of the small and shrewd, ideas by aims, symbols by programs. The expansion-element common to all Civilizations, the imperialistic substitution of outer space for inner spiritual space, characterizes this also. Quantity replaces quality, spreading replaces deepening. We must not confuse this hurried and shallow activity with the Faustian will-to-power. All it means is that creative inner life is at an end and intellectual existence can only be kept up materially, by outward effect in the space of the City. Diatribe belongs necessarily to the "religion of the irreligious" and is the characteristic form that the "cure of souls" takes therein. It appears as the Indian preaching, the Classical rhetoric, and the Western journalism. It appeals not to the best but to the most, and it values its means according to the number of successes obtained by them. It substitutes for the old thoughtfulness an *intellectual male-prostitution* by speech and writing, which fills and dominates the halls and the market-places of the megalopolis.

C. VIRGIL GHEORGHIU: *The Twenty-fifth Hour* *

The Twenty-fifth Hour, a novel by the Rumanian Gheorghiu (1916–   ), created a furor when it was first published in Paris in

* Reprinted from *The Twenty-fifth Hour* by C. Virgil Gheorghiu; by permission of Alfred A. Knopf, Inc.; copyright 1950 by C. Virgil Gheorghiu. Pp. 41–2, 45–6, 48–9.

1949. It became a best-seller, and the subject of a great many news-paper articles and conferences. In the selection that follows, the hero, Traian Koruga, discusses his plans for a novel with a friend, the lawyer George Damian.

"Joking aside, George," said Traian, "I feel that something of immense import is taking shape around us. I know neither when it started nor where it first broke out, nor how long it will last, but I am conscious of its presence. We are caught up in a vortex, and it will tear away the flesh from our limbs and crush every bone in our bodies. I feel this thing coming, as rats feel it when they abandon a sinking ship. But we cannot swim ashore; for us there is no shore."

"What is this 'thing' you allude to?"

"Call it revolution, if you like," said Traian. "A revolution of inconceivable proportions, to which all human beings will fall victim.". . .

"And what is this great danger threatening us all?" asked the attorney.

"The mechanical slave," answered Traian Koruga. "You know him, too, George. The mechanical slave is the servant who waits on us daily in a thousand ways. He drives our car, switches on our light, pours water on our hands when we wash, gives us massage, tells us funny stories when we turn on the radio, lays out roads, breaks up mountains.". . .

"A society which contains million of millions of mechanical slaves and a mere two thousand million humans—even if it happens to be the humans who govern it—will reveal the characteristics of its proletarian majority.". . .

"We are learning the laws and the jargon of our slaves, so that we can give them orders. And so, gradually and imperceptibly, we are renouncing our human qualities and our own laws. We are dehumanizing ourselves by adopting the way of life of our slaves. The first symptom of this dehumanization is contempt for the human being. Modern man assesses by technical standards his own value and that of his fellow men; they are replaceable component parts. Contemporary society, which numbers one man to every two or three dozen mechanical slaves, must be organized in such a way as to function according to technological laws. Society is now created for technological, rather than for human, requirements. And that's where tragedy begins.". . .

"This slow process of dehumanization is at work under many different guises, making man renounce his emotions and reducing social relationships to something categorical, automatic, and precise, like the relationship between different parts of a machine. The rhythm and the jargon of the mechanical slaves, or robots, if you like, finds echoes in our social relationships and our administration, in painting, literature, and dancing. Men are becoming the apes of robots.". . .

"Technological Civilization can create comforts, but it cannot create the Spirit. And without the Spirit there is no genius. A society without men of genius is doomed. This new Civilization, which is now superseding Western Civilization and which will eventually conquer the entire world, will perish in its turn.". . .

"The downfall of technocracy will be followed by a rebirth of human and spiritual values. This great light will probably come from the East, from Asia. But not from Russia. The Russians have bowed down and worshipped the electric light of the West and will suffer the same fate as the West. It is the Orient that, at length, will conquer this technocracy of ours and will keep electricity for lighting streets and houses instead of building altars to it and bowing down before it as Western society, in its barbarism, is doing today. The men from the East will not try to floodlight the hidden ways of life and the soul by means of neon tubes. They will subdue and control the machines of Technological Civilization by the power of their own spirit and genius, as a conductor controls his orchestra by means of an instinctive sense of musical harmony. But we shall not live to see those times—in our age man worships the electric sun like a barbarian."

"So we shall die in chains?" said the attorney.

"We ourselves almost certainly shall—as prisoners of the technological barbarians. My novel will be the epilogue of this phase of man's existence—this chapter of man's history."

"What will it be called?"

"*The Twenty-fifth Hour*," said Traian. "The hour when mankind is beyond salvation—when it is too late even for the coming of the Messiah. It is not the last hour; it is one hour past the last hour. It is Western Civilization at this very moment. It is NOW."

ARNOLD TOYNBEE: *A Study of History* *

Since 1925 the English historian Arnold Toynbee (1889–1975) has served as Director of Studies of the Royal Institute of International Affairs, London. The first three volumes of his *Study of History*, immensely popular in D. C. Somervell's abridgment, appeared in 1934. "Mr. Toynbee's study," says Crane Brinton, "belongs . . . with such

* From *A Study of History* by Arnold J. Toynbee, abridged by D. C. Somervell, published under the auspices of the Royal Institute of International Affairs. Copyright 1946 by Oxford University Press, Inc. Pp. 245, 247–8, 251, 253–4, 552–4.

works as those of . . . St. Augustine, Vico, Buckle, and Spengler. It is philosophy of history, metaphysics, even theology, not narrative history."

The Breakdowns of Civilizations

FOR our present purpose it is enough to observe that of the living civilizations every one has already broken down and is in process of disintegration except our own.

And what of our Western Civilization? It has manifestly not yet reached the stage of a universal state. But we found, in an earlier chapter, that the universal state is not the first stage in distintegration any more than it is the last. It is followed by what we have called an 'interregnum,' and preceded by what we have called a 'time of troubles,' which seems usually to occupy several centuries; and if we in our generation were to permit ourselves to judge by the purely subjective criterion of our own feeling about our own age, the best judges would probably declare that our 'time of troubles' had undoubtedly descended upon us.

*   *   *

What, then, causes the breakdowns of civilizations? Before applying our own method, which involves the marshalling of the relevant concrete facts of history, we had better pass in review certain solutions of the problem which soar higher in search of their evidence and rely for proof either on unprovable dogmas or else on things outside the sphere of human history.

One of the perennial infirmities of human beings is to ascribe their own failure to forces that are entirely beyond their control. This mental manoeuvre is particularly attractive to sensitive minds in periods of decline and fall; and in the decline and fall of the Hellenic Civilization it was a commonplace of various schools of philosophers to explain the social decay which they deplored but could not arrest as the incidental and inevitable effect on an all-pervasive onset of 'cosmic senescence.' This was the philosophy of Lucretius (cf. *De Rerum Natura*, Bk. II, ll. 1144–74) in the last generation of the Hellenic time of troubles, and the same theme recurs in a work of controversy written by one of the Fathers of the Western Church, St. Cyprian, when the Hellenic universal state was beginning to break up three hundred years later. He writes:

'You ought to be aware that the age is now senile. It has not now the stamina that used to make it upstanding, nor the vigour and robustness that used to make it strong. . . . There is a diminution in the winter rains that give nourishment to the seeds in the earth, and in the summer heats that ripen the harvests. . . . This is the sentence that has been passed upon the World; this is the law of God; that what has been must die, and what has grown up must grow old.'

* * *

However, our latter-day Western advocates of a predestinarian or deterministic explanation of the breakdowns of civilization do not attempt to link up the destinies of these human institutions with the destiny of the Physical Universe as a whole. They appeal instead to a law of senescence and death with a shorter wave-length, for which they claim jurisdiction over the whole kingdom of life on this planet. Spengler, whose method is to set up a metaphor and then proceed to argue from it as if it were a law based on observed phenomena, declares that every civilization passes through the same succession of ages as a human being; but his eloquence on this theme nowhere amounts to proof, and we have already noticed that societies are not in any sense living organisms. In subjective terms societies are the intelligible fields of historical study. In objective terms, they are the common ground between the respective fields of activity of a number of individual human beings, who are themselves living organisms but who cannot conjure up a giant in their own image out of the intersection of their own shadows and then breathe into this unsubstantial body the breath of their own life. The individual energies of all the human beings who constitute the so-called 'members' of a society are the vital forces whose operation works out the history of that society, including its time-span. To declare dogmatically that every society has a predestined time-span is as foolish as it would be to declare that every play is bound to contain just so many acts.

We may dismiss the theory that breakdowns occur when each civilization draws near the close of its biological life-span, because civilizations are entities of a kind that is not subject to the laws of biology; but there is another theory which suggests that, for some reason unexplained, the biological quality of the individuals whose mutual relations constitute a civilization mysteriously declines after a certain or uncertain number of generations; in fact, that the experience of civilization is in the long run essentially and irremediably dysgenic.

* * *

We have now disposed of three deterministic explanations of the breakdowns of civilizations: the theory that they are due to the 'running down' of the 'clockwork' of the Universe or to the senscence of the Earth; the theory that a civilization, like a living organism, has a life-span determined by the biological laws of its nature; and the theory that the breakdowns are due to a deterioration in the quality of the individuals participating in a civilization, as a result of their pedigrees' accumulating too long a tale of 'civilized' ancestors. We have still to consider one further hypothesis, generally referred to as the cyclical theory of history.

The invention of this theory of cycles in the history of Mankind was a natural corollary to the sensational astronomical discovery, apparently made in the Babylonic Society at some date between the eighth and sixth centuries B.C., that the three conspicuous and familiar cycles—the day-and-night, the lunar month and the solar year—were not the only examples of periodic recurrence in the movements of the heavenly bodies; that there was also a larger co-ordination of stellar movements embracing all the planets as well as Earth, Moon and Sun; and that 'the music of the spheres', which was made by the harmony of this heavenly chorus, came round full circle, chord for chord, in a great cycle which dwarfed the solar year into insignificance. The inference was that the annual birth and death of vegetation, which was manifestly governed by the solar cycle, had its counterpart in a recurrent birth and death of all things on the time-scale of the cosmic cycle.

*   *   *

Does reason constrain us to believe, quite apart from any alleged influence of the stars, in a cyclic movement of human history? Have we not, in the course of this Study, ourselves given encouragement to such a supposition? What of those movements of Yin and Yang, Challenge and Response, Withdrawal and Return, Apparentation and Affiliation, which we have elucidated? Are they not variations on the trite theme that 'History repeats itself'? Certainly, in the movement of all these forces that weave the web of human history, there is an obvious element of recurrence. Yet the shuttle which shoots backwards and forwards across the loom of Time in a perpetual to-and-fro is all this time bringing into existence a tapestry in which there is manifestly a developing design and not simply an endless repetition of the same pattern. This, too, we have seen again and again. The metaphor of the wheel in itself offers an illustration of recurrence being concurrent with progress. The movement of the wheel is admittedly repetitive in relation to the wheel's own axle, but the wheel has only been made and fitted to its axle in order to give mobility to a vehicle of which the wheel is merely a part, and the fact that the vehicle, which is the wheel's *raison d'être*, can only move in virtue of the wheel's circular movement round its axle does not compel the vehicle itself to travel like a merry-go-round in a circular track.

This harmony of two diverse movements—a major irreversible movement which is born on the wings of a minor repetitive movement—is perhaps the essence of what we mean by rhythm; and we can discern this play of forces not only in vehicular traction and in modern machinery but likewise in the organic rhythm of life.

* * *

Thus the detection of periodic repetitive movements in our analysis of the process of civilization does not imply that the process itself is of the same cyclic order as they are. On the contrary, if any inference can legitimately be drawn from the periodicity of these minor movements, we may rather infer that the major movement which they bear along is not recurrent but progressive. Humanity is not an Ixion bound for ever to his wheel nor a Sisyphus for ever rolling his stone to the summit of the same mountain and helplessly watching it roll down again.

This is a message of encouragement for us children of the Western Civilization as we drift to-day alone, with none but stricken civilizations around us. It may be that Death the Leveller will lay icy hand on our civilization also. But we are not confronted with any *Saeva Necessitas.* The dead civilizations are not dead by fate, or 'in the course of nature,' and therefore our living civilization is not doomed inexorably in advance to 'join the majority' of its species. Though sixteen civilizations may have perished already to our knowledge, and nine others may be now at the point of death, we—the twenty-sixth—are not compelled to submit the riddle of our fate to the blind arbitrament of statistics. The divine spark of creative power is still alive in us, and, if we have the grace to kindle it into flame, then the stars in their courses cannot defeat our efforts to attain the goal of human endeavor.

* * *

The Disintegrations of Civilizations

These considerations and comparisons suggest that we are already far advanced in our time of troubles; and, if we ask what has been our most conspicuous and specific trouble in the recent past, the answer clearly is: nationalistic internecine warfare, reinforced, as has been pointed out in an earlier part of this Study, by the combined 'drive' of energies generated by the recently released forces of Democracy and Industrialism. We may date the incidence of this scourge from the outbreak of the French Revolutionary wars at the end of the eighteenth century. But, when we examined this subject before, we were confronted by the fact that, in the modern chapter of our Western history, this bout of violent warfare was not the first but the second of its kind. The earlier bout is represented by the so-called Wars of Religion which devastated Western Christendom from the middle of the sixteenth to the middle of the seventeenth century, and we found that between these two bouts of violent warfare there intervenes a century in which warfare was a comparatively mild disease, a 'sport of kings,' not exacerbated by fanaticism in either the religious sectarian or the democratic national vein. Thus, in our own history too, we find what we have come to recognize as the typical pattern of a time of troubles: a breakdown, a rally and a second relapse.

We can discern why the eighteenth-century rally in the course of our time of troubles was abortive and ephemeral; it was because the toleration achieved by 'the Enlightenment' was a toleration based not on the Christian virtues of faith, hope and charity but on the Mephistophelian maladies of disillusionment, apprehension and cynicism. It was not an arduous achievement of religious fervour but a facile by-product of its abatement.

Can we at all foresee the outcome of the second and still more violent bout of warfare into which out Western World has fallen in consequence of the spiritual inadequacy of its eighteenth-century Enlightenment? If we are to try to look into our future, we may begin by reminding ourselves that, though all the other civilizations whose history is known to us may be either dead or dying, a civilization is not like an animal organism, condemned by an inexorable destiny to die after traversing a predetermined life-curve. Even if all other civilizations that have come into existence so far were to prove in fact to have followed this path, there is no known law of historical determinism that compels us to leap out of the intolerable frying-pan of our time of troubles into the slow and steady fire of a universal state where we shall in due course be reduced to dust and ashes. At the same time, such precedents from the histories of other civilizations and from the life-course of nature are bound to appear formidable in the sinister light of our present situation. This chapter itself was written on the eve of the outbreak of the General War of 1939–45 for readers who had already lived through the General War of 1914–18, and it was recast for re-publication on the morrow of the ending of the second of these two world wars within one lifetime by the invention and employment of a bomb in which a newly contrived release of atomic energy has been directed by man to the destruction of human life and works on an unprecedented scale. This swift succession of catastrophic events on a steeply mounting gradient inevitably inspires a dark doubt about our future, and this doubt threatens to undermine our faith and hope at a critical eleventh hour which calls for the utmost exertion of these saving spiritual faculties. Here is a challenge which we cannot evade, and our destiny depends on our response.

'I dreamed, and behold I saw a man cloathed with rags, standing in a certain place, with his face from his own house, a book in his hand and a great burden upon his back. I looked, and saw him open the book and read therein; and as he read he wept and trembled; and, not being able longer to contain, he broke out with a lamentable cry saying "What shall I do?"

It was not without cause that Bunyan's 'Christian' was so greatly distressed.

'I am for certain informed (said he) that this our city will be burned with fire from Heaven—in which fearful overthrow both myself with thee my wife and you my sweet babes shall miserably come to ruine, except (the which yet I see not) some way of escape can be found, whereby we may be delivered.'

What response to this challenge is Christian going to make? Is he going to look this way and that as if he would run, yet stand still because he cannot tell which way to go? Or will he begin to run—and run on crying 'Life! Life! Eternal Life!'—with his eye set on a shining light and his feet bound for a distant wicket-gate? If the answer to this question depended on nobody but Christian himself, our knowledge of the uniformity of human nature might incline us to predict that Christian's imminent destiny was Death in his City of Destruction. But in the classic version of the myth we are told that the human protagonist was not left entirely to his own resources in the decisive hour. According to John Bunyan, Christian was saved by his encounter with Evangelist. And, inasmuch as it cannot be supposed that God's nature is less constant than Man's, we may and must pray that a reprive which God has granted to our society once will not be refused if we ask for it again in a humble spirit and with a contrite heart.

TEILHARD DE CHARDIN: *The Phenomenon of Man* *

Not all twentieth-century philosophies of history are pessimistic. In *The Phenomenon of Man* (published posthumously in France in 1955) Pierre Teilhard de Chardin views history in the long time perspective of evolution and comes to decidedly optimistic conclusions. Teilhard (1881–1955), Jesuit Father and noted paleontologist, was professor of geology at the Catholic Institute of Paris, corresponding member of the Académie des Sciences, and for many years scientific adviser to the Geological Survey of China.

A New Phase of Evolution

WE ARE, at this very moment, passing through an age of *transition*. . . .

. . . To us, in our brief span of life, falls the honour and good fortune of coinciding with a critical change of the noosphere.

In these confused and restless zones in which present blends with future in a world of upheaval, we stand face to face with all the grandeur, the unprecedented grandeur, of the phenomenon of man. Here if anywhere, now if ever, have we, more legitimately than any of our predecessors, the right to think that we can measure the importance and detect the direction of the process of hominisation. Let us look carefully and try to understand. And to do so let us probe beneath the surface and try to decipher the particular form of mind which is coming to birth in the womb of the earth today. . . .

In the last century and a half the most prodigious event, perhaps, ever recorded by history since the threshold of reflection has been taking place in our minds: the definitive access of consciousness to a *scale of new dimensions;* and in consequence the birth of an entirely renewed universe, without any change of line or feature by the simple transformation of its intimate substance.

Until that time the world seemed to rest, static and fragmentable, on the three axes of its geometry. Now it is a casting from a single mould.

What makes and classifies a 'modern' man (and a whole host of our contemporaries is not yet 'modern' in this sense) is having become capable of seeing in terms not of space and time alone, but also of duration, or—and it comes to the same thing—of biological space-time; and above all having become incapable of seeing anything otherwise—anything—*not even himself.* . . .

. . . Man discovers that *he is nothing else than evolution become conscious of itself,* to borrow Julian Huxley's concise expression. It seems to me that our modern minds (because and inasmuch as they are modern) will never find rest until they settle down to this view. On this summit and on this summit alone are repose and illumination waiting for us. . . .

[However, it is not enough to say] that evolution, by becoming conscious of itself in the depths of ourselves, only needs to look at itself in the mirror to perceive itself in all its depths and to decipher itself. In addition it becomes free to dispose of itself—it can give itself or refuse itself. Not only do we read in our slightest acts the secret of its proceedings; but for an elementary part *we hold it in our hands,* responsible for its past to its future.

Is this grandeur or servitude? Therein lies the whole problem of action.

A Feeling to Be Overcome: Discouragement

The reasons behind the scepticism regarding mankind which is fashionable among 'enlightened' people today are not merely of a representative order. Even when the intellectual difficulties of the mind in conceiving the collective and visualising space-time have been overcome, we are left with another and perhaps a still more serious form of hesitation which is bound up with the incoherent aspect presented by the world of man today. The nineteenth century had lived in sight of a promised land. It thought that we were on the threshold of a Golden Age, lit up and organised by science, warmed by fraternity. Instead of that, we find ourselves slipped back into a world of spreading and ever more tragic dissension. Though possible and even perhaps probable in theory, the idea of a spirit of the earth does not stand up to the test of experience. No, man will never succeed in going beyond man by uniting with himself. That Utopia must be abandoned as soon as possible and there is no more to be said.

To explain or efface the appearances of a setback which, if it were true, would not only dispel a beautiful dream but encourage us to weigh up a radical absurdity of the universe, I would like to point out in the first place that to speak of experience—of the results of experience—in such a connection is premature to say the least of it. After all half a million years, perhaps even a million, were required for life to pass from the pre-hominids to modern man. Should we now start wringing our hands because, less than two centuries after glimpsing a higher state, modern man is still at loggerheads with himself? Once again we have got things out of focus. To have understood the immensity around us, behind us, and in front of us is already a first step. But if to this perception of depth another perception, that of *slowness*, be not added, we must realise that the transposition of values remains incomplete and that it can beget for our gaze nothing but an impossible world. Each dimension has its proper rhythm. Planetary movement involves planetary majesty. Would not humanity seem to us altogether static if, behind its history, there were not the endless stretch of its prehistory? Similarly, and despite an almost explosive acceleration of noogenesis at our level, we cannot expect to see the earth transform itself under our eyes in the space of a generation. Let us keep calm and take heart.

In spite of all evidence to the contrary, mankind may very well be advancing all round us at the moment—there are in fact many signs whereby we can reasonably suppose that it is advancing. But, if it is doing so, it must be—as is the way with very big things—doing so almost imperceptibly.

Love as Energy

We are accustomed to consider (and with what a refinement of analysis!) only the sentimental face of love, the joy and miseries it causes us. It is in its natural dynamism and its evolutionary significance that I shall be dealing with it here, with a view to determining the ultimate phases of the phenomenon of man.

Considered in its full biological reality, love—that is to say the affinity of being with being—is not peculiar to man. It is a general property of all life and as such it embraces, in its varieties and degrees, all the forms successively adopted by organised matter. In the mammals, so close to ourselves, it is easily recognised in its different modalities: sexual passion, parental instinct, social solidarity, etc. Farther off, that is to say lower down on the tree of life, analogies are more obscure until they become so faint as to be imperceptible. But this is the place to repeat what I said earlier when we were discussing the '*within* of things.' If there were no internal propensity to unite, even at a prodigiously rudimentary level—indeed in the molecule itself—it would be physically impossible for love to appear higher up, with us, in 'hominised' form. By rights, to be certain of its presence in ourselves, we should assume its presence, at least in an inchoate form, in everything that is. And in fact if we look around us at the confluent ascent of consciousnesses, we see it is not lacking anywhere. . . .

Mankind, the spirit of the earth, the synthesis of individuals and peoples, the paradoxical conciliation of the element with the whole, and of unity with multitude—all these are called Utopian and yet they are biologically necessary. And for them to be incarnated in the world all we may well need is to imagine our power of loving developing until it embraces the total of men and of the earth.

The Ultimate Earth

With that said, we have now to ask: *along what lines* of advance, among others—judging from the present condition of the noosphere—are we destined to proceed from the planetary level of psychic totalisation and evolutionary upsurge we are now approaching?

I can distinguish three principal ones in which we see again the predictions to which we were already led by our analysis of the ideas of science and humanity. They are: the organisation of research, the concentration of research upon the subject of man, and the conjunction of science and religion. These are three natural terms of one and the same progression. . . .

We can envisage a world whose constantly increasing 'leisure' and heightened interest would find their vital issue in fathoming everything, trying everything, extending everything; a world in which giant telescopes and atom smashers would absorb more money and excite more spontaneous admiration than all the bombs and cannons put together; a world in which, not only for the restricted band of paid research-workers, but also for the man in the street, the day's ideal would be the wresting of another secret or another force from corpuscles, stars, or organised matter; a world in which, as happens already, one gives one's life to be and to know, rather than to possess. That, on an estimate of the forces engaged, is what is being relentlessly prepared around us.

In some of the lower organisms the retina is, as it were, spread over the whole surface of the body. In somewhat the same way human vision is still diffuse in its operation, mixed up with industrial activity and war. Biologically it needs to individualise itself independently, with its own distinct organs. It will not be long now before the noosphere finds its eyes. . . .

. . . Man, the knowing subject, will perceive at last that man, 'the object of knowledge,' is the key to the whole science of nature. . . .

. . . So far we have certainly allowed our race to develop at random, and we have given too little thought to the question of what medical and moral factors *must replace the crude forces of natural selection* should we suppress them. In the course of the coming centuries it is indispensable that a nobly human form of eugenics, on a standard worthy of our personalities, should be discovered and developed.

Eugenics applied to individuals leads to eugenics applied to society. . . . Points involved are: the distribution of the resources of the globe; the control of the trek towards unpopulated areas; the optimum use of the powers set free by mechanisation; the physiology of nations and races; geo-economy, geo-politics, geo-demography; the organisation of research developing into a reasoned organisation of the earth. Whether we like it or not, all the signs and all our needs converge in the same direction. We need and are irresistibly being led to create, by means of and beyond all physics, all biology and all psychology, *a science of human energetics.*

It is in the course of that creation, already obscurely begun, that science, by being led to concentrate on man, will find itself increasingly face to face with religion.

To outward appearance, the modern world was born of an antireligious movement: man becoming self-sufficient and reason supplanting belief. Our generation and the two that preceded it have heard little but talk of the conflict between science and faith; indeed it seemed at one moment a foregone conclusion that the former was destined to take the place of the latter.

But, inasmuch as the tension is prolonged, the conflict visibly seems to need to be resolved in terms of an entirely different form of equilibrium—not in elimination, nor duality, but in synthesis. After close on two centuries of passionate struggles, neither science nor faith has succeeded in discrediting its adversary. On the contrary, it becomes obvious that neither can develop normally without the other. And the reason is simple: the same life animates both. Neither in its impetus nor its achievements can science go to its limits without becoming tinged with mysticism and charged with faith.

Firstly *in its impetus.* We touched on this point when dealing with the problem of action. Man will only continue to work and to research so long as he is prompted by a passionate interest. Now this interest is entirely dependent on the conviction, strictly undemonstrable to science, that the universe has a direction and that it could—indeed, if we are faithful, it *should*—result in some sort of irreversible perfection. Hence comes belief in progress. . . .

In short, as soon as science outgrows the analytic investigations which constitute its lower and preliminary stages, and passes on to synthesis—synthesis which naturally culminates in the realisation of some superior state of humanity—it is at once led to foresee and place its stakes on the *future* and on the *all*. And with that it out-distances itself and emerges in terms of *option* and *adoration*.

Thus Renan and the nineteenth century were not wrong to speak of a Religion of Science. Their mistake was not to see that their cult ΄of humanity implied the re-integration, in a renewed form, of those very spiritual forces they claimed to be getting rid of. . . .

Always pushing forward in the three directions we have just indicated, and taking advantage of the immense duration it has still to live, mankind has enormous possibilities before it.

Bibliographical Note[*]

1. *On Intellectuals and Intellectual History*

Intellectual history, the history of ideas, and the sociology of knowledge are closely related but not entirely synonymous fields of study. J. H. Robinson's *Mind in the Making* (Harper, 1921) was one of the first books to introduce intellectual history to Americans. A. O. Lovejoy elucidated the working concepts and methods of the history of ideas in many articles and books, notably in *The Great Chain of Being* (Harvard, 1936; Harper, 1965), chap. 1, and in "Reflections on the History of Ideas," *Journal of the History of Ideas*, 1 (1940). An article by R. K. Merton in *Isis*, 27 (1937) gives the viewpoint of "The Sociology of Knowledge."

A number of more recent articles, some of them critical particularly of the history of ideas as expounded by Lovejoy, are the following: Franklin L. Baumer, "Intellectual History and its Problems," *Journal of Modern History*, 21 (1949) (also available in the Bobbs-Merrill Reprint Series in History); Maurice Mandelbaum, "The History of Ideas, Intellectual History, and the History of Philosophy," *History and Theory*, Beiheft 5 (1965); Hajo Holborn, "The History of Ideas," *American Historical Review*, 73 (1968); Quentin Skinner, "Meaning and Understanding in the History of Ideas," *History and Theory*, 8 (1969); Felix Gilbert, "Intellectual History: Its Aims and Methods," *Daedalus*, 100 (1971); and Leonard Krieger, "The Autonomy of Intellectual History," *Journal of the History of Ideas*, 34 (1973).

No bibliography of intellectual history should fail to include F. M. Cornford's brilliant essay on unwritten assumptions in *The Unwritten Philosophy and Other Essays* (Cambridge, 1950), and Carl Becker's equally brilliant discussion of "climates of opinion" in *The Heavenly City of the Eighteenth-Century Philosophers* (Yale, 1932, 1968). See also W. Warren Wagar's discussion of "world views" in his *World Views: A Study in Comparative History* (Dryden, 1977). Articles by Karl Mannheim in *Essays on the Sociology of Culture* (Routledge & Paul, 1956) and the compilation by George B. de Huszar entitled *The Intellectuals* (Free Press, 1960) supply interesting and controversial views of the intellectuals, their history and role in society.

[*] This bibliography consists primarily of general works in English, and includes few monographs or studies of individual thinkers. Dates of publication refer to the first edition of a book (or to the date when it was first translated into English) and to the most recent edition known to the author of *Main Currents of Western Thought*. Publishers' names have been abbreviated and translators' names omitted for the sake of brevity.

2. *General*

Since J. H. Randall's pioneering *The Making of the Modern Mind* (Houghton Mifflin, 1926, 1940), general surveys of the intellectual history of the West have been coming thick and fast. Crane Brinton's *Ideas and Men* (Prentice-Hall, 1950, 1963) cuts the widest swath, beginning with the Greeks and ending with the mid-twentieth century. P. Smith's two-volume *A History of Modern Culture* (Holt, 1930–34; Collier, 1962) and J. Bronowski's *The Western Intellectual Tradition* (Harper, 1960, 1962) go only, respectively, from 1543 to 1776 and from Leonardo da Vinci to Hegel. The two-volume intellectual history by W. R. Coates, H. V. White, and J. S. Schapiro, *The Emergence of Liberal Humanism* and *The Ordeal of Liberal Humanism* (McGraw-Hill, 1966–70), commences with the Renaissance, whereas Roland Stromberg's *An Intellectual History of Modern Europe* (Appleton, 1966) commences about 1590. Franklin L. Baumer's *Modern European Thought* (Macmillan, 1977) pursues the theme "from being to becoming" from 1600 to 1950.

For religious ideas, see Basil Willey's suggestive little book, *Christianity Past and Present* (Cambridge, 1952); my *Religion and the Rise of Scepticism* (Harcourt, 1960, 1969), which traces the history of "the sceptical tradition" from the seventeenth century to the present "Age of Longing"; and *God in Modern Philosophy* by James Collins (Regnery, 1959, 1967), which commences wih Cusanus and Calvin. Two particularly fine histories of philosophy have appeared in recent years: Frederick Copleston's *A History of Philosophy*, 8 vols. (Newman, 1963–66), and J. H. Randall's *The Career of Philosophy*, 2 vols. (Columbia, 1962, 1965), of which the latter is much the more broadly gauged. W. T. Jones's *A History of Western Philosophy* (Harcourt, 1952, 1969) is a useful one-volume work. For scientific ideas and theories of nature, see R. G. Collingwood's *The Idea of Nature* (Oxford, 1945, 1960) and W. C. Dampier's *A History of Science* (Cambridge, 1929, 1958), the latter notable for relating science to philosophy and religion. In the realm of political ideas G. Sabine's *A History of Political Theory* (Holt, 1937; Dryden, 1973) still stands out, as does Hans Kohn's *The Idea of Nationalism* (Macmillan, 1944, 1948) which, however, comes down only to the end of the eighteenth century. The following books are suggestive for philosophies of history: R. G. Collingwood's *The Idea of History* (Oxford, 1946, 1957); Karl Löwith's *Meaning in History* (Chicago, 1949); and Bruce Mazlish's *The Riddle of History: The Great Speculators from Vico to Freud* (Harper, 1966; Minerva, 1968).

Students are also referred to pertinent articles in the *Dictionary of the History of Ideas, International Encyclopedia of the Social Sciences, Encyclopedia of Philosophy, Catholic Encyclopedia, Schaff-Herzog Encyclopedia of Religious Knowledge, Hastings Encyclopaedia of Religion and Ethics;* also to the following journals: *Journal of the History of Ideas, Isis* (for science and "its cultural influences"), and *History and Theory* (for the philosophy of history). *Political Theory* includes some articles on the history of political ideas.

of the chief presuppositions of seventeenth-century thought. So does Paul Hazard's classic *The European Mind, 1680–1715* (Yale, 1953; World Publishing Co., 1967) which was originally published in 1935 under the much more exciting title of *La crise de la conscience européenne*. Meyrick Carré's *Phases of Thought in England* (Clarendon, 1949) deals with more than English thought, and with more than the seventeenth century. Gerald Cragg's *Freedom and Authority* (Westminster, 1975) is the most recent overview of seventeenth-century English thought.

The Origins of Modern Science by Herbert Butterfield (G. Bell, 1949; Free Press, 1968) is perhaps the best single book on the "scientific revolution" as such. A. R. Hall's *The Scientific Revolution 1500–1800* (Longmans, 1954; Beacon, 1970) and Crombie's *Augustine to Galileo*, mentioned above under "The Middle Ages," provide excellent reviews of the specifically scientific achievements of the sixteenth and seventeenth centuries. Thomas Kuhn's *The Structure of Scientific Revolutions* (Chicago, 1962, 1970) deals in general with "the nature, causes, and consequences of revolutions in basic scientific concepts." M. Ornstein's *The Role of Scientific Societies in the Seventeenth Century* (Chicago, 1928; Archon, 1963) is a good general book on the new scientific academies, and Mark Curtis' *Oxford and Cambridge in Transition 1558–1642* (Oxford, 1959) has an interesting chapter on science and the universities.

For the interconnection between the new science and philosophy E. A. Burtt's *The Metaphysical Foundations of Modern Physical Science* (Harcourt, 1927; Doubleday, 1955) is indispensable, as are Alexandre Koyré's *From the Closed World to the Infinite Universe* (Johns Hopkins, 1957) and A. O. Lovejoy's *The Great Chain of Being*, mentioned above under "On Intellectuals and Intellectual History": the former especially for the new ideas about infinity and the plurality of worlds, the latter for its discussion of Copernicus and Giordano Bruno. For the impact of science on other areas of thought, see Basil Willey's *The Seventeenth Century Background* (Chatto & Windus, 1934; Doubleday, 1953) which examines "the thought of the age in relation to Religion and Poetry"; Richard S. Westfall's *Science and Religion in Seventeenth-Century England* (Yale, 1958); Marjorie Nicolson's *The Breaking of the Circle: Studies in the Effect of the "New Science" upon Seventeenth-Century Poetry* (Northwestern, 1950; Columbia, 1960); and G. N. Clark's *Science and Social Welfare in the Age of Newton* (Clarendon, 1937, 1949). R. F. Jones' *Ancients and Moderns* (Washington University, St. Louis, 1936; California, 1965) examines new educational ideas and attitudes toward history in the light of the new science. See also on seventeenth-century interpretations of history Victor Harris, *All Coherence Gone* (Chicago, 1949) and Ernest Tuveson, *Millenium and Utopia: A Study in the Background of the Idea of Progress* (California, 1949).

Good books on other important aspects of seventeenth-century thought are these: on philosophy, Richard Popkin's *The History of Skepticism from Erasmus to Descartes* (Van Gorcum, 1960; Harper, 1968); on religion, Jan Miel, *Pascal and Theology* (Johns Hopkins, 1969); and on political thought J. N. Figgis, *The Divine Right of Kings* (Cambridge, 1914; Harper, 1965),

3. The Middle Ages

The Mind of the Middle Ages by F. B. Artz (Knopf, 1953, 1959) is a useful survey with extensive bibliography. David Knowles' *The Evolution of Medieval Thought* (Helicon, 1962; Random House, 1964), and Gordon Leff's *Medieval Thought* (Penguin, 1958; Quadrangle, 1959) are also good general accounts. William J. Brandt's *The Shape of Medieval History: Studies in Modes of Perception* (Yale, 1966) calls attention to some fundamental assumptions of medieval thinking.

See especially C. N. Cochrane's *Christianity and Classical Culture* (Clarendon, 1940, 1957) for the relationship between medieval and classical thought. The first volume of Jaroslav Pelikan's projected five-volume history of Christian doctrine deals with the early Middle Ages: *The Emergence of the Catholic Tradition* (Chicago, 1971). Religious dissent has attracted much attention in recent years. See on this subject Jeffrey B. Russell, *Religious Dissent in the Middle Ages* (Wiley, 1971), Austin B. Evans, *Heresies of the High Middle Ages* (Columbia, 1969), and Gordon Leff, *Heresy in the Later Middle Ages* (Barnes & Noble, 1967).

On medieval philosophy, studies by Etienne Gilson and F. C. Copleston rank at the top: *The History of Christian Philosophy in the Middle Ages* (Random House, 1955) and *The Spirit of Medieval Philosophy* (Scribner's, 1936, 1940) by Gilson, and *A History of Medieval Philosophy* (Methuen, 1972; Harper, 1974) by Copleston. See A. C. Crombie's *Augustine to Galileo: The History of Science A. D. 400–1650* (Falcon, 1952; Penguin, 1969) for science; Herschel Baker's *The Dignity of Man* (Harvard, 1947) for conceptions of the nature of man; C. H. McIlwain's *The Growth of Political Thought in the West* (Macmillan, 1932, 1959) and W. Ullman's *A History of Political Thought: The Middle Ages* (Penguin, 1965) for political and social ideas. J. N. Figgis's classic *The Political Aspects of St. Augustine's 'City of God'* (Longmans, 1921; Peter Smith, 1963) is still worth consulting for philosophy of history, as are two stimulating articles by, respectively, G. La Piana and T. Mommsen: "Theology of History," in *The Interpretation of History*, J. R. Strayer (ed.) (Princeton, 1943), and "St. Augustine and the Christian Idea of Progress," *Journal of the History of Ideas*, 12 (1951).

4. The Renaissance

W. K. Ferguson's *The Renaissance in Historical Thought* (Houghton Mifflin, 1948) describes the major interpretations of the Renaissance from the fourteenth century to the twentieth. See also on interpretation Federico Chabod's brilliant essay "The Concept of the Renaissance" in *Machiavelli and the Renaissance* (Harvard, 1958) and Douglas Bush's *The Renaissance and English Humanism* (Toronto, 1939).

Denis Hay's *The Italian Renaissance in its Historical Background* (Cambridge, 1961, 1977) is a good general study. See also *The Renaissance: Six essays* (Metropolitan Museum of Art, 1953; Harper, 1962). Eugenio Garin's

Italian Humanism and Civic Life in the Renaissance (Basil Blackwell, 1965) is particularly good on Italy, Lewis Spitz's *The Religious Renaissance of the German Humanists* (Harvard, 1963) on Germany, Werner Gundersheimer (ed.), *French Humanism 1470–1600* (Harper, 1969, 1970) on France, and A. L. Rowse's *The Elizabethan Renaissance* (Scribner's, 1972) on England. Roland Bainton's *Erasmus of Christendom* (Scribner's, 1969) is the best recent book on Erasmus and Christian humanism.

For the role of the classics in Renaissance thought see further R. R. Bolgar's *The Classical Heritage and its Beneficiaries* (Cambridge, 1954); for philosophy, Paul Kristeller's *Renaissance Thought* (Harper, 1961, 1965) and *Eight Philosophers of the Italian Renaissance* (Stanford, 1964); for cosmology and conceptions of the nature of man, E. M. W. Tillyard's *The Elizabethan World Picture* (Chatto & Windus, 1943), Theodore Spencer's *Shakespeare and the Nature of Man* (Macmillan, Ltd., 1942, 1949), Ernst Cassirer (ed.), *The Renaissance Philosophy of Man* (Chicago, 1948, 1969), and Charles Trinkaus's *In Our Image and Likeness: Humanity and Divinity in Italian Humanist Thought*, 2 vols. (Chicago, 1970); for art and the growing prestige of art, the appropriate chapters in Leonardo Olschki's *The Genius of Italy* (Oxford, 1949; Cornell, 1964).

By now the literature on Machiavelli is enormous. J. W. Allen's *A History of Political Thought in the Sixteenth Century* (Methuen, 1928, 1957) is still well worth reading on the subject. Articles by Eric Cochrane ("Machiavelli: 1940–1960," *Journal of Modern History*, 33, 1961) and John Geerken, "Machiavelli Studies since 1969," *Journal of the History of Ideas*, 37, 1976) review the more recent literature. For those interested in the tangled web of the Renaissance and science, Marie Boas Hall's *The Scientific Renaissance, 1450–1630* (Harper, 1962) is indispensable. On the same subject see also the interesting discussion by Dana Durand and Hans Baron in the *Journal of the History of Ideas*, 4 (1943), and Eric Cochrane's article "Science and Humanism in the Italian Renaissance" in the *American Historical Review*, 81 (1976).

5. The Confessional Age

H. J. Grimm's *The Reformation Era* (Macmillan, 1954, 1973), a general work, includes an excellent bibliography summarizing the latest work in Reformation thought. Ernst Troeltsch's *Protestantism and Progress* (Williams & Norgate, 1912; Beacon Hill, 1958) is still basic reading for interpretation. Robert M. Kingdon (ed.), *Transition and Revolution: Problems and Issues of European Renaissance and Reformation History* (Burgess, 1974) contains valuable interpretative essays. E. H. Harbison's *The Christian Scholar in the Age of the Reformation* (Scribner's, 1956) interprets the Reformation as a "scholars' revolution" and is also notable for linking Protestant scholarship to the patristic age and the Renaissance.

A. C. McGiffert's *Protestant Thought before Kant* (Scribner's, 1911; Harper, 1962) stands up as an excellent brief survey of the main strands of Protestant thought. Lewis W. Beck deals briefly but well with Protestant

philosophy in *Early German Philosophy* (Harvard, 1969). James Mackinnon's *Luther and the Reformation*, vol. 1 (Longmans, Green, 1925) is particularly good on the relationship between Lutheran and medieval thought. Other more recent works on Luther are Roland Bainton's *Here I Stand* (Abingdon-Cokesbury, 1950; New American Library, 1963) and Gerhard Ebeling's *Luther: An Introduction to His Thought* (Fortress, 1970).

J. T. McNeill's *The History and Character of Calvinism* (Oxford, 1954, 1967) surveys the whole movement. François Wendel focuses on Calvin in *Calvin: The Origins and Development of His Religious Thought* (Harper, 1963). Marshall Knappen's *Tudor Puritanism* (Chicago, 1939; P. Smith, 1963) is still the best comprehensive study of that subject. But see further John New's *Anglican and Puritan* (Stanford, 1964) for the ideas that divided these two groups from 1558 to 1640.

In recent years there has been growing interest in what has been called the left wing of the Reformation. Roland Bainton's general article by that title in the *Journal of Religion*, 21 (1941) is especially recommended. Oher studies of note are James Stayer's *Anabaptists and the Sword* (Coronado, 1972) and Steven Ozment's *Mysticism and Dissent: Religious Ideology and Social Protest in the Sixteenth Century* (Yale, 1973). P. Janelle's *The Counter Reformation* (Bruce, 1949) remains one of the best books on that subject. E. M. Burns' book by the same title (Van Nostrand, 1964) is another.

Troeltsch's *The Social Teaching of the Christian Churches*, vol. 2 (George Allen & Unwin, 1931) is the classic on that subject, distinguishing between "church-type" and "sect-type." J. W. Allen's book, mentioned under "The Renaissance," is still the best general study of the political thought of the reformers, but see also A. S. P. Woodhouse's *Puritanism and Liberty* (Dent, 1938) and Perez Zagorin's book, mentioned below under "The Scientific Revolution." Detailed studies of the toleration controversy abound, among them Bainton's *The Travail of Religious Liberty* (Westminster, 1951; Harper, 1958), J. Lecler's *Toleration and the Reformation* (Association, 1960), and W. K. Jordan's *The Development of Religious Toleration in England* (Harvard, 1932–40). See also Keith Thomas' *Religion and the Decline of Magic* (Scribner's, 1971) which deals with contemporary witchcraft in England and how it was tolerated. For the interconnection between economic ideas and religion Max Weber's *The Protestant Ethic and the Spirit of Capitalism* (Scribner's, 1930, 1958) is, of course, prescribed reading, as is also R. H. Tawney's *Religion and the Rise of Capitalism* (Murray, 1926; New American Library, 1963). See also in this connection B. N. Nelson's *The Idea of Usury* (Princeton, 1949; Chicago, 1969).

6. The Scientific Revolution

G. N. Clark's *The Seventeenth Century* (Clarendon, 1929; Oxford, 1961) and Carl Friedrich's *The Age of the Baroque, 1610–1660* (Harper, 1952) both have chapters on seventeenth-century thought, including scientific thought. Louis Bredvold's *The Intellectual Milieu of John Dryden* (Michigan, 1934, 1956) does much more than its title describes; it delves into some

Perez Zagorin, *A History of Political Thought in the English Revolution*
(Routledge & Paul, 1954), and Richard Aaron's *John Locke* (Oxford, 1937,
1971) which also treats Locke's thought as a whole. Hugh Honour's *The
New Golden Land: European Images of America from the Discoveries to
the Present Time* (Pantheon, 1975) deals with both the art and the literature
of the subject.

7. *The Enlightenment*

Everybody should read for its thesis Carl Becker's *The Heavenly City of
the Eighteenth-Century Philosophers* (Yale, 1932, 1969). See, however, the
reassessment of it in R. O. Rockwood (ed.), *Carl Becker's Heavenly City
Revisited* (Cornell, 1958), and the reexamination of recent interpretations in
general in Franco Venturi's *Utopia and Reform in the Enlightenment*
(Cambridge, 1971).

General works of merit include Paul Hazard's *European Thought in the
Eighteenth Century* (Yale, 1954); Ernst Cassirer's *The Philosophy of the
Enlightenment* (Princeton, 1951; Beacon, 1960) which covers all areas of
thought, not only philosophy; A. Cobban (ed.), *The Eighteenth Century:
Europe in the Age of the Enlightenment* (Thames & Hudson, 1969); Peter
Gay's *The Enlightenment*, 2 vols. (Knopf, 1966, 1969); and Norman Hamp-
son's *The Enlightenment* (Penguin, 1968).

For individual countries see: on England, Gerald Cragg's *Reason and
Authority in the Eighteenth Century* (Cambridge, 1964); on Scotland, A. C.
Chitnis, *The Scottish Enlightenment* (Rowman, 1976); on France, George
Havens, *The Age of Ideas* (Holt, 1955; Free Press, 1965) and Ira Wade, *The
Intellectual Origins of the French Enlightenment* (Princeton, 1971). R. R.
Palmer's *Catholics and Unbelievers in Eighteenth Century France* (Prince-
ton, 1939; Cooper Square, N. Y., 1961) presents "the intellectual position of
those who opposed the new thinkers." Lewis Beck's *Early German Philoso-
phy*, mentioned above under "The Reformation," is particularly good on
the German Enlightenment. Roy Pascal's *The German Sturm und Drang*
(Manchester, 1953) and W. H. Bruford's *Culture and Society in Classical
Weimar* (Cambridge, 1962) cover the "Weimar culture" of Goethe, Schiller,
and Herder.

Most of the above books discuss religious ideas, but see also Frank Manuel's
The Eighteenth Century Confronts the Gods (Harvard, 1959). Basil Willey's
The Eighteenth Century Background (Chatto & Windus, 1940; Columbia,
1953) and Aram Vartanian's *Diderot and Descartes* (Princeton, 1953) are
particularly illuminating on ideas of nature, as is Lester Crocker's *The Age
of Crisis: Man and World in Eighteenth Century French Thought* (Johns
Hopkins, 1959) on ideas of human nature. On political thought, Kingsley
Martin's *French Liberal Thought in the Eighteenth Century* (Little, Brown,
1929; revised edition retitled *The Rise of French Liberal Thought*, New
York University, 1954) is still useful, though one should also consult more
recent works such as John Plamenatz's *Man and Society, Political and Social
Theory*, vol. 1, *Machiavelli through Rousseau* (McGraw-Hill, 1963) and

Harry Payne's *The Philosophes and the People* (Yale, 1976). J. B. Bury's *The Idea of Progress* (Macmillan, 1920; Dover, 1960) and Charles Frankel's *The Faith of Reason* (King's Crown, 1948) are standard works on Enlightenment conceptions of history but need to be balanced by Henry Vyverberg's *Historical Pessimism in the French Enlightenment* (Harvard, 1958). See also the eighteenth-century chapters in John Passmore's *The Perfectibility of Man* (Duckworth, 1970). Friedrich Meinecke's *Historism* (Routledge and Paul, 1972) is the classic account of the rise of historicism. Peter Reill's *The German Enlightenment and the Rise of Historicism* (California, 1975) is a more recent but more limited study.

8. *Age of Becoming*

The most comprehensive account is still J. T. Merz's *The History of European Thought in the Nineteenth Century*, 4 vols. (Blackwood, 1896–1914, 1912–1928). The following works are also helpful on nineteenth-century thought in general: Ernst Cassirer's *The Problem of Knowledge: Philosophy, Science, and History since Hegel* (Yale, 1950, 1974); George Mosse's *The Culture of Western Europe: The Nineteenth and Twentieth Centuries* (Rand McNally, 1961); Karl Löwith's *From Hegel to Nietzsche* (Holt, 1964); and Maurice Mandelbaum's *History, Man, and Reason; a Study in Nineteenth-Century Thought* (Johns Hopkins, 1971). Walter Houghton's *The Victorian Frame of Mind 1830–1870* (Yale, 1957) is outstanding for England alone. D. C. Somervell's *English Thought in the Nineteenth Century* (Longmans, 1938; Methuen, 1957) is a useful survey.

For the different "periods" singled out in this book, see (1) on Romanticism: A. O. Lovejoy's *Essays in the History of Ideas* (Johns Hopkins, 1948; Putnam's, 1960), important for interpretation, but to be counterbalanced by René Wellek's essay on the concept of romanticism in *Concepts of Criticism* (Yale, 1963). Other interesting general studies are Jacques Barzun's *Romanticism and the Modern Ego* (Little, Brown, 1943; reprinted as *Classic, Romantic and Modern*, Doubleday, 1961); H. G. Schenk's *The Mind of the European Romantics* (Constable, 1966; Doubleday, 1969); and Meyer Abrams's *Natural Supernaturalism: Tradition and Revolution in Romantic Literature* (Norton, 1971).

For (2), the New Enlightenment, Elie Halévy's *The Growth of Philosophic Radicalism* (Faber, 1928; Beacon, 1955) is the classic study of the Benthamites but should be supplemented by a good comprehensive book on the younger Mill, such as J. M. Robson's *The Improvement of Mankind: The Social and Political Thought of J. S. Mill* (Toronto, 1968). The two best general books on Positivism are Walter Simon's *European Positivism in the Nineteenth Century* (Cornell, 1963) and D. G. Charlton's *Positivist Thought in France during the Second Empire* (Clarendon, 1963). F. A. von Hayek's *The Counter-Revolution of Science* (Free Press, 1952) is important for its discussion of "scientism." On the Hegelian movement see Sidney Hook's *From Hegel to Marx* (Reynal & Hitchcock, 1936; Michigan, 1962) and William Brazill's *The Young Hegelians* (Yale, 1970).

(3) The approach of the centenary celebration of *The Origin of Species* produced a spate of important new studies of the Darwinian world, including Loren Eiseley's *Darwin's Century* (Doubleday, 1958, 1961), Gertrude Himmelfarb's *Darwin and the Darwinian Revolution* (Doubleday, 1959; Norton, 1968), and John C. Greene's *The Death of Adam: Evolution and its Impact on Western Thought* (Iowa State, 1959). J. W. Burrow's *Evolution and Society* (Cambridge, 1966) showed that theories of social evolution antedated Darwin. Thomas Glick (ed.), *The Comparative Reception of Darwinism* (Texas, 1974) is particularly noteworthy for showing how Darwinism fared in countries other than England.

Looking "Toward the Twentieth Century" (4), Holbrook Jackson's *The Eighteen Nineties* (Richards, 1913; Knopf, 1927) still makes lively reading, but should be supplemented by weightier studies like Erich Heller's *The Disinherited Mind* (Farrar, 1957; Harcourt, 1975), which contains essays on Burckhardt and Nietzsche as well as some other nineteenth- and twentieth-century figures; and Koenraad Swart's *The Sense of Decadence in Nineteenth Century France* (M. Nijhoff, 1964) for the "Decadents."

For the upheaval in religious ideas, see Claude Welch's *Protestant Thought in the Nineteenth Century* (Yale, 1972) and Basil Willey's *Nineteenth Century Studies* (Chatto & Windus, 1949; Harper, 1966) and *More Nineteenth Century Studies* (Columbia, 1956). Albert Schweitzer's classic *The Quest of the Historical Jesus* (Macmillan, 1948, 1968) deals with the Higher Criticism. For free thought and free thinkers see Owen Chadwick's *The Secularization of the European Mind in the Nineteenth Century* (Cambridge, 1975), and D. G. Charlton's *Secular Religions in France 1815–1870* (Oxford, 1963). Frank Turner's *Between Science and Religion* (Yale, 1974) examines the thought of those in late Victorian England who found neither Christianity nor scientific naturalism congenial and sought an alternative.

Crane Brinton's *English Political Thought in the Nineteenth Century* (E. Benn, 1933; Harvard, 1949) and Roger Soltau's *French Political Thought in the Nineteenth Century* (Yale, 1931; Russell & Russell, 1959) are standard studies. Leonard Krieger studies German political thought, particularly the liberal tradition in *The German Idea of Freedom* (Beacon, 1957; Chicago, 1972). John Plamenatz provides a more recent analysis of selected political and social theorists in *Man and Society: Political and Social Theory, Bentham through Marx* (McGraw-Hill, 1963). The section in Mulford Sibley's *Political Ideas and Ideologies* (Harper, 1970) entitled "The Modern Liberal Tradition" is particularly useful on the consequences of Utilitarianism and the "liberal split" between Herbert Spencer and T. H. Green. Carlton Hayes' *The Historical Evolution of Modern Nationalism* (R. R. Smith, 1931; Macmillan, 1964) is important for distinguishing different types of nationalism. See also on nationalism Hans Kohn's *Prophets and People* (Macmillan, 1946), and on "race-thinking" Jacques Barzun's *Race: A Study in Superstition* (Harcourt, 1937; Harper, 1965). The first three volumes of G. D. H. Cole's *History of Socialist Thought* (St. Martin's, 1953–1960) deal with the nineteenth century. Recent studies of imperialist thought include A. P. Thornton's *Doctrines of Imperialism* (Wiley, 1965) and Bernard

Semmel's *Imperialism and Social Reform: English Social-imperial Thought,
1895–1914* (Harvard, 1960).

G. P. Gooch's *History and Historians in the Nineteenth Century* (Longmans, 1935, 1967) has never been replaced as a general survey of the various
schools of historical thought. Georg Iggers's *The German Conception of
History* (Wesleyan, 1968) deals particularly with the theoretical assumptions of the German historians; W. Warren Wagar's *Good Tidings* (Indiana, 1972) with the idea of progress "from Darwin to Marcuse." Hayden
White writes about realism in nineteenth-century historiography and the
reaction against it in *Metahistory: The Historical Imagination in Nineteenth-Century Europe* (Johns Hopkins, 1973, 1975).

9. Age of Anxiety

For the difficult "transition" from the old century to the new, see, in
addition to works mentioned in the previous section (Mosse, Heller, etc.),
H. Stuart Hughes' *Consciousness and Society: The Reorientation of European Social Thought, 1890–1930* (Knopf, 1958, 1961) and John Weiss (ed.),
The Origins of Modern Consciousness (Wayne State, 1965), both of which
emphasize the "generation of the '90's"; and the essays collected and edited
by W. Warren Wagar under the title *European Intellectual History since
Darwin and Marx* (Harper, 1966). For overall views of twentieth-century
thought, see Paul Tillich's *The Courage To Be* (Yale, 1952, 1959) for his
conception of an Age of Anxiety; Paul Fussell's *The Great War and Modern
Memory* (Oxford, 1975) for the impact of World War I, particularly in
English "memory"; C. B. Cox and A. E. Dyson (eds.), *The Twentieth
Century Mind* (Oxford, 1972), 3 vols., which deals with continental European ideas as well as with "History, Ideas, and Literature in Britain"; and,
for those who read French, René Marill (pseudonym R. Albérès), *L'Aventure
intellectuelle du XXᵉ siècle* (A. Michel, 1969, 1970). George Lichtheim's
Europe in the Twentieth Century (Praeger, 1972) also includes much ma-
terial on intellectual developments. Three recent books concentrate on new
departures in German thought, particularly in the 1920's: Peter Gay's
Weimar Culture (Harper, 1968), Walter Laqueur's *Weimar: A Cultural
History 1918–1933* (Putnam's 1974), and Fritz Ringer's *The Decline of the
German Mandarins: The German Academic Community, 1890–1933* (Har-
vard, 1969). See also the volume edited by Donald Fleming and Bernard
Bailyn which treats *The Intellectual Migration: Europe and America, 1930–
1960* (Harvard, 1969).

For new developments in theology and religious thought, see W. M.
Horton's twin volumes, still indispensable, *Contemporary English Theology*
and *Contemporary Continental Theology* (Harper, 1936, 1938); Philip E.
Hughes (ed.), *Creative Minds in Contemporary Theology* (Eerdmans,
1966); and William R. Hughes (ed.), *The New Christianity: An Anthology
of the Rise of Modern Religious Thought* (Delacorte, 1967). John Mac-
quarrie's *The Scope of Demythologizing: Bultmann and his Critics* (Harper,
1960, 1961) describes the great debate over the "demythologizing" of the
New Testament.

Albert W. Levi's *Philosophy and the Modern World* (Indiana, 1959) deals imaginatively with some of the great issues in philosophy from Bergson to Whitehead. John Passmore's *A Hundred Years of Philosophy* (Basic Books, 1966, 1967) identifies and describes recent "schools" of philosophy. On existentialism in particular, see F. H. Heinemann's *Existentialism and the Modern Predicament* (Harper, 1953) and William Barrett's *What is Existentialism?* (Grove, 1964). Frederick Copleston's *Contemporary Philosophy* (Burns & Oates, 1956) is especially good on the varieties of existentialism. It also treats logical positivism, as also does Allan Janik and Stephen Toulmin's *Wittgenstein's Vienna* (Simon & Shuster, 1973) which is, however, a much more broadly gauged book than its title indicates.

On the new views of "nature" and the philosophy of science, see in addition to Collingwood's *The Idea of Nature*, mentioned in the "General" section above, A. N. Whitehead's classic *Science and the Modern World* (Macmillan, 1925, 1967), and especially Milič Čapek's *The Philosophical Impact of Contemporary Physics* (Princeton, 1961), which describes the new concepts against the background of "The Classical Picture of the Physical World." Several books by Ernst Cassirer also bear interestingly on this subject: part 1 of *The Problem of Knowledge* (see under "Century of Becoming") and *Determinism and Indeterminism in Modern Physics* (Yale, 1956).

Books on the leading psychologists and their ideas about the nature of man naturally abound in what Otto Rank called the "Psychological Age." Lancelot Whyte's *The Unconscious before Freud* (Basic Books, 1960; Doubleday, 1962) is an important pioneering work. Henri Ellenberger's *The Discovery of the Unconscious* (Basic Books, 1970) is impressive and full on the psychoanalytical movement. *Freud and the 20th Century*, Benjamin Nelson (ed.), (Meridian, 1957) is a good collection of essays on the "Freudian Revolution." B. B. Wolman's *Contemporary Theories and Studies in Psychology* (Harper, 1960) is useful in identifying other "schools" of psychological thought. Ira Progoff discusses the "search for meaning" by modern psychologists, principally Jung, Adler, and Rank in *The Death and Rebirth of Psychology* (Julian, 1956).

The literature on political and social ideas is vast, and there is room here for only a few titles. Arnold Brecht's *Political Theory: The Foundations of Twentieth-Century Political Thought* (Princeton, 1959) is an impressive work at a high level. H. Stuart Hughes' *The Obstructed Path: French Social Thought in the Years of Desperation, 1930–1960* (Harper, 1968) is the sequel to *Consciousness and Society*, listed in the first paragraph of this section. On fascism and its intellectual background, see especially Ernst Nolte's *Three Faces of Fascism* (Holt, 1965, 1966) and George Mosse's *The Crisis of German Ideology* (Grosset & Dunlap, 1964, 1972). The chapters in G. D. H. Cole's *History of Socialist Thought*, mentioned under "Century of Becoming," and L. Rabedz (ed.), *Revisionism: Essays on the History of Marxist Ideas* (Praeger, 1962) are useful for new developments in socialist and Marxist thought. On communism and the intellectuals, see the appropriate chapters in George B. de Huszar's *The Intellectuals*, mentioned in the first section "On Intellectuals and Intellectual History," and David Caute's *Communism and the French Intellectuals* (Macmillan, 1964).

The Philosophy of History in our Time, Hans Meyerhoff (ed.), (Doubleday, 1959) is an excellent introduction to that subject, consisting of essays by historians and philosophers of history ranging from "historicism" to "the meaning of history." Both Iggers and Wagar, mentioned in the last paragraph of the bibliography for "Century of Becoming," carry over into the twentieth century. See also E. H. Carr's *What is History?* (Knopf, 1961, 1962) and Geoffrey Barraclough's *History in a Changing World* (Blackwell, 1956, 1957), the latter especially for its discussion of historical relativism and European history in world perspective. Pierre-Henri Simon's *L'Esprit et l'histoire* (Cohn, Paris, 1954) is a fascinating "essay on the historical conscience in twentieth-century literature."

No bibliography of twentieth-century ideas should fail to include "literature" and the literary intellectuals who have deliberately engaged themselves in the great ideological battles. The following books are among the more suggestive and informative: on the novelists, E. B. Burgum's *The Novel and the World's Dilemma* (Oxford, 1947; Russell & Russell, 1963), R. W. B. Lewis' *The Picaresque Saint: Representative Figures in Contemporary Fiction* (Lippincott, 1959), which includes studies of the Italians, and Henri Peyre's *The Contemporary French Novel* (Oxford, 1955); and on the dramatists, J. W. Krutch's *"Modernism" in Modern Drama* (Cornell, 1952) and Martin Esslin's *The Theatre of the Absurd* (Doubleday, 1961). Fritz Pappenheim's *The Alienation of Modern Man* (Monthly Review, 1959) also makes interesting reading in this connection.

Italian Humanism and Civic Life in the Renaissance (Basil Blackwell, 1965) is particularly good on Italy, Lewis Spitz's *The Religious Renaissance of the German Humanists* (Harvard, 1963) on Germany, Werner Gundersheimer (ed.), *French Humanism 1470–1600* (Harper, 1969, 1970) on France, and A. L. Rowse's *The Elizabethan Renaissance* (Scribner's, 1972) on England. Roland Bainton's *Erasmus of Christendom* (Scribner's, 1969) is the best recent book on Erasmus and Christian humanism.

For the role of the classics in Renaissance thought see further R. R. Bolgar's *The Classical Heritage and its Beneficiaries* (Cambridge, 1954); for philosophy, Paul Kristeller's *Renaissance Thought* (Harper, 1961, 1965) and *Eight Philosophers of the Italian Renaissance* (Stanford, 1964); for cosmology and conceptions of the nature of man, E. M. W. Tillyard's *The Elizabethan World Picture* (Chatto & Windus, 1943), Theodore Spencer's *Shakespeare and the Nature of Man* (Macmillan, Ltd., 1942, 1949), Ernst Cassirer (ed.), *The Renaissance Philosophy of Man* (Chicago, 1948, 1969), and Charles Trinkaus's *In Our Image and Likeness: Humanity and Divinity in Italian Humanist Thought*, 2 vols. (Chicago, 1970); for art and the growing prestige of art, the appropriate chapters in Leonardo Olschki's *The Genius of Italy* (Oxford, 1949; Cornell, 1964).

By now the literature on Machiavelli is enormous. J. W. Allen's *A History of Political Thought in the Sixteenth Century* (Methuen, 1928, 1957) is still well worth reading on the subject. Articles by Eric Cochrane ("Machiavelli: 1940–1960," *Journal of Modern History*, 33, 1961) and John Geerken, "Machiavelli Studies since 1969," *Journal of the History of Ideas*, 37, 1976) review the more recent literature. For those interested in the tangled web of the Renaissance and science, Marie Boas Hall's *The Scientific Renaissance, 1450–1630* (Harper, 1962) is indispensable. On the same subject see also the interesting discussion by Dana Durand and Hans Baron in the *Journal of the History of Ideas*, 4 (1943), and Eric Cochrane's article "Science and Humanism in the Italian Renaissance" in the *American Historical Review*, 81 (1976).

5. *The Confessional Age*

H. J. Grimm's *The Reformation Era* (Macmillan, 1954, 1973), a general work, includes an excellent bibliography summarizing the latest work in Reformation thought. Ernst Troeltsch's *Protestantism and Progress* (Williams & Norgate, 1912; Beacon Hill, 1958) is still basic reading for interpretation. Robert M. Kingdon (ed.), *Transition and Revolution: Problems and Issues of European Renaissance and Reformation History* (Burgess, 1974) contains valuable interpretative essays. E. H. Harbison's *The Christian Scholar in the Age of the Reformation* (Scribner's, 1956) interprets the Reformation as a "scholars' revolution" and is also notable for linking Protestant scholarship to the patristic age and the Renaissance.

A. C. McGiffert's *Protestant Thought before Kant* (Scribner's, 1911; Harper, 1962) stands up as an excellent brief survey of the main strands of Protestant thought. Lewis W. Beck deals briefly but well with Protestant

3. *The Middle Ages*

The Mind of the Middle Ages by F. B. Artz (Knopf, 1953, 1959) is a useful survey with extensive bibliography. David Knowles' *The Evolution of Medieval Thought* (Helicon, 1962; Random House, 1964), and Gordon Leff's *Medieval Thought* (Penguin, 1958; Quadrangle, 1959) are also good general accounts. William J. Brandt's *The Shape of Medieval History: Studies in Modes of Perception* (Yale, 1966) calls attention to some fundamental assumptions of medieval thinking.

See especially C. N. Cochrane's *Christianity and Classical Culture* (Clarendon, 1940, 1957) for the relationship between medieval and classical thought. The first volume of Jaroslav Pelikan's projected five-volume history of Christian doctrine deals with the early Middle Ages: *The Emergence of the Catholic Tradition* (Chicago, 1971). Religious dissent has attracted much attention in recent years. See on this subject Jeffrey B. Russell, *Religious Dissent in the Middle Ages* (Wiley, 1971), Austin B. Evans, *Heresies of the High Middle Ages* (Columbia, 1969), and Gordon Leff, *Heresy in the Later Middle Ages* (Barnes & Noble, 1967).

On medieval philosophy, studies by Etienne Gilson and F. C. Copleston rank at the top: *The History of Christian Philosophy in the Middle Ages* (Random House, 1955) and *The Spirit of Medieval Philosophy* (Scribner's, 1936, 1940) by Gilson, and *A History of Medieval Philosophy* (Methuen, 1972; Harper, 1974) by Copleston. See A. C. Crombie's *Augustine to Galileo: The History of Science A. D. 400–1650* (Falcon, 1952; Penguin, 1969) for science; Herschel Baker's *The Dignity of Man* (Harvard, 1947) for conceptions of the nature of man; C. H. McIlwain's *The Growth of Political Thought in the West* (Macmillan, 1932, 1959) and W. Ullman's *A History of Political Thought: The Middle Ages* (Penguin, 1965) for political and social ideas. J. N. Figgis's classic *The Political Aspects of St. Augustine's 'City of God'* (Longmans, 1921; Peter Smith, 1963) is still worth consulting for philosophy of history, as are two stimulating articles by, respectively, G. La Piana and T. Mommsen: "Theology of History," in *The Interpretation of History*, J. R. Strayer (ed.) (Princeton, 1943), and "St. Augustine and the Christian Idea of Progress," *Journal of the History of Ideas*, 12 (1951).

4. *The Renaissance*

W. K. Ferguson's *The Renaissance in Historical Thought* (Houghton Mifflin, 1948) describes the major interpretations of the Renaissance from the fourteenth century to the twentieth. See also on interpretation Federico Chabod's brilliant essay "The Concept of the Renaissance" in *Machiavelli and the Renaissance* (Harvard, 1958) and Douglas Bush's *The Renaissance and English Humanism* (Toronto, 1939).

Denis Hay's *The Italian Renaissance in its Historical Background* (Cambridge, 1961, 1977) is a good general study. See also *The Renaissance: Six essays* (Metropolitan Museum of Art, 1953; Harper, 1962). Eugenio Garin's